Contemporary Authors®

NEW REVISION SERIES

Contemporary Authors
was named an
*"Outstanding
Reference Source"* by
*the American Library
Association Reference
and Adult Services
Division after its 1962
inception.
In 1985 it was listed by
the same organization
as one of the
twenty-five most
distinguished reference
titles published in the
past twenty-five years.*

ISSN 0275-7176

Contemporary Authors®

A Bio-Bibliographical Guide to
Current Writers in Fiction, General Nonfiction,
Poetry, Journalism, Drama, Motion Pictures,
Television, and Other Fields

JAMES G. LESNIAK
SUSAN M. TROSKY
Editors

NEW REVISION SERIES
volume **38**

 **Gale Research Inc.** · *DETROIT · LONDON*

STAFF

James G. Lesniak and Susan Trosky, *Editors, New Revision Series*

Elizabeth A. Des Chenes, Kevin S. Hile, Susan M. Reicha, Kenneth R. Shepherd,
and Thomas Wiloch, *Associate Editors*

Bruce Ching, David Johnson, Margaret Mazurkiewicz, Tom Pendergast,
Cornelia A. Pernik, Pamela L. Shelton, and Deborah A. Stanley, *Assistant Editors*

Marilyn K. Basel, Anne Janette Johnson, Sharon Malinowski, Diane Telgen, and Michaela Swart Wilson,
Contributing Editors

Hal May, *Senior Editor, Contemporary Authors*

Victoria B. Cariappa, *Research Manager*

Mary Rose Bonk, *Research Supervisor*

Reginald A. Carlton, Clare Collins, Andrew Guy Malonis, and Norma Sawaya, *Editorial Associates*

Mike Avolio, Patricia Bowen, Rachel A. Dixon, Shirley Gates,
Sharon McGilvray, and Devra M. Sladics, *Editorial Assistants*

℗™ This book is printed on acid-free paper that meets the minimum requirements
of American National Standard for Information Sciences—
Permanence Paper for Printed Library Materials, ANSI Z39.48-1984.

Library of Congress Catalog Card Number 81-640179
ISBN 0-8103-1992-6
ISSN 0275-7176

Printed in the United States of America.

Published simultaneously in the United Kingdom
by Gale Research International Limited
(An affiliated company of Gale Research Inc.)

Contents

Indexing note: All *Contemporary Authors New Revision Series* entries are indexed in the *Contemporary Authors* cumulative index, which is published separately and distributed with even-numbered *Contemporary Authors* original volumes and odd-numbered *Contemporary Authors New Revision Series* volumes.

As always, the most recent *Contemporary Authors* cumulative index continues to be the user's guide to the location of an individual author's listing.

Preface

The *Contemporary Authors New Revision Series* (*CANR*) provides completely updated information on authors listed in earlier volumes of *Contemporary Authors* (*CA*). Entries for individual authors from *any* volume of *CA* may be included in a volume of the *New Revision Series. CANR* updates only those sketches requiring significant change.

Authors are included on the basis of specific criteria that indicate the need for significant revision. These criteria include bibliographical additions, changes in addresses or career, major awards, and personal information such as name changes or death dates. All listings in this volume have been revised or augmented in various ways. Some sketches have been extensively rewritten, and many include informative new sidelights. As always, a *CANR* listing entails no charge or obligation.

How to Get the Most out of *CA* and *CANR:* Use the Index

The key to locating an author's most recent listing is the *CA* cumulative index, which is published separately and distributed with even-numbered original volumes and odd-numbered revision volumes. It provides access to *all* entries in *CA* and *CANR*. Always consult the latest index to find an author's most recent entry.

For the convenience of users, the *CA* cumulative index also includes references to all entries in these related Gale literary series: *Authors and Artists for Young Adults, Authors in the News, Bestsellers, Black Literature Criticism, Black Writers, Children's Literature Review, Concise Dictionary of American Literary Biography, Concise Dictionary of British Literary Biography, Contemporary Authors Autobiography Series, Contemporary Authors Bibliographical Series, Contemporary Literary Criticism, Dictionary of Literary Biography, Drama Criticism, Hispanic Writers, Major 20th Century Writers, Poetry Criticism, Short Story Criticism, Something about the Author, Something about the Author Autobiography Series, Twentieth-Century Literary Criticism, World Literature Criticism,* and *Yesterday's Authors of Books for Children.*

A Sample Index Entry:

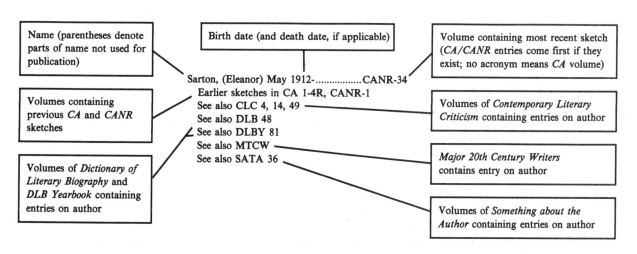

For the most recent *CA* information on Sarton, users should refer to Volume 34 of the *New Revision Series,* as designated by "CANR-34"; if that volume is unavailable, refer to CANR-1. And if CANR-1 is unavailable, refer to CA 1-4R, published in 1967, for Sarton's First Revision entry.

How Are Entries Compiled?

The editors make every effort to secure new information directly from the authors. Copies of all sketches in selected *CA* and *CANR* volumes published several years ago are routinely sent to listees at their last-known addresses, and returns from these authors are then assessed. For deceased writers, or those who fail to reply to requests for data, we consult other reliable biographical sources, such as those indexed in Gale's *Biography and Genealogy Master Index,* and bibliographical sources, such as *National Union Catalog, LC Marc,* and *British National Bibliography.* Further details come from published interviews, feature stories, and book reviews, and often the authors' publishers supply material.

What Kinds of Information Does an Entry Provide?

Sketches in *CANR* contain the following biographical and bibliographical information:

- **Entry heading:** the most complete form of author's name, plus any pseudonyms or name variations used for writing

- **Personal information:** author's date and place of birth, family data, educational background, political and religious affiliations, and hobbies and leisure interests

- **Addresses:** author's home, office, or agent's addresses as available

- **Career summary:** name of employer, position, and dates held for each career post; résumé of other vocational achievements; military service

- **Awards and honors:** military and civic citations, major prizes and nominations, fellowships, grants, and honorary degrees

- **Membership information:** professional, civic, and other association memberships and any official posts held

- **Writings:** a comprehensive list of titles, publishers, dates of original publication and revised editions, and production information for plays, television scripts, and screenplays

- **Adaptations:** a list of films, plays, and other media which have been adapted from the author's work

- **Work in progress:** current or planned projects, with dates of completion and/or publication, and expected publisher, when known

- **Sidelights:** a biographical portrait of the author's development; information about the critical reception of the author's works; revealing comments, often by the author, on personal interests, aspirations, motivations, and thoughts on writing

- **Biographical and critical sources:** a list of books and periodicals in which additional information on an author's life and/or writings appears

Related Titles in the *CA* Series

Contemporary Authors Autobiography Series complements *CA* original and revised volumes with specially commissioned autobiographical essays by important current authors, illustrated with personal photographs they provide. Common topics include their motivations for writing, the people and experiences that shaped their careers, the rewards they derive from their work, and their impressions of the current literary scene.

Contemporary Authors Bibliographical Series surveys writings by and about important American authors since World War II. Each volume concentrates on a specific genre and features approximately ten writers; entries list works written by and about the author and contain a bibliographical essay discussing the merits and deficiencies of major critical and scholarly studies in detail.

Suggestions Are Welcome

The editors welcome comments and suggestions from users on any aspects of the *CA* series. If readers would like to suggest authors whose entries should appear in future volumes of the series, they are cordially invited to write: The Editors, *Contemporary Authors,* 835 Penobscot Bldg., Detroit, MI 48226-4094; call toll-free at 1-800-347-GALE; or fax to 1-313-961-6599.

CA Numbering System and Volume Update Chart

Occasionally questions arise about the *CA* numbering system and which volumes, if any, can be discarded. Despite numbers like "29-32R," "97-100" and "137," the entire *CA* series consists of only 102 physical volumes with the publication of *CA New Revision Series* Volume 38. The following chart notes changes in the numbering system and cover design, and indicates which volumes are essential for the most complete, up-to-date coverage.

CA First Revision	• 1-4R through 41-44R (11 books) *Cover:* Brown with black and gold trim. There will be no further First Revision volumes because revised entries are now being handled exclusively through the more efficient *New Revision Series* mentioned below.
CA Original Volumes	• 45-48 through 97-100 (14 books) *Cover:* Brown with black and gold trim. • 101 through 137 (37 books) *Cover:* Blue and black with orange bands. The same as previous *CA* original volumes but with a new, simplified numbering system and new cover design.
CA Permanent Series	• *CAP*-1 and *CAP*-2 (2 books) *Cover:* Brown with red and gold trim. There will be no further *Permanent Series* volumes because revised entries are now being handled exclusively through the more efficient *New Revision Series* mentioned below.
CA New Revision Series	• *CANR*-1 through *CANR*-38 (38 books) *Cover:* Blue and black with green bands. Includes only sketches requiring extensive changes; **sketches are taken from any previously published *CA*, *CAP*, or *CANR* volume.**

If You Have:	**You May Discard:**
CA First Revision Volumes 1-4R through 41-44R **and** *CA Permanent Series* Volumes 1 and 2	*CA* Original Volumes 1, 2, 3, 4 Volumes 5-6 through 23-24 Volumes 25-28 through 41-44
CA Original Volumes 45-48 through 97–100 and 101 through 137	NONE: These volumes will not be superseded by corresponding revised volumes. Individual entries from these and all other volumes appearing in the left column of this chart will be revised and included in the various volumes of the *New Revision Series*.
CA New Revision Series Volumes *CANR*-1 through *CANR*-38	NONE: The *New Revision Series* does not replace any single volume of *CA*. Instead, volumes of *CANR* include entries from many previous *CA* series volumes. All *New Revision Series* volumes must be retained for full coverage.

A Sampling of Authors and Media People
Featured in This Volume

Woody Allen
As both a writer and Academy Award-winning film-maker, Allen is recognized for his ability to balance comedy and drama with his own offbeat brand of modern angst. His works include *Manhattan* and *Zelig*.

Natalie Babbitt
Babbitt has carved a niche for herself as both an author and illustrator whose works for young people, such as *Tuck Everlasting,* are defined by their originality, humor, and challenging themes.

Amiri Baraka
Adept at writing in a number of genres, Baraka examines the political concerns of black America in many of his works, including *The Dutchman* and *Afrikan Revolution: A Poem*.

Nigel Calder
A specialist in writing popular works about scientific issues, Calder explores topics ranging from outer space colonization in *Spaceships of the Mind* to population growth and food production in *Eden Was No Garden*.

Frederick Forsythe
An Edgar Allan Poe Award-winner, Forsythe is widely considered the originator of the "documentary thriller" genre represented by titles such as *The Day of the Jackal* and *The Odessa File*.

Ken Kesey
In works such as *One Flew Over the Cuckoo's Nest* and *Sometimes a Great Notion,* Kesey examines the struggle of the human spirit in conflict with modern-day values.

Maxine Hong Kingston
Kingston combines legend, stories, and myth to chronicle both her family history and the experiences of other Chinese Americans. Among her most popular works are *The Woman Warrior* and *China Men*.

Mercer Mayer
A versatile author and illustrator, Mayer has been lauded for popularizing the wordless picture book and developing several beginning reader series, including "Little Monsters" and "Little Critters."

Desmond Morris
Morris's lifelong fascination with wildlife has led him to write a number of best-selling books about animal behavior, including *Dogwatching, Catwatching,* and *The Naked Ape*.

Piers Paul Read
Although perhaps best-known for his nonfiction bestseller *Alive: The Story of the Andes Survivors,* Read has also produced a number of highly stylized novels that explore caste, crime, and Catholicism in modern society.

Alexandra Ripley
Romance novelist Ripley gained instant notoriety for writing *Scarlet,* the much-debated sequel to Margaret Mitchell's novel *Gone with the Wind*.

Emma Tennant
Tennant's wide-ranging body of fiction offers a satirical but penetrating vision of conditions in modern England. Her books include *The Colour of Rain* and *The Magic Drum*.

Lewis Thomas
In books like *The Lives of a Cell* and *The Medusa and the Snail,* medical pathologist Thomas explores natural phenomena in a philosophical context.

Chris Van Allsburg
Van Allsburg's Caldecott Medal-winning illustration style—a mixture of technical detail and surprising images—is displayed in works such as *Swan Lake* and *The Polar Express*.

Phyllis Whitney
Once called "America's queen of romantic suspense" for titles like *Spindrift* and *The Singing Stones,* Whitney has been praised for her ability to mix the lure of exotic locales with intricate and suspenseful plots.

Contemporary Authors ®

NEW REVISION SERIES

AARON, Chester 1923-

PERSONAL: Born May 9, 1923, in Butler, PA; son of Albert (a grocer and farmer) and Celia (Charleson) Aaron; married Margaurite Kelly (a jeweler), April 17, 1954 (divorced, 1973); stepchildren: Louis Daniel Segal. *Education:* Attended University of California, Los Angeles; University of California, Berkeley, B.A., 1966; San Francisco State University, M.A., 1972.

ADDRESSES: Home—P.O. Box 388, Occidental, CA 95465. *Office*—Department of English, St. Mary's College of California, Moraga, CA 94575. *Agent*—Kathi J. Paton Literary Agency, 19 West 55th St., New York, NY 10019.

CAREER: St. Mary's College of California, Moraga, began as assistant professor, became professor of English, 1980—; writer. Kaiser Permanente, San Francisco, CA, x-ray technician, 1957-58; Alta Bates Hospital, Berkeley, CA, chief x-ray technician, 1957-75; MKI Engineering, San Francisco, technical writer, 1972. Also served as a volunteer at the California Marine Mammal Center in Marin County. *Military service:* U.S. Army, 1943-46.

AWARDS, HONORS: Grants from Huntington Hartford Foundation, 1951, the Chapelbrook Foundation, 1970, and the National Endowment for the Arts, 1976; *Duchess* was named a 1982 notable children's trade book in the field of social studies by a joint committee of the National Council for the Social Studies and the Children's Book Council.

WRITINGS:

About Us (novel), McGraw, 1967.

YOUNG ADULT FICTION

Better Than Laughter, Harcourt, 1972.
An American Ghost, illustrations by David Lemon, Harcourt, 1973.

Hello to Bodega, Atheneum, 1976.
Spill, Atheneum, 1978.
Catch Calico! (Junior Literary Guild selection), Dutton, 1979.
Gideon, Lippincott, 1982.
Duchess, Lippincott, 1982.
Out of Sight, Out of Mind, Lippincott, 1985.
Lackawana, Lippincott, 1986.
Alex, Who Won His War, Walker, 1991.

OTHER

The Cowbank (play), produced at University of California, Berkeley, 1955.

Also author of unpublished novel entitled *Axel.* Contributor of short stories to *Amistad, Coastlines, Highlights for Children, North American Review,* and *Texas Quarterly.*

ADAPTATIONS: Cougar, based on *An American Ghost,* was released by ABC-TV as a weekend special in 1984; *Lackawanna* was optioned for a feature film by Moonlight Productions in association with ITC Productions.

SIDELIGHTS: Chester Aaron's desire to become a writer originated in his childhood. An early and avid reader, Aaron remembers an incident that would shape his ultimate career. For his eleventh birthday, he received a copy of Jack London's *White Fang* from one of his brothers. Rushing through the book, the young Aaron rendered an exciting account of it to a spellbound group of children. "But as good as my story was," he recounts in an essay in *Something about the Author Autobiography Series,* "its impact did not approach the impact the original writing, the words and the sentences Jack London had composed, had had on me. . . . 'Someday,' I promised the kids as well as myself, 'I'm going to write stories.'" Although he has written throughout his life, he was in his middle forties when he published his first book. Drawing strongly upon the experience of his youth, Aaron crafts realistic fiction primarily for young adults, and earns much praise for its uncompromising honesty. The critical reception of his work has often surpassed its popular success with readers; however, Aaron's "books belong to the sterling old adventure genre, though with more inner subtleties," as Naomi Lewis describes them in *Twentieth-Century Children's Writers.*

Aaron's parents, Jews from Poland and Russia, emigrated at the turn of the twentieth century to settle in the Pennsylvania mining town of North Butler where they operated a small grocery store. Aaron's five brothers and one sister were nearly adults when he was born in 1923. And the Great Depression of the 1930s threw the region and their family into upheaval. His parents, generous to those who were unable to pay for their groceries, refused food to no one; and their philanthropy included preparing and delivering packages of meat, vegetables, and bread to the poorest of the unemployed at Christmas. "Before long we were as impoverished as the poorest worker's family," recalls Aaron. "We had no food. I went, with other kids, to trail along behind the occasional coal trains, gathering fallen lumps of coal for our stove. I hiked many miles with my father to pick wild mushrooms and nuts and berries to supplement the potatoes that composed our meals. . . . As difficult as it was we never went on welfare, as did almost all of the other families. When our taxes fell due my father insisted on paying them off by working in the hot sun digging ditches, while kids and grown-ups sitting on the porch tried to make sense out of that old Jew's code of morality." With the onset of World War II came a cultural clash and many ethnic slurs to Aaron and his family—insensitive, childish remarks and pranks as well as Nazi swastikas painted on their store. "The jokes and curses I received from the kids could no longer be forgiven so easily," recalls Aaron. "I was driven not just to fight back but to fight and hurt, and even, if necessary, to maim. Driven by a mix of fear and anger I learned the reputation of being a kid it was no longer wise to tease with epithets suggesting Jews were stingy and biblically convicted Christ-killers."

Following high school graduation, Aaron was deferred from the military draft since four of his brothers were already in the service and his parents were both old and ill. He worked in the steel mills for a while but impulsively decided to join the Army. "Fighting ignorant and insensitive kids for their stupid little epithets was no longer enough. I had to kill Germans." He fought in southern Germany and as the war drew to a close, he describes an event that changed him as a human being. As his military unit approached Dachau, they detected a hovering gray-orange cloud and an increasing stench which they soon realized emanated from burning human flesh. "We stormed

the gates of Dachau and overwhelmed the few remaining German troops. I helped open the doors of the various gray wooden barracks that contained the living and the dead, one indistinguishable from the other. We remained at Dachau two days. Those two days changed whatever direction my life, up until then, might have been traveling. I was never the same man. I still dream about those two days at Dachau. I have struggled to convince myself that I am more than a Jew, I am a man, a human being, like Catholic and Protestant and Moslem men. But it doesn't work. I find myself listening to words of Gentiles, even of those I love, waiting to hear the denunciation that might precede a fist or a rifle butt or knocks at my door in the middle of the night."

He was twenty-two when he returned from the war, and his parents had died. For a while, he worked variously at odd jobs while studying creative writing at the University of California, Los Angeles, on the G.I. Bill. He submitted several stories for publication; and although he was generally unsuccessful, he continued to receive encouragement by professors who considered him to have a powerful voice and one that needed to be heard. With the help of a Hartford Foundation grant, he began work on a praised, but ultimately unpublished novel; discouraged, Aaron set aside his plans to write full-time and trained instead as an x-ray technician—a profession he worked at for nearly fifteen years while continuing to write part-time. In the late 1960s, though, he published his first book, a critically acclaimed autobiographical novel, *About Us.*

Calling *About Us* "a beautiful and original book," Donald Fanger praises it in the *Nation* as being "lyrical without mushiness and tough without posing, full of a truth that cannot be abstracted from the words that carry it." Richard G. Lillard describes the book as "a rich cross-section of attitudes and conflicts in America during the Depression and World War II," adding in the *Los Angeles Times Calendar,* "Its radiant insight illuminates a wide circumference of human joy and suffering." Regarding it as a novel about the disintegration of a family, Fanger notes that it records "the scarcely perceptible stages through a pure present tense that becomes gradually complicated with a past and with intimations of a future." As Fanger concludes, "It is a remarkable first novel, able in its authenticity to hear comparison with the best of its kind."

Shortly thereafter, Aaron also began teaching at Saint Mary's College in Moraga, California, which gave him more time to pursue writing. When he discovered sadly that his students were ignorant of the Nazi concentration camps, however, he understood that the time had come to write about the Holocaust. The resulting *Gideon* chronicles the story of a brave fourteen-year-old boy who survives the Warsaw ghetto and later the death camp at Treblinka through his own resourcefulness. Lewis labels it a "powerful and important book." And a contributor to *Bulletin of the Center for Children's Books* deems it a "moving and terrible story, written with craft and conviction."

Aaron explains in his autobiographical essay that in his fiction for adults and young adults alike, "I use the same vocabulary, the same reliance on clear prose, the same insistence on direct narrative (with as little complexity as possible in the structure) that I learned from Jack London." However, with young adults, Aaron discovered a unique and challenging audience—"readers who not merely expressed their enthusiasm for my own work but expressed as well that voracious hunger for literature (stories) that adds depth and color to their world." Pointing out that "they admit to an unrestrained thrill, they do not censor or sublimate, they yield to the writer, they willingly suspend disbelief and accept what the writer offers them," Aaron adds that "if the writer stumbles, or deceives, or concocts lies to describe truths, the young readers will quietly but surely turn away, put the book down, shrug off the writer."

BIOGRAPHICAL/CRITICAL SOURCES:

BOOKS

Something about the Author Autobiographical Series, Volume 12, Gale, 1991, pp. 1-17.
Twentieth-Century Children's Writers, 3rd edition, St. James Press, 1989.

PERIODICALS

Bulletin of the Center for Children's Books, November, 1977; June, 1982.
Horn Book, December, 1977.
Los Angeles Times Calendar, July 16, 1967.
Nation, June 26, 1967.
Publishers Weekly, October 28, 1983.

*   *   *

ABBOTT, Sarah
    See Zolotow, Charlotte S(hapiro)

*   *   *

ADAM, Jan 1920-

PERSONAL: Born August 24, 1920, in Malcov, Czechoslovakia; married wife, Zuzana, 1945; children: Julie. *Education:* School for Political and Social Studies, Prague, Czechoslovakia, graduated, 1949, Dr.Rs., 1953.

ADDRESSES: Home—5855 Dalridge Hill N.W., Calgary, Alberta, Canada T3A 1M1. *Office*—Department of

Economics, University of Calgary, 2500 University Dr. N.W., Calgary, Alberta, Canada T2N 1N4.

CAREER: Czechoslovak Ministry of Foreign Affairs, Czechoslovak Embassy, Vienna, Austria, 1949-51; Charles University, Prague, Czechoslovakia, assistant, 1959-63, docent in political economy, 1963-68; McGill University, Montreal, Quebec, visiting associate professor of economics, 1968-69; University of Calgary, Alberta, professor, 1969-88, professor emeritus of economics, 1988—.

MEMBER: American Association for the Advancement of Slavic Studies, Canadian Association of Slavists, British Association for Soviet and East European Studies.

WRITINGS:

Wage, Price, Taxation Policies in Czechoslovakia: 1948-1970, Duncker & Humbolt, 1974.
Wage Control and Inflation in Soviet Bloc Countries, Macmillan, 1979, Praeger, 1980.
(Editor) *Employment Policies in the Soviet Union and Eastern Europe,* St. Martin's, 1982, 2nd revised edition, 1987.
Employment and Wage Policies in Poland, Czechoslovakia, and Hungary since 1950, St. Martin's, 1984.
Economic Reforms in the Soviet Union and Eastern Europe since the 1960s, St. Martin's, 1989.
(Editor) *Economic Reforms and Welfare Systems in the U.S.S.R., Poland, and Hungary,* St. Martin's, 1991.

WORK IN PROGRESS: "I am in the process of finishing a book on the development of theoretical views on planning and market in the U.S.S.R. and East European countries since the 1960s. I am also involved in gathering materials for a new book on the causes of the collapse of the socialist system in Eastern Europe."

BIOGRAPHICAL/CRITICAL SOURCES:

PERIODICALS

Times Literary Supplement, January 10, 1986, p. 31.

*   *   *

AHLBERG, Allan 1938-

PERSONAL: Born June 5, 1938, in England; married Janet Hall (an illustrator), July, 1969; children: Jessica. *Education:* Sunderland Teacher Training College, Certificate in Education.

ADDRESSES: Home—Leicester, England. *Agent*—Penguin Books Ltd., 27 Wrights Lane, London W8 5TZ, England.

CAREER: Worked at various jobs, including postman, soldier, grave digger, schoolteacher, and plumber's mate; writer, 1975—.

AWARDS, HONORS: Commendation from Library Association (England), 1977, for *Burglar Bill;* Kate Greenaway Medal from Library Association (England), 1979, selected by the Notable Children's Book Committee of the Association for Library Service to Children, 1979, and named to the International Board on Books for Young People (IBBY) 1980 Honors List, all for *Each Peach Pear Plum: An "I Spy" Story;* Other Award from Children's Rights Workshop, 1980, for *Mrs. Plug the Plumber;* Best Books of the Year Award, *School Library Journal,* 1981, for *Funnybones; Peek-a-boo!* was a 1981 selection of the Notable Children's Book Committee of the Association for Library Service to Children, and recipient of *Parents Magazine* Best Book for Babies Award, 1985; commendation from Library Association (Great Britain), 1982, Best Books of the Year Award, *School Library Journal,* 1983, Teacher's Choice Award, National Council of Teachers of English, 1983, and citation, Notable Children's Book Committee of the Association for Library Service to Children, 1983, all for *The Baby's Catalogue;* Emil/Kurt Maschler Award, 1986, Children's Book Award of the Federation of Children's Book Groups, 1986, Golden Key (Holland), 1987, Prix du Livre pour la Jeunesse (France), 1987, all for *The Jolly Postman; or, Other Peoples Letters;* Silver Paint Brush (Holland), 1988, for *Funnybones;* Signal Poetry Award, 1990, for *Heard It on the Playground.*

WRITINGS:

FOR CHILDREN; ILLUSTRATED BY WIFE, JANET AHLBERG

The Old Joke Book, Kestrel Books, 1976, Viking, 1977.
Burglar Bill, Greenwillow, 1977.
The Vanishment of Thomas Tull, Scribner, 1977.
Jeremiah in the Dark Woods, Kestrel Books, 1977, Viking, 1978.
The One and Only Two Heads, Collins, 1979.
Two Wheels, Two Heads, Collins, 1979.
Son of a Gun, Heinemann, 1979.
Little Worm Book, Granada, 1979, Viking, 1980.
Funnybones, Heinemann, 1980, Greenwillow, 1981.
The Ha Ha Bonk Book, Penguin, 1982.
The Baby's Catalogue, Kestrel Books, 1982.
The Jolly Postman; or, Other People's Letters, Little, Brown, 1986.
The Cinderella Show, Viking, 1986, Penguin, 1987.
The Clothes Horse and Other Stories, Penguin, 1987.
Starting School, Penguin, 1988.
Bye Bye Baby, Little, Brown, 1989.
The Jolly Christmas Postman, Little, Brown, 1991.
The Bear Nobody Wanted, Penguin, in press.
It Was a Dark and Stormy Night, Penguin, in press.

CHILDREN'S VERSE

Cops and Robbers, illustrated by J. Ahlberg, Heinemann, 1978, Greenwillow, 1979.
Each Peach Pear Plum: An "I Spy" Story, illustrated by J. Ahlberg, Kestrel Books, 1978, Viking, 1979.
Peek-a-boo!, illustrated by J. Ahlberg, Viking, 1981 (published in England as *Peepo!,* Kestrel Books, 1981).
Please Mrs. Butler (see also below), illustrated by Fritz Wegner, Kestrel Books, 1983.
The Mighty Slide, illustrated by Charlotte Voake, Penguin, 1988.
Heard It in the Playground (see also below), illustrated by Wegner, Viking, 1989.

"BRICK STREET BOYS" SERIES; ILLUSTRATED BY WIFE JANET AHLBERG

Here Are the Brick Street Boys, Collins, 1975.
A Place to Play, Collins, 1975.
Sam the Referee, Collins, 1975.
Fred's Dream, Collins, 1976.
The Great Marathon Football Match, Collins, 1976.

"DAISYCHAIN" SERIES

Ready, Teddy, Go!, illustrated by J. Ahlberg, Heinemann, 1983.
Summer Snowman, illustrated by J. Ahlberg, Heinemann, 1983.
That's My Baby, illustrated by J. Ahlberg, Heinemann, 1983.
Which Witch?, illustrated by J. Ahlberg, Heinemann, 1983.
Clowning About, illustrated by Andre Amstutz, Heinemann, 1984.
The Good Old Dolls, illustrated by Amstutz, Heinemann, 1984.
Monster Munch, illustrated by Amstutz, Heinemann, 1984.
Rent-a-Robot, illustrated by Amstutz, Heinemann, 1984.
One True Santa, illustrated by J. Ahlberg, Heinemann, 1985.

"FOLDAWAYS" SERIES; ILLUSTRATED BY COLIN MCNAUGHTON

Circus, Granada, 1984.
Families, Granada, 1984.
Monsters, Granada, 1984.
Zoo, Granada, 1984.

"FUNNYBONES" SERIES; ILLUSTRATED BY ANDRE AMSTUTZ

The Black Cat, Heinemann, 1990.
The Pet Shop, Heinemann, 1990.
Dinosaur Dreams, Heinemann, 1991.
Mystery Tour, Heinemann, 1991.
Skeleton Crew, Heinemann, 1991.

Bumps in the Night, Heinemann, 1991.
Give the Dog a Bone, Heinemann, 1991.
The Ghost Train, Heinemann, in press.

"HAPPY FAMILY" SERIES

Mr. Biff the Boxer, illustrated by J. Ahlberg, Puffin, 1980, published in "Wacky Family" series, Western Publishing, 1982.
Mr. Cosmo the Conjuror, illustrated by Joe Wright, Puffin, 1980.
Miss Jump the Jockey, illustrated by Amstutz, Puffin, 1980.
Master Salt the Sailor's Son, illustrated by Amstutz, Puffin, 1980, published in "Wacky Family" series, Western Publishing, 1982.
Mrs. Plug the Plumber, illustrated by Wright, Puffin, 1980, published in "Wacky Family" series, Western Publishing, 1982.
Mrs. Wobble the Waitress, illustrated by J. Ahlberg, Puffin, 1980.
Miss Brick the Builder's Baby, illustrated by McNaughton, Puffin, 1981, published in "Wacky Family" series, Western Publishing, 1982.
Mr. Buzz the Beeman, illustrated by Faith Jaques, Puffin, 1981, published in "Wacky Family" series, Western Publishing, 1982.
Mr. and Mrs. Hay the Horse, illustrated by McNaughton, Puffin, 1981, published in "Wacky Family" series, Western Publishing, 1982.
Mrs. Lather's Laundry, illustrated by Amstutz, Puffin, 1981, published in "Wacky Family" series, Western Publishing, 1982.
Master Money the Millionaire, illustrated by Amstutz, Puffin, 1981.
Mr. Tick the Teacher, illustrated by Jaques, Puffin, 1981.
Master Bun the Baker's Boy, illustrated by Wegner, Puffin, 1988.
Mr. Creep the Crook, illustrated by Amstutz, Puffin, 1988.
Miss Dose the Doctor's Daughter, illustrated by Jaques, 1988.
Mrs. Jolly's Joke Shop, illustrated by McNaughton, Puffin, 1988.

"HELP YOUR CHILD TO READ" SERIES

Bad Bear, illustrated by Eric Hill, Granada, 1982.
Double Ducks, illustrated by Hill, Granada, 1982.
Fast Frogs, illustrated by Hill, Granada, 1982.
Poorly Pigs, illustrated by Hill, Granada, 1982.
Rubber Rabbit, illustrated by Hill, Granada, 1982.
Silly Sheep, illustrated by Hill, Granada, 1982.
Hip-Hippo-Ray, illustrated by Amstutz, Granada, 1983.
King Kangaroo, illustrated by Amstutz, Granada, 1983.
Mister Wolf, illustrated by Amstutz, Granada, 1983.
Spider Spy, illustrated by Amstutz, Granada, 1983.

Tell-Tale Tiger, illustrated by Amstutz, Granada, 1983.
Travelling Moose, illustrated by Amstutz, Granada, 1983.

"RED NOSE READERS" SERIES; ILLUSTRATED BY COLIN McNAUGHTON

Bear's Birthday, Walker Books, 1985.
Big Bad Pig, Walker Books, 1985.
Fe Fi Fo Fum, Walker Books, 1985.
Happy Worm, Walker Books, 1985.
Help!, Walker Books, 1985.
Jumping, Walker Books, 1985.
Make a Face, Walker Books, 1985.
So Can I, Walker Books, 1985.
Blow Me Down!, Walker Books, 1986.
Crash! Bang! Wallop!, Walker Books, 1986.
Look Out for the Seals!, Walker Books, 1986.
Me and My Friend, Walker Books, 1986.
One, Two, Flea!, Walker Books, 1986.
Push the Dog, Walker Books, 1986.
Shirley's Shops, Walker Books, 1986.
Tell Us a Story, Walker Books, 1986.

"SLOT BOOKS" SERIES; ILLUSTRATED BY JANET AHLBERG

Playmates, Viking Kestrel, 1984.
Yum, Yum, Viking Kestrel, 1984.

OTHER

(With John Lawrence) *The History of a Pair of Sinners: Forgetting Not Their Ma Who Was One Also* (verse), Granada, 1981.
Ten in a Bed (stories for children), illustrated by Amstutz, Granada, 1983.
Woof! (novel), illustrated by Wegner, Penguin, 1986.
Mrs. Butler Song Book (based on poems from *Please Mrs. Butler* and *Heard It in the Playground*), music by Colin Matthews, illustrations by Wegner, Viking, in press.

ADAPTATIONS: Several of Allan and Janet Ahlberg's books have been adapted for audiocassette, including *A Place to Play, Fred's Dream,* and *Each Peach Pear Plum.*

WORK IN PROGRESS: The Giant's Baby, a book for children.

SIDELIGHTS: Janet and Allan Ahlberg are something of an anomaly within the realm of children's book publishing, and their mercurial ride to popularity is a testimony to the dedication with which they apply themselves to their chosen profession. While some authors of children's books fall into anonymity relative to the characters which they create, the Ahlbergs are well-recognized by most young bookworms throughout England and the United States. Recently, they found themselves unwittingly propelled into legitimate respectability in their native England when seven of their books were included among a list of fifty-one titles which the British government recommended as preparation for national curriculum tests. To be considered, according to a London *Times* contributor, "[both] comic and naughty," and still merit the approval of educators, shows that the Ahlbergs take their responsibility to their young audience seriously, yet not *too* seriously.

Both Janet and Allan Ahlberg went to school with the intention of being schoolteachers. Before his entry into Teachers College at the age of twenty-five, Allan filled his time with various jobs, such as postman, gravedigger, and plumber's mate, rounding out a life-experience that would be reflected in his later writing. After completing his own education, he taught at the primary school level for over ten years. Janet, on the other hand, discovered that she had little aptitude for the demands of teaching and though she completed her certificate in education, under the encouragement of one of her lecturers, Charles Bray, she went on to develop her abilities in drawing and painting by studying graphic design for three more years. The Ahlbergs were now married, and while Allan continued to teach, Janet did free-lance designing of educational visual-aids for another few years, until they made the decision to combine her talent for children's illustration with Allan's long-harbored desire to write. For eighteen months the Ahlbergs put all their energy into creating picture books, but received only rejection slips. They refused to give up on their creative partnership, knowing that they had the capability of producing better books than those they found on the shelves at local booksellers. The couple was close to running out of money to support themselves, necessitating Allan's return to teaching, when the "Brick Street Boys" series was accepted for publication by Collins. Published books authored by the Ahlbergs followed thereafter in rapid succession, and Janet and Allan have since produced more than one hundred books for children between them.

After the Ahlbergs moved to their current home bordering a quiet Leicestershire village, a way of working evolved that has taken into account the divergent aspects of their partnership. Allan is at his most creative in the early morning, and repairs to a converted garden shed to do his writing, while Janet begins her studio work later in the day. However, there is a great deal of interaction between author and illustrator. As Allan says in Douglas Martin's *The Telling Line*, "The story flows from the words into the pictures and back again. The story in the pictures is a counterpoint . . . to the story in the words." The couple tosses around ideas for new books together, with Allan proposing rough outlines, and then starting work on a full text if Janet likes the idea. He also contributes ideas for pictorial jokes and visual suggestions, but

the unwritten story is hers to bring to life with her whimsical line-drawings and watercolor washes.

"Children's books may not be a major art form, but they are not trivial or insignificant," says Allan in the London *Times*. One of the many unique aspects of the Ahlbergs' partnership is the great attention to detail that they bring to their work, and which extends to a relatively comprehensive understanding of the many steps involved in the business of book production, an industry which has become quite sophisticated over the past several years. From creating the book 'dummy' and deciding upon the visual interplay between illustration and text, to the selection of paper, novel design elements (such as punch-outs or bound-in envelopes) and typeface, the Ahlbergs' use of new technology has been, according to Martin, "restrained and individual." An innovative illustrator, Janet employs a great deal of hand-lettered elements within her drawings, and her illustrations are characterized by their use of margin artwork, which threads through or clusters around hand-lettered texts, sometimes replacing words altogether. "There are precedents for a lot of these techniques in children's books from many lands and long ago," Martin continues, "but the Ahlbergs have combined and added to them with great virtuosity and inventiveness, bringing fresh variations and insights to each subsequent book."

The first books that the Ahlbergs produced were parodies of "Dick and Jane" readers, which they designed to assist older children with reading difficulties who did not want to be stigmatized for reading "baby books." "Here is Sam. Here is Fred. Here is the ball. Fred kicks the ball. Sam kicks the ball. Fred kicks Sam. Here is the referee" reads the text of one of the "Brick Street Boys" books. As the *Times* contributor notes, "[The books by the Ahlbergs] are also refreshingly free from the standards of the po-faced ideologues who pontificate on children's books." Whether they are writing fanciful children's stories of their own creation, such as *The Vanishment of Thomas Tull* and *Burglar Bill,* or parodying the conventions of established genres and the fairy tale tradition of wicked witches, dark forests, and beautiful princesses, as in *Ten in a Bed* and *Jeremiah in the Dark Woods,* the Ahlbergs invoke a warm, humorous nostalgia in their books. In Allan Ahlberg's collection of poems for junior school children, *Heard It in the Playground,* the setting is a primary school with no real sense of period, but full of observed details—wooden coat-pegs, marbles, the broad expanse of polished hallway floors, the class hamster—that render it timeless and never-changing. In the *Times Literary Supplement,* George Szirtes describes the setting as "a stage we pass through in which the differences between individual lives are reduced and blurred. We are communal but nuclear; we the class, we the teachers, and we the parents waiting at the school gates. Ahlberg's sympathy extends to all three sides in the eternal triangle." That quality of nostalgia is also reflected in the illustrations accompanying the texts, whether drawn by Janet, or by one of the other artists with whom the couple works on certain projects for the sake of variety, such as Andre Amstutz, Colin McNaughton, Faith Jaques, Eric Hill, and Fritz Wegner. Commenting on the book *Bye Bye Baby* for example, Toronto *Globe and Mail* critic Elizabeth MacCallum describes Janet Ahlberg's contribution as "winning illustrations, with light airy watercolors of postwar England, when social roles were still well-defined."

Although many of the ideas for their stories come from recollections of their own childhoods and experiences, sometimes existing circumstances come into play and a story is born. For example, the idea for the book *Starting School* grew out of a booklet that the couple had drafted under the guidance of a staff member at their daughter Jessica's school, for use by the parents of newly-enrolling students. Similarly, one of the Ahlberg's most popular books thus far, *The Jolly Postman; or, Other People's Letters,* was inspired by Jessica Ahlberg's babyhood fascination with putting bits of paper in and out of envelopes.

However inspirations come to Allan and Janet Ahlberg, their ability to relate to a child's perception of the world, with humor and a bit of irreverence, has made them one of the most popular of "bookmakers" for young people. As Aiden Chambers writes in *Horn Book,* "Their books are dramatic, not because they pack them with thrills and spills or popeyed goings on but because they know how to select from life and make a pattern of what they select that changes everydayness from dull routine to an excitement."

BIOGRAPHICAL/CRITICAL SOURCES:

BOOKS

Martin, Douglas, *The Telling Line,* Julia MacRae Books, 1989, pp. 264-78.

PERIODICALS

Commonweal, November 11, 1977.
Globe and Mail (Toronto), July 14, 1990.
Horn Book, December, 1982.
Los Angeles Times Book Review, May 31, 1981.
New Statesman, November 28, 1975; November 21, 1980; December 4, 1981; December 3, 1982.
New York Times Book Review, April 10, 1977; April 22, 1979; April 29, 1979; May 20, 1979; March 1, 1981; August 14, 1988, p. 28; February 11, 1990, p. 23.
Observer, July 19, 1981; December 6, 1981.
Punch, November 17, 1982.
Saturday Review, May 28, 1977; May 26, 1979.
Spectator, July 16, 1977.

Times (London), March 5, 1980; November 29, 1986; October 1, 1988; March 8, 1991, p. 18.
Times Educational Supplement, November 23, 1979; January 18, 1980; March 7, 1980; June 20, 1980, November 21, 1980; January 2, 1981; July 24, 1981; November 20, 1981; November 19, 1982; March 11, 1983; June 3, 1983; September 30, 1983.
Times Literary Supplement, March 25, 1977; December 1, 1978; March 28, 1980; November 21, 1980; September 18, 1981; March 26, 1982; November 26, 1982; July 22, 1983; November 30, 1984; August 15, 1986, p. 898; November 28, 1986, p. 1345; April 3, 1987, p. 357; October 9, 1987, p. 1120; April 1, 1988, p. 368; September 9, 1988, p. 1000; November 24, 1989, p. 1310.
Tribune Books (Chicago), November 16, 1986, p. 4.
Washington Post Book World, February 11, 1979.

—*Sketch by Pamela Shelton*

*   *   *

AITMATOV, Chingiz (Torekulovich)   1928-

PERSONAL: Born December 12, 1928, in Sheker Village, Kirghizia, U.S.S.R. (now Kyrgyzstan); son of Torekul and Nahima Aitmatov; married; wife's name, Keres (a physician); children: three sons and one daughter. *Education:* Received degree in animal husbandry from Kirghiz Agricultural Institute; attended Moscow Literary Institute of the Union of Soviet Writers.

ADDRESSES: Home—43 Dzerzhinsky Flat 1, Frunze, Kyrgyzstan. *Office*—c/o Kirghiz Branch of the Union of Writers, Ulitsa Pushkina 52, Frunze, Kyrgyzstan.

CAREER: Novelist, short story writer, and playwright, 1952—. Communist Party of the Soviet Union, assistant to the secretary of Sheker Village Soviet, c. 1943, member, beginning in 1959. People's Writer of Kirghiz Soviet Socialist Republic, 1968. Candidate member of Central Committee of Kirghiz Soviet Socialist Republic; vice-chairman of committee of Solidarity with Peoples of Asian and African Countries; deputy of U.S.S.R. Supreme Soviet. Cinema Union of Kirghiz Soviet Socialist Republic, first secretary, 1964-69, chairman, beginning in 1969.

MEMBER: World Academy of Art and Science, European Academy of Arts, Science, and Humanity.

AWARDS, HONORS: Lenin Prize for literature and the fine arts, 1963, for *Povesti gor i stepei;* Order of the Red Banner of Labor (twice); U.S.S.R. State Prize, 1968, for *Proshchai, Gulsary!;* Hero of Socialist Labor, 1978.

WRITINGS:

IN ENGLISH TRANSLATION

Dzhamilia (novel), Pravda, 1959, translation published as *Jamila,* Foreign Languages Publishing House (Moscow).

Povesti gor i stepei, Sovetskii Pisatel, 1963, translation published as *Tales of the Mountains and Steppes,* Progress Publishers, 1969.

Proshchai, Gulsary! (novella), Molodia Guardiia, 1967, translation by John French published as *Farewell, Gulsary!,* Hodder & Stoughton, 1970.

Posle skazki, Belyi parokhod (novel), 1970, translation by Mirra Ginsburg published as *The White Steamship,* Crown, 1972, translation by Tatyana Feifer and George Feifer published in England as *The White Steamship,* Hodder & Stoughton, 1972.

(With Kaltai Mukhamedzhanov) *Voskhozhdenie na Fudzhiamu* (play; produced in Moscow, 1973; produced as "The Ascent of Mount Fuji" in Washington, D.C., 1975), translation by Nicholas Bethell published as *The Ascent of Mount Fuji,* Farrar, Straus, 1975.

The Day Lasts More than a Hundred Years, translated by John French, Macdonald, 1983.

The Cranes Fly Early, translation by Eve Manning, Imported Publications, 1983.

(With others) *You Have to Treat Your Heart,* Imported Publications, 1986.

A Time to Speak, International Publishing, 1989.

The Place of the Skull (novel), translated by Natasha Ward, Grove, 1989.

Also author of *Tri povesti* (novel), translation published as *Short Novels,* Progress Publishers.

OTHER

Rasskazy (title means "Stories"), Sovetskii Pisatel, 1958.

Verbliuzhii glaz (short stories and novellas; title means "The Camel's Eye"), Sovetskii Pisatel, 1962.

Materinskoe Pole (novel; title means "The Field of Mothers"), Pravda, 1963.

Samanchy zholu (short stories and novellas), Basmasy, 1963.

Povesti (title means "Novellas"), Izvestia, 1967.

Pervyi uchitel (novel; title means "The First Master"), Detskaia Literatura, 1967.

Atadan kalgan tuiak, Mektep, 1970.

Povesti i rasskazy (title means "Novellas and Stories"), Molodaia Guardiia, 1970.

Pegil pes, begushchij kraem moria, Sovetskii Pisatel, 1977.

V soavtostve s zemleiu i vodoiu (essays and lectures), Kyrgyzstan, 1978.

Contributor of articles to *Pravda* and other major newspapers and periodicals.

SIDELIGHTS: Unlike such dissident Soviet writers as Solzhenitsyn and Tsabour, Chingiz Aitmatov has managed to remain in the U.S.S.R. and write of life in the republic of his birth, Kirghizia. A member of one of the Soviet Union's central Asian minorities, he is the first Kirghiz author to become known outside the U.S.S.R. Several of his books have been translated into French, German, Polish, English, and Arabic editions. His work has also been the focus of several Soviet films. His play, *The Ascent of Mount Fuji,* is probably his most famous work in the West. His novella, *Farewell, Gulsary!* and novel *The White Steamship* have also received favorable critical attention outside his homeland.

Surprising to many readers in the Western world, although he has been critical of the Soviet government, Aitmatov has always remained an active and prominent member of the Communist party. "Aitmatov himself is an impressive but curious figure," points out Bohdan Nahaylo in the *Spectator.* "Over the years he has gone further than most Soviet writers in condemning the horrors of the Stalin era and examining social, cultural and philosophical questions raised by the Soviet experience. Despite his reputation as a bold and independently minded 'liberal', he has skillfully managed to avoid getting into serious trouble and has risen to the heights of the Soviet establishment."

Aitmatov's style of drawing heavily on folklore and parables to present his ideas may be one reason his writings have not put him in disfavor with his government and party. As *Newsweek*'s Jay Axelbank noted, Aitmatov "tries to steer clear of political ideology and concentrate on psychological portraits" in his writing. He incorporates aspects of the Kirghiz oral tradition into the reality of Soviet society and culture.

One of the best examples of this quality of Aitmatov's work is to be found in *Farewell, Gulsary!* This novella recounts the story of an old draughthorse, once a magnificent steed, and his aged master, Tanabai. The tale is strongly reminiscent of the old oral epics that focus on the cultural importance of horses and horseback riding. As Gulsary and his master contemplate their shared past, Aitmatov illustrates the interwoven destinies of man and animal, the concordance of man and nature so vital to the Kirghiz oral heritage. The horse suffers a long, agonizing death which prompts deep soul-searching in his master. In the end, Tanabai accepts the passing of his old companion and the passing of the old days.

Underlying Aitmatov's support of the Soviet system is a strong determination to uphold the freedom of artistic expression. "Clearly among the things he believes," said

Frank Getlein of *Commonweal,* "is the efficacy of facing facts, however unpleasant." These two aspects of Aitmatov's character have led him, occasionally, to violate certain literary taboos of the Soviet state. In *The White Ship,* for example, Aitmatov depicts the suicide of a seven-year-old boy who becomes despondent after witnessing the brutal slaying and consumption of a rare deer.

Some Soviet readers were offended by the pessimism of the story, and the outcry against it prompted the author to defend his artistic integrity in the *Literaturnaya Gazeta.* Countering suggested changes in the tale, Aitmatov was quoted in the *New York Times:* "I had a choice, either to write or not to write the story. And if to write it, then only as I did." The author also asserted that evil is inexorable and, lacking the capacity to overcome the adult evil surrounding him, the boy had to sacrifice his life or his childhood ideals. As Rosemarie Keiffer explained in *Books Abroad,* Aitmatov intended to provoke thought by allowing the young protagonist to take his own life: "The boy's fate is aimed at elucidating certain human faults: Who has been faithful to the most positive of childhood dreams? Who has measured up to the moral aspirations of adolescence? Who has remained truthful in his relations with children? Aitmatov does not pretend here to teach men how to live up to their most cherished and human ideals, only to prick their consciences with the disparities between those ideals and the realities of most people's lives."

Another of Aitmatov's more daring and well-known works is *The Ascent of Mount Fuji,* a play he co-authored with Kaltai Mukhamedzhanov, another native of Kirghizia. This drama caused a sensation when it premiered in Moscow in 1973 because it openly treats the delicate subject of Soviet suppression of dissidents. The drama does not recount the many horrors suffered by dissidents in the Soviet state; instead, it is a psychological study of betrayal and quiescence. Four old schoolmates meet on a mountaintop to renew their friendship but find they must first confront and reconcile the absence of a fifth friend, Sabur, a poet who questioned some Red Army tactics. Sabur had been betrayed by one of his four friends while the other three remained silent. Each must now acknowledge his own portion of guilt in the case. "The authors, both members of minority republics in the U.S.S.R., conceivably had in mind the wartime arrest of Solzhenitsyn when writing their drama," notes a reviewer for *Publishers Weekly.* "Severe underwriting fills the drama with overtones that suggest what may, or should, trouble the Russian soul today." And a reviewer for *Library Journal* comments that "what is particularly absorbing, however, is the questioning attitude the authors take toward such issues as atheism, scientific research, and the necessity of war."

Assessing Aitmatov's appeal for both Western and Eastern readers, Rosemarie Keiffer declared: "Like the classi-

cal poets and epic bards, he is a patriot and a historian of his nation. He is an ardent lover of life and nature, possesses a deep understanding of such varied human passions as love and despair, admires the Leninist society's ideals of order and progress, and is optimistic about that society's potential for bringing prosperity to his native region. And permeating all his writing is a serene harmony between past and present, between man and nature, between joy and sadness, a spirit which unequivocally condemns such aberrations of the human ideal as war or personal cruelty but which also holds to the hope that such ideals will at least endure and possibly one day even be attained."

BIOGRAPHICAL/CRITICAL SOURCES:

PERIODICALS

Books Abroad, summer, 1975.
Commonweal, July 18, 1975.
Globe and Mail (Toronto), July 8, 1989.
Library Journal, August, 1975.
Los Angeles Times Book Review, June 18, 1989.
Newsweek, June 24, 1974; June 30, 1975.
New York Times, July 30, 1970; May 6, 1989.
New York Times Book Review, April 30, 1989.
Publishers Weekly, June 9, 1975.
Spectator, November 5, 1983.
Times (London), August 18, 1983.
Times Literary Supplement, June 26, 1987.
UNESCO Courier, October, 1972.*

* * *

ALBAUM, Gerald (Sherwin) 1933-

PERSONAL: Born November 2, 1933, in Los Angeles, CA; son of Leslie and Edith (Elster) Albaum; married Carol Weinstein, October 10, 1954; children: Marc, Lisa, Daniel. *Education:* University of Washington, Seattle, B.A., 1954, M.B.A., 1958; University of Wisconsin, Ph.D., 1962. *Religion:* Jewish.

ADDRESSES: Home—720 Fair Oaks Dr., Eugene, OR 97401. *Office*—College of Business Administration, University of Oregon, Eugene, OR 97403.

CAREER: University of Wisconsin—Madison, instructor in marketing, 1960-62; University of Pittsburgh, Pittsburgh, PA, assistant professor of marketing, 1962-64; University of Arizona, Tucson, associate professor of marketing, 1964-67; University of Massachusetts—Amherst, associate professor of marketing, 1967-69; University of Oregon, Eugene, associate professor, 1969-72, professor of marketing, 1972—. University of Hawaii, visiting associate professor, 1968-69, visiting professor of marketing,

1971; visiting professor of marketing, Arizona State University, 1976, University of Texas at Austin, 1983; Institute for Constructive Capitalism, University of Texas at Austin, senior research fellow, 1984—; visiting professor, Institute of International Economics and Management, Copenhagen Business School, Denmark, 1986, 1989, University of Auckland, New Zealand, 1988, Helsinki School of Economics and Business Administration, Finland, 1990, Bilkent University, Turkey, 1990, University of Technology, Sydney, Australia, 1991, University of Aalborg, Denmark, 1991. *Military service:* U.S. Army, 1954-56.

MEMBER: Academy of International Business, American Marketing Association, Association for Consumer Research, Academy of Marketing Science.

WRITINGS:

(Editor with J. H. Westing) *Modern Marketing Thought,* Macmillan, 1964, 3rd edition, 1975.
Price Formulation, Division of Economics and Business Research, University of Arizona, 1965.
(With F. L. W. Richardson) *Human Interaction and Sales Success,* Division of Economics and Business Research, University of Arizona, 1967.
(With Gordon E. Miracle) *International Marketing Management,* Irwin, 1970.
(Editor with M. Venkatesan) *Scientific Marketing Research,* Free Press, 1971.
(With Donald S. Tull) *Survey Research: A Decisional Approach,* Intext, 1973.
(Editor with Gilbert A. Churchill, Jr.) *Critical Issues in Sales Management: State-of-the-Art and Future Research Needs,* Division of Research, College of Business Administration, University of Oregon, 1979.
(With Paul E. Green and Tull) *Research for Marketing Decisions,* 5th edition, Prentice-Hall, 1988.
(With J. Strandskov, E. Duerr, and L. Dowd) *International Marketing and Export Management,* Addison-Wesley, 1989.
(With R. Peterson and G. Kozmetsky) *Modern American Capitalism,* Quorum Books, 1990.

Contributor of articles to marketing, management, and social science journals.

WORK IN PROGRESS: Studying research methodology and international activities of business organizations.

*   *   *

ALEXANDER, Lloyd (Chudley) 1924-

PERSONAL: Born January 30, 1924, in Philadelphia, PA; son of Alan Audley (a stockbroker and importer) and Edna (Chudley) Alexander; married Janine Denni, January 8, 1946; children: Madeleine (Mrs. Zohair Khalil). *Education:* Attended West Chester State Teachers College, 1942; Lafayette College, 1943; and Sorbonne, University of Paris, 1946. *Avocational interests:* Music (particularly violin, piano, and guitar), printmaking.

ADDRESSES: Home—1005 Drexel Ave., Drexel Hill, PA 19026. *Agent*—Brandt & Brandt, 1501 Broadway, New York, NY 10036.

CAREER: Author of children's books; free-lance writer and translator, 1946—. Author-in-residence, Temple University, 1970-74. Also worked as cartoonist, layout artist, advertising copywriter, and editor of an industrial magazine. *Military service:* U.S. Army, Intelligence, 1943-46; became staff sergeant.

MEMBER: Authors Guild, Authors League of America, PEN, Amnesty International, Carpenter Lane Chamber Music Society (member of board of directors).

AWARDS, HONORS: Isaac Siegel Memorial Juvenile Award, 1959, for *Border Hawk: August Bondi;* notable book citation, American Library Association (ALA), 1964, for *The Book of Three;* Newbery Honor Book, ALA, 1965, for *The Black Cauldron;* "Best Books" citations, *School Library Journal,* 1967, for *Taran Wanderer,* 1971, for *The King's Fountain,* and 1982, for *Westmark;* citation from American Institute of Graphic Arts Children's Books, 1967-68, for *The Truthful Harp;* "Children's Book of the Year" citation, Child Study Association of America, 1968, for *The High King,* 1971, for *The King's Fountain,* 1973, for *The Cat Who Wished to Be A Man,* 1974, for *The Foundling and Other Tales of Prydain,* 1975, for *The Wizard in the Tree,* 1982, for *The Kestrel,* and 1985, for *The Black Cauldron* and *Time Cat;* Newbery Medal, ALA, and National Book Award nomination, both 1969, both for *The High King;* "Best Books of the Year" citation, Library of Congress, 1970, and National Book Award, 1971, both for *The Marvelous Misadventures of Sebastian;* Drexel Award, 1972 and 1976, for outstanding contributions to literature for children; *Boston Globe-Horn Book* Award, 1973, for *The Cat Who Wished to Be a Man;* "Outstanding Books of the Year" citation, *New York Times,* 1973, for *The Foundling and Other Tales of Prydain;* Laura Ingalls Wilder Award nomination, 1975; CRABbery Award, Oxon Hill Branch of Prince George's County Library (Maryland), 1979, National Book Award nomination, 1979, Silver Pencil Award, 1981, and Austrian Children's Book Award, 1984, all for *The First Two Lives of Lukas-Kasha.*

American Book Award nomination, 1980, for *The High King,* and 1982, for *The Wizard in the Tree;* "Best Books for Young Adults" citation, ALA, 1981, for *Westmark,* 1982, for *The Kestrel,* and 1984, for *The Beggar Queen;*

American Book Award, 1982, for *Westmark;* Parents' Choice Award, 1982, for *The Kestrel,* 1984, for *The Beggar Queen,* and 1986, for *The Illyrian Adventure;* Golden Cat Award, Sjoestrands Foerlag (Sweden), 1984, for excellence in children's literature; Regina Medal, Catholic Library Association, 1986; Church and Synagogue Library Association Award, 1987; Field Award, Pennsylvania Library Association, 1987, for *The Illyrian Adventure;* Lifetime Achievement Award, Pennsylvania Center for The Book in Philadelphia, 1991.

WRITINGS:

And Let the Credit Go, Crowell, 1955.
My Five Tigers, Crowell, 1956.
Janine Is French, Crowell, 1958.
My Love Affair with Music, Crowell, 1960.
(With Louis Camuti) *Park Avenue Vet,* Holt, 1962.
Fifty Years in the Doghouse, Putnam, 1963 (published in England as *Send for Ryan!,* W. H. Allen, 1965).
My Cats and Me: The Story of an Understanding, Running Press, 1989.

JUVENILES

Border Hawk: August Bondi (biography), Farrar, Straus, 1959.
Aaron Lopez and Flagship Hope (biography), Farrar, Straus, 1960.
Time Cat: The Remarkable Journeys of Jason and Gareth, Holt, 1963 (published in England as *Nine Lives,* Cassell, 1963).
Coll and His White Pig, Holt, 1965.
The Truthful Harp, Holt, 1967.
The Marvelous Misadventures of Sebastian, Dutton, 1970.
The King's Fountain, Dutton, 1971.
The Four Donkeys, Holt, 1972.
The Foundling and Other Tales of Prydain, Holt, 1973.
The Cat Who Wished to Be a Man, Dutton, 1973.
The Wizard in the Tree, Dutton, 1975.
The Town Cats and Other Tales, Dutton, 1977.
The First Two Lives of Lukas-Kasha, Dutton, 1978.
The Remarkable Journey of Prince Jen, Dutton, 1991.
The Fortune-tellers, Dutton, 1992.

THE "PRYDAIN CHRONICLES" SERIES

The Book of Three, Holt, 1964.
The Black Cauldron, Holt, 1965.
The Castle of Llyr, Holt, 1966.
Taran Wanderer, Holt, 1967.
The High King, Holt, 1968.

THE WESTMARK TRILOGY

Westmark, Dutton, 1981.
The Kestrel, Dutton, 1982.
The Beggar Queen, Dutton, 1984.

THE VESPER HOLLY ADVENTURES

The Illyrian Adventure, Dutton, 1986.
The El Dorado Adventure, Dutton, 1987.
The Drackenberg Adventure, Dutton, 1988.
The Jedera Adventure, Dutton, 1989.
The Philadelphia Adventure, Dutton, 1990.

TRANSLATOR FROM THE FRENCH

Jean-Paul Sartre, *The Wall and Other Stories,* New Directions, 1948, published as *Intimacy and Other Stories,* Peter Nevill, 1949, New Directions, 1952.
Sartre, *Nausea,* New Directions, 1949 (published in England as *The Diary of Antoine Roquentin,* Lehmann, 1949).
Paul Eluard, *Selected Writings,* New Directions, 1951, published as *Uninterrupted Poetry: Selected Writings,* 1975.
Paul Vialar, *The Sea Rose,* Neville Spearman, 1951.

CONTRIBUTOR

Elinor Whitney Field, editor, *Horn Book Reflections on Children's Books and Reading,* Horn Book, 1969.
Cricket's Choice, Open Court, 1974.
Betsy Hearne and Marilyn Kaye, editors, *Celebrating Children's Books,* Lothrop, 1981.
Barbara Harrison and Gregory Macguire, editors, *Innocence and Experience,* Lothrop, 1987.
Charlotte F. Otten and Gary D. Schmidt, editors, *The Voice of the Narrator in Children's Literature,* Greenwood, 1989.
Ann Durell and Margaret Sachs, editors, *The Big Book for Peace,* Dutton, 1990.

OTHER

Also author of afterword to *Five Children and It* by E. Nesbit. Work included in New Directions anthologies. Contributor to *Contemporary Poetry;* also contributor of articles to *School Library Journal, Harper's Bazaar, Horn Book,* and other periodicals. Member of editorial board, *Cricket.*

ADAPTATIONS: The Cat Who Wished to Be a Man and *The Wizard in the Tree* have been produced on stage in Japan. *The Marvelous Misadventures of Sebastian* was produced as a television serial in Japan. *The Black Cauldron,* an animated film produced by Walt Disney Productions in 1985, is based on parts of Alexander's Prydain novels.

SIDELIGHTS: Lloyd Alexander is widely regarded as a master of twentieth-century children's literature. He is best-known for his fantasy fiction and modern fables: imaginative and adventurous stories, often rooted in historical fact and legend, which explore universal themes such as good versus evil and the quest of individuals for self-identity. Among Alexander's best-known works are the five novels which comprise his "Prydain Chronicles"—culminating with *The High King,* which in 1969 received the prestigious Newbery Medal for children's literature. Among Alexander's numerous other awards are the National Book Award for *The Marvelous Misadventures of Sebastian* and the American Book Award for his imaginative 1981 novel, *Westmark.* "At heart, the issues raised in a work of fantasy are those we face in real life," Alexander stated in his Newbery Award acceptance speech printed in *Horn Book.* "In whatever guise—our own daily nightmares of war, intolerance, inhumanity; or the struggles of an Assistant Pig-Keeper against the Lord of Death—the problems are agonizingly familiar. And an openness to compassion, love, and mercy is as essential to us here and now as it is to any inhabitant of an imaginary kingdom."

Alexander was born in 1924 in Philadelphia, Pennsylvania, and was also raised there. His father, a former stockbroker who was bankrupted by the Stock Market Crash of 1929, struggled to support the Alexander family through a number of largely unsuccessful business ventures. Money was scarce, and little was available for lessons in an early love of Alexander's, the piano. Eventually he became impassioned with books, scouring the odd assortment that lay about his household. "I learned to read quite young and have been an avid reader ever since, even though my parents and relatives were not great readers," he was quoted by Lee Bennett Hopkins in *More Books by More People.* "I was more or less left to my own devices and interests, which, after all, may not be such a bad idea." Alexander became very fond of Greek and Celtic mythologies, in addition to the Welsh tales and legends contained in the *Mabinogion.* He also discovered the novels of Charles Dickens, and was particularly impressed with *Nicholas Nickleby.* "Dickens was one of many authors who helped me grow up (and are still helping)," Alexander wrote in *Top of the News.* "For a long while he was both refuge and encouragement. If he helped me escape from my daily life, . . . he also sent me back somehow better able to face up to it."

At the age of fifteen, Alexander announced to his parents that he wished to become a poet—a decision which greatly concerned his father. As Alexander recalled in *More Books by More People,* "poetry, my father warned, was no practical career; I would do well to forget it." His mother interceded, however, and it was agreed upon that Alexander could pursue poetry—granted he also find practical work. "For my part, I had no idea how to find any sort of work—or, in fact, how to go about being a poet. For more than a year I had been writing long into the night and studying verse forms to the scandalous neglect of my homework." Upon graduation, Alexander's poor grades and his family's limited finances ruled out the possibility

of college or a scholarship, and his prospects of becoming a successful writer looked equally dim. "In addition to poor marks, I collected rejection slips," Alexander recollected in *My Love Affair with Music.* "My goal was to become an author and it appeared that I would reach it only if I inserted the qualifying word 'unpublished'." Alexander was able to find work as a messenger boy in a bank, a job which, although low-paying and one he found miserable, allowed him to continue writing.

Alexander eventually saved enough money to enroll in a local college to formally study writing, yet he found the coursework inadequate. Instead, as he wrote in *My Love Affair with Music,* he decided that "adventure . . . was the best way to learn about writing," and he enlisted in the army. The year was 1942 and the United States was already in the Second World War. Alexander was eventually assigned to military intelligence, and his unit was sent off to the country of Wales for combat training. "Wales was an enchanted world," Alexander has stated. "The Welsh language fascinated me, as did English spoken with a Welsh lilt, more song than speech. . . . It seemed I recognized faces from all the hero tales of my childhood. . . . The Companions of Arthur might have galloped from the mountains with no surprise to me. Wales, to my eyes, appeared still a realm of bards and heroes; even the coal-tips towered like dark fortresses. Not until years afterwards did I realize I had been given, without my knowing, a glimpse of another enchanted kingdom."

Alexander was assigned to the Seventh Army in the Alsace-Lorraine region of France, and worked as an interpreter-translator. When the war ended in 1945, he was sent to work with a counter-intelligence unit in Paris, and, as he wrote in *My Love Affair with Music,* "fell in love with the city at first sight and sound." The same year he met his future wife, a young Parisian named Janine Denni, and the two were married three months later in January of 1946. Alexander requested a discharge from the army to resume his education, and received a scholarship from the French Foreign Ministry, with which he attended the Sorbonne, University of Paris. Feeling, however, that he needed to be closer to his roots if he were to succeed as a writer, Alexander returned to the United States with his wife and her small daughter Madeleine, whom he had adopted. The three initially lived with Alexander's parents, until they were moved into their own home, an old farmhouse in Drexel Hill, just outside of Philadelphia.

Alexander began writing novels, the first three of which were promptly rejected by publishers. Between 1948 and 1955, he worked a variety of jobs to support his family, including being a cartoonist, advertising writer, layout artist, and an associate editor for an industrial magazine; he also translated several works from French, including Jean-Paul Sartre's *The Wall* and *Nausea.* Alexander was on the verge of giving up on writing when his fourth novel, *And Let the Credit Go,* was published. Based on his own experiences as a struggling writer, the book launched a number of biographical-based adult books by Alexander. "One thing I had learned during those seven years was to write about things I knew and loved," he explained in *Horn Book.* "Our cats delighted me. So did music; I had . . . tried to learn the violin, piano, and guitar. I relished Janine's war with the English language and her bafflement at the peculiar customs of Americans. All this found its way into books and was published. I was writing out of my own life and experience. But nearly ten years passed before I learned a writer could know and love a fantasy world as much as his real one."

Alexander made his first venture into children's fantasy with *Time Cat: The Remarkable Journeys of Jason and Gareth.* The story of a magical black cat which is able to transport a young boy into different historical periods, *Time Cat* brought Alexander into contact once again with ancient Wales. "Surely everyone cherishes a secret, private world from the days of childhood. Mine was Camelot, and Arthur's Round Table, Malory, and the *Mabinogion,*" Alexander wrote in *Horn Book.* "The Welsh research brought it all back to me. Feeling like a man who has by accident stumbled into an enchanted cavern lost since boyhood, both terrified and awestruck, I realized I would have to explore further." Originally intending to include a Welsh episode in *Time Cat,* Alexander decided to replace it with an Irish one, and began plans to devote a future book to his beloved Wales. "Not to the beautiful land of Wales I knew in reality," he told *Horn Book,* "but an older, darker one."

Alexander didn't expect that his exploration would result in the five-novel Prydain Chronicles. In the first novel, *The Book of Three,* Alexander's intent was to retell the convoluted tales of the *Mabinogion.* "I tried this at first, but strange things happened to me," he stated in an interview for *The Pied Pipers.* "I found I had been kidding myself: I didn't want simply to retell anybody's mythology. What I really wanted to do was invent my own, or at least use my own in some way. . . . The more I worked on *The Book of Three* the more I realized the personal importance it was taking on. . . . It was a tremendously liberating decision. I found myself, to my amazement, tapping into various areas of my personality that I never even knew existed." The subsequent books of the series, *The Black Cauldron, The Castle of Llyr, Taran Wanderer,* and *The High King,* relate the adventures of a young hero, Taran, on a quest which leads him to understand the true meaning of heroism, goodness, and also evil. "Prydain grew into something much more than a thinly disguised ancient Wales," Laura Ingram commented in *Dictionary of Literary Biography.* "Undeniably, it was similar to that land,

but reshaped by the addition of contemporary realism, modern values, and a generous dose of humor, as well as the special depth and insight provided by characters who not only act, but think, feel, and struggle with the same kinds of problems that confuse and trouble people in the twentieth century." *The Black Cauldron* was a runner-up for the Newbery Medal in 1966, while *The High King* received the prestigious honor in 1969.

Alexander followed the Prydain Chronicles with several simpler tales geared more towards younger children. Some of these books, including *Coll and His White Pig, The Truthful Harp,* and *The Foundling and Other Tales of Prydain,* are special introductions for young readers into the world of Prydain. In 1970, Alexander went in a different direction with another children's book, *The Marvelous Misadventures of Sebastian,* which was honored with the National Book Award. The story, set in a country similar to eighteenth-century Europe, charts the adventures of a young fiddler as he assists an orphaned princess who is trying to escape marriage to the repressive ruler of the land. As Alexander describes in *The Pied Pipers,* the boy "comes into the possession of a fiddle that allows him to play and hear music as he has never done before. It changes his life." Alexander added that the story has parallels to his own discovery of the joys of writing for children. "The fiddle . . . is a mixed blessing because it also drains his life away the more he understands his magnificent discovery. Without being pretentious about it, I suppose *Sebastian* attempts to say something about what it feels like to be an artist."

In 1981, Alexander published a new novel, *Westmark,* the first of a trilogy which would include *The Kestrel* (1982) and *The Beggar Queen* (1984). These novels became known as "The Westmark Trilogy," through which Alexander explores the political development of an imaginary land called Westmark, "a cross between colonial America and feudal Europe," writes Ingram. "Quite different in tone and setting from the *Prydain* series," according to Jill P. May in *Twentieth Century Children's Writers,* Alexander's Westmark trilogy depicts "the horrors of revolution and unrest, and the conflicts caused by corrupt leadership." A subsequent series of five books by Alexander recounts the adventures of a spirited young character named Vesper Holly. The first novel in the series, *The Illyrian Adventure,* was "in every way different from anything I'd written before," Alexander was quoted in *Something about the Author.* "It was intended as an entertainment— for its author as much as anyone—with a gloriously fearless heroine, legendary heroes, inscrutable mysteries, and fiendish villains. What surprised me shouldn't have surprised me at all. In what was meant as sheer amusement, below the surface I realized that my own concerns and questions were still there, even though set in different terms."

In her book *The Green and Burning Tree: On the Writing and Enjoyment of Children's Books,* Eleanor Cameron describes Alexander as "a perfect example of one who, before he could come into his own as a writer, had to discover that place which was, for him, the spiritual symbol or expression of something hidden." Alexander's varied contributions to children's literature have earned him not only many awards and critical accolades, but also a devoted and diverse readership. "I am amazed and delighted by how many adults read the 'Prydain Chronicles,' " Alexander was quoted in *The Pied Pipers.* "I don't think adults stop growing, or at least they shouldn't. If you stop growing you're dead. At any rate, I've never tried to pull any punches with the kids." For Alexander, the world of the imagination and fantasy has been a way to explore that which is most real. "Using the device of an imaginary world allowed me in some strange way to go to the central issues," he added in *The Pied Pipers.* "In other worlds I used the imaginary kingdom not as a sentimentalized fairyland, but as an opening wedge to express what I hoped would be some very hard truths. I never saw fairy tales as an escape or a cop out. . . . On the contrary, speaking for myself, it is the way to understand reality."

BIOGRAPHICAL/CRITICAL SOURCES:

BOOKS

Alexander, Lloyd, *My Love Affair with Music,* Crowell, 1960.
Authors and Artists for Young Adults, Volume 1, Gale, 1989.
Attebery, Brian, *The Fantasy Tradition in American Literature: From Irving to LeGuin,* Indiana University Press, 1980.
Cameron, Eleanor, *The Green and Burning Tree: On the Writing and Enjoyment of Children's Books,* Little, Brown, 1962.
Children's Literature Review, Gale, Volume 1, 1976; Volume 5, 1983.
Contemporary Literary Criticism, Volume 35, Gale, 1985.
Crouch, Marcus, *The Nesbit Tradition: The Children's Novel in England, 1945-1970,* Rowman, 1972.
Dictionary of Literary Biography, Volume 52: *American Writers for Children since 1960: Fiction,* Gale, 1986.
Hopkins, Lee Bennett, *More Books by More People,* Citation, 1974.
Jacobs, James S., and Michael O. Tunnell, *Lloyd Alexander: A Bio-Bibliography,* Greenwood, 1991.
Livingston, Myra Cohn, *A Tribute to Lloyd Alexander,* Drexel Institute, 1976.
May, Jill P., *Lloyd Alexander,* Twayne, 1991.

Something about the Author, Volume 49, Gale, 1987, p. 21-35.
Twentieth Century Children's Writers, 3rd edition, St James, 1989, pp. 16-18.
Tymn, Marshall B. and others, *Fantasy Literature: A Core Collection and Reference Guide,* Bowker, 1979.
Wintle, Justin and Emma Fisher, editors, *The Pied Pipers: Interviews with the Influential Creators of Children's Literature,* Paddington Press, 1974.

PERIODICALS

Chicago Tribune Book World, November 26, 1967.
Christian Science Monitor, May 2, 1968; November 7, 1973.
Cricket, January, 1974; December, 1976; September, 1983.
Elementary English, December, 1971.
Horn Book, October, 1964; April, 1965; June, 1965; December, 1965; June, 1966; June, 1967; April, 1968; August, 1969; December, 1970; August, 1971; October, 1971; December, 1972; October, 1973; August, 1975; February, 1978; August, 1981; August, 1982; August, 1983; August, 1984; October, 1984.
Junior Bookshelf, October, 1966; June, 1967.
Los Angeles Times, July 24, 1985; July 27, 1985.
New Yorker, December 3, 1973.
New York Review of Books, December 3, 1964.
New York Times Book Review, March 23, 1958; April 14, 1963; December 3, 1964; June 19, 1966; April 9, 1967; March 24, 1968; November 15, 1970; July 25, 1971; November 5, 1972; September 30, 1973; November 4, 1973; May 4, 1975; November 13, 1977; December 10, 1978; May 10, 1981; April 25, 1982; June 7, 1987.
Philadelphia Sunday Bulletin, March 22, 1959.
Saturday Review, March 18, 1967; April 20, 1968; June 19, 1971.
School Library Journal, December, 1967; February, 1968; October, 1970; December, 1972; May, 1975; November, 1977; May, 1981; April, 1982; April, 1988.
Times Literary Supplement, November 24, 1966; May 25, 1967; October 3, 1968; April 6, 1973.
Top of the News, November, 1968.
Washington Post Book World, August 21, 1966; May 5, 1968; November 8, 1970; November 12, 1978; May 10, 1981; January 9, 1983.
Wilson Library Bulletin, October, 1970; June, 1974.
Writer, May, 1971.
Writer's Digest, April, 1973.

*   *   *

ALEXANDER, Meena 1951-

PERSONAL: Born February 17, 1951, in Allahabad, India; came to the United States in 1979; daughter of

George and Mary Alexander; married David Lelyveld; children: Adam Kuruvilla, Svati Mariam. *Education:* University of Khartoum, B.A. (with first-class honors), 1969; University of Nottingham, Ph.D., 1973.

ADDRESSES: Home—541 West 113th St., No. 4C, New York, NY 10025. *Office*—Department of English, Hunter College, City University of New York, 695 Park Ave., New York, NY 10021.

CAREER: University of Khartoum, Khartoum, Sudan, tutor in English, 1969; University of Delhi, Delhi, India, lecturer in English, 1974; Jawaharlal Nehru University, Delhi, lecturer in English and French, 1975; Central Institute of English and Foreign Language, Hyderabad, India, lecturer in English, 1975-77; University of Hyderabad, Hyderabad, lecturer, 1977-79, reader in English, 1979; Fordham University, Bronx, NY, assistant professor of English, 1980-87; Hunter College, City University of New York, New York City, assistant professor of English, 1987-89; Hunter College and Graduate Center, City University of New York, associate professor, 1989—; Columbia University, New York City, lecturer in writing program, 1990—. Lecturer at University of Stirling, 1973, and Osmania University, 1978; visiting fellow at Centre de Recherches en Litterature et Civilization Nord-Americaines, Sorbonne, University of Paris, autumn, 1979; visiting assistant professor at University of Minnesota—Twin Cities, summer, 1981; writer in residence at Center for American Culture Studies, Columbia University, 1988. Gives poetry readings.

WRITINGS:

The Bird's Bright Ring (poems), Writers Workshop (Calcutta, India), 1976.
Without Place (poems), Writers Workshop (Calcutta, India), 1977.
I Root My Name (poems), United Writers, 1977.
In the Middle Earth (one-act play), Enact, 1977.
The Poetic Self: Towards a Phenomenology of Romanticism, Arnold-Heinemann, 1979, Humanities, 1981.
Stone Roots (poems), Arnold-Heinemann, 1980.
House of a Thousand Doors (poems), Three Continents, 1989.
The Storm: A Poem in Five Parts, Red Dust, 1989.
Women in Romanticism, Macmillan, 1989.
Nampally Road (novel), Mercury House, 1991.
Fault Lines (memoir), Feminist Press, 1992.

SIDELIGHTS: Meena Alexander told *CA:* "In *Fault Lines,* the memoir which has just gone to press, I move back and forth between India, the Sudan, and New York City. I have lived in the city since 1979 and it provides the framework within which I remember, within which I write, fabricate, make fictive worlds. In my present poems, for instance 'Paper Filled with Light' forthcoming in *Grand Street,* I write a back-and-forth line, the lyrics of dislocation."

BIOGRAPHICAL/CRITICAL SOURCES:

PERIODICALS

Los Angeles Times Book Review, January 27, 1991, p. 7.

*　　*　　*

ALLARD, Harry
　　See ALLARD, Harry G(rover), Jr.

*　　*　　*

ALLARD, Harry G(rover), Jr. 1928-
(Harry Allard)

PERSONAL: Born January 27, 1928, in Evanston, IL; son of Harry Grover (in sales) and Gladys (Bedford) Allard. *Education:* Northwestern University, B.S., 1948; Middlebury College, M.A., 1960; Yale University, Ph.D., 1973. *Politics:* "Anarchist. I don't know. Maybe a monarchist." *Religion:* Russian Orthodox. *Avocational interests:* Drawing, reading, listening to classical music, and learning languages.

ADDRESSES: Home—Apdo. Postal 454, 68000 Oaxaca, Oax., Mexico.

CAREER: Wabash College, Crawfordsville, IN, instructor in French, 1959-60; Trinity University, San Antonio, TX, instructor in French, 1962-65; associated with Yale University, New Haven, CT, 1965-68; Salem State College, Salem, MA, 1968-87, began as assistant professor, became associate professor of French; retired. Taught English at Berlitz School in Paris; worked as legal translator in Paris. Author and translator of children's books. *Military service:* U.S. Army Signal Corps, 1951-52.

AWARDS, HONORS: The Tutti-Frutti Case was selected as one of the *New York Times*'s best illustrated children's books of the year, 1975; *The Stupids Step Out* was selected for the Children's Book Showcase, 1975, and was included on *School Library Journal*'s list, "Best of the Best 1966-1978," 1979; *Miss Nelson Is Missing!* was a runner-up for the Edgar Allan Poe Award, and was selected as an outstanding book of the year by the *New York Times,* both in 1977, received the Georgia Children's Book Award from the University of Georgia in 1980, and received the California Young Readers Medal and was named a Buckeye honor book, both in 1982; Academy Award nomination for best animated film from Academy of Motion Picture Arts and Sciences, 1978, for movie adaptation of *It's So Nice to Have a Wolf around the House;* International

Reading Association's "Children's Choices" selections, 1979, for *The Stupids Have a Ball,* and 1982, for *There's a Party at Mona's Tonight* and *The Stupids Die; I Will Not Go to Market Today* was selected for the American Institute of Graphics Arts Book Show, 1980; *The Stupids Die* was chosen one of *School Library Journal's* Best Books, 1981, was runner-up for First Kentucky Bluegrass Award, 1983, and won the Arizona Book Award, 1985; Parents' Choice award for literature, 1982, "Golden Sower" award, 1984, and Colorado Children's Book Award, 1985, all for *Miss Nelson Is Back;* "Golden Sower" award, 1987, for *Miss Nelson Has a Field Day.*

WRITINGS:

FOR CHILDREN; UNDER NAME HARRY ALLARD

The Stupids Step Out, illustrated by James Marshall, Houghton, 1974.

The Tutti-Frutti Case: Starring the Four Doctors of Goodge, illustrated by Marshall, Prentice-Hall, 1975.

(Translator from the German) Luis Murschetz, *A Hamster's Journey,* Prentice-Hall, 1976.

Crash Helmet, illustrated by Jean-Claude Suares, Prentice-Hall, 1977.

It's So Nice to Have a Wolf around the House, illustrated by Marshall, Doubleday, 1977.

Miss Nelson Is Missing!, illustrated by Marshall, Houghton, 1977.

(With Marshall) *The Stupids Have a Ball,* illustrated by Marshall, Houghton, 1978.

(Adapter and translator from the German) *May I Stay?* (fairy tale), illustrated by F. A. Fitzgerald, Prentice-Hall, 1978.

Bumps in the Night, illustrated by Marshall, Doubleday, 1979.

I Will Not Go to Market Today, illustrated by Marshall, Dial, 1979.

(Translator from the German) Friedrich Karl Waechter, *Three Is Company,* illustrated by Waechter, Doubleday, 1980.

The Stupids Die, illustrated by Marshall, Houghton, 1981.

There's a Party at Mona's Tonight, illustrated by Marshall, Doubleday, 1981.

Miss Nelson Is Back, illustrated by Marshall, Houghton, 1982.

Miss Nelson Has a Field Day, illustrated by Marshall, Houghton, 1985.

The Stupids Take Off, illustrated by Marshall, Houghton, 1989.

The Cactus Flower Bakery, illustrated by Ned Delaney, HarperCollins, 1991.

OTHER

(Under name Harry G. Allard) *Anna de Noailles, Nun of Passion: A Study of the Novels of Anna de Noailles,* [New Haven, CT], 1973.

ADAPTATIONS:

It's So Nice to Have a Wolf Around the House (full-length television cartoon feature), Learning Corporation of America, 1978.

Miss Nelson Is Missing (motion picture) Learning Corporation of America, 1979.

Miss Nelson Is Back (TV segment), introduced by LeVar Burton and narrated by Ruth Buzzi on "Reading Rainbow," PBS-TV, 1983.

WORK IN PROGRESS: Miss Nelson Meets Her Match; In a Spanish Inn; a novel for children; *Lullaby,* an adult horror novel; translation of an adult novel from the French.

SIDELIGHTS: Harry G. Allard, Jr. is best known for his comic children's book series: one featuring the Stupids, a family of morons, and the other about a schoolteacher named Miss Nelson. Allard shares the same birthday, January 27, with another famous children's author: Lewis Carroll. "I was born in Evanston, Illinois," Allard told *Something about the Author (SATA).* "I now look upon sharing a birthday with the creator of Alice as a good omen."

"I went to high school in Chicago," Allard explains to *SATA.* "My favorite subject was Latin. I majored in art at Northwestern University, and was graduated from there in 1949 with a B.S. A limbo of misdirected efforts followed, from which I was at last saved by the Korean War (Signal Corps in Japan and in Korea). Chicago again, but only for one year. To shake the dust of Chicago from my heels forever, I went to live in Paris for four years. When I came back to the U.S.A. the only thing I could do was teach French, so I taught French. . . . To make it official I got an M.A. from Middlebury College in 1960 and a Ph.D. in French from Yale in 1973."

In 1968, Allard began teaching in the department of foreign languages at Salem State College in Salem, Massachusetts. Upon moving to nearby Charlestown, Allard met author-illustrator James Marshall, whose artwork provided the inspiration for Allard's first book, *The Stupids Step Out.* "James Marshall started it. . . . He did all the spade work, as it were," the author tells Jean Ross in his *Contemporary Authors (CA)* interview. "He started with the 'George and Martha' series, which was a success, and then I gave him *The Stupids Step Out* and he took it to Houghton Mifflin. . . . I never had to do anything. It was always easy."

The Stupids Step Out describes a typical day in the life of Stanley Q. Stupid and his family—Mrs. Stupid and the children Buster and Petunia. The Stupids engage in such silly practices as wearing cats on their heads or socks on their ears, taking baths without water, and sleeping with their feet on their pillows. "It was an accident that *The Stupids Step Out* worked so well and was so well received," Allard tells Ross. However, he also states in his *CA* interview that he believes the Stupids became popular "because children are always under the thumb of somebody—adults, whether they are parents or priests or nuns or whatever—and here the children can make fun of adults and feel superior to them and know more than they do. Also because the Stupids are such a wild family . . . there's something anarchistic about them. And . . . so many books seem to be socially manipulative. They're either telling children to love children of other races or to respect old people or to understand blind people and dying people. There are too many messages. With the Stupids there is no message at all. They just seem to do what they want to do." The Stupid family returns in *The Stupids Have a Ball*, in which the family throws a costume party to celebrate the children's having failed all their subjects at school, *The Stupids Die*, in which the Stupids assume they are dead when their house lights go out unexpectedly, and *The Stupids Take Off*.

The Stupids Step Out was followed by *Miss Nelson Is Missing!*, which was a runner-up for a 1977 Edgar Allan Poe Award. Miss Nelson is a good-natured teacher who disguises herself as a demanding battleaxe substitute called Miss Viola Swamp in the hopes that her unruly class will mend its ways and come to appreciate her. Miss Nelson and her counterpart reappear in *Miss Nelson Is Back* and *Miss Nelson Has a Field Day*. *It's So Nice to Have a Wolf around the House* was published in the same year as *Miss Nelson Is Missing!*, and tells of Cuthbert Q. Devine, a professional bank robber and wolf. Cuthbert takes a position as housekeeper and companion to an old man and his three old pets, abandons his old ways, and enriches his companions' lives. *I Will Not Go to Market Today* is the story of Fenimore B. Buttercrunch, a well-fed rooster whose jam supply is running alarmingly low, but whose attempt to go marketing are foiled by natural catastrophes such as blizzards, hurricanes, and floods.

"James Marshall and I work very closely together and we fight a lot about things," Allard told Ross. "It's text first, but then we work a lot on the illustrations. I make suggestions, and of course anything that's in the drawing gets deleted from the text. I have to redo the text because I don't want it to say what the picture is already saying, so the text gets shorter and smaller. Sometimes if I have an idea for a visual gag I bracket it in the text and suggest a visual idea.

"Once I get the idea, I write in a white heat, like [one] night when I got up at three. It was all done by seven or eight and then I went to Cambridge to have it photocopied. But if something is accepted, if it is going to become a book, then I keep doing it, doing it, doing it. And I think the polishing shows, because it's always obviously towards simplicity, to make the sentences as simple and almost transparent as possible. There's no way to show off in children's books. You know, you're not showing off your vocabulary. The only thing you can really work with is rhythm, as in the sense of the English Bible. The words are so simple, but very often the rhythm is mysterious and beautiful.

"When I get an idea, I want to write immediately. I might not have an idea for a long time, so then I do other things. I'm writing a book for adults now and I write in my diary and I write a lot of letters; I'm always writing something. I suppose if I lived exclusively from this I would get up every morning and sit down at nine o'clock to write, whether I was inspired or not. I don't really believe in inspiration. I think you just do it, that's all. If you wait for inspiration you might wait forever."

BIOGRAPHICAL/CRITICAL SOURCES:

BOOKS

Contemporary Authors, Volume 113, Gale, 1985, pp. 20-23.
Holtze, Sally Holmes, editor, *Fifth Book of Junior Authors and Illustrators*, H. W. Wilson, 1983.
Something about the Author, Volume 42, Gale, 1986, pp. 23-28.
Ward, Martha E., and Dorothy A. Marquardt, *Authors of Books for Young People*, 2nd edition, Scarecrow, 1971.

PERIODICALS

Commonweal, November 11, 1977.
Newsweek, July 18, 1977; December 19, 1977; December 6, 1982.
New Yorker, December 2, 1974.
New York Times, December 12, 1974; December 8, 1977.
New York Times Book Review, May 5, 1974; April 17, 1977; November 6, 1977; November 13, 1977; May 21, 1978; April 22, 1979; April 12, 1981; April 26, 1981; November 14, 1982.
Saturday Review, May 27, 1978.
Washington Post Book World, May 19, 1974; July 12, 1981.

ALLCHIN, A(rthur) M(acdonald) 1930-

PERSONAL: Born April 20, 1930, in England; son of Frank Macdonald (a physician) and Louise (Wright) Allchin. *Education:* Christ Church, Oxford, B.A., 1951, B.Litt. and M.A., 1955; Cuddesdon College, theology study, 1954-56. *Politics:* Socialist.

ADDRESSES: Home—2, Canterbury Rd., Oxford OX2 6LU, England.

CAREER: Priest of Church of England; St. Mary Abbots, Kensington, London, England, curate, 1956-60; Pusey House, Oxford, England, librarian, 1960-69; Canterbury Cathedral, Canterbury, England, residentiary canon, 1973-87, honorary canon, 1988; St. Theosevia Centre for Christian Spirituality, Oxford, director, 1987—. Cuddesdon College, Oxford, visiting lecturer in church history, 1962—; visiting lecturer in theology, General Theological Seminary, New York City, 1967, 1968, and Catholic Theological Faculty, Lyons, France, 1980; visiting professor, Nashotah House, Wisconsin, 1984-85, and at University of Dallas, 1985. University of Aarhus, Centre for Grundtvig Studies, Denmark, research fellow, 1990. Warden of community, Sisters of the Love of God, Oxford, 1967—. Member of the Doctrine Commission of the Church in Wales. Has participated in symposia.

AWARDS, HONORS: Honorary Doctorate of Divinity from Bucharest Theological Institute, 1977, and Nashotah House, Wisconsin, 1985.

WRITINGS:

The Silent Rebellion, S.C.M. Press, 1958.
Abbe Paul Couturier, Faith Press, 1960.
(Editor) *Dialogue: East and West,* Faith Press, 1963.
The Spirit and the Word: Two Studies in Nineteenth-Century Anglican Theology, Faith Press, 1963.
(With John Coulson and Meriol Trevor) *Newman, a Portrait Restored: An Ecumenical Revaluation,* Sheed, 1965.
(With H. A. Hodges) *A Rapture of Praise,* Hodder & Stoughton, 1966.
(Editor with Coulson) *The Rediscovery of Newman: An Oxford Symposium,* Sheed, 1967.
(Editor) *Sacrament and Image: Essays in the Christian Understanding of Man,* Fellowship of St. Alban and St. Sergius, 1967.
(Editor) *The Tradition of Life: Romanian Essays in Spirituality and Theology,* Fellowship of St. Alban and St. Sergius, 1971.
(Editor) *Orthodoxy and the Death of God: Essays in Contemporary Theology,* Fellowship of St. Alban and St. Sergius, 1971.
(With A. M. Ramsey and Robert E. Terwilliger) *The Charismatic Christ,* Morehouse, 1973.

The Theology of the Religious Life: An Anglican Approach, S.L.G. Press, 1974.
Eucharist and Unity: Thoughts on the Anglican-Roman Catholic International Commissions Agreed Statement on Eucharistic Doctrine, Together with Full Text of That Statement, S.L.G. Press, 1974.
(Editor) *Theology and Prayer: Essays on Monastic Themes Presented at the Orthodox-Cistercian Conference, Oxford, 1973,* Fellowship of St. Alban and St. Sergius, 1975.
Wholeness and Transfiguration: Illustrated in the Lives of St. Francis of Assisi and St. Seraphim of Sarov, S.L.G. Press, 1975.
Ann Griffiths, University of Wales Press, 1976.
(Editor) *Solitude and Communion: Papers on the Hermit Life Given at St. David's, Wales, in the Autumn of 1975,* S.L.G. Press, 1977.
The World Is a Wedding: Explorations in Christian Spirituality, Oxford University Press, 1978.
The Kingdom of Love and Knowledge: The Encounter between Orthodoxy and the West, Darton, Longman, & Todd, 1979, Seabury, 1982.
The Living Presence of the Past: The Dynamic of Christian Tradition, Seabury, 1981 (published in England as *The Dynamic of Tradition,* Darton, Longman, & Todd, 1981).
A Taste of Liberty, S.L.G. Press, 1983.
The Joy of All Creation, Darton, Longman, & Todd, 1984.
Participation in God, Darton, Longman, & Todd, 1988.
Praise above All, University of Wales Press, 1991.
Profitable Wonders, Morehouse, 1991.

Also author of numerous pamphlets, published lectures, and addresses on theological subjects. Contributor to theology journals, including *Studia Liturgica, Irenikon, Theology,* and *Eastern Churches Review.*

WORK IN PROGRESS: Research on the Danish theologian N. F. S. Grundtvig for an introductory study in English.

*   *   *

ALLEN, Woody 1935-

PERSONAL: Given name, Allen Stewart Konigsberg; born December 1, 1935, in Brooklyn, NY; son of Martin (a waiter and jewelry engraver) and Nettie (Cherry) Konigsberg; married Harlene Rosen, 1954 (divorced, 1960); married Louise Lasser (an actress), February 2, 1966 (divorced); children: (with Mia Farrow) Satchel. *Education:* Attended New York University and City College (now City College of the City University of New York), 1953. *Politics:* Democrat.

ADDRESSES: Agent—Jack Rollins, Rollins & Joffe, 130 West 57th St., New York, NY 10019.

CAREER: Comedian, actor, director, and writer for television, films, and the stage. Began writing jokes for columnists and celebrities while in high school; regular staff writer for National Broadcasting Corp., 1952, writing for such personalities as Herb Shriner, Sid Caesar, Art Carney, Kaye Ballard, Buddy Hackett, Carol Channing, Pat Boone, Jack Paar, and Garry Moore. Performer in nightclubs, on television, and on the stage in 1960s.

AWARDS, HONORS: Sylvania Award, 1957, for script of a *Sid Caesar Show*; Academy Awards for best director and best original screenplay from the Academy of Motion Picture Arts and Sciences, National Society of Film Critics award, and New York Film Critics Circle award, all 1977, for *Annie Hall*; British Academy Award and New York Film Critics award, both 1979, for *Manhattan*; Academy Award nomination for best director, 1984, for *Broadway Danny Rose*; Academy Award for best original screenplay, Golden Globe Award for best motion picture comedy or musical, New York Film Critics award, and Los Angeles Film Critics award, all 1987, all for *Hannah and Her Sisters*; Academy Award nominations for best director and best original screenplay, both 1989, for *Crimes and Misdemeanors*; Academy Award nomination and Writers Guild Award nomination, both 1991, both for *Alice*.

WRITINGS:

Getting Even (humor collection), Random House, 1971.
Without Feathers (humor collection), Random House, 1975.
Non-Being and Somethingness (collections from comic strip *Inside Woody Allen*), Random House, 1978.
Side Effects (humor collection), Random House, 1980.
The Lunatic's Tale, Redpath Press, 1986.

SCREENPLAYS

(And actor) *What's New, Pussycat?,* United Artists, 1965.
(With Frank Buxton, Len Maxwell, Louise Lasser, and Mickey Rose, and actor) *What's Up, Tiger Lily?,* American International, 1966.
(With Rose, and actor and director) *Take the Money and Run,* Palomar, 1969.
(With Rose, and actor and director) *Bananas* (also see below), United Artists, 1971.
(And actor and director) *Everything You Always Wanted to Know about Sex But Were Afraid to Ask* (based on the book by David Ruben), United Artists, 1972.
(And actor) *Play It Again, Sam* (also see below; based on the play), Paramount, 1972.
(With Marshall Brickman, and actor and director) *Sleeper* (also see below), United Artists, 1973.

(And actor and director) *Love and Death* (also see below), United Artists, 1975.
(With Brickman, and actor and director) *Annie Hall* (also see below), United Artists, 1977.
(And director) *Interiors* (also see below), United Artists, 1978.
Four Screenplays: Sleeper, Love and Death, Bananas, Annie Hall, Random House, 1978.
(With Brickman, and actor and director) *Manhattan* (also see below), United Artists, 1979.
(And actor and director) *Stardust Memories* (also see below), United Artists, 1980.
(And actor and director) *A Midsummer Night's Sex Comedy,* Warner Brothers, 1982.
Four Films of Woody Allen (includes *Annie Hall, Manhattan, Stardust Memories,* and *Interiors*), Random House, 1982.
(And actor and director) *Zelig,* Orion, 1983.
(And actor and director) *Broadway Danny Rose,* Orion, 1984.
(And director) *The Purple Rose of Cairo,* Orion, 1985.
(And actor and director) *Hannah and Her Sisters* (produced by Orion, 1986), Random House, 1986.
(And narrator and director) *Radio Days,* Orion, 1987.
(And director) *September,* Orion, 1987.
(And director) *Another Woman,* Orion, 1988.
(And actor and director) *Oedipus Wrecks* in *New York Stories,* Touchstone, 1989.
(And actor and director) *Crimes and Misdemeanors,* Orion, 1989.
(And director) *Alice,* Orion, 1990.

PLAYS

(With Herbert Farjeon, Hermoine Gingold, and others) *From A to Z,* produced in New York at Plymouth Theatre, April 20, 1960.
Don't Drink the Water (produced in New York at Morosco Theatre, November 17, 1966), Samuel French, 1967.
Play It Again, Sam (produced on Broadway at Broadhurst Theatre, February 12, 1969), Random House, 1969.
Death: A Comedy in One Act, Samuel French, 1975.
God: A Comedy in One Act, Samuel French, 1975.
The Floating Light Bulb (produced in New York at Vivian Beaumont Theatre, April 27, 1981), Random House, 1982.

Author of radio production of *God,* produced by National Radio Theatre of Chicago, 1978. Featured on recording *Woody Allen, Stand-up Comic: 1964-1968,* United Artists Records, 1978.

WORK IN PROGRESS: Another film.

SIDELIGHTS: Woody Allen falls into one of the most rarified categories of artist—the *auteur* filmmaker, one whose vision pervades every aspect of his work. Allen is also one of the world's best-recognized cinematic figures; indeed, he has more "name value" as a writer or director than do many of the stars of his pictures. But for all his acclaim and fame, he maintains a relatively balanced perspective on his own importance. As he told Natalie Gittelson in a *New York Times* piece, "I'm not holed up in my apartment every night poring over Russian literature and certain Danish philosophers. I'm really hardly a recluse. When a half-dozen *paparazzi* follow me down the street, naturally, I don't like that very much. But I do go out all the time—to movies, to shop, to walk around in the street, to those parties I think I'll enjoy."

The object of substantial media attention was born Allen Stewart Konigsberg in pre-World War II Brooklyn, New York. In many ways, the growing boy resembled his peers: "I was out in the streets from 8 o'clock in the morning," Allen tells *Newsweek*'s Jack Kroll, "playing baseball and basketball. At lunchtime I'd race into the house, eat a tuna-fish sandwich by myself and read a comic book—Superman, Batman or Mickey Mouse. I'd run back out on the street and play ball. Then I'd run back in for dinner, read another comic book, run back out again for two hours, come in and watch the St. Louis Cardinals beat the Dodgers on television."

Young Allen hated school. In a *Rolling Stone* interview, the writer recalls the "equally bad" experience of attending public school and Hebrew school, in a neighborhood that, though primarily Jewish, was filled with "teachers [who] were backward and anti-Semitic." With that kind of academic background, it's not surprising that Allen shunned higher education as well. He briefly attended New York's City College and entered into an equally brief teenage marriage to childhood sweetheart Harlene Rosen.

By this time Allen was also submitting jokes and one-liners, some of which caught the attention of columnists like Earl Wilson. From there it was a quick foray into television, where Allen was among the youngest—and quietest—staff writers for shows starring Sid Caesar, Art Carney, and Jack Paar, among others. During the early 1960s Allen worked as a comedian in nightclubs, where he began to create the persona that would bring him fame—that of the intellectual bumbler, unlucky in love, adversary of nature and small appliances, a perpetual victim of his own urban angst. His comedy was embraced by a generation of city sophisticates, but the persona didn't exactly reflect its creator. "People always associated me with Greenwich Village and sweaters with holes in them and things like that," Allen remarks to Tom Shales in an *Esquire* piece. "And I've never been that kind of person. Never. I never lived in the Village. I always lived on the Upper East Side of Manhattan."

Film producer Charles Feldman discovered Allen in 1964 and offered him a screenwriting job on a movie called *What's New, Pussycat?* The story of a man who simply cannot stay faithful to the woman he loves, the movie also marked Allen's acting debut as a neurotic psychiatric patient. In a *Dictionary of Literary Biography* profile, Alan S. Horowitz notes that even in this knockabout farce, the "conflict between security and freedom, and its related problem of freedom versus commitment, recurs in later Allen films."

While *What's New, Pussycat?* "was a great financial success, Allen was not entirely pleased with the finished film," continues Horowitz. The writer "began looking for a project over which he would have more creative control. He acquired the Japanese-made spy film 'Dagi no Kagi' (1964), reedited it, and dubbed in a sound track written and performed by himself, [second wife Louise] Lasser, Frank Buxton, and Len Maxwell, changing the film to a spy spoof about a search for an egg salad recipe." The film, *What's Up, Tiger Lily?,* has enjoyed cult status to this day.

The success of Allen's first two films marked the onset of an era, between the late 1960s and the mid-1970s, that saw him writing, directing, and/or starring in six more free-wheeling comedies. Beginning with *Take the Money and Run,* the comedies reinforced the Allen persona, a kind of modern version of Charlie Chaplin's Little Tramp. *Bananas,* Allen's next outing, features him as products-tester Fielding Mellish, who rises—through a series of misadventures—from soldier to president of the tiny banana-republic San Marcos (a country that "leads the world in hernias").

"Both 'Bananas' and 'Take the Money and Run' boast sharp bits of parody (of prison movies, TV commercials, courtroom dramas), with Allen kidnapping the cliches and transporting them into wildly inappropriate settings," finds *Film Comment*'s Richard Zoglin, who adds: "The underlying message of Allen's comedy is the tyranny of the cliche, which threatens to dehumanize us, to turn us into reflexive automatons. This is not random gag-writing but social comedy of a subtle subversiveness."

Allen the playwright had written and starred in the Broadway production of *Play It Again, Sam,* a romantic farce about identity and commitment, with Allen's character, Allan Felix, fantasizing about being as tough and irresistible as Humphrey Bogart. When Felix finds himself increasingly attracted to his best friend's wife, the spirit of the real Bogey appears periodically to explain the mysteries of the female mind. *Play It Again, Sam* enjoyed a prosperous stage run and was adapted by Allen for his fifth produced screenplay.

1972, the same year of the film *Play It Again, Sam,* was also the year of *Everything You Always Wanted to Know about Sex But Were Afraid to Ask,* Allen's film derived—only slightly—from Dr. David Ruben's controversial bestseller. Allen's film takes an anecdotal approach: "Do Aphrodisiacs Work?," for instance, features Allen as a medieval court jester who uses a love potion to get his hands on "the royal tomatoes" (i.e., the queen). According to *Film Comment* contributor Michael Dempsey, Allen's version of *Sex* approximates a "savage dissection of sexual absurdity."

Allen's next film, *Sleeper,* presents him as health-food store owner Miles Monroe, whose disastrous ulcer operation results in his being frozen alive. *Sleeper* recounts what happens when this urban specimen defrosts 200 years later. In 2173 technology has taken over, with robots serving as servants, Jewish-accented tailors, and even cordial home pets. The time-traveling Miles, with his memory of a more natural earth, is perceived as a threat by the dictatorial government. Miles joins a rebel force that includes Luna (Diane Keaton), an anthem-spouting free spirit who helps him escape his foes.

Sleeper explores themes familiar to Allen works, including the search for cultural identity (Miles has to be cued to his time by being shown artifacts of his own epoch, including a beauty pageant and a picture of Richard Nixon, whom Miles cannot identify). Sex also plays a role in Miles's identity crisis—after Luna comments that he has gone two hundred years without it, Miles corrects her: "Two hundred and four, if you count my marriage." But in the new age, sex has been replaced by machinery-made stimuli, a concept that Miles samples but ultimately rejects. "During the conclusion of 'Sleeper' Miles Monroe comes right out with his total disbelief in science and politics, opting for 'sex and death, two things which come once in my life—but at least after death you're not nauseous,' " as Dempsey quotes.

Allen's next movie, *Love and Death,* is both a spoof of Russian literature and an examination into the meaning of life. The movie opens in nineteenth-century Czarist Russia, where the citizens of a small village are preparing to join in the fight against Emperor Napoleon's invading forces—all except Boris (Allen), a "militant coward" in love with his cousin Sonia (Keaton). Pressured into joining the army after Sonia decides to marry the town's herring merchant, Boris, as klutzy as ever, becomes a quite inadvertent war hero ("*You* should have such inadvertent heroism," he sniffs to a rival). By this time Sonia is again unmarried, for the herring merchant has expired. She and Boris marry and each finds happiness—until they devise a plot to kill the visiting Napoleon. The plan backfires, Boris is captured, and is sentenced to die the next morning at six o'clock. "It was supposed to be five o'clock, but I had a smart lawyer," he remarks. At film's end, the dead Boris dances with Death.

"Although the story sounds tragic, 'Love and Death' is a comedy," Horowitz says. "The dead Boris appears at the beginning, joking about death and setting the story in flashback. By letting the audience know what Boris's fate will be, Allen makes the film lighter and more amenable to humor." The critic also finds that *Love and Death* has "other literary and theatrical devices which Allen has used in many of his films. Frequently he speaks directly to the audience in absurdist fashion. The film is filled with allusions to Russian literature [specifically, the works of Leo Tolstoy and Feyodor Dostoevsky] and to the films of Ingmar Bergman, one of Allen's favorite filmmakers. Finally, Allen's discussion of death leads him to examine the rationale behind death, which brings him to explore the existence and nature of God."

In *Annie Hall* Allen wrestled further with serious themes. The setting for this film is contemporary New York, the characters are witty and self-motivated, and the plot goes back farther than *Pygmalion:* a highly sophisticated man uses education and culture to create the perfect mate out of a simple, small-town woman and then watches in mounting disbelief as the newly liberated female breaks from his influence and forms a life of her own. With its insights into the way romances blossom and wilt in the 1970s, *Annie Hall* was embraced by many as a representative film of its age. The movie, declares *Newsweek*'s Janet Maslin, "is a perverse self-help manual about How to Be Your Own Worst Enemy, and even its most uproarious moments ride an undercurrent of wistfulness."

Allen himself noted *Annie Hall*'s biggest departure from his previous works in the interview with Natalie Gittelson: " 'Sleeper' and 'Love and Death' were cartoon-style films. I was still struggling to develop a sense of cinema, a better feeling for technique. But even though those films tried for some satirical content, they were still cartoon. I had intended to be very serious in 'Love and Death.' But the serious intent underlying the humor was not very apparent to most audiences. Laughter submerges everything else. That's why I felt that, with 'Annie Hall,' I would have to reduce some of the laughter. I didn't want to destroy the credibility for the sake of the laugh."

Allen's efforts were richly rewarded, for *Annie Hall* swept the 1978 Academy Awards, taking best picture, best director for Allen, best original screenplay for Allen and Marshall Brickman, and best actress for Keaton. America's newest *auteur,* however, made headlines as much for his boycotting of the ceremony as for his Oscar triumphs. While Allen had made no secret of his disregard for awards, he noted that the Oscars were held on Monday and thus conflicted with his previous commitment playing clarinet with the New Orleans Funeral and Ragtime Band at a New York City nightclub.

In his next film, *Interiors,* Allen broke completely from comedy. The film deals with a family in trouble: The parents, Eve and Arthur, are at the breaking point in their marriage. Their three enigmatic daughters, Flyn, Joey, and Renata, "are like [Anton] Chekhov's *Three Sisters,*" as *Dictionary of Literary Biography*'s Horowitz sees it. "Chekhov's women talk about 'going to Moscow' but never go anywhere. Allen's women talk of becoming artists and achieving self-fulfillment, yet manage only to wallow in their own despair. Arthur leaves Eve and romances vivacious and lively Pearl. . . . The family, particularly Eve, cannot accept this, and Eve commits suicide." Horowitz echoes many critics in his view that with this work Allen's "conscious avoidance of laughter gives the film a stilted, unnatural quality, and his dialogue is unrealistic, filled with psychological jargon."

Manhattan, released in 1979, is the movie many people see as a truer follow-up to *Annie Hall.* Certainly there are many similarities. Like *Annie Hall, Manhattan* follows the romantic foibles of New York's intellectual elite. The movie again stars Allen and Keaton as nervous lovers; this time, however, Allen plays a disgruntled television hack yearning to write the Great American Novel, and Keaton portrays an overeducated critic who cranks out movie novelizations on the side. Their romance is doomed, though, by the lovers and ex-spouses who surround them: Keaton's Mary Wilke has had a long-running affair with a married college professor; Allen's Issac Davis must cope with a 17-year-old girlfriend as well as an ex-wife (bisexual when they married, but who left Issac shortly afterward for another woman) publishing a tell-all account of their relationship called *Marriage, Divorce and Selfhood.*

In *New York Times* critic Vincent Canby's opinion, *Manhattan* "moves on from both 'Interiors' and 'Annie Hall,' being more effectively critical and more compassionate than the first and more witty and clear-eyed than the second." As Canby adds, the film is "mostly about Issac's efforts to get some purchase on his life after he initiates a breakup with his illegal, teenage mistress . . . and his attempt to forge a relationship with the deeply troubled Mary Wilke. Unlike all of his friends except the still-learning [teenager] Tracy, Issac believes in monogamy. 'I think people should mate for life,' he says, 'like pigeons and Catholics.' "

Most critics and scholars considered *Annie Hall* and *Manhattan* Allen's two best films to date. But the movie Allen himself is most proud of, from that period, is one that offended many of his fans. "The best film I ever did, really, was *Stardust Memories,*" the director tells Tom Shales. "It was my least popular film. That may automatically mean it was my best film. It was the closest that I came to achieving what I set out to achieve." In *Stardust Memories,* famous film director Sandy Bates (played by Allen) spends a weekend at an upstate New York resort where a collection of critics and fans pay homage to his work. Along the way he meets a mysterious woman and anticipates a visit from his French mistress (married with children, but no less accessible to Sandy's advances). He also confronts his current girlfriend, a neurotic actress. Besieged, Sandy contemplates his future while every one in his life pulls him in opposite directions. Eventually, fantasy and reality become a blur.

Whether meant satirically or sincerely, *Stardust Memories* nonetheless bore the wrath of insulted patrons. Critics generally panned the film, citing uneven pacing and overall sourness. One *Washington Post* writer calls the work an example of the "self-pitying tradition" of Federico Fellini's *8 1/2,* which *Stardust Memories* distinctly resembles. The critic adds that the spectacle of "the celebrity artist [envisioning] himself as a potential victim of this freak show of admirers and supplicants" doesn't help Allen's case. "Allen even shows [Sandy] Bates fantasizing his own murder at the hands of some blandly psychotic fan. There's no satiric distancing to soften or contradict the impression of fundamental distaste."

Whether or not Allen was truly influenced by the negative press he received for *Stardust Memories,* his next effort, *A Midsummer Night's Sex Comedy,* certainly changed direction. This film is a pastoral comedy centering on love, adultery, and the spirit world in a turn-of-the-century setting. Appraising the story of a crackpot inventor, played by Allen, who brings a group of friends and lovers to a country retreat where couplings and recouplings abound, critics generally agreed that *Midsummer Night's* is a pleasant diversion. *New York Times* writer Janet Maslin even commended Allen for his willingness to pursue new directions.

1983's *Zelig* showed Allen once again trying to broaden his artistry. This film presents Allen as a rather nondescript urban Jew who amazingly adopts the looks and characteristics of any distinct individual or group he encounters. Among fat men, for instance, Zelig's weight balloons; among black jazz musicians, Zelig's skin darkens. Eventually, "The Human Chameleon" catches the fancy of a fickle Roaring Twenties America, and Leonard finds himself the subject of songs, dances, and movies. Exploited by his ruthless sister, however, Leonard is miserable. Then a psychiatrist, Eudora Fletcher, becomes convinced that she can cure Zelig of his tendencies. But his public doesn't want cured the man who inspired the hit tune "You May Be Six People But I Love You." The resulting backlash drives Leonard out of the country and into Nazi Germany—in effect an entire nation of conformists, led by Hitler. Fortunately for Leonard, Eudora spots his face among the masses in a newsreel film and embarks on a daring rescue.

Zelig, set in the 1920s, used a myriad of modern technological magic to evoke the jumpy, crackling film footage of that era. By shooting black-and-white film and then running it through a gauntlet of edits and scratches, Allen and cinematographer Gordon Willis created authentic looking action. Willis also succeeded in editing Allen's image into actual old footage, thus showing the character of Leonard Zelig with such notables as Babe Ruth, Calvin Coolidge, and even Adolph Hitler.

Critics disagreed on the merits of *Zelig.* John Simon finds it "a curious example of a film with too much cleverness for its own good." Assessing the film in *National Review,* Simon goes on to say that "though the kaleidoscopic fortunes of the protagonist are aptly mirrored in the collage-like quality of the movie, the art of assemblage, instead of enhancing the semblance of reality, proves an inadequate way of dissembling: the cunningly joined snippets challenge us to peer behind them and discover the central hollowness." London *Times* writer David Robinson, however, finds no reason not to include *Zelig* in the company "of great comedies, like *Candide* or *Verdoux* or *Viridiana,*" adding that in all such narratives the "seemingly transparent simplicity leave you with quite as many questions about the condition of man as do great tragedies. When you recover from the laughter, this pure, perfect, beautiful comedy leaves a trail of reflections about truth and fiction and the difficulty of preserving one's own personality in a society which offers so many off-the-peg models for being which are so much easier to wear."

Embarking on yet another narrative form, Allen next brought out *Broadway Danny Rose.* A Damon Runyonesque showbiz romance, *Broadway Danny Rose* features Allen as Danny Rose, a very-small-time theatrical agent to such acts as a skating rabbi, a blind xylophonist, a woman who plays the rims of drinking glasses, and a parrot who warbles standards like "I Gotta Be Me." The film's heroine is Tina Vitale, ex-moll of an unsuccessful gangster, current girlfriend of Lou Canova, an Italian lounge-singer whose career Danny is trying to resuscitate. Lou is married, so he asks Danny to be his stand-in and accompany Tina to a nightclub opening where Lou is making a comeback. A series of misunderstandings and betrayals results in Danny and Tina on the run from the mob, discovering their feelings for one another in the process.

Some critics see *Broadway Danny Rose* as a throwback to Allen's earlier comedies like *Sleeper;* others find it gratifying in a way they hadn't expected from such a modern filmmaker. Richard Corliss, for one, thinks the movie "is free of the Post-Funny School's hip condescension toward mediocrity. In the melancholy perseverance of these 'entertainers,' Danny and Woody find something admirable, even lovable. So should the movie audience," says the

Time reviewer. Similarly, Canby observes that the movie "is a love letter not only to American comedy stars and to all of those pushy hopefuls who never quite make it to the top in show biz, but also to the kind of comedy that nourished the particular genius of Woody Allen."

For *The Purple Rose of Cairo,* his fifteenth film, Allen turned to Depression-era New Jersey. The film centers on Cecilia, a destitute and abused wife who consoles herself by repeatedly seeing the adventure film *The Purple Rose of Cairo.* One day, the film's clean-cut hero, Tom Baxter, actually leaves the screen and enters Cecilia's life. Finding herself the love interest of a fictional character proves both confusing and exhilarating to Cecilia. But back in Hollywood, studio executives are panicked. It seems that Tom Baxters have begun to leave their movies all across America. The executives decide that only Gil Shepard, the actor who plays Tom, might convince the make-believe adventurer to return to the *Purple Rose* so that the movie can proceed. Gil is dispatched to New Jersey, where he quickly becomes Tom's rival for Cecilia's love. She accepts Gil's invitation to follow him back to Hollywood. Rebuffed, Tom Baxter returns to the *Purple Rose* movie. But when Cecilia, bags packed, goes to the movie house to meet Gil, he doesn't show up. He has left without her. Evidently he only pretended to love Cecilia in order to get Tom Baxter to return to the big screen. The movie's final image is of Cecilia, sitting in the audience once again, waiting for a movie to bring her out of her misery.

Canby wrote in the *New York Times* that *The Purple Rose of Cairo* is "pure enchantment, [a] sweet, lyrically funny, multilayered work that again demonstrates that Woody Allen is our premier film maker." To *Time*'s Schickel, the comedy "is not merely one of the best movies about movies ever made. It is still more unusual, because it comes at its subject the hard way, from the front of the house, instead of from behind the scenes. Its subject is not how movies work but how they work on the audience. Or more accurately, how they once did." And *New Yorker*'s Pauline Kael declares *Purple Rose* to be "the most purely charming" of Allen's films to date, perhaps "the fullest expression yet of his style of humor."

Hannah and Her Sisters, a 1986 comedy-drama, proved yet another high point of Allen's career. It tells the story of how shifting allegiances and marital strife affect the lives of three grown sisters and their families. Hannah, the eldest, is a Broadway actress married to Elliott, a financial adviser. Elliott, however, has a desperate passion for Lee, the youngest sister, who herself lives with an alienated artist, Frederick. Holly, the middle sister, aspires to both acting and writing, depending on her mood. She ends up in a romance with Mickey, Hannah's first husband and, as played by Allen, a rampant hypochondriac.

Several critics praise *Hannah and Her Sisters* as a full-bodied, uplifting work. In the *Washington Post,* Paul Attanasio deems the movie "an encyclopedia of the emotions of ordinary life, not a movie so much as a prayer, if prayers could be so funny and tortured and full of love." "It is one of the extraordinary aspects of the film that 'Hannah and Her Sisters' is most secure when it's being least self-consciously funny," notes Canby in his *New York Times* column. *Newsweek*'s David Ansen wrote, "Anyone bemoaning the disappearance of adult matter from the movies need look no farther," he writes. "Here Allen single-handedly restores glamour and substance to middle age. He juggles these overlapping stories with novelistic finesse, counterpointing hilarity and pathos with almost faultless tact."

It is generally believed that *Radio Days,* Allen's next self-directed screenplay, is pulled from events in its creator's early years. But, as usual, Allen wasn't telling the press how much of the movie was fact and how much fiction. An anecdotal film with Allen providing a voice-over narration, *Radio Days* follows two narratives: one featuring young Joe and his family, the other tracing the rise of Sally White, a cigarette girl with more spunk than talent but one who nonetheless becomes the toast of radio high-society, thanks to some influential friends and a brace of elocution lessons. With *Radio Days,* Canby is once again among Allen's most vocal supporters. "Never has Mr. Allen been so steadily in control," he wrote, "as 'Radio Days' slides from low blackout sketch to high satire to family drama that's as funny as it is moving," he writes in the *New York Times.* Devoting two articles to *Radio Days,* Canby also states that the film "is so densely packed with vivid detail of place, time, music, event and character that it's virtually impossible to take them all in in one sitting."

But even Canby admits that the director's next feature, *September,* "has big problems." This straight drama is notable for the fact that Allen, after seeing a first version of the film, "went out and filmed it all over again—rethought, rewritten and . . . substantially recast," as Eric Lax relates in a *New York Times* report. But to hear critics tell it, the new version is no more successful. "Gloomy" and "claustrophobic" are common adjectives the reviewers use to describe *September,* which takes place in one house and centers around infidelity, suicide, and scandal. *New Yorker*'s Kael calls it "profoundly derivative and second-rate." She added: "When [a character] lifts up a large bouquet of wilting wildflowers and complains that her mother picked them but didn't bother to put them in water, some part of you refuses to believe that Woody Allen thought this up and that it survived the months of writing and shooting and reshooting and editing."

Another Woman, Allen's similarly ponderous account of a philosophy professor who realizes a greater understand-

ing and acceptance of life, fared better with critics, some of whom found it more relaxed, less stilted. Much better received was *Oedipus Wrecks,* Allen's contribution to the 1988 omnibus *New York Stories.* In his contribution, Allen plays a lawyer beleaguered by his hyper-critical mother. After the woman vanishes during a botched magic trick, she reappears—to her son's considerable mortification—as a giant figure in the New York sky. There she continues to offer her humiliating recollections and criticisms of her son.

Even more successful was Allen's 1989 work, *Crimes and Misdemeanors,* which comprises both dramatic and comedic storylines. The dramatic narrative concerns an ophthalmologist plagued with a destructive mistress. The comedic plot deals with the efforts of a modest filmmaker (played by Allen) to complete a serious documentary—about a philosophy professor—while begrudgingly preparing a film about his egomaniacal brother-in-law, a successful television producer. This film, which many critics consider one of Allen's finest, earned several Oscar nominations, including one for best film. Michael Wilmington, in his *Los Angeles Times* review, hails *Crimes and Misdemeanors* as "a film that stands apart" and adds that it consists of "real comic savagery and dramatic grace."

In *Alice,* Allen writes of a fragile, starry-eyed woman who finds release from a stifling marriage through magic, literally turning herself invisible or flying through the air by taking potions dispensed by a Chinese herbologist. Several critics note a Fellini-like touch to the film, a whimsical quality, that makes it a charming though slight film. "Much of 'Alice,' " writes Peter Rainer in the *Los Angeles Times,* "is pleasantly out of whack. . . . Allen may consider 'Alice' to be a minor jest before his next Big One, but there are pleasures in its small-time ambitions that sometimes elude him on his more ambitious projects." *Alice* was nominated for both the Academy Award and Writers Guild Award.

While Allen has made himself known in many artistic categories—not just films, but television, theatre, print, and others—the movies are his most familiar and succesful genre. And yet the writer-director-actor has said that he doesn't enjoy the physical process of filmmaking, the early hours, the reshooting. "I wish somebody would come in and tell me I can't make films anymore," Allen revealed to Tom Shales in *Esquire.* He also told Shales, "There's never been a film of mine that I've been really satisfied with," and he added that he won't watch his films once they are released because "I think I would hate them."

BIOGRAPHICAL/CRITICAL SOURCES:

BOOKS

Adler, Bill and Jeff Feinman, *Woody Allen: Clown Prince of American Humor,* Pinnacle, 1975.

Anobile, Richard, editor, *Woody Allen's "Play It Again, Sam,"* Grosset, 1977.

Brode, Douglas, *Woody Allen: His Films and Career,* Citadel, 1985.

Cohen, Sarah Blacher, editor, *From Hester Street to Hollywood: The Jewish-American Stage and Screen,* Indiana University Press, 1983.

Contemporary Literary Criticism, Gale, Volume 16, 1981, Volume 52, 1989.

De Navacelle, Thierry, *Woody Allen on Location,* Morrow, 1987.

Dictionary of Literary Biography, Volume 44: *American Screenwriters, Second Series,* Gale, 1986.

Guthrie, Lee, *Woody Allen: A Biography,* Drake, 1978.

Hirsch, F., *Love, Sex, Death, and the Meaning of Life: Woody Allen's Comedy,* McGraw, 1981.

Kael, Pauline, *Reeling,* Little, Brown, 1976.

Lahr, John, *Automatic Vaudeville: Essays on Star Turns,* Knopf, 1984.

Lax, Eric, *On Being Funny: Woody Allen and Comedy,* Charterhouse, 1975.

Lax, Eric, *Woody Allen,* Knopf, 1991.

Palmer, M., *Woody Allen,* Proteus Press, 1980.

Yacowar, Maurice, *Loser Take All: The Comic Art of Woody Allen,* Ungar, 1979.

PERIODICALS

Atlantic, August, 1971; December, 1982; May, 1985.

Chicago Tribune, April 30, 1977; May 11, 1979; October 3, 1980; April 30, 1981; May 31, 1981; June 1, 1981; August 19, 1983; January 27, 1984; January 29, 1984; March 25, 1985; February 7, 1986; February 4, 1987; March 3, 1989; December 25, 1990.

Chicago Tribune Book World, October 17, 1971.

Commentary, July, 1979; June, 1982; November, 1983.

Commonweal, November 7, 1980; September 24, 1982; September 9, 1983; March 23, 1984; April 19, 1985; March 14, 1986; February 27, 1987.

Comparative Drama, winter, 1980-81.

Dissent, fall, 1985.

Encounter, June, 1988.

Esquire, April, 1987.

Film Comment, March/April, 1974; March/April, 1978; May/June, 1979; May/June, 1986.

Film Quarterly, winter, 1972; March/April, 1987.

Los Angeles Times, June 24, 1982; March 22, 1983; July 29, 1983; March 1, 1985; January 30, 1987; December 18, 1987; March 3, 1989; October 13, 1989; October

17, 1989; October 22, 1989; December 25, 1990; February 20, 1991.

Midstream, June-July, 1979.

Nation, September 11, 1982; September 17, 1983; March 17, 1984; February 21, 1987.

National Review, June 22, 1979; September 17, 1982; August 5, 1983; May 3, 1985; March 14, 1986; March 27, 1987.

New Leader, May 26, 1975.

New Republic, May 23, 1981; August 16, 1982; August 15, 1983; February 20, 1984; April 1, 1985; February 10, 1986; March 9, 1987.

Newsweek, June 23, 1975; May 2, 1977; April 24, 1978; May 11, 1981; July 19, 1982; July 18, 1983; January 30, 1984; February 25, 1985; February 3, 1986; February 2, 1987; January 4, 1988.

New Yorker, May 15, 1971; June 16, 1975; April 25, 1977; July 26, 1982; July 8, 1983; February 6, 1984; March 25, 1985; February 24, 1986; March 9, 1987; January 25, 1988.

New York Review of Books, June 29, 1978.

New York Times, June 29, 1975; July 9, 1975; August 2, 1978; April 29, 1979; September 19, 1980; September 20, 1980; September 28, 1980; October 19, 1980; March 19, 1981; July 16, 1982; July 25, 1982; October 19, 1982; July 15, 1983; July 17, 1983; July 18, 1983; January 27, 1984; January 29, 1984; June 4, 1984; March 1, 1985; February 7, 1986; February 9, 1986; January 25, 1987; January 30, 1987; February 1, 1987; May 14, 1987; November 24, 1987; December 16, 1987; December 18, 1987; March 1, 1989; March 12, 1989; October 13, 1989; October 15, 1989; October 22, 1989; December 25, 1990; January 15, 1991.

New York Times Book Review, October 26, 1980.

New York Times Magazine, January 7, 1973; April 22, 1979; January 19, 1986.

Rolling Stone, April 9, 1987.

Saturday Review, January 6, 1979; May, 1986.

Time, April 25, 1977; April 30, 1979; August 2, 1982; July 11, 1983; January 23, 1984; March 4, 1985; February 3, 1986; February 2, 1987; December 21, 1987.

Times (London), May 24, 1990; July 21, 1990.

Washington Post, May 2, 1979; September 25, 1979; October 3, 1980; June 2, 1981; August 7, 1983; January 27, 1984; March 22, 1985; February 7, 1986; January 30, 1987; April 1, 1987; March 11, 1988; March 3, 1989; October 13, 1989; January 25, 1991.

Washington Post Book World, September 21, 1980.

*   *   *

AMADI, Elechi (Emmanuel) 1934-

PERSONAL: Born May 12, 1934, in Aluu, Nigeria; son of Daniel Wonuchuku and Enwere (Weke) Amadi; married Dorah Nwonne Ohale, December, 1957; children: Eberechi, Chinyere, Ejimole, Nyege, Okachi, Aleru, Nwerenda (daughters), and Wonukwuru (son). *Education:* University College of Ibadan (now University of Ibadan), B.Sc., 1959. *Politics:* Independent. *Religion:* Protestant. *Avocational interests:* Music, lawn tennis, table tennis, hockey.

ADDRESSES: Home—Mbodo, Aluu, Rivers State, Nigeria. *Office*—Department of Nigerian Languages, Rivers State College of Education, Rivers State, Nigeria.

CAREER: Surveyor in Enugu, Nigeria, 1959-60; science teacher in Nigerian schools, 1960-63, and headmaster, 1966-67; Government of Rivers State of Nigeria, Ahoada and Port Harcourt, government divisional officer, 1968-69, senior administrative officer, 1969-83, commissioner of education, 1987-89, commissioner of lands and housing, 1989-90; Rivers State College of Education, Rivers State, writer in residence, dean of arts, and director of general studies, 1984-87, head of department of Nigerian languages, 1991—. *Military service:* Nigerian Army, 1963-66; became captain; rejoined in 1968 and served with Marine Commandos during the Civil War.

WRITINGS:

The Concubine (novel), Humanities, 1966.
The Great Ponds (novel), Humanities, 1969.
Okpukpe (prayerbook in Ikwerre), C.S.S. Printers (Port Harcourt), 1969.
(With Obiajunwo Wali and Greensille Enyinda) *Okwukwo Eri* (hymnbook in Ikwerre), C.S.S. Printers, 1969.
Isiburu (play; produced in Ibadan, Port Harcourt, and Aiyetoro), Heinemann, 1973.
Sunset in Biafra (Civil War diary), Humanities, 1973.
Peppersoup [and] *Ibadan* (plays), Onibonoje, 1977.
The Slave (novel), Humanities, 1979.
Ethics in Nigerian Culture (philosophy), Heinemann, 1982.
Estrangement (novel), Humanities, 1985.
Kaydara, Heinemann, in press.

Author of *Speaking and Singing,* a collection of papers and poems. Also author of twenty-two poems.

WORK IN PROGRESS: Chei! Calabar, a play; *Nancy Go Home,* a novella for young readers; *Golden Road,* a novel; translating the entire Protestant prayerbook into Ikwerre.

SIDELIGHTS: Elechi Amadi once told *CA* that he is "preoccupied with matter, space, life's purpose (if any), and man." He usually sets novels, plays, and poems in his own country of Nigeria. He has traveled to Britain, western Germany, and the United States.

BIOGRAPHICAL/CRITICAL SOURCES:

BOOKS

Eko, Ebele, *Elechi Amadi: The Man and His Work,* Kraft Books, 1989.

PERIODICALS

Spectator, September 20, 1969.
West Africa, March 14, 1970.

*   *   *

AMBLER, Eric 1909-
(Eliot Reed, a joint pseudonym)

PERSONAL: Born June 28, 1909, in London, England; son of Alfred Percy (a music hall performer) and Amy Madeline (Andrews) Ambler; married Louise Crombie, October 5, 1939 (divorced May, 1958); married Joan Harrison, October 11, 1958. *Education:* Attended University of London, 1924-27.

ADDRESSES: Agent—Linder AG, Jupiterstrasse 1, 8032 Zurich, Switzerland.

CAREER: Writer, 1937—. Engineering apprentice, London, England, 1927-28; actor, comedian, and songwriter in vaudeville, 1929-30; advertising copywriter and agency director, 1930-37. Producer of several films, including "October Man," 1947; worked on 96 educational and training films for the British Army. *Military service:* British Army, Artillery, 1940-46; served in North Africa and Italy; assistant director of Army Kinematography, 1944-46; became lieutenant colonel; awarded Bronze Star.

MEMBER: Authors League of America, Writers Guild of America, West (council member, 1961-64), Garrick Club (London).

AWARDS, HONORS: Academy Award nomination, 1953, for screenplay "The Cruel Sea"; Golden Dagger Award, Crime Writers Association, 1959, for *A Passage of Arms,* 1962, for *The Light of Day,* 1967, for *Dirty Story,* and 1973, for *The Levanter;* Mystery Writers of America, Edgar Allan Poe Award for best mystery novel, 1963, for *The Light of Day,* and for best critical/biographical work, 1987, for *Here Lies: An Autobiography;* Grand Master Award, Mystery Writers of America, 1975; Svenska Deckarakademins Grand Master Award, 1975; Order of the British Empire, 1981; Golden Dagger Award (first presented), Veterans of the OSS (Office of Strategic Services), 1989.

WRITINGS:

NOVELS

The Dark Frontier, Hodder & Stoughton, 1936.

Background to Danger (also see below), Knopf, 1937, reprinted, Berkley Publishing, 1985 (published in England as *Uncommon Danger,* Hodder & Stoughton, 1937).

Cause for Alarm (also see below), Hodder & Stoughton, 1938, Knopf, 1939, reprinted, Berkley Publishing, 1985.

Epitaph for a Spy, Hodder & Stoughton, 1938, Knopf, 1952, reprinted, Berkley Publishing, 1987.

A Coffin for Dimitrios (Book-of-the-Month Club selection; also see below), Knopf, 1939 (published in England as *The Mask of Dimitrios,* Hodder & Stoughton, 1939).

Journey Into Fear (also see below), Knopf, 1940, reprinted, Berkley Publishing, 1987.

Intrigue (contains *Journey Into Fear, A Coffin for Dimitrios, Cause for Alarm,* and *Background to Danger*), introduction by Alfred Hitchcock, Knopf, 1943.

Judgment on Deltchev (also see below), Knopf, 1951, reprinted, Berkley Publishing, 1985.

The Schirmer Inheritance (also see below), Knopf, 1953, reprinted, Berkley Publishing, 1984.

State of Siege (also see below), Knopf, 1956, reprinted, Berkley Publishing, 1985 (published in England as *The Night-Comers,* Heinemann, 1956).

Passage of Arms (also see below), Heinemann, 1959, Knopf, 1960, reprinted, Berkley Publishing, 1985.

The Light of Day, Heinemann, 1962, Knopf, 1963, reprinted, Berkley Publishing, 1985, published as *Topkapi,* Bantam, 1964.

A Kind of Anger, Atheneum, 1964.

Dirty Story: A Further Account of the Life and Adventures of Arthur Abdel Simpson (Literary Guild alternate selection), Atheneum, 1967.

The Intercom Conspiracy, Atheneum, 1969, reprinted, Berkley Publishing, 1987.

The Levanter (also see below), Atheneum, 1972.

Doctor Frigo (also see below), Atheneum, 1974.

The Siege of the Villa Lipp, Random House, 1977 (published in England as *Send No More Roses,* Weidenfeld & Nicolson, 1977).

The Care of Time, Farrar, Straus, 1981.

The Levanter [and] *Dr. Frigo,* Atheneum, 1982.

SCREENPLAYS

(With Peter Ustinov) *The Way Ahead,* Two Cities, 1944.

United States, British Army, 1945.

The October Man, Two Cities, 1947.

(With David Lean and Stanley Haynes) *One Woman's Story,* Cineguild, 1949 (released in England as *The Passionate Friends*).

Highly Dangerous, J. Arthur Rank Organization, 1950.

The Clouded Yellow, General Film Distributors, 1950.

(With others) *Encore,* Paramount, 1951.

The Magic Box, J. Arthur Rank Organization, 1951.

The Promoter, Universal, 1952 (released in England as *The Card*).

Shoot First, United Artists, 1953 (released in England as *Rough Shoot*).

The Cruel Sea (based on the novel by Nicholas Monsairat), Ealing Pictures, 1953.

Lease of Life, Ealing Pictures, 1954.

The Purple Plain, United Artists, 1954.

Battle Hell, Distributors Corp. of America, 1957 (released in England as *Yangtse Incident*).

A Night to Remember, J. Arthur Rank Organization, 1958.

The Wreck of the Mary Deare, Metro-Goldwyn-Mayer, 1960.

Love, Hate, Love, American Broadcasting Company, 1970.

Creator of television series *Checkmate,* 1961-62.

WITH CHARLES RODDA UNDER JOINT PSEUDONYM ELIOT REED; NOVELS

Skytip, Doubleday, 1950.

Tender to Danger, Doubleday, 1951 (published in England as *Tender to Moonlight,* Hodder & Stoughton, 1952).

The Maras Affair, Doubleday, 1953.

Passport to Panic, Collins, 1958.

OTHER

(Contributor) *The Queen's Book of the Red Cross,* Hodder & Stoughton, 1939.

Eric Ambler's Double Decker, World Publishing, 1945.

The Ability to Kill, and Other Pieces (essays), Bodley Head, 1963, reprinted, Mysterious Press, 1987.

(Editor, author of introduction, and contributor) *To Catch a Spy: An Anthology of Favourite Spy Stories,* Bodley Head, 1964, Atheneum, 1965.

The Intriguers: A Second Omnibus (contains *A Passage of Arms, State of Siege, The Schirmer Inheritance,* and *Judgment on Deltchev*), Knopf, 1965.

(Contributor of essay) Dorothy Salisbury Davis, editor, *Crime Without Murder: An Anthology of Stories by the Mystery Writers of America,* Scribner, 1970.

(Contributor) George Hardinge, editor, *Winter's Crimes 2,* Macmillan, 1970.

(Author of introduction) Arthur Conan Doyle, *The Adventures of Sherlock Holmes,* Murray-Cape, 1974.

Here Lies: An Autobiography, Weidenfeld & Nicolson, 1985, Farrar, Straus, 1986.

Waiting for Orders: Short Stories, Mysterious Press, 1991.

Contributor of articles and short stories to *London Times, Sketch,* and other publications.

A collection of Ambler's manuscripts, correspondence, and reviews is at the Department of Special Collections, Mugar Memorial Library, Boston University.

ADAPTATIONS: Journey into Fear was filmed by RKO in 1942; *Background to Danger* was filmed by Warner Brothers in 1943; *The Mask of Dimitrios* was filmed by Warner Brothers in 1944; *Epitaph for a Spy* was filmed as *Hotel Reserve* by RKO in 1944; *The Light of Day* was filmed as *Topkapi* by United Artists in 1964; *Epitaph for a Spy* appeared as a television episode of the *Climax!* series for the Columbia Broadcasting System.

SIDELIGHTS: In the field of espionage fiction Eric Ambler is known as the writer who first created realistic stories about intelligence operations. Writing in the *Hollins Critic,* Paxton Davis states: "Ambler's world, far from being the projection of an adolescent's fantasies of spies who foil master-plots while they wallow in booze and broads, is very much the world we live in. It is Eric Ambler's distinctive contribution to 20th-century fiction that he was able both to discard [the espionage genre's] preposterous conventions, which were strangling the literature of espionage, and to establish a believable world, shabby, gritty, devious, threatening, but compellingly interesting, to replace them." As Joan DelFattore explains in the *Dictionary of Literary Biography,* "In Ambler's world people do things to gain something or to avoid something. There are very few real idealists or patriots in these stories, and their survival rate is close to zero."

Ambler first turned to writing espionage novels when he realized that there were no books in the genre worth a second reading. "It was the villains who bothered me most," he recounts in *Here Lies: An Autobiography.* "Power-crazed or coldly sane, master criminals or old-fashioned professional devils, I no longer believed a word of them." His first novel, *The Dark Frontier,* was meant as a parody of the spy thriller, but reviewers found it to be so good that Ambler stuck with the genre, turning out a series of thrillers during the late 1930s.

It was in his first six novels that Ambler established his reputation as a writer of this new kind of realistic espionage story. "He acquired," Julian Symons writes in *Critical Occasions,* "the sort of reputation that has about it almost a legendary nature." George Grella writes that Ambler "occupies an enviable position in the field of suspense literature. Along with Somerset Maugham and Graham Greene, he changed the spy novel from the jolly-good-fellows, sporting tale of hearty English Fascism to a sophisticated examination of the methods and moralities of modern international intrigue." Grella particularly notes Ambler's "disenchanted, liberal political views which were innovative in a form previously dominated by a provincial, upper-class vision—the world through a mono-

cle." Symons also sees Ambler's political stance as something new to the genre. "Writers of spy stories, from John Buchan onwards," Symons writes, "have almost always been staunch right wingers, proudly unaware of political subtleties: Mr. Ambler seemed to many readers refreshingly aware of the world's changed political climate."

In his book *Mortal Consequences,* Symons elaborates further on Ambler's political perspective. Ambler, he writes, "infused warmth and political color into the spy story by using it to express a Left Wing point of view." Ralph Harper points out in *The World of the Thriller* that Ambler was the first in his genre to display "a critical attitude toward capitalism." Robert Gillespie of *Salmagundi* judges all of Ambler's books to be "political and economic novels but they are something else first. Before they are socialist realism they are democratic realism and before that they are romances."

Over the years, Ambler's political views have changed and his novels have reflected this evolution. As he tells Symons in the London *Times,* "Before the war I was very much an anti-Fascist writer, and after August 1939 and the Nazi-Soviet pact I'd really lost my subject matter. I was of the Thirties, and long after the tears had been wiped away there was still a sense of loss, a loss of belief." "In the 1930s a staunch anti-Fascist, in the 1950s suspicious in turn of Soviet policy," Davis writes, "Ambler [revealed] himself in 1969 [with *The Intercom Conspiracy*] as purged of faith in the wisdom, good intentions or competence of either of the great post-war powers, . . . echoing the antipathy to political action that has become so common, East and West, in these post-Hungary, post-Vietnam years."

Although his politics have evolved over the years, Ambler's novels usually concern "invariably decent, intelligent, well bred men more or less unwittingly enmeshed in Gorgonian webs of political and financial conspiracy," as a reviewer for *Time* notes. Symons sees a recurring situation in Ambler's novels. "The central character," he writes in *Mortal Consequences,* "is an innocent figure mixed up in violent events who slowly comes to realize that the agents and spies working on both sides are for the most part unpleasant but not important men. They murder casually and without passion on behalf of some immense corporation or firm of armaments manufacturers whose interests are threatened. These, rather than any national group, are the enemy."

Some reviewers find this use of a non-professional spy to be one reason for the popularity of Ambler's work. "The amateur as protagonist," Ronald Ambrosetti writes in *Dimensions of Detective Fiction,* "succeeds for Ambler by reducing all of the angst of international intrigue to a very personal level. Ambler gets the edge on suspense by making his spy-detective an average person—the reader identifies easily. In this sense, the Ambler novel is more of a 'thriller' than the . . . professional-spy novels."

In evaluations of his career as a writer, Ambler is often referred to as a "master of suspense" or a "Grand Master." His influence in the genre of espionage fiction has been substantial for many years, and his work has received the highest awards the field has to offer. "To say he is held in high esteem by his writing colleagues would be an understatement," Symons remarks in an article for the London *Times.* At a lunch held in honor of Ambler, Symons reports, such writers as John le Carre, Frederick Forsyth, Gavin Lyall, and Lionel Davidson were in attendance. Le Carre said that Ambler's novels "were the well into which everybody had dipped," while Graham Greene cabled a greeting: "To the master from one of his disciples."

Phoebe Adams of *Atlantic* claims that "Ambler probably could not write badly if he tried." In similar terms, Frederick Busch of the *Chicago Tribune Book World* states: "I think that Ambler cannot write a seriously flawed novel. And I think that his best are among the genre's best." In conclusion, Busch believes that "Ambler has magnificently stood the test of time."

After a near-fatal automobile accident in 1985—an accident brought on when, overcome by fumes, he spun his car off a road in Switzerland—Ambler decided that it was time to write his autobiography. Ironically titled *Here Lies: An Autobiography,* the book follows Ambler's life from his childhood spent among his family's music hall friends (his parents were stage performers), through his careers as vaudeville performer, advertising copywriter, playwright and engineer, until just after the Second World War. "Ambler turns out to write as well about domesticities as he does about exotic intrigue," John Gross notes in the *New York Times.* "He has his chosen areas of reticence, of course," James Fenton writes in the London *Times,* "but the general approach is anti-pretentious and sardonic."

BIOGRAPHICAL/CRITICAL SOURCES:

BOOKS

Contemporary Literary Criticism, Gale, Volume 4, 1975, Volume 6, 1976, Volume 9, 1978.

Dictionary of Literary Biography, Volume 77: *British Mystery Writers, 1920-1939,* Gale, 1989.

Eames, Hugh, *Sleuths, Inc.,* Lippincott, 1978.

Haffmans, Gerd, editor, *Uber Eric Ambler,* Diogenes (Zurich), 1979.

Harper, Ralph, *The World of the Thriller,* Press of Case Western Reserve University, 1969.

Lambert, Gavin, *The Dangerous Edge,* Grossman, 1976.

Landrum, Larry N., Pat Browne, and Ray B. Browne, editors, *Dimensions of Detective Fiction,* Popular Press, 1976.

Symons, Julian, *Critical Occasions,* Hamish Hamilton, 1966.

Symons, *Mortal Consequences: A History—From the Detective Story to the Crime Novel,* Harper, 1972.

PERIODICALS

Atlantic, January, 1941; July, 1972; October, 1974.

Best Sellers, September 15, 1969; September, 1977.

Books, October 22, 1939; October 13, 1940; April, 1970.

Books and Bookmen, April, 1970.

Boston Transcript, September 18, 1937.

Chicago Tribune, August 7, 1986.

Chicago Tribune Book World, September 13, 1981; October 28, 1981; March 14, 1982.

Commonweal, August 7, 1953.

Economist, January 13, 1973.

Globe & Mail (Toronto), November 16, 1985.

Guardian, February 2, 1970; September 23, 1972.

Hollins Critic, February, 1971.

Journal of Popular Culture, fall, 1975.

Life, January 23, 1972.

Listener, August 31, 1972; December 8, 1977.

Los Angeles Times Book Review, February 10, 1991.

Manchester Guardian, August 13, 1940.

National Observer, October 16, 1967; September 22, 1969.

National Review, December 20, 1974.

New Review, September, 1974.

New Statesman, February 20, 1970; July 1, 1977.

Newsweek, June 12, 1961; July 10, 1972; October 14, 1974; June 20, 1977; August 31, 1981.

New Yorker, January 28, 1939; October 19, 1940; March 2, 1963; November 21, 1964; July 15, 1972; October 7, 1974; June 20, 1977.

New York Herald Tribune Book Review, March 23, 1952; August 2, 1953; September 16, 1956.

New York Times, August 8, 1937; January 29, 1939; October 22, 1939; July 18, 1943; September 23, 1956; September 16, 1969; July 3, 1972; November 16, 1974; June 6, 1977; September 11, 1981; July 29, 1986.

New York Times Book Review, October 18, 1964; October 8, 1967; September 21, 1969; July 16, 1972; September 13, 1981.

Observer, February 22, 1970; August 27, 1972; November 17, 1974; June 26, 1977.

Publishers Weekly, July 24, 1967; September 9, 1974.

Punch, March 11, 1970.

Rolling Stone, March 25, 1976.

Salmagundi, summer, 1970.

Saturday Review, September 18, 1937; January 28, 1939; October 25, 1969; August 5, 1972.

Spectator, July 19, 1940; February 28, 1970.

Time, June 26, 1972; November 11, 1974; June 6, 1977; September 14, 1981.

Times (London), January 7, 1970; June 13, 1985; June 23, 1989.

Times Literary Supplement, July 20, 1956; March 5, 1970; November 10, 1972; November 22, 1974; July 29, 1977.

Tribune Books (Chicago), February 3, 1991.

Washington Post, October 22, 1981.

Washington Post Book World, January 14, 1968; July 20, 1969; September 14, 1969; July 2, 1972; September 29, 1974; September 6, 1981.

Weekly Book Review, February 28, 1943.

Wilson Library Bulletin, June, 1943.

*   *   *

ASHERON, Sara
See MOORE, Lilian

*   *   *

AYDY, Catherine
See TENNANT, Emma

B

BABBITT, Natalie (Zane Moore) 1932-

PERSONAL: Born July 28, 1932, in Dayton, OH; daughter of Ralph Zane (a business administrator) and Genevieve (Converse) Moore; married Samuel Fisher Babbitt (vice-president of Brown University), June 26, 1954; children: Christopher Converse, Thomas Collier II, Lucy Cullyford. *Education:* Smith College, B.A., 1954. *Politics:* Democrat. *Avocational interests:* Needlework, piano, word puzzles.

ADDRESSES: Home—26 Benefit St., Apt. 4, Providence, RI, 02904, and 63 Seaside Ave., Dennis, MA 02638.

CAREER: Children's book writer and illustrator.

MEMBER: Authors Guild, Authors League of America, PEN (American Center).

AWARDS, HONORS: Best Book of 1969 for Children Ages Nine to Twelve citation, *New York Times,* for *The Search for Delicious;* American Library Association (ALA) Notable Book citation, 1970, John Newbury Honor Book citation, 1971, and *Horn Book* Honor citation, all for *Kneeknock Rise;* Children's Spring Book Festival Honor Book citation, sponsored by *Book World,* 1971, Children's Book Council Showcase title, 1972, and *School Library Journal* Honor List citation, all for *Goody Hall;* ALA Notable Book citation, *School Library Journal* Best Book of the Year citation, *Horn Book* Honor List citation, and National Book Award nomination, 1974, all for *The Devil's Storybook;* ALA Notable Book citation, *Horn Book* Honor List citation, Christopher Award for juvenile fiction, 1976, International Reading Association choices list citation, U.S. Honor Book citation, Congress of the International Board on Books for Young People citation, all 1978, for *Tuck Everlasting;* ALA Notable Book citation, 1977, for *The Eyes of the Amaryllis;* George C.

Stone Center for Children's Books award, 1979; Hans Christian Anderson Medal nomination, 1981.

WRITINGS:

SELF-ILLUSTRATED VERSE

Dick Foote and the Shark (Junior Literary Guild selection), Farrar, Straus, 1967.
Phoebe's Revolt, Farrar, Straus, 1968.

SELF-ILLUSTRATED FICTION

The Search for Delicious, Farrar, Straus, 1969.
Kneeknock Rise (Junior Literary Guild selection), Farrar, Straus, 1970.
The Something (Junior Literary Guild selection), Farrar, Straus, 1970.
Goody Hall, Farrar, Straus, 1971.
The Devil's Story Book, Farrar, Straus, 1974.
Tuck Everlasting, Farrar, Straus, 1975.
The Eyes of the Amaryllis, Farrar, Straus, 1977.
Herbert Rowbarge, Farrar, Straus, 1982.
The Devil's Other Storybook, Farrar, Straus, 1987.
Nellie—A Cat on Her Own, Farrar, Straus, 1989.

ILLUSTRATOR

Samuel Fisher Babbitt, *The Forty-Ninth Magician,* Pantheon, 1966.
Valerie Worth, *Small Poems,* Farrar, Straus, 1972.
Worth, *More Small Poems,* Farrar, Straus, 1976.
Worth, *Still More Small Poems,* Farrar, Straus, 1978.
Worth, *Curlicues: The Fortunes of Two Pug Dogs,* Farrar, Straus, 1980, also published as *Imp and Biscuit: the Fortunes of Two Pugs,* Chatto & Windus, 1981.
Worth, *Small Poems Again,* Farrar, Straus, 1985.
Worth, *Other Small Poems Again,* Farrar, Straus, 1986.
Worth, *All the Small Poems,* Farrar, Straus, 1987.

OTHER

Contributor to *Redbook, Publishers Weekly, Horn Book, New York Times Book Review, Cricket, School Library Journal, USA Today,* and *Washington Post Book World.*

Babbitt's books have been translated into several languages.

WORK IN PROGRESS: Bub, a picture book.

SIDELIGHTS: A man who has lost his identical twin, a family who has discovered the secret to eternal life, and a boy who must save his kingdom from evil are all subjects of novels written by Natalie Babbitt. Primarily known as a children's book writer, she is also appreciated by older readers as a gifted storyteller. In entertaining narratives, her characters confront many basic human needs, including the need to be loved, the need for growth, change, and independence, the need to overcome fear, and the need to believe in something unexplainable. Her orignality, sense of humor, and courage when facing challenging themes has also established her reputation as an important children's book author.

The author's mother encouraged her early interest in art and reading. Genevieve Moore read children's books aloud to her daughters, and they decided Natalie would become an artist and her sister a writer. Impressed with Brazilian artist Luis de Vargas's airbrushed figures of glamorous women popular during the second World War, the young artist imitated them using colored pencils. Discouraged by the difference between Vargas's finished drawings and hers, she was inspired by Sir John Tenniel's illustrations in *Alice in Wonderland* to work with pen and ink, which became her specialty.

Babbitt received brief training in a summer fashion illustration course at Cleveland School of Art. There she realized she enjoyed creative drawing more than drawing sketches of alligator bags. Later, in art classes at Smith College where she competed with other artists for the first time in her life, she saw that success as an illustrator required more than creativity. In *Something about the Author Autobiography Series (SAAS),* she explained, "It was . . . the best lesson I learned in four years of college: to wit, you have to work hard to do good work. I had always done what came easily, and what came easily had always been good enough. It was not good enough at Smith, and would never be good enough again."

While at Smith, she met Samuel Babbitt, whom she married in 1954. She kept busy working and raising a family of three children while her husband, an aspiring writer, wrote a novel. The many hours alone with the novel did not suit him, however, and he went back to work as a college administrator. Her sister also produced a comic novel, for which Babbitt supplied illustrations, but abandoned the project when an editor asked for a substantial rewriting. "I learned three valuable things from observing what happened to my mother, sister and husband with their forays into the writer's world," she said in her autobiographical essay. "You have to give writing your full attention, you have to like the revision process, and you have to like to be alone. But it was years before I put any of it to good use." After reading Betty Freidan's *The Feminine Mystique,* she realized that while her career as a homemaker had been successful, she had neglected to develop her other talents. After discussions with other women making similar discoveries, she decided to pursue a second career as an illustrator.

In 1966, *The Forty-Ninth Magician,* written by her husband, was published with her illustrations with the help of Michael di Capua at Farrar, Straus & Giroux. Di Capua's encouragement helped Babbitt to continue producing children's books even after her husband became too busy to write the stories. She wrote *Dick Foote and the Shark* and *Phoebe's Revolt,* two picture books in which the stories are told in rhyming poetry.

Babbitt's ideas for books sometimes start with her meditations on a single image, such as a mountain and what can be found behind it, or on a single word. While thinking about the image or the word, she imagines characters whose personalities allow her to develop dialogue and plots for each story. The final result is often very different from her first idea.

Goody Hall started with Babbitt's thinking about the word "smuggler," yet it became a conversation with her mother. Her Grandmother Converse was a woman who supported herself and a daughter by dressmaking. In *SAAS,* Babbitt wrote, "I loved my Grandma Converse. . . . I doubt she ever had an ambitious thought in her life. But my mother not only wanted things, she knew what to want—what, that is, in terms of a Great American Dream of wealth, accomplishment, and social acceptiblity. . . . Like the heores of Horatio Alger, my mother was never afraid of hard work, and many of the things she wanted were worth wanting. . . . She died when I was twenty-four and not yet mature enough to have figured it all out and discussed it with her. So I put it all into my story *Goody Hall* instead."

Goody Hall is a Gothic mystery set in the English countryside. A large Victorian house decorated with "gingerbread" woodcarvings belongs to Midas Goody, whose disappearance spurs a young tutor to investigate. His encounters with an empty tomb, a hollow statue stuffed with precious stones, a gypsy, a rich youngster and his eccentric mother, and other surprises leads to a happy ending where confusing disguises are abandoned and the Goody family is reunited. Though the plot, like the old house with its hints of secret passageways and hidden closets, can frighten and bewilder, "in the end we feel the way the Goodys did about their house," Jean Fritz remarks in the *New York Times Book Review.*

In *The Devil's Storybook,* the title character is a trickster who is fooled as often as he tries to fool others. For example, he gives the power of speech to a goat who then annoys the Devil with his constant complaining. In another story, the Devil sneaks into the bedroom of a pretty lady who outwits him. Babbitt's Devil is middle-aged and pot-bellied and often fails to reach his goal of causing trouble for others. In light of this, his continued meddling in others' lives makes the stories interesting to read, says Selma G. Lanes in *Horn Book.* The sequel, *The Devil's Other Story Book,* also pits the devil against animals and humans who leave the trickster in the dust. There is a moral lesson even in the stories where the devil gives "hell, literally, to those who deserve it," Laurel Graeber remarks in the *New York Times Book Review,* adding that "Ms. Babbitt's ethical lessons . . . rarely undermine her narrative gifts."

In *Tuck Everlasting,* a family who has discovered a secret spring that makes the drinkers immortal find out that living forever without ever growing or changing is not very pleasant; this is explained to a ten-year-old girl who discovers the family by accident. Tuck's explanation of the role of mortality in the cycle of nature "is one of the most vivid and deeply felt passages in American children's literature," *Ms.* reviewer Michele Landsberg declares. A *Horn Book* reviewer says it is a book that rewards a second reading and appeals to adults as well as younger readers.

Babbitt believes that writers don't always have an audience of a specific age group in mind. The source of any book is a writer's sense of urgency that something needs to be said in print, she said in a symposium held at PEN Headquarters in 1987, published in *PEN Newsletter.* The choice to write either for children or for adults comes more from a writer's temperament, or is suggested by the age of the main character, she added. She once told *CA,* "I write for children because I am interested in fantasy and the possibilities for experience of all kinds before the time of compromise. I believe that children are far more perceptive and wise than American books give them credit for being."

In a recent *Horn Book* essay, however, she expressed her concern about the final effect of fantasy stories on impressionable minds. She wrote, "On a recent school visit a fifth-grader asked me if the magic spring water in *Tuck Everlasting* . . . was real. 'No,' I said, 'it isn't real.' 'But,' said the fifth-grader, 'didn't you ever think that when you described it so well, as if it was real, we might believe you?' I have lain awake over that question. Are we somehow implying in our books that the unreal, the impossible, is more greatly to be desired than the real and the possible? Are we maybe whispering that there are instant metamorphoses to be had somewhere, that everyone can and should be a hero? I am only trying to say that we had better tread lightly." In an age when television characters and glamorous celebrities are the most visible role models, she said, writers need to be aware of how children's self-esteem can plummet when they compare themselves to fictional wizards and beauty queens: "It is absolutely true that in America anyone can grow up to be president, but the word is *can,* not *will.* We'd better be sure our children know that while luck is always a factor in how things turn out, there will be no magic, no fairy godmother, no hag on the road with her basket of charms." Babbitt believes young readers also need to be reminded that in the real world, growth and change can take a long time to achieve.

Looking back on her published work, Babbitt recognizes that many of her own childhood memories are in the stories. The childhood experiences recalled in Babbitt's books remain meaningful into adulthood, Anita Moss comments in *Dictionary of Literary Biography.* This quality makes her books enjoyable for readers of all ages. A *Horn Book* reviewer summarizes, "Babbitt's infectious sense of humor, her wisdom and perspective on life, and her ability not to take herself too seriously—but to take what she writes and her audience very seriously—have shaped a magnificent body of work."

BIOGRAPHICAL/CRITICAL SOURCES:

BOOKS

Children's Literature Review, Volume 2, Gale, 1976, pp. 5-8.

Dictionary of Literary Biography, Volume 52: *American Writers for Children since 1960: Poets, Writers, Illustrators, and Non-Fiction Authors,* Gale, 1987, pp. 22-29.

Hopkins, Lee Bennett, *More Books by More People,* Citation Press, 1974, pp. 24-29.

Something about the Author Autobiography Series, Volume 5, Gale, 1988, pp. 41-52.

Twentieth-Century Children's Writers, 3rd edition, St. Martin's, 1989, p. 48.

PERIODICALS

Book World, December 12, 1982, p. 8.

Cricket, April, 1974.

Horn Book, August, 1969, p. 407; June, 1970, p. 295; August, 1971, pp. 380-381; November, 1984, pp. 779-783; July, 1987, pp. 509-511; September, 1987, pp. 607-608; May, 1988, pp. 329-331; September, 1988, pp. 582-589; March, 1989, pp. 133-134; November, 1989, pp. 728-731.

Library Journal, May 15, 1969, p. 2096; June 15, 1970, p. 2306.

Ms., May 11, 1990, p. 74.

New Statesman, November, 1968.

New Yorker, December 4, 1971, p. 199.

New York Times Book Review, July 2, 1967, p. 16; November 9, 1969, p. 62; May 2, 1971, p. 18; July 28, 1974, p. 8; November 16, 1975, p. 32; November 13, 1977, p. 37; November 14, 1982, pp. 44, 54; November 1, 1987, p. 36.

PEN Newsletter, September, 1988, pp. 16-26.

Redbook, December, 1971.

Times Literary Supplement, April 4, 1975, p. 365; July 16, 1976, p. 882; March 25, 1977, p. 348; June 29, 1984, p. 737; August 31, 1984, p. 977.

Top of the News, summer, 1987, pp. 376-382.

Writer, June, 1971.

*   *   *

BAILEY, George 1919-

PERSONAL: Born November 28, 1919, in Chicago, IL; son of George Theodore (a steward) and Ila Ruth (Jacobson) Bailey; married Beate Ross, September 27, 1949; children: Ariane Eliza. *Education:* Columbia University, B.A., 1943; Magdalen College, Oxford, B.A. and M.A., 1949.

ADDRESSES: Agent—Carl Brandt, Brandt & Brandt Literary Agents, Inc., 1501 Broadway, New York, NY 10036.

CAREER: U.S. Army, civilian employee in Germany, 1950-55, resettlement officer, 1950-51, Russian liaison officer at Supreme Headquarters, Berlin, 1951-55; *Reporter,* New York City, foreign correspondent, 1956-67, executive editor, 1967-68; *Harper's,* New York City, foreign correspondent, 1968-70; special correspondent and liaison officer for Axel Springer Verlag, beginning 1973; director of Radio Liberty, 1982-85; coordinating editor of international Russian magazine, *Kontinent,* based in Berlin. Commentator on television and radio. *Military service:* U.S. Army, 1943-46; became first lieutenant; received Bronze Star.

AWARDS, HONORS: Overseas Press Club award for best magazine reporting of foreign affairs, 1960; D.H.L., University of Tampa, 1986.

WRITINGS:

(With Seymour Freidin) *The Experts,* Macmillan, 1968.

(With Owen Barfield and others) *C. S. Lewis, Speaker and Teacher,* Zondervan, 1971.

Germans: The Biography of an Obsession, World Publishing, 1972, 2nd revised and enlarged edition, Macmillan, 1991.

Auf der Suche nach den Deutschen, Molden Verlag (Vienna), 1973, Avon/Discus, 1974.

(With others) *Munich,* Time-Life, 1981.

(Editor) *Kontinent Four: Contemporary Russian Writers,* Avon, 1982.

Armageddon in Prime Time, Avon, 1984.

Zacharow, der Weg zur Perestroika, Herbig (Munich), 1988.

The Making of Andrei Sakharov, Allen Lane/Penguin, 1989.

Galileo's Children, Arcade Publishing, 1990.

SIDELIGHTS: George Bailey told *CA:* "[I have] spent the last half-century in linguistic vagabondage in Europe, most of it in and around Germany. I married into a German-Jewish-Austrian family at the end of the forties and have borne the consequences of that audacity with manly cheerfulness ever since. I served seven years as U.S. Army liaison officer to the Red Army during and after the Second World War and was present at the surrender negotiations in Reims and Berlin. I spent one harrowing year (1950) as a resettlement officer for Soviet Army defectors in the D.P. camps of Germany and Austria. I covered the Hungarian Revolution for ABC out of Vienna and was alternately ABC's resident correspondent in Berlin and Vienna."

By the mid-1950s Bailey began working in various jobs as an editor and foreign correspondent for magazines like *Reporter* and *Harper;* and during the early 1980s he was the director for Radio Liberty. In addition to Europe, he has been to the Middle and Far East. Bailey speaks Russian, German, French, Hungarian, Greek, Czech, Italian, Serbo-Croat, and Spanish.

BIOGRAPHICAL/CRITICAL SOURCES:

PERIODICALS

Christian Science Monitor, June 20, 1968.

New York Times, June 29, 1968.

Times Literary Supplement, September 29, 1989, p. 1058.

Washington Post, July 18, 1968.

*   *   *

BAKER, Alan 1951-

PERSONAL: Born November 14, 1951, in London, England; son of Bernard Victor (a welder) and Barbara Joan (a tracer; maiden name, Weir) Baker. *Education:* Attended Croydon Technical College, 1969-71, Hull University, 1971-72, and Croydon Art College, 1972-73; Brighton Art College, B.A., 1976. *Religion:* "Agnostic."

ADDRESSES: Home and office—St. Michaels, Telscombe Village, near Lewes, East Sussex, England.

CAREER: Author and free-lance illustrator of children's books. Part-time teacher of illustration at Brighton Polytechnic.

AWARDS, HONORS: First class honorary degree in art and design, Brighton Art College, 1976; five awards for Books of the Year, 1989; Silver Campaign Press Award, 1990; Gold Creative Circle Award, 1990.

WRITINGS:

SELF-ILLUSTRATED JUVENILES

Benjamin and the Box, Deutsch, 1977.
Benjamin Bounces Back, Harper, 1978.
Benjamin's Dreadful Dream, Harper, 1980.
Benjamin's Portrait, Deutsch, 1986.
One Naughty Boy, Deutsch, 1989.
Goodnight William, Deutsch, 1990.
Benjamin's Balloon, Deutsch, 1990.
Two Tiny Mice, Kingfisher, 1990.
Jason's Dragon, BBC Publications, 1992.
Where's Mouse?, Kingfisher, 1992.
Both Sides Now: Joni Mitchel, Scholastic Inc., 1992.

JUVENILES

Mythical Beasts, Hutchinson, 1981.
Benjamin's Book, Deutsch, 1982, Lothrop, 1983.
A Fairyland Alphabet, Deutsch, 1984.
Dinosaurs, F. Watts, 1984.
Snakes, F. Watts, 1984.
Spiders, F. Watts, 1985.
Hairy Tales and Nursery Crimes, Deutsch, 1985.

ILLUSTRATOR

Ann Philippa Pearce, *The Battle of Bubble and Squeak,* Deutsch, 1978.
Heritage of Flowers, Hutchinson, 1980.
Rudyard Kipling, *The Butterfly That Stamped,* Macmillan, 1982.
Robin Lister, *The Odyssey,* Kingfisher, 1987.
Robin Lister, *The Story of King Arthur,* Kingfisher, 1988.
Kate Petty, *Stop, Look and Listen, Mr. Toad!,* Hodder & Stoughton, 1991.

ADAPTATIONS: Benjamin and the Box has been featured on the Canadian Broadcasting Corp. (CBC-TV) series, "The Friendly Giant," in March and April of 1980, and on British and Norwegian television.

SIDELIGHTS: Alan Baker told *CA* that his free-lance work "tends to be very different from the books that I do, and I think of it as a separate career. This work is greatly influenced by my environment." He adds: "I live in the country just outside a small village in a very quiet corner of England. My illustrations are mostly plant, animal and fantasy (pixies, dragons, etc.). I get great inspiration from travel, which I used to do a lot of (living very simply which I think is important in order to really 'see' things). As a child, I had a pet hamster—hence the 'Benjamin' books.

"Although I enjoy writing for children, the illustration comes first. I tend to think of certain pictures I would like to create and then link them with a simple story. I like to think of the writing as adding a further dimension to the illustrations. The words hold the storyline when the idea cannot be illustrated. I now teach illustration part-time at Brighton Polytechnic—for me a nice day out!"

BIOGRAPHICAL/CRITICAL SOURCES:

PERIODICALS

Times Literary Supplement, December 2, 1979.

*   *   *

BAKER, Betty Lou   1928-1987

PERSONAL: Born June 20, 1928, in Bloomsburg, PA; died November 6, 1987, in Tuscon, AZ; daughter of Robert Weidler and Mary (Wentling) Baker; married Robert George Venturo, 1947 (divorced, 1965); children: Christopher Patrick. *Education:* Attended school in Orange, NJ. *Avocational interests:* Western history, wildlife and, "of course, Indians."

ADDRESSES: 4127 East Indian School, Apt. 20, Phoenix, AZ 85018.

CAREER: Writer. Worked as a dental assistant and owner of gift shop. Lecturer to groups and instructor of writing for children.

MEMBER: Arizona Press Women.

AWARDS, HONORS: Western Heritage Award, 1963, for *Killer-of-Death,* and 1970, for *And One Was a Wooden Indian;* Spur Award, Western Writers of America, 1966, for *Walk the World's Rim;* Western Writers Award (fiction), 1968, for *The Dunderhead War;* Children's Book Showcase Award, 1977, for *Dupper.*

WRITINGS:

The Sun's Promise, Abelard, 1962.
Little Runner of the Longhouse, Harper, 1962.
The Shaman's Last Raid, Harper, 1963, revised edition published as *The Medicine Man's Last Stand,* Scholastic, 1965.
Killer-of-Death, Harper, 1963.
The Treasure of the Padres, Harper, 1964.

Walk the World's Rim, Harper, 1965.
The Blood of the Brave, Harper, 1966.
The Dunderhead War, Harper, 1967.
Great Ghost Stories of the Old West, Four Winds, 1968.
Do Not Annoy the Indians, Macmillan, 1968.
The Pig War, Harper, 1969.
Arizona, Coward, 1969.
And One Was a Wooden Indian, Macmillan, 1970.
A Stranger and Afraid, Macmillan, 1972.
The Big Push, Coward, 1972.
At the Center of the World: Based on Papago and Pima Myths, Macmillan, 1973.
The Spirit is Willing, Macmillan, 1974.
Three Fools and a Horse (Apache folktale), Macmillan, 1975.
Dupper, Greenwillow, 1976.
Settlers and Strangers: Native Americans in the Desert Southwest and History as They Saw It, Macmillan, 1977.
Save Sirrushany!, Macmillan, 1978.
No Help at All (Mayan legend), Greenwillow, 1978.
Partners, Greenwillow, 1978.
Latki and the Lightening Lizard (Indian folktale), Macmillan, 1979.
All-By-Herself, Greenwillow, 1980.
Rat is Dead, Harper, 1980.
The Great Desert Race, Macmillan, 1980.
Santa Rat, Greenwillow, 1980.
And Me, Coyote! (Indian folktales), Harper, 1981.
Worthington Botts and the Steam Machine, Macmillan, 1981.
Danby and George, Greenwillow, 1981.
Rat is Dead and Ant is Sad (Pueblo folktale), Harper, 1981.
The Turkey Girl, Macmillan, 1983.
Seven Spells to Farewell, Macmillan, 1982.
My Sister Says, Macmillan, 1984.
The Night Spider Case, Macmillan, 1984.

Baker's papers are housed at the University of California Library, Los Angeles; and in the Kerlan Collection, University of Minnesota, Minneapolis.

SIDELIGHTS: Betty Lou Baker specialized in writing historical fiction about the southwestern United States. Many of her books were retellings of American Indian legends and myths; other works featured themes tied to historical events, such as the Mexican War of 1846. Baker was inspired to write, in part, by the "boring sketchiness and occasional inaccuracies" of her son's history books. In an essay for the *Third Book of Junior Authors,* Baker further explained what inspired her work: "Though I usually begin with an intriguing historical situation, people soon involve me and history is relegated to the background. . . . Primarily, I write the sort of book I liked to read, about interesting people involved in lots of action and none of the boring stuff I skip when I read."

Critics have praised Baker's work both for its historical context and colorful characterizations. A reviewer for *Horn Book* called *And One Was a Wooden Indian* "profoundly humorous." "A nicely crafted fantasy," noted Zena Sutherland, writing in the *Chicago Tribune Book World* of *Seven Spells to Farewell.* And a *Bulletin of the Center for Children's Books* reviewer extolled *The Spirit is Willing* by saying: "The writing style is vivacious, the characters come alive, the details of the period and locale are vivid, and the author has created a family and community that are believable and enjoyable."

Baker was a disciplined writer who produced five thousand words a day; she also lectured and travelled extensively. During her travels, Baker continually looked for new book ideas. "Writing is the only job I've ever had that doesn't bore me," she once commented. "Every book is different, not just different in background and characters, but different problems to be solved. Somehow what you learn on one book never applies to the next. And the subject matter can always change to suit my interests."

BIOGRAPHICAL/CRITICAL SOURCES:

BOOKS

de Montreville, Doris, and Donna Hill, editors, *Third Book of Junior Authors,* Wilson, 1972, pp. 24-25.
Kirkpatrick, D. L., editor, *Twentieth Century Children's Writers,* 1978, St. Martin's, pp. 53-54.

PERIODICALS

Bulletin of the Center for Children's Books, July-August, 1974; March, 1978; May, 1982.
Chicago Tribune Book World, June 6, 1982.
Horn Book, April, 1971; October, 1978.

*　　*　　*

BALDWIN, Stan(ley C.) 1929-

PERSONAL: Born December 17, 1929, in Bend, OR; son of Leonard Rite (a cowboy) and Irma Mae (Brown) Baldwin; married Marjorie Antoinette Iverson, December 17, 1948; children: Kathleen (Mrs. Morton Holland), Krystal (Mrs. Arthur W. Brown), Steven, Karen (Mrs. Donald Kraus), Gregory Laverne Todd. *Education:* Attended Powellhurst College, Prairie Bible Institute, and Oregon State University. *Avocational interests:* Sports, fishing, property development, automobile mechanics, home and yard work, boating, water skiing, travel (has toured Mexico, Israel, Asia, Africa, and Europe).

ADDRESSES: Home—7610 S.E. Dolinda St., Milwaukie, OR 97267.

CAREER: Village Church, Carol Stream, IL, pastor, 1970-75. Scripture Press, Wheaton, IL, managing editor, *Power for Life* series, 1970-72, and *Power for Living* series, 1971-73, executive editor, *Freeway* series, 1973-74, editor, *Victor Books* series, 1974-75. Free-lance writer and lecturer, 1975—. Pastor of community church in Albany, OR, 1955-62; pastor of Baptist churches in Corvallis, OR, 1962-65, and Burns, OR, 1965-69.

MEMBER: Oregon Association of Christian Writers (president, 1965-66, 1976-77, 1988-1990).

WRITINGS:

Will the Real Good Guys Please Stand?, Victor Books, 1971.
Games Satan Plays, Victor Books, 1971.
(With wife, Marjorie Baldwin) *Tough Questions Boys Ask,* Victor Books, 1972.
(With M. Baldwin) *Tough Questions Girls Ask,* Victor Books, 1972.
(With James D. Mallory) *The Kink and I,* Victor Books, 1973.
(With Hank Aaron and Jerry Jenkins) *Bad Henry,* Chilton, 1974.
What Did Jesus Say About That?, Victor Books, 1975.
What Makes You So Special, Baker Books, 1977.
(With Malcolm MacGregor) *Your Money Matters,* Bethany House, 1977.
(With Jerry Cook) *Love, Acceptance, and Forgiveness,* Regal Books, 1979.
A True View of You, Regal Books, 1982, reprinted as *If I'm Created in God's Image, Why Does it Hurt to Look in the Mirror?,* 1989.
How to Build Your Christian Character, Victor Books, 1982.
Bruised But Not Broken, Multnomah, 1985.

Also author of *When Death Means Life,* 1986, *The Overflowing Life,* 1987, *Take This Job and Love It,* 1988, and, with J. Cook, *A Few Things I've Learned Since I Knew It All,* 1989.

Contributor of articles and stories to periodicals, including *Christianity Today, Decision, Eternity, War Cry, Virtue, Discipleship Journal, Charisma, Christian Life, Pentecostal Evangel, Eternity, Moody Monthly,* and *Guideposts.*

WORK IN PROGRESS: A book, tentatively titled *At Cross Purposes,* for Multnomah; a book on Christian attitudes toward the secular workplace; an update and total revision of *Your Money Matters,* with Malcolm MacGregor; and a second book with Jerry Cook.

SIDELIGHTS: Stan Baldwin told *CA:* "I write as a ministry: to influence people, teach them, communicate to them. I suppose I'm nothing but a preacher at heart, only I've found a bigger pulpit—the printed page.

"It was an awesome experience for me, early in my career, to attend a Billy Graham crusade in Chicago and see 25,000 people gathered to hear the evangelist. I realized then that everything I write reaches an audience that large and maybe ten times larger.

"So I must write, I suspect, for the same reason Graham must preach. It's the most effective use I can make of my talents and represents an opportunity I cannot neglect. How else could I reach such multitudes, including people who read only German, Spanish, French, Japanese, or Indonesian, into all of which at least some of my works have been translated?

"As a co-author, I am able to provide an important service by teaming with people who have something vitally important to say but lack the skill or the time to say it in writing. The large success of my books of this type has brought many people to seek my services as a co-author. I try to limit my involvement to those people with whom I feel a strong kinship.

"I find writing hard work. I'm an active person, and it's difficult to sit inside at a computer keyboard when the whole world beckons outside. Often I spend the earliest hours of my day writing and then give in to the call of other things. But I keep at the writing relentlessly, slow as the progress seems, because I know something worthwhile will eventually emerge."

*   *   *

BALTIMORE, J.
  See CATHERALL, Arthur

*   *   *

BARAKA, Amiri 1934-
  (LeRoi Jones)

PERSONAL: Born October 7, 1934, in Newark, NJ; original name Everett LeRoi Jones; name changed to Imamu ("spiritual leader") Ameer ("blessed") Baraka ("prince"); later modified to Amiri Baraka; son of Coyette Leroy (a postman and elevator operator) and Anna Lois (Russ) Jones; married (divorced August, 1965); married Sylvia Robinson (Bibi Amina Baraka), 1966; children: (first marriage) Kellie Elisabeth, Lisa Victoria Chapman; (second marriage) Obalaji Malik Ali, Ras Jua Al Aziz, Shani Isis, Amiri Seku, Ahi Mwenge. *Education:* Attended Rutgers University, 1951-52; Howard University, B.A., 1954; Columbia University, M.A. (philosophy); New School for Social Research, M.A. (German literature).

ADDRESSES: Office—Department of Africana Studies, State University of New York at Stony Brook, Long Island, NY 11794-4340. *Agent*—Joan Brandt, Sterling Lord Agency, 660 Madison Ave., New York, NY 10021.

CAREER: Yugen magazine and Totem Press, founder and editor, 1958; New School for Social Research, New York City, instructor, 1961-64; State University of New York at Stony Brook, associate professor, 1983-85, professor of Afro-American studies, 1985—. Visiting professor, University of Buffalo, summer, 1964, Columbia University, fall, 1964, and 1966-67, Yale University, 1977-78, George Washington University, 1978-79, Rutgers University, 1988, and San Francisco State University. Founder and director, 1964-66, of Black Arts Repertory Theatre (disbanded, 1966); currently director of Spirit House (a black community theater; also known as Heckalu Community Center), and head of advisory group at Treat Elementary School, both in Newark. Member, Political Prisoners Relief Fund, and African Liberation Day Commission. Candidate, Newark community council, 1968. *Military service:* U.S. Air Force, 1954-57; weather-gunner; stationed for two and a half years in Puerto Rico with intervening trips to Europe, Africa, and the Middle East.

MEMBER: All African Games, Pan African Federation, Black Academy of Arts and Letters, National Black Political Assembly (secretary general; co-governor), National Black United Front, Congress of African People (cofounder; chairman), Black Writers' Union, League of Revolutionary Struggle, United Brothers (Newark), Newark Writers Collective.

AWARDS, HONORS: Longview Best Essay of the Year award, 1961, for *Cuba Libre;* John Whitney Foundation fellow (poetry and fiction), 1962; Obie Award, *Village Voice,* Best American Off-Broadway Play, 1964, for *Dutchman;* Guggenheim fellowship, 1965-66; Yoruba Academy fellow, 1965; second prize, International Art Festival, Dakar, 1966, for *The Slave;* National Endowment for the Arts grant, 1966; Doctorate of Humane Letters, Malcolm X College (Chicago, IL), 1972; Rockefeller Foundation fellow (drama), 1981; Poetry Award, National Endowment for the Arts, 1981; New Jersey Council for the Arts award, 1982; American Book Award, Before Columbus Foundation, 1984, for *Confirmation: An Anthology of African-American Women;* Drama Award, 1985.

WRITINGS:

PLAYS UNDER NAME LEROI JONES

A Good Girl Is Hard to Find, produced in Montclair, NJ, at Sterington House, 1958.

Dante (one act; based on an excerpt from the novel *The System of Dante's Hell;* also see below), produced in New York at Off-Bowery Theatre, 1961; later pro-

duced as *The Eighth Ditch* at the New Bowery Theatre, 1964.

Dutchman (produced Off-Broadway at Village South Theatre, 1964; produced Off-Broadway at Cherry Lane Theater, 1964; produced in London, 1967; also see below), Faber & Faber, 1967.

The Baptism: A Comedy in One Act (produced Off-Broadway at Writers' Stage Theatre, 1964; produced in London, 1970-71; also see below), Sterling Lord, 1966.

The Toilet (produced with *The Slave: A Fable* Off-Broadway at St. Mark's Playhouse, 1964; produced at International Festival of Negro Arts at Dakar, Senegal, 1966; also see below), Sterling Lord, 1964.

J-E-L-L-O (one-act comedy; produced in New York by Black Arts Repertory Theatre, 1965; also see below), Third World Press, 1970.

Experimental Death Unit #1 (one act; also see below), produced Off-Broadway at St. Mark's Playhouse, 1965.

The Death of Malcolm X (one act; produced in Newark at Spirit House, 1965), published in *New Plays from the Black Theatre,* edited by Ed Bullins, Bantam, 1969.

A Black Mass (also see below), produced in Newark at Proctor's Theatre, 1966.

PLAYS

Slave Ship (produced as *Slave Ship: A Historical Pageant* at Spirit House, 1967; produced in New York City, 1969; also see below), Jihad, 1967.

Madheart: Morality Drama (one-act; also see below), produced at San Francisco State College, 1967.

Arm Yourself, or Harm Yourself, A One-Act Play (produced at Spirit House, 1967; also see below), Jihad, 1967.

Great Goodness of Life (A Coon Show) (one-act; also see below), produced at Spirit House, 1967; produced Off-Broadway at Tambellini's Gate Theater, 1969.

Home on the Range (one-act comedy; also see below), produced at Spirit House, 1968; produced in New York City at a Town Hall rally, 1968.

Junkies Are Full of SHHH . . . (produced at Spirit House, 1968; produced with *Bloodrites* Off-Broadway at Henry Street Playhouse, 1970), both published in *Black Drama Anthology,* edited by Woodie King and Ron Milner, New American Library, 1971.

Board of Education (children's play), produced at Spirit House, 1968.

Resurrection in Life (one-act pantomime), produced under the title *Insurrection* in Harlem, NY, 1969.

Black Dada Nihilism (one-act), produced Off-Broadway at Afro-American Studio, 1971.

A Recent Killing (three-act), produced Off-Broadway at the New Federal Theatre, 1973.

Columbia the Gem of the Ocean, produced in Washington, DC, by Howard University Spirit House Movers, 1973.

The New Ark's A-Moverin, produced in Newark, 1974.

The Sidnee Poet Heroical, in Twenty-Nine Scenes, (one-act comedy; produced Off-Broadway at the New Federal Theatre, 1975; also see below), Reed & Cannon, 1979.

S-1: A Play with Music in 26 Scenes (also see below), produced in New York at Washington Square Methodist Church, 1976; produced at Afro-American Studio, 1976.

(With Frank Chin and Leslie Siko) *America More or Less* (musical), produced in San Francisco at Marine's Memorial Theater, 1976.

The Motion of History (four-act; also see below), produced at New York City Theatre Ensemble, 1977.

What Was the Relationship of the Lone Ranger to the Means of Production?: A Play in One Act, (produced in New York at Ladies Fort, 1979; also see below), Anti-Imperialist Cultural Union, 1978.

Dim Cracker Party Convention, produced in New York at Columbia University, 1980.

Boy and Tarzan Appear in a Clearing, produced Off-Broadway at New Federal Theatre, 1981.

Money: Jazz Opera (libretto), produced in New York at Kool Jazz Festival, 1982.

Money, produced Off-Broadway at La Mama Experimental Theatre Club, 1982.

Song: A One Act Play about the Relationship of Art to Real Life, produced in Jamaica, NY, 1983.

Also author of the plays *Home on the Range* and *Police,* published in *Drama Review,* summer, 1968; *Rockgroup,* published in *Cricket,* December, 1969; *Revolt of the Moonflowers,* 1969, lost in manuscript; *The Coronation of the Black Queen,* published in *Black Scholar,* June, 1970; *Black Power Chant,* published in *Drama Review,* December, 1972; and *Vomit and the Jungle Bunnies,* unpublished. Contributor of plays to books, including *Spontaneous Combustion: Eight New American Plays,* edited by Rochelle Owens, Winter House, 1972.

PLAY COLLECTIONS

(Under name LeRoi Jones) *Dutchman* [and] *The Slave,* Morrow, 1964.

The Baptism [and] *The Toilet,* Grove, 1967.

Four Black Revolutionary Plays: All Praises to the Black Man (contains *Experimental Death Unit #1, A Black Mass, Great Goodness of Life,* and *Madheart*), Bobbs-Merrill, 1969.

The Motion of History and Other Plays (contains *Slave Ship* and *S-1*), Morrow, 1978.

Selected Plays and Prose of LeRoi Jones/Amiri Baraka, Morrow, 1979.

SCREENPLAYS

Dutchman, Gene Persson Enterprises, Ltd., 1967.

Black Spring, Jihad Productions, 1968.

A Fable (based on *The Slave*), MFR Productions, 1971.

Supercoon, Gene Persson Enterprises, Ltd., 1971.

POETRY UNDER NAME LEROI JONES

April 13 (broadside Number 133), Penny Poems (New Haven), 1959.

Spring & So Forth (broadside Number 141), Penny Poems, 1960.

Preface to a Twenty Volume Suicide Note, Totem/Corinth, 1961.

The Disguise (broadside), [New Haven], 1961.

The Dead Lecturer (also see below), Grove, 1964.

Black Art (also see below), Jihad, 1966.

POETRY

Black Magic (also see below), Morrow, 1967.

A Poem for Black Hearts, Broadside Press, 1967.

Black Magic: Sabotage; Target Study; Black Art; Collected Poetry, 1961-1967, Bobbs-Merrill, 1969.

It's Nation Time, Third World Press, 1970.

Spirit Reach, Jihad, 1972.

Afrikan Revolution: A Poem, Jihad, 1973.

Hard Facts: Excerpts, People's War, 1975, 2nd edition, Revolutionary Communist League, 1975.

Spring Song, Baraka, 1979.

AM/TRAK, Phoenix Book Shop, 1979.

Selected Poetry of Amiri Baraka/Leroi Jones (includes "Poetry for the Advanced"), Morrow, 1979.

In the Tradition: For Black Arthur Blythe, Jihad, 1980.

Reggae or Not! Poems, Contact Two, 1982.

ESSAYS UNDER NAME LEROI JONES

Cuba Libre, Fair Play for Cuba Committee (New York City), 1961.

Blues People: Negro Music in White America, Morrow, 1963, published in England as *Negro Music in White America,* MacGibbon & Kee, 1965.

Home: Social Essays (contains *Cuba Libre,* "The Myth of a 'Negro Literature,' " "Expressive Language," "the legacy of malcolm x, and the coming of the black nation," and "state/meant"), Morrow, 1966.

ESSAYS

Black Music, Morrow, 1968.

Raise, Race, Rays, Raze: Essays since 1965, Random House, 1971.

Strategy and Tactics of a Pan-African Nationalist Party, Jihad, 1971.

Kawaida Studies: The New Nationalism, Third World Press, 1972.

Crisis in Boston!, Vita Wa Watu People's War, 1974.

Daggers and Javelins: Essays, 1974-1979, Morrow, 1984.

(With wife, Amina Baraka) *The Music: Reflections on Jazz and Blues,* Morrow, 1987.

EDITOR UNDER NAME LEROI JONES

January 1st 1959: Fidel Castro, Totem, 1959.

Four Young Lady Poets, Corinth, 1962.

(And co-author) *In-formation,* Totem, 1965.

Gilbert Sorrentino, *Black & White,* Corinth, 1965.

Edward Dorn, *Hands Up!,* Corinth, 1965.

(And contributor) *Afro-American Festival of the Arts Magazine,* Jihad, 1966, published as *Anthology of Our Black Selves,* 1969.

Also editor and author of introduction of *The Moderns: An Anthology of New Writing in America,* 1963, published as *The Moderns: New Fiction in America,* 1964.

EDITOR

(With Larry Neal and A. B. Spellman) *The Cricket: Black Music in Evolution,* Jihad, 1968, published as *Trippin': A Need for Change,* New Ark, 1969.

(And contributor; with Larry Neal) *Black Fire: An Anthology of Afro-American Writing,* Morrow, 1968.

A Black Value System, Jihad, 1970.

(With Billy Abernathy [under pseudonym Fundi]) *In Our Terribleness (Some Elements of Meaning in Black Style),* Bobbs-Merrill, 1970.

(And author of introduction) *African Congress: A Documentary of the First Modern Pan-African Congress,* Morrow, 1972.

(With Diane DiPrima) *The Floating Bear, A Newsletter, No. 1-37, 1961-1969,* McGilvery, 1974.

(With Amina Baraka) *Confirmation: An Anthology of Afro-American Women,* Morrow, 1983.

OTHER

(Contributor under name LeRoi Jones) Herbert Hill, editor, *Soon, One Morning,* Knopf, 1963.

(Under name LeRoi Jones) *The System of Dante's Hell* (novel; includes the play *Dante;* also see below), Grove, 1965.

(Author of introduction) David Henderson, *Felix of the Silent Forest,* Poets Press, 1967.

Striptease, Parallax, 1967.

Tales (short stories; also see below), Grove, 1967.

(Author of preface), *Black Boogaloo (Notes on Black Liberation),* Journal of Black Poetry Press, 1969.

Focus on Amiri Baraka: Playwright LeRoi Jones Analyzes the 1st National Black Political Convention (sound recording), Center for Cassette Studies, 1973.

Three Books by Imamu Amiri Baraka (LeRoi Jones) (contains *The System of Dante's Hell, Tales,* and *The Dead Lecturer*), Grove, 1975.

The Autobiography of LeRoi Jones/Amiri Baraka, Freundlich Books, 1984.

(Contributor of commentary) Larry Neal, *Visions of A Liberated Future: Black Arts Movement Writings,* Thunder's Mouth Press, 1989.

The LeRoi Jones/Amiri Baraka Reader, edited by William J. Harris, Thunder's Mouth, 1991.

Works represented in more than seventy-five anthologies, including *A Broadside Treasury, For Malcolm, The New Black Poetry, Nommo,* and *The Trembling Lamb.* Baraka's works have been translated into German, French, and Spanish. Contributor to *Evergreen Review, Poetry, Downbeat, Metronome, Nation, Negro Digest, Saturday Review,* and other periodicals. Editor with Diane Di Prima, *The Floating Bear,* 1961-1963. Papers by and about Amiri Baraka/LeRoi Jones are housed in the Dr. Martin Sukov Collection at Yale University's Beinecke Rare Book and Manuscript Library; numerous letters to and from the author, and several of Baraka's manuscripts are collected at Indiana University's Lilly Library; the author's letters to Charles Olson are housed at the University of Connecticut's Special Collections Library; other manuscripts and materials are collected at Syracuse University's George Arents Research Library.

WORK IN PROGRESS: "Why's/Wise," an epic poem; four books of poetry.

SIDELIGHTS: Amiri Baraka (known as LeRoi Jones until 1967) is a major author whose strident social criticism and incendiary style have made it difficult for audiences and critics to respond with objectivity to his works. His art stems from his Afro-American heritage. His method in poetry, drama, fiction and essays is confrontational, calculated to shock and awaken audiences to the political concerns of black Americans. Baraka's own political stance has changed several times, each time finding expression in his plays, poems, and essays so that his works can be divided into periods; a member of the avant garde during the 1950s, Baraka became a black nationalist, and later a Marxist with socialist ideals. Critical opinion has been sharply divided between those who feel, with *Dissent* contributor Stanley Kaufman, that Baraka's race and political moment account for his fame, and those who feel that Baraka stands among the most important writers of the age. In *American Book Review,* Arnold Rampersad counts Baraka with Phyllis Wheatley, Frederick Douglass, Paul Laurence Dunbar, Langston Hughes, Zora Neale Hurston, Richard Wright, and Ralph Ellison "as one of the eight figures . . . who have significantly affected the course of African-American literary culture."

Baraka did not always identify with radical politics, nor did he always train his writing to be their tool. He was born in Newark, New Jersey, and enjoyed a middle-class education. During the 1950s he attended Rutgers University and Howard University. Then he spent two years in the Air Force, stationed for most of that time in Puerto Rico. When he returned to New York City, he attended Columbia University and the New School of Social Research, where he took a degree in German literature. He lived in Greenwich Village's lower east side where his friends were the Beat poets Allen Ginsberg, Frank O'Hara, and Gilbert Sorrentino. The white avant garde—primarily Ginsberg, O'Hara, and leader of the Black Mountain poets Charles Olson—taught Baraka that writing poetry is a process of discovery rather than an exercise in fulfilling traditional expectations of what poems should be. Baraka learned much from the projectivist poets who believed that a poem's form should follow the shape determined by the poet's own breath and intensity of feeling. In 1958 Baraka founded *Yugen* magazine and Totem Press, important forums for new verse. His first play, *A Good Girl Is Hard to Find,* was produced at Sterington House in Montclair, New Jersey, that same year.

Preface to a Twenty Volume Suicide Note, Baraka's first published collection of poems, appeared in 1961. M. L. Rosenthal wrote in *The New Poets: American and British Poetry* that these poems show Baraka's "natural gift for quick, vivid imagery and spontaneous humor." The reviewer also praised the "sardonic or sensuous or slangily knowledgeable passages" that fill the early poems. While the cadence of blues and many allusions to black culture are found in the poems, the subject of blackness does not predominate. Throughout, rather, the poet shows his integrated, Bohemian social roots. For example, the poem "Notes for a Speech" states, "African blues / does not know me . . . Does / not feel / what I am," and the book's last line is "You are / as any other sad man here / american."

With the rise of the civil rights movement, however, Baraka's works took on a more militant tone, and he began a reluctant separation from his Bohemian beginnings. His trip to Castro's Cuba in July of 1960 marked an important turning point in his life. His view of his role as a writer, the purpose of art, and the degree to which ethnic awareness deserved to be his subject changed dramatically. In Cuba he met writers and artists from Third World countries whose political concerns included the fight against poverty, famine, and oppressive governments. They felt he was merely being self-indulgent, "cultivating his soul" in poetry while there were social problems to solve in America. In *Home: Social Essays,* Baraka explains how he tried to defend himself against these accusations, and was further challenged by Jaime Shelley, a Mexican poet, who had said, " 'In that ugliness you live in, you want to cultivate your soul? Well, we've got millions of starving people to feed, and that moves me enough to make poems out of.' " Soon Baraka began to identify with Third World writers and to write poems and plays that had strong ethnic and political messages.

Dutchman, a play of entrapment in which a white woman and a middle-class black man both express their murderous hatred on a subway, was first performed Off-Broadway in New York City in 1964. The one-act play makes many references to sex and violence and ends in the black man's murder. While other dramatists of the time were using the techniques of naturalism, Baraka used symbolism and other experimental techniques to enhance the play's emotional impact. Lula, the white woman, represents the white state, and Clay, the black man in the play, represents ethnic identity and non-white manhood. Lula kills Clay after taunting him with sexual invitations and insults such as "You ain't no nigger, you're just a dirty white man. Get up, Clay. Dance with me, Clay." The play established Baraka's reputation as a playwright and has been often anthologized and performed. Considered by many to be the best play in America, it won the *Village Voice* Obie Award in 1964. Later, Anthony Harvey adapted it for a film made in Britain, and in the 1990s it was revived for several productions in New York City. Darryl Pinckney comments in the *New York Times Book Review* that *Dutchman* has survived the test of time better than other protest plays of the 1960s due to its economic use of vivid language, its surprise ending, and its quick pacing.

The plays and poems following *Dutchman* expressed Baraka's increasing disappointment with white America and his growing need to separate from it. Baraka wrote in *Cuba Libre* that the Beat generation had become a counterculture of drop-outs, which did not amount to very meaningful politics. Baraka felt there had to be a more effective alternative to disengagement from the political, legal, and moral morass that the country had become. In *The Dead Lecturer,* Baraka explored the alternatives, finding that there is no room for compromise: if he identifies with an ethnic cause, he can find hope of meaningful action and change; but if he remains in his comfortable assimilated position, writing "quiet" poems, he will remain "a dead lecturer." The voice in these poems is more sure of itself, led by a "moral earnestness" that is wedded to action, Baraka wrote in a 1961 letter to Edward Dorn. Critics observed that as the poems became more politically intense, they left behind some of the flawless technique of the earlier poems. *Nation* review contributor Richard Howard commented, "These are the agonized poems of a man writing to save his skin, or at least to settle in it, and so urgent is their purpose that not one of them can trouble to be perfect."

To make a clean break with the Beat influence, Baraka turned to writing fiction in the mid 1960s. He wrote *The System of Dante's Hell,* a novel, and *Tales,* a collection of short stories. The novel echoes the themes and structures found in earlier poems and plays. The stories, like the poems in *Black Magic,* also published in 1967, are "fugitive narratives" that "describe the harried flight of an intensely self-conscious Afro-American artist/intellectual from neo-slavery of blinding, neutralizing whiteness, where the area of struggle is basically within the mind," Robert Eliot Fox writes in *Conscientious Sorcerers: The Black Post-Modernist Fiction of LeRoi Jones/Baraka, Ishmael Reed, and Samuel R. Delany.* The role of violent action in achieving poilitical change is more prominent in these stories. Unlike Shakespeare's Hamlet, who deliberates at length before taking violent action, during this period Baraka sought to stand with "the straight ahead people, who think when that's called for, who don't when they don't have to," he wrote in *Tales.* The role of music in black life is seen more often in these books, also. In the story "Screamers," the screams from a jazz saxophone galvanize the people into a powerful uprising.

Baraka's classic history *Blues People: Negro Music in White America,* published in 1963, traces black music from slavery to contemporary jazz. The blues, a staple of black American music, grew out of the encounter between African and American cultures in the South to become an art form uniquely connected to both the African past and the American soil. Finding indigenous black art forms was important to Baraka at this time, for he was searching for a more authentic ethnic voice for his own poetry. In this important study, Baraka became known as an articulate jazz critic and a perceptive observer of social change. As Clyde Taylor states in *Amiri Baraka: The Kaleidoscopic Torch* by James B. Gwynne, "The connection he nailed down between the many faces of black music, the sociological sets that nurtured them, and their symbolic evolutions through socio-economic changes, in *Blues People,* is his most durable conception, as well as probably the one most indispensible thing said about black music."

Baraka will also be long remembered for his other important studies, *Black Music,* which expresses black nationalist ideals, and *The Music: Reflections on Jazz and Blues,* which expresses his Marxist views. In *Black Music,* John Coltrane emerges as the patron saint of the black arts movement, for replacing "weak Western forms" of music with more fluid forms learned from a global vision of black culture. Though some critics feel that Baraka's essay writing is not all of the same quality, Lloyd W. Brown comments in *Amiri Baraka* that his essays on music are flawless: "As historian, musicological analyst, or as a jour-

nalist covering a particular performance Baraka always commands attention because of his obvious knowledge of the subject and because of a style that is engaging and persuasive even when the sentiments are questionable and controversial."

After Black Muslim leader Malcolm X was killed in 1965, Baraka moved to Harlem and became a black nationalist. He founded the Black Arts Repertory Theatre/School in Harlem and published the collection *Black Magic.* Poems in *Black Magic* chronicle Baraka's divorce from white culture and values and display his mastery of poetic techniques. In *Amiri Baraka: The Kaleidoscopic Torch,* Taylor observed, "There are enough brilliant poems of such variety in *Black Magic* and *In Our Terribleness* to establish the unique identity and claim for respect of several poets. But it is beside the point that Baraka is probably the finest poet, black or white, writing in this country these days." There was no doubt that Baraka's political concerns superceded his just claims to literary excellence, and the challenge to critics was to respond to the political content of the works. Some critics who felt the best art must be apolitical, dismissed his new work as "a loss to literature." Kenneth Rexroth wrote in *With Eye and Ear,* "In recent years [Baraka] has succumbed to the temptation to become a professional Race Man of the most irresponsible sort. . . . His loss to literature is more serious than any literary casualty of the Second War." For the next ten years, Baraka hated whites and Jews, including the whites who had once been his friends. In 1966 he moved back to Newark, New Jersey, and a year later changed his name to the Bantuized Muslim appellation Imamu ("spiritual leader," later dropped) Ameer (later Amiri, "blessed") Baraka ("prince").

A new aesthetic for black art was being developed in Harlem and Baraka was its primary theorist. Black American artists should follow African, not North American standards of beauty and value, he maintained, and should stop looking to white culture for validation. The black artist's role, he wrote in *Home: Social Essays,* was to "aid in the destruction of America as he knows it." Foremost in this endeavor was the imperative to portray society and its ills faithfully so that the portrayal would move people to take necessary corrective action.

By the early 1970s Baraka was recognized as "a teacher of great talent" by Broadside Press publisher Dudley Randall and many others. Randall noted in *Black World* that younger black poets Nikki Giovanni and Don. L. Lee (now Haki R. Madhubuti) were "learning from LeRoi Jones, a man versed in German philosophy, conscious of literary tradition . . . who uses the structure of Dante's *Divine Comedy* in his *System of Dante's Hell* and the punctuation, spelling and line divisions of sophisticated contemporary poets." More importantly, Rampersad writes in the *American Book Review,* "More than any other black poet, however, he taught younger black poets of the generation past how to respond poetically to their lived experience, rather than to depend as artists on embalmed reputations and outmoded rhetorical strategies derived from a culture often substantially different from their own."

After coming to see black nationalism as a destructive form of racism, Baraka denounced it in 1974 and became a Third World Socialist. Hatred of non-whites, he declared in the *New York Times,* "is sickness or criminality, in fact, a form of fascism." Since 1974 he has produced a number of Marxist poetry collections and plays. His new poilitical goal is the formation of socialist communities and a socialist state. *Daggers and Javelins* and the other books produced during this period lack the emotional power of the works from the black nationalist period, say the American critics. However, critics who agree with his new politics such as exiled Philipino leftist intellectual E. San Juan praise his work of the late 1970s. San Juan wrote in *Amiri Baraka: The Kaleidoscopic Torch* that Baraka's 1978 play *Lone Ranger* was "the most significant theatrical achievement of 1978 in the Western hemisphere." Joe Weixlmann responds in the same source to the tendency to categorize the radical Baraka instead of analyze him: "At the very least, dismissing someone with a label does not make for very satisfactory scholarship. Initially, Baraka's reputation as a writer and thinker derived from a recognition of the talents with which he is so obviously endowed. The assaults on that reputation have, too frequently, derived from concerns which should be extrinsic to informed criticism."

Baraka's standing as a major poet is matched by his importance as a cultural and political leader. His influence on younger writers has been so significant and widespread that it would be difficult to discuss American literary history without mentioning his name. As leader of the Black Arts movement of the 1960s, Baraka did much to define and support black literature's mission into the twenty-first century. His experimental fiction of the 1960s is yet considered the most significant contribution to black fiction since that of Jean Toomer, who wrote during the Harlem Renaissance of the 1920s. Writers from other ethnic groups credit Baraka with opening "tightly guarded doors" in the white publishing establishment, notes Native American author Maurice Kenney in *Amiri Baraka: The Kaleidoscopic Torch.* Kenny adds, "We'd all still be waiting the invitation from the *New Yorker* without him. He taught us how to claim it and take it."

BIOGRAPHICAL/CRITICAL SOURCES:

BOOKS

Allen, Donald M., and Warren Tallman, editors, *Poetics of the New American Poetry,* Grove, 1973.

Baraka, Amiri, *The Autobiography of LeRoi Jones/Amiri Baraka,* Freundlich Books, 1984.

Baraka, and Larry Neal, editors, *Black Fire: An Anthology of Afro-American Writing,* Morrow, 1968.

Baraka, *Black Magic: Sabotage; Target Study; Black Art; Collected Poetry, 1961-1967,* Bobbs-Merrill, 1969.

Baraka, *Tales,* Grove, 1967.

Benston, Kimberly A., editor, *Baraka: The Renegade and the Mask,* Yale University Press, 1976.

Benston, *Imamu Amiri Baraka (LeRoi Jones): A Collection of Critical Essays,* Prentice-Hall, 1978.

Bigsby, C. W. E., *Confrontation and Commitment: A Study of Contemporary American Drama, 1959-66,* University of Missouri Press, 1968.

Bigsby, *The Second Black Renaissance: Essays in Black Literature,* Greenwood Press, 1980.

Brown, Lloyd W., *Amiri Baraka,* Twayne, 1980.

Concise Dictionary of American Literary Biography, Volume 1: *The New Consciousness,* Gale, 1987.

Contemporary Literary Criticism, Gale, Volume 1, 1973; Volume 2, 1974; Volume 3, 1975; Volume 5, 1976; Volume 10, 1979; Volume 14, 1980; Volume 33, 1985.

Dace, Letitia, *LeRoi Jones (Imamu Amiri Baraka): A Checklist of Works by and about Him,* Nether Press, 1971.

Dictionary of Literary Biography, Gale, Volume 5: *American Poets since World War II,* 1980; Volume 7: *Twentieth Century American Dramatists,* 1981; Volume 16: *The Beats: Literary Bohemians in Postwar America,* two parts, 1983; Volume 38: *Afro-American Writers after 1955: Dramatists and Prose Writers,* 1985.

Dukore, Bernard F., *Drama and Revolution,* Holt, 1971.

Ellison, Ralph, *Shadow and Act,* New American Library, 1966.

Fox, Robert Elliot, *Conscientious Sorcerers: The Black Post-Modernist Fiction of LeRoi Jones/Baraka, Ishmael Reed and Samuel R. Delany,* Greenwood Press, 1987.

Gwynne, James B., editor, *Amiri Baraka: The Kaleidoscopic Torch,* Steppingstones Press, 1985.

Hall, Veronica, *Chicorel Theater Index to Plays in Anthologies, Periodicals, Discs and Tapes,* Chicorel Library Publishing, 1970.

Harris, William J., *The Poetry and Poetics of Amiri Baraka: The Jazz Aesthetic,* University of Missouri Press, 1985.

Henderson, Stephen E., *Understanding the New Black Poetry: Black Speech and Black Music as Poetic References,* Morrow, 1973.

Hudson, Theodore, *From LeRoi Jones to Amiri Baraka: The Literary Works,* Duke University Press, 1973.

Jones, LeRoi, *Blues People: Negro Music in White America,* Morrow, 1963.

Jones, *The Dead Lecturer,* Grove, 1964.

Jones, *Dutchman,* Faber & Faber, 1967.

Jones, *Home: Social Essays,* Morrow, 1966.

Jones, *Preface to a Twenty Volume Suicide Note,* Totem Press/Corinth Books, 1961.

Kofsky, Frank, *Black Nationalism and the Revolution in Music,* Pathfinder, 1970.

Lacey, Henry C., *To Raise, Destroy, and Create: The Poetry, Drama, and Fiction of Imamu Amiri Baraka (LeRoi Jones),* Whitson Publishing Company, 1981.

O'Brien, John, *Interviews with Black Writers,* Liveright, 1973.

Ossman, David, *The Sullen Art: Interviews with Modern American Poets,* Corinth, 1963.

Rexroth, Kenneth, *With Eye and Ear,* Herder and Herder, 1970.

Rosenthal, M. L., *The New Poets: American and British Poetry since World War II,* Oxford University Press, 1967.

Sollors, Werner, *Amiri Baraka/LeRoi Jones: The Quest for a "Populist Modernism,"* Columbia University Press, 1978.

Stepanchev, Stephen, *American Poetry since 1945,* Harper, 1965.

Weales, Gerald, *The Jumping-Off Place: American Drama in the 1960s,* Macmillan, 1969.

Whitlow, Roger, *Black American Literature: A Critical History,* Nelson Hall, 1973.

PERIODICALS

American Book Review, February, 1980; May-June, 1985.

Atlantic, January, 1966; May, 1966.

Avant Garde, September, 1968.

Black American Literature Forum, spring, 1980; spring, 1981; fall, 1982; spring, 1983; winter, 1985.

Black World, April, 1971; December, 1971; November, 1974; July, 1975.

Book Week, December 24, 1967.

Book World, October 28, 1979.

Boundary 2, number 6, 1978.

Chicago Defender, January 11, 1965.

Chicago Tribune, October 4, 1968.

Contemporary Literature, Volume 12, 1971.

Detroit Free Press, January 31, 1965.

Detroit News, January 15, 1984; August 12, 1984.

Dissent, spring, 1965.

Ebony, August, 1967; August, 1969; February, 1971.

Educational Theatre Journal, March, 1968; March, 1970; March, 1976.

Esquire, June, 1966.

Essence, September, 1970; May, 1984; September, 1984; May, 1985.

Jazz Review, June, 1959.

Journal of Black Poetry, fall, 1968; spring, 1969; summer, 1969; fall, 1969.

Los Angeles Free Press, May 3, 1968.

Los Angeles Times, April 20, 1990.

Los Angeles Times Book Review, May 15, 1983; March 29, 1987.

Nation, October 14, 1961; November 14, 1961; March 13, 1964; April 13, 1964; January 4, 1965; March 15, 1965; January 22, 1968; February 2, 1970.

Negro American Literature Forum, March, 1966; winter, 1973.

Negro Digest, December, 1963; February, 1964; August, 1964; March, 1965; April, 1965; March, 1966; April, 1966; June, 1966; April, 1967; April, 1968; January, 1969; April, 1969.

Newsweek, March 13, 1964; April 13, 1964; November 22, 1965; May 2, 1966; March 6, 1967; December 4, 1967; December 1, 1969; February 19, 1973.

New York, November 5, 1979.

New Yorker, April 4, 1964; December 26, 1964; March 4, 1967; December 30, 1972.

New York Herald Tribune, March 25, 1964; April 2, 1964; December 13, 1964; October 27, 1965.

New York Post, March 16, 1964; March 24, 1964; January 15, 1965; March 18, 1965.

New York Review of Books, May 22, 1964; January 20, 1966; July 2, 1970; October 17, 1974; June 11, 1984; June 14, 1984.

New York Times, April 28, 1966; May 8, 1966; August 10, 1966; September 14, 1966; October 5, 1966; January 20, 1967; February 28, 1967; July 15, 1967; January 5, 1968; January 6, 1968; January 9, 1968; January 10, 1968; February 7, 1968; April 14, 1968; August 16, 1968; November 27, 1968; December 24, 1968; August 26, 1969; November 23, 1969; February 6, 1970; May 11, 1972; June 11, 1972; November 11, 1972; November 14, 1972; November 23, 1972; December 5, 1972; December 27, 1974; December 29, 1974; November 19, 1979; October 15, 1981; January 23, 1984; February 9, 1991.

New York Times Book Review, January 31, 1965; November 28, 1965; May 8, 1966; February 4, 1968; March 17, 1968; February 14, 1971; June 6, 1971; June 27, 1971; December 5, 1971; March 12, 1972; December 16, 1979; March 11, 1984; July 5, 1987; December 20, 1987.

New York Times Magazine, February 5, 1984.

Salmagundi, spring-summer, 1973.

Saturday Review, April 20, 1963; January 11, 1964; January 9, 1965; December 11, 1965; December 9, 1967; October 2, 1971; July 12, 1975.

Studies in Black Literature, spring, 1970; Volume 1, number 2, 1970; Volume 3, number 2, 1972; Volume 3, number 3, 1972; Volume 4, number 1, 1973.

Sunday News (New York), January 21, 1973.

Time, December 25, 1964; November 19, 1965; May 6, 1966; January 12, 1968; April 26, 1968; June 28, 1968; June 28, 1971.

Times Literary Supplement, November 25, 1965; September 1, 1966; September 11, 1969; October 9, 1969; August 2, 1991.

Tribune Books, March 29, 1987.

Washington Post, August 15, 1968; September 12, 1968; November 27, 1968; December 5, 1980; January 23, 1981; June 29, 1987.

Washington Post Book World, December 24, 1967; May 22, 1983.*

* * *

BARCLAY, Bill
See MOORCOCK, Michael (John)

* * *

BARCLAY, William Ewert
See MOORCOCK, Michael (John)

* * *

BARKER, George Granville 1913-

PERSONAL: Born February 26, 1913, in Essex, England; son of George and Marion Frances (Taaffe) Barker; married Jessica Woodward, 1935 (divorced, 1940); married 1942; wife's name, Elizabeth; married Elspeth Langlands, January 10, 1964; children: Raffaella-Flora, Alexander, Roderick, Samuel, Lily. *Education:* Attended Regents Street Polytechnic, 1927-30. *Politics:* None. *Religion:* Roman Catholic.

ADDRESSES: Home—Bintry House, Itteringham, Aylsham, Norfolk, England. *Agent*—John Johnson, Clerkenwell House, 45-47 Clerkenwell Green, London EC1 R0HT, England.

CAREER: Writer. Professor of English literature, Imperial Tohoku University, Sendai, Japan, 1939-41; visiting professor of English literature, State University of New York College at Buffalo, 1965-66, University of Wisconsin, 1971-72, and Florida International University, 1974. Has given poetry readings throughout the United States. Arts fellow, York University, 1966.

AWARDS, HONORS: Royal Society of Literature bursary, 1950; Guiness Prize, 1962; Levinson Prize from *Poetry* magazine, 1965; Borestone Mountain Poetry Prize, 1967; Arts Council bursary, 1968; Commonwealth Prize, 1988.

WRITINGS:

POEMS

Thirty Preliminary Poems, Archer Press, 1933.

Poems, Faber, 1935.

Calamiterror, Faber, 1937.

Elegy on Spain, Contemporary Bookshop, 1939.

Lament and Triumph, Faber, 1940.

Selected Poems, Macmillan, 1941.

Sacred and Secular Elegies, New Directions, 1943.

Eros in Dogma, Faber, 1944.

Love Poems, Dial, 1947.

News of the World, Faber, 1950.

The True Confession of George Barker (long autobiographical poem), Fore Publications, 1950, New American Library, 1964.

A Vision of Beasts and Gods, Faber, 1954.

Collected Poems, 1930-1955, Faber, 1957, Criterion, 1958.

The View from a Blind I, Faber, 1962.

(With Martin Bell and Charles Causley) *Penguin Modern Poets Number Three,* Penguin, 1962.

Collected Poems, 1930-1965, October House, 1965.

Dreams of a Summer Night, Faber, 1966.

The Golden Chains, Faber, 1968.

Runes and Rhymes and Tunes and Chimes, Faber, 1969.

At Thurgarton Church: A Poem with Drawings, Trigram Press, 1969.

What Is Mercy and a Voice, Poem-of-the-Month Club, 1970.

To Aylsham Fair, Faber, 1970.

Poems of People and Places, Faber, 1971.

III Hallucination Poems, Helikon Press, 1972.

The Alphabetical Zoo, Faber, 1972.

In Memory of David Archer, Faber, 1973.

Dialogues, Merrimack Book Service, 1976 (published in England as *Dialogues Etc.,* Faber, 1976).

Seven Poems, Greville Press, 1977.

Villa Stellar, Faber, 1978, Merrimack Book Service, 1979.

Anno Domini, Faber, 1983.

Collected Poems, Faber, 1987.

Seventeen, Greville, 1988.

Street Ballads, Faber, 1991.

OTHER

Alanna Autumnal (novel), Wishart & Co., 1933.

Janus (stories), Faber, 1935.

The Dead Seagull (novel), Lehmann, 1950, Farrar, Straus, 1951.

Two Plays (contains *Seraphina* and *In the Shade of the Old Apple Tree*), Faber, 1958.

(Author of foreword) Alfred, Lord Tennyson, *Idylls of the King, and a Selection of Poems,* New American Library, 1962.

Essays, Macgibbon & Kee, 1970.

(Author of introduction) Maurice Carpenter, *The Black Ballads and the Love Words,* Quaker Press, 1971.

Contributor to *Nation, New Verse, Life and Letters Today,* and *New Republic.*

SIDELIGHTS: George Granville Barker "must be the oldest living enfant terrible in the world," according to Robert Nye in the London *Times.* A writer and poet who began publishing at the age of twenty, Barker's work is marked by rebellion, erotic imagery, and a high romantic outlook. Though sometimes criticized for his lack of consistency, Barker's best works have been described as being among the finest written in the English language. Jo Marie Gulledge in the *Dictionary of Literary Biography* allows that "whether one finds Barker's poetry 'plain-speaking' or marred by obscurity, honest or blasphemous, the astonishing images will last." In his review of *Collected Poems* for *Agenda,* Jonathan Barker notes that "even Barker's staunchest admirers do not dispute the unevenness of his writing, but he is also one of those few English poets who need to be read entire for the full range and comprehensiveness of his vision to be properly appreciated. [Barker] remains a major figure for me, one of the few living poets in our language whose best work really matters and is sure to endure."

Throughout much of his work, Barker deals with such themes as sexuality, uncertainty, and despair. *Poetry* critic E. G. Burrows comments in his review of *The True Confession of George Barker:* "Barker confesses in middle-age to those typical ills of mid-twentieth century man: the failure to relate to one's fellowman, the obsession with and distortion of sex, rootlessness and Godlessness, the loss of human love and its effect on art. These are the weightiest of themes and though Barker treats them jocularly and without respect at times, we know that he knows he is whistling in the dark. Behind the clever lines there is a tense battle being waged and it is Barker's genius to show us the value of this struggle and the toll it has taken even in the midst of his most urbane verses."

Many reviewers feel that one of Barker's most impressive traits as a writer is the emotional intensity he brings to his work. It is this emotional intensity that grabs the reader, drawing him in and involving him in the experience of the poetry. Terry Eagleton writes in *Stand* that "the authenticity of the emotional impulse is impressive. Barker is willing to reveal himself, and while the unstaunched flow of that confessionalism leaves a good many ragged edges, it also conveys the sense of an individual voice rather than of an anonymous ('timeless') Naturepoet." Commenting in the festschrift *Homage to George Barker on His Sixtieth Birthday,* Paul Potts notes that Barker's writings truly reflect the man as well as the poet. As Potts writes, Barker "is capable of spoiling a good poem by a noisy line, but

never of trying to make one out of any emotion that is not an integral part of his own deep feeling."

Religion also plays an important role in Barker's writings. In the chapter he contributed to *Homage to George Barker on His Sixtieth Birthday,* Patrick Swift writes: "I doubt if it is possible to discuss Barker's work at all seriously without penetrating to some extent into the world of religious belief. He himself asserts the supreme importance of religion. For him poetry cannot usurp the responsibilities of religion. The poet cannot operate without the sanction of the religious man, whereas the religious man can pray without reference to the poet. The category of prayer being of a higher order than that of the poem." Writing in *PN Review,* Sebastian Barker calls the collection *Anno Domini,* in which most of the poems are addressed to God, a "great achievement" because in this work the poet was able "to suggest a human shambles which seems a little more divine and a divine shambles which seems a little more human. . . . Within this serious framework, compassion and wit make delightful and satisfying combination in a deity."

However, Roger Garfitt of *London Magazine* claims that "Barker's quality as a religious poet is that he is an impenitent, as most of us are. The poems hold in tension the conflicts basic to any relationship, spiritual or personal: the recognition of need, for instance, and the reaction of defiance that immediately follows." And Potts writes that "the world of George Barker is a place for sinners. It is not a street of barricades, nor is it a house where one prays. Yet the nature of the poetry in him is the plentifulness of forgiveness. His is original without being unique. He is very much of this world, in so far as it is a vale of tears, without being seduced by worldliness. His technique is in advance of his maturity. He is married to poetry, he is not just having an affair with words. But he is still waiting for the cock to crop whereas, according to the calendar of his achievements, he should be getting ready for the gift of tongues."

In an evaluation of Barker's poetry for *PN Review,* David Gascoyne states: "I recognise and salute in George Barker a poet whose work has never ceased to develop, who has been almost uninterruptedly prolific, whose themes have been basic and perennial, and who has remained faithful to his exceptional gift, enriching our language and literature to an extent that remains to be estimated." In another article for *PN Review,* Robert Fraser looks back on Barker's career and concludes that "what has survived is the courage of one for whom the struggle against social and linguistic complacency had endlessly to be renewed with weapons which wear themselves out in use, to be replaced by others, which are sharper, even if initially cruder." In a review for *London Magazine* of Barker's *Collected Poems, 1930-1955,* Anthony Cronin notes that "the best of these verses can stand comparison with the best poetry of our time, with Yeats and Auden. . . . They seem to me to be, at their best, among the most honest and agonizing, and therefore reconciling, consolatory and elating poems written in English in this century."

BIOGRAPHICAL/CRITICAL SOURCES:

BOOKS

Contemporary Literary Criticism, Gale, Volume 8, 1978, Volume 48, 1988.

Dictionary of Literary Biography, Volume 20: *British Poets, 1914-1945,* Gale, 1983.

Feder, Lillian, *Ancient Myth in Modern Poetry,* Princeton University Press, 1971.

Fodaski, Martha, *George Barker,* Twayne, 1969.

Heath-Stubbs, John and Martin Green, editors, *Homage to George Barker on His Sixtieth Birthday,* Martin Brian & O'Keefe, 1973.

Scarfe, Francis, *Auden and After: The Liberation of Poetry, 1930-1941,* Routledge, 1942.

PERIODICALS

Agenda, summer, 1987.

Criterion, July, 1935.

Durham University Journal, December, 1940.

Encounter, August, 1971.

Library Journal, February 1, 1979.

Life and Letters Today, June, 1940.

London Magazine, October, 1954; September, 1956; May, 1958; May, 1962; June, 1966; May, 1968; August/ September, 1976.

London Mercury, June, 1935; June, 1937.

Nation, December 13, 1941.

New Statesman, September 25, 1970.

Parnassus, Volume 8, number 2, 1980.

PN Review, Volume 9, number 5, 1983.

Poetry, December, 1941; April, 1944; April, 1948; December, 1964.

Punch, March 27, 1968.

Saturday Review, July 4, 1964; December 25, 1965.

Scrutiny, June, 1934.

Sewanee Review, summer, 1968.

Spectator, August 2, 1957.

Stand, Volume XV, number 4, 1974.

Times (London), June 25, 1987.

Times Literary Supplement, April 14, 1966; April 16, 1970.

Yale Review, winter, 1948.

BARKER, Ralph 1917-

PERSONAL: Born October 21, 1917, in Feltham, Middlesex, England; son of Frederick Charles and Alma (Golding) Barker; married Joan Muriel Harris, 1948; children: Sarah Geraldine. *Education:* Attended Hounslow College, 1926-34. *Religion:* Church of England. *Avocational interests:* Aviation, cricket, tennis, and duplicate bridge.

ADDRESSES: Home—Old Timbers, 16 Aldercombe Lane, Caterham, Surrey, England.

CAREER: Writer. *Sporting Life* (newspaper), London, England, sub-editor, 1935; Barclays Bank, Ltd., London, clerk and cashier, 1936-48; Royal Air Force, aircrew, 1940-46, intelligence, 1948-61, retired as flight lieutenant.

MEMBER: Royal Aeronautical Society (associate member), Society of Authors.

WRITINGS:

Down in the Drink, Chatto & Windus, 1955.
The Ship-Busters, Chatto & Windus, 1957.
The Last Blue Mountain, Chatto & Windus, 1959, Doubleday, 1960, reprinted, Mountaineers, 1979.
Strike Hard, Strike Sure, Chatto & Windus, 1963.
Ten Great Innings, Chatto & Windus, 1964.
The Thousand Plan, Chatto & Windus, 1965.
Ten Great Bowlers, Chatto & Windus, 1966.
Great Mysteries of the Air, Chatto & Windus, 1966, Macmillan (New York), 1967.
Aviator Extraordinary, Chatto & Windus, 1969.
Test Cricket: England vs. Australia, Batsford, 1969.
Verdict on a Lost Flyer, Harrap, 1969, St. Martin's, 1971.
The Schneider Trophy Races, Chatto & Windus, 1971.
Against the Sea, Chatto & Windus, 1972.
One Man's Jungle, Chatto & Windus, 1975.
The Blockade Busters, Chatto & Windus, 1976, Norton, 1977.
Survival in the Sky, Kimber, 1976.
The Cricketing Family Edrich, Pelham Books, 1976.
The Hurricats, Pelham Books, 1978.
Not Here, But in Another Place, St. Martin's, 1980.
The RAF at War, Time-Life, 1981.
Innings of a Lifetime, Collins, 1982.
Goodnight, Sorry for Sinking You: The Story of the SS City of Cairo, Collins, 1984.
Purple Patches, Collins, 1987.
Children of the Benares, Methuen, 1987.
That Eternal Summer, Collins, 1990.

Contributor to *Sunday Express* (London).

ADAPTATIONS: The Thousand Plan was made into the movie *The Thousand Plane Raid* by United Artists in 1969. A five-part television series based on *Verdict on a Lost Flyer* is available on videotape. The story concerns the love affair between pioneer aviators Bill Lancaster and Chubbie Miller that climaxed in a sensational murder trial in Miami and ended with the disappearance of Lancaster during an attempted record flight.

WORK IN PROGRESS: The Glory Shall Remain: The Story of the Royal Flying Corps in France, 1914-1918, for Constable.

BIOGRAPHICAL/CRITICAL SOURCES:

PERIODICALS

Guardian, June 23, 1990.
Times Literary Supplement, January 28, 1983; May 31, 1985.

*   *   *

BARRATT-BROWN, Michael 1918-

PERSONAL: Born March 15, 1918, in Birmingham, England; son of Alfred (a college principal) and Doris Eileen (Cockshott) Barratt-Brown; married Frances Mary Lloyd, August 8, 1940 (divorced June, 1946); married Eleanor Mary Singer (a medical practitioner), July 15, 1946; children: Christopher John, Richard Rollo, Daniel, Deborah. *Education:* Corpus Christi College, Oxford, B.A., 1940, M.A., 1945. *Politics:* Labour. *Religion:* None.

ADDRESSES: Home—Robin Hood Farm, Baslow, near Bakewell, Derbyshire, England.

CAREER: Special assistant to chief of Balkan and Yugoslavian missions, United Nations Relief and Rehabilitation Administration, 1944-47; Cambridge University, Cambridge, England, part-time tutor, 1947-61; University of Sheffield, Sheffield, England, lecturer, 1961-66, senior lecturer in extra-mural studies, 1966-77; Northern College, Barnsley, England, principal, 1977-83. Institute for Workers' Control, member of council; Bertrand Russell Peace Foundation, member of board of directors; chairman, Third World Information Network Ltd. and Twin Trading Ltd. Spokesman Books, member of editorial board.

MEMBER: Royal Statistical Society (fellow), Society of Industrial Tutors (chairman, 1965-77; president, 1978—).

AWARDS, HONORS: Associate fellow of Institute for Developmental Studies, University of Sussex, 1976; fellow of Sheffield City Polytechnic, 1984; honorary doctorate, Open University, 1985.

WRITINGS:

(With John Hughes) *Britain's Crisis and the Common Market,* New Left, 1962.
After Imperialism, Heinemann, 1963, 3rd edition, 1970.

Adult Education for Industrial Workers, National Institute of Adult Education, 1969.
What Economics Is About, Weidenfeld & Nicolson, 1970.
Trade Unions and Rising Prices, Institute for Workers' Control, 1971.
Essays on Imperialism, Spokesman Books, 1972.
From Labourism to Socialism: The Political Economy of Labour in the 1970s, Spokesman Books, 1972.
The Economics of Imperialism, Penguin Books, 1974.
(With Ken Coates) *Accountability and Industrial Democracy: Evidence to the Bullock Committee,* Institute for Workers' Control, 1976.
Resources and the Environment: A Socialist Perspective, Spokesman Books, 1976.
Full Employment: Priority, Spokesman Books, 1978.
Information at Work, Arrow Books, 1978.
(With Coates) *What Went Wrong,* Spokesman Books, 1978.
(With Coates) *The Right to Useful Work,* Spokesman Books, 1979.
(With Su Shaozhi and others) *Democracy and Socialism in China,* Spokesman Books, 1982.
(With John Eaton and Coates) *An Alternative Economic Strategy for the Labour Movement,* Spokesman Books, 1982.
Models in Political Economy, Penguin Books, 1984.
European Union: Fortress or Democracy, Spokesman Books, 1990.
Fair Trade: A Piece of the Action for the Third World, Zed Books, 1992.
What Hope for Africa?, Transnational Institute, 1992.
A Future for Socialism?, New Left Books, in press.

EDITOR

Red Paper: A Response to the Labour Party's Green Paper, Institute for Workers' Control, 1972.
Europe: Time to Leave—and How to Go, Spokesman Books, 1973.
Anatomy of Underdevelopment: Documents on Economic Policy in the Third World, Spokesman Books, 1974.
(With Coates) *Trade Union Register,* Spokesman Books, 1973 edition, 1975, 1974 edition, 1976.
Social and Economic Study Packs, Greater London Council, 1984-85.

OTHER

Contributor to books, including *Introduction to the Sociology of Developing Societies,* edited by Teodor Shanin, Macmillan, 1980; and *Planning the Planners: How to Control the Recovery—An Examination of the 1982 TUC-Labour Party Report on Economic Planning and Industrial Democracy,* edited by Anthony Topham, Spokesman Books, 1983. Contributor to *Socialist Encyclopaedia.* Member of editorial board, *Universities, Left Review, New Reasoner,*

New Left Review, May Day Manifesto, New Socialist, and *European Labour Forum.*

SIDELIGHTS: Michael Barratt-Brown told *CA:* "I write because I am driven to try to explain to others in simple terms what I believe to be the right way of understanding the complex society we live in. Writing is an extension of my role as a teacher."

*   *   *

BARRINGTON, Michael
See MOORCOCK, Michael (John)

*   *   *

BARRY, William A(nthony) 1930-

PERSONAL: Born November 22, 1930, in Worcester, MA; son of William (a steelworker) and Catherine (a housewife; maiden name, McKenna) Barry. *Education:* Boston College, A.B., 1956; Fordham University, M.A., 1960; Weston School of Theology, S.T.L., 1963; University of Michigan, Ph.D., 1968.

ADDRESSES: Home—775 Harrison Ave., Boston, MA 02118. *Office*—Provincial Office of New England, Society of Jesus, 775 Harrison Ave., Boston, MA 02118.

CAREER: Entered Society of Jesus (Jesuits), 1950; ordained Roman Catholic priest, 1962; teacher of Latin, English, and German at private secondary school in Fairfield, CT, 1956-58; University of Michigan, Ann Arbor, staff psychologist and lecturer in psychology, 1968-69; Weston School of Theology, Cambridge, MA, assistant professor, 1969-73, associate professor of pastoral psychology, 1973-78, member of staff at Center for Religious Development, 1971-78, director of center, 1971-75, member of board of directors, 1979-84; Society of Jesus, Provincial Office of New England, Boston, MA, vice-provincial, 1978-84, assistant novice director, 1985-88; Boston College, Boston, rector of Jesuit Community, 1988-91, trustee, 1988-91; Society of Jesus, Provincial Office of New England, Boston, provincial, 1991—. Ecumenical Counseling Service, Melrose, MA, staff psychologist, 1970-71, member of board of directors, 1971-81.

MEMBER: American Psychological Association, Society for the Scientific Study of Religion, Society for the Psychological Study of Social Issues.

AWARDS, HONORS: Grant from Association of Theological Schools, 1975-76.

WRITINGS:

(With Harold L. Rausch, Richard K. Hertel, and Mary Ann Swain) *Communication, Conflict, and Marriage:*

Explorations in the Theory and Study of Relationships, Jossey-Bass, 1974.

(With William J. Connolly) *The Practice of Spiritual Direction,* Seabury, 1982.

God and You: Prayer as a Personal Relationship, Paulist Press, 1987.

"Seek My Face": Prayer as a Personal Relationship in Scripture, Paulist Press, 1989.

Paying Attention to God: Discernment in Prayer, Ave Maria Press, 1990.

"Now Choose Life": Conversion as a Way to Life, Paulist Press, 1990.

Finding God in All Things: A Companion to the Spiritual Exercises of St. Ignatius, Ave Maria Press, 1991.

(Editor with Kerry Maloney) *A Hunger for God: Ten Approaches to Prayer,* Sheed and Ward, 1991.

Spiritual Direction and the Encounter with God: A Theological Inquiry, Paulist Press, 1992.

Contributor to religious and psychology journals.

SIDELIGHTS: William A. Barry once told *CA:* "I originally decided on doctoral studies in clinical psychology because of a conviction that there is an intimate connection between human intra- and interpersonal dynamics and the human reaction to God. While at the University of Michigan I became part of a research project on interpersonal relationships headed by Harold L. Rausch. We analyzed data from newlywed couples engaged in improvisational conflict. Our premise was that the inevitable conflict in intimate relationships could be handled in ways that were constructive or destructive depending on the strength of the affective bond between the couple and the flexibility of the personality structures of the individuals. If the bond was strong and both parties relatively flexible and adaptable as persons, then they could face conflict and communicate in ways that led to constructive resolution of the conflict. On the other hand, if the bond was not strong and/or each party had relatively inflexible personalities, then conflict would either be avoided entirely, leading to less and less intimacy, or escalate sooner or later into a pitched battle with destructive consequences for the individuals, their relationship, and probably their children.

"In the research and in my work as a psychotherapist I noted the strength of the resistance to newness, difference, and change, but I was also aware of the human capacity and desire for growth, health, freedom, and a less neurotic life. Few psychologists focus on the latter and fewer still wonder about the sources of this capacity for transcendence. I certainly enjoyed doing psychotherapy and helping people uncover hidden, neurotic motivation, but I found myself more and more fascinated and deeply moved by the courage of people to face their own conflicts and darkness. I became convinced that whether they could name the sources of such confidence or not, that source was a trust, a faith in the power of light over darkness, of love over fear and hate. As I helped people to look at this source, they became more articulate about experiences of transcendence, of a sense of hope in midst of despair and darkness, of a Presence that promised life, of a wholeness that was possible and desirable. People were helped by talking about such experiences and found themselves more and more conscious of their relationship with God.

"All my training as a clinical psychologist became focused on helping people to develop that relationship through paying attention to their experiences of God in their daily lives [and] through trying to describe these experiences. We discovered together that such a focus not only gave more meaning to our lives but also gradually forced us to examine our other relationships, our work and the direction of our lives in the light of this relationship. Whereas psychology tends to reduce human experience to its explanation in past history, a laudable enterprise in itself, the type of pastoral counseling I call spiritual direction, and the theological reflection based on it, tend to expand the way of looking at human experience to include the mysterious Other we call God as participant in it.

"Consistently, through all my writing, I have tried to pay close attention to human experience and to tie theory to such experience."

*   *   *

BASU, Kaushik 1952-

PERSONAL: Born January 9, 1952, in Calcutta, India; son of Keshab C. (a solicitor) and Usha (a housewife; maiden name, Ghosh) Basu; married Alaka Malwade (a demographer), July 21, 1977; children: Karna (son), Diksha (daughter). *Education:* University of Delhi, B.A. (with honors), 1972; London School of Economics and Political Science, London, M.Sc., 1974, Ph.D., 1976.

ADDRESSES: Office—Centre for Advanced Studies in Economic History and Economic Development, Delhi School of Economics, University of Delhi, Delhi, India 110 007.

CAREER: University of Delhi, Delhi, India, reader in economics, 1978-85, professor of economics, 1985—. Visiting associate professor at Centre for Operations Research and Econometrics, Louvain-la-Neuve, Belgium, 1981-82; visiting professor at Centre d'economie mathematique et d'econometrie, Brussels, Belgium, 1981-82; visiting professor of economics, Princeton University, Princeton, NJ, 1989-91. Joint managing editor of *Journal of Quantitative Economics.*

MEMBER: United States Econometric Society (fellow), Royal Economic Society (England), Centre for Operations Research and Econometrics (fellow).

WRITINGS:

Revealed Preference of Government, Cambridge University Press, 1980.
The Less Developed Economy: A Critique of Contemporary Theory, Basil Blackwell, 1984.
Agrarian Structure and Economic Underdevelopment, Harwood, 1990.
Economic Graffiti: Essays for Everyone, Oxford University Press, 1991.

Author of biweekly column "An Economist's Diary" for *Indian Express* newspaper. Contributor to economic journals. Member of board of editors of *Indian Economic Review, Journal of Public Economics,* and *World Bank Economic Review.*

WORK IN PROGRESS: Lectures in Industrial Organization Theory, for Basil Blackwell, 1993.

SIDELIGHTS: Kaushik Basu once told *CA:* "The person whose writings have influenced me the most is Bertrand Russell. I have always enjoyed abstract reasoning and deductive logic. Like Russell, I believe that one should speak the truth as far as possible. It follows—and this is my advice to fellow human beings—that if you do not have enough courage to criticize an evil man to his face, at least have the courage to do it behind his back!"

*   *   *

BB

See WATKINS-PITCHFORD, Denys James

*   *   *

BELL, David Victor John 1944-

PERSONAL: Born in 1944, in Toronto, Ontario, Canada; son of Herbert McLean and Violet (Bryan) Bell; married Kaaren Cambelle Macdonald, 1966; children: Kristin Cassandra, Jason David. *Education:* Attended York University, 1962-65; University of Toronto, B.A. (first class honors), 1965; Harvard University, A.M., 1967, Ph.D., 1969. *Avocational interests:* Tennis, squash, touch football, music (has been a professional chorister and jazz bassist).

ADDRESSES: Home—5 Shaindell St., Thornhill, Ontario, Canada L3T 3X5. *Office*—Department of Political Science, York University, 4700 Keele St., Downsview, Ontario, Canada M3J 1P3.

CAREER: Michigan State University, East Lansing, assistant professor of political science, 1969-71; York University, Downsview, Ontario, assistant professor, 1971-73, associate professor, 1973-81, professor of political science, 1981—, dean of graduate studies, 1981—, chairperson of Department of Political Science, 1991-92. Visiting professor of peace studies, Juniata College, spring, 1978. Cofounder and president, Grindstone Cooperative Ltd., 1976-81; chairman, Leave Fellowship Selection Committee, Social Science and Humanities Research Council, 1978. Lecturer; has appeared on television and radio programs. Varsity women's soccer coach.

MEMBER: Canadian Political Science Association, Association of Cinema, Television, and Radio Artists.

AWARDS, HONORS: Woodrow Wilson fellowships, 1965, 1967; Canada Council leave fellowship, 1976-77; grants from Canadian Department of Transport, 1977-78, Transport Canada, 1978-79, Social Science and Humanities Research Council, 1979-80, 1984, and Canadian Department of Labour, 1980-81.

WRITINGS:

(With Karl W. Deutsch) *Instructor's Manual to Accompany "Politics and Government"*, Houghton, 1970, 2nd edition (with wife, Kaaren C. M. Bell), 1974.

(Editor with Deutsch and Seymour Martin Lipset) *Issues in Politics and Government*, Houghton, 1970.

(Contributor) Jack Bumsted, editor, *Canadian History before Confederation*, Irwin, 1972.

Resistance and Revolution, Houghton, 1973.

Power, Influence, and Authority, Oxford University Press, 1975.

(Contributor) Paul Fox, editor, *Politics Canada*, 4th edition, McGraw, 1977.

(Contributor) Joseph S. Tulchin, editor, *Hemispheric Perspectives on the United States*, Greenwood Press, 1978.

(With Lorne J. Tepperman) *The Roots of Disunity: A Study of Canadian Political Culture*, McClelland & Stewart, 1979, revised edition, Oxford University Press, 1992.

(Author of foreword) H. Darling, *The Politics of Freight Rates*, McClelland & Stewart, 1980.

(With M. Goodstadt and others) *Alcohol: Public Education and Social Policy*, Addiction Research Foundation, 1981.

(Author of foreword) David Brooks, *Zero Energy Growth*, McClelland & Stewart, 1981.

(Contributor) Michael Whittington and Glen Williams, editors, *Canadian Politics in the 1980s*, Methuen, 1981.

(Contributor) G. Dlugos and others, editors, *Management under Differing Value Systems*, De Gruyter, 1981.

(Contributor) M. M. Rosenberg, W. B. Shaffir, A. Turowetz, and M. Weinfeld, editors, *An Introduction to Sociology*, Methuen, 1983, 2nd edition, 1989.

(Author of foreword) Williams, *Not for Export: Toward a Political Economy of Canada's Arrested Industrialization*, McClelland & Stewart, 1983.

(Contributor) Whittington and Williams, editors, *Canadian Politics in the 1990's*, Methuen, 1990.

(Editor with Frederick Fletcher, and contributor) *Reaching the Voter: Constituency Level Campaigning in Canada*, [Toronto], 1991.

Co-editor of a series of monographs, "Canada in Transition: Crises in Development," McClelland & Stewart, 1975—. Contributor of articles and reviews to periodicals, including *Issues in Politics and Government, Journal of Canadian Studies, Yale Review, Newsletter* of Association for Canadian Studies in American Universities, *Windsor Review, Harvard Alumni Bulletin, Negotiation Journal, American Political Science Review, Peace Magazine,* and *Canadian Journal of Political Science.* Member of editorial board, *Teaching Political Science* and *International Interactions,* both 1972—; guest editor of a special issue of *International Interactions,* 1979.

SIDELIGHTS: David Victor John Bell told *CA:* "In 1989, I was asked to write some television scripts for a TV Ontario series on Canadian political parties and ideologies ('Left, Right, and Centre.') The producer explained that writing for television was very different than writing for radio. 'You have to keep it simple, and say everything three times,' he explained. 'Viewers aren't paying attention to the words because they're too busy watching the pictures.'"

*   *   *

BELLE, Pamela 1952-

PERSONAL: Born June 16, 1952, in Ipswich, England; daughter of Brian Henry (a teacher) and Sylvia (a housewife; maiden name, Wilkinson) Belle; married Alan David Fincher, July 3, 1976 (divorced, 1984); married Stephen Thomas, August 6, 1990; children: Hugh. *Education:* University of Sussex, B.A. (with honors), 1975; Coventry College of Education, postgraduate certificate in education, 1976. *Politics:* "Slightly left of center!" *Religion:* None.

ADDRESSES: Home—"Brambledown," 61, New Rd., Bromham, Wiltshire, England. *Agent*—Vivienne Schuster, John Farquharson Ltd., 162-168 Regent St., London W.1, England.

CAREER: Northchurch St. Mary's First School, Berkhamsted, England, teacher, 1978-85; writer, 1985—.

MEMBER: National Union of Teachers, Richard III Society.

WRITINGS:

The Moon in the Water (novel), Berkley Publishing, 1984.
The Chains of Fate (novel), Berkley Publishing, 1984.
Alathea (novel), Berkley Publishing, 1985.
The Lodestar, St. Martin's, 1988.
Wintercombe, St. Martin's, 1988.
Herald of Joy, St. Martin's, 1989.
A Falling Star, St. Martin's, 1990.

WORK IN PROGRESS: A fourth book in the "Wintercombe" series, set in the Glorious Revolution of 1688, for St. Martin's.

SIDELIGHTS: Pamela Belle told *CA:* "Originally I wrote purely for my own enjoyment. Successful publication was a bonus! I have no particular viewpoint to put forth or axe to grind, although I tend to fill my books with all the things I find enjoyable: poetry, music, magic, food, animals, children, humor, and the fascination of entering a world long vanished. My characters also tend to reflect my own beliefs and prejudices on the equality of women and the importance of love, tolerance, and compassion, my distrust of organized religion, and my love of the world of imagination. Nevertheless, my main concern is to tell my story entertainingly and convincingly, and more serious considerations are by the way. I would rather have my books read and enjoyed by many and ignored by serious reviewers than write more difficult and obscure works that, like many 'classics,' people think they ought to read, but haven't.

"I do, however, place great importance on proper historical research. I think this is because my characters seem so real to me that I cannot bear to destroy the illusion by falsifying the picture. Everything I write about *could* have happened or existed, even if it never did in reality. I want my characters to be sufficiently real and alive to lead my readers into my own enjoyment and study of history."

BIOGRAPHICAL/CRITICAL SOURCES:

PERIODICALS

Washington Post, October 9, 1984.
Washington Post Book World, November 6, 1988, p. 8.

* * *

BEYERHAUS, Peter (Paul Johannes) 1929-

PERSONAL: Born February 1, 1929, in Hohenkraenig, Germany; son of Siegfried (a minister) and Fridel (a nurse; maiden name, Korweck) Beyerhaus; married Ingegard Kalen (a teacher), August 6, 1955; children: Karolina, Jo-

hannes, Maria, Christoph, Gunilla. *Education:* University of Uppsala, L.Th., 1956, D.Th., 1957.

ADDRESSES: Home—Stiffurtstrasse 5, D-7400 Tuebingen, Germany. *Office*—Institute of Missiology, Hausserstrasse 43, D-7400 Tuebingen, Germany.

CAREER: Ordained Lutheran minister, 1955; German Missionary Council, Hamburg, Germany, theological assistant, 1953-54; pastor of Lutheran churches in Berlin, Germany, 1955, and Norrkoeping, Sweden, 1956; missionary in Transvaal, South Africa, 1957-60; Lutheran Theological College, Mapumulo, Natal, lecturer, 1960-65; Tuebingen University, Tuebingen, Germany, professor of missiology and ecumenics, 1966—, director of Institute of Missiology, 1966—. Freie Hochschule fuer Mission (graduate school of missiology and Biblical studies), Korntal, rector. Chairman of International Christian Network.

WRITINGS:

Die Selbstaendigkeit der jungen Kirchen als missionarisches Problem, Rheinischen Missions Gesellschaft, 1956, revised and condensed version (with Henry Lefever) published as *The Responsible Church and the Foreign Mission,* Eerdmans, 1964.

(Editor) *Begegnung mit messianischen Bewegungen in Afrika,* Evangelischer Missionsverlag, 1967, translation published as *The Encounter with Messianic Movements in Africa,* Scottish Institute of Missionary Studies, 1968.

Humanisierung: Einzige Hoffnung der Welt?, MKB-Verlag, 1969, translation by Margaret Clarkson published as *Missions: Which Way? Humanization or Redemption,* Zondervan, 1971.

The Church Crossing Frontiers, [Uppsala], 1969.

Allen Voelkern zum Zeugnis: Biblisch-theologische Besinnung zum Wesen der Mission, R. Brockhaus, 1972.

In Ostasien erlebt (also see below), Evangelischer Missionsverlag, 1972.

Shaken Foundations: Theological Foundations for Mission (lectures), Zondervan, 1972.

In der Inselwelt Suedostasiens erlebt: Zweiter Teil des Reiseberichts (continuation of *In Ostasien erlebt*), Evangelischer Missionsverlag, 1973.

Bangkok '73: Anfang oder Ende der Weltmission (includes selections of Eighth World Missionary Conference, 1972-73), Liebenzeller Mission, 1973, translation published as *Bangkok '73: The Beginning or End of World Mission?,* Zondervan, 1974.

(Editor with Walter Kuenneth) *Reich Gottes oder Weltgemeinschaft,* Liebenzeller Mission, 1975.

(Editor with Ulrich Betz) *Oekumene im Spiegel von Nairobi '75* (title means "Ecumenism in the Mirror of Nairobi"), Liebenzeller Mission, 1976.

Ideologien: Herausforderung an den Glauben (title means "Ideologies as Challenge to the Faith"), Bad Liebenzell, 1979.

(Editor) *Weg und Zeugnis: Bekennende Gemeinschaften im gegenwaertigen Kirchenkampf 1965-1980* (title means "Way and Witness: Confessing Fellowships in the Present Church Struggle 1965-1980"), Bad Liebenzell, 1980.

Aufbruch der Armen: Die neue Missionsbewegung nach Melbourne (title means "The Poor on the Move: The New Mission Movement after Melbourne"), Bad Liebenzell, 1981.

(Editor) *Frauen im theologischen Aufstand: Eine Orientierungshilfe zur Feministischen Theologie* (title means "Women in Theological Rebellion: Orientation about Feminist Theology"), [Stuttgart], 1983.

(Editor with Lutz V. Padberg) *Eine Welt, eine Religion?* (title means "One World, One Religion?: A Critical Assessment of the New Age Movement"), Bad Liebenzell, 1988.

(Editor with Padberg) *Der Konziliare Prozess: Utopie und Realitaet*, Bad Liebenzell, 1990.

The Utopian Error: Discerning the Biblical Kingdom of God from Its Political Counterfeits, Crossway, 1992.

*   *   *

BILLS, Scott L(aurence) 1948-

PERSONAL: Born October 20, 1948, in Latrobe, PA; son of Robert H. (a chemical engineer) and Dolores E. (an artist; maiden name, Bloom) Bills; married Kristi Dixon (a reading specialist), December, 1978; children: Seth Holland. *Education:* West Virginia University, B.A. (with honors), 1970; Kent State University, M.A., 1976, Ph.D., 1981.

ADDRESSES: Home—1720 East Austin St., Nacogdoches, TX 75961. *Office*—Department of History, P.O. Box 13013, SFA Station, Stephen F. Austin University, Nacogdoches, TX 75962-3013.

CAREER: Library of Congress, Congressional Research Service, Washington, DC, research assistant in Foreign Affairs and National Defense Division, 1978; Kent State University, Kent, OH, lecturer in American history, 1979-80; Kent State University Press, Kent, assistant editor, 1981-82; West Virginia University, Morgantown, visiting assistant professor of history, 1982-83; Stephen F. Austin State University, Nacogdoches, TX, assistant professor, 1983-89, associate professor of history, 1989—. Walsh College, Canton, OH, lecturer, fall, 1980. Has presented papers at and participated in conferences and annual meetings. Research consultant for television movie *Kent State*, summer, 1980.

MEMBER: American Historical Association, Organization of American Historians, Society for Historians of American Foreign Relations, Atlantic Council (academic associate), Council on Peace Research in History, Southern Historical Association, Phi Beta Kappa.

AWARDS, HONORS: Research Council grant, Stephen F. Austin State University, 1985, 1986, 1990.

WRITINGS:

(Editor and author of introduction) *Kent State/May 4: Echoes through a Decade*, Kent State University Press, 1982, revised edition, 1988.

Empire and Cold War: The Roots of U.S.-Third World Antagonism, 1945-47, St. Martin's, 1990.

Also author of a novella and several short stories. Contributor to *NATO after Thirty Years*, edited by Lawrence S. Kaplan and others, Scholarly Resources, 1981; *Public History: An Introduction*, edited by Barbara J. Howe and Emory L. Kemp, Robert E. Krieger, 1986; and *East-West Rivalry in the Third World: Security Issues and Regional Perspectives*, edited by Robert W. Clawson, Scholarly Resources, 1986. Also contributor to periodicals, including *Vietnam Generation, Left Review*, and *Real People*.

WORK IN PROGRESS: "A book dealing with big-power wrangling over the disposition of former Italian colonies during the early cold war years, with the focus on Libya."

SIDELIGHTS: Scott L. Bills told *CA:* "I teach and write history, especially in the area of post-1945 America, with emphasis on the Cold War and domestic society of the 1960s. I guess my real aspiration is to be a writer as well as a historian. It is to this end that I am continuing to work on fiction in addition to more conventional academic research and writing."

About *Kent State/May 4: Echoes through a Decade*, Bills commented: "I was not in Kent in May, 1970, but I well recall the emotional impact of the shootings on myself and the people around me. I feel that the Kent State shootings were an important historical event, pulling together the different threads of political and social conflict of the latter 1960s, exemplifying the divisions in American society that were so intense, so murderous—that now seem so distant. As someone who was part of the youth counterculture of the 1960s, I think that era deserves better and closer scrutiny than it has so far received.

"In my fiction writing, I like to use a science fiction motif to elaborate on such themes as personal character and vision, human relationships, and an existential approach to life. My interest in the genre is in its use as a device to suspend belief and allow for a different kind of discussion of the contemporary world."

In discussing his *Empire and Cold War: The Roots of U.S.-Third World Antagonism, 1945-47,* Bills explained to *CA:* "This book examines the source of American policy toward nationalist movements in colonial areas at the end of World War II through 1947, considering events in French North Africa, the Middle East, and Southeast Asia in the context of the emerging cold war. The Second World War shattered and remade the world. Two great powers—the United States and the Soviet Union—warily confronted each other across the smoking ruins of Europe. But the end of war for Europeans prompted a surge of renewed struggle in colonial areas, as nationalist groups sought greater autonomy or independence. American policymakers were no longer afforded the luxury of ignoring colonial problems as they began to fashion a new globalism to counter Soviet influence. Anti-Western unrest in colonies threatened to create a hostile bloc of non-white peoples, convinced that their future lay with leftist creeds. Anti-colonial upheaval also threatened to undermine the reconstruction of Western Europe. Throughout the southern rimlands of Eurasia, flashpoint areas engaged U.S. attention and pressed American officials to forge a policy inconsistent with the American self-image of a freedom-loving republic intent upon self-determination for all peoples. Self-determination, if it did not involve an evolutionary path to self-rule under the tutelage of Western powers, was no more acceptable to U.S. leaders than to European officials long schooled in the imperial way.

"The onset of cold war ensured that the United States would take a steadily more conservative view of such issues as Algerian unrest, the disposition of Italian colonies, and guerrilla warfare in Vietnam and Indonesia. During the key years 1945-47, the United States did not appear to carry out its wartime promises of independence for colonial peoples. The year 1947 marked the trial flight of a colonial policy based primarily upon cold war priorities, applied consistently through the various Third World theaters of big-power contention and convulsion. The immediate postwar years also comprised an era of new myth-making, one in which the failure of American leaders to champion colonial self-determination marked the beginning of deep-rooted Third World antagonism toward the United States."

*   *   *

BLAIS, Marie-Claire 1939-

PERSONAL: Born October 5, 1939, in Quebec, Quebec, Canada; daughter of Fernando and Veronique (Nolin) Blais. *Education:* Attended Pensionnat St. Roch in Quebec; studied literature and philosophy at Laval University in Quebec. *Religion:* Catholic.

CAREER: Full-time writer.

MEMBER: PEN.

AWARDS, HONORS: Prix de la Langue Francaise, L'Academie Francaise, 1961, for *La Belle Bete;* Guggenheim fellowships, 1963 and 1964; Le Prix France-Quebec and Prix Medicis (Paris), both 1966, both for *Une Saison dans la vie d'Emmanuel;* Prix du Gouverneur General du Canada, 1969, for *Les Manuscrits de Pauline Archange,* and 1979, for *Le Sourd dans la ville;* elected member of Order of Canada, 1972; honorary doctorate from York University (Toronto), 1975; Prix Belgique, 1976; named honorary professor at Calgary University, 1978; Prix Athanase David, 1982; Prix de l'Academie Francaise, 1983.

WRITINGS:

La Belle Bete (novel), Institut Litteraire du Quebec, 1959, translation by Merloyd Lawrence published as *Mad Shadows,* Little, Brown, 1961.

Tete Blanche (novel), Institut Litteraire du Quebec, 1960, translation by Charles Fullman under same title, Little, Brown, 1961.

Le Jour est noir (novella; also see below), Editions du Jour (Montreal), 1962.

Pays voiles (poems; also see below), Garneau (Quebec), 1963.

Existences (poems; also see below), Garneau, 1964.

Une Saison dans la vie d'Emmanuel (novel), Editions du Jour, 1965, translation by Coltman published as *A Season in the Life of Emmanuel,* introduction by Edmund Wilson, Farrar, Straus, 1966.

Les Voyageurs sacres (novella; also see below), HMH, 1966.

L'Insoumise (novel), Editions du Jour, 1966, translation by David Lobdell published as *The Fugitive,* Oberon, 1978.

The Day Is Dark [and] *The Three Travelers* (contains Derek Coltman's translations of *Le Jour est noir* and *Les Voyageurs sacres*), Farrar, Straus, 1967.

David Sterne (novel), Editions du Jour, 1967, translation by Lobdell under same title, McClelland & Stewart, 1973.

Les Manuscrits de Pauline Archange (novel), Editions du Jour, 1968, translation by Coltman published with translation of *Vivre! Vivre!: La Suite des Manuscrits de Pauline Archange* (also see below) as *The Manuscripts of Pauline Archange,* Farrar, Straus, 1970.

Vivre! Vivre!: La Suite des Manuscrits de Pauline Archange (novel), Editions du Jour, 1969.

Les Apparences (novel), Editions du Jour, 1970, translation by Lobdell published as *Durer's Angel,* McClelland & Stewart, 1974.

Le Loup (novel), Editions du Jour, 1972, translation by Sheila Fischman published as *The Wolf,* McClelland & Stewart, 1974.

Un Joualonais sa Joualonie (novel), Editions du Jour, 1973, reprinted as *A coeur joual,* Robert Laffont, 1977, translation by Ralph Manheim published as *St. Lawrence Blues,* Farrar, Straus, 1974.

Une Liaison parisienne (novel), Robert Laffont, 1976, translation by Fischman published as *A Literary Affair,* McClelland & Stewart, 1979.

Le Sourd dans la ville (novel), Stanke, 1979, translation by Carol Dunlop published as *Deaf to the City,* General Publishing, 1979.

(Editor with Richard Teleky) *The Oxford Book of French-Canadian Short Stories,* Oxford University Press, 1980.

Les Nuits de l'underground (novel), Stanke, 1982, translation by Ray Ellenwood published as *Nights in the Underground,* General Publishing, 1982.

Visions d'Anna (novel), Stanke, 1982, translation by Fischman published as *Anna's World,* Lester, Orpen & Dennys, 1985.

Pays voiles—Existences, Stanke, 1983, translation by Michael Harris published as *Veiled Countries in Veiled Countries* [and] *Lives,* Vehicule Press, 1984.

Pierre, la guerre du printemps 81, Primeur, 1984.

PLAYS

La Roulotte aux Poupees, produced in Quebec at Theatre de L'Estoc, 1960.

L'Execution (two-act; produced in Montreal at Theatre du Rideau Vert, 1967), Editions du Jour, 1968, translation by David Lobdell published as *The Execution,* Talon Books, 1976.

Fievre, Editions du Jour, 1974.

La Nef des sorcieres, Quinze Editeurs, 1976.

L'Ocean murmures, Quinze Editeurs, 1977.

Also author of *Eleanor,* produced in Quebec at Theatre de L'Estoc, and *Sommeil d'Hiver,* 1985, and *Fiere,* 1985.

TELEVISION SCRIPTS

L'Ocean, Radio-Canada, 1976.

Journal en images froides, Radio-Canada, 1978.

L'Exil, L'Escale, Radio-Canada, 1979.

RADIO SCRIPTS

Le Disparu, Radio-Canada, 1971.

L'Envahisseur, Radio-Canada, 1972.

Deux Destins, Radio-Canada, 1973.

Fievre, Radio-Canada, 1973.

Une Autre Vie, Radio-Canada, 1974.

Un Couple, Radio-Canada, 1975.

Une Femme et les autres, Radio-Canada, 1976.

L'Enfant Video, Radio-Canada, 1977.

Murmures, Radio-Canada, 1977.

Le Fantome d'une voix, Radio-Canada, 1980.

SIDELIGHTS: Marie-Claire Blais, according to Edmund Wilson in *O Canada: An American's Notes on Canadian Culture,* is "a writer in a class by herself." Although each of her novels is written in a different style and mood, "we know immediately," writes Raymond Rosenthal, "that we are entering a fully imagined world when we start reading any of her books." Wilson wrote that Blais is a "true 'phenomenon'; she may possibly be a genius. At the age of twenty-four, she has produced four remarkable books of a passionate and poetic force that, as far as my reading goes, is not otherwise to be found in French Canadian fiction." That was in 1964; when Wilson read *A Season in the Life of Emmanuel* in 1965, he compared the novel to works by J. M. Synge and William Faulkner.

"*A Season in the Life of Emmanuel* is a particularly Canadian work of art," writes David Stouck, "for the sense of winter and of life's limitations (especially defined by poverty) are nowhere felt more strongly. Yet . . . these physical limitations serve to define the emotional deprivation that is being dramatized. That eroding sense of poverty is never externalized as a social issue, nor is the harshness of the Quebec landscape seen as an existentialist 'condition.' Rather, in the oblique and relentless manner of her writing Miss Blais remains faithful stylistically to the painful vision of her imagination and in so doing has created both a fully dramatic and genuinely Canadian work of art."

Writing in the *New York Times Book Review,* Robertson Davies claims that *The Day Is Dark* and *Three Travelers* are "less substantial than *A Season in the Life of Emmanuel,*" but, he adds, "all the writing of this extraordinary young woman is so individual, so unlike anything else being written on this continent, that admirers of her poetic vision of life may find them even more to their taste." Laurent LeSage, writing in *Saturday Review,* says of the two novellas: "Although the basic structures of fiction are still recognizable, they have been weakened and distorted to prevent any illusion of realistic dimension or true-to-life anecdote from distracting us from the author's intention. Without warning the narrative shifts from one character to another, chronology is jumbled, events are sometimes contradictory, and the fancied is never clearly separated from the real. By a series of interior monologues Mlle. Blais works along the lower levels of consciousness, and only rarely does she come to the surface. The world of her revery is the somber, shadowy one of primitive urges and responses. . . . Each [character] obeys a force that resembles a tragic predestination, leading [him] in a lonely quest through life to [his] final destruction." The novellas are actually prose poems, similar in some respects to works by Walter de la Mare. Rosenthal defines the genre as "a piece of prose that should be read more than once, preferably several times. If after reading it in the prescribed fashion," says Rosenthal, "the work assumes depth and color and value it did not have at the first reading, then the author has written a successful prose poem. In a prose poem each word counts and Mlle. Blais generally doesn't waste a syllable."

Several critics comment on the pain found in Blais's works. In his study of Canadian literature, Wilson comments that "these novels of Marie-Claire Blais are the most unrelievedly painful that I remember ever to have read, and one questions . . . the inevitability of so much pain." L. Clark Keating, writing in *Romance Notes,* finds that Blais's "characters and situations, with but few exceptions, are hateful, perverse and repulsive. No crime, no meanness, no indecent thought, no deliberate breaking of the Ten Commandments are alien to her characters young or old, male or female." Keating concludes that Blais's writings are "as shocking as Zola's or the films used as evidence in the Nuremburg trials."

But Irving Wardle, although he admits that "harshness and squalor are there," sees that, at least in *A Season in the Life of Emmanuel,* these elements "are transformed in the writing into the material of adolescent fantasy. [Blais] has the myth-making faculty, and it is an exciting thing to watch." LeSage writes: "Marie-Claire Blais lets her words pour forth in a rhapsodic torrent. In *Three Travelers* they often form into verses, but everywhere they have the poetic qualities of image and cadence as they create laments and paeans, cries of love, lust, and hate for the wretched characters whose affliction is the sickness of life. The power of her writing is terrific." Wilson explains that "Blais has grown up in this cult, and the idea that man is born to sorrow, the agony of expiation, is at the base of her tragic consciousness. [Her work] is the refinement to a purer kind of poetry than that of the protesting patriots of the desperate cry that arises from the poverty, intellectual and material, the passionate self-punishing piety and the fierce defeated pride of Quebec."

Daniel M. Murtaugh observes that *A Season in the Life of Emmanuel* "has at its center an autobiographical sketch by a consumptive child whose writing is a cry of defiance against the misery of his life and the approach of his death. The manuscripts of a suffering child, a structural detail of that novel, are the sum and substance of its successor. *The Manuscripts of Pauline Archange* takes us through memories of almost unmitigated horror rendered bearable, redeemed even, for us as for the novel's heroine, by the fluid, re-creative medium of her prose. . . . What Pauline remembers does not fall into a conventional plot or lend itself easily to summary. Her life is lived out in the mental and physical squalor of a French Canadian slum, under the tyranny of repressed, frustrated adults who visit their failures in blows upon their consumptive, lamed offspring. To survive is to escape, to rebel, above all, to avoid pity.

Pity 'stinks of death,' and only leads to torture and rape of the victims it cannot help. Pauline writes her manuscripts because, as her family tells her, she 'has no heart.' Only at such a cost does she live and speak to us."

Rosenthal emphasizes that Blais has done much to "put Canada on the literary map." He says of her work: "Mlle. Blais leaves out a great deal, almost all the familiar furniture of fiction, and yet her characters have a tenacious life and her themes, though often convoluted and as evanescent as the mist that dominates so much of her imagination, strike home with surprising force." "With *David Sterne,*" writes Brian Vintcent, "Mlle. Blais has placed herself firmly and uncompromisingly in the literary tradition of the French moralists leading back through Camus, Genet and Gide to Baudelaire. The book deals in one way or another with many of the themes explored by these writers, and this makes it somewhat derivative. It owes most, perhaps, to the more abstract and less sensational works of Jean Genet, in which the passionate existential wranglings, the rebellion, the life of crime and sensation are so prominent. The confessional and didactic style of the book will also strike echoes in the reader's mind. But *David Sterne* survives and transcends these comparisons. What allows it to do so is the immense compassion and tenderness Mlle. Blais displays for her characters in their whirlwind of struggle and suffering. The hard cold eye she casts on the cruel world of *Mad Shadows* has grown into one full of pity and profound sadness for the fate of men condemned to do battle with themselves."

In 1980, Blais published *Deaf to the City,* a novel told in one book-length paragraph. "Blais," Marjorie A. Fitzpatrick explains in the *French Review,* "brings to life—and then to death—the inhabitants of the gloomy little Montreal hotel that serves as the novel's setting. Like voices in a fugue or threads in a well-made tapestry, their lives weave in and out through each other to form a harmonious (though depressing) whole." Writing in the *Dictionary of Literary Biography,* Eva-Marie Kroeller states that *Deaf to the City* "fuses prose and poetry even more radically than Blais's earlier works." Fitzpatrick concludes that "If Blais can sustain in future works the combination of human authenticity and tight technical mastery that she found in [*A Season in the Life of Emmanuel*] and has achieved again in [*Deaf to the City*], she may well come to stand out as one of the most powerful fiction writers of French expression of this generation."

The *Virginia Quarterly Review* writer concludes that Blais's novels are "to be read slowly and carefully for the unusual insights they present in often difficult but provocative images and sometimes demanding but intriguing technical innovations. This is a serious, talented and deeply effective writer." Kroeller calls Blais "one of the most prolific and influential authors of Quebec's literary scene since the late 1950s." Blais, Kroeller believes, "has firmly established an international reputation as a writer who combines strong roots in the literary tradition of her province with an affinity to existentialist fiction of Western Europe and the United States."

BIOGRAPHICAL/CRITICAL SOURCES:

BOOKS

Contemporary Authors Autobiography Series, Volume 4, Gale, 1986.
Contemporary Literary Criticism, Gale, Volume 2, 1974, Volume 3, 1975, Volume 6, 1976, Volume 13, 1980, Volume 22, 1982.
Dictionary of Literary Biography, Volume 53: *Canadian Writers since 1960, First Series,* Gale, 1986.
Fabi, Therese, *Le Monde perturbe des jeunes dans l'oeuvre romanesque de Marie-Claire Blais: sa vie, son oeuvre, la critique,* Editions Agence d'Arc (Montreal), 1973.
Goldmann, Lucien, *Structures mentales et creation culturelle,* Editions Anthropos (Paris), 1970.
Marcotte, Gilles, *Notre roman a l'imparfait,* La Presse (Montreal), 1976.
Meigs, Mary, *Lily Briscoe: A Self-Portrait,* Talonbooks, 1981.
Meigs, *The Medusa Head,* Talonbooks, 1983.
Nadeau, Vincent, *Marie-Claire Blais: le noir et le tendre,* Presses de l'Universite de Montreal, 1974.
Stratford, Philip, *Marie-Claire Blais,* Forum House, 1971.
Wilson, Edmund, *O Canada: An American's Notes on Canadian Culture,* Farrar, Straus, 1965.

PERIODICALS

Books Abroad, winter, 1968.
Books in Canada, February, 1979.
Book Week, June 18, 1967.
Canadian Literature, spring, 1972.
Chatelaine, August, 1966.
Cite libre, July-August, 1966.
Coincidences, May-December, 1980.
Culture, March, 1968.
La Dryade, summer, 1967.
Etudes, February, 1967.
French Review, March, 1981.
Globe and Mail (Toronto), March 30, 1985.
Journal of Canadian Fiction, Number 25-26, 1979.
Lettres Quebecoises, winter, 1979-80.
Livres et Auteurs Quebecois, 1972.
Los Angeles Times, September 18, 1987.
New Statesman, March 31, 1967.
New York Times Book Review, April 30, 1967; September 20, 1987.
Nous, June, 1973.
Novel, autumn, 1972.
Observer, April 2, 1967.

Recherches Sociographiques, September-December, 1966.
Revue de l'Institut de Sociologie, Volume 42, number 3, 1969.
La Revue de Paris, February, 1967.
Romance Notes, autumn, 1973.
Saturday Review, April 29, 1967.
Times Literary Supplement, March 30, 1967.
Virginia Quarterly Review, autumn, 1967.
Voix et Images, winter, 1983.
Weekend Magazine, October 23, 1976.

*　　*　　*

BLOOM, Ken(neth) 1949-

PERSONAL: Born November 28, 1949, in Silver Spring, MD; son of George (an accountant) and Florence (an accountant; maiden name, Berkowitz) Bloom. *Education:* Attended University of Maryland, 1969-72.

ADDRESSES: Home—532 West 50th St., No. 4AR, New York, NY 10019. *Office*—Heide Lange, Sanford J. Greenburger Associates, Inc., 55 Fifth Ave., New York, NY 10003.

CAREER: New Playwrights Theatre, Washington, DC, associate producer and director, 1970-79; *Washington Post,* Washington, DC, editor of "Washington Season," 1979-81; Broadway correspondent for Canadian Broadcasting and National Public Radio, 1981-83; Harbinger Records, New York City, president, 1983—. Assistant company manager of the Joffrey Ballet, spring, 1985. Consultant to Wolf Trap Farm Park, Smithsonian Institution's Division of Performing Arts, Theatre Collection of the Museum of the City of New York, Library of Performing Arts at Lincoln Center, Brooklyn Academy of Music, American Society of Composers, Authors, and Publishers, Twentieth Century-Fox.

MEMBER: National Academy of Recording Arts and Sciences, Dramatists Guild.

WRITINGS:

American Song, Volume 1: *The Complete Musical Theatre Companion, 1900-1984,* Facts on File, 1985.
Broadway: An Encyclopedic Guide to the History, People and Places of Times Square, Facts on File, 1991.
American Song, Volume 2: *The Complete Hollywood Musical,* Facts on File, 1991.

Also author of musical comedies.

SIDELIGHTS: Ken Bloom told *CA* that he is especially interested in musical theatre and popular song. As the president of Harbinger Records, he has co-produced with partner Bill Rudman the original cast album of Geraldine

Fitzgerald's *Streetsongs, Maxine Sullivan Sings the Songs of Harold Arlen and Ted Koehler* (Grammy nomination), *Together: Maxine Sullivan Sings Jule Styne, The Lady's in Love with You: Maxine Sullivan Sings Burton Lane,* and an album of unpublished Harold Arlen songs sung by Peggy Lee.

Bloom has also written and directed musical revues based on the works of Arlen, Cole Porter, Dietz and Schwartz, and Jerome Kern. The Kern revue was adapted for a series of programs broadcast by Pennsylvania Public Television. Bloom has also directed original musical comedies, both in Washington, DC, and New York City.

* * *

BLY, Peter A(nthony) 1944-

PERSONAL: Born July 31, 1944, in King's Lynn, England; became Canadian citizen; son of Phillip William (a butcher) and Mollie Irene (a homemaker; maiden name, Rye) Bly; married Margaret Philomena O'Dwyer (a legal aid assessment officer), July 25, 1968; children: Siobhain Montserrat, Declan Santiago. *Education:* University of London, B.A., 1966, M.A., 1967, Ph.D., 1978. *Religion:* Anglican.

ADDRESSES: Home—288 Frontenac Street, Kingston, Ontario, Canada K7L 3S8. *Office*—Department of Spanish and Italian, Queen's University at Kingston, Kingston, Ontario, Canada K7L 3N6.

CAREER: Dalhousie University, Halifax, Nova Scotia, lecturer, 1968-69, assistant professor of Spanish, 1969-71; Queen's University at Kingston, Kingston, Ontario, lecturer, 1971-72, assistant professor, 1972-79, associate professor, 1979-83, professor of Spanish, 1983—, head of department, 1984—.

MEMBER: International Association of Hispanists, International Galdos Association (secretary-treasurer, 1990-95), Canadian Association of Hispanists (president 1981-84), British Association of Hispanists, American Association of Teachers of Spanish and Portuguese.

AWARDS, HONORS: Awards from Canadian Association of Hispanists, 1978, for "Fortuna and No. 11, Cava de San Miguel," 1979, for "Beards in the *Poema de Mio Cid:* Structural and Converted Patterns," and 1980, for "Sex, Egotism, and Social Regeneration in Galdos's *El caballero encantado.*"

WRITINGS:

Perez Galdos: La de Bringas, Critical Guides to Spanish Texts, Volume 30, Grant & Cutler/Tamesis Books, 1981.

Galdos's Novel of the Historical Imagination, Francis Cairns, 1983.

(With C. Blanco, Peter Goldman, and John Kronik) *Fortunata and Feijoo: Four Studies of a Chapter by Perez Galdos,* Tamesis Books, 1984.

Vision and the Visual Arts in Galdos: A Study of the Novels and Newspaper Articles, Francis Cairns, 1985.

(Editor) *Galdos y la historia,* Ottawa Hispanic Studies, Volume 1, Dovehouse Editions Canada, 1988.

Perez Galdos: Nazarin, Critical Guides to Spanish Texts, Volume 54, Grant & Cutler/Tamesis Books, 1991.

Editor of *Anales Galdos,* 1990-95.

WORK IN PROGRESS: A critical study of Perez Galdos's *Angel Guerra.*

SIDELIGHTS: In *Galdos's Novel of the Historical Imagination,* Peter A. Bly examines the most influential novels of Spain's Benito Perez Galdos, whose literary achievement is tied to the body of work he produced during the decade of the 1880s. Adapted from Bly's Ph.D. Thesis, the book was called "very readable" by *Times Literary Supplement* reviewer A.F. Lambert, who also found it a "skillful study" despite "traces of the . . . One-tracked thinking characteristic of the doctoral thesis." "Peter Bly's book is not at all trivial," the critic continued, "Galdos's greatest novels . . . explore and meditate upon the interrelationship between public and private life, and Bly focuses thorough and expert attention upon this relationship in its historical dimension."

Bly told *CA:* "My aim in writing on Galdos is to spread the message to other Hispanists and general readers about Galdos's superb literary art and the relevance of his studies on people and society for twentieth-century humanity."

BIOGRAPHICAL/CRITICAL SOURCES:

PERIODICALS

Times Literary Supplement, August 5, 1983.

* * *

BOND, Edward 1934-

PERSONAL: Born July 18, 1934, in London, England; married Elizabeth Pable, 1971. *Education:* Attended state schools in England until fifteen. *Politics:* Socialist. *Religion:* Atheist.

ADDRESSES: Agent—Margaret Ramsey Ltd., 14A Goodwin's Ct., St. Martin's Lane, London WC2N 4LL, England.

CAREER: Spent early years working in factories and offices; now full-time writer; member of the writers group of the Royal Court Theatre. *Military service:* British Army; served two years with the infantry.

AWARDS, HONORS: George Devine Award, English Stage Society, 1968, for *Early Morning;* co-recipient, with Peter Barnes, of the John Whiting Playwrights Award, Arts Council, 1969, for *Narrow Road to the Deep North;* Best New Play awards, *Plays and Players,* 1976, for *The Fool,* and 1985, for *The War Plays;* D.Litt., Yale University.

WRITINGS:

PLAYS

The Pope's Wedding and Other Plays (includes *The Pope's Wedding* [also see below], produced in the West End, 1962 and 1984; *Mr. Dog, The King with Golden Eyes,* and *Sharpeville Sequence*), Methuen, 1971.

Saved (produced in the West End at Royal Court Theatre, 1965; produced in New Haven, CT, at Yale School of Drama Repertory Theatre, on a triple bill with plays by David Epstein and Anthony Scully, 1968; produced Off-Broadway, 1970; also see below), Hill & Wang, 1966, Heinemann, 1984.

Early Morning (produced in the West End, 1968; produced Off-Broadway, 1970; also see below), Calder & Boyars, 1968, Hill & Wang, 1969.

Narrow Road to the Deep North (written for the Peoples and Cities Conference in Coventry and produced there at Belgrade Theatre, 1968; produced in the West End, 1969; produced in Boston at Charles Playhouse, 1969; produced on Broadway, 1972; also see below), Methuen, 1968, Hill & Wang, 1969.

Black Mass (also see below), produced in Sheffield, England, at Sheffield Playhouse, 1970.

Lear (produced in the West End, 1971; produced at Yale School of Drama Repertory Theatre, 1973; also see below), Hill & Wang, 1972, student edition with notes and commentary, Methuen, 1983.

Bingo: Scenes of Money and Death; and Passion (contains *Passion* [also see below], produced in the West End, 1971, produced at Yale School of Drama Repertory Theatre, 1972; and *Bingo* [also see below], produced in the West End, 1974), Methuen, 1974.

The Sea (comedy; produced in the West End, 1973; produced at Source Theater, 1984; also see below), Hill & Wang, 1973.

Bingo [and] *The Sea* (also see below), Hill & Wang, 1975.

The Fool (produced in London, 1975; also see below), Dramatic Club Publications (Chicago, IL), 1978.

(Author of libretto) *We Come to the River* (opera; produced in London at Covent Garden, 1976; also see below), music by Hans Werner Henze, published as *We Come to the River: Actions for Music,* Schott, 1976.

A-A-America! [and] *Stone* (two plays), Methuen, 1976, revised edition, Heinemann, 1982.

The Fool [and] *We Come to the River* (two plays), Eyre Methuen, 1976.

Plays, Methuen, 1977, published as *Plays One: Saved, Early Morning, The Pope's Wedding,* 1983.

Plays Two (includes *Lear, The Sea, Narrow Road to the Deep North, Black Mass,* and *Passion*), Methuen, 1978.

The Woman: Scenes of War and Freedom (produced in London at National Theatre, 1978; produced in Baltimore, MD, at Center Theater, 1983), Hill & Wang, 1979.

The Bundle: or, New Narrow Road to the Deep North (produced in London by Royal Shakespearean Company, 1978; produced at Yale Repertory Theatre, 1979), Heinemann, 1978.

The Worlds, with The Activists Papers (two plays; includes *The Worlds,* produced by Newcastle University Theatre Society, 1979), Methuen, 1980.

(Translator) Frank Wedekind, *Spring Awakening,* Methuen, 1980.

Restoration [and] *The Cat* (includes *Restoration: A Pastoral,* a musical, with music by Nick Bicat, produced in London at the Royal Court Theatre, 1981, produced in Washington, DC at Arena Theatre, 1986; and *The Cat,* libretto for opera with music by Henze, performed by Stuttgart Opera, 1983), Eyre Methuen, 1982, 2nd edition, Methuen, 1982.

Summer (produced in London at National Theatre, 1982; produced in New York at Manhattan Theatre Club, 1983; also see below), Methuen, 1982.

Summer [and] *Fables,* Methuen, 1983.

Derek [and] *Choruses from after the Assassinations,* Methuen, 1984.

The War Plays; Part 1: Red, Black and Ignorant, Part 2: The Tin Can People, Part 3: Great Peace (produced by Royal Shakespeare Company, 1985), Methuen, 1985, published in two volumes, Methuen, 1985, and in one volume, 1991.

Human Cannon (produced in South Wales), Methuen, 1985.

Jackets 2 (produced in double-bill with *Sugawara* [adapted from kabuki drama] at Bush Theatre, 1990), Methuen, 1990.

In the Company of Men [and] *Notes on Post Modernism,* Methuen, 1990.

Also author of *Jackets 1,* and *Orpheus* (a libretto for ballet), 1982.

SCREENPLAYS

Blow-Up (based on a short story by Julio Cortazar), Premier Productions, 1969.

(With Clement Biddle-Wood and Schlondorff) *Michael Kohlhaas* (based on a novella by Heinrich Von Kleist), Columbia, 1969.

Laughter in the Dark (based on a novel by Vladimir Nabokov), Lopert, 1969.

Walkabout (based on a novel by James Vance Marshall), Twentieth Century-Fox, 1971.

(Author of additional dialogue) *Nicholas and Alexandria* (based on a book by Robert K. Massie), screenplay by James Goldman, Columbia, 1971.

OTHER

Theatre Poems and Songs, edited by Malcolm Hay and Philip Roberts, Methuen, 1978.

Bond: Poems, 1978 to 1985, Heinemann, 1988.

Plays by Bond have been translated into twenty-five languages.

SIDELIGHTS: "Edward Bond . . . is distinguished by his historical perspective and his social awareness. In his plays, a scrutiny of the past enables us to comprehend injustice of the present—and vice versa," Mel Gussow observes in the *New York Times.* In the 1970 play *Black Mass,* for example, which was written to commemorate the tenth anniversary of the Sharpeville Massacre in South Africa, Bond's Christ gives the South African Prime Minister poison at the communion table during the Eucharist. *Restoration* also addresses issues of freedom and interracial justice as they affect the lives of a wealthy murderer's valet and his black wife. And *The Woman,* set against the backdrop of the Trojan War, is an allegory about a state's abuses of power.

Bond made his debut as an original playwright in 1965 with *Saved,* a play in which a street gang stones an infant to death. Conceived in a casual affair between two working-class youths, the child has failed to elicit affection from its grandparents, who share their home with the couple. The child's father makes an attempt to establish meaningful communication with others in the household, but the young mother finds a gang leader less boring. The infanticide has little effect on the family, who have been numbed by years of repressed aggression and exploitation.

With *Saved,* Bond's name quickly became associated with disturbing depictions of violence. His next play, *Early Morning,* was a farce in which Queen Victoria, a lesbian Florence Nightingale, Prince Albert, and Benjamin Disraeli destroy each other and continue to attack each other in the afterlife. The violence in *Saved* and *Early Morning* resulted in both plays being banned by the Lord Chamberlain; it was not until the fall of 1968, when official censorship of the English stage was ended, that Bond could even hope to produce his plays without difficulty.

Bond says that the reception of *Saved* outraged him. During an interview with Ronald Bryden published in the *London Observer,* Bond declared: "It didn't knock me out exactly, it surprised me. I was a very simple person. I'd spent a long time learning to write, and do it well. I knew I'd finally done it—written just what I intended; got it right. And suddenly all these people who set themselves up as custodians of art, of artistic opinion, were sounding off in every direction except that. They weren't involved with art at all. . . . But it didn't affect me as a writer. Art is the most private of all activities, and the theatre is the most private of all arts." In a letter published in the *Guardian,* Bond explained, "I chose to show violence in an inarticulate, working-class group because this brings out clearly our general social position vis-a-vis violence. Socially we are as confused about our own larger use of violence as my characters are about theirs," he said in 1965.

Bond's preface to the published play *Saved* explains that he believes people have been dehumanized by cultural institutions so that individuals try to reclaim some sense of personal power by acts of violence, which require energy and passion to execute. Furthermore, he believes audiences desensitized by daily exposure to violence should be shocked awake by representations of violence on the stage; he reasons that feelings of outrage or disgust are better than no feeling at all. Indeed, some critics and viewers were appalled by the violence in his plays and denounced the playwright for portraying murder on stage.

In *Plays and Players,* John Russell Taylor notes that "in the 'Author's Note' [Bond] wrote for the published text of *Saved* . . . he offers what may well be the key to most of the difficulties people . . . have often found in his work. 'Like most people,' he says, 'I am a pessimist by experience, but an optimist by nature, and I have no doubt that I shall go on being true to my nature. Experience is depressing, and it would be a mistake to be willing to learn from it.' " Taylor believes that in Bond's early plays "some sort of hope gleams through, if only because some sort of basic goodness survives indestructibly the horrors of experience and steadfastly refuses to learn from them."

Commenting on Bond's career, Bryden states: "Serious critics generally agree that he is the foremost of the new wave of dramatists who followed Osborne and his contemporaries in the 1960s. When his play *Saved* was staged at the Court in 1965, it was more or less howled down for its violence. . . . But when it was revived in 1969, in repertory with Bond's subsequent plays *Early Morning* and *Narrow Road to the Deep North,* recantations poured in and the consensus was that a formidable talent had been savagely misjudged. The conversion of the critics was completed by the arrival of Bond's *Lear* in 1971."

The evil that Bond's Lear suffers is more horrifying than that of his Shakespearean antecedent because it stems not from individual greed but from a society's collective renunciation of all natural human compassion. *Library Journal* reviewer J. H. Crouch relates that Bond's skill "transmutes the stuff of classic tragedy into horrifying, yet splendid melodrama." A *Variety* reviewer, on the other hand, believes that "the play's psychopathy of stupidity and violence is repeated and repeated. There is apostrophized humor, but it's an otherwise unremittingly downbeat piece, of longish (almost three hours) and grueling evening of allegorical drama." Writing in the *New York Times,* Walter Kerr concurs: "There had been no controlling principle to account for the deeds being done, nothing intimately human or narratively necessary to engage us. We were only being invited to watch violence as violence, to accept it as the occasion's *sole* activity. . . . Mr. Bond, whose earlier *Saved* was a relatively realistic play . . . has here become so obsessed with the idea of violence that he has neglected to give it plausible, or even theatrically coherent, organization."

Meaningless violence does not play a leading role in Bond's 1973 play *The Sea,* which some critics feel is his best work. The passive indifference of a small village toward the drowning death of a young man is rather the subject of *The Sea.* Critics appreciate two lively comic scenes and a wider emotional range than is found in his earlier plays. Clive Barnes, reviewing *Bingo,* a 1971 production, in the *Times Literary Supplement,* writes: "Mr. Bond's new play is about the death of Shakespeare. It is his most direct play since *Saved,* avoiding both absurdism and symbolism, and dealing with a man at the point of death, literally a man at point of accounting. The man happens to be William Shakespeare, and Mr Bond is artistically honest with the basic facts known of the poet's life and character. But it could almost be any man of feeling, nervously aware of love and hate, and significance and insignificance of worldly goods, coming naked and fearful to that final summing up that is the only thing certain after birth."

Though Bond's plays received largely negative reviews when first produced because of misunderstandings about the presentation of violence, they won the respect of critics and audiences in the 1970s and 1980s. Because of different approaches to character, Bond's working relationships with actors also came under strain during the late '70s, culminating in his withdrawl from the Royal Shakespeare Company production of *The War Plays* in 1985 and a long sabbatical from the London stage. Instead, Bond produced his play about the Spanish Civil War, *Human Cannon,* with a group of amateur actors in South Wales. London *Times* reveiwer Jim Hiley said of the play with which Bond returned to the London stage in 1990, "*Jackets 2* seems unlikely to diminish the combative aura that sur-

rounds [Bond]. But his return to the London theatre is surely to be welcomed. However abrasive his character and elusive his vision, Edward Bond's talent is too rare to be left in the wilderness."

Speaking of his mission as a dramatist to a *Twentieth Century Literature* interviewer, Bond said, "It seems to me to be the job of rational people, of writers, of dramatists to plead for a just society, in their plays to rationally argue for a just society, to state clearly the conditions under which we live and try to make everybody understand that they must bear the consequences of the sort of life they lead. To show that our society is irrational and therefore dangerous—and that it maintains itself by denegating and corrupting human beings—that is what *Bingo* is about. If you are an unjust person it doesn't matter how cultured you are, how civilized you are, how capable you are of producing wonderful sayings, wonderful characters, wonderful jokes, you will still destroy yourself. And so a writer, nowadays, has to, as it were, put the cards on the table for the public and say: 'These are the consequences of your life; they are inescapable. If you want to escape violence you don't say "violence is wrong," you alter the conditions that create violence.' If you don't do that, then you are like somebody who says 'Well, the children in our village are dying of diptheria, but we will not do anything about the drains!' "

Concerning his formal schooling, Bond once said that he is glad that his education was "deplorable." "It was marvellous for me. [Schools make] children . . . competitive, aggressive. People are not born violent by nature. Society . . . makes men animals in order to control them. I write because I want to change the structure of society. I think that society as it exists is primitive, dangerous and corrupt—that it destroys people. . . . I've no Utopia, no image of the society I want to see emerge. It would simply be people being themselves, happy in their own way— what could be more natural?"

BIOGRAPHICAL/CRITICAL SOURCES:

BOOKS

Bond, Edward, *Saved,* Hill & Wang, 1966, Heinemann, 1984.
Contemporary Literary Criticism, Gale, Volume 4, 1975; Volume 6, 1976; Volume 13, 1980; Volume 23, 1983.
Coult, Tony, *The Plays of Edward Bond,* Methuen, 1978.
Dictionary of Literary Biography, Volume 13: *British Dramatists since World War II,* Gale, 1982.
Edward Bond: A Companion to the Plays, TQ Publications, 1978.

PERIODICALS

Choice, September, 1967.
Christian Science Monitor, July 6, 1968.

Cue, December 14, 1968.
Guardian, November 12, 1965; January, 1978.
Library Journal, December 1, 1972.
Listener, April 18, 1968; August 8, 1968; June 18, 1970.
Los Angeles Times, April 9, 1983.
Nation, November 16, 1970.
Newsweek, November 9, 1970.
New York, November 9, 1970.
New York Times, November 26, 1970; October 24, 1971; January 7, 1972; April 29, 1973; May 13, 1973; August 19, 1974; August 25, 1974; March 11, 1979; June 3, 1979; February 11, 1983; February 20, 1983; February 2, 1986.
Observer Review, November 9, 1969.
Plays and Players, August, 1970.
Prompt, Number 13, 1969.
Show Business, January 4, 1969.
Stage, October 7, 1971; May 31, 1973.
Stand, summer, 1989.
Time, November 9, 1970; January 17, 1972.
Times (London), July 27, 1985; February 23, 1987; February 28, 1990; March 5, 1990.
Twentieth Century Literature, February 28, 1990; March 5, 1990.
Variety, December 18, 1968; January 29, 1969; March 12, 1969; November 18, 1970; October 20, 1971; March 1, 1972; July 4, 1973.
Washington Post, January 24, 1986; May 18, 1984.

*   *   *

BOOKMAN, Charlotte
See Zolotow, Charlotte S(hapiro)

*   *   *

BRADBURY, Edward P.
See MOORCOCK, Michael (John)

*   *   *

BRAND, Garrison
See BRANDNER, Gary

*   *   *

BRANDNER, Gary 1933-
(Garrison Brand, Phil Garrison, Barnaby Quill; joint pseudonyms: Clayton Moore, Lee Davis Willoughby)

PERSONAL: Born May 31, 1933, in Sault Ste. Marie, MI; son of Henry Phil and Beada (Gehrman) Brandner; married Martine Wood, 1988. *Education:* University of Washington, B.A., 1955.

ADDRESSES: Home—9000 Vanalden Ave., #121, Northridge, CA 91324. *Agent*—Sharon Jarvis & Co., 260 Willard Ave., Staten Island, NY 10314.

CAREER: Dan B. Miner (advertising agency), Los Angeles, CA, copywriter, 1955-57; Douglas Aircraft, Santa Monica, CA, technical writer, 1957-59; North American Rockwell, Downey, CA, technical writer, 1959-67; full-time free-lance writer, 1969—.

MEMBER: Mystery Writers of America, Private Eye Writers of America, Horror Writers of America, Writers Guild of America West.

WRITINGS:

Vitamin E: Key to Sexual Satisfaction, Nash Publishing, 1971, revised edition, Paperback Library, 1972.
Living off the Land, Nash Publishing, 1971.
Off the Beaten Track in London, Nash Publishing, 1972.
(With Clayton Matthews) *Saturday Night in Milwaukee,* Curtis Books, 1973.
(Under pseudonym Clayton Moore) *Wesley Sheridan,* Berkley Publishing, 1974.
The Aardvark Affair, Zebra Publications, 1975.
The Beelzebub Business, Zebra Publications, 1975.
The Players, Pyramid Publications, 1975.
London, Pocket Books, 1976.
Billy Lives!, Manor, 1976.
The Howling, Fawcett, 1977.
The Howling II, Fawcett, 1978.
Offshore, Pinnacle Books, 1978.
Walkers, Fawcett, 1980.
The Sterling Standard, Fawcett/Popular Library, 1980.
Hellborn, Gold Medal, 1981.
A Rage in Paradise, Playboy Paperbacks, 1981.
Cat People, Gold Medal, 1982.
(Under pseudonym Lee Davis Willoughby) *The Express Riders,* Bryans, 1982.
Quintana Roo, Ballantine/Fawcett, 1984.
The Brain Eaters, Ballantine/Fawcett, 1985.
The Howling III, Ballantine/Fawcett, 1985.
Carrion, Ballantine/Fawcett, 1986.
Cameron's Closet, Ballantine/Fawcett, 1987.
Floater, Ballantine/Fawcett, 1988.
Doomstalker, Ballantine/Fawcett, 1989.

SCREENPLAYS

(Co-author) *The Howling II* (based on his novel of the same title), Granite Productions, 1982.
Cameron's Closet (based on his novel of the same title), Smart Egg Productions, 1987.

OTHER

Contributor to anthologies, including *Year's Best Horror Stories*, edited by Richard Davis, Sphere Books, 1971. Contributor of over fifty short stories, sometimes under pseudonyms, to periodicals, including *Ellery Queen's Mystery Magazine, Alfred Hitchcock's Mystery Magazine, Mike Shayne Mystery Magazine, Cavalier, Gem, New Blood,* and *Twilight Zone.*

ADAPTATIONS: A movie based on *The Howling* was filmed by Avco Embassy Pictures Corp., 1981; an Australian-made movie based on *The Howling III* was released by Square Pictures, 1987; a movie based on *Cameron's Closet* was filmed and released in 1989; a mini-series based on *Walkers* was produced by NBC, 1990.

WORK IN PROGRESS: Three novels, *Head Game, Stigmata,* and *Night Eyes;* a screenplay, *The Living End.*

SIDELIGHTS: Gary Brandner told *CA:* "More than twenty years as a writer has taught me that you had better kiss security goodbye. No more paid vacations, sick leave, health insurance, Christmas bonuses. In return you get to create your own fictional world, reward the good guys, and punish the bad as doesn't always happen in real life.

"My advice to a writer starting out: Get it on paper and get it out to market and start the next one. Don't talk it away. And respect your reader. Without him you do not exist."

BIOGRAPHICAL/CRITICAL SOURCES:

PERIODICALS

Los Angeles Times, May 25, 1989.
New York Times, November 13, 1987.

*   *   *

BREMNER, Geoffrey   1930-

PERSONAL: Born August 22, 1930, in London, England. *Education:* Oxford University, M.A., 1953; University of Reading, Ph.D, 1977.

ADDRESSES: Home—12 College Rd., Reading RG6 1QB, England.

CAREER: Schoolmaster in southern England, 1954-66; University of the West Indies, St. Augustine, Trinidad, lecturer in French, 1966-69; University of Khartoum, Khartoum, Sudan, senior lecturer in French, 1969-74; teacher at Reading University and Open University, 1974-78; University of Wales, University College of Wales, Aberystwyth, lecturer in French, 1978-89.

WRITINGS:

Order and Chance: The Pattern of Diderot's Thought, Cambridge University Press, 1983.
Diderot: Jacques le Fatalist (critical guide to French texts), Grant & Cutler, 1985.
(Editor) *Aberystwyth Word Lists,* (semi-annual), privately printed, 1986—.
(Editor) *New French Words,* privately printed, 1991.

Contributor to learned journals.

WORK IN PROGRESS: English translation of *Diderot: Writings on Art and Literature* for Penguin Classics.

SIDELIGHTS: Geoffrey Bremner told *CA:* "Wanting to produce something which would have an appeal beyond a limited circle of eighteenth-century French specialists and have some practical value, I began in 1986, with the help of some colleagues, to produce *Aberystwyth Word Lists,* a regular series of updates of the standard French-English dictionaries, recording new words and meanings in French and providing English translations. These word lists are sent out twice a year on subscription to French departments in universities and other educational establishments, translation units of companies and international organizations, freelance translators and dictionary publishers. This year the most useful material from the issues for the first four years was collected and published as *New French Words.* The number of subscribers increases regularly and the lists, as well as being, so far as I know, the sole reference work recording new French vocabulary with English translations, also reflect the latest developments in French political, social and cultural life."

*   *   *

BREUER, Reinhard   1946-

PERSONAL: Born August 3, 1946, in Regensburg, West Germany. *Education:* Attended University of Michigan, 1969; University of Wuerzburg, M.H., 1971, Ph.D., 1974; attended University of Maryland at College Park, 1972, and Oxford University, 1973; University of Munich, habilitation, 1979.

ADDRESSES: Office—Daimler-Benz AG, Postbach 80 02 30, 7000 Stuttgart 80, West Germany.

CAREER: Max-Planck-Institut fuer Astrophysik, Munich, West Germany, scientist, 1974-80; Max-Planck-Institut fuer Plasmaphysik, Munich, press officer, 1980-84; *GEO* magazine, Hamburg, West Germany, editor, 1984-90; affiliated with Daimler-Benz AG, Stuttgart, 1990—. Lecturer and astrophysicist at University of Munich; lecturer at Hamburg University, 1984, and Tubingen University, 1990.

MEMBER: Astronomical Society of West Germany.

WRITINGS:

Das anthropische Prinzip, Meyster, 1981, translation published as *The Anthropic Principle,* Birkhaeuser, 1984, revised edition, 1991.
Contact with the Stars, W. H. Freeman, 1982.
Der lautlose Schlag (title means "The Silent Strike"), Meyster, 1982.
Die Pfeile der Zeit (title means "The Arrows of Time"), Meyster, 1984.
Mensch and Kosmos (title means "Man and Universe"), Gruner and Jahr, 1990.

Also author of articles and of science features for television.

WORK IN PROGRESS: The End of the World: From Apocalypse to the Death of Matter.

SIDELIGHTS: Reinhard Breuer once told *CA* that his first two books, "*Contact with the Stars* and *The Anthropic Principle,* are concerned with the role of mankind and intelligence in the universe. There is the question of extraterrestrial life forms and communication with them if they exist, which seems unlikely, then the structure of the laws of nature and the universe, which seemingly had to be quite special in order to bring forward intelligence. The long-term prospects for intelligence in the universe—survival, influence—are investigated in my work in progress, presumably boiling down to the suspicion that life and intelligence have only a marginal role to play in the universe."

*   *   *

BROOK, Peter (Stephen Paul) 1925-

PERSONAL: Born March 21, 1925, in London, England; son of Simon (a chemist) and Ida (a chemist; maiden name, Jansen) Brook; married Natasha Parry (a stage and film actress), November 3, 1951; children: one son, one daughter. *Education:* Magdalen College, Oxford, B.A., 1944. *Avocational interests:* Painting, piano playing, traveling.

ADDRESSES: Office—International Center of Theatre Creation, 56 rue de l'Universite, 7500 Paris, France.

CAREER: Writer, producer, and director. Director of numerous stage productions for Birmingham Repertory Theatre, including *Man and Superman,* 1945, and *The Lady From the Sea,* 1946; for Stratford Theatre, including *Love's Labour's Lost,* 1947, *Measure for Measure,* 1950, and *Romeo and Juliet;* for Royal Opera House, including *Boris Godunov,* 1947, *Marriage of Figaro,* 1949, and *Sa-*

lome, 1950; for Metropolitan Opera, including *Faust,* 1953, and *Eugene Onegin,* 1957; for Royal Shakespeare Theatre Co., including *King Lear,* 1962, and *The Persecution and Assassination of Marat as Performed by the Inmates of the Asylum of Charenton under the Direction of the Marquis de Sade* (also called *Marat/Sade*), 1964; and for Avignon Theater Festival, including *The Mahabharata,* 1985. Also director of plays produced in such cities as New York, Paris, and Glasgow. Director of motion pictures for Crown Film Unit, 1945, and director of many motion pictures, including *The Beggar's Opera,* 1953, *Lord of the Flies,* 1962, *Marat/Sade,* 1967, *Tell Me Lies,* 1968, *King Lear,* 1969, *Meetings with Remarkable Men,* 1979, *La Tragedie de Carmen,* 1983, and *Mahabharata,* 1989. Director of television productions, including *Box for One,* 1949, *King Lear,* 1953, and *Heaven and Earth,* 1957. Lecturer on drama. Founding member, International Center of Theatre Creation, 1970.

MEMBER: Association of Cinematographers and Allied Technicians.

AWARDS, HONORS: Named best director by London Critics' Poll, 1964, and New York Drama Critics' Poll, 1965, and received Antoinette Perry ("Tony") Award for best director from League of New York Theatres and Producers, and Outer Circle Award, both 1965, all for *The Persecution and Assassination of Marat as Performed by the Inmates of the Asylum of Charenton Under the Direction of the Marquis de Sade;* Commander of the Order of the British Empire and Chevalier de l'Ordre des Arts et des Lettres, both 1965; Drama Desk Award for best director, Antoinette Perry Award for best director, and named best director by New York Drama Critics' Poll, all 1970, all for *A Midsummer Night's Dream;* Shakespeare Award from Freiherr von Stein Foundation, 1973; elected to Theater Hall of Fame at Uris Theater, 1983; award from Society of West End Theatre for contribution to American theater, 1983; Legion d'honneur, 1987; special Antoinette Perry Award for achievement in lyric theater for *La Tragedie de Carmen;* honorary D.Litt. from University of Birmingham; and other awards.

WRITINGS:

(And director) *U.S.* (play), first produced on West End, 1966.
The Empty Space (nonfiction), Atheneum, 1968.
(With Marius Constant and Jean-Claude Carriere) *La Tragedie de Carmen* (adapted from the opera by Georges Bizet), produced in New York City, 1983.
The Shifting Point, 1946-1987 (collection of essays), Harper, 1987.

Also author and director of screenplays, including *Lord of the Flies,* adapted from the novel by William Golding, 1962; *King Lear,* adapted from the play by William Shakespeare, 1971; (with Jeanne de Salzmann) *Meetings With Remarkable Men,* 1979; (with Carriere and Marie-Helene Estienne) *Swann in Love,* adapted from the Marcel Proust novel *Remembrance of Things Past,* 1984; and (with Carriere) *Mahabharata,* based on Indian epic poem, 1989. Also co-author of *Moderato Cantabile,* 1960.

SIDELIGHTS: Many theatre critics rank Peter Brook among the most influential figures of the twentieth-century stage. According to Jonathan Lieberson in the *New York Review of Books,* "Brook is one of the most imaginative theater directors to have emerged since World War II. He began directing plays while a student at Oxford University in the 1940s, and for his early productions he edited the texts, selected the music, and designed the costumes and sets. In a long career he has displayed a gift for creating disturbing and exciting images and situations on the stage."

Brook's revolutionary productions of Shakespearean works such as *A Midsummer Night's Dream* and *King Lear,* both of which employed spare settings and offbeat costuming to spark fresh interpretations, revealed Brook's interest in the Absurdist theatre of Samuel Beckett and the political didacticism of Bertolt Brecht. The modern theatre's strength, Brook contended, "lies in making certain little concentrated events in which one can participate—the unique quality of living events that technology makes more and more inaccessible." This twin interest in art and social relevance has endeared Brook to reviewers such as *New York Times*'s Anthony Lewis. "In an increasingly technological world, of huge abstractions, he sees the theater supplying the elements of community and life for which people yearn," wrote Lewis. "It is almost a religious experience."

Brook's initiation to the theatre was fairly auspicious. After graduating from Magdalen College at age twenty, he created brief advertising films for Crown Film Unit. He then involved himself in a production of George Bernard Shaw's *Pygmalion* by the Entertainments National Service Organization. While directing a dress rehearsal, Brook was observed by William Armstrong, a prominent British stage director. Armstrong referred Brook to the Birmingham Repertory Theatre, where the latter made his debut in 1945 as director of Shaw's *Man and Superman.* The following year, critics raved about his direction of Shakespeare's *Romeo and Juliet,* in which his casting of youthful actors was considered a welcome departure from the stodgy productions that had plagued recent presentations of Shakespeare's work.

Brook scored again with his 1953 production of Gounod's opera *Faust* for the Metropolitan Opera. Rejecting the opera's medieval setting, he placed the action in the nineteenth century and emphasized the customs of that period.

Faust was therefore more subtly unconventional than Brook's previous efforts. He also directed his first film, *The Beggar's Opera,* in 1953. His grasp of cinematic technique was deemed sufficient by most critics, but some complained that scenes were alternately too cinematic and too stage-like. Less successful was Brook's second film, *Moderato Cantabile,* an experimental work described by Andrew Sarris as "an exercise in languorous introspection of the Resnais—*Hiroshima Mon Amour* school."

In 1964 Brook implemented improvisation and aspects of Antonin Artaud's "Theatre of Cruelty" in the play *The Persecution and Assassination of Marat as Performed by the Inmates of Charenton Under the Direction of the Marquis de Sade (Marat/Sade).* Brook was extremely successful in instilling an obsession with deranged and violent behavior in his actors, and the subsequent performances shocked audiences. "The *Marat/Sade,*" noted Lewis, "with its unforgettable evocation of the inmates of the Asylum at Charenton, left some in its audience physically ill." Brook repeated his success in 1967 when he directed the film version of the play.

Two other works Brook directed in the 1960s were not as well received. Both the play *U.S.* and the motion picture *Tell Me Lies* suffered, according to reviewers, from their contrived attempts at relevance to the Vietnam War. And Sarris complained that "*Tell Me Lies* provides an entirely new set of cinematic conceptions that miscarry in the messiest ways imaginable."

Throughout the 1960s Brook also lectured on drama at universities. In 1968 his comments were collected and published as *The Empty Space.* In the book, Brook divides the theatre into four categories: he calls conventional theatre "deadly," dubs ritualistic works "holy," accessible works "rough," and considers his own style "immediate." The "immediate" approach, according to Gerald Weales, is one "in which the creativity happens at that moment and is shared by performers and audience alike." Weales added that "performers must constantly walk the line between discipline and discovery, avoiding a sealed and finished production, creating the play fresh with each performance."

The Empty Space was generally welcomed by critics as thought-provoking insight into the modern theatre. Weales called it "an exploration." In *Drama,* Edward Argent observed that "it is essential reading for anyone seriously interested in the drama—infuriating to some, baffling maybe, but essential." *New Leader*'s Albert Bermel praised Brook's "tact and eclecticism" and called *The Empty Space* "an absorbing document."

Brook continued directing in the 1970s. His most notable works were the motion pictures *King Lear* and *Meetings With Remarkable Men. New York Times*'s Vincent Canby called *King Lear* a film "of lovely surprises." He noted, "It's a downhill journey, but one that, by the flash of the lightning that the play provides, illuminates, for a very brief time, the essence of existence without comprehensible moral order, and makes it bearable." John Simon disagreed, contending that "there is almost no poetry at all in the film." He charged that "Brook will do anything for an effect, however nonsensical."

Meetings With Remarkable Men was less successful. Brook's biography of Russian mystic G. I. Gurdjieff concentrated on the philosopher's search for enlightenment in the Near East. *Newsweek*'s Jack Kroll complained that Brook's solemn approach overwhelmed the drama. "The ineffable is indeed ineffable," Kroll conceded, "but surely a film on this subject should get under your skin, disrupt your complacency, make you feel the possibility of another kind of inner life." Janet Maslin in the *New York Times* similarly charged, "Watching this handsome, affectless effort feels a little like receiving a series of postcards in the mail, each one beautiful but missing a message on the back." She added, "Certainly *Meetings With Remarkable Men* is a film that requires supplementary energy, whether it comes from the curiosity, or the prior knowledge that the right audience may provide."

In 1987, Brook's collection of essays entitled, *The Shifting Point, 1946-1987,* was published. In this book Brook shares the wisdom and experiences he gained in his over forty years producing and directing plays for the theatre. Many reviewers have pointed to the historical and cultural importance of Brook's book in understanding the impact of the theatre on society. Erika Hunk commented in the *Village Voice* that books such as Brook's *The Shifting Point, 1946-1987* are immensely valuable. Hunk explained that these books "do make us think, remind us of the value of seeing their productions, remind us, finally, that there's value to the entire enterprise of arguing about theatre: after all, it *is* arguing about the world."

Francis King stated in the *New York Times Book Review* that Brook is theater's "most original and creative theoretician." King continued to remark that "there is hardly a piece in *The Shifting Point, 1946-1987* that does not have something fascinating to say—not merely to those who look to the theater for their livelihood but to those who go to it for enjoyment, instruction, and above all, for the 'interest' that, in his final essay, Mr. Brook interprets as taking in all those aspects of living that are directly related to essential questions of being and becoming."

BIOGRAPHICAL/CRITICAL SOURCES:

BOOKS

Sattis, Andrew, *The American Cinema: Directors and Direction, 1929-1968,* Dutton, 1968.

PERIODICALS

Book World, December 29, 1968.
Chicago Tribune, September 26, 1984.
Cue, February 13, 1971.
Drama, spring, 1969.
London, November, 1968.
New Leader, December 2, 1968.
New Statesman, October 18, 1968.
Newsweek, September 3, 1979.
New York, May 26, 1980.
New York Review of Books, March 3, 1988.
New York Times, October 4, 1955; May 18, 1958; January 15, 1971; December 5, 1971; December 22, 1971; August 5, 1979; May 25, 1980; November 27, 1983; March 22, 1984; July 31, 1985; September 30, 1987; October 19, 1987; November 26, 1987; September 28, 1989; December 26, 1989.
New York Times Book Review, November 17, 1968; October 18, 1987.
New York Times Magazine, October 4, 1987.
Times (London), April 14, 1988.
Village Voice, December 29, 1987.
Vogue, November 15, 1968.
Washington Post, December 11, 1983; October 5, 1984; November 27, 1989.

*   *   *

BROWN, Richard H(arvey) 1940-

PERSONAL: Born May 12, 1940, in New York, NY; son of Samuel Robert and Sylvia Brown; married Nathalie Babel (a dealer in art and antiques), April 5, 1967; children: Ramiro. *Education:* University of Lausanne, certificate, 1960; University of California, Berkeley, B.A., 1961; Columbia University, M.A., 1965; University of California, San Diego, Ph.D., 1973. *Politics:* Democratic Socialist. *Religion:* Jewish.

ADDRESSES: Home—Washington, DC *Office*—Department of Sociology, 2112 Art Sociology Bldg., University of Maryland, College Park, MD 20742.

CAREER: Community Development Foundation (consultants), New York City, regional director for Latin America, 1965-67; Hudson Institute, Harmon, NY, member of senior research staff, 1967; Human Resources Administration, Community Development Agency, New York City, assistant commissioner for planning and budgeting, 1968-69; Social Engineering Technology (consulting firm), Los Angeles, CA, principal, 1969-74; University of Maryland, College Park, professor of sociology, 1975—, and professor of comparative literature, 1985—. Founder and president of Washington Institute for Social

Research, 1978—. Visiting instructor at New School for Social Research, 1968; lecturer at University of California, San Diego, 1971-72; guest professor or lecturer at universities in France, Germany, the United Kingdom, Canada, People's Republic of China, and Latin America. Consultant to various governmental, private sector, and international organizations.

MEMBER: International Society for the Comparative Study of Civilizations, International Sociological Association, Society for International Development, American Sociological Association, American Academy of Political and Social Science, American Association of University Professors, Democratic Socialists of America, Union for Democratic Communication.

AWARDS, HONORS: Resident fellow, National Center for Alcohol Education, 1974-75; grant, National Institutes of Health, 1976; Legion of Honor Award, Chapel of the Four Chaplains, Temple University, 1983; Fulbright fellow in Latin America, 1985.

WRITINGS:

A Poetic for Sociology: Toward a Logic of Discovery for the Human Sciences, Cambridge University Press, 1977.

(Editor with Stanford M. Lyman) *Structure, Consciousness, and History,* Cambridge University Press, 1978.

(Editor) *American Society: Essays on the Political Economy and Cultural Psychology of an Advanced Capitalist System,* Ginn, 1981.

(Editor with George Coelho) *Traditions and Transformations: Asian Indians in America,* Studies in Third World Societies, Volume 38, 1986.

Society as Text: Essays on Rhetoric, Reason, and Reality, University of Chicago Press, 1987.

(Editor with Coelho) *Migration and Modernization: The Indian Diaspora in Comparative Perspective,* Studies in Third World Societies, 1987.

Social Science as Civic Discourse: Essays on the Invention, Uses, and Legitimation of Social Theory, University of Chicago Press, 1989.

(Editor) *Writing the Social Text: Poetics and Politics in Social Science Discourse,* Aldine, 1992.

(Editor with W. Liu) *Modernization in East Asia: Economic, Political, and Social Perspectives,* Praeger, 1992.

El Postmodernismo y la sociologia, Revista Colombiana de la Sociologia, 1992.

Discourse and Dominion: Knowledge, Power, and Civic Discourse in a Democratic Society, University of Chicago Press, 1993.

(Editor) *Cultural Perspectives on Modernization in East Asia,* Studies in Third World Societies, 1993.

(Editor) *Truth and Mimesis in Art and Social Science,* University of Illinois Press, 1993.

Also author, with Remi Clignet, of *America at the Edge of the Millennium: Decline and Renewal in the Abstract Society,* 1992. Contributor of more than seventy articles and reviews to social science and humanities journals.

Some of Brown's books have been published in French, German, Italian, Spanish, Japanese. and Russian.

WORK IN PROGRESS: La Retour de la rhetorique: Poetique et persuasion dans les sciences sociales, for Meridiens Klincksieck; *Self and Sensibility in Indian Culture: A Journey of Recovery; Forbidden Substances: The Political Economy and Moral Phenomenology of Drugs; Modernism and Modernization: Cultural Psychology, State Formation, and Economic Growth in Comparative Historical Perspective.*

SIDELIGHTS: In the preface to *A Poetic for Sociology,* Richard H. Brown writes: "After receiving a statistical functionalist version of social science at Berkeley and Columbia, I spent a number of years 'applying' this knowledge in programs of intentional social change—economic development planning in Latin America, antipoverty activities in New York City, stints with think-tanks and consulting firms. What struck me most in this work was the dissonance between social theory as I had learned it and political reality as I was experiencing it. . . .

"In the hands of conservatives the social systems models encouraged efforts to control society much in the manner that experiments are controlled. When liberals were in charge their reluctance to exercise such control insured that programs simply failed. In either case the intention of helping people was vitiated by the manipulativeness of the helping techniques; the increasing demand for experts to run larger and more complex organizations violated the increasing need for nonalienating forms of work and of governance.

"While I was out in the field there had emerged in America a 'new' sociology that promised to be true to the data as existentially enacted. . . . Yet the problems that interested me most were still the old-fashioned ones—class conflict, social mobility, and institutional change. I wanted a macrotheory of action but instead found microtheories of consciousness."

Brown continues in his preface: "In trying to bridge these two realms, I discovered that the conflicts between schools are not so much a war of armies as an anarchy in the streets. . . . Thus, no bridge could carry the weight I wanted to put on it unless its foundations were set in the deeper, epistemological substrata that underlies the conflicts between sociological schools. . . .

"I set out to find a conceptual vocabulary that could justify interpretive procedures as a rigorous way of knowing and under which, at the same time, the epistemology of positive sociology could be subsumed. Cognitive aesthetics, or what might be called a critical poetic, provided the beginnings of such a vocabulary."

Brown told *CA:* "*Society as Text* and *Social Science as Civic Discourse* continue my studies into the relations between theory and practice. These works are at once philosophical critiques of social theory and social theoretical critiques of politics. Philosophy seeks to define our nature and destiny—what we are, what we can know, and what we should become. Social thought concerns the scarcities inherent in any social order, and the possibilities and constraints that these provide for human freedom. Politics is the creation of reality through conflictual action, the determining of who gets what. The 'utopias' of philosophy or fiction are never far from 'reality,' however, because yesterday's utopias provide the warrant for present practices. Today's fictions become tomorrow's factions.

"These three domains of human experience—the utopian 'ought,' the theoretical description of what 'is,' and the political practice seeking to bring the 'is' closer to the 'ought'—all are conducted through language, all are modes of persuasive discourse. By focusing on the shaping of experience through language, therefore, we become able to see that the dehumanizing segregations of modern life need not be absolute. Art and science are both communitarian, symbolic constructions. Moral discourse and objective descriptions both are products of situationally-constrained, socially-embedded, rhetorical performance. Knowledge of experts and the understandings of ordinary folks both are 'worlds' created through socially communicative interaction. Such reformulations may encourage a less alienated, fragmented vision of our politics and our culture, and a more authentic understanding of ourselves. These dilemmas and possible responses also are addressed in *Discourse and Dominion: Knowledge, Power, and Civic Discourse in a Democratic Society.*

"I have sought to infuse humane values into the social sciences by reformulating their epistemological foundations. At the same time, I am exploring ways to link humanistic theories of society with practical interventions. The Washington Institute for Social Research was formed in 1978 for this purpose. We sponsor public debates on current issues, prepare tapes of symposia for broadcast on national public radio, consult with governmental, business, and community service organizations, and conduct practically-directed social research on problems that invite theoretical reconceptualization and institutional redirection.

"The broad intellectual framework for these activities is a conception of the emerging world political economy and America's role in it. On the one hand, we are faced with potential apocalyptic catastrophes on a global scale—ecological disasters, nuclear wars, food/population imbal-

ances, and the like. On the other hand, our collective means for addressing these difficulties are limited to nationalistic and technocratic interventions which, even if successful, would buy physical survival for some by sacrificing the human dignity of all.

"In addition, the United States is experiencing a special crisis. In our first century, we had a frontier to conquer; in our second we made an industrial revolution and gained world economic and military domination. But with the rise and collapse of Soviet power, the emergence of Europe and Japan as competitors, and the diffusion of power through formerly placid Third World nations, the days of continuous easy growth for America are over. This has led to a decline of American influence, deepening economic scarcity, and a crisis of legitimacy of our cultural values. Moreover, advanced capitalism itself has generated enormous economic concentrations, a hugely expanded role for the state, and the destruction of traditional communities and values, thereby further eroding our democratic institutions and commitments. These are themes that I explore in *America at the Edge of the Millennium* and in *Modernism and Modernization.*

"I believe that the agenda of democratic socialism—though still halting and incomplete—can provide some solutions. To cite but one example, in former times it was thought that economic efficiency required the authoritarian control of workers. Indeed this was accepted even in so-called Marxist states. Such an assumption is no longer tenable. Experience with job enrichment, co-management, and worker's direct control of the means of production has been proven successful as a way not only to deepen democracy by extending it to the economic realm, but also to enhance productive efficiency and political legitimacy. This is only one illustration. Many other experiments in this spirit have already shown their practical effectiveness and moral worth in numerous countries and settings. But even if such democratic socialist ideas were purely 'utopian,' we should remember that mass material comfort also was utopian before the industrial revolution, and that political democracy was itself a utopian dream before its realization for many in our American Revolution."

*   *   *

BRUGGER, Robert J(ohn) 1943-

PERSONAL: Surname is pronounced *Broo*-ger; born February 8, 1943, in New Haven, CT; son of John R. (an educational broadcasting consultant) and Angeline M. (a Montessori teacher) Brugger; children: Laura, Rebecca, Mary Eleanor. *Education:* University of Notre Dame, A.B., 1965; University of Maryland, M.A., 1967; Johns Hopkins University, Ph.D., 1974.

ADDRESSES: Home—223 Chancery Rd., Baltimore, MD 21218. *Office*—701 W. 40th St., Ste. 275, Baltimore, MD 21211.

CAREER: University of Virginia, Charlottesville, assistant professor of history, 1974-80, *Papers of James Madison,* associate editor, 1980-83, consultant, 1983—; author and research director, Maryland Historical Society Maryland textbook project, 1983-85. Eliot House, visiting scholar and tutor. Johns Hopkins University Press, history editor. Lectures extensively at meetings, symposia, and conferences. *Military service:* U.S. Marine Corps, 1967-70; became captain.

MEMBER: American Historical Association, Organization of American Historians, Southern Historical Association.

AWARDS, HONORS: Daniel Coit Gilman fellowship, 1970-71; Phi Alpha Theta Graduate Essay Award, 1971; Ford Foundation fellowship, 1971-72; Woodrow Wilson dissertation fellowship, 1972-73; Wilson Gee Institute faculty research grant, University of Virginia, 1975, 1976, and 1978; Andrew W. Mellon Faculty Fellowship in the Humanities, Harvard University, 1978-79; nomination for Frederick Jackson Turner Prize, Organization of American Historians, 1979, for *Beverley Tucker: Heart over Head in the Old South;* nomination for Pulitzer Prize, for *Maryland: A Middle Temperament, 1634-1980.*

WRITINGS:

Beverley Tucker: Heart over Head in the Old South, Johns Hopkins University Press, 1978.
Ourselves/Our Past: Psychological Approaches to American History, Johns Hopkins University Press, 1981.
Maryland: A Middle Temperament, 1634-1980, Johns Hopkins University Press, 1988.

Contributor to *Legal Education in Virginia, 1779-1979: A Biographical Approach,* edited by William Hamilton Bryson, [Virginia]. Editor, "Secretary of State" series, University of Virginia, 1980-83. Contributor to numerous periodicals, including *Journal of Southern History, Virginia Quarterly, Civil War History, Review of Politics,* and *American Historical Review.*

WORK IN PROGRESS: A comparative study of intellectual life in antebellum America, north and south.

BIOGRAPHICAL/CRITICAL SOURCES:

PERIODICALS

Washington Post Book World, October 30, 1988, p. 3.

BUEHLMANN, Walbert 1916-

PERSONAL: Born August 6, 1916, in Lucerne, Switzerland; son of Jacob (a butcher) and Elisabeth (Sigrist) Buehlmann. *Education:* Attended Capuchin Theological Union, 1935-43; University of Fribourg, D.D., 1949.

ADDRESSES: Home—Kapuzinerkloster, CH-6415 Arth, Switzerland.

CAREER: Entered Order of Franciscan Capuchins, 1935, ordained Roman Catholic priest, 1942; Roman Catholic missionary in Tanzania, 1950-53; University of Fribourg, Fribourg, Switzerland, professor of missiology, 1954-70; Generalate of Order of Franciscan Capuchins, Rome, Italy, general secretary for mission, 1970-82; writer, 1983—.

WRITINGS:

The Coming of the Third Church, Orbis, 1977.
Courage, Church, Orbis, 1977.
The Missions on Trial, Orbis, 1978.
The Search for God, Orbis, 1979.
God's Chosen Peoples, Orbis, 1982.
The Church of the Future: A Model for the Year 2001, Orbis, 1986.
Dreaming about the Church, Sheed & Ward, 1987.
With Eyes to See: Church and World in the Third Millennium, Orbis, 1990.

SIDELIGHTS: Walbert Buehlmann told *CA:* "Since I have been a missionary in Tanzania, under colonial rule and in the pre-conciliar church, mission has changed tremendously. In that time, we had 'our missions,' for which we were fully responsible. Now 'our missions' have become 'local churches' with the missionaries in their service. In that time we aimed first at the 'conversion of pagans.' Now we try to announce God's universal love for all people in all religions, and consequently to build up a better world, together with all people of good will. In that time we had the only European (Roman) model of Church. Now we stress on inculturation and hope to have—in the future—a more pluriform, more decentralized Church of six continents. After all, I try to show in my books a worldwide, open-minded, updated Church, for which it is worthwhile to be engaged."

BIOGRAPHICAL/CRITICAL SOURCES:

PERIODICALS

Commonweal, March 3, 1978.

BULLOCK, Michael 1918-
(Michael Hale)

PERSONAL: Born April 19, 1918, in London, England; son of Herbert Stanley Billingsley (an insurance manager) and Katherine (Wortham) Bullock; married Catherine Schneller (a novelist), January 10, 1941 (deceased); children: Miriam Raya, Marcus Paul. *Education:* Attended Stowe School, Bucks, England, and Hornsey School of Art.

ADDRESSES: Home—3836 West 18th Ave., Vancouver, British Columbia, V6S 1B5 Canada. *Agent*—Joan Daves, 59 East 54th St., New York, NY 10022; and International Copyright Bureau, 26 Charing Cross Rd., London WC2H 0DG, England.

CAREER: Free-lance literary translator and writer, 1954—; University of British Columbia, Vancouver, professor of creative writing and translation, 1969-83, professor emeritus, 1983—. McGuffey Visiting Professor, Ohio University, Athens, 1968. Artist; has exhibited his drawings and paintings in Canada, England and Germany.

MEMBER: International PEN (member of executive committee of English Centre), Translators Association (committee member, 1961-66; chairman, 1964-66), Society of Authors (member of committee of management, 1967-68).

AWARDS, HONORS: Schlegel-Tieck German Translation Prize, administered by the Translators Association for the German Government, German Publishers Association, and British publishers, 1965, for *Report on Bruno* by Joseph Breitbach, and *The Thirtieth Year* by Ingeborg Bachmann; Commonwealth fellowship, 1968; French Translation Award, Canada Council, 1979, for *Stories for Late Night Drinkers* by Michel Tremblay; Social Sciences and Humanities Research Council fellowship, 1981; Okanagan Short Fiction Award, 1986, for story "The Forest Pool."

WRITINGS:

POETRY

(Under pseudonym Michael Hale) *Transmutations,* Favil Press, 1938.
Sunday Is a Day of Incest, Abelard, 1960.
World without Beginning, Amen!, Favil and Barrie & Rockliff, 1963, reprinted, Third Eye, 1987.
Zwei Stimmen in meinem Mund (Two Voices in My Mouth) (bilingual selection), Atelier Verlag, 1967.
A Savage Darkness, Sono Nis, 1969.
Black Wings, White Dead, Fiddlehead, 1978.
Lines in the Dark Wood, Third Eye, 1981.
Prisoner of the Rain: Poems in Prose, Third Eye, 1982.
Quadriga for Judy, Third Eye, 1982.

Brambled Heart, Third Eye, 1985.
Vancouver Moods, Third Eye, 1986.
Poems on Green Paper, Third Eye, 1987.

FICTION

Sixteen Stories as They Happened, Sono Nis, 1969.
Green Beginning Black Ending, Sono Nis, 1971.
Randolph Cranstone and the Pursuing River, Rainbird, 1974.
Randolph Cranstone and the Glass Thimble, Marion Boyers, 1977.
The Man with Flowers Through His Hands, Third Eye, 1985.
The Double Ego: An Autocollage, Third Eye, 1985.
Randolph Cranstone and the Veil of Maya, Third Eye, 1986.
The Story of Noire, Third Eye, 1987.
Randolph Cranstone Takes the Inward Path, Third Eye, 1988.
The Burning Chapel, Ekstasis, 1990.
The Secret Garden, Ekstasis, 1990.
The Walled Garden: A Fantasia, Ekstasis, 1990.

PLAYS

The Raspberry Picker (adapted from a play by Fritz Hochwaelder), produced in London, England, 1967.
Not to Hong Kong, produced in London, England, 1972.
The Island Abode of Bliss, produced in Vancouver, British Columbia, 1972.
The Coats, produced in London, Ontario, 1975.
Biography: A Game (adapted from a play by Max Frisch), produced in New York City, 1979.

TRANSLATOR

Willibald Klinke, *Kant for Everyman,* Macmillan, 1952.
Wilhelm Worringer, *Abstraction and Empathy: A Contribution to the Psychology of Style,* International Universities Press, 1953.
(With Ronald Gregor) Martin Buber, *Good and Evil: Two Interpretations,* Scribner, 1953.
Karl Jaspers, *Origin and Goal of History,* Yale University Press, 1953.
Josef Pieper, *End of Time: A Meditation on the Philosophy of History,* Pantheon, 1954.
Walter Jens, *Blind Man,* Macmillan, 1954.
Paul Herrmann, *Conquest by Man,* Harper, 1954.
Gustav Schenk, *Book of Poisons,* Rinehart, 1955.
Theodor Heuss, *Preludes to Life: Early Memoirs,* Citadel, 1955.
Georges Houot and P. H. Willm, *Fathoms Down,* Dutton, 1955.
Gustav von Koenigswald, *Meeting Prehistoric Man,* Thames & Hudson, 1956.

Rene von Nebesky-Wojkowitz, *Where the Gods Are Mountains,* Weidenfeld & Nicholson, 1956, Reynal, 1957.

Alfred Metraux, *Easter Island,* Oxford University Press, 1957.

Reinhard Lullies, *Greek Sculpture,* Abrams, 1957, revised edition, 1960.

Walter Erben, *Marc Chagall,* Praeger, 1957, revised edition, 1966.

Marcellin Boule, *Fossil Men,* Macmillan, 1957.

Will Berthold, *Sinking of the Bismarck,* Longmans, Green, 1958.

Max Frisch, *I'm Not Stiller,* Abelard, 1958.

Anton Luebke, *World of Caves,* Weidenfeld & Nicholson, 1958, Coward, 1959.

Herbert Wendt, *Out of Noah's Ark,* Houghton, 1959.

Zoe Oldenbourg, *Chains of Love,* Pantheon, 1959.

Joachim Leithaeuser, *Inventors' Progress,* World Publishing, 1959.

Erben, *Joan Miro,* Lund, 1959, Braziller, 1960.

Gilbert Cesbron, *Lost Children of Paris,* Abelard, 1959.

Pierre Rousseau, *Man's Conquest of the Stars,* Jarrolds, 1959, Norton, 1961.

Frisch, *Homo Faber: A Report,* Abelard, 1959.

Joachim Maass, *Gouffe Case,* Barrie & Rockliff, 1960.

Andersch, *The Redhead,* Heinemann, 1960.

Siegfried Lenz, *The Lightship,* Hill & Wang, 1960.

Will Grohmann, *Art of Henry Moore,* Abrams, 1960.

(And editor with Jerome Ch'en) *Poems of Solitude* (from the Chinese), Abelard, 1960.

Eduard Trier, *The Sculpture of Marino Marini,* Praeger, 1961.

(With Johanna Capra) Giovanni Mariacher, *Italian Blown Glass,* McGraw, 1961.

Bernhard Bultmann, *Oskar Kokoschka,* Abrams, 1961.

Ulrich Schamoni, *Their Fathers' Sons,* Barrie & Rockliff, 1962.

Otto Walter, *The Mute,* Grove, 1962.

(With Alisa Jaffa) Frederic Neuberg, *Ancient Glass,* Barrie & Rockliff, 1962.

Frisch, *The Fire Raisers,* Methuen, 1962.

Frisch, *Andorra,* Methuen, 1962, Hill & Wang, 1963.

Frisch, *Count Oederland,* Methuen, 1962.

Robert Neumann, *Festival,* Barrie & Rockliff, 1963.

(And editor) Ernst Theodor Hoffmann, *The Tales of Hoffmann,* Ungar, 1963.

Lenz, *The Survivor,* Hill & Wang, 1963.

Roger Goepper, *The Essence of Chinese Painting,* Lund, 1963, Boston Book Co., 1964.

Ingeborg Bachmann, *The Thirtieth Year,* Deutsch, 1964.

Joseph Breitbach, *Report on Bruno,* Knopf, 1964.

Wali al-Din Samih, *Daily Life in Ancient Egypt,* McGraw, 1964.

Johan Henrik Langaard and Reider Revold, *Edvard Munch,* McGraw, 1964.

Lenz, *Time of the Guiltless,* B.B.C., 1965.

Frisch, *Wilderness of Mirrors,* Methuen, 1965.

Klaus Berger, *Odilon Redon: Fantasy and Colour,* McGraw, 1965.

(With Ch'en) *Mao and the Chinese Revolution, with 37 Poems by Mao Tse-Tung,* Oxford University Press, 1965.

(With Henry Mins) Charles De Tolnay, *Hieronymous Bosch,* Methuen, 1966.

Walter August Staehelin, *The Book of Porcelain,* Macmillan, 1966.

Friedrich Duerrenmatt, *The Marriage of Mr. Mississippi* (published with an essay, *Problems of the Theatre,* translated by Gerhard Nellhaus), Grove, 1966.

Rolf Schneider, *Bridges and Bars,* J. Cape, 1967.

Charles Chasse, *The Nabis and Their Period,* Lund Humphries, 1969.

Cecile and Michel Beurdeley, *Giuseppe Castiglione,* Lund Humphries, 1969.

Georges Boudaille, *Courbet,* New York Graphic Society, 1969.

Karl Krolow, *Invisible Hands,* Grossman, 1969.

Krolow, *Foreign Bodies,* Ohio University Press, 1969.

Andre Busza, *Astrologer in the Underground,* Ohio University Press, 1970.

Joachim C. Fest, *Face of the Third Reich: Portraits of the Nazi Leadership,* Pantheon, 1970.

Francoise Cachin, *Paul Signac,* New York Graphic Society, 1971.

Michel Tremblay, *Stories for Late Night Drinkers,* Intermedia, 1978.

Rolf Schneider, *November,* Knopf, 1981.

Ornella Volta, *Satie,* Marion Boyars, 1989.

Also translator of *The Persian Mirror* by Thomas Pavel, 1987, and of other works. Contributor of translations to anthologies and periodicals.

OTHER

Lifelines: My Life in Art, Ekstasis, 1990.

Contributor of poems, fiction and articles to periodicals, including *Canadian Fiction Magazine, West Coast Review* and *Kayak.* Founding editor, *Expression;* member of editorial board, *Canadian Fiction Magazine.*

WORK IN PROGRESS: A volume of short fiction; two volumes of poems; further translations.

SIDELIGHTS: Michael Bullock told *CA:* "In my own writing and drawing, I try to express and foster a view of life and literature that is imaginative and personal and opposed to the mechanization and alienation of much contemporary art." This intention has led Bullock to combine elements from surrealism, imagism, and expressionism into a literary language all his own. Jack F. Stewart, writing in *Canadian Literature,* quotes Bullock describing his poetry: "My poetry is made up of images; therefore it is *imagist.* The images are surreal . . . ; therefore my poetry is *surrealist.* The images are drawn from the natural world but shown in the distorting mirror of a personality and used as a means of expressing this personality; therefore my poetry is *expressionist.* . . . I feel that the designation surrealist is the most all-embracing and affords the highest degree of freedom; therefore I embrace it. But if ever I felt that surrealism had assumed the significance of a dogma, I should at once discard it."

Bullock's early poems were strongly influenced by a visit to the International Exhibition of Surrealism held in London in 1936. Organized by the painter Roland Penrose and art critic Herbert Read, the exhibition introduced the English public to surrealism. Bullock, then a nineteen year old student, was enthusiastic over the surrealists' use of fantastic imagery in their work. He began to write poems in which he experimented with free-form imagery and automatic writing. His first collection, *Transmutations,* appeared in 1938 under the pseudonym of Michael Hale.

After this initial publication, Bullock turned his attention to working as a free-lance translator. During the next two decades he translated well over 100 books, usually from the original German into English. It was not until the 1960s that Bullock once again began to publish his poetry. Several collections of his work appeared in England and Germany at this time. In the late 1960s he moved to Canada, settling in British Columbia to teach at the University of British Columbia.

Bullock's poetry ranges in form from free verse to the prose poem, but always exhibits a surrealist sensibility. John Ditsky, writing in *Canadian Forum,* states that Bullock's "surrealism is neither occasional nor accidental, but thoroughgoing—and impressive." Bullock draws his images from the natural world and describes them with quiet power, creating poems both mysterious and vibrantly visual. As Stewart explains, Bullock's "poems have an enigmatic clarity that does not yield up their secrets to casual reading; they delight and puzzle."

Bullock's fiction shares many of the qualities admired in his poetry. In his Ralph Cranstone books, Bullock narrates "a succession of wild dreams, subtly interlocked, which haunt the mind with a series of possible meanings," as a critic for *New Fiction* explains. In her review of *The Man with Flowers Through His Hands* for the Toronto *Globe and Mail,* Nancy Wigston explains that the collection "opens the door on [a] kind of dreamscape world. . . . We witness a series of intricate unravelings and repatternings, underscored by an ever-present irony. . . . The fabulist behind these fantastic realities is providing a feast for the benefit of all the bedazzled searchers in the world who may long to escape, but in the meantime are fascinated by the ceaseless and sensual movement of life's mysteries." Writing of the same book for *Fantasy Review,* Jessica Amanda Salmonson claims that "as dark fantasy, or as a surprisingly linear and accessible form of surrealism, Michael Bullock is in either category Canada's finest exponent of the macabre."

As a poet and fiction writer, Bullock has gained a reputation as a creator of imaginative work which draws on the surrealist tradition to express a personal vision. Andrew Parkin, writing in *Issue,* concludes that Bullock "is one of the most vivid, mysterious and technically proficient poets writing in English today." Writing in the *San Jose Mercury News,* Brown Miller states: "Bullock has been quietly, unassumingly producing an original and highly skilled poetry that has gradually made a permanent place in Canadian and world literature."

BIOGRAPHICAL/CRITICAL SOURCES:

BOOKS

Bullock, Michael, *Lifelines: My Life in Art,* Ekstasis, 1990.
Stewart, Jack, *The Incandescent Word: The Surrealist Art of Michael Bullock,* Third Eye, 1987.

PERIODICALS

Author, summer, 1966.
Books in Canada, October, 1975.
British Columbia Library Quarterly, January, 1972; April, 1973; June, 1973.
Canadian Fiction Magazine, Number 50/51, 1984.
Canadian Forum, February, 1971.
Canadian Literature, Number 94, 1983; Number 105, 1985; Number 108, 1986; Number 115, 1987.
Fantasy Review, February, 1986.
Globe and Mail (Toronto), November 29, 1986.
Issue, March/April, 1985.
Madame, January 1, 1967.
Montreal Gazette, October 25, 1969.
New Fiction, January, 1977.
Quarry, Volume 34, number 2, 1985.
Quill and Quire, July, 1975.
San Francisco Review of Books, January/February, 1983; May/June, 1983.
San Jose Mercury News, December 30, 1984.
Vancouver Sun, July 25, 1969; May 29, 1970.
Washington Post Book World, August 9, 1981.
Waves, Volume 13, number 2/3, 1985.
West Coast Review, June, 1978.

BURNHAM, Sophy 1936-

PERSONAL: Born December 12, 1936, in Baltimore, MD; daughter of George Cochran (an attorney) and Sophy Tayloe (Snyder) Doub; married David Bright Burnham (a journalist), March 12, 1960 (divorced, 1984); children: Sarah Tayloe, Molly Bright. *Education:* Attended University of Florence, 1956-57; Smith College, B.A. (cum laude), 1958.

ADDRESSES: Home—1405 31st St. N.W., Washington, DC 20007.

CAREER: Author and playwright. Smithsonian Institution, Washington, DC, assistant curator for Museum Services, 1962-64; David McKay Co., Inc., New York City, associate editor, 1972-74; Fund for New American Plays, Kennedy Center, New York City, project director, 1992—. Volunteer with numerous organizations, including Studio Theatre, Washington, DC, founding member, 1978, interim chairman of board, 1978-80; DC Community Humanities Council, regranting arm of National Endowment for the Humanities, founding member, 1979-85, vice chairman, 1979-80; and The Octagon, Architects Institute of America, board of directors, 1984-89. Consultant to numerous organizations, including Arts International, National Park Service, Environmental Protection Agency, Institute for Law and Social Research, Department of Housing and Urban Development, and Mitre Corporation.

MEMBER: Authors Guild, Authors League of America, Playwrights Forum.

AWARDS, HONORS: Best magazine feature award, National Steeplechase and Hunt Association, 1970; Daughter of Mark Twain, Mark Twain Society, 1974; Third Prize, Episcopal Drama Award, Episcopal Foundation for Drama, 1979, for *Penelope;* Best Children's Radio Play, National Association of Community Broadcasters, 1980, for *The Witch's Tale;* Award of Excellence, *Communications Arts* magazine, 1980, for article "Machu Picchu"; First Prize, Women's Theatre Award, 1981, for *Penelope.* Grant award from Office of Advanced Drama Research, University of Minnesota, 1976, for *Penelope;* grants from DC Arts and Humanities Council, 1980-81, and Helene Wurlitzer Foundation of Taos, NM, 1981, 1983, 1991.

WRITINGS:

BOOKS

The Art Crowd, McKay, 1973.
(Editor) C. D. Brennan and others, *Threat to Licensed Nuclear Facilities,* Mitre Corp. (Washington, DC), 1975.
Buccaneer (young adult novel), Warne, 1977.
The Landed Gentry, Putnam, 1978.

The Dogwalker (young adult novel), Warne, 1979.
A Book of Angels: Reflections on Angels Past and Present and True Stories of How They Touch Our Lives, Ballantine, 1990.
Angel Letters, Ballantine, 1991.
Revelations (novel), Ballantine, in press.

PLAYS

Penelope, first produced by New Playwrights Theatre, 1976, broadcast on Pacifica National Radio, 1977.

Also author of radio plays *The Witch's Tale, Beauty and the Beast,* and *The Nightingale,* first broadcast on National Public Radio for Children's Radio Theatre; author of play, *The Study,* staged readings performed at Center Stage, Baltimore, produced for the Women's Project, New York City.

OTHER

Music of Shakespeare's England (television screenplay), Smithsonian Institution, 1962.
The Smithsonian's Whale (short film), Smithsonian Institution, 1963.
The Leaf Thieves (short film), Smithsonian Institution, 1964.

Also contributor of numerous essays and articles to magazines, including *Esquire, New York, New York Times Magazine, Realites, Redbook,* and numerous foreign magazines. Contributing editor to *Town and Country,* 1975-1980, and to *New Woman,* 1984—.

WORK IN PROGRESS: For Writers Only, for Ballantine; *The President's Angel,* a novel, for Ballantine; *Love Stories: Men I Have Known,* a collection of short stories; and *The Birthday Present,* a play.

SIDELIGHTS: Sophy Burnham told *CA:* "I first knew I was a writer at the age of ten, when I failed my fifth grade English exam. I failed because the first question was: 'Finish this paragraph.' Forty-five minutes and two bluebooks later, when the bell rang, I was still writing and came out of my trance astonished and confused. I had never gotten to the second question. It took another fifteen years to take the dare and begin to write.

"If I don't write for a certain amount of time in a given period I get ugly, like a junkie without a fix. . . . The fact that people sometimes pay me to write is a surprise bonus of the craft. But sometimes they do not. I write anyway. Still, I sometimes go through periods of drought, and if I have any suggestion on what a writer needs, it is to cultivate the sensitivity of a butterfly (for observation), a skin of a rhino (for rejection) and the tenacity of a bulldog (for keeping on keeping on). Most of writing is revision—I rewrite, rewrite, rewrite. My question: How to make it clearer? My immediate aim is to forge sentences so clear and compelling that the reader's eye keeps moving to the next page. For me, the writing itself, the singing of the song, gives pleasure. If the finished song touches another man's heart or mind, that's a miracle: I am filled with humility."

A brush with death led to the writing of *A Book of Angels*. In the book, Burnham recounts a skiing accident from which she was rescued by a stranger. Her tumble toward a cliff was interrupted by a skier dressed in black who positioned himself in front of her, allowing her to run into him to stop, and then disappeared. Burnham told *CA*, "I did not grow up believing in miracles or angels, but when I was twenty-eight an angel saved my life. For years I hid the fact from myself, and nearly twenty years later I began collecting stories of people who had seen angels and had their lives saved by them. In *A Book of Angels* I explore not only present-day encounters but also the understanding of angels throughout history and in different cultures. The stories appear along with quotations from poets, mystics, and saints, including Milton, Dante, Goethe, [and] Blake, [as well as] the Koran, the Bible, and others."

"A book about angels could easily go wrong," said *Tribune Books* reviewer Phyllis Theroux, "being too sentimental, unscholarly, unfocused or badly written. The author avoids all these pitfalls. . . . Like all good books, it exceeds its subject and illuminates the tough, tiring and sometimes miraculous business of living, where angels sometimes help out. 'Are there really forces,' Burnham asks, 'that dive, invisible, into our petty affairs?' She makes an awfully good case for it."

Burnham told *CA* that her latest work, the novel *Revelations*, took twelve years to write. She describes it as "a story of friendship and betrayal, of love and fear, and of the junction of spiritual and erotic love. It concerns an Episcopal minister, a love affair, a mystical revelation of God, and ultimately the ecclesiastical trial to which [the minister] is brought." Narrated by the minister's best friend as he recalls the events now thirty years past, *Revelations*, Burnham noted, "explores the spiritual journey that all people undertake."

BIOGRAPHICAL/CRITICAL SOURCES:

PERIODICALS

Los Angeles Times, May 1, 1990.
Milwaukee Journal, May 20, 1973.
Newsday, March 22, 1973; July 9, 1978.
Newsweek, April 9, 1973.
New York Times, March 27, 1973.
New York Times Book Review, March 25, 1973; July 2, 1978.
Progressive, September, 1978.
Tribune Books (Chicago), August 12, 1990.

Washington Post, April 15, 1990.
Washington Post Book World, March 25, 1973.

*   *   *

BUTLER, Octavia E(stelle) 1947-

PERSONAL: Born June 22, 1947, in Pasadena, CA; daughter of Laurice and Octavia M. (Guy) Butler. *Education:* Pasadena City College, A.A., 1968; attended California State University, Los Angeles, 1969, and University of California, Los Angeles.

ADDRESSES: Home—P.O. Box 6604, Los Angeles, CA 90055.

CAREER: Free-lance writer, 1970—.

MEMBER: Science Fiction Writers of America.

AWARDS, HONORS: Hugo Award, World Science Fiction Convention, 1984, for short story "Speech Sounds"; Hugo Award, Nebula Award, Science Fiction Writers of America, Locus Award from *Locus* magazine, and award for best novelette from *Science Fiction Chronicle Reader,* all 1985, all for novelette "Bloodchild"; Nebula Award nomination, 1987, for novelette "The Evening and the Morning and the Night."

WRITINGS:

SCIENCE FICTION

Patternmaster, Doubleday, 1976.
Mind of My Mind, Doubleday, 1977.
Survivor, Doubleday, 1978.
Kindred, Doubleday, 1979, 2nd edition, Beacon Press, 1988.
Wild Seed, Doubleday, 1980.
Clay's Ark, St. Martin's, 1984.
Dawn: Xenogenesis (first novel in the "Xenogenesis" trilogy), Warner Books, 1987.
Adulthood Rites (second novel in the "Xenogenesis" trilogy), Warner Books, 1988.
Imago (third novel in the "Xenogenesis" trilogy), Warner Books, 1989.

Contributor to anthologies, including *Clarion,* 1970, and *Chrysalis 4,* 1979; contributor to *Isaac Asimov's Science Fiction Magazine, Future Life, Transmission,* and other publications.

SIDELIGHTS: Concerned with genetic engineering, psionic powers, advanced alien beings, and the nature and proper use of power, Octavia E. Butler's science fiction presents these themes in terms of racial and sexual awareness. "Butler consciously explores the impact of race and sex upon future society," Frances Smith Foster explains in *Extrapolation.* As one of the few black writers in the science fiction field, and the only black woman, Butler's racial and sexual perspective is unique. This perspective, however, does not limit her fiction or turn it into mere propaganda. "Her stories," Sherley Anne Williams writes in *Ms.*, "aren't overwhelmed by politics, nor are her characters overwhelmed by racism or sexism." Speaking of how Butler's early novels deal with racial questions in particular, John R. Pfeiffer of *Fantasy Review* maintains that "nevertheless, and therefore more remarkably, these are the novels of character that critics so much want to find in science fiction—and which remain so rare. Finally, they are love stories that are mythic, bizarre, exotic and heroic and full of doom and transcendence."

Among Butler's strengths as a writer, according to some reviewers, is her creation of believable, independent female characters. "Her major characters are black women," Foster explains, and through these characters Butler explores the possibilities for a society open to true sexual equality. In such a society Butler's female characters, "powerful and purposeful in their own right, need not rely upon eroticism to gain their ends." Williams also believes that Butler posits "a multiracial society featuring strong women characters." In addition to her unique characters, critics praise Butler's controlled, economical prose style. Writing in the *Washington Post Book World,* Elizabeth A. Lynn calls the author's prose "spare and sure, and even in moments of great tension she never loses control over her pacing or over her sense of story." "Butler," Dean R. Lambe of the *Science Fiction Review* similarly attests, "has a fine hand with lean, well-paced prose."

Butler's stories have been well received by science fiction fans. In 1985 she won three of the field's top honors—the Nebula Award, the Hugo Award, and the Locus Award— for her novella "Bloodchild," the story of human males on another planet who bear the children of an alien race. "Bloodchild," Williams explains, "explores the paradoxes of power and inequality, and starkly portrays the experience of a class who, like women throughout most of history, are valued chiefly for their reproductive capacities."

It is through her novels, however, that Butler reaches her largest audience; and, of these, she is best known for her books set in the world of the "Patternists," including *Patternmaster, Mind of My Mind, Survivor,* and *Wild Seed.* The Patternist series tells of a society dominated by an elite, specially-bred group of telepaths who are mentally linked together into a hierarchical pattern. Originally founded by a four thousand-year-old immortal Nubian named Doro who survives by killing and then taking over younger bodies, these telepaths seek to create a race of superhumans. But Doro's plans are repeatedly thwarted in *Wild Seed* by Anyanwu, an immortal woman who does not need to kill to survive; and in *Mind of My Mind* Mary,

Doro's daughter, organizes all the other telepaths to defeat him, thus giving the Patternists an alternative to Doro's selfish and murderous reign. As *Dictionary of Literary Biography* contributor Margaret Anne O'Connor says, "this novel argues for the collective power of man as opposed to individual, self-interested endeavor."

The Patternist novels cover hundreds of years of human history. *Wild Seed* takes place in the eighteenth and nineteenth centuries and *Mind of My Mind* is set in a Los Angeles of the near future, but the other books in the series are set in the distant future. *Patternmaster,* like *Mind of My Mind,* addresses the theme of the importance of compassion and empathy between people over the ambitions of the individual. In this tale Butler describes an Agrarian society now ruled by the telepaths whose communities are at constant risk of attack from humans who have been monstrously mutated by a genetic disease—just how this disease is brought to Earth by an astronaut is explained in *Clay's Ark.* During one of these raids, a Patternist ruler is wounded and becomes an invalid. His two sons vie for his position, and Butler shows how the younger son, Teray, learns from a woman healer named Amber that compassion is necessary to maintain and control the communal Pattern. By learning—as Mary did in *Mind of My Mind*—the benefits of the community over the individual, Teray defeats his brother and takes his father's place.

Although many of Butler's protagonists in the Patternist books are black women, the novelist does not display any particular favoritism towards either blacks or women. Instead, she emphasizes the need for breaking down race and gender barriers by illustrating the inability of those hindered by prejudice and narrow vision to progress and evolve. According to Foster, for "the feminist critic, Octavia Butler may present problems. Her female characters are undeniably strong and independent; but whether, as Joanna Russ insists is crucial, 'the assumptions underlying the entire narrative are feminist,' is uncertain, for 'who wins and who loses' is less clear than that a compromise has been made which unifies the best of each woman and man. For Afro-American literary critics, Butler can present problems as well, for their attention has been focused upon the assumptions and depictions about the black experience of the past and the present; yet the implications of Butler's vision should be a significant challenge."

In *Survivor,* another Patternist novel, and Butler's more recent *Xenogenesis* trilogy, the author uses alien beings to help illustrate her themes: the differences between humans and aliens magnifies the issue of cultural misunderstanding and prejudice-inspired antipathy. With *Survivor,* the character Alanna survives on a distant world by learning to understand and love one of the alien Kohn's. The *Xenogenesis* books explore the interrelationships between two peoples in greater depth by creating a race called the Oankali, nomadic aliens who interbreed with other sentient species in order to improve their gene pool. Arriving on Earth after a nuclear holocaust has wiped out almost all of humanity, the Oankali offer mankind a second chance through the combination of the best characteristics of both species. They accomplish this through a third sex called ooloi, whose function is to manipulate the two races' genes into a new species. Here, according to *Analog* reviewer Tom Easton, "we may have Butler's [main] point: The ooloi are the means for gene transfer between species, but they also come between, they are intermediaries, moderators, buffers, and Butler says that the human tragedy is the unfortunate combination of intelligence and hierarchy."

One book that Butler has written that has nothing to do with either her Patternist or her Xenogenesis series is *Kindred,* which, except for its time-travel theme, diverges enough from the science fiction genre that her publisher marketed it as a mainstream novel. *Kindred* concerns Dana, a contemporary black woman who is pulled back in time by her great-great-grandfather, a white plantation owner in the antebellum American South. To insure that he will live to father her great-grandmother, and thus insure her own birth in the twentieth century, Dana is called upon to save the slave owner's life on several occasions. "Butler makes new and eloquent use of a familiar science-fiction idea, protecting one's own past, to express the tangled interdependency of black and white in the United States," Joanna Russ writes in the *Magazine of Fantasy and Science Fiction.* Williams calls *Kindred* "a startling and engrossing commentary on the complex-actuality and continuing heritage of American slavery."

Butler currently enjoys a solid reputation among both readers and critics of science fiction, and Williams notes that Butler has a "cult status among many black women readers." She also notes that "Butler's work has a scope that commands a wide audience." Many of her books have been recommended by critics as examples of the best that science fiction has to offer. For example, speaking of *Kindred* and *Wild Seed,* Pfeiffer argues that with these books Butler "produced two novels of such special excellence that critical appreciation of them will take several years to assemble. To miss them will be to miss unique novels in modern fiction." And Easton asserts that with *Dawn* "Butler has gifted SF with a vision of possibility more original than anything we have seen since [Arthur C.] Clarke's *Childhood's End.*" Nevertheless, Foster believes that Butler's novels deserve more recognition because they fill a void in the science fiction genre, which often neglects to explore sexual, familial, and racial relationships. "Since Octavia Butler is a black woman who writes speculative fiction which is primarily concerned with social relationships, where rulers include women and nonwhites," Foster concludes, "the neglect of her work is startling."

BIOGRAPHICAL/CRITICAL SOURCES:

BOOKS

Contemporary Literary Criticism, Volume 38, Gale, 1986.
Dictionary of Literary Biography, Volume 33: *Afro-American Fiction Writers after 1955,* Gale, 1984.

PERIODICALS

Analog: Science Fiction/Science Fact, January 5, 1981; November, 1984; December 15, 1987; December, 1988.
Black American Literature Forum, summer, 1984.
Black Scholar, March/April, 1986.
Equal Opportunity Forum Magazine, Number 8, 1980.
Essence, April, 1979.
Extrapolation, spring, 1982.
Fantasy Review, July, 1984.
Janus, winter, 1978-79.
Los Angeles Times, January 30, 1981.
Magazine of Fantasy and Science Fiction, February, 1980; August, 1984.
Ms., March, 1986; June, 1987.
Salaga, 1981.
Science Fiction Review, May, 1984.
Thrust: Science Fiction in Review, summer, 1979.
Washington Post Book World, September 28, 1980; June 28, 1987; July 31, 1988; June 25, 1989.*

—*Sketch by Kevin S. Hile*

*   *   *

BUTLER, William E(lliot II)   1939-

PERSONAL: Born October 20, 1939, in Minneapolis, MN; son of William Elliott (a public accountant) and Maxine (Elmberg) Butler; married Darlene Mae Johnson (an economist), September 2, 1961 (died, 1989); children: William Elliott III, Bradley Newman. *Education:* Hibbing State Junior College (now Hibbing Community College), A.A., 1959; American University, B.A., 1961; Johns Hopkins University, M.A., 1963, Ph.D., 1970; Harvard University, J.D., 1966; London University, LL.D., 1979. *Religion:* Protestant. *Avocational interests:* Book collecting, bookplate collecting.

ADDRESSES: Home—20 Ainger Road, London NW3 3AS, England. *Office*—Faculty of Laws, University College, University of London, 4-8 Endsleigh Gardens, London WC1, England.

CAREER: Member of Bar of U.S. District Court, U.S. Court of Appeals for District Columbia, and U.S. Supreme Court. Johns Hopkins University, Washington Center of Foreign Policy Research, Washington, DC, research assistant in international relations, 1966-68; Catholic University of America, Washington, DC, lecturer in international law, 1967-68; Harvard University, Cambridge, MA, research associate in law and associate of Russian Research Center, 1968-70; University College, University of London, London, England, reader, 1970-76, professor of comparative law, 1976—, dean of Faculty of Laws, 1977-79, 1988-90, director of Centre for the Study of Socialist Legal Systems, 1982—, vice dean of Faculty of Laws, 1986-88. Guest senior scholar, Department of International Law, Faculty of Laws, Moscow State University, U.S.-U.S.S.R. cultural exchange agreement, 1971-72, 1981; guest scholar, Faculty of Law, Moscow State University, 1972, 1980, Institute of State and Law, U.S.S.R. Academy of Sciences, Anglo-Soviet cultural exchange agreement, 1976, 1980, 1982, 1984, 1988, Mongolian Academy of Sciences, 1979, and Harvard Law School, 1982; visiting professor of law, New York University Law School, 1978, Ritumeikan University, 1985, and Harvard Law School, 1986-87; lecturer at the Hague Academy of International Law, 1985. Member of the first British lawyers' delegation to China, 1979-80; coordinator of the UCL-USSR Academy of Sciences Protocol on Cooperation, 1981—; vice-chairman of the Council of the School of Slavonic and East European Studies at the University of London, 1982-88; chairman of the civil rights in Russia Advisory Panel at the University of London, 1983-87; member of committee of management at the Institute of Advanced Legal Studies, 1985-88; member of the court of governors of City of London Polytechnic, 1985-89; honorary member of the All-Union Society of Bibliophiles, 1989; member of special counsel for the Commission on Economic reform for the USSR Council of Ministers, 1989—.

MEMBER: International Law Association, International Association of Mongolists (secretariat, 1987—), American Society of International Law, American Association for the Advancement of Slavic Studies, American Foreign Law Association, British Institute of International and Comparative Law, United Kingdom National Committee for Comparative Law, National Association for Soviet and East European Studies, Federal International des Societes d'Amateurs d'Ex-Libris (vice president, 1984-86; executive secretary, 1988—), Society of Public Teachers of Law, Bookplate Society (secretary, 1978-86; foreign secretary, 1988—), Private Libraries Association, Bibliographical Society, Anglo-Mongolian Society, Cosmos Club.

AWARDS, HONORS: Royal Society of Arts fellow; Associe, International Academy of Comparative Law.

WRITINGS:

The Law of Soviet Territorial Waters: A Case Study of Maritime Legislation and Practice, Praeger, 1967.

(With Donald W. Wainhouse, Bernhard G. Bechhoefer, Anne P. Simons, and Arnold Wolfers) *Alternative Methods for Dealing with Breaches of Arms Control Agreements,* five volumes, U.S. Arms Control and Disarmament Agency, 1968.

(Co-editor and translator) *The Merchant Shipping Code of the U.S.S.R. (1968),* Johns Hopkins Press, 1970.

The Soviet Union and the Law of the Sea, Johns Hopkins Press, 1971.

(Translator and author of introduction) G. I. Tunkin, *Theory of International Law,* Harvard University Press, 1975.

(With John N. Hazard and Peter B. Maggs) *The Soviet Legal System,* 3rd edition, Oceana, 1977.

Northeast Arctic Passage, A. W. Sijthoff, 1978.

(Compiler and translator) *The Soviet Legal System: Legislation and Documentation,* Oceana, 1978.

The Mongolian Legal System, Martinus Nijhoff, 1982.

Commercial, Business and Trade Laws: The Soviet Union and Mongolia, Oceana, 1982.

Soviet Law, Butterworths, 1983, 2nd edition, 1988.

(Translator) A. Kuznetsov, *The Journey,* Transnational/ Horizon, 1984.

(With Hazard and Maggs) *The Soviet Legal System: The Law in the 1980s,* Oceana, 1984.

Bibliography on the Soviet Union and the Development of the Law of the Sea, Oceana, 1985.

Anglo-American and Socialist Legal Systems, Horitsun-bunka-sha, 1986.

Leslie C. Benenson, Exlibristen, 1986.

(With Darlene J. Butler) *The Golden Era of American Bookplate Design, 1890-1940,* Exlibristen, 1986.

Bookshop Memories, Arethusa, 1987.

Arbitration in the Soviet Union, Oceana, 1989.

EDITOR

(And translator) *Russian Family Law,* Hazen, 1965.

(With Vaclav Mostecky, and contributor) *Soviet Legal Bibliography,* Harvard Law School Library, 1965.

Writings on Soviet Law and Soviet International Law, Harvard Law School Library, 1966.

(And translator) *Customs Code of the USSR,* Hazen, 1966.

Microfiche Project on Russian-Soviet Law, Inter Documentation Co. (Leiden), 1972.

(And author of introduction) P. P. Shafirov, *A Discourse Concerning the Just Causes of the War between Sweden and Russia: 1700-1721,* Oceana, 1973.

(With Donald D. Barry and George Ginsburgs, and contributor) *Contemporary Soviet Law: Essays in Honor of John N. Hazard,* Martinus Nijhoff, 1974.

(And compiler) *Russian and Soviet Law: An Annotated Catalogue of Reference Works, Legislation, Court Reports, Serials, and Monographs on Russian and Soviet*

Law (Including International Law), Inter Documentation Co., 1976.

(And contributor) *Russian Law: Historical and Political Perspectives,* A. W. Sijthoff, 1977.

(And translator) *A Source Book on Socialist International Organizations,* A. W. Sijthoff, 1978.

(And compiler and translator) *Collected Legislation of the U.S.S.R. and Constituent Union Republics,* seven volumes, Oceana, 1979—.

(And contributor) *International Law in Comparative Perspective,* A. W. Sijthoff, 1980.

(And compiler) *Soviet Commercial and Maritime Arbitration,* Oceana, 1980.

Law in the Mongolian People's Republic: Mongolian Law on Microfiche, Inter Documentation Co., 1980.

(And author of introduction) *Anglo-Polish Legal Essays,* Transnational, 1982.

Microfiche Project on Public International Law, Inter Documentation Co., 1982.

(And contributor) *The Legal System of the Chinese Soviet Republic, 1931-1934,* Transnational, 1983.

(And compiler with A. J. Nathanson) *Mongolian-English-Russian Dictionary of Legal Terms and Concepts,* Martinus Nijhoff, 1983.

(And compiler and translator) *The USSR, Eastern Europe, and the Development of the Law of the Sea,* Oceana, 1983—.

(And compiler and translator) *Basic Documents on the Soviet Legal System,* Oceana, 1983, 2nd edition, 1990.

(And contributor) *Legislative Reform and East-West Trade,* Condyne, 1984.

(With V. N. Kudriavtsev, and contributor) *Comparative Law and Legal System: Historical and Socio-Legal Perspectives,* Oceana, 1985.

The Law of the Sea and International Shipping: Anglo-Soviet Post-UNCLOS Perspectives, Oceana, 1985.

(And contributor) *Justice and Comparative Law: Anglo-Soviet Perspectives on Criminal Law, Evidence, Procedure, and Sentencing Policy,* Martinus Nijhoff, 1986.

(With B. Hepple and Alan C. Neal, and contributor) *Comparative Labour Law: Anglo-Soviet Perspectives,* Gower, 1987.

(And contributor) *International Law and the International System,* Martinus Nijhoff, 1987.

(With Peter B. Maggs and John B. Quigley, Jr., and contributor) *Law after Revolution: Essays on Socialist Law in Honor of Harold J. Berman,* Oceana, 1988.

(And translator) V. E. Grabar, *The History of International Law in Russia, 1647-1917,* Clarendon Press, 1989.

The Non-Use of Force in International Law, Martinus Nijhoff, 1989.

Control over Compliance with International Law, Martinus Nijhoff, 1990.

Perestroika and International Law, Nijhoff, 1990.

OTHER

Contributor to books, including *The Law of the Sea: The United Nations and Ocean Management,* edited by L. M. Alexander, University of Rhode Island, 1971; *A Treatise on International Criminal Law,* edited by M. Cherif Bassiouni and V. P. Nanda, C. C. Thomas, 1973; *Limits to National Jurisdiction over the Sea,* edited by G. T. Yeats and J. H. Young, University of Virginia Press, 1974; *Environmental Law: International and Comparative Aspects,* edited by J. Nowak, Oceana, 1976; *The Soviet Codes of Law,* edited by W. B. Simons, A. W. Sijthoff, 1980; *Perspectives on Soviet Law for the 1980s,* edited by F. J. M. Feldbrugge and Simons, Martinus Nijhoff, 1982; *Russia and the West in Eighteenth Century,* edited by A. G. Cross, Oriental Research Partners, 1983; *The Soviet Union and Eastern Europe,* edited by G. Schopflin, Muller, Blond & White, 1986; *The Soviet Union under Gorbachev,* edited by M. McCauley, Macmillan, 1987; and *The Weightier Matters of the Law,* edited by J. Witte and F. S. Alexander, Scholars Press, 1988. Also contributor of over five hundred articles, translations, and reviews to journals, including *International Legal Materials* and *Soviet Statutes and Decisions.*

Also author of *Contemporary Soviet Bookplate Design,* 1982. Editor and translator of *Vignettes of Bookplate Collecting in Leningrad,* 1981, and *The Graphic Work of A. I. Kalashnikov,* 1982; also editor of *Collected Works on Socialist Legal Systems on Microfiche,* 1981. Editor of "Legal Systems of the World" series, Butterworth & Co.; editor of *Harvard International Law Journal,* 1965-66, member of editorial advisory committee, 1983—; editor of *Soviet Statutes and Decisions,* 1969-76, member of editorial board, 1977—; editor of *Bookplate Journal,* 1983-86, member of editorial board, 1986—, co-editor, 1989—; editor of *Yearbook on Socialist Legal System,* 1986—. Contributing editor to *International Journal of Politics,* 1969—; member of editorial board of *Earth Law,* 1975-77; member of editorial board of *Review of Socialist Law,* 1975—; editorial advisor for *International Legal Materials,* 1982—; member of editorial board for *Coexistence,* 1984—; member of editorial board for *Marine Policy,* 1988—.

WORK IN PROGRESS: Russian international legal history; the systematization of Soviet law; selected documents on socialist international organizations; Russian and Soviet legal history; socialist legal systems; international and comparative law; history of Russian bookplates.

SIDELIGHTS: William E. Butler once told *CA* that he "has travelled in the Soviet Union on more than thirty-six occasions since 1960 and was the first Western jurist ever

to undertake legal research in Mongolia during 1979, and
again in 1987."*

C

CALDER, Angus 1942-

PERSONAL: Born February 5, 1942, in Sutton, Surrey, England; son of Ritchie (a writer) and Mabel (McKail) Calder; married Jennifer Daiches (a writer), October 1, 1963 (marriage dissolved); married Kate Kyle, 1986; children: (first marriage) Rachel Elizabeth, Gowan Lindsay, Gideon James; (second marriage) Douglas William. *Education:* King's College, Cambridge, M.A., 1963; University of Sussex, D.Phil., 1968. *Politics:* "International Revolutionary Socialist." *Religion:* "None." *Avocational interests:* Cookery, cricket, curling, music of all kinds, cinemagoing, theatre, and looking at paintings.

ADDRESSES: Home—15 Leven Terrace, Edinburgh 3, Scotland. *Office*—Open University, 60 Melville St., Edinburgh EH3 7HF, Scotland. *Agent*—A. D. Peters & Co., 10 Buckingham St., London WC2N 6BV, England.

CAREER: University of East Africa, University College, Nairobi, Kenya, lecturer in literature, 1968-71; part-time tutor and counsellor, Open University in Scotland, 1972-79, staff tutor in arts, 1979—.

MEMBER: Scottish Poetry Library Association, Society of Authors, Scottish PEN.

AWARDS, HONORS: Gregory Award, 1967, for an unpublished collection of poems; John Llewellyn Rhys Memorial Prize, 1970, for *The People's War: Britain, 1939-1945;* Scottish Arts Council Book Award, 1981, for *Revolutionary Empire: The Rise of the English-Speaking Empires from the Fifteenth Century to the 1780s.*

WRITINGS:

(Editor) Charles Dickens, *Great Expectations,* illustrations by Marcus Stone and others, Penguin, 1965, Greenwich House, 1982.

(With former wife, Jenni Calder) *Scott,* Evans Brothers, 1969, also published as *Sir Walter Scott,* Arco, 1969.

The People's War: Britain, 1939-1945, Pantheon, 1969.

(Compiler) *Britain At War,* Jackdaw Publications, 1973.

(Co-editor) *Writers in East Africa,* East African Literature Bureau, 1974.

(Editor and author of introduction) Walter Scott, *Old Mortality,* Penguin, 1974.

Russia Discovered: Nineteenth-Century Fiction from Pushkin to Chekhov, Heinemann, 1976.

(Contributor) *Literature and Western Civilisation,* Volume 6, Aldus Books, 1976.

Revolutionary Empire: The Rise of the English-Speaking Empires from the Fifteenth Century to the 1780s, Dutton, 1981.

(Editor with Jack Mapanje and Cosmo Pieterse) *Summer Fires: New Poetry of Africa,* Heinemann, 1983.

(Editor with Dorothy Sheridan) *Speak for Yourself: A Mass Observation Anthology, 1937-1949,* J. Cape, 1984.

T. S. Eliot, Humanities Press, 1987.

Byron, Open University Press, 1987.

(Editor) *Byron and Scotland: Radical or Dandy?,* Edinburgh University Press, 1989.

The Myth of the Blitz, J. Cape, 1991.

(Editor with William Donnelly) *Burns,* Penguin, 1991.

Also author of television script, "Home Fires," for *World at War* series, 1973. Contributor of reviews to *Cencrastus, London Review of Books, New Statesman* and other publications, and of poems to journals. Editor, *Granta,* 1962-63; co-editor, *Journal of Commonwealth Literature,* 1981-87.

WORK IN PROGRESS: Books on mass-observation and on imperial history.

SIDELIGHTS: Angus Calder once told *CA:* "I try to express, as well as I can, my humanist values, which commit me to international, libertarian, revolutionary socialism. This is not narrowly 'political,' and I doubt if writers should get mixed up in political parties. My humanism involves every aspect of life which prose and poetry can cover. Ideology is, precisely, the writer's medium and his business. Writing is a form of action designed to affect the way people think. But is also a form of exploration and research, and I think the acceptance as binding of any received set of ideas (Methodism, say, or a party political programme) is bound to hamper exploration and research."

American critics have been almost unanimous in viewing *The People's War: Britain, 1939-1945* as a marvelously comprehensive record of Britain's home front in World War II. Almost as unanimously, though, they have implied that the book punctured the traditional picture—"the image," as Thomas Lask comments in the *New York Times,* "of a tight little island, without division or complaint, silently united under Churchill, stoic under the bombing, patient with shortages, girded only for war. . . . If this book has a thesis, it is that the average Briton's desire for change (a muted revolutionary impulse) was thwarted during the war." Eric Forbes-Boyd, in his *Christian Science Monitor* review of *The People's War,* mentions that at times in his "gripping narrative" of Britons under siege, Calder looks "back from the viewpoint of his own postwar, disillusioned generation" and "observes with a too sardonic eye that quite fails to perceive what is there." Forbes-Boyd also notes that the book was drawn and sifted from official documents, Mass Observation Reports, diaries, memoirs, newspapers, and anything that offered an authentic piece of evidence. But Calder regards himself as a writer, from a family of writers, "not as a 'critic' or 'historian' or 'scholar' or any kind of specialist."

Praising Calder's "wealth of social, political and gossipy detail that most of us previously knew nothing of," C. H. Rolph calls *The People's War* a "marvelous book," concluding in his *Nation* review: "There is another whole volume of information buried in the end notes. I relived the London war in these pages. And I salute a man who can combine the industry, the eclecticism and the literary grace to make one read compulsorily more than a quarter of a million words almost nonstop." According to a *Times Literary Supplement* contributor, "This second generation critic is doing his formidable best to ensure that the third and fourth generations know the sins of the fathers, as well as their virtues."

More recently, Calder indicated to *CA:* "I grow more and more interested in myth, its relationship to history and to human action in the present. . . . Why do people create

their heroes—Jefferson, Burns, Churchill, Lenin—and how do these creations affect the historical process? . . . I value the art of story-telling which many scholars—though few ordinary people—seem to think old-fashioned and embarrassing." Calder also expressed that he practiced this approach on his book on the British Empire, *Revolutionary Empire: The Rise of the English-Speaking Empires from the Fifteenth Century to the 1780s,* adding: "It will seem pretentious to say that Scott and Tolstoy have latterly been the chief influences on my technique of which I am conscious, but I will be content if I can produce a large volume, like one of theirs, which people will read through, in sequence, from cover to cover. Narrative isn't in conflict with 'analysis'; for a historian, I think, it should be the means by which insight is conveyed."

Regarding Calder's *Revolutionary Empire,* John Keegan writes in the *New York Review of Books:* "This enormous book tells the story of the English imperial effort from the fifteenth century to the American Revolution." Describing Calder's narrative style, D. K. Fieldhouse points out in the *Times Literary Supplement* that he divides his three-hundred-year history into periods of about a generation in length: "Like the individual frames in a cartoon, one period set-piece dissolves into the next, creating the illusion of continuous movement. . . . The virtue of this method is that it recreates a strong sense of chronology. Contemporary events fit into a coherent historical situation and suggest their own logical outcome." Praising Calder's "extremely agreeable literary style," Keegan notes that "the eye runs on, pleasurable and effortlessly, while the mind absorbs acres of information without the least sensation of force-feeding." Noting the author's obviously extensive reading in the preparation for such a book, an *Economist* contributor says Calder "wears his scholarship lightly." And remarking on the book's "formidable wealth of detail," John Spuring adds in the *New Statesman* that it "is worth anybody's time and money, as hard to put down, one might say, as it is to balance on one's knee."

BIOGRAPHICAL/CRITICAL SOURCES:

PERIODICALS

Books, November, 1969.
Choice, May, 1987.
Christian Science Monitor, November 1, 1969.
Economist, June 18, 1981.
Esquire, April, 1970.
Nation, November 24, 1969.
National Observer, January 26, 1970.
New Leader, February 2, 1970.
New Statesman, May 22, 1981.
New Yorker, January 17, 1979.
New York Review of Books, December 17, 1981.
New York Times, December 20, 1969.

New York Times Book Review, December 21, 1969.
Observer Review, September 7, 1969.
Time, February 2, 1970.
Times (London), September 14, 1991, p. 39.
Times Literary Supplement, September 18, 1969; July 24, 1981; March 23, 1984; January 1, 1988.
William & Mary Quarterly, June, 1985.

*   *   *

CALDER, Jenni 1941-

PERSONAL: Born December 3, 1941, in Chicago, IL; daughter of David (a literary critic) and Isabel (Mackay) Daiches; married Angus Calder (a writer), October 1, 1963 (marriage dissolved); children: Rachel Elizabeth, Gowan Lindsay, Gideon James. *Education:* Cambridge University, B.A. (first class honors), 1963; University of London, M.Phil., 1965. *Politics:* Socialist. *Religion:* Atheist. *Avocational interests:* Walking, cooking, music.

CAREER: University of Nairobi, Nairobi, Kenya, lecturer in literature, 1968-69; author and part-time lecturer, 1969-78; Royal Scottish Museum (now National Museums of Scotland), Edinburgh, lecturer in education department, 1978-87, museum editor, 1987—.

WRITINGS:

Chronicles of Conscience: A Study of George Orwell and Arthur Koestler, University of Pittsburgh Press, 1968.
(With former husband, Angus Calder) *Scott,* Evans Brothers, 1969, also published as *Sir Walter Scott,* Arco, 1969.
There Must Be a Lone Ranger, Hamish Hamilton, 1974, also published as *There Must Be a Lone Ranger: The Myth and Reality of the American Wild West,* Taplinger, 1975.
Women and Marriage in Victorian Fiction, Thames & Hudson, 1976, also published as *Women and Marriage in Nineteenth-Century Fiction,* Oxford University Press, 1976.
Huxley and Orwell, "Brave New World" and "Nineteen Eighty-four", Edward Arnold, 1976.
Heroes: From Byron to Guevara, Hamish Hamilton, 1977.
The Victorian Home, Batsford, 1977.
(Compiler) *The Victorian and Edwardian Home from Old Photographs,* Thames & Hudson, 1977, Hippocrene, 1979.
(Editor and author of introduction) Robert Louis Stevenson, *The Strange Case of Dr. Jekyll and Mr. Hyde, and Other Stories,* Penguin, 1979.
RLS: A Life Study, Hamish Hamilton, 1980, published as *Robert Louis Stevenson: A Life Study,* Oxford University Press, 1980.

(Editor) *Robert Louis Stevenson: A Critical Celebration* (essays), Barnes & Noble, 1980.
(Editor) *The Robert Louis Stevenson Companion* (essays), P. Harris, 1980.
(Editor) *Stevenson and Victorian Scotland* (essays), Edinburgh University Press, 1981.
(Editor) *The Enterprising Scot: Scottish Adventure and Achievement,* Royal Museum of Scotland, 1986.
"Animal Farm" and "Nineteen Eighty-four", Open University Press, 1987.
(Editor and author of introduction) Stevenson, *Island Landfalls: Reflections from the South Seas* (selections), Canongate, 1987.
(Editor) *The Wealth of a Nation,* National Museum of Scotland, 1989.
(Editor) *Scotland in Trust,* Preservation Press, 1991.
Co-editor) Stevenson, *St. Ives,* Richard Drew, 1991.

Also author of *Royal Scottish Museum: The Early Years,* 1984, and author/editor of publications for the National Museums of Scotland, including *If It Wasnae for the Weaver,* 1986, *Bonny Fighters: The Story of the Scottish Soldier 1600-1914,* 1987, and *Museum Publishing Problems and Potential,* 1988.

WORK IN PROGRESS: Research on museum history; Margaret Oliphant.

SIDELIGHTS: Jenni Calder once told *CA:* "My motivations in writing are compounded of curiosity, a love of writing and reading, and an urge to communicate. I am a socialist, an internationalist and a feminist in instinct and intellect, and most of my interests and activities, professional or recreational, stem from this. I have a deep concern for the fates of Israel and Scotland, disbelieve in patriotism."

The subject of Victorian England particularly interests Calder and has provided material for several of her books. In *Women and Marriage in Victorian Fiction,* for example, she examines the social structure of the period as it is reflected in literary texts through their depiction of marriage and the role of women. Although Naomi Bliven calls it "an intelligent and entertaining study," in the *New Yorker,* Walter Allen suggests in the *Times Literary Supplement* that "to use novels as source-materials for social history, is to inevitably to distort and diminish them." Bliven notes that, as literary criticism, the book "does not illuminate writers' intentions or achievements . . . [but] succeeds and holds the reader in quite another way: it illuminates our lives because she puts her finger on matters that trouble us as much as they troubled the Victorians." According to Bliven: "The Victorians, like us, were climbers. Along with their romantic demands, they harbored the ambition that the perfect marriage would result in a family that would become great and powerful and enduring. . . . Yet this aspiration became ever less plausible as the industrial revolution proceeded on its way, first assailing the families of the poor and then stripping wealthier families of a multiplicity of functions that they had once assumed: school, hospital, bank, business, employment agency." In novels addressed mainly to women, writers presented lives of perfection in their fiction, which bore no resemblance to reality, notes Bliven; however, toward the end of the nineteenth century, "writers began expressing dissatisfaction with the Victorian ideals of womanhood and marriage. . . . Writers began to propose that women be active . . . and receive better educations, either to make them interesting spouses (the ideal Victorian wife often bored the ideal Victorian husband) or to enable them to support themselves if they did not marry."

BIOGRAPHICAL/CRITICAL SOURCES:

PERIODICALS

America, October 17, 1981.
Best Seller, August, 1975.
British Book News, January, 1981; January, 1982; November, 1986.
Choice, February, 1976; October, 1976.
New Statesman, August 22, 1980.
New Yorker, November 15, 1976.
New York Times Book Review, February 1, 1981.
Spectator, July 26, 1980.
Times Literary Supplement, August 27, 1976; August 5, 1977; October 21, 1977; June 6, 1980; November 20, 1981.
Washington Post Book World, September 14, 1980.

*   *   *

CALDER, Nigel (David Ritchie) 1931-

PERSONAL: Born December 2, 1931, in London, England; son of (Peter) Ritchie (Lord Ritchie-Calder of Balmashannar; a writer) and Mabel Jane Forbes (McKail) Calder; married Elisabeth Palmer (a research assistant and literary agent), May 22, 1954; children: Sarah, Penelope, Simon, Jonathan, Katharine. *Education:* Attended Merchant Taylors' School; Sidney Sussex College, Cambridge, B.A., 1954, M.A., 1957. *Avocational interests:* Sailing.

ADDRESSES: Home and office—8 The Chase, Furnace Green, Crawley, West Sussex RH10 6HW, England. *Agent*—Elisabeth Calder, 8 The Chase, Furnace Green, Crawley, West Sussex RH10 6HW, England.

CAREER: Writer. Mullard Research Laboratories, Redhill, Surrey, England, research physicist, 1954-56; *New Scientist,* London, England, staff writer, 1956-60, science editor, 1960-62, editor, 1962-66. *Military service:* British Army, 1950-51; became lieutenant.

MEMBER: Association of British Science Writers (chairman, 1962-64), Cruising Association (London; vice-president).

AWARDS, HONORS: UNESCO Kalinga Prize for the popularization of science, 1972.

WRITINGS:

Electricity Grows Up, Phoenix House, 1958.
Robots, Roy, 1958.
Radio Astronomy, Roy, 1959, revised edition, Phoenix House, 1964.
(Editor) *The World in 1984,* Penguin, 1964.
Eden Was No Garden: An Inquiry Into the Environment of Man, Holt, 1967, published in England as *The Environment Game,* Secker & Warburg, 1967.
(Editor) *Unless Peace Comes: A Scientific Forecast of New Weapons,* Viking, 1968.
Technopolis: Social Control of the Uses of Science, MacGibbon & Kee, 1969, Simon & Schuster, 1970.
Violent Universe: An Eye-Witness Account of the Commotion in Astronomy, 1968-1969, British Broadcasting Corporation, 1969, published as *Violent Universe: An Eyewitness Account of the New Astronomy,* Viking, 1970.
Living Tomorrow: Planning for the Future, Penguin, 1970.
The Mind of Man: An Investigation into Current Research on the Brain and Human Nature, Viking, 1970.
Restless Earth: A Report on the New Geology, Viking, 1972.
The Life Game, British Broadcasting Corporation, 1973, published as *The Life Game: Evolution and the New Biology,* Viking, 1974.
(Editor) *Nature in the Round: A Guide to Environmental Science,* Weidenfield & Nicolson, 1973, Viking, 1974.
The Weather Machine: How Our Weather Works and Why It Is Changing, British Broadcasting Corporation, 1974, Viking, 1975.
The Human Conspiracy, Viking, 1976.
The Key to the Universe: A Report on the New Physics, Viking, 1977.
Spaceships of the Mind, Viking, 1978, Penguin, 1979.
Einstein's Universe, Viking, 1979.
Nuclear Nightmares: An Investigation into Possible Wars, British Broadcasting Corporation, 1979, Viking, 1980.
The Comet Is Coming!: The Feverish Legacy of Mr. Halley, British Broadcasting Corporation, 1980, Viking, 1981.
Timescale: An Atlas of the Fourth Dimension Viking, 1984.
1984 and Beyond: Nigel Calder Talks to His Computer About the Future, Viking, 1984.

The English Channel, Penguin, 1986.
(Editor with John Newell) *Future Earth: Exploring the Frontiers of Space,* Croom Helm, 1989.

Also author of *The Green Machine,* 1986. Author of television documentaries produced by British Broadcasting Corp., some in conjunction with Public Broadcasting System: *Russia: Beneath the Sputniks,* 1967; *The World in a Box,* 1968; *The Violent Universe,* 1969; *The Mind of Man,* 1970; *The Restless Earth,* 1972; *The Life Game,* 1973; *The Weather Machine,* 1974; *The Human Conspiracy,* 1975; *The Key to the Universe,* 1977; *The Whole Universe Show,* 1977; *Spaceships of the Mind,* 1978; *Einstein's Universe,* 1979; *Nuclear Nightmares,* 1979; *The Comet Is Coming!,* 1981. *The Comet Is Coming* was recorded on audio cassette by Recorded Books, 1988.

Science correspondent for *New Statesman,* 1959-62 and 1966-71. Contributor to science journals in England and the United States.

SIDELIGHTS: Nigel Calder has gained a reputation as a writer of popular works on scientific topics. Calder's books, often published as companion pieces to his television documentaries, cover a wide range of subject matter, including the continental drift, the human mind, and recent discoveries in subatomic physics. In several of his books he speculates on the future and on humanity's place in a changing world.

In *Eden Was No Garden: An Inquiry into the Environment of Man,* Calder examines the problem of providing food for a rapidly growing earth population. He proposes that large-scale factory food production, not traditional agricultural methods, is the best way to supply food in the future and discusses how new technology would aid the preservation of the environment. R. C. Cowen, in a *Christian Science Monitor* review, says, "Perhaps the book will appeal as a review of today's scientific and technical developments as they bear on man's basic problems." *Library Journal* critic Harold Bloomquist praises Calder's offering of a "full-blown Utopian vision of what the world might be; truthfully, it looks pretty good."

Calder's interest in the future is not limited to earthly matters. His book *Spaceships of the Mind* explores the possibilities of outer space colonization. He includes a study of physicist Gerard O'Neill, who is working on a space superstructure capable of housing its own atmosphere, environment, and populace. "Calder's book is on the borderline between science and fantasy, but no matter," writes Martin Gardner in the *New York Review of Books,* "Calder knows his science, and between discussions of outrageous plans there are solid facts about the universe, and informed speculation about the awesome possibilities that lie ahead as population pressures and energy needs propel us into what O'Neill calls the High Frontier." According

to Phillip Morrison in *Scientific American:* "There is nowhere else to go for so up-to-date, wide-ranging and specific an overview of this remarkable field. That the detail is not deep, and that it is not made easy for a reader to move beyond what is here into more technical material, should be no surprise. This is a new style of introduction to a science, and it is hugely successful in its own terms."

Two of Calder's books, *Unless Peace Comes: A Scientific Forecast of New Weapons* and *Nuclear Nightmares: An Investigation into Possible Wars,* focus on what he perceives to be an immediate threat to the future of humanity. *Unless Peace Comes,* which Calder edited, contains the thoughts of fifteen scientists from around the world who predict the warfare that may result unless nations can resolve their conflicts peacefully. *Nation* critic John Gliedman finds the book "rather conservative in its approach. No attention is given to the future technology of guerrilla war and counter insurgency. And yet, even with these important omissions, the book illuminates perhaps the greatest of the many ironies of the arms race: that it often feeds upon breakthroughs in civilian fields." In a *New York Times Book Review* article, D. S. Greenberg says that the scientists' contributions "are clearly intended to shock and appall. The intention is achieved, not through raucous prophecy and admonition, but rather through a fairly detached, even-toned recitation of technically attainable possibilities for conducting wars of the next decade, and, equally important, the political tensions that may be created simply because of the existence of unfamiliar and potentially devastating means of warfare." According to a *Harper's* contributor, "The quiet restraint, the general excellence of the writing, added to the expertise of the authors, lend all too real a sense of absolute authority and conviction to this important book."

Calder's concern with atomic warfare is continued in *Nuclear Nightmares.* In this book, the author lists four circumstances—"nightmares"—that might trigger nuclear war: worldwide nuclear arms proliferation, imperfections of command systems, escalation of a conflict in Europe, and the fear of one superpower that the other is about to attempt a disabling first strike. "Calder's particular and enviable talent is for turning abstruse technicalities into everyday language, without damage to the subtlety of the specialists' language," comments John Keegan in *New Republic.* "He demonstrates it once again here and, after reading the book, no layman will be able to take refuge in the comforting belief that he doesn't understand the issues." Keegan continues: "Proliferation is, in the author's view, a problem which the superpowers still could solve between themselves, by forbidding nuclear testing of any sort and making life impossible for states that broke the ban. Inevitably his conclusion has a utopian ring. But what appeal against the apparently inexorable tightening of the nuclear collar around all of our throats has not? At least critics will not be able to accuse him of mere hand-wringing. He knows the facts almost as well as those whose daily round it is to deal with them. He has concrete suggestions to make for setting limits on a trend which no sane person can wish to see continue." According to Denys Blakeway in a *New Statesman* review of *Nuclear Nightmares,* "Calder is a reluctant pessimist with whose vision of the future it is, sadly, difficult to disagree."

Published during the centenary year of the birth of Albert Einstein, Calder's *Einstein's Universe* interprets the physicist's theories for the nonspecialist reader. David Quammen writes in the *Christian Science Monitor* that "Calder's book is casual in style but not condescending, abundantly thought-provoking, and concise. He has held himself to a high standard of lucidity, while juggling a prodigiously complex assemblage of fact and theory and paradox and conjecture." However, some critics find the work still too specialized for its intended audience. For instance, *Chicago Tribune Book World* reviewer Guy Murchie notes that while the author "explains all these [theories], and without using academic or technological jargon, not many of us will be able to comprehend how 'all physical processes' are 'governed by the speed of light' or will accept without challenge that 'incest among the gravitons produces the curvature of space.' " *Village Voice* critic Eliot Fremont-Smith comments on Calder's simplified approach to Einstein's theory of relativity: "The trouble is that at crucial points it isn't simple at all; it's horrendously complex, convoluted, and contradictory. This makes one fret—not so much over the difficulties of relativity as over the accumulating evidence that, as a layman, one isn't measuring up." According to Edmund Fuller in the *Wall Street Journal,* however, the author "is a singularly lucid writer with a gift for the memorable metaphors which, for the general reader, must take the place of the physicist's equations."

Among Calder's other books dealing with natural science are *The Weather Machine: How Our Weather Works and Why It Is Changing* and *The Comet Is Coming!: The Feverish Legacy of Mr. Halley.* In *The Weather Machine,* the author discusses how changes in climate can affect everything from literature (a particularly wet, gloomy summer influenced Mary Shelley's writing of the gothic classic *Frankenstein*) to politics (an overly hot summer in 1788 shriveled the grain crops in France, causing bread riots in 1789 and, ultimately, the French Revolution). But, more alarmingly, Calder reports, recent climactic studies indicate a new ice age is imminent—which is "ominous for the human species," as the author puts it. Expressing a belief that "in attempting the often highly complicated theories of past climates and meteorological processes, Nigel Calder has sometimes over-simplified to the extent of misrep-

resentation," T. J. Chandler writes in the *Times Literary Supplement:* "The book will be of use to those looking for a lightly written, copiously illustrated review of recent research into the general circulation of the atmosphere of the more dramatic weather phenomena and of glacial periods." In the words of the *New York Times*'s Christopher Lehmann-Haupt, "Thanks to his elegantly diagrammed book with its chilly forecast, Mr. Calder has me worrying about the weather for a change."

The phenomenon of Halley's comet is explored in Calder's 1981 book, *The Comet Is Coming!* The comet, which appears once every seventy-six years, has historically induced suicide, human sacrifice, and predictions of Armageddon. "In addition to the army of soothsayers and astrologers who heretofore have interpreted it for us," writes Michael Collins in the *Washington Post Book World,* "Halley is preceded by a first-rate PR man. . . . Nigel Calder has put together a potpourri of fact and fancy, a fascinating compendium of all we would ask about comets, if we only knew the right questions." Both Collins and *New Republic* reviewer Katha Pollitt note that Calder himself takes a dim view of the fervor caused by the comet. Praising Calder's "wealth of fascinating comet lore," Pollitt concludes, "All in all, this is a handy little book, stuffed with odd tid bits of information and with just enough science to challenge the casual reader."

Calder has also written on the subject of space and time. *1984 and Beyond* offers a reassessment of *The World in 1984,* the predictions presented by scholars in 1964 about what they perceived the world to be like in the year of George Orwell's classic *Nineteen Eighty-four.* Scholars did not foresee such occurrences as the energy crisis or the "disenchantment with nuclear power," says Frederic Golden in *Discover,* later adding that "some forecasts were unerring," such as human organ transplants and cloning. *Timescale* covers the catastrophic events that have occurred in the cosmos over the past thirteen billion years to change life on this planet in ways more significant than the gradual evolutionary process described by scientists twenty years ago. "Popularizing complicated ideas is a difficult . . . task," writes Geoffrey Sampson in *British Book News,* adding that although Calder sometimes "errs on the side of flippancy," the book itself "represents a very good idea well executed."

More recently, Calder's *Future Earth: Exploring the Frontiers of Space,* "tells of our understanding of processes like climate, disease and ageing, with the implication that burgeoning knowledge will soon unwrap new benefits and bring new responsibilities," writes F. W. Taylor in the *Times Literary Supplement.* According to Colin Ward in the *London Review of Books,* "This is one of those superlatively produced and illustrated popular accounts of current science that are food and drink for the enquiring young."

BIOGRAPHICAL/CRITICAL SOURCES:

BOOKS

Calder, Nigel, *The Comet Is Coming!: The Feverish Legacy of Mr. Halley,* Viking, 1981.
Calder, Nigel, *Einstein's Universe,* Viking, 1979.
Calder, Nigel, *The Weather Machine: How Our Weather Works and Why It Is Changing,* Viking, 1975.

PERIODICALS

Atlantic, June, 1981.
British Book News, April, 1984; November, 1986.
Chicago Tribune Book World, March 11, 1979.
Choice, June, 1988.
Christian Science Monitor, June 22, 1967; May 23, 1977; April 9, 1979; May 11, 1981.
Discover, March, 1984.
Globe and Mail (Toronto), June 4, 1988.
Harper's, August, 1968.
Library Journal, June 1, 1967; September 1, 1986.
Listener, April 8, 1976.
London Review of Books, January 19, 1989.
Los Angeles Times Book Review, September 21, 1980; December 18, 1983; February 5, 1984.
Nation, October 28, 1968.
Natural History, August/September, 1972.
New Republic, January 7, 1978; September 27, 1980; September 23, 1981.
New Statesman, February 29, 1980.
New Yorker, July 14, 1986.
New York Review of Books, September 29, 1977; November 23, 1978.
New York Times, April 17, 1975; March 12, 1979.
New York Times Book Review, July 28, 1968; March 11, 1979; November 23, 1980.
Observer, August 17, 1986.
Saturday Review, June 14, 1975.
Scientific American, May, 1971; July, 1972.
Times Literary Supplement, December 20, 1974; June 16-June 22, 1989.
Village Voice, March 19, 1979.
Wall Street Journal, March 19, 1979.
Washington Post Book World, March 25, 1979; May 10, 1981; February 2, 1984.*

* * *

CANNON, Curt
See HUNTER, Evan

CAREY, M. V.
See CAREY, Mary V(irginia)

* * *

CAREY, Mary V(irginia) 1925-
(M. V. Carey)

PERSONAL: Born May 19, 1925, in New Brighton, England; brought to the United States in 1925, naturalized citizen in 1955; daughter of John Cornelius (an engineer) and Mary Alice (Hughes) Carey. *Education:* College of Mount St. Vincent, B.S., 1946. *Religion:* Roman Catholic.

ADDRESSES: Home—3748 Birch St., Ventura, CA 93003.

CAREER: Coronet, New York City, editorial associate, 1948-55; Walt Disney Productions, Burbank, CA, assistant editor of publications, 1955-69; free-lance writer, 1969—.

MEMBER: PEN, Mystery Writers of America, Society of Children's Book Writers.

AWARDS, HONORS: Southern California Council on Literature for Children and Young People Award, 1986, for *A Place for Allie.*

WRITINGS:

NOVELIZATIONS OF WALT DISNEY MOTION PICTURES

(With George Sherman) *Walt Disney's "Babes in Toyland,"* Golden Press, 1961.
Walt Disney's "The Sword in the Stone," Whitman Publishing, 1963.
The Story of Walt Disney's Motion Picture "Mary Poppins," Whitman Publishing, 1964.
Walt Disney's "The Misadventures of Merlin Jones," Whitman Publishing, 1964.
Walt Disney's "Donald Duck and the Lost Mesa Ranch," Whitman Publishing, 1966.
The Story of Walt Disney's Motion Picture "Jungle Book," Whitman Publishing, 1967.
The Story of Walt Disney's Motion Picture "Blackbeard's Ghost," Whitman Publishing, 1968.
Mrs. Brisby's Important Package (adapted from film *The Secret of NIMH*), Golden Press, 1982.

JUVENILES

Raggedy Ann and the Glad and Sad Day, Golden Press, 1972.
Little Lulu and the Birthday Surprise, Whitman Publishing, 1973.
The Tawny, Scrawny Lion and the Clever Monkey, Golden Press, 1974.
Alonzo Purr, the Seagoing Cat, Western Publishing, 1974.

The Owl Who Loved Sunshine, Golden Press, 1977.
The Gremlins Storybook, Golden Press, 1984.

"THE THREE INVESTIGATORS" JUVENILE MYSTERY SERIES; UNDER NAME M. V. CAREY

The Mystery of the Flaming Footprints, Random House, 1971.
The Mystery of the Singing Serpent, Random House, 1972.
The Mystery of Monster Mountain, Random House, 1973.
The Secret of the Haunted Mirror, Random House, 1974.
The Mystery of the Invisible Dog, Random House, 1975.
The Mystery of Death Trap Mine, Random House, 1976.
The Mystery of the Magic Circle, Random House, 1978.
The Mystery of the Sinister Scarecrow, Random House, 1979.
The Mystery of the Scar-Faced Beggar, Random House, 1981.
The Mystery of the Blazing Cliffs, Random House, 1981.
The Mystery of the Wandering Cave Man, Random House, 1982.
The Mystery of Missing Mermaid, Random House, 1984.
The Mystery of the Trail of Terror, Random House, 1984.
The Mystery of the Creep-Show Crooks, Random House, 1985.
The Mystery of the Cranky Collector, Random House, 1987.
The Case of the Savage Statue, Random House, 1987.

OTHER

(Editor) Jane Black, *The Indispensables,* Hewitt House, 1971.
Step-by-Step Candlemaking, Golden Press, 1972.
Step-by-Step Winemaking, Golden Press, 1973.
Love Is Forever (collection of prose and poetry), C. R. Gibson, 1975.
(With George Sherman) *A Compendium of Bunk,* C. C Thomas, 1976.
(Editor) *Grandmothers Are Very Special People,* C. R. Gibson, 1977.
A Place for Allie (young adult novel), Dodd, 1985.

SIDELIGHTS: Mary V. Carey told *CA:* "More and more I don't have any philosophy about writing, except that it is something we can do if God is good to us. Of course *we* are the ones who have to do the paperwork.

"A couple of years ago an old friend came visiting and reminded me of how it was when we were children. She told how we used to sit on my front porch and every day we read, and since we tackled some great long books, we couldn't finish them at a sitting. So each day I would tell her what had happened the day before, condensing the story and leaving out the parts that weren't really important. 'And then sometimes you told your own stories,' she said. So I am lucky. I have gotten back to where I was when I was nine. The long detour I took on the way en-abled me to learn how to spell—I don't think I spelled that well at nine."

* * *

CARKEET, David 1946-

PERSONAL: Surname is accented on second syllable; born November 15, 1946, in Sonora, CA; son of Ross Albert (a judge) and Mary (Hill) Carkeet; married Barbara Lubin (a social worker), August 16, 1975; children: Anne, Laurie, Molly. *Education:* University of California, Davis, A.B. (cum laude), 1968; University of Wisconsin—Madison, M.A., 1970; Indiana University, Ph.D., 1973.

ADDRESSES: Home—23 Ridgemoor, St. Louis, MO 63105. *Office*—Department of English, University of Missouri, St. Louis, MO 63121.

CAREER: University of Missouri, St. Louis, assistant professor, 1973-79, associate professor, 1979-87, professor of English, 1987—.

AWARDS, HONORS: James D. Phelan Award in literature from San Francisco Foundation, 1976, for *Double Negative;* Edgar Award nomination, Mystery Writers of America, 1980, for *Double Negative;* O. Henry Award, 1982; National Endowment for the Arts fellowship, 1983.

WRITINGS:

Double Negative (novel), Dial, 1980.
The Greatest Slump of All Time (novel), Harper, 1984.
I Been There Before (novel), Harper, 1985.
The Silent Treatment (young adult novel), HarperCollins, 1988.
The Full Catastrophe (novel), Simon & Schuster, 1990.
Quiver River (young adult novel), HarperCollins, 1991.

Contributor to language and literature journals. Contributor of short stories to *Kansas Quarterly, North American Review,* and *Carolina Quarterly.*

SIDELIGHTS: Emphasizing the humorous aspects of contemporary society, David Carkeet's novels have garnered praise from fans and critics alike. "Carkeet seems to make a habit of producing remarkable volumes," writes Tom Nolan in the *Los Angeles Times Book Review.* His first novel, *Double Negative,* introduces Jeremy Cook, a linguist who applies his knowledge of language to such varied uses as solving murder mysteries and, in *The Full Catastrophe,* resolving marital difficulties. Carkeet's other novels include *The Greatest Slump of All Time,* a baseball story which won raves from sports and literary buff Larry King, and *I Been There Before,* a fantasy which features Mark Twain returning to Earth in modern times.

Rating Carkeet's work alongside that of classic humorists Stephen Leacock and Robert Benchley, Nolan calls *The*

Full Catastrophe "eccentric, hilarious, wildly inventive and eerily accurate." Speaking of the novel in the *New York Times Book Review,* Maxine Chernoff finds Carkeet's views on what men and women want from marriage "troubling," but notes that "there is also much truth to his observations." Those observations are made by eccentric, emotionally bankrupt Jeremy Cook, who attempts to diagnose the linguistic troubles in the unhappy marriage of Beth and Dan Wilson. Labelling the Wilson's troubles "complementary schismogenesis," Cook begins to uncover his own needs and desires while addressing his patients' lack of communication. "Carkeet has examined this contemporary predicament with humor, insight and sympathy," writes Chernoff.

BIOGRAPHICAL/CRITICAL SOURCES:

PERIODICALS

Los Angeles Times Book Review, April 8, 1990, p. 1.
New York Times Book Review, February 18, 1990, p. 12.

*   *   *

CARLISE, Carris
See PEMBERTON, Margaret

*   *   *

CARNER, Mosco   1904-1985

PERSONAL: Surname originally Cohen; born November 15, 1904, in Vienna, Austria; died of a heart attack, August 3, 1985; son of Rudolph and Selma (Liggi) Cohen; married Elisabeth Rode (a physician), February 17, 1962 (died, 1970); married Hazel Sebag-Montefione, April 25, 1976. *Education:* Vienna Music Conservatory, diploma, 1926; University of Vienna, Ph.D., 1928. *Avocational interests:* Reading, travel, motoring, and swimming.

ADDRESSES: Home—14 Elsworthy Rd., London NW3, England.

CAREER: State Theatre, Free City of Danzig (now in Poland), operatic conductor, 1930-33; conductor of major symphony orchestras in London, England, 1938-55; musical author and critic, London, 1949-85. Member of British Broadcasting Corporation score reading panel, 1944-48, 1957-62, 1963-72.

MEMBER: Society for the Promotion of New Music (executive board, 1948-58), London Critics' Circle (honorary member).

AWARDS, HONORS: Silver medal of Italian government, 1963, for *Puccini: A Critical Biography.*

WRITINGS:

(Author of preface) Rene Lenormand, *A Study of Twentieth-Century Harmony: A Treatise and Guide for the Student Composer of To-day,* Volume 1: *Harmony in France to 1914,* B. F. Wood Music, 1940, published as *A Study of Twentieth-Century Harmony: Harmony in France to 1914 and Contemporary Harmony,* two volumes, Da Capo, 1975.
Dvorak, Novello, 1940.
A Study of Twentieth-Century Music, Joseph Williams, 1942.
Of Men and Music, Joseph Williams, 1944.
A History of the Waltz, Parrish, 1948.
Puccini: A Critical Biography, Duckworth, 1958, Knopf, 1959, 2nd edition, Holmes & Meier, 1977.
(Translator and author of introduction) Giuseppe Adami, editor, *Letters of Giacomo Puccini: Mainly Connected with the Composition and Production of His Operas,* new edition, Harrap, 1974.
Alban Berg: The Man and His Work, Duckworth, 1975, Holmes & Meier, 1977, revised and enlarged edition, Duckworth, 1983.
Madame Butterfly, Barrie & Jenkins, 1979.
Major and Minor, Holmes & Meier, 1980.
The Songs of Hugo Wolf, BBC Music Guides, 1982.
Puccini's Tosca, Cambridge University Press, 1985.

Contributor to books, including *Schubert Symposium,* edited by G. Abraham, Lindsay Drummond, 1946; *Schumann Symposium,* edited by Abraham, Oxford University Press, 1952; *The Concerto,* edited by R. Hill, Penguin, 1952; *Chamber Music,* edited by A. Robertson, Penguin, 1957; *Choral Music,* edited by A. Jacobs, Penguin, 1963; *New Oxford History of Music,* 1975; and *Grove's Dictionary of Music,* 5th and 6th editions. Contributor to British newspapers and periodicals, including *Daily Telegraph, London Times,* and *Musical Times.* Music critic, *Time and Tide,* 1949-61, and *Evening News* (London), 1957-61.

WORK IN PROGRESS: A new edition of *Puccini: A Critical Biography.*

SIDELIGHTS: "The reputation that Mosco Carner has achieved by his full-length studies of Puccini and Berg has naturally thrown into the shade his achievements in other fields of musicology," Martin Cooper stated in the *Times Literary Supplement.* Carner's *Major and Minor,* a collection of essays, said Cooper, "is an excellent reminder of the catholicity of [the author's] taste and the versatility of his mind."

"By far the longest and most significant of this collection is the essay on Beethoven's 'Fidelio'—its history, the comparison of the three versions and the sources on which the composer drew in planning the musical presentation of Bouilly's original drama," Cooper continued. "By detailed examination, Dr. Carner shows the specific qualities of each of Beethoven's librettists—Sonnleithner's dramatically diffuse original version corrected by Stephan von Breuning in the short-lived second version, and Treitschke's almost completely successful re-shaping of the work as we know it today."

Puccini: A Critical Biography and *Alban Berg: The Man and His Work* have been published in French and Italian editions. An obituary in the *New York Times* noted that London music critic Edward Greenfield regarded *Puccini: A Critical Biography* as "indispensable."

BIOGRAPHICAL/CRITICAL SOURCES:

PERIODICALS

Listener, June 12, 1980.
Times Literary Supplement, July 11, 1980.

OBITUARIES:

PERIODICALS

Daily Variety, August 8, 1985.
New York Times, August 7, 1985.
Times (London), August 6, 1985.

[Sketch reviewed by wife, Hazel Carner.]

* * *

CARPENTER, Frederic Ives (Jr.) 1903-1991

PERSONAL: Born February 1, 1903, in Chicago, IL; died of pneumonia, March 16, 1991, in Walnut Creek, CA; son of Frederic Ives (an educator) and Emma (Cook) Carpenter; married Lillian Moore Cook (a psychologist), February 6, 1926; children: Barbara Carpenter Fleischman, Alan Frederic, Anne Carpenter Robertson, John Randell. *Education:* Harvard University, A.B., 1924, M.A., 1927; University of Chicago, Ph.D., 1929.

MEMBER: Modern Language Association, University of California Faculty Club.

CAREER: Educator, editor, and author. University of Chicago, instructor, 1924-26, 1927-29; Harvard University, Cambridge, MA, instructor and tutor, 1929-34; University of California, Berkeley, lecturer, 1946-51, research associate in English, beginning 1951.

WRITINGS:

Emerson and Asia, Harvard University Press, 1930.
(Editor) *Ralph Waldo Emerson: Representative Selections,* American Book Co., 1934.
Emerson Handbook, Hendricks House, 1953.
American Literature and the Dream, Philosophical Library, 1955.
Robinson Jeffers, Twayne, 1962.

Eugene O'Neill, Twayne, 1964, revised edition, 1979.
Laurens Van der Post, Twayne, 1969.
Robinson Jeffers Today: Beyond Good and Beneath Evil, Duke University Press, 1977.

Also contributor to numerous academic and literary publications. Editor, *New England Quarterly,* 1929-37. Carpenter's works have been translated into Italian, Spanish, and Chinese.

SIDELIGHTS: Frederic Ives Carpenter, Jr., was known as an authority on the American writers Ralph Waldo Emerson, Robinson Jeffers, and Eugene O'Neill. Carpenter's son, John Randell Carpenter, who is also an author, told *CA* that his father's forty years of correspondence with O'Neill and Jeffers are collected in the University of California's Bancroft Library in Berkeley, as well as correspondence with other literary figures including Van Wyck Brooks, Perry Miller, Bernard De Voto, Laurens Van Der Post, William Everson, Walter Van Tilburg Clark, Conrad Richter, Alex Haley, and Maxine Hong Kingston.

OBITUARIES:

PERIODICALS

Chicago Tribune, March 25, 1991, section 4, p. 12.
New York Times, March 20, 1991, p. B9.
San Francisco Chronicle, March 19, 1991.

[Sketch reviewed by son, John Randell Carpenter.]

* * *

CARPENTER, John (Randell) 1936-

PERSONAL: Born April 14, 1936, in Cambridge, MA; son of Frederic Ives (a writer) and Lillian (a psychologist; maiden name, Cook) Carpenter; married Bogdana Marie-Magdalena Chetkowska (a professor), April 15, 1963; children: Michael Randell, Magdalena Maria-Anna. *Education:* Harvard University, B.A. (cum laude), 1958; Sorbonne, University of Paris, Dr. d'Universite, 1964. *Politics:* Independent.

ADDRESSES: Home—1606 Granger Ave., Ann Arbor, MI 48104.

CAREER: Poet, translator, critic, and teacher. Free-lance translator and editor, Berkeley, CA, 1966-74; University of Washington, Seattle, and Seattle Public Schools, poet in residence, teacher, lecturer, 1975-77, 1977-80; University of Michigan, Ann Arbor, assistant professor, lecturer, 1982-88. Co-organizer of "Seattle Poetry," a series of readings; member of Berkeley Civic Arts Commission, 1968-73; artist in residence for Seattle Arts Commission, 1975. *Military service:* U.S. Air Force Reserve, 1960-62.

MEMBER: PEN, Poetry Society of America, Poets and Writers, American Literary Translators Association.

AWARDS, HONORS: National Endowment for the Arts fellowships, 1976-77, 1979, 1980-81, 1987-88; Witter Bynner Poetry Translation Award, 1979, and second prize of Islands and Continents Translation Award, 1979, both for *Selected Poems* by Zbigniew Herbert; Andrew Mellon Foundation Award, 1986, for *Creating the World: Poetry, Art, and Children.*

WRITINGS:

Historie de la litterature francaise sur la Louisiane, 1683-1763 (title means "History of the French Literature of Louisiana, 1683-1763"), Nizet, 1965.
Gathering Water (poems), Red Cedar, 1972.
Putting the Loon Together (poems), Seattle Arts Commission, 1975.
(Translator, editor, and author of introduction with wife, Bogdana Carpenter) Zbigniew Herbert, *Selected Poems,* Oxford University Press, 1977.
Egret (poems), Seattle Arts Commission, 1979.
Hammering, Seattle Arts Commission, 1984.
(Translator, editor, and author of introduction and notes with B. Carpenter) Herbert, *Report from the Besieged City and Other Poems,* Ecco Press, 1985.
Creating the World: Poetry, Art, and Children, University of Washington Press, 1986.
(Translator) Herbert, *Still Life with a Bridle,* Ecco Press, 1991.

Poems and translations have been anthologized in *The New York Times Book of Verse,* edited by Thomas Lask, Macmillan, 1972; *Selected Poems of Czeslaw Milosz,* Seabury Press, 1974; and *Iron Country: Anthology of Washington State Writers,* Copper Canyon Press, 1979. Contributor of poems, translations, and articles to literary journals, including *Abraxas, Cross Currents, Encounter, Epoch, Kenyon Review, London Review, Magill's Annual, Modern Poetry in Translation, New Yorker, New York Review of Books, Paris Review, Parnassus: Poetry in Review, Perspective, Poetry, Poetry Nation,* and *Poetry Northwest;* contributor to newspapers. Editor of anthologies of children's work, published by Seattle Public Schools: *Chimineys, the Wind, and the Three Giants,* 1978; *The Dreamer on His Back,* 1978; *The Birth of the World,* 1979; *Scowler,* 1979; *Stealing the Moon and Stars,* 1979.

WORK IN PROGRESS: "I am currently working on a critical study of the literature of World War II; it covers the literature of most European countries, and is extremely synthetic. It has grown out of my interest in translation, especially from Polish, French, and Russian, and my interest in contemporary history."

SIDELIGHTS: John Carpenter told *CA:* "I have always been passionately attached to two themes in literature: first, ethics, and how people—myself included—can and might act. Second, the quest for what is real. In whatever

genre these have always seemed to be the most interesting matters. I have no beautiful soul to show, and my marketability is low—but these are, really, excellent handicaps to have."

*   *   *

CARR, Robyn 1951-

PERSONAL: Born July 25, 1951, in St. Paul, MN; daughter of Ronald E. and Bette (Crandall) Henrichs; married James R. Carr; children: Brian, Jamie. *Education:* Attended Arthur B. Anker School of Nursing, 1969-71.

ADDRESSES: Home—Arizona. *Agent*—c/o St. Martin's Press, 175 5th Ave., New York, NY 10010.

CAREER: Writer, 1975—.

WRITINGS:

NOVELS

Chelynne, Little, Brown, 1980.
The Blue Falcon, Little, Brown, 1981.
The Bellerose Bargain, Little, Brown, 1982.
The Braeswood Tapestry, Little, Brown, 1984.
The Troubadour's Romance, Little, Brown, 1985.
The Chappington Affair, Pinnacle Books, 1985.
By Right of Arms, Little, Brown, 1986.
The Everlasting Covenant, Little, Brown, 1987.
Tempted, Bantam, 1987.
Rogue's Lady, Zebra Books/Pinnacle Books, 1988.
Informed Risk, Silhouette Books, 1989.
Woman's Own, St. Martin's, 1990.
To Mother, with Love, Silhouette Books, 1991.
Mind Tryst, St. Martin's, 1992.

NONFICTION

Practical Tips for Writers of Popular Fiction, Writer's Digest Books, 1992.

Also contributor to *Writer's Digest.*

SIDELIGHTS: Robyn Carr told *CA:* "It seems to me that writing is more of a lifestyle than a career. My family tells me that writers are strange, unpredictable people. They argue about when I'm the most difficult to live with—when I'm waiting for an offer on a proposal, or trying to finish the book on time, or waiting for the final manuscript to be read and accepted. Undoubtedly, I'm difficult at all those times.

"There is a space of time in the process that is my favorite to occupy. That is the brief point between the satisfactory (by my standards) completion of a manuscript and the very beginning of the next novel—the *very* end of one and the *very* beginning of the next. There is not much actual typing happening in this space of time. One book is gone and cannot be touched or improved any further, and the next exists only as a seedling, not even planted onto paper. It is during this time that I talk aloud to myself, page through phone books and maps, leave myself unintelligible notes, read voraciously, and daydream constantly. My family feels that I'm not really working, since I'm not stacking up pages or typing. This is the most important thing I do, though; and this initial enthusiasm for the story, this first spark will, after a great deal of technical and mechanical manipulation, become a novel. Writing, from beginning to end, might be a long, creative process. For me it is this flicker of excitement at the start that is creation. Then I do my work.

"What seems to make my books work well and maintain popularity has largely to do with the heroines. The women in my works adhere to the customs of their time but are possessed of some contemporary values. While they might indeed marry their father's choice or seem to hold their men as 'heads of households,' they regard their own strength, independence, and self-esteem highly. There were women in historical periods whose actions and values were far ahead of their time and who strongly resemble our most admired contemporary women. Eleanor of Aquitaine, for instance, endowed a convent as a shelter for abused women. My heroines are fun to create because of the delicate balance between the way they seem to fit the period into which they are drawn and the way they hold a strong identity with the contemporary woman in their strength of conviction, their determination to succeed despite the odds, their affirmation of their own power."

BIOGRAPHICAL/CRITICAL SOURCES:

PERIODICALS

New York Times Book Review, August 5, 1990, p. 18.
Washington Post, July 29, 1985.
Washington Post Book World, August 3, 1986, p. 6.

*   *   *

CARRUTH, Hayden 1921-

PERSONAL: Surname accented on final syllable; born August 3, 1921, in Waterbury, CT; son of Gorton Veeder (an editor) and Margery (Barrow) Carruth; married Sara Anderson, March 14, 1943; married Eleanore Ray, November 29, 1952; married Rose Marie Dorn, October 28, 1961; married Joe-Anne McLaughlin, December 29, 1989; children: (first marriage) Martha Hamilton; (third marriage) David Barrow. *Education:* University of North Carolina, A.B., 1943; University of Chicago, M.A., 1948. *Politics:* Abolitionist.

ADDRESSES: Home—RD 1, Box 128, Munnsville, NY 13409.

CAREER: Poet; free-lance writer and editor. Associate editor, University of Chicago Press, 1951-52; project administrator, Intercultural Publications, Inc., 1952-53. Poet-in-residence, Johnson State College, 1972-74; adjunct professor, University of Vermont, 1975-78; visiting professor, St. Michael's College, Winooskie, VT; professor of English, Syracuse University, 1979-85; professor, Bucknell University, 1985-86; professor, Syracuse University, 1986-91. Owner and operator, Crow's Mark Press, Johnson, VT. *Military service:* U.S. Army Air Forces, World War II; became staff sergeant; spent two years in Italy.

AWARDS, HONORS: Bess Hokin Prize, 1954, Vachel Lindsay Prize, 1956, Levinson Prize, 1958, and Morton Dauwen Zabel Prize, 1967, all from *Poetry* magazine; Harriet Monroe Poetry Prize, University of Chicago, 1960, for *The Crow and the Heart;* grant-in-aid for poetry, Brandeis University, 1960; Bollingen Foundation fellowship in criticism, 1962; Helen Bullis Award, University of Washington, 1962; Carl Sandburg Award, *Chicago Daily News,* 1963, for *The Norfolk Poems;* Emily Clark Balch Prize, *Virginia Quarterly Review,* 1964, for *North Winter;* Eunice Tietjens Memorial Prize, 1964; Guggenheim Foundation fellow, 1965 and 1979; National Endowment for the Humanities fellow, 1967; Governor's Medal, State of Vermont, 1974; Shelley Memorial Award, Poetry Society of America, 1978; Lenore Marshall Poetry Prize, 1978, for *Brothers, I Loved You All; The Voice That Is Great within Us: American Poetry of the Twentieth Century* was selected as one of the New York Public Library's Books for the Teen Age, 1981 and 1982; Whiting Writers Award, Whiting Foundation, 1986; senior fellowship, National Endowment for the Arts, 1988; Ruth Lilly Poetry Prize, 1990.

WRITINGS:

POETRY

The Crow and the Heart, 1946-1959, Macmillan, 1959.
In Memorium: G. V. C., privately printed, 1960.
Journey to a Known Place (long poem), New Directions, 1961.
The Norfolk Poems: 1 June to 1 September 1961, Prairie Press, 1962.
North Winter, Prairie Press, 1964.
Nothing for Tigers; Poems, 1959-1964, Macmillan, 1965.
Contra Mortem (long poem), Crow's Mark Press, 1967.
(Contributor) *Where Is Vietnam?: American Poets Respond,* Anchor Books, 1967.
For You: Poems, New Directions, 1970.
The Clay Hill Anthology, Prairie Press, 1970.
From Snow and Rock, From Chaos: Poems, 1965-1972, New Directions, 1973.

Dark World, Kayak, 1974.

The Bloomingdale Papers, University of Georgia Press, 1975.

Loneliness: An Outburst of Hexasyllables, Janus Press, 1976.

Aura, Janus Press, 1977.

Brothers, I Loved You All, Sheep Meadow Press, 1978.

Almanach du Printemps Vivarois, Nadja, 1979.

The Mythology of Dark and Light, Tamarack, 1982.

The Sleeping Beauty, Harper, 1983, revised edition, Copper Canyon Press, 1990.

If You Call This Cry a Song, Countryman Press, 1983.

Asphalt Georgics, New Directions, 1985.

Lighter Than Air Craft, edited by John Wheatcroft, Press Alley, 1985.

The Oldest Killed Lake in North America, Salt-Works Press, 1985.

Mother, Tamarack Press, 1985.

The Selected Poetry of Hayden Carruth, Macmillan, 1986.

Sonnets, Press Alley, 1989.

Tell Me Again How the White Heron Rises and Flies Across the Nacreous River at Twilight toward the Distant Islands, New Directions, 1989.

EDITOR

(With James Laughlin) *A New Directions Reader,* New Directions, 1964.

The Voice That Is Great within Us: American Poetry of the Twentieth Century, Bantam, 1970.

The Bird/Poem Book: Poems on the Wild Birds of North America, McCall, 1970.

OTHER

Appendix A (novel), Macmillan, 1963.

After "The Stranger": Imaginary Dialogues with Camus, Macmillan, 1964.

(Contributor) *The Art of Literary Publishing,* Pushcart Press, 1980.

Working Papers: Selected Essays and Reviews, edited by Judith Weissman, University of Georgia Press, 1981.

Effluences from the Sacred Caves: More Selected Essays and Reviews, University of Michigan Press, 1984.

Sitting In: Selected Writings on Jazz, Blues, and Related Topics (includes poetry), University of Iowa Press, 1986.

Contributor to periodicals, including *Poetry, Hudson Review, New Yorker,* and *Partisan Review.* Editor-in-chief, *Poetry,* 1949-50; member of editorial board, *Hudson Review,* 1971—; poetry editor, *Harper's,* 1977-83.

SIDELIGHTS: Though known primarily as a critic and editor, Hayden Carruth is also, according to the *Virginia Quarterly Review,* "a poet who has never received the wide acclaim his work deserves and who is certainly one of the most important poets working in this country today. . . . [He is] technically skilled, lively, never less than completely honest, and as profound and deeply moving as one could ask." Characterized by a calm, tightly controlled, and relatively "plain" language that belies the intensity of feeling behind the words, Carruth's poetry elicits praise from those who admire its wide variety of verse forms and criticism from those who find its precision and restraint too impersonal and academic.

Commenting in his book *Babel to Byzantium,* James Dickey speculates that these opposing views of Carruth's work may result from the occasionally uneven quality of his poetry. In a discussion of *The Crow and the Heart,* for example, Dickey notes "a carefulness which bursts, once or twice or three times, into a kind of frenzied eloquence, a near-hysteria, and in these frightening places sloughing off a set of mannerisms which in the rest of the book seems determined to reduce Carruth to the level of a thousand other poets. . . . [He] is one of the poets (perhaps all poets are some of these poets) who write their best, pushing past limit after limit, only in the grip of recalling some overpowering experience. When he does not have such a subject at hand, Carruth amuses himself by being playfully skillful with internal rhyme, inventing bizarre Sitwellian images, being witty and professionally sharp."

American Poetry Review critic Geoffrey Gardner, who characterizes Carruth as "a poet who has always chosen to make his stand just aside from any of the presently conflicting mainstreams," says that such linguistic playfulness is typical of the poet's early work. He attributes it to Carruth's struggle "to restore equilibrium to the soul [and] clarity to vision, through a passionate command of language," a struggle that gives much of his poetry "a Lear-like words-against-the-storm quality." Continues Gardner: "I won't be the first to say Carruth's early work is cumbered by archaisms, forced inversions, sometimes futile extravagances of vocabulary and a tendency of images and metaphors to reify into a top heavy symbolism. . . . But the courage of [his] poems can't be faulted. From the earliest and against great odds, Carruth made many attempts at many kinds of poems, many forms, contending qualities of diction and texture. . . . If the struggle of contending voices and attitudes often ends in poems that don't quite succeed, it remains that the struggle itself is moving for its truthfulness and intensity. . . . Carruth uniformly refuses to glorify his crazies. They are pain and pain alone. What glory there is—and there are sparks of it everywhere through these early poems—he keeps for the regenerative stirrings against the storm of pain and isolation."

Like many poets, Carruth turns to personal experience for inspiration; however, with the possible exception of *The Bloomingdale Papers* (a long poetic sequence Carruth wrote in the 1950s while confined to a mental hospital for treatment of alcoholism and a nervous breakdown), he does not indulge in the self-obsessed meditations common among some of his peers. Instead, Carruth turns outward, exploring such "universal opposites" as madness (or so-called madness) and sanity or chaos and order. He then tries to balance the negative images—war, loneliness, the destruction of the environment, sadness—with mostly nature-related positive images and activities that communicate a sense of stability—the cycle of the seasons, performing manual labor, contemplating the night sky, observing the serenity of plant and animal life. But, as Gardner points out, "Carruth is not in the least tempted to sentimentality about country life. . . . [He recognizes] that it can be a life of value and nobility in the midst of difficult facts and chaos." Nor is he "abstractly philosophical or cold," according to the critic. "On the contrary," Gardner states, "[his poems] are all poems about very daily affairs: things seen and heard, the loneliness of missing friends absent or dead, the alternations of love for and estrangement from those present, the experiences of a man frequently alone with the non-human which all too often bears the damaging marks of careless human intrusion." Furthermore, he says, "Carruth comes to the politics of all this with a vengeance. . . . [His poems] all bear strong public witness against the wastes and shames of our culture that are destroying human value with a will in a world where values are already hard enough to maintain, in a universe where they are always difficult to discover. Carruth does not express much anger in [his] poems. Yet one feels that an enormous energy of rage has forced them to be."

Concludes Alastair Reid in the *Saturday Review:* "[Carruth's] poems have a sureness to them, a flair and variety. . . . Yet, in their dedication to finding an equilibrium in an alien and often cruel landscape, Vermont, where the poet has dug himself in, they reflect the moods and struggles of a man never at rest. . . . His work teems with the struggle to live and to make sense, and his poems carve out a kind of grace for us."

Carruth once told *CA:* "I have a close but at the same time uncomfortable relationship with the natural world. I've always been most at home in the country probably because I was raised in the country as a boy, and I know something about farming and woodcutting and all the other things that country people know about. That kind of work has been important to me in my personal life and in my writing too. I believe in the values of manual labor and labor that is connected with the earth in some way. But I'm not simply a nature poet. In fact, I consider myself and I consider the whole human race fundamentally alien. By evolving into a state of self-consciousness, we have separated ourselves from the other animals and the plants and from the very earth itself, from the whole universe. So

there's a kind of fear and terror involved in living close to nature. My poems, I think, exist in a state of tension between the love of natural beauty and the fear of natural meaninglessness or absurdity.

"I think there are many reasons for poets and artists in general to be depressed these days. . . . They have to do with a lot . . . [of] things that are going on in our civilization. They have to do with the whole evolution of the sociology of literature during the last fifty years. Things have changed; they've turned completely around. I don't know if I can say it briefly but I'll try. When I was young and starting to write poetry seriously and to investigate the resources of modern poetry, as we called it then, we still felt beleaguered; modern poetry was still considered outrageous by most of the people in the publishing business and in the reading audience at large. We still spoke in terms of the true artists and the philistines. We felt that if we could get enough people to read T. S. Eliot and Wallace Stevens and e e cummings and William Carlos Williams and other great poets of that period, then something good would happen in American civilization. We felt a genuine vocation, a calling, to try and make this happen. And we succeeded. Today thousands of people are going to colleges and attending workshops and taking courses in twentieth-century literature. Eliot and Stevens are very well known, very well read; and American civilization has sunk steadily, progressively, further and further down until most of the sensible people are in a state of despair. It's pretty obvious that good writing doesn't really have very much impact on social events or national events of any kind. We hope that it has individual impact, that readers here and there are made better in some way by reading our work. But it's a hope; we have no proof."

BIOGRAPHICAL/CRITICAL SOURCES:

BOOKS

Contemporary Literary Criticism, Gale, Volume 4, 1975, Volume 7, 1977, Volume 10, 1979, Volume 18, 1981.
Dickey, James, *Babel to Byzantium,* Farrar, Straus, 1968.
Dictionary of Literary Biography, Volume 5: *American Poets since World War II,* Gale, 1980.

PERIODICALS

American Poetry Review, May, 1979; January, 1981.
Chicago Tribune Book World, December 26, 1982.
Los Angeles Times, December 12, 1986.
Los Angeles Times Book Review, June 3, 1984.
Nation, February 15, 1965; October 25, 1971.
New York Times, January 3, 1976.
New York Times Book Review, May 12, 1963; April 6, 1975; September 2, 1979; May 23, 1982; August 21, 1983; January 22, 1984; July 14, 1985; May 11, 1986.
Poetry, August, 1963; May, 1974.

Saturday Review, October 27, 1979.
Seneca Review, spring, 1990.
Times Literary Supplement, July 23, 1971.
Virginia Quarterly Review, summer, 1963; summer, 1971; summer, 1979.
Washington Post Book World, January 1, 1984; April 13, 1986.

*   *   *

CARWELL, L'Ann
   See McKISSACK, Patricia (L'Ann) C(arwell)

*   *   *

CATHERALL, Arthur 1906-1980
   (J. Baltimore, A. R. Channel, Dan Corby, Peter Hallard, Trevor Maine, Linda Peters, Margaret Ruthin)

PERSONAL: Born February 6, 1906, in Bolton, Lancashire, England; died January 6, 1980; married Elizabeth Benson, 1936; children: Margaret Ruth, John Arthur. *Religion:* Congregationalist.

ADDRESSES: Home—26 Florence Ave., Bolton, Lancashire, England. *Agent*—Hope, Leresche & Steele, 11 Jubilee Pl., Chelsea, London SW3 3TE, England.

CAREER: Worked in cotton-spinning industry before becoming a free-lance writer, mainly of books for children. Founder of a society which maintains a residential school for spastic children. *Military service:* Royal Air Force, 1940-45; served in India, Burma, Ceylon; became flight lieutenant; staff officer to Commander in Chief, Royal Air Force, South East Asia Command.

MEMBER: Society of Authors, North Regional Authors (chairman).

WRITINGS:

Tomorrow's Hunter, Jenkins, 1950.
Vibrant Brass, Dent, 1954.
(Under pseudonym J. Baltimore) *Singapore Sari,* Fiction House, 1958.
No Bouquets for These, Tempest Press, 1958.
(With David Reade) *Step in My Shoes* (play), produced in Southport, Lancashire, 1958.

FOR CHILDREN

Rod o' the Rail, Pearson, 1935.
The Rival Tugboats, A. & C. Black, 1936.
Adventurer's Ltd., A. & C. Black, 1938.
Black Gold, Pearson, 1939.
Vanished Whaler, illustrations by S. Drigin, Nelson, 1939.

Keepers of the Khyber, Nelson, 1940.
Lost with All Hands, Nelson, 1940.
Raid on Heligoland, Collins, 1940.
The Flying Submarine, Collins, 1942.
The River of Burning Sand, Collins, 1947.
The Bull Patrol, Lutterworth Press, 1949.
Riders of the Black Camel, Venturebooks, 1949.
Cock o' the Town, illustrations by Kenneth Brookes, Boy Scouts Association (London), 1950.
Wings for a Gull, Warne, 1951.
Pirate Sealer, Collins, 1953.
Shanghaied!, Collins, 1954.
Ten Fathoms Deep, illustrations by Geoffrey Whittam, Dent, 1954, Criterion, 1968.
Jackals of the Sea, illustrations by Whittam, Dent, 1955.
The Scuttlers, illustrations by A. Bruce Cornwell and Drake Brookshaw, Nelson, 1955.
Sea Wraith, Lutterworth Press, 1955.
Wild Goose Saboteur, illustrations by Brookes, Dent, 1955.
Forgotten Submarine, illustrations by Whittam, Dent, 1956.
Land under the White Robe, illustrations by Whittam, Dent, 1956.
Jamboree Challenge, illustrations by Brookes, Roy, 1957.
Java Sea Duel, illustrations by Whittam, Dent, 1957.
Java Trap, illustrations by Paul Hogarth, Dent, 1958, Roy, 1967.
Tenderfoot Trapper, illustrations by Edward Osmond, Dent, 1958, Criterion, 1959.
Sea Wolves, illustrations by Whittam, Dent, 1959, Roy, 1960.
Dangerous Cargo, illustrations by Whittam, Dent, 1960, Roy, 1961.
Lapland Outlaw, illustrations by Fred Wood, Dent, 1960, Lothrop, 1966.
(Under pseudonym Trevor Maine) *Blue Veil and Black Gold,* illustrations by Richard Kennedy, Odhams Press, 1961, Roy, 1965.
China Sea Jigsaw, illustrations by Whittam, Dent, 1961, Roy, 1962.
Orphan Otter, illustrations by N. Osten-Sacken, Dent, 1962, Harcourt, 1963.
Vagabond Ape, illustrations by Osten-Sacken, Dent, 1962.
Yugoslav Mystery, illustrations by Stuart Tresilian, Dent, 1962, Lothrop, 1964.
Prisoners under the Sea, illustrations by Whittam, Dent, 1963.
Lone Seal Pup, illustrations by Osmond, Dent, 1964, Dutton, 1965.
The Strange Invader, illustrations by Tresilian, Dent, 1964, published as *The Strange Intruder,* Lothrop, 1965.

Tanker Trap, illustrations by Whittam, Dent, 1965, Roy, 1966.

(Under pseudonym Linda Peters) *Reindeer Rescue,* illustrations by F. M. Johnson, E. J. Arnold, 1966.

Sicilian Mystery, illustrations by Tresilian, Dent, 1966, Lothrop, 1967.

A Zebra Came to Drink, illustrations by Osmond, Dutton, 1967.

Prisoners in the Snow, illustrations by Victor Ambrus, Lothrop, 1967.

Death of an Oil Rig, illustrations by Whittam, Dent, 1967, Phillips, 1969.

Night of the Black Frost, illustrations by Roger Payne, Lothrop, 1968.

Camel Caravan, illustrations by Joseph Papin, Seabury Press, 1968, published in England as *Desert Caravan,* Macdonald, 1969.

Kidnapped by Accident, illustrations by Ambrus, Dent, 1968, Lothrop, 1969.

Island of Forgotten Men, illustrations by Whittam, Dent, 1968.

Duel in the High Hills, illustrations by Stanley Smith, Dent, 1968, Lothrop, 1969.

Red Sea Rescue, illustrations by Ambrus, Dent, 1969, Lothrop, 1970.

Antlers of the King Moose, illustrations by Edward Mortelmans, Dutton, 1970.

The Big Tusker, illustrations by Douglas Phillips, Lothrop, 1970.

Keepers of the Cattle, illustrations by Bernard Brett, Dent, 1970.

Freedom for a Cheetah, illustrations by Shyam Varma, Lothrop, 1971.

Barracuda Mystery, illustrations by Gavin Rowe, Dent, 1971.

The Unwilling Smuggler, illustrations by Whittam, Dent, 1971.

Last Horse on the Sands, illustrations by David Farris, Dent, 1972, Lothrop, 1973.

Cave of the "Cormorant," Dent, 1973.

A Wolf from the Sky, illustrations by Derek Lucas, Dent, 1974.

Stranger of Wreck Buoy Sands, Dent, 1975.

Twelve Minutes to Disaster and Other Stories, illustrations by Lucas, Dent, 1977.

The Ghost Elephant, Abelard-Schuman, 1977.

The Last Run and Other Stories, Dent, 1977.

No Surrender! and Other Stories, Dent, 1979.

The Thirteen Footprints and Other Stories, Dent, 1979.

Smuggler in the Bay, Dent, 1980.

CHILDREN'S BOOKS UNDER PSEUDONYM A. R. CHANNEL

Phantom Patrol, Collins, 1940.

The Tunnel Busters, Collins, 1960.

The Million-Dollar Ice Floe, illustrations by Eric Mudge-Marriott, Dobson, 1961.

Operation V.2., Collins, 1961.

Arctic Spy, illustrations by Horace Gaffron, Collins, 1962.

The Forgotten Patrol, Collins, 1962.

The Rogue Elephant, illustrations by D. J. Watkins-Pitchford, Dobson, 1962, Macrae Smith, 1963.

Mission Accomplished, Collins, 1964.

Red Ivory, illustrations by Watkins-Pitchford, Macrae Smith, 1964.

Jungle Rescue, illustrations by Watkins-Pitchford, Dobson, 1967, Phillips, 1968.

CHILDREN'S BOOKS UNDER PSEUDONYM MARGARET RUTHIN

Kidnapped in Kandy, illustrations by C. Cane, Blackie, 1951.

The Ring of the Prophet, Warne, 1953.

White Horse of Hungary, Warne, 1954.

Strange Safari, Warne, 1955.

The Secret Pagoda, Warne, 1960.

Jungle Nurse, illustrations by Hugh Marshall, F. Watts, 1960.

Reindeer Girl, illustrations by Marie Whitby, Dobson, 1961, published as *Elli of the Northland,* Farrar, Straus, 1968.

Lapland Nurse, illustrations by Whitby, Dobson, 1962.

Secret of the Shetlands, illustrations by Gwen Gibson, Dobson, 1963.

Katrina of the Lonely Isles, illustrations by Gibson, Dobson, 1964, Farrar, Straus, 1965.

Kidnapped on Stromboli, Dobson, 1966.

Hungarian Rebel, Dobson, 1970.

CHILDREN'S BOOKS UNDER PSEUDONYM PETER HALLARD

Coral Reef Castaway, illustrations by Terence Greer, Phoenix House, 1958, Criterion, 1960.

Barrier Reef Bandits, illustrations by Marshall, Criterion, 1960.

Guardian of the Reef, illustrations by Marshall, Dobson, 1961.

Boy on a White Giraffe, illustrations by Shelia Bewley, Seabury Press, 1969, published in England as *White Giraffe,* Macdonald, 1969.

Lost in Lapland, illustrations by Judith Ann Lawrence, Macdonald, 1970, published as *Puppy Lost in Lapland,* F. Watts, 1971.

Kalu and the Wild Boar, illustrations by W. T. Mars, F. Watts, 1973.

CHILDREN'S BOOKS UNDER PSEUDONYM DAN CORBY; U.S. EDITIONS UNDER NAME ARTHUR CATHERALL

A Shark on the Saltings, Parrish, 1959.

The Little Sealer, Parrish, 1960, published as *The Arctic Sealer,* Criterion, 1961.

Lost Off the Grand Banks, Parrish, 1961, Criterion, 1962.

Man-Eater, illustrations by Richard Lewis, Parrish, 1963, Criterion, 1964.

Thunder Dam, illustrations by Omar Davis, Parrish, 1964, Criterion, 1965.

Conqueror's Gold, Parrish, 1965.

OTHER

Camp-Fire Stories and How to Tell Them, Jenkins, 1935.

(With George W. Blow) *The Steam and Steel Omnibus,* illustrations by Blow, Collins, 1950.

The Scout Story Omnibus, Collins, 1954.

The Young Baden-Powell, illustrations by William Randell, Parrish, 1961, Roy, 1962.

Vanishing Lapland, F. Watts, 1972.

Catherall contributed over a thousand short stories to numerous publications, including *Boy's Life of America,* and was a regular Boy Scouts columnist for the *Bolton Evening News* for thirty-five years. His adult novel *Vibrant Brass* has been optioned for filming.

SIDELIGHTS: Arthur Catherall set a high standard for himself as a children's writer: he wanted to write realistic stories that contained honest, worthy characters for young boys and girls to emulate. His legacy of nearly a hundred books and over a thousand short stories is a monument to his success in achieving those goals. Throughout his works Catherall presents characters who encounter difficulties in all parts of the world and overcome the difficulties through their resourcefulness and their courage. Gwen Marsh, writing in *Twentieth-Century Children's Writers,* said that Catherall "always held up to his readers an image of a hero or heroine with courage, kindness, loyalty, and spirit."

Catherall was a world traveler who vowed that he went out and searched for material to fill his books. "I have shoveled coal on small fishing vessels off the coast of Iceland and in the north east Atlantic," he once said. "I have traveled on tramp steamers, and gone with members of their crews to the dives on many a waterfront. . . . My travels have taken me to Algeria, and across the Atlas mountains into the desert. I have camped and climbed in a number of European countries, walked across Lapland and climbed Sweden's highest mountain. I spent some time in the Faroe Islands, pony trekked in Austria—at heights varying from 4 to 6,000 feet. I traveled the length of Finnish Lapland in 1969 and I have walked over Norwegian and Swedish Lapland." His stories have been justly praised for their authenticity and for their attention to the geography of the land in which they are set.

Catherall wrote primarily for boys, he said, because he worked with the Boy Scouts in England for all his life, contributing a regular column on Scout activities to his local newspaper. "You don't find any unnecessary clubbing or shooting in my books," he was quoted in *Twentieth-Century Children's Writers.* "Boys can be little savages without the inspiration of a story to start them off. They look for heroes in a story. I try to give them the right kind of heroes, for boys are great imitators." The author has written for girls as well, under the pseudonym Margaret Ruthin. "The dozen books I have written for girls," he once commented, "were done immediately on my return from service with the Royal Air Force when publishers were stacked up with boys manuscripts, and had very few stories for girls." Catherall also wrote under a number of other pseudonyms.

Catherall once said: "I write because I must. There are so many things I want to write about that the business has become almost a disease. I recently received among my fan mail a letter from a boy in Chicago who said, 'Please keep on writing, I think you are the best writer in the world.' I wish I could believe him, but letters of appreciation from youngsters makes me keep on telling stories I think they like."

BIOGRAPHICAL/CRITICAL SOURCES:

BOOKS

Chevalier, Tracy, editor, *Twentieth-Century Children's Writers,* 3rd edition, St. James Press, 1989, pp. 177-79.

PERIODICALS

Books and Bookmen, September, 1969.
Library Journal, July, 1970.
Saturday Review, March 22, 1969.
Times (London), July 2, 1980.
Times Literary Supplement, May 25, 1967, p. 459; June 26, 1969; April 16, 1970.*

*   *   *

CHANDLER, David Leon 1937(?)-

PERSONAL: Born c. 1937; married; wife's name, Mary Voelz Chandler. *Education:* Attended Boston University.

ADDRESSES: *Home and office*—390 Holly St., Denver, CO 80220. *Agent*—Jed Mattes, 175 West 73rd St., New York, NY 10023.

CAREER: Has worked as merchant seaman and farm laborer; *Panama City News-Herald,* Panama City, FL, reporter, 1959-61; *New Orleans States-Item,* New Orleans, LA, reporter, 1961-64; *Life* (magazine), New York City, contract reporter and correspondent, 1965-71; free-lance writer, 1972-78; *Ledger-Star,* Norfolk, VA, investigative reporter, 1979-81; *People* (magazine), New York City, correspondent, 1982-90.

MEMBER: Dramatists Guild, Authors League of America.

AWARDS, HONORS: Shared Pulitzer Prize for investigative reporting, 1962; Sigma Delta Chi prize for national magazine reporting, 1970; named outstanding journalist by Virginia chapter of Sigma Delta Chi, 1979; Virginia Press Association Investigative Reporting Award, 1980; Scripps Howard Distinguished Journalism Citation, 1980.

WRITINGS:

Dragon Variation, Dutton, 1974.
Brothers in Blood: The Rise of the Criminal Brotherhoods, Dutton, 1975.
The Natural Superiority of Southern Politicians: A Revisionist History, Doubleday, 1977.
One Hundred Tons of Gold, Doubleday, 1978.
Dialing for Data, Random House, 1984.
Henry Flagler: The Astonishing Life and Times of the Visionary Robber Baron Who Founded Florida, Macmillan, 1985.
(With wife, Mary Voelz Chandler) *Binghams of Louisville: The Dark History Behind One of America's Great Fortunes,* Crown, 1988.

WORK IN PROGRESS: A history for Random House.

SIDELIGHTS: Pulitzer Prize-winning journalist David Leon Chandler used his investigative skills to look into the life of Henry Flagler, "one of the more remarkable of the major carnivores who stalked the American economy in the late 19th and early 20th centuries," as John Gross describes him in the *New York Times.* The facts of Flagler's life resulted in Chandler's writing not one, but two biographies about him. In researching the first book, *Henry Flagler: The Astonishing Life and Times of the Visionary Robber Baron Who Founded Florida,* Chandler discovered a separate story in the life of Flagler's widow, whom Chandler believes was murdered by her second husband. Her story is told in *The Binghams of Louisville: The Dark History Behind One of America's Great Fortunes.*

One of only two biographies on Henry Flagler, Chandler's book follows Flagler's career from his partnership in Standard Oil with John D. Rockefeller to his pioneering development of Florida. Almost single-handedly, Flagler transformed Florida from "the most backward state in the union," according to Gross, by constructing numerous hotels, pushing the railroad system south to Key West, founding the city of Palm Beach, and fostering tourism and agriculture.

While critics welcomed a biography on Flagler, one of history's overlooked figures, not all admired Chandler's ap-

proach. "Chandler's effort to do [Flagler] justice," writes Jonathan Yardley in the *Washington Post,* "has resulted in an awkward book that, although it contains a great deal of interesting information, is patchily constructed and flat. There's a very good story in Flagler's life, but not in Chandler's book." Gross suggests that perhaps Flagler was "a sphinx without a riddle" and compliments Chandler on piecing together "a lively picture of the outward trappings of [Flagler's] glory."

Having completed his biography of Flagler, Chandler next turned to the mysterious circumstances surrounding the death of Flagler's wealthy widow, Mary Lily. The richest woman in America, Mary Lily died less than a year after her marriage to Robert Worth Bingham. Based on evidence that Mary Lily's body showed exposure to morphine and arsenic, combined with the fact that Bingham originally agreed to be left out of his wife's will but later produced a secret codicil granting him five million dollars, Chandler concludes that Robert Worth Bingham murdered his wife for her money.

Chandler's conclusions were disputed by Barry Bingham, Sr., son of Robert Worth Bingham, in an eight-pound legal document. The family's challenges may have caused the biography's original publisher, Macmillan, to drop the book, which was later published by Crown. Critics, as well, received Chandler's theory with skepticism. In the *Los Angeles Times Book Review,* Digby Diehl writes that "Chandler's solid job of investigative reporting does not support his damning conclusion." Although James Duffy of the *New York Times Book Review* finds that Chandler has written "an entertaining crime book," he wonders "whether it represents clever deduction based on solid research, or a fictionalized yarn selectively using the historical materials." "The evidence Chandler presents to support [his] conclusion is impressive," Yardley admits, "though in the end, of course, he and the reader are engaged in pure speculation."

BIOGRAPHICAL/CRITICAL SOURCES:

PERIODICALS

Best Sellers, April, 1977.
Los Angeles Times, December 4, 1987.
Los Angeles Times Book Review, February 6, 1983; March 20, 1988.
National Review, July 8, 1977.
New Republic, January 22, 1977.
New York Times, July 18, 1986.
New York Times Book Review, January 16, 1977; January 10, 1988.
People, June 8, 1987.
Washington Post, June 25, 1986; December 23, 1987.

CHANNEL, A. R.
See CATHERALL, Arthur

*   *   *

CHILVER, Peter 1933-

PERSONAL: Born November 18, 1933, in Southend, Essex, England; son of A. H. and A. E. (Mack) Chilver. *Education:* St. Edmund Hall, Oxford, B.A. (with honors), 1956, M.A., 1964; Royal Academy of Dramatic Art, London, England, Diploma in Speech and Drama (with honors), 1963; University of London, Postgraduate Certificate of Education (with distinction), 1965, Academic Diploma in Education (with distinction), 1969, M.Phil., 1973, Ph.D., 1976.

ADDRESSES: Home—27 Cavendish Gardens, Barking, Essex, England. *Office*—Department of English, Langdon School, London, England.

CAREER: Southend Education Authority, Southend, England, teacher, 1957-60; Inner London Education Authority, London, England, teacher, 1964-68; Acton College of Education, London, lecturer in English and drama, 1968-70; Thomas Huxley College, London, senior lecturer in drama, 1970-77; University of London, London, member of faculty of education, 1974-77; Langdon School, London, head of department of English, 1977—. Visiting lecturer, Ontario Conference of Teachers of English, 1980, 1981, 1982, 1985, and 1987.

AWARDS, HONORS: W. H. Page scholarship, English-Speaking Union, 1974; British Council travel award, 1985.

WRITINGS:

Staging a School Play, Batsford, 1967, Harper, 1968.
Improvised Drama, Batsford, 1967.
Dirty Bertie (musical play), Evans Brothers, 1968.
The Nine Scandalous Lives of Dick Turpin, Highwayman (musical play), Evans Brothers, 1968.
Talking: Discussion, Improvisation, and Debate in Schools, Batsford, 1968.
(With Eric Jones) *Designing a School Play,* Batsford, 1968, Taplinger, 1970.
Stories for Improvisation in Primary and Secondary Schools, Batsford, 1969.
Producing a Play, Batsford, 1974.
Teaching Improvised Drama: A Handbook for Secondary Schools, Batsford, 1978.
(With Gerard Gould) *Learning and Language in the Classroom: Discursive Talking and Writing across the Curriculum,* Pergamon, 1982.
Spotlight, Thornes, 1986.
Insight, Thornes, 1986.

Contributor to *Drama and the Whole Curriculum,* Hutchinson, 1982, and *Perspectives on Small Group Learning,* Rubicon, 1990.

WORK IN PROGRESS: The role of literature in the school curriculum.

*   *   *

CLEARMAN, Brian (Patrick Joseph) 1941-

PERSONAL: Born March 19, 1941, in Longview, WA; son of W. Wade (a carpenter and builder) and Ethel K. (a beautician and homemaker; maiden name, Sauers) Clearman. *Education:* Attended Lower Columbia College, 1959-60, 1964, and Saint Martin's College, 1960-62; Portland State University, B.S., 1965; graduate study at Western State College of Colorado, 1972; University of Oregon, M.S., 1975.

ADDRESSES: Home and office—Mount Angel Abbey, Saint Benedict, OR 97373.

CAREER: Entered Order of St. Benedict (Benedictines), 1964, took monastic vows, 1966; Mount Angel Abbey, Saint Benedict, OR, teacher at preparatory school, 1968-76, staff member of abbey's business office, 1976—.

WRITINGS:

"TRANSPORTATION MARKINGS: A STUDY IN COMMUNICATION" SERIES

First Studies in Transportation Markings, Part A: *Foundations,* University Press of America, 1981, 2nd edition, Mount Angel Abbey, 1991, Part B: *A First Study in Transportation Marking: The United States,* University Press of America, 1981, Part C: *International Transportation Markings: Floating and Fixed Marine,* University Press of America, 1981, 2nd edition, Mount Angel Abbey, 1988, Part D: *International Marine Aids to Navigation,* University Press of America, 1981, 2nd edition, Mount Angel Abbey, 1988; *Further Studies in Transportation Markings,* Mount Angel Abbey, Part E: *International Traffic Control Devices,* 1984, Part F: *International Railway Signals,* 1991, Part G: *International Aeronautical Aids to Navigation,* in press, Part H: *Comprehensive Classification of Transportation Markings,* in press.

SIDELIGHTS: Brian Clearman once told *CA:* "Transportation markings are those devices—external to a means of transportation—that aid the safety of motorists, navigators, and engineers. They include buoys, lighthouses, fog signals, unlighted beacons, road and rail signals, safety signs, electronic mechanisms, aeronautical lights, and road and runway markings. My interest in them began more than twenty-five years ago with the lighthouses and river lights of the Washington and Oregon coasts and of the Columbia River and Puget Sound. Gradually it expanded to include all other forms of transportation markings. My writings survey markings less as technical phenomena and more as communications and as applied semiotics.

"The preparation of the studies has taken place, to a considerable extent, within a monastic context. That milieu has greatly influenced, not only the form, but also the content of the research and writing. Hopefully the end product will provide an introductory compendium of the whole range of markings."

*　　*　　*

CLEAVER, Bill
See CLEAVER, William J(oseph)

*　　*　　*

CLEAVER, Vera 1919-

PERSONAL: Born January 6, 1919, in Virgil, SD; daughter of Fortis Alonzo and Beryl Naiome (Reininger) Allen; married William Joseph (Bill) Cleaver (an author), October 4, 1945 (died, 1981). *Education:* Educated at schools in Kennebeck, SD, and Perry and Tallahassee, FL.

ADDRESSES: Home—600 East Lake Elbert Dr., Winter Haven, FL 33881. *Office*—Harper & Row Junior Books Group, 10 East 53rd St., New York, NY 10022.

CAREER: Author of books for children with husband, Bill Cleaver. Free-lance accountant, 1945-54; accountant (civilian), United States Air Force, Tachikawa, Japan, 1954-56, and Chaumont, France, 1956-58.

AWARDS, HONORS: Horn Book Honor List, 1967, for *Ellen Grae; Horn Book* Honor List, 1969, American Library Association (ALA) notable book, 1970, Newbery Honor Book, and National Book Award nomination, all for *Where the Lilies Bloom;* National Book Award nomination, 1971, for *Grover; New York Times* outstanding book, ALA notable book, 1973, for *Me Too;* National Book Award nomination, 1974, all for *The Whys and Wherefores of Littabelle Lee;* Golden Spur Award, Western Writers of America, Lewis Carroll Bookshelf award, and *New York Times* outstanding book citation, all 1975, all for *Dust of the Earth;* National Book Award nomination, 1979, for *Queen of Hearts;* Children's Choice Award, 1986, for *Sweetly Sings the Donkey.*

WRITINGS:

CHILDREN'S FICTION

Sugar Blue, illustrated by Eric Nones, Lothrop, 1984.

Sweetly Sings the Donkey, Lippincott, 1985.
Moon Lake Angel, Lothrop, 1987.
Belle Pruitt (Junior Library Guild selection), Lippincott, 1988.

CHILDREN'S FICTION; WITH HUSBAND, BILL CLEAVER

Ellen Grae (also see below), illustrated by Ellen Raskin, Lippincott, 1967.
Lady Ellen Grae (also see below), illustrated by E. Raskin, Lippincott, 1968.
Where the Lilies Bloom, illustrated by Jim Spanfeller, Lippincott, 1969.
Grover, illustrated by Frederic Marvin, Lippincott, 1970.
The Mimosa Tree, Lippincott, 1970.
I Would Rather Be a Turnip, Lippincott, 1971.
The Mock Revolt, Lippincott, 1971.
Delpha Green and Company, Lippincott, 1972.
The Whys and Wherefores of Littabelle Lee, Atheneum, 1973.
Me Too, Lippincott, 1973.
Ellen Grae [and] *Lady Ellen Grae,* Hamish Hamilton, 1973.
Dust of the Earth, Lippincott, 1975.
Trial Valley, Lippincott, 1977.
Queen of Hearts, Lippincott, 1978.
A Little Destiny, Lothrop, 1979.
The Kissimmee Kid, Lothrop, 1981.
Hazel Rye, Lippincott, 1983.

OTHER

The Nurse's Dilemma (adult fiction), Avalon Books, 1966.

Contributor of stories to numerous magazines and periodicals, including *McCall's* and *Woman's Day.* A collection of Cleaver's manuscripts is at the Kerlan Collection, University of Minnesota, Minneapolis, and at the University of North Carolina, Chapel Hill.

ADAPTATIONS: Where the Lilies Bloom was filmed by United Artists, 1974.

SIDELIGHTS: For almost twenty-five years, Vera and Bill Cleaver wrote as a team—one developing and researching the ideas, the other doing the actual writing. After her husband's death in 1981, Vera continued to write the type of novels that she and her husband had jointly produced—novels that depict young people accepting responsibility beyond their years and coming to terms with the harsh circumstances of life. "Despite what for many would be overwhelming circumstances, they preserve and exert their newly found individuality with uncommon, but not unbelievable, resourcefulness and intelligence," writes Jane Harper Yarbrough in an essay in *Dictionary of Literary Biography.* "The Cleavers offer young adult readers sensitive, insightful characters with whom to identify, with whom to join on the turbulent voyage of growing up responsible."

Born in Virgil, South Dakota, Vera began writing at the early age of six under the influence of her maternal grandfather, who published a newspaper at the time; she received her education in schools in South Dakota and Florida, and eventually worked as a free-lance accountant. She met Bill during World War II. A native of Seattle, Washington, Bill had been educated in private schools in British Columbia before joining the United States Air Force. In 1945 they married and Vera worked as an accountant for the Air Force in Tachikawa, Japan, and Chaumont, France. Unable to complete their formal education, the Cleavers taught themselves in public libraries and got their literary start by publishing almost 300 stories about children for adults in various pulp magazines. Later, they wrote for periodicals such as *McCall's* and *Woman's Day,* and in the late 1960s, they turned to writing for young adult readers. Their work is popular and well-received critically, regularly earning American Library Association notable book citations; four of their novels have been finalists in the National Book Award competition: *Where the Lilies Bloom, Grover, The Whys and Wherefores of Littabelle Lee,* and *Queen of Hearts.*

In *Where the Lilies Bloom,* which was also named a Newbery Honor Book, fourteen-year-old Mary Call Luther's father dies, leaving her with the responsibility of holding together their impoverished and parentless family, of guiding and providing for herself and her siblings in the mountains of Appalachia. Yarbrough praises the heroine, "whose inner strength, love of family, irrepressible dignity, pragmatic resourcefulness, indomitable will, and joy for life combine to provide readers with a vividly memorable character whose uplifting story is of one young woman's victories over the oppressive forces of nature and society." Compelled to keep their father's death a secret lest they be dispatched to separate foster homes, they bury him in a mountainside grave and sustain themselves by "wildcrafting," or collecting medicinal herbs that grow wild. Calling it "a story of good people, with real natures, living under conditions of hardship, in poverty, in the midst of bereavement, maintaining their independence, wit and dignity," William Saroyan, in a *New York Times Book Review* critique of the novel, concludes: "Reading the book has been like eating a good meal of bread, cheese, onion and cold water. I tend to have this feeling of hunger satisfied when I read very good writing."

Grover is the story of Grover Ezell, an eleven-year-old boy who struggles with his mother's suicide, and his father's emotional instability as well. Although he had not been told that his mother was dying, Grover somehow knew. When his mother's surgery was followed by his father's sudden attentive attempts to provide her with the things

she had long wanted, Grover suspected that his mother's health would not improve; however, he was unprepared for her death by a self-inflicted gunshot wound. Grover does not believe his father when he tells him that his mother's death was accidental; he struggles to understand the meaning of death, eventually gaining insight into the incident. Calling it "a sad, but not a somber story, in which there is humor to counterbalance sorrow, and action as well as introspection," Diane Farrell remarks in her *Horn Book* review that it is also "a profoundly wise and real tale." Although she deems it "a raw book," Joan Murphy remarks in the *School Librarian* that it is "one which is much nearer to everyman's, or every child's, experience than we care to think."

The Whys and Wherefores of Littabelle Lee tells the story of a sixteen-year-old girl who lives in the Ozark Mountains with her elderly grandparents and her Aunt Sorrow, whose income as a doctor of natural medicine supports them all. When her aunt falls from a horse and injuries prevent her from maintaining her practice, she marries her longtime suitor and Littabelle Lee is left with the responsibility of caring for herself and her grandparents. "To read this book, full of truth and the natural life of the country, is a rewarding experience," remarks M. H. Miller in the *Children's Book Review.* "It contains much eventful incident, and much simple, wise reflection." Although Ruth Pegau, in a *Library Journal* review, finds the story "predictable, talky, and dull," Jonathan Yardley believes that the Cleavers offer "morals without belaboring them," suggesting in the *New York Times Book Review* that the book is more "about the dignity of poor people who struggle to live on a demanding mountain land that they love. . . . It is about children who are faithful to family, and children who are not. It is about a law in which there is mercy and true justice. Most of all, it is about growing up, about meeting the responsibilities that are one's 'whys and wherefores.' "

In *Queen of Hearts,* twelve-year-old Wilma Lincoln agrees to stay with her seventy-nine-year-old grandmother who is recovering from a mild stroke. Granny Lincoln, who has gone through three hired women before Wilma arrives and resents depending upon others, tries to humiliate Wilma, who responds in anger; however, writes Jean Fritz in the *New York Times Book Review,* "Wilma learns to stand up to the cantankerous old soul, to follow her into her past, and she even finds a way to make her grandmother feel useful." Referring to it as "a devastatingly honest tragicomedy," Ethel Heins, in a *Horn Book* review, praises the novel as "a brave, humane book, wholly individual in conception and style."

"The Cleavers know human nature and they portray many facets of it in a truly believable and arousing manner," writes Patricia J. Cianciolo in *Top of the News.*

"Their stories highlight the humor as well as the pathos characteristic of the human experience. . . . The human experiences they portray are done with an honesty, a sensitivity, and a realism that are unique in children's literature today." Critics agree that although the Cleaver novels are relentlessly realistic, they are not depressing. "The fight must be fought, but if the end is defeat, very well then, the end is defeat and there is no disgrace in it," observes John Rowe Townsend in his *A Sounding of Storytellers.* "It is better to have fought and lost than not to have fought. . . . This sense of the indomitability of the human spirit is undoubtedly the major reason why in the end the Cleaver books are more likely to lift up than cast down the reader, to offer an astringent yet stimulating experience."

BIOGRAPHICAL/CRITICAL SOURCES:

BOOKS

Children's Literature Review, Volume 6, Gale, 1984.
Dictionary of Literary Biography, Gale, Volume 52: *American Writers for Children since 1960: Fiction,* Gale, 1986, pp. 91-97.
Townsend, John Rowe, *A Sounding of Storytellers: New and Revised Essays on Contemporary Writers for Children,* Harper, 1979, pp. 30-40.
Twentieth-Century Children's Writers, 3rd edition, edited by Tracy Chevalier, St. James Press, 1989.

PERIODICALS

Children's Book Review, summer, 1974, p. 64.
Horn Book, April, 1970, pp. 158-59; June, 1978, p. 275; October, 1979.
Library Journal, June 15, 1973, p. 2000.
New York Times Book Review, September 28, 1969, p. 34; March 4, 1973, pp. 6-7; April 30, 1978, p. 51.
School Librarian, December, 1971, p. 370.
Top of the News, June, 1976, pp. 338-50.*

*   *   *

CLEAVER, William J(oseph) 1920-1981
(Bill Cleaver)

PERSONAL: Born March 24, 1920, in Hugo, OH; died August 20, 1981, in Winter Haven, FL; married wife, Vera Allen (a writer), October 4, 1945. *Education:* Educated at private schools in Vancouver, British Columbia, and Seattle, WA.

ADDRESSES: Home—600 East Lake Elbert Dr., Winter Haven, FL 33881.

CAREER: Author of books for children with wife, Vera Cleaver. Jeweler and watchmaker, 1950-54. *Military ser-*vice: U.S. Army Air Corps, 1942-45; U.S. Air Force in Japan, 1954-56, and in France, 1956-58.

AWARDS, HONORS: Horn Book Honor List, 1967, for *Ellen Grae; Horn Book* Honor List, 1969, American Library Association (ALA) notable book, 1970, Newbery Honor Book, and National Book Award nomination, all for *Where the Lilies Bloom;* National Book Award nomination, 1971, for *Grover; New York Times* outstanding book, ALA notable book, 1973, for *Me Too;* National Book Award nomination, 1974, all for *The Whys and Wherefores of Littabelle Lee;* Golden Spur Award, Western Writers of America, and Lewis Carroll Bookshelf award, and *New York Times* outstanding book citation, all 1975, all for *Dust of the Earth;* National Book Award nomination, 1979, for *Queen of Hearts.*

WRITINGS:

CHILDREN'S FICTION UNDER NAME BILL CLEAVER; WITH WIFE, VERA CLEAVER

Ellen Grae (also see below), illustrated by Ellen Raskin, Lippincott, 1967.
Lady Ellen Grae (also see below), illustrated by E. Raskin, Lippincott, 1968.
Where the Lilies Bloom, illustrated by Jim Spanfeller, Lippincott,1969.
Grover, illustrated by Frederic Marvin, Lippincott, 1970.
The Mimosa Tree, Lippincott, 1970.
I Would Rather Be a Turnip, Lippincott, 1971.
The Mock Revolt, Lippincott, 1971.
Delpha Green and Company, Lippincott, 1972.
The Whys and Wherefores of Littabelle Lee, Atheneum, 1973.
Me Too, Lippincott, 1973.
Ellen Grae [and] *Lady Ellen Grae,* Hamish Hamilton, 1973.
Dust of the Earth, Lippincott, 1975.
Trial Valley, Lippincott, 1977.
Queen of Hearts, Lippincott, 1978.
A Little Destiny, Lothrop, 1979.
The Kissimmee Kid, Lothrop, 1981.
Hazel Rye, Lippincott, 1983.

OTHER

Contributor of stories to numerous magazines and periodicals, including *McCall's* and *Woman's Day.* A collection of Cleaver's manuscripts is at the Kerlan Collection, University of Minnesota, Minneapolis, and at the University of North Carolina, Chapel Hill.

ADAPTATIONS: Where the Lilies Bloom was filmed by United Artists, 1974.

SIDELIGHTS: See entry on wife, Vera Cleaver, for joint "Sidelights" on Bill and Vera Cleaver.

OBITUARIES:

PERIODICALS

Publishers Weekly, September 18, 1981, p. 90.
School Library Journal, January, 1982, p. 19.*

*   *   *

CLINTON, (Lloyd) D(eWitt) 1946-
(Witt Lowidski)

PERSONAL: Born August 29, 1946, in Topeka, KS; son of John J. and Natalie (Mathews) Clinton; married Jacqueline Fay Hollebeck Sobin (a nurse researcher); children: Melissa Elizabeth Sobin (stepchild). *Education:* Southwestern College, Winfield, KS, B.A., 1968; Wichita State University, M.A., 1972; Bowling Green State University, M.F.A., 1975, Ph.D., 1981.

ADDRESSES: Home—3567 North Murray Ave., Shorewood, WI 53211. *Office*—Department of English, University of Wisconsin—Whitewater, 800 West Main St., Whitewater, WI 53190-1790.

CAREER: Wayne State University, Detroit, MI, instructor in English, 1975-77; University of Wisconsin—Whitewater, lecturer, 1981-85, assistant professor, 1985-88, associate professor of English, 1988—. University of Wisconsin System teaching fellow, 1989-90. Fellow in poetry at the Ragdale Foundation, 1984, and at the MacDowell Colony, 1988. Coordinator of Poetry-in-the-Schools Project, Kansas Arts Commission, 1972-73. Poet in residence with Poetry-in-the-Schools Projects in Kansas, Montana, South Carolina, Ohio and Michigan, 1973-81. Member of literature panel, Ohio Arts Council, 1982-84, and of Wisconsin Arts Board, 1985-86. Coordinator of university sponsored creative writing workshops, festivals and retreats. Gives poetry readings. *Military service:* U.A. Army, Artillery, computer operator, 1968-70; served in Vietnam.

MEMBER: Associated Writing Programs.

AWARDS, HONORS: Honorable mention for Elliston Book Award from University of Cincinnati, 1976; grant from Michigan Council for the Arts, 1981; grant from Wisconsin Arts Board, 1987.

WRITINGS:

The Conquistador Dog Texts (poems), New Rivers Press, 1976.
The Coyot. Inca Texts (poems), New Rivers Press, 1979.
Das Illustrite Mississippithal Revisited (chapbook), Browns Mill Review, 1983.
Night Jungle Bird Life (chapbook), 02 Press, 1983.

(Editor with Tom Montag and C. W. Truesdale) *An Americas Anthology: A Geopoetics Landmark,* Volume I, New Rivers Press, 1983.
Furnace: A Ballet Performance (chapbook), Kawabata Press, 1984.
(Under pseudonym Witt Lowidski) *Active Death: Unholy Rhymes,* Count Dracula Fan Club, 1986.
(Editor) *Eleven Wisconsin Poets,* Kendall/Hunt, 1987.

Work represented in anthologies, including: *Heartland II: Poets of the Midwest,* 1975; *New BkMk Poets,* BookMark Press, 1977; *Center,* Center Press, 1983; *Poetry Ohio: Art of the State,* 1984; *Wisconsin Poetry,* 1991. Contributor of articles and poems to magazines, including *Mid-American Review, Overland Journal, Stone Country, Worcester Review, Contact II, Wisconsin Review, Apalachee Quarterly, Birmingham Poetry Review, Kenyon Review, Great River Review,* and *Gulf Stream Magazine.*

SIDELIGHTS: D. Clinton told *CA:* " 'Geopoetics' is a term coined by Tom Montag to describe the early issues of *Salthouse.* I've used the term as a subtitle to a large anthology, *An Americas Anthology,* as well as a 'catch phrase' to describe my own work in historical improvisation.

"My interest in re-writing history, especially American conquistador history, began in 1975 when Howard McCord introduced me to the holy texts of the ancient Mayas, Aztecs, Incas, as well as tales of singular 'heroic' conquistadors, including deVaca and Coronado.

"One of the more recent historical improvisations was *Das Illustrite Mississippithal Revisited,* a short poetic history of Mississippi travelers and explorers. All of this work is part of an on-going project called the Conquistador Dog Texts Series. My work in 'geopoetics' then is to re-tell, reconstruct, and re-imagine our past histories, putting a new light on long ago, almost forgotten stories of the Americas."

*   *   *

COLES, Don 1928-

PERSONAL: Born April 12, 1928, in Woodstock, Ontario, Canada; son of John Langdon and Alice Margaret (Brown) Coles; married Heidi Goelnitz; children: Sarah, Luke. *Education:* University of Toronto, M.A., 1952; Cambridge University, M.A., 1954.

ADDRESSES: Home—122 Glenview Ave., Toronto, Ontario, Canada M4R 1P8. *Office*—Vanier College, York University, North York, Ontario, Canada.

CAREER: Lived as a translator in Scandinavia, Italy, and Germany, 1954-65; York University, Vanier College,

North York, Ontario, instructor, 1965-66, lecturer, 1966-68, assistant professor, 1968-71, associate professor, 1971-81, professor of humanities and creative writing, 1981—, director of Programme in Creative Writing, 1981-86.

MEMBER: League of Canadian Poets.

AWARDS, HONORS: Prize from Canadian Broadcasting Corp. Literary Competition, 1980, for poem "Landslides"; Gold Medal, National Magazine Awards, 1986, for "Dark Fields"; runner-up, Arvon International Poetry Competition.

WRITINGS:

Sometimes All Over (poetry), Macmillan, 1975.
Anniversaries (poetry), Macmillan, 1979.
The Prinzhorn Collection (poetry), Macmillan, 1982.
Landslides: Selected Poems 1975-1985, McClelland & Stewart, 1986.
K. in Love (poetry), Vehicule Press, 1989.
Little Bird (poetry), Vehicule Press, 1991.

Work is represented in anthologies, including *The Poets of Canada,* edited by John Robert Colombo, Hurtig, 1978; *The Oxford Book of Canadian Verse,* Oxford University Press, 1983; and *Penguin Anthology of Canadian Poetry,* Penguin Books, 1984. Contributor to periodicals, including *Saturday Night, Poetry, Canadian Forum, Ariel, London Review of Books, Arc,* and *London Magazine.*

SIDELIGHTS: Don Coles lived in Scandinavia, Italy, and Germany from 1954-1965.

BIOGRAPHICAL/CRITICAL SOURCES:

BOOKS

Contemporary Literary Criticism, Volume 46, Gale, 1988.

PERIODICALS

Globe & Mail (Toronto), August 9, 1986.

*   *   *

COLLINGS, I. J(illie)

PERSONAL: Born in Adelaide, Australia; daughter of George Collings; married; children: Kean Christopher Buckley. *Education:* University of Adelaide, B.A., 1955; London School of Palmistry, F.S.S.P.P., 1968; Mayo School of Astrology, D.M.S. (with honors), 1978; British Institute of Graphologists, diploma, 1985.

ADDRESSES: Home—6 Woodstock House, 11 Marylebone High St., London W.1, England. *Office*—14 Highbourne House, 13-15 Marylebone High St., London W.1, England.

CAREER: Woman, London, England, feature writer, 1969-70, deputy features editor, 1970, author of "The *Woman Magazine* Astrology Column," 1975-85. Television broadcaster, public speaker.

WRITINGS:

The Malevolent Despot (novel), Gollancz, 1968.
Astrology and Your Child, twelve volumes, Mayflower, 1980.
Around the Next Corner, New English Library, 1990.
Life Forces: Guidelines for a Healthy Life on a Polluted Planet, New English Library, 1991.

Author of astrology columns in *Mother,* 1981-85.

WORK IN PROGRESS: More writings on health.

*   *   *

COLLINS, Hunt
See HUNTER, Evan

*   *   *

COLVIN, James
See MOORCOCK, Michael (John)

*   *   *

CONRAD, Paul (Francis) 1924-

PERSONAL: Born June 27, 1924, in Cedar Rapids, IO; son of Robert H. (a freight and passenger agent) and Florence G. (Lawler) Conrad; married Barbara Kay King (an information officer), February 27, 1953; children: David, James, Carol, Elizabeth. *Education:* University of Iowa, B.A., 1950. *Politics:* Democrat. *Religion:* Roman Catholic.

ADDRESSES: Home—Rancho Palos Verdes, CA. *Office*—*Los Angeles Times,* Times Mirror Sq., Los Angeles, CA 90053. *Agent*—Pauline Buck and Natalie Goodman, BG, 1362 North Doheny Dr., Los Angeles, CA 90069.

CAREER: Denver Post, Denver, CO, editorial cartoonist, 1950-64; *Los Angeles Times,* Los Angeles, CA, editorial cartoonist, 1964—. Cartoons syndicated by Register and Tribune Syndicate, 1953-63, and Los Angeles Times Syndicate, 1964—. Cartoons and bronze sculptures exhibited at Los Angeles County Museum of Art, 1979. Held first Richard M. Nixon Lecture Chair at Whittier College, 1977-78. Lecturer on cartoons for Cooke-Daniels Lecture Tours at Denver Art Museum, 1964. Has appeared on radio and television programs. *Military service:* U.S.

Army, 1942-45, served with Corps of Engineers in Pacific theater of operations.

MEMBER: Society of Professional Journalists (fellow), Phi Delta Theta.

AWARDS, HONORS: Distinguished service award, Sigma Delta Chi, 1963, 1969, 1971, 1981, 1982, 1987, all for editorial cartooning; Pulitzer Prize in editorial cartooning, 1964, 1971, 1984, runner-up, 1982; Overseas Press Club award, 1970, 1981; journalism award, University of Southern California, 1972; Robert F. Kennedy Journalism Award, 1985, for editorial cartooning; Joseph Quinn Memorial Award, Greater Los Angeles Press Club, 1988; second place, John Fischetti Editorial Cartoon Competition, 1989; Hugh Hefner First Amendment Award, 1990, for print journalism.

WRITINGS:

(With Malcolm Boyd) *When in the Course of Human Events* (cartoons and prayers), Sheed & Ward, 1973.

The King and Us: Editorial Cartoons, edited by Les Guthman, Clymer Publications, 1974.

Pro and Conrad, introduction by Art Buchwald, Neff-Kane, 1979.

Drawn and Quartered, Abrams, 1985.

The Gang of Eight, Faber & Faber, 1985.

ADAPTATIONS: When in the Course of Human Events was released as recording of the same title, University of Southern California, School of Library Science.

SIDELIGHTS: Paul Conrad began his cartooning career in college, where he drew for the *Daily Iowan.* During the 1950s and 1960s he worked as cartoonist for the *Denver Post,* focusing on such topics as the Cold War, Korea, the Kennedy presidency, and social issues including integration. Conrad's popularity increased at this time, prompting one *Time* reporter to describe him as "probably the nation's hottest new cartooning property." By 1977 Harlan Lebo of the *Writer's Digest* labeled the cartoonist "one of the most respected practitioners of his trade."

Critics recognize in Conrad's cartoons extensive research, attention to detail and technical accuracy, simplicity, and strong editorial content. Known for investigating issues and for studying characters before he creates a cartoon, Conrad explained to John Grecny of *University Magazine* that cartoonists should possess sufficient background on and knowledge of their subjects to be effective. For example, he researched the physiological changes experienced by the aging Dwight D. Eisenhower and pictured him accordingly. Though a *Time* writer claimed the resulting caricature depicted Eisenhower as "progressively older and near-senile," the same writer conceded that the character was technically accurate as well as familiar to Conrad's audience.

Likewise, Grecny suggested that Conrad's caricatures capture the souls of his subjects. Conrad agreed, citing his drawing of Ronald Reagan as Napoleon captioned "The War Powers Actor" as an example of a drawing that illustrates its subject's temperament. "You can get the entire personality of the person in the caricature itself," the cartoonist maintained. "If that's the soul, fine, and it probably is—it's the personality of the man, what he is, how he thinks, how he would react, what makes him go. You can put all that into a caricature."

The *Time* reporter also commented that the simplicity of Conrad's cartoons allows readers to absorb them with one look. He observed that the cartoonist imparts his whole message in pictures; captions, if they exist at all, are brief. Another interviewer stated in *Target* that Conrad's "cartoons sound a single note—a trumpet blast that is over in a moment but that resonates in the mind." The writer attributed this instant comprehension to Conrad's ability to capture the very essence of his opinions. "The look of his cartoons reinforce . . . [his] directness—they're black and white with minimal shading, bold images cut into the pages," stated the *Target* critic. "Few cartoonists' work arrest the eye that scans America's grey editorial pages the way Paul Conrad's work does."

The *Time* writer, like others, also acknowledged the weighty editorial content of the cartoons, which Conrad has claimed as his final goal. Conrad contended in *University Magazine* that no substantial difference exists between editorial writing and editorial cartooning. He further explained in *Target* that the cartoonist, like the editorial writer, crusades against injustice and illustrates inequities. Thus, as he told Lebo, editorial cartoons should be more than mere illustrations of contemporary events. Rather, they should express an opinion, usually controversial, pictorially. Conrad commented that to be effective, "a cartoonist should get out of bed mad and stay mad." In a *Time* interview, he revealed that "the cartoonist's function is essentially a negative one, and the cartoon that advocates something usually says nothing."

Conrad stresses the importance of editorial content in his cartoons. He advises other cartoonists to have an issue and opinion on a situation firmly in mind before beginning to draw, asserting that "what a cartoonist has to do is try and take a story and capture the issues in a personal way." He explained further in the *Writer's Digest:* "I decide who's right and who's wrong, and go from there. But I can't just comment on an issue. I've got to take an editorial position. Too many cartoonists simply illustrate the news. Well, the readers *know* the news, and a cartoon that illustrates doesn't tell them a thing they don't already know. So, I formulate an opinion *and draw it.*" As he elaborated to Grecny: "God, I can't imagine waking up every morning and *not* stating an opinion. I'd go absolutely *bananas!*"

Grecny maintains that Conrad's opinions deeply impress his readers. The writer remarked that Conrad criticizes life- and liberty-threatening political pretensions—including greed, pride, and hypocrisy—while forcing Americans to reflect on these timely issues, either by inspiring them or enraging them. Grecny suggested that Americans "prepare a simple breakfast consisting of cereal, coffee, and Conrad. Think about it. At that time of the morning when most of us are still wiping the sleep from our eyes, words can be a bit hard to digest, especially opinions and things that need to be thought about. But to wake up to an opinion, deftly expressed, not in words, but in pictures is a pleasure, even a luxury. There are some mornings when he will make you smile, even laugh; at other times he will make you angry—if not at him, then at what is going on in the world. Still, he will always give you a thought for the day."

Some may view proof of Conrad's impact and success by his 1973 inclusion on Richard M. Nixon's "Enemies List," the president's roll of media figures critical of or threatening to his administration. Grecny recalled that Conrad was one of the nation's cartoonists "most occupied with toppling a presidency," and *Los Angeles Times* national news editor Ed Guthman observed that Conrad drew Nixon (whom the cartoonist once called "an abject mistake") as a dark-eyed, hunched, and secretive scoundrel. Conrad told Lebo that he "was ready to trade . . . Pulitzer Prizes for a place on the list," explaining, "I thought it would have been a complete waste of time to draw Nixon for two and a half years and not make the enemies list. I was elated, but also a little depressed that this sort of thing would go on."

BIOGRAPHICAL/CRITICAL SOURCES:

PERIODICALS

Los Angeles Times, November 26, 1987; October 24, 1988.
Newsweek, September 12, 1977.
Target, spring, 1983.
Time, June 13, 1960; April 30, 1984.
University Magazine, fall, 1983.
Writer's Digest, December, 1977.

*　　　*　　　*

CORBY, Dan
See CATHERALL, Arthur

*　　　*　　　*

CORNEBISE, Alfred E(mile) 1929-

PERSONAL: Surname is pronounced *Corn*-a-beeze; born May 3, 1929, in Brownfield, TX; son of Fred Marcel (a farmer) and Mattie Bell (a housewife; maiden name, Williams) Cornebise; married Jan Miller (a teacher and artist), August 9, 1957; children: Michael Wayne, Tanya Renee, Mark Alfred. *Education:* Wayland Baptist College (now University), B.A., 1955; Texas Technological College (now Texas Tech University), M.A., 1958; University of North Carolina at Chapel Hill, Ph.D., 1965; also attended University of Wyoming, 1959, and Oxford University, 1978. *Politics:* Democrat. *Religion:* Congregational.

ADDRESSES: Home—1815 24th Ave. Pl., Greeley, CO 80631. *Office*—Department of History, University of Northern Colorado, Greeley, CO 80631.

CAREER: Wayland Baptist College (now University), Plainview, TX, instructor in European history, 1959-60; Valdosta State College, Valdosta, GA, associate professor of modern European history, 1965-67; University of Northern Colorado, Greeley, assistant professor, 1967-71, associate professor, 1971-75, professor of modern European history, 1975—, chairman of department of history, 1984-86. *Military service:* U.S. Marine Corps, 1951-53; served in Korea; became sergeant. U.S. Naval Reserve, intelligence officer, 1958-68; became lieutenant.

MEMBER: German Studies Association, American Journalism Historians Association.

WRITINGS:

The Weimar in Crisis: Cuno's Germany and the Ruhr Occupation, University Press of America, 1977.
The Amaroc News: The Daily Newspaper of the American Forces in Germany, 1919-1923, Southern Illinois University Press, 1981.
Typhus and Doughboys: The American Polish Typhus Relief Expedition, 1919-1921, University of Delaware Press, 1982.
The Stars and Stripes: Doughboy Journalism in World War I, Greenwood Press, 1984.
War as Advertised: The Four Minute Men and America's Crusade, 1917-1918, American Philosophical Society, 1984.
(Editor) *Doughboy Doggerel: Verse of the American Expeditionary Force, 1918-1919,* Ohio University Press, 1985.
Art from the Trenches: America's Uniformed Artists in World War I, Texas A&M University Press, 1991.
(Editor) *War Diary of a Combat Artist: Captain Harry Everett Townsend,* University Press of Colorado, 1991.

Contributor to history and philosophy journals.

WORK IN PROGRESS: History of the American Military Press, for Greenwood Press.

SIDELIGHTS: Alfred E. Cornebise told *CA:* "It is my belief that the historian should be particularly interested in developing a clear, coherent narrative which tells the story of the past, rather than over-analyzing historical events. In addition, emphasis needs to be placed upon what the common people were doing when documentary evidence exists to illustrate this. Newspapers are good sources that can be turned to this end. My books, especially those on the U.S. Army newspapers, are intended to be examples of this approach to history. I've attempted, in these cases, to make the American doughboy of the World War I era 'come alive' as a historical character. I have been concerned with his general attitudes, his loves, hates, and what his daily life was like. Many of these things are revealed in the soldier newspapers that he read. It has also been my intent to write history that can be read, understood, and appreciated by the general reader, while maintaining the scholarly mode and apparatus for the benefit of academics.

"My first book was based on research in several German archives, including the Bundesarchiv in Coblenz and the Berlin Document Center in West Berlin. Additional research was done in the Public Record Office and the British Library in London. I have a competency in the German language and used this in connection with my researches. I have traveled worldwide, including such places as Korea, Japan, Mexico, the United Kingdom, Denmark, Belgium, the Netherlands, France, West Germany, East Germany, Finland, and the Soviet Union."

*　　*　　*

COSNER, Shaaron 1940-

PERSONAL: Born February 10, 1940, in Albuquerque, NM; daughter of Roy F. (a U.S. Air Force officer) and Louise (a housewife; maiden name, Brian) Bigelow; married Ron Cosner (a teacher), March 3, 1962 (divorced February, 1992); children: Bob, Vikki. *Education:* Arizona State University, B.A., 1965, M.A., 1982. *Religion:* Roman Catholic.

ADDRESSES: Home—2162 East Aspen Dr., Tempe, AZ 85282. *Office*—Corona del Sol High School, 1101 Knox Rd., Tempe, AZ 85284.

CAREER: Corona del Sol High School, Tempe, AZ, English teacher, 1982—; writer.

WRITINGS:

JUVENILES

American Windmills: Harnessers of Energy, McKay, 1978.
American Cowgirls: Yesterday and Today, McKay, 1979.
Masks around the World and How to Make Them, McKay, 1980.
How to Be Your Own Weather Forecaster, Messner, 1981.
The Light Bulb, Walker & Co., 1984.

The History of Paper, Carolrhoda, 1984.
Special Effects in Movies and Television, Messner, 1985.
Lunar Bases, F. Watts, 1990.
War Nurses, Walker & Co., 1990.
Dinosaur Dinners, F. Watts, 1991.
Underground Railroad, F. Watts, 1991.

Contributor of more than sixty articles to periodicals, including *Arizona, Arizona Highways, Americana, Mankind, Early American Life,* and *Antiques.*

SIDELIGHTS: Shaaron Cosner told *CA:* "I was the type of person who always did everyone's term papers in high school and college. Then I took a course at Arizona State University from Ken Donelson, an expert in children's literature. I wrote a paper on Nancy Drew, and he commented, 'This deserves publication.' Until then, it had never dawned on me that I could get paid for doing something I loved. I took a few courses at a local junior college and was soon on my way to becoming a paid writer. Some of the things I learned very quickly were not to expect undue attention from friends, family, and relatives, not to think because one piece sells you can give up your job and just write, and not to think that because one piece was not edited, the next piece will be perfect, too. It just isn't so.

"I have become a writer of science topics by accident. My first book was on windmills after I had done an article on them for a magazine. I sold it to the first person I sent it to, which, I soon learned, also doesn't happen very often. After that the topics that kept popping up all seemed to be somewhat scientific. I'm most fascinated by inventors. I think, like writers, they are very special people who are unappreciated.

"Since my father was in the Air Force, I spent my childhood traveling around the world. I went to elementary schools in the Philippines and Germany, and high school was spent in Vicenza, Italy. I think always being new in school gave me the skills I need now to get to know and evaluate people quickly in interviews, although I would much rather be in the library researching.

"I think the most important thing a writer can learn, besides the limitations of the job already mentioned, is what he or she does best. I know I am good at research and putting in layman's language some of the more difficult or confusing descriptions of scientific terms. Yet, people are always asking, 'Why don't you try fiction? That's where the money is.' I would love to try fiction and maybe someday when I'm really established I will, but right now I think I should stick with what I know I do best. Since I think in outlines and three-by-five cards, it would be very difficult to make the transition to creative make-believe."

CREWS, Clyde F. 1944-

PERSONAL: Born November 20, 1944, in Louisville, KY; son of Clyde S. (an electrician) and Nell (a secretary; maiden name, Graboske) Crews. *Education:* Bellarmine College, B.A., 1966; Fordham University, M.A., 1968, Ph.D., 1972. *Avocational interests:* Photography, baseball, regional history, pre-1950 films.

ADDRESSES: Office—Department of Theology, Bellarmine College, Newburg Rd., Louisville, KY 40205.

CAREER: Ordained Roman Catholic priest, 1973; Bellarmine College, Louisville, KY, member of theology department, 1973-84, professor of theology, 1984—, chairperson of department, 1977—, special assistant to president, 1980-84. Curator of Cathedral Museum of Louisville, 1975—. Member of board of trustees of Saint Meinrad College and School of Theology, 1978-85. Consultant to Leadership Louisville, 1980—. Co-founder of Louisville Historical League.

MEMBER: American Catholic Historical Association, Catholic Theological Society of America.

AWARDS, HONORS: Woodrow Wilson fellow, 1966-67; Danforth fellow, 1967-71.

WRITINGS:

Fundamental Things Apply: Reflecting on Christian Basics, Ave Maria Press, 1983.
English Catholic Modernism: Maude Petre's Way of Faith, University of Notre Dame Press, 1984.
Ultimate Questions: A Primer, Paulist Press, 1986.
An American Holy Land, Michael Glazier Press, 1987.
Seasons of the Spirit, Liturgical Press, 1992.

Contributor to periodicals, including *America, Christian Century, Commonweal, National Catholic Reporter,* and *Catholic Historical Review.*

WORK IN PROGRESS: A popular history of American Catholicism.

SIDELIGHTS: In *English Catholic Modernism: Maude Petre's Way of Faith,* Clyde F. Crews examines the life of Maude Petre, an English member of the Roman Catholic Modernist movement. Although Petre did not contribute new ideas to the movement, according to Crews, she actively spread the doctrine of other Modernists such as George Tyrrell, an Irish priest whose opinions caused his dismissal from the Society of Jesus and barred him from the Sacraments. Crews notes, however, that while others were excommunicated or alienated from the Church, Petre remained a devout Catholic, participating in public service efforts and working to reconcile traditional Catholicism with Modernity.

Crews told *CA:* "I see writing as a task: usually a pleasure to have done, almost never to do. It does offer entrees into new inner, outer and historical worlds. Occasionally it brings us to the rims, at least, of depth. The imaginative work of making the past—its personalities, conflicts, drives, and complexities—our contemporary: this I find is the special challenge of my own kind of teaching and writing."

BIOGRAPHICAL/CRITICAL SOURCES:

PERIODICALS

Times Literary Supplement, September 21, 1984.

*   *   *

CROSS, Gillian (Clare) 1945-

PERSONAL: Born December 24, 1945, in London, England; daughter of (James) Eric (a scientist and musician) and Joan (an English teacher; maiden name, Manton) Arnold; married Martin Cross (an examinations director), May 10, 1967; children: Jonathan George, Elizabeth Jane, Colman Anthony Richard, Katherine Clare. *Education:* Somerville College, Oxford, B.A. (with first class honors), 1969, M.A., 1972; University of Sussex, D.Phil., 1974.

ADDRESSES: Home—41 Essex Rd., Gravesend, Kent DA11 OSL, England.

CAREER: Writer. Worked previously as a teacher, an assistant to an old-style village baker, and an assistant to a member of Parliament.

MEMBER: Society of Authors.

WRITINGS:

JUVENILE FICTION

The Runaway, illustrated by Reginald Gray, Methuen, 1979.
The Iron Way, illustrated by Tony Morris, Oxford University Press, 1979.
Revolt at Ratcliffe's Rags, illustrated by Morris, Oxford University Press, 1980, published as *Strike at Ratcliffe's Rags,* Magnet, 1987.
Save Our School, illustrated by Gareth Floyd, Methuen, 1981.
A Whisper of Lace, Oxford University Press, 1981.
The Dark behind the Curtain, illustrated by David Parkins, Oxford University Press (Oxford), 1982, (New York), 1984.
The Demon Headmaster, illustrated by Gary Rees, Oxford University Press, 1982.
The Mintyglo Kid, illustrated by Floyd, Methuen, 1983.
Born of the Sun, illustrated by Mark Edwards, Oxford University Press, 1983, Holiday House, 1984.

On the Edge, Oxford University Press, 1984, Holiday House, 1985.

The Prime Minister's Brain, illustrated by Sally Burgess, Oxford University Press, 1985.

Swimathon!, illustrated by Floyd, Methuen, 1986.

Chartbreak, Oxford University Press, 1986, published in the United States as *Chartbreaker,* Holiday House, 1987.

Roscoe's Leap, Holiday House, 1987.

A Map of Nowhere, Oxford University Press, 1988, Holiday House, 1989.

Rescuing Gloria, Methuen, 1989.

Twin and Super-Twin, illustrated by Maureen Bradley, Holiday House, 1990.

Wolf, Oxford University Press, 1990, Holiday House, 1991.

Gobbo the Great, illustrated by Philippe Dupasquier, Methuen, 1991.

Rent-a-Genius, illustrated by Glenys Ambrus, Hamish Hamilton, 1991.

WORK IN PROGRESS: The Ghost From under the Ground, a short novel about the ghost of a dinosaur.

SIDELIGHTS: Gillian Cross once told *CA:* "When I was a child, for as far back as I can remember, there was always a great divide between the 'official' writing I did for school and the 'private' writing that I did for myself. At school, I was busy being a model student, studying English literature, French, history and Latin as my main subjects. Then I went to University to take an English degree and write a doctoral thesis. But in private, I scribbled. I remember having a tremendous lust for clean, blank sheets of paper. When I was fifteen that's what I asked everyone to give me for my birthday and, to this day, I find it difficult to pass a stationer's shop without going in and buying something. But I never finished anything I wrote. There was always the shadow of the other books—the great books that I studied at school—to remind me how bad my own writing was.

"I told stories as well. When my brother was small, I told him cowboy stories and when I had to travel to school on the train for half an hour every day I told my friends an endless serial story—it was very popular because *they* were the heroines. But it never occurred to me that I wanted to be a writer. I thought that everyone else wrote in secret, too, and I assumed that they all did it better. So I just scrawled my half-stories and my 'Chapter One's' and kept quiet about them.

"Then, when I was nineteen, things started to happen to me. Between school and University I worked as a volunteer in England, helping on a course for educationally-subnormal teenagers and teaching in a fairly poor part of London, quite different from the suburbs where I had always lived. I began to see that life was more varied and more demanding than I had realized. I married early, while I was still at University, and took a year off to have my first child. During that year, I worked for an old-style baker in a village outside Oxford, helping him to make the bread. I used this experience later on, to describe the Victorian village bakery in *The Iron Way.*

"What really made me into a writer was finishing my doctoral thesis. Suddenly, I was no longer a student. For the first time in my life I had lots of free time and no 'official' writing to do. And I was up to the knees in stories. I had two children by then, and I was always making up stories for them and making them small, illustrated books. I'd also helped to start a children's book group in Lewes, the small town where I was living by then. So I decided it was time I had a go at some proper writing. Thanks to my thesis I knew how to handle something long and, very tentatively, I began my first real book. It has never been published (quite rightly!) but by the time I'd finished it I was hooked and I went straight on to the next one. Four years later, when I had five finished books and a whole host of rejections slips, two of my books were accepted, simultaneously, by two different publishers.

"I have often asked myself why it took me so long to begin properly. Partly, I think, it was the effect of studying English literature. I enjoyed it immensely and learned a vast amount from it, but it was very intimidating. But I was also put off by sheer lack of time. Until I was nearly twenty-eight I was a student, and for most of my grownup life I'd been a student with small children. I could have written short stories—and that's where aspiring authors are often told to begin. I think it's very bad advice. Writing good short stories is a very special skill, and it's not one that interests me at all. I like to be absorbed in a *long* story. I like the fascinating contrast between the wide sweep of the structure and the small details, both of which affect each other.

"It's very important to me that the writing I do now is 'private' writing and not 'official' writing. Writing fiction is the one thing that anyone can do. The quality is not the crucial thing. The crucial thing is that you control it *yourself* and decide exactly what you want to do and how you want to do it. A sort of freedom.

"I like to write for children and young people because then I feel free to write about important things: love, death, moral decisions. I find a lot of adult fiction is cynical and despairing, concerned with illustrating the powerlessness and unimportance of ordinary people. I believe that ordinary people *are* important and that everyone has the power to influence his own life. I think the young know that too.

"I have done one or two other things since I began writing seriously. For a while I taught part time at a university and I spent some time as an assistant to a member of Parliament. But although I enjoyed these things, writing was my major activity." Cross recently added that with two young children again, "writing is still crucially important to me, although I have only twelve hours a week to devote to it. I don't think I'll ever like writing short stories, but I'm beginning to see all sorts of interesting possibilities in short *books,* for very young children."

BIOGRAPHICAL/CRITICAL SOURCES:

PERIODICALS

Times Literary Supplement, July 24, 1981; July 23, 1982; September 17, 1982; February 1, 1985; March 14, 1986; May 23, 1986; November 20, 1987; November 25, 1988.*

*   *   *

CROSS, Nigel   1942-

PERSONAL: Born June 4, 1942, in Bristol, England; son of Wilfred and Phyllis (Lewis) Cross; married Anita Lyn Clayburn, April 13, 1963; children: Natasha. *Education:* University of Bath, B.Sc., 1966; Victoria University of Manchester, M.Sc., 1967, Ph.D., 1974.

ADDRESSES: Office—Design Discipline, Open University, Walton Hall, Milton Keynes MK7 6AA, England.

CAREER: University of London, London, England, research assistant, 1967-68; University of Manchester Institute of Science and Technology, Manchester, England, lecturer in design technology, 1968-70; Open University, Milton Keynes, England, lecturer, 1970-75, senior lecturer in design, 1975-88, head of Design Discipline, 1981—, professor of design studies, 1988—. Visiting professor of design methodology, Delft University, Nederlands, 1990—. Design consultant to builders and developers in England and abroad.

MEMBER: Design Research Society (honorary general secretary, 1971-74, vice-chairman, 1977-79, chairman, 1979-82).

WRITINGS:

(Editor) *Design Participation,* Academy Editions, 1972.
(Editor with David Elliot and Robin Roy) *Man-Made Futures: Readings in Society, Technology, and Design,* Hutchinson, 1974.
Design and Technology, Open University Press, 1975.
(With Roy) *Design Methods Manual,* Open University Press, 1975.
The Automated Architect, Pion Ltd., 1977.
Methods Guide, Open University Press, 1978.

Home, Open University Press, 1979.
Developments in Design Methodology, Wiley, 1984.
Computer Aided Design, Open University Press, 1987.
Engineering Design Methods, Wiley, 1989.
Product Planning and the Design Brief, Open University Press, 1992.

SIDELIGHTS: Nigel Cross told *CA:* "My writing is academic, addressed principally to students, researchers, and other academics in the broad field of design. In particular, my Open University publications are teaching texts, intended to bring knowledge, skills, and awareness of design to a large, non-specialized audience.

"After studying architecture I became interested in new design techniques such as computer-aided design (CAD) and design methods. I became especially interested in adapting these techniques to promote the participation of users and laypeople generally in the design process, The Open University teaching context allows me to develop this interest with respect to a large, non-specialist audience."

*   *   *

CROWTHER, (Francis) Bosley   1905-1981

PERSONAL: Born July 13, 1905, in Lutherville, MD; died of heart failure, March 7, 1981, in Mount Kisco, NY; son of Francis Bosley (a merchant) and Eliza (Leisenring) Crowther; married Florence Ellinger Marks (a literary agent), January 20, 1933; children: F. Bosley III, John M., Jefferson H. *Education:* Princeton University, B.A., 1928. *Avocational interests:* Sailing, wood carving, gardening.

CAREER: New York Times, New York City, general reporter and rewrite man, 1928-32, assistant drama editor, 1932-37, assistant screen editor, 1937-40, screen editor and film critic, 1940-68; Columbia Pictures Industries, Inc., New York City, creative consultant, 1968-73; independent consultant and writer, 1973-81. Lecturer.

MEMBER: New York Film Critics (chairman, 1944, 1951-67), Century Club (New York City).

AWARDS, HONORS: New York Times intercollegiate current events winner, 1928; Screen Directors Guild of America award for film criticism, 1953; New York Film Critics honorary special award, 1968.

WRITINGS:

(With William Du Bois) *East of the Sun* (three-act play), first produced in Philadelphia at the Broad Street Theatre, 1935.
(Contributor) Jack Goodman, editor, *While You Were Gone,* Simon & Schuster, 1946.

The Lion's Share: The Story of an Entertainment Empire, Dutton, 1957.
Hollywood Rajah: The Life and Times of Louis B. Mayer, Holt, 1960.
Movies and Censorship, Public Affairs Pamphlets, 1962.
The Great Films: Fifty Golden Years of Motion Pictures, Putnam, 1967.
Vintage Films, Putnam, 1977.
Reruns: Fifty Memorable Films, Putnam, 1978.

Also author of play *Royal Stuff.*

SIDELIGHTS: "In an era when television was growing up and movies were still the major cultural force in American life," wrote Robert D. McFadden of the *New York Times,* "[Bosley] Crowther was perhaps the most influential commentator in the country on the art and industry of motion pictures." Although films with social content, like *Citizen Kane, The Grapes of Wrath* and *Gone with the Wind* were his favorites, Crowther defended such lightweight films as *Gigi* and *Ben-Hur* as well. In the 1950s, when Senator Joseph McCarthy led attacks on the Hollywood film industry, Crowther was a strong opponent, speaking out against government censorship. In the 1960s, when films like *Bonnie and Clyde* brought an unprecedented level of violence to the screen, Crowther attacked what he saw as dangerous sensationalism. During his long tenure as *New York Times* film critic, Crowther also championed foreign films. His kind words about film directors Ingmar Bergman and Federico Fellini, among others, helped establish their reputations in the United States.

"There is, I am told, a vagrant notion that all we members of the screen department do is go to movies and sit around drinking in plush cafes with voluptuous Hollywood stars," Crowther once commented. "To be sure, we do go to movies. But if any invidious outsider has the notion that this is all we do, he has another notion coming." In fact, Crowther viewed three or four films a week. He wrote some 200 film reviews a year, about half the total printed by the *New York Times,* and wrote articles for the Sunday edition as well.

Crowther's book *The Lion's Share: The Story of an Entertainment Empire* traces the history of the Metro-Goldwyn-Mayer film studio. In doing so, it also provides a history of the motion pictures from the early days of peep-shows to the sweeping historical epics of its heyday. *Hollywood Rajah: The Life and Times of Louis B. Mayer* focuses on the eccentric head of MGM.

In *The Great Films: Fifty Golden Years of Motion Pictures* Crowther chooses what he considers to be the fifty "breakthrough" films of motion picture history. Included on the list are *The Birth of a Nation, King Kong,* and *Blow-Up.* Reviewing the book in the *New York Times Book Review,* John Grierson stated: "There is on the face of it much to

enjoy in a many-faceted book of this kind, and much to enjoy along the way in its author's warm, liberal and wide-ranging testament. His 50 films represent a classical choice. Give or take half a dozen, few serious film observers will greatly demur."

Crowther once told *CA:* "Throughout my career as a film critic, I was a persistent opponent of film censorship and thus an ardent advocate of freedom of the screen, and I strongly urged and applauded the distribution of worthy foreign-language films in the United States." In addition, Crowther remarked, "I openly condemned the attempted restraints on filmmakers by the congressional committees, and I early deplored excessive violence in films."

BIOGRAPHICAL/CRITICAL SOURCES:

BOOKS

Beaver, Frank E., editor, *Bosley Crowther: Social Critic of the Film,* University of Michigan Press, 1970.

PERIODICALS

Best Sellers, December 1, 1967, p. 357; May, 1977, p. 44.
Film Quarterly, fall, 1968, p. 79.
Films in Review, January, 1968.
New York Times, November 25, 1967, p. 37.
New York Times Book Review, February 6, 1977, p. 8.
Saturday Review, April 6, 1957.
Time, December 1, 1967.
Wall Street Journal, December 4, 1967, p. 20.

OBITUARIES:

PERIODICALS

Chicago Tribune, March 9, 1981, Section 5, p. 9.
Newsweek, March 16, 1981.
New York Times, March 8, 1981, p. 36.
Time, March 23, 1981, p. 61.
Washington Post, March 9, 1981.*

*   *   *

CUPPLEDITCH, David 1946-

PERSONAL: Born January 2, 1946, in Louth, England; son of George Alfred and Mary Barton (Hall) Cuppleditch; married Sylvia Lynn Phillips (a nurse), May 7, 1981. *Education:* Attended Ruskin School of Drawing and Fine Art, Oxford.

ADDRESSES: Home—7, Horncastle Rd., Louth, Lincolnshire LN11 9LB, England.

CAREER: London Sketch Club, London, England, secretary, 1974-76; writer and artist, 1976—.

WRITINGS:

The London Sketch Club, Dilke Press, 1978.
The John Hassall Lifestyle, Dilke Press, 1979.
Phil May: The Artist and His Wit, Fortune Press, 1981.
(Contributor) William Feaver, editor, *Masters of Caricature,* Weidenfeld & Nicolson, 1981.
Louth in Old Picture Postcards, European Library, 1983.
Lincoln in Old Picture Postcards, European Library, 1984.
(Author of introduction) Robert Machray, *The Night Side of London,* illustrations by Tom Browne, Paul Harris, 1984.
(Author of introduction) R. N. Benton, *Louth in Early Days,* Skilton, 1985.
Mablethorpe in Old Picture Postcards, European Library, 1985.
Louth in Old Picture Postcards, Volume 2, European Library, 1986.
Joseph Willey: A Victorian Lincolnshire Photographer, Skilton, 1987.
H. L. Howe: A Twentieth-Century Louth Photographer, Dilke Press, 1988.
(Author of introduction) Andrew Ware, *Louth Grammar School,* Skilton, 1989.
Around Louth in Old Photographs, Alan Sutton, 1989.
(Author of introduction) John Lill, *Louth Playgoers: The First Sixty Years,* Dilke Press, 1992.

Contributor of articles and reviews to magazines, including *Artist.*

*   *   *

CYLWICKI, Albert 1932-

PERSONAL: Surname is pronounced Sill-*wick*-ee; born June 20, 1932, in Detroit, MI; son of Vincent J. (an automobile factory foreman) and Victoria (a housewife; maiden name, Buszek) Cylwicki. *Education:* Assumption University, Windsor, Ontario, B.Sc., 1955; University of St. Michael's College, Toronto, Ontario, S.T.B., 1961; University of Detroit, M.A.T.M., 1964. *Avocational interests:* Jogging, golf, writing.

ADDRESSES: Home—402 Augustine St., Rochester, NY 14613. *Office*—Aquinas Institute, 1127 Dewey Ave., Rochester, NY 14613.

CAREER: Entered Congregation of St. Basil (Basilians), 1950, ordained Roman Catholic priest, 1960; Catholic Central High School, Detroit, MI, teacher of mathematics and theology, 1955-56, 1957-58; St. Michael's College School, Toronto, Ontario, teacher of science, 1960-61; Aquinas Institute, Rochester, NY, teacher of mathematics, science, and theology, 1961-63; University of St. Michael's College, Toronto, instructor in mathematics,

1964-66; Andrean High School, Merrillville, IN, teacher of mathematics and theology, 1966-72, 1973-77, chairman of department of mathematics, 1973-76; St. Thomas High School, Houston, TX, teacher of mathematics and theology, 1977-81, chairman of department of mathematics, 1977-80; Catholic Central High School, Detroit, teacher of mathematics and theology, 1981-86; Aquinas Institute, Rochester, teacher of mathematics, 1987-92.

MEMBER: National Council of Teachers of Mathematics (life member).

WRITINGS:

If Today You Hear His Voice, Alba House, 1981.
His Word Resounds, Alba House, 1988.

Contributor to *Our Sunday Visitor, Homiletic Pastoral Review, My Daily Visitor,* and *Pulpit Resource.*

WORK IN PROGRESS: A book of daily reflections on the Scripture.

SIDELIGHTS: Albert Cylwicki told *CA: "If Today You Hear His Voice* is a collection of essays that relates Scripture to everyday life, with examples from movies and television, newspapers and books, and the lives of entertainers and other public figures. I compiled the essays at the encouragement of people who heard me preach or had read some of the things I wrote. The book was published as a preaching aid for other priests, but the flowing text and popular style have led critics to recommend it to the general reader as well.

"An example would be the essay using the movie 'Lawrence of Arabia.' In the film there is an unforgettable scene in which Colonel Lawrence and a company of Arabs are traveling across the desert in a sandstorm under a scorching sun. When it is discovered that one of their companions, Jasmin, has disappeared, Lawrence risks leaving the group to go back by himself in search of Jasmin. Lawrence finds Jasmin—blind from the sand, delirious from the sun, and dying from thirst. When Lawrence brings Jasmin back alive, the amazed Arabs exclaim: 'Here is Jasmin, not worth a half crown, but saved at his own risk by Lawrence, our Lord.'

"This episode gives us some insight about what Jesus has done for us. For, as St. Paul writes in Romans 5:6-11, 'Christ died for us godless men. It is rare that anyone should lay down his life for a just man, though it is barely possible that for a good man someone may have the courage to die. It is precisely in this that God proves his love for us: that while we were still sinners, Christ died for us.'

"Through examples like the above, I try to attune readers' ears to hear God's voice in our everyday experiences of reading books and newspapers, viewing films, and sharing in people's lives. It is a book of stories, not abstractions. It searches the Scriptures, without getting too technical."

D

DALE, (Mary) Alzina Stone 1931-

PERSONAL: Born February 23, 1931, in Chicago, IL; daughter of Raleigh Webster (a professor of economics) and Ursula (a professor of economics; maiden name, Batchelder) Stone; married Charles Herrick Dale (a manager and advisory consultant), December 26, 1956; children: Elizabeth, Alexander, Kenneth. *Education:* Swarthmore College, B.A. (with high honors), 1952; University of Chicago, M.A., 1957, postgraduate study, 1963, 1968. *Politics:* Republican. *Religion:* Episcopalian.

ADDRESSES: Home and office—5548 South Kenwood Ave., Chicago, IL 60637.

CAREER: Free-lance editor and writer, 1975-82, clients included Midway Editorial Research, Science Research Associates, and *American Journal of Sociology;* free-lance writer and lecturer, 1978—; Illinois Citizens for Better Care, Chicago, in charge of public relations, development, and fund-raising, 1982-83. Consultant to and leader of workshops on researching and writing, including Illinois Gifted Program Writing Workshops, 1980-89, Mystery Writers of America Midwest Workshops on Research and Writing Techniques, 1983, 1985, 1986, 1992, and Newberry Library Lyceum courses, 1989-92. Officer of local organizations, including Illinois Parent-Teacher Association and Cub Scouts. *Urban Gateways* artist in residence, 1984—, consultant for High School Humanities Project, 1989-90. Conference participant and invited speaker at colleges and universities.

MEMBER: Mystery Writers of America, Authors Guild, Authors League of America, British Crime Writers Association, Children's Reading Roundtable, Sayers Society, C. S. Lewis Society, Chesterton Society, Conference of Christianity and Literature, Society of Midwest Authors, Phi Beta Kappa.

AWARDS, HONORS: Quality of Design and Production Award, Catholic Book Awards, 1986, for *The Art of G. K. Chesterton;* finalist, Crime Writers' Association Dagger Award and MRA Macavity Award, both for *Mystery Readers Walking Guide: England.*

WRITINGS:

Maker and Craftsman: The Story of Dorothy L. Sayers, Eerdmans, 1978, updated version, Harold Shaw, 1992.

(Contributor) Margaret P. Hannay, editor, *As Her Whimsey Took Her: Critical Essays on the Work of Dorothy L. Sayers,* Kent State University Press, 1979.

The Outline of Sanity: A Life of G. K. Chesterton, Eerdmans, 1983.

(Editor and author of introduction) Dorothy L. Sayers, *Love All* [and] *Busman's Honeymoon* (plays), Kent State University Press, 1984.

The Art of G. K. Chesterton, Loyola University Press, 1985.

(With Barbara Sloan Hendershott) *Mystery Readers Walking Guide: London,* Passport Press, 1986.

(Coauthor) *Mystery Readers Walking Guide: England,* Passport Press, 1988.

T. S. Eliot, the Philosopher Poet, Harold Shaw, 1988.

(Editor) *Collected Works of G. K. Chesterton,* Volume 15, Ignatius, 1989.

Mystery Readers Walking Guide: New York, Passport, 1992.

(Editor) *Dorothy L. Sayers Centennial Book,* Walker & Co., 1992.

Also contributor to *A Taste of the Pineapple,* Bowling Green University Press, 1988, and *The Riddle of Joy,* Eerdmans, 1989. Contributor of articles and book reviews to periodicals, including *Anglican Theological Review, Books and Religion, Chicago Sun-Times, Chicago Tribune,*

Christianity Today, Episcopalian, Hyde Park Herald, Journal of Medievalism, Living Church, and *Sayers Review.*

SIDELIGHTS: Alzina Stone Dale once told *CA:* "I began as a history major with an interest in writing historicals. . . . I am a born tourist, especially in places of historical interest." These interests, along with a love of mystery stories, led to her work as coauthor of *Mystery Readers Walking Guide: London* and *Mystery Readers Walking Guide: England,* which highlight locations featured in more than one hundred mystery novels. In a review of the London guide, the *Chicago Tribune*'s Harriet Choice noted that readers can retrace the steps of Sherlock Holmes and other famous sleuths by following eleven different walks and sixteen maps. "The very details that so delight fans of this genre are the heart and soul of *Mystery Reader's Walking Guide: London,*" Choice declared.

BIOGRAPHICAL/CRITICAL SOURCES:

PERIODICALS

Armchair Detective, winter, 1991; fall, 1992.
Chicago Tribune, November 2, 1986.
Chicago Tribune Book World, January 9, 1983.
Globe and Mail (Toronto), December 24, 1983.
Time, February 14, 1983.
Times Literary Supplement, June 3, 1983.
Washington Post Book World, February 27, 1983.

*   *   *

DARBY, Michael   1944-

PERSONAL: Born September 2, 1944, in Northampton, England; son of Arthur Douglas (a company director) and Ilene Doris (a housewife; maiden name, Eatwell) Darby; married Elisabeth Done (a lecturer). *Education:* University of Reading, Ph.D., 1974. *Avocational interests:* Entomology.

ADDRESSES: Office—Carroll Foundation, Carroll House, 2-6 Catherine Pl., London SW1E 6HF, England.

CAREER: Victoria and Albert Museum, London, England, 1964-71, began as museum assistant, became senior museum assistant in textile department, research assistant in prints and drawings department, 1971-76, director of museum's exhibition program, 1976-83, deputy director of museum, 1983-88; Carroll Foundation, London, surveyor general, 1989—. Member of Council of the National Trust.

MEMBER: Royal Society of the Arts, Royal Entomological Society, Royal Geographical Society.

WRITINGS:

(With John Physick) *Marble Halls,* Victoria and Albert Museum, 1973.
Early Railway Prints, Victoria and Albert Museum, 1974.
The Islamic Perspective: An Aspect of British Architecture and Design in the Nineteenth Century, World of Islam Festival Trust, 1983.
British Art in the Victoria and Albert Museum, Philip Wilson, 1983.
(With Anthony Burton, John Ayers, and Susan Haskins) *The Victoria and Albert Museum: England's Treasury of the World's Finest Decorative Arts,* Viking, 1983.
John Pollard Seddon, Victoria and Albert Museum, 1989.

Author of quarterly publication *Biographical Dictionary of British Coleopterists,* 1981—. Contributor to periodicals, including *Country Life, Saturday Book, Discovering Antiques,* and *Observer.*

WORK IN PROGRESS: A work on architect and design theoretician Owen Jones (1809-1874); research on phylogeny of Ptiliidae, the smallest known beetles.

SIDELIGHTS: Michael Darby told *CA:* "I have long found it difficult to come to terms with the idea of art historical research as a profession, but have enjoyed it in my spare time. For this reason I have increasingly thrown myself into arts administration and to my entomological research. Working on one has helped to throw light on the other, and vice versa, so that comparative studies of art and natural science, particularly in the nineteenth century, interest me more and more."

*   *   *

DARLING, Lois MacIntyre   1917-1989

PERSONAL: Maiden name originally spelled McIntyre; born August 15, 1917, in New York, NY; died of leukemia, December 19, 1989; daughter of Malcolm (a mechanical engineer) and Grace (Hamilton) McIntyre; married Louis Darling, Jr. (a writer and illustrator), June 3, 1946 (died January 21, 1970). *Education:* Attended Grand Central School of Art, 1935-40, and Columbia University, 1947-51; studied privately with artists Frank Reilly and Frank V. DuMond, 1938-41. *Avocational interests:* Sailing, walking.

ADDRESSES: Home—c/o Julie Zickefoose, Box 410, Hadlynne, CT 06439.

CAREER: Riverside Yacht Club, Riverside, CT, sailing instructor and head of junior program, 1940-41; Boucher Manufacturing Co., New York City, maker of ship models for war effort, 1942-43; American Museum of Natural History, New York City, staff artist, 1951-53; writer and illustrator, 1953—. Treasurer, Connecticut Conservationists, Inc., 1955-56. *Military service:* U.S. Navy, WAVES, 1943-45.

MEMBER: American Institute of Biological Sciences, Nature Conservancy, National Audubon Society, Authors Guild, Society of Illustrators, Thames Science Center, Valley Shore Audubon Society, Westport Audubon Society (conservation chairman, 1953-60), Catboat Association.

AWARDS, HONORS: National woman's sailing championship, 1941.

WRITINGS:

AUTHOR AND ILLUSTRATOR WITH HUSBAND, LOUIS DARLING, JR.

Before and after Dinosaurs, Morrow, 1959.
Sixty Million Years of Horses, Morrow, 1960.
The Science of Life, World Publishing, 1961.
Bird, Houghton, 1962.
Turtles, Morrow, 1962.
Coral Reefs, World Publishing, 1963.
The Sea Serpents around Us, Little, Brown, 1965.
General Ecology, Morrow, 1967.
A Place in the Sun: Ecology and the Living World, Morrow, 1968.
Worms, Morrow, 1972.

ILLUSTRATOR

Llewellyn Howland, *Sou' West and by West,* Harvard University Press, 1948.
Edwin H. Colbert, *Evolution of the Vertebrates,* Wiley, 1955.
(With L. Darling, Jr.) Rachel Carson, *Silent Spring,* Houghton, 1962.
(With L. Darling, Jr.) Roger Tory Peterson, *Birds,* Life Nature Library, 1963.
(With L. Darling, Jr.) Niko Tinbergen, *Animal Behavior,* Life Nature Library, 1965.
(With L. Darling, Jr.) Maurice Brooks, *The Appalachians,* Houghton, 1965.
Corey Ford, *Where the Sea Breaks Its Back,* Little, Brown, 1966.

OTHER

Also author and illustrator of *H.M.S. Beagle: Further Research, or Twenty Years a-Beagling,* 1977, and *The Mariner's Mirror,* 1978.

Lois Darling's papers are housed in permanent collections at the Beinecke Library, Yale University; and at the Kerlan Collection, University of Minnesota.

SIDELIGHTS: For more information on Lois and Louis Darling, please see entry on Louis Darling.

BIOGRAPHICAL/CRITICAL SOURCES:

BOOKS

More Junior Authors, edited by Muriel Fuller, Wilson, 1963.

*　　　*　　　*

DARLING, Louis, Jr.　1916-1970

PERSONAL: Born April 26, 1916, in Stamford, CT; died of cancer, January 21, 1970, in Norwich, CT; son of Louis and Llanceley (Lockwood) Darling; married Lois MacIntyre (a writer and illustrator), June 3, 1946. *Education:* Attended Grand Central School of Art, 1936-37; studied privately with artists Frank V. DuMond and Frank Reilly, 1938-40. *Politics:* Democrat.

ADDRESSES: Home—c/o Julie Zickefoose, Box 410, Hadlynne, CT 06439.

CAREER: Writer and illustrator. Worked as a commercial artist. *Military service:* U.S. Army Air Forces, 1942-45; became staff sergeant.

MEMBER: American Association for the Advancement of Science, American Ornithological Society, National Audubon Society, Authors Guild of Authors League of America, Ecological Society of America, Nature Conservancy, Animal Behavior Society, Catboat Association, Coffee House Club (New York).

AWARDS, HONORS: John Burroughs Medal, 1966, for *The Gull's Way.*

WRITINGS:

AUTHOR AND ILLUSTRATOR WITH WIFE, LOIS MACINTYRE DARLING

Before and after Dinosaurs, Morrow, 1959.
Sixty Million Years of Horses, Morrow, 1960.
The Science of Life, World Publishing, 1961.
Turtles, Morrow, 1962.
Bird, Houghton, 1962.
Coral Reefs, World Publishing, 1963.
The Sea Serpents around Us, Little, Brown, 1965.
General Ecology, Morrow, 1967.
A Place in the Sun: Ecology and the Living World, Morrow, 1968.
Worms, Morrow, 1972.

SELF-ILLUSTRATED

Greenhead, Morrow, 1954.
Chickens, Morrow, 1955.
Seals and Walruses, Morrow, 1955.
Penguins, Morrow, 1956.
Kangaroos and Other Animals with Pockets, Morrow, 1958.

The Gull's Way, Morrow, 1965.

ILLUSTRATOR

Margaret E. Bell, *Watch for a Tall White Sail,* Morrow, 1948.

Elizabeth Howard, *North Winds Blow Free,* Morrow, 1949.

Ruth Dudley, *Hank and the Kitten,* Morrow, 1949.

Beverly Cleary, *Henry Huggins,* Morrow, 1950.

E. Howard, *Peddler's Girl,* Morrow, 1951.

Jerrold Beim, *Swimming Hole,* Morrow, 1951.

B. Cleary, *Ellen Tebbits,* Morrow, 1951.

B. Cleary, *Henry and Beezus,* Morrow, 1952.

J. Beim, *Country Garage,* Morrow, 1952.

B. Cleary, *Otis Spofford,* Morrow, 1953.

J. Beim, *Erick on the Desert,* Morrow, 1953.

Carl L. Biemiller, *Magic Ball from Mars,* Morrow, 1953.

B. Cleary, *Henry and Ribsy,* Morrow, 1954.

J. Beim, *Shoeshine Boy,* Morrow, 1954.

B. Cleary, *Beezus and Ramona,* Morrow, 1955.

J. Beim, *Country School,* Morrow, 1955.

J. Beim, *Thin Ice,* Morrow, 1956.

Delia Goetz, *Deserts,* Morrow, 1956.

Oliver Butterworth, *The Enormous Egg,* Little, Brown, 1956.

B. Cleary, *Henry and the Paper Route,* Morrow, 1957.

J. Beim, *Time for Gym,* Morrow, 1957.

D. Goetz, *Tropical Rain Forests,* Morrow, 1957.

Eleanor Cameron, *Mister Bass's Planetoid,* Little, Brown, 1958.

D. Goetz, *Arctic Tundra,* Morrow, 1958.

Lucy Gallup, *Independent Bluebird,* Morrow, 1959.

D. Goetz, *Grasslands,* Morrow, 1959.

Alberta W. Constant, *Miss Charity Comes to Stay,* Crowell, 1959.

Robert M. McClung, *Shag, Last of the Plains Buffalo,* Morrow, 1960.

D. Goetz, *Swamps,* Morrow, 1961.

D. Goetz, *Mountains,* Morrow, 1962.

(With L. M. Darling) Rachel Carson, *Silent Spring,* Houghton, 1962.

B. Cleary, *Henry and the Clubhouse,* Morrow, 1962.

(With L. M. Darling) Roger Tory Peterson, *Birds,* Life Nature Library, 1963.

B. Cleary, *Ribsy,* Morrow, 1964.

D. Goetz, *Islands of the Ocean,* Morrow, 1964.

B. Cleary, *Mouse and the Motorcycle,* Morrow, 1965.

(With L. M. Darling) Niko Tinbergen, *Animal Behavior,* Life Nature Library, 1965.

(With L. M. Darling) Maurice Brooks, *The Appalachians,* Houghton, 1965.

B. Cleary, *Ramona the Pest,* Morrow, 1968.

B. Cleary, *Runaway Ralph,* Morrow, 1970.

SIDELIGHTS: With his wife, Lois MacIntyre Darling, Louis Darling, Jr. wrote and illustrated a number of books that introduced young readers to the natural sciences. Avid conservationists, the Darlings continually stressed the importance of understanding how individual actions affected the environment. Both Darlings had backgrounds in the sciences; they used this knowledge when writing books such as *Worms,* which tried to show that even the smallest of creatures was useful and, in many ways, beautiful. The Darlings's best-known work includes illustrations for Roger Tory Peterson's reference book, *Birds,* and art for Rachel Carson's landmark environmental treatise, *Silent Spring.*

BIOGRAPHICAL/CRITICAL SOURCES:

BOOKS

More Junior Authors, edited by Muriel Fuller, Wilson, 1963, pp. 60-62.

PERIODICALS

New York Herald Tribune, April 4, 1966.

*   *   *

DAVIDSON, Michael
See RORVIK, David M(ichael)

*   *   *

DEVINE, (Mary) Elizabeth 1938-

PERSONAL: Born August 12, 1938, in Evanston, IL; daughter of William P. (an engineer) and Helen (a homemaker; maiden name, Sullivan) Devine. *Education:* Loyola University of Chicago, A.B., 1960, Ph.D., 1964. *Politics:* Democrat. *Religion:* Agnostic.

ADDRESSES: Home—28 Village St., Marblehead, MA 01945. *Office*—Department of English, Salem State College, Salem, MA 01970.

CAREER: Michigan State University, East Lansing, assistant professor of English, 1964-69; Salem State College, Salem, MA, associate professor, 1969-76, professor of English, 1976—. St. James Press, business editor, 1983-84.

MEMBER: Modern Language Association of America, American Association of University Professors (president, 1971-75).

WRITINGS:

(Editor with Carl J. Stratman and David G. Spencer) *Restoration and Eighteenth-Century Theatre Research: A*

Bibliography of Criticism, 1900-1968, Southern Illinois University Press, 1971.

Appearances: A Complete Guide to Cosmetic Surgery, Piatkus Books, 1982.

(With Nancy L. Braganti) *The Travelers' Guide to European Customs and Manners,* Meadowbrook Press, 1984, revised edition published as *European Customs and Manners,* 1992.

(Editor) *The Annual Obituary, 1983,* St. James Press, 1984.

(With Braganti) *The Travelers' Guide to Asian Customs and Manners,* St. Martin's, 1986.

(With Braganti) *The Travelers' Guide to Latin American Customs and Manners,* St. Martin's, 1989.

(With Braganti) *The Travelers' Guide to Middle Eastern and North African Customs and Manners,* St. Martin's, 1991.

WORK IN PROGRESS: The Black Sox: After the Scandal, with Philip C. Hockins.

SIDELIGHTS: Elizabeth Devine told *CA:* "My first book, *Appearances: A Complete Guide to Cosmetic Surgery,* was a complete fluke. I had shown a publisher a proposal for a travel book; he didn't want that book but said that the proposal showed that I have good research skills. He then asked if I would like to write a book on cosmetic surgery. Deciding that one who is new at free-lance writing does not turn down such a proposition, I said yes. I spent the better part of a year researching and writing the book. When I started, I was completely uninterested in cosmetic surgery. I remain so. Since the book had very positive reviews, the experience proved that with enough perseverance, one can write about anything.

"The book about European customs and manners was really a labor of love. I had lived in England and France for extended periods and had visited about half the countries about which Nancy Braganti and I wrote. Since one of the things I find most interesting is observing how people behave in their ordinary, daily activities, I really enjoyed writing *The Travelers' Guide to European Customs and Manners.*

"Writing about Asia was even more fascinating, because customs are so utterly different from those in Europe and America. The French shake hands *constantly;* the Japanese rarely do and resent being touched by other people.

"My greatest pleasure in writing—and in traveling—is letting my curiosity take over and following where it leads."

DILLENBERGER, John 1918-

PERSONAL: Born July 11, 1918, in St. Louis, MO; son of Charles and Bertha (Hoffman) Dillenberger; children: Eric, Paul. *Education:* Elmhurst College, B.A., 1940; Union Theological Seminary, B.D., 1943; Columbia University, Ph.D., 1948.

ADDRESSES: Home—322 Hanover Ave. #201, Oakland, CA 94606.

CAREER: Ordained minister, United Church of Christ, 1943; Union Theological Seminary, New York City, tutor, 1947-48; Princeton University, Princeton, NJ, instructor, 1948-49; Columbia University, New York City, 1949-54, began as assistant professor, became associate professor; Harvard University, Divinity School, Cambridge, MA, associate professor, 1954-57, Parkman Professor of Theology, 1957-58; Drew University, Madison, NJ, professor, 1958-62; San Francisco Theological Seminary, San Francisco, CA, professor and dean of graduate studies, 1962-64; Graduate Theological Union, Berkeley, CA, professor, dean, and president, 1964-78, professor emeritus, 1983—; Hartford Seminary, Hartford, CT, professor and president, 1978-83.

MEMBER: Society for Values in Higher Education.

AWARDS, HONORS: D.D., University of Vermont, 1957, and Elmhurst College, 1959; S.T.D., Church Divinity School of the Pacific, 1965; L.H.D., University of San Francisco, 1966.

WRITINGS:

God Hidden and Revealed, Muhlenberg, 1953.

(With Claude Welch) *Protestant Christianity: Interpreted through Its Development,* Scribner, 1954, revised and enlarged edition, Macmillan, 1987.

Protestant Thought and Natural Science, Doubleday, 1960.

(Editor) *Martin Luther: Selections from His Writings,* Doubleday/Anchor, 1961.

Contours of Faith, Abingdon, 1969.

(Editor) *John Calvin: Selections from His Writings,* Doubleday/Anchor, 1971.

Benjamin West: The Context of His Life's Work, Trinity University Press, 1977.

Perceptions of the Spirit in Twentieth-Century American Art, [Indianapolis], 1977.

The Visual Arts and Christianity in America, Scholars Press, 1984, revised and enlarged edition, Crossroad, 1988.

A Theology of Artistic Sensibilities, Crossroad, 1986.

(Editor) Paul Tillich, *On the Visual Arts and Architecture,* Crossroad, 1987.

Contributor to books, including *The Old Testament and Christian Faith,* edited by Anderson, Harper, 1963; *The New Hermeneutic,* edited by Cobb and Robinson, Harper, 1964; *D-Days at Dayton,* edited by Jerry R. Tompkins, Louisiana State University Press, 1965; and *Humanities, Religion, and the Arts Tomorrow,* Holt, 1972.

*   *   *

DILLON, Eilis 1920-

PERSONAL: Given name is pronounced El-*eesh;* born March 7, 1920, in Galway, Ireland; daughter of Thomas (a university professor) and Geraldine (Plunkett) Dillon; married Cormac O'Cuilleanain (a university professor), March 28, 1940 (died, 1970); married Vivian Mercier (a professor and critic), April 5, 1974 (died, 1989); children: (first marriage) Eilean, Maire (died, 1990), Cormac. *Education:* Educated in Ireland. *Politics:* Irish Nationalist. *Religion:* Roman Catholic. *Avocational interests:* Music, travel, the theatre.

ADDRESSES: Home—7 Templemore Ave., Rathgar, Dublin 6, Ireland. *Agent*—Georges Borchardt, Inc., 136 East 57th St., New York, NY 10022; and David Bolt Associates, 12 Heath Dr., Send, Surrey, GU23 7EP England.

CAREER: Writer. Lecturer on creative writing, Trinity College, Dublin University, 1971-72, and University College, Dublin, 1988; lecturer at American universities and colleges on three tours, speaking on writing for children and Anglo-Irish literature, especially poetry.

MEMBER: Societa Dante Alighieri (Cork), Royal Society of Literature (fellow), Irish Writers Center (executive board member), Irish Writers Union (chairperson), Irish Children's Book Trust (chairperson), Irish Copyright Collection Agency (secretary).

AWARDS, HONORS: New York Herald Tribune Children's Spring Book Festival Honorable Mention citations, 1960, for *The Singing Cave,* 1964, for *The Coriander,* and 1970, for *A Herd of Deer;* German Juvenile Book Prize Honor List citation, 1968, for *A Family of Foxes;* Notable Book citation, American Library Association, and Lewis Carroll Shelf Award, both 1970, both for *A Herd of Deer;* Irish Book of the Year Award, 1991, for *The Island of Ghosts;* D.Litt., National University of Ireland, 1992.

WRITINGS:

CHILDREN'S FICTION

Midsummer Magic, illustrated by Stuart Tresilian, Macmillan, 1949.

The Lost Island, illustrated by Richard Kennedy, Faber & Faber, 1952, Funk, 1954.

The San Sebastian, illustrated by Kennedy, Faber & Faber, 1953, Funk, 1954.

The House on the Shore, illustrated by Kennedy, Faber & Faber, 1955, Funk, 1956.

The Wild Little House, illustrated by V. H. Drummond, Faber & Faber, 1955.

The Island of Horses, illustrated by Kennedy, Faber & Faber, 1956, Funk, 1957.

Plover Hill, illustrated by Prudence Seward, Hamish Hamilton, 1957.

Aunt Bedelia's Cats, illustrated by Christopher Brooker, Hamish Hamilton, 1958.

The Singing Cave, illustrated by Kennedy, Faber & Faber, 1959, Funk, 1960.

The Fort of Gold, illustrated by Kennedy, Faber & Faber, 1961, Funk, 1962.

King Big-Ears, illustrated by Kveta Vanecek, Faber & Faber, 1961, Norton, 1963.

A Pony and a Trap, illustrated by Monica Braisier-Creagh, Hamish Hamilton, 1962.

The Cats' Opera (also see below), illustrated by Vanecek, Faber & Faber, 1962, Bobbs-Merrill, 1963.

The Coriander, illustrated by Kennedy, Faber & Faber, 1963, illustrated by Vic Donahue, Funk, 1964.

A Family of Foxes, illustrated by Kennedy, Faber & Faber, 1964, Funk, 1965.

The Sea Wall, illustrated by Kennedy, Farrar, Straus, 1965.

The Lion Cub, illustrated by Kennedy, Hamish Hamilton, 1966, Duell, Sloan & Pearce, 1967.

The Road to Dunmore (also see below), illustrated by Kennedy, Faber & Faber, 1966.

The Key (also see below), illustrated by Kennedy, Faber & Faber, 1967.

The Cruise of the Santa Maria, illustrated by Kennedy, Funk, 1967, F. M. O'Brien, 1991.

Two Stories: The Road to Dunmore [and] *The Key,* illustrated by Kennedy, Meredith, 1967.

The Seals, illustrated by Kennedy, Faber & Faber, 1968, Funk, 1969.

Under the Orange Grove, illustrated by Kennedy, Faber & Faber, 1968, Meredith, 1969.

A Herd of Deer, illustrated by Kennedy, Faber & Faber, 1969, Funk, 1970.

The Wise Man on the Mountain, illustrated by Gaynor Chapman, Hamish Hamilton, 1969, Atheneum, 1970.

The Voyage of Mael Duin, illustrated by Alan Howard, Faber & Faber, 1969.

The King's Room, illustrated by Kennedy, Hamish Hamilton, 1970.

The Five Hundred, illustrated by Gareth Floyd, Hamish Hamilton, 1972, F. M. O'Brien, 1991.

The Shadow of Vesuvius, Thomas Nelson, 1978.

Down in the World, illustrated by Kennedy, Hodder & Stoughton, 1983.
The Horse Fancier, Macmillan, 1985.
The Seekers, Macmillan, 1986.
The Island of Ghosts, Macmillan, 1989.

ADULT FICTION

Death at Crane's Court (mystery novel), Faber & Faber, 1953, Walker & Co., 1963.
Sent to His Account (mystery novel), Faber & Faber, 1954, Walker & Co., 1969.
Death in the Quadrangle (mystery novel), Faber & Faber, 1956, Walker & Co., 1968.
The Bitter Glass, Faber & Faber, 1958, Appleton-Century-Crofts, 1959.
The Head of the Family, Faber & Faber, 1960.
Bold John Henebry, Faber & Faber, 1965.
Across the Bitter Sea, Simon & Schuster, 1973.
Blood Relations, Simon & Schuster, 1977.
Wild Geese, Simon & Schuster, 1980.
Citizen Burke, Hodder & Stoughton, 1984.
The Interloper, Hodder & Stoughton, 1987.

PLAYS

Manna, produced on Radio Eireann, Dublin, Ireland, 1962.
A Page of History, produced in Dublin at the Abbey Theatre, 1966.
The Cats' Opera (for children; adapted from novel of the same title), produced at the Abbey Theatre, 1981.

IN GAELIC

An Choill bheo (title means "The Living Forest"), Oifig an tSolathair (Government Publications Sale Office), 1948.
Oscar agus an Coiste se nEasog (title means "Oscar and the Six-Weasel Coach"), Oifig an tSolathair, 1952.
Ceol na Coille (title means "The Song of the Forest"), Oifig an tSolathair, 1955.

OTHER

(Editor) *The Hamish Hamilton Book of Wise Animals,* Hamish Hamilton, 1973.
Living in Imperial Rome, Faber & Faber, 1974, Thomas Nelson, 1975, published as *Rome under the Emperors,* Thomas Nelson, 1976.
Inside Ireland (travel), photographs by Tom Kennedy, Hodder & Stoughton, 1982, Beaufort Books, 1984.
(Author of introduction) Pat Donion, editor, *The Lucky Bag: Classic Irish Children's Stories,* F. M. O'Brien, 1984.

Dillon's books have been translated into French, German, Dutch, Swedish, Czech, Polish, Hebrew, and Norwegian.

WORK IN PROGRESS: Children of Bach, a children's book to be published by Faber & Faber and Scribner, and a new novel.

SIDELIGHTS: Eilis Dillon "is simply a good writer," a critic for the *Times Literary Supplement* states, "loving and understanding people, and concerned to tell stories that are as exciting as adventure stories should be but in which the events are tied firmly to human possibility." Dillon, who speaks Gaelic, English, French, and Italian, most often sets her adventure stories on the Irish seacoast and writes of the fishermen and farmers who make that region their home. In *Use of English,* Winifred Whitehead emphasizes the sense of community that Dillon creates in her novels: "Her books are remarkable for their distinctive recreation of rural Ireland; the men living close to the land or sea, as farmworkers or fishermen; the women working equally hard in their small houses, caring for their men-folk and their children; and the children themselves, seen essentially as a part of the community with their own place in it and their own chores to carry out at home, having only so much liberty to range the countryside, with its rich wildlife and its possibilities of adventure."

Dillon once explained to *CA* how she learned about her subject: "My father was professor of chemistry at a university. We lived in a village on the sea coast a few miles west of Galway, where the common language of the people was Irish. From visiting our neighbors, from going to the village school, and mainly from my early knowledge of the Irish language and the old Irish songs, I came gradually to know the mind of these people. Later I spent summers in the Aran Islands and also in the remote parts of Connemara where we used to camp in tents. My school was the Ursuline Convent in Sligo, where William Butler Yeats lived as a boy. It is beautiful country, dominated by two mountains, Benbulben and Knocknarea, whose names are associated with the oldest of the Irish folk tales.

"I never remember a time when I did not want to write. I composed my first story at the age of seven, about a mouse called Harry who got into bad company, committed murder and was hanged. I would not choose such a subject for a children's book now."

Dillon was not fond of Sligo, and she left the school after her first year. She then went to live with her grandparents and attended an Irish-speaking school. She kept busy studying literary classics with her grandfather and attending cello lessons, but she was often alone and relished the time she had to herself. She began to write poetry and at sixteen saw her work published under a pseudonym in a small magazine.

After a year away, Dillon returned to Sligo, where a teacher suggested she try her hand at writing novels. Dillon studied literary theory and found that the prefaces to many classics contained helpful guidelines. She worked at this, "practising every day as I would on a musical instrument," she wrote in an essay for *Contemporary Authors Autobiography Series* (*CAAS*). Her first success was written in Irish, the language she had learned at home and as manager of an Irish language school owned by a friend of her father's.

Dillon related, "I began to write in Irish, a children's book—not about mice behind the walls but rabbits underground. I used the beautiful old script that was still standard in Ireland. It was all handwritten, of course, since typewriters with that script were rare. The story ran to about 30,000 words and was well-plotted. I sent it to the Government Publications Sale Office, which had a program of publishing as well as distributing official documents. It was accepted at once. By the time I was notified of this, I was one-third the way through the next one."

Dillon explained why breaking into print was so easy for her: "Publishing was almost an unknown business in Ireland at that time. One or two houses existed, mainly for producing school texts, and occasionally they published a novel of guaranteed respectability. But England, always a great publishing country, was frantically looking for material after the long years of the war when no one had the time or inclination to write. I decided to make one attempt and to stand or fall by that. . . . I had written a very old-fashioned children's book about a magic loaf of bread that gave animals the power of speech. The river figured in it, and the burned out castle on the opposite bank, and the lovely house that we had left so long ago. Macmillan in London accepted it and published it with black and white drawings by an artist who knew how to give character to animals. Then Macmillan decided against publishing children's books and handed me on to Faber and Faber, who had always had Irish writers on their list."

In 1940 Dillon married Dr. Cormac O'Cuilleanain, a professor of Irish at the University of Cork who later became the Warden there. With plenty of space in the Warden's House, Dillon was able to devote her mornings to writing while taking care of her family of three children. Believing that Irish novels were possessed of typically weak plots, she chose to write mysteries, a form that requires "perfect plotting," she said. Dillon next turned to writing mainstream fiction, beginning with what she considers to be her first novel, *The Bitter Glass*. This story of a young couple's survival after the destruction of a railroad bridge during the Irish Civil War was highly acclaimed in England and the United States. In Ireland, however, readers were stunned that Dillon would expose that period of her nation's history in fiction.

In the early 1960s, Dillon's husband developed rheumatoid arthritis which hindered his work at the university.

Following her mother's advice, the couple moved to Rome. Still disciplining herself to write daily, Dillon wrote the play, *A Page of History,* which was produced in Dublin's Abbey Theatre in 1966. The play was a success; however, the theater was destroyed by fire and further productions were cancelled.

In 1970, after the death of her husband, Dillon moved back to Dublin and finished writing *Across the Bitter Sea,* a novel about a nineteenth-century landlord's attempts to improve the lives of working-class people in the context of violent social change. A *Times Literary Supplement* reviewer writes that, in addition to Dillon's insights on the social class divisions and religious intolerance of its times, "What gives *Across the Bitter Sea* its distinction is Miss Dillon's deep sympathy with her own people and their sufferings. She comes from a family of politicians and has the Irish capacity for making yesterday's wrongs as alive as today's."

In 1974, Dillon married fellow writer Vivian Mercier and moved to Santa Barbara, California, where Mercier took a professorship. When not in California or Ireland, the couple visited a rented retreat near Perugia, Italy. They returned to live in Dublin after Mercier retired in 1987; Dillon was again widowed in 1989.

Dillon's recent work includes the historical novel *Citizen Burke,* which she describes in *CAAS* as "a psychological novel," and *The Interloper*. She has also used American history as a subject. Her 1986 book, *The Seekers,* follows an Englishman's pursuit of romance across the Atlantic to the Pilgrim settlement at Plymouth and his return to his homeland with his bride.

In 1991, Dillon became the first author to receive the Irish Book of the Year award, presented to her for *The Island of Ghosts*. The honor was especially pleasing to her, considering the way the Irish feel about awards. In 1986 Dillon wrote in *CAAS,* "The Irish make sure that no one will become conceited and they slap down any tendency in that direction unhesitatingly. I have a great many admirers there, but I have never been honored in any way. . . . Still, the Irish do love their writers, though one has an impression that they feel, as [Anton] Chekhov said, that a country which nurtures writers is like a farmer who owns a granary and breeds rats."

Dillon told *CA:* "Coming back to live permanently in Ireland has been enormously stimulating. The company and conversation are so good that I feel my life as a writer has been restarted."

BIOGRAPHICAL/CRITICAL SOURCES:

BOOKS

Books for Children, 1900-1965, American Library Association, 1966.
Contemporary Literary Criticism,
Books for Children, 1900-1965,
Dillon, Eilis, essay in *Contemporary Authors Autobiography Series,* Volume 3, Gale, 1986, pp. 49-67.
Eyre, Frank, *British Children's Books in the Twentieth Century,* Longman, 1971.
Fisher, Margery, *Intent Upon Reading: A Critical Appraisal of Modern Fiction for Children,* Hodder & Stoughton, 1961.
Larrick, Nancy, *A Parents' Guide to Children's Reading,* 3rd edition, Doubleday, 1969.

PERIODICALS

Best Sellers, October 1, 1967.
Books and Bookmen, December, 1967; August, 1968; March, 1970; May, 1970.
Book World, December 31, 1967.
Chicago Tribune, November 12, 1960.
Commonweal, August 18, 1978.
Creation, August, 1962.
Listener, November 16, 1967; March 14, 1974.
New Statesman, November 8, 1963; May 15, 1970.
New York Herald Tribune Book Review, June 17, 1956; November 17, 1957.
New York Times Book Review, November 17, 1957; October 4, 1959; April 27, 1969.
Punch, December 19, 1969.
Saturday Review, November 13, 1954.
Spectator, July 8, 1955; March 25, 1978.
Times Literary Supplement, November 27, 1953; December 9, 1965; May 25, 1967, p. 443; March 1, 1974, p. 201; July 11, 1975; April 7, 1978; November 19, 1987, p. 1248.
Use of English, spring, 1979, pp. 58-62.
Washington Post Book World, January 4, 1981, p. 6.

—*Sketch by Marilyn K. Basel and Deborah A. Stanley*

*   *   *

DRAKE, David (Allen) 1945-

PERSONAL: Born September 24, 1945, in Dubuque, IA; son of Earle Charles (a maintenance foreman) and Maxine (Schneider) Drake; married Joanne Kammiller (a teacher), June 5, 1967; children: Jonathan. *Education:* University of Iowa, B.A., 1967; Duke University, J.D., 1972.

ADDRESSES: Home—P.O. Box 904, Chapel Hill, NC 27514. *Agent*—Kirby McCauley Ltd., 432 Park Ave. S., New York, NY 10016.

CAREER: Town of Chapel Hill, NC, assistant town attorney, 1972-80; part-time bus driver, 1981; full-time freelance writer, 1982—. Partner of Carcosa (publisher). *Military service:* U.S. Army, 1969-71; served in Viet Nam and Cambodia.

MEMBER: International Fortean Organization, Science Fiction Writers of America, Phi Beta Kappa.

WRITINGS:

"HAMMER'S SLAMMERS" SERIES

Hammer's Slammers (science fiction), Ace Books, 1979.
Cross the Stars, Tor Books, 1984.
At Any Price, Baen, 1985.
Counting the Cost, Baen, 1987.
Rolling Hot, Baen, 1989.
The Warrior, Baen, 1991.

"KELLY" SERIES

Sky Ripper, Tor Books, 1983.
Fortress, Tor Books, 1986.

"YATES" SERIES; WITH JANET MORRIS

Kill Ratio, Ace Books, 1987.
Target, Ace Books, 1989.

"NORTHWORLD" SERIES

Northworld, Ace Books, 1990.
Vengeance, Ace Books, 1991.
Justice, Ace Books, 1992.

OTHER

The Dragon Lord (fantasy novel), Putnam, 1979, revised edition, Tor Books, 1982.
Time Safari, Tor Books, 1982.
From the Heart of Darkness, Tor Books, 1984.
The Forlorn Hope, Tor Books, 1984.
Birds of Prey, Baen, 1984.
(With Karl Edward Wagner) *Killer,* Baen, 1984.
(With Janet Morris) *Active Measures,* Baen, 1985.
Bridgehead, Tor Books, 1986.
Ranks of Bronze, Baen, 1986.
Lacey and His Friends, Baen, 1986.
Dagger, Ace Books, 1988.
The Sea Hag, Baen, 1988.
(With Janet Morris) *Explorers in Hell,* Baen, 1989.
Vettius and His Friends, Baen, 1989.
Surface Action, Ace Books, 1990.
(With Jim Kjelgaard) *The Hunter Returns,* Baen, 1991.

The Jungle, Tor Books, 1991.
The Military Dimension, Baen, 1991.
Old Nathan, Baen, 1991.
Starliner, Baen, 1992.

Contributor of more than fifty stories to magazines. Assistant editor of *Whispers.*

WORK IN PROGRESS: "Seven novels under contract. Odds and ends of short stories and editing chores."

E

ECKERT, Horst 1931-
(Janosch)

PERSONAL: Born March 11, 1931, in Zaborze, Germany (now Poland); son of Johann (a shopkeeper) and Hildegard E. (Glodny) Eckert. *Education:* Attended gymnasium in Zaborze, 1940-43, and textile design school in Krefeld, Germany, 1947-49. *Religion:* None.

ADDRESSES: Home—Munich, Germany.

CAREER: Author and illustrator of children's books. Once worked as an industrial designer. *Exhibitions:* Wilhelm-Busch-Museum, Germany, 1980; Stadt-und Schiffahrtsmuseum Kiel, Germany, 1981; Stadtgeschichtliche Museen Nuernberg, Duererhaus, Germany, 1981.

AWARDS, HONORS: Hans Christian Andersen highly commended illustrator, German Federal Republic, 1972; German Children's Book Prize Honor List.

WRITINGS:

(With Wolfgang Menz) *Absatzplanung und Verkaufssteuerung in der Druckindustrie: ein Leitfaden* (nonfiction), Graphische Gewerbe, 1973.

UNDER PSEUDONYM JANOSCH

Cholonek; oder, Der liebe Gott aus Lehm (adult novel; title means "Cholonek, or, the God of Clay"), Bitter, 1970.
Sacharin im Salat (novel), Guetersloh, 1975.
Sandstrand (novel), Beltz, 1979.

UNDER PSEUDONYM JANOSCH; FOR CHILDREN

Das Regenauto, illustrations by Caroline Sommer, Ellermann, 1969, translation published as *The Magic Auto,* Crown, 1971.
Autos Autos viel Autos, illustrations by Friedrich Kohlsaat, Beltz, 1971.

UNDER PSEUDONYM JANOSCH; FOR CHILDREN; SELF-ILLUSTRATED

Historia de Valek, el caballo, Editorial Lumen, 1963.
Valek y Jarosch, Editorial Lumen, 1963.
Onkel Poppoff kann auf Baeume fliegen, Domino, 1964.
Das Auto hier heisst Ferdinand, Deutscher Buecherbund, 1965, translation published as *The Yellow Auto Named Ferdinand,* Carolrhoda, 1973.
Das Apfelmaennchen, Parabel, 1965, translation published as *Just One Apple,* Walck, 1966.
Heute um neune hinter der Scheune, Parabel, 1965, translation published as *Tonight at Nine,* Walck, 1967.
Rate mal, wer suchen muss, Parabel, 1966, Austrian and Swiss editions published as *Rat einmal, wer suchen muss,* Domino, 1966, translation by Margaret Green published as *Has Anyone Seen Paul? Who Will Be He?: A Story and Counting Rhymes,* Dobson, 1969.
Leo Zauberfloh; oder, Wer andern eine Grube graebt, Domino, 1966.
Poppoff und Piezke, Parabel, 1966.
Hannes Strohkopp und der unsichtbare Indianer, Parabel, 1966.
Schlafe, lieber Hampelmann, Parabel, 1967.
Rabenkoenig Muckelbass, Domino, 1967.
Der Josa mit der Zauberfiedel, Parabel, 1967, translation published as *Joshua and the Magic Fiddle,* World Publishing, 1968.
Herr Wuzzel und sein Karussell, Parabel, 1968, Swiss edition published as *Herr Wuzzel und sein Zauber-Karussell,* Globi-Verlag, 1968, adaptation and translation by Judy Lester published in England as *Mr. Wuzzle,* Longman, 1969.
Lukas Kuemmel, Zauberkuenstler, Paulus, 1968, translation by Anthea Bell published as *Luke Caraway: Master Magician or Indian Chief,* Andersen, 1977.

Boellerbam und der Vogel, Middelhauve, 1968, translation by Refna Wilkin published as *Bollerbam,* Walck, 1969.

Wir haben einen Hund zu Haus, Parabel, 1968.

Der Maeuse-Sheriff: Luegengeschicten aus dem Wilden Westen, erlogen von einer Maus, Bitter, 1969.

Ach lieber Schneemann, Parabel, 1969, translation published as *Dear Snowman,* World Publishing, 1970, published in England as *Oh Dear, Snowman!,* Dobson, 1972.

3 Raeuber und 1 Rabenkoenig, Parabel, 1969, translation by Elizabeth Shub published as *The Thieves and the Raven,* Macmillan, 1970.

Leo Zauberfloh; oder, Die Loewenjagd in Oberfimmel, Bitter, 1970, translation by A. Bell published as *Leon the Magic Flea; or, The Lion Hunt in Upper Fimmel,* Abelard-Schuman, 1974.

Komm nach Iglau Krokodil, Parabel, 1970, translation published as *The Crocodile Who Wouldn't Be King,* Putnam, 1971.

Flieg Vogel, flieg, Parabel, 1971.

Loewe spring durch den Ring, Parabel, 1971.

Ene bene Bimmelbahn, Parabel, 1971.

Lari Fari Mogelzahn; jeden Abend eine Geschichte, Beltz & Gelberg, 1971.

Bilder und Gedichte fuer Kinder, Westermann, 1972.

Schulfiebel 1, Westermann, 1972.

Wohin Rast die Feuerwehr, [Munich], 1972.

Janosch erzaehlt Grimm's Maerchen und zeichnet fuer Kinder von heute; fuenfzig ausgewaehlte Maerchen, Beltz & Gelberg, 1972, translation by Patricia Crampton published as *Not Quite as Grimm,* Abelard-Schuman, 1974.

One-Eye, Ginger, and Lefty, Dobson, 1972.

Ich bin ein grosser Zottelbaer, Parabel, 1972, translation by James Dobson published as *I Am a Great Big Hairy Bear,* Dobson, 1973.

Tales of the Lying Nutcracker, translation from the German by Erika Hyams, Abelard-Schuman, 1973.

Time for Bed, Dobson, 1973.

Familie Schmidt, Rowohlt, 1974.

Hottentotten gruene Motten, Rowohlt, 1974.

Baerenzirkus Zampano, Parabel, 1975, translation by J. Dobson published as *Zampano's Performing Bear,* Dobson, 1976.

Oh, wie schoen ist Panama, Beltz & Gelberg, 1976, translation by A. Bell published as *The Trip to Panama,* Andersen, 1978, Little, Brown, 1981.

Das starke Auto Ferdinand, Parabel, 1976.

Die Globeriks, Globi-Verlag, 1976.

Die Loewenreise, Beltz & Gelberg, 1976.

Das grosse Janosch Buch: Geschicten und Bilder, Beltz & Gelberg, 1976, translation by A. Bell published as *The Big Janosch Book of Fun and Verse,* Andersen, 1980.

Kasper Loeffel und seine gute Oma, Parabel, 1977, translation by J. Dobson published as *Crafty Caspar and His Good Old Granny,* Dobson, 1979.

Ich sag, du bist ein Baer, Beltz & Gelberg, 1977, translation by Klaus Flugge published as *Hey Presto! You're a Bear!,* Little, Brown, 1980.

Die Maus hat rote Struempfe an Beltz, Beltz & Gelberg, 1978.

Ein Mann ein Kahn die Maus das Haus, Parabel, 1978.

Das kleine Hasenbuch, Parabel, 1978.

Schnuddelbuddel sagt gutnacht, Parabel, 1978.

Traumstunde fuer Siebenschlaefer, Beltz & Gelberg, 1978.

The Rain Car, translation from the German by J. Dobson, Dobson, 1978.

The Treasure-Hunting Trip, translation from the German by A. Bell, Andersen, 1980.

A Letter for Tiger, Andersen, 1981.

Animal Antics, in Words and Pictures, translation of *Leben der Thiere* by A. Bell, Andersen Press, 1982.

See You in the Morning!, translation from the German by A. Bell, Methuen, 1983.

The Higher and Higher House, translation from the German by A. Bell, Methuen, 1984.

Das grosse Panama-Album, Beltz & Gelberg, 1984.

Herr Korbes will Klein Huehnchen kuessen, Diogenes, 1984.

Die Fiedelgrille und der Maulwurf, Diogenes, 1985, translation by Elizabeth D. Crawford published as *The Cricket and the Mole,* Bradbury Press, 1987.

"I'll Make You Well, Tiger," Said the Bear, translation of *Ich mach dich gesund, sagte der Baer* by Elisabeth Muhlemann, Adama Books, 1985, also published in England as *Little Tiger, Get Well Soon!,* Andersen, 1986.

The Old Man and the Bear, Bradbury Press, 1987, originally published as *Der Alte Mann und der Baer.*

Schimanski; die Kraft der inneren Maus, Diogenes, 1989.

Also author and illustrator of numerous other children's books, including *Ich male einen Bauernhof,* Parabel, *The Curious Tale of Hare and Hedgehog,* 1988, *Hello, Little Pig,* 1988, and *The Little Hare Book,* 1988.

ILLUSTRATOR; UNDER PSEUDONYM JANOSCH

Mischa Damjan (pseudonym), *Filipo und sein Wunderpinsel,* Nord-Sued, 1967, translation published as *The Magic Paintbrush,* Walck, 1967.

Jozef Wilkon, *Die Loewenkinder,* Middelhauve, 1968.

Hans-Joachim Gelberg, *Die Stadt der Kinder,* Bitter, 1969.

Jack Prelutsky, *Lazy Blackbird, and Other Verses,* Macmillan, 1969.

Hans Baumann, *Der wunderbare Ball Kadalupp,* Betz, 1969, translation published as *Gatalop the Wonderful Ball,* Walck, 1971.

Herbert Heckmann, *Geschicten vom Loeffelchen,* Middel-hauve, 1970.

Beverly Cleary, *Die Maus auf dem Motorrad,* Union, 1972.

B. Cleary, *Mauserich Ralf Haut ab,* Union, 1972.

Walter D. Edmonds, *Das Mausehaus,* Loewes, 1972.

Paul Maar, *Kikerikiste,* Deutscher Taschenbuch, 1973.

Anne K. Rose, *How Does a Czar Eat Potatoes?,* Lothrop, 1973.

Yuri Koval, *A Pig in a Poke,* translation from the Russian, Abelard-Schuman, 1975.

James Kruss, *Der Kleine Flax,* Oetinger, 1975.

Bombo, Parabel, 1978.

Bombo kann alles, Parabel, 1978.

Wasja kauft den Hund im Sack, Thienemann, 1978.

Der Weihnachtsstern, Oetinger, 1978.

Kaese Kaese, Mosaik, 1978.

Christine Noestlinger, *Einer,* Beltz & Gelberg, 1980.

Herbert Rosendorfer, *Die Herberge zum irdischen Paradies: ein Plaeydoyer fuer das unsterbliche Wirtschaus,* Etcetera, 1982.

Also illustrator of *Bonko,* by H. Baumann, 1972, *Yosi vekhinor ha-kesamim,* by Tzvi Rozen, 1972, and *Die lustigen Abenteur des Kasperl larifari,* by Franz-Graf von Pocci, 1972. An exhibition catalog of Janosch's illustrations entitled *Janosch: Gemalde and Grafik* was published by Merlin, 1980.

SIDELIGHTS: Horst Eckert has written and illustrated over seventy books under the name Janosch, and his books are familiar to children all over the world through their translations from German into many different languages. Most of his books are populated by animals, and the animated expressions and carefree antics of the author's bears, pigs, and other creatures delight young children. Eckert was highly commended for his skills as an illustrator by the Hans Christian Andersen jury in 1972 for the body of his work, but his popularity can best be measured by the over half a million copies of his books that have sold worldwide.

Eckert was born in 1931 in the Polish town of Zaborze, which was under German rule until after World War II. He attended school until he was thirteen, when he left to work in a blacksmith's shop and later in different factories. In 1953 he tried to study at the Academy of Art in Munich, Germany, but in his autobiographical sketch for *Fourth Book of Junior Authors and Illustrators* he says, "I had to leave the academy. I had no talent." Eckert stayed on in Munich, living on the little money he earned doing odd jobs. A chance conversation gave him the idea to write a children's book, but he had no success until he wrote his seventh book, which sold ninety thousand copies. From that point on he has made his living writing and illustrating his own children's books and illustrating

books for other authors. "And now I succeed too in painting," he comments in his autobiographical sketch. "I have had many exhibitions, and it doesn't matter so much whether the pictures are all sold every time because now I don't need money. But to be a painter—that was what I wanted to become when it began."

Naomi Lewis, writing in the *Observer,* called *The Big Janosch Book of Fun and Verse* (originally *Das grosse Janosch Buch*) "the nursery book of the season." The volume contains hundreds of illustrations, numerous poems and fables, and even some mini-novels; all contain a lesson, though none are overtly moralistic. *Hey Presto! You're a Bear!* (originally *Ich sag, du bist ein Baer*) is a picture-book fantasy in which a young boy discovers that he has the power to turn people into any animal he wants by saying "Hey Presto!" The story resembles Dr. Seuss's *The Cat in the Hat,* but in Eckert's version the young boy's parents join in the game, and parent and child alike enjoy the playful fantasy.

BIOGRAPHICAL/CRITICAL SOURCES:

BOOKS

Fourth Book of Junior Authors and Illustrators, H. W. Wilson, 1978, pp. 196-97.

PERIODICALS

Library Journal, September 15, 1967, p. 110; September 1, 1970.

National Observer, November 4, 1968.

New York Times, November 3, 1968.

New York Times Book Review, May 22, 1966; November 7, 1971.

Observer, December 7, 1980; July 19, 1987.

School Library Journal, February, 1981, pp. 57-58; October, 1981, p. 130; August, 1987, p. 70.

Times Literary Supplement, April 12, 1969; July 2, 1970; April 6, 1973; June 15, 1973, p. 687.*

*   *   *

ECONOMOU, George 1934-

PERSONAL: Surname pronounced Ee-con-*oh*-moo; born September 24, 1934, in Great Falls, MT; son of Demetrios G. and Amelia (Ananiadis) Economou; married Rochelle Owens (a poet and playwright) June 17, 1962. *Education:* Colgate University, A.B., 1956; Columbia University, M.A., 1957, Ph.D., 1967.

ADDRESSES: Office—Department of English, University of Oklahoma, Norman, OK 73019.

CAREER: Wagner College, New York City, lecturer in English, 1958-60; Long Island University, Brooklyn, NY, assistant professor, 1961-69, associate professor, 1969-73, professor of English, 1973-83, chairman of department, 1982-83; University of Oklahoma, Norman, professor of English, 1983—, chairman of department, 1983-90.

AWARDS, HONORS: American Council of Learned Societies fellow, 1975-76; Creative Artists Public Service Program fellow in poetry, 1977, National Endowment for the Arts fellow in poetry, 1988.

WRITINGS:

The Georgics, Black Sparrow Press, 1968.
Landed Natures, Black Sparrow Press, 1969.
Poems for Self Therapy, Perishable Press, 1972.
The Goddess Natura in Medieval Literature, Harvard University Press, 1972.
(Co-editor and contributor) *In Pursuit of Perfection: Courtly Love in Medieval Literature,* Kennikat, 1975.
(Editor and contributor) *Geoffrey Chaucer,* McGraw, 1975.
Ameriki: Book One and Selected Earlier Poems, Sun, 1977.
Philodemos, His Twenty-Nine Extant Poems, Perishable Press, 1983.
Voluntaries, Corycian Press, 1984.
(Editor) *Proensa: An Anthology of Troubadour Poetry,* translated by Paul Blackburn, Paragon, 1986.
harmonies and fits, Point Riders Press, 1987.

Contributor of translation of Euripides's *Cyclops* to *The Tenth Muse,* edited by Charles Doria, Ohio University Press, 1980. Also contributor of poems, stories, reviews, and translations from modern Greek poetry and ancient Greek drama to numerous magazines. Editor, *Chelsea Review,* 1958-60, and *Trobar,* 1960—.

WORK IN PROGRESS: A translation of William Langland's *Piers Plowman, C-Text.*

*   *   *

EDWARDS, Anne-Marie 1932-

PERSONAL: Born October 29, 1932, in York, England; daughter of Wilfrid (an engineer) and Margaret (an artist; maiden name, Jackson) Calvert; married Michael Edwards (a pilot and writer), January 8, 1955; children: Julie, Christopher. *Education:* Victoria University of Manchester, B.A. (with honors), 1954; University of Southampton, M.A., 1967.

ADDRESSES: Home and office—2 Woodlands Rd., Ashurst, Southampton SO4 2AD, England.

CAREER: High school English teacher and department head in Romford, England, 1959-62; Northeast Essex Technical College, Colchester, England, lecturer in En-

glish, 1965-66; University of Southampton, School of Navigation, Southampton, England, lecturer in English, 1969; Workers Educational Association, Southampton and Kendal, England, lecturer in English, 1969—. Radio broadcaster for British Broadcasting Corp. Founder with husband, Michael Edwards, of Arcady Books, a publishing house.

MEMBER: Society of Authors, Thomas Hardy Society, Jane Austen Society, Southampton Poets.

WRITINGS:

New Forest Walks, British Broadcasting Corp., 1975.
Discovering Hardy's Wessex, British Broadcasting Corp., 1978.
In the Steps of Jane Austen, British Broadcasting Corp., 1979.
New Forest Walks 2, British Broadcasting Corp., 1979.
(Editor) *New Forest Cookery,* Arcady Books, 1983.
(Editor) *The Island Cookbook,* Arcady Books, 1984.
(Editor) *The Family Outdoor Book,* Arcady Books, 1984.
(Contributor) *Jane Austen Handbook,* Scribner, 1985.
The New Forest Companion, Countryside Books, 1987.
In the Steps of Thomas Hardy, Countryside Books, 1989.

Contributor to *Out and About,* 1990—. Also contributor to magazines and newspapers, including *She, Country Life,* and *This England.* Co-editor of *Mayflower.*

SIDELIGHTS: Anne-Marie Edwards once told *CA:* "My husband and I both feel it is important that people should have vision as a saving factor in ordinary life. By relating authors to their worlds and involving the reader personally as a visitor to these worlds we hope to help people realize their own potential abilities and derive more pleasure and fulfillment from their own surroundings. My husband's book involves his readers in the world of flying. I hope that mine involve the reader in a deeper appreciation of man and nature."

*   *   *

el HAJJAM, Mohammed ben Chaib 1940-
(Mohammed Mrabet)

PERSONAL: Born March 25, 1940, in Tangier, Morocco; son of Chaib and Rahma bent Bouchta (Tuzani) el Hajjam; married Zohra bent Ali ben Allal, 1964; children: Mohammed Larbi, Hadija, Ahmed, Aicha. *Religion:* Muslim.

ADDRESSES: Home—Souami, Rue 10, No. 26, Tangier, Morocco. *Agent*—Roberto de Hollanda, P.O. Box 180136, 53 Bonn 1, Germany.

CAREER: Writer, 1967—.

WRITINGS:

UNDER NAME MOHAMMED MRABET; TRANSLATED BY PAUL BOWLES FROM THE ORIGINAL MAGHREBI

Love with a Few Hairs (novel), P. Owen, 1967, Braziller, 1968.
The Lemon (novel), P. Owen, 1969.
M'Hashish, City Lights, 1969.
The Boy who Set the Fire and Other Stories, Black Sparrow Press, 1974.
Look and Move On (autobiographical novel), Black Sparrow Press, 1976.
Harmless Poisons, Blameless Sins (short stories), Black Sparrow Press, 1976.
The Big Mirror (novella), Black Sparrow Press, 1977.
The Beach Cafe and the Voice, Black Sparrow Press, 1979.
(Contributor) *Five Eyes* (anthology), Black Sparrow Press, 1979.
The Chest (short stories), Tombouctou Books, 1983.
Three Tales, School of Visual Arts Press, 1983.
Marriage with Papers (novella), Tombouctou Books, 1985.

Also author of one-act play, *Earth,* 1980.

SIDELIGHTS: The fiction of Mohammed ben Chaib el Hajjam—better known as Mohammed Mrabet—often illustrates the disruptive influences of Western culture on the ancient patterns of Moroccan life. The author's direct, stylistic simplicity promotes a narrative efficiency comparable to "some of the most sophisticated new fiction," observed J. H. Stern in *Saturday Review.* In Mrabet's first novel, *Love with a Few Hairs,* the "confrontation of cultures is beautifully dramatized," Stern wrote, involving what *New York Times Book Review* critic J. M. Edelstein described as "a mixture of Western sophistication and ancient beliefs, of naivete and guile, of strict morality and easy promiscuity." The story concerns a young Moroccan who comes close to madness after he deserts the wife he had won with a magic love potion concocted from a few hairs. In the end, he is saved by an English hotelkeeper, Mr. David, who has loved him all the while. Calling it a somber book, Edelstein wrote that it shows a "world where love is a commodity and perfunctory, where the gulfs between human beings are not only vast but are also taken for granted as permanent." According to J. A. Phillips in *Best Sellers,* the reader glimpses "an ancient people rebelling against the ignorance, tradition, and superstition which keep them from becoming a part of the Western sophistication they see about them."

In later works, Mrabet draws widely from traditional sources. *Harmless Poisons, Blameless Sins* is a collection of tales based on the adventures of Hadidan Aharam, a legendary picaresque hero in Moroccan folklore. Whether pitted against rich men, sheiks, animals, or wives, the wily Aharam always emerges the victor, usually by means of a clever ruse which neatly defeats his adversaries and gives him the last laugh. In another work, *The Big Mirror,* Mrabet tells of a beautiful sorceress whose malevolent occult powers are turned against her husband. "A gruesome vendetta ensues, but the catharsis is suitably mysterious and inconclusive," a *Booklist* reviewer remarked.

Look and Move On, an autobiographical novel, recounts Mrabet's own adventures with Americans in Morocco and the cultural disjunction he experienced as a visitor in the United States. "It moves from scene to scene, year to year, at tremendous speed," noted Robert Bonazzi in *Library Journal.* "It makes for fast reading, exciting reading." As in his other writings, Mrabet's technique and presentation "lend immediate appeal," a *Booklist* reviewer maintained. Although Bonazzi believes some "gratuitous violence and melodrama need deletion," he nevertheless concluded: "[Mrabet] sums up Los Angeles's airless lifestyle perfectly, chillingly. . . . Most of it works beautifully."

BIOGRAPHICAL/CRITICAL SOURCES:

PERIODICALS

Best Sellers, March 15, 1968.
Booklist, June 1, 1976; September 1, 1977.
Library Journal, July, 1976.
New Statesman, January 27, 1967.
New York Times Book Review, September 8, 1968.
Saturday Review, April 6, 1968.
Times Literary Supplement, February 2, 1967.
Transatlantic Review, Spring, 1971.

*   *   *

ELLEN, Jaye
   See NIXON, Joan Lowery

*   *   *

ELLIS, Howard W(oodrow) 1914-

PERSONAL: Born February 19, 1914, in Linton, IN; son of Lee (a merchant) and Effie May Ellis; married Susanna Goldsmith, August 27, 1942; children: Patricia Sue, Mary Lou. *Education:* Evansville College (now University of Evansville), A.B., 1941; Garrett Biblical Institute (now Garrett Evangelical Theological Seminary), B.D., 1946; studied art at American Art Academy, Chicago Art Institute, Peabody College, and University of Tennessee. *Politics:* Democrat.

ADDRESSES: Home—Ann Robe House, 605 Anderson St., Greencastle, IN 46135.

CAREER: Ordained Methodist minister, Indiana Annual Conference, 1946; Methodist Church, member of staff of

General Board of Evangelism, 1946-66, associate secretary and director of Cooperative Department of Youth Evangelism, 1952-64, director of unconventional evangelism, 1964-66; Central Methodist Church, Indianapolis, IN, minister of witness and outreach, 1966-68; Main Street United Methodist Church, Booneville, IN, senior pastor, 1974-78; Gobin Memorial United Methodist Church, Greencastle, IN, associate pastor for pastoral care, beginning 1978; itinerate gospel art evangelist in United States, Great Britain, Mexico, Scandinavia, and India, 1978—. Artist, with several one-man shows; work has been exhibited at Parthenon Galleries, Nashville, TN, 1958, Smithsonian Institute, Washington, DC, 1960, Mexican Institute for North American Cultural Relations, Mexico City, 1960, and at other art festivals in the United States, Korea, Mexico, and Japan.

MEMBER: Disciplined Order of Christ, Tennessee Art League, Kappa Chi, Kappa Alpha, Pi Gamma Mu.

AWARDS, HONORS: H.H.D., Evansville College, 1962; awards for graphic art, Tennessee Art League and Nashville Arts Festival; Denman Evangelism Award, South Indiana Conference, 1984.

WRITINGS:

Evangelism for Teen-Agers, Abingdon, 1958, published as *Evangelism for Teen-Agers for a New Day,* 1966.
The Witnessing Fellowship, Abingdon, 1961.
How to Draw and Speak, Warner, 1961.
(Editor and illustrator) *He Took the Cup,* Upper Room, 1961.
(With Ted McEachern) *Reflections on Youth Evangelism,* Methodist Board of Education, 1963.
The Last Supper, Upper Room, 1963.
The Marks of the Christian, Christian Literary Society, 1984.
Sallman's Christ in Words and Pictures, Warner Press, 1992.
Warner Sallman: His Portrait, Warner Press, 1992.

WORK IN PROGRESS: The Good Life, a poetic version of the Sermon on the Mount; *Celebrating the Nativity Story; Reliving the Passion Story.*

SIDELIGHTS: Howard W. Ellis told *CA:* "My purpose in my Christian painting, preaching, printmaking, and writing is to make Christ known, trusted, loved, and obeyed. I have worked exclusively with the Gospel in art throughout my career because this is my gift—to give them my Christ. I think of my work not as a gift but a calling."

*　　　*　　　*

EWBANK, Walter F(rederick) 1918-

PERSONAL: Born January 29, 1918, in Poona, India; son of Sir Robert (in Indian civil service) and Frances Helen (Simpson) Ewbank; married Ida Margaret Whitworth, April 5, 1941; married Josephine Alice Williamson, October 9, 1976; children: Jane Margaret (Mrs. Andrew Colin Renfrew), Clare Caroline (Mrs. John Henry Fryer Fryer-Spedding), Anthea Mary. *Education:* Balliol College, Oxford, B.A. (with honors), 1946, B.Th., 1952. *Avocational interests:* Greek and Latin classical literature, walking, bird-watching, meteor-watching.

ADDRESSES: Home—7 Castle Court, Castle St., Carlisle CA3 8TO, England.

CAREER: Ordained clergyman of Church of England, 1946; youth chaplain of Diocese of Carlisle, 1949-52; Casterton School, Westmorland, chaplain, 1952-62; administrative chaplain to Bishop of Carlisle, 1962-66; St. Cuthbert's Church, Carlisle, vicar, 1966-71; archdeacon of Westmorland and Furness and vicar of Winster, 1971-77; canon residentiary of Carlisle Cathedral, 1977-82; archdeacon of Carlisle, 1977-84; honorary canon, 1982—. Member of Convocation of York and the Church Assembly, 1957-70; diocesan director of ordinands, 1962-70; member of Canon Law Standing Commission, 1968-70, and Faculty Jurisdiction Commission, 1979-84; rural dean of Carlisle, 1969-71; chairman, diocesan board of finance, 1977-82.

AWARDS, HONORS: Winter War Remembrance Medal, 1940.

WRITINGS:

Salopian Diaries, Wilding & Son, 1961.
Morality without Law, World Publishing, 1969.
Charles Euston Nurse: A Memoir, World Publishing, 1982

Also author of *Thomas Bloomer, Bishop of Carlisle: A Memoir,* 1984, *Ellen Margaret Cartwright: A Memoir,* 1990, and *Memories of the Border Regiment in the First World War,* 1991.

Contributor of articles to periodicals.

F

FARADAY, M. M.
  See RORVIK, David M(ichael)

*　　*　　*

FERRIS, Jean 1939-

PERSONAL: Born January 24, 1939, in Fort Leavenworth, KS; daughter of Jack W. (a major general in the armed services) and Jessie (a housewife; maiden name, Wickham) Schwartz; married Alfred G. Ferris (an attorney), September 8, 1962; children: Kerry Ordway, Gillian Anne. *Education:* Stanford University, B.A., 1961, M.A., 1962.

ADDRESSES: Home—2278 San Juan Rd., San Diego, CA 92103.

CAREER: Veterans Administration Hospital, San Francisco, CA, clinical audiologist, 1962-63; San Diego Speech and Hearing Association, San Diego, CA, clinical audiologist, 1963-65; clinical audiologist in a doctor's office in San Diego, 1975-76; secretary and office assistant in San Diego, 1979-84.

MEMBER: Society of Children's Book Writers, Southern California Council on Literature for Children and Young People, Authors Guild, Authors League of America.

AWARDS, HONORS: Grant from Society of Children's Book Writers, 1984, 1987; American Library Association Best Book for Young Adults, *Booklist* Editor's Choice, *School Library Journal* Best Book of the Year, and Southern California Council on Literature for Children and Young People award for a distinguished work of fiction, all for *Invincible Summer;* International Reading Association Young Adults Choice, Iowa Young Readers Award, and Virginia Young Readers Award nomination, all for

Looking for Home; American Library Association Best Book for Young Adults and California Young Readers Medal nomination, both for *Across the Grain.*

WRITINGS:

Amen, Moses Gardenia, Farrar, Straus, 1983.
The Stainless Steel Rule, Farrar, Straus, 1986.
Invincible Summer, Farrar, Straus, 1987.
Looking for Home, Farrar, Straus, 1988.
Across the Grain, Farrar, Straus, 1990.
Relative Strangers, Farrar, Straus, 1993.

WORK IN PROGRESS: *Taking Pictures,* an adult mystery; *Music from the Moon,* a historical romance; *Why My Mother Is Green,* a middle-grade art book about self-portraits.

SIDELIGHTS: Jean Ferris told *CA:* "I'm very interested in the future of our young people. I try, in my work, to give them hope for the future and some guideposts for achieving a satisfying life, even when circumstances seem bleak and/or dismaying.

"I'm fascinated by the teenage years. There's so much going on then, so many emotional changes, decisions for the future, social problems. I remember my own teenage years vividly and they weren't all beer and skittles.

"I believe that what every youngster needs the most is *one* person who is absolutely bonkers about him or her, who attaches no strings to the love he or she offers the child. You'd think every child would have two such people—parents. Unfortunately, not so. Incidentally, this one loving person does not have to be a parent. It can be anybody—even me, at long distance, through my books.

"I feel certain that I will continue to write for young people because I care so much about them and find them so brave and complex. I've recently been working on a couple of novels for adults, but my first love will always be writing for kids."

*   *   *

FINE, Anne 1947-

PERSONAL: Born December 7, 1947, in Leicester, England; daughter of Brian (a chief scientific experimental officer) and Mary Laker; married Kit Fine (a university professor), 1968; children: two daughters. *Education:* University of Warwick, B.A. (with honors), 1968.

ADDRESSES: Home—County Durham, England. *Agent*—Murray Pollinger, 222 Old Brompton Rd., London SW5 0BZ, England.

CAREER: English teacher at Cardinal Wiseman Girls' Secondary School, 1968-70; Oxford Committee for Famine Relief, Oxford, England, assistant information officer, 1970-71; Saughton Jail, Edinburgh, Scotland, teacher, 1971-72; free-lance writer, 1973—. Volunteer for Amnesty International.

AWARDS, HONORS: Guardian/Kestrel Award nominations, 1978, for *The Summer-House Loon,* and 1987, for *Madame Doubtfire;* Scottish Arts Council Book Award, 1986, for *The Killjoy; Observer* Prize for Teenage Fiction nomination, 1987, for *Madame Doubtfire;* Smarties (6-8) Award, 1989, for *Bill's New Frock; Guardian* Award for Children's Fiction, 1989, and Carnegie Medal, 1990, both for *Goggle Eyes;* Children's Author of the Year, British Book Awards, 1990.

WRITINGS:

FICTION FOR CHILDREN

The Summer-House Loon, Methuen, 1978, Crowell, 1979.
The Other, Darker Ned, Methuen, 1979.
The Stone Menagerie, Methuen, 1980.
Round behind the Ice-House, Methuen, 1981.
The Granny Project, Farrar, Straus, 1983.
Scaredy-Cat, illustrated by Vanessa Julian-Ottie, Heinemann, 1985.
Anneli the Art Hater, Methuen, 1986.
Madame Doubtfire, Hamish Hamilton, 1987, published as *Alias Madame Doubtfire,* Little, Brown, 1988.
Crummy Mummy and Me, illustrated by David Higham, Deutsch, 1988.
A Pack of Liars, Hamish Hamilton, 1988.
My War with Goggle Eyes, Little, Brown, 1989 (published in England as *Goggle Eyes,* Hamish Hamilton, 1989).
Stranger Danger?, illustrated by Jean Baylis, Hamish Hamilton, 1989.
Bill's New Frock, illustrated by Philippe Dupasquier, Methuen, 1989.

A Sudden Puff of Glittering Smoke, illustrated by Adriano Gon, Picadilly Press, 1989.
Only a Show, illustrated by Valerie Littlewood, Hamish Hamilton, 1990.
A Sudden Swirl of Icy Wind, illustrated by Higham, Picadilly Press, 1990.
The Country Pancake, illustrated by Dupasquier, Methuen, 1990.
Poor Monty, illustrated by Clara Vulliamy, Clarion Books, 1991.
A Sudden Glow of Gold, Picadilly Press, 1991.
The Book of the Banshee, Hamish Hamilton, 1991, Little, Brown, 1992.
The Worst Child I Ever Had, illustrated by Vulliamy, Hamish Hamilton, 1991.
Design-A-Pram, Heinemann, 1991.

OTHER

The Granny Project (play; based on her story), Collins, 1986.
The Killjoy (adult novel), Bantam (London), 1986, Mysterious Press, 1987.
Taking the Devil's Advice (adult novel), Viking, 1990.

Also author of radio play *The Captain's Court Case,* 1987. Contributor of short stories to periodicals.

SIDELIGHTS: In such children's books as *The Summer-House Loon, Alias Madame Doubtfire,* and *My War with Goggle-Eyes,* novelist Anne Fine brings a keen comic insight to bear on family problems. "I was brought up in the country, in a family of five girls, including one set of triplets," Fine once related. "My husband was brought up in a family of six boys, including twins. Family relationships have always interested me and it is with the close members of their families that the characters in my books are either getting, or not getting, along."

Fine's first book, *The Summer-House Loon,* presents teenager Ione Muffet, the daughter of a blind college professor who is sometimes oblivious to her. The novel portrays a single, farcical day in Ione's life as she attempts to match her father's secretary with an intelligent yet fumbling graduate student. Calling the novel "original and engaging . . . , mischievous, inventive and very funny," *Times Literary Supplement* writer Peter Hollindale praises Fine for "a fine emotional delicacy which sensitively captures, among all the comic upheaval, the passionate solitude of adolescence." *The Summer-House Loon* is "not just a funny book, although it is certainly that," Marcus Crouch of *Junior Bookshelf* likewise comments. "Here is a book with deep understanding, wisdom and compassion. It tosses the reader between laughter and tears with expert dexterity."

A sequel, *The Other, Darker Ned,* finds Ione organizing a charity benefit for famine victims. "Through [Ione's] observations of other people" in both these works, Margery Fisher comments in *Growing Point,* "we have that delighted sense of recognition which comes in reading novels whose characters burst noisily and eccentrically out of the pages." While these books "are not for everyone, requiring a certain amount of sophistication," Anthea Bell remarks in *Twentieth-Century Children's Writers,* for readers "in command of that sophistication they are stylishly light-hearted entertainment."

Some of Fine's next novels directly examine such social issues as homelessness and care of the elderly. *The Stone Menagerie,* in which a boy discovers that a couple is living on the grounds of a mental hospital, is "devised with a strict economy of words, an acute sense of personality and a shrewd, ironic humour that once more shows Anne Fine to be one of the sharpest and humorous observers of the human condition writing today for the young," Fisher writes in *Growing Point.* And in using humor while "tackling the aged and infirm," Fine's *The Granny Project* "against all the odds contrives to be both audacious and heart-warming," Charles Fox remarks in *New Statesman.* The story of how four siblings conspire to keep their grandmother out of a nursing home by making her care a school assignment, *The Granny Project* is "mordantly funny, ruthlessly honest, yet compassionate in its concern," Nancy C. Hammond notes in *Horn Book.*

Alias Madame Doubtfire brings a more farcical approach to a serious theme, this time the breaking up of a family. "Novels about divorce for children are rarely funny," Roger Sutton observes in the *Bulletin of the Center for Children's Books,* but Fine's work "will have readers laughing from the first page." To gain more time with his children, out-of-work actor Daniel poses as Madame Doubtfire, a supremely capable housekeeper, and gets a job in his ex-wife Miranda's household. Miranda remains blind to her housekeeper's identity while the children quickly catch on, leading to several amusing incidents. But "beneath the farce, the story deals with a serious subject," Mark Geller states in *New York Times Book Review:* "the pain children experience when their parents divorce and then keep on battling." "The comedy of disguise allows the author to skate over the sexual hates and impulses inherent in the situation without lessening the candour of her insights into the irreconcilable feelings of both adults and children," Fisher concludes. "Readers of the teenage novel, weary of perfunctory blue-prints of reality, should be thankful to Anne Fine for giving them such nourishing food for thought within an entertaining piece of fiction."

Crummy Mummy and Me and *A Pack of Liars* "are two more books whose prime intent is to make young people laugh," Chris Powling of the *Times Educational Supplement* observes. "Both exploit the standard comic techniques of taking a familiar situation, turning it on its head, and shaking it vigorously to see what giggles and insights fall into the reader's lap." *A Pack of Liars* recounts how a school assignment to write to a pen pal turns into a mystery of sorts, while *Crummy Mummy and Me* presents a role-reversal in the relationship between an irresponsible mother and her capable daughter. "Details of the plots, though neatly worked out, may sometimes seem a little farfetched in the abstract," Bell notes; "in practice, however, the sheer comic verve of the writing carries them off." Powling agrees, commenting that "once again the narrative shamelessly favours ingenuity over plausibility on the pretty safe assumption that a reader can't complain effectively while grinning broadly." Both books, the critic concludes, "offer welcome confirmation that humour is closer to humanity than apostles of high seriousness care to admit."

In *My War with Goggle-Eyes,* Fine offers yet another "comic yet perceptive look at life after marriage," Ilene Cooper states in *Booklist.* From the opening, in which young Kitty relates to a schoolmate how her mother's boyfriend "Goggle-Eyes" came into her life, "to the happy-ever-after-maybe ending, Fine conveys a story about relationships filled with humor that does not ridicule and sensitivity that is not cloying," Susan Schuller comments in *School Library Journal.* In showing how Kitty gradually learns to accept her mother's new relationship, "Anne Fine writes some of the funniest—and truest—family fight scenes to be found," Sutton observes in *Bulletin of the Center for Children's Books.* The result is "a book that is thoroughly delightful to read," Schuller concludes.

Fine has also written fiction for adults, including the award-winning novel *The Killjoy.* Unlike the sharply witty portraits of family life of her children's books, *The Killjoy* "is an unsettling tale of suspense and a horrific psychological study of a suffering, deformed man," as Elena Brunet describes it in the *Los Angeles Times Book Review.* In detailing the twisted, increasingly debasing relationship between a physically scarred professor and a student, Fine "never falters," *New York Times* critic John Gross comments. "You feel that every aspect of the drama has been thought through and fully imagined, that every detail belongs in its place." "Fine happily eschews generalisations in favour of a zest for understanding human particulars," Valentine Cunningham comments in the *Observer.* "It promises great fictional things to come."

BIOGRAPHICAL/CRITICAL SOURCES:

BOOKS

Children's Literature Review, Volume 25, Gale, 1991, pp. 27-36.
Twentieth-Century Children's Writers, 3rd edition, St. James Press, 1989, pp. 336-337.

PERIODICALS

Booklist, April 15, 1989, p. 1465.
Bulletin of the Center for Children's Books, April, 1988, p. 155; May, 1989, p. 222.
Growing Point, September, 1980, p. 3756; September, 1987, p. 4858; September, 1988, p. 5037; May, 1990, pp. 5343-44.
Horn Book, October, 1983, p. 573.
Junior Bookshelf, August, 1978, pp. 202-203.
Los Angeles Times Book Review, March 13, 1988, p. 14.
New Statesman, December 2, 1983, p. 26; May 2, 1986, p. 27; June 5, 1987, p. 35.
New York Times, March 27, 1987, p. 21.
New York Times Book Review, May 1, 1988, p. 34.
Observer, May 4, 1986, p. 23.
School Library Journal, May, 1989, p. 104.
Spectator, July 4, 1987, pp. 34-36.
Times Educational Supplement, June 3, 1988, p. 49.
Times Literary Supplement, July 7, 1978, p. 767; November 20, 1981, p. 1355; June 22, 1990, p. 674.
Wilson Library Bulletin, February, 1990, pp. 84-85.

—*Sketch by Diane Telgen*

*   *   *

FOREMAN, Michael 1938-

PERSONAL: Born March 21, 1938, in Lowestoft, England; son of Walter Thomas (a crane operator) and Gladys (Goddard) Foreman; married Janet Charters, September 26, 1959 (divorced, 1966); married Louise Phillips, 1980; children: (first marriage) Mark; (second marriage) Ben Shahn, Jack. *Education:* Lowestoft School of Art, National Diploma in Design (painting), 1958; Royal College of Art, A.R.C.A. (with first honors), 1963.

ADDRESSES: Home—5 Church Gate, London SW6, England. *Agent*—John Locke, 15 East 76th St., New York, NY 10021.

CAREER: Graphic artist, children's author. Lecturer in graphics at St. Martin's School of Art, London, England, 1963-66, London College of Printing, 1966-68, Royal College of Art, London, 1968-70, and Central School of Art, London, 1971-72. Art director of *Ambit,* 1960—, *Playboy,* 1965, and *King,* 1966-67. Work exhibited at individual

show, Royal Festival Hall, London, 1985, and in Europe, America, and Japan.

AWARDS, HONORS: Schweppes traveling scholarship to United States, 1961-63; Gimpel Fils Prize for young painters, 1962; Festival International du Livre Silver Eagle Award, France, 1972; Francis Williams Memorial Award, Victoria and Albert Museum, 1972, and 1977, for *Monkey and the Three Wizards;* Kate Greenaway Commended Book, British Library Association, 1978, for *The Brothers Grimm: Popular Folk Tales;* Carnegie Medal, British Library Association, 1980, Kate Greenaway Highly Commended Book, 1980, and Graphics Prize, International Children's Book Fair, Bologna, Italy, 1982, for *City of Gold and Other Stories from the Old Testament;* Kate Greenaway Medal and Kurt Maschler/Emil Award, Book Trust of England, both 1982, for *Sleeping Beauty and Other Favourite Fairy Tales;* Kate Greenaway Medal, 1982, for *Longneck and Thunderfoot;* Federation of Children's Book Groups award, England, 1983, for *The Saga of Erik the Viking;* Kate Greenaway Commended Book and *New York Times* Notable Book, both 1985, for *Seasons of Splendour: Tales, Myths and Legends of India;* runner-up, Maschler Award, 1985, for *Shakespeare Stories;* runner-up, Maschler Award, 1986, and *Signal* Poetry award, 1987, for *Early in the Morning: A Collection of New Poems;* Kate Greenaway Medal and W. H. Smith/Books in Canada Award, both 1990, for *War Boy: A Country Childhood..*

WRITINGS:

SELF-ILLUSTRATED

The Perfect Present, Coward, 1967.
The Two Giants, Pantheon, 1967.
The Great Sleigh Robbery, Hamish Hamilton, 1968, Pantheon, 1969.
Horatio, Hamish Hamilton, 1970, published as *The Travels of Horatio,* Pantheon, 1970.
Moose, Hamish Hamilton, 1971, Pantheon, 1972.
Dinosaurs and All That Rubbish, Hamish Hamilton, 1972, Crowell, 1973.
War and Peas, Crowell, 1974.
All the King's Horses, Hamish Hamilton, 1976, Bradbury, 1977.
Panda's Puzzle, and His Voyage of Discovery, Hamish Hamilton, 1977, Bradbury, 1978.
Panda and the Odd Lion, Hamish Hamilton, 1979.
Trick a Tracker, Philomel, 1981.
Land of Dreams, Holt, 1982.
Panda and the Bunyips, Hamish Hamilton, 1984, Schocken, 1988.
Cat and Canary, Andersen, 1984, Dial, 1985.
Panda and the Bushfire, Prentice-Hall, 1986.
Ben's Box, Hodder and Stoughton, 1986.

Ben's Baby (picture book), Andersen, 1987, Harper, 1988.

The Angel and the Wild Animal, Andersen, 1988, Atheneum, 1989.

One World, Andersen, 1990.

War Boy: A Country Childhood, Arcade, 1990.

(Editor) *Michael Foreman's Mother Goose,* Harcourt, 1991.

The Boy Who Sailed with Columbus, Pavilion, 1991.

(Editor) *Michael Foreman's World of Fairy Tales,* Arcade, 1991.

Jack's Fantasic Voyage, Andersen, 1992.

ILLUSTRATOR

Janet Charters, *The General,* Dutton, 1961.

Cledwyn Hughes, *The King Who Lived on Jelly,* Routledge & Kegan Paul, 1963.

Eric Partridge, *Comic Alphabets,* Routledge & Kegan Paul, 1964.

Derek Cooper, *The Bad Food Guide,* Routledge & Kegan Paul, 1966.

Leonore Klein, *Huit Enfants et un Bebe,* Abelard, 1966.

Mabel Watts, *I'm for You, You're for Me,* Abelard, 1967.

Sergei Vladimirovich Mikalkov, *Let's Fight!, and Other Russian Fables,* Pantheon, 1968.

Donald Davie, *Essex Poems,* 1969.

William Ivan Martin, *Adam's Balm,* Bowmar, 1970.

C. O. Alexander, *Fisher v. Spassky,* Penguin, 1972.

William Fagg, editor, *The Living Arts of Nigeria,* Studio Vista, 1972.

Barbara Adachi, *The Living Treasures of Japan,* Wildwood House, 1973.

Janice Elliott, *Alexander in the Land of Mog,* Brockhampton Press, 1973.

Elliott, *The Birthday Unicorn,* Penguin, 1973.

Sheila Burnford, *Noah and the Second Flood,* Gollancz, 1973.

Jane H. Yolen, *Rainbow Rider,* Crowell, 1974.

Georgess McHargue, *Private Zoo,* Viking, 1975.

Barbara K. Walker, *Teeny-Tiny and the Witch-Woman,* Pantheon, 1975.

Cheng-en Wu, *Monkey and the Three Wizards,* translated by Peter Harris, Collins & World, 1976.

Alan Garner, *The Stone Book,* Collins & World, 1976.

Garner, *Tom Fobble's Day,* Collins & World, 1976.

Garner, *Granny Reardun,* Collins & World, 1977.

Hans Christian Andersen, *Hans Christian Andersen: His Classic Fairy Tales,* translated by Erik Haugaard, Gollancz, 1977.

K. Bauman, *Kitchen Stories,* Nord Sud, 1977, published as *Mickey's Kitchen Contest,* Andersen, 1978.

Garner, *The Aimer Gate,* Collins & World, 1978.

Bryna Stevens, reteller, *Borrowed Feathers and Other Fables,* Random House, 1978.

Brian Alderson, translator, *The Brothers Grimm: Popular Folk Tales,* Gollancz, 1978.

Oscar Wilde, *The Selfish Giant,* Kaye & Ward, 1978.

Seven in One Blow, Random House, 1978.

Garner, *Fairy Tales of Gold,* Collins & World, 1979, Volume 1: *The Golden Brothers,* Volume 2: *The Girl of the Golden Gate,* Volume 3: *The Three Golden Heads of the Well,* Volume 4: *The Princess and the Golden Mane.*

Bill Martin, *How to Catch a Ghost,* Holt, 1979.

Anthony Paul, *The Tiger Who Lost His Stripes,* Andersen Press, 1980.

Ernest Hemingway, *The Faithful Bull,* Emme Italia, 1980.

Aldous Huxley, *After Many a Summer,* Folio Society, 1980.

Allen Andrews, *The Pig Plantagenet,* Hutchinson, 1980.

Peter Dickenson, *City of Gold and Other Tales from the Old Testament,* Gollancz, 1980.

Terry Jones, *Terry Jones' Fairy Tales,* Pavilion, 1981, Puffin, 1986.

John Loveday, editor, *Over the Bridge,* Penguin, 1981.

Robert McCrum, *The Magic Mouse and the Millionaire,* Hamish Hamilton, 1981.

Rudyard Kipling, *The Crab That Played with the Sea: A Just So Story,* Macmillan, 1982.

Angela Carter, selector and translator, *Sleeping Beauty and Other Favourite Fairy Tales,* Gollancz, 1982, Schocken, 1984.

Helen Piers, *Longneck and Thunderfoot,* Kestrel, 1982.

McCrum, *The Brontosaurus Birthday Cake,* Hamish Hamilton, 1982.

Jones, *The Saga of Erik the Viking,* Pavilion, 1983, Puffin, 1986.

Charles Dickens, *A Christmas Carol,* Dial, 1983.

Nanette Newman, *A Cat and Mouse Love Story,* Heinemann, 1983.

Robert Louis Stevenson, *Treasure Island,* Penguin, 1983.

Kit Wright, editor, *Poems for 9-Year-Olds and Under,* Puffin, 1984.

Helen Nicoll, editor, *Poems for 7-Year-Olds and Under,* Puffin, 1984.

Wright, editor, *Poems for 10-Year-Olds and Over,* Puffin, 1985.

Roald Dahl, *Charlie and the Chocolate Factory,* Puffin, 1985.

Madhur Jaffrey, *Seasons of Splendour: Tales, Myths and Legends of India,* Pavilion, 1985.

McCrum, *Brontosaurus Superstar,* Hamish Hamilton, 1985.

Leon Garfield, *Shakespeare Stories,* Gollancz, 1985, Houghton, 1991.

William McGonagall, *Poetic Gems,* Folio Society, 1985.

Stevenson, *A Child's Garden of Verses,* Delacorte, 1985.

Nigel Gray, *I'll Take You to Mrs. Cole!* (picture book), Bergh, 1986, Kane/Miller, 1992.

Edna O'Brien, *Tales for the Telling: Irish Folk and Fairy Tales,* Pavilion, 1986, Puffin, 1988.

Eric Quayle, *The Magic Ointment and Other Cornish Legends,* Andersen, 1986.

Jones, *Nicobobinus,* Pavilion, 1986.

Michael Moorcock, *Letters from Hollywood,* Harrap, 1986.

Charles Causley, *Early in the Morning,* Kestrel, 1986, Viking, 1987.

Kipling, *Just So Stories,* Kestrel, 1987.

Kipling, *The Jungle Book,* Kestrel, 1987.

Jan Mark, *Fun,* Gollancz, 1987, Viking, 1988.

Daphne du Maurier, *Classics of the Macabre,* Gollancz, 1987.

Clement C. Moore, *The Night before Christmas,* Viking, 1988.

Jones, *The Curse of the Vampire's Socks,* Pavilion, 1988.

J. M. Barrie, *Peter Pan and Wendy,* Pavilion, 1988.

Martin Bax, *Edmond Went Far Away,* Harcourt, 1989.

David Pelham, *Worms Wiggle,* Simon & Schuster, 1989.

Eric Quayle, editor, *The Shining Princess and Other Japanese Legends,* Arcade, 1989.

Ann Turnbull, *The Sand Horse* (picture book), Macmillan, 1989.

Kiri Te Kanawa, *Land of the Long White Cloud,* Arcade, 1990.

Alderson, translator, *The Arabian Nights,* Gollancz, 1992.

Also illustrator of *Making Music* by Gwen Clemens, 1966; *The Birthday Unicorn* by Janet Elliott, 1970; *The Pushcart War* by Jean Merrill, 1976; *The Nightingale and the Rose* by Oscar Wilde, 1981; and *The Young Man of Cury* by Charles Causley, Macmillan.

OTHER

Winter's Tales, illustrated by Freire Wright, Doubleday, 1979.

Also creator of animated films for television in England and Scandinavia.

SIDELIGHTS: Children's author Michael Foreman draws upon his real-life experiences when writing and illustrating books. Foreman once told *CA,* "I was born in a fishing village on the east coast [of England] and grew up there during the war. My first book, *The General,* was set there and the local people recognise the church, the ice cream hut, and other scenes in the pictures. By the time *The General* was published, I was living in London and my second book, *The Perfect Present,* contained many London scenes. Since then I have been to many parts of the world and the sketches I bring back become the backgrounds for new books. *Rainbow Rider* is set in New Mex-

ico and Arizona, for example, *Panda and the Odd Lion* in Africa and Venice.

"Sometimes the story is about travelling to many places, as with *Horatio* or *Trick a Tracker.* Occasionally, I get the idea for a story while travelling, but usually it takes a long time to get the right place, the right story, and the right character to meet. Much of my time I am illustrating the work of other writers, and the subject matter varies from the Bible to Shakespeare to stories set in contemporary Britain or the future. My own books are never really about a place or country, but about an idea which is hopefully common to the dreams of everyone, one which works best, however, against a particular background."

War Boy: A Country Childhood received the Kate Greenaway Medal in 1990. The book is a memoir of Foreman's boyhood growing up in England during World War II. Said reviewer Christopher Lehmann-Haupt in the *New York Times,* "Though his memories are haunted by enemy bombers and V1 and V2 rockets, the author recalls in delicate watercolors the many joys of being a shopkeeper's child under siege: the licorice comforts that left your teeth stained black, or the millions of flower seeds that were exploded out of gardens and showered around the district so that 'the following spring and summer, piles of rubble burst into bloom.' "

Foreman's village, Pakefield, is Britain's closest town to Germany; he writes, "The memory of those who passed through our village on the way to war will remain forever with the ghosts of us children in the fields and woods of long ago." "Foreman's recollections are sharp and graphic," said *School Library Journal* reviewer Phyllis G. Sidorsky, "as he poignantly recalls the servicemen who crowded into his mother's shop, grateful for her welcoming cup of tea and a place to chat."

"My books are not intended for any particular age group," Foreman once commented, "but the type is large and inviting for young readers who like to explore the pages after the story has been read to them. In addition I want the story to have some relevance for the adult reader. Less a question of age—more a state of mind."

BIOGRAPHICAL/CRITICAL SOURCES:

PERIODICALS

Isis, November, 1966.
New Statesman, November 27, 1987, p. 34.
New York Times, December 3, 1990.
New York Times Book Review, April 28, 1985, p. 26.
School Library Journal, May, 1990, p. 116.
Times (London), August 29, 1991, p. 14.
Times Educational Supplement, November 14, 1986, p. 41; March 11, 1988, p. 24; June 3, 1988, p. 46; October 13, 1989, p. 28; September 21, 1990, p. R22.

Times Literary Supplement, November 26, 1982; November 30, 1984, p. 1379; June 6, 1986, p. 630; November 25, 1988, p. 1321; August 3, 1990, p. 833.
Washington Post Book World, September 11, 1988, p. 9.

*   *   *

FORSYTH, Frederick 1938-

PERSONAL: Born in 1938 in Ashford, Kent, England; son of a furrier, shopkeeper, and rubber tree planter; married wife, Carole ("Carrie"; a model), September, 1973; children: Frederick Stuart, Shane Richard. *Education:* Attended University of Granada. *Avocational interests:* Sea fishing, snooker.

ADDRESSES: Home—St. John's Wood, London, England. *Office*—c/o Hutchinson Publishing Group, 62-65 Chandos Pl., London WC2N 4NW, England.

CAREER: Novelist. *Eastern Daily Press,* Norwich, England, and King's Lynn, Norfolk, England, reporter, 1958-61; Reuters News Agency, reporter in London, England, and Paris, France, and bureau chief in East Berlin, East Germany, 1961-65; British Broadcasting Corp. (BBC), London, England, reporter, 1965-67, assistant diplomatic correspondent, 1967-68; free-lance journalist in Nigeria, 1968-70. *Military service:* Royal Air Force, pilot, 1956-58.

AWARDS, HONORS: Edgar Allan Poe Award, Mystery Writers of America, 1971, for *The Day of the Jackal.*

WRITINGS:

NOVELS

The Day of the Jackal (also see below), Viking, 1971.
The Odessa File (also see below), Viking, 1972.
The Dogs of War (also see below), Viking, 1974.
The Shepherd, Hutchinson, 1975, Viking, 1976.
The Novels of Frederick Forsyth (contains *The Day of the Jackal, The Odessa File,* and *The Dogs of War*), Hutchinson, 1978, published as *Forsyth's Three,* Viking, 1980, published as *Three Complete Novels,* Avenel Books, 1980.
The Devil's Alternative (also see below), Hutchinson, 1979, Viking, 1980.
The Four Novels (contains *The Day of the Jackal, The Odessa File, The Dogs of War,* and *The Devil's Alternative*), Hutchinson, 1982.
The Fourth Protocol (also see below), Viking, 1984.
The Negotiator, Bantam, 1989.
The Deceiver, Bantam, 1991.

OTHER

The Biafra Story (nonfiction), Penguin, 1969, revised edition published as *The Making of an African Legend: The Biafra Story,* 1977.
(Contributor) *Visitor's Book: Short Stories of Their New Homeland by Famous Authors Now Living in Ireland,* Arrow Books, 1982.
Emeka, Spectrum Books, 1982.
No Comebacks: Collected Short Stories, Viking, 1982.
The Fourth Protocol (screenplay), Lorimar, 1987.

Also author of *The Soldiers,* a documentary for BBC. Contributor of articles to newspapers and magazines, including *Playboy.*

ADAPTATIONS: The Day of the Jackal was filmed by Universal in 1973; *The Odessa File* was filmed by Columbia in 1974; *The Dogs of War* was filmed by United Artists in 1981; *The Fourth Protocol,* 1987, was filmed by Lorimar and executive produced by Forsyth. The Mobil Showcase Network filmed two of Forsyth's short stories ("A Careful Man" and "Privilege") under the title *Two by Forsyth* in 1984; "A Careful Man," was also videotaped and broadcast on Irish television.

SIDELIGHTS: Realism is the key word behind the novels of Frederick Forsyth. Often credited as the originator of a new genre, the "documentary thriller," Forsyth found sudden fame with the publication of his smash best-seller, *The Day of the Jackal,* a book that combines the suspense of an espionage novel with the detailed realism of the documentary novel, first made popular by Truman Capote's *In Cold Blood.* The detail in Forsyth's novels depends not only on the months of research he spends on each book, but also on his own varied personal experiences which lend even greater authenticity to his writing. As *Dictionary of Literary Biography* contributor Andrew F. Macdonald explains, "the sense of immediacy, of an insider's view of world affairs, of all-too-human world figures," as well as quick-paced plots, are the keys to the author's popularity. Critics, however, have sometimes faulted the novelist for shallow characterization and a simplistic writing style. Forsyth does not deny his emphasis on plotting over other considerations. In a *Los Angeles Times* interview he remarks: "My books are 80% plot and structure. The remaining 20% is for characters and descriptions. I try to keep emotions out. Occasionally a personal opinion will appear in the mouth of one of my characters, but only occasionally. The plot's the thing. This is how it works best for me."

For Forsyth the road to becoming a best-selling novelist was a long, circuitous route filled with adventurous detours that would later work their way into his writing. Early in his life, Forsyth became interested in becoming a foreign correspondent when his father introduced him to the world news as reported in the London *Daily Express.* In a London *Times* interview with John Mortimer, Forsyth relates how his father "would get out the atlas and show me where the trouble spots were. And, of course, father had been to the Orient, he told me about tiger shoots and the headhunters in Borneo." Impatient to experience life for himself, Forsyth left school at the age of seventeen and went to Spain, where he briefly attended the University of Granada while toying with the idea of becoming a matador. However, having previously trained as a Tiger Moth biplane pilot, Forsyth decided to join the Royal Air Force in 1956. He learned to fly a Vampire jet airplane, and—at the age of nineteen—he was the youngest man in England at the time to earn his wings.

But Forsyth still dreamed of becoming a foreign corespondent, and towards that end he left the service to join the staff of the *Eastern Daily Press.* His talent for languages (Forsyth is fluent in French, German, Spanish, and Russian) later landed him his dream job as a correspondent for Reuters News Agency and then for the British Broadcasting Corp. (BBC). It was during an assignment for the BBC that Forsyth's career took a sudden turn. Assigned to cover an uprising in the Nigerian region of Biafra, Forsyth began his mission believing he was going to meet an upstart rebellious colonel who was misleading his followers. He soon realized, though, that this leader, Colonel Ojukwu, was actually an intelligent man committed to saving his people from an English-supported government whose corrupt leaders were allowing millions to die of starvation in order to obtain their oil-rich lands. When Forsyth reported his findings, he was accused of being unprofessional and his superiors reassigned him to covering politics at home. Outraged, Forsyth resigned, and he tells Henry Allen in a *Washington Post* article that this experience destroyed his belief "that the people who ran the world were men of good will." This disillusionment is reflected in his writing. Forsyth reveals to Mortimer that he prefers "to write about immoral people doing immoral things. I want to show that the establishment's as immoral as the criminals."

Going back to Africa, Forsyth did free-lance reporting in Biafra and wrote an account of the war, *The Biafra Story,* which *Spectator* critic Auberon Waugh asserts "is by far the most complete account, from the Biafran side [of the conflict], that I have yet read." In 1970, when the rebels were finally defeated and Ojukwu went into exile, Forsyth returned to England to find that his position on the war had effectively eliminated any chances he had of resuming a reporting career. He decided, however, that he could still put his journalism experience to use by writing fiction. Recalling his days in Paris during the early 1960s when rumors were spreading that the Secret Organization Army had hired an assassin to shoot President Charles de

Gaulle, Forsyth sat down and in just over a month wrote *The Day of the Jackal* based on this premise.

Forsyth had problems selling the manuscript at first because publishers could not understand how there could be any suspense in a plot about a presidential assassination that had obviously never come to pass. As the author explains to Allen, however, "The point was not whodunit, but how, and how close would he get?" The fascinating part of *The Day of the Jackal* lies in Forsyth's portrayal of the amoral, ultra-professional killer known only by his code name, "Jackal," and detective Claude Lebel's efforts to stop him. Despite what *New York Times Book Review* critic Stanley Elkin calls Forsyth's "graceless prose style," and characterization that, according to J. R. Frakes in a *Book World* review, uses "every stereotype in the filing system," the author's portrayal of his nemesis weaving through a non-stop narrative has garnered acclaim from many critics and millions of readers. By boldly switching his emphasis from the side of the law to the side of the assassin, Forsyth adds a unique twist that gives his novel its appeal. "So plausible has Mr. Forsyth made his implausible villain . . . and so exciting does he lead him on his murderous mission against impossible odds," says Elkin, "that even saintly readers will be hard put not to cheer this particular villain along his devious way." The author, however, notes that he considered the positive response to his villain a distinctly American response. "There is this American trait of admiring efficiency," he explains to a *Washington Post* interviewer, "and the Jackal is efficient in his job."

"*The Day of the Jackal* established a highly successful formula," writes Macdonald, "one repeated by Forsyth and a host of other writers." Using a tight, journalistic style, Forsyth creates an illusion of reality in his writing by intermixing real-life people and historical events with his fictional characters and plots; "the ultimate effect is less that of fiction than of a fictional projection into the lives of the real makers of history," Macdonald attests. The author also fills his pages with factual information about anything from how to assemble a small nuclear device to shipping schedules and restaurant menus. But the main theme behind the author's novels is the power of the individual to make a difference in the world, and even change the course of history. Macdonald describes the Forsyth protagonist as "a maverick who succeeds by cutting through standard procedure and who as a result often has difficulty in fitting in, [yet he] lives up to his own high professional standards. Forsyth suggests that it is the lone professionals, whether opposed to the organization or part of it, who truly create history, but a history represented only palely on the front pages of newspapers."

Since Forsyth had a three book contract with Viking, he quickly researched and wrote his next two novels, *The*

Odessa File, about a German reporter's hunt for a Nazi war criminal, and *The Dogs of War,* which concerns a mercenary who orchestrates a military coup in West Africa. Forsyth drew on his experience as a reporter in East Berlin for *The Odessa File,* as well as interviewing experts like Nazi hunter Simon Wisenthal, to give the novel authenticity. Background to *The Dogs of War* also came from the author's personal experiences—in this case, his time spent in Biafra. When it comes to details about criminal doings, however, Forsyth goes right to the source. In a *Globe and Mail* interview with Rick Groen, Forsyth says, "There are only two kinds of people who really know the ins and outs of illegal activities: those who practice them and those who seek to prevent them from being practiced. So you talk to cops or criminals. Not academics or criminologists or any of those sorts." This tactic has gotten Forsyth into some dangerous situations. In a *Chicago Tribune* interview the author regales Michael Kilian with one instance when he was researching *The Dogs of War.* Trying to learn more about gun trafficking in the black market, Forsyth posed as a South African interested in buying arms. The ploy worked until one day when the men he was dealing with noticed a copy of *The Day of the Jackal* in a bookstore window. It was "probably the nearest I got to being put in a box," says the author.

The Dogs of War became a highly controversial book when a London *Times* writer accused Forsyth of paying two-hundred-thousand dollars to mercenaries attempting a coup against the President of Equatorial Guinea, Francisco Marcias Nguema. At first, the novelist denied any involvement. Later, however, David Butler and Anthony Collins reported in *Newsweek* that Forsyth admitted to having "organized a coup attempt for research purposes, but that he had never intended to go through with it." The controversy did not hurt book sales, though, and *The Dogs of War* became Forsyth's third best-seller in a row.

After *The Dogs of War* Forsyth did not attempt another thriller for several years. He credits exhaustion to this lengthy hiatus. "Those first three novels had involved a lot of research, a lot of traveling, a half-million words of writing, a lot of promotion," the novelist tells *New York Times Book Review* contributor Tony Chiu. "I was fed up with the razzmatazz. I said I would write no more." To avoid heavy English taxes, Forsyth moved to Ireland, where tax laws are lenient on writers. One explanation as to why he returned to writing has been offered by *New York Times Book Review* critic Peter Maas, who records that when a tax man came to Forsyth's door one day and explained that only actively writing authors were eligible for tax breaks, Forsyth quickly told him that he was working on a novel at that moment. "I hasten to say," Maas writes, "that all this may be apocryphal, but in the interests of providing us a greater truth, I like to think it happened.

It's a wonderful thought, the idea of a tax person forcing a writer into more millions."

Forsyth made his comeback with *The Devil's Alternative,* an intricately plotted, ambitious novel about an American president who must choose between giving in to the demands of a group of terrorists and possibly causing a nuclear war in the process, or refusing their demands and allowing them to release the biggest oil spill in history from the tanker they have hijacked. "The vision is somewhat darker than in Forsyth's earlier works, in which a moral choice was possible," notes Macdonald. "Here, . . . somebody must get hurt, no matter which alternative is chosen." The usual complaints against Forsyth's writing have been trained against *The Devil's Alternative.* Peter Gorner, for one, argues in the *Chicago Tribune Book World* that "his characters are paper-thin, the pages are studded with cliches, and the plot is greased by coincidence." But Gorner adds that " . . . things move along so briskly you haven't much time to notice." *Los Angeles Times* critic Robert Kirsch similarly notes that "Forsyth's banal writing, his endless thesaurus of cliches, his Hollywood characters do not interfere with page turning." Nevertheless, *New York Times Book Review* contributor Irma Pascal Heldman expresses admiration for Forsyth's abilities to accurately predict some of the political crises that came to pass not long after the book was published. She also praises the "double-whammy ending that will take even the most wary reader by surprise. *The Devil's Alternative* is a many-layered thriller."

As with *The Devil's Alternative,* Forsyth's *The Fourth Protocol* and *The Negotiator* offer intrigue on a superpower scale. *The Fourth Protocol* is the story of a Soviet plot to detonate a small atomic device in a U.S. airbase in England. The explosion is meant to be seen as an American error and help put the leftist, antinuclear Labour Party into power. Reviews on the novel have been mixed. *Time* magazine reviewer John Skow faults the author for being too didactic: "[Forsyth's] first intention is not to write an entertainment but to preach a political sermon. Its burden is that leftists and peaceniks really are fools whose habitual prating endangers civilization." Michiko Kakutani of the *New York Times* also feels that, compared to Forsyth's other novels, *The Fourth Protocol* "becomes predictable, and so lacking in suspense." But other critics, like *Washington Post Book World* reviewer Roderick MacLeish, maintain a contrary view. MacLeish asserts that it is Forsyth's "best book so far" because the author's characters are so much better developed. "Four books and a few million pounds after *Jackal* Frederick Forsyth has become a well-rounded novelist."

Of *The Negotiator,* Forsyth's tale of the kidnapping of an American president's son, *Globe and Mail* critic Margaret Cannon declares that "while nowhere nearly as good as

The Day of the Jackal or *The Odessa File,* it's [Forsyth's] best work in recent years." Harry Anderson, writing in *Newsweek,* also calls the novel "a comparative rarity; a completely satisfying thriller." Some critics like *Washington Post* reviewer John Katzenbach have resurrected the old complaints that Forsyth "relies on shallow characters and stilted dialogue," and that while "the dimensions of his knowledge are impressive, rarely does the information imparted serve any greater purpose." Acknowledging that *The Negotiator* has "too many characters and a plot with enough twists to fill a pretzel factory," Cannon nevertheless adds that ". . . the endless and irrelevant descriptive passages are gone and someone has averted Forsyth's tendency to go off on tiresome tangents."

It has always been the plots and technical details in his novels that have most fascinated Forsyth, however. "Invention of the story is the most fun," the author tells Peter Gorner in the *Chicago Tribune.* "It's satisfying, like doing a jigsaw or a crossword." He admits to Groen that he loves the research: "I quite enjoy going after the facts. I put into my books a pretty heavy diet of factuality." Recognizing that Forsyth is aiming to entertain his audience with these techniques, Macdonald writes that a "common element in all the criticism [against the author] is a refusal to accept Forsyth's docudrama formula for what it is, but rather to assume it should be more conventionally 'fictional.' " Forsyth has sold over thirty million books to readers who know, as Jay Carr of the *Detroit News* puts it, that the thrill of the author's books lies not in finding out how "Forsyth is going to defuse the bomb whose wick he ignites, but rather to see how he works out the details."

BIOGRAPHICAL/CRITICAL SOURCES:

BOOKS

Bestsellers 89, Issue 4, Gale, 1990.
Contemporary Literary Criticism, Gale, Volume 2, 1974, Volume 5, 1976, Volume 36, 1986.
Dictionary of Literary Biography, Volume 87: *British Mystery and Thriller Writers since 1940, First Series,* Gale, 1989.

PERIODICALS

Armchair Detective, May, 1974; winter, 1985.
Atlantic, December, 1972; August, 1974.
Book and Magazine Collector, June, 1989.
Book World, September 5, 1971.
Chicago Tribune, October 16, 1984; April 16, 1989; June 14, 1989.
Chicago Tribune Book World, March 2, 1980.
Christian Science Monitor, September 7, 1984.
Daily News (New York), September 30, 1984.
Detroit News, February 10, 1980; August 15, 1982; April 30, 1989.

Globe and Mail (Toronto), September 8, 1984; August 29, 1987; April 29, 1989.
Life, October 22, 1971.
Listener, June 17, 1971; September 28, 1972; January 10, 1980.
Los Angeles Times, March 19, 1980; March 28, 1980; May 7, 1982; August 28, 1987.
Los Angeles Times Book Review, April 16, 1989.
National Observer, October 30, 1971.
National Review, August 2, 1974.
New Leader, April 7, 1980.
New Statesman, September 20, 1974; January 15, 1988.
Newsweek, July 22, 1974; May 1, 1978; April 24, 1989.
New York Post, September 21, 1974.
New York Times, October 24, 1972; April 18, 1978; January 17, 1980; August 30, 1984; August 28, 1987.
New York Times Book Review, August 15, 1971; December 5, 1971; November 5, 1972; July 14, 1974; October 16, 1977; February 24, 1980; March 2, 1980; May 9, 1982; September 2, 1984; April 16, 1989.
Observer, June 13, 1971; September 24, 1972; September 22, 1974.
People, October 22, 1984.
Publishers Weekly, August 9, 1971; September 30, 1974; March 17, 1989.
Saturday Review, September 4, 1971; September 9, 1972.
Spectator, August 2, 1969.
Time, September 3, 1984.
Times (London), August 22, 1982; March 17, 1987; May 13, 1989.
Times Literary Supplement, July 2, 1971; October 25, 1974; December 19, 1975.
Wall Street Journal, April 12, 1989; April 18, 1989.
Washington Post, August 19, 1971; September 26, 1971; December 12, 1978; February 13, 1981; March 28, 1984; August 29, 1987; April 21, 1989.
Washington Post Book World, February 3, 1980; August 26, 1984.
World Press Review, March, 1980; May, 1987.*

*   *   *

FOULDS, Elfrida Vipont 1902-
(Elfrida Vipont; Charles Vipont, a pseudonym)

PERSONAL: Born July 3, 1902, in Manchester, England; daughter of Edward Vipont (a physician) and Dorothy (Crowley) Brown; married Robinson Percy Foulds, April 21, 1926 (died 1954); children: Robin, Carolyn, Dorothy, Ann. *Education:* Attended Mount School, York, England. *Religion:* Society of Friends (Quaker).

ADDRESSES: Home—Green Garth, Yealand Conyers, near Carnforth, Lancashire LA5 9SG, England.

CAREER: Writer of children's books. Lecturer on writing books for children and on Quaker history; Quaker Evacuation School, Yealand Manor, Lancashire, headmistress, 1939-45; member and chairman of Yealand Conyers Parish Council (local government) until 1983.

MEMBER: PEN, Society of Authors.

AWARDS, HONORS: Carnegie Medal from the British Library Association, 1951, for *The Lark on the Wing;* *Book World*'s Children's Spring Book Festival Honor Book, 1970, for *The Elephant and the Bad Baby;* D.H.L., Earlham College, 1984.

WRITINGS:

FOR CHILDREN; UNDER NAME ELFRIDA VIPONT, EXCEPT WHERE INDICATED

Good Adventure: The Quest of Music in England, illustrated by Estella Canziani, Heywood, 1931.

Colin Writes to Friends House, illustrated by Elisabeth Brockbank, Friends Book Centre, 1934, revised edition, Bannisdale Press, 1957.

(Under pseudonym Charles Vipont) *Blow the Man Down,* illustrated by Norman Hepple, Oxford University Press, 1939, Lippincott, 1951.

The Lark in the Morn, illustrated by Terrence Reginald Freeman, Oxford University Press, 1948, Bobbs-Merrill, 1950, 2nd edition, Holt, 1970.

The Lark on the Wing, illustrated by Freeman, Oxford University Press, 1948, Bobbs-Merrill, 1951, 2nd edition, Holt, 1970.

A Lily among Thorns: Some Passages in the Life of Margaret Fell of Swarthmore Hall, Friends Home Service Committee, 1950.

Sparks among the Stubble (short stories), illustrated by Patricia Lambe, Oxford University Press, 1950.

The Family at Dowbiggins, illustrated by Freeman, Bobbs-Merrill, 1955.

(Under pseudonym Charles Vipont), *The Heir of Craigs,* illustrated by Tessa Theobald, Oxford University Press, 1955.

(Coauthor) *Five More,* Blackwell, 1957.

(Editor) *The High Way: An Anthology,* Oxford Univerity Press, 1957.

The Secret of Orra, illustrated by D. J. Watkins-Pichford, Blackwell, 1957.

The Spring of the Year, illustrated by Freeman, Oxford University Press, 1957.

(Editor) *Bless This Day: An Anthology of Prayers for Young Children,* Harcourt, 1958.

More about Dowbiggins, illustrated by Freeman, Lutterworth, 1958, reprinted as *A Win for Henry Conyers,* Hamish Hamilton, 1969.

Henry Purcell and His Times, illustrated by L. J. Broderick, Lutterworth, 1959.

Changes at Dowbiggins, illustrated by Freeman, Lutterworth, 1960, reprinted as *Boggarts and Dreams,* Hamish Hamilton, 1969.

Flowering Spring, illustrated by Shirley Hughes, Oxford University Press, 1960.

The Story of Christianity in Britain, illustrated by Gaynor Chapman, M. Joseph, 1960.

What about Religion?, illustrated by Peter Roberson, Museum Press, 1961.

Search for a Song, illustrated by Peter Edwards, Oxford University Press, 1962.

(Editor) *The Bridge: An Anthology,* illustrated by Trevor Brierley Lofthouse, Oxford University Press, 1962.

Larry Lopkins, illustrated by Pat Marriot, Hamish Hamilton, 1965.

Rescue for Mittens, illustrated by Jane Paton, Hamish Hamilton, 1965.

Stevie, illustrated by Raymond Briggs, Hamish Hamilton, 1965.

The Offcomers, illustrated by Janet Duchesne, Hamish Hamilton, 1965, McGraw, 1967.

Terror by Night: A Book of Strange Stories, Hamish Hamilton, 1966, published as *Ghosts' High Noon,* Walck, 1967.

Weaver of Dreams: The Girlhood of Charlotte Bronte, Walck, 1966.

A Child of the Chapel Royal, illustrated by John Lawrence, Oxford University Press, 1967.

(Coauthor) *People of the Past,* Oxford University Press, 1967.

The China Dog, illustrated by Constance Marshall, Hamish Hamilton, 1967.

The Secret Passage, illustrated by Ian Ribbons, Hamish Hamilton, 1967.

Children of the Mayflower, illustrated by Evadne Rowan, Heinemann, 1969, Watts, 1970.

Michael and the Dogs, illustrated by Marriot, Hamish Hamilton, 1969.

The Elephant and the Bad Baby, illustrated by Briggs, Coward, 1969.

The Pavilion, illustrated by Prudence Seward, Oxford University Press, 1969, Holt, 1970.

Towards a High Attic: The Early Life of George Elliot, Hamish Hamilton, 1970, Holt, 1971.

(Coauthor) *My England,* Heinemann, 1973.

A Little Bit of Ivory: A Life of Jane Austen, Hamish Hamilton, 1977.

FOR YOUNG PEOPLE OR ADULTS

Quakerism: An International Way of Life, 1930 Committee, 1930.

Lift Up Your Lamps: The Pageant of a Friends Meeting, 1930 Committee, 1939.

The Birthplace of Quakerism: A Handbook for the 1652 Country, Friends Home Service Committee, 1952, revised edition, 1987.

Let Your Lives Speak: A Key to the Quaker Experience, Pendle Hill, 1953.

(Under name Elfrida Vipont) *The Story of Quakerism 1652-1952,* Bannisdale Press, 1954, reprinted as *The Story of Quakerism through Three Centuries,* 1960, revised edition, Friends United Press, 1977.

(Under name Elfrida Vipont) *Arnold Rowntree: A Life,* Bannisdale Press, 1955.

Living in the Kingdom, Young Friends Movement, 1955.

The Quaker Witness: Yesterday and Today, Friends United Press, 1955.

(Editor under name Elfrida Vipont) *The High Way: An Anthology,* Oxford University Press, 1957.

(Under name Elfrida Vipont) *Ackworth School: From Its Foundation in 1779 to the Introduction of Co-Education in 1946,* Lutterworth, 1959.

(Under name Elfrida Vipont) *A Faith to Live By,* Friends General Conference, 1962, published in England as *Quakerism: A Faith to Live By,* Bannisdale Press, 1965.

(Editor under name Elfrida Vipont) *The Bridge: An Anthology,* illustrated by Trevor Brierley, Oxford University Press, 1962.

(Under name Elfrida Vipont) *Some Christian Festivals,* M. Joseph Ltd., 1963, Roy, 1964.

(Under name Elfrida Vipont) *Bed in Hell* (novel), Hamish Hamilton, 1974, St. Martin's Press, 1975.

(Under name Elfrida Vipont) *George Fox and the Valiant Sixty,* Hamish Hamilton, 1975.

Swarthmore Hall, Quaker Home Service, 1979.

The Candle of the Lord, Pendle Hill, 1983.

OTHER

Foulds is also author of short radio plays for school broadcasting, including *A True Tale,* 1952; *John Crook, Quaker,* 1954; *Kitty Wilkinson,* 1956; *Dr. Dinsdale in Russia,* 1956. Contributor to many journals and periodicals. Foulds's manuscripts compose part of the Kerlan Collection at the University of Minnesota.

WORK IN PROGRESS: A novel for young people set during World War II.

SIDELIGHTS: Elfrida Vipont Foulds is perhaps best known for *The Lark in the Morn,* and its Carnegie Medal-winning sequel, *The Lark on the Wing.* As in all her books, these two stories for young children are interwoven with a strong Quaker sentiment and an enduring love of music, recalling Foulds's training as a professional singer.

Although describing herself as an avid storyteller throughout her childhood, Foulds credited a chance meeting with a volume of Robert Louis Stevenson's *Treasure Island* with making her aware of the magic of books at a young age. "A book is a living world, and the characters in it are living people," she once told *CA.* Foulds further stated that "life is the essential thing. A story, a setting, a group of characters must be given time to come alive; otherwise you have an ephemeral, dead-alive story. They will not come to life of themselves; patient research is needed, until you know your characters and their settings as well as you know your closest friends and probably better." She continued, "Characters are like people; they have a life of their own, and once they come alive, you cannot impose your will on them. If you have drawn your plot too tightly, they can make hay of it."

Foulds has found her writing for young people to be one of the most rewarding jobs imaginable, but also breaks away into other areas of interest to her: biography, history, religion, music. "These are not a whit less exacting," she pointed out, "but they involve a different kind of discipline which I seem to need from time to time." The steady outpouring of volumes of all different genres attests to Foulds' commitment as a writer. "I found out by experience that hard work and self-discipline were essential to my craft. I soon learnt that the humility to take criticism and learn from it was another necessary ingredient, as well as the courage to recognize failure, and pick myself up and begin again. There was, however, another kind of criticism which must be resisted at all costs: the criticism which strikes at what your book has to say about life, which—take it or leave it—is what you were born to say."

BIOGRAPHICAL/CRITICAL SOURCES:

BOOKS

Twentieth–Century Children's Writers, 3rd edition, St. James Press, 1989.

PERIODICALS

Books and Bookmen, July, 1969.
Christian Science Monitor, January 23, 1956.
Junior Bookshelf, July, 1951.
Library Association Record, May, 1951.
Library Journal, May 15, 1970.
New York Times Book Review, July 9, 1967; March 22, 1970.
Times Literary Supplement, October 16, 1969.
Young Reader's Review, June, 1967.

*   *   *

FRENCH, Peter A(ndrew) 1942-

PERSONAL: Born March 19, 1942, in Newburgh, NY; son of Ernest C. (a Lutheran minister) and Gretchen (Schillke) French; married Sandra Schall, June 1, 1961;

children: Sean Trevor, Shannon Elizabeth. *Education:* Gettysburg College, B.A., 1963; University of Southern California, M.A., 1965; University of Miami, Coral Gables, FL, Ph.D., 1971.

ADDRESSES: Home—15807 Wolf Creek, San Antonio, TX 78232. *Office*—Department of Philosophy, Trinity University, 715 Stadium Dr., San Antonio, TX 78284.

CAREER: Northern Arizona University, Flagstaff, instructor, 1965-66, assistant professor, 1966-68; Miami-Dade Junior College, Miami, FL, assistant professor, 1968-71, chairman, 1970-71; University of Minnesota-Morris, assistant professor, 1971-72, associate professor, 1972-76, professor of philosophy, 1976-81, coordinator of philosophy department, 1972-73, 1977-78; Trinity University, San Antonio. TX, Lennox Distinguished Professor of the Humanities and professor of philosophy, 1981—, chairman of department of philosophy, 1982-88. Visiting professor, Dalhousie University, 1976. University of Delaware, Center for the Study of Values, distinguished research professor, 1980-81, senior fellow, 1981-90. Member, Minnesota Humanities Commission.

MEMBER: American Philosophical Association, Society for Philosophy and Public Affairs, Royal Institute of Philosophy, North American Society for Social Philosophy, Minnesota Philosophical Society.

AWARDS, HONORS: Horace T. Morse-Amoco Foundation Award, 1979, for outstanding contribution to undergraduate education; Governor of Minnesota's certificate of honor, 1982, for outstanding contribution to education.

WRITINGS:

Exploring Philosophy, Schenkman, 1970, revised edition, 1972.
Individual and Collective Responsibility: Massacre at My Lai, Schenkman, 1972, 2nd edition, 1992.
Conscientious Actions, General Learning Press, 1974.
Philosophical Explorations, General Learning Press, 1975.
Philosophers in Wonderland, Llewellyn, 1975.
(With H. K. Wettstein and T. E. Uehling) *Contemporary Perspectives in the Philosophy of Language,* University of Minnesota Press, 1978.
The Scope of Morality, University of Minnesota Press, 1979.
Ethics in Government, Prentice-Hall, 1983.
Collective and Corporate Responsibility, Columbia University Press, 1984.
(With Brent Fisse) *Corrigible Corporations and Unruly Laws,* Trinity University Press, 1985.
Shame, Responsibility, and the Corporations, edited by Hugh Curtler, Haven Publishing, 1986.
(With Curtis Brown) *Puzzles, Paradoxes, and Problems,* St. Martin's, 1987.

The Spectrum of Responsibility, St. Martin's, 1991.
Corporations in the Mortal Community, Harcourt, 1991.
Responsibility Matters, University Press of Kansas, 1992.

Computer software designer for *Stalking the Ripper with Reason,* St. Martin's, 1991, and *Treasure Haunt,* St. Martin's, 1991. Senior editor, *Midwest Studies in Philosophy,* 1976—. Contributor to philosophy journals, including *American Philosophical Quarterly, Philosophy, Ethics,* and *Southern Journal of Philosophy.* Editor, *Journal of Social Philosophy,* 1989—.

WORK IN PROGRESS: A video series, "Beyond the Answers."

*   *   *

FRIEDMAN, Kathy V(allone) 1943-

PERSONAL: Born September 26, 1943, in Rochester, NY; daughter of Joseph Anthony (an attorney) and Nina (a school teacher; maiden name, Lauricella) Vallone; divorced. *Education:* Cornell University, A.B., 1965; University of North Carolina at Chapel Hill, M.A., 1970, Ph.D., 1979.

ADDRESSES: Home—P.O. Box 1251, Washington, DC 20013. *Office*—U.S. Census Bureau, Data User Services Division, Washington DC 20233.

CAREER: Civic Music Association, Rochester, NY, publicity director, 1965-67; Tulane University, New Orleans, LA, instructor in sociology, 1971-73; independent researcher in London, England, 1974-75; Battelle Human Affairs Research Centers, Human Resources Planning Institute, Seattle, WA, research analyst, 1975-79; staff aide to U.S. Representative Richard Gephardt, Washington, DC, 1981; Joint Economic Committee, Washington, DC, staff assistant, 1981-82; legislative assistant to U.S. Representative Louis Stokes, Washington, DC, 1982-85; independent researcher in Washington, DC, 1986-87; U.S. Census Bureau, survey statistician, census promotion specialist, and data user services specialist, 1988—.

MEMBER: American Sociological Association.

AWARDS, HONORS: Guldin Award in Journalism, 1962, for article, "Science and Religion: Can They Coexist?"; National Defense Education Act fellowship, 1968-70.

WRITINGS:

(Contributor) Reece McGee, editor, *Introduction to Sociology,* Dryden, 1977.
Legitimation of Social Rights and the Western Welfare State: A Weberian Perspective, University of North Carolina Press, 1981.

(Contributor) Ronald M. Glassman, William H. Swatos, Jr., and Paul L. Rosen, editors, *Bureaucracy against Democracy and Socialism,* Greenwood Press, 1987.

WORK IN PROGRESS: Capital Credit: The Ultimate Right for Twenty-First Century Citizens for University of North Carolina Press.

SIDELIGHTS: Kathy V. Friedman told *CA:* "After publication, in 1981, of *Legitimation of Social Rights and the Western Welfare State: A Weberian Perspective,* I moved to Washington, DC, and worked on Capitol Hill for several years. It became apparent to me that, despite the rise and expansion of the welfare state, Americans were still having trouble bringing sufficient income into their households from labor force participation. . . . Although in the mid-1980s, forty-two percent of every U.S. budget dollar went as a direct transfer to individuals, Americans were suffering from a declining standard of living relative to the immediately preceding decades. Why?

"I began to rethink the rise of the welfare state. While in *Legitimation of Social Rights* I was concerned with the justifications that were articulated by policymakers in order to make the welfare state possible, in my current work, *Capital Credit: The Ultimate Right for Twenty-First Century Citizens,* I am concerned with the distributional problem that the welfare state was instituted to address. That problem is the relationship among people, work, and income, and specifically, the social institutions for allocating wealth to societal members in an age of increasing technological advance and attendant economic dislocations. From a distributional standpoint, the welfare state was a response to the declining opportunity for people to derive income from labor force participation. Due to the intense productivity generated by the application of technology, Western economies began undergoing vicissitudes in the business cycle, vicissitudes that periodically threw people out of the labor force because their productivity was not needed. Then, the enormous societal wealth generated by the application of technology was taxed by the welfare state and redistributed through an increasing series of programs to individuals, households, and communities in American society.

"To be sure, when the welfare state was instituted, policymakers assumed it would be a temporary phenomenon, redistributing income until economies 'righted' themselves. Economies did not do so. In fact, the problem of income distribution in American society became more complicated with the rise of robotics, increasing international competition, and the deterioration of economies worldwide due to inflation and debt. Moreover, income inequalities have not substantially narrowed for the last few decades. Finally, the political popularity/legitimacy of the welfare state has declined, though not the actual dollar volume of redistributions. Where do we go from here? Have we been trying to solve the wrong problem?"

Friedman credits Norman G. Kurland of the Center for Economic and Social Justice in Arlington, Virginia, with introducing her to a concept of employee ownership based on the ideas of Louis Kelso, originator of the Employee Stock Ownership Principle (ESOP). "The central notion to which [Kurland] introduced me," Friedman said, "was, 'Why not redistribute the opportunity for individuals in society to own the technology that has replaced their labor?'

"This idea has many advantages, chief among which is that ownership of stock shares in the technology of our times would allocate income to individuals through the primary income distribution, not through the 'extra' societal steps of taxing and redistribution. This would be extremely efficient relative to the complex—and inflationary—apparatus of the welfare state. Second, this approach recognizes explicitly that technology is the major producer of wealth in society, not human labor power, and therefore, future sources of income should be sought in the relationship of a society's citizens to the society's technology, not exclusively in the relationship of an individual to his or her labor force participation. Third, and most importantly for this argument, technology today is bought on credit, and specifically 'self-liquidating credit.' 'Self-liquidating' credit is credit for a commodity that pays for itself—for example, a hotel, or machinery that stamps out a marketable product. Indeed, when American business and industry take out loans for expansion, these loans are paid back from future profits, and the loan 'self liquidates.'

"That modern society's wealth-producing technology is purchased through self-liquidating credit has revolutionary implications for the future allocation of wealth in society and for the institution of citizenship. If credit, not prior wealth, is needed to buy into the chief wealth-producing commodity of our time, then those without prior wealth could become participants in the productive process. By democratizing access to credit—through imaginative variations of the ESOP—participation in the productive process could become an economic right of citizenship, paralleling the civil, political, and social rights created in earlier centuries."

Friedman's next book, *Capital Credit,* will address this issue. "My current work outlines the specific institutional mechanisms as well as the bases of legitimation for economic rights in credit as a potential fourth right of citizenship," Friedman said. "The liberal state, the welfare state, and the capital credit state may be thought of as three points on a continuum of relating individuals to economy and society in a way that honors and expands democratic principles while preserving democratic freedoms from encroachments by the state, including a highly pervasive welfare state."

*   *   *

FRIEDMAN, Thomas L(oren) 1953-

PERSONAL: Born July 20, 1953, in Minneapolis, MN; son of Harold Abraham and Margaret (a retired real estate broker; maiden name, Philips) Friedman; married Ann Louise Bucksbaum (a copy editor), November 23, 1978. *Education:* Brandeis University, B.A. (summa cum laude), 1975; St. Antony's College, Oxford, M.Phil., 1978. *Religion:* Jewish.

ADDRESSES: Office—New York Times, Washington, DC, bureau, 1627 I Street NW, Washington, DC 20006.

CAREER: Correspondent in London, England, and Beirut, Lebanon, for United Press International, 1978-81; *New York Times,* New York City, business reporter, 1981-82, Beirut bureau chief, 1982-84, Jerusalem bureau chief, 1984-89, Washington, DC, bureau, chief diplomatic correspondent, 1989—.

MEMBER: Phi Beta Kappa.

AWARDS, HONORS: Overseas Press Club award, 1980, for best business reporting from abroad; George Polk Award, 1982, and Pulitzer Prize and Livingston Award for Young Journalists, both 1983, all for coverage of war in Lebanon; Pulitzer Prize, 1988, for coverage of Israel; Page One Award, New York Newspaper Guild, 1984; Colonel Robert D. Heinl, Jr., Memorial Award in Marine Corps History, Marine Corps Historical Foundation, 1985; National Book Award, National Book Foundation, 1989, for *From Beirut to Jerusalem;* New Israel Fund Award for Outstanding Reporting from Israel.

WRITINGS:

(Text) *War Torn* (photo collection), Pantheon, 1984.
From Beirut to Jerusalem, Farrar, Straus, 1989.

Contributor to *New York Times Magazine.*

SIDELIGHTS: Having survived five years of reporting from one of the most war-torn areas of the Middle East, Thomas L. Friedman decided he had had enough when he awoke one night in 1984 to find his Beirut neighborhood under mortar attack. *Chicago Tribune* reporter Kenneth R. Clark related Friedman's reaction: "I said to myself, 'This is really crazy. I'm the *New York Times* bureau chief in Beirut and my neighborhood is being shelled and it's not news. It's time to go home.' " From his assignment in Beirut Friedman moved on to a posting in Jerusalem, where he remained until 1989. Two Pulitzer Prizes and innumerable war stories later, Friedman returned to the United States, as chief diplomatic correspondent for the Washington, DC, bureau of the *New York Times.*

From Beirut to Jerusalem represents the culmination of Friedman's experiences covering the Middle East, with glimpses of his youth and background. As a Jewish American, Friedman brings an enlightening perspective to discussions of Middle Eastern affairs. Barbara Newman said in the *Los Angeles Times Book Review* that Friedman "has written an intimate portrait of his ten years of reporting in the Middle East, chronicling his change from awestruck lover of Israel to outspoken critic." Friedman's infatuation with Israel began at the age of fifteen, when he visited the country with his parents. In the introductory chapter of *From Beirut to Jerusalem,* Friedman relates an anecdote from his high school days: "I was insufferable. When the Syrians arrested thirteen Jews in Damascus, I wore a button that said, 'Free the Damascus 13,' which most of my classmates thought referred to an underground offshoot of the Chicago 7."

From Beirut to Jerusalem is divided into two sections, discussions of Beirut and of Jerusalem, corresponding to Friedman's assignments first as Beirut bureau chief and later as Jerusalem bureau chief for the *New York Times.* "Mr. Friedman is different when writing of Beirut than he is when writing of Jerusalem," said Roger Rosenblatt in the *New York Times Book Review.* "When he arrives in Jerusalem for the second stage of his assignment, and for the second half of the book, he becomes the political and historical analyst. Reporting from Beirut, he is, for the most part, Pandemonium's correspondent, detailing scenes of pathos and hysteria."

Rosenblatt praised Friedman's treatment of his subject. "For a writer to appear evenhanded discussing the Jews and Arabs in this situation takes little more than giving each equal space in print and ascribing as many errors and atrocities to one as to the other. Mr. Friedman, who leaves no question as to the ardor of his Jewishness, is more interestingly evenhanded in that he rarely makes judgments on specific actions. When he delivers opinions, the judgments are so cosmic and melancholy that the question of fairness does not arise. First and last he is a reporter."

Conor Cruise O'Brien of the *New York Times* said, "I warmly recommend *From Beirut to Jerusalem.* But I do have some reservations. Mr. Friedman is splendid when he is interpreting events of which he has firsthand experience. His grasp on the previous history of the Arab-Israeli conflict is not so sure." O'Brien cited a section of the book which documents Egyptian President Anwar el-Sadat's efforts to negotiate a peace treaty with Israel only after waging war in 1973. O'Brien contends that Sadat made an unreciprocated attempt for peace in 1971. "Most Israelis have forgotten that episode," O'Brien said. "It is odd that so staunch a critic of Israel as Mr. Friedman should share in that Israeli amnesia."

Friedman concluded in *From Beirut to Jerusalem* that the situation in the Middle East is not hopeless, but will require the intervention of the United States for its resolution. "Only a real friend tells you the truth about yourself," he wrote. "An American friend has to help jar these people out of their fantasies by constantly holding up before their eyes the mirror of reality."

BIOGRAPHICAL/CRITICAL SOURCES:

BOOKS

Friedman, Thomas L., *From Beirut to Jerusalem,* Farrar, Straus, 1989.

PERIODICALS

Chicago Tribune, December 1, 1989.
Detroit News, April 19, 1983.
Los Angeles Times Book Review, July 16, 1989, p. 2.
Newsweek, July 24, 1989, p. 57.
New York Times, February 27, 1983; April 19, 1983; July 6, 1989.
New York Times Book Review, July 9, 1989, pp. 1, 26.
Publishers Weekly, April 15, 1988; June 2, 1989, pp. 73-74; July 14, 1989.
Time, July 10, 1989, p. 62.
Times (London), February 22, 1990.
Times Literary Supplement, June 29, 1990.
Washington Post Book World, July 16, 1989, pp. 1, 11.

*　　*　　*

FRISBIE, Richard P(atrick) 1926-

PERSONAL: Born November 27, 1926, in Chicago, IL; son of Chauncey Osborn and Pearl (Harrison) Frisbie; married Margery Rowbottom (a writer), June 3, 1950; children: Felicity, Anne, Thomas, Ellen, Paul, Patrick, Teresa, Margaret. *Education:* Attended University of Chicago, 1944; University of Arizona, B.A., 1948. *Religion:* Roman Catholic.

ADDRESSES: Home—631 North Dunton Ave., Arlington Heights, IL 60004. *Office*—Frisbie Communications, 333 North Michigan Ave., Chicago, IL 60601.

CAREER: Chicago Daily News, Chicago, IL, staff writer, 1948-53, assistant feature editor, 1953-55; advertising agency creative director at Wentzel, Wainwright, Poister & Poore, Chicago, 1955-58, Cunningham & Walsh, Chicago, 1958-61, Hill, Rogers, Mason & Scott, Chicago, 1961-63, and Campbell-Ewald, Chicago, 1964-66; Frisbie Communications, Chicago, editorial and advertising consultant, 1966—. Arlington Heights Public Library, mem-

ber of board of directors, 1967-93, treasurer, 1971-73, president, 1973-79; North Suburban Library System, member of board of directors, 1976-81, treasurer, 1978-79, president, 1979-81. Illinois Center for the Book, president, 1991—. Member of executive board, Cana Conference of Chicago, 1953, 1954.

MEMBER: Society of Midland Authors (treasurer, 1980-81 and 1983-85; president, 1985-88; recording secretary, 1990—).

AWARDS, HONORS: Catholic Press Association Award for best article in a general interest magazine, for article "Let's Be Serious about the Comics."

WRITINGS:

(With wife, Margery Frisbie) *The Do-It-Yourself Parent,* Sheed, 1963.
Family Fun and Recreation, Abbey Press, 1964.
How to Peel a Sour Grape, Sheed, 1965.
Who Put the Bomb in Father Murphy's Chowder?, Doubleday, 1968.
It's a Wise Woodsman Who Knows What's Biting Him, Doubleday, 1969.
Basic Boat Building, Henry Regnery, 1975.
Bicentennial Biographies, Marquis, 1976.
Looking Back, 1877-1977, Marquis, 1977.
Future Gazing, Marquis, 1978.
Second Starts: It's Never as Late as You Think, Marquis, 1979.
Vanished Glory: Towns Where the Date Is Always Yesterday, Marquis, 1980.
The Lure of the Islands: Appointments with Dreams, Marquis, 1981.
Legends That Came to Life, Marquis, 1982.
Speculations for Starry Nights, Marquis, 1983.
Epic Escapes and Rescues, Marquis, 1984.
Winners and Losers, Marquis, 1985.
Traces of Adventure, Marquis, 1986.
Adventure: The Art of Living Dangerously, Marquis, 1987.
Larger-Than-Life Americans, Marquis, 1988.
Mansions Haunted by History, Marquis, 1989.
Under the Farthest Horizon, Marquis, 1990.
The Inconstant Earth, Marquis, 1991.
Encore for the Gay Nineties, Marquis, 1992.

OTHER

Contributor of about 400 articles to periodicals. Former editor, *Events, Chrysler Owners' Magazine,* and *Town and Country News;* former co-editor, *Couplet;* editor, *Chicago,* 1971-72.

BIOGRAPHICAL/CRITICAL SOURCES:

PERIODICALS

Chicago Daily News, June 8, 1955.
Newsweek, December 12, 1952.
New York Times, March 2, 1965.
St. Jude, March, 1963.
Sign, April, 1963.

*   *   *

FULLER, Robert C(harles) 1952-

PERSONAL: Born May 6, 1952, in Grand Rapids, MI; son of Charles Richard (a real estate appraiser) and Bette (a teacher; maiden name, De Good) Fuller; married Kathy Lange (a university development officer), September 6, 1975; children: Bryan Lawrence, Matt Lawrence. *Education:* Denison University, B.A. (summa cum laude), 1974; University of Chicago, M.A., 1975, Ph.D., 1978.

ADDRESSES: Home—1126 Pembrook Dr., Peoria, IL 61614. *Office*—Department of Religious Studies, Bradley University, Peoria, IL 61625.

CAREER: Bradley University, Peoria, IL, assistant professor, 1978-83, associate professor, 1983-88, professor of religious studies, 1988—.

MEMBER: Phi Beta Kappa.

AWARDS, HONORS: Grants from Midwest Faculty Seminar, 1982-84, and National Endowment for the Humanities, 1984.

WRITINGS:

Mesmerism and the American Cure of Souls, University of Pennsylvania Press, 1982.
Religion and the Life Cycle, Fortress, 1988.
Alternative Medicine and American Religious Life, Oxford University Press, 1989.
Ecology of Care, Westminster, 1992.

Contributor to *Journal of Humanistic Psychology* and *Church History.*

WORK IN PROGRESS: Visions of the Anti-Christ: Fear and Hatred in American Religion.

SIDELIGHTS: Robert C. Fuller told *CA:* "Most of my research stems from my ambivalence toward the two major sources of Americans' ideas about human nature—religion and psychology. I suppose that I have never really decided whether I am ultimately trying to critique psychology from a religious point of view or vice versa. I identify with both Ralph Waldo Emerson and William James in believing that a 'radically empirical' analysis of human experience is capable of articulating a religious outlook in a way that is compatible with the modern, scientific world view.

"My books on mesmerism and the unconscious are intellectual histories and do not advance any normative thesis of their own. The reader will, however, detect a subtle advocacy of the religious and cultural importance of psychological models which depict the human capacity to encounter the sacred.

"I am now working on two writing projects. The first is a philosophical study of religious belief. The second is a historical and psychological study of the concept of the Anti-Christ in American religious thought."

*   *   *

FULTON, Robin 1937-

PERSONAL: Born May 6, 1937, on the Isle of Arran, Scotland. *Education:* University of Edinburgh, M.A., 1959, Ph.D., 1972.

ADDRESSES: Home—Postboks 467, N 4001 Stavanger, Norway.

CAREER: Poet and translator.

AWARDS, HONORS: Eric Gregory Award, 1966; University of Edinburgh writer's fellowship, 1969-71; Scottish Arts Council bursary, 1972; Artur Lundkvist Award, 1977, and Swedish Academy award, 1978, both for Swedish translations.

WRITINGS:

POETRY

A Manner of Definition, and Other Poems, Giles Gordon, 1963.
Instances, Macdonald, 1967.
Inventories, Caithness Books, 1969.
The Spaces between the Stones, New Rivers Press, 1971.
Quarters, Castlelaw Press, 1971.
The Man and the Surbahar, Macdonald, 1971.
Tree-Lines, New Rivers Press, 1974.
Music and Flight, Sceptre Press, 1975.
Between Flights, Interim Press, 1976.
Places to Stay In, Sceptre Press, 1978.
Following a Mirror, Oasis Books, 1980.
Selected Poems, 1963-1978, Macdonald, 1980.
Fields of Focus, Anvil Press, 1982.
Coming Down to Earth and Spring Is Soon, Shearsman Books with Oasis Books, 1990.

TRANSLATOR

An Italian Quartet: Versions after Saba, Ungaretti, Montale, Quasimodo, Dufor, 1966.

(From the Russian) Aleksandr Aleksandrovich Blok, *Twelve,* Akros Publications, 1968.

(From the Swedish) Lars Gustafsson, *Selected Poems,* New Rivers Press, 1972.

Five Swedish Poets, Seton Hall University, 1972.

Gunnar Harding, *They Killed Sitting Bull and Other Poems,* London Magazine Editions, 1973.

(From the Swedish) Tomas Transtroemer, *Selected Poems,* Penguin, 1973, expanded edition, Ardis, 1981.

(With Anselm Hollo) *Paavo Haavikko and Tomas Transtroemer,* Penguin, 1974.

Oesten Sjoestrand, *The Hidden Music and Other Poems,* Oleander Press, 1975.

Werner Aspenstroem, *Selected Poems,* Oasis Books, 1976.

Aspenstroem, *The Blue Whale and Other Prose Pieces,* Oasis Books, 1981.

Transtroemer, *The Wild Square,* Oasis Books, 1984.

(From the Norwegian) Olav Hauge, *Don't Give Me the Whole Truth* (selected poems), Anvil Press, 1985.

(From the Swedish) Kjell Espmark, *Bela Bartok against the Third Reich* (selected poems), Oasis Books and Norstedts, 1985.

Transtroemer, *Collected Poems,* Bloodaxe Books, 1987.

Stig Dagerman, *German Autumn,* Quartet Books, 1988.

Sjoestrand, *Toward the Solitary Star,* edited by S. P. Sondrup, Brigham Young University Press, 1988.

Paer Lagerkvist, *Guest of Reality,* Quartet Books, 1989.

Preparations for Flight, and Other Swedish Stories, Forest Books, 1990.

Four Swedish Poets: Kjell Espmark, Lennart Sjoegren, Eva Stroem & Tomas Transtroemer, White Pine Press, 1990.

EDITOR

Trio: New Poets from Edinburgh, New Rivers Press, 1971.

Ian Crichton Smith, *Selected Poems,* Macdonald (Edinburgh), 1982.

A Garioch Miscellany, Macdonald, 1984.

OTHER

Contemporary Scottish Poetry: Individuals and Contexts (criticism), Macdonald, 1974.

The Way the Words Are Taken, Selected Essays, Macdonald, 1989.

Editor, *Lines Review,* 1967-76; also editor of special Scottish issue of *Spirit,* 1971, and *Literary Review,* 1975.

SIDELIGHTS: A prominent British poet, Robin Fulton has consistently received high critical praise for his own volumes of verse as well as for his translations of works in other languages. Although Fulton's reliance on small presses somewhat limited the general public's awareness of his early work, recommendations by the Poetry Book Society for *Fields of Focus* earned publicity and healthier sales figures for the highly acclaimed poet.

Fulton's early poetry, reminiscent of the work of poet E. E. Cummings in its lack of punctuation, is characterized by a "desire to stretch the boundary of poetic construction," observes Martin Booth in the *Dictionary of Literary Biography.* Although fresh and creative in his use of language, Fulton never resorts to gimmicks in his poetry. "His is not a poetry concerned with word games," Booth states. "He is not a poet who loves language for its own sake, but one who uses it simply as a means of intellectual expression."

In the collection of poems entitled *Coming Down to Earth and Spring Is Soon,* Fulton "invests the metaphors of seasonal change as a reflection of human life with new vitality," writes Robert L. Kindrick in *World Literature Today.* Pointing to Fulton's themes and imagery, Kindrick calls the volume "an especially pleasurable one that provides a splendid sampling of his mature voice." Booth, too, praises Fulton's mature poems. "Fulton's vision is in recent years a more refined one, plumbing depths in his poetry in a more concise and exacting way," Booth states. Calling Fulton "a poet of importance and considerable promise," Booth concludes that "one has to wonder what he has yet to produce."

BIOGRAPHICAL/CRITICAL SOURCES:

BOOKS

Dictionary of Literary Biography, Volume 40: *Poets of Great Britain and Ireland Since 1960,* Gale, 1985.

PERIODICALS

Choice, March, 1975.
Saturday Review/World, September 7, 1974.
Stand, winter 1990, p. 65.
Times Literary Supplement, August 14, 1969; May 20, 1977; August 8, 1980; April 8, 1983.
World Literature Today, summer 1990, p. 489.

G

GACKENBACH, Dick 1927-

PERSONAL: Born February 9, 1927, in Allentown, PA; son of William and Gertrude (Reichenbach) Gackenbach. *Education:* Attended Jameson Franklin School of Art, NY, and Abbott School of Art, Washington, DC. *Avocational interests:* Classical music, gourmet cooking, dogs.

ADDRESSES: Home and office—Washington Depot, CT. *Agent*—McIntosh & Otis, Inc., 475 Fifth Ave., New York, NY 10017.

CAREER: J. C. Penney Co., New York City, 1950-72, began as paste-up artist, became creative director; free-lance author and illustrator, 1972—. Consultant on art education for children with learning disabilities, 1988—.

AWARDS, HONORS: Children's Choice designation, International Reading Association and Children's Book Council, 1978, for *Mother Rabbit's Son Tom;* Garden State Children's Book Award from New Jersey Library Association, 1979, for *Hattie Rabbit; New York Times* Outstanding Book citation, 1981, for *McGoogan Moves the Mighty Rock;* Book of the Year citation, Child Study Association of America, 1985, for *Mag the Magnificent.*

WRITINGS:

FOR CHILDREN; SELF-ILLUSTRATED

Claude the Dog: A Christmas Story (Junior Literary Guild selection), Seabury, 1974.
Do You Love Me?, Seabury, 1975.
Claude and Pepper, Seabury, 1976.
Hattie Rabbit, Harper, 1976.
Hound and Bear, Seabury, 1976.
Harry and the Terrible Whatzit (Junior Literary Guild selection), Seabury, 1977.
Hattie Be Quiet, Hattie Be Good, Harper, 1977.

The Leatherman (Junior Literary Guild selection), Seabury, 1977.
Mother Rabbit's Son Tom, Harper, 1977.
Ida Fanfanny, Harper, 1978.
Pepper and All the Legs, Seabury, 1978.
The Pig Who Saw Everything, Seabury, 1978.
Crackle Gluck and the Sleeping Toad, Seabury, 1979.
More From Hound and Bear (Junior Literary Guild selection), Clarion Books, 1979.
Hattie, Tom, and the Chicken Witch: A Play and a Story, Harper, 1980.
A Bag Full of Pups, Clarion Books, 1981.
Little Bug, Clarion Books, 1981.
McGoogan Moves the Mighty Rock, Harper, 1981.
Annie and the Mud Monster, Lothrop, 1982.
(Adapter) *Arabella and Mr. Crack: An Old English Tale,* Macmillan, 1982.
Binky Gets a Car (Junior Literary Guild selection), Clarion Books, 1982.
Mr. Wink and His Shadow Ned, Harper, 1983.
(Adapter) *The Princess and the Pea,* Macmillan, 1983.
What's Claude Doing? (Junior Literary Guild selection), Clarion Books, 1984.
Poppy the Panda (Junior Literary Guild selection), Clarion Books, 1984.
The Dog and the Deep Dark Woods, Harper, 1984.
King Wacky, Crown, 1984.
(Reteller) *The Perfect Mouse,* Macmillan, 1984.
Mag the Magnificent, Clarion Books, 1985.
(Adapter) *Timid Timothy's Tongue Twisters,* Holiday House, 1986.
Hurray for Hattie Rabbit!, Harper, 1986.
Dog for a Day (Junior Literary Guild selection), Clarion, 1987.
Harvey the Foolish Pig, Ticknor & Fields, 1988.
Supposes, Harcourt, 1989.
With Love from Gran, Houghton, 1989.

Beauty, Brave and Beautiful, Houghton, 1990.

Hattie Rabbit, HarperCollins Children's Books, 1990.

Alice's Special Room, Houghton, 1991.

Mighty Tree, Harcourt, 1992.

Claude Has a Picnic, Clarion, in press.

ILLUSTRATOR

Gertrude Norman, *The First Book of Music,* F. Watts, 1954.

Steven Kroll, *Is Milton Missing?* (Junior Literary Guild selection), Holiday House, 1975.

Sally Cartwright, *What's in a Map?,* Coward, 1977.

Miriam Anne Bourne, *What Is Papa Up To Now?,* Coward, 1977.

Jim Murphy, *Rat's Christmas Party,* Prentice-Hall, 1979.

Kroll, *Amanda the Giggling Ghost,* Holiday House, 1980.

Marjorie N. Allen, *One, Two, Three—Ah-Choo!* (Junior Literary Guild selection), Coward, 1980.

Kroll, *Friday the Thirteenth,* Holiday House, 1981.

Janice Lee Smith, *The Monster in the Third Dresser Drawer and Other Stories about Adam Joshua,* Harper, 1981.

Barbara Isenberg and Susan Wolf, *The Adventures of Albert, the Running Bear,* Clarion Books, 1982.

Crescent Dragonwagon, *I Hate My Brother Barry,* Harper, 1983.

Smith, *The Kid Next Door and Other Headaches: Stories about Adam Joshua,* Harper, 1984.

David A. Adler, *My Dog and the Green Sock Mystery,* Holiday House, 1986.

Adler, *My Dog and the Birthday Mystery,* Holiday House, 1987.

Mary Calhoun, *Jack and the Whoopee Wind,* Morrow, 1987.

Kathleen Harris, *The Wonderful Hay Tumble,* Morrow, 1988.

Smith, *It's Not Easy Being George: Stories about Adam Joshua (and His Dog),* HarperCollins Children's Books, 1989.

Smith, *The Show-And-Tell War: And Other Stories about Adam Joshua,* HarperCollins Children's Books, 1990.

Smith, *The Turkey's Side of It: Adam Joshua's Thanksgiving,* HarperCollins Children's Books, 1990.

Smith, *There's A Ghost in the Coat Room,* HarperCollins Children's Books, 1991.

Trinka Enell, *Roll Over, Rosie,* Clarion, 1991.

ADAPTATIONS: The audio version of *Timid Timothy's Tongue Twisters* (four cassettes and a guide) was issued by Live Oak Media in 1989.

SIDELIGHTS: Dick Gackenbach had a career in advertising with J. C. Penney in New York City for twenty years before choosing his second career as a children's book illustrator and author. His books contain a variety of subjects and techniques including stories based on childhood experiences, jokebooks, and stories about mysterious events. Their themes emphasize the importance of affection, generosity, courage, and tolerance. Since 1954, he has illustrated more than twenty books by other children's authors, including David Adler's *My Dog and the Birthday Mystery* and the Adam Joshua stories by Janice Lee Smith.

Gackenbach was born in Allentown, Pennsylvania. When he was young, his family lived on a farm. They were hard workers who had no books and no time to read. They listened to the radio, which at that time broadcast many entertaining shows such as "The Shadow," which was his favorite. He also liked to trace the comics from the newspapers and watch horror films, running home afterward through the frightening dark. Other than that, the children made up their own entertainments. "The fun, along with the love I received, and the values I learned during those difficult times, have been the source of many of my books," he wrote in *Fifth Book of Junior Authors and Illustrators.*

The family moved to town where the author attended high school. After graduation at age seventeen in 1944, he enlisted in the Navy and was stationed near San Francisco. "I had a terrific time, meeting interesting people, discovering museums, galleries, big city libraries, theatres, concerts," he recalled. "I saw my first Van Gogh and my first Impressionists in San Francisco on weekend leave. I read *Madame Bovary* and other classics. I was very fortunate to make a good friend whose guidance into the world of books and culture changed my life."

He planned to go to New York and become a fashion illustrator when his time in the Navy was up. In school with the help of the G.I. Bill at Abbott School of Art in Washington, D.C., he discovered his talents lay elsewhere. "I had trouble with the special washes one must master," he explained. "The rendering of texture was crucial. Velvet has to look like velvet and silk like silk. But art school exposed me to all kinds of art. I gravitated toward design and decided to go into advertising instead. I transferred to the Jameson Franklin School of Art in New York City and studied for two years. I would not have learned to render in classical style anywhere but in art school, but in many ways, the best art education I received was on the job."

He began as a paste-up artist in J. C. Penney's corporate headquarters in New York City, laying out ads and display signs for the store. Eventually, he became one of three creative directors there. He lived in Greenwich Village, visited galleries and museums, and traveled often, visiting Europe and Turkey. In the 1950s, he started building his collection of children's books, which now contains all of

Maurice Sendak's works, an early edition of *The Wizard of Oz,* and contemporary books by Shel Silverstein and others. He sent his first children's book out for publication and it was almost accepted by *Parent's Magazine.* His illustrations were published in Gertrude Norman's *The First Book of Music* in 1954, but he would not try again at publishing until he left his job at Penney's and moved to Washington Depot, an artist's and writer's community in Connecticut. Ten years later, he decided to make it his permanent home.

Gackenbach wrote, "In 1972, I decided to enter the field of children's literature for several reasons. One was that over the years I collected many children's books; as a child I never had any because I grew up during the Great Depression and my family was poor. I later developed a great love for children's books. Also, I like children and as a writer and illustrator I have become somewhat like a grandfather to many, many children: I get a chance to tell them stories and draw pictures for them. The best way I can explain is just to say that my writing is a lot of fun.

"At first I planned only to illustrate children's books. After trying to get illustration assignments with no success, I decided to try to write my own books. I was very lucky and my first book was accepted by Seabury in 1974. Whenever I get letters from people who tell me they want to illustrate children's books, I advise them to try to write their own."

Gackenbach's first book *Claude the Dog* reflects his interest in dogs. He owns two Dachshunds that he says have not yet forgiven him for not using them as a model for the illustration of God in the book *Harvey, the Foolish Pig.* Thinking himself unequal to the task of representing God's actual features, the illustrator drew a lion king for the book instead, he explains in a *Juvenile Literary Guild* brochure. *Claude the Dog* shows a well-cared-for pet giving all his Christmas presents to a homeless mutt and counting it as no loss since he keeps his cherished family. A *Publishers Weekly* reviewer says the book's "large, droll pictures are love made visible." In a more recent book, *A Bag Full of Pups,* a Mr. Mullin's dozen puppies find homes with various strangers, including a hunter and a policewoman, and a boy who simply wants the dog to become his friend.

Claude the Dog was quickly published in 1974 partly because Gackenbach's prior career had given him the skill of color separation, a technique used in publishing books in color that makes book production costly. "Anyone who works as an artist in advertising will tell you that separations are the first thing they teach you. When I stop to consider that advertising gave me precious training for what I really wanted to do, I feel a lot better about my long haul as a corporate executive," he wrote.

Gackenbach's book ideas begin with stories. Describing his writing process, he said, "I get out the typewriter and just see what comes. It comes easily; in that regard, I am a very, very lucky writer. I'll do an entire draft and then go back and revise and polish. A short story for a picture book generally takes five or six drafts which I do over a period of several days. As I'm writing I begin to visualize pictures. Once the story is in shape, I begin work on the dummy. Most of my illustrations are essentially line drawings—my strongest asset. I then do the overlay of gray ink and water mix, followed by the wash, which may be in color. I have the reputation of sending very finished dummies to the publisher. It's easier for me this way to make changes later and gives the editor a much clearer idea of what I would like the book to look like. I usually do three books a year and take two months off to relax and 'recharge.' "

He said he enjoys doing research in libraries to be sure the details in his books about the past are accurate, but mostly he draws from memory or his imagination. "Having grown up in the country, birds, animals, trees, and flowers are a part of me. I can draw an animal or a tree without any reference at all. I especially like to draw chickens—and there are lots of them in my books—maybe because we always had chickens on the farm in Allentown."

Gackenbach's works in several genre feature animals as main characters. *Harvey, the Foolish Pig* presents the tragedy of an ambitious porker whose greediness leads him to an untimely death instead of wealth. On his way to ask the wise King of the Animals how to become rich, he is delayed by a wolf, a lonely rich sow, and a thirsty tree, who also have questions for the King. Not seeing the opportunities before him, he returns with answers to the tree (under which there is a pot of gold), the sow (who proposes), and the wolf (who makes a meal of the pig on the King's advice). The story is based on an Armenian folk tale in which the main character was a man. Gackenbach made the character a pig because he likes to draw animals and knows that children enjoy seeing them in books. The author also illustrated his adaptations of *The Princess and the Pea* and *Arabella and Mr. Crack: An Old English Tale.*

The Leatherman, about a wanderer dressed all in leather who mysteriously arrives in Ben Pickett's town every thirty-four days, is based on stories about a real person who lived in the small towns of Connecticut. An informal investigation shows the wary townspeople that this stranger is not at all harmful. *School Library Journal* contributor Judith Weedman Mackie believes that the story's moral—"the importance of respect for others' differences and the harmful results of fear based on ignorance"—are the book's strongest feature. *Beauty, Brave and Beautiful* presents another outcast—an ugly runt made uglier by abuse—whose resilience, loyalty, and heroic deeds are valued by some wise children. Beauty can't be found in her woodland retreat after helping children escape from an attacking bear. Eventually, however, she returns to see the children and wins the town's approval, which she has deserved all along.

More than a dozen of Gackenbach's books have been Junior Literary Guild selections. Critics recommend his books, with their large, colorful drawings, for reading aloud to small groups. *McGoogan Moves the Mighty Rock* is particularly entertaining for the Irish brogue voice of the main character, George A. Woods relates in the *New York Times Book Review.* McGoogan, a kind man who meets a huge talking rock, agrees to help the rock reach the sea. Once there, the rock promises to give him the gold nugget at its center. Along the way, the rock gives parts of itself away until it is the size of a small stone. McGoogan decides he would rather keep the stone as a friend than make it keep the bargain regarding its heart of gold.

Gackenbach now lives in a condominium in Washington Depot where he spends less time taking care of his garden and more time working on books. For aspiring writers, he suggests keeping a notebook of ideas and sketches. Whether or not they become books, he says these notes are helpful information about one's inner life and development as an artist—and "an awful lot of fun."

BIOGRAPHICAL/CRITICAL SOURCES:

BOOKS

Fifth Book of Junior Authors and Illustrators, Wilson, 1983, pp. 118-19.
Marquardt, Dorothy A., and Martha E. Ward, *Authors of Books for Young People, Supplement* to the 2nd edition, Scarecrow, 1979.

PERIODICALS

Bulletin of the Center for Children's Books, February, 1985; February, 1987; April, 1988.
Juvenile Literary Guild (brochure), April-September, 1988.
New York Times Book Review, May 1, 1977, pp. 29, 43; December 9, 1979; February 22, 1981, p. 31.
Publishers Weekly, October 28, 1974, p. 48.
School Library Journal, November, 1977, pp. 46-47; August, 1988, p. 80.
Times Literary Supplement, March 30, 1984, p. 339.*

*   *   *

GALLAGHER, Vera   1917-

PERSONAL: Born August 1, 1917, in Calgary, Alberta, Canada; daughter of Dominic (a teacher) and Teresa (a teacher; maiden name, Price) Gallagher. *Education:* Received B.A. from College of St. Thomas; received M.A. from Seattle University; received D.Minn. from Jesuit School of Theology, Berkeley, CA.

ADDRESSES: Home—11544 Phinney Ave. N., Seattle, WA. 98133.

CAREER: Roman Catholic nun. Principal of schools to which juvenile courts sent teenager adjudicated delinquent, 1939-70. Founder and executive director of Shepherd's Associates, Inc. (non-profit organization which provides affordable therapy to women survivors of childhood sexual abuse). Educator and consultant to United Indians of All Tribes in the direction of their Healing Project (for men, women, teens, children survivors of childhood sexual abuse). Washington state certified mental health counselor.

WRITINGS:

Hearing the Cry of the Poor, Liguori Publications, 1983.
(With William F. Dodds) *Speaking Out, Fighting Back: Personal Experiences of Women Who Survived Childhood Sexual Abuse in the Home,* Madrona, 1985.
Becoming Whole Again, McGraw, 1991.

Also author of *Little Nellie of Holy God,* Bruce Publishing, and *Shepherdess for Christ,* Catechetical Guild. Contributor of numerous articles to religious and secular periodicals.

WORK IN PROGRESS: A book dealing with addiction of drugs and alcohol.

SIDELIGHTS: Sister Vera Gallagher recently told *CA:* "I've always longed for time to write, never had it, so I have earned how to write at high speed. I snatch a few minutes here, a few minutes there, and the pages pile up. Currently, I have contracts for two more books and was recently offered a contract for a third which I refused. Two books behind are enough for me."

*   *   *

GARFIELD, Leon   1921-

PERSONAL: Born July 14, 1921, in Brighton, Sussex, England; son of David Kalman (a businessman) and Rose (Blaustein) Garfield; married Vivien Dolores Alcock (an artist), October 23, 1948; children: Jane Angela. *Education:* Attended grammar school in Brighton, England. *Politics:* "Somewhere between Labour and Liberal." *Religion:* Jewish. *Avocational interests:* Eighteenth-century music, collecting paintings and china, films, theatre (mainly Shakespeare).

ADDRESSES: Home—59 Wood Lane, Highgate, London N6, England. *Agent*—The Ellen Levine Literary Agency

Inc., Suite 906, 370 Lexington Ave., New York, NY 10017; Jo Stewart, 201 East 66th St., New York, NY 10021; and Winant, Towers, Ltd., Clerkenwell House, 45-47 Clerkenwell Green, London ECIR OHT, England.

CAREER: Whittington Hospital, London, England, biochemical technician, 1946-66; part-time biochemical technician in a hospital in London, England, 1966; novelist, 1966—. *Military service:* British Army, Medical Corps, 1940-46; served in Belgium and Germany.

MEMBER: International PEN.

AWARDS, HONORS: Gold Medal, Boys' Clubs of America, 1966, for *Jack Holborn;* first *Guardian* Award for children's fiction, 1967, for *Devil-in-the-Fog;* Arts Council of Great Britain Award for the best book for older children, and American Library Association (ALA) Notable Book citation, both 1967, *Boston Globe-Horn Book* honor book citation, 1968, and Phoenix award, 1987, all for *Smith;* Carnegie Medal runner-up, 1967, for *Smith,* 1968, for *Black Jack,* and 1970, for *The Drummer Boy; New York Times* Best Illustrated book citation, 1968, for *Mister Corbett's Ghost;* Carnegie Medal for the most outstanding book of the year, and Kate Greenaway Medal commendation, both 1970, both for *The God beneath the Sea;* Kate Greenaway Medal commendation, and ALA Notable Book citation, both 1972, both for *The Ghost Downstairs;* Child Study Association of America's Children's Books of the Year citation, 1976, for *The House of Hanover: England in the Eighteenth Century;* Whitbread Literary Award, 1980, for *John Diamond; Boston Globe-Horn Book* Fiction Honor citation, 1981, for *Footsteps;* Federation of Children's Book Groups awards, 1981, for *Fair's Fair;* Hans Christian Andersen Award nomination, 1981; Golden Cat Award, 1985; runner-up for Maschler awards, 1985, for *Shakespeare Stories* and *The Wedding Ghost.*

WRITINGS:

JUVENILE NOVELS

Jack Holborn, illustrated by Antony Maitland, Constable, 1964, Pantheon, 1965.
Devil-in-the-Fog, illustrated by Maitland, Pantheon, 1966.
Smith, illustrated by Maitland, Pantheon, 1967.
Mr. Corbett's Ghost, illustrated by Alan E. Cober, Pantheon, 1968.
Black Jack, illustrated by Maitland, Longman, 1968, Pantheon, 1969.
The Drummer Boy, illustrated by Maitland, Pantheon, 1969.
The Ghost Downstairs, illustrated by Maitland, Longman, 1970, Pantheon, 1972.
The Strange Affair of Adelaide Harris, illustrated by Fritz Wegner, Pantheon, 1971.

The Captain's Watch, illustrated by Trevor Ridley, Heinemann, 1971.
Lucifer Wilkins, illustrated by Ridley, Heinemann, 1973.
(With Edward Blishen) *The Sound of Coaches* (Junior Literary Guild selection), illustrated by John Lawrence, Viking, 1974.
The Prisoners of September, Viking, 1975.
The Pleasure Garden, illustrated by Wegner, Viking, 1976.
An Adelaide Ghost, Ward, Lock, 1977.
The Confidence Man, Kestrel, 1978, Viking, 1979.
The Night of the Comet: A Comedy of Courtship Featuring Bostock and Harris, Delacorte, 1979.
Footsteps: A Novel, illustrated by Maitland, Delacorte, 1980, published in England as *John Diamond,* Kestrel, 1980.
Fair's Fair, illustrated by Margaret Chamberlain, Macdonald, 1981, American edition illustrated by S. D. Schindler, Doubleday, 1983.
Guilt and Gingerbread, illustrated by Wegner, Kestrel, 1984.
The Wedding Ghost, illustrated by Charles Keeping, Oxford University Press (Oxford), 1985, (New York), 1987.
The December Rose, Kestrel, 1986, Viking Kestrel, 1987.
The Empty Sleeve, Delacorte, 1988.
Blewcoat Boy, Gollancz, 1988, published as *Young Nick and Jubilee,* illustrated by Ted Lewin, Delacorte, 1989.
Revolution!, Collins, 1989.

"APPRENTICES" SERIES

The Lamplighter's Funeral, illustrated by Maitland, Heinemann, 1976.
Mirror, Mirror, illustrated by Maitland, Heinemann, 1976.
Moss and Blister, illustrated by Faith Jaques, Heinemann, 1976.
The Cloak, illustrated by Jaques, Heinemann, 1977.
The Valentine, illustrated by Jaques, Heinemann, 1977.
Labour in Vain, illustrated by Jaques, Heinemann, 1977.
The Fool, illustrated by Jaques, Heinemann, 1977.
Rosy Starling, illustrated by Jaques, Heinemann, 1977.
The Dumb Cake, illustrated by Jaques, Heinemann, 1977.
Tom Titmarsh's Devil, illustrated by Jaques, Heinemann, 1977.
The Enemy, illustrated by Jaques, Heinemann, 1978.
The Filthy Beast, illustrated by Jaques, Heinemann, 1978.
The Apprentices (collection of series titles), Viking, 1978.

ADULT NOVELS

The Mystery of Edwin Drood (completion of the novel begun by Charles Dickens), Deutsch, 1980, Pantheon, 1981.

The House of Cards, Bodley Head, 1982, St. Martin's, 1983.

JUVENILE SHORT STORIES

The Restless Ghost: Three Stories by Leon Garfield, illustrated by Saul Lambert, Pantheon, 1969.

Mister Corbett's Ghost, and Other Stories, illustrated by Maitland, Longman, 1969.

The Boy and the Monkey, illustrated by Ridley, Heinemann, 1969, F. Watts, 1970.

(Reteller with Blishen) *The God beneath the Sea,* illustrated by Keeping, Longman, 1970, American edition illustrated by Zevi Blum, Pantheon, 1971.

(Reteller with Blishen) *The Golden Shadow,* illustrated by Keeping, Pantheon, 1973.

(Reteller) *King Nimrod's Tower,* illustrated by Michael Bragg, Lothrop, 1982.

(Reteller) *The Writing on the Wall,* illustrated by Bragg, Methuen, 1982, Lothrop, 1983.

(Reteller) *The King in the Garden,* illustrated by Bragg, Methuen, 1984, Lothrop, 1985.

(Reteller) *Tales from Shakespeare,* illustrated by Michael Foreman, Schocken, 1985.

(Reteller) *Shakespeare Stories,* illustrated by Foreman, Houghton, 1991.

Also author of short stories, "The Questioners" in *Winter's Tales for Children, 4,* Macmillan, 1968, and the title story in *The Restless Ghost and Other Encounters and Experiences,* edited by Susan Dickinson, Collins, 1970.

EDITOR

Baker's Dozen: A Collection of Stories, Ward, Lock, 1973, published as *Strange Fish and Other Stories,* Lothrop, 1974.

The Book Lovers: A Sequence of Love-Scenes, Ward, Lock, 1977, Avon, 1978.

A Swag of Stories: Australian Stories, illustrated by Caroline Harrison, Ward, Lock, 1977.

(With Mervyn Peake and Blishen) *Sketches from Bleak House,* Methuen, 1983.

OTHER

(With David Proctor) *Child O'War: The True Story of a Sailor Boy in Nelson's Navy,* illustrated by Maitland, Holt, 1972.

The House of Hanover: England in the Eighteenth Century (nonfiction), Seabury, 1976.

Also author, with Patrick Hardy, of the play *The Cabbage and the Rose,* published in *Miscellany Four,* edited by Blishen, Oxford University Press, 1967.

ADAPTATIONS: John Diamond was filmed for BBC-TV, 1981; *Jack Holborn* was made into a Taurus Film (shown on German television), 1982; *The Ghost Downstairs* and *The Restless Ghost* were both dramatized for TV in 1982 and 1983, respectively; a six-part series based on *The December Rose* was shown on BBC-TV, 1986-87; *Mr. Corbett's Ghost* was filmed in 1987. Several of Garfield's other books have been dramatized for film and television. *Devil-in-the Fog, Smith* and *The Strange Affair of Adelaide Harris* have been adapted as television serials for British TV, and *Black Jack* was made into a full-length feature film, produced by Tony Garnett and directed by Ken Loach.

SIDELIGHTS: Leon Garfield's works have been categorized as books for children, but he writes for readers of all ages. Inspired by Victorian novels, Greek myths, and Biblical tales, his fiction evokes the mystery that attends antiquity. His retellings of old stories take readers back to ancient Greece, Babylon, and the scenes of Shakespeare's plays; his novels are most often set in 17th- and 18th-century Britain. *Times Literary Supplement* contributor H. R. Woudhuysen comments, "Garfield's strength lies in creating memorable minor characters, a vivid sense of time and place, and a distinctive atmosphere of smells and tastes, with great skill and economy."

Titles in *The Apprentices* series, twelve illustrated books about various 18th-century apprentices, were first published separately as stories for children. Later, however, an American publisher marketed them under one cover as a collection for adults. The stories, none of which are longer than thirty pages, show young adults learning all-but-forgotten skills such as lamplighting and mirror-silvering in historic London. Because Garfield's heroes confront problems that belong to a past era, they are perhaps more interesting as historical fiction than as moral tales for children, Nicholas Tucker suggests in the *Times Literary Supplement.* Tucker concludes, however, that "our own age, like any other, should always be grateful for effective moral tales illustrating the need for greater love and understanding."

Garfield's retellings of ancient stories appeal to both children and adult readers. According to *New York Times Book Review* contributor Barbara Wersba, *The God beneath the Sea* is "like a mosaic of fiery, precious jewels," keeping all the excitement of the original Greek myths. Speaking of *The Golden Shadow,* a collection of mythical tales from the life of Heracles, *New Statesman* contributor Gerard Benson writes, "Here the myth is transmuted into something new: utterly modern in its writing and still Greek in feeling."

Garfield's retelling of Bible stories is also masterful. In *The King in the Garden,* a little girl helps the cursed Old Testament King Nebuchadnezzar regain his bearings after a season of madness. He returns to Babylon to find out he hasn't even been missed, and all is well. This parable of the theme that "people can get along just fine without a king, but neither people nor a king can get along without the help of God" is told in language that sounds beautiful when read aloud, Elizabeth Crow relates in the *New York Times Book Review.* Garfield gives the Old Testament story of the Tower of Babel a new angle in *King Nimrod's Tower.* While crowds of people bicker about the building of the Tower of Babel, a "ladder" they hope will help them to reach God, God's attention centers on a boy who is trying to understand his stray puppy. At the point in the story when the languages become confused and work on the tower stops, suddenly the boy and the dog can understand each other.

Shakespeare Stories retells twelve of the playwright's most famous plays in a way that both young readers and adults can enjoy. Pared down to their essential actions, the form of the stories preserves a sense of the plays in performance. When relating what the characters say, Garfield uses Shakespeare's original words. Because of this, says D. J. R. Bruckner of the *New York Times Book Review,* readers can savor the dramatic power of the plays "and learn something new about English at the same time."

The Drummer Boy looks at the aftermath of a massacre during the Napoleonic Wars from the viewpoint of a boy who leads thousands of men to their deaths on the battlefield. Love figures importantly in the boy's future encounters with a general's daughter and her maid. More important is the boy's discovery of a mentor in the person of a brave and kindly surgeon. In the *New York Times Book Review* Robert Hood writes that this ambitious novel "instructs youngsters on the nature of glory, love and illusion as they clash with death and reality." And a *Times Literary Supplement* reviewer recommends it to readers of all ages for its memorable themes and scenes.

House of Cards, written specifically for adults, can be appreciated by younger readers who have a taste for elaborate suspense novels popularized during the Victorian era. "A good Victorian novel is like a suite of rooms deliciously furnished for our comfort; they open into each other—the plots and subplots—and are each decorated with all manner of captivating objects, that is, the descriptions and flourishes of the text. Virtue is rewarded, evil is banished and the merely unpleasant are made to slink away," Michele Slung explains in a *Washington Post* review. With its gradually revealed secrets about a beautiful young girl's past, including her abduction from Poland in 1847, *House of Cards* promises to be a satisfying reading experience even for those "who think they don't like Dickens," Bruce Allen writes in the *Christian Science Monitor. Times Literary Supplement* contributor Peter Lewis recommends it to readers who wish Dickens had penned a few more suspense novels before his death. Says Lewis, "It is an entertainment, plotted with great skill and ingenuity, peopled by vivid, boldly drawn and memorable characters, and

narrated by a master storyteller with verve, wit, and a delight in the well-turned phrase and the expressive possibilities of language."

The plot of *John Diamond* is not as complicated as that of *House of Cards,* yet at every turn it displays the author's craftiness, Jacky Gillott remarks in the London *Times.* A boy seeking to make amends for his late father's sins finds he must also evade a gang of ill-intentioned street urchins. By the time these mysteries unravel, "something more than tale-telling has been accomplished. A deeper reassurance is delivered," Gillott intimates. Like the works of Dickens, the story of the boy's quest sheds light on guilt and love in the context of an exciting adventure story.

Garfield paid further homage to Dickens by providing a new ending to *The Mystery of Edwin Drood,* the novel Dickens left half-finished when he died in 1870. Sporting a missing corpse, opposite-sex twins, and a mystery-man who may or may not be an investigator, the novel's first half provides many loose ends for Garfield to tie up. Critics suggest Garfield's offering is more successful than prior attempts to complete the manuscript. They attribute this to his ability to imitate the earlier novelist's style. "The language is nearly always believable as being that of Dickens himself," Angus Wilson comments in the *New York Times Book Review.* "His prose is everywhere alive in the right way." J. I. M. Stewart writes in the *Times Literary Supplement* that Garfield "has, for example, caught the trick of bizarre simile and analogy in which Dickens's work untiringly abounds. All in all, here is a notable achievement in a tricky literary genre."

Many critics praise Garfield's achievements as a writer. Carolyn See concludes in the *Los Angeles Times* that *House of Cards* is a delightfully well-crafted Victorian novel. "Beyond that," she adds, "Garfield has written award-winning children's books and possesses that priceless ability to create a make-believe picture and let you walk into it, to let you be there, and he makes that world so sweetly inviting that you put down the book with a sigh of regret, sorry to be back in this real world."

BIOGRAPHICAL/CRITICAL SOURCES:

BOOKS

Blishen, Edward, editor, *The Thorny Paradise,* Kestrel Books, 1975.
Children's Literature Review, Volume 21, Gale, 1990.
Contemporary Literary Criticism, Volume 12, Gale, 1980.
Townsend, John Rowe, *A Sense of Story,* Lippincott, 1971.
Wintle, Justin, and Emma Fisher, *The Pied Pipers,* Paddington, 1974.

PERIODICALS

Books and Bookmen, June, 1967.

Children's Book World, November 5, 1967.
Children's Literature in Education, winter, 1978.
Christian Science Monitor, November 2, 1967; February 9, 1983, p. 15.
Commonweal, November 10, 1967.
Contemporary Children's Literature, Number 54, 1989.
Growing Point, May, 1982.
Guardian, June 9, 1971.
Horn Book, December, 1968; February, 1971; February, 1972; October, 1974; March, 1990.
Los Angeles Times, February 24, 1983, pp. 2, 20.
National Observer, January 15, 1968.
New Statesman, May 26, 1967; November, 1968; May 25, 1973, p. 782.
New York Times Book Review, November 26, 1967; May 17, 1970, p. 26; March 1, 1981, p. 7; April 14, 1985, p. 43; January 26, 1986, p. 32.
Publishers Weekly, September 30, 1988.
Time, October 27, 1980.
Times (London), July 2, 1980.
Times Literary Supplement, May 25, 1967; April 16, 1970, p. 411; March 28, 1980, p. 355; July 20, 1980; October 3, 1980, p. 1087; May 21, 1982, p. 566; November 26, 1982, p. 1301; June 24, 1988, p. 716.
Variety, March 19, 1969.
Washington Post, March 26, 1983.
Washington Post Book World, March 15, 1981, p. 7; December 1, 1985, p. 11.
Writer, April, 1969.
Young Reader's Review, April, 1966.

OTHER

Leon Garfield, Conn Films, Inc., 1969.*

*   *   *

GARRISON, Phil
See BRANDNER, Gary

*   *   *

GIBB, Lee
See WATERHOUSE, Keith (Spencer)

*   *   *

GLICKMAN, Susan 1953-

PERSONAL: Born April 21, 1953, in Baltimore, MD; daughter of Buddy Irwin (a physician) and Roslyn Wolfe (a social worker) Glickman; married Toan Klein (a glass artist), 1985; children: Jesse (son). *Education:* Tufts University, B.A., 1974; Oxford University, M.A., 1976; University of Toronto, Ph.D., 1984.

ADDRESSES: Office—Department of English, University of Toronto, Toronto, Ontario, Canada M5S 1A1.

CAREER: Sidgwick & Jackson Ltd. (publisher), London, England, reader and permissions editor, 1976-77; NC Press, Toronto, Ontario, assistant editor, 1977-78; University of Toronto, Toronto, assistant professor of English, 1982—.

MEMBER: P.E.N. International, Writers' Union of Canada, League of Canadian Poets, Association of Canadian University Teachers of English, Amnesty International.

AWARDS, HONORS: Social Sciences and Humanities Research Council of Canada doctoral fellowship, 1978-82; grants from Ontario Arts Council, 1982, 1983, 1991-92; Canada Research fellowship, 1987—; Canada Council arts grant, 1991-92.

WRITINGS:

Complicity (poems), Vehicule Press, 1983.
The Power to Move (poems), Vehicule Press, 1986.
Henry Moore's Sheep, and Other Poems, Vehicule Press, 1990.

Work represented in anthologies, including *The Inner Ear,* Quadrant Editions, 1983; *Full Moon,* Quadrant Editions, 1983; *Anything Is Possible,* Mosaic Press, 1984. Contributor of poems, book reviews, and literary criticism to periodicals.

WORK IN PROGRESS: Love and Hunger, poems; *On the Poetics of Landscape,* criticism; *The Canadian Sublime: Essays.*

SIDELIGHTS: Susan Glickman told *CA:* "Poetry for me is a way of expressing being in the world: not just talking *about* the world, but re-experiencing it, untangling the multiple layers of sensation, perception, emotion, thought, and memory that flash by in one instant of existence, and clarifying their relatedness by eliciting it more fully. It is a worshipful attendance to the totality of experience, a process of discovery that is also a process of invention.

"My first book, *Complicity,* was written from a particular perspective—that of the individual alone in the city—and is a meditation on the network of familial and social responsibilities that are ours even in solitude. In some ways it attempts to discover how the personal becomes the political. As a first book, it is partly also a statement of poetic allegiances and perhaps too solemn and polemical.

"My next book, *The Power to Move,* was a lot freer and also a lot more fun to write. Its governing metaphor is travel, although some of the poems are about the exploration of people or ideas rather than places. The poems are more extroverted and more engaged with the physical world. Perhaps they are a little *too* playful, not engaging deeply enough with the more painful and profound sources of experience. My third book, *Henry Moore's Sheep,* attempts to conjoin the seriousness of the first book with the exuberance of the second: it centres on the family as the model of world.

"My collections of poetry *do* tend to be 'books,' in that they are thematic units, not anthologies of discrete pieces. Whatever preoccupies me for a while tends to generate a lot of related writing, which eventually emerges as some kind of sustained exploration. The next step, logically enough, it very long poems. I'm writing a book now of four or five long (i.e., 15-page) poems, all intimately related to each other."

*　　　*　　　*

GOFFART, Walter (Andre) 1934-

PERSONAL: Born February 22, 1934, in Berlin, Germany; son of Francis-Leo (a Belgian diplomat) and Andree (Steinberg) Goffart; married Roberta Frank (a university professor), December 31, 1977; children: (first marriage) Vivian (Mrs. Lewis Humphreys), Andrea Judith. *Education:* Harvard University, A.B. (magna cum laude), 1955, A.M., 1956, Ph.D., 1961; attended Ecole Normale Superieure and Ecole des Hautes Etudes (Paris), 1957-58.

ADDRESSES: Home—Toronto, Ontario, Canada. *Office*—Department of History, University of Toronto, Toronto, Ontario, Canada M5S 1A1.

CAREER: University of Toronto, Toronto, Ontario, lecturer, 1960-63, assistant professor, 1963-66, associate professor, 1966-71, professor of history, 1971—, coordinator of graduate studies in department of history, 1986-88, Centre for Medieval Studies, academic secretary, 1969-71, 1972—, acting director, 1971-72. University of California, Berkeley, visiting assistant professor of history, 1965-66; visiting fellow, Institute for Advanced Studies, 1967-68, and Dumbarton Oaks Center for Byzantine Studies, 1973-74.

MEMBER: International Society of Anglo-Saxonists, American Historical Association, Medieval Academy of America (councillor, 1977-78; fellow, 1982—), Haskins Society.

AWARDS, HONORS: American Council of Learned Societies fellow, 1973-74; Guggenheim fellow, 1979-80; Connaught research fellow in the humanities, University of Toronto, 1983-84; standard research grant, Social Sciences and Humanities Research Council of Canada,

1990-92; Haskins Medal, Medieval Academy of America, 1991, for *The Narrators of Barbarian History (A.D. 550-800).*

WRITINGS:

The Le Mans Forgeries: A Chapter from the History of Church Property in the 9th Century, Harvard University Press, 1966.

Caput and Colonate: Towards a History of Late Roman Taxation, University of Toronto Press, 1974.

(Translator with Marshall Baldwin) Carl Erdmann, *The Origin of the Idea of Crusade,* Princeton University Press, 1978.

Barbarians and Romans, A.D. 418-584: The Techniques of Accommodation, Princeton University Press, 1980.

The Narrators of Barbarian History (A.D. 550-800): Jordanes, Gregory of Tours, Bede, and Paul the Deacon, Princeton University Press, 1988.

Rome's Fall and After (collected studies), Hambledon Press, 1990.

Contributor to books, including *The Dating of "Beowulf,"* edited by Colin Chase, University of Toronto Press, 1981; and *Das Reich und die Barbaren,* by E. K. Chrysos and A. Schwartz, Boehlau, 1989. Contributor to professional journals.

WORK IN PROGRESS: Mapping the Middle Ages: Historical Atlases and Medieval Europe (1568-1870).

SIDELIGHTS: Walter Goffart's *Barbarians and Romans, A.D. 418-584: The Techniques of Accommodation* "is an important discussion of one of the most basic aspects of the transition from late antiquity to the Middle Ages, written by a scholar who has investigated problems of Visigothic, Burgundian, Frankish, and Lombard history since the inception of his academic career," asserts Walter Emil Kaegi, Jr., in *American Historical Review.* In his book, Goffart investigates the fifth-century Roman institution of *hospitalas* whereby Goths and Burgundians lodged on Roman soil with governmental and civilian cooperation in exchange for protecting the landowners from peasant uprisings. The author argues that, in this instance, the barbarians were not accorded large percentages of land held by Roman civilians, as is commonly believed, but instead were given tax revenues normally paid to the government on those land portions, rather than having the government pay the mercenaries. Therefore, Goffart claims that this policy of *hospitalas* was not the origin of later land-sharing arrangements.

E. A. Thompson describes the work in the *Times Literary Supplement* as "stimulating," adding, "It is very detailed. It forces us to look at old problems in a new way, and it has a lot to teach us incidentally. But its main theses are very much open to question." John Beeler comments in

Historian that "the evidence, admittedly, is scanty. . . . But Goffart's arguments are convincing, and while they are certain to provoke controversy, they go far to explain the absence of any popular outcry over the barbarian settlement."

BIOGRAPHICAL/CRITICAL SOURCES:

PERIODICALS

American Historical Review, April, 1982; October, 1990.
Catholic Historical Review, October, 1990.
Historian, May, 1982.
Speculum, October, 1990.
Times Literary Supplement, April 10, 1981; May 5, 1989, p. 492.

*   *   *

GOUDIE, Andrew Shaw 1945-

PERSONAL: Born August 21, 1945, in Cheltenham, England; son of William (a pharmacist) and Mary (Pulman) Goudie. *Education:* Trinity Hall, Cambridge, B.A., 1970, Ph.D., 1971. *Religion:* Christian.

ADDRESSES: Home—57 Linkside Ave., Oxford, England. *Office*—School of Geography, Oxford University, Mansfield Rd., Oxford, England.

CAREER: Oxford University, St. Edmund Hall and Hertford College, Oxford, England, lecturer and demonstrator in geography, 1970-76, fellow of Hertford College, 1976—, professor of geography, 1984—.

MEMBER: Institute of British Geographers, British Geomorphological Research Group, Geographical Club.

WRITINGS:

Duricrusts of Tropical and Sub-Tropical Landscapes, Clarendon Press, 1973.
Environmental Change, Clarendon Press, 1977, new edition, 1992.
The Warm Desert Environment, Cambridge University Press, 1977.
The Prehistory and Paleo-geography of the Great Indian Desert, Academic Press, 1978.
The Human Impact, Basil Blackwell, 1981, new edition, 1990.
Geomorphological Techniques, Allen & Unwin, 1981, new edition, 1990.
Chemical Sediments and Geomorphology, Academic Press, 1983.
The Nature of the Environment, Basil Blackwell, 1984, new edition, 1992.
Discovering Landscape in England and Wales, Allen & Unwin, 1985.

The Land Forms of England and Wales, Basil Blackwell, 1990.
Techniques for Desert Reclamation, Wiley, 1990.

Contributor to professional journals.

WORK IN PROGRESS: Research on the landforms and history of deserts.

*   *   *

GRACE, William J(oseph), Jr. 1948-

PERSONAL: Born July 18, 1948, in Watertown, NY; son of William J. (a surgeon) and Mary E. (Feeley) Grace; married Valerie Ruebush; children: Emily Claire. *Education:* University of Colorado, B.A., 1971.

ADDRESSES: Home—Chevy Chase, Maryland. *Office*—Merrill Lynch, 1850 K St. NW, Washington, DC 20006.

CAREER: Stowe School, Stowe, VT, high school teacher of English and sociology, 1971-74; Merrill Lynch, Washington, DC, account executive, 1975-83, vice-president, 1983-88, first vice-president, 1988—.

WRITINGS:

NONFICTION

The ABCs of IRAs, Dell, 1982, 2nd edition, 1984.
The Phoenix Approach, Bantam, 1984.
What Are You Worth?, Weidenfeld & Nicolson, 1989.

Also contributor to the *Washington Post.*

SIDELIGHTS: William J. Grace, Jr., told *CA* that after spending fifteen years as a full-time investment broker, he now gets to spend more time managing private investments of his own and with his family. While his first three books were drawn from his field of expertise, Grace hopes to write his next book on a non-financial subject.

*   *   *

GREEN, Edwin 1948-

PERSONAL: Born May 16, 1948, in Wanstead, England; married; children: two. *Education:* University of Sussex, B.A. (with honors), 1969, M.Phil., 1977.

ADDRESSES: Office—Archivist, Midland Bank, Poultry, London EC2P 2BX, England.

CAREER: City University, London, England, researcher for insurance records survey, 1972-74; Midland Bank, London, archivist, 1974—. City University, visiting research fellow, 1990—. Lutyens Trust, member, honorary treasurer, 1984—.

MEMBER: Business Archives Council (member of executive council, 1975—; deputy chairman, 1984—).

WRITINGS:

(With Hugh Cockerell) *The British Insurance Business, 1547-1970: An Introduction and Guide to Historical Records in the United Kingdom,* Heinemann, 1976.

(With John Orbell and Michael Moss) *From Cape to Cape: A History of Lyle Shipping,* Paul Harris, 1977.

Debtors to Their Profession: A History of the Institute of Bankers, 1879-1979, Methuen, 1979.

The Making of a Modern Banking Group: A History of the Midland Bank since 1900, St. George's Press, 1979.

(With Moss) *A Business of National Importance: The Royal Mail Shipping Group, 1902-1937,* Methuen, 1982.

(With A. R. Holmes) *Midland: 150 Years of Banking Business,* Batsford, 1986.

Banking: An Illustrated History, Phaidon Press, 1989.

Contributor to *Dictionary of Business Biography.* Contributor to business journals.

BIOGRAPHICAL/CRITICAL SOURCES:

PERIODICALS

Banking World, April, 1990.
Business Archives, November, 1987.
Business History, April, 1988.
History Today, August, 1979.
Times Literary Supplement, May 6, 1983.

*   *   *

GREENE, Constance C(larke) 1924-

PERSONAL: Born October 27, 1924, in New York, NY; daughter of Richard W. (a newspaper editor) and Mabel (a journalist; maiden name, McElliott) Clarke; married Philip M. Greene (a radio station owner), June 8, 1946; children: Sheppard, Philippa, Stephanie, Matthew, Lucia. *Education:* Attended Skidmore College, 1942-44. *Politics:* Democrat. *Religion:* Roman Catholic.

ADDRESSES: Home—East Hampton, Long Island, NY 11937. *Agent*—Marilyn Marlow, Curtis Brown Ltd., 575 Madison Ave., New York, NY 10022.

CAREER: Associated Press, New York City, began as mail-room clerk, became reporter, 1944-46; writer, 1968—.

AWARDS, HONORS: A Girl Called Al was named a *Washington Post Book World*'s Spring Book Festival Honor Book, 1969, and listed as an American Institute of Graphic Arts Children's Book, 1970; *A Girl Called Al,*

Beat the Turtle Drum and *The Love Letters of J. Timothy Owen* were all named American Library Association Notable Books.

WRITINGS:

A Girl Called Al, illustrated by Byron Barton, Viking, 1969.

Leo the Lioness, Viking, 1970.

The Good-Luck Bogie Hat, Viking, 1971.

Unmaking of Rabbit, Viking, 1972.

Isabelle the Itch, illustrated by Emily McCully, Viking, 1973.

The Ears of Louis, illustrated by Nola Langner, Viking, 1974.

I Know You, Al, illustrated by Barton, Viking, 1975.

Beat the Turtle Drum, illustrated by Donna Diamond, Viking, 1976.

Getting Nowhere, Viking, 1977.

I and Sproggy, illustrated by McCully, Viking, 1978.

Your Old Pal, Al, Viking, 1979.

Dotty's Suitcase, Viking, 1980.

Double-Dare O'Toole, Viking, 1981.

Al(exandra) the Great, Viking, 1982.

Ask Anybody, Viking, 1983.

Isabelle Shows Her Stuff, Viking, 1984.

Star Shine, Viking, 1985.

Other Plans (adult novel), St. Martin's, 1985.

The Love Letters of J. Timothy Owen, Harper, 1986.

Just Plain Al, Viking, 1986.

Isabelle and Little Orphan Frannie, Viking, 1988.

Monday I Love You, Harper, 1988.

Al's Blind Date, Viking/Kestrel, 1989.

Funny You Should Ask (short story collection), Delacorte, 1992.

Odds on Oliver, Viking, 1992.

Contributor to periodicals, including New York *Daily News.*

ADAPTATIONS: Beat the Turtle Drum was presented as "Very Good Friends" on *ABC Afternoon Special,* 1976; "Very Good Friends" and *A Girl Called Al* are available on audiocassette, both distributed by Listening Library, both 1985.

SIDELIGHTS: Since both of her parents worked for the New York *Daily News,* children's and young adult fiction writer Constance C. Greene was born with the "tools" of her trade readily accessible. "I grew up with typewriters, newspapers, books, magazines, and conversation all around," Greene related in an interview for *Authors and Artists for Young Adults (AAYA).* "So while it wasn't inevitable that I'd become a writer, that background certainly influenced me.

"My father was a long-time editor of the paper, and my mother reviewed movies for them. The *Daily News* was much more powerful in those days and had the largest circulation in the country. They didn't call themselves journalists back then; they were newspaper people. I've always thought that newspaper work was the best possible profession because it led to a very interesting life. A friend of mine whose father was a businessman said that she used to be so impressed because my family talked about all kinds of ideas and things that weren't discussed at her house."

Greene grew up in the suburbs, but her family eventually moved to the city. "I lived in Larchmont, and that was about twenty-five minutes from New York," she recalled in her *AAYA* interview. "But shortly after I turned fifteen, the *Daily News* made my father their managing editor. He began to work all night long, which was why we moved into the city. This was just before World War II, so New York City was still comparatively safe, but exciting."

Greene completed her secondary schooling in Manhattan, but then left Skidmore College after only two years. She explained to *AAYA*: "Not a serious student, I tired of wasting my time and my father's money. I really wanted to get a job in newspapers. I tried the *Sun, World Telegram,* and *Time,* but nobody would hire me. I finally asked the Associated Press [AP] if they needed help and they put me to work in the mailroom—the bottom rung of the ladder, a very lowly job, indeed. I worked nights for $16.50 a week. At midnight, I would go home by myself on the subway. Always nervous, my mother gave me a whistle to wear around my neck. Fortunately, I had a rapid climb at the AP."

"Since all the young men had gone off to war by 1945, I worked hard and finally got onto the City Desk, which had to be the most exciting job anyone of my age ever had. I did a lot of interviews and went out to Staten Island to meet the incoming troopships. Since the *Baltimore Sun* papers were big AP clients, I would ask the troops where they were from and write about those from Baltimore. . . . There were also the tiresome things, like interviewing 4-H Club members from Iowa. I can't be thankful enough for the year and a half at AP. The job taught me a lot. Working for a wire service, you learn to cram as much as you can into the smallest space possible. I rarely have to cut anything."

Greene left the Associated Press after she married in 1946 to move to Connecticut and concentrate on raising her family. "It's very difficult to write when you have a bunch of kids around," she revealed to *AAYA*. "With so many interruptions, I found myself putting a lot of things on hold. I wrote short stories because I could do those in one sitting. My mother suggested that I write a book for chil-

dren, but that was the furthest thing from my mind at that time. I didn't believe that I could sustain the interest of a reader throughout a book, and really wanted, most of all, to write my short stories. I published a series of these one-page short stories in the *Daily News.* I wrote a lot about little kids, especially one named Charlie, but always from an adult's point of view. They were very easy for me."

"When we were living in Connecticut and the children were still growing up," Greene recalled in an article in *50 Plus,* "I joined a short-story writing group at the Darien Community Association. Everyone was very serious about their writing and a few had even been published. I got so tired of the rejection slips that our teacher—who, by the way, was excellent—suggested that I try for the juvenile market. I started writing my first book, *A Girl Called Al,* and it felt right from the beginning. When I showed the teacher the first few chapters, she said, 'This is what you should do.' "

"I should forget all the other stuff, and that my book was good, she told me," Greene continued her story with *AAYA.* "So I sent it to a publisher where a friend's daughter was a reader. The daughter wrote back and said that although they liked my book, they didn't think that it was complete. 'The heck with this,' I decided, and wrote Phyllis McGinley, a friend of my mother's. McGinley had written a lot of children's books and had won a Pulitzer Prize for her poetry. I asked her if there were any agents who handled just children's books. She gave me the name of her agent, Marilyn Marlow, one of the foremost children's book agents in New York. I sent Marilyn my material. She returned my manuscript and said that she also didn't think it was complete, but was interested in my writing. If I finished the book off a little, she would send it out.

"The first publisher to receive it suggested that I make so many changes that I left saying, 'Oh my God, I don't know what to do.' Marilyn advised we try someone else. She sent it to Velma Varner at Viking, who called me in and said, 'You've got the bones, just flesh them out.' That did it for me. I went home absolutely exhilarated to flesh out the bones. It was the best piece of advice I've ever heard. It demonstrated the differences between those two publishers: the first was too wordy and left me discouraged; Velma had the right touch. She said simply, 'Just do this.' It is the same advice that I now give."

A Girl Called Al was published in 1968. Greene discussed the character of Al in her *AAYA* interview: "The special thing about Al is that she describes herself. She has a high I.Q. but doesn't work to capacity. She's also very nonconformist. At the time I invented her, the terminology of a 'latch-key' kid hadn't been created, but that's what Al was. Her mother and father were divorced and she came home every day to an empty place because her mother worked. Those kids, who often have to take care of younger brothers and sisters, have a great weight of responsibility on their shoulders, but Al's nonconformity is what made her different. The narrator of the book is the opposite of Al; she's really the straight man. Her family has a mother, father, and little brother, and she is relatively unsophisticated. Al has traveled to a lot of places and has done all kinds of things like riding on airplanes. The narrator's family can't afford to do all those things, so she and Al make a nice contrast. The narrator is about as close to me as anything I've done, or maybe I just remember myself being like that."

Louise Fitzhugh's *Harriet the Spy* provided Greene with the needed inspiration that led to the "Al" series. "I'm almost positive that I started writing *Al* after reading that book," Greene explained to *AAYA*. "It opened doors for me. I set out to write about a city kid because they have such a different life from suburban or country kids, and I enjoyed the idea of moving those two kids around the city.

"Al was thirteen when I started out and after six books, I've reluctantly made her fourteen. Maybe I should not have tampered with her age at all. Although Al and her friend have wandered all over New York City, they have remained relatively unsophisticated. I have always expected somebody to call me out on that fact, but, so far, nobody has."

Throughout the "Al" series, as well as in the rest of her writings, Greene has tried to keep her prose and ideas fresh and enduring. "I read the newspapers and that still gives me a feeling for language," she told *AAYA*. "I also listen to kids." Indeed, "eavesdropping—in the nicest possible way—can be very productive," she wrote in a *Writer* magazine article. Greene admits that while window-shopping she heard one young friend say to another "Have a weird day." She was intrigued by the play on the common "Have a good day" and later used its slangy form in *I Know You, Al* and other "Al" books. Now she receives letters from young fans who sign off with "Have a weird day."

Greene has based many of the ideas for her other books on her own children. For instance, *Leo the Lioness* was inspired by her daughter Lucia. She told *50 Plus:* "[When] our youngest was a teenager, she was an astrology freak. She was always studying the signs and talking about how Leo was the best sign, the lion, the king! So I built a story around it." Other people and events have also inspired her, as well, but Greene interprets those with a writer's eye. The character of Gran in *The Unmaking of Rabbit* is modeled on her own mother-in-law. *Double-Dare O'Toole* was based on a phase in her son-in-law's life when he

couldn't resist a dare. He consequently found himself in dangerous or humorous situations because of that.

Despite Greene's distaste for heavy fiction, one of her most popular books remains *Beat the Turtle Drum,* based the story of her older sister's death at age thirteen. She wrote the book after the death of her parents. "That is the only book that I have taken directly from my own life," she explained to *AAYA*. "I wrote that story of two sisters many, many years after in order to try and recreate what had happened. I was only eleven at the time and couldn't remember much about how my mother or father felt, or how people reacted. It was difficult in the beginning but, as with most of my books, I started with a real idea and character and then let my imagination take over. *Beat the Turtle Drum* might have been a better story if I'd recited everything exactly the way it happened, but oftentimes I don't remember it that way. Though I'm not sure that everything in the story actually happened, writing it did make me feel a little better. When I go to schools, this is the book all kids seem to want to talk about. I would really rather not have it be the one thing that I'm known for."

Beat the Turtle Drum was eventually adapted as "Very Good Friends" for an *ABC Afterschool Special* in 1976. Also in the mid-1970s, Greene moved from Connecticut to Maine, where her husband owned a radio station. The sudden peace and quiet disturbed her concentration, she told *AAYA*. "All my kids were in or through with college and I didn't have any friends. Although I could never understand how anyone could write with little kids around, I could do so once mine were reasonably grown up. Having been used to telephones ringing, people coming and going, and lots of friends, I found that serenity was not really good for me."

Greene and her husband sold their radio station after six years of living in Maine and settled happily in East Hampton, Long Island. "Now we live on North Main Street, smack in the middle of town with the fire engines, the ambulances, and never mind the tourists," she informed her *AAYA* interviewer. "I used to be fairly rigid in my writing hours, but either I've changed, or I was doing it wrong all the time. I've found that I work better if I'm not too rigid. I write a little in the afternoon, maybe do something else, and then go back to it.

"I like writing for the middle-grade kids, ages nine to twelve. I think that those kids have changed less from when I or my children were their age than any of the others. The publishers have been wanting funny books for boys that age, so I've been working on that. I've written a couple of books already that have been popular with boys, such as *Double Dare O'Toole. The Love Letters of J. Timothy Owen* was the ideal situation of a lighthearted book with serious overtones."

"I would like to write another adult book. My first was published in 1986 and was called *Other Plans.* It was a story about a boy who didn't get along with his father and although it got some good reviews, it didn't do very well. If I had that one to do all over again, I probably would have written it as a young adult and it probably would have been a heck of a lot more successful. But I have written another adult novel that I started a long time ago that had a very good plot. I used to think that if you had a good plot, the rest was easy, but the book didn't turn out to be saleable. I'd like to go back to it, which is sometimes harder than starting afresh, but the book still intrigues me. It is a murder mystery—the sort I like to read, so it might be fun to do. Writing should not be all drudgery."

BIOGRAPHICAL/CRITICAL SOURCES:

BOOKS

Authors and Artists for Young Adults, Volume 7, Gale, 1991, pp. 93-100.
Something about the Author Autobiography Series, Volume 11, Gale, 1991, pp. 129-147.

PERIODICALS

50 Plus, June, 1981, pp. 74-75.
Horn Book, August, 1969; February, 1971; April, 1973; February, 1974; April, 1975.
New York Times Book Review, January 21, 1973; November 15, 1975; February 15, 1981.
Saturday Review, April 19, 1969.
Teacher, April, 1975.
Writer, August, 1982, pp. 23-26.

*　　　*　　　*

GREENHILL, Basil (Jack) 1920-

PERSONAL: Born February 26, 1920, in Weston-super-Mare, Somerset, England; son of Basil Jack and Edith (Holmes) Greenhill; married Gillian Stratton, 1950 (died, 1959); married Ann Giffard, 1961; children: (first marriage) Richard Basil Stratton; (second marriage) James Giffard. *Education:* University of Bristol, B.A., 1946, Ph.D., 1981. *Religion:* Anglican. *Avocational interests:* Boating, travel.

ADDRESSES: Office—West Boetheric Farm, St. Dominic, Saltash, Cornwall, PL12 G52, England.

CAREER: British Government, Diplomatic Service, 1946-67, served in Pakistan, 1950-54, New York, NY, 1954, Tokyo, Japan, 1955-58, and Geneva, Switzerland, 1958, high commissioner in East Pakistan (now Bangladesh), 1958-59, and Ottawa, Ontario, 1961-64; National Maritime Museum, Greenwich, London, England, direc-

tor, 1967-83. Member of Ancient Monuments Board for England, 1972-82; trustee, Royal Naval Museum, 1973-83; Dulwich College, member of board of governors, 1974-86, chairman of picture gallery committee, 1977-86; chairman of *SS Great Britain* project, 1982—; chairman of maritime of history, Exeter University, 1985—; chairman of government advisory committee on historic wreck sites, 1986—. Principal historical advisor for BBC television series "The Commanding Sea," 1980, and "Trade Winds," 1985, and for BBC radio series "The British Seafarer," 1981. *Military service:* British Navy, 1941-45; became lieutenant.

MEMBER: International Congress of Maritime Museums (president, 1975—), Royal Historical Society (fellow), Society for Nautical Research (vice-president), National Museum Directors Conference.

AWARDS, HONORS: Named companion of St. Michael and St. George, 1967; American Association Award, 1968, for *Westcountrymen in Prince Edward's Isle;* Order of the White Rose of Finland, 1980; named companion of the Bath, 1981; honorary fellowship, University of Exeter, 1985.

WRITINGS:

The Merchant Schooners, Percival Marshall, Volume 1, 1951, revised edition, 1968, Volume 2, 1958, revised edition, 1978.
Out of Appledore, Percival Marshall, 1959, 4th edition, 1980.
Sailing for a Living, Percival Marshall, 1962.
(With wife, Ann Giffard) *Westcountrymen in Prince Edward's Isle,* David & Charles, 1967, revised edition, University of Toronto Press, 1975.
(With A. Giffard) *The Merchant Sailing Ship,* David & Charles, 1970.
Boats and Boatmen of Pakistan, David & Charles, 1971.
(With A. Giffard) *Women under Sail,* David & Charles, 1971.
(With A. Giffard) *Travelling by Sea in the Nineteenth Century,* A. & C. Black, 1972.
Steam and Sail, David & Charles, 1973.
A Victorian Maritime Album, Patrick Stephens, 1974.
(With W. J. Slade) *Westcountry Coasting Ketches,* Conway Maritime Press, 1974.
A Quayside Camera, David & Charles, 1975.
The Coastal Trade, Phaidon, 1975.
Archaeology of the Boat, A. & C. Black, 1976.
(With A. Giffard) *Victorian and Edwardian Sailing Ships,* Batsford, 1976.
(Editor and author of preface) Georg Kahres, *The Last Tall Ships,* Conway Maritime Press, 1978, 2nd edition, 1989.

(With A. Giffard) *Victorian and Edwardian Ships and Harbours,* Batsford, 1978.

(With A. Giffard) *Victorian and Edwardian Steamships,* Batsford, 1979.

Schooners, Batsford, 1980.

The British Sea Farer Discovered, British Broadcasting Corp. and Hutchinson, 1980.

The Life and Death of the Sailing Ship, H.M.S.O., 1981.

(With A. Giffard) *Towards Quebec,* H.M.S.O., 1981.

Karlsson, H.M.S.O., 1983.

The Grain Races, Conway Maritime Press, 1986.

The Woodshipbuilders, Batsford, 1986.

(With A. Giffard) *The British Assault on Finland,* Conway Maritime Press, 1989.

(Editor and author of preface with E. Eglinton) *The Navy Fletcher,* Exeter University Press, 1990.

The Herzog in Cecilie, Conway Maritime Press, 1991.

Also author of numerous pamphlets. Contributor of more than two hundred articles and reviews on maritime history subjects to a variety of publications, including *Times* (London), *Christian Science Monitor, Geographical Magazine, Lloyd's List,* and *Country Life.*

ADAPTATIONS: Westcountrymen in Prince Edward's Isle was filmed for television; *The Herzog in Cecilie* has been the subject of a BBC radio feature program.

WORK IN PROGRESS: A research project on the Royal Navy, 1820-1855.

SIDELIGHTS: Basil Greenhill once told *CA:* "The maritime aspects of history have been greatly neglected. Most of my writing is intended to make people more widely aware of the importance and interest of the maritime dimension."

*   *   *

GREENMAN, Robert 1939-

PERSONAL: Born December 11, 1939, in Brooklyn, NY; son of Bert B. (a frozen foods broker) and Martha (Ehrlich) Greenman; married Carol Sokolov (a medical administrator), May 28, 1960; children: Lisa, Sara, Rachel. *Education:* Emerson College, B.S., 1961. *Religion:* Jewish.

ADDRESSES: Home—4272 Bedford Ave., Brooklyn, NY 11229.

CAREER: High school teacher of English and journalism, 1961-91; writer, 1991—. Adjunct member of faculty, Kingsborough Community College of the City University of New York, 1980.

AWARDS, HONORS: Gold Key Award from Columbia Scholastic Press Association, 1984.

WRITINGS:

The Rap Book, Price, Stern, 1979.

The New York Times Captive Vocabulary, New York Times, 1980, revised edition, 1982.

Words in Action, Times Books, 1983, revised edition published as *Words That Make a Difference,* Farragut Publishing, 1989.

Journalism: A Teacher's Guide, Newsday, 1990.

The Adviser's Companion, Columbia Scholastic Press Association, 1991.

SIDELIGHTS: Robert Greenman told *CA:* "*Captive Vocabulary* is a promotional book I produced for the *New York Times.* For it I collected one thousand sentences from the *Times,* each of which featured a 'vocabulary' word that high school students are likely to encounter while reading the *Times.* A brief definition and a pronunciation accompany each word. The book's title derives from the fact that, despite its reputation as a newspaper for the well educated, the *Times* uses a core of less than two thousand 'educated' words again and again to such an extent that mastery of them means, virtually, mastery of the *Times* (in terms of its word usage). In fact, almost every word in the book can be found on high school vocabulary lists. The book is given free to students and teachers with in-school subscriptions to the *Times.*

"*Captive Vocabulary* led me to write *Word in Action* (now *Words That Make a Difference*), which is composed of fifteen hundred passages from the *Times,* each featuring a word that should be a part of everyone's writing and speaking vocabularies. Unlike *Captive Vocabulary, Words That Make a Difference* was written for a general audience and contains not only the usual type of enrichment word, such as *obfuscate* and *punctilious,* but also Yiddish words and slang. The common theme among all the book's entries is that they make one's communication more precise, alive, and colorful. I end the book with a series of short chapters on different aspects of today's language, such as slang, allusions, and questions of good usage.

"*The Adviser's Companion* is the result of what I learned during my thirteen years advising a student newspaper. It deals with hundreds of major and minor problems, questions, and situations encountered by every high school newspaper adviser. Subjects range from reporting to layouts, and from advertising to libel—with an emphasis on the need for advisers and staffs to professionalize their attitudes and practices. I consider the book's most important chapter to be the one in which I suggest ways to attract or recruit minority students to the school newspaper staff and journalism class. The number of minority students in school journalism has a direct influence on the number of minority professionals in the future.

"A school newspaper should exist not to enhance the school's image or promote the administration's goals, but to report truthfully the way things are in school and to help students better cope with the problems they encounter in and out of school. I urge advisers to think of their newspapers as adversaries of the administration, which is much the same role professional papers play with respect to government. I also show advisers how to live with this kind of relationship."

* * *

GROSSMAN, Allen (R.) 1932-

PERSONAL: Born January 7, 1932, in Minneapolis, MN; son of Louis S. and Beatrice (Berman) Grossman; children: Adam, Jonathan, Bathsheba, Lev, Austin. *Education:* Harvard University, B.A., 1955, M.A., 1957; Brandeis University, Ph.D., 1959.

ADDRESSES: Home—4 Jeffrey Ter., Lexington, MA. *Office*—Department of English, Johns Hopkins University, Baltimore, MD 21217.

CAREER: Brandeis University, Waltham, MA, beginning 1967, assistant professor, professor of English, Paul E. Prosswimmer Professor of Poetry and General Education, 1983-91; Johns Hopkins University, Baltimore, MD, professor of English, 1991—.

AWARDS, HONORS: Golden Rose Trophy, New England Poetry Club, 1969; Witter Bynner Prize for Poetry, American Academy and Institute of Arts and Letters, 1981; Guggenheim fellowship, 1983-84; fellowship for creative writers, National Endowment for the Arts, 1985-86, for poetry; MacArthur fellowship, 1989; Sheaffer-PEN Award, 1989.

WRITINGS:

A Harlot's Hire, Walker-de Berry, 1962.
The Recluse, Pym-Randall, 1965.
Poetic Knowledge in the Early Yeats (prose), University Press of Virginia, 1969.
And the Dew Lay All Night upon My Branch, Aleph, 1973.
The Woman on the Bridge over the Chicago River, New Directions, 1979.
Of the Great House, New Directions, 1981.
Against Our Vanishing: Winter Conversations on Poetry and Poetics, Rowan Tree, 1981.
The Bright Nails Scattered on the Ground, New Directions, 1986.
The Ether Dome and Other Poems New and Selected, New Directions, 1991.
The Sighted Singer: Two Works on Poetry for Readers and Writers, Johns Hopkins University Press, 1991.

BIOGRAPHICAL/CRITICAL SOURCES:

BOOKS

Williamson, Alan, *Introspection and Contemporary Poetry,* Harvard University Press, 1984.

PERIODICALS

New Republic, December, 1978.
Virginia Quarterly Review, autumn, 1969.

* * *

GROTEN, Dallas 1951-

PERSONAL: Born April 10, 1951, in Albert Lea, MN; son of John H. (a contractor) and Viola (a housewife; maiden name, Backlund) Groten; married Caroline Griebel (a registered nurse), December 25, 1981. *Education:* Augsburg College, B.A., 1973; St. Mary's College of Minnesota, M.A.

ADDRESSES: Home—Oak Hill Dr., Box 144A, Spring Valley, MN 55975.

CAREER: Lay minister and youth counselor at Lutheran church in Fort Wayne, IN, 1974-76; Good Earth Village (American Lutheran Church camp), Spring Valley, MN, program director, 1977-79; Wykoff Public Schools, Wykoff, MN, Title I instructor, counselor, and head track coach, 1978-90; career counselor, Southeastern Minnesota Private Industry Council, 1990—. Writer.

AWARDS, HONORS: Winning Isn't Always First Place won the *Group* magazine award for the best book of the year.

WRITINGS:

Winning Isn't Always First Place (stories for young people), Bethany House, 1983.
Will the Real Winner Please Stand?, Bethany House, 1985.
So What Do I Do Now? (stories), Bethany House, 1989.
Ordinary Champions (stories for youth), Augsburg, 1989.

SIDELIGHTS: Dallas Groten told *CA:* "I have always enjoyed participating in the creative process. This interest became a decision in 1975 when I decided to become a professional writer.

"The road to publication was never easy. In my struggle to be a writer, I read as many of the world's great books as I could, in hope that some of the 'greatness' would rub off on me. I wrote thousands of pages of prose, poetry, and song, relying strongly upon my excellent literary background at Augsburg College. At last, after eight years of work and study, with only a poem and brief magazine article in print, Bethany House released *Winning Isn't Always First Place.*

"Though in the past I had written about many different subjects in both fiction and nonfiction, I could not get a book published until I wrote about my own practical experiences as a track coach. *Winning Isn't Always First Place* is a book of short stories, based upon true events, that string together in a novelistic and thematic unity. Each story sets the stage for a Christian devotional lesson and Bible verse. Questions are included at the end of each chapter for personal dissection. My other books *Will the Real Winner Please Stand, So What Do I Do Now?,* and *Ordinary Champions* are all written for young people and follow a similar format as *Winning Isn't Always First Place.*

"I never realized when I first decided to become a writer how isolating writing can be. Nor did I imagine how difficult it is to make a living in my chosen profession. To be a writer is to be blessed, but the blessing sometimes is disguised as a curse."

H

HAIG-BROWN, Roderick (Langmere) 1908-1976

PERSONAL: Born February 21, 1908, in Lancing, Sussex, England; died October 9, 1976, in Campbell River, British Columbia, Canada; son of Alan Roderick (an Army officer) and Violet M. (Pope) Haig-Brown; married Anne Elmore (a high school librarian), January 20, 1934; children: Valerie Joan, Mary Charlotte, Alan Roderick, Evelyn Celia. *Education:* Attended Charterhouse School, Godalming, England.

ADDRESSES: Home—2250 Campbell River Rd., Campbell River, British Columbia V9W 4N7, Canada. *Agent*—Harold Ober Associates, Inc., 40 East 49th St., New York, NY 10017.

CAREER: Naturalist and author. Logger, guide, fisherman, and trapper in Washington State and British Columbia, 1926-30, and 1931-34; Family and Children's Court, Campbell River, judge, 1941-75. University of Victoria (British Columbia), chancellor, 1971-73. Federal Electoral Boundary Commission, commissioner, 1965-66, member, 1972-73, and 1975; International Salmon Commission, member, 1970—. Member, Federal Saltwater Sports Advisory Committee. Consultant, National Film Board, Canadian Broadcasting Company, and Vancouver Public Aquarium. *Military service:* Canadian Army, 1939-45; served overseas; became major; assigned to Royal Canadian Mounted Police, 1944.

MEMBER: Authors Guild, Canadian Writers Association, Society of Authors.

AWARDS, HONORS: Canadian Library Association medals, 1947, for *Starbuck Valley Winter,* and 1963, for *The Whale People;* Governor General's Award, 1948, for *Saltwater Summer;* LL.D., University of British Columbia, 1952; Crandall Conservation Trophy, 1955; National Award in Letters, University of Alberta, 1956; Barien Library Award, 1964, for *Fisherman's Fall;* Vicky Metcalf Award (juvenile writing), 1965; Conservation Award, Trout Unlimited, 1965; J. B. Harkin Award, 1977.

WRITINGS:

Silver: The Life Story of an Atlantic Salmon, A. & C. Black, 1931.

Pool and Rapid, J. Cape, 1932.

Ki-Yu: A Story of Panthers, Houghton, 1934, revised edition published as *Panther: The Story of a North American Mountain Lion,* Collins, 1967.

The Western Angler: An Account of Pacific Salmon and Western Trout in British Columbia, Derrydale, 1939.

Return to the River: The Story of the Chinook Run, Morrow, 1941.

Timber: A Novel of Pacific Coast Loggers, Morrow, 1942.

Starbuck Valley Winter, Morrow, 1943.

A River Never Sleeps (autobiography), Morrow, 1946.

Saltwater Summer, Morrow, 1948.

On the Highest Hill, Morrow, 1949.

Measure of the Year, Morrow, 1950.

Fisherman's Spring, Morrow, 1951.

Mounted Police Patrol, Morrow, 1954.

Fisherman's Winter, Morrow, 1954.

Captain of the Discovery: The Story of Captain George Vancouver, Macmillan, 1956.

Fabulous Fishing in Latin America: Your Guide to the 60 Best Fishing Areas in Mexico, the Caribbean, Central and South America, Pan American World Airways, 1956.

Fisherman's Summer, Morrow, 1959.

(Contributor) *The Face of Canada,* Clarke, Irwin, 1959.

The Farthest Shores, Longmans, Green, 1960.

The Living Land: An Account of the Natural Resources of British Columbia, Macmillan, 1961.

Fur and Gold, Longmans, Green, 1962.

The Whale People, Collins, 1962.

(Contributor) Anthony Netboy, editor, *The Pacific Northwest,* Doubleday, 1963.

A Primer of Fly-Fishing, Morrow, 1964.

Fisherman's Fall, Morrow, 1964.

(Contributor) J. M. S. Careless and R. Craig Brown, editors, *The Canadians,* Macmillan, 1967.

(With Ralph Wahl) *Come Wade the River,* Superior Publishing, 1971.

The Salmon, Fisheries Marine Service, 1974.

The Master and His Fish: From the World of Roderick Haig-Brown, University of Washington Press, 1981.

Writings and Reflections: From the World of Roderick Haig-Brown, University of Washington Press, 1982.

Also contributor to numerous periodicals, including *Atlantic Monthly, Sports Illustrated,* and *Life.*

SIDELIGHTS: Roderick Haig-Brown was well known for his numerous writings about the Canadian wilderness. In books such as *Fisherman's Spring* and *The Living Land,* he mixed scientific facts with almost poetic descriptions of his adopted country; in novels such as *Saltwater Summer* and *On the Highest Hill,* Haig-Brown explored the complex, and sometimes unhealthy, relationship between man and nature. All of Haig-Brown's work stressed the need for conservation of natural resources, whether these resources be wildlife or the land itself. In an article for *Canadian Children's Literature,* Heather Kirk noted that the author "challenged children to think hard about life and to feel profoundly by presenting them with a complete view of the world to which they could relate which was exciting yet sobering."

BIOGRAPHICAL/CRITICAL SOURCES:

BOOKS

Dictionary of Literary Biography, Volume 88: *Canadian Writers, 1920-1959, Second Series,* Gale, 1989, pp. 104-108.

PERIODICALS

British Columbia Library Quarterly, July, 1958.

Canadian Children's Literature, Number 51, 1988, pp. 25-42.

Globe and Mail (Toronto), June 22, 1991.

*   *   *

HALE, Michael
See BULLOCK, Michael

HALLARD, Peter
See CATHERALL, Arthur

*   *   *

HANNON, Ezra
See HUNTER, Evan

*   *   *

HARTMANN, Frederick Howard   1922-

PERSONAL: Born July 6, 1922, in New York, NY; son of Frederick Herman and Grace (MacNamara) Hartmann; married Regina Lou Kiracofe, December 26, 1943; children: Lynne Merry, Vicky Carol, Peter Howard. *Education:* University of California, A.A., 1942, A.B., 1943; Princeton University, M.A., 1947, Ph.D., 1949; University of Geneva, graduate study, 1948.

ADDRESSES: Home—8457 Twin Rocks Rd., Loomis, CA 95650.

CAREER: Princeton University, Princeton, NJ, instructor, 1946-47; University of Florida, Gainesville, assistant professor, 1948-52, associate professor, 1952-56, professor of political science, 1956-66, director of Institute of International Relations, 1963-66; Naval War College, Newport, RI, Alfred Thayer Mahan Professor of Maritime Strategy, 1966-88, professor emeritus, 1988—, special academic advisor to the president, 1966-86. Occasional lecturer at Air War College, 1963—, and at Army War College, 1964, 1965, 1966, Naval War College, 1964, 1965, 1966, National War College, and Inter-American Defense College; visiting professor, Wheaton College, 1967-69, Brown University, 1968, University of Rhode Island, 1970, Texas Tech University, 1974-75, and University of California, Berkeley, 1979-80; visiting scholar, Hoover Institution, Stanford University, 1979-80, and Technical University, Ankara, 1989. University of Florida, Fulbright advisor, 1950-53, secretary of Fulbright Committee, 1951-59, chairman of Fulbright Committee, 1962-66. Member of National Selection Committee for the Fulbright Program, 1954-56. U.S. delegate to Naval War Colleges of America, 4th Conference, 1966, 6th Conference, 1970, 10th Conference, 1980, 12th Conference, 1985. Civic Action Association of Greater Gainesville, founding member and vice-president, 1963-64. *Military service:* U.S. Naval Reserve, active duty, 1943-46; received seven battle stars; retired as captain.

MEMBER: International Studies Association (vice-president of New England Division, 1970-71; president, 1971-72), Foreign Policy Association, American Political

Science Association, American Association of University Professors (member of national council, 1963-66), Southern Political Science Association, New England Political Science Association (member of executive committee, 1982-84), Pi Sigma Alpha, Delta Phi Epsilon, Blue Key.

AWARDS, HONORS: Fulbright research scholar at University of Bonn, Germany, 1953-54; Rockefeller grant for research in Germany on reunification, 1959; U.S. Naval War College Foundation research grant, 1973; Exxon Corp. research grant, 1973; Meritorious Civilian Service Medal, U.S. Department of the Navy, 1985.

WRITINGS:

(Editor) *Basic Documents of International Relations,* McGraw, 1951.
(Editor) *Readings in International Relations,* McGraw, 1952, revised edition published as *World in Crisis: Readings in International Relations,* Macmillan, 1967, 4th edition, 1973.
The Relations of Nations, Macmillan, 1957, 6th edition, 1983.
The Swiss Press and Foreign Affairs in World War II (monograph), University of Florida Press, 1960.
Germany between East and West: The Reunification Problem, Prentice-Hall, 1965.
The New Age of American Foreign Policy, Macmillan, 1970.
The Conservation of Enemies, Greenwood Press, 1982.
(With Robert L. Wendzel) *To Preserve the Republic,* Macmillan, 1985.
(With Wendzel) *Defending America's Security,* Pergamon-Brassey, 1988, 2nd edition, Brassey's Defence Publishers, 1990.
Naval Renaissance: The U.S. Navy in the 1980s, Naval Institute Press, 1990.

Contributor to *System for Educating Military Officers in the U.S.,* 1976. Contributor of articles to professional journals.

WORK IN PROGRESS: America the Superpower.

*   *   *

HARWICK, B. L.
See KELLER, Beverly

*   *   *

HATFIELD, Elaine (Catherine) 1937-
(Elaine Hatfield Walster)

PERSONAL: Born October 22, 1937, in Detroit, MI; daughter of Charles E. (a police officer) and Eileen (Kala-

har) Hatfield. *Education:* University of Michigan, B.A., 1959; Stanford University, Ph.D., 1963. *Religion:* None.

ADDRESSES: Home—3334 Ano'Ai, Honolulu, HI 96822. *Office*—334 Porteus, Honolulu, HI 96822.

CAREER: University of Minnesota, Minneapolis, assistant professor, 1963, associate professor of psychology, 1963-66; University of Rochester, Rochester, NY, associate professor of psychology, 1966-67; University of Wisconsin—Madison, associate professor, 1969-70, professor of sociology and psychology, 1970-81; University of Hawaii at Manoa, Honolulu, professor of psychology and chairperson of department, 1981—. Guest research professor at Sonderforschungsbereich 24, Mannheim, West Germany, 1972.

MEMBER: International Society for the Study of Personal Relationships, International Society for Research on Emotions, International Network on Personal Relationships, American Psychological Association (fellow), Society of Experimental Social Psychology (member of executive committee, 1970-73).

AWARDS, HONORS: Grants from National Institute of Mental Health, 1965-68, 1969-72, 1976-78, and 1982-83, National Science Foundation, 1966-68, 1967-69, 1970-72, and 1971-75, and National Institutes of Health, 1979-80; National Media Award from American Psychological Association, 1979, for *A New Look at Love,* 1986, for *Mirror, Mirror: The Importance of Looks in Everyday Life.*

WRITINGS:

(Under name Elaine Hatfield Walster with Ellen Berscheid) *Interpersonal Attraction,* Addison-Wesley, 1969, 2nd edition, 1978.
(With William Griffitt) *Human Sexual Behavior,* Scott, Foresman, 1974.
(With G. W. Walster) *A New Look at Love,* University Press of America, 1978.
(Under name Elaine Hatfield Walster with Berscheid and G. W. Walster) *Equity: Theory and Research,* Allyn & Bacon, 1978.
(With Susan Sprecher) *Mirror, Mirror: The Importance of Looks in Everyday Life,* State University of New York Press, 1986.
(With J. Carlson) *Psychology of Emotion,* Harcourt, 1992.
(With R. Rapson) *Love, Sex, and Intimacy,* Harper, 1992.

Contributor to numerous books, including *Altruism, Sympathy, and Helping,* edited by Lauren Wispe, Academic Press, 1978, *Equity and Justice in Social Behavior,* edited by Gerald Greenberg and R. L. Cohen, Academic Press, 1982, and *Compatible and Incompatible Relationships,* edited by William Ickes, Springer-Verlag, 1985. Also contributor of more than 150 articles to psychology journals.

HAUG, C(harles) James 1946-

PERSONAL: Born April 14, 1946, in Minot, ND; son of Philip N. (a farmer) and Marie (a teacher; maiden name, McLaughlin) Haug; married Ruth Severson (an administrative coordinator), September 7, 1967; children: Stopher, Martin, James. *Education:* University of North Dakota, B.A., 1968; attended Universitie de Bordeaux, 1968-69; University of Kansas, Ph.D., 1976.

ADDRESSES: Home—P.O. Box 257, Mississippi State, MS 39762. *Office*—Department of History, Mississippi State University, Mississippi State, MS 39762.

CAREER: Mississippi State University, Mississippi State, MS, assistant professor, 1976-80, associate professor, 1980-91, professor of modern European history, 1991—. Senior fellow, Center for International Security and Strategic Studies.

MEMBER: American Historical Association, Society for French Historical Studies, Southern Historical Association.

AWARDS, HONORS: Fulbright fellow, 1968; Wesley Ballaine Award from Travel Research Association, 1976, for the year's outstanding essay in travel research; National Endowment for the Humanities fellow, 1979; Atlantic Council of the United States and German Marshall Fund of the United States travel award, 1988.

WRITINGS:

(Contributor) Dennis J. Mitchell and Peyton W. Williams, editors, *The Humanities and Public Policy,* Mississippi Committee on the Humanities, 1979.
Leisure and Urbanism in Nineteenth-Century Nice, Regents Press of Kansas, 1983.
The Strategic Defense Initiative: An International Perspective, Columbia University Press, 1987.
The Mechanical Feature: 100 Years of Engineering at Mississippi State University, University of Mississippi Press, 1992.

Contributor to history journals, including *North Dakota Quarterly, History Teacher,* and *French History Studies.*

WORK IN PROGRESS: The Revolution in Bacteriology in Nineteenth-Century France, publication expected in 1993; researching the history of low-speed flight.

SIDELIGHTS: In *Leisure and Urbanism in Nineteenth-Century Nice* C. James Haug examines the French city of Nice during the years of its greatest popularity and growth. Planned as a tourist mecca for wealthy Europeans, the city was an innovator in urban planning as well as an enclave of comfort and luxury. Georges Dupeux of the Universite de Bordeaux III assesses *Leisure and Urbanism* for the *European History Quarterly,* stating: "The role of tourism as a factor in urbanization has seldom received from historians the attention it deserves. In choosing the town of Nice as a field of study James Haug has succeeded in developing the theme perfectly." But, according to Dupeux, while the "pressure of tourism on the economy and society of Nice is admirably understood and analysed by James Haug," there are two gaps in his "otherwise well-informed and original study." One gap concerns the demographics of Nice's permanent population, the other "relates to the city's political life," particularly the conflicts faced by municipal authorities between the wants and needs of the tourist population of Nice and those of the city's permanent residents. Charlene M. Leonard similarly argues in the *American Historical Review* that a "more thorough analysis of the group [Nice's municipal council] responsible for formulating policy would lend greater authority to [Haug's] judgments." Nonetheless, Leonard concludes: *Leisure and Urbanism* "provides an excellent introduction of interest both to social historians and urban analysts. In addition to being informative, it is well written and entertaining to read, with useful charts, graphs, and illustrations."

Haug told *CA:* "It is clear that the major issues of contemporary society have their origins in Europe of the nineteenth century. It is thus doubly important that we understand this part of our past. In my writing I try to clarify these issues and make their implications understood to modern readers." More recently, Haug added that he has "expanded my research areas to include major concentrations in the history of technology and engineering."

BIOGRAPHICAL/CRITICAL SOURCES:

PERIODICALS

American Historical Review, October, 1983.
European History Quarterly, January, 1984.
Times Literary Supplement, January 28, 1983.

*   *   *

HAUGAARD, Erik Christian 1923-

PERSONAL: Born April 13, 1923, in Frederiksberg, Denmark; came to the United States in March, 1940; son of Gotfred Hans Christian (a professor of biochemistry) and Karen (Pedersen) Haugaard; married Myrna Seld (a writer), December 23, 1949 (died, 1981); married Masako Taira (a professor); children: (first marriage) Mikka Anja, Mark. *Education:* Attended Black Mountain College, 1941-42, and New School for Social Research, 1947-48. *Avocational interests:* Reading the Icelandic sagas.

ADDRESSES: Home—Toad Hall, Ballydehob, County Cork, Ireland.

CAREER: Author of children's books, drama and poetry. Worked as a farm laborer in Fyn, Denmark, 1938-40, and later as a sheep herder in Wyoming. *Military service:* Royal Canadian Air Force, 1943-45; became flight sergeant; received War Service Medal from Christian X of Denmark.

AWARDS, HONORS: John Golden Fund fellowship, 1958, for *The Heroes;* honorable mentions, *New York Herald Tribune* Children's Spring Book Festival, 1962, for *Hakon of Rogen's Saga,* and 1967, for *The Little Fishes;* American Library Association (ALA) Notable Book Awards citations, 1963, for *Hakon of Rogen's Saga,* 1965, for *A Slave's Tale,* and 1971, for *The Untold Tale; Boston Globe*-Horn Book Award, 1967, Jane Addams Children's Book Award, 1968, and Danish Cultural Minister's Prize, 1970, all for *The Little Fishes;* ALA Best Books for Young Adults citation, 1980, for *Chase Me! Catch Nobody!;* Phoenix Award, 1988, for *The Rider and His Horse.*

WRITINGS:

Twenty-five Poems, Squire Press, 1957.
Portrait of a Poet: Hans Christian Andersen (pamphlet), Library of Congress, 1974.

FOR YOUTH

Hakon of Rogen's Saga, Houghton, 1963.
A Slave's Tale (sequel to *Hakon of Rogen's Saga*), Houghton, 1965.
Orphans of the Wind, Houghton, 1966.
The Little Fishes, illustrated by Milton Johnson, Houghton, 1967.
The Rider and His Horse, Houghton, 1968.
The Untold Tale, Houghton, 1971.
A Messenger for Parliament, Houghton, 1976.
Cromwell's Boy, Houghton, 1978.
Chase Me! Catch Nobody!, Houghton, 1980.
Leif the Unlucky, Houghton, 1982.
A Boy's Will, illustrated by Troy Howell, Rinehardt, 1983.
The Samurai's Tale, Houghton, 1984.
Prince Boghole, illustrated by Julie Downing, Macmillan, 1987.
Princess Horrid, illustrated by Diane Dawson Hearne, Macmillan, 1990.
The Boy and the Samurai, Houghton, 1991.
The Story of Yuriwaka, Rinehart, 1991.

TRANSLATOR

Complete Fairy Tales and Stories of Hans Christian Andersen, Doubleday, 1973.
Hans Christian Andersen: His Classical Fairy Tales, illustrated by Michael Foreman, Doubleday, 1978.
Hans Christian Andersen, *The Emperor's Nightingale,* Schocken Books, 1979.

Hans Christian Andersen: The Complete Fairy Tales & Stories, Doubleday, 1983.

OTHER

Also author of unpublished adult novel, "The Last Heathen"; author of plays *The Heroes, The President Regrets,* and *An Honest Man.* Translator of Eskimo poetry, collected by Knud Rasmussen, for *American Scandinavian Review.*

WORK IN PROGRESS: A novel about pirates; translations of Japanese fairy tales.

SIDELIGHTS: Erik Christian Haugaard's novels for young readers present young people in wartime settings who encounter hardship and violence and learn the difference between mere physical power and inner strength. A seven-year-old orphaned in Denmark during the early 1600s is the main character of *The Untold Tale.* A thirteen-year-old orphan who becomes a spy for the notorious General Cromwell in seventeenth-century England narrates *A Messenger for Parliament.* In *The Rider and His Horse,* a Jewish young adult survives the destruction of Jerusalem and the mass suicide of the Zealots at Masada during a period of Roman conquest described by the historian Josephus (an actual survivor of the battle of Masada). And *Chase Me! Catch Nobody!* is set in Germany during the late 1930s, where its fourteen-year-old protagonist is caught up in the fight between Nazi fascists and their enemies. Like the rebel hero of *Chase Me! Catch Nobody!,* Haugaard's young heroes encounter two kinds of people: the vulnerable, and "the strong men" who "have no kindness and they wear themselves out, without ever having enjoyed the beauty of strength, which is to protect the weak, not to threaten them." The other picture of strength that emerges in the novels belongs to adults who choose to nurture the young and anyone who depends on their help for survival. In Haugaard's books, "nurturing men, not traditional heroes, are the most highly honored. The virtue most highly honored in turn is not the traditional male *courage,* but the godly type of love for all that is the original meaning of *charity,*" Lois R. Kuznets comments in *Children's Literature in Education.* Kuznets remarks, "Haugaard's message . . . is unequivocally clear: *every* child in *every* place and time is of *equal* value."

Haugaard was born in Denmark but fled his homeland when he was seventeen to escape the German invasion during World War II. "Like driftwood, like any of my own heroes, I was caught up, my choices limited and determined by events over which I had absolutely no control, or even understanding. . . . Being uprooted because of war, I suppose that is the basic situation in most of my books," he tells *Language Arts* interviewers Shelton L. Root, Jr., and M. Jean Greenlaw. Readers of Haugaard's books find in them a new "appreciation of the often neglected powerless," Kuznets adds. "Generally, he sees the powerless as people who manage, despite all hindrances, to make important moral decisions and to achieve emotional and spiritual growth that the powerful rarely perceive, understand, or attain." In this way, readers can better understand the gaps in histories which focus on conquerors and kings, and their wars which also changed the fortunes of millions of poorer people. Kuznets observes that all of Haugaard's novels "are about periods of extreme violence and armed conflict," portrayed vividly to display the horrors of war. Presenting this sometimes shocking material, she suggests, "allows [him] to 'sing,' as stated in [*Hakon of Rogen's Saga*], 'the song of the battlefield that no one dares tell' and to write 'the hitherto unspoken, unwritten truth' [cited from *A Slave's Tale*] ignored by standard histories, hoping someone will at last listen to the 'sparrow's song [and learn from it the truth the eagle flies too high to hear].' "

The Danish author, who has lived and worked in the United States, Italy, and Japan, tells Root and Greenlaw that as he sees it, all children with imagination try "to conceive of a world without hypocrisy and war." In their attempt to understand if such a world is possible, they come up against many questions that are essentially answerless, and resign themselves to accepting a world wherein war and deception are inevitable. "But," he adds, "the artistic child persists, at least partly because he is fascinated by the journey, he delights in his make believe world." The novelist further explains that people keep trying to imagine a world without war for reasons beyond escapism—because they actually desire to live in peace.

Hakon of Rogen's Saga features a teen orphaned in the violent times of the end of the Viking period of Scandinavian history. When his stepmother is stolen by pirates, his father fights for revenge, but dies in the battle. Hakon survives to protect his inheritance from a greedy uncle, and wins a moral victory with the help of the slave girl Helga (whose story is told in *A Slave's Tale*). Marcus Crouch comments in *The Nesbit Tradition: The Children's Novel in England, 1945-1970,* "All the best historical novels are stories of change. The change in *Hakon's Saga* is a small one—a change of ruler in a tiny island—but it has importance because it represents a change of heart." Hakon's determination to abandon violent conquest as a means of personal gain represents a change of attitude that brought a more peaceful life to many Scandinavians at the end of the 10th century.

"Haugaard consistently chooses to write about periods shown in historical perspective to be turning points in human thought and feeling, periods that mark the end of an era, forcing those born into them to reassess traditional values and ideas," Kuznets observes. This scenario affords a look at inner conflicts that are behind violence as well as the few humane people alive during such times whose ideas and values are more advanced than that of their brutal neighbors. The moral development of humane leaders and "their capacity to cherish other people's children," she says, is Haugaard's central theme and the key to understanding his writing.

The Little Fishes follows three Italian orphans through the period of German occupation in Naples in 1943. The novel is based on experiences with beggar children he met in Italy and on stories told to him by survivors of the war. One young beggar visited Haugaard's apartment persistently to receive food, money, or clothing. After taking home a pair of expensive boots to shield him from the snow, he returned wearing his tennis shoes. When Haugaard accused him of selling the boots, the beggar presented a five-year-old boy who had the oversized boots tied to his legs to keep them from sliding off. The beggar claimed to be taking good care of the boy, who was his brother. The protagonist of *The Little Fishes,* a similar boy in his teens, becomes an enemy of the Nazis when he delivers a package of passports for an anti-Fascist. To the German soldiers, he is a dirty "little fish" born to be victimized, but he refuses to accept their world view which classifies people as either bullies or victims.

In an acceptance speech quoted in *Horn Book* for the first *Boston Globe*-Horn Book Award for Excellence in Text, Haugaard says *The Little Fishes* was intended to make "a significant comment on humanity. . . . I wanted to tell not only what happened to the victims of war but also how . . . [a person] in degradation could refuse to be degraded. Our history books tell about the victories and defeats of armies; I wanted to tell about the defeat and victory of a human being." Kuznets summarizes that such novels challenge young adults in difficult situations, sometimes without the needed help from adults, "to do *more than merely survive*" by becoming nurturing adults who are able to assist others.

Haugaard's themes and the historical content in the books make them attractive to adult readers as well as young people. This is partly because his first intent was to write for adults. His first novel, "The Last Heathen," an unpublished book about a Norwegian who tries to reestablish the Old Norse religion long after his country had been Christianized, came back from a Houghton Mifflin editor with a suggestion that he should use the same material to write a book for young adults. After reading Scott O'Dell's *Island of the Blue Dolphins,* he saw what could be accomplished in that genre and has written for young readers ever since.

To explain why he writes historical novels, Haugaard tells Root and Greenlaw, "I probably write historical novels because they are the kind of books that I liked as a child.

I found my own times dull; . . . I loved to daydream, I still do. When I am writing a book, I am totally immersed in the [historical] period. I want to know what my characters would be doing in every situation, even though I may have no reason to write about them. I talk about nothing else."

Literature, he once told *CA,* is one of man's best and most important friends. "Man is forever lonely; but he has two friends whom he cannot lose, for though he may be unfaithful to them, they will never desert him. Nature and Art: ageless and eternal, they were there before we were born and will remain when we are gone. We are a part of nature which no end of scientific development can change, though it can distance us from it. Art: literature, music, painting, sculpture are the immortal parts of mortal man. This, too, we can deny; but only at the cost of greater loneliness. Hans Christian Andersen died long ago; but the fairy tales he wrote remain; if we do not read them the loss is not his but ours."

He continued, "No author can know whether his stories have enough truth in them to make them live forever. But if this is not his ambition, then I would not call him a humble man but a fraud. Once words are printed they take on a far greater importance than when they are spoken; therefore, especially when we write for children, we must only write what we consider to be the truth. Platitudes and lies are not harmless when they are disguised as truth and served to that audience which has the least experience with which to expose them. . . . My hope has always been that my books will help some other human being—some other child—to feel a little less lonely, a little less lost, a little more comforted."

BIOGRAPHICAL/CRITICAL SOURCES:

BOOKS

Children's Literature Review, Volume 11, Gale, 1986.
Crouch, Marcus, *The Nesbit Tradition: The Children's Novel in England, 1945-1970,* Ernest Benn Limited, 1972.
Haugaard, Erik Christian, *Hakon of Rogen's Saga,* Houghton, 1963.
Haugaard, Erik Christian, *A Slave's Tale,* Houghton, 1965.
Haugaard, Erik Christian, *The Little Fishes,* Houghton, 1967, pp. 66-67.
Haugaard, Erik Christian, *Chase Me! Catch Nobody!,* Houghton, 1980.
Something about the Author Autobiography Series, Volume 12, Gale, 1986.

PERIODICALS

Children's Literature in Education, summer, 1980, pp. 62-68.

Horn Book, February, 1968, p. 14.
Language Arts, May, 1979, pp. 549-61.

*   *   *

HAUSMAN, Gerald 1945-
(Gerry Hausman)

PERSONAL: Born October 13, 1945, in Baltimore, MD; son of Sidney (an engineer) and Dorothy (Little) Hausman; married Lorry Wright, June, 1968; children: Mariah Fox, Hannah. *Education:* New Mexico Highlands University, B.A., 1968. *Avocational interests:* Reading, athletics.

ADDRESSES: Home—P.O. Box 517, Tesuque, NM 87501.

CAREER: Poetry teacher in Lenox, MA, 1969-72; Bookstore Press, Lenox, editor, 1972-77; Sunstone Press, Santa Fe, NM, vice-president, 1979-83; Santa Fe Preparatory School, Santa Fe, teacher of English, 1983-87. Poet-in-residence in public schools, 1970-76, and at Central Connecticut State College, 1973.

MEMBER: Poets and Writers.

AWARDS, HONORS: Union College poetry prize, 1965, for *Quebec Poems;* Gerald Hausman Scholarship awarded in author's name to two Native American high-school students at Santa Fe Preparatory School, 1985.

WRITINGS:

(With David Kherdian) *Eight Poems,* Giligia, 1968.
(Editor) *Shivurrus Plant of Mopant and Other Children's Poems,* Giligia, 1968.
New Marlboro Stage, Giligia, 1969, 2nd edition, Bookstore Press, 1971.
Circle Meadow, Bookstore Press, 1972.
The Boy with the Sun Tree Bow, Berkshire Traveller Press, 1973.
Beth: The Little Girl of Pine Knoll, Bookstore Press, 1974.
Sitting on the Blue-Eyed Bear, Lawrence Hill, 1975.
(Under name Gerry Hausman with wife, Lorry Hausman) *The Pancake Book,* Persea Books, 1976.
(Under name Gerry Hausman with L. Hausman) *The Yogurt Book,* Persea Books, 1977.
The Day the White Whales Came to Bangor, Cobblesmith, 1977.
Night Herding Song, Copper Canyon Press, 1979.
No Witness, Stackpole, 1980.
Runners, Sunstone Press, 1984.
Meditations with Animals: A Native American Bestiary, Bear & Co., 1986.
Meditations with the Navajo, Bear & Co., 1988.
Turtle Dream, Mariposa, 1989.
Stargazer, Lotus Press, 1989.
Ghost Walk, Mariposa, 1991.

Turtle Island Alphabet, St. Martin's, 1992.
The Navajo Way, Simon & Schuster, 1992.
Coyote Walks on Two Legs, Philomel, 1993.
Eagle Boy, Harper-Collins, 1993.
Turtle Island Alphabet for Young Readers, Harper-Collins, 1993.

Contributor to *Poets in the Schools,* edited by Kathleen Meagher, Connecticut Commission on the Arts, 1973. Contributor to anthologies, including *Contemporaries: 28 New American Poets,* Viking; *Desert Review Anthology,* Desert Review Press; and *Poetry Here and Now,* edited by Kherdian, Morrow. Some of Hausman's work has been recorded on audiotapes and released by Lotus Press, including "Navajo Nights," 1987, "Stargazer," 1989, "Native American Animal Stories," 1990, and "Ghost Walk," 1991.

SIDELIGHTS: Gerald Hausman told *CA:* "For the past twenty-five years I have been collecting Native American and other ethnic tales. For the next twenty-five I hope, God willing, to do the same."

*   *   *

HAUSMAN, Gerry
See HAUSMAN, Gerald

*   *   *

HENKES, Kevin 1960-

PERSONAL: Born November 27, 1960, in Racine, WI; son of Bernard E. and Beatrice (Sieger) Henkes; married Laura Dronzek, May 18, 1985. *Education:* Attended University of Wisconsin—Madison.

ADDRESSES: Home—Madison, WI.

CAREER: Writer and illustrator.

AWARDS, HONORS: A Weekend with Wendell was named a Children's Choice Book by the Children's Book Council and the International Reading Association, 1986; *Chester's Way* was named a notable book by the American Library Association, 1988.

WRITINGS:

Once Around the Block, illustrated by Victoria Chess, Greenwillow, 1987.

SELF-ILLUSTRATED

All Alone, Greenwillow, 1981.
Clean Enough, Greenwillow, 1982.
Margaret and Taylor, Greenwillow, 1983.
Return to Sender, Greenwillow, 1984.

Bailey Goes Camping, Greenwillow, 1985.
Grandpa and Bo, Greenwillow, 1986.
Two Under Par, Greenwillow, 1987.
Sheila Rae, the Brave, Greenwillow, 1987.
A Weekend with Wendell, Greenwillow, 1987.
The Zebra Wall, Greenwillow, 1988.
Chester's Way, Greenwillow, 1988.
Jessica, Greenwillow, 1989.
Shhhh, Greenwillow, 1989.
Julius, the Baby of the World, Greenwillow, 1990.
Chrysanthemum, Greenwillow, 1991.

SIDELIGHTS: Kevin Henkes' fiction and picture books for young readers have been praised by many critics for their light-hearted, yet sensitive portrayal common occurrences in young children's lives. In her review of *Jessica,* Mary Harris Veeder suggests in *Tribune Books* that Henkes' ability to represent with accuracy, sensitivity, and good-humor, many of the events children experience in day-to-day life one reason for Henkes's popularity with young readers. Veeder writes, "Henkes' children are full of the imperfections and emotions which mark real life."

Henkes explains in his autobiographical sketch for *Sixth Book of Junior Authors and Illustrators* his feeling on being an author of children's books: "I'm a very lucky person. I've known for a very long time that I wanted to be an artist and a writer—and that's exactly what I do for a living. Making books is my job, but more importantly, it is what I love doing more than anything else.

"My first book—*All Alone*—was published in 1981. Since then, I've tried to create different kinds of books, even novels. I like trying new ways to fill the pages between two covers. Experimenting with words and paint and ink keeps my job interesting."

BIOGRAPHICAL/CRITICAL SOURCES:

BOOKS

Sixth Book of Junior Authors and Illustrators, H. W. Wilson, 1989, p. 123-24.

PERIODICALS

New York Times Book Review, April 28, 1991, p. 22.
Publishers Weekly, December 18, 1981, p. 70.
Tribune Books, May 14, 1989, p. 5.

*   *   *

HINSON, (Grady) Maurice 1930-

PERSONAL: Born December 4, 1930, in Marianna, FL; son of Bartlett A. and Willie (Blackman) Hinson; married Margaret Hume, June 16, 1952; children: Jane Leslie, Susan Elizabeth. *Education:* Attended Juilliard School of

Music, 1947-48; University of Florida, B.A., 1952; graduate study, Conservatoire National, University of Nancy, 1953; University of Michigan, M.M., 1955, D.M.A., 1958.

ADDRESSES: Home—1201 Wellington Pl., Louisville, KY 40207. *Office*—School of Church Music, Southern Baptist Theological Seminary, 2825 Lexington Rd., Louisville, KY 40280.

CAREER: University of Michigan, Ann Arbor, teacher of piano, 1953-57; Southern Baptist Theological Seminary, School of Church Music, Louisville, KY, professor of piano, 1957—. Guest lecturer in piano at National Music Camp, Interlochen, MI, summers, 1960-70; lecturer and recitalist at universities, conventions, and workshops throughout the United States, Canada, England, Japan, Taiwan, Germany, Australia, and other countries. *Military service:* U.S. Army, 1952-54.

MEMBER: American Liszt Society, Music Teachers National Association (president of southern division, 1966-68), American Guild of Organists, Kentucky Music Teachers Association (president, 1962-64; former chairman of piano and of certification board), Greater Louisville Music Teachers Association (president, 1960-62), Pi Kappa Lambda.

AWARDS, HONORS: Outstanding Alumnus, University of Michigan, 1988; Medal of Excellence, American Liszt Society; Liszt Medal, Hungarian Liszt Society.

WRITINGS:

Keyboard Bibliography, Music Teachers National Association, 1968.
Contemporary Piano Literature, two volumes, Belwin Mills, 1969.
Duets of Early American Music, Belwin-Mills, 1969.
Early American Music, Belwin-Mills, 1969.
Guide to the Pianist's Repertoire (also see below), edited by Irwin Freundlich, Indiana University Press, 1973, 2nd revised and enlarged edition, 1987.
The Piano Teacher's Sourcebook: An Annotated Bibliography of Books Related to the Piano and Piano Music, Belwin-Mills, 1974, 3rd edition, 1986.
An Adventure in Ragtime, Belwin-Mills, 1975.
The Piano in Chamber Ensemble: An Annotated Guide, Indiana University Press, 1978.
Supplement to Guide to the Pianist's Repertoire, Indiana University Press, 1979.
Music for Piano and Orchestra: An Annotated Guide, Indiana University Press, 1981.
Music for More Than One Piano: An Annotated Guide, Indiana University Press, 1983.
The Pianist's Reference Guide, Alfred Publishing, 1987.
The Pianist's Guide to Transcriptions, Arrangements, and Paraphrases, Indiana University Press, 1990.

EDITOR OF MUSICAL COMPOSITIONS

(And annotator with Anne McClenny) *A Collection of Early American Keyboard Music,* Willis Music, 1971.
Piano Music in Nineteenth-Century America, two volumes, Hinshaw Music, 1975.
Arthur Farwell, *American Indian Melodies,* Hinshaw Music, 1977.
(With McClenny) *Dances of the Young Republic,* Hinshaw Music, 1977.
Presto d'incerto autore, Hinshaw Music, 1977.
(With Charlotte Martin) *Piano Music of Viceregal Mexico,* Hinshaw Music, 1979.
Twelve by Eleven, Alfred Publishing, 1991.

Also editor of *Classical Music in the Worship Service,* two volumes, G. Schirmer, and of musical compositions by Muzio Clementi, Edward MacDowell, Alexander Reinagle, Raynor Taylor, Hector Berlioz, Samuel Coleridge-Taylor, Anton Diabelli, and Johann Anton Andre, all published by Alfred Publishing.

OTHER

Contributor to *The New Grove Dictionary of Music in the United States.* Contributor of articles to periodicals, including *American Music Teacher, Clavier, English Liszt Society Journal,* and *Piano Quarterly.* Founding editor, *Journal of the American Liszt Society;* editor for articles and reviews, *American Music Teacher;* contributing editor, *Piano Quarterly.*

WORK IN PROGRESS: Editing of teaching editions of the classical piano repertoire for Alfred Publishing.

*   *   *

HOFF, Syd(ney) 1912-

PERSONAL: Born September 4, 1912, in New York, NY; son of Benjamin (a salesman) and Mary (Barnow) Hoff; married Dora Berman, 1937. *Education:* Studied fine art at National Academy of Design, New York City.

ADDRESSES: Agent—Scott Meredith Literary Agency, 845 Third Ave., New York, NY 10022.

CAREER: Cartoonist, 1928—. Originator of daily cartoon panels, "Tuffy," William Randolph Hearst Syndicate, 1939-49, and "Laugh It Off," King Features Syndicate, 1958-77. Also star of a series of television shows, *Tales of Hoff,* Columbia Broadcasting System (CBS). National advertising commissions include Standard Oil, Chevrolet, Maxwell House Coffee, and Arrow Shirts.

MEMBER: Authors League of America, Authors Guild, Magazine Cartoonists Guild.

AWARDS, HONORS: Irving and Me was selected as one of the year's ten best children's books by the *New York Times*, 1967.

WRITINGS:

Military Secrets, Hillair, 1943.
It's Fun Learning Cartooning, Stravon, 1952.
Learning to Cartoon, Stravon, 1966.
Irving and Me (young adult novel), Harper, 1967.
Syd Hoff's Joke Book, Putnam, 1972.
The Art of Cartooning, Stravon, 1973.
Jokes to Enjoy, Draw and Tell, Putnam, 1974.
Dinosaur Do's and Don'ts, Windmill, 1975.
Editorial and Political Cartooning: From Earliest Times to the Present . . . , Stravon, 1976.
Syd Hoff's Best Jokes Ever, Putnam, 1978.
Syd Hoff Shows You How to Draw Cartoons, Scholastic, 1979, reprinted as *How to Draw Cartoons,* 1991.
Mighty Babe Ruth, Scholastic, 1980.
Syd Hoff's How to Draw Dinosaurs, Windmill, 1981.
The Man Who Loved Animals (biography of Henry Bergh), Putnam, 1982.
The Young Cartoonist: The ABC's of Cartooning, Stravon, 1983.
Syd Hoff's Animal Jokes, Lippincott Junior Books, 1985.

Also creator of comic strip, "Tuffy." Contributor of short fiction to *Alfred Hitchcock* and *Ellery Queen.* Also contributor to *Esquire, Look, New Yorker, Saturday Evening Post, Playboy,* and other periodicals.

CARTOON COLLECTIONS

Feeling No Pain: An Album of Cartoons, Dial, 1944.
Mom, I'm Home!, Doubleday, 1945.
Oops! Wrong Party!, Dutton, 1951.
Oops! Wrong Stateroom!, Ives Washburn, 1953.
Out of Gas!, Ives Washburn, 1954.
Okay—You Can Look Now!, Duell, 1955.
The Better Hoff, Holt, 1961.
Upstream, Downstream, and Out of My Mind, Bobbs-Merrill, 1961.
So This Is Matrimony, Pocket Books, 1962.
'Twixt the Cup and the Lipton, Bobbs-Merrill, 1962.
From Bed to Nurse; or, What a Way to Die, Dell, 1963.
Hunting, Anyone?, Bobbs-Merrill, 1963.

SELF-ILLUSTRATED; FOR CHILDREN

Muscles and Brains, Dial, 1940.
Eight Little Artists, Abelard-Schuman, 1954.
Patty's Pet, Abelard-Schuman, 1955.
Danny and the Dinosaur, Harper, 1958.
Julius, Harper, 1959.
Sammy, the Seal, Harper, 1959.
Ogluk, the Eskimo, Holt, 1960.
Oliver, Harper, 1960.

Where's Prancer?, Harper, 1960.
Who Will Be My Friends?, Harper, 1960.
Albert the Albatross, Harper, 1961.
Chester, Harper, 1961.
Little Chief, Harper, 1961.
Stanley, Harper, 1962.
Grizzwold, Harper, 1963.
Lengthy, Putnam, 1964.
Mrs. Switch, Putnam, 1967.
Wanda's Wand, C. R. Gibson, 1968.
The Witch, the Cat, and the Baseball Bat, Grosset, 1968.
Baseball Mouse, Putnam, 1969.
Herschel the Hero, Putnam, 1969.
Jeffrey at Camp, Putnam, 1969.
Mahatma, Putnam, 1969.
Roberto and the Bull, McGraw, 1969.
The Horse in Harry's Room, Harper, 1970.
The Litter Knight, Putnam, 1970.
Palace Bug, Putnam, 1970.
Siegfried, Dog of the Alps, Grosset, 1970.
Wilfred the Lion, Putnam, 1970.
The Mule Who Struck It Rich, Little, Brown, 1971.
Thunderhoof, Harper, 1971.
Ida the Bareback Rider, Putnam, 1972.
My Aunt Rosie, Harper, 1972.
Pedro and the Bananas, Putnam, 1972.
A Walk Past Ellen's House, McGraw, 1973.
Amy's Dinosaur, Windmill Books, 1974.
Kip Van Wrinkle, Putnam, 1974.
Katy's Kitty, Windmill, 1975.
Pete's Pup, Windmill, 1975.
Barkley, Harper, 1976.
Henrietta Lays Some Eggs, Garrard, 1977.
How to Make Up Jokes, Grosset, 1977.
The Littlest Leaguer, Windmill Books, 1977.
Walpole, Harper, 1977.
Henrietta, Circus Star, Garrard, 1977.
Henrietta, the Early Bird, Garrard, 1978.
Henrietta Goes to the Fair, Garrard, 1979.
Nutty Noodles, Scholastic, 1979.
Santa's Moose, Harper, 1979.
Slugger Sal's Slump, Windmill, 1979.
Henrietta's Halloween, Garrard, 1980.
Merry Christmas, Henrietta, Garrard, 1980.
Scarface Al and His Uncle Sam, Coward, 1980.
Henrietta's Fourth of July, Garrard, 1981.
Soft Skull Sam, Harcourt, 1981.
Happy Birthday, Henrietta!, Garrard, 1983.
Barney's Horse, Harper, 1987.
Mrs. Brice's Mice, Harper, 1988.

ILLUSTRATOR; FOR CHILDREN

Arthur Kober, *Thunder over the Bronc,* Simon & Schuster, 1935.

A. Kober, *Parm Me,* Constable, 1945.

Allan Sherman, *Hello Muddah, Hello Fadduh!,* Harper, 1964.

A. Sherman, *I Can't Dance!,* Harper, 1964.

Joan M. Lexau, *I Should Have Stayed in Bed!,* Harper, 1965.

J. M. Lexau, *The Homework Caper,* Harper, 1966.

J. M. Lexau, *The Rooftop Mystery,* Harper, 1968.

Tom Mac Pherson, editor, *Slithers,* Putnam, 1968.

Jerome Coopersmith, *A Chanukah Fable for Christmas,* Putnam, 1969.

John Peterson, *Mean Max,* Scholastic, 1970.

Mildred Wright, *Henri Goes to Mardi Gras,* Putnam, 1971.

Ruth B. Gross, *A Book about Christopher Columbus,* Scholastic, 1974.

Edward R. Ricciuti, *Donald and the Fish That Walked,* Harper, 1972.

Peggy Bradbury, *The Snake That Couldn't Slither,* Putnam, 1976.

Joan Lowery Nixon, *The Boy Who Could Find Anything,* Harcourt, 1978.

Clare Gault and Frank Gault, *A Super Fullback for the Super Bow,* Scholastic, 1978.

Louise Armstrong, *Arthur Gets What He Spills,* Harcourt, 1979.

J. L. Nixon, *Bigfoot Makes a Movie,* Putnam, 1979.

Al Campanis, *Play Ball with Roger the Dodger,* Putnam, 1980.

J. M. Lexau, *Don't Be My Valentine,* Harper, 1985.

Alvin Schwartz, editor, *I Saw You in the Bathtub, and Other Folk Rhymes,* HarperCollins, 1991.

OTHER

Little Red Riding-Hood (for children), illustrated by Charles Mikolaycak, C. R. Gibson, 1968.

When Will It Snow? (for children), illustrated by Mary Chalmers, Harper, 1971.

Giants and Other Plays for Kids (includes *Lion in the Zoon, Children on the Moon, The Family,* and *Wild Flowers*), Putnam, 1973.

Gentleman Jim and the Great John L., Coward, 1977.

Boss Tweed and the Man Who Drew Him, Coward, 1978.

Hoff's manuscripts are housed at the Kerlan Collection, University of Minnesota, Minneapolis; University of California, Los Angeles; de Grummond Collection, University of Southern Mississippi, Hattiesburg; Syracuse University, New York; and the Library of Congress, Washington, D.C.

ADAPTATIONS: Danny and the Dinosaur was made into a filmstrip by Weston Woods.

SIDELIGHTS: Syd Hoff, who launched his career as a cartoonist in 1928, has become one of the most prolific of contemporary author/illustrator/graphic humorists. Like most artists, he began sketching in childhood, and in *Something about the Author Autobiography Series* he relates an incident that influenced his desire to become an artist: "I remember one day when we came home from a trolley-car ride; I drew a picture of the conductor, resplendent in his uniform with brass buttons. 'Sydney is the artist of the family,' my mother proclaimed, immediately hammering the picture into the wall with a three-inch nail." Later, when he was a high school student, cartoonist Milt Gross appeared as guest speaker at a student assembly and Hoff was asked to participate on stage as illustrator during another student's presentation. When he finished his illustrations, "Gross leaped to my side and embraced me. 'Kid, someday you'll be a great cartoonist!' he proclaimed, loud enough for the whole school to hear. Later, he made a sketch in my notebook, while everyone was begging him for autographs. It was all like a dream." Although Hoff excelled in drawing, he was less than a stunning student academically and eventually dropped out of school at the age of sixteen. He lied about his age and enrolled in the National Academy of Design in New York City "in the hope of becoming a fine artist," Hoff once commented, "but a natural comic touch in my work caused my harried instructors to advise me to try something else. I did. At eighteen I sold my first cartoon to the *New Yorker,* and have been a regular contributor to that magazine ever since."

His humorous work is hallmarked by simplicity. Preferring to work in ink, washes, crayon, and watercolor, Hoff draws upon the New York neighborhoods in which he grew up for the characters in his cartoons; however, his humor is not dependent upon cliche or stereotype. Asked in 1939 to create a comic strip for the William Randolph Hearst Syndicate, Hoff worked on "Tuffy," about a little girl, for the next ten years. And in 1958, he began what would become nearly twenty years of work on another comic strip entitled "Laugh It Off." He also starred in a series of television shows called *Tales of Hoff* for CBS, was commissioned by national sponsors for cartoons for their advertisements, and had begun to write short mystery fiction for such publications as *Alfred Hitchcock* and *Ellery Queen.*

By this time, Hoff was married with a family. One of his daughters, though, had been stricken with a physically debilitating condition; and one day he drew some pictures to take her mind off her physical therapy. These pictures formed the basis of *Danny and the Dinosaur,* one of Hoff's earliest books for children. Translated into half a dozen languages with more than ten million copies sold, the book has become a classic in children's fare. "Becoming a children's author meant making personal appearances," Hoff indicates in his autobiographical essay. "I traveled all over the country, meeting young people and giving them pointers in the art of cartooning." Hoff believes that "the best humor has to do with events that people can identify as having happened to them, or something that has been in the subconscious. As Humor, for some reason, is basically sad. There's some sort of affinity between the sad and the funny that makes it all the funnier."

BIOGRAPHICAL/CRITICAL SOURCES:

BOOKS

Contemporary Graphic Artists, Volume 1, Gale, 1986, pp. 138-41.
Something about the Author Autobiography Series, Volume 4, Gale, 1987, pp. 211-31.
Twentieth-Century Children's Writers, St. Martin's Press, 1989, pp. 459-60.

PERIODICALS

Best Sellers, September 1, 1967.
New York Times Book Review, October 8, 1967.
Washington Post, February 8, 1981.
Young Readers' Review, April, 1967.

*   *   *

HOOK, J(ulius) N(icholas) 1913-

PERSONAL: Born December 25, 1913, in Macoupin County, IL; son of Charles E. and Rose (Engel) Hook; married second wife, Rachel Grace Gerhart, 1955; children: Edward N., Julian Lee. *Education:* University of Illinois, A.B., 1933, A.M., 1934, Ph.D., 1941. *Religion:* Presbyterian.

ADDRESSES: Home—318 Old Mill Trace, Crawfordsville, IN 47933.

CAREER: High school teacher in Forrest, IL, 1934-36; Mankato State College (now University), Mankato, MN, 1941-46, began as instructor, became associate professor of English; University of Illinois at Urbana-Champaign, professor of English, 1946-71, professor emeritus, 1971—. Summer school teacher in Texas, New York, Rhode Island, Wisconsin, and Missouri. Coordinator of Project English, U.S. Office of Education, 1961.

MEMBER: National Council of Teachers of English (executive secretary, 1953-60), Conference on College Composition and Communication (treasurer, 1953-60), Modern Language Association of America, Conference on English Education (chairman, 1966-68), Illinois Association of Teachers of English (president, 1961).

AWARDS, HONORS: Twice honored by National Council of Teachers of English in 1960, with W. Wilbur Hat-

field Award and by establishment of research foundation in his honor; named Illinois Author of the Year, 1981.

WRITINGS:

(With William F. Ekstrom) *Toward Better English,* Lippincott, 1941, 2nd edition, 1949.
(With Elizabeth Collette, Tom Peete Cross, and Elmer Stauffer) *Writers in America,* Ginn, 1949.
(With Collette, Cross, and Stauffer) *Writers in England,* Ginn, 1949.
Teaching of High School English, Ronald, 1950, 5th edition, 1982.
(With Max Herzberg, Florence Guild, and Robert L. Stevens) *Better English,* six volumes, Ginn, 1952-53.
(With Ekstrom) *Guide to Composition,* Lippincott, 1953.
(With E. G. Mathews) *Modern American Grammar and Usage,* Ronald, 1956.
(With others) *Literature for High Schools,* four volumes, Ginn, 1957.
How to Take Examinations in College, Barnes & Noble, 1958.
(With Guild and Stevens) *English Skills,* four volumes, Ginn, 1959.
(With Stevens) *Harbrace Guide to Sentence-Building,* Harcourt, 1961.
Guide to Good Writing, Ronald, 1961.
Writing Creatively, Heath, 1964, 2nd edition, 1967.
(With William H. Evans) *Individualized English,* Follett, 1965, 2nd edition, 1974.
(With Stevens) *Competence in English,* Harcourt, 1967, 2nd edition, 1977.
Spelling 1500, Harcourt, 1967, 3rd edition, 1985.
Testmanship, Barnes & Noble, 1967.
(Editor) *Publishers and English Teachers,* American Textbook, 1967.
The Story of American English, Harcourt, 1972.
The Story of British English, Scott, Foresman, 1974.
People Say Things Different Ways, Scott, Foresman, 1974.
History of the English Language, Ronald, 1975.
English Today, Ronald, 1976.
A Long Way Together, National Council of Teachers of English, 1979.
The Grand Panjandrum, and 1,999 Other Rare, Useful, and Delightful Words, Macmillan, 1980, 2nd edition, 1990.
Two-Word Verbs in English, Harcourt, 1981.
Family Names: How Our Surnames Came to America, Macmillan, 1982.
The Book of Names, F. Watts, 1983.
The Appropriate Word, Addison-Wesley, 1990.
(With others) *Portable Writing Lab,* Harcourt, 1991.
All Those Wonderful Names, Wiley, 1991.

Also author, with Ryoji Inoue, of *Determiners, Prepositions, Two-Word Verbs, and Verbs.* Contributor to professional journals. Editor, *Illinois English Bulletin,* 1949-59.

WORK IN PROGRESS: A series on towns.

SIDELIGHTS: J. N. Hook told *CA:* "The English language has many sideroads not familiar to the general public. In the past decade or so I've been exploring some of them and sharing what I've found."

*   *   *

HOPKINS, Robert S(ydney)
(Robert Rostand)

PERSONAL: Born in Los Angeles, CA. *Education:* Educated in Los Angeles, CA.

ADDRESSES: P.O. Box 11164, Torrance, CA 90510.

CAREER: Writer. Worked as lecturer in geography and with U.S. State Department in Washington, DC.

WRITINGS:

(With Albert B. Carr) *Islands of the Deep Sea* (juvenile nonfiction), John Day, 1967.
Darwin's South America (nonfiction), John Day, 1969.
I've Had It: A Practical Guide to Moving Abroad, Holt, 1972.
The Raid on Villa Joyosa (novel), Putnam, 1973.
Riviera: A Novel about the Cannes Film Festival, Morrow, 1980.

NOVELS UNDER PSEUDONYM ROBERT ROSTAND

The Vengeance Run, Berkley, 1972.
The Killer Elite, Delacorte, 1973.
Viper's Game, Delacorte, 1974.
The D'Artagnan Signature, Putnam, 1976.
A Killing in Rome, Delacorte, 1977.
Cross Currents, Pinnacle, 1985.
October Kill, Pocket Books, 1989.

ADAPTATIONS: The film adaptation of *The Killer Elite* starred James Caan and Robert Duvall and was released by United Artists in 1975.

BIOGRAPHICAL/CRITICAL SOURCES:

PERIODICALS

New York Times Book Review, February 6, 1977, p. 12.

*   *   *

HOPPER, Nancy J.   1937-

PERSONAL: Born July 25, 1937, in Lewistown, PA; daughter of David L. (a school superintendent) and Joyce (Beaver) Swartz; married James A. Hopper (a professor and artist), August 20, 1960; children: Christopher J., Jennifer A. *Education:* Juniata College, B.A., 1959. *Avocational interests:* Reading, bird-watching, walking, going to zoos, attending concerts, travel in U.S. and abroad, volunteer work in schools.

ADDRESSES: Home—2341 Ridgewood, Alliance, OH 44601.

CAREER: Housewife and writer. High school English teacher at public schools in Tyrone, PA, 1959-60; Freeport Public Schools, Freeport, NY, high school English teacher, 1960-62.

MEMBER: Authors Guild.

AWARDS, HONORS: American Library Association recommended book for the reluctant young adult reader citation, 1988, for *Wake Me When the Band Starts Playing.*

WRITINGS:

JUVENILE NOVELS

Secrets, Elsevier/Nelson, 1979.
The Seven-and-One-Half Sins of Stacey Kendall, Dutton, 1982.
Just Vernon, Lodestar, 1982.
Hang On, Harvey!, Dutton, 1983.
Lies (young adult), Lodestar, 1984.
Ape Ears and Beaky, Dutton, 1984.
Rivals (young adult), Lodestar/Dutton, 1985.
The Truth or Dare Trap, Dutton, 1985.
Carrie's Games (young adult), Lodestar/Dutton, 1987.
Wake Me When the Band Starts Playing (young adult), Lodestar, 1988.
The Interrupted Education of Huey B. (young adult), Lodestar, 1991.
The Queen of Put-Down, Four Winds Press/Macmillan, 1991.

SIDELIGHTS: Nancy J. Hopper once told *CA:* "I like to work from character, the character coming first, the story happening at least partially as a result of that character. The largest part of my writing is both for and about people between the ages of nine and sixteen. I find individuals in this age group to be fascinating. They have a fresh, critical eye on life and are quite often endowed with a great sense of humor. They are engaged in the all-encompassing battle to grow up, to mature, to understand; and I think that is, to a great extent, what life is about, at either age one month or age eighty years. It seems to me that between the ages of nine and sixteen, individuals make a frontal attack on this issue, acting with determination, courage, and a willingness to take their bumps and to write off their losses. This enables them as real people, and as people in books, to move in and out of situations that offer much in the way of opportunity for excitement, and, best of all, to regard life as what it really is: an adventure."

Hopper's novels have been translated into both Danish and German.

*　　*　　*

HOUSTON, James A(rchibald) 1921-

PERSONAL: Born June 12, 1921, in Toronto, Ontario, Canada; came to the United States in 1962; son of James Donald (a clothing importer) and Gladys Maud (Barbour) Houston; married Alma G. Bardon, 1950 (divorced, 1966); married Alice Daggett Watson, December 9, 1967; children: John James, Samuel Douglas. *Education:* Attended Ontario College of Art, 1938-40, Ecole Grand Chaumiere, Paris, 1947-48, Unichi-Hiratsuka, Tokyo, 1958-59, and Atelier 17, 1961. *Religion:* Anglican. *Avocational interests:* Fishing, sketching.

ADDRESSES: Home—24 Main St., Stonington, CT 06378 (winter); P.O. Box 43, Tlell, Queen Charlotte Islands, British Columbia, V0T 1Y0, Canada (summer). *Office*—717 Fifth Ave., New York, NY 10022.

CAREER: Author and illustrator. Canadian Guild of Crafts, Arctic adviser, 1949-52; Government of Canada, West Baffin, Northwest Territories, first civil administrator, 1952-62; Steuben Glass, New York City, associate director of design, 1962-72, master designer, 1972—. Visiting lecturer at Wye Institute and Rhode Island School of Design. Chairman of board of directors of Canadian Arctic Producers, 1976-77, and American Indian Art Center; member of board of directors of Canadian Eskimo Arts Council; president of Indian and Eskimo Art of the Americas; vice-president of West Baffin Eskimo Cooperative and Eskimo Art, Inc. Member of primitive art committee of Metropolitan Museum of Art. *Exhibitions:* Canadian Guild of Crafts, 1953, 1955, 1957; Robertson Galleries, Ottawa, 1953; Calgary Galleries, 1966; Canadiana Galleries, Edmonton, 1977; Yaneff Gallery, Toronto, 1983, 1986; Steuben Glass, 1987; represented in collections of Glenbow-Alberta Museum of Art, Montreal Museum of Fine Arts, National Gallery of Art, Ottawa. *Military service:* Canadian Army, Toronto Scottish Regiment, 1940-45; became warrant officer.

MEMBER: Producers Guild of America, Writers' Union of Canada, Canadian Eskimo Arts Council, Canadian Arctic Producers, American Indian Arts Center, Indian and Eskimo Art of the Americas, Explorers Club, Century Association, Grolier Club, Leash.

AWARDS, HONORS: American Indian and Eskimo Cultural Foundation award, 1966; Canadian Library Association Book of the Year awards, 1966, for *Tikta'liktak: An Eskimo Legend,* 1968, for *The White Archer: An Eskimo Legend,* 1980, for *River Runners: A Tale of Hardship and Bravery,* and runner-up, 1982, for *Long Claws: An Arctic Adventure;* American Library Association Notable Books awards, 1967, for *The White Archer,* 1968, for *Akavak: An Eskimo Journey,* and 1971, for *The White Dawn: An Eskimo Saga;* decorated officer of Order of Canada, 1972; Amelia Frances Howard-Gibbon award runner-up, 1973, for *Ghost Paddle: A Northwest Coast Indian Tale;* Vicky Metcalf award, 1977; Inuit Kuavati Award of Merit, 1979; Vicky Metcalf Short Story award, 1980, for "Long Claws" in *The Winter Fun Book;* Canadian nominee, Hans Christian Andersen Award, 1987; Citation of Merit Award, Royal Canadian Academy of Arts, 1987; Max and Gretta Ebel Award, Canadian Society of Children's Authors, Illustrators, and Performers, 1989; D.Litt., Carleton University, 1972; D.H.L., Rhode Island College, 1975; D.F.A., Rhode Island School of Design, 1979; D.D.L., Dalhousie University, 1987; honorary fellow, Ontario College of Art, and fellow, Royal Society of Art, London, 1981.

WRITINGS:

Canadian Eskimo Art, Queen's Printer, 1955.
Eskimo Graphic Art, Queen's Printer, 1960.
Eskimo Prints, Barre Publishing, 1967, 2nd edition, 1971.
The White Dawn: An Eskimo Saga (novel; Book-of-the-Month Club selection), Harcourt, 1971.
(Editor and illustrator) *Songs of the Dream People: Chants and Images from the Indians and Eskimos of North America,* Atheneum, 1972.
Ojibwa Summer, photographs by B. A. King, Barre Publishing, 1972.
Ghost Fox (novel), Harcourt, 1977.
Spirit Wrestler (novel), Harcourt, 1980.
Eagle Song (novel), Harcourt, 1983.
Running West (novel), Crown, 1989.

FOR CHILDREN; SELF-ILLUSTRATED

Tikta'liktak: An Eskimo Legend, Harcourt, 1965.
Eagle Mask: A West Coast Indian Tale, Harcourt, 1966.
The White Archer: An Eskimo Legend, Harcourt, 1967.
Akavak: An Eskimo Journey, Harcourt, 1968.
Wolf Run: A Caribou Eskimo Tale, Harcourt, 1971.
Ghost Paddle: A Northwest Coast Indian Tale, Harcourt, 1972.
Kiviok's Magic Journey: An Eskimo Legend, Atheneum, 1973.
Frozen Fire: A Tale of Courage, Atheneum, 1977.
River Runners: A Tale of Hardship and Bravery, Atheneum, 1979.
Long Claws: An Arctic Adventure, Atheneum, 1981.

Black Diamonds: A Search for Arctic Treasure, Atheneum, 1982.

Ice Swords: An Undersea Adventure, Atheneum, 1985.

The Falcon Bow: An Arctic Legend, McElderry, 1986.

Whiteout, Key Porter, 1988.

The White Dawn: An Eskimo Saga (also see below), Harcourt, 1989.

ILLUSTRATOR

Shoot to Live, 1944.

Alma Houston, *Nuki,* 1955.

Raymond de Coccola and Paul King, *Ayorama,* 1956.

Tuktut/Caribou, 1957.

Elizabeth Pool, *The Unicorn Was There,* Bauhan, 1966.

(And author of introduction) George Francis Lyon, *The Private Journal of Captain G. F. Lyon of H.M.S. Hecla, During the Recent Voyage of Discovery under Captain Parry, 1921-23,* Imprint Society, 1970.

M. J. Wheeler, *First Came the Indians,* Atheneum, 1983.

R. de Coccola and P. King, *The Incredible Eskimo,* Hancock House, 1986.

SCREENPLAYS

The White Dawn, Paramount Pictures, 1973.

The Mask and the Drum, Swannsway Productions, 1975.

So Sings the Wolf, Devonian Group, 1976.

Kalvak, Devonian Group, 1976.

Houston has also adapted *Art of the Arctic Whaleman,* 1978, and *Legends of the Salmon People,* 1978, for the screen.

OTHER

Contributor of short stories to periodicals. Houston's manuscripts are collected at the National Library of Canada, Ottawa.

ADAPTATIONS: Ghost Fox has been recorded on eight cassettes by Crane Memorial Library, 1978.

SIDELIGHTS: James A. Houston is "probably the most popular and influential authority on Arctic culture that Canada has produced," according to T. F. Rigelhof in the Toronto *Globe and Mail.* Houston derives his authority as an author, illustrator, glass designer, and filmmaker from his remarkable experiences living with the Inuit people in the Canadian Arctic. Combining art school training with a life worthy of an adventure movie, he grounds his stories, whether for adults or for children, in the legends and myths of his beloved Inuit. His books explore the challenges of living close to the land, and detail the changes that an environment can make upon the character of its inhabitants.

Houston was born on June 12, 1921, in Toronto, Ontario, the son of an adventurous clothing importer and an artis-tic mother. His father took advantage of his traveling salesman status to visit the far reaches of the Canadian wilderness, where he traded with Eskimos and Indians. In "A Primitive View of the World" (his May Hill Arbuthnot lecture delivered at Northern Illinois University and reprinted in *Top of the News*), Houston recalls that his father, on returning home, "would give us each a hug, then produce two pairs of delicious-smelling, smoked, moosehide moccasins." Houston and his sister would crawl into bed with their parents and their father would tell stories and "draw Sioux pulling toboggans south of Moose Jaw, Saskatchewan, and Sarcee teepees pitched on the plains near Medicine Hat, painted ponies and feathered riders coming to collect their treaty money. . . . I didn't care what other children's fathers did because I would never have traded theirs for mine."

If his father prepared Houston for a life of adventure, his mother prepared him for life as an artist. When he was eight or nine, Houston was quarantined for three weeks with a case of scarlet fever, and his mother brought him a book: "I eagerly opened the cover," he recalls in his Arbuthnot lecture, "only to find that it was entirely blank—no words, no pictures. My mother smiled, 'If you want a book, make one yourself.' " He did, writing and illustrating a story about a shipwrecked boy cast away on a small island. When he was nine, he illustrated a poem for a Canadian magazine and was paid three dollars.

Houston's love of drawing continued into his adolescence, and at age twelve he was enrolled in classes at the Toronto Art Gallery (now the Art Gallery of Ontario). Houston recalls that his teacher, Dr. Arthur Lismer, a famous Canadian artist, left for Africa for some time and returned with a surprise for his students: "He arrived on a Saturday morning amidst wild West African drumming and singing. The recorded music resounded through the galleries as he danced among us, his face hidden by a huge Congo mask. I remember thinking who made that mask, who is beating those exciting rhythms on the drums? I was hooked forever on the lives of primitive people. I trembled to think of my own teacher, Dr. Lismer, treading on the soil of Africa, perhaps paddling on the Congo River with big crocodiles around him. I determined at that moment that I, too, would go to see the wildest corners of the earth." Houston would fulfill his dream, but not before he served in the Canadian Army during World War II and continued his art training in Paris, France.

Houston returned to Toronto via Montreal in 1948, remembering in his Arbuthnot lecture that "after Paris, both cities struck me a being far too proper, with men in gray baggy suits and girls tightly bound in girdles. I asked myself where should I go?" Fueled by his desire to find a "suitable people to draw," Houston hopped aboard a train that would take him as far north as a train would go for nineteen dollars: Moosonee, Ontario, which lay at the south end of James Bay. He lived on an island called Moose Factory, making hundreds of drawings of Cree Indians, who were "dressed in braids, tartan shawls and knee-high moccasins." But Houston longed to explore the vast, nearly uninhabited area that loomed to the north of him, the great Arctic.

When a small plane rushing medical assistance to a village deep in the Arctic landed to refuel, Houston saw his chance. He remembers the co-pilot bursting into his room with this offer: "If you'll help me woggle the gas, you can fly into the Arctic with us—free! We're leaving now! The doctor has an emergency." Houston expected to stay just four days, but when it was clear that the doctor would have to fly the wounded child back to civilization right away, he made a sudden decision: he was staying. As he stood on the shore of the Hudson Bay, surrounded by all he owned—a sleeping bag, a sketch pad, and a can of peaches—and watching the plane disappear, he had no idea that he would live in the Arctic for fourteen years.

At first, Houston knew nothing of the Inuit language, but found that his sketches enabled him to communicate and build the people's confidence in him, for with drawings they shared the same language. The young artist lived with the semi-nomadic tribe in their winter igloos and summer tents, and was astounded by the soapstone carvings crafted by some of the tribesmen. Fascinated by the stories that the carvings told, and by the quality of the workmanship, Houston took a collection of the works to the Canadian Handicraft Guild in Montreal. He has been credited with the "discovery" of this art form, and his discovery led the Canadian government to set up subsidies for Inuit sculptors, which allowed the Inuits to develop a market for their work and made them less dependent on the declining fur trade. Later, Houston taught the Eskimos to make prints from their original stone cuts, further enhancing the spread of their art. Now, many art museums have collections of Eskimo art.

Houston married in 1949, and continued to live in the Hudson Bay area, working for the Canadian Handicraft Guild, and for the Canadian government. In 1955, he became the first federal civil administrator of West Baffin Island, most of which lies within the Arctic Circle. Houston traveled the 65,000-square-mile territory by dog sled, making friends with the 341 Eskimos who earned their living on the desolate island. Camped with these people, he became familiar with their distinctive means of telling stories. These mythic stories commemorated heroic deeds from the Eskimos' shared past, using "that age-old art of oral storytelling which involves the breathtaking excitement of the human voice mixed with animal sounds and shouts often accompanied by dancing and the rhythm of the drum or the howling Arctic winds," Houston told the

Arbuthnot lecture audience. "There were, of course, no special stories for children. Every modern story, myth, or legend was told to suit all ages." Houston soon wanted to tell his own tales, for good storytellers were prized in his adopted culture. This desire eventually found its expression in his books for children and adults, which he began to write after leaving the Arctic for the very different world of New York City.

Houston's children's books are known for their sympathetic treatment of native peoples living in the Arctic and the Pacific Northwest, where he maintains a writing and fishing cottage. His early stories have mythic qualities, stressing the importance of human endurance and resourcefulness in the face of overwhelming odds. In *Wolf Run*, for example, a young boy sets out into the Arctic to find food for his starving family. On the point of collapse, the boy is visited by two helpful wolves that he believes to be the spirits of his deceased grandparents, and he then finds food. While the earlier books focus only on native peoples, the later works explore the reaction of primitive cultures to the modern world. In works such as *River Runners, Frozen Fire, Black Diamonds,* and *Ice Swords,* Houston places a white and an Indian boy in a situation that allows them to trust each other and, according to John Robert Sorfleet in *Twentieth-Century Children's Writers,* "the white boys learn respect and affection for the northern environment and native ways, and the native boys learn some practical advantages of modern technology and education." In all of his children's books, Houston's spare yet vivid illustrations set the mood for the story.

Sheila Egoff writes in *The Republic of Childhood: A Critical Guide to Canadian Children's Literature in English* that Houston "has not only been the most prolific spokesman for the Eskimo in children's literature, but also the most artistic writer." Similarly, Alice E. Kane, in *In Review: Canadian Books for Children,* commends Houston's "almost magical power of making the strange, hard world of the Eskimo believable to the city dweller." In his Arbuthnot lecture, Houston stated: "I believe having a direct living experience with the culture about which one is writing is invaluable. This has long been my method of relating northern stories, and I believe it would apply to other cultures around the world."

BIOGRAPHICAL/CRITICAL SOURCES:

BOOKS

Children's Literature Review, Volume 3, Gale, 1978, pp. 83-88.

Egoff, Sheila, *The Republic of Childhood: A Critical Guide to Canadian Children's Literature in English,* Oxford University Press, 1975.

Twentieth-Century Children's Writers, 3rd edition, St. James Press, 1989, pp. 468-470.

PERIODICALS

Canadian Children's Literature, Volume 31/32, 1983.
Globe and Mail (Toronto), November 30, 1985; November 12, 1988.
In Review: Canadian Books for Children, winter, 1969, pp. 26-27.
New York Times Book Review, October 8, 1967; December 13, 1981, p. 39.
Top of the News, summer, 1987, pp. 391-402.
Washington Post, April 15, 1983.*

—*Sketch by Tom Pendergast*

*   *   *

HUDNUT, Robert K(ilborne) 1934-

PERSONAL: Born January 7, 1934, in Cincinnati, OH; son of William Herbert (a clergyman) and Elizabeth (Kilborne) Hudnut; married Constance Conklin; married Janet Lee Morlan; children: (first marriage) Heidi, Robert, Jr., Heather, Matthew. *Education:* Princeton University, B.A. (summa cum laude), 1956; Union Theological Seminary, New York, NY, M.Div., 1959.

ADDRESSES: Home—1078 Elm St., Winnetka, IL 60093. *Office*—1225 Willow Rd., Winnetka, IL 60093.

CAREER: Ordained Presbyterian minister, 1959; Westminster Presbyterian Church, Albany, NY, assistant pastor, 1959-62; St. Luke Presbyterian Church, Wayzata, MN, pastor, 1962-73; Minnesota Public Interest Research Group, Minneapolis, executive director, 1973-75; Winnetka Presbyterian Church, Winnetka, IL, pastor, 1975—. Fusion candidate for mayor of Albany, 1961; member of board of directors for Minnesota Council of Churches, 1964-70; co-chairman of Minneapolis Board of Welfare Task Force on Homeless Alcoholics, 1967, and Minnesota Joint Religious Legislative Committee, 1970-75; chairman of Democratic Party, 33rd Senatorial District, MN, 1970-72, and Minnetonka Democratic Party, 1970-72; president, Greater Metropolitan Federation of Twin Cities, 1970-72; national chairman of Presbyterians for Church Renewal, 1971; trustee, Princeton University, 1972-76, and Asheville (NC) School, 1979—.

MEMBER: Phi Beta Kappa.

AWARDS, HONORS: Rockefeller Foundation fellow, 1956; Distinguished service award, Minnetonka Teachers Association, 1969.

WRITINGS:

Surprised by God—What It Means to Be a Minister in Middle-Class America Today, Association Press, 1967.

A Thinking Man and the Christ, Fortress, 1971.
The Sleeping Giant: Arousing Church Power in America, Harper, 1971.
A Sensitive Man and the Christ, Fortress, 1971.
An Active Man and the Christ, Fortress, 1972.
Arousing the Sleeping Giant: How to Organize Your Church for Action, Harper, 1973.
Church Growth Is Not the Point, Harper, 1975.
The Bootstrap Fallacy: What the Self-Help Books Don't Tell You, William Collins, 1978.
This People, This Parish, Zondervan, 1986.
Meeting God in the Darkness, Regal, 1989.

Contributor to *Our Sunday Visitor* (Catholic weekly), *Christian Century, Presbyterian Life, Minneapolis Star,* and other publications.

*   *   *

HUNGRY WOLF, Adolf 1944-

PERSONAL: Name originally Adolf Gutohrlein; born February 16, 1944, in Germany; son of Swiss and Hungarian parents; married Beverly Little Bear (a writer), October, 1971; children: Adolf, Jr., Okan, Iniskim, Star. *Education:* Long Beach State College (now University of California, Long Beach), B.A., 1966.

ADDRESSES: Home—P.O. Box 844, Skookumchuck, British Columbia, Canada V0B 2E0.

CAREER: Writer, 1962—. Union Pacific Railroad, Los Angeles, CA, locomotive fireman, 1962-65; high school history teacher in Long Beach, CA, 1967; longshoreman, 1968-69.

MEMBER: Crazy Dogs Society (traditional Blackfoot warrior group).

AWARDS, HONORS: Preis der Leseratten from German Scholastic Association, 1983, for *Der Rabe weiss wo die Sonne wohnt: Wie ich eine indianische Familie bekam.*

WRITINGS:

The Good Medicine Book, Warner Paperback Library, 1973.
(With wife, Beverly Hungry Wolf) *Blackfoot Craftworker's Book,* Good Medicine Books, 1977.
The Blood People, Harper, 1977.
Rails in the Canadian Rockies, Good Medicine Books, 1979.
(With Ben Calf Robe and B. Hungry Wolf) *Siksika: A Blackfoot Legacy,* Good Medicine Books, 1979.
A Good Medicine Collection: Life in Harmony with Nature (previously published as parts of the Good Medicine

Books series, Volumes 1, 2, 4, 6, and 8), Good Medicine Books, 1983.

Canadian Railway Scenes, Good Medicine Books, 1983.

(With B. Hungry Wolf) *Pow-wow,* Good Medicine Books, 1983.

(With B. Hungry Wolf) *Shadows of the Buffalo: A Family Odyssey among the Indians,* Morrow, 1983.

Der Rabe weiss wo die Sonne wohnt: Wie ich eine indianische Familie bekam (title means "The Raven Knows Where the Sun Lives: How I Became Part of an Indian Family"), Sauerlander, 1983.

(With son, Okan Hungry Wolf) *Canadian Railway Stories: 100 Years of History and Lore,* Good Medicine Books, 1985.

(Editor with B. Hungry Wolf) *Children of the Sun: Stories by and about Indian Kids,* Morrow, 1987.

Off on a Wild Caboose Chase: True Adventures, Folklore, and a Farewell Tribute to the Old Train Caboose by a Writer Who Lives Aboard One, Morrow, 1989.

Teachings of Nature, Good Medicine Books, 1989.

Legends Told by the Old People, Book Publishing, 1990.

Traditional Dress, Book Publishing, 1990.

Canadian Railway Scenes No. 4, Good Medicine Books, 1991.

Canadian Sunset: A Farewell Look at North America's Last Great Train, Interurban Press, 1991.

(With B. Hungry Wolf) *Indian Tribes of the Northern Rockies,* Book Publishing, 1991.

(With Star Hungry Wolf) *Children of the Circle: Photos and Essays of Indian Kids,* Good Medicine Books, 1991.

WORK IN PROGRESS: A novel; research on Native American culture, western history, railways, and photographic history.

SIDELIGHTS: Adolf Hungry Wolf practices "life in harmony with nature." He and his family live in the wilderness of the Canadian Rockies, without telephones, electricity, or formal schools. Hungry Wolf, his wife, Beverly, and their children have adopted traditions passed on by Native American forebears, and participate in Blackfoot Indian tribal events. Hungry Wolf's interest in railroads is evidenced by his four cabooses, five box cars, and tracks. He writes from an office he constructed in one of his railroad cars.

Off on a Wild Caboose Chase is Hungry Wolf's tribute to his favorite type of train car, now falling into disuse. The book features a guide to scenic rail trips, train-oriented songs and poems, and stories of his experiences as a railroad employee and caboose owner. A *Publishers Weekly* reviewer calls the book "a relaxing and enjoyable reading experience."

BIOGRAPHICAL/CRITICAL SOURCES:

PERIODICALS

Los Angeles Times Book Review, April 5, 1987, p. 4.
New York Times Book Review, February 26, 1989, p. 35.
Publishers Weekly, September 17, 1973, p. 58; December 19, 1986, p. 37; November 18, 1988, p. 58.
Washington Post Book World, May 8, 1988, p. 12.

*   *   *

HUNGRY WOLF, Beverly   1950-

PERSONAL: Born April 1, 1950, in Cardston, Alberta, Canada; daughter of Edward (an artist) and Ruth (Beebe) Little Bear; married Adolf Hungry Wolf (a writer), October, 1971; children: Adolf, Jr., Shane, Okan, Iniskim, Star. *Education:* Attended Lethbridge Community College, 1969-70.

ADDRESSES: Home—P.O. Box 844, Skookumchuck, British Columbia, Canada V0B 2E0.

CAREER: St. Mary's Indian School, Blood Reserve, Alberta, teacher's assistant, 1970-71; mother, housewife, homesteader, and publisher of family-owned business, Good Medicine Books.

WRITINGS:

(With husband, Adolf Hungry Wolf) *Blackfoot Craftworker's Book,* Good Medicine Books, 1977.

(With Ben Calf Robe and A. Hungry Wolf) *Siksika: A Blackfoot Legacy,* Good Medicine Books, 1979.

The Ways of My Grandmothers, Quill, 1980.

(With A. Hungry Wolf) *Pow-wow,* Good Medicine Books, 1983.

(With A. Hungry Wolf) *Shadows of the Buffalo: A Family Odyssey among the Indians,* Morrow, 1983.

(Editor with A. Hungry Wolf) *Children of the Sun: Stories by and about Indian Kids,* Morrow, 1987.

(With A. Hungry Wolf) *Indian Tribes of the Northern Rockies,* Book Publishing, 1991.

WORK IN PROGRESS: Daughters of the Buffalo Women, to be published in 1993.

SIDELIGHTS: Beverly Hungry Wolf is a member of the Blood tribe of the Blackfoot people. She did not learn to speak English until she went to reservation boarding school. She once told *CA:* "I am actively involved in the traditional culture of the Blackfoot tribe, and I am trying to bridge the culture of our tribe and those of neighboring people of all races. I also practice a basic lifestyle in harmony with nature. I teach our four children at home, where we live without a telephone or electricity. I plan to share some of the results in future writings. We are now living on an isolated homestead in the British Columbia Rockies but continuing our cultural life within the tribal society by traveling back and forth a lot.

"Prejudice and lack of understanding among differing people and differing generations are the greatest challenges in trying to bridge my tribal culture with others. This problem exists on both sides. Through my work and writings I hope I'm contributing to a very slow improvement."

Hungry Wolf recorded the recollections and opinions of the older women living on a Blackfoot Indian reserve in western Canada in *The Ways of My Grandmothers.* Members of the Bloods, the women hold strong ideas about tradition, religion, and the modern world. A writer for the *New York Times Book Review* calls the book "a rare record of the American Indian heritage."

BIOGRAPHICAL/CRITICAL SOURCES:

PERIODICALS

Los Angeles Times Book Review, April 5, 1987, p. 4.
New York Times Book Review, August 17, 1980, p. 12; June 14, 1981, p. 35.
Publishers Weekly, May 2, 1980, p. 70; December 19, 1986, p. 37.
Washington Post Book World, May 8, 1988, p. 12.

*   *   *

HUNT, David C(urtis) 1935-

PERSONAL: Born December 7, 1935, in Oswego, KS; son of Burl H. and Julia (a piano teacher; maiden name, Long) Hunt; married Carol Beth Keene, February 2, 1969; children: Laura Allison, Anne Elizabeth, Matthew David. *Education:* University of Tulsa, B.A., 1958, M.A., 1968. *Politics:* Democrat. *Religion:* Roman Catholic.

ADDRESSES: Home—4808 Magnolia, Omaha, NE 68137. *Office*—Joslyn Art Museum, 2200 Dodge St., Omaha, NE 68102.

CAREER: KTUL-TV, Tulsa, OK, part-time production artist, 1956-58; KTSM-TV, El Paso, TX, production artist, 1960-62; KOTV-TV, Tulsa, studio camera operator, 1962; Bendix Radio Corp., Kailua, HI, illustrator in Publications Division, 1962-63; Douglas Aircraft (now McDonnell-Douglas Aircraft), Tulsa, illustrator and designer in Publications Division, 1963-65; Thomas Gilcrease Institute of American History and Art, Tulsa, exhibits specialist, 1965-67, curator of art, production manager, and associate editor of museum publications, 1967-72; Nelda C. and H. J. Lutcher Stark Foundation, Orange, TX, curator and design consultant for Stark Museum of Art,

1972-76; Tulsa City-County Library System, Tulsa, coordinator of audio-visual services, 1976-77; Missoula Museum of the Arts, Missoula, MT, director, 1977-80; Joslyn Art Museum, Center for Western Studies, Omaha, NE, curator of western American art and department head, 1980—.

Co-curator of nationally-touring Bodmer-Maxmilian exhibition, "Views of a Vanishing Frontier," sponsored by Joslyn Art Museum and the InterNorth Art Foundation, 1984-85; curator or co-curator of numerous other exhibitions throughout the United States. Instructor at University of Tulsa, 1970-72. Artist (including commissioned murals). Member of Orange Community Players. *Military service:* U.S. Army, technical illustrator for publications and training aids, 1958-60; served in Korea.

MEMBER: International Council of Industrial Editors, American Association for State and Local History, American Association of Museums, Montana Art Gallery Directors Association, Humane Education Council of Southeast Texas, Tulsa Arts Guild, Sabine Audubon Society, Theta Alpha Phi.

AWARDS, HONORS: Margaret C. Hewgley Award, Oklahoma Artists Annual, 1963, for representational painting; Certificate of Craftsmanship, Weyerhaeuser Paper Corp., 1966, for "Discovery in Meso America" in *American Scene;* 3M Printing Job of the Year awards, 3M Corp., 1966, for "Naturalists in America," and 1968, for "W. R. Leigh: The Artist's Studio Collection," both in *American Scene;* Award of Excellence, Simpson Lee Paper Co., 1968, for work in *American Scene;* Wrangler Award, National Cowboy Hall of Fame and Western Heritage Center, 1969, for "W. R. Leigh: The Artist's Studio Collection," and 1972, for *The Art of the Old West;* Printing Industries of America, Certificates of Merit in graphic arts competition, 1969, for "The Plains of Philippi" and "W. R. Leigh: The Artist's Studio Collection," and Certificate of Merit, 1984, for Joslyn publications; Awards of Excellence, International Council of Industrial Editors, both 1969, for *American Scene* and *The Thomas Gilcrease Institute: A National Treasury;* Mead Award, Mead Paper Co., 1970, for "The Missouri River: Waterway West"; Certificate of Excellence, American Institute of the Graphic Arts, 1984, for catalogue to *Views of a Vanishing Frontier;* Award of Excellence, Art Museum Association of America, 1984, George Wittenborn Memorial Award, Art Libraries of North America, 1985, and Silver Medal in International Book Exhibition, Leipzig, Germany, 1989, all for *Karl Bodmer's America;* Addison E. Sheldon Memorial Award, Nebraska State Historical Society, 1984, for exhibition "Views of a Vanishing Frontier"; Award of Merit in museums publications competition, American Association of Museums, 1985, for Joslyn publications; Oklahoma

Book Award, Oklahoma Library Association, 1989, for *The Lithographs of Charles Banks Wilson.*

WRITINGS:

The Thomas Gilcrease Institute: A National Treasury (monograph), Thomas Gilcrease Institute, 1969.

(With Paul A. Rossi) *The Art of the Old West,* Knopf, 1971, 4th edition, Promontory Press, 1981.

Guide to Oklahoma Museums, University of Oklahoma Press, 1981.

(With William H. Goetzmann and others) *Karl Bodmer's America,* University of Nebraska Press, 1984.

The Lithographs of Charles Banks Wilson, University of Oklahoma Press, 1989.

CATALOGUES

The Great American Documents Gallery, Thomas Gilcrease Institute, 1968.

(With Joel Bernstein) *Images of the West: Myth and Reality,* Missoula Museum of the Arts and University of Montana Department of Art, 1979.

(With Goetzmann and Joseph C. Porter) *The West as Romantic Horizon,* Joslyn Art Museum, 1980.

Legacy of the West, Joslyn Art Museum, 1981.

(With John C. Ewers and others) *Views of a Vanishing Frontier,* University of Nebraska Press, 1984.

(With Graham Beal and J. G. Studholme) *Bodmer's America: The Aquatint Atlas,* Alecto Historical Editions, 1991.

OTHER

Contributor to *Reader's Encyclopedia of the American West,* edited by Howard R. Lamar, Crowell, 1977. Contributor to periodicals, including *American History Illustrated, Nebraskaland Magazine, Four Winds Magazine,* and *Gilcrease Magazine.* Past associate editor, *American Scene.*

SIDELIGHTS: David C. Hunt told *CA:* "I did not set out to be a writer. Writing and publishing both resulted from professional interests and activities associated with the occupation of a museum curator, but having gotten into the field, I now find that there are more and more subjects I'd like to research and write about. American art and history remain the chief areas of my interest.

"Growing up in the oilfields of northeastern Oklahoma, I was early exposed to public collections of fine art and western Americana assembled by oilmen such as Thomas Gilcrease, Waite Phillips, and Frank Phillips. My dad worked for Phillips Petroleum Co. at the time, and we often visited the Phillips's ranch and museum at Woolaroc, west of Bartlesville. Later, I was employed at the Gilcrease Museum in Tulsa, where a professional interest in such collections developed.

"One of my duties at Gilcrease was that of production manager for the museum quarterly and related publications. I soon went from designing the quarterly to writing articles for same. Eventually, articles for other publications resulted. The highlight of my writing experience at Gilcrease was co-authoring *The Art of the Old West* for Alfred Knopf. Based entirely upon the resources of the vast Gilcrease collection, it has sold extremely well—'for an art book.' Nearly everything I have done since in the writing field has derived from that first success.

"Having taken only one class in journalism at the University of Tulsa as part of the general requirements for a commercial art degree, I necessarily developed subsequent writing skills on the job. I'm not sure what my 'philosophy' with respect to writing might be, other than to say that I try to write the way I like to read. Other than imparting information, a line or paragraph has to 'sound right' to me. A certain rhythm in phrasing and overall organization is important. It's not unlike writing music or dialogue for a play. I've done some of that, too.

"Natural history remains a secondary, non-professional interest of mine. As with writing, my introduction to nature and the wilderness ideal resulted from activities associated with the arts. I also admit to a lasting affection for the theatre and for amateur dramatics, in which I was once active."

BIOGRAPHICAL/CRITICAL SOURCES:

PERIODICALS

Washington Post Book World, October 21, 1984, p. 5.

*   *   *

HUNTER, Evan 1926-
(Curt Cannon, Hunt Collins, Ezra Hannon, Richard Marsten, Ed McBain)

PERSONAL: Born October 15, 1926, in New York, NY; son of Charles and Marie (Coppola) Lombino; married Anita Melnick, October 17, 1949 (divorced); married Mary Vann Finley, June, 1973; children: (first marriage) Ted, Mark, Richard; (second marriage) Amanda Eve Finley (stepdaughter). *Education:* Hunter College (now Hunter College of the City University of New York), B.A., 1950. *Politics:* Democrat.

ADDRESSES: Agent—William Morris Agency, 1350 Avenue of the Americas, New York, NY 10019.

CAREER: Writer. Taught at two vocational high schools in New York City for a short time, about 1950; held various jobs, including answering the telephone at night for American Automobile Association and selling lobsters for a wholesale lobster firm, both New York City; worked for Scott Meredith Literary Agency, New York City, for about six months. *Military service:* U.S. Navy, 1944-46.

MEMBER: Phi Beta Kappa.

AWARDS, HONORS: Mystery Writers of America Award, 1957, for short story "The Last Spin"; Grand Master Award, Mystery Writers of America, 1986, for lifetime achievement.

WRITINGS:

The Evil Sleep, Falcon, 1952.
The Big Fix, Falcon, 1952, published under pseudonym Richard Marsten as *So Nude, So Dead,* Fawcett, 1956.
Find the Feathered Serpent, Winston, 1952, reprinted, Gregg, 1979.
Don't Crowd Me, Popular Library, 1953, published in England as *The Paradise Party,* New English Library, 1968.
(Under pseudonym Hunt Collins) *Cut Me In,* Abelard, 1954, published as *The Proposition,* Pyramid, 1955.
The Blackboard Jungle, Simon & Schuster, 1954, reprinted, Avon, 1976.
(Contributor) David Coxe Cook, editor, *Best Detective Stories of the Year 1955,* Dutton, 1955.
(Under pseudonyn Hunt Collins) *Tomorrow's World,* Bouregy, 1956, published as *Tomorrow and Tomorrow,* Pyramid Books, 1956, published in England under pseudonym Ed McBain, Sphere, 1979.
Second Ending, Simon & Schuster, 1956, published as *Quartet in H,* Pocket Books, 1957.
The Jungle Kids (short stories), Pocket Books, 1956.
(With Craig Rice, under pseudonym Ed McBain) *April Robin Murders* (crime novel), Random House, 1958.
(Under pseudonym Curt Cannon) *I'm Cannon—For Hire* (crime novel), Fawcett, 1958.
Strangers When We Meet (also see below), Simon & Schuster, 1958.
(Under pseudonym Curt Cannon) *I Like 'Em Tough* (short stories), Fawcett, 1958.
A Matter of Conviction, Simon & Schuster, 1959, reprinted, Avon, 1976, published as *Young Savages,* Pocket Books, 1966.
The Remarkable Harry (juvenile), Abelard, 1960.
The Last Spin and Other Stories, Constable, 1960.
The Wonderful Button (juvenile), Abelard, 1961.
Mothers and Daughters, Simon & Schuster, 1961.
Happy New Year, Herbie, and Other Stories, Simon & Schuster, 1963.
Buddwing, Simon & Schuster, 1964.
(Under pseudonym Ed McBain) *The Sentries* (crime novel), Simon & Schuster, 1965.
The Paper Dragon, Delacorte, 1966.

A Horse's Head, Delacorte, 1967.
(Editor under pseudonym Ed McBain) *Crime Squad,* New English Library, 1968.
(Editor under pseudonym Ed McBain) *Homicide Department,* New English Library, 1968.
Last Summer, Doubleday, 1968.
(Editor under pseudonym Ed McBain) *Downpour,* New English Library, 1969.
(Editor under pseudonym Ed McBain) *Ticket to Death,* New English Library, 1969.
Sons, Doubleday, 1969.
Nobody Knew They Were There, Doubleday, 1971.
The Beheading and Other Stories, Constable, 1971.
Every Little Crook and Nanny, Doubleday, 1972.
The Easter Man (a Play), and Six Stories (also see below), Doubleday, 1972.
Seven, Constable, 1972.
Come Winter, Doubleday, 1973.
Streets of Gold, Harper, 1974.
(Under pseudonym Ed McBain) *Where There's Smoke* (crime novel), Random House, 1975.
(Under pseudonym Ezra Hannon) *Doors* (crime novel), Stein & Day, 1975.
The Chisholms: A Novel of the Journey West (also see below), Harper, 1976.
(Under pseudonym Ed McBain) *Guns* (crime novel), Random House, 1976.
Me and Mr. Stenner (juvenile), Lippincott, 1977.
Walk Proud (also see below), Bantam, 1979.
Love, Dad, Crown, 1981.
(Under pseudonym Ed McBain) *The McBain Brief* (short stories), Hamish Hamilton, 1982, Arbor House, 1983.
Far From the Sea, Atheneum, 1983.
Lizzie, Arbor House, 1984.
(Under pseudonym Ed McBain) *Another Part of the City,* Mysterious Press, 1987.
(Under pseudonym Ed McBain) *Downtown,* Morrow, 1989.
(Under pseudonym Ed McBain) *Gangs,* Avon, 1989.

UNDER PSEUDONYM ED McBAIN; "87TH PRECINCT" SERIES

Cop Hater (also see below), Simon & Schuster, 1956.
The Mugger (also see below), Simon & Schuster, 1956.
The Pusher (also see below), Simon & Schuster, 1956.
The Con Man (also see below), Simon & Schuster, 1957.
Killer's Choice, Simon & Schuster, 1957.
Killer's Payoff, Simon & Schuster, 1958.
Lady Killer, Simon & Schuster, 1958.
Killer's Wedge, Simon & Schuster, 1959.
'Til Death, Simon & Schuster, 1959.
King's Ransom, Simon & Schuster, 1959.
Give the Boys a Great Big Hand, Simon & Schuster, 1960.
The Heckler, Simon & Schuster, 1960.
See Them Die, Simon & Schuster, 1960.

Lady, Lady, I Did It!, Simon & Schuster, 1961.

Like Love, Simon & Schuster, 1962.

The Empty Hours (three novellas), Simon & Schuster, 1962.

Ten Plus One, Simon & Schuster, 1963.

Ax, Simon & Schuster, 1964.

He Who Hesitates, Delacorte, 1965.

Doll, Delacorte, 1965.

Eighty Million Eyes, Delacorte, 1966.

The 87th Precinct (includes *Cop Hater, The Mugger, The Pusher,* and *The Con Man*), Boardman, 1966.

Fuzz (also see below), Doubleday, 1968.

Shotgun, Doubleday, 1969.

Jigsaw, Doubleday, 1970.

Hail, Hail, the Gang's All Here, Doubleday, 1971.

Sadie When She Died, Doubleday, 1972.

Let's Hear It for the Deaf Man, Doubleday, 1972.

87th Precinct: An Ed McBain Omnibus, Hamish Hamilton, 1973.

Hail to the Chief, Random House, 1973.

Bread, Random House, 1974.

The Second 87th Precinct Omnibus, Hamish Hamilton, 1975.

Blood Relatives, Random House, 1975.

So Long as You Both Shall Live, Random House, 1976.

Long Time No See, Random House, 1977.

Calypso, Viking, 1979.

Ghosts, Viking, 1980.

Heat, Viking, 1981.

Ice, Arbor House, 1983.

Lightning, Arbor House, 1984.

Eight Black Horses, Avon, 1986.

Poison, Morrow, 1987.

Tricks, Morrow, 1987.

McBain's Ladies: The Women of the 87th Precinct, Mysterious Press, 1988.

Lullaby, Morrow, 1989.

McBain's Ladies, Too, Mysterious Press, 1989.

Vespers, Morrow, 1990.

Widows: A Novel of the 87th Precinct, Morrow, 1991.

UNDER PSEUDONYM ED McBAIN; "MATTHEW HOPE" SERIES; CRIME NOVELS

Goldilocks, Arbor House, 1978.

Rumpelstiltskin, Viking, 1981.

Beauty and the Beast, Hamish Hamilton, 1982, Holt, 1983.

Jack and the Beanstalk, Holt, 1984.

Snow White and Rose Red, Holt, 1986.

Puss in Boots, Holt, 1987.

The House That Jack Built, Holt, 1988.

Three Blind Mice, Mysterious Press, 1991.

UNDER PSEUDONYM RICHARD MARSTEN

Rocket to Luna (juvenile), Winston, 1953.

Danger: Dinosaurs (juvenile), Winston, 1953.

Runaway Black (crime novel), Fawcett, 1954.

Murder in the Navy (crime novel), Fawcett, 1955, published under pseudonym Ed McBain as *Death of a Nurse,* Pocket Books, 1968.

The Spiked Heel (crime novel), Holt, 1956.

Vanishing Ladies (crime novel), Pocket Books, 1957.

Even the Wicked (crime novel), Permabooks, 1957, published in England under pseudonym Ed McBain, Severn House, 1979.

Big Man (crime novel), Pocket Books, 1959, published in England under pseudonym Ed McBain, Penguin, 1978.

(Contributor) Leo Marguiles, editor, *Dames, Danger, and Death,* Pyramid, 1960.

PLAYS; UNDER NAME EVAN HUNTER

"The Easter Man," produced in Birmingham, England, at Birmingham Repertory Theatre, 1964, produced under title "A Race of Hairy Men!" on Broadway at Henry Miller's Theater, April, 1965.

"The Conjuror," produced in Ann Arbor, Mich., at Lydia Mendelssohn Theatre, November 5, 1969.

"Stalemate," produced in New York, 1975.

SCREENPLAYS AND TELEVISION SCRIPTS; UNDER NAME EVAN HUNTER

"Strangers When We Meet" (based on author's novel of same title), Columbia Pictures Industries, Inc., 1960.

"The Birds" (based on short story by Daphne du Maurier), Universal Pictures, 1963.

"Fuzz" (based on author's novel of same title), United Artists Corp., 1972.

"Walk Proud" (based on author's novel of same title), Universal, 1979.

"The Chisholms" (Columbia Broadcasting System television series), Alan Landsburg Productions, 1979-80.

OTHER

Also author of "Appointment at Eleven" for "Alfred Hitchcock Presents," 1955-61. The Mulgar Memorial Library of Boston University holds Hunter's manuscripts.

ADAPTATIONS: Several of Hunter's novels have been made into movies, including "The Blackboard Jungle," Metro-Goldwyn-Mayer, Inc., 1955; "Cop Hater," United Artists Corp., 1958; "The Muggers" (based on *The Mugger*), United Artists, 1958; "The Pusher," United Artists, 1960; "The Young Savages" (based on *A Matter of Conviction*), United Artists, 1961; "High and Low" (based on *King's Ransom*), Toho International, 1963; "Mr. Buddwing" (based on *Buddwing*), Metro-Goldwyn-Mayer, 1967; "Last Summer," Twentieth Century-Fox Film Corp., 1969; "Sans Mobile apparent" (title means "Without Apparent Motive"; based on *Ten Plus One*), President

Films, 1971; "Le Cri du cormoran le soir au-dessus des jonques" (title means "The Cry of the Cormorant at Night Over the Junks"; based on *A Horse's Head*), Gaumont International, 1971; and "Every Little Crook and Nanny," Metro-Goldwyn-Mayer, 1972.

SIDELIGHTS: With numerous novels, short stories, plays, and film scripts to his credit, Evan Hunter ranks as one of today's most versatile and prolific writers. Known to millions throughout the world under his pseudonym, Ed McBain (originator of the "87th Precinct" detective series), Hunter is also the author (under his own name) of such thought-provoking best-sellers as *The Blackboard Jungle, Strangers When We Meet, Mothers and Daughters,* and *Last Summer.* He prefers to keep these two identities strictly separate, he explains, because "I don't like to confuse critics who are very easily confused anyway. I also do not like to confuse readers. I wouldn't like a woman, for example, who had read *Mothers and Daughters* by Evan Hunter, to pick up *The Heckler* by Evan Hunter and find that it's about mayhem, bloodshed and violence. I think this would be unfair to her and unfair to me as well."

Though it appeared some ten years after Hunter made his first serious attempts to write for publication, *The Blackboard Jungle* caused the twenty-eight-year-old author to be labeled an "overnight" success. A semi-autobiographical work, *The Blackboard Jungle* tells the story of an idealistic young man who confronts the often violent realities of trying to teach a group of sullen, illiterate, delinquent teenagers in a big-city vocational high school. Written in what was then politely termed the "vernacular," Hunter's dramatic indictment of both the inadequacies of teacher training colleges and of the New York City school system is "a nightmarish but authentic first novel," according to a *Time* critic. The *New York Herald Tribune Book Review*'s Barbara Klaw points to Hunter's "superb ear for conversation," "competence as a storyteller," and "tolerant and tough-minded sympathy for his subject" as some of the book's best features, while Nathan Rothman of the *Saturday Review* feels that it is free of the "distortions and dishonesty" of many newspaper articles on the same topic. And even though the *Nation*'s Stanley Cooperman believes that Hunter "makes only cursory attempts to probe the wellsprings of the action he photographs so well," he concludes that the ex-substitute teacher "succeeds in dramatizing an area heretofore neglected in fiction."

Hunter is frequently praised for the consistently high standard of professionalism evident in his writing. He told *CA:* "When I was beginning to write, I wrote a great many detective stories for the pulp magazines. I wrote not only police stories, but private eye and man-on-the-run and woman-in-jeopardy, the whole gamut. After *The Blackboard Jungle* was published, Pocket Books did the reprint

of it. I had an old mystery novel kicking around that I had not yet sold, and there was a pseudonym on it, but not Ed McBain. We sent it to Pocket Books as a possibility for a paperback original. The editor there at the time, a man named Herbert Alexander, was a very bright guy. He recognized the style and called my agent and said, 'Is this our friend Hunter?' My agent said, 'Yes, it is,' and Alexander said, 'Well, I'd like to talk to him.'

"We had lunch one day," Hunter continues, "and the gist of the conversation was that the mainstay of Pocket Books was Erle Stanley Gardner; he had sold millions of books and they would just republish each title every three or four years with new jackets. They kept selling as if they were new books all the time. But he was getting old and they were looking for a mystery writer who could replace him, so they asked me if I had any ideas about a mystery series. I said I would think about it. I got back to them and I said that it seemed to me—after all the mysteries I'd written—that the only *valid* people to deal with crime were cops, and I would like to make the lead character, rather than a single *person,* a *squad* of cops instead—so it would be a *conglomerate* lead character. They said, 'OK, we'll give you a contract for three books and if it works we'll renew it.' I started writing the series."

Hunter's "87th Precinct" novels are known as "police procedurals" in the mystery trade. "The nice thing about the '87th Precinct' is that I can deal with any subject matter so long as it's criminally related," Hunter told *CA.* "With the Ed McBain novels, I only want to say that cops have a tough, underpaid job, and they deal with murder every day of the week, and that's the way it is, folks. With the Hunters, the theme varies and I'll usually ponder the next book for a long, long time—until it demands to be written."

Most of Hunter's other novels exhibit definite thematic concerns, occasionally inspired by biographical or autobiographical material, but often just "intellectual concepts that come to me and take a while to develop before they're put down on paper." He has written a great deal about young people, especially the relationship between the young and the old (usually parents). "I don't know why I've been attracted to writing about young people," he once remarked to a *Publishers Weekly* interviewer. "I guess from *Blackboard Jungle,* it's been a situation that's always appealed to me, the idea of adults in conflict with the young. I think part of my fascination is with America as an adolescent nation and with our so-called adult responses that are sometimes adolescent."

Often these same novels contain elements of current topical interest as well—the state of the American educational system in *The Blackboard Jungle,* the emptiness of post-World War II middle-class life in *Mothers and Daughters,* the Vietnam War in *Sons,* and the anti-Establishment "hippie" movement of the late 1960s and early 1970s in *Love, Dad.* The *New York Times Book Review*'s Ivan Gold concludes, "Mr. Hunter is a serious and honorable writer trying to entertain us, and also trying to tell us, now and again, some useful things about our lives." As Hunter himself once explained to the *Publishers Weekly* interviewer, "The whole reason I write anything is so that someone somewhere will say, 'Oh, yeah. I feel that way too. I'm not alone.' "

BIOGRAPHICAL/CRITICAL SOURCES:

BOOKS

Contemporary Literary Criticism, Gale, Volume 11, 1979; Volume 31, 1985.
Dictionary of Literary Biography Yearbook: 1982, Gale, 1982.
Newquist, Roy, *Conversations,* Rand McNally, 1967.

PERIODICALS

Best Sellers, June 15, 1968; August 15, 1969; March 15, 1971.
Books, June, 1970.
Books and Bookmen, January, 1969.
Catholic World, August, 1958.
Chicago Sunday Tribune, January 22, 1956; June 8, 1958; May 28, 1961.
Choice, June, 1970.
Detroit News, January 16, 1983.
Globe and Mail (Toronto), October 19, 1985; June 21, 1986; February 28, 1987.
Harper's, December, 1967; June, 1968.
Los Angeles Times, May 14, 1981; February 4, 1983.
Nation, December 4, 1954.
New Yorker, January 13, 1975.
New York Herald Tribune Book Review, October 17, 1954; January 15, 1956; July 20, 1958.
New York Herald Tribune Lively Arts, May 21, 1961.
New York Times, January 8, 1956; June 15, 1958; June 12, 1968; April 10, 1981; April 19, 1985; February 20, 1987; July 3, 1987.
New York Times Book Review, May 28, 1961; October 20, 1968; July 16, 1969; September 28, 1969; September 19, 1976; May 6, 1979; May 10, 1981.
New Statesman, January 10, 1969.
Newsweek, March 8, 1971.
Observer (London), April 5, 1970.
People, December 19, 1977.
Publishers Weekly, April 3, 1981.
San Francisco Chronicle, July 9, 1961.
Saturday Review, October 9, 1954; January 7, 1956; April 24, 1971; September 9, 1972.
Springfield Republican, July 9, 1961.
Time, October 11, 1954; June 9, 1958; March 8, 1971.
Times (London), August 20, 1981; September 11, 1982; July 11, 1985.
Times Literary Supplement, November 21, 1958; July 28, 1961; January 25, 1968; May 28, 1970; July 13, 1973.
Virginia Quarterly Review, summer, 1968.
Washington Post Book World, March 29, 1981; January 19, 1983; June 24, 1984.
Writer, April, 1969.
Writer's Digest, April, 1971.

I-J

ISHIDA, Takeshi 1923-

PERSONAL: Born June 7, 1923, in Aomori, Japan; son of Kaoru (a governor) and Kyo (Ohtsuka) Ishida; married Reiko Oinuma, 1950; children: Hiroshi, Ken. *Education:* University of Tokyo, Hogaku-shi, 1949.

ADDRESSES: Home—2-13-7 Nishikata, Bunkyo-ku, Tokyo 113, Japan. *Office*—Faculty of Political Economy, Yachiyo International University, Yachiyo City 276, Japan.

CAREER: University of Tokyo, Tokyo, Japan, research assistant in political science, 1949-52, researcher at Institute of Social Science, 1952-53, associate professor, 1953-67, professor of political science, 1967-84, professor emeritus, 1984—; Chiba University Faculty of Law and Economics, Chiba City, Japan, professor of political science, 1984-89; Yachiyo International University, Faculty of Political Economy, Yachiyo City, Japan, professor of comparative politics, 1990—. Research associate at Harvard University, 1962-63; senior specialist at East-West Center, University of Hawaii, 1965; visiting professor at Colegio de Mexico, 1971-72, St. Anthony's College, Oxford, 1974, University of Arizona, 1976-77, University of Dares-Salaam, 1978, and Free University, Berlin, 1981-82; fellow, Institute for Advanced Study, Berlin, 1985-86.

MEMBER: International Peace Research Association (member of executive council, 1974-76), Japan Political Science Association (member of executive council, 1975-77).

AWARDS, HONORS: Rockefeller Foundation fellow, 1961-63; cultural award from government of Australia, 1975.

WRITINGS:

Japanese Society, Random House, 1971.
Japanese Political Culture: Change and Continuity, Transaction Books, 1983.
(Editor with Ellis Krauss) *Democracy in Japan,* University of Pittsburgh Press, 1989.

Chairperson of editorial board of Japan Political Science Association, 1975-77; member of international advisory board of *Comparative Political Studies.*

WORK IN PROGRESS: A collection of articles in English, *Japan: Her Culture, Society, and Politics.*

SIDELIGHTS: Takeshi Ishida told *CA:* "In recent years, there has been a considerable growth in the number of Western scholarly works on Japan, but works by Japanese authors rarely appear in English. My works in English seek to describe and analyze the essential features of Japanese society as perceived by a Japanese social scientist. I have been trying to produce something different from the books on Japan written by foreign scholars, particularly emphasizing the cultural tradition of Japanese society.

"While writing along this line, I should be careful to avoid two difficulties. The first is that, if we put too much emphasis on the uniqueness of culture, we tend to fall into the trap of cultural determination. The second is that, by identifying a certain characteristic as a national trait, we tend to be ahistorical. In order to avoid the first difficulty, we need to clarify to what extent the same scheme can be applied to other societies and to what extent there is a difference between Japanese society and others. To avoid the second difficulty, we need to analyze historical development. This is the reason why I have been trying to integrate the social scientific approach and historical approach."

JACOBS, Louis 1920-

PERSONAL: Born July 17, 1920, in Manchester, England; son of Harry and Lena (Myerstone) Jacobs; married Shulamith Lisagorsky, 1944; children: Ivor, Naomi, David. *Education:* University College, London, B.A. (with honors), 1946, Ph.D., 1952; Manchester Talmudical College, rabbinical diploma, 1941.

ADDRESSES: Home—27 Clifton Hill, St. John's Wood, London NW8 0QE, England.

CAREER: Central Synagogue, Manchester, England, rabbi, 1948-52; New West End Synagogue, London, England, rabbi, 1952-60; Jews' College, London, tutor, 1960-62; New London Synagogue, London, rabbi, 1964—. Harvard University Divinity School, visiting professor of Jewish thought, 1985-86; Lancaster University, visiting professor in department of religious studies, 1986—.

AWARDS, HONORS: Commander of the British Empire, 1990.

WRITINGS:

We Have Reason to Believe, Vallentine, Mitchell, 1959, 3rd edition, 1965.
Jewish Values, Vallentine, Mitchell, 1960, 2nd edition, Hartmore, 1969.
Studies in Talmudic Logic, Vallentine, Mitchell, 1962.
(Translator) Dobh Baer Schneor Zalman, *Tract on Ecstasy,* Vallentine, Mitchell, 1963.
Principles of the Jewish Faith, Basic Books, 1964.
Seeker of Unity: The Life and Works of Aaron of Starosselje, Basic Books, 1966.
Jewish Law, Behrman, 1968.
Faith, Basic Books, 1968.
(Editor) *Jewish Ethics, Philosophy and Mysticism,* Behrman, 1969.
Jewish Thought Today, Behrman, 1970.
Hasidic Prayer, Schocken, 1972.
What Does Judaism Say About . . . ?, Quadrangle, 1973.
Jewish Biblical Exegesis, Behrman, 1973.
A Jewish Theology, Behrman, 1973.
Theology in the Responsa, Routledge & Kegan Paul, 1975.
Hasidic Thought, Behrman, 1976.
Jewish Mystical Testimony, Schocken, 1977.
TEKYU: The Unsolved Problem in the Babylonian Talmud, Cornwell, 1981.
A Tree of Life: Divinity, Flexibility and Creativity in Jewish Law, Oxford University Press, 1984.
The Talmudic Argument, Cambridge University Press, 1984.
The Book of Jewish Belief, Behrman, 1984.
Structure and Form of the Babylonian Talmud, Cambridge University Press, 1991.

Religion and the Individual: A Jewish Perspective, Cambridge University Press, 1991.

Contributor to theology publications.

WORK IN PROGRESS: Talmudic reasoning and literary analysis of the Talmud; theological studies.

SIDELIGHTS: Louis Jacobs told *CA:* "In my works I have tried to follow the style of English theological writing, ever mindful of the warning addressed to those tho imagine that obscurity is evidence of depth: 'You don't have to be fat to drive fat oxen!' Some of my books are technical but often belong to the *genre* of popular theology. To engage in which I do not consider to be unworthy or embarrassing; quite the opposite."

BIOGRAPHICAL/CRITICAL SOURCES:

PERIODICALS

Judaism, winter, 1979.
Times (London), July 29, 1989.
Times Literary Supplement, February 2, 1967.

*   *   *

JAMES, Philip
See MOORCOCK, Michael (John)

*   *   *

JANOSCH
See ECKERT, Horst

*   *   *

JANSSON, Tove Marika 1914-

PERSONAL: Name is pronounced "*Toh*-vay *Yan*-son"; born August 9, 1914, in Helsinki, Finland; daughter of Viktor (a sculptor) and Signe (a designer; maiden name, Hammarsten) Jansson. *Education:* Studied book design in Stockholm, 1930-33; studied painting in Helsinki, 1933-36, and at Atelier Adrien Holy, Paris, France, 1938, and in Florence, Italy.

ADDRESSES: Home—Helsinki 13, Finland.

CAREER: Finnish artist and illustrator whose oil paintings have been exhibited in Helsinki; *London Evening News,* writer and designer of "Moomins" cartoon strip, 1953-60; writer and illustrator of children's and adult books.

MEMBER: PEN, Painter's Society (Helsinki), Authors Club (Helsinki; director).

AWARDS, HONORS: Stockholm Award for best children's book, 1952, Nils Holgersson Plaque and Selma Lagerloef Medal, 1953, all for *The Book about Moomin, Mymble and Little My;* nominated for International Hans Christian Andersen Award, 1956, for *Moominsummer Madness;* Finnish Academy Award, Hans Christian Andersen Diploma of the International Council of Youth (Florence), Elsa Beskow Award (Malmoe, Sweden), and Rudolf Koivu plaquette (Finland), all 1958, all for *Moominland Mid-Winter;* Swedish Culture Prize (Helsinki), 1958, 1963, and 1970, for body of work; Hans Christian Andersen Diploma, 1962, for *Who Will Comfort Toffle?,* and 1964, for *Tales from Moomin Valley;* Finnish State Literature Prize, 1963; Anni Swan Prize (Finland), 1964, for *Tales from Moomin Valley;* Langman's Prize, 1965; named to International Board on Books for Young People (IBBY) 1966 Honors List; Hans Christian Andersen Medal, Author Award, 1966; *Expressen* (Stockholm daily paper) Winnie-the-Pooh Prize, 1970, and Finnish State Prize, 1971, both for *Moominvalley in November;* Selma Lagerloef Prize, 1972, for *Sculptor's Daughter;* Bonniers Publishing House (Sweden) scholarship award, 1972; Swedish Academy Prize, 1972; Werner Soederstroem Publishing House/Grafia Society (Finland) scholarship and medal for illustration, 1973; awarded Order of Smile Medal of Polish children and Pro-Finlandia Medal, both 1976; Austrian State Prize for Children's and Juvenile Literature, 1978, for *Who Will Comfort Toffle?;* honorary doctorate, Abo Academy, 1978; Le Grand Prix des Treize, 1979, for *The Summer Book;* Dunce's Cap Prize, Finnish Comic Strip Society, 1980; Suomen Kulttuurirahaston Palkinto, 1989; Tupilak's Kulturpris, 1990.

WRITINGS:

JUVENILE FICTION; SELF-ILLUSTRATED

Smaatrollen och den stora oeversvaemningen (title means "The Small Trolls and the Large Flood"), Soederstroem, 1945.

Kometjakten, Soederstroem, 1945 (also published in Sweden as *Mumintrollet och kometjakt,* Sorlins, 1946), revised edition published as *Kometen komer,* Schildt, 1968, translation by Elizabeth Portch published as *Comet in Moominland* (also see below), Benn, 1951, Walck, 1968.

Trollkarlens hatt, Schildt, 1949, translation by Portch published as *The Finn Family Moomintroll* (also see below), Benn, 1950, Walck, 1965, published as *The Happy Moomins,* Bobbs-Merrill, 1952.

Moominpappans bravader, Schildt, 1950, published as *The Exploits of Moominpappa,* Walck, 1966, revised edition published as *Muminppans memoar,* Schildt, 1968.

Hur gick det sen?, Schildt, 1952, published as *The Book about Moomin, Mymble and Little My,* Benn, 1953.

Farlig midsommar, Schildt, 1954, published as *Moominsummer Madness* (also see below), Walck, 1961.

Trollvinter, Schildt, 1957, translation by Thomas Warburton published as *Moominland Midwinter* (also see below), Benn, 1958, Walck, 1962.

Vem ska troesta Knyttet?, Schildt, 1960, translation by Kingsley Hart published as *Who Will Comfort Toffle?,* Benn, 1961, Walck, 1969.

Det osynliga barnet och andra beraettelser, Schildt, 1962, translation by Warburton published as *Tales from Moominvalley* (also see below), Walck, 1964.

Pappan och havet, Schildt, 1965, translation by Hart published as *Moominpapa at Sea* (also see below), Walck, 1967.

Sent i November, Schildt, 1970, translation by Hart published as *Moominvalley in November* (also see below), Walck, 1971.

Den farliga resan, Schildt, 1977, translation by Hart published as *The Dangerous Journey,* Benn, 1978.

Moominstroll (multi-volume set containing *Comet in Moominland, Finn Family Moomintroll, Moominland Midwinter, Moominpappa at Sea, Moominsummer Madness, Moominvalley in November, Tales from Moominvalley*), Avon, 1978.

Skurken i muminhuset, Schildt, 1980.

ILLUSTRATOR

Lewis Carroll (pseudonym of Charles Lutwidge Dodgson), *Alice's Adventures in Wonderland,* Delacorte, 1977.

Also illustrator of Swedish editions of *Alice in Wonderland, The Hobbit,* and *The Hunting of the Snark.*

OTHER

Bildhuggarens dotter (autobiography), Schildt, 1968, translation by Hart published as *Sculptor's Daughter,* Benn, 1969, Avon, 1976.

Lyssnerskan (adult short stories; title means "The Listener"), Schildt, 1971.

Sommarboken (adult fiction), Schildt, 1972, translation by Thomas Teal published as *The Summer Book,* Pantheon, 1975.

Solstaden (adult fiction), Schildt, 1974, translation by Teal published as *Sun City,* Pantheon, 1976.

Dockskapet (adult short stories), Schildt, 1978.

Den a'rliga bedragaren (adult novel), Schildt, 1982.

Stenakern (adult novel), Schildt, 1984.

Resa med laett bagage (adult short stories), Schildt, 1987.

Rent spel (adult novel), Schildt, 1989.

Author of screenplays for Finnish television, including *Orm i salongen,* 1974; *Foenstret,* 1976; *Kvinnan som lanade minnen,* 1977; *Filitjonkan sem trodde pa katastrofer,* 1978, published as *The Fillyjonk Who Believed* in Disasters, 1989; *Sommar'on,* 1978; *Den a'rliga bedra-garen,* 1985; *Dockskapet,* 1986; *White Lady,* 1986. Author of radio plays, including *Lyssnerskan,* 1976; *Tio fo're fyra,* 1977; author of two plays for children.

All of Jansson's children's books, with the exception of *Smaatrollen och den stora oeversvaemningen,* have been translated from her native Swedish into German, Italian, Norwegian, Danish, Polish, Hebrew, Japanese, Spanish, Finnish, Icelandic, Dutch, French, Yugoslavian, Czech, Russian, Ukrainian, in the Faroe Islands, Persian, Portu-guese, Lithuanian, and English.

ADAPTATIONS: Adult and juvenile novels and short story collections that have been issued in talking-book for-mat for the handicapped include: *Sent i november, Solsta-den, Den farliga resan, Skurken i muminhuset, Den a'rliga bedragaren, Resa med ha'tt bagage, Farlig midsommar, Trollvinter, Rent spel, Sommarboken.*

SIDELIGHTS: "We lived in a large, dilapidated studio in Helsinki," says author Tove Jansson in Eva von Zweigberg-gk's *Barnboken i sverige 1750-1950,* recalling her early childhood in Finland, "and I pitied other children who had to live in ordinary flats, who had living-rooms without staircases, and sleeping compartments up close to the ceil-ing, nothing like the mysterious jumble of turn-tables, sacks with plaster and cases with clay, pieces of wood and iron constructions where one could hide and build in peace. A home without sculptures seemed as naked to me as one without books." The creative environment sparked by the activities of her artistic parents greatly influenced the young Tove, for as she recalls in *Illustrators of Chil-dren's Books: 1957-1966,* "To get peace for their work, they gave me a pencil to handle as soon as I was old enough to hold it." The encouragement she received as a child toward reading and drawing led her to create the in-habitants of Moominland, a collection of some of the most successful and beloved characters within the world of chil-dren's literature.

Reading was one of Jansson's favorite activities as a young girl, and books were always in abundance. When she was approximately nine years old, she rejected what she con-sidered to be girls' books in favor of books by Edgar Allan Poe, Rudyard Kipling, Robert Louis Stevenson, Selma Lagerloef, Joseph Conrad, and Jack London. "After I was thirteen, I became a bookworm," she writes in *Min vaeg till barnboken.* "I read everything I could get my hands on. My mother 'Ham,' in her work, made book covers. She obtained free samples of many to bring home and I read them all from cover to cover. When I was forced to go out-side for fresh air, I would continue reading behind a trash container in the yard. At night I would read by flashlight under the covers. I read a lot of Victor Hugo and Thomas Hardy." Although she received formal training in paint-

ing and book design, Jansson's abilities as a writer, espe-cially of children's literature, eventually came to fulfill-ment in 1939, when she wrote and illustrated her first book for young people. Since that time, Jansson has con-tinued to expand her world of imagination, supplementing it with several works for adults, as well as her autobio-graphical work, *Sculptor's Daughter.*

"Tove Jansson is one of the legend-makers. To impose on the world a new concept, a dimension developed in every detail, is one of the most precious achievements of any writer," writes Marcus Crouch in *Junior Bookshelf.* In the tradition of such authors as Lewis Carroll, Edith Nesbit, C. S. Lewis, and Mary Norton, Jansson has opened the doorway to a land where the unlikely is commonplace, and a child's imaginary vision is not hindered by the impo-sition of everyday reason and logic. Behind the Moomins, the leading characters that inhabit this mythical land, fall the long shadows of trolls and elves which dwell within the Scandinavian folklore of the author's own childhood. Jansson once recalled for *Cricket* moments from her youth which eventually formed part of the inspiration for the creation of Moominland. Her family had taken a sailing trip to an uninhabited island off the Finnish coast, when a thunderstorm suddenly sprang up, and they were forced to spend the night anchored off the island's rocky shore. "The gale was full of strange noises, shouts, whispers, and something scurrying over the sailcloth, and I was certain the island was full of trolls. So I asked how big and angry trolls were. 'They're small,' my mother said, 'small and nice. They like gales, just as we do.' "

Moominland is a place inhabited by characters of many different sorts: not only a family of Moomintrolls, but Snufkin, Hemulen, Toffle, the Muddler, Fillyjonk, Mym-ble, Grandpa-Grumble, and the villainous Groke—unique names for the curious assemblage of creatures who wander in and out of the Moomin stories. Jansson's books are not so much separate novels as they are handfuls of stories drawn from a continuous saga threading its way through the forest of an idyllic valley near the sea, and eventually coming to rest at a lighthouse keeping watch from a small seabound island. Like a thunderstorm suddenly appearing on the horizon, Jansson's stories are characterized by an overshadowing menace, oftentimes taking the form of some type of natural disaster. Whether it be a flood, a hur-ricane, volcanic eruptions, or a comet descending menac-ingly towards earth, such disasters carry with them the potential for sending her character's world into chaos without warning. But in the realm of Moominland, all misfortunes are more than balanced by the strengthening of the familial ties between these curious characters; the love of friends and neighbors, and the love of freedom. "The Moomin books depict the insecurity of contempo-rary man," writes Mary Orvig in *Horn Book;* "at the same time, they show a genuine way to live. The most important thing is to cut loose from acquisitiveness and to love one's neighbor without expecting anything in return." The author's underlying message throughout the Moomin books is that it is necessary for one to accept physical objects as merely transient possessions. Only with that understanding do her characters attain inner peace and stability. In *Moominland Midwinter,* the character Tootick reiterates this theme, saying "Everything is so uncertain and that is what I find so reassuring."

"Miss Jansson clothes the undoubted seriousness of her vision in rich wit and humor," reports a *Times Literary Supplement* contributor. The unique pen-and-ink illustrations drawn by the author further serve to illuminate her fantastic world, adding another degree of lushness to its landscape. In an interview with *Top of the News,* she provided insight into her role as illustrator of the Moomin books. "The world of children is a landscape in strong colors where safety and catastrophe run on parallel courses . . . there is room for anything . . . [and] the illustrations are simply an attempt at explaining what I have perhaps failed to express in words, a kind of footnote," Jansson explains. "Sometimes lines and planes can say more than words. And in the blessed blacks of China ink the child can see its own enchanted danger, tempered to the desired degree of terror."

Entering the world of Tove Jansson is not only finding one's own "enchanted danger," but experiencing for oneself the magic, mystery and happiness of the author's enchanted youth. "We lived in Finland . . . during the summer in the archipelago farthest out into the sea—as we do now. If something has influenced my books it may be these summer islands and, of course, the sea," she recalls in *Illustrators of Children's Books: 1957-1966.* The wild stretch of ocean beyond a rocky coastline, and the plaintive moan of the wind through a tangle of island trees; such scenes reminiscent of the northern Finnish landscape so close to Jansson's heart are ever-present in Moominland. The grounding of Moominland in the world of nature gives the Moomin books a universal appeal to young people. All of Jansson's children's books, with the exception of *Smaatrollen och den stora oeversvaemningen,* have been translated into many languages, reaching the imaginations of children around the world. But the Moomin books speak also to a universal humanity through their funny and wholesome little creatures. "The warm, kindly, generous world of Tove Jansson is a world like our own, yet strange," writes Crouch, "a world in which exciting things happen, perils are faced bravely, and at the end of every adventure there await Moominhouse and the calm constant loving kindness of Moominmamma. And always there is the promise of another day."

BIOGRAPHICAL/CRITICAL SOURCES:

BOOKS

Cameron, Eleanor, *The Green and Burning Tree,* Little, Brown, 1969.
Children's Literature Review, Volume 2, Gale, 1976.
Crouch, Marcus, *The Nesbit Tradition: The Children's Novel in England 1945-1970,* Benn, 1972, pp. 136-137.
Doyle, Brian, *The Who's Who of Children's Literature,* Schocken Books, 1968.
Fisher, Margery, *Who's Who in Children's Books: A Treasury of the Familiar Characters of Childhood,* Holt, 1975, pp. 234, 238.
Fisher, Margery, *Intent Upon Reading: A Critical Appraisal of Modern Fiction for Children,* Watts, 1962, pp. 160-162.
Hurlimann, Bettina, *Three Centuries of Children's Books in Europe,* translated and edited by Brian W. Alderson, Oxford University Press, 1967, p. 381.
Jansson, Tove, *Moominland Midwinter,* Walck, 1962.
Jansson, Tove, *Sculptor's Daughter,* Avon, 1976.
Kingman, Lee, and others, compilers, *Illustrators of Children's Books: 1957-1966,* Horn Book, 1968.
Kingman, Lee, and others, compilers, *Illustrators of Children's Books: 1967-1976,* Horn Book, 1978.
Orvig, Mary, *Children's Books in Sweden 1945-1970,* Austrian Children's Book Club (Vienna), 1973.
Stroemstedt, B., editor, *Min vaeg till barnboken,* Bonniers, 1964.
von Zweigbergk, Eva, *Barnboken i sverige 1750-1950,* Raben & Sjoegren, 1965.

PERIODICALS

Bookbird, Number 4, 1966.
Book World, June 2, 1968, p. 20.
Bulletin of the Center for Children's Books, June, 1952, p. 74; June, 1967, p. 154; September, 1967, pp. 9-10; May, 1970, p. 145; March, 1972, p. 108; July-August, 1975, p. 178.
Christian Science Monitor, May 2, 1968, p. B5.
Cricket, December, 1980.
Horn Book, June, 1967, pp. 341-342; February, 1972, pp. 48-49; February, 1973, pp. 17-23.
Junior Bookshelf, June, 1966, pp. 173-174; December, 1966, pp. 353-357.
New York Review of Books, December 9, 1965, p.38.
New York Times Book Review, May 14, 1961, p. 28; May 5, 1968, p. 43.
Saturday Review, May 11, 1968, pp. 38-39.
Times Literary Supplement, November 17, 1950; November 23, 1951; November 28, 1952; May 19, 1961; October 22, 1971.

Top of the News, April, 1967.*

—Sketch by Pamela L. Shelton

*   *   *

JENNISON, C. S.
    See STARBIRD, Kaye

*   *   *

JONES, LeRoi
    See BARAKA, Amiri

*   *   *

JUDD, Robert   1939-

PERSONAL: Born June 16, 1939, in OH; son of Clarence Howard (a newspaper editor) and Cora Harris Judd; married in 1964; wife's name Karen (divorced). *Education:* Williams College, B.A. (honors), 1961. *Politics:* "Skeptic."

CAREER: J. Walter Thompson Co., New York City, copywriter, 1961-78; free-lance writer, 1978-82; J. Walter Thompson Co., London, England, creative director and vice-president, 1982-87. Member of the board, Big Apple Circus, 1978-79.

MEMBER: Amnesty International, Hampstead Cricket Club, London Library.

WRITINGS:

(With Deborah Phillips) *How to Fall Out of Love,* Houghton, 1979.
(With D. Phillips) *Sexual Confidence,* Houghton, 1980.
Formula One, Morrow, 1990.
The Race, Morrow, 1991.
Monza, Morrow, 1992.
Phoenix, Viking, 1992.

SIDELIGHTS: Speaking of his novels about auto racing, Robert Judd told *CA:* "Beyond the sensation, motor racing is a brilliant metaphor. Call it the way we live our lives or would like to live or are forced to live our lives. The drivers go round and round, faster and faster, on the leading edge of technology, taking prodigious risks, paid millions a year, and the international demands of a sport that covers five continents. Add the conflicting forces of the largest corporations on earth and a devoted following of four billion fans, and you will find the novel fills a larger screen than film ever dreamed of."

BIOGRAPHICAL/CRITICAL SOURCES:

PERIODICALS

New York Times Book Review, April 15, 1990, p. 19.

K

KAJENCKI, Francis C(asimir) 1918-

PERSONAL: Surname is pronounced Ka-*yent*-ski; born November 15, 1918, in Erie, PA; son of Antoni A. (a laborer) and Antonina (a homemaker; maiden name, Stasewska) Kajencki; married Virginia T. Bierasinski (deceased); children: Francis C., Jr., Anthony A. II, Miriam Kajencki-Orton, AnnMarie. *Education:* U.S. Military Academy, B.S., 1943; University of Southern California, M.S., 1949; University of Wisconsin—Madison, M.S. (journalism), 1967; George Mason University, M.A., 1976. *Politics:* Independent. *Religion:* Roman Catholic.

ADDRESSES: Home—3308 Nairn St., El Paso, TX 79925.

CAREER: Writer. U.S. Army, career officer, 1943-73; served in the Pacific theater during World War II; instructor in guided missiles at Air Defense School, Ft. Bliss, TX, 1949-53; commanded U.S. Nuclear Warhead Support Group, Turkey, 1961-62; on general staff, Department of Army, 1963-66; chief of public information division, Allied Land Forces Southeast Europe, Izmir, Turkey, 1967-69; assistant chief of information, department of Army, 1972-73, retired as colonel, 1973. Member of advisory board of trustees of El Paso Community Foundation.

MEMBER: National Press Club, Polish National Alliance, Polish American Congress of Texas (president 1984-88), U.S. Military Association of Graduates.

AWARDS, HONORS: Two Meritorious Service Medals and Legion of Merit for military service.

WRITINGS:

Star on Many a Battlefield: Brevet Brigadier General Joseph Karge in the American Civil War, Fairleigh Dickinson University Press, 1980.

"Uncle Billy's" War: General William T. Sherman's Changing Concept of Military-Civilian Relations During the Civil War—From Staunch Civilian Protector to "Cruel Plunderer," University Microfilms International, 1989.

Poles in the 19th Century Southwest, Southwest Polonia Press, 1990.

Contributor of articles and reviews to journals, including *Louisiana History, Arizona and the West, Polish American Studies,* and *New Mexico Historical Review,* and newspapers.

WORK IN PROGRESS: Writing "Kajencki Family History."

SIDELIGHTS: Francis C. Kajencki told *CA:* "I enjoyed my military career of thirty-six years. Nevertheless, I had found it somewhat technical and restrictive, and felt an urge to be more expansive and creative. Writing seemed to be the vehicle for releasing my suppressed energy.

"I turned to the field in which I had some knowledge and experience—military history. While a student at the U.S. Army Command and General Staff College, Ft. Leavenworth, Kansas (1957-58), I found an unusual amount of data on Polish-born Brevet Brigadier General Joseph Karge, a cavalry commander in the Civil War. As an American of Polish descent, I took a keen interest in Karge and wondered why no historian had rescued him from obscurity. I wanted to tell about Karge's contribution to the Northern victory—among other things, General Karge was the first Union commander to beat Confederate General ('That Devil') Nathan Bedford Forrest—and the result was *Star on Many a Battlefield: Brevet Brigadier General Joseph Karge in the American Civil War.*

"After relocating to El Paso, Texas, in 1975, following my active military service, I 'discovered' a number of Poles who made significant contributions to the history of New Mexico Territory. Among them, two were prominent and successful merchants. A third ran a hostelry on the famous Santa Fe Trail, and his ranch, during the Civil War, served as the field headquarters for the Union forces. And yet another Pole was a high-ranking member of the joint U.S.-Mexican Boundary Commission that set the new boundary between the two countries following the war with Mexico, 1846-48. My purpose was to document their contributions and to establish their place in New Mexico history. I accomplished my purpose with the publication of *Poles in the 19th Century Southwest.*"

*   *   *

KAUFELT, David Allan 1939-

PERSONAL: Born September 8, 1939, in Elizabeth, NJ; son of Julius Louis (founder of supermarket chain) and Irene (Meyer) Kaufelt; married Lynn Higashi (a real estate agent), 1974; children: Jackson. *Education:* University of Pennsylvania, B.S.E., 1961; New York University, M.A., 1962.

ADDRESSES: Home—P.O. Box 153, Sugarloaf Shores, FL 33044. *Agent*—Dick Duane, Pinder Lane Productions, 159 West 53rd St., New York, NY 10019.

CAREER: Advertising copywriter, 1965-75; Henry Street Settlement, New York City, director of the public interest, 1975-77; Upsala College, East Orange, NJ, instructor in creative writing, 1975-77. Executive board member, Florida Humanities Council, 1986-90; member of steering committee, Council for Florida Libraries; member, Mayor's Blue Ribbon Task Force on the Arts; cofounder and president, Key West Literary Festival; former president, Founders Society of the Tennessee Williams Fine Arts Center. *Military service:* U.S. Army, public information specialist, 1963-65.

WRITINGS:

Six Months with an Older Woman, Putnam, 1973.
The Bradley Beach Rumba, Putnam, 1974.
Spare Parts, Warner Books, 1978.
Late Bloomer, Harcourt, 1979.
Midnight Movies, Delacorte, 1980.
The Wine and the Music, Delacorte, 1981.
Silver Rose, Delacorte, 1982.
Souvenir, New American Library, 1983.
American Tropic, Poseidon, 1986.
The Fat Boy Murders, Pocket Books, 1992.

ADAPTATIONS: Six Months with an Older Woman was filmed for television by the Columbia Broadcasting System.

WORK IN PROGRESS: The Radium Girl Murders, for Pocket Books.

*   *   *

KAVANAUGH, James J(oseph) 1934-
(Father Stephen Nash)

PERSONAL: Born September 17, 1934, in Kalamazoo, MI; son of Frank P. (a salesman) and Hazel Ann (Wendell) Kavanaugh. *Education:* Xavier University, Cincinnati, OH, B.A., 1954; Catholic University of America, M.A., 1963, Ph.D., 1966; U.S. International University, Ph.D., 1973. *Avocational interests:* Tennis, golf, and the theater.

ADDRESSES: c/o Steven J. Nash Publishing, P.O. Box 2115, Highland Park, IL 60035.

CAREER: Ordained Roman Catholic priest, 1956, resigned priesthood, 1967; licensed clinical psychologist in state of California, 1971. Flint Intercollegiate Newman Club, Flint, MI, chaplain, 1958-64; Catholic University of America, Washington, DC, nursing school instructor, 1961-63, instructor in theology, 1964; Trinity College, Washington, DC, instructor in theology, 1964-66; Human Resources Institute, La Jolla, CA, marriage counselor and educational director, 1966-72; U.S. International University, San Diego, CA, professor of graduate psychology, 1970-72; Los Gatos, CA, private practice in clinical psychology, 1974-76. University of Toronto, visiting professor of religious studies; seminar instructor, 1970—. Gives poetry readings and lectures; conducts workshops; guest on television and radio programs; stage and television actor.

WRITINGS:

POETRY

There Are Men Too Gentle to Live among Wolves (also see below), Dutton, 1971, 2nd edition, Steven J. Nash, 1990.
Will You Be My Friend? (also see below), Steven J. Nash, 1971, 2nd edition, 1990.
Faces in the City, Steven J. Nash, 1972.
Today I Wondered about Love, Nash Publishing (Los Angeles), 1972, revised edition, Steven J. Nash, 1990.
The Poetry of James Kavanaugh, Steven J. Nash, 1974.
Sunshine Days and Foggy Nights, Dutton, 1975, 2nd edition, Steven J. Nash, 1990.
America, Dutton, 1976.
Winter Has Lasted Too Long, Dutton, 1977, 2nd edition, Steven J. Nash, 1990.
Walk Easy on the Earth, Dutton, 1979, 2nd edition, Steven J. Nash, 1990.

Maybe If I Loved You More, Dutton, 1982, 2nd edition, Steven J. Nash, 1990.

Mystic Fire: The Love Poems of James Kavanaugh (also see below), Steven J. Nash, 1991.

Quiet Water: The Inspirational Poems of James Kavanaugh (also see below), Steven J. Nash, 1991.

Tears and Laughter of a Man's Soul (also see below), Steven J. Nash, 1991.

RECORDINGS

There Are Men Too Gentle (cassette recording; contains selections from the book, *There Are Men Too Gentle to Live among Wolves*), original score by Elmer Bernstein, Karo, 1972.

Of Love, Life and Laughter (cassette recording; includes selections from *Mystic Fire, Quiet Water, Tears and Laughter of a Man's Soul,* and *Will You Be My Friend?*), Steven J. Nash, 1991.

Search: A Guide for Those Who Dare (cassette recording; also see below; readings based on the book, *Search: A Guide for Those Who Dare to Ask of Life Everything Good and Beautiful*), Steven J. Nash, 1991.

Also performer in audio and video cassettes of lectures, poetry, and inspirational messages.

OTHER

There's Two of You, Newman, 1964.

Man in Search of God, Paulist Press, 1967.

A Modern Priest Looks at His Outdated Church, Trident, 1967.

The Struggle of the Unbeliever, Trident, 1968.

The Birth of God, Trident, 1969.

The Crooked Angel (for children), Steven J. Nash, 1970, 2nd edition, 1990.

(With Everett L. Shostrom) *Between Man and Woman,* Steven J. Nash, 1971.

Celebrate the Sun: A Love Story, Steven J. Nash, 1973, 2nd edition, 1990.

(With Darrell Fetty) *Street Music* (musical review), first performed in Los Angeles at Theatre 40, 1974.

A Coward for Them All (novel; also see below), Bantam, 1979.

A Village Called Harmony: A Fable, Dutton, 1980, 2nd edition, Steven J. Nash, 1990.

Laughing Down Lonely Canyons, Harper, 1984, 2nd edition, Steven J. Nash, 1990.

The Celibates (novel), Harper, 1985.

Search: A Guide for Those Who Dare to Ask of Life Everything Good and Beautiful, Harper, 1985, 2nd edition, Steven J. Nash, 1990.

From Loneliness to Love, Harper, 1986, 2nd edition, Steven J. Nash, 1990.

Also author of screenplays "A Coward for Them All," based on his novel of the same title, 1980, and "The Metamorphosis of Mort Meekin"; author of lyrics for Burt Bacharach album *Futures,* 1979. Contributor to psychology journals and popular magazines, including *Look, Playboy, Psychology Today,* and *Ladies' Home Journal;* contributor to *Saturday Evening Post,* under the pseudonym Father Stephen Nash, 1966.

SIDELIGHTS: James J. Kavanaugh's *A Modern Priest Looks at His Outdated Church,* which began as an article published in the *Saturday Evening Post* under the pseudonym Father Stephen Nash, became a controversial 1967 bestseller. A critique of Catholicism as it existed during the 1960s, the book "argues that [Catholic] ideals have been frozen into law, abstractions have been given primacy over persons, arbitrary traditions (such as compulsory clerical celibacy) have trampled the uniqueness of the individual, and produced misery and guilt on a systematic basis," said John Leo in the *New York Times Book Review.*

A *Time* reviewer predicted that "many Catholics who hope and pray for renewal may have cause to suspect that Kavanaugh's angry and oversimplified criticism can only hurt rather than help the forces of change within the church." *Christian Century*'s C. M. Smith defended Kavanaugh, however, saying, "Fr. Kavanaugh does not write with sweet reasonableness, but then neither did Luther. And, like Luther, he insists he is interested not in destroying the church but in saving it." Kavanaugh left the priesthood shortly after completing the book.

After *A Modern Priest Looks at His Outdated Church,* Kavanaugh continued to write, producing poetry, novels, and inspirational works including *Search: A Guide for Those Who Dare to Ask of Life Everything Good and Beautiful.* While many of his books could be described as "self-help" literature, Kavanaugh's views on that genre are strong. In an article in the newsletter of the James Kavanaugh Institute, Kavanaugh said that "I burn all self-help books or tapes in which hyped heroes tell me how easy it is to put one's life together. . . . I heed those who are still wading through pain, who must struggle at times just to hang on. I don't believe in quick fixes and I'm outraged when anyone promises one."

BIOGRAPHICAL/CRITICAL SOURCES:

BOOKS

Kavanaugh, James J., *A Modern Priest Looks at His Outdated Church,* Trident, 1967.

Kavanaugh, *Search: A Guide For Those Who Dare to Ask of Life Everything Good and Beautiful,* Harper, 1985.

PERIODICALS

Best Sellers, July 1, 1967.

Christian Century, August 2, 1967.
Christian Science Monitor, July 6, 1967.
Commonweal, July 28, 1967.
Los Angeles Times, November 7, 1980.
New York Times Book Review, July 30, 1967.
Saturday Review, July 29, 1967.
Time, July 7, 1967.
Walk Easy on the Earth: The Voice of the James Kavanaugh Institute, fall, 1991.
Washington Post, May 14, 1967.

*   *   *

KELLER, Beverly
(B. L. Harwick)

PERSONAL: Born in San Francisco, CA; daughter of Wearne E. and Ruth (Burke) Harwick; married William Jon Keller, June 18, 1949 (died, 1964); children: Lisa, Kristen, Michele. *Education:* University of California, Berkeley, B.A., 1950. *Avocational interests:* Politics and animals' rights.

ADDRESSES: Home—Davis, CA.

CAREER: Author, newspaper columnist, and feature writer.

AWARDS, HONORS: Harcourt, Brace & World fellow, University of Colorado, 1969; "Best Book" citation, *School Library Journal,* for *Fiona's Bee* and *No Beasts! No Children!;* "Notable Book" citation, American Library Association, 1981, for *The Sea Watch;* "Pick of the Lists" citation, *American Bookseller,* for *A Small, Elderly Dragon;* "Best Books of Spring" citation, *School Library Journal,* and voted one of "The Year's Ten Best," *Philadelphia Enquirer,* both for *No Beasts! No Children!;* nomination for California Young Reader's Medal, Sunshine State Young Reader's Award, and South Carolina Young Reader's Award, all 1990, for *Desdemona, Twelve Going on Desperate.*

WRITINGS:

ADULT FICTION

The Baghdad Defections (suspense novel), Bobbs-Merrill, 1973.

JUVENILE FICTION

Fiona's Bee (Junior Literary Guild selection), Coward, 1975.
The Beetle Bush (Junior Literary Guild selection), Coward, 1976.
Don't Throw Another One, Dover!, Coward, 1976.
(Under name B. L. Harwick) *The Frog Prints,* Raintree Editions, 1976.

The Genuine, Ingenious Thrift Shop Genie, Clarissa Mae Bean and Me, Coward, 1977.
Pimm's Place (Junior Literary Guild selection), Coward, 1978.
The Sea Watch, Four Winds Press, 1980.
Fiona's Flea (Junior Literary Guild selection), Coward, 1981.
The Bee Sneeze (Junior Literary Guild selection), Coward, 1982.
My Awful Cousin Norbert, Lothrop, 1982.
No Beasts! No Children!, Lothrop, 1983.
A Small, Elderly Dragon, Lothrop, 1984.
When Mother Got the Flu (Junior Literary Guild selection), Coward, 1984.
A Garden of Love to Share, Parker Brothers, 1984.
Rosebud, with Fangs, Lothrop, 1985.
Desdemona, Twelve Going on Desperate, Lothrop, 1986.
Fowl Play, Desdemona, Lothrop, 1989.
Only Fiona, Harper/Collins, 1988.
No Mummies in the Pool, Desdemona, Bradbury, 1992.
Phoebe at Dead Weeds, Scholastic Inc., in press.
Phoebe and the Guest Rat, Scholastic Inc., in press.

OTHER

Hide and Seek (textbook), Scott, Foresman, 1985.
Consumer Skills, Quercus, 1986.
A Car Means Out, Quercus, 1987.
Cliffhanger, Quercus, 1987.
Beam Me Up, He Said, Quercus, 1987.

Also contributor to textbooks. Contributor to anthologies, including *The Best from Fantasy and Science Fiction,* edited by Edward Ferman, Doubleday, 1974; and *The Random House Book of Humor for Children,* Random House, 1988. Contributor to periodicals, including *Atlantic, Fantasy and Science Fiction, Cosmopolitan,* and *American Voice. Fiona's Bee* has been produced as an audio recording by Listening Library in 1976, renewal, 1991.

Some of Keller's books have been published in Japanese and Spanish.

ADAPTATIONS: A Small, Elderly Dragon was optioned for film by Walt Disney Pictures, 1990.

WORK IN PROGRESS: Two novels.

SIDELIGHTS: Beverly Keller told *CA:* "As a child, I didn't live anywhere, but travelled with my parents. Wherever we stayed, my father let it slip that he was really Lawrence Tibbett, the great Metropolitan Opera star, secretly married to my mother, who was really Gertrude Ederle, the first woman to swim the English Channel. My mother weighed ninety pounds and was terrified of any body of water larger than a bathtub.

"I knew what it was to be treated like a star. We had flowers and fruit baskets and prime tables. Now and then the band leader in a hotel dining room would beg my father to honor the guests with an aria. Now and then my father obliged.

"So we changed hotels often. By the time I finished high school, I'd attended thirteen schools, and in the process missed English grammar entirely. One compensates.

"In my junior year at the University of California at Berkeley I married Bill Keller. He joined the foreign service, and we lived for the next years in Baghdad and Beirut. I got caught in a camel migration in Iraq and arrived in Lebanon in time for the Suez Crisis. At its height, we drove through the Middle East and Europe, losing a wheel in Turkey, sleeping in abandoned villas on the Aegean, arriving in Rome at the outbreak of the Hungarian Revolution.

"We rented a penthouse which had belonged to Count Ciano, Mussolini's son-in-law. It wound around the building—vast terraces, marble floors, an enormous den full of assegais, spears, shields, guns . . . and there were rooms I never cared to enter.

"Afterward, we travelled third class by rail through Europe with our two small children, which explains why I have looked my age for many years.

"The Booth cartoon *Write about Dogs* gives some inkling of my working conditions. I live with five dogs, most of them large to enormous, and a wolf cross who has no idea he is supposed to be difficult."

BIOGRAPHICAL/CRITICAL SOURCES:

PERIODICALS

Chicago Tribune Book World, June 9, 1985.
Washington Post Book World, May 13, 1984.

           *   *   *

KERSEY, Katharine C(lark) 1935-

PERSONAL: Born February 8, 1935, in Winchester, VA; daughter of Edward Thomas (a Baptist minister) and Katherine Fahr (Essex) Clark; married L. Wilbur Kersey (a Baptist minister); children: Barbara Leigh, David, Marc. *Education:* University of Richmond, B.S., 1956; Old Dominion University, M.S., 1969; University of Virginia, Ed.D., 1973.

ADDRESSES: Home—3805 Shoreline Dr., Portsmouth, VA 23703. *Office*—Department of Education, Old Dominion University, 5215 Hampton Blvd., Norfolk, VA 23508.

CAREER: Director of private school in Portsmouth, VA, 1965-71; Old Dominion University, Norfolk, VA, instructor, 1969-73, assistant professor, 1973-77, associate professor, 1977-83, professor of education and director of graduate program for early childhood education, 1983—, chairperson of department of child study, 1985—, director of university nursery school and kindergarten, 1970-72, 1980—. Teacher at public school in Portsmouth, 1966-69; Hampton Institute, instructor, summer, 1969. Member of Tidewater Advisory Board for the Prevention of Child Abuse and Portsmouth Service League. Guest on television programs.

MEMBER: National Association for the Education of Young Children, Southern Association for Children under Six, Virginia Association for the Education of Young Children. Tidewater Association for Early Childhood Education, Delta Kappa Gamma.

WRITINGS:

Sensitive Parenting: From Infancy to Adulthood, Acropolis Books, 1983.
Heading Off Problems: A Primer for Parents, Acropolis Books, 1985.
Helping Your Child Handle Stress, Acropolis Books, 1985.
Don't Take It Out on Your Kids, Acropolis Books, 1988.

Author of weekly column "Raising Children (and Parents, Too)," *Virginia Pilot/Ledger Star* and *Roanoke Times and World News,* 1978—. Contributor to *Ladycom.*

SIDELIGHTS: Katharine C. Kersey told *CA:* "I began writing a newspaper column, 'Raising Children (and Parents, Too),' in June, 1978. As soon as the column began, I received more and more questions from readers, and I realized there was a crying need for someone to be available to whom they could turn.

"Parents are confused trying to raise children in today's world. The methods that their own parents found successful no longer work. Their questions deal with the problems in today's society: divorce, working mothers, drugs, latchkeyism, step-arrangements, daycare, illness, hospitalization, death, alcoholism, and child abuse.

"My writings deal with positive alternatives which parents can use to bring about positive outcomes. I challenge parents to remember the goal of parents: to work ourselves out of a job; to raise independent, competent, and confident children."

KESEY, Ken (Elton) 1935-
(O. U. Levon, a joint pseudonym)

PERSONAL: Born September 17, 1935, in La Junta, CO; son of Fred A. and Geneva (Smith) Kesey; married Faye Haxby, May 20, 1956; children: Shannon, Zane, Jed (deceased), Sunshine. *Education:* University of Oregon, B.A., 1957; Stanford University, graduate study, 1958-61, 1963.

ADDRESSES: Home—85829 Ridgeway Rd., Pleasant Hill, OR 97401. *Agent*—Sterling Lord Literistic, Inc., 660 Madison Ave., New York, NY 10021.

CAREER: Multi-media artist and farmer. Night attendant in psychiatric Veterans Administration Hospital, Menlo Park, CA, 1961; president, Intrepid Trips, Inc. (motion picture company), 1964.

AWARDS, HONORS: Woodrow Wilson fellowship; Saxton Fund fellowship, 1959; Distinguished Service award, State of Oregon, 1978.

WRITINGS:

One Flew Over the Cuckoo's Nest (novel), Viking, 1962, new edition with criticism, edited by John C. Pratt, 1973.
Sometimes a Great Notion (novel), Viking, 1964.
(Contributor) *The Last Whole Earth Catalog: Access to Tools,* Portola Institute, 1971.
(Editor with Paul Krassner and contributor) *The Last Supplement to the Whole Earth Catalog,* Portola Institute, 1971.
(Compiler and contributor) *Kesey's Garage Sale* (interviews and articles, including "Tools from My Chest," "An Impolite Interview with Ken Kesey," and the screenplay "Over the Border"), introduction by Arthur Miller, Viking, 1973.
(Author of introduction) Paul Krassner, editor, *Best of "The Realist": The Sixties' Most Outrageously Irreverent Magazine,* Running Press, 1984.
Demon Box (essays, poetry, and stories, including "The Day Superman Died," "Good Friday," "Finding Doctor Fung," "Run into the Great Wall," and "The Search for the Secret Pyramid"), Viking, 1986.
Little Trickler the Squirrel Meets Big Double the Bear (juvenile), Penguin, 1988.
(Under joint pseudonym O. U. Levon [an anagram for "University of Oregon novel"] with Robert Bluckner, Ben Bochner, James Finley, Jeff Forester, Bennett Huffman, Lynn Jeffress, Neil Lindstrom, H. Highwater Powers, Jane Sather, Charles Varani, Meredith Wadley, Lidia Yukman, and Ken Zimmerman, and author of introduction) *Caverns* (mystery novel), Penguin, 1989.
The Further Inquiry (autobiographical screenplay), Viking, 1990.

Also author of two unpublished novels, "End of Autumn" and "Zoo," and "Seven Prayers by Grandma Whittier," an unfinished novel serialized between 1974 and 1981 in *Spit in the Ocean,* a magazine Kesey published sporadically during the 1970s and 1980s. Work included in anthologies, including *Stanford Short Stories 1962,* edited by Wallace Stegner and Richard Scowcroft, Stanford University Press, 1962. A collection of Kesey's manuscripts is housed at the University of Oregon.

WORK IN PROGRESS: Sailor Song, a novel set in Alaska, for Viking, excerpts of which have been published in *Life* and *Esquire.*

ADAPTATIONS: One Flew Over the Cuckoo's Nest was adapted for the stage by Dale Wasserman and produced on Broadway at the Cort Theatre on November 13, 1963, revived in 1971, and adapted for film by United Artists in 1975; *Sometimes a Great Notion* was adapted for film by Universal in 1972.

SIDELIGHTS: Ken Kesey, a writer and cultural hero of the psychic frontier, is best known as the author of the widely-read play *One Flew Over the Cuckoo's Nest* and the insightful contemporary novel *Sometimes a Great Notion.* His works are set in California and Oregon, two locations representing two facets of Kesey's experience that provide the major tensions in his works. Oregon represents traditional rural family values and self-reliance inherited from Baptist pioneer stock; California is associated with the countercultural revolution in which Kesey played an important role. Therefore Kesey's name is often associated with the American West Coast and the hippie movement that centered itself there during the 1960s. Though he has since taken a more critical stance in regard to the alternative lifestyle he once championed, Kesey's later works remain haunted by fond references to the uninhibited life he enjoyed as a member of The Merry Pranksters, a group who traveled America in a bus when experimental drug use was at its peak. His novels, plays, screenplays and essays express the author's intrepid quest for heightened consciousness in which he has explored magic, hypnotism, mind-altering or psychoactive drugs, the occult, Eastern religions, and esoteric philosophies. His works also carry forward the American literary traditions of the Transcendentalists and the Beats as well as the frontier humor and vernacular style established by Mark Twain.

Kesey was born and raised "a hard-shell Baptist" in Colorado and Oregon, he tells Linda Gaboriau in a *Crawdaddy* interview. He accompanied his father on many hunting and fishing trips in the Pacific Northwest and developed a deep respect for nature. His love of the outdoors was matched by his fascination with extraordinary experience. After receiving a book of magic in the mail with a set of mail-order Batman decals, he studied theatrical magic and learned to perform illusions. "I . . . did shows all through high school and in college," he tells Gaboriau. "I went from this into ventriloquism (and even had a show on TV), and from ventriloquism into hypnotism. And from hypnotism into dope. But it's always been the same trip, the same kind of search," he says, referring to his quest for heightened consciousness.

Kesey auditioned for film roles in Hollywood before entering college at the University of Oregon in Eugene, where he majored in speech and communications, gaining experience in acting and writing for radio and television. An active athlete during both high school and college, he won a scholarship as the outstanding college wrestler in the Northwest. Each of Kesey's interests figure largely in his works. Hunting and fishing are strategically important events in the two major works that established his literary reputation. His characters are physically strong and ready to compete against overwhelming pressure to conform to standards or submit to authorities that oppose their well-being. His style incorporates techniques borrowed from theatre and film such as flashbacks, fade-outs, and jump cuts, and it shows familiarity with the conventions of horror films and popular Westerns.

Kesey married his high school sweetheart, Faye Haxby, while at the University of Oregon, and moved to California where he enrolled in Stanford's creative writing program. There he met Wallace Stegner, Richard Scowcroft, Malcolm Cowley, and Frank O'Connor—writers who were also literary critics—and fellow students Wendell Berry, Larry McMurtry and Robert Stone. He also encountered the cultural radicalism that was developing in Perry Lane, a section of Stanford patterned after the haven of the Beat movement in San Francisco's North Beach. According to *Free You* contributor Vie Lovell, to whom Kesey dedicated *One Flew Over the Cuckoo's Nest*, the Perry Lane group "pioneered what have since become the hall-marks of hippie culture: LSD and other psychedelics too numerous to mention, body painting, light shows and mixed media presentations, total aestheticism, be-ins, exotic costumes, strobe lights, sexual mayhem, freakouts and the deification of psychoticism, eastern mysticism, and the rebirth of hair." Like many others, Kesey said in a speech on tape from the Kesey archives at the University of Oregon that events at Perry Lane and similar places were a watershed, at the same time both the culmination of civilization to that point, and the fulmination of volatile social forces that would have some impact on all the years to come.

When Lovell suggested Kesey take part in the drug experiments being conducted at the Veterans Administration Hospital at Menlo Park, he accepted. There he was paid to ingest various psychoactive drugs and to report their effects. This experience, together with his experiences as an aide at the VA Hospital, led him to write *One Flew Over the Cuckoo's Nest*. Before finishing this play, now considered a classic representation of American values in conflict, he also produced an unpublished novel about his North Beach experience titled "Zoo," written at Stanford, and eighty pages of story outline for a novel about Perry Lane.

One Flew Over the Cuckoo's Nest is a celebration of the resilience of the human spirit as seen in the characteristically American resistance to corrupt authority. The novel tells how Randle Patrick McMurphy, a cocky, fast-talking inmate of a prison farm who has had himself committed to a mental hospital to avoid work, creates upheaval in the ward that is so efficiently and repressively directed by Nurse Ratched. His self-confidence and irrepressible sense of humor inspire the passive, dehumanized patients to rebel against Big Nurse and the "Combine" of society she represents. McMurphy ultimately sacrifices himself in the process of teaching his fellow patients the saving lessons of laughter and self-reliance.

Contemporary audiences have received the work with notable enthusiasm for several decades. In the early 1960s, the novel supplied a critique of an American society that had been portrayed in the 1950s as a lonely crowd of organization men who could achieve affluence only through strict conformity. That critique continued to suit the mood of the 1970s and 1980s because larger themes were involved: the modern world as technologized and consequently divorced from nature; contemporary society as repressive; authority as mechanical and destructive; contemporary man as weak, frightened, and sexless, a victim of rational but loveless forces beyond his control. The novel's message that people need to get back in touch with their world, to open doors of perception, to enjoy spontaneous sensuous experience, and to resist the manipulative forces of a technological society was particularly appealing to the young, but not just to them. An admiration for self-reliant action as its own source of authority runs deep in the American psyche.

One Flew Over the Cuckoo's Nest was a resounding critical success. It became quite popular among young people, and by the 1970s, when it became the contemporary novel most frequently used in college courses, more than a million copies had been sold. American audiences have appreciated the work in each of its incarnations as play, novel, and film. The play version by Dale Wasserman appeared on Broadway with Kirk Douglas starring as McMurphy in 1963 and was revived in 1971; campus productions continue to draw attentive audiences. The film version, directed by Milos Forman and starring Jack Nicholson, was a box office hit and won six Academy Awards in 1975.

The novel is widely appreciated for the range of subjects, issues, and disciplines it includes. A 1977 double-issue of *Lex et Scientia,* the official journal of the International Academy of Law and Science, contains essays on *One Flew Over the Cuckoo's Nest* described by editor Ralph Porzio as "a cornucopia of source material from disciplines so numerous and varied as to challenge the mind and imagination." He observes that it treats the areas of psychology, psychiatry, medicine, literature, human relations, drama, art, cosmology, law, religion, American culture, and folk culture through a kaleidoscopic blend of tragedy, pathos, and humor. This rich variety explains why *One Flew Over the Cuckoo's Nest* is used as a text for college courses in many disciplines.

The multitude of interests the book has attracted is of course paralleled by the large number of responses it has evoked. A partial list of topics that show up in treatments of *One Flew Over the Cuckoo's Nest* includes the following diverse items: the patterns of romance, the patterns of comedy, the patterns of tragedy, black humor, the absurd, the hero in modern dress, the comic Christ, the folk and western heroes, the fool as mentor, the Grail Knight, attitudes toward sex, abdication of masculinity, the politics of laughter, mechanistic and totemistic symbolization, the comic strip, the ritualistic father-figure, and the psychopathic savior.

Ronald Wallace, writing in *The Last Laugh: Form and Affirmation in the Contemporary American Comic Novel,* connects the novel directly to Kesey's early interest in comic books by pointing out that its main characters are drawn from ancient conventions of comedy. Wallace perceives in Nurse Ratched and McMurphy respectively the *aiazon*—the boastful, deluded fool—and the *eiron*—the witty self-deprecator who defeats his opponent by hiding his skill and intelligence. Furthermore, Wallace sees McMurphy as a "Dionysian Lord of Misrule" who "presides over a comic fertility ritual and restores instinctual life to the patients." In a *Critique* review, Terry G. Sherwood notices the balance between comic strip conventions and those belonging to the serious novel, since its major confrontation is between the forces of good and evil. *Journal of Narrative Technique* reviewer Michael Boardman points out the novel's power as a classic tragedy because it portrays a character opposed by forces from within himself as well as from others. The conflict between Big Nurse and McMurphy becomes a struggle between McMurphy's need for freedom as an individual and his need to survive in a hostile environment by conforming to oppressive standards. The conventions of the Western novel with its characters, colloquialisms, and frontier values are also present in *One Flew Over the Cuckoo's Nest,* observes Richard Blessing in the *Journal of Popular Culture.* Blessing writes, "Essentially, the McMurphy who enters the ward

is a frontier hero, an anachronistic paragon of rugged individualism, relentless energy, capitalistic shrewdness, virile coarseness and productive strength. He is Huck Finn with muscles, Natty Bumppo with pubic hair. He is the descendant of the pioneer who continually fled civilization and its feminizing and gentling influence."

The brand of individualism and freedom presented in McMurphy's behavior approaches anarchy too closely for some critics. The mayhem he raises by throwing plates and butter at walls, shouting obscenities, breaking windows, sneaking prostitutes into the ward, and stealing boats, claims Bruce E. Wallis in *Cithara,* is not a foundation for lasting sanity and self-esteem beyond reproach. The best opposition to society's more repressive forces, he feels, may not, after all, be man's sexual and nonrational capacities.

Other critics are alarmed by the novel's portrayal of women. Leslie Horst says in *Lex et Scientia* that Kesey's depiction of Nurse Ratched is demeaning; more importantly, she continues, "considerable hatred of women is justified in the logic of the novel. The plot demands that the dreadful women who break the rules men have made for them become the targets of the reader's wrath." Viewing the novel primarily from the aspect of gender, Robert Forrey's negative assessment of the novel in *Modern Fiction Studies* claims that "the premise of the novel is that women ensnare, emasculate, and, in some cases, crucify men." On the other hand, Wallace contends that there is no misogyny intended in Kesey's reversal of traditionally-assigned gender-appropriate roles, which he relates to all comic literature "from Aristophanes to Erica Jong." Boardman suggests that the Big Nurse is not meant to represent womankind, but to be the incarnation of evil required by the novel's dramatic action. In *The Art of Grit: Ken Kesey's Fiction,* M. Gilbert Porter reports Kesey's comment that any good story needs a villain that is truly recognizably evil if the writer is to fulfill his ethical purpose, that of standing "between the public and evil. . . . The good writer in [Kesey's] opinion is a person of 'power' and character who guards faithfully that axis of human choice." Ronald Billingsley, in an unpublished dissertation, also maintains that Kesey's book does not define women as generally evil: "Big Nurse and her emasculating ilk are no more truly feminine than the Acutes and Dr. Spivey are truly masculine. Like machines, these women are neuter, asexual devices that respond to *power.*"

Kesey's next book, *Sometimes a Great Notion,* reflects Kesey's Oregon background and the concerns of the upper Northwest region. The title refers to the folk song refrain "Sometimes it seems a great notion / to jump in the river and drown," and signals one of the book's themes, the relatively high suicide rate in the Wakonda logging town and others like it. Independent loggers Hank and Leland

Stamper are at odds with their union-dominated community and with each other. After Hank involves his Ivy-league educated half-brother's mother in a sexual relationship, Leland seeks revenge by seducing Hank's wife. The novel approaches these events from a variety of points of view to reveal what the brothers learn from each other.

Like William Faulkner, a writer Kesey greatly admires, Kesey comments on the subjectivity of perception by using the cinematic device of multiple perspectives. To make the medium of fiction more fit for his purpose, he liberates himself from the chronological order used in most conventional novels. He also employs conscious authorial intrusion. Innovative use of italics, capital letters, and parentheses help him replicate in print the confusion, moral bankruptcy, and future shock that his characters face.

In many ways, the conflict between the Stamper brothers corresponds to Kesey's own inner conflicts. During his college years, the conflict between his down-home athletic nature and his more artistic and intellectual side became more obvious. He could socialize with both intellectuals and more active groups, but they did not usually find each other mutually acceptable. The brothers in *Sometimes a Great Notion* embody these conflicting impulses. Gordon Lish asks in a *Genesis West* interview: "Where are you going in *Great Notion*? What is it you're testing?" Kesey answers: "For one thing, I want to find out which side of me really is: the woodsy, logger side—complete with homespun homilies and crackerbarrel corniness, a valid side of me that I like—or its opposition. The two Stamper brothers in the novel are each one of the ways I think I am."

In 1963 when Kesey was finishing *Sometimes a Great Notion,* a developer forced the evacuation of Perry Lane, and the Keseys bought a house in La Honda where he continued as a leader of the psychedelic movement. For the next few years, he set aside the writing life as too far removed from first-hand experience, and sought an alternative with Neal Cassady and other kindred spirits in a group called The Merry Pranksters. After his curiosity about altered states of consciousness was stimulated by the experiments at the VA Hospital, Kesey continued his experimental drug use together with the group at La Honda. They devised games and a variety of audio-visual aids to enhance their sensory perceptions while under the influence of drugs. Evolving from private parties to public parties to large-scale public events, these "acid-tests" introduced light shows, psychedelic art, mixed-media presentations, and acid rock music to the growing hippie culture.

Headed for the New York World's Fair and the events surrounding the publication of *Sometimes a Great Notion,* the Pranksters crossed the country in a 1939 International

Harvester bus. Decorated with bright colors applied at random, the bus carried two plackards, one on the front announcing its name "Further" and one on the back saying "Caution: Weird Load." The events of the trip are recorded in several works using a variety of media. A documentary film of the trip in progress is stored in Los Angeles, California. Tom Wolfe's *The Electric Kool-Aid Acid Test* became an underground classic and a paragon of the New Journalism, a style of nonfiction that includes the observer's responses as a participant in the events described. Though Wolfe's book contains some factual errors and distortions, the Keseys say that it accurately captures the spirit and atmosphere of the Merry Prankster period. Kesey's own accounts of those days appear in *Kesey's Garage Sale, Demon Box,* and *The Further Inquiry.*

Critics refer to *Kesey's Garage Sale* as the book in which the destructive potential of drugs catches up with the author. It contains his screenplay "Over the Border," based on his 1967 flight to Mexico to avoid prosecution for marijuana possession. After witnessing the squalor and anti-American sentiments of small Mexican towns, and after his son survived a brush with death, Kesey returned to California to serve a short sentence at the San Mateo County Jail and the San Mateo Sherriff's Honor Camp. When released, he moved to a farm in Pleasant Hill, near Eugene, Oregon. Wolfe's book preserved and extended Kesey's reputation as a drug culture guru so that many visitors sought him out at the farm, looking for drug experiences or a place to live. Numbering in the hundreds per week during the seventies, the number of visitors has since decreased, leaving Kesey with more time for writing, teaching, farming, family, and community service.

Demon Box, Kesey's 1986 collection of shorter works written in the '70s and '80s, reflects on both his pleasant and unpleasant experiences in the counterculture. "There are nostalgic memories of meeting the Beatles in London and the Nazi gestalt therapy of Dr. Woofner, the Charismatic Manipulator of the Big Sur Institute of Higher Light," yet, the image it leaves of the '60s on Deboree's farm is "not Aquarius the truth-seeker, but the infantile Venus-ruled Taurus gunned into fertilizer because he got too big for his fences," Ronald Curran comments in a *Western American Literature* review. Curran sees Kesey's elegy for Neal Cassady, "The Day After Superman Died," as an "ambivalent" tribute to the friend who died of a drug overdose and exposure in 1968. "[The narrator's] lament for his friend evolves into a chronicle of fear over [the] dark forces" beyond his understanding and control, which appear in the story as various corpses, a raven, and the animal-like copulation of Sandy and the two bums he has banished from his farm, Porter relates.

The other pieces in *Demon Box*—fictionalized autobiographical sketches, travelogues to Egypt and China, and essays, most of them previously published in underground magazines—are held together by the presence of a narrative persona, Devlin Deboree. Kesey first used this version of himself in "Over the Border," along with fictional names for his family and friends. He has employed this cast of characters consistently ever since. The name Devlin Deboree (note the alliterating consonants and the end sounds similar to Ken Kesey) suggests "devil" and "debris," which could be taken to refer to bedeviling ruins and rubble or to one who bedevils ruins and rubble (that is, one who raises the devil with the debris in American culture). Or it may be an updated version of Thomas Carlyle's Teufelsdroeckh ("devil's dirt"), who in *Sartor Resartus* is an earlier seeker of higher consciousness. In any case, this persona allows Kesey fictional latitude for shaping actual events into suggestive patterns of meaning.

Being a guru of psychedelic experience can have its dark side, a fact apparent in several of the works collected in this book. Porter explains, "The problem years seem mainly to be those between the publication of *Sometimes a Great Notion* in 1964 and Kesey's move to the farm in Pleasant Hill in 1968. Troubled areas from those years come up repeatedly in the new work: the experiments with drugs and group living that sometimes exploited family and friends, the vision of altering consciousness and establishing revolution, the lure of power, the scrapes with the law, the rasping polarities of freedom and responsibility, the frustrating attempts to establish universal connections. The tone in these pieces shifts from self-indulgence to self-criticism to self-congratulation, but underlying every movement is an intense quest for understanding, for direction, for form." *Los Angeles Times Book Review* contributor Daniel Pyne observes, "In his strong, lucid new collection of stories and essays, . . . Kesey wrestles with those 20 years—with the contradictions that the last two decades have engendered—and with the terrifying possibility that he came away from his Great Quest empty-handed. . . . Or at least not with the kind of universal truths and solutions that [he] seemed to be seeking." Oliver Harris sums up in the *New Statesman* that as a final assessment of the outcome of those years, *Demon Box* "raises more questions than it answers."

Critics are also ambivalent about the uneven quality of Kesey's style in *Demon Box*. "Kesey is at his best when out of Oregon on magazine assignments abroad, producing comic masterpieces of New Journalism on location in Egypt and China, or when returning to mourn the fallen idols of the Sixties," which include John Lennon and the late Cassady, Harris notes. He attributes the uneven style to Kesey's ability to master language while faithfully displaying its inherent limitations. Because *Demon Box* was not published until thirteen years after *Kesey's Garage Sale*, some critics speculates that the author's experimen-

tal drug use had adversely affected his literary creativity. Other explanations for the hiatus include the author's previously-expressed preference for immediate sensory experience over "literary" experience (which is more reflective), and his awareness of the limits of language as a tool for expanding or heightening consciousness.

The Further Inquiry, Kesey's 1990 retrospective on the Merry Prankster years, is also introspective. Structured as a mock trial, the screenplay pits a prosecutor named Chest against the testimony of the various Pranksters. Dierdre English observes in the *New York Times Book Review* that for the author, "the Pranksters were not pioneers but 'unsettlers,' and their destination was no destination. And one not need blame LSD and marijuana for the sins of heroin and cocaine to admit that the acid revolution did leave some dead Indians behind." In this trial, Kesey "is at once confessing to the damage done and asking for equal consideration of the righteous fun the Pranksters wreaked," English explains. "Uptight America was in desperate need of what they provided: an astoundingly successful communal exorcism of the stifling spirits of the '50s' conformity. In the current cultural atmosphere, a new puritanism about sex, drugs and rebellious play, it would be liberating to quaff a hit of what the Pranksters had—their all-out excitement, spontaneity and spoofing. But some of their ideas of fun no longer amuse." English concludes that the group is only partly acquitted by this defense, especially when compared to other accounts of their activities such as Paul Perry's *On the Bus: The Complete Guide to the Legendary Trip of Ken Kesey and the Merry Pranksters and the Birth of the Counterculture*. For skirting some of the more disturbing issues and events that Perry presents in detail, English says of Kesey's *Further Inquiry*, "The Prankster rides again."

Continuing to take experimental risks in the 1980s, Kesey wrote a children's book, *Little Trickler the Squirrel Meets Big Double the Bear*. In this story as in his other books, good conquers evil. When a little squirrel decides to stop the bullying of a local tyrant, the Ozark mountains become safe again for the animals who live there. Kesey also worked with thirteen creative writing graduate students to write *Caverns*, a mystery novel. It was their responsibility to see that it was published. The plot begins in 1934 when an itinerant evangelist named Loach discovers a cave decorated with archetypical "drawings that will challenge conventional ideas about American archaeology and Western religion," Alfred Bendixen relates in the *New York Times Book Review*. The story follows Loach from his discovery of the cave, to the murder of a photographer and a subsequent prison term, and finally to his quest to rediscover the cave. Loach is accompanied on his quest by an archaeologist, a reporter, a priest, two mediums, and a large cast of motley characters. Bendixen adds, "The book is probably best described as a partly successful attempt to fuse the adventures of Indiana Jones with the cosmic spirit and multiple perspectives of 'The Canterbury Tales.'" However, Madison Smartt Bell comments in the *Voice Literary Supplement,* "The result less resembles *The Canterbury Tales* than an uneven day at the Mingus Jazz Workshop. It's fun to isolate the solos; Kesey's seem the strongest, probably because they are the most recognizable. . . . Most scenes and characters are slightly overdrawn, giving the book a cartoon quality which is nonetheless appealing—it has the same amiably sarcastic relation to the junk adventure novels of the '30s and '40s that the Indiana Jones movies have to old serials. At the same time there are some moving and revealing moments." Bendixen observes that the novel is troubled by the lack of a unified authorial voice, its large cast of mostly unsympathetic characters, and its emphasis on plot and comic misadventures, yet it succeeds in being "a revolutionary model for the teaching of creative writing" by "reminding us . . . that the novel requires an individual voice, fully realized characters and a clear sense of time and place."

The novel would have been more fragmented if the students had produced chapters for it individually as originally planned. Kesey recalls in the *New York Times Book Review* that a more unified voice was achieved by requiring everyone to write and discuss plot developments while together in class. It also had helped to be sent out together on a common journey toward an unknown finish so that no single writer's vision would take precedent over another's. He recalls telling the class, "One of the dumbest things you were ever taught was to write what you know. Because what you know is usually dull. Remember when you first wanted to be a writer? Eight or [ten] years old, reading about thin-lipped heroes flying over mysterious viny jungles toward untold wonders? That's what you wanted to write about, about what you *didn't* know." Kesey tells David Weddle in an article on the class for *Rolling Stone,* "The fun in writing is like jazz—where you're singing, where suddenly the voice is going forward and you're riding it, you're surfing on top of it. That is the art of writing. . . . It's as hard to find it as it is to teach somebody to find it." Under these guidelines the class produced an interesting novel that found a publisher in 1989 and fulfilled their mandate. Work on this project also helped break the writer's block Kesey encountered halfway through his novel *Sailor's Song* when interrupted by the tragic death of his son Jed in 1984.

Though Kesey's works are few in number, they are significant additions to American literature and that body of writing that seeks to explore and extend the limits of the human spirit. Kesey's fiction displays a distinctive blending of American traditions. As an extension of the Beat movement, it reflects the concerns and attitudes of Ameri-

can Transcendentalism. A number of parallels link Kesey with a tradition that found its most complete expression in Ralph Waldo Emerson, Henry David Thoreau, and Walt Whitman. Emerson defined Transcendentalism as Idealism in 1842; Kesey's search was Idealism in the 1960s. Kesey shared with the Transcendentalists such attitudes as these: love of nature, with the expectation that nature teaches the most important truths; an eclectic approach to finding knowledge, with conventions and institutions largely ignored or resisted; an impatience with the limitations of language; a confidence in intuitive knowledge and an obsession with a transcendental experience; an attraction to the vernacular hero; a feeling that reform must begin with the self; and a predisposition toward mysticism.

In addition to *One Flew Over the Cuckoo's Nest,* critics regard Kesey as an accomplished writer for other achievements. His approach to cherished American traditions and values is original and engaging, and his humor grows naturally out of the situations and idioms of his characters. Kesey displays a skill for creating the revealing anecdote. He readily perceives both the rational and more complex sides of human nature, giving his characters a spiritual depth necessary to carry his themes of freedom and the moral responsibilities of creativity. His innovative fictional technique and self-criticism are notable. Furthermore, in keeping with his often-cited declaration that he would "rather live a novel than write one," his personal quests have made him an influential leader in culture as well as literature.

BIOGRAPHICAL/CRITICAL SOURCES:

BOOKS

Acton, Jay, Alan Le Mond, and Parker Hodges, *Mug Shots: Who's Who in the New Earth,* World Publishing, 1972.

Allen, Mary, *The Necessary Blankness: Women in Major American Fiction of the Sixties,* University of Illinois Press, 1976.

Billingsley, Ronald G., *The Artistry of Ken Kesey,* University of Oregon, 1971.

Concise Dictionary of American Literary Biography, 1968-1988, Gale, 1989.

Contemporary Literary Criticism, Gale, Volume 1, 1973; Volume 3, 1975; Volume 6, 1976; Volume 11, 1979; Volume 46, 1987.

Cook, Bruce, *The Beat Generation,* Scribner, 1971.

Dictionary of Literary Biography, Gale, Volume 2: *American Novelists since World War II,* 1978; Volume 16: *The Beats: Literary Bohemians in Postwar America,* 1983.

Harris, Charles B., *Contemporary American Novelists of the Absurd,* College & University Press, 1971.

Kesey, Ken, *One Flew Over the Cuckoo's Nest,* Viking, 1962, new edition with criticism, edited by John C. Pratt, 1973.

Kesey, *Sometimes a Great Notion* (novel), Viking, 1964.

Kesey, *Kesey's Garage Sale,* Viking, 1973.

Kesey, *Demon Box,* Viking, 1986.

Kesey, *The Further Inquiry,* Viking, 1990.

Krassner, Paul, *How a Satirical Editor Became a Yippie Conspirator in Ten Easy Years,* Putnam, 1971.

Labin, Suzanne, *Hippies, Drugs, and Promiscuity,* Arlington House, 1972.

Leeds, Barry H., *Ken Kesey,* Ungar, 1981.

Perry, Paul, *On the Bus: The Complete Guide to the Legendary Trip of Ken Kesey and the Merry Pranksters and the Birth of the Counterculture,* Thunder's Mouth Press, 1990.

Porter, M. Gilbert, *The Art of Grit: Ken Kesey's Fiction,* University of Missouri Press, 1982.

Wallace, Ronald, *The Last Laugh: Form and Affirmation in the Contemporary American Comic Novel,* University of Missouri Press, 1971.

Wolfe, Tom, *The Electric Kool-Aid Acid Test,* Farrar, Straus, 1968.

PERIODICALS

Annals of the American Academy of Political and Social Science, Volume 376, 1968.

CEA Critic, Volume 37, 1975.

Cithara, Volume 12, 1972.

Crawdaddy, Volume 29, 1972.

Critique, Volume 5, 1962; Volume 13, 1971.

Free You, Volume 2, 1968.

Genesis West, fall, 1963.

Journal of American Studies, Volume 5, 1971.

Journal of Narrative Technique, Volume 9, 1979.

Journal of Popular Culture, winter, 1971.

Lex et Scientia, Volume 13, issues 1-2, 1977.

Los Angeles Times Book Review, August 31, 1986.

Modern Fiction Studies, Volume 19, 1973; Volume 21, 1975.

Nation, February 23, 1974.

New Statesman, October 10, 1986.

New Yorker, April 21, 1962; December 1, 1975.

New York Herald Tribune, February 25, 1962; July 27, 1964; August 2, 1964.

New York Review of Books, September 10, 1964.

New York Times, July 27, 1964; January 18, 1966; March 12, 1966; October 21, 1966; August 4, 1986.

New York Times Book Review, February 4, 1962; August 2, 1964; August 18, 1968; October 7, 1973; August 4, 1986; September 14, 1986; December 31, 1989; January 21, 1990; December 9, 1990.

Northwest Review, spring, 1963; spring, 1977.

People, March 22, 1976.

Rocky Mountain Review, Volume 43, number 1, 1989.

Rolling Stone, March 7, 1970; September 27, 1973; July 18, 1974; October 5, 1989.

Time, February 16, 1962; July 24, 1964; February 12, 1965; September 8, 1986.

Times Literary Supplement, February 24, 1966; February 25, 1972.

Voice Literary Supplement, February 2, 1990.

Washington Post, June 9, 1974.

Washington Post Book World, August 10, 1986.

Western American Literature, Volume 9, 1974; Volume 10, 1975; Volume 22, 1987.

Wisconsin Studies in Contemporary Literature, Volume 5, 1964; Volume 7, 1966.*

*   *   *

KEY, Mary Ritchie 1924-

PERSONAL: Born March 19, 1924, in San Diego, CA; daughter of George Lawrence (an inventor) and Iris (a teacher; maiden name, Lyons) Ritchie; married Harold Hayden Key (divorced, 1968); married A. E. Patton; children: (first marriage) Mary Helen Ellis, Harold Hayden, Jr. (deceased), Thomas George. *Education:* Summer studies at University of Oklahoma, 1946, 1949, University of Chicago, 1954, University of Michigan, 1959, University of California, Los Angeles, 1966; University of Texas, M.A., 1960, Ph.D., 1963.

ADDRESSES: Office—Department of Linguistics, University of California, Irvine, CA 92717.

CAREER: Chapman College, Orange, CA, assistant professor of linguistics, 1963-66, bibliographer, Summer Institute of Linguistics, 1964-66; University of California, Irvine, assistant professor, 1966-71, associate professor, 1971-78, professor of linguistics, 1978—, linguistics program chairman, 1969-71, 1975-77, 1987. Has conducted field research on eight American English dialects, Spanish, and American Indian languages in Mexico, Bolivia, and Chile. Lecturer in linguistics in Bolivia, 1956, Kiel, Germany, 1968, Chile, 1975, and Japan, 1986. Consultant to Center for Applied Linguistics, Washington, DC.

MEMBER: International Reading Association (member of board of directors of Orange County chapter, 1968-72), Linguistic Society of America, American Dialect Society, Delta Kappa Gamma (chapter president, 1974-76).

AWARDS, HONORS: Regent's grant, University of California, 1974; Vice Chancellor of Academic Affairs award, University of California, Irvine, 1975; Fulbright-Hays research award and lectureship in comparative linguistics, Chile, 1975; Friends of the Library book award, University of California, Irvine, 1976, for *Paralanguage and Ki-*

nesics; Kentucky Colonel award, Frankfort, 1977; University of California, Irvine, faculty research fellowship, 1984-85; honorable mention, Rolex Awards for Enterprise, 1990, for project "Computerizing Languages of the World."

WRITINGS:

(Editor with Harold Key) *Vocabulario Mejicano de la Sierra de Zacapoaxtla, Puebla,* Summer Institute of Linguistics, 1953.

(Editor) *Notas Linguisticas de Bolivia,* six volumes, Summer Institute of Linguistics, 1959-62.

(Editor) *Vocabularios Bolivianos,* five volumes, Summer Institute of Linguistics, 1962-66.

(With H. Key) *Bolivian Indian Tribes: Classification, Bibliography, and Map of Present Language Distribution,* Summer Institute of Linguistics, 1967.

Comparative Tacanan Phonology: With Cavinena Phonology and Notes on Pano-Tacanan Relationship, Mouton, 1968.

(Editor with Adam Kendon and Richard M. Harris) *The Organization of Behavior in Face-to-Face Interaction,* Mouton, 1975.

Male/Female Language, Scarecrow, 1975.

Paralanguage and Kinesics (Nonverbal Communication): With a Bibliography, Scarecrow, 1975.

Nonverbal Communication: A Research Guide and Bibliography, Scarecrow, 1977.

The Grouping of South American Indian Languages, Gunter Narr, 1979.

(Coeditor) *The Relationship of Verbal and Nonverbal Communication,* Mouton, 1980.

Catherine the Great's Linguistic Contribution, Linguistic Research, 1980.

(Coeditor) *Nonverbal Communication Today: Current Research,* Mouton, 1982.

Polynesian and American Linguistic Connections, Jupiter Press, 1984.

(Editor with Henry M. Hoenigswald) *General and Amerindian Ethnolinguistics: In Remembrance of Stanley Newman,* Mouton, 1989.

(Editor) *Language Change in South American Indian Languages,* University of Pennsylvania Press, 1991.

BIOGRAPHICAL/CRITICAL SOURCES:

BOOKS

Longacre, Robert E., *Current Trends in Linguistics Four: Ibero-American and Caribbean Linguistics,* Mouton, 1968.

KILREON, Beth
See WALKER, Barbara (Jeanne) K(erlin)

*   *   *

KINGSTON, Maxine (Ting Ting) Hong   1940-

PERSONAL: Born October 27, 1940, in Stockton, CA; daughter of Tom (a scholar, a manager of a gambling house, and a laundry worker) and Ying Lan (a practitioner of medicine and midwifery, a field hand, and a laundry worker; maiden name, Chew) Hong; married Earll Kingston (an actor), November 23, 1962; children: Joseph Lawrence Chung Mei. *Education:* University of California, Berkeley, A.B., 1962, teaching certificate, 1965.

ADDRESSES: Home—Oakland, CA.

CAREER: Writer. Sunset High School, Hayward, CA, teacher of English and mathematics, 1965-67; Kahuku High School, Kahuku, HI, teacher of English, 1967; Kahaluu Drop-In School, Kahaluu, HI, teacher, 1968; Honolulu Business College, Honolulu, HI, teacher of English as a second language, 1969; Kailua High School, Kailua, HI, teacher of language arts, 1969; Mid-Pacific Institute, Honolulu, teacher of language arts, 1970-77; University of Hawaii, Honolulu, visiting associate professor of English, beginning 1977.

AWARDS, HONORS: General nonfiction award, National Book Critics Circle, 1976, for *The Woman Warrior: Memoirs of a Girlhood among Ghosts; Mademoiselle* Magazine Award, 1977; Anisfield-Wolf Race Relations Award, 1978; *The Woman Warrior* was named one of the top ten nonfiction works of the decade by *Time* magazine, 1979; National Education Association writing fellow, 1980; named Living Treasure of Hawaii, 1980; *China Men* was named to the American Library Association Notable Books List, 1980; American Book Award for general nonfiction, 1981, for *China Men;* Stockton (Calif.) Arts Commission Award, 1981; Hawaii Writers Award, 1983.

WRITINGS:

The Woman Warrior: Memoirs of a Girlhood among Ghosts, Knopf, 1976, Lane, 1977.

China Men (Book-of-the-Month Club selection), Knopf, 1980.

Hawaii One Summer, Meadow Press, 1987.

Tripmaster Monkey: His Fake Book, Knopf, 1988.

Contributor to books, including *Your Reading,* edited by Jerry Walker, National Council of Teachers of English, 1975. Contributor of stories and articles to periodicals, including *New York Times Magazine, Ms., New Yorker, New West, New Dawn, American Heritage,* and *Washington Post.*

SIDELIGHTS: Maxine Hong Kingston "blends myth, legend, history, and autobiography into a genre of her own invention," writes Susan Currier in the *Dictionary of Literary Biography Yearbook: 1980.* Her books *The Woman Warrior: Memoirs of a Girlhood among Ghosts* and *China Men* are classified as nonfiction, but, according to Anne Tyler in *New Republic,* "in a deeper sense, they are fiction at its best—novels, fairytales, epic poems." Both books are based on the history and myth imparted to Kingston by members of her family and other Chinese-American "story-talkers" who lived in her childhood community in Stockton, California. In *Tripmaster Monkey: His Fake Book,* Kingston weaves history and myth into a massive novel filled with humor and extravagant escapades.

The Woman Warrior is described by Currier as "a personal work, an effort to reconcile American and Chinese female identities." *Washington Post Book World* reviewer William McPherson comments that it is "a strange, sometimes savagely terrifying and, in the literal sense, wonderful story of growing up caught between two highly sophisticated and utterly alien cultures, both vivid, often menacing and equally mysterious." Primarily a memoir of Kingston's childhood, *The Woman Warrior* also concerns itself with the lives of other women in her family, as embellished or imagined by the author. According to *Washington Post* critic Henry Allen, "in a wild mix of myth, memory, history and a lucidity which verges on the eerie," Kingston describes "their experiences as women, as Chinese coming to America and as Americans." "Its companion volume, *China Men* . . . attempts a broader synthesis," indicates Currier, "dealing with male Chinese 'sojourners' in North America and Hawaii, but it is inextricably tied to the autobiographical interests of *The Woman Warrior.*" Kingston's mother dominates *The Woman Warrior,* her father, *China Men,* writes Currier. "In both books," she comments, "additional characters flesh out the social, political, and cultural history Kingston introduces." *China Men* also includes the fictionalized histories of several members of Kingston's family and the community in which she grew up.

Harper's critic Frances Taliaferro remarks that the books' "titles plainly speak their ostensible subjects, female and male; just as plainly the books must be read together. Though I have no inherited command of the terms yin and yang, it seems to me that like those opposing principles the two books form one whole, for the shaping imagination is indivisible." Kingston told *New York Times Book Review* critic Timothy Pfaff that she considers the two works "one big book. I was writing them more or less simultaneously. The final chapter in 'China Men' began as a short story that I was working on before I even started 'The Woman Warrior.' "

Many of the stories included in *The Woman Warrior* are reconstructed from those Kingston's mother related to her as "lessons 'to grow up on,' " writes Currier. Kingston's mother, referred to as Brave Orchid in the book, married her father in China, before he immigrated to New York City. For fifteen years he worked in a laundry and sent part of the money he earned back to China, enabling Brave Orchid to study for certifications in medicine and midwifery, which eventually provided her with a good income and respect in what *Ms.* critic Sara Blackburn calls "a starving society where girl children were a despised and useless commodity." She came to the United States when her husband sent for her, having to give up her medical practice to work for the benefit of her family as a laundress and field hand. Her first two children had died in China while she was alone, but within her first year in the United States, at the age of forty-five, she gave birth to Maxine in Stockton, California, where the family later settled.

Maxine was named after a lucky blonde American gamester in a gambling parlor her father managed. The first of her mother's six American-born children, she grew up surrounded not only by the ghosts of the ancestors and characters who peopled her mother's tales, but also by Americans who, as "foreigners," were considered "ghosts" by her mother. And, according to *New York Times Book Review* critic Jane Kramer, the young Maxine, "in a country full of ghosts, is already a half-ghost to her mother." Kingston's memoir, described by *Time* critic Paul Gray as "drenched in alienation," is also characterized by ambiguity, since, as he points out, it "haunts a region somewhere between autobiography and fiction." It is difficult to distinguish whether the narrator of the book's stories "is literally Maxine Hong Kingston," Gray comments. "Art has intervened here. The stories may or may not be transcripts of actual experience."

The book is divided into five different sections; Kingston's character is central to the second and fifth sections, in each instance, identifying herself with a legendary warrior woman. The tales Kingston's mother told her about heroines and swordswomen were "especially appealing," writes Currier, since the actual status of females in Chinese culture was so low. Such myths had long coexisted with an ancient tradition of female oppression. As *New York Review of Books* critic Diane Johnson remarks, "messages which for Western girls have been confusingly obscured by the Victorian pretense of woman worship are in the Chinese tradition elevated to epigram: 'When fishing for treasures in the flood, be careful not to pull in girls.' " Furthermore, points out Johnson, Maxine "has been given hints of female power, and also explicit messages of female powerlessness from her mother, who in China had been a doctor and now toiled in the family laundry." Kingston dreamed of becoming an avenger, "like Fa

Mu Lan," writes Kramer, "the girl of her mother's chants who fought gloriously in battle centuries ago and became a legend to the Chinese people . . . and then . . . took off her armor to be a perfect, obedient wife in her husband's house." The fantasy was impractical in Kingston's childhood community, but, as an adult, she eventually fights a more solitary, unconventional battle by coming to terms with her family through her writing.

For example, in *The Woman Warrior,* she tells the story of her father's sister whose name was never revealed to her American nephews and nieces. "No Name" aunt became pregnant with an illegitimate child while her husband was in America. Villagers raided and destroyed the family compound on the day she bore the child, and she committed "spite suicide" with the baby in the family well. Since the aunt was regarded as a curse to the family, discussed only within the context of a homily, Kingston had to imagine the circumstances of her life, retelling the story in several possible variations. Sympathy for this relative was an act of rebellion: as Currier writes, "Deliberately forgotten by her family, 'No Name' aunt has an avenger in the niece, who, fifty years later, devotes 'pages of paper to her, though not origamied into houses and clothes.' " Kingston tells her mother's story in part three, concentrating on the fifteen-year interval between her husband's departure and her own arrival in the United States. Currier comments that "of the . . . women of her generation whose stories are told in this book, she is the most heroic."

Kingston turns to the men of her family in *China Men,* a book which also "span(s) two continents and several generations," according to Currier. *New York Times* reviewer John Leonard comments that it is "framed, on the one hand, by a wedding and a funeral, and, on the other, by the birth of boys. . . . In between is sheer magic: poetry, parable, nightmare, the terror and exhilaration of physical labor, the songs of survival, the voices of the dead, the feel of wood and blood, the smell of flowers and wounds. History meets sensuality." In *China Men,* writes Allen, Kingston "describes the men slaving for a dollar a week building sugar plantations; smuggling themselves into America in packing crates; building the railroads; adopting new names, such as Edison, Roosevelt and Worldster." Although women are not prominent as characters in *China Men,* Kingston told Pfaff, "There still are women who take the role of storyteller. The women are not centerstage, but without the female storyteller, I couldn't have gotten into some of the stories."

In order to "understand the men with whom she is connected," Kingston adopts many of the same techniques she used in *The Woman Warrior,* indicates *New York Times Book Review* critic Mary Gordon, "the blend of myth, legend and history, the fevered voice, relentless as a truth-seeking child's." She begins with the story of her father, who has trained as a scholar in China, and, according to Gray, "is subject to black moods and bitterness over his low estate" during much of Maxine's childhood. Perhaps in reflection of his heritage, "his angriest curses vilify women's bodies," writes Gray. "The girl both understands and is bewildered." But, since her father was not a "story-talker" like Brave Orchid, and was silent about his past, Kingston must "piece together the few facts she has and invent the rest," Gordon writes. *Newsweek* critic Jean Strouse comments that "in a dreamlike mix of memory and desire, she tries out versions of her father's life, weaving them through her narrative." Not only does the author recreate his life in China and provide five different versions of how he entered the United States; she also widely separates the story of "the father from China" from that of the man she knew and refers to as "the American father."

In Kingston's tale, "the father from China" found his skills in calligraphy and poetry useless in the United States. After emigrating, he became part-owner of a laundry in New York City, writes Frederick Wakeman, Jr. in the *New York Review of Books,* "along with three other China Men who spend their salaries on $200 suits, dime-a-dance girls, motorcycles, and flying lessons." Kingston follows this account of idyllic bachelor existence with an ancient Chinese ghost story about a beautiful spirit woman who, writes Wakeman, "beguiles a handsome traveler until he loses nearly all memory of his family back home." Eventually, the man is "released from her spell" and returns to his wife. "In the same way," points out Wakeman, "the father from China turns away from the lure of his three high-living friends, and puts the temptations of bachelorhood behind him after his wife joins him in New York." But, according to Kingston, soon after Brave Orchid arrived in the United States and weaned her husband away from his companions—she cooked the men elaborate meals and insisted they keep the Chinese holidays—the partners cheated the father from China out of his share of the business. The couple then left for California where "the American father" had to struggle to support his family.

The book, comments Strouse, "is about a great deal more than sexual warfare, however. It tells of emigration, persecution, work, endurance, ritual, change, loss and the eternal invention of the new." In a later section of the book, Kingston presents the story of the father she knew in Stockton, and she ends *China Men* with characters of her own generation, relating the tale of a brother's tour of duty in Vietnam and his attempts to locate relatives in Hong Kong. Rounding out the book are the highly representative, embellished histories of earlier China Men who preceded her father to America. She tells of a greatgrandfather who traveled to Hawaii to clear the land and work on a sugar plantation. The overseers forbade talking, she relates, and Gordon maintains that "nowhere is Mrs. Kingston's technique—the close focus, the fascination with the details of survival strategies, the repetitive fixated tone—more successful than in her description of the plantation workers' talking into the earth in defiance of the silence imposed upon them by white bosses. The men dig holes and shout their longings, their frustrations, down the hole to China, frightening their overseers, who leave them alone." "The poignancy of that moment is the fruit of stunning historical reconstruction coupled with the imagination of a novelist," Gray indicates.

Another grandfather was hired by the Central Pacific Railroad in the 1860's to work in the Sierra Nevadas, helping to link the continent by rail, she writes. *Los Angeles Times Book Review* critic Phyllis Quan remarks that Kingston portrays this grandfather "as part of that band of migrant workers who fled the white demons' ceremonial photograph sessions held upon the completion of the tracks and were bound to other destinations, leaving a network of steel trails as the only evidence of their presence." In Taliaferro's words, he "comes closest of all these China Men to the strange essentials. Deep in the tunneled rock, he sees immovable time. Riding the wickerwork basket of the dynamiter's trade, he swings athwart cliffs and ravines, overcome by beauty and fear." Gordon indicates that Kingston's "success at depicting the world of men without women must be the envy of any woman writer who has tried to capture this foreign territory. Her understanding of the lacerations of crushing physical work and the consolations of community is expressed in nearly perfect prose." She adds: "In comparison with these tales of her ancestors, the story of the brother who goes to Vietnam is a disappointment. . . . Since Mrs. Kingston's particular genius is most suited to illuminating incomprehensible lives, the brother's life, being more understandable, does not call up her highest gifts."

Quan has similar criticisms, commenting that the second half of the book loses "the cohesion and vitality of myth of the first half," but she believes that this discontinuity is due to the fact that Kingston interrupts her narrative with a section called "The Laws," "a somewhat rude but informative overview of the immigration and naturalization policies affecting Chinese people." Kingston discussed this section with Pfaff, commenting that "the mainstream culture doesn't know the history of Chinese-Americans, which has been written and written well. That ignorance makes a tension for me. So all of a sudden, right in the middle of the stories, plunk—there is an eight-page section of pure history. It starts with the Gold Rush and then goes right through the various exclusion acts, year by year. . . . It really affects the shape of the book, and it might look quite clumsy. But on the other hand, maybe

it will affect the shape of the novel in the future. Now maybe another Chinese-American writer won't have to write that history." And, as Kingston writes, "the reason the second half of the book has fewer myths is that our modern daily life has lost its myths. I am exploring how we live without nature, how we live with machines and battleships."

Throughout the rest of the work, Kingston often blends history with pure fantasy. "What makes the book more than nonfiction," writes Tyler, "are its subtle shifts between the concrete and the mythical." *Washington Post Book World* critic Edmund White comments that "by delving into her own girlhood memories, by listening to the tall tales her Chinese immigrant parents told her . . . by researching the past in books and by daydreaming her way into other lives, the author has stitched together a unique document so brightly colored that it seems to be embroidery sewn in brilliant silk threads, a picture of fabulous dragons sinuously coiling around real people, a mandarin square of triumph and privation, of memorable fact and still more vivid fancy." Kingston, he indicates, has "freely woven fairy tales into her recital of facts and rendered her account magical." As Tyler comments, "Edges blur; the dividing line passes unnoticed. We accept one fact and then the next, and then suddenly we find ourselves believing in the fantastic. Is it true that when one of the brothers was born, a white Christmas card flew into the room like a dove?"

In her imaginative fervor, Kingston often alters and even popularizes classical Chinese myths. Although, in general, Wakeman finds *China Men* praiseworthy, he writes that "as Kingston herself has admitted, many of the myths she describes are largely her own reconstructions. Often, they are only remotely connected with the original Chinese legends they invoke; and sometimes they are only spurious folklore, a kind of self-indulgent fantasy that blends extravagant personal imagery with appropriately *voelkisch* themes." He adds that "precisely because the myths are usually so consciously contrived, her pieces of distant China lore often seem jejune and even inauthentic—especially to readers who know a little bit about the original high culture which Kingston claims as her birthright."

However, Kingston writes that, as a sinologist, Wakeman "is a scholar on what he calls the 'high tradition,' and so he sees me as one who doesn't get it right, and who takes liberties with it. In actuality, I am writing in the peasant talk-story Cantonese tradition ('low,' if you will), which is the heritage of Chinese Americans. Chinese Americans have changed the stories, but Mr. Wakeman compares our new stories to the ancient, scholarly ones from the old country, and finds them somehow inauthentic." Furthermore, claims Gordon, "the straight myth and the straight history are far less compelling than the mixture [Kingston] creates." As Kingston told Pfaff, "I have come to feel that the myths that have been handed down from the past are not something that we should be working toward, so I try to deal with them quickly—get them over with—and then return to a realistic kind of present. This time I'm leaving it to my readers to figure out how the myths and the modern stories connect. Like me, and I'm assuming like other people, the characters in the book have to figure out how what they've been told connects—or doesn't connect—with what they experience." "This sort of resurrection," concludes Wakeman, "is an important way for Kingston to establish a link between her present Americanness and the China of her ancestor's past. The myths—which by their very nature mediate the irreconcilable—initially make it possible for her to rediscover an otherwise lost China, and then summoning it, lay that spirit to rest."

Tripmaster Monkey: His Fake Book presents Chinese history and myth with a wild humor through the character of Wittman Ah Sing, a young Chinese-American whose philosophy of life calls for doing as one pleases whatever the consequences. Herbert Gold, in his review for *Tribune Books,* believes that the novel "blends the kind of magic realism familiar to readers of Latin American fiction with the hard-edged black humor of flower-epoch comic writers and performers—a little bit of Lenny Bruce and a whole lot of Gabriel Garcia Marquez. Kingston's energy, talent and unique perspective make an odd dish work, like some sort of hefty Chinese *nouvelle maxi-cuisine* stew." Writing in the *New Republic,* Anne Tyler calls *Tripmaster Monkey* "a great, huge sprawling beast of a novel, over 400 pages densely packed with the rantings and ravings and pranks and high jinks of one Wittman Ah Sing. . . . That Wittman is Chinese gives his story depth and particularity. That he's American lends his narrative style a certain slangy insouciance. That he's Chinese-American, with the self-perceived outsider's edgy angle of vision, makes for a novel of satisfying complexity and bite and verve."

BIOGRAPHICAL/CRITICAL SOURCES:

BOOKS

Contemporary Literary Criticism, Gale, Volume 12, 1980, Volume 19, 1981, Volume 58, 1990.
Dictionary of Literary Biography Yearbook: 1980, Gale, 1981.
Kingston, Maxine Hong, *China Men,* Knopf, 1980.
Kingston, *The Woman Warrior: Memoirs of a Girlhood among Ghosts,* Knopf, 1976.
Rainwater, Catherine, and William J. Scheick, *Contemporary American Women Writers: Narrative Strategies,* University Press of Kentucky, 1985.
Smith, Sidonie, *A Poetics of Women's Autobiography: Marginality and the Fictions of Self-Representation,* Indiana University Press, 1987.

PERIODICALS

America, February 26, 1976.
Belles Lettres, summer, 1989.
Christian Science Monitor, August 11, 1980.
Harper's, October, 1976; August, 1980.
Horizon, July, 1980.
Hudson Review, spring, 1990.
International Fiction Review, January, 1978.
Los Angeles Times Book Review, June 22, 1980; April 23, 1989; July 2, 1989; June 10, 1990.
Mademoiselle, March, 1977.
Michigan Quarterly Review, winter, 1987.
Ms., January, 1977; August, 1980.
Nation, June 5, 1989.
New Republic, June 21, 1980; April 17, 1989.
Newsweek, October 11, 1976; June 16, 1980.
New Yorker, November 15, 1976.
New York Review of Books, February 3, 1977; August 14, 1980.
New York Times, September 17, 1976; June 3, 1980; April 14, 1989.
New York Times Book Review, November 7, 1976; June 15, 1980; April 23, 1989.
San Francisco Review of Books, September 2, 1980.
Saturday Review, July, 1980.
Southwest Review, spring, 1978.
Time, December 6, 1976; June 30, 1980; May 1, 1989.
Times Literary Supplement, January 27, 1978; April 16, 1989; September 15, 1989.
Tribune Books (Chicago), April 16, 1989.
Washington Post, June 26, 1980.
Washington Post Book World, October 10, 1976; June 22, 1980; April 16, 1989.

*   *   *

KOCHANEK, Stanley A(nthony) 1934-

PERSONAL: Born May 10, 1934, in Bayonee, NJ; son of Anthony John and Wanda (Wronski) Kochanek; married Priscilla Boughton, September 8, 1984 (died, April 30, 1990); children: (previous marriage) Christopher, Kevin. *Education:* Rutgers University, B.A., 1956, M.A., 1957; University of Pennsylvania, Ph.D., 1963.

ADDRESSES: Home—333 South Allen St., Apt. 303, State College, PA 16801. *Office*—Department of Political Science, Pennsylvania State University, University Park, PA 16802.

CAREER: Pennsylvania State University, University Park, assistant professor, 1963-67, associate professor,

1967-73, professor of political science, 1973—. Consultant to Commission on the Organization for the Conduct of Foreign Policy. *Military service:* U.S. Army, 1957.

MEMBER: American Political Science Association, Association for Asian Studies, Southern Political Science Association.

AWARDS, HONORS: Fulbright fellow in India, 1959-61; grant from National Science Foundation, 1966; fellow of American Institute of Indian Studies, 1967-68, 1972, 1981-82; senior Fulbright fellow in Pakistan, 1976-77; fellow, American Institute of Bangladesh Studies, 1990-91.

WRITINGS:

The Congress Party of India, Princeton University Press, 1968.
Business and Politics in India, University of California Press, 1974.
Interest Groups and Development: Business and Politics in Pakistan, Oxford University Press, 1983.
(With Robert L. Hardgrave, Jr.) *India: Government and Politics in a Developing Nation,* Harcourt, 1992.

Contributor to political science journals. Member of board of editors, *Asian Survey* and *Journal of Commonwealth and Comparative Studies.*

WORK IN PROGRESS: Patron Client Politics and Business in Bangladesh.

BIOGRAPHICAL/CRITICAL SOURCES:

PERIODICALS

American Historical Review, December, 1969.

*　　*　　*

KOSTELANETZ, Richard (Cory) 1940-

PERSONAL: Born May 14, 1940, in New York, NY; son of Boris (a lawyer) and Ethel (Cory) Kostelanetz; divorced. *Education:* Brown University, A.B. (with honors), 1962; King's College, London, graduate study, 1964-65; Columbia University, M.A., 1966. *Politics:* Libertarian; registered Democrat.

ADDRESSES: Home—P.O. Box 444, Prince Street Station, New York, NY 10012-0008.

CAREER: Writer, visual artist, critic, poet, composer, filmmaker, holographer, video artist, and lecturer. British Broadcasting Corp. (BBC), London, England, producer-interviewer of program "New Release," 1965-66; Assembling Press, New York City, co-founder and president, beginning 1970; City University of New York, John Jay College of Criminal Justice, New York City, program asso-

ciate in thematic studies. 1972-73; Future Press, New York City, literary director, 1976—; co-editor/publisher, *Precisely: A Critical Magazine,* 1977-84; RK Editions, New York City, sole proprietor, 1978—; coordinator-interviewer, "American Writing Today," Voice of America Forum Series, 1979-81.

Visiting professor of American studies and English at University of Texas at Austin, spring, 1977; guest of Mishkenot Sha'ananim, Jerusalem, 1979, and 1986, and DAAD Kunstlerprogramm, West Berlin, 1981-83. Guest artist at WXXI-FM, Rochester, NY, 1975-76, Synapse, Syracuse University, 1975, Cabin Creek Center for Work and Environmental Studies, 1978, Electronic Music Studio of Stockholm, 1981, 1983, 1984, 1986, and 1988, Brooklyn College Center for Computer Music, 1982, WGBH-FM, Boston, 1983, Public Access Synthesizer Studio, New York City, 1983, Dennis Gabor Laboratory, Museum of Holography, 1985, 1989, Experimental TV Center, Owego, New York, 1985, 1986, 1987, 1989, and 1990, and Film/Video Arts, 1989. Has lectured and given readings of his poetry and fiction at numerous colleges and universities, including New York University, Cooper Union, Brown University, Harvard University, University of Iowa, Antioch College, Carnegie-Mellon University, University of Southern California, Rutgers University, Detroit Institute of Arts, and Barnard College. One-man exhibitions of visual art at Washtenaw Community College, 1975, University of Toledo, 1977, Bertha Urdang Gallery, New York City, 1977, Long Island University, 1978, University of South Carolina, 1978, Simon Fraser University, 1978, University of Alberta, 1978, Cornell College, 1979, California State College, Bakersfield, 1980, University of North Dakota, 1980, Miami-Dade Community College, 1980, and Vassar College, 1981. Has exhibited his holograms at the Museum of Holography in New York City, 1978, 1986. Has exhibited his book art, visual poetry, and other works in over 60 group exhibitions.

MEMBER: American PEN, International Association of Art Critics, Audio Independents, Foundation for Independent Video and Film, National Artworkers, Artists Equity, American Society of Composers, Authors, and Publishers (ASCAP), National Writers Union, Society for Origination of Horspiel in America, Phi Beta Kappa.

AWARDS, HONORS: Woodrow Wilson fellow, 1962-63; Fulbright fellow, 1964-65; Pulitzer fellow in critical writing, 1965-66; Guggenheim fellow, 1967; *Numbers: Poems and Stories* was selected one of the Best Books of 1976 by the American Institute of Graphic Arts; National Endowment for the Arts grants in visual arts, 1976, 1978, 1979, and 1985, and in media arts, 1981, 1982, 1985, 1986, 1989, and 1990; Pushcart Prize, 1977; Southern Alberta Art Gallery art prize, 1978; Ludwig Vogelstein Foundation grant, 1980; Fund for Investigative Journalism grant,

1980; Coordinating Council of Literary Magazines editors' fellow, 1981; New York State Council on the Arts Media Services grant (through Future Press), 1982, and 1984; American Society of Composers, Authors, and Publishers (ASCAP) Award in serious music composition, annually, 1983-1991; Kitchen Media Bureau grant, 1983; Freunde der Deutschen Kinemathek grant, 1983; Inter Nationes (German translation agency) grants, 1983, 1984, 1985, and 1986; American Public Radio Program Fund grant, 1985; Ann Arbor Film Festival prize, 1986.

WRITINGS:

POEMS

Visual Language, Assembling Press, 1970.
I Articulations/Short Fictions, Kulchur, 1974.
Portraits from Memory, Ardis, 1975.
Numbers: Poems and Stories, Assembling Press, 1976.
Rain Rains Rain, Assembling Press, 1976.
Illuminations, Laughing Bear, 1977.
Numbers Two, Luna Bisonte, 1977.
Richard Kostelanetz, RK Editions, 1980.
Turfs/Arenas/Fields/Pitches, High/Coo Press, 1980.
Arenas/Fields/Pitches/Turfs, BkMk Press/University of Missouri at Kansas City, 1982.
Fields/Pitches/Turfs/Arenas, Runaway Spoon Press, 1990.
Solos, Duets, Trios & Choruses, Membrane Press, 1991.

FICTION

In the Beginning (novel), Abyss Publications, 1971.
Accounting, Amodulo (Brescia, Italy), 1972, Poetry Newsletter (Sacramento), 1973.
Ad Infinitum: A Fiction, International Artists' Cooperation (Friedrichsfehn, West Germany), 1973.
Metamorphosis, Membrane Press, 1974.
Obliterate, Ironwhorsebook, 1974.
Come Here, Cookie (Des Moines), 1975.
Constructs, West Coast Poetry Review, 1975.
Extrapolate, Cookie, 1975.
Modulations, Assembling Press, 1975.
Openings and Closings, D'Arc, 1975.
One Night Stood (novel), Future Press, 1977.
Constructs Two, Membrane Press, 1978.
Foreshortenings and Other Stories, Tuumba Press, 1978.
Inexistences: Constructivist Fictions, RK Editions, 1978.
Milestones in a Life, Lethbridge Herald, 1978.
Tabula Rasa: A Constructivist Novel, RK Editions, 1978.
And So Forth, Future Press, 1979.
Exhaustive Parallel Intervals (novel), Future Press, 1979.
More Short Fictions, Assembling Press, 1980.
Epiphanies, Literarisches Colloquium Berlin, 1983.
Constructs Three: Stories, RK Editions, 1991.
Constructs Four: Stories, RK Editions, 1991.
Constructs Five: Stories, RK Editions, 1991.

Constructs Six: Stories, RK Editions, 1991.
Fifty Untitled Constructivist Fictions, RK Editions, 1991.
Intermix, RK Editions, 1991.
Flipping, RK Editions, 1991.
March, Generator Press, 1991.

NONFICTION

Music of Today, Time-Life Records, 1967.
The Theatre of Mixed Means: An Introduction to Happenings, Kinetic Environments, and Other Mixed-Means Performances, Dial Press, 1968.
Master Minds: Portraits of Contemporary American Artists and Intellectuals, Macmillan, 1969.
Recyclings: A Literary Autobiography, Volume 1, Assembling Press, 1974, Volume 2, Future Press, 1984, augmented edition published as *Recyclings, 1959-61,* Future Press, 1984.
The End of Intelligent Writing: Literary Politics in America, Sheed & Ward, 1974, published as *Literary Politics in America: The End of Intelligent Writing,* Andrews & McMeel, 1977.
Prunings/Accruings, Ecart Publications (Geneva), 1977.
Grants and the Future of Literature, RK Editions, 1978.
Wordsand: 1967-1978: Art with Words, Numbers, and Lines, in Several Media: An Unillustrated Catalog with Related Documents, RK Editions, 1978.
"The End" Appendix: "Intelligent Writing" Reconsidered / "The End" Essentials: "Intelligent Writing" Epitomized (extracts from *The End of Intelligent Writing*), Scarecrow, 1979.
Twenties in the Sixties: Previously Uncollected Critical Essays, Greenwood Press, 1979.
Metamorphosis in the Arts, Assembling Press, 1980.
Arts History, RK Editions, 1981.
Autobiographies, Mudborn, 1981.
The Old Poetries and the New, University of Michigan Press, 1981.
Reincarnations, Future Press, 1981.
American Imaginations, Merve Verlag, 1983.
Autobiographien New York Berlin, Merve Verlag, 1986.
The Grants-Fix: Publicly Funded Literary Granting in America, RK Editions, 1987.
The Old Fictions and the New, McFarland & Co., 1987.
Prose Pieces/Aftertexts, Atticus Press, 1987.
Conversing with Cage, Limelight Editions, 1988.
On Innovative Music(ian)s, Limelight Editions, 1989.
Unfinished Business: An Intellectual Nonhistory, RK Editions, 1990.
Twenty-Two Years of References (chapbook of letters), Ghost Dance, 1991.
Uninflected, Nonsyntactic Prose, goodbooqpress, 1991.
The New Poetries and Some Old, Southern Illinois University Press, 1991.

Politics in the African-American Novel, Greenwood Press, 1991.

Published Encomia, 1967-91, RK Editions, 1991.

On Innovative Art(ist)s, McFarland, 1992.

EDITOR

On Contemporary Literature: An Anthology of Critical Essays on the Major Movements and Writers of Contemporary Literature, Avon, 1964.

The New American Arts, Horizon Press, 1965.

Twelve from the Sixties, Dell, 1967.

The Young American Writers: Fiction, Poetry, Drama, and Criticism, Funk, 1967.

Beyond Left & Right: Radical Thought for Our Time, Morrow, 1968.

(With Henry Korn) *Assembling: A Collection of Otherwise Unpublishable Manuscripts,* Gnilbmessa, 1970.

Imaged Words & Worded Images, Outerbridge & Dienstfrey, 1970.

John Cage, Praeger, 1970, reprinted, Da Capo, 1991.

Moholy-Nagy, Praeger, 1970, reprinted, Da Capo, 1991.

Possibilities of Poetry: An Anthology of American Contemporaries, Delta/Dell, 1970.

Young Writers in North America, American PEN, 1971.

Future's Fictions, Panache, 1971.

Human Alternatives: Visions for Us Now, Morrow, 1971.

(With Korn and Mike Metz) *Second Assembling: A Collection of Otherwise Unpublishable Manuscripts,* Assembling Press, 1971.

Social Speculations: Visions for Our Time, Morrow, 1971.

In Youth, Ballantine, 1972.

Seeing through Shuck, Ballantine, 1972.

(With Korn and Metz) *Third Assembling: A Collection of Otherwise Unpublishable Manuscripts,* Assembling Press, 1972.

Breakthrough Fictioneers: An Anthology, Something Else Press, 1973.

The Edge of Adaptation: Man and the Emerging Society, Prentice-Hall, 1973.

(With Korn and Metz) *Fourth Assembling: A Collection of Otherwise Unpublishable Manuscripts,* Assembling Press, 1973.

(With Korn and Metz) *Fifth Assembling: A Collection of Otherwise Unpublishable Manuscripts,* Assembling Press, 1974.

Essaying Essays: Alternative Forms of Exposition, Out of London Press, 1975.

Language and Structure in North America: The First Large Definitive Survey of North American Language Art, November 4-30, 1975, Kensington Arts Association (Toronto), 1975.

(With Korn and Metz) *Sixth Assembling: A Collection of Otherwise Unpublishable Manuscripts,* Assembling Press, 1975.

Younger Critics in North America: Essays on Literature and the Arts, Margins, 1976.

(With Korn) *Seventh Assembling: A Collection of Otherwise Unpublishable Manuscripts,* Assembling Press, 1977.

Assembling Assembling, Assembling Press, 1978.

Eighth A-J Assembling, Assembling Press, 1978.

Eighth K-Z Assembling, Assembling Press, 1978.

Esthetics Contemporary, Prometheus Books, 1978, revised edition, 1989.

(With others) *Complete Assembling,* Assembling Press, 1979.

A Critical (Ninth) Assembling, Assembling Press, 1979.

Visual Literature Criticism: A New Collection, Southern Illinois University Press, 1979.

Scenarios, Assembling Press, 1980.

Tenth Assembling, Assembling Press, 1980.

Text-Sound Texts, Quill/Morrow, 1980.

(And author of introduction) *The Yale Gertrude Stein,* Yale University Press, 1980.

American Writing Today, two volumes, Voice of America Forum Series, 1981, revised edition, Whitston, 1991.

Aural Literature Criticism, Precisely/RK Editions, 1981.

Eleventh Assembling: Pilot Proposals, Assembling Press, 1981.

The Avant-Garde Tradition in Literature, Prometheus Books, 1982.

The Literature of SoHo, Shantih, 1983.

(With Benjamin Hrushovski) *The Poetics of the New Poetry,* RK Editions, 1983.

(With Stephen Scobie) *Precisely Complete,* six volumes, RK Editions, 1985.

Gertrude Stein Advanced: An Anthology of Criticism, McFarland & Co., 1990.

John Cage Criticism, University of Michigan Press, 1992.

FILMS

(With Bart Weiss) *Openings and Closings,* 1976.

(With Peter Longauer) *Constructivist Fictions,* 1979.

Epiphanies, 1983-91.

(With Martin Koerber) *A Berlin Lost,* 1984.

(With Koerber) *Berlin Sche-Einena Jother,* 1988.

A Berlin Lost has been translated into German, French, Spanish, and other languages.

RECORDINGS

Experimental Prose, Assembling Press, 1976.

Foreshortenings and Other Stories, RK Editions, 1976.

Openings and Closings, RK Editions, 1976.

Audio Art, RK Editions, 1977.

Asdescent and Anacatabasis, RK Editions, 1978.

Monotapes, RK Editions, 1978.

Praying to the Lord, RK Editions, 1981.

Seductions, RK Editions, 1981.

The Gospels/Die Evangelien, Westdeutscher Rundfunk, 1982.

Conversations and Dialogues, RK Editions, 1983.

The Eight Nights of Hanukah, Canadian Broadcasting Corporation, 1983.

Invocations, Folkways Records, 1983.

Relationships, RK Editions, 1983.

Two German Hoerspiele, RK Editions, 1983.

Audio Writing, RK Editions, 1984.

New York City, Westdeutscher Rundfunk, 1984.

Complete Audio Writing, nine audiocassettes, RK Editions, 1985.

A Special Time, American Public Radio, 1985.

Le Bateau Ivre/The Drunken Boat, edited by Maya Reed, RK Editions, 1986.

Americas' Game, RK Editions, 1988, Curious Music, 1992.

Resume, Illuminati, 1988.

Turfs/Arenas/Fields/Pitches, RK Editions, 1988.

Onomatopoeia, RK Editions, 1988.

More Complete Audio Writing (audio-only VHS video cassettes), RK Editions, 1989.

The Gospels Abridged, Peter Norton Family Foundation, 1990.

Kaddish, Westdeutscher Rundfunk, 1991.

RADIO SCRIPTS

Audio Art, Australian Broadcasting, 1978.

Text-Sound in North America, Australian Broadcasting, 1981.

Glenn Gould as a Radio Artist, Westdeutscher Rundfunk, 1983.

Hoerspiel USA: Radio Comedy, Westdeutscher Rundfunk, 1983.

Audio Writing, Australian Broadcasting, 1984.

(With Koerber and Michael Maassen) *Nach Weissensee,* Rundfunk im Amerikanischen Sektor Berlins, 1984.

Radio Comedy Made in America Today, Westdeutscher Rundfunk, 1986.

Hoerspielmaschner Tony Schwartz, Westdeutscher Rundfunk, 1987.

New York City Radio, Sender Freies Berlin, 1988.

Orson Welles as a Radio Artist, Westdeutscher Rundfunk, 1988.

Horspiel USA auf Schallplatte, Westdeutscher Rundfunk, 1990.

Pionere der US-Radiokunst: Norman Corwin, Westdeutscher Rundfunk, 1991.

VIDEOTAPES

(And narrator) *Poetry to See and Poetry to Hear,* WCBS-Camera Three/New York State Department of Education, 1974.

Openings and Closings, RK Editions, 1975.

Three Prose Pieces, RK Editions, 1975.

Declaration of Independence, KENW (Portales, NM), 1979.

Epiphanies, RK Editions, 1980.

Partitions, RK Editions, 1986.

Home Movies Reconsidered: My First Twenty-Seven Years, RK Editions, 1987.

Seductions and Relationships, RK Editions, 1987.

(And narrator) *Video Writing,* RK Editions, 1987.

Video Strings, RK Editions, 1989.

Kinetic Writings, RK Editions, 1989.

Onomatopoeia, RK Editions, 1989.

Stringsieben, RK Editions, 1989.

Stringtwo, RK Editions, 1990.

Kaddish, RK Editions, 1991.

Video Fictions, RK Editions, 1992.

Video Poems, RK Editions, 1992.

OTHER

Numbers One (art portfolio), Cory Gallery (San Francisco), 1974.

Word Prints (art portfolio), RK Editions, 1975.

Epiphanies (play), first produced in Grand Forks, ND, 1980.

Lovings (play), first produced in New York City, 1991.

Contributor to over 70 anthologies. Contributor of fiction, poems, reviews, articles, and essays to numerous periodicals, including *New York Times Magazine, National Review, Esquire, Commonweal, Tri-Quarterly, Holiday, Chicago Review, New Republic, Village Voice, Nation, Hudson Review, Partisan Review, Rolling Stone, North American Review, Transatlantic Review, Publishers Weekly,* and *Harper's Bazaar.* Contributing editor, *Lotta Poetica,* 1970-71, *Arts in Society,* 1970-75, *Humanist,* 1970-78, *Pushcart Prize Anthology,* 1977—, *New Lazarus,* 1980—, *New York Arts Journal,* 1980-82, *Literature in Performance,* 1980-83, *Rampike,* 1987—, *Avant-Garde: Interdisciplinary and International Journal,* 1988—, and *Liberty,* 1989—. Advisory editor, *Contemporary Dramatists,* St. James, 1973, 1976, and *Performing Arts Journal,* 1976-81.

SIDELIGHTS: Richard Kostelanetz is a leading advocate of contemporary avant-garde literature. Jamake Highwater, writing in *Shadow Show: An Autobiographical Insinuation,* states that Kostelanetz "remains today one of the most articulate and influential spokesmen for the avant-garde." His own creative work, usually of a highly innovative nature, includes fiction, verbal and visual poetry, radio scripts, videotapes, holograms, and graphic art. In addition, Kostelanetz has edited a score of anthologies featuring the work of young writers, written critical studies, edited collections of work by John Cage and Gertrude Stein, and run the avant-garde Assembling Press, Future Press and RK Editions.

Writing in *Seneca Review,* Donald Hall describes Kostelanetz as a "publicist and statesman of the new. . . . He locates his attention on poetry that falls between genres, on 'intermedia' as he calls it, like visual poetry and sound-text. His energy is vast, his output prolific. As editor of *Assembling* (the most remarkable magazine of its day, an invention of conceptual art); as Cicero to Jason Epstein's Cato; as tireless promoter of eccentric poets, unacceptable poets, outlandish poets, weird poets, and good poets—he is unlike anyone else in contemporary literature." As Rochelle Ratner notes in the *Soho Weekly News,* "It's hard to think about experimental writing without the name Richard Kostelanetz coming to mind."

Perhaps Kostelanetz's most outspoken literary book has been *The End of Intelligent Writing: Literary Politics in America,* an examination of the New York-centered literary business and how it resists the work of younger, more innovative writers. The book outlines the interconnections existing between leading New York publishing houses, major book reviews, East Coast universities, and literary magazines, showing an almost incestual relationship in American publishing.

Kostelanetz's charges of a powerful, although loosely organized, New York literary conspiracy were not dismissed. In fact, some reviewers, like Roger Sale in the *New York Times Book Review,* found little new in the charges. "Kostelanetz's recital of the sins of his powerful elders, which is probably what this book will become noted for, just isn't news," writes Sale. "His own epigraphs show similar conditions operating in earlier days." Similarly, John W. Aldridge, writing in the *Michigan Quarterly Review,* states: "However vigorously we may deplore the fact, it is simply in the nature of literary groups in all times and places that they will protect and promote their own and, with one degree or another of malevolent calculation, will exclude or ignore those who are not their own." Benjamin DeMott of the *Atlantic* acknowledges that, for instance, Kostelanetz "presents a battery of statistics supporting his charge that the choice of books to be noticed reflects the closeness of relationship between the [*New York Review of Books*] and Random House."

In the book's second half, Kostelanetz discusses the work of younger, more experimental, writers that he feels have been neglected by the literary establishment. Sale, for one, found this section "much better. . . . I'm glad to have his recommendations. . . . There is . . . a mine of information in the second half of this book, and once one gets clear those whom Kostelanetz will speak of with highest praise, and why, one can learn a lot from it." Thomas Powers of *Harper's* finds that "Kostelanetz is a witty, committed, engaging writer. He is not meanspirited. . . . He is tireless, informed, and often perceptive. He wants to further the cause of literature and encourage all those young writers

who live a long way from and don't know how to approach the centers of literary power. It seems to me that anyone interested in literature, or in the practical business of writing, or in the creative crisis of artists to whom nothing is forbidden, ought to read his book."

In an attempt to circumvent the problems of literary publishing today, Kostelanetz created the innovative *Assembling* anthologies during the 1970s. Unlike other anthologies in which works are chosen by editors, the *Assembling* anthologies consisted of work submitted by writers and artists in already-printed form. As Kostelanetz explains in his article for the *Contemporary Authors Autobiography Series:* "Initially a reaction to the artificial authoritarianism of most literary magazines, [*Assembling*] invited artist and writers whom we knew to be doing 'otherwise unpublishable work' to contribute a thousand copies of whatever they wanted to include. In return, we promised to bind their submissions into a thousand books, returning two to each contributor. My feeling was that if anyone felt strongly enough about their work to make a thousand copies of it, they deserved membership in *Assembling*'s community." Contributions were bound in alphabetical order according to contributor's name, creating an egalitarian structure of presentation, and, since all work submitted was used, only the readers themselves were the judges of the contributors' work. The editorial middleman was bypassed. Blair H. Allen in the *Small Press Review* calls *Assembling* "an international avant-garde magazine which innovated the editorial and publishing process. . . . It's a waker-upper for those bored with innocuous convention in literature playing it 'safe,' a chance to see how avant-garde art injects freshness in literary presentation."

Among Kostelanetz's other anthologies of experimental writing is *Breakthrough Fictioneers,* a collection of work from nearly 100 different writers. Tom Montag, writing in *Margins,* calls *Breakthrough Fictioneers* "a landmark anthology, though it has been nearly universally neglected by the established reviewing powers." "The book," Richard Mathews writes in *Style,* "washes us in a consciousness unlike anything in fiction since the invention of the novel in the Eighteenth Century, and perhaps parallels that century in a literary, critical, anti-romantic reaffirmation of classic values. There is a renewed interest in invention, form and proportion, avoidance of extravagant personal expression or emotion, and a neoteric abstract approach to time, space and consciousness. The book presents a new sensibility, coupled with a new style—intermedia—and the result is a rich, intriguing, suggestive anthology."

Kostelanetz has also written or edited several books on the works and ideas of avant-gardists Gertrude Stein and John Cage. He edited *The Yale Gertrude Stein,* which presents a generous sampling of Stein's experimental writing ranging from the most complex to the matter-of-fact. A "massive, useful book," as a *Choice* reviewer describes it, *The Yale Gertrude Stein* should, according to the *Antioch Review* critic, "win more admirers for Stein, who has produced some of the most extraordinary writing of our time, and a good deal of appreciation for Kostelanetz." *Conversing with Cage* is a collection of interviews with the noted avant-garde composer mixed with his statements about music, performance, and other topics. "A book ingeniously put together by Richard Kostelanetz," as Alan Rich notes in the *Los Angeles Herald-Examiner, Conversing with Cage* is "valuable for advanced students of music, visual and literary artists, and general readers interested in the avant-garde," according to the *Choice* critic.

"Although perhaps best known as a prolific anthologist whose books cover the avant-garde of many of the new arts and cultural thought, and as a critic whose profiles, for example, of John Cage and other major figures are still sought after," Larry McCaffery writes in *Postmodern Fiction,* "Richard Kostelanetz has also staked out for himself a particularly original kind of fiction which is expressed not only through literary means, but also through other arts. This province is the area of pure sequence (or sometimes counter-sequence, if the ordering of the materials defies any logical trajectory)." Kostelanetz's fiction follows a formalist approach, "a radically formalist approach," as Philip G. Leggiere explains in *State(s) of the Art.* Leggiere continues: "Paring his narratives down to fundamental elements—a single word, a phrase, a geometrical design, or a sentence—Kostelanetz charts the unfolding sequences, patterns, relationships, and permutations inherent in the original chosen element. More than clever (though they almost always manage to be that), these stories will open the reader's mind to an array of perceptually and conceptually intricate forms."

Examples of Kostelanetz's fiction cover a wide range of formats and styles. *In the Beginning,* for example, consists of the alphabet spread out over 30 pages, rendered in single and double letter combinations. *Tabula Rasa: A Constructivist Novel* contains 1,000 blank pages, the reader expected to infer the story from the title page alone. Kostelanetz's minimal fictions consist of single sentences arranged one after the other (although the reader is told they can be rearranged as he or she pleases), which can form any number of interweaving stories.

Kostelanetz's creative work in other genres displays similar innovations. His visual poetry links language and sequence to create meaning. The poem "Disintegration," for example, features the one title word repeated again and again, slowly fading from black to white and then disappearing. Other works feature series of numbers or stenciled letters and focus attention on formal patterns rather than on semantic content. "In [Kostelanetz's] poetry,"

Dick Higgins writes in *Newsart,* "as in his criticism, he takes the extreme of objective positions. His words are visual and self-contained. They have no lyric effect whatsoever. To find anything that resembles them one must go to the visual arts, to the lineage of Mondrian and van Doesberg, of the Swiss geometric abstractionists."

Kostelanetz employs similar strategies in his nonfiction as well. The book *Recyclings* contains essays which are, according to Welch D. Everman in *Small Press Review,* "words in themselves, devoid of connection, syntax, and guidelines. Performance is controlled by the printed page but remains infinite in interpretation, for the elements of these important texts are simply what they are: words as openness, words as freedom, words as possibility, words as words, offered up by Kostelanetz, and free and open to the play of thought."

Critical reaction to Kostelanetz's experiments typically praise his adventurous spirit. Blair H. Allen, reviewing the poetry collection *Illuminations* in the *Los Angeles Times Book Review,* finds that "Kostelanetz's ultravisual approach (via innovative typography) provokes the imagination into personally found meanings. The superb design structure of his word and letter choices fuses art and language, creating mind-challenging effects equally at home in art gallery or book." Higgins calls Kostelanetz "one of our liveliest poets."

During a career spanning over 25 years, Kostelanetz has earned a reputation as a prominent avant-garde artist and writer, as well as a promoter of radically innovative and experimental work. He is "still essential," as Edward Butscher writes in *Booklist,* "still fighting the 'good fight' against the literary cabals and commercial barkers that have our literature by the neck." Kostelanetz, Allen concludes, "is most certainly a most ardent and eloquent proponent and defender of freedom of expression and ideas in the literary marketplace." Michael Joseph Phillips in *Small Press Review,* pointing to the wide range of work produced by the author/artist, claims that "Kostelanetz really staggers the imagination."

Writing in his biographical note to *Published Encomia, 1967-1991,* Kostelanetz speaks of his varied career: "Unable to get a doctorate, or any of the emoluments promised to holders of that degree, I have since been unemployed, nonetheless publishing articles, books, poetry, fiction, plays and experimental prose, as well as composing audiotapes and videotapes, producing films and holograms, that have been exhibited and broadcast around the world. Such work is acknowledged in histories of both American literature and modern music; my art, along with my critical interests, are customarily characterized as 'avant-garde' and 'anarchist libertarian.' Deliciously single for the past twenty-five years, I have resided in downtown

Manhattan since 1966 and leave my cluttered studio as infrequently as possible. My favorite hobbies are swimming and reading in the sunshine. From time to time I try to disprove characterizations of me as unemployable and unmarriageable; invariably I fail."

BIOGRAPHICAL/CRITICAL SOURCES:

BOOKS

American Literary Scholarship: 1987, Duke University Press, 1989.

Berman, Ronald S., *America in the Sixties,* Free Press, 1967.

Bory, Jean-Francois, editor, *Once Again,* New Directions, 1968.

Columbia Literary History of the United States, Columbia University Press, 1988.

Contemporary Authors Autobiography Series, Volume 8, Gale, 1989.

Contemporary Literary Criticism, Volume 28, Gale, 1984.

Contemporary Novelists, fifth edition, St. James Press, 1989.

Contemporary Poets, fifth edition, St. James Press, 1991.

Dencker, Klaus Peter, *Test-Bilder/Visuelle Poesie International,* DuMont Schauberg, 1972.

Frank, Peter, *Something Else Press: An Annotated Bibliography,* McPherson, 1983.

Harvard Guide to Contemporary American Writing, Harvard University Press, 1979.

Hassan, Ihab, *Contemporary American Literature, 1945-1972,* Ungar, 1973.

Highwater, Jamake, *Shadow Show: An Autobiographical Insinuation,* Harper, 1986.

Holmes, Thomas B., *Electronic and Experimental Music,* Scribner, 1985.

Johnson, Tom, *The Voice of New Music,* Het Apollohuis (Eindhoven, Netherlands), 1989.

Kostelanetz, Richard, *Published Encomia, 1967-1991,* RK Editions, 1991.

Letter and Image, Van Nostrand, 1970.

May, Charles E., *Short-Story Theories,* Ohio University Press, 1976.

McCaffery, Larry, editor, *Postmodern Fiction: A Biobibliographical Guide,* Greenwood Press, 1986.

Myers, George, Jr., *An Introduction to Modern Times,* Lunchroom Press, 1982.

Robson, Ernest, *Poetry as a Performance Art On and Off the Page,* Primary Press, 1976.

Woodress, James, editor, *American Literary Scholarship: 1980,* Duke University Press, 1981.

PERIODICALS

American Book Review, March, 1981.

American Literature, December, 1982.

Antioch Review, summer, 1975, p. 114; summer, 1978; winter, 1982.

Artweek, April 24, 1971.

Asylum, Number 20, 1987.

Atlantic, February, 1975.

Ballet Review, Volume II, number 4, 1968.

Book Forum, March, 1977.

Booklist, October 1, 1977; December 15, 1978; May 1, 1979; June 15, 1979.

Choice, December 4, 1980.

Christian Science Monitor, December 2, 1965; March 28, 1968.

Commonweal, February 14, 1975.

Cultural Information Service, April 30, 1979.

Drama Review, fall, 1981.

Esquire, May, 1975.

Factsheet Five, Number 36, 1990; Number 38, 1990; Number 40, February, 1991; Number 42, 1991.

Georgia Review, summer, 1975.

German Studies, February, 1974.

Harper's, November, 1974.

Intermedia, December, 1975; winter-spring, 1976.

Library Journal, December 15, 1974.

Lightworks, Number 13, 1981; Number 17, 1985.

Los Angeles Times, October 21, 1969; December 5, 1974.

Los Angeles Times Book Review, October 16, 1977; June 15, 1980.

Margins, December, 1973-January, 1974; April-May, 1974; October-November, 1974; October, 1975.

Michigan Quarterly Review, summer, 1975.

Nation, June 24, 1978.

National Review, May 23, 1975.

Newsart, June, 1980.

New Letters, September, 1974.

New Yorker, August 30, 1982.

New York Times, February 16, 1968; September 5, 1985.

New York Times Book Review, November 21, 1965; October 21, 1973; December 29, 1975; December 21, 1980.

Northwest Review, Volume XXVI, number 2, 1986.

Progressive, May, 1975.

Recordings of Experimental Music, February/March, 1984.

Salmagundi, summer, 1975.

San Francisco Review of Books, January, 1976.

Saturday Review, May 20, 1967; December 2, 1967; January 30, 1971.

Seneca Review, Volume XI, number 2, 1981.

Sewanee Review, October, 1974; January, 1975.

Small Press Review, April, 1975; June-July, 1976; March, 1979; February, 1980; July, 1981.

Soho Weekly News, August 28, 1975; December 30, 1976.

Southwest Review, winter, 1981.

State(s) of the Art, Number 1, 1991.

Style, summer, 1975.

Times Literary Supplement, January 21, 1972; February 18, 1972; September 11, 1981.
Village Voice, February 2, 1976; December 20, 1976; May 10, 1988.
Washington Monthly, November, 1973.
Washington Post Book World, January 22, 1978.
West Coast Poetry Review, summer, 1974.
World Literature Today, autumn, 1981.

—Sketch by Thomas Wiloch

*   *   *

KROETSCH, Robert   1927-

PERSONAL: Born June 26, 1927, in Heisler, Alberta, Canada; son of Paul (a farmer) and Hilda (Weller) Kroetsch; married Mary Jane Lewis, January 13, 1956 (divorced, 1979); married Smaro Kamboureli, July 17, 1982; children: (first marriage) Laura Caroline, Margaret Ann. *Education:* University of Alberta, B.A., 1948; McGill University, graduate study, 1954-55; Middlebury College, M.A., 1956; University of Iowa, Ph.D., 1961.

ADDRESSES: Home—4081 Cedar Hill Rd., Victoria, British Columbia, Canada. *Office*—Department of English, University of Manitoba, Winnipeg, Manitoba, Canada R3T 2N2. *Agent*—MGA Agency, 10 St. Mary St., Suite 510, Toronto, Ontario, M4Y 1P9, Canada.

CAREER: Yellowknife Transportation Co. (riverboats), Northwest Tertitories, Canada, laborer and purser, 1948-50; U.S. Air Force, Goose Bay, Labrador, civilian information and education specialist, 1951-54; State University of New York at Binghamton, assistant professor, 1961-65, associate professor, 1965-68, professor of English, 1968-78; University of Manitoba, Winnipeg, professor of English, 1978-85, Distinguished Professor, 1985—.

MEMBER: Modern Language Association of America, American Association of University Professors.

AWARDS, HONORS: Fellowship to Bread Loaf Writers' Conference, 1966; Governor General's Award for fiction, 1969; Royal Society of Canada fellow.

WRITINGS:

NOVELS

But We Are Exiles, St. Martin's, 1966.
The Words of My Roaring, St. Martin's, 1966.
The Studhorse Man, Simon & Schuster, 1970.
Gone Indian, New Press, 1973.
Badlands, New Press, 1975.
What the Crow Said, General Publishing, 1978.
Alibi, Beaufort Books, 1983.

POEMS

The Stone Hammer Poems, 1960-1975, Oolichan Books, 1975.
Seed Catalogue: Poems, Turnstone Press, 1978.
The Ledger, Brick/Nairn, 1979.
The Sad Phoenician, Coach House Press, 1979.
The Criminal Intensities of Love as Paradise, Oolichan Books, 1981.
Field Notes, General Publishing, 1981.
Advice to My Friends: A Continuing Poem, Stoddart, 1985.
Excerpts from the Real World: A Prose Poem in Ten Parts, Oolichan Books, 1986.
The Complete Field Notes: The Long Poems of Robert Kroetsch, McClelland, 1989.

OTHER

Alberta: Description and Travel, St. Martin's, 1959.
(With James Bacque and Pierre Gravel) *Creation,* New Press, 1970.
(Author of introduction) Glen Sorestad, *Prairie Pub Poems,* Thistledown, 1976.
(Editor) *Sundog: Stories from Saskatchewan,* Coteau Books, 1980.
The Crow Journals, NeWest Press, 1980.
(Author of preface) Eli Mandel, *Dreaming Backwards,* General Publishing, 1981.
(Editor) Daphne Marlatt, *How Hug a Stone,* Turnstone, 1983.
Letters to Salonika, Grand Union Press, 1983.
(Editor with Smaro Kamboureli) Douglas Barbour, *Visible Visions: The Selected Poetry of Douglas Barbour,* NeWest Press, 1984.
(Editor with Reingard M. Nischik) *Gaining Ground: European Critics on Canadian Literature,* NeWest Press, 1985.
The Lovely Treachery of Words: Essays Selected and New, Oxford University Press, 1989.

Contributor to *Montrealer, Maclean's, Globe and Mail, Books in Canada, Essays on Canadian Writing, Journal of Canadian Fiction, Canadian Review of American Studies, Canadian Literature,* and other publications.

ADAPTATIONS: The Words of My Roaring was adapted for the stage and first produced in Calgary at Theatre Calgary in 1980; *The Studhorse Man* was adapted for the stage and first produced in Toronto at Theatre Passe Muraille in 1981.

SIDELIGHTS: "I'm interested in sharing with the reader the fact that I'm making a fiction," Canadian novelist and poet Robert Kroetsch told Geoff Hancock in an interview for *Canadian Fiction Magazine.* Abandoning what he calls "the old style realism," Kroetsch has adopted an approach that pulls the reader into the fiction-making process. Connie Harvey writing in *Essays on Canadian Writing* explains, "Kroetsch wants to force the reader into a direct perceptual approach to the material so that he, as well as the narrator, creates the work."

According to Harvey, Kroetsch's use of language helps create a "voice" that allows for this direct perceptual experience. "With gerunds and participles, verbals that operate as nouns, and adjectives, Kroetsch is able to list the details of a scene without interrupting the flow of action, thereby creating an immediate experience for the reader's perception," Harvey says. In thus engaging the reader, notes Louis MacKendrick in *Essays on Canadian Writing,* Kroetsch hopes to overcome "the tyranny of language." He breaks free of "the word's received meaning and absolutes into a contemporary world of fresh usage" by "demythologizing, deconstructing, unnaming, uncreating, or uninventing," MacKendrick says.

In an *Essays on Canadian Writing* interview, Kroetsch justifies this novel approach by pointing out that "creation and destruction go hand in hand." But, he continues, "my destruction takes the form of trying to make an old story work, for instance having almost to destroy the old story to tell it anew." According to Kroetsch, the old stories, instead of illuminating the world, sometimes stop people from seeing it. "It's like a pair of glasses that don't quite fit anymore," he explains later in that interview. To improve vision, Kroetsch has said he wants to "uninvent" a mythology and to set another one in its place.

The theme of Kroetsch's first novel *But We Are Exiles* is drawn from the ancient myth of Narcissus. (Son of a river-god, Narcissus was a vain creature who loved only himself. When the wood-nymph Echo fell in love with him, he scorned her, and, as punishment for his vanity Nemesis, goddess of law and justice, caused him to fall in love with his own reflection seen in a pool. Narcissus gazed at his image until he wasted away.) In Kroetsch's story, protagonist Peter Guy pilots a work boat up Canada's MacKenzie River in search of the drowned body of the boat owner, Mike Hornyak. Accompanying him is Kettle Fraser, Hornyak's wife and Guy's former lover. Writing in *Canadian Literature,* Peter Thomas says that in loving both Hornyak and Guy, Fraser recognizes the two faces of Narcissus. The faceless condition in which Guy finds Hornyak's body is a revelation of his own emptiness, according to Thomas who writes that Guy "joins with the image he has tried to reject" when he climbs into the barge which holds the corpse. It is the myth of Narcissus, concludes Thomas now writing in *Essays on Canadian Writing,* which "provides the main structural symbolism in the relations of Peter Guy/Mike Hornyak, two faces of self-love embracing at the conclusion, and their Echo Kettle Fraser."

The Studhorse Man, described by Kroetsch as the *Odyssey* retold on dry land, is another example of an old tale that has been infused with new life. Narrated by Demeter Proudfoot, a lunatic who spends much of his time in an asylum bathtub, the story is an account of how the last of the studhorse men, Hazard Lepage, takes a perfect virgin stallion (named Poseidon) across Alberta in search of a perfect mare. Lepage's fiance, Martha Proudfoot, remains at home. By the book's end, the horse has trampled Lepage to death and Demeter has gone mad under the strain of knowing Lepage and trying to tell his story. Martha, however, survives. "The book's pattern is circular, as is Hazard's journey," observes *New York Times Book Review* critic Paul West, "and the point—made in a manner that fuses prairie tall-tale with Odyssean myth—is that perfectionists procrastinate and thus waste their lives while life in general goes muddling on around them."

Despite the unhappy fate of its main character, *The Studhorse Man* is "flanked by bouts of farce," according to West. Writing in *Canadian Literature,* critic Peter Thomas describes the work as a "complex and essentially comic confabulation" and thinks this "tale told by an idiot" is an assault on realism: "The myths of Demeter and Poseidon . . . are fragmented and distorted schemes of reference in *The Studhorse Man.* Their order is mocked as it is realized." And yet, *Essays on Canadian Writing*'s MacKendrick observes, in this as in his other novels, "Kroetsch's unrestraint is more idea than performance, for he retains all the virtues of story and storytelling while imitating their conventions and parodying their devices. . . . In his hands, the possibilities and improbabilities of [this technique] have an exciting life."

"Kroetsch's reputation in Canada continues to grow," Robert R. Wilson writes in the *Dictionary of Literary Biography.* "His novels, especially *The Studhorse Man,* have become standard texts in university courses and his nonacademic audience . . . is large."

BIOGRAPHICAL/CRITICAL SOURCES:

BOOKS

Bessai, Diane, and David Jackel, editors, *Figures in a Ground: Canadian Essays on Modern Literature Collected in Honour of Sheila Watson,* Western Producer Prairie Books, 1978.

Contemporary Literary Criticism, Volume 5, Gale, 1976.

Dictionary of Literary Biography, Gale, Volume 53: *Canadian Writers since 1960,* 1986.

Keith, W. J., editor, *A Voice in the Land: Essays by and about Rudy Wiebe,* NeWest Press, 1982.

Lecker, Robert, *Robert Kroetsch,* Twayne, 1986.

Neuman, Shirley, and Robert R. Wilson, *Labyrinths of Voice: Conversations with Robert Kroetsch,* NeWest Press, 1982.

Stephens, Donald G., editor, *Writers of the Prairies,* University of British Columbia Press, 1973.

Thomas, Peter, *Robert Kroetsch,* Douglas & McIntyre, 1980.

Twigg, Alan, *For Openers,* Harbour, 1981.

PERIODICALS

Arts Manitoba, January/February, 1977.

Books in Canada, October, 1983.

Canadian Fiction Magazine, spring/summer, 1977.

Canadian Forum, October-November, 1978; June-July, 1981.

Canadian Literature, summer, 1974; summer, 1978.

Canadian Studies, fall, 1982.

Compass, spring, 1979.

Dandelion, Volume 10, number 2, 1983.

Essays on Canadian Writing, fall, 1977; summer, 1978; summer/fall, 1980.

Grain, May, 1982.

Island, Number 7, 1980.

Journal of Canadian Fiction, summer, 1972.

Kunapipi, Number 2, 1979.

Mosaic, spring, 1981.

New Quarterly, spring, 1985.

New York Times Book Review, April 26, 1970.

Open Letter, spring, 1978; spring, 1983; summer/fall, 1984.

Red Cedar Review, spring, 1985.

Studies in Canadian Literature, winter, 1976; summer, 1977.

University of Windsor Review, spring, 1972.

L

LaGATTUTA, Margo 1942-

PERSONAL: Born September 18, 1942, in Detroit, MI; daughter of Edwin Olaf (a designer) and Elizabeth (a painter; maiden name, True) Grahn; married Stephen La-Gattuta (a creative director at an advertising agency), November 14, 1964 (divorced, June, 1988); children: Mark, Erik, Adam. *Education:* Attended Western Michigan University, 1960-62, and Pratt Institute, 1962-64; Oakland University, B.A. (with honors), 1980; attended Warren Wilson College, 1981-82; Vermont College, M.F.A., 1984.

ADDRESSES: Home—2134 West Gunn Rd., Rochester, MI 48306. *Office*—Inventing the Invisible, 29 West Lawrence, Pontiac, MI 48342.

CAREER: Paint Creek Center for the Arts, Rochester, MI, writing teacher, 1983—; Upland Hills Awareness Center, writing teacher, 1983—; teacher, Oakland Community College; producer and host of radio show "Art in the Air" on WPON. Creator and director of Detroit Poets reading series, 1979-80; teacher at Oakland Writers Conference, 1984; assistant director and member of board of trustees of Cranbrook Writers Conference; gives seminars in creativity for education and business under title "Inventing the Invisible"; gives poetry readings at libraries, museums, colleges, and universities, and on WDET-Radio.

MEMBER: Poets and Writers, Poetry Society of America, Detroit Women Writers, Metro-Detroit Book and Author Society.

AWARDS, HONORS: Gwendolyn Brooks Award, Midwest Poetry Festival, 1990; first place award, Ohio Poetry Day, 1990; Ragdale Writers Colony fellow.

WRITINGS:

Diversion Road (poems), State Street Press, 1983.

(With Chris Reising) *Noedgelines* (poems and visual art collaboration), Earhart Press, 1986.
The Dream Givers (poems), Lake Shore Publishing, 1990.

Also author of *Embracing the Fall* (poems). Work represented in anthologies, including *1984 Anthology of Magazine Verse, State Street Press Anthology,* 1989, and *Passages North Anthology,* 1990.

WORK IN PROGRESS: The Usual and the Unsung (poems); *The Seven Magic Elephants of Creativity* (nonfiction book on creative approaches to learning and teaching).

SIDELIGHTS: Margo LaGattuta told CA: "I am motivated by the energy of active imagination. My recently completed manuscript, *The Blue Fox,* was created over a period of three years in graduate school (at Warren Wilson College and Vermont College), during which my study was directed toward the understanding of the creative process in myself and others. I have sought the balance of the intuitive and logical modes of thinking and have learned the importance of leading with the intuitive energy in my own poetry. I find I must begin with an overall pattern of wholeness, then work with the critical mind to fill in the parts. My work is also inspired by the music and suggestibility of language and might be called lyrical surrealism.

"I write for the joy of seeing, for the sense of connecting my inner and outer landscapes, for that moment of awareness in which I feel most truly alive. I write so that I may connect to you."

BIOGRAPHICAL/CRITICAL SOURCES:

PERIODICALS

Adrian Telegram, February 28, 1986.

Daily Press, (Escanaba, MI), March 18, 1989; September 25, 1989.
Detroit Free Press, October 10, 1979.
Detroit Monthly Magazine, March, 1990.
Detroit News, October 21, 1979.
Eccentric, June 26, 1986; April 20, 1989; March 29, 1990.
Grosse Pointe News, February 22, 1986.
Kalamazoo Gazette, May 17, 1987.
Michigan Daily, (Ann Arbor), September 25, 1989.
Oakland Press Sunday Magazine, October 18, 1987,
Oxford Leader, March 28, 1990.
Rochester Clarion, May 26, 1988.
Windsor Star, August 10, 1987.

*   *   *

LANG, T. T.
See TAYLOR, Theodore

*   *   *

LASKER, Joe
See LASKER, Joseph Leon

*   *   *

LASKER, Joseph Leon 1919-
(Joe Lasker)

PERSONAL: Born June 26, 1919, in Brooklyn, NY; son of Isidore (a tailor) and Rachel (Strollowitz) Lasker; married Mildred Jaspen (a teacher), November 28, 1949; children: David Raymond, Laura, Evan.

ADDRESSES: Home—20 Dock Road, Norwalk, CT 06854. *Office*—c/o Kraushaar Galleries, 724 Fifth Avenue, New York, NY 10019.

CAREER: Artist; author and illustrator of children's books. Oil paintings contained in numerous permanent collections, including Whitney Museum of American Art, Philadelphia Museum of Art, Baltimore Museum, and Joseph Hirschorn Museum. Art teacher, City College (now of the City University of New York), 1947-48, visiting associate professor of art, University of Illinois, 1953-54. *Military service:* U.S. Army, 1941-45.

MEMBER: National Academy of Design, Connecticut Association for Children with Learning Disabilities (president, 1964-65).

AWARDS, HONORS: Edwin Austin Abbey Memorial fellowship, 1947, 1948; Prix de Rome fellowship, 1950, 1951; Guggenheim fellowship, 1954; purchase award, American

Academy of Arts and Letters, 1965, 1968; grant, National Institute of Arts and Letters, 1968; Best Illustrated Children's Book Award and Outstanding Children's Book Award, both *New York Times,* 1976, Art Books for Children citation, Brooklyn Museum, 1976, Notable Book of the Year Award, American Library Association (ALA), 1977 and award from Brooklyn Library, 1979, all for *Merry Ever After: The Story of Two Medieval Weddings;* first Altman prize, National Academy of Design, 1980; ALA Notable Book of the Year Award, 1980, for *The Boy Who Loved Music.*

WRITINGS:

JUVENILE; SELF-ILLUSTRATED

Mothers Can Do Anything, Albert Whitman, 1972.
He's My Brother, Albert Whitman, 1974.
Tales of a Seadog Family, Viking, 1974.
Merry Ever After: The Story of Two Medieval Weddings, Viking, 1976.
The Strange Voyage of Neptune's Car, Viking, 1977.
Nick Joins In, Albert Whitman, 1980.
The Do-Something Day, Viking, 1981.
The Great Alexander the Great, Viking, 1983.
A Tournament of Knights, Crowell, 1986.

ILLUSTRATOR

Miriam Schlein, *The Sun, the Wind, the Sea, and the Rain,* Abelard, 1960.
Charlotte Zolotow, *The Man with the Purple Eyes,* Abelard, 1961.
Schlein, *Snow Time,* Albert Whitman, 1962.
Schlein, *The Way Mothers Are,* Albert Whitman, 1963.
Norma Simon, *What Do I Say?,* Albert Whitman, 1967.
Simon, *What Do I Do?,* Albert Whitman, 1969.
Simon, *How Do I Feel?,* Albert Whitman, 1970.
Joan Fassler, *Howie Helps Himself,* Albert Whitman, 1974.
Judy Delton, *Carrot Cake,* Crown, 1975.
Delton, *Rabbit Finds a Way,* Crown, 1975.
Simon, *All Kinds of Families,* Albert Whitman, 1976.
David Lasker, *The Boy Who Loved Music,* Viking, 1979.
Wesley Porter, reteller, *Kate Shelley and the Midnight Express: An American Folk Legend,* F. Watts, 1979.
Dorothy Van Woerkom, *Pearl in the Egg: A Tale of the Thirteenth Century,* Crowell, 1980.
Shirley Climo, *The Cobweb Christmas,* Crowell, 1982.

SIDELIGHTS: Author-illustrator Joe Lasker has been widely praised for his historical picture books for children. Inspired by the panorama of history, he has opened many windows to the past with rich, romantic illustrations and careful attention to period detail. Joyous wedding festivities in feudal Europe, riding into battle with Alexander the Great, a woman's historic voyage around Cape Horn, the pageantry of jousting tournaments in the Middle Ages—all have been brought to life within the pages of his books.

"Painting is my first love," Joe Lasker once told *CA.* "I illustrate and write to support my 'habit' and family. As it must to (practically) all illustrators of children's books, I, too, have become an 'author.'" Lasker's illustrations reflect not only skillful artistic technique but a well-rounded knowledge of art history. The story *The Great Alexander the Great* is brought to life with pictures styled after famous Pompeiian murals of the Battle of Issus, and *A Tournament of Knights* contains all the richness and texture of a medieval tapestry. "Being the artist that he is, Mr. Lasker convinces us that color has never been as bright or as clear as it was in those days," comments Jean Fritz in the *New York Times Book Review.* "Surely blue has never been *that* blue."

The Great Alexander the Great recounts the life of the great Macedonian king. Lasker enables children to relate to Alexander by focusing his story on the warrior-king's love of his horse Bucephalus. "If Mr. Lasker's previous books have sometimes lacked strong narrative interest, that complaint cannot be made here," writes Joyce Milton in the *New York Times Book Review.* "Moreover, the romantic style of the pictures is nicely balanced by a straightforward text that tells its story without prettying up Alexander's character."

Winner of several awards, Lasker's *Merry Ever After: The Story of Two Medieval Weddings* makes the works of the master painters of the medieval period accessible to young readers. Depicting the social structure of fifteenth-century Europe within a period motif, the book has been commended for its balanced portrayal of feudal society. "[Lasker] has written a story of a stimulating and faintly cautionary sort," writes John Russell in the *New York Times Book Review.* He concludes, "*Merry Ever After* is a very good book. Even if the youthful reader never looks at an Old Master painting, he or she will have learned of an alternative social structure . . . And if the images give a new immediacy to the next museum visit—well, so much the better."

BIOGRAPHICAL/CRITICAL SOURCES:

BOOKS

Goodrich, Lloyd, and John Bauer, *American Art of Our Century,* Praeger, 1961.
Kingman, Lee, and others, compilers, *Illustrators of Children's Books: 1957-1976,* Horn Book, 1978.

PERIODICALS

Horn Book, December, 1983, p. 59.
Life, March 20, 1950.

Los Angeles Times Book Review, November 23, 1986, p. 12.
New York Times Book Review, Octoberg20, 1974, p. 8; October 17, 1976, p. 40; October 23, 1977, p. 32; November 13, 1983, p. 41; November 9, 1986, p. 58.
Parade, September 1, 1963.
School Library Journal, March, 1983, p. 29; January, 1986, p. 31.

*   *   *

LAUBER, Patricia (Grace) 1924-

PERSONAL: Born February 5, 1924, in New York, NY; daughter of Hubert Crow (an engineer) and Florence (Walker) Lauber; married Russell Frost III, 1981. *Education:* Wellesley College, B.A., 1945. *Avocational interests:* Theatre, music, animals, sailing, and travel.

ADDRESSES: Agent—c/o Bradbury Press, 866 Third Ave., New York, NY 10022.

CAREER: Writer of children's books, 1954—. *Look,* New York City, writer, 1945-46; *Scholastic Magazines,* New York City, writer and editor, 1946-55; Street & Smith, New York City, editor in chief of *Science World,* 1956-59; Grolier, Inc., New York City, chief editor, science and mathematics, *The New Book of Knowledge,* 1961-67; consulting editor, *Scientific American Illustrated Library,* 1977-80. Consultant, National Science Resources Center, National Academy of Sciences-Smithsonian Institution.

AWARDS, HONORS: New York Times Notable Book citation, 1982, for *Journey to the Planets;* American Book Award nomination for children's nonfiction, 1982, for *Seeds: Pop, Stick, Glide,* and 1983, for *Journey to the Planets; Washington Post*/Children's Book Guild Award, 1983, for overall contribution to children's nonfiction literature; New York Academy of Sciences Honor Book, 1986, for *Tales Mummies Tell,* 1987, for *Volcano: The Eruption and Healing of Mount St. Helens,* 1988, for *From Flower to Flower,* and 1990, for *The News about Dinosaurs;* Newbery Honor Book, and *Horn Book* Fanfare Book, both 1987, both for *Volcano: The Eruption and Healing of Mount St. Helens;* Award for Outstanding Contribution to Children's Literature, Central Missouri State University, 1987; Eva L. Gordon Children's Science Author Award, American Nature Study Society, 1988; Orbis Pictus Honor Book, National Council of Teachers of English, 1989, for *The News about Dinosaurs,* 1990, for *Seeing Earth from Space,* and 1991, for *Summer of Fire;* Lifetime Achievement Commendation, National Forum on Children's Science Books, Carnegie-Mellon University, 1992.

WRITINGS:

JUVENILE NONFICTION

Magic up Your Sleeve, Teen-Age Book Club, 1954.

(Editor) *Jokes and More Jokes,* Scholastic, 1955.

Battle against the Sea: How the Dutch Made Holland, Coward, 1956 (published in England as *Battle against the Sea: The Challenge of the Dutch and the Dikes,* Chatto & Windus, 1963), revised edition, 1971.

Highway to Adventure: The River Rhone of France, Coward, 1956.

Valiant Scots: People of the Highlands Today, Coward, 1957.

Penguins on Parade, illustrated by Douglas Howland, Coward, 1958.

Dust Bowl: The Story of Man on the Great Plains, Coward, 1958.

Rufus, the Red-Necked Hornbill, illustrated by Polly Cameron, Coward, 1958.

The Quest of Galileo, illustrated by Lee J. Ames, Doubleday, 1959.

Changing the Face of North America: The Challenge of the St. Lawrence Seaway, Coward, 1959, revised edition, 1968.

All about the Ice Age, Random House, 1959.

Our Friend the Forest: A Conservation Story, illustrated by Anne Marie Jauss, Doubleday, 1959.

All about the Planets, Random House, 1960.

The Quest of Louis Pasteur, illustrated by Ames, Doubleday, 1960.

Getting to Know Switzerland, illustrated by J. L. Pellicer, Coward, 1960.

The Story of Numbers, Random House, 1961.

Icebergs and Glaciers, Garrard, 1961.

The Mississippi: Giant at Work, Garrard, 1961.

Famous Mysteries of the Sea, Thomas Nelson, 1962.

All about the Planet Earth, Random House, 1962.

Your Body and How It Works, Random House, 1962.

The Friendly Dolphins, Random House, 1963.

Penguins, Garrard, 1963.

The Congo: River into Central Africa, Garrard, 1964.

The Surprising Kangaroos and Other Pouched Mammals, Random House, 1965.

Big Dreams and Small Rockets: A Short History of Space Travel, Crowell, 1965.

Volcanoes, Garrard, 1965.

The Story of Dogs, Random House, 1966.

The Look-It-Up Book of Mammals, illustrated by Guy Coheleach, Random House, 1967.

The Look-It-Up Book of Stars and Planets, illustrated by John Polgreen, Random House, 1967.

The Look-It-Up Book of the Fifty States, illustrated by Herbert Borst, Random House, 1967.

Bats: Wings in the Night, Random House, 1968.

The Planets, Random House, 1969.

This Restless Earth, Random House, 1970.

Who Discovered America: Settlers and Explorers of the New World before the Time of Columbus, Random House, 1970.

Of Man and Mouse: How House Mice Became Laboratory Mice, Viking, 1971.

Earthquakes: New Scientific Ideas about How and Why the Earth Shakes, Random House, 1972.

Everglades: A Question of Life or Death, photographs by Patricia Caulfield, Viking, 1973.

Cowboys and Cattle Ranching, Crowell, 1973.

Who Needs Alligators?, Garrard, 1974.

Life on a Giant Cactus, Garrard, 1974.

Too Much Garbage, illustrated by Vic Mays, Garrard, 1974.

Great Whales, Garrard, 1975.

Earthworms: Underground Farmers, Garrard, 1976.

Sea Otters and Seaweed, Garrard, 1976.

Mystery Monsters of Loch Ness, illustrated by Mays, Garrard, 1978.

Tapping Earth's Heat, illustrated by Edward Malsberg, Garrard, 1978.

What's Hatching out of That Egg?, Crown, 1979.

Seeds: Pop, Stick, Glide, photographs by Jerome Wexler, Crown, 1981.

Journey to the Planets, Crown, 1982, 4th revised edition, 1993.

Tales Mummies Tell, Crowell, 1985.

Volcanoes and Earthquakes, Scholastic, Inc., 1985.

What Big Teeth You Have!, illustrated by Martha Weston, Crowell, 1986.

Get Ready for Robots!, illustrated by True Kelley, Crowell, 1986.

Volcano: The Eruption and Healing of Mount St. Helens, Bradbury, 1986.

From Flower to Flower: Animals and Pollination, photographs by Wexler, Crown, 1986.

Dinosaurs Walked Here and Other Stories Fossils Tell, Bradbury, 1987.

Snakes Are Hunters, illustrated by Holly Keller, Crowell, 1987.

Lost Star: The Story of Amelia Earhart, Scholastic, Inc., 1988.

Voyagers from Space: Meteors and Meteorites, illustrated by Mike Eagle, Crowell, 1989.

The News about Dinosaurs, illustrated by John Gurche, Douglas Henderson, and Gregory Paul, Bradbury, 1989.

Seeing Earth from Space, Orchard Books, 1990.

An Octopus Is Amazing, illustrated by Keller, Crowell, 1990.

How We Learned the Earth Is Round, illustrated by Megan Lloyd, Crowell, 1990.

Living with Dinosaurs, illustrated by Henderson, Bradbury, 1991.

Great Whales, the Gentle Giants, illustrated by Pieter Folkens, Henry Holt, 1991.

Summer of Fire: Yellowstone 1988, Orchard Books, 1991.

JUVENILE FICTION

Clarence, the TV Dog, Coward, 1955.

Clarence Goes to Town, Coward, 1957, Random House, 1967.

Found: One Orange-Brown Horse, Random House, 1957.

The Runaway Flea Circus, Random House, 1958.

Clarence Turns Sea Dog, Coward, 1959, Random House, 1965.

Adventure at Black Rock Cave, Random House, 1959.

Champ, Gallant Collie, Random House, 1960.

Curious Critters, Garrard, 1969.

Clarence and the Burglar, illustrated by Paul Galdone, Coward, 1973.

Clarence and the Cat, illustrated by Galdone, Coward, 1977.

Home at Last: A Young Cat's Tale, illustrated by Mary Chalmers, Coward, 1980.

OTHER

Contributor of short stories and light essays to adult magazines. Former editor, Coward-McCann's "Challenge Books" series, and Garrard's "Good Earth Books" series; free-lance editor, *Scientific American Illustrated Library.*

WORK IN PROGRESS: A book of light fiction and three nonfiction works.

SIDELIGHTS: Through such award-winning books as *Volcano: The Eruption and Healing of Mount St. Helens* and *Journey to the Planets,* Patricia Lauber has made science an entertaining as well as enriching reading experience for children. "Children are born curious, wanting and needing to understand the world around them, wanting to know why, how, and what: the very questions that scientists ask," the author remarked in *The Lion and the Unicorn.* Contrary to the popular perception of science as dry and lifeless, Lauber continued, "I believe that the best science books have a story line: that one thing leads to another, that it is possible to build tension so that the reader really wants to find out what happens next." Lauber's own work, whether describing nature's marvels, animals both prehistoric and living, or technological matters, informs readers with clear explanations, up-to-date information, and illustrations carefully selected by the author for their interest and accuracy.

In *The Quest of Galileo,* for instance, "the story of the man who destroyed the Aristotelian view of the universe is told clearly and forthrightly," Isaac Asimov writes in *Horn Book,* and "extraordinarily good is the description of the

experiments Galileo conducted and the conclusions he drew therefrom." Similarly, in *Tales Mummies Tell* Lauber makes science accessible to children "by illustrating how it can answer questions any normal youngster would find interesting," *Washington Post Book World* contributor Michael Guillen notes. With her uncomplicated yet interesting explanations of scientific principles, the critic adds, "Lauber makes science more attractive and not, thank goodness, merely more respectworthy."

Lauber earned her first American Book Award nomination for 1982's *Seeds: Pop, Stick, Glide,* a book Steve Matthews of *School Library Journal* calls "the Mercedes of the introductory seed books." The critic explains: "The text is vivid and assumes very little on the part of readers, except a willingness to perceive the natural world." "The text is remarkable," Marion P. Hassis similarly comments in *Appraisal: Children's Science Books.* "It manages to go into sufficient depth to surprise and fascinate an adult reader, yet uses sentence structure and vocabulary that will allow comfortable reading by intermediate readers." As Matthews concludes: "*Seeds* not only informs, it fosters an appreciation of the plant world and makes wondrous what is too often seen as commonplace."

Journey to the Planets has received similar praise; a *Kirkus Reviews* writer calls it "a stimulating experience for the eyes, mind, and imagination." In her review, Margaret L. Chatham of *School Library Journal* predicts that Lauber's colorfully illustrated guide to our solar system will become popular "because Lauber has the rare ability to explain things simply without compromising scientific accuracy." The critic's forecast proved accurate, for *Journey to the Planets* has already inspired three additional updates; *Appraisal* contributor Diane F. Holzheimer notes of one that Lauber's "metaphors and concrete examples draw the reader in and make these remote and awesome places real."

A less remote but equally awesome event was the 1980 volcanic eruption of Mount St. Helens in the state of Washington, and Lauber's *Volcano: The Eruption and Healing of Mount St. Helens* "is told in a gripping style and with extraordinary photographs," Elizabeth S. Watson describes in *Horn Book.* "Evident throughout the book are Patricia Lauber's careful scholarship and talent for distilling material to present it in an extremely smooth narrative." "Not only is the eruption carefully explained, but nature's slow rebuilding process is delineated," Frances Bradburn recounts in *Wilson Library Bulletin.* As a result, the critic continues, "children are given the privilege of experiencing a year in the life of a volcano and its surrounding areas, a year in which they witness the miraculous power of two of nature's greatest forces—an active volcano and life's resilient rebirth."

Although Lauber had kept abreast of the developments in the volcano's eruption, "I had not thought of doing a book specifically on Mount St. Helens—until I saw the photo," the author related in a Junior Literary Guild publicity article. "It was a close-up of a hardy green plant that had pushed its way up through a crack in the crust of ash and put out a pink flower. It made me think about doing a book that would explain not only why and how the volcano erupted but also how life came back to a region as barren as the moon." This portrayal of the area's renewal makes *Volcano,* "while written for children, [a book] that will appeal to the curious and full of wonder of all ages," Bradburn writes. "From Patricia Lauber's masterly book we learn that solid information can be captivating in the hands of a gifted writer," Jo Carr comments in *Horn Book.* The judges for the 1987 Newbery Awards, the critic concludes, "showed great wisdom in choosing this perfect book for a Newbery Honor Book."

Although she is best known for her award-winning nonfiction, Lauber has also written several stories for children. Her first, *Clarence, the TV Dog,* came from her experiences with her own dog and proved popular enough to inspire four more "Clarence" books. A friendly dog who watches television and catches a burglar by untying his shoelaces, Clarence, as well as his family, is "believable and funny, simpler than life and twice as natural," *New York Times Book Review* writer Marjorie Fischer comments of the first book. *Clarence Goes to Town* is similarly funny, the critic adds in another review, "a fine mixture of the probable and improbable—sensible nonsense."

Speaking of her origins as an author, Lauber once commented: " 'How did you become a writer?' is a question that I long found very difficult to answer. Finally, I realized what the problem was: I don't think that I 'became' a writer; I think I was born wanting to write. As a very small child, I loved stories and being read to and soon learned to read myself, because then I could have as many stories as I wanted.

"When I had learned to read, and also to print and to spell a few words, I made a wonderful discovery—I could make up stories and poems myself and put them on paper. The spelling wasn't very good, but people seemed to enjoy what I wrote anyhow. This encouraged me. . . .

"I write about anything that interests me—dogs, horses, forests, birds, mysteries, life in other countries. Some of my books are fiction, and some are nonfiction, but all are based on what I've seen around me. I like to stand and stare at things, to talk with people, and to read a lot. From this I'm always learning something I didn't know before. Some time later, when I've had a chance to think things over, I write down what I heard, saw, felt, and thought."

"And that," the author concluded, "is about as close as I can come to answering another question people often ask me. 'Where do you get your ideas?' My ideas come from everywhere—from things I read, from things people tell me about, from things I see about me, from things I experience. The important aspect is that they must interest me very much, because then I want to share them with other people."

BIOGRAPHICAL/CRITICAL SOURCES:

BOOKS

Children's Literature Review, Volume 16, Gale, 1989.

PERIODICALS

Appraisal: Children's Science Books, fall, 1981, pp. 24-25; winter, 1988, pp. 39-40.
Bulletin of the Center for Children's Books, September, 1986, p. 12.
Horn Book, October, 1959, p. 396; September-October, 1986, p. 609; November-December, 1987, pp. 710-713.
Junior Literary Guild publicity packet, April-September, 1986, p. 33.
Kirkus Reviews, May 15, 1982, pp. 606-607.
The Lion and the Unicorn, Volume 6, 1982, pp. 5-9.
New York Times, November 30, 1982.
New York Times Book Review, November 13, 1955, p. 36; November 17, 1957, p. 38; April 26, 1959, p. 38; May 24, 1970, pp. 28, 30; August 1, 1982.
School Library Journal, April, 1981, p. 114; August, 1982, p. 118.
Washington Post Book World, May 12, 1985.
Wilson Library Bulletin, April, 1987, pp. 48-49.

—*Sketch by Diane Telgen*

*   *   *

LAWRENCE, Louise
See MACE, Elizabeth Rhoda

*   *   *

LAXALT, Robert P(eter) 1923-

PERSONAL: Born September 24, 1923, in Alturas, CA; son of Dominique (a sheepman) and Theresa (Alpetche) Laxalt; married Joyce Nielsen (a schoolteacher), May 29, 1949; children: Bruce, Monique, Kristin. *Education:* Attended Santa Clara University, 1941-43; University of Nevada, B.A., 1947. *Politics:* Republican. *Religion:* Roman Catholic.

ADDRESSES: Home—650 Cardinal Way, Reno, NV 89509. *Office*—University of Nevada, Reno, NV 89557.

Agent—Curtis Brown Ltd., 575 Madison Ave., New York, NY 10022.

CAREER: U.S. Consular Service, Belgian Congo, 1943-45; United Press Associations, correspondent in Reno, NV, 1948-53; University of Nevada, Reno, director of University Press, 1954—. U.S. Library of Congress, consultant on Basque history and culture.

MEMBER: Sigma Delta Chi.

AWARDS, HONORS: Fulbright research fellow in Basque history and culture.

WRITINGS:

Sweet Promised Land, Harper, 1957, new edition illustrated by George Carlson with foreword by William A. Douglass, University of Nevada Press, 1986 (published in England as *Dominique*).
A Man in the Wheatfield, Harper, 1964.
Nevada, Coward, 1970.
In a Hundred Graves: A Basque Portrait, University of Nevada Press, 1972.
A Cup of Tea in Pamplona (novel), illustrated by Carlson, University of Nevada Press, 1985.
The Basque Hotel (novel), University of Nevada Press, 1989.
(Author of text) *A Time We Knew: Images of Yesterday in the Basque Homeland,* photographs by William Albert Allard, University of Nevada Press, 1990.

Contributor of articles and short stories to periodicals, including *American Weekly, Atlantic Monthly, Bluebook, Cosmopolitan, Mademoiselle, Saturday Evening Post,* and *True.*

SIDELIGHTS: Robert P. Laxalt speaks French and Basque.

BIOGRAPHICAL/CRITICAL SOURCES:

PERIODICALS

New Statesman, March 26, 1965, p. 500.
New York Times Book Review, May 18, 1986, p. 25; September 24, 1989, p. 48.
Times Literary Supplement, March 11, 1965, p. 201.
Virginia Quarterly Review, spring, 1965, p. 41.
Washington Post Book World, October 1, 1989, p. 10.
West Coast Review of Books, Number 1, 1989, p. 69.*

*   *   *

LEASE, Gary   1940-

PERSONAL: Born September 27, 1940, in Hollywood, CA; son of Rex Lloyd (an actor) and Isabelle (Riehle) Lease; married Patricia Metkovich (a secretary), Septem-

ber 10, 1966 (divorced, 1986); married Dorothea Ann Ditchfield, August 26, 1988; children: (first marriage) Dylan. *Education:* Loyola University of Los Angeles, B.A., 1962; University of Munich, Dr.Theol., 1968.

ADDRESSES: Office—University of California, Santa Cruz, Santa Cruz, CA 95064.

CAREER: St. Xavier College, Chicago, IL, assistant professor of theology, 1968-69; Loyola University of Los Angeles, Los Angeles, CA, assistant professor of religious studies, 1969-73, acting chairman of department, 1971; University of California, Santa Cruz, assistant professor, 1973-74, associate professor of religious studies, 1974—, chairman of department, 1974-76, chairman of history of consciousness, 1976-77, acting provost of Kresge College, 1977-78, professor of history of consciousness, 1984—, chair, environmental studies, 1986-89, chair, history of consciousness, 1988-89, associate chancellor, 1989-90, dean of humanities, 1990—. John XXIII Institute for Ecumenical Theology, research director, 1968-69; University of California Education Abroad Program Study Center, director, 1980-82. California Department of Fish and Game hunter safety instructor, 1971—; investigator for various archaeological excavations, 1974, 1976, 1980, 1981.

MEMBER: American Academy of Religion, American Historical Association, American Society for the Study of Religion, American Schools of Oriental Research, American Research Center in Egypt, International Association for Coptic Studies, Gesellschaft fuer Geistesgeschichte.

AWARDS, HONORS: National Defense Foundation fellow, 1962; Danforth Foundation fellow, 1967; Younger humanist fellow at University of Munich, National Endowment for the Humanities, 1971; Fulbright fellow, 1984; American Philosophical Society research grant, 1986; DAAD study grant, 1987; American Council of Learned Societies grant-in-aid, 1988; National Endowment for the Humanities summer grant, 1990.

WRITINGS:

Witness to the Faith, Irish University Press, 1971.

Contributor to books, including *Vecchi e Nuovi Dei,* edited by R. Caporale, Valentino (Turin), 1976; *Jewish Tradition in the Diaspora: Studies in Memory of Professor Walter J. Fischel,* edited by M. M. Caspi, Berkeley Publishing, 1981; *Religion and Politics in the Modern World,* edited by Peter Merkl and Ninian Smart, New York University Press, 1983; *Newman and the Modernists,* edited by Mary Jo Weaver, University Press of America, 1985; and *The Roots of Egyptian Christianity,* edited by Birger Pearson and James Goehring, Fortress, 1986. Contributor to various periodicals and journals, including *Religious and Theological Abstracts, Newman-Studien, Biblical Archae-*

ologist, *Metanoia: An Interdisciplinary Review, Journal of the American Academy of Religion, Religious Studies Review, Goettinger Miszellen, Downside Review, Loyola,* and *Journal of Ecumenical Studies.*

WORK IN PROGRESS: Research on the history of nineteenth-century religious thought in Germany; studying problems of Christian origins and Hellenistic mystery religions; a study of the relationship of religion and political ideologies; a biography of Merry del Val.

BIOGRAPHICAL/CRITICAL SOURCES:

PERIODICALS

Times Literary Supplement, July 14, 1972, p. 638.

*   *   *

LEONI, Edgar (Hugh) 1925-

PERSONAL: Surname pronounced "Lee-*own*-ee"; born May 6, 1925, in New York, NY; son of Paul G. (a business executive) and Nelly (a housewife; maiden name, Duval) Leoni. *Education:* Harvard University, B.A., 1947; Columbia University, M.A., 1952.

ADDRESSES: Home—42 West 88th St., New York, NY 10024.

CAREER: American International Underwriters, New York City, marine insurance claims examiner, 1951-64; Pageant Book Co., Inc., New York City, editor-in-chief, 1964-66; Oxford Book Co., Inc. (a textbook publisher), New York City, associate editor, 1967-72; semi-retired bookdealer, 1972—. *Military service:* U.S. Army, translator, (Japanese) 1943-46, (Russian) 1950-51; became sergeant.

WRITINGS:

Nostradamus: Life and Literature, Exposition Press, 1961, reprinted as *Nostradamus and His Prophecies,* Bell Publishing, 1982.

SIDELIGHTS: Edgar Leoni worked many years as an insurance claims examiner and then as a textbook editor until a merger thrust him into semi-retirement at the age of 47, and he became a bookdealer in out-of-print books. He was a teenager, though, when he began his work on the sixteenth-century prophet Michel Nostradamus after discovering that despite tremendous interest in the man and his prophecies, there was a dearth of comprehensive and reliable texts in English on the subject. According to Leoni, the only complete English translation of Nostradamus's prophecies available was an inadequate 1672 work by French physician Garencieres and a deficient adaptation of that work published in 1947. However, Leoni's

own prime academic interests—history, classical and romance languages, and classical geography—provided the prerequisites for a competent treatment of Nostradamus and his prophecies. Aided by the massive resources at Harvard University's libraries, Leoni completed his work in 1948 as an alternative to the then-optional thesis; in 1961, he published his study as *Nostradamus: Life and Literature,* which was reprinted twenty-one years later as *Nostradamus and His Prophecies.*

Interest in Nostradamus has spanned the centuries primarily because the prophecies project far into the future and are open to countless interpretations, remarks Leoni in his introduction to *Nostradamus.* "The number of works on Nostradamus in the English language is second only to that in French, and they range in quality from the very impressive to the utterly ridiculous," he continues. "And yet, surprisingly, in the four hundred years since the prophecies were first published, there had been no *truly complete* translation, with even the minimum of scholarly precision that the term implies." Aiming, as he says in the introduction, "to fill the void and to provide a complete and definitive work," Leoni presents parallel text in English and the original French with explicatory notes, a series of indexes, historical background for the prophecies, biographical and bibliographical material on both Nostradamus and his commentators, plus a guide to extant criticism. He even includes Nostradamus's will and some letters. Calling the work "definitive" and praising its "meticulous scholarship," Crane Brinton, professor of history at Harvard University, wrote in the *American Historical Review* in 1962 that "Leoni has assembled almost all traces left by Nostradamus." Noting its obvious worth to historians, Brinton added that it also "makes surprisingly interesting reading."

"The prophecies that Nostradamus alleged extended to 3797 A.D. were published, with minor exceptions, between 1555 and 1568," Leoni explained to *CA.* "They consist of ten Centuries—collections of one hundred rhymed quatrains, or four-line verses—to which Nostradamus gave the collective name 'Milliade.' Due to various irregularities, though, there are somewhat less than one thousand verses. In addition to the 'Milliade' there are two long prose prefaces that include prophecies." Outside the focal Centuries collection, says Leoni, are 141 four-line verses, called the "Presages," collected from the almanacs Nostradamus published between 1555 and 1567, which his book offers in the same format as the quatrains. "Somewhat different in style from the quatrains," adds Leoni, "the verses of the 'Presages' each have a dating by year or month and year." Comparing Nostradamus to such diverse political figures as Karl Marx and Ronald Reagan, Leoni also told *CA* that "Nostradamus provides one of history's classic examples of a 'byword' reputation that persists in clear contradiction to [his having been proven] wrong about practically everything."

Although Leoni's scholarly work on Nostradamus has sold more than two hundred thousand copies in twenty printings, it has not generated the critical response, media attention, or bookstore presence of more recent translations, which Leoni believes borrow heavily from his own work. Remarking on this to *CA,* Leoni observed: "Never before has a definitive work on a subject of perennial interest to millions remained in such essential obscurity."

BIOGRAPHICAL/CRITICAL SOURCES:

BOOKS

Leoni, Edgar, *Nostradamus and His Prophecies,* Bell Publishing, 1982.

PERIODICALS

American Historical Review, July, 1962.

* * *

LESTER, Helen 1936-

PERSONAL: Born June 12, 1936, in Evanston, IL; daughter of William Howard (a businessman) and Elizabeth (Sargent) Doughty; married Robin Lester (a headmaster of a private school), August 26, 1967; children: Robin Debevoise, James Robinson. *Education:* Bennett Junior College, A.A.S., 1956; Wheelock College, B.S., 1959. *Religion:* Protestant. *Avocational interests:* Cooking, running, tennis, writing country and western songs.

ADDRESSES: Home—2230 Lincoln Park W., Chicago, IL 60614.

CAREER: Elementary school teacher in Lexington, MA, 1959-62; Francis W. Parker School, Chicago, IL, teacher of second grade, 1962-69; Hamlin School, San Francisco, CA, teacher of first grade, 1987-89; Francis W. Parker School, teacher, 1989—; writer. Volunteer worker in New York City soup kitchen.

AWARDS, HONORS: Colorado Children's Book Award, 1990, California Young Reader Medal, 1990-91, Nebraska Children's Book Award, 1990-91, all for *Tacky the Penguin.*

WRITINGS:

JUVENILES

Cora Copycat (self-illustrated), Dutton, 1979.
The Wizard, the Fairy, and the Magic Kitchen, Houghton, 1983.
It Wasn't My Fault, Houghton, 1985.
A Porcupine Named Fluffy, Houghton, 1986.
Pockins Gets Her Way, Houghton, 1987.

Tacky the Penguin, Houghton, 1988.
The Revenge of the Magic Chicken, Houghton, 1990.

WORK IN PROGRESS: Me First and *Three Cheers for Tacky,* both for Houghton; several short stories for a Scott, Foresman reading series.

SIDELIGHTS: Helen Lester told *CA:* "My books are written for the three-to-six-year-old age group. As a mother of young children I felt a need for more short but satisfying bedtime stories, and that need spurred me into writing. My stories are humorous approaches to a message (*The Wizard* involves cooperation; *It Wasn't My Fault* is about guilt and is written for the clumsy of the world). Life's pretty serious sometimes, and I feel the heavier concepts are better received if given a lighter touch.

"Although I illustrated my own first book, I now have a superb illustrator in Lynn Munsinger, who draws what I would if I could. Though we never need to confer, each of us is delighted with the other's work."

Lester adds: "Thanks to *Tacky the Penguin* I've recently had some excitement! *Tacky* won the 1990 Colorado Children's Book Award, the 1990-91 California Young Reader Medal, and the 1990-91 Nebraska Children's Book Award (the Golden Sower). The fact that the winner of these awards is the choice of the children of each state is especially gratifying."

BIOGRAPHICAL/CRITICAL SOURCES:

PERIODICALS

New York Times Book Review, April 6, 1986, p. 21.

* * *

LEVON, O. U.
See KESEY, Ken (Elton)

* * *

LEWIN, Hugh 1939-

PERSONAL: Born December 3, 1939, in Lydenburg, South Africa; son of William (a priest) and Muriel (a nurse; maiden name, Paynter) Lewin; married Patricia Davidson (a lawyer), September 24, 1972; children: Thandi, Tessa. *Education:* Rhodes University, B.A., 1960; University of South Africa, B.A., 1968, Diploma in Library Science, 1970.

ADDRESSES: Home—Box HG236, Highlands, Harare, Zimbabwe. *Office*—Friedrich Naumann Foundation, P.O. Box 1636, Harare, Zimbabwe.

CAREER: Drum, Johannesburg, South Africa, assistant editor, 1963-64; *Observer,* London, England, sub-editor,

1972-73; Nigerian Publications, London, 1974-75; *Guardian,* London, sub-editor, 1976-78; *South,* London, production editor, 1979-81; Friedrich Naumann Foundation, Harare, Zimbabwe, media training officer, 1981—.

WRITINGS:

Bandiet: Seven Years in a South African Prison, Barrie & Jenkins, 1974, Heinemann Educational Books, 1981.

(Editor with Don Rowlands) *Reporting Africa: A Manual for Reporters in Africa,* Thomson Foundation, 1985.

(Compiler) *A Community of Clowns: Testimonies of People in Urban Rural Mission,* WCC Publications (Switzerland), 1987.

CHILDREN'S BOOKS

Jafta, illustrated by Lisa Kopper, Evans Brothers, 1981, Carolrhoda, 1983.

Jafta: My Father, illustrated by Kopper, Evans Brothers, 1981, published in United States as *Jafta's Father,* Carolrhoda, 1983.

Jafta: My Mother, illustrated by Kopper, Evans Brothers, 1981, published in United States as *Jafta's Mother,* Carolrhoda, 1983.

Jafta: The Wedding, illustrated by Kopper, Evans Brothers, 1981, published in United States as *Jafta and the Wedding,* Carolrhoda, 1983.

Jafta: The Journey, illustrated by Kopper, Evans Brothers, 1983, Carolrhoda, 1984.

Jafta: The Town, illustrated by Kopper, Evans Brothers, 1983, Carolrhoda, 1984.

(With Tony Namata) *An African Elephant,* Zimbabwe Publishing House, 1984.

An Elephant Came to Swim, illustrated by Kopper, Hamish Hamilton, 1985.

"Second Chance" Series (includes *A Bamboo in the Wind, A Flower in the Forest, A Shell on the Beach,* and *A Well in the Desert*), illustrated by Kopper, Hamish Hamilton, 1989.

OTHER

Contributor to books, including *Apartheid: Calibrations of Color,* edited by Paul Weinburg, Rosen Publishing, 1991. Work represented in anthologies, including *Poets to the People,* Heinemann, 1980.

ADAPTATIONS: The "Jafta" books were adapted for the Public Broadcasting Service (PBS-TV) *Reading Rainbow* series, 1989.

SIDELIGHTS: Hugh Lewin presents a positive portrait of childhood in contemporary South Africa through his "Jafta" series. The picture books in the series focus on the daily life of Jafta, a lively little boy living in an unspecified village of South Africa. Originally intending to portray Jafta's father as a political prisoner, Lewin decided that

the complex subject of life under apartheid was too difficult for his selected audience. The illustrations, however, occasionally supply details not mentioned in the text, such as picturing Jafta's father working behind bars. Using simple, yet lyrical prose, Lewin describes Jafta's feelings about himself and his surroundings, and introduces children of other countries to an unfamiliar culture through his descriptions and use of regional terms. "This is the kind of depicting image children need of cultures other than their own," points out Gillian Klein in the *Times Educational Supplement.* "These are the kind of children's books of which there can never be enough—comprehensible yet enriching, widening horizons, enchanting and delighting."

Lewin spent his own childhood in South Africa, and began the "Jafta" series in an attempt to teach his daughters about his homeland. The son of an Anglican parish priest, Lewin originally intended to pursue the same career. While in college, though, he visited a destitute black community and found himself questioning the contradictory relationship between the laws of apartheid and his Christian beliefs. Soon after, he became an active member of the Liberal Party, and in 1962, he joined the National Committee for Liberation (N.C.L.), later renamed the African Resistance Movement. The nonviolent policy of the N.C.L., which called for shocking lawmakers into awareness without using physical force, appealed to Lewin, and he was involved in three subversive acts during his eighteen months with the group.

In 1964, Lewin was arrested and imprisoned when South African police made mass raids on Leftist sympathizers. Because he was a political prisoner, Lewin was considered inferior and received harsher treatment, but managed to earn degrees in both English and librarianship through correspondence courses. Released in 1971, he was given the choice to remain in South Africa under twenty-four hour house arrest, or to leave the country. Moving to London, Lewin remained politically active, worked as a journalist, and wrote his first book, *Bandiet: Seven Years in a South African Prison.* In 1981 he began the "Jafta" series, writing the first four books before moving to Zimbabwe. "I wrote *Bandiet* to give people some idea of the peculiarly nasty way in which political prisoners are treated in South Africa," explains Lewin. "My more recent children's books began as an attempt to explain to my English-born children something about life in Africa. Then I wanted to provide a broad picture of the South African experience for all children."

Interracial Books for Children Bulletin contributor Geraldine L. Wilson criticizes this approach. She maintains that Lewin should identify the society in which Jafta lives, and also sees him as failing to deal with the issue of apartheid and its effects on the inhabitants of South Africa. "If books about South Africa cannot reveal some of the realities of life there, perhaps they should not be done at all." Other critics, however, praise the "Jafta" series for introducing children to a new culture, and for including those experiences which are familiar to all children. "That which is different is clearly articulated and explained. . . . But there are also the common experiences," observes Klein. And Leila Berg writes in the *Times Educational Supplement* that throughout the series there is "a *flavour* of Africa, generalised and idealised, but setting the mind free to wander, to leap, and to reflect."

In the first book of the series, *Jafta,* the young title character expresses his feelings by relating them to the animals living around him. The subsequent books consist of Jafta's descriptions of other aspects of his life, including his mother, his father, his older sister's wedding, and a visit to the town in which his father works. The universal elements of childhood, such as bedtime stories and the teasing of younger siblings, are a part of Jafta's life, as are elements specific to South Africa, such as living in a one-room village house and having an absent father who must work in a distant town because of apartheid laws. "Knowing South Africa, I welcomed the images of the land so unerringly evoked on every page," comments Klein. "Between them, Hugh Lewin and Lisa Kopper have brought another continent within the grasp of . . . children's imaginations."

Lewin explains that the main thrust of the stories in the series "is to describe through the everyday experiences of a child something of his own African environment and what makes it different (e.g., indigenous birds and animals, local village activities and ceremonies, rural and town life in South Africa) as well as what is similar for any child anywhere (e.g., relationships with close family, emotions and responses, youthful enthusiasms and excitements). If the books explain the differences and enliven the similarities, I feel that they will have achieved something and will incidentally have helped diminish the dearth of decent material on black Africa."

BIOGRAPHICAL/CRITICAL SOURCES:

BOOKS

Chambers, Nancy, editor, *The Signal Review of Children's Books 2: A Selective Guide to Picture Books, Fiction, Plays, Poetry, Information Books Published during 1983,* Thimble Press, 1984, p. 54.
Children's Literature Review, Volume 9, Gale, 1985, pp. 89-92.

PERIODICALS

Booklist, November 1, 1984, p. 370.
Bulletin of the Center for Children's Books, May, 1983, p. 171; January, 1985.
Children's Book Review Service, April, 1983, p. 87.
Curriculum Review, February, 1984, p. 95.
Growing Point, July, 1981, p. 3909.
Interracial Books for Children Bulletin, Volume 15, numbers 7, 8, pp. 30-31.
Language Arts, September, 1983, pp. 771-72.
New Statesman, November 8, 1985, p. 25.
Publishers Weekly, February 4, 1983, p. 70.
School Librarian, December, 1981, p. 333; February, 1990, p. 15.
School Library Journal, May, 1983, p. 63; November, 1984, p. 112.
Times Educational Supplement, June 5, 1981, p. 37; October 2, 1981, pp. 20-21; March 12, 1982, p. 38.
Times Literary Supplement, October 25, 1985, p. 1218.*

*   *   *

LEYVA, Ricardo
See VALDES, Nelson P.

*   *   *

LIEBERSON, Stanley   1933-

PERSONAL: Born April 20, 1933, in Montreal, Quebec, Canada; son of Jack (a garment worker) and Ida (Cohen) Lieberson; married Patricia Beard, 1960; children: Rebecca, David, Miriam, Rachel. *Education:* Attended Brooklyn College (now Brooklyn College of the City University of New York), 1950-52; University of Chicago, M.A., 1958, Ph.D., 1960.

ADDRESSES: Home—5 Mystic Lake Dr., Arlington, MA 02174. *Office*—Department of Sociology, Harvard University, William James Hall #580, Cambridge, MA 02138.

CAREER: State University of Iowa, Iowa City, 1959-61, began as instructor, became professor of sociology; University of Wisconsin—Madison, assistant professor, 1961-63, associate professor, 1963-66, professor of sociology, 1966-67; University of Washington, Seattle, professor of sociology and director of Center for Demography and Ecology, 1967-71; University of Chicago, Chicago, IL, professor of sociology and associate director of Population Research and Training Center, 1971-74; University of Arizona, Tucson, professor of sociology, 1974-83; University of California, Berkeley, professor of sociology, 1983-88; Harvard University, Cambridge, MA, professor of sociology, 1988—, Abbott Lowell Lawrence Professor of Sociology, 1991—. University of Toronto, Claude Bissell Visiting Professor, 1979-80. Iowa Urban Community Research Center, associate director, 1959-61.

MEMBER: International Population Union, American Sociological Association, Population Association of America, Pacific Sociological Society.

WRITINGS:

(With others) *Metropolis and Region,* Johns Hopkins University Press, 1960.

Ethnic Patterns in American Cities, Free Press of Glencoe, 1963.

(Editor) *Explorations in Sociolinguistics,* Indiana University Press, 1967.

Language and Ethnic Relations in Canada, Wiley, 1970.

(With Beverly Duncan) *Metropolis and Region in Transition,* Sage Publications, 1970.

A Piece of the Pie: Blacks and White Immigrants since 1880, University of California Press, 1980.

Language Diversity and Language Contact, Stanford University Press, 1981.

Making It Count: The Improvement of Social Research and Theory, University of California Press, 1985.

(With Mary C. Waters) *From Many Strands: Ethnic and Racial Groups in Contemporary America* (monograph), Russell Sage, 1988.

*   *   *

LINDOP, Edmund 1925-

PERSONAL: Born August 31, 1925, in Chicago, IL; son of Edmund Frank (a realtor) and Sarah (Vaughn) Lindop; married Esther Crabtree (a writer and teacher), July 29, 1962; children: Laurie. *Education:* University of Southern California, B. A. (summa cum laude), 1947, M. A., 1950; additional study at National University of Mexico and University of California, Los Angeles. *Religion:* Methodist.

ADDRESSES: Home—920 Las Pulgas Rd., Pacific Palisades, CA 90272.

CAREER: Social studies teacher in Torrance, CA, 1948-49, and Los Angeles, CA, 1949-56; University High School, Los Angeles, history and government teacher, 1957-1986, chairman of social studies department, 1959-60, 1971-84; University of California, Los Angeles, training teacher, 1957-86.

MEMBER: PEN, National Council for the Social Studies, Phi Beta Kappa, Phi Delta Kappa, Chi Phi.

WRITINGS:

(With others) *Understanding Latin America,* Ginn & Co., 1960, revised edition, 1967.

Jumbo, King of Elephants, Little, Brown, 1960.

Hubert, the Traveling Hippopotamus, Little, Brown, 1961.

Life in Latin America, Ginn & Co., 1962.

Pelorus Jack, Dolphin Pilot, Little, Brown, 1964.

George Washington and the First Balloon Flight, Albert Whitman, 1964.

(With Joseph Jares) *White House Sportsmen,* Houghton, 1964.

War Eagle: The Story of a Civil War Mascot, Little, Brown, 1966.

The First Book of Elections, F. Watts, 1968, revised edition, 1972.

Modern America: The Dazzling Twenties, F. Watts, 1970.

Modern America: The Turbulent Thirties, F. Watts, 1970.

An Album of the Fifties, F. Watts, 1978.

Our Neighbors in Latin America, Ginn & Co., 1980.

Cuba, F. Watts, 1980.

Latin America, Ginn & Co., 1983.

All about Republicans, Enslow Publications, 1985.

(With Joy Thornton) *All about Democrats,* Enslow Publications, 1985.

Birth of the Constitution, Enslow Publications, 1987.

By a Single Vote! One-Vote Decisions that Changed American History, Stackpole Books, 1987.

The Bill of Rights and Landmark Cases, F. Watts, 1989.

(Contributor) *Geography: Our Changing World,* West, 1990.

Presidents by Accident, F. Watts, 1991.

Contributor to professional journals.

SIDELIGHTS: Edmund Lindop told *CA:* "Why is history the source for much of my writing? It is because I see the past as an exciting drama performed by colorful, intriguing people, whose adventures and accomplishments were far more fascinating than anything recorded in fiction.

"More than 1,016,000 copies of my books have been sold. I attribute their success primarily to my lengthy teaching experience that gave me the opportunity to learn how and what to write for young readers."

*   *   *

LIONNI, Leo(nard) 1910-

PERSONAL: Born May 5, 1910, in Amsterdam, Holland; came to United States, 1939; naturalized citizen, 1945; son of Louis and Elisabeth (a concert soprano; maiden name Grossouw) Lionni; married Nora Maffi, December, 1931; children: Louis, Paolo. *Education:* Attended schools in Holland, Belgium, United States, Italy, and Switzerland; University of Genoa, Ph.D. (economics), 1935. *Politics:* "Sometimes on the left—sometimes beyond." *Religion:* "None."

ADDRESSES: Home—New York, NY; and Porcignano, 53017 Radda in Chianti, Siena, Italy. *Agent*—Agenzia Letteraria Internazionale, Corso Matteotti 3, Milan, Italy.

CAREER: Free-lance writer, designer, and painter, 1930-39; N. W. Ayer & Sons, (advertising agency), Philadelphia, PA, art director, 1939-47; Olivetti Corporation of America, San Francisco, CA, design director, 1949-59; *Fortune* magazine, New York City, art director, 1949-62; Parsons School of Design, New York City, head of graphics design department, 1952-54; author and illustrator of children's books, 1959—. Has exhibited his paintings and sculpture at numerous individual and group shows in galleries, museums, and at universities throughout the U.S. and Europe. Individual shows include: Worcester Museum, MA, 1958; Philadelphia Art Alliance, 1959; Naviglio, Milan, 1963; Obelisco, Rome, 1964; Galleria dell'Ariete, Milan, 1966; Galleria del Milione, Milan, 1972; Linea 70, Verona, 1973; Il Vocolo, Genoa, 1973; Baukunst Galerie, Cologne, 1974; Klingspor Museum Offenback, 1974; and Galleria CIAK, Rome, 1975. Group shows include: Museum of Modern Art, New York City, 1954; Bratislava Biennale, 1967; and Venice Biennale, 1972.

MEMBER: Alliance Graphique Internationale, American Institute of Graphic Arts (president, 1956), Society of Typographic Arts (honorary member), Bund Deutscher Buchkunstler (honorary member), Authors League of America, Artists Equity.

AWARDS, HONORS: National Society of Art Directors Award, 1955; Architectural League Gold Medal, 1956; *New York Times* Best Illustrated award, 1959, for *Little Blue and Little Yellow;* Caldecott Honor Book, 1960, Lewis Carroll Shelf Award, 1962, and Children's Book Prize (Germany), 1963, all for *Inch by Inch; New York Times* Best Illustrated award, 1963, Caldecott Honor Book and American Library Association (ALA) Notable Book citation, both 1964, German Government Illustrated Book Award, 1965, and Bratislava Biennale Golden Apple, 1967, all for *Swimmy;* Spring Book Festival picture book honor, 1968, for *The Biggest House in the World; New York Times* Best Illustrated award, 1967, Caldecott Honor Book and ALA Notable Book citation, both 1968, all for *Frederick;* ALA Notable Book citation, 1970, for *Fish Is Fish;* Caldecott Honor Book, ALA Notable Book citation, and Christopher Book Award, all 1970, all for *Alexander and the Wind-Up Mouse;* five manor awards at Teheran Film Festival in 1970 for two animated films; elected to Art Directors Hall of Fame, 1974; George G. Stone Center for Children's Books Award for body of work, 1976; American Institute of Graphic Arts Gold Medal, 1984; Jane Addams Children's Book Award, 1988, for *Nicholas, Where Have You Been?.*

WRITINGS:

SELF-ILLUSTRATED WORKS FOR CHILDREN

Little Blue and Little Yellow, McDowell Obolensky, 1959.

Inch by Inch, Obolensky, 1960.
On My Beach There Are Many Pebbles, Obolensky, 1961.
Swimmy, Pantheon, 1963.
Tico and the Golden Wings, Pantheon, 1964.
Frederick, Pantheon, 1967.
The Alphabet Tree, Pantheon, 1968.
The Biggest House in the World, Pantheon, 1968.
Alexander and the Wind-Up Mouse, Pantheon, 1969.
Fish Is Fish, Pantheon, 1970.
Theodore and the Talking Mushroom, Pantheon, 1971.
The Greentail Mouse, Pantheon, 1973.
In the Rabbitgarden, Pantheon, 1975.
A Colour of His Own, Abelard, 1975, published as *A Color of His Own,* Pantheon, 1976.
Pezzettino, Pantheon, 1975.
A Flea Story: I Want to Stay Here! I Want to Go There!, Pantheon, 1977.
Geraldine, the Music Mouse, Pantheon, 1979.
Let's Make Rabbits: A Fable, Pantheon, 1982.
Cornelius, Pantheon, 1983.
Frederick's Fables: A Leo Lionni Treasury of Favorite Stories, introduction by Bruno Bettelheim, Pantheon, 1985, published in England as *Frederick's Tales,* Andersen Press, 1986.
It's Mine!, Pantheon, 1986.
Nicholas, Where Have You Been?, Pantheon, 1987.
Six Crows, Knopf, 1988.
Tillie and the Wall, Knopf, 1989.
Frederick and His Friends, Knopf, 1989.
Matthew's Dream, Knopf, 1991.

"PICTURES TO TALK ABOUT" SERIES

Who?, Pantheon, 1983.
What?, Pantheon, 1983.
Where?, Pantheon, 1983.
When?, Pantheon, 1983.

"COLORS, LETTERS, NUMBERS, AND WORDS TO TALK ABOUT" SERIES

Colors to Talk About, Pantheon, 1985.
Letters to Talk About, Pantheon, 1985.
Numbers to Talk About, Pantheon, 1985.
Words to Talk About, Pantheon, 1985.

OTHER

Design for the Printed Page, Fortune Magazine, 1960.
(And illustrator) *Il Taccuino di Leo Lionni* (title means "Leo Lionni's Notebook"), Electa (Milan), 1972.
La Botanica Parallela (essays), Adelphi (Milan), 1976, translated by Patrick Creagh as *Parallel Botany,* Knopf, 1977.
(Illustrator) Hannah Solomon, *Mouse Days: A Book of Seasons,* Pantheon, 1981.
(Illustrator) Naomi Lewis, *Come With Us,* Andersen Press, 1982.

Also illustrator of *Mouse Days Calendar 1981,* 1980. Contributor to *Fortune, Casabella, Domus, Print, Architecture Plus, Wilson Library Bulletin,* and *Horn Book.* Editor, *Print,* 1955-57, *Panorama* (Italy), 1964-65. All of Lionni's books have been translated into other languages.

ADAPTATIONS: Five Lionni Classics, based on Lionni's stories, was released on video cassette by Random House and was an award winner in the American Film and Video Festival in 1988.

SIDELIGHTS: Born into a creative family, Leo Lionni knew at an early age that he wanted to become an artist and spent much of his adolescence at the art museums of his native Amsterdam teaching himself to draw. And although his education did not include formal art classes, he did study throughout Europe before earning a doctorate in economics from the University of Genoa in 1935 and simultaneously establishing himself as a painter. Emigrating to the United States in 1939, Lionni became a naturalized citizen in 1945 and was soon recognized as a "dynamic talent in commercial design," notes Lesley S. Potts in the *Dictionary of Literary Biography.* A pioneer in the field of advertising art and design, Lionni also began exhibiting his paintings and sculpture internationally in individual and group shows; and, according to Potts, "Reviewers of his work described Lionni as a phenomenon, genuinely versatile, and one of the world's most original designers."

Lionni's career as an author and illustrator of children's books began by chance in the late 1950s. While travelling by train with his grandchildren, he improvised an entertaining story to pass the time and later worked the material into a book—*Little Blue and Little Yellow,* which has since become an acknowledged classic in children's literature. "Among the varied things I have done in my life few have given me more and greater satisfactions than my children's books," states Lionni in his essay, "My Books for Children" in *Authors and Illustrators of Children's Books.* Recognized as a master of art and design, Lionni has also succeeded in creating award-winning fables that focus on individuality, self-reliance, and esthetic values. "Artistically and thematically, Lionni's books have developed in ways that reflect his own childhood and its influences, as well as his life as a designer, artist, and thinker," writes Potts, adding that "Lionni's work is further characterized by a deep concern for quality. He believes that children must grow up with a sense of excellence and pride in workmanship."

Little Blue and Little Yellow is a tale about two blobs of color who happen to be close friends but become a single blob of green when they embrace each other too closely. Problems ensue when their parents no longer recognize them, but the story ends happily and the blobs are able to return to their original colors. "Illustrated entirely with torn-paper collage, a dramatically innovative technique for its day, the theme of the book is the unfairness of judging by appearances," writes Potts, who notes that critical reception of the book was "uniformly enthusiastic." Although some critics found the story to be social commentary on race relations, Lionni denies that this was his intent. However, Potts observes that "it was the first picture book to tell an allegorical tale about human problems and human situations using neither humans nor animals as its protagonists, but merely bits of torn paper distributed across the picture space in such a way as to denote specific actions, purposes, and emotions."

Lionni's next book for children, *Inch by Inch,* was a Caldecott Honor Book and received the Lewis Carroll Shelf Award and the German Children's Book Prize. It tells of a little caterpillar who escapes being eaten by various birds in a clever ploy that involves measuring their tails, necks, and legs for them. Although most birds, whatever their size, present little difficulty for the caterpillar, he must use greater ingenuity when the nightingale asks that his song be measured. "As the little green worm travels across the pages of this book, his ingenuity and that of the artist become more and more apparent," writes Linda Kauffman Peterson in *Newbery and Caldecott Medal and Honor Books.* Illustrated in crayon and textured collage, the book influenced other artists to use this medium, says Potts, who notes, however, that it "has seldom been equaled in the areas of collage design and technique." Potts relates that, according to Lionni, "*Inch by Inch* reflected his life in advertising. 'When I had to make a living, I had to survive and I really made a living telling people things that they didn't need to know. That's what the inchworm did and he managed, very cleverly, to survive.'"

"If *Inch by Inch* reflects Lionni's pragmatic period of survival in the world of advertising . . . ," suggests Potts, *Swimmy,* with its Marxist overtones, "mirrors his increasing involvement in politics." A Caldecott Award Honor Book and the first picture book by an American illustrator to win the Bratislava Biennale Golden Apple, *Swimmy* is about a little black fish whose family is eaten by a large, ravenous tuna. The sole survivor, Swimmy finds another school of fish and devises a scheme for their safety whereby they all swim in one enormous fish-shaped formation in which Swimmy is the eye. Critics praise the beautifully textured watercolor washes and prints that Lionni used to render the undersea world, as well as the text that accompanies the illustrations. "Though Lionni's text is simple and direct, the economy of words makes the illustrations highly important in extending and embellishing the story," observes Peterson. "The artist's inventive style remains a popular one within the realm of picture books, and the underlying themes have a relevancy that wears well with time."

In *Frederick,* which was also named a Caldecott Honor Book and is considered by many critics to be Lionni's best work, he uses what has since become almost a trademark—a mouse as the main character. In the book, a family of field mice gather food throughout the summer to sustain them during the coming winter. Frederick, on the other hand, spends his time enjoying the sunshine. When winter comes and the stored food is depleted, the other mice fear for their future, but Frederick entertains them with rhymes and stories about summer and gets the entire family through the remainder of winter. Like its predecessors, the story utilizes collage illustrations; and in its stressing of the importance of the artist to society, says Potts, it mirrors Lionni's own concerns at the time of its creation—his questioning of whether the artist's responsibility is to oneself or to one's society. Suggesting that *"Frederick* is one of the most autobiographical of Lionni's fables, going back to his early childhood development as an artist," Potts describes the story as "one of the progression from feelings to images and finally to words—an emergence into literacy—as he experiences the warmth of the sunlight and the colors of nature, then the poetic expression of all that he has felt and seen." Noting that each of Lionni's books is "unique, varied in artistic expression," George A. Woods states in the *New York Times Book Review,* "As Frederick's friends tell him, 'You are a poet'; so is Lionni—with a palette."

Another of Lionni's stories to feature a mouse is *Alexander and the Wind-Up Mouse,* a Caldecott Honor Book and recipient of the Christopher Book Award. Alexander is a mouse whose friend is a toy mechanical mouse named Willy, the favorite toy of the children in the house. Alexander envies the attention his friend receives and wishes that he, too, were mechanical. However, when Willy is broken and tossed into the trash, Alexander asks a magical lizard to make Willy into a real mouse instead. "Alexander's story illustrates the importance of remaining human, of thinking for oneself, and of the transforming power of love," writes Potts. And although Sada Fretz, in a *School Library Journal* review of the book, found that it "lacks the depth and resonance of Lionni's previous mouse fable, *Frederick,*" Mary Hobbs declares in the *Junior Bookshelf* that it "deserves to become a classic among picture books."

Lionni differs from many artists in that he has avoided the development of a consistent style; in "My Books for Children," he remarks that he finds "greater joy and satisfaction in developing a form for each idea." Potts believes that Lionni's books for children reflect his evolving attitude about art and the artist in society: *Little Blue and Little Yellow* expressed his belief that young children could

comprehend images devoid of detail; *Inch by Inch* presented his thoughts about his early career in advertising; *Swimmy* asserted his early political position that the artist must also be an activist; *Frederick* demonstrated his later belief that the artist contributes to society apart from any political considerations; and *Alexander and the Wind-Up Mouse* articulated the theme that is most important to him—the exercising of personal choice. Potts suggests that this theme "remains Lionni's prime area of concern in his books: 'It's no accident that exactly those books which pose basic problems of choice are my favorite books—*Inch by Inch; Swimmy; Frederick* and *Alexander.* They are the ones which, I find, say the most to me."

Lionni explains in "My Children's Books" that his "characters are humans in disguise and their little problems and situations are human problems, human situations." Continuing, Lionni says: "The protagonist of my books is often an individual who is, because of special circumstances, an outcast, a rebel, a victim, or a hero. His story ends happily because of his intelligence . . . , his vitality and resourcefulness . . . , his goodness . . . , or simply because his will and patience turn the laws of averages to his advantage. Often he has to learn through suffering . . . , but it is always his own vitality, his discovery that life is a positive, exciting fact, that makes him come out on top." And although critics occasionally wonder whether his themes are intended for children, Lionni holds that he is not aware of the age of his readers: "I believe, in fact, that a good children's book should appeal to all people who have not completely lost their original joy and wonder in life. . . . The fact is that I really don't make books for children at all. I make them for that part of us, of myself and of my friends, which has never changed, which is still child."

BIOGRAPHICAL/CRITICAL SOURCES:

BOOKS

Bader, Barbara, *American Picture Books from Noah's Ark to the Beast Within,* Macmillan, 1976, pp. 525-43.
Chevalier, Tracy, editor, *Twentieth-Century Children's Writers,* 3rd edition, St. James Press, 1989.
Children's Literature Review, Volume 7, Gale, 1984.
Dictionary of Literary Biography, Volume 61: *American Writers for Children since 1960: Poets, Illustrators, and Nonfiction Authors,* Gale, 1987, pp. 139-52.
Hoffman, Miriam, and Eva Samuels, editors, *Authors and Illustrators of Children's Books: Writers on Their Lives and Works,* Bowker, 1972, pp. 302-06.
Hopkins, Lee Bennett, *Books Are by People,* Citation Press, 1969.
Newbery and Caldecott Medal and Honor Books: An Annotated Bibliography, G. K. Hall, 1982, pp. 319-20, 326-27.

PERIODICALS

American Artist, April, 1953, p. 30.
Globe and Mail (Toronto), May 28, 1988.
Junior Bookshelf, December, 1971, p. 364.
Library Journal, March 15, 1964, p. 100.
Los Angeles Times Book Review, March 27, 1988; May 22, 1988.
New York Times Book Review, June 11, 1967, p. 32; May 29, 1983; December 22, 1985; September 20, 1987.
School Library Journal, May, 1970, p. 60.
Time, December 22, 1958, p. 53.
Times Literary Supplement, April 11, 1986.
Top of the News, October, 1962, pp. 65-67.
Tribune Books (Chicago), September 13, 1987.
Washington Post Book World, May 9, 1982.
Wilson Library Bulletin, October, 1964; May, 1970, pp. 947-50.*

—*Sketch by Sharon Malinowski*

*   *   *

LIU, Sarah   1943-

PERSONAL: Born December 14, 1943, in Shanghai, China; came to the United States in 1960, naturalized citizen, 1973; daughter of David (a missionary) and Mary (Feng) Lamb; married Kenneth Liu (a clergyman), August 14, 1965; children: Sharene Janelle. *Education:* Wheaton College, B.S., 1964; University of Dayton, M.S., 1979.

ADDRESSES: Home—1454 Roamont Dr., Centerville, OH 45459.

CAREER: Centerville City Schools, Centerville, OH, teacher, 1966—.

WRITINGS:

WITH MARY LOU VITTITOW

Games without Losers, Incentive Publications, 1975.
Creative Bible Activities for Children, Victor Books, 1977.
Every Day Is a Special Day, Incentive Publications, 1978.
Christians Celebrate, Christian Publications, 1981.
Learning Games without Losers, Incentive Publications, 1985.
Fun Things for Kids at Christmas Time, Standard Publications, 1991.

SIDELIGHTS: Sarah Liu once told *CA:* "All of my books include games and activities for school children to make learning more fun."

LOWIDSKI, Witt
See CLINTON, (Lloyd) D(eWitt)

*   *   *

LUBIN, Leonard
See LUBIN, Leonard B.

*   *   *

LUBIN, Leonard B.   1943-
(Leonard Lubin)

PERSONAL: Born November 27, 1943, in Detroit, MI; son of Arnold and Annette (Wexler) Lubin. *Education:* John Herron School of Art, diploma, 1965.

ADDRESSES: Home—367 6th St., Brooklyn, NY 11215. *Agent*—Dilys Evans, 1123 Broadway, New York, NY 10010.

CAREER: Artist, author, and illustrator of books. Worked variously as an antique shop owner, free-lance artist, window dresser, and bookstore salesman, 1965-75.

AWARDS, HONORS: Lewis Carroll Shelf Award and *New York Times* best-illustrated book of the year citation, both 1975, and Children's Book Council's Children's Book Showcase selection, 1976, all for *The Pig-Tale; The Little Swineherd, and Other Tales* was included in the American Institute of Graphic Arts Book Show and was a National Book Award finalist, both 1979; American Book Award for illustration, 1980, and *School Library Journal* best books of the year citation, 1981, both for *The Birthday of the Infanta.*

WRITINGS:

SELF-ILLUSTRATED CHILDREN'S BOOKS

(Reteller) Madame d'Aulnoy, *The White Cat,* Little, Brown 1978.
(Under name Leonard Lubin) *The Elegant Beast,* Viking, 1981.
(Reteller under name Leonard Lubin) *Aladdin and His Wonderful Lamp,* translation from the Arabic by Richard F. Burton, Delacorte, 1982.
This Little Pig: A Mother Goose Favorite, Lothrop, 1985.
Sing a Song of Sixpence: A Favorite Mother Goose Rhyme, Lothrop, 1987.
Christmas Gift-Bringers, Lothrop, 1989.

ILLUSTRATOR

Lewis Carroll, *The Pig-Tale,* Little, Brown, 1975.
Veronica S. Hutchinson, reteller, *Henny Penny,* Little, Brown, 1976.
Stephen Schwartz, *The Perfect Peach: A Story,* Little, Brown, 1977.

ILLUSTRATOR UNDER NAME LEONARD LUBIN

Paula Fox, *The Little Swineherd, and Other Tales,* Dutton, 1978.

Oscar Wilde, *The Birthday of the Infanta,* Viking, 1979.

W. S. Gilbert, *Gilbert without Sullivan* (libretti selection; contains *H.M.S. Pinafore, The Pirates of Penzance, The Mikado,* and *The Gondoliers*), Viking, 1981.

Isabelle Holland, *Kevin's Hat,* Lothrop 1984.

Jane Leslie Conly, *Racso and the Rats of NIMH,* Harper, 1986.

Diane Muldrow, editor, *My Little Book of Mother Goose Rhymes,* Western Publishing, 1989.

Conly, *RT, Margaret, and the Rats of NIMH,* Harper, 1990.

SIDELIGHTS: Leonard B. Lubin fills the pages of his own works and those of others with rich, luxuriant illustrations. In such works as *The Elegant Beast* and *Henny Penny,* he furnishes the pages with drawings of animals dressed in elaborately detailed and historically accurate costumes. By dressing his characters in such clothing and placing them in corresponding settings, Lubin is able to introduce children to a variety of other cultures and time periods. Marsha Miro maintains in the *Detroit Free Press* that "technically" Lubin's "illustrations are almost fanatically perfect—exquisitely drawn, beautifully colored, subtly modeled. There is a lush aesthetic beauty to the pictures that must stimulate and educate a child's eye."

Born in Detroit, Michigan, Lubin was the eldest of three children and began drawing at an early age. Even in grade school his art teachers, along with the librarian, were very encouraging, and his interest in illustration grew as he entered high school. "In my last three years of high school, Raymond De Vleeschouwer came to teach art. He was an artist, and it was fantastic to work with him," Lubin once recalled. At the same time, he was also involved in a Saturday morning art class sponsored by the Detroit Institute of Art. "We used the museum to get historical as well as artistic background. It taught us that we had to constantly reinterpret what we were seeing from the past in order to apply it to the present," wrote Lubin.

Despite a family conflict over his future career, Lubin began applying for art scholarships and won a full scholarship to John Herron School of Art in Indianapolis. "I had a hard time in art school," revealed Lubin. The city itself was a welcome change, but the school was far more conservative than he had expected. Because the faculty consisted of mainly Herron alumni there were ingrained methods of teaching which, along with the small town attitudes of the school itself, Lubin saw as stiflers of creativity. "The emphasis was on technique to the absurd extent that we would spend weeks learning the different grades of graphite—and even the methods of sharpening pen-

cils," he explained. "I felt this had nothing to do with art." Some of the other students at the school shared Lubin's views, and the challenges the experience presented eventually taught Lubin a lot about himself. "I might have learned faster at another school, but I don't have any regrets. In any case, most of what I do know about art, I've come by naturally," maintained Lubin.

Following graduation, Lubin began working in a friend's antique shop, eventually opening one of his own. He continued drawing and painting for private buyers, setting up an easel in the shop and working between customers, but soon found he wasn't being challenged. "Yet, all I was qualified to do was paint and draw. I had what was called a 'fine art' education, and hadn't learned the aspects of commercial art because I wanted no part of it," recounted Lubin. Working at the shop enabled Lubin to meet a number of new people, members of the Metropolitan Opera Company among them. Upon seeing his drawings, one of the costume designers encouraged him to come to New York, telling him the details in the drawings were so precise and accurate that she could make costumes from them. Lubin eventually did move to New York, and quickly discovered he could not rely on such "connections."

It wasn't until he arrived in New York City that the thought of doing children's books occurred to Lubin, and he didn't know where to start. He got a job in a display house where he stayed for a few years, working in the studio, the design area, and finally in a smaller studio where he did a lot of costume designing. Lubin's interest in costumes, particularly those from seventeenth and eighteenth century France, had originated in high school, where he learned about them from an art teacher and from a number of books. After leaving his studio job, Lubin designed window displays for a while before deciding to focus his energy toward breaking into the publishing industry. He took his portfolio around, but when nothing came of it he got a job at a Doubleday bookstore, hoping to move up to the art and editorial department. Lubin's first break came when he ran into an old friend who was working for Little, Brown and Houghton-Mifflin in Boston. After returning home from a short visit to Massachusetts, Lubin received a call from Little, Brown informing him they had work, and he was assigned the illustrations for Lewis Carroll's *The Pig-Tale.*

"I feel the reason I had trouble finding assignments in New York was because the publishers didn't know what to do with me," remarked Lubin. "Although they were enthusiastic about my work, they didn't know how to apply my particular talents to book illustration. In fact many of the books I have illustrated are not specifically children's books." *The Elegant Beast,* for example, is a history of costumes in which Lubin uses animal characters as his models. "I look at animals and I laugh and see people," Lubin once commented. "Though many of the expressions on animal faces are not human at all—they do *look* human. Many of the characters I created in the book were suggested by the costumes of each period. I just couldn't picture any other animal than the one I chose to draw in that costume. The attitudes and ambiance of each period, what went on back then, who they were, what they were doing, what they looked like, suggested definite animal counterparts." In a *School Library Journal* review of *The Elegant Beast* Patricia Dooley points out: "This original, opulent and witty book ought to enjoy a long run in the 'new books' rack before being consigned to the relative obscurity of the history-of-costume shelf. It will amuse and instruct anyone who is interested in that curious veneer called 'culture,' as much as it will the student of couture."

A number of Lubin's subsequent works have also centered around animals, so he has developed a method of dealing with the problems involved in bringing them to life. "You can't find reference material on a pig singing, but you can find pictures of pigs with their mouths open," he pointed out. "I combine a number of things and adapt my reference to the situation. I can get a sense of movement and how clothes might hang on an animal by looking at a person. I have a huge reference library of my own—books and books." Lubin's interest in books carries over into his free time too. Many of the books he enjoys, such as historical fiction and biographies, can also be used as references for his work, lending his drawings the historical authenticity for which they are known. "Sometimes too much imagination in illustration is just that: too much," explained Lubin. "Perhaps what I do is too literal sometimes. I do love detail, but I still feel there is enough left to the imagination so that kids can dream about what's in the picture. There's also enough going on in the illustrations for kids to be able to make up little stories of their own, as well as go back and find details they have missed."

BIOGRAPHICAL/CRITICAL SOURCES:

PERIODICALS

Children's Book Review Service, September, 1989, p. 8.
Detroit Free Press, December 9, 1990, p. 5G.
New York Times Book Review, April 26, 1981, p. 43; November 14, 1982.
Parents' Choice, spring, 1988, pp. 1-2.
Publishers Weekly, March 20, 1978, p. 68.
School Library Journal, May, 1978, p. 58; October, 1981, p. 152; February, 1983, p. 79.*

LUDWIG, Lyndell 1923-

PERSONAL: Born December 6, 1923, in Berkeley, CA; daughter of Albert Philip (a college professor) and Gladys (a child development teacher; maiden name, Newman) Ludwig. *Education:* University of Washington, Seattle, B.A., 1945; attended University of California, Berkeley, 1945-46, and California College of Arts and Crafts, 1948-56.

ADDRESSES: Home—Berkeley, CA. *Office*—15 Lenox Road, Kensington, CA 94707.

CAREER: University of California, Berkeley, secretary at Associated Students Store, 1947-64; researcher and writer, 1964—; founder and publisher, Star Dust Books, 1989—. Free-lance lettering and poster work, 1958-64.

AWARDS, HONORS: Ts'ao Chung Weighs an Elephant was a finalist at the Prix International du Livre pour Enfants, Geneva, Switzerland, 1987.

WRITINGS:

JUVENILE; SELF-ILLUSTRATED

Ts'ao Chung Weighs an Elephant, Creative Arts Book Co., 1983.
The Shoemaker's Gift (also see below), Creative Arts Book Co., 1983.
The Little White Dragon, Star Dust Books, 1989.

OTHER

An abridged version of *The Shoemaker's Gift* was included in the Harcourt Brace Jovanovich Reading Program Series.

WORK IN PROGRESS: Children's books, based on Chinese stories: *Ring a Bell to Catch a Thief; How the Rabbit Got His Long Ears; The Country Goose; One Can Always Find a Way to Do Anything; Why the Cock Crows When the Sun Comes Up; "Kerplunk"; The Tree, and the Foolish King.*

SIDELIGHTS: Lyndell Ludwig once told *CA:* "My father taught at Nan Kai School in Tientsin, China, from 1916 to 1918, and returned with a love for the Chinese people and their culture. Exposed to things Chinese from my earliest years, I, too, developed similar interests.

"I subscribe to several magazines and periodicals from mainland China which help me to understand present conditions there. Also, for the past several years I have been studying T'ang poems and ancient Chinese essays with a Chinese friend. Character by character, line by line, the ideas unfold, and I am continually impressed by the richness and beauty of the Chinese language."

Ludwig more recently added: "For many years now I have been working at interpreting and illustrating Chinese stories for children in English. Since I began studying Chinese many years ago as a student at the University of Washington in Seattle, and later in ordering books from Hong Kong and mainland China, I have been deeply impressed by the fascinating tales of this wonderful, ancient land. Much to my surprise I also came across many stories written in Chinese from Hans Christian Andersen, Charles Dickens, Mark Twain and other Western writers. But why were these Chinese tales not available in English for children in the West? So began a rewarding journey.

"Children are important! The world is changing and cultures are blending. Stories from China should become known and enjoyed in the West. As such they are enormously valuable by broadening the scope for growth and understanding. And, they are also fun to read."

*   *   *

LUNCH, Lydia 1959-
[A pseudonym]

PERSONAL: Born June 2, 1959, in Rochester, NY; daughter of Leonard L. and Lucy (Viccari) Koch.

ADDRESSES: P.O. Box 1085, Canal Street Station, New York, NY, 10013-1085.

CAREER: Actress, guitarist, songwriter, storyteller, and poet.

WRITINGS:

(With Exene Cervenka) *Adulterers Anonymous* (poetry collection), Grove, 1982.
(Contributor) Charles Neal, editor, *Tape Delay,* SAF Publishing, 1987.
(Author of introduction) *Visual Addiction* (survey of art by Robert Williams), Last Gasp, 1991.
Incriminating Evidence (stories, monologues, and a play), Last Gasp, 1992.
AS-FIX-E-8 (comic/stories), Last Gasp, 1992.
(Contributor) Andrea Juno and V. Vale, editors, *Angry Women,* Re/Search Publications, 1992.

Also author of the prose work *The Right Side of My Brain,* 1990, and the screenplay *Psychomenstruum,* 1990.

WORK IN PROGRESS: A collection of autobiographical writings, *My Father's Daughter.*

SIDELIGHTS: Writing in the *Village Voice Literary Supplement,* Jessica Hagedorn described the poetry in *Adulterers Anonymous* as "pure rock and roll, moving from page to page with a certain shallow urgency." Hagedorn praised Lydia Lunch's "sustained rage" and concluded that Lunch and co-author Exene Cervenka "work well together." The critic also noted that "these ladies obviously

had some fun with this book, in spite of their deliberate, black-on-black flirtation with a doomed and bankrupt landscape."

Lunch told *Contemporary Authors:* "I am besieged. Mediocrity, complacency, apathy, and rot refuse to leave me alone and force me to strike out artistically. I'm basically a confrontationalist. My job is not one of responsibility, but one to make people question how they feel, why they feel that way, and how they behave."

BIOGRAPHICAL/CRITICAL SOURCES:

PERIODICALS

Village Voice Literary Supplement, December, 1982.

*   *   *

LUNDBERG, Erik F(ilip) 1907-1987

PERSONAL: Born August 13, 1907, in Stockholm, Sweden; died September 14, 1987, in Saltsjoebaden, Sweden; son of Filip and Astrid (Stedt) Lundberg; married Gertrud Nebelung, March 28, 1937; children: Britta Lundberg Tschinkel, Klas, Gunnar. *Education:* Attended University of Chicago, 1931-32, and Columbia University, 1932-33; University of Stockholm, D.Phil., 1937. *Avocational interests:* Tennis, swimming, hiking.

ADDRESSES: Home—Syrenparken 13, S-13300 Saltsjoebaden, Sweden. *Office*—Skandinaviska Enskilda Banken, 10322 Stockholm, Sweden.

CAREER: Government Economic Research Institute, Stockholm, Sweden, director, 1937-55; University of Stockholm, Stockholm, professor of economics, 1946-65; Stockholm School of Economics, Stockholm, professor of economics, 1965-76, professor emeritus, 1976-87. Visiting professor at University of Washington, Seattle, 1950, and University of California, Berkeley, 1960-61; guest professor, Chinese University of Hong Kong, 1983. Head of World Bank Mission to Portugal, 1964; president of Royal Swedish Academy of Sciences, 1973-76; chairman of Nobel Committee for Economics, 1974-79. Member of State Power Board, Stockholm, 1946-87, and Swedish Government Planning Council, 1960-87. Member of board of directors, Fagersta Stell Co., 1948-68, and Dagens Nyheters Publishing Co., 1964-72. Economic advisor to government of Iceland, 1935, Central Bank of Australia, 1955-56, and government of Portugal, 1974-77; scientific advisor to Scandinavian Bank, 1955-87.

MEMBER: International Economic Association (president, 1969-79), Royal Swedish Academy of Sciences (president, 1973-76), American Economic Association.

AWARDS, HONORS: Arnberg Prize, 1946, and Soederstrom Prize, 1980, both from the Royal Swedish Academy of Sciences; Bernhard Harms Prize, Institut fuer Weltwirtschaft an der Universitaet Kiel, 1980; honorary Ph.D., University of Oslo, 1981.

WRITINGS:

Studies in the Theory of Economic Expansion, P. S. King & Son, 1937.

Konjunkturer och ekonomisk politik, 1953, translation published as *Business Cycles and Economic Policy,* Allen & Unwin, 1955.

Produktivitet och Raentabilitet (title means "Productivity and Profitability"), Norstedt, 1961.

Instability and Economic Growth, Yale University Press, 1968.

Svensk finanspolitik i teori och praktik (title means "Swedish Fiscal Policy in Theory and Practice"), Aldus/Bonnier, 1971.

(With Lars Calmfors) *Inflation och arbetsloeshet* (title means "Inflation and Unemployment"), Studiefoerbundet Naeringsliv och samhaelle, 1974.

(With Bengt Ryden) *Svensk ekonomisk politik: Laerdomar fran 70-talet,* Studiefoerbundet Naeringsliv och samhaelle, 1980.

Ekonomiska Kriser foer och nu (title means "Economic Crisis in Past Times and Now"), Studiefoerbundet Naeringsliv och samhaelle, 1983.

Kriserna & economerna, Liber, 1984.

Also author of *Wages in Sweden, 1860-1930,* 1933. Contributor to periodicals, including *Journal of Economic Literature.*

EDITOR

Richard Stone and others, *Income and Wealth: Series One,* Bowes & Bowes, 1951.

The Business Cycle in the Post-War World: Proceedings of a Conference Held by the International Economic Association, St. Martin's, 1955.

Ekonomisk politik i foervandling, Norstedt, 1970.

Inflation Theory and Anti-Inflation Policy: Proceedings of a Conference Held by the International Economic Association at Saltsjoebaden, Sweden, Westview, 1977.

(With Sven Grassman) *The World Economic Order: Past and Prospects,* St. Martin's, 1981.

WORK IN PROGRESS: Studies in Economic Instability and Change, for Studiefoerbundet Naeringsliv och samhaelle/Oxford University Press.

BIOGRAPHICAL/CRITICAL SOURCES:

BOOKS

Henriksson, Rolf G. H., editor, *Konjunkturinstitutet under Erik Lundbergs tid,* Konj Instituet, 1987.

Jonung, Lars, editor, *The Stockholm School Revised: Proceedings from a Symposium in 1987,* Studiefoerbundet Naeringsliv och samhaelle, 1987.

On Incomes Policy: Papers and Proceedings from a Conference in Honor of Erik Lundberg, Studiefoerbundet Naeringsliv och samhaelle/Industrial Council for Social and Economic Studies, 1969.

Seligman, Ben, *Main Currents in Modern Economics,* Macmillan, 1962.

[Sketch reviewed by wife, Gertrud Lundberg.]

M

MACE, Elizabeth Rhoda 1943-
(Louise Lawrence)

PERSONAL: Born June 5, 1943, in Leatherhead, England; daughter of Fred (a bricklayer) and Rhoda Edith (a cook; maiden name, Cowles) Holden; divorced first husband; married second husband, Graham Mace, 1987; children: (first marriage) Rachel Louise, Ralph Lawrence, Rebecca Jane. *Education:* Attended high school in Lydney, England. *Politics:* "Unaffiliated to, and critical of, all political systems." *Religion:* "Unaffiliated to, and critical of, all religious sects."

ADDRESSES: Home—22 Church Road, Cinderford, Gloucestershire GL14 2EA, England. *Agent*—A. M. Heath & Co., 40-42 William IV St., London WC2N 4DD, England.

CAREER: Gloucestershire County Library, Forest of Dean Branches, Gloucestershire, England, assistant librarian, 1961-63, 1969-71; writer, 1971—.

WRITINGS:

SCIENCE FICTION AND OCCULT NOVELS; UNDER PSEUDONYM LOUISE LAWRENCE

Andra, Collins, 1971.
The Power of Stars, Collins, 1972.
The Wyndcliffe, Collins, 1974.
Sing and Scatter Daisies, Harper, 1977.
Star Lord, Pocket Books, 1980.
Cat Call, Harper, 1980.
Earth Witch, Harper, 1981.
Calling B for Butterfly, Harper, 1982.
Dram Road, Harper, 1983.
Children of the Dust, Bodley Head, 1985.
Moonwind, Bodley Head, 1986.
The Warriors of Taan, Bodley Head, 1988.
Extinction Is Forever, Bodley Head, 1990.

Ben-Harran's Castle, Bodley Head, 1992.

SIDELIGHTS: Elizabeth Rhoda Mace, who writes under the pseudonym Louise Lawrence, once told *CA:* "What motivated me into writing my first (unpublished) book at the age of twenty-two was fear of mental stagnation. What gave rise to that fear was being married with small children, totally isolated socially and environmentally in a remote farmhouse, with a husband who had no time for me. I didn't choose to become a writer. An idea came to me and I felt compelled to set it down, and in six weeks I had written a very bad book.

"I wrote to occupy my mind, as a hobby, as a way of escaping from unhappy reality into worlds of fantasy. I wrote because I was compelled to write . . . and it got a hold on me like a drug.

"When I left my husband I wrote to survive and support my children. Writing was no longer an escape. It was a process of self-realization, an expression of experiences, and ideas come to me unsought. I think it is not I who write books, but books that make me write them. Perhaps I'm an open mind and things flow through me, are channeled through my fingertips and into words.

"I have viewpoints on many subjects, but I find my opinions constantly change. I suppose like all people I search for meaning and something to believe in. I ask questions that have no answers and want to know the purpose of human existence. My books are little inroads, blind alleys often, excursions I have made into vast subjects. To me they are important, and I guess one day I would like to write a book that is important to other people, too—because I care about the future of this earth and those who are born to live on it."

MAHY, Margaret 1936-

PERSONAL: Born March 21, 1936, in Whakatane, New Zealand; daughter of Frances George (a builder) and May (a teacher; maiden name, Penlington) Mahy; children: Penelope Helen, Bridget Frances. *Education:* University of New Zealand, B.A., 1958. *Politics:* "Anarchist." *Religion:* "Humanist." *Avocational interests:* Reading, gardening.

ADDRESSES: Home—R.D. 1, Lyttelton, New Zealand. *Agent*—Vanessa Hamilton, The Summer House, Woodend, West Stoke Chichester, West Suzzex PO18 9BP England.

CAREER: Writer. Petone Public Library, Petone, New Zealand, assistant librarian, 1958-59; School Library Service, Christchurch, New Zealand, librarian in charge, 1967-76; Canterbury Public Library, Christchurch, children's librarian, 1976-80. Writer in Residence, Canterbury University, 1984, and Western Australian College of Advanced Education, 1985.

MEMBER: New Zealand Library Association.

AWARDS, HONORS: Esther Glenn Medals, New Zealand Library Association, 1969, for *A Lion in the Meadow*, 1973, for *The First Margaret Mahy Story Book*, and 1983, for *The Haunting;* Een Zilveren Griffel, 1978; Best Children's Books of 1982 citation, and *School Library Journal* Best Book citation, both 1982, both for *The Haunting;* Carnegie Medals, British Library Association, 1982, for *The Haunting*, 1986, for *The Changeover: A Supernatural Romance*, and 1987 for *Memory;* 1984 Notable Children's Book citation, Association for Library Service to Children (ALSC), Children's Book of the Year citation, and Best Books for Young Adults award, American Library Association (ALA), all 1986, for *The Changeover;* Honor List citation, *Horn Book*, 1985, for *The Changeover*, and 1987, for *The Catalogue of the Universe; 17 Kings and 42 Elephants* was named one of the year's ten best illustrated books in 1987 by the *New York Times Book Review;* Best Books of 1987 citation, Young Adult Services Division (ALA), for *The Tricksters*, and Best Books of 1989 citation for *Memory;* Society of School Librarians International Book award (Language Arts, Science and Social Studies category), and *Boston Globe/Horn Book* award, both 1988, for *Memory;* May Hill Arbuthnot Lecturer, ALSC, 1989.

WRITINGS:

PICTURE BOOKS

A Lion in the Meadow (verse; also see below), illustrations by Jenny Williams, F. Watts, 1969, new edition, 1986.

A Dragon of an Ordinary Family, illustrations by Helen Oxenbury, F. Watts, 1969.

Pillycock's Shop, illustrations by Carol Barker, F. Watts, 1969.

The Procession, illustrations by Charles Mozley, F. Watts, 1969.

Mrs. Discombobulous, illustrations by Jan Brychta, F. Watts, 1969.

The Little Witch, illustrations by Mozely, F. Watts, 1970.

Sailor Jack and the 20 Orphans, illustrations by Robert Bartlett, Picture Puffin, 1970.

The Princess and the Clown, F. Watts, 1971.

The Railway Engine and the Hairy Brigands, Dent, 1972.

17 Kings and 42 Elephants (verse), Dent, 1972, 2nd edition edited by Phyllis J. Fogelman with illustrations by Patricia MacCarthy, Dial, 1987.

The Boy with Two Shadows, illustrations by Williams, F. Watts, 1972, Lippincott, 1989.

The Man Whose Mother was a Pirate, illustrations by Brian Froud, Atheneum, 1972, illustrations by Margaret Chamberlain, Viking Kestrel, 1986.

Rooms to Let, F. Watts, 1974, published in the United States as *Rooms to Rent.*

The Rare Spotted Birthday Party, F. Watts, 1974.

The Witch in the Cherry Tree, illustrations by Williams, Parents' Magazine Press, 1974, Dent, 1984.

Stepmother, F. Watts, 1974.

Ultra-Violet Catastrophe! Or, The Unexpected Walk with Great-Uncle Mangus Pringle, Parents' Magazine Press, 1975.

David's Witch Doctor, F. Watts, 1975.

The Wind between the Stars, Dent, 1976.

The Boy Who Was Followed Home, illustrations by Steven Kellogg, F. Watts, 1976.

Leaf Magic (also see below), Parents' Magazine Press, 1976.

Jam: A True Story, illustrations by Helen Craig, Little, Brown, 1986.

JUVENILE FICTION

The Great Millionaire Kidnap, illustrations by Brychta, Dent, 1975.

The Nonstop Nonsense Book, illustrations by Quentin Blake, Dent, 1977.

The Great Piratical Rumbustification, and The Librarian and the Robbers, illustrations by Blake, Dent, 1978.

The Birthday Burglar and A Very Wicked Headmistress, Dent, 1984, new edition with illustrations by Chamberlain, Godine, 1988.

The Adventures of a Kite, illustrations by David Cowe, Arnold-Wheaton, 1985.

Sophie's Singing Mother, illustrations by Jo Davies, Arnold-Wheaton, 1985.

The Earthquake, illustrations by Dianne Perham, Arnold-Wheaton, 1985.

The Cake, illustrations by Cowe, Arnold-Wheaton, 1985.

The Catten, illustrations by Davies, Arnold-Wheaton, 1985.

A Very Happy Bathday, illustrations by Elizabeth Fuller, Arnold-Wheaton, 1985.

Clever Hamburger, illustrations by Rodney McRae, Arnold-Wheaton, 1985.

My Wonderful Aunt (four volumes), illustrations by Dierdre Gardiner, Wright Group, 1986, revised edition in one volume, Children's Press, 1988.

When the King Rides By, Thornes, 1988.

Seven Chinese Brothers, illustrations by Jean and Mousien Tseng, Scholastic, 1990.

The Great White Man-Eating Shark: A Cautionary Tale, illustrations by Jonathan Allen, Dial Books for Young Readers, 1990.

Making Friends, illustrations by Wendy Smith, McElderry Books, 1990.

Keeping House, Macmillan, 1991.

Pumpkin Man and the Crafty Creeper, Greenwillow Books, 1991.

The Queen's Goat, illustrations by Emma Chichester Clark, Dial Books for Young Readers, 1991.

Also author of *Ups and Downs, Wibble Wobble, The Dragon's Birthday,* and *The Spider in the Shower,* all 1984; author of *Out in the Big Wild World,* 1985, *The Three Wishes,* 1986, and *How Mr. Rooster Didn't Get Married,* illustrations by Fuller, Arnold-Wheaton.

JUVENILE FICTION WITH JOY COWLEY AND JUNE MELSER

Roly-Poly, illustrations by Gardiner, Shortland (New Zealand), 1982, Arnold-Wheaton, 1985.

Cooking Pot, illustrations by Gardiner, Shortland, 1982, Arnold-Wheaton, 1985.

Fast and Funny, illustrations by Lynette Vondrusha, Shortland, 1982, Arnold-Wheaton, 1985.

Sing to the Moon, illustrations by Isabel Lowe, Shortland, 1982, Arnold-Wheaton, 1985.

Tiddalik, illustrations by Philip Webb, Shortland, 1982, Arnold-Wheaton, 1985.

JUNIOR NOVELS

Clancy's Cabin, illustrations by Trevor Stubley, Dent, 1974.

The Bus under the Leaves, illustrations by Margery Gill, Dent, 1974.

The Pirate Uncle, illustrations by Mary Dinsdale, Dent, 1977.

Raging Robots and Unruly Uncles, illustrations by Peter Stevenson, Dent, 1981.

The Pirates' Mixed-Up Voyage: Dark Doings in the Thousand Islands, illustrations by Chamberlain, Dent, 1983.

The Blood-and-Thunder Adventure on Hurricane Peak, illustrations by Smith, Dent, 1989.

Dangerous Spaces, Viking Children's Books, 1991.

YOUNG ADULT NOVELS

The Haunting (also see below), illustrations by Bruce Hogarth, Atheneum, 1982.

The Changeover: A Supernatural Romance, Atheneum, 1984.

The Catalogue of the Universe, Atheneum, 1985.

Aliens in the Family, Scholastic, 1986 (first hard-cover edition published in England by Methuen, 1986).

The Tricksters, Margaret McElderry Books, 1987.

Memory, Margaret McElderry Books, 1988.

FOR SCHOOLS; PUBLISHED BY SCHOOL PUBLICATIONS BRANCH, DEPARTMENT OF EDUCATION (WELLINGTON, NEW ZEALAND)

The Crocodile's Christmas Jandals, 1982.

The Bubbling Crocodile, 1983.

Mrs. Bubble's Baby, 1983.

Shopping with a Crocodile, 1983.

Going to the Beach, 1984.

The Great Grumbler and the Wonder Tree, 1984.

Fantail, Fantail, 1984.

A Crocodile in the Garden, 1985.

The Crocodile's Christmas Thongs, 1985.

Horrakopotchin, 1985.

THE "SUNSHINE SERIES"; PUBLISHED BY THE WRIGHT GROUP

Level 6: The Trouble with Heathrow [illustrations by McRae]; *The Pop Group* [illustrations by Madeline Beasley]; *Baby's Breakfast* [illustrations by McRae]; *The Man Who Enjoyed Grumbling,* illustrations by Wendy Hodder, 1986, revised edition, Heinemann Educational, 1987.

Level 7: Muppy's Ball [illustrations by Jan Vander Voo]; *The Garden Party* [illustrations by McRae]; *The Tree Doctor* [illustrations by Hodder]; *Feeling Funny,* illustrations by McRae, 1986, revised edition, Heinemann Educational, 1986.

Level 8: A Pet to the Vet, The King's Treasure, The New House Villain, The Funny Funny Clown Face, illustrations by Miranda Whitford, 1986, revised edition, Heinemann Educational, 1987.

Level 9: Tai Taylor is Born, [illustrations by Nick Price]; *Grow Up Sally Sue, Trouble on the Bus,* [illustrations by Hodder]; *Shuttle 4, Mr. Rumfitt,* [illustrations by Price]; *The Terrible Topsy-Turvy, Tissy-Tossy Tangle,* 1986, revised edition, Heinemann Educational, 1987.

Level 11: The Mad Puppet; Iris La Bonga and the Helpful Taxi Driver; The Haunting of Miss Cardamon; The Girl Who Washed in Moonlight; Elliott and the Cats Eating Out, 1987.

NONFICTION

New Zealand: Yesterday and Today, F. Watts, 1975.

Also author of *Look under 'V',* 1977.

COLLECTIONS

The First Margaret Mahy Story Book: Stories and Poems, Dent, 1972.
The Second Margaret Mahy Story Book: Stories and Poems, Dent, 1973.
The Third Margaret Mahy Story Book: Stories and Poems, illustrations by Shirley Hughes, Dent, 1975.
A Lion in the Meadow and Five Other Favorites, illustrations by Williams, Bartelt, Brychta, Mozley, and Froud, 1976.
The Chewing-Gum Rescue and Other Stories, illustrations by Jan Ormerod, Dent, 1982, Methuen, 1984.
Leaf Magic and Five other Favourites, illustrations by Chamberlain, Dent, 1984.
The Downhill Crocodile Whizz and Other Stories, illustrations by Ian Newsham, Dent, 1986.
Mahy Magic: A Collection of the Most Magical Stories from the Margaret Mahy Story Books, illustrations by Shirley Hughes, Dent, 1986.
The Door in the Air and Other Stories, illustrations by Diana Catchpole, Dent, 1988, Delacorte, 1991.
Chocolate Porridge and Other Stories, illustrations by Hughes, 1989.

Also author of *The Horrible Story and Others,* 1987.

OTHER

(Adaptor) *The Haunting of Barney Palmer* (screenplay based on *The Haunting*), [New Zealand], 1987.
The Tin Can Band and Other Poems, illustrations by Honey De Lacey, 1989.

Author of scripts "A Land Called Happy," "Wooly Valley," "Once upon a Story," and "The Margaret Mahy Story Book Theatre" for Television New Zealand, and scripts for the Gibson Group television series *Cuckooland.*

ADAPTATIONS: Cassette versions of Mahy's works include *The Haunting,* 1986, *The Chewing Gum Rescue and Other Stories,* 1988, and *The Pirate's Mixed-Up Voyage,* all read aloud by Richard Mitchley, and *Nonstop Nonsense,* read by Kenneth Stanley, all published by G. K. Hall.

SIDELIGHTS: Fantastical adventures that tell about how people get along in family life have made New Zealand author Margaret Mahy well-known around the world. In more than fifty separate titles since her first book *A Lion in the Meadow,* Mahy has written about a world full of unexpected possibilities, a world familiar to children, that she insists remains real for adults. Her younger characters help each other to learn about the world of adults; through

friendship tested by adventure, teens and preteens wounded by childhood experiences find healing. This healing helps them to continue their journeys into adulthood. Critics place Mahy's work, which appeals to readers of all ages, with the best in the field of young people's literature. Mahy "has deserved her reputation as queen of the light fantastic with stories and picture-book texts which erupt with delightful visions," states *Times Literary Supplement* critic Sarah Hayes. When writing about aliens with unusual powers, intelligent adolescents, or "a primeval New Zealand of immense rain-forests and sulphorous volcanoes, . . . she writes with all the force and precision and richness of a poet," Elizabeth Ward observes in the *Washington Post Book World.*

The first of many books concerned with the relationship between fantasy and reality, *A Lion in the Meadow* shows a mother in trouble because she refuses to take her son seriously when he relates a report that seems incredible to her. Annoyed by his warnings that there is a lion in the meadow, and thinking that he is playing an imaginative game with her, the busy mother gives the child a box of matches. Inside it, she says, is a little dragon that can grow large enough to scare the lion away. She soon regrets having lied to the child and vows not to lie to her children again. The fable illustrates that though fantasy is important to children, it is dangerous for adults not to recognize and teach the difference between fantasy and reality.

In addition to being valued for their themes, Mahy's books for children are popular and highly acclaimed because of her skills as a poet. The rhythmic verses in *17 Kings and 42 Elephants* such as "Watchers in the jungle, moist and mistilline, Bibble-bubble-babbled to the bing-bang-bong!" are as memorable as "The Congo" and other masterpieces by American poet Vachel Lindsay. The parade of kings, elephants, tigers, and other jungle animals winds from an un-named beginning to an un-named destination, making a journey that is enjoyable for its own sake, say the critics. The book's "language is a miraculous mixture of concision and freedom, joy and mystery, silliness and seriousness, all rolled into one," Arthur Yorinks comments in the *New York Times Book Review.*

More of Mahy's enjoyable wordplay is found in *The Birthday Burglar and A Very Wicked Headmistress.* Puns and alliterations of the letter B abound in this story of a rich but lonely man who steals birthday parties. Confronted with the family and friends of an elderly woman who intend to reclaim her stolen birthday party, he returns all the stolen birthdays and becomes a bee-keeper. Mahy's artistry as a wordsmith is most noticeable in her collected short stories, writes Mary M. Burns in *Horn Book.* The comic wordplay in *The Great Millionaire Kidnap* helps the plots along, says a reviewer for the *Spectator.* For instance, the two crooks who kidnap a kind rich man are named

Scarcely and Hardly Likely, and their mother's name is Pretty. In addition to Mahy's sense of humor, delightful comic names, and a matter-of-fact presentation of improbable sights such as a roller-skating alligator, "her wonderful sense of words and timing" make her one of the best short story writers writing today, a reviewer comments in a *Junior Bookshelf* review of *The Downhill Crocodile Whizz.*

The family relationships of young adults is the focus of Mahy's books for that age group. She uses characters of different age groups from a wide range of backgrounds to demonstrate this theme. New problems faced by teens everywhere are given special attention in each new book. The author also makes use of many different fictional techniques from fantasy to dramatic dialogue.

In *The Haunting,* a young man finds out he is in line to inherit psychic powers that he feels are a curse more than a blessing. Barney Palmer describes a sequence of mealtime family discussions and ties them together with explanations of his own thoughts and feelings. In the end, Barney needs the help of his older sisters to ward off a series of aunts and uncles who determine to make him accept his inheritance. Critics praise Mahy's ability to develop likeable characters and an ambitious theme within this framework. Barney and his family "are beautifully drawn, and perhaps because they care so much for each other, readers care for them, too," Michael Cart comments in *School Library Journal.* Hayes observes in the *Times Literary Supplement,* "*The Haunting* manages to combine a realistic approach to family life—in which how you feel about your parents and yourself is actually important—with a strong and terrifying line in fantasy."

"The book is in fact a powerful demonstration of the perils and rewards of imagination as it works through the Scholar family," Margery Fisher notes in *Growing Point.* Marcus Crouch, writing in a *Junior Bookshelf* review, feels that the book's strength "lies in the way Miss Mahy relates the fantasy to the relationships of ordinary life. The Scholars and the Palmers may be unusual but they are real people, and it matters greatly to the reader that the harmony of their lives should not be destroyed."

Aliens in the Family combines elements of science fiction and drama. The story begins with a broken family group made up of twelve-year-old Jake's father, stepmother, and a new brother and sister who do not accept her. When an alien from outer space appeals to them for help in his escape from his pursuers, the children become allies and friends through the process of problem-solving. Unexpected time-travel helps the group to find a new starting point from which they learn to define themselves by looking forward to common goals instead of hanging onto roles that defined them in the past. Penny Blubaugh sum-marizes in *Voice of Youth Advocates,* "Using Bond and Jake as aliens in their own situations, Mahy has written a story of families learning to accept and believe in each other in spite of, and even because of, their differences."

The Tricksters provides an insightful look at the inner lives of people who celebrate Christmas together at a New Zealand beach house. The Hamiltons share their celebration with their British friend Anthony. During his visit, the seven family members take turns telling him the story of the house and the family who built it (the Cardinals), each giving a new twist to the story of a boy who had died by drowning. Anthony suspects the legends he hears about the boy's death and the house are not completely factual. Helen J. Hinterberg remarks in the *Christian Science Monitor* that "Mahy creates an eerie atmosphere worthy of a classic gothic novel and suspense worthy of a first-rate thriller." The group's interactions become even more interesting with the arrival of three young men, the Cardinal brothers, who claim to be related to the family who built the house. The Hamiltons suspect something more sinister explains their visit. Perhaps they are ghosts, or the ghost of the drowned boy returned, incarnated in three different aspects of his personality. Seventeen-year-old Ariadne fears that she has called them into being by writing a romantic novel that she hides from the rest of the family. The Cardinal brothers' unnerving similarity to her characters helps to convince her that they are tricksters with harmful plans. "Just when it seems evil is going to win, Mahy throws in a surprising ending" which is tidy if not completely satisfying, Kristie A. Hart writes in a *Voice of Youth Advocates* review.

Keeping whimsy "just a step away," here Mahy also offers "the solidity of a robust and affectionate family, with its shared language, its traditional squabbles, accepted rivalries and secrets," Hayes sums up. Hayes also remarks that "the ability to combine a dazzling fantasy with painfully real emotions is a particular gift." According to Robin McKinley in the *New York Times Book Review,* Ariadne's thoughts in the novel express Mahy's theme that convincing storytellers have a dangerous skill. Critics recommend it to adult readers of contemporary fantasy as well as to young adults.

Dangerous Spaces presents one young woman's struggle to control her habit of trying to avoid life's difficulties by escaping to a private world inhabited by her great-uncle's ghost. Anthea's own parents have died suddenly and she lives with relatives whose complicated and noisy lives are no comfort to her. Soon she is retreating to the spacious dream-world Viridian every night, and her trips become so dangerous that her life is threatened. Compared to the dream-worlds in other books, Mahy's Viridian "is unique in its slow slide from . . . a place of beauty to one of menace and danger," writes Patricia Manning in the *School Library Journal.*

Down-to-earth Flora, the cousin who resents the glamorous Anthea at first, charges in to Viridian to rescue her and puts an end to the haunting that has plagued the family for generations. Descriptions of Viridian that are challenges at the book's beginning make more sense to the reader when Mahy brings the book to a memorable close. The skillful weaving of adventure with insights into family relationships for which Mahy is known rewards readers who finish the book, a *Publishers Weekly* reviewer comments.

Family relationships and their importance to young adults is just one of the author's major themes. Hayes writes in the *Times Literary Supplement,* "the double aspect of things—man and beast, [good] and evil, young and old—intrigues Margaret Mahy." *The Catalogue of the Universe* finds a balance between rational thinking and idealistic belief. The main characters are high school seniors working out the problems of identity common to that age group. Angela has lived without a father for many years, and feels that the blessings of beauty, a loving mother, and intelligence have not compensated for his absence. Tycho, her friend since early childhood, who is looking to science and astronomy to provide a rational basis for his life, helps Angela in her search for her missing father. When they encounter the lost parent, a disappointment leaves Angela to find out who she is apart from family ties.

"Angela and Tycho learn what they have suspected all along, that neither idealism nor rationalism [alone] is the key to coping with an existence that must be made up minute by minute," Colin Greenland notes in the *Times Literary Supplement.* Furthermore, their story shows that while forgiveness can help relationships to survive, it does not always change the imperfections of others, and it is difficult to forgive. Mahy's story makes these points without becoming pessimistic or sentimental. "Angela shares with her friend Tycho a fascination with matters like the square root of two and the moons of Jupiter which outlast emotional pains and the novel moves lightly," Gillian Wilce maintains in the *New Statesman.*

The Changeover: A Supernatural Romance, presents a fourteen-year-old girl's collaboration with adult witches who have told her that magic is the only way to save her three-year-old brother from death. The child's health had begun to fail at about the same time that Laura's divorced mother took a growing interest in a man she does not trust. Soon after, Laura becomes convinced that an evil warlock has cast a spell on her brother, and she determines to break the spell in a ritual that turns her into a witch. Set in contemporary New Zealand, the story copes realistically with Laura's feelings and "reconciles a num-

ber of disparate elements," says *Horn Book* reviewer Paul Heins, who relates that Mahy keeps the supernatural and realistic components of the story well-balanced.

Critics believe the supernatural elements in *The Changeover* are secondary to what it teaches about growing up in a threatening environment. "The author's insights into the jagged tensions of family life in contemporary New Zealand count for much more than her world of witches," Robert Dunbar remarks in the *School Librarian.* "In the manner of all good supernaturalists, [Mahy's] stories always have a perfectly possible rational explanation," Hayes observes in the *Times Literary Supplement.* "This one could be about the products of a young girl's fevered imagination during a period of physical and emotional turmoil; or about the influence of a boy traumatized by a cruel foster father and years of psychotherapy; or about a miracle cure, a single parent, and a dirty old man." The story of entrapment and rescue lends itself to many such interpretations. In addition, Laura's changeover coincides with her passage through puberty. Hayes concludes, "It is rare to find a novel which captures so well the changeover from child to adult, and from what is real in the mind to what is real outside."

Mahy compares the powers and limitations of magic and science in the well-received junior novel *The Blood-and-Thunder Adventure on Hurricane Peak.* Michael Dirda of the *Washington Post Book World* remarks, "In my book you can't beat a slapstick novel starring an evil industrialist, a beautiful scientist and a bumbling sorcerer, two talking cats, a supernatural forest and plot mixups right out of [Shakespeare's comedy] *A Midsummer Night's Dream.*" The threads of the entertainingly-tangled plot take as many unexpected turns as the book's roller-skating policemen. *Horn Book* reviewer Nancy Vasilakis added, "We are also the beneficiaries of some discerning Mahy wisdom regarding the truth of fairy tales and forests, enchanted or otherwise, as well as the meaning of the imagination and art and its application to science." *Times Literary Supplement* reviewer John Mole explains, "There is a romance between the acting principal of the school and the scientist Belladonna Doppler, in which the rival claims of magic and science argue their way towards a happy marriage." The scientist sums up near the end that though sorcery had brought them into the forest, they needed science to come back out.

Memory explores how the ability to remember can be both a curse and a blessing. Main character Jonny Dart blames himself for the accidental death of his sister, and the passage of five years has not helped to ease his sense of loss. For the old woman he lives with, however, a better memory would solve problems. Because she suffers from Alzheimer's disease, Sophie forgets where she is, wakes Jonny at night thinking he is someone else, and wears a tea cozy instead of a hat. These challenges bring Jonny's attention to present realities and help him to discover that he is kind-hearted.

Mahy wrote *Memory* while thinking of her own experiences with caring for the elderly. She explains in the May Hill Arbuthnot Lecture published in *Journal of Youth Services in Libraries,* "For a number of years I was in charge of my aunt, and though my aunt and Sophie are not the same person, they are similar in many ways. A lot of the happenings, a lot of the conversations, in *Memory* are directly transposed from life with my aunt, and if the story lacks the nastiness, the sheer fatigue of response involved in looking after a demented person, it is partly because, though these elements were present, they were not a commanding part of my life with [my] aunt."

Like her other books, *Memory* contains material that communicates to adults as well as to children. Doug Anderson sees "a well-defined political context" for the book. He writes in the *Times Literary Supplement,* "it is full of allusions to issues in contemporary New Zealand politics; Maori rights, the social complexities of a racially mixed nation, the disintegration of a traditional culture in the face of rampant commercialism (references that non-New Zealanders are unlikely to understand are carefully footnoted). Above all, Mahy raises the idea that anger at injustice is a good thing, something to be nurtured and focused."

Mahy's ability to combine themes relevant to young adults with fantasy is matched by her consistently non-sexist perspective on roles and relationships. Jan Dalley, writing in the *Times Literary Supplement,* points out that Mahy "continually pushes at the boundaries of [fairy-tale] conventions," and "roots out the sexism that used to be integral" to fiction for young readers. For example, though the roles of rescuer, leader, and problem-solver have been traditionally assigned to males, she gives these roles as often to females of various ages and levels of social status. In Mahy's books, the roles of home economist and nurturer, traditionally assigned to women, is also assigned to men. Growth to sexual maturity is equally exciting and frightening to her male and female adolescents. Adults of both sexes are equally subject to weakness and failure to discern the needs of their children. All her characters face the same challenges to strike a balance between freedom and commitment, reason and emotion. And they all benefit from recognizing the power of the imagination, which they learn to celebrate as well as to contain.

While many of her books explore the need to keep fantasy in its proper proportion to reality, Mahy indulges fantasy most freely in *The Door in the Air and Other Stories.* In "The Bridge Builder," for example, the main character creates bridges that double as bird cages, musical instruments, and aquariums. "Best of all are the quality and texture of her fantasy: vivid, dreamlike, seldom whimsical, with images that last," Dalley comments in the *Times Literary Supplement.* Keeping the collection in perspective as whimsy is the humorous story "A Work of Art," in which two young men exhibit a home-baked birthday cake as a sculpture in a local gallery. There, the fruitcake receives praise for its "passionate equilibrium." The presence of this story suggests that while *A Door in the Air* entertains readers of one age group, they also can be appreciated by older readers as a study of the purpose of art and art criticism.

In her work as a librarian, Mahy is called upon to distinguish works of fact from works of fiction by shelving them separately, as if imagined stories somehow do not contain elements of truth about life. Unlike the many fault lines that score the geography of her homeland, she believes the distinction is an imaginary rift. This "dislocation," as she calls it in her lecture, comes from the contrast between the British culture she learned from books and the tropical New Zealand environment in which she lived. The "imaginative truth" seemed to be more true than "the facts and images of my everyday life," she recalls. The celebration of Christmas, for example, which she has always observed in the sunny islands, is not complete for her without stories of England's snow drifts and holly. "The imaginative truth and the factual truth are at odds with one another but I still need those opposites to make Christmas come alive for me," she explains. She finds that the same kind of paradox applies to differences between make-believe and science. Pointing to changes in scientific theories about how the world began, she comments that what we think of as scientific fact sometimes proves to be wrong in the light of new discoveries, "and the truest thing in science is wonder just as it is in story. And I never forget that story is as important to human beings as science, more powerful at times because it is more subversive."

In her lecture, she says that one does not have to impose the truth onto children, because "they demand to be told. When a child writes and asks me 'Do you believe in supernatural things?' they may be asking me to confirm that a story like *The Haunting* is literally true. But mostly they are asking 'Just where am I to fit this story in my view of the world?' . . . Part of giving them the truest answer we can give also involves telling stories of desire: once there was a man who rode on a winged horse, once there was a boy who spoke to the animals, and the animals talked back to him, once there was a girl who grew so powerful that she was able not only to overcome her enemy but to overcome the base part of herself. Beware or the wolf will eat you and then you will become part of the wolf until something eats the wolf and so on. . . . It is a gamble because we cannot tell just what is going to happen in the individual head when the story gets there and starts working." Commenting on her own work, she sums up, "I have told the children all the truth I know from personal experience."

She concludes by explaining that what has always driven her to read and write is a fascination with what can be known through stories, a fascination that she believes has always been an important part of human nature. She emphasizes, "*The mere cadence of six syllables—A* Tale of Adventure—*instantly conjures up in the mind a jumbled and motley host of memories. Memories not only personal but we may well suspect racial; and not only racial but primeval. Ages before history had learned its letters, there being no letters to learn, ages before the children of men builded the city and the tower called Babel and their language was confounded, the rudiments of this kind of oral narrative must have begun to flourish. Indeed the greater part of even the largest of dictionaries, every page of the most comprehensive atlases consists of relics and records in the concisest shorthand from bygone chapters of the tale whereof we know neither the beginning nor the end—that of Man's supreme venture into the world without and into the world within.*"

BIOGRAPHICAL/CRITICAL SOURCES:

BOOKS

Children's Literature Review, Volume 7, Gale, 1984, pp. 176-188.
Mahy, Margaret, *17 Kings and 42 Elephants,* Dent, 1972, 2nd edition, Dial, 1987.
Mahy, Margaret, *The Door in the Air and Other Stories,* Dent, 1988, Delacorte, 1991.
Mahy, Margaret, *The Great Millionaire Kidnap,* Dent, 1975.

PERIODICALS

Christian Science Monitor, June 6, 1986, p. B6; November 4, 1988, p. B3; January 25, 1989, p. 13.
Fantasy Review, March, 1985, p. 27.
Growing Point, November, 1982, p. 3985.
Horn Book, November/December, 1984, p. 764; November/December, 1989, pp. 772-773; March, 1991, p. 201.
Journal of Youth Services in Libraries, summer, 1989, p. 313-329.
Junior Bookshelf, February, 1983, p. 45; August, 1986, pp. 144-145.
Listener, November 8, 1984, p. 27.
New Statesman, November 8, 1985, pp. 27-28.
New York Times Book Review, July 13, 1986, p. 22; May 17, 1987, pp. 31, 44; November 8, 1987, p. 40.
Publishers Weekly, February 1, 1991, p. 80.

School Librarian, September, 1984, p. 260; April, 1991, p. 121.
School Library Journal, August, 1982, p. 119; April, 1991, p. 98.
Spectator, December 6, 1975, p. 732.
Times Literary Supplement, September 17, 1982, p. 1001; July 13, 1984, p. 794; November 8, 1985, p. 1274; December 13, 1985, p. 1435; August 1, 1986, p. 850; October 9, 1987, p. 1120; October 30, 1987, p. 1205; November 25, 1988, p. 1323; April 7, 1989, p. 378.
Voice of Youth Advocates, April, 1987, p. 39; June, 1987, p. 80.
Washington Post Book World, October 12, 1986, p. 11; January 14, 1990, p. 10.

*　　*　　*

MAINE, Trevor
See CATHERALL, Arthur

*　　*　　*

MAITLAND, David J(ohnston) 1922-

PERSONAL: Born May 11, 1922, in Medford, MA; son of John Todd (a machinist) and Jane (a housewife; maiden name, Campbell) Maitland; married Elizabeth Burton Green (a housewife), September 1, 1945; children: Margaret Todd Maitland-Bachhuber, James Campbell. *Education:* Amherst College, B.A., 1943; Union Theological Seminary, New York, NY, M.Div., 1946; University of Wisconsin—Madison, M.S., 1953; Columbia University, Ph.D., 1959. *Politics:* Democrat.

ADDRESSES: Home—600 East First St., Northfield, MN 55057. *Office*—Department of Religion, Carleton College, Northfield, MN 55057.

CAREER: Ordained minister of United Church of Christ, 1946; University of Wisconsin—Madison, campus minister, 1946-52; Beloit College, Beloit, WI, chaplain and assistant professor of religion, 1952-54; Carleton College, Northfield, MN, chaplain, 1956—, associate professor, 1956-67, professor of religion, 1967-86, professor emeritus, 1986—.

WRITINGS:

Against the Grain: Coming through Mid-Life Crisis, Pilgrim Press (New York, NY), 1981.
Looking Both Ways: A Theology for Mid-Life, John Knox, 1985.
Aging: A Time for New Learning, John Knox, 1987.
Aging as Counter-Culture: A Vocation for the later Years, Pilgrim Press, 1991.

Contributor to *Religion and Aging,* edited by Mel Kimble, Fortress Press, 1992.

WORK IN PROGRESS: Ministry and Aging.

SIDELIGHTS: David J. Maitland told *CA:* "Both *Against the Grain* and *Looking Both Ways* were the result of efforts to make sense out of some of the disillusionments of my own middle years. They reflect the understandings of human development and Christian faith to which I came in the course of these struggles. In my present writing I am attempting to apply these understandings to life's last years.

"While the major crisis of mid-life is the gradual awareness of one's mortality, there are numerous losses that are intrinsic to that stage of life: of one's youthfulness, of no longer being the parent of small children, the death of peers, and especially, the death of parents. All of these have ramifications for a person's understanding of life. It is my intent to be intentionally aware of these realities and to discover what gains may be latent in the losses. A 'theology for mid-life' reflects my assumption that one's understanding of God is unavoidably influenced by such traumas.

"The premise of my work in progress is that, because of societal aversion to the inescapable reality of aging, there are very few images available that enable men and women to be positive about what is happening in their lives as they grow older. I wish to affirm—both for individuals and for the sake of the wisdom of which society is now largely deprived—the values latent in aging."

*   *   *

MAJOR, Kevin (Gerald) 1949-

PERSONAL: Born September 12, 1949, in Stephenville, Newfoundland, Canada; son of Edward (a fisherman and boiler-room worker) and Jessie (Headge) Major; married Anne Crawford (a librarian), July 3, 1982; children: Luke, Duncan. *Education:* Memorial University of Newfoundland, B.Sc., 1973. *Religion:* Anglican.

ADDRESSES: Home—Box 85, Eastport, Newfoundland, Canada A0G 1Z0. *Agent*—Nancy Colbert, 303 Davenport Rd., Toronto, Ontario, Canada M5R 1K5.

CAREER: Teacher, Roberts Arm, Newfoundland, 1971-72, and Carbonear, Newfoundland, 1973; Eastport Central High School, Eastport, Newfoundland, teacher of special education and biology, 1974-76; writer, 1976—. Substitute teacher, 1976—. Guest on television and radio programs.

MEMBER: Writers Union of Canada.

AWARDS, HONORS: Children's Literature Prize from Canada Council, Book-of-the-Year Award from Canadian Association of Children's Librarians, and Ruth Schwartz Children's Book Award from Ruth Schwartz Charitable Foundation and Ontario Arts Council, all 1979, all for *Hold Fast; Hold Fast* was also named to the Hans Christian Andersen Honor List by the International Board on Books for Young People, and to the *School Library Journal* list of Best Books of the Year, both 1980; *Far from Shore* received the Canadian Young Adult Book Award from the Young Adult Caucus of the Saskatchewan Library Association, and was named to the *School Library Journal* list of Best Books of the Year, both 1981.

WRITINGS:

YOUNG ADULT NOVELS

Hold Fast, Clarke, Irwin, 1978, Delacorte, 1980.
Far from Shore, Clarke, Irwin, 1980, Delacorte, 1981.
Thirty-six Exposures, Delacorte, 1984.
Dear Bruce Springsteen, Doubleday/Delacorte, 1987.
Blood Red Ochre, Doubleday/Delacorte, 1989.
Eating between the Lines, Doubleday, 1991.

OTHER

(Editor and contributor of illustrations) *Doryloads: Newfoundland Writings and Art,* Breawater Books, 1974.
(With James A. Tuck) *Terra Nova National Park: Human History Study,* Parks Canada, 1983.

Hold Fast has been translated into French, German, and Danish.

SIDELIGHTS: Kevin Major has been recognized as one of the most important figures in Canadian young adult literature. Often dealing with problems encountered by youth in the author's native province of Newfoundland, Major's novels are known for their frank treatment of profane language and sexuality—for which they have sometimes been banned from school libraries and curricula. "Sex and strong language play no greater or no lesser a part in my work than they do in real life," Major stated in *School Libraries in Canada.* "The truth is both are preoccupations of adolescents as is their family life, school, their relationships with their friends. So why the great fear?"

In an interview with Sherie Posesorski for *Books in Canada,* Major related his start in writing: "As a substitute teacher, I saw that young people were voraciously reading the new genre of American realistic young adult fiction by Judy Blume, Robert Cormier, and S. E. Hinton. . . . I saw that there were no comparable stories for a similar age group situated in Newfoundland, so I decided to write a story about young people growing up in the outports, dramatizing situations that would be relevant to their lives." Major's first novel, *Hold Fast,* won three of Canada's major awards for books for young people and was also named a Hans Christian Andersen honor book. The author once commented, "In *Hold Fast* I wanted to capture the Newfoundland way of life, its way of speaking and manner of dealing with people, and I wanted to convey some of my pride in our traditions—fishing, hunting, and the general closeness to nature."

However, such traditions are challenged by modern trends. Major told Posesorski that "Newfoundland society is in the midst of tremendous changes. The young are caught between the old traditional values of Newfoundland outport society and the onslaught of American popular culture." More generally commenting on situations encountered by youth, Major stated in *School Libraries in Canada* that "Adolescence is often a worrisome period of pressures—pressure to do well in school, to gain acceptance from friends, to cope with problems without the fund of experience that adults often take for granted."

After writing *Hold Fast,* Major produced several books that experimented with writing style. In an interview with *CA,* Major had declared: "One of the things I am interested in doing is trying to tell stories in different ways. I think a lot of books for young people are very similar in that they are told through the first person. There are not many chances taken in narrative form." *Far From Shore* uses five characters' points of view in depicting a family's disintegration and reunification. *Thirty-six Exposures,* a story about a high school student with interests in poetry and photography, employs a more radical narrative structure. "The story is episodic, at times to a fault (perhaps an attempt to unfold it like frames from a roll of film)," asserted *Booklist* reviewer Sally Estes. *Dear Bruce Springsteen* is an epistolary novel about a Newfoundland boy whose letters to the rock star of the title are a substitute for communication with his own absent father. Major deals with the European settlers' destruction of Native American tribes in *Blood Red Ochre,* in which narratives of a modern high school student and a nineteenth-century young man of the Beothuk tribe alternate until, mysteriously, the protagonists meet at a Beothuk burial ground. Major "continues to be one of our strongest and most technically innovative writers for young adults," asserts Sarah Ellis in an article for *Horn Book.*

Although the protagonists of Major's novels are young adults, in his interview with *CA* the author declared dissatisfaction with the way his works are categorized: "I've never really been content with the term 'young adult book,' which is usually how they're labeled, because it tends to place a limit on the readership, on the kind of audience the labelers think the books would appeal to. I'd like to think of them as being good novels to begin with,

to be enjoyed by readers of any age; and it does seem that a fair number of adults are reading the books and enjoying them."

For a previously published interview, see entry in *Contemporary Authors New Revision Series,* Gale, Volume 21, 1988, pp. 263-266.

BIOGRAPHICAL/CRITICAL SOURCES:

BOOKS

Children's Literature Review, Volume 11, Gale, 1986, pp. 123-133.
Contemporary Literary Criticism, Volume 26, Gale, 1983.
Dictionary of Literary Biography, Volume 60: *Canadian Writers since 1960, Second Series,* Gale, 1987.
Gallo, Donald R., editor and compiler, *Speaking for Ourselves,* National Council of Teachers of English, 1990, pp. 133-134.
Moss, John, *A Reader's Guide to the Canadian Novel,* McClelland & Stewart, 1981.
Twentieth-Century Children's Writers, 3rd edition, St. James Press, 1989, pp. 629-631.

PERIODICALS

Atlantic Insight, November, 1984.
Best Sellers, January, 1982.
Booklist, November 1, 1984, p. 361.
Books in Canada, December, 1980; December, 1984, pp. 24-25.
Canadian Children's Literature: A Journal of Criticism and Review, Number 14, 1979, pp. 81-83.
Children's Literature Association Quarterly, Fall, 1985, pp. 140-141.
Globe and Mail (Toronto), March 26, 1988; March 11, 1989.
Horn Book, September/October 1989, pp. 659-661.
In Review: Canadian Books for Children, summer, 1978; February, 1981.
Maclean's, December 17, 1979; December 15, 1980.
Ottawa Journal, June 19, 1979.
Quill and Quire, November, 1980; November, 1984.
Saturday Night, October, 1978.
School Libraries in Canada, spring, 1984, pp. 15-16.
Toronto Sun, June 29, 1978.
World of Children's Books, fall, 1978, pp. 56-59.*

*   *   *

MAKOWSKY, Veronica A(nn) 1954-

PERSONAL: Born November 29, 1954, in New Haven, CT; daughter of John S. (a U.S. Army Reserve administrator) and Olga (a steel company shipping clerk; maiden name, Popylisen) Makowsky; married Jeffrey C. Gross (a systems engineer for International Business Machines Co.), June 30, 1978. *Education:* Connecticut College, B.A. (summa cum laude), 1976; Princeton University, M.A., 1978, Ph.D., 1981.

ADDRESSES: Home—Baton Rouge, LA. *Office*—Department of English, Louisiana State University, Baton Rouge, LA 70803.

CAREER: Textual Center, Princeton, NJ, textual assistant for *The Writings of Henry D. Thoreau,* 1978-79; assistant for descriptive catalog of the papers of F. Scott Fitzgerald in Princeton, NJ, 1979-80; Middlebury College, Middlebury, VT, assistant professor of American literature, 1981-85; Louisiana State University, Baton Rouge, LA, assistant professor, 1985-89, associate professor of English, 1989—.

MEMBER: Modern Language Association of America, Society for the Study of Southern Literature, Phi Beta Kappa.

AWARDS, HONORS: National Endowment for the Humanities grant, 1979-80, fellowship, 1984-85; National Book Critics Circle Award nomination, 1980, for *Henry Adams;* Newberry fellowship, 1985; Louisiana State University summer grants, 1986, 1990; short fiction prize, *Southern Review.*

WRITINGS:

(Editor and author of introduction) R. P. Blackmur, *Henry Adams,* Harcourt, 1980.
(Editor and author of introduction) Blackmur, *Studies in Henry James,* New Directions, 1983.
Caroline Gordon: A Biography, Oxford University Press, 1989.
Susan Glaspell's Century of American Women, Oxford University Press, 1992.

Contributor to periodicals, including *Review, Southern Quarterly, Southern Review,* and *Princeton University Library Chronicle. Henry James Review,* associate editor, 1988-89, acting editor, 1989-90, co-editor, 1990-91.

WORK IN PROGRESS: A book on the writings of Varina Davis (Mrs. Jefferson Davis).

SIDELIGHTS: Veronica A. Makowsky told *CA:* "My general fields are women's biography and southern literature. In particular, I am interested in the dynamics of literary and historic couples, such as novelist Caroline Gordon and poet Allen Tate, playwright Susan Glaspell and Provincetown Players founder George Cram Cook, and letter writer and memoirist Varina Howell Davis and her husband, Confederate President Jefferson Davis. Are such partnerships fruitful or destructive, particularly for the women? Do power struggles predominate, or is mutual support more common? Do we need to revise our definitions of literature and success when we look at the career of a nineteenth-century woman like Varina Davis, who was not a conventional belles-lettriste? These questions are of particular interest today when so many women have careers; the interest is compounded when the issues are creativity and fame."

BIOGRAPHICAL/CRITICAL SOURCES:

PERIODICALS

Choice, October, 1989, p. 315.
Sewanee Review, October, 1989, p. 572.
Times Literary Supplement, November 17, 1989, p. 1260.

*   *   *

MANJON, Maite
  See MANJON DE READ, Maria Teresa

*   *   *

MANJON DE READ, Maria Teresa   1931-
  (Maite Manjon)

PERSONAL: Born November 11, 1931, in Madrid, Spain; daughter of Bruno (a businessman) and Maria (Alonso-Martin) Manjon-Capitan; married Jan Read (a writer), November 21, 1956; children: John Carlos. *Education:* University of Madrid, Practicante, 1953.

ADDRESSES: Home—1 Donaldson Gardens, St. Andrews, Fife KY16 9DH, Scotland. *Agent*—Curtis Brown Ltd., 162-168 Regent St., London W1R 5TA, England.

CAREER: Casa de Salud Valdecilla, Santander, Spain, nurse, 1954-56; medical interpreter for the British Council, 1956-73; Hispanic Council, London, England, librarian, 1973-82; writer and translator, 1982—.

WRITINGS:

UNDER NAME MAITE MANJON

(With Catherine O'Brien) *Spanish Cooking at Home and on Holiday,* Pan Books, 1973.
The Home Book of Portuguese Cookery, Faber, 1974.
(With husband, Jan Read) *Paradores of Spain,* Macmillan, 1977.
(With Read) *Flavours of Spain,* Cassell, 1978.
(With Read) *Visitors' Scotland,* Macmillan, 1979.
(With Read) *The Great British Breakfast,* M. Joseph, 1981.
(Translator) Lalo Grosso de Macpherson, *Cooking with Sherry,* Espasa-Calpe, 1983.
(With Read and Hugh Johnson) *Spanish Wine and Food,* Weidenfeld, 1986.
(Contributor) Read and Johnson, *Chilean Wine,* Sotheby, 1986.

Gastronomy of Spain and Portugal, Prentice-Hall, 1990.
(With Read) *Catalonia: Traditions, Places, Wine and Food,* Herbert Press, 1992.

Contributor to *Decanter* and *Journal of the International Wine and Food Society.*

SIDELIGHTS: Maria Teresa Manjon De Read told *CA:* "After taking a medical degree at the University of Madrid and working as a theater sister for a leading Spanish surgeon, I came to London to improve my English and to translate medical texts. Like many Spanish girls from my milieu, I had never learned to cook, but soon I developed a vivid interest in the subject. With encouragement from my husband, the writer Jan Read, I wrote the first of a number of books on Spanish cuisine. I have since collaborated with him on a series of books on travel and gastronomy and helped him, by interpreting, with notes on food and at tastings, with his books on Spanish, Portuguese, and Chilean wines."

＊　　＊　　＊

MANSUR, Ina　1910-1988

PERSONAL: Born January 5, 1910, in Peru, ME; died November 20, 1988; daughter of Marshall H. (a farmer) and Daisy M. (Conant) Babb; married Lawrence Cutler Mansur (a teacher and physicist), July 8, 1930. *Education:* Boston University, A.B., 1930. *Religion:* Unitarian-Universalist.

ADDRESSES: Home—320 Concord Rd., Bedford, MA 01730.

CAREER: Massachusetts Institute of Technology, Cambridge, member of radar research staff, 1941-45; U.S. Army Air Force, Cambridge, civilian microwave scientist, 1945-47; Town of Bedford, MA, town historian, 1975-88.

MEMBER: National Trust for Historical Preservation, Association for the Preservation of Technology, Society for the Preservation of New England Antiquities, New England Historical Genealogical Society, Maine Historical Society, Connecticut Society of Genealogists, Friends of Chesterwood.

WRITINGS:

A New England Church, 1730-1834, Cumberland Press, 1974.
(With husband Lawrence Mansur) *A Pictorial History of Bedford, Massachusetts, 1729 to Modern Times,* Modern Printing, 1992.

Columnist for weekly newspaper, *Bedford Minute-Man.* Contributor to periodicals.

WORK IN PROGRESS: Continuing research on the area around Bedford, MA.

SIDELIGHTS: Ina Mansur once told *CA:* "I wrote my book [*A New England Church, 1730-1834*] to answer the question of descendants, 'Why did my ancestors quarrel and divide our church into two congregations?' As town historian of Bedford, Massachusetts, I answer questions about this community's people, buildings, and events from 1729 to about 1920. I have traced the origins of buildings, the influence of families, and the growth of industry.

"From 1729, when Bedford became a town, until 1833 the local government was a theocracy. All of the taxpayers supported one church, the town's Congregational church. However, the members of the church had grown into two opposing religious philosophies.

"One part of the church believed in the emotional appeal of born-again Christianity, life after death, the constant supervision or companionship of divine power, and the trinitarian composition of that power. Members of this persuasion planned week-long revival meetings which were held in the town's meetinghouse. Religious persons who could not believe all of these tenets were outcasts. They were to be shunned. They enjoyed a dim future.

"The other part of the church rejected emotionalism and the trinitarian concept of divinity. Universalist lectures were being given in neighboring towns and a Universalist speaker was invited to Bedford. The message was the ability of every person to improve his own understanding, to develop whatever talent he had been given at birth, and to contribute in his own way to the community. If he could not believe that divine power was divided into three parts, he was free to believe what he would.

"The quarrel spread from religious tenets to the use of the town's meetinghouse by either of the church's parties, then to the principle of paying a minister out of tax funds while he condemned part of the inhabitants. The tension became legal, and at last the Trinitarians (as they wished to be known) erected a church for their own use; the Universalists (or Unitarians as they preferred to be called) retained the town's meetinghouse through a majority-vote of the inhabitants, and the town used a schoolhouse for its business.

"The separation of one church into two churches was an example of the beginning of protestant sectarianism in America. It occurred before some parts of this nation were settled. Pioneers in western areas of the United States, coming later, could base their religious life on denominations of their choice, services they had known before they traveled west. Freedom of choice in these matters still goes on today."＊

MARCUS, Mordecai 1925-

PERSONAL: Born January 18, 1925, in Elizabeth, NJ; son of Sidney (a bookdealer) and Mary (Swerdlow) Marcus; married Erin Jenean Gasper, June 3, 1955; children: Paul, Emily. *Education:* Brooklyn College (now Brooklyn College of the City University of New York), B.A., 1949; New York University, M.A., 1950; University of Kansas, Ph.D., 1958. *Politics:* Liberal Democrat. *Religion:* "Unaffiliated humanist."

ADDRESSES: Home—822 Mulder Dr., Lincoln, NE 68510. *Office*—Department of English, University of Nebraska, Lincoln, NE 68588-0333.

CAREER: University of Kansas, Lawrence, instructor in English, 1953-58; Purdue University, West Lafayette, IN, instructor, 1958-60, assistant professor of English, 1960-65; University of Nebraska, Lincoln, assistant professor, 1965-66, associate professor, 1966-72, professor of English, 1972—. Has given poetry readings at Hastings College, 1978, Wayne State College, 1979, and University of Nevada, Reno, 1979.

WRITINGS:

(Editor with Henry F. Salerno) *Cross-Section: Essays on Contemporary America,* Holt, 1963.
Five Minutes to Noon (poems), Best Cellar Press, 1971.
Return from the Desert (poems), Newedi Press, 1977.
Conversational Basketball (poems), Nebraska Review, 1980.
Talismans (chapbook of poems), Sparrow Press, 1981.
Emily Dickinson: Selected Poems (monograph), Cliff's Notes, 1982.
Restorations (poems), Ali Baba Press, 1984.
The Poems of Robert Frost: An Explication (critical study), G.K. Hall, 1991.

Also contributor to numerous books, including *The Red Badge of Courage: Text and Criticism,* edited by Richard Lettis, Robert F. McDonnell, and William E. Morris, Harcourt, 1960; *Stephen Crane's Career: Perspectives and Evaluations,* edited by Thomas A. Gullason, New York University Press, 1972; and *Bartleby, the Inscrutable,* edited by M. T. Inge, Archon Books, 1979. Contributor to anthologies, including *The Dimensions of Literature: A Critical Anthology,* edited by James E. Miller, Jr., and Bernice Slote, Dodd, 1967; *Borestone Mountain Poetry Awards: Best Poems of 1971,* Pacific Books, 1972; and *Seventy on the Seventies,* edited by R. McGovern, Ashland Poetry Press, 1981. Contributor of articles, poems, and book reviews to more than 170 periodicals, including *Christian Century, Journal of Aesthetics and Art Criticism, North American Review, Modern Fiction Studies, Poet and Critic, Shenandoah,* and *Literature and Psychology.*

WORK IN PROGRESS: Poems; studying the theme of love-and-death in literature for possible articles; studies in American and modern poetry.

BIOGRAPHICAL/CRITICAL SOURCES:

PERIODICALS

Nantucket Review, May, 1975.

*   *   *

MARLAND, Christina
See PEMBERTON, Margaret

*   *   *

MARSHALL, Edward
See MARSHALL, James (Edward)

*   *   *

MARSHALL, James (Edward) 1942-
(Edward Marshall)

PERSONAL: Born October 10, 1942, in San Antonio, TX; son of George E. (an insurance salesman) and Cecille (Harrison) Marshall. *Education:* Attended New England Conservatory of Music, 1960-61; Southern Connecticut State College, B.A., 1967; also attended Trinity College, 1967-68. "No art school (self-taught)."

ADDRESSES: Home—93 Mansfield Hollow Rd., Mansfield Center, CT 06250. *Agent*—Sheldon Fogelman, 10 East 40th St., New York, NY 10016.

CAREER: Cathedral High School, Boston, MA, French and Spanish teacher, 1968-70; free-lance writer and illustrator, 1970—.

AWARDS, HONORS: Several books selected to list of *New York Times* Outstanding Books of the Year, including *George and Martha,* 1972, and *Miss Nelson Is Missing!* and *A Summer in the South,* both 1977; several books selected to list of *New York Times* Ten Best Illustrated Books of the Year, including *George and Martha,* 1972, *George and Martha Encore,* 1973, and *The Tutti-Frutti Case: Starring the Four Doctors of Goodge,* 1975; *George and Martha* was selected as a Children's Book Showcase title of the Children's Book Council, 1973, as were *All the Way Home,* 1974, *The Stupids Step Out,* 1975, and *Bonzini! The Tattooed Man,* 1977; the American Institute of Graphic Arts Children's Book Show included *All the Way Home* and *The Piggy in the Puddle,* 1973-74, and *I Will Not Go to Market Today,* 1980; Academy Award nomination for best animated film from the Academy of Motion Picture Arts and Sciences, 1978, for movie adaptation of *It's So Nice to Have a Wolf around the House;* Edgar Allan Poe Award runner-up from the Mystery Writers of America, 1978, Georgia Children's Picture Storybook Award from the University of Georgia College of Education, 1980, Younger Reader Medal from the California Reading Association, 1982, and Buckeye Children's Book Award honor book citation from the State Library of Ohio, 1982, all for *Miss Nelson Is Missing!;* Children's Choice Award from the International Reading Association, 1979, for *The Stupids Have a Ball* and *George and Martha One Fine Day,* and 1982, for *The Stupids Die* and *There's a Party at Mona's Tonight; The Stupids Step Out* was included on *School Library Journal*'s "Best of the Best 1966-1978" list, 1979; *The Stupids Die* was chosen one of *School Library Journal*'s Best Books, 1981, and was runner-up for the Kentucky Bluegrass Award from Northern Kentucky University, 1983; Arizona Young Readers Award, 1981, for *Miss Nelson Is Missing!,* and 1985, for *The Stupids Die;* California Young Reader Medal, California Reading Association, 1982, for *Miss Nelson Is Missing!;* Golden Sower Award, University of Nebraska Center for Curriculum and Instruction, 1984, and Colorado Children's Book Award from the University of Colorado, 1985, both for *Miss Nelson is Back;* Parents' Choice Award for literature from the Parents' Choice Foundation, 1982, for *Miss Nelson is Back* and *Roger's Umbrella,* 1983, for *Rapscallion Jones;* Colorado Children's Book Award from the University of Colorado, Washington Children's Choice Picture Book Award from the Washington Library Media Association, and California Young Reader Medal from the California Reading Association, all 1983, all for *Space Case;* Golden Sower Award, University of Nebraska Center for Curriculum and Instruction, and Kentucky Bluegrass Award, second-place winner, 1987, both for *Miss Nelson Has a Field Day;* Caldecott honor book citation, American Library Association, 1989, for *Goldilocks and the Three Bears.*

WRITINGS:

SELF-ILLUSTRATED

What's the Matter with Carruthers?, Houghton, 1972.
Yummers!, Houghton, 1973.
Miss Dog's Christmas Treat, Houghton, 1973.
Willis, Houghton, 1974.
The Guest, Houghton, 1975.
Four Little Troubles (also see below), Volume I: *Eugene,* Volume II: *Someone Is Talking about Hortense,* Volume III: *Sing Out Irene,* Houghton, 1975.
Speedboat, Houghton, 1976.
A Summer in the South, Houghton, 1977.
(Selector) *James Marshall's Mother Goose,* Farrar, Straus, 1979.

Portly McSwine, Houghton, 1979.
(Under name Edward Marshall) *Troll Country* (Junior Literary Guild selection), Dial, 1980.
(Under name Edward Marshall) *Space Case* (Junior Literary Guild selection), Dial, 1980.
Taking Care of Carruthers, Houghton, 1981.
Rapscallion Jones, Viking, 1983.
The Cut-Ups, Viking, 1984.
Wings: A Tale of Two Chickens, Viking, 1986.
Yummers Too: The Second Course, Houghton, 1986.
Three Up a Tree, Dial, 1986.
Merry Christmas, Space Case, Dial, 1986.
(Reteller) *Red Riding Hood,* Dial, 1987, published as *Little Red Riding Hood,* Collins, 1987.
The Cut-Ups Cut Loose, Viking, 1987.
(Reteller) *Goldilocks and the Three Bears,* Dial, 1988, published as *Goldilocks,* Collins, 1988.
(Reteller) *Hey, Diddle, Diddle,* Heath, 1989.
My Friends the Frogs, Heath, 1989.
(Reteller) *The Three Little Pigs,* Dial, 1989.
The Cut-Ups at Camp Custer, Viking Kestrel, 1989.
The Cut-Ups Carry On, Viking, 1990.
(Reteller) *Hansel and Gretel,* Dial, 1990.
Rats on the Roof: And Other Stories, Dial, 1991.
Mother Hubbard & Her Wonderful Dog, Farrar, Straus, 1991.

"GEORGE AND MARTHA" SERIES; SELF-ILLUSTRATED

George and Martha (ALA Notable Book; *Horn Book* honor list), Houghton, 1972.
George and Martha Encore, Houghton, 1973.
George and Martha Rise and Shine, Houghton, 1976.
George and Martha One Fine Day, Houghton, 1978.
George and Martha, Tons of Fun, Houghton, 1980.
George and Martha Back in Town, Houghton, 1984.
George and Martha 'Round and 'Round, Houghton, 1988.

"THE STUPIDS" SERIES; SELF-ILLUSTRATED

(With Harry Allard) *The Stupids Step Out,* Houghton, 1974.
(With Allard) *The Stupids Have a Ball,* Houghton, 1978.
(With Allard) *The Stupids Die,* Houghton, 1981.
(With Allard) *The Stupids Take Off,* Houghton, 1989.

"FOX" SERIES; SELF-ILLUSTRATED

(Under name Edward Marshall) *Three by the Sea,* Dial, 1981.
(Under name Edward Marshall) *Fox and His Friends,* Dial, 1982.
(Under name Edward Marshall) *Fox in Love,* Dial, 1982.
(Under name Edward Marshall) *Fox on Wheels,* Dial, 1983.
(Under name Edward Marshall) *Fox at School,* Dial, 1983.

(Under name Edward Marshall) *Fox All Week*, Dial, 1984.

(Under name Edward Marshall) *Four on the Shore*, Dial, 1985.

Fox on the Job, Dial, 1988.

Fox Be Nimble, Dial, 1990.

ILLUSTRATOR

Byrd Baylor, *Plink, Plink, Plink*, Houghton, 1971.

Lore Segal, *All the Way Home*, Farrar, Straus, 1973.

Norma Klein, *Dinosaur's Housewarming Party* (Junior Literary Guild selection), Crown, 1974.

Charlotte Pomerantz, *The Piggy in the Puddle*, Macmillan, 1974.

Jakob Grimm and Wilhelm Grimm, *The Frog Prince*, retold by Edith H. Tarcov, Four Winds Press, 1974.

Harry Allard, *The Tutti-Frutti Case: Starring the Four Doctors of Goodge*, Prentice-Hall, 1975.

Russell Hoban, *Dinner at Alberta's* (ALA Notable Book; Junior Literary Guild selection), Crowell, 1975.

Cynthia Jameson, *A Day with Whisker Wickles*, Coward, 1975.

Jeffrey Allen, *Mary Alice, Operator Number 9*, Little, Brown, 1975.

Laurette Murdock, *Four Little Troubles*, Volume IV: *Snake—His Story*, Houghton, 1975.

Allen, *Bonzini! The Tattooed Man*, Little, Brown, 1976.

Diane Wolkstein, reteller, *Lazy Stories*, Seabury, 1976.

Allard, *It's So Nice to Have a Wolf around the House* (Junior Literary Guild selection), Doubleday, 1977.

Allard, *Miss Nelson Is Missing!*, Houghton, 1977.

Frank Asch, *MacGoose's Grocery*, Dial, 1978.

Jan Wahl, *Carrot Nose*, Farrar, Straus, 1978.

Allard, *I Will Not Go to Market Today* (Junior Literary Guild selection), Dial, 1979.

Allard, *Bumps in the Night*, Doubleday, 1979.

Jane Yolen, *How Beastly! A Menagerie of Nonsense Poems*, Philomel, 1980.

John McFarland, reteller, *The Exploding Frog: And Other Fables from Aesop*, Little, Brown, 1981.

Allard, *There's a Party at Mona's Tonight* (Junior Literary Guild selection), Doubleday, 1981.

Allard, *Miss Nelson Is Back*, Houghton, 1982.

Daniel Pinkwater, *Roger's Umbrella*, Dutton, 1982.

Allard, *Miss Nelson Has a Field Day*, Houghton, 1985.

Clement C. Moore, *The Night before Christmas*, Scholastic, 1985.

Allen, *Nosey Mrs. Rat* (*Horn Book* honor list), Viking, 1985.

Allen, *Mary Alice Returns*, Little, Brown, 1986.

Louis Phillips, *Haunted House Jokes*, Viking Kestrel, 1987.

Barbara Karlin, reteller, *Cinderella*, Little, Brown, 1989.

OTHER

(Contributor) *Once Upon a Time . . . : Celebrating the Magic of Children's Books in Honor of the Twentieth Anniversary of Reading Is Fundamental*, Putnam, 1986.

(With Richard Beach) *Teaching Literature in the Secondary School*, Harcourt, 1990.

Marshall's manuscripts are included in the Kerlan Collection of the University of Minnesota, the de Grummond Collection of the University of Southern Mississippi, the University of Oregon Library, and the University of Connecticut at Storrs.

ADAPTATIONS:

It's So Nice to Have a Wolf around the House (full-length television cartoon feature), Learning Corporation of America, 1978.

Miss Nelson Is Missing (motion picture), Learning Corporation of America, 1979, (filmstrip), Weston Woods, 1984.

Miss Nelson Is Back (TV segment; introduced by LaVar Burton and narrated by Ruth Buzzi), Reading Rainbow, PBS-TV, 1983.

Three by Sea, Reading Rainbow, PBS-TV, 1983 (follow the reader series; cassette with paperback book and teacher's guide), Listening Library, 1985.

The Night before Christmas (filmstrip with cassette), Listening Library, 1986.

I Will Not Go to Market Today (filmstrip with cassette), Random House, 1984.

Fox and His Friends (cassette), Random House, 1986.

Fox at School (cassette), Random House, 1986.

Fox in Love (cassette), Random House, 1986.

Fox on Wheels (cassette), Random House, 1986.

Miss Nelson Is Missing (cassette with paperback book), Houghton, 1987.

George and Martha (cassette with paperback book), Houghton, 1987.

Random House has released *James Marshall's Mother Goose* as a cassette, and the following titles as filmstrip with cassette: *George and Martha, George and Martha Encore, George and Martha Rise and Shine, George and Martha One Fine Day, The Stupids Step Out* (also available as read-along cassette), *The Stupids Have a Ball* (also available as read-along cassette), and *The Stupids Die* (also available as read-along cassette).

SIDELIGHTS: James Marshall, author and illustrator of several popular series of children's books, relied on books for entertainment while growing up on an isolated farm near San Antonio, Texas. His family later moved to Beaumont, Texas. "Beaumont is deep south and swampy and I hated it," the author declared in an interview with Rachel Koenig for *Something about the Author*. "I knew I would die if I stayed there, so I diligently studied the viola, and eventually won a scholarship to the New England Conservatory in Boston." Marshall earned praise there, but his music study was cut short by injury. "I flew out of my seat on a plane and injured my hand, but ignored the injury and continued to play," he explained. "As a result I developed a condition which forbad me to play more than twenty minutes a day. . . . Looking back, I think this turn of events was all for the good. It helped me realize something that had before been only subconscious. That is, I did not want to be a professional musician, and having the injury made it easier for me to stop."

Marshall then attended several colleges in Texas and Connecticut, eventually receiving a degree in French and history. He returned to Boston, where he taught French and Spanish at a private school. Not having studied Spanish previously, Marshall learned the language from Puerto Rican students in his Spanish class. While teaching, Marshall resumed his hobby of drawing, which he had abandoned in the second grade when a teacher laughed at his artwork. A friend who saw his sketches brought them to the attention of a neighbor who worked in publishing; the neighbor contacted the director of children's books at Houghton-Mifflin, and advised him of Marshall's skills. Marshall met with the director, and the next day was offered a contract to illustrate *Plink Plink Plink*.

A year later, Marshall wrote and illustrated *George and Martha*, the first book in a widely acclaimed series featuring a pair of hippopotamus friends. The author took the names of the protagonists from Edward Albee's play *Who's Afraid of Virginia Wolf?*, which was broadcast on television at the time that sketches for *George and Martha* were being made. However, "Albee's gladiatorial marriage partners are a far cry from the gently prankish hippo pals that Marshall describes as 'innocent, crafty and courtly' with 'exquisite manners and a sense of fun,' " asserted Leonard Marcus, who interviewed Marshall for *Publishers Weekly*. Marshall told Marcus about a dream in which his character Martha complained about the stories: "She had become very cross with me. She wanted better stories, better *lines*. And I distinctly remember her telling me that if she didn't get them she was going to a certain other illustrator's house. I woke up in a cold sweat!"

Marshall has also coauthored and illustrated a series of books about "the Stupids," described by Marcus as "a family of noodle-heads whose talent for getting backwards what every four-year-old can plainly understand is matched only by their boundless *joie de vivre*." The books

"satirize the antics of the nuclear American family in the mass media of the 1950's," wrote *Twentieth-Century Children's Writers* contributor Hugh T. Keenan, who also asserted that the stories of the Stupids "are calculated to amuse adults and children, though on different levels." A few critics have complained that "The Stupids" series derides stupid people. However, evaluating *The Stupids Step Out*, Nora L. Magid asserted in the *New York Times Book Review* that "these particular Stupids are so safe, snug and amiable in their context as to make the condition enviable."

Under the pseudonym Edward Marshall, the author began to produce his "Fox" books, which a *Bulletin of the Center for Children's Books* reviewer called "a justifiably popular easy-to-read series." As described by Keenan in *Dictionary of Literary Biography*, "Fox tries for the upper hand, but more often than not . . . is outfoxed by his younger sister Louise or by fate." Marshall related to Koenig his reason for using a pseudonym: "I wanted to do an easy-to-read book, but I was under an exclusive contract at a publishing house so I made up Edward, supposedly a cousin of mine from San Antonio. One day an editor called me and said, 'we're having so much trouble reaching your cousin to get publicity material, could *you* tell me something about him?' 'Well,' I said, 'It's very difficult for him living way out there near the crematorium with his eighteen children. . . .' I just spun a whole yarn about this so-called cousin, and before I knew it, it was printed in a publication."

Marshall's work as illustrator of Harry Allard's "Miss Nelson" series, about a nice teacher who disguises herself as a mean substitute in order to bring her class under control, has received attention from teachers as well as young readers. Referring to Miss Nelson's harsh alter ego, Marshall told Marcus that "all over America, teachers are dressing up as Viola Swamp." Marshall has also been involved with retellings of classic stories, such as *Little Red Riding Hood, Cinderella,* and *Goldilocks and the Three Bears*, which was named a Caldecott honor book in 1989.

Marshall told Koenig: "A book must have a good beginning and a strong middle, but without a knockout ending, you're shot. I've done books which featured wonderful characters, and some of the funniest lines I've ever written, but I blew the endings and they just don't work. You have to make a full circle because ending is emotionally satisfying. If not, everything valuable which precedes your bad ending will go out the window, no matter how hard you worked on it. I also teach that pacing is essential. You don't kill a story from page to page, you kill it by stalling. You have to make a book *move*, there always has to be a reason to turn the next page."

BIOGRAPHICAL/CRITICAL SOURCES:

BOOKS

Dictionary of Literary Biography, Volume 61: *American Writers for Children since 1960: Poets, Illustrators, and Nonfiction Authors,* Gale, 1987, pp. 189-199.
Keenan, *Twentieth-Century Children's Writers,* 3rd edition, St. James Press, 1989, pp. 637-639.
Something about the Author, Volume 51, Gale, 1988, pp. 109-121.

PERIODICALS

Bulletin of the Center for Children's Books, April, 1988, p. 161.
New York Times Book Review, May 5, 1974, p. 19.
Publishers Weekly, July 28, 1989, pp. 202-203.*

*   *   *

MARSHALL, Thomas Archibald   1938-
(Tom Marshall)

PERSONAL: Born April 9, 1938, in Niagara Falls, Ontario, Canada; son of Douglas Woodworth (a chemical engineer) and Helen (Kennedy) Marshall. *Education:* Queen's University, B.A., 1961, M.A., 1965.

ADDRESSES: Home—Kingston, Ontario, Canada. *Office*—Department of English, Queen's University, Kingston, Ontario, Canada.

CAREER: Queen's University, Kingston, Ontario, instructor, 1964-66, lecturer, 1966-69, assistant professor, 1969-73, associate professor, 1973-85, professor of English, 1985—.

WRITINGS:

ALL UNDER NAME TOM MARSHALL

(With Tom Eadie and Colin Norman) *The Beast with Three Backs* (poems), Quarry Press, 1965.
The Silences of Fire (poems), Macmillan, 1969.
The Psychic Mariner (critical study of poems by D. H. Lawrence), Viking, 1970.
A. M. Klein (criticism), Ryerson, 1970.
Magic Water (poems), Quarry Press, 1971.
(Editor with David Helwig) *Fourteen Stories High* (anthology), Oberon, 1971.
The Earth-Book (poems), Oberon, 1974.
The White City (poems), Oberon, 1976.
Rosemary Goal (novel), Oberon, 1978, HarperCollins, 1992.
Harsh and Lovely Land (critical study), University of British Columbia Press, 1979.
The Elements (poems), Oberon, 1980.
Dance of the Particles (poems), Quarry Press, 1984.

Playing with Fire (poems), Oberon, 1984.
Glass Houses (stories), Oberon, 1985.
Adele at the End of the Day (novel), Macmillan, 1987, Faber & Faber, 1988, Random House, 1990.
Voices on the Brink (novel), Macmillan, 1989.
Changelings (novel), Macmillan, 1991, McClelland & Stewart, 1992.
Ghost Safari (poems), Oberon, 1991.
Travelling Light (novella), Quarry Press, 1992.
Multiple Exposures, Promised Lands (critical essays), Quarry Press, 1992.

Former chief editor of *Quarry;* poetry editor of *Canadian Forum,* 1973-78; contributor to numerous anthologies.

ADAPTATIONS: With David Helwig, Gail Fox, and Stuart MacKinnon, Marshall has made a sound recording of his own work, *Four Kingston Poets,* Quarry Recordings, 1972.

WORK IN PROGRESS: A large historical novel.

SIDELIGHTS: Thomas Archibald Marshall told *CA:* "A poet attempts to make sense of the world, to discover what is real, for himself and others." He continues, "I am very concerned about Canada's national identity and the future of Canada, but more optimistic about it then some of my contemporaries seem to be. I am also interested in foreign countries and cultures, and enjoy travelling."

Describing Marshall's novel *Adele at the End of the Day* as "a bittersweet masterpiece quite unlike anything being written in Canada today," Thomas S. Woods of the Toronto *Globe and Mail* praises Marshall's poetic language as well as the book's "adroitly" constructed plot. Although Marshall is best known for his poetry and literary criticism, Woods states that *Adele at the End of the Day* "will confirm a permanent place for him at the head table of Canadian literati."

BIOGRAPHICAL/CRITICAL SOURCES:

PERIODICALS

Globe and Mail (Toronto), May 30, 1987.

*   *   *

MARSHALL, Tom
See MARSHALL, Thomas Archibald

*   *   *

MARSTEN, Richard
See HUNTER, Evan

MARTIN, Brian P(hilip) 1947-
(Rusticus)

PERSONAL: Born October 6, 1947, in Gosport, England; son of Albert (an innkeeper) and Ena (Petworth) Martin; married Carol Rose Payne, March 9, 1968; children: Spencer John, Ross Brian. *Education:* Attended grammar school in Gosport, England.

ADDRESSES: Home—4 Upper Birtley, Brook, Godalming, Surrey, England.

CAREER: National Health Service, Portsmouth, England, hospital administrator, 1964-77; *Shooting Times and Country Magazine,* Windsor, England, assistant editor and commissioning editor, 1977-91; free-lance writer, 1992—.

AWARDS, HONORS: Prix Litteraire, International Council for Game and Wildlife Conservation, 1986, for *Sporting Birds of the British Isles.*

WRITINGS:

Sporting Birds of the British Isles, David & Charles, 1984.
(With Rosemary Wadey) *Game Cook: From Field to Table,* Burlington Publishing, 1984.
The Great Shoots, David & Charles, 1986.
World Birds, Guinness, 1987.
British Gameshooting, Wildfowling and Roughshooting, Ward, Lock, 1987.
Tales of the Old Gamekeepers, David & Charles, 1989.
The Glorious Grouse, David & Charles, 1990.
Birds of Prey of the British Isles, David & Charles, 1992.
Tales of the Old Countrymen, David & Charles, 1992.

Author of column "Country Scene," under pseudonym Rusticus, in *Shooting Times and Country Magazine.* Contributor to magazines and newspapers.

WORK IN PROGRESS: Wildfowl of the British Isles and North-West Europe, a revised edition of *Sporting Birds of the British Isles,* and two other books.

*　　　*　　　*

MARTIN, Ged
See MARTIN, Gerald Warren

*　　　*　　　*

MARTIN, Gerald Warren 1945-
(Ged Martin)

PERSONAL: Born May 22, 1945, in Hornchurch, England; son of Percival Joseph Willing (a hospital administrator) and Edith Dorothy (Wheel) Martin. *Education:*

Magdalene College, Cambridge, B.A. (with first class honors), 1967, Ph.D., 1972.

ADDRESSES: Office—Centre of Canadian Studies, 21 George Square, University of Edinburgh, Edinburgh EH8 9LD, Scotland.

CAREER: Cambridge University, Magdalene College, Cambridge, England, Charles Kingsley Bye Fellow in History, 1969-70, research fellow, 1970-72; Australian National University, Canberra, Australia, research fellow in history, 1972-77; University College, Cork, Ireland, lecturer in modern history, 1977-83; University of Edinburgh, Centre of Canadian Studies, Edinburgh, Scotland, director, 1983—. Has made broadcasts in Great Britain, North America, and New Zealand.

MEMBER: Historical Association (England), Cambridge Historical Society, British Association for Canadian Studies (president, 1990-92).

AWARDS, HONORS: Riddell Prize, Ontario Historical Society, 1981; Canadian High Commissioner's Award for Contribution to British-Canadian Relations, 1989; Five Continents Award, International Council for Canadian Studies, 1990.

WRITINGS:

UNDER NAME GED MARTIN

Durham Report and British Policy: A Critical Essay, Cambridge University Press, 1972.
(With Ronald Hyam) *Reappraisals in British Imperial History,* Macmillan, 1975.
(Editor) *The Founding of Australia,* Hale & Iremonger, 1978.
Episodes of Old Canberra, Australian National University Press, 1978.
(With Jeffrey Simpson) *The Canadian Guide to Britain,* Volume 1, Macmillan, 1985.
Bunyip Aristocracy, Croom Helm, 1986.
(With Simpson) *Canada's Heritage in Scotland,* Dundurn Press, 1989.
(With Gillian Martin) *Waltzing Britannia: A Guide to Britain for Australians,* Hale & Iremonger, 1989.
History As Science or Literature: Explaining Canadian Confederation 1858-1867, Canadian High Commission (London), 1989.
(Editor) *The Causes of Canadian Confederation,* Acadiensis Press, 1990.

Contributor to *From Rebellion to Patriation: Canada and Britain in the Nineteenth and Twentieth Centuries,* edited by C. C. Eldridge, Lampeter, 1989; *The Origins of Australia's Capital Cities,* edited by Pamela Statham, Cambridge University Press, 1989; and *Imperialism and Its Legacy: Issues and Perspectives,* edited by Benjamin Kline and S.

Payne, University Press of America, 1990. Founding coeditor, *British Journal of Canadian Studies* and *British Review of New Zealand Studies;* contributor to *Albion, Australian Economic History Review, British Journal of Canadian Studies, Higher Education Review, Historical Journal, Irish Historical Studies, Journal of American Studies, Journal of Imperial and Commonwealth History, New Zealand Journal of History, Ontario History,* and *Times Higher Education Supplement.*

WORK IN PROGRESS: Research on British attitudes to constitutional development in British North America between 1837 and 1867 and on British imperial history; a biography of Sir Francis Bond Head.

BIOGRAPHICAL/CRITICAL SOURCES:

PERIODICALS

Globe and Mail (Toronto), May 25, 1985.
Times Literary Supplement, March 30, 1990, p. 336.

*   *   *

MARTIN, Kenneth R(obert)   1938-

PERSONAL: Born February 12, 1938, in Upper Darby, PA; son of Kenneth Edward (a chemist) and Evelyn (Rankin) Martin. *Education:* Dickinson College, A.B., 1959; University of Pennsylvania, M.A., 1961, Ph.D, 1965. *Avocational interests:* Travel, American primitive antiques and folk art, nautical painting and jazz.

ADDRESSES: Home—Days Ferry, ME. *Office*—P.O. Box 284, Woolwich, ME 04579.

CAREER: Gettysburg College, Gettysburg, PA, instructor, 1965-66, assistant professor of history, 1966-68; Slippery Rock State College, Slippery Rock, PA, associate professor of history, 1968-74; Kendall Whaling Museum, Sharon, MA, director, 1974-80; History Associates, Inc., Rockville, MD, senior historian, 1981-84; self-employed author, 1984—. *Military service:* U.S. Army Reserve, 1959-67; became first lieutenant.

MEMBER: American Folk Art Society.

AWARDS, HONORS: Hagley Foundation research grant-in-aid, 1972.

WRITINGS:

Delaware Goes Whaling, Eleutherian Mills-Hagley Foundation, 1974.
Whalemen and Whaleships of Maine, Harpswell Press, 1975.
"Naked and a Prisoner": Captain Edward Barnard's Journal of Shipwreck in Palau, Kendall Whaling Museum/Pacific Trust Territory, 1980.

Home Port: A History of the Navy Federal Credit Union, Dorrance, 1983.
Whalemen's Paintings and Drawings, Associated University Presses, 1983.
(With N. Lipfert) *Lobstering and the Maine Coast,* Maine Maritime Museum, 1985.
(With E. Reynolds) *"A Singleness of Purpose": The Skolfields and Their Ships,* Maine Maritime Museum, 1987.
(With R. L. Snow) *Maine Odyssey: Good Times and Hard Times in Bath,* Patten Free Library, 1988.
(Editor with Snow) *"I Am Now a Soldier!": The Civil War Diaries of Lorenzo Vanderhoef,* Patten Free Library, 1990.
(With Philip R. Thomas) *Competitiveness Through Total Cycle Time,* McGraw-Hill, 1990.
(With Thomas) *Getting Competitive,* McGraw-Hill, 1991.
"Some Very Handsome Work": Scrimshaw at the Cape Cod National Seashore, Eastern National Park & Monument Association, 1991.

Editor, Kendall Whaling Museum series, 1977-80. Contributor of articles and reviews to numerous periodicals, including *Mankind, Victorian Studies, Journal of Popular Culture, Pennsylvania History, Hawaiian Journal of History,* and *Technology and Culture.*

*   *   *

MASON, Herbert Warren, Jr.   1932-

PERSONAL: Born April 20, 1932, in Wilmington, DE; son of Herbert Warren (a paper manufacturer) and Mildred Jane (a paper manufacturer; maiden name, Noyes) Mason; married Mary Stauffer Grimley (a professor of English), September 11, 1954 (divorced); married Jeanine Young (a psychiatric nurse clinician), June 25, 1982; children: (first marriage) Cathleen, Paul, Sarah. *Education:* Harvard University, A.B., 1955, A.M., 1965, Ph.D., 1969. *Politics:* "Registered Democrat." *Religion:* Roman Catholic. *Avocational interests:* Travel (Europe, the Middle East, Turkey, Egypt, North Africa, Japan), sailing, walks, baseball, music (Bach to "soft" rock).

ADDRESSES: Home—The Common, Phillipston, MA 01331. *Office*—Department of University Professors, Boston University, 745 Commonwealth Ave., Boston, MA 02215.

CAREER: Wentworth Institute, Boston, MA, teacher of English, 1956-57; American School of Paris, Paris, France, teacher of English, 1959-60; St. Joseph's College, North Windham, ME, instructor in English, 1960-62; Simmons College, Boston, instructor in comparative literature, 1962-63; Tufts University, Medford, MA, visiting professor of Islamic history, 1966-67; Harvard University, Cambridge, MA, lecturer in Islamic history, 1967-68; worked as translator on series project for Bollingen Foundation, New York, 1968-72; Boston University, Boston, university professor of religion and Islamic history, 1972—. Member of faculty at University of Maine in Gorham, spring, 1962, and in Portland, summer, 1967; resident of Cummington Community for the Arts, autumn, 1978. Has given readings at colleges and universities all over the United States; conducted writing and translating workshops. Crew member on a schooner, 1950; semi-professional baseball player, summer, 1951; actor for summer theater, 1952; private detective, 1956. Member of board of trustees of Board of the Charity of Edward Hopkins; member of Boston Athenaeum.

MEMBER: International PEN, International Congress of Orientalists, Medieval Academy of America, American Oriental Society, American Academy of Religion, Society for Values in Higher Education (fellow).

AWARDS, HONORS: Award from Kittredge Fellowship, 1957, for play, "Empty Houses"; National Book Award nomination, 1971, for *Gilgamesh*.

WRITINGS:

(Editor) *Reflections on the Middle East Crisis*, Mouton, 1970.
(Author of adaptation) *Gilgamesh: A Verse Narrative*, Houghton, 1971.
Two Statesmen of Medieval Islam, Mouton, 1972.
The Death of al-Hallaj: A Dramatic Narrative (poem), University of Notre Dame Press, 1979.
Summer Light (novel), Farrar, Straus, 1980.
Moments in Passage (memoirs), Morning Star Press, 1980.
(Editor and translator) Louis Massignon, *The Passion of al-Hallaj*, four volumes, Princeton University Press, 1983.
A Legend of Alexander (narrative poems), Notre Dame University Press, 1987.
Memoir of a Friend: Louis Massignon, Notre Dame University Press, 1988. *Testimonies and Reflections* (essays), Notre Dame University Press, 1989.

Contributor of articles, stories, and poems to magazines, including *American Poetry Review, American Scholar, Psychology Today,* and *Sewanee Review.* Coeditor of *Humaniora Islamica,* 1973, 1974. *Gilgamesh: A Verse Narrative, The Death of al-Hallaj: A Dramatic Narrative,* and *Memoir of a Friend: Louis Massignon* have been translated into several languages, including French, Arabic, German, Urdu, and Japanese.

WORK IN PROGRESS: Where the Rivers Meet, a novel; a book on Islamic mysticism; a collection of new verse narratives.

SIDELIGHTS: Herbert Warren Mason, Jr.'s, novel *Summer Light* is described by Doris Grumbach in the *Washington Post Book World* as "a lovely, evocative [work], Chekovian in size and tone, and written with discreet charm and unusual taste."

BIOGRAPHICAL/CRITICAL SOURCES:

PERIODICALS

Washington Post Book World, June 15, 1980.

*   *   *

MASON, Philip (Parker)   1927-

PERSONAL: Born April 28, 1927, in Salem, MA; son of Homer Philip (an engineer) and Mildred (a nurse; maiden name, Trask) Mason; married Henrietta Dow, June 16, 1951 (divorced, 1991); children: Catherine, Susan, Steven, Jonathan, Christopher. *Education:* Boston University, B.A., 1950; University of Michigan, M.A., 1951, Ph.D., 1956. *Religion:* Unitarian Universalist.

ADDRESSES: Home—630 Merrick, #410, Detroit, MI 48202. *Office*—Walter P. Reuther Library, Wayne State University, Detroit, MI 48202.

CAREER: Michigan State Archives, Lansing, director, 1953-58; Wayne State University, Detroit, MI, professor of history, 1958-90, distinguished professor, 1990—, university archivist, 1958—, director of archives of labor history and urban affairs, 1959—. Detroit Historical Society, trustee and historian, 1963—. *Military service:* U.S. Naval Reserve, 1945-46.

MEMBER: American Historical Association, Organization of American Historians, American Association for State and Local History, Oral History Association, Society of American Archivists (executive secretary, 1963-68; president, 1970-71; fellow), Historical Society of Michigan (president, 1965-66), Prismatic Club.

WRITINGS:

(Editor) *Schoolcraft's Expedition to Lake Itasca: The Discovery of the Source of the Mississippi,* Michigan State University Press, 1958.
(With Paul J. Pentecost) *From Bull Run to Appomattox: Michigan's Role in the Civil War,* Wayne State University Press, 1961.
(Editor) *Schoolcraft: Literary Voyager or Muzzeniengun,* Michigan State University Press, 1962.
(With Frank B. Woodford) *Harper of Detroit: Origin and Growth of a Great Metropolitan Hospital,* Wayne State University Press, 1964.
Detroit, Fort Lernoult and the American Revolution, Wayne State University Press, 1964.
A History of American Roads, Rand McNally, 1967.

Prismatic of Detroit, Edwards Brothers, 1970.

The Ambassador Bridge: A Monument to Progress, Wayne State University Press, 1987.

Copper Country Journal, Wayne State University Press, 1991.

WORK IN PROGRESS: Grace Hospital of Detroit.

*   *   *

MAYER, Mercer 1943-

PERSONAL: Born in December 30, 1943, Little Rock, AR; married first wife, Marianna (divorced); married second wife, Jo; children: Len, Jessie. *Education:* Studied at the Honolulu Academy of Arts and the Art Students League. *Avocational interests:* Guitar playing, painting, walking in the woods, sitting by the river, and listening to opera.

ADDRESSES: Home—Bridgewater, CT.

CAREER: Author and illustrator of children's books. Has worked as an art director for an advertising agency.

AWARDS, HONORS: Citation of Merit, Society of Illustrators Annual National Exhibit, 1970, for *A Boy, A Dog, and A Frog,* 1975, for *What Do You Do with a Kangaroo?,* and 1976, for *Frog Goes to Dinner;* Children's Book Award, American Institute of Graphic Arts, 1971, for *A Special Trick;* Brooklyn Art Books for Children citation, 1973, for *A Boy, A Dog, and A Frog,* 1975, for *What Do You Do with a Kangaroo?,* and 1977, for *Frog Goes to Dinner;* International Books for Children Award, Association for Childhood Education, 1974, for *A Boy, A Dog, and A Frog;* Best Books of the Year citation, Child Study Association, 1974, for *You're the Scaredy-Cat;* Best Illustrated Books of the Year citation, *New York Times,* Ten Best Books citation, *Learning* magazine, and Irma Simonton Black Award, Bank Street College of Education, all 1977, all for *Everyone Knows What a Dragon Looks Like;* Brooklyn Art Books for Children Award, 1977, for *Frog Goes to Dinner;* Michigan Young Readers Award, 1982, for *Beauty and the Beast;* California Young Reader Medal, 1983, for *Liza Lou and the Yeller Belly Swamp.*

WRITINGS:

SELF-ILLUSTRATED

A Boy, a Dog, and a Frog, Dial, 1967.
There's a Nightmare in My Closet, Dial, 1968.
Terrible Troll, Dial, 1968.
If I Had. . . . Dial, 1968.
I Am a Hunter, Dial, 1969.
Frog, Where Are You?, 1969.
A Special Trick, Dial, 1970.

The Queen Always Wanted to Dance, Simon & Schuster, 1971.
A Silly Story, Parents' Magazine Press, 1972.
Frog on His Own, Dial 1973.
Bubble, Bubble, Parents' Magazine Press, 1973.
Mrs. Beggs and the Wizard, Parents' Magazine Press, 1973.
A Frog and a Friend, Golden Press, 1974.
What Do You Do with a Kangaroo?, Four Winds, 1974.
Two More Moral Tales (contains *Just a Pig at Heart* and *Sly Fox's Folly*), Four Winds, 1974.
Walk, Robot, Walk, Ginn, 1974.
You're the Scaredy-Cat, Parents' Magazine Press, 1974.
Frog Goes to Dinner, Dial, 1974.
Just for You, Golden Press, 1975.
The Great Cat Chase: A Wordless Book, Four Winds, 1975.
Professor Wormbog in Search of the Zipperump-a-Zoo, Golden Press, 1976.
Liza Lou and the Great Yeller Belly Swamp, Parents' Magazine Press, 1976.
Ah-Choo, Dial, 1976.
Four Frogs in a Box, Dial, 1976.
Hiccup, Dial, 1976.
There's a Nightmare in My Cupboard, Dent, 1976.
Just Me and My Dad, Western, 1977.
Oops, Dial, 1977.
Professor Wormbog's Gloomy Kerploppus: A Book of Great Smells, Western, 1977.
Mercer's Monsters, Western, 1977.
How the Trollusk Got His Hat, Western, 1979.
Herbert, the Knightly Dragon, Western, 1980.
East of the Sun and West of the Moon, Four Winds, 1980.
Professor Wormbog's Cut It, Glue It, Tape It, Do-It Book, Western, 1980.
Professor Wormbog's Crazy Cut-Ups, Western, 1980.
Herbert, the Timid Dragon, Western, 1980.
Play with Me, Golden Press, 1982.
The Sleeping Beauty, Macmillan, 1984.
Dr. Critter, Simon & Shuster, 1987.
Construction Critter, Simon & Shuster, 1987.
The Pied Piper of Hamlin, Macmillan, 1987.
What Do You Do with a Kangaroo?, Scholastic, 1987.
There's Something in My Attic, Dial, 1988.
When I Grow Up, Golden Books, 1991.
Thrills and Spills, Delmar, 1991.

"LITTLE MONSTER" SERIES

Little Monster's Word Book, Western, 1977.
Little Monster at Work, Western, 1978.
Little Monster's You-Can-Make-It Book, Western, 1978.
Little Monster's Bedtime Book, Western, 1978.
Little Monster's Counting Book, Western, 1978.
Little Monster's Neighborhood, Western, 1978.

Mercer Mayer's Little Monster's Library (set of six books), Western, 1978.

Little Monster's Mother Goose, Western, 1979.

Little Monster's Scratch and Sniff Mystery, Western, 1980.

"LITTLE CRITTER" SERIES

The New Baby, Golden Press, 1983.

When I Get Bigger, Golden Press, 1983.

I Was So Mad, Golden Press, 1983.

All By Myself, Golden Press, 1983.

Me Too!, Golden Press, 1983.

Just Grandma and Me, Golden Press, 1983.

Just a Snowy Day, Golden Press, 1983.

Just Me and My Puppy, Golden Books, 1985.

Just Grandpa and Me, Golden Books, 1985.

Just Go to Bed, Golden Books, 1985.

Just Me and My Babysitter, Golden Books, 1986.

Just Me and My Little Sister, Golden Books, 1986.

Astronaut Critter, Simon & Shuster, 1986.

Cowboy Critter, Simon & Shuster, 1986.

Fireman Critter, Simon & Shuster, 1986.

Policeman Critter, Simon & Shuster, 1986.

Sailor Critter, Simon & Shuster, 1987.

Just a Mess, Golden Books, 1987.

Baby Sister Says No!, Golden Books, 1987.

Little Critter's Little Sister's Birthday, Golden Books, 1988.

Little Critter's Picnic, Golden Books, 1988.

Staying Overnight, Golden Books, 1988.

This Is My House, Golden Books, 1988.

The Trip, Golden Books, 1988.

These Are My Pets, Golden Books, 1988.

Just My Friend and Me, Golden Books, 1988.

Happy Easter, Little Critter, Golden Books, 1988.

This Is My Friend, Golden Books, 1989.

Christmas Book, Golden Books, 1989.

Just a Daydream, Golden Books, 1989.

The Fussy Princess, Golden Books, 1989.

Play with Me, Golden Books, 1989

Just a Nap, Golden Books, 1989.

Just Camping Out, Golden Books, 1989.

Just a Rainy Day, Golden Books, 1990.

Just Me and My Mom, Golden Books, 1990.

Just Going to the Dentist, Golden Books, 1990.

This Is My School, Golden Books, 1990.

Two-Minute Little Critter Stories, Golden Books, 1990.

Little Critter at Scout Camp, Golden Books, 1991.

Just Me and My Little Brother, Golden Books, 1991.

WITH MARIANNA MAYER

Mine, Simon & Schuster, 1970.

A Boy, a Dog, a Frog, and a Friend, Dial, 1971.

Me and My Flying Machine, Parents' Magazine Press, 1971.

One Frog Too Many, Dial, 1975.

There's An Alligator under My Bed, Dial, 1987.

ILLUSTRATOR

John D. Fitzgerald, *The Great Brain,* Dial, 1967.

Liesel M. Skorpen, *Outside My Window,* Harper, 1968.

George Mendoza, *The Gillygoofang,* Dial, 1968.

Sidney Offit, *The Boy Who Made a Million,* St. Martin's, 1968.

G. Mendoza, *The Crack in the Wall, and Other Terribly Weird Tales,* Dial, 1968.

Sheila LaFarge, *Golden Butter,* Dial 1969.

J. D. Fitzgerald, *More Adventures of the Great Brian,* Dial, 1969.

Kathryn Hitte, *Boy, Was I Mad!.* Parents' Magazine Press, 1969.

Warren Fine, *The Mousechildren and the Famous Collector,* Harper, 1970.

Jean R. Larson, *Jack Tar,* M. Smith, 1970.

Barbara Wersba, *Let Me Fall before I Fly,* Atheneum, 1971.

Jane H. Yolen, *The Bird of Time,* Crowell, 1971.

Jan Wahl, *Margaret's Birthday,* Four Winds, 1971.

J. D. Fitzgerald, *Me and My Little Brain,* Dial, 1971.

Candida Palmer, *Kim Ann and the Yellow Machine,* Ginn, 1972.

Mildred Kantrowitz, *Good-Bye Kitchen,* Parents' Magazine Press, 1972.

J. Walh, *Grandmother Told Me,* Little, Brown 1972.

J. D. Fitzgerald, *The Great Brain at the Academy,* Dial, 1972.

Mabel Watts, *While the Horses Galloped to London,* Parents' Magazine Press, 1973.

J. D. Fitzgerald, *The Great Brain Reforms,* Dial, 1973.

B. Wersba, *Amanda Dreaming,* Atheneum, 1973.

J. D. Fitzgerald, *The Return of the Great Brain,* Dial, 1974.

J. D. Fitzgerald, *The Great Brain Does It Again,* Dial, 1975.

John Bellairs, *The Figure in the Shadows,* Dial, 1975.

Jay Williams, *Everyone Knows What a Dragon Looks Like,* Four Winds, 1976.

J. Williams, *The Reward Worth Having,* Four Winds, 1977.

M. Mayer, reteller, *Beauty and the Beast,* Four Winds, 1978.

Nancy Garden, reteller, *Favorite Tales from Grimm,* Four Winds, 1982.

OTHER

(Editor) *The Poison Tree and Other Poems,* Scribner, 1977.

Appelard and Liverwurst, illustrated by Steven Kellogg, Four Winds, 1978.

Liverwurst Is Missing, illustrated by S. Kellogg, Four Winds, 1982.

Whinnie the Lovesick Dragon, illustrated by Diane Dawson Hearne, Macmillan, 1986.

(Reteller) Charles Dickens, *A Christmas Carol: Being a Ghost Story of Christmas,* Macmillan, 1986.

Also author of *Tiny Tink! Tonk! Tales,* 1984, and *Zoomer Builds a Racing Car,* 1985.

SIDELIGHTS: Popular children's author Mercer Mayer is well-known for his versatility, humor, and artistic skill. Noted as one of the first creators of wordless picture books, Mayer also writes and illustrates nonsense fiction, fantasy, and folktales. In both his writing and illustrating, Mayer emphasizes the unconventional; his language can be simple or sophisticated, while his illustrations run the gamut of artistic styles. Despite his notoriety, Mayer is still a bit surprised that his works are so popular with young readers. "I find it quite odd to be included amongst authors. For it is hard to conceive of myself as one. I tell stories with pictures, and quite often I even add words," he notes in an essay for the *Fourth Book of Junior Authors.* "I am now at home with what I do. Children's books are a good place to call home."

Because his father was in the Navy, Mayer moved around a great deal as a child. The family eventually settled in Hawaii, where Mayer attended Theodore Roosevelt High School; upon graduation, he continued his studies at the Honolulu Academy of Arts. In 1964, Mayer moved to New York City for instruction at the Art Student's League. Over time, he began to put together an art portfolio, which he hoped to use to land illustration jobs. Unfortunately, Mayer had little luck. He relates in his essay: "I pounded the streets of New York . . . and received a polite smile everywhere I went. Finally I received some good advice from an art director. He told me to throw my portfolio away because it was so bad." Although initially upset by this evaluation, Mayer decided to take the advice; in his spare time, he began to refine his sketching. Mayer soon quit his job with an advertising agency in order to peddle his artwork to various publishers. Eventually, he was able to secure a number of illustration contracts.

Mayer published his first picture book in 1967. *A Boy, a Dog, and a Frog* was praised by many critics for its imaginative use of pictures. Mayer "expresses the boy's frustration with economy . . . and the range of emotions the frog experiences, bafflement, annoyance, amusement, melancholy, and finally, joy, with a few deft pen strokes," writes George A. Woods in the *New York Times Book Review.* And Robert Cohen, writing in *Young Readers Review,* calls the book "delightful . . . most heartily recommended for all picture book collections."

Mayer has repeated the success of *A Boy, a Dog, and a Frog* with a number of colorful volumes. Also writing in *Young Readers Review,* Phyllis Cohen describes *There's a Nightmare in My Closet* as a "magnificently funny book," one that "must be seen to be fully appreciated." Barbara Karlin of the *West Coast Review of Books* praises *Little Monster's Word Book* by saying "Mayer remembers what it was like to be a little kid. . . . This is a book with which a lot of little people are going to spend many happy hours." "The narrative is smooth. . . . Illustrations, boldly executed with rich use of color and careful attention to detail, . . . are graphically gripping," concludes Barbara Elleman in a *Booklist* review of *East of the Sun and West of the Moon.*

In spite of his own busy writing schedule, Mayer has found time to illustrate books for a number of other authors. His pictures for Marianne Mayer's retelling of *Beauty and the Beast* are applauded by P. Gila Reinstein of the *Dictionary of Literary Biography* as having a "wealth of detail" that is "full and lavish." And Bonita Brodt, writing in the *Chicago Tribune,* calls Mayer's adaptation of *A Christmas Carol* a "wonderful interpretation . . . because it makes the tale accessible to young children and also remains true to the older ones as well." In summing up Mayer's success, Reinstein notes: "Reflecting the world . . . from the child's point of view has been a hallmark of [Mayer's] work from the beginning of his career, and whatever changes come in his approach to children and their books, the honesty and emotional intensity that are essential to his work will remain unchanged."

BIOGRAPHICAL/CRITICAL SOURCES:

BOOKS

Contemporary Literary Criticism, Volume 11, Gale, 1979, pp. 159-176.

Dictionary of Literary Biography, Volume 61: *American Writers for Children since 1960: Poets, Illustrators, and Nonfiction Authors,* Gale, 1987, pp. 208, 209.

Fourth Book of Junior Authors, edited by Doris de Montreville and Elizabeth D. Crawford, Wilson, 1978, pp. 259-60.

PERIODICALS

Booklist, November 1, 1980, p. 407.

Chicago Tribune, December 7, 1986, section 14, p. 3.

New York Times Book Review, November 26, 1967, p. 62.

West Coast Review of Books, September, 1977, p. 55.

Young Readers Review, December, 1967, p. 12; June, 1968, p. 10.*

McBAIN, Ed
  See HUNTER, Evan

*   *   *

McCLOSKEY, Patrick   1948-

PERSONAL: Born May 23, 1948, in Howell, MI; son of Gerald Richard (a dentist) and Gertrude (a teacher; maiden name, Devereaux) McCloskey. *Education:* Duns Scotus College, B.A. (magna cum laude), 1971; University of Dayton, M.A. (theology), 1974; St. Leonard College, M.Div., 1975; St. Bonaventure University, M.A. (Franciscan studies), 1981.

ADDRESSES: Home—42 Calhoun St., Cincinnati, OH 45219.

CAREER: Entered Order of Friars Minor (Franciscans), 1967, ordained Roman Catholic priest, 1975; Roger Bacon High School, Cincinnati, OH, teacher of religion and English, 1975-84, academic dean, 1978-84; St. Anthony Messenger Press, Cincinnati, assistant promotion director, 1984-85; General Cuvia, Order of Friars Minor, Rome, Italy, director of communications, 1986-91.

WRITINGS:

(Contributor) Leonard Foley, editor, *Saint of the Day,* St. Anthony Messenger Press, Volume I, 1974, Volume II, 1975.
St. Anthony of Padua: Wisdom for Today, St. Anthony Messenger Press, 1977.
Franciscan Saint of the Day, St. Anthony Messenger Press, 1981.
When You Are Angry with God, Paulist Press, 1987.
Naming Your God: The Search for Mature Images, Ave Maria Press, 1991.

SIDELIGHTS: Since the late 1970s, Patrick McCloskey has been involved in a massive research project on the origins of the Franciscan province of St. John the Baptist in Cincinnati, Ohio. He began by editing and translating the letters of Father William Unterthiner, founder of the province. He then proceeded to work with others on translating materials for a history of the province, beginning in 1840. This ongoing project, which McCloskey has edited and footnoted, has so far resulted in more than fifteen hundred pages of manuscript.

McCloskey spent the summer of 1982 in Italy and Austria, where he conducted research for his history project and participated in a Franciscan renewal program. There he was able to see the originals of some letters he had worked on only from transcripts.

McCloskey told *CA:* "History of all kinds is one of my life-long interests. Human beings are mixed bags of noble and ignoble motives, but history leaves me optimistic.

"*Naming Your God* was written mostly between 2 and 4 p.m. in Rome, due to office hours I needed to keep."

*   *   *

McCORD, David (Thompson Watson)   1897-

PERSONAL: Born November 15, 1897, in New York, NY; son of Joseph Alexander and Eleanore Baynton (Reed) McCord. *Education:* Harvard University, B.A. (physics), 1921, M.A. (romance languages), 1922. *Politics:* Republican. *Religion:* Episcopalian. *Avocational interests:* Traveling, theater, fishing, baseball, watercolor painting, collecting owls, wood engravings, amateur radio operator.

ADDRESSES: c/o Harvard Club of Boston, 374 Commonwealth Ave., Boston, MA 02215.

CAREER: Harvard Alumni Bulletin, Cambridge, MA, associate editor, 1923-25, editor, 1940-46; *Boston Evening Transcript,* Boston, MA, member of the drama staff, 1923-28; Harvard Fund Council, Cambridge, executive director, 1925-63; poet, editor, and humorist. Phi Beta Kappa poet at Harvard University, 1938, Tufts College, 1938 and 1978, College of William and Mary, 1950, Massachusetts Institute of Technology, 1973, and Colby College, 1979; Lowell Institute, lecturer, 1950; Bread Loaf Writers Conference, staff member, 1958, 1960, 1962, 1964; Harvard University, summer instructor of advanced writing courses, 1963, 1965, 1966; Framingham State College, visiting professor, 1974. Association of Harvard Alumni, member of board of directors, 1965-68; Harvard Society of Advanced Study and Research, councilor, 1967-72. Poetry and Farnsworth Rooms of the Harvard College Library, honorary curator; Harvard University, honorary life associate of Dudley House and honorary member of Senior Common Room of Lowell House; Boston Center for Adult Education, honorary trustee; trustee of Historic Boston, Inc., Peter Bent Brigham Hospital, Boston, Charity of Edward Hopkins, New England College, and Boston Athenaeum; overseer, Old Sturbridge Village, MA, and Perkins Institute for the Blind; *American Heritage Dictionary,* member of usage panel. Has had several one-man shows of his watercolors. *Military service:* Field Artillery, U.S. Army, 1918; became second lieutenant.

MEMBER: International PEN, American Alumni Council, American Council of Learned Societies, American Academy of Arts and Sciences (fellow), Royal Society of Arts, Colonial Society of Massachusetts, Massachusetts Historical Society, Phi Beta Kappa (honorary), Harvard

Club, St. Botolph Club, Tavern Club, Club of Odd Volumes (Boston, MA), Faculty Club, Signet Club (Cambridge, MA), Century Club (New York City).

AWARDS, HONORS: Golden Rose, New England Poetry Club, 1941; William Rose Benet award, 1952; Guggenheim fellowship, 1954; National Institute of Arts and Letters grant, 1961; Sarah Josepha Hale medal, 1962; Miriam Kallen award, 1976; first recipient of the National Council of Teachers of English Award for Excellence in Poetry for Children, 1977; Littauer Foundation grant, 1983; Harvard Medal, 1984. Litt.D., Northwestern University, 1954, University of New Brunswick, 1963, Williams College, 1971, Keene State College, 1983, and Skidmore College, 1986; LL.D., Washington and Jefferson College, 1955; L.H.D., Harvard University, 1956, Colby College, 1968, Framingham State College, 1975, and Fitchburg State College, 1986; Art.D., New England College, 1956; Ed.D., Suffolk University, 1979; D.C.L., Simmons College, 1983.

WRITINGS:

POETRY FOR CHILDREN

Far and Few: Rhymes of the Never Was and Always Is (also see below), illustrated by Henry B. Kane, Little, Brown, 1952.

Take Sky (one poem), privately printed, 1961.

Take Sky: More Rhymes of the Never Was and Always Is (also see below), illustrated by Kane, Little, Brown, 1962.

All Day Long: Fifty Rhymes of the Never Was and Always Is (also see below), illustrated by Kane, Little, Brown, 1966.

Every Time I Climb a Tree (contains selections from *Far and Few, Take Sky,* and *All Day Long*), illustrated by Marc Simont, Little, Brown, 1967.

For Me to Say: Rhymes of the Never Was and Always Is, illustrated by Kane, Little, Brown, 1970.

Mr. Bidery's Spidery Garden, illustrated by Kane, Harrap, 1972.

Pen, Paper and Poem, Rinehart, 1973.

Away and Ago: Rhymes of the Never Was and Always Is, illustrated by Leslie Morrill, Little, Brown, 1975.

The Star in the Pail, illustrated by Simont, Little, Brown, 1975.

One at a Time: His Collected Poems for the Young, illustrated by Kane, Little, Brown, 1980.

Speak Up: More Rhymes of the Never Was and Always Is, illustrated by Simont, Little, Brown, 1980.

All Small, illustrated by Madelaine Gill Linden, Little, Brown, 1986.

Also author of text for recording *The Pickety Fence and 51 Other Poems,* Pathways of Sound.

POETRY FOR ADULTS

Floodgate, Washburn & Thomas, 1927.

Oxford Nearly Visited: A Fantasy, Cygnet Press, 1929.

Chocorua, privately printed, 1932.

The Crows, Scribner, 1934.

Bay Window Ballads, illustrated by John Lavalle, Scribner, 1935.

The Stretch, privately printed, 1937.

Twelve Verses from XII Night, privately printed, 1938.

The Knowing, privately printed, 1938.

Reflection in Blue, privately printed, 1939.

And What's More, Coward-McCann, 1941.

The Legend of St. Botolph, privately printed, 1942.

Christmas 1943, privately printed, 1943.

On Occasion, Harvard University Press, 1943.

Remembrance of Things Passed, Club of Odd Volumes (Boston), 1947.

Midway in This Middle Year of the Twentieth Century, privately printed, 1950.

A Star by Day, Doubleday, 1950.

Poet Always Next But One, College of William and Mary, 1951.

Blue Reflections on the Merchants Limited, Club of Odd Volumes, 1952.

The Old Bateau, and Other Poems, Little, Brown, 1953.

Ten Limericks, privately printed, 1953.

Odds without Ends, Little, Brown, 1954.

By Swancote Pool, privately printed, 1954.

Whereas to Mr. Franklin, Old South Association (Boston), 1954.

60 Lines for Three-Score Hatch, India Wharf Rats Club (Boston), 1957.

Sonnets to Baedeker, illustrated by Lavalle, Scribner, 1963.

In Memory of Sir Winston Churchill, 25 January, 1965, privately printed, 1965.

H.R.H. H.H.R., privately printed, 1965.

Observation Tower, Club of Odd Volume, 1966.

Roland Hayes, privately printed, 1967.

Poem for the Occasion, Colonial Society of Massachusetts (Boston), 1970.

Spree Fever, privately printed, 1970.

Thomas Dudley Cabot, privately printed, 1972.

R.R.: Lines, Sharp as Serifs, on the By-Passing of His Ninetieth Birthday, privately printed, 1973.

Sestina for the Queen, Bostonian Society, 1976.

The Children's World, privately printed, 1979.

EDITOR

Once and For All (essays), Coward-McCann, 1929.

What Cheer: An Anthology of American British Humorous and Witty Verse, Coward-McCann, 1945, published as *The Pocket Book of Humorous Verse,* Pocket

Books, 1946, published as *The Modern Treasury of Humorous Verse,* Garden City Books, 1951.

Arthur Griffin, *New England Revisited,* Houghton, 1966.

Bibliotheca Medica: Physician for Tomorrow, Harvard Medical School, 1966.

Stow Wengenroth, *Stow Wengenroth's New England,* Barre Publishers, 1969.

OTHER

Oddly Enough (essays), Washburn & Thomas, 1926.

Stirabout (essays), Washburn & Thomas, 1928.

Alice in Botolphland (play), St. Botolph Club (Boston), 1932.

H.T.P.: Portrait of a Critic, Coward McCann, 1935.

Notes on the Harvard Tercentenary, Harvard University Press, 1936.

An Acre for Education, Being Notes on the History of Radcliffe College, Radcliffe College, 1938, 4th revised edition, 1963.

(And illustrator) *About Boston: Sight, Sound, Flavor, and Inflection,* Doubleday, 1948.

The Camp at Lockjaw (short story), illustrated by Gluyas Williams, Doubleday, 1952.

. . . As Built with Second Thoughts, Centennial Commission of the Boston Public Library, 1953.

The Related Man, American Academy of Arts and Sciences, 1953.

David McCord's Oregon, Massachusetts Historical Society, 1959.

On the Frontier of Understanding, University of New Brunswick, 1959.

The Language of Request: Fishing with a Barbless Hook (essay), American Alumni Council (Washington, DC), 1961.

The Fabric of Man: Fifty Years of the Peter Bent Brigham Hospital, Hospital Celebration Committee (Boston), 1963.

In Sight of Sever: Essays from Harvard, Harvard University Press, 1963.

(With David B. Little and Sinclair H. Hitchings) *Art and Education* (lecture), University of Chicago Press, 1966.

Children and Poetry (lecture), University of Chicago Press, 1966.

Notes from Four Cities, 1927-1953, A. J. St. Onge, 1969.

Celebration: 1925-1975, privately printed, 1975.

Harvard: A Living Portrait, Foremost Publishers, 1982.

Also contributor to *Atlantic Monthly, Harper's, Ladies' Home Journal, New Yorker, Saturday Evening Post, Saturday Review of Literature, Theatre Arts Monthly, Virginia Quarterly,* and *Yale Review.* Collections of McCord's manuscripts are located at the Boston Public Library, Houghton Library, Harvard University, and other collections.

SIDELIGHTS: Considered by many critics to be the leading poet for children of his day, David McCord "has produced a body of work which ranks highest among all poetry written for children in this country," according to Myra Cohn Livingston in a *Horn Book* commentary. McCord has written verses ranging from the humorous and nonsensical to the instructive and the lyrical. A Harvard graduate who spent almost his entire working career as an administrator for his alma mater, McCord has regarded his poetry to be of only secondary interest. "It is a tribute to his talent and to his extraordinary energy," *Dictionary of Literary Biography* contributor Priscilla N. Grundy therefore proclaims, "that he achieved his high rank among children's poets in this context."

Although McCord was born in New York City and lived for a time in Princeton, New Jersey, it was the three years he spent in Oregon that influenced much of his later poetry. Moving with his family to the American Northwest when he was twelve, McCord lived on his uncle's farm on land that was still mostly unexplored wilderness. There was no heat, electricity, or running water on the farm, and the young McCord received no formal schooling except for one year when he visited a tutor once a week. With very little contact with children his own age, McCord spent his time doing chores and, as he says in a *Library Quarterly* article, learning "the language of the wild." He later adds, "I am very grateful for that rare experience. It taught me more, I think, than anything else about the essential poetry of life. It taught me, in a profusion of wildflowers, in a time of drought, in the terror of a forest fire, to honor the earth itself."

After leaving his uncle's farm when he was fifteen, McCord moved to Portland, Oregon, where he attended high school and wrote for his school newspaper. He then worked for a time in Des Moines, Iowa, before moving once again, this time to Washington, Pennsylvania. Despite his disjointed education, McCord managed to pass his entrance examinations to Harvard University, where he decided to major in physics even though he had almost failed the physics portion of the test. He went on to graduate with a bachelor's degree in physics and a master's in romance languages and became the executive director of the Harvard Fund Council for thirty-seven years.

Much of the writing McCord did while he was at Harvard was in the form of light essays, poetry for adults, book reviews, and some plays, short stories, and nonfiction. The majority of his poetry for children, for which he would become best known, was not published until after he left Harvard. He did, however, try his hand at juvenile poetry as early as 1924, when he wrote several such verses and was able to publish one in the *Saturday Review of Literature.* But McCord's first collection, *Far and Few: Rhymes of the Never Was and Always Is,* was not published until

1952, and his second collection was not published until ten years after that. From his retirement in 1963 and until the early 1980s, McCord became a prolific author of children's verse.

During this time he also read his poems to children at their schools and entertained them with exciting stories, telling them, according to X. J. Kennedy in *Horn Book*, "a few blood-curdling yarns about snakes and man-eating fish he had known in his boyhood." He would also read the poetry that children had written and offer them suggestions as to how they could improve their verses. For this McCord earned the respect of his young audience. "They acknowledged that he was a man who took their work seriously, who cared enough about it to want to improve it."

McCord's respect for children has been one of the primary inspirations for his writing. Although his poems often are designed to impart information to his young audience, he strives to compose entertaining verses that do not preach a moral lesson. "His poems describe everything from fifty legs of a centipede to hornets' nests, fishing, and how to write verse," Livingston observes. "What rescues all this from being moralistic, didactic, and encyclopedic is his ability to present his enthusiasms and discoveries with respect for the child's intelligence as well as his glorious wordplay."

McCord credits his fascination with language to his grandmother. "My grandmother read me the Bible through—the King James Version, all the magnificent parts of it—twice before I was twelve," he recalls in *Library Quarterly*. "That had a great deal to do with conditioning my instinctive feeling for rhythm and passionate love of words." Although McCord writes on a variety of topics ranging from verses about animals and the adventures of childhood to nonsense limericks and verses that teach about the different types of poetry, his love of words is a unifying force. "McCord," declares Grundy, "stands out among twentieth-century poets for children—indeed among those for adults as well—in his emphasis on sounds and sound patterns." Calling this the "primary characteristic" of his work, Grundy later adds that it "is not just that the poems have meter and rhyme (some do not), but that the author clearly enjoys his acrobatics with sounds." In Lee Bennett Hopkins's *Books Are by People*, McCord reasons that "poetry for children should keep reminding them, without any feeling on their part that they are being reminded, that the English language is a most marvelous and availing instrument."

In addition to showing children some of the delights of language, McCord is concerned with reacquainting them with nature and their surroundings in general. Modern technology, McCord feels, has deprived children of the direct contact with nature that he experienced as a boy. He

states in *Library Quarterly*, for instance, that "one of the tragedies of our time is that a boy will have flown to the height of thirty thousand feet before he ever climbs a mountain. All the wonder of going up on his own two feet will come long after he first took wing. Why bother?" McCord therefore tries to inspire an interest in nature through his verses.

But not only should children become more attuned to nature, they should also strive to be more aware of the whole world around them, the poet feels. "What David McCord has added [to the work of the poets who have preceded him]," Livingston concludes, "is the invitation to the young people of this country to look about, to be aware, to learn and grow, as he himself has done, with a keen eye and ear for the American landscape, its rhythms, its vernacular, and its subject matter from sky to earth below. He has never lost the sensitivities of childhood, the love of children, or the knowledge that curiosity and wonder are the lifeblood of the young."

BIOGRAPHICAL/CRITICAL SOURCES:

BOOKS

Children's Literature Review, Volume 9, Gale, 1978, pp. 93-104.
Dictionary of Literary Biography, Volume 61: *American Writers for Children since 1960: Poets, Illustrators, and Nonfiction Authors,* Gale, 1987, pp. 209-213.
Hopkins, Lee Bennett, *Books Are by People,* Citation Press, 1969.
Sutherland, Zena, Dianne L. Monson, and May Hill Arbuthnot, *Children and Books,* 6th edition, Scott, Foresman, 1981, pp. 255-307.

PERIODICALS

Children's Literature Association Quarterly, summer, 1980, pp. 22-24.
Growing Point, March, 1973, pp. 2101-2102.
Horn Book, February, 1971, p. 58; October, 1974; April, 1976, p. 173; February, 1979, pp. 25-39; February, 1981, p. 63; June, 1981, pp. 273-279; August, 1983, p. 507.
Language Arts, March, 1978, pp. 379-387.
Library Quarterly, January, 1967, pp. 53-66.
The Lion and the Unicorn, winter, 1980-81, pp. 75-82.
New York Herald Tribune Book Review, September 7, 1952, p. 6.
New York Times Book Review, September 7, 1952, p. 12; November 11, 1962, pp. 3, 61; November 6, 1966, pp. 6, 67; February 11, 1968, p. 26; November 9, 1980, pp. 50-51, 62.
Saturday Review of Literature, November 18, 1950, p. 17.
Time, June, 29, 1962.
Virginia Kirkus Service, July 15, 1966, p. 685.

Washington Post Book World, November 9, 1980, pp. 11-16.*

—*Sketch by Kevin S. Hile*

*   *   *

McELROY, Colleen J(ohnson) 1935-

PERSONAL: Born October 30, 1935, in St. Louis, MO; daughter of Jesse O. (an army officer) and Ruth (Long) Johnson; married David F. McElroy (a writer), November 28, 1968 (divorced); children: Kevin D., Vanessa C. *Education:* Attended University of Maryland, 1953-55; Harris Teachers College, A.A., 1956; Kansas State University, B.S., 1958, M.S., 1963; graduate study at University of Pittsburgh, 1958-59, and Western Washington State College (now Western Washington University), 1970-71; University of Washington, Ph.D., 1973.

ADDRESSES: Home—Seattle, WA. *Office*—Department of English, University of Washington, Seattle, WA 98105.

CAREER: Rehabilitation Institute, Kansas City, MO, chief speech clinician, 1963-66; Western Washington State College (now Western Washington University), Bellingham, assistant professor of English, 1966-73; University of Washington, Seattle, 1973—, began as assistant professor, currently professor of English. Affiliate member of speech faculty, University of Missouri—Kansas City, 1965-66; summer instructor, Project Head Start and Project New Careers. Moderator of "Outlook," KVOS-TV, 1968-72. Artist; watercolors and pen-ink sketches displayed at gallery exhibit, 1978. Member of board, Washington State Commission for the Humanities.

MEMBER: American Speech and Hearing Association, National Council of Teachers of English, Conference on College Composition and Communication, Writers Guild of America East, Writers Union, Author's Guild, Dramatist Guild, United Black Artists Guild (Seattle).

AWARDS, HONORS: Carnation teaching incentive award, 1973; Breadloaf scholarship for fiction, 1974; Best of Small Presses award for poetry, Pushcart Book Press, 1976; National Endowment for the Arts fellowship in creating writing, 1978 and 1991; Matrix Women of Achievement Award, 1985; Before Columbus American Book Award, 1985, for *Queen of the Ebony Isles;* Fulbright Creative Writing fellowship, 1990; Rockefeller fellowship, 1991; Jessie Ball DuPont Distinguished Black Scholar Residency, 1992.

WRITINGS:

Speech and Language Development of the Preschool Child: A Survey, C. C. Thomas, 1972.
The Mules Done Long Since Gone (poems), Harrison-Madronna Press, 1973.

Music from Home: Selected Poems, Southern Illinois University Press, 1976.
(Contributor) *Iron Country* (anthology), Copper Canyon Press, 1978.
(Contributor) Dexter Fisher, editor, *The Third Woman* (anthology), Houghton, 1980.
(Contributor) *Backbone 2* (anthology), Seal Press, 1980.
Winters without Snow (poems), I. Reed, 1980.
Looking for a Country under Its Original Name (poems), Blue Begonia Press, 1985.
Queen of the Ebony Isles (poems), Wesleyan University Press, 1985.
Jesus and Fat Tuesday and Other Short Stories, Creative Arts Book Company, 1987.
Bone Flames (poems), Wesleyan University Press, 1987.
Lie and Say You Love Me (poems), Circinatum Press, 1988.
Blue Flames (poems), Wesleyan University Press, 1989.
What Madness Brought Me Here: New and Selected Poems, 1968-1988, University Press of New England, 1990.

Also author of *Driving under the Cardboard Pines.* Contributor to anthology *Black Sister: Poems by Black American Women, 1946-1980,* 1981. Contributor of essays, poems, and short fiction to numerous literary reviews and little magazines, including *Wormwood Review, Poetry Northwest, Choice, Seneca Review, Southern Poetry Review, Confrontation, Massachusetts Review, Georgia Review, Manhattan Review, Kenyon Review, Southern Poetry Review,* and *Black Warrior Review.*

WORK IN PROGRESS: Study War No More, a novel; *Halfway to Nosybe,* a collection of essays.

*   *   *

McKISSACK, Patricia (L'Ann) C(arwell) 1944-
(L'Ann Carwell)

PERSONAL: Born August 9, 1944, in Nashville, TN; daughter of Robert (a civil servant) and Erma (a civil servant) Carwell; married Fredrick L. McKissack (a writer), December 12, 1965; children: Fredrick L., Jr., Robert and John (twins). *Education:* Tennessee Agricultural and Industrial State University (now Tennessee State University), B.A., 1964; Webster University, M.A., 1975. *Avocational interests:* World travel, entertaining, and touring old houses.

ADDRESSES: Home—5900 Pershing Ave., St. Louis, MO 63112. *Office*—All-Writing Services, 225 South Meramec, #506, St. Louis, MO 63105.

CAREER: Junior high school English teacher in Kirkwood, MO, 1968-75; Forest Park College, St. Louis, MO, part-time instructor in English, 1975—. Children's book editor at Concordia Publishing House, 1976-81, and Institute of Children's Literature, 1984—; instructor at University of Missouri—St. Louis, 1978—; co-owner of All-Writing Services. Educational consultant on minority literature.

MEMBER: Society of Children's Book Writers.

AWARDS, HONORS: Helen Keating Ott Award from National Church and Synagogue Librarians Association, 1980, for editorial work at Concordia Publishing House; C. S. Lewis Silver Medal awards from *Christian School* magazine, 1984, for *It's the Truth, Christopher* and *Abram, Abram, Where Are We Going?;* Coretta Scott King Award, and Jane Addams Peace Award, both 1990, both for *Long Hard Journey: Story of the Pullman Car Porter;* Parent's Choice Award, 1990, for *Nettie Jo's Friends.*

WRITINGS:

FOR CHILDREN

(Under name L'Ann Carwell) *Good Shepherd Prayer,* Concordia, 1978.

(Under name L'Ann Carwell) *God Gives New Life,* Concordia, 1979.

Ask the Kids, Concordia, 1979.

Who Is Who?, Children's Press, 1983.

Martin Luther King, Jr.: A Man to Remember, Children's Press, 1984.

Paul Laurence Dunbar: A Poet to Remember, Children's Press, 1984.

Michael Jackson, Superstar, Children's Press, 1984.

Lights Out, Christopher, illustrated by Bartholomew, Augsburg, 1984.

It's the Truth, Christopher, illustrated by Bartholomew, Augsburg, 1984.

The Apache, Children's Press, 1984.

Mary McLeod Bethune: A Great American Educator, Children's Press, 1985.

Aztec Indians, Children's Press, 1985.

The Inca, Children's Press, 1985.

The Maya, Children's Press, 1985.

Flossie and the Fox, illustrated by Rachel Isadora, Dial, 1986.

Our Martin Luther King Book, illustrated by Rachel Isadora, Child's World, 1986.

Who Is Coming?, illustrated by Clovis Martin, Children's Press, 1986.

Give It with Love, Christopher: Christopher Learns about Gifts and Giving, illustrated by Bartholomew, Augsburg, 1988.

Speak Up, Christopher: Christopher Learns the Difference between Right and Wrong, illustrated by Bartholomew, Augsburg, 1988.

A Troll in a Hole, Milliken, 1988.

Nettie Jo's Friends, illustrated by Scott Cook, Knopf, 1988.

Mirandy and Brother Wind, illustrated by Jerry Pinkney, Knopf, 1988.

Monkey-Monkey's Trick: Based on an African Folk-Tale, illustrated by Paul Meisel, Random House, 1989.

Jesse Jackson: A Biography, Scholastic, 1989.

(With Ruthilde Kronberg) *A Piece of the Wind and Other Stories to Tell,* Harper, 1990.

No Need for Alarm, Milliken, 1990.

A Million Fish—More or Less, illustrated by Dena Schutzer, Knopf, 1992.

The Dark Thirty: Southern Tales of the Supernatural, illustrated by Brian Pinkney, 1992.

Christmas in the Big House—Christmas in the Quarters, Scholastic, 1992.

Sojourner Truth: "Ain't I a Woman?," Scholastic, 1992.

WITH HUSBAND, FREDRICK L. McKISSACK

Look What You've Done Now, Moses, illustrated by Joe Boddy, David Cook, 1984.

Abram, Abram, Where Are We Going?, illustrated by Boddy, David Cook, 1984.

Cinderella, illustrated by Tom Dunnington, Children's Press, 1985.

Country Mouse and City Mouse, illustrated by Anne Sikorski, Children's Press, 1985.

The Little Red Hen, illustrated by Dennis Hockerman, Children's Press, 1985.

The Three Bears, illustrated by Virginia Bala, Children's Press, 1985.

The Ugly Little Duck, illustrated by Peggy Perry Anderson, Children's Press, 1986.

When Do You Talk to God? Prayers for Small Children, illustrated by Gary Gumble, Augsburg, 1986.

King Midas and His Gold, illustrated by Dunnington, Children's Press, 1986.

Frederick Douglass: The Black Lion, Children's Press, 1987.

A Real Winner, illustrated by Quentin Thompson and Ken Jones, Milliken, 1987.

The King's New Clothes, illustrated by Gwen Connelly, Children's Press, 1987.

Tall Phil and Small Bill, illustrated by Kathy Mitter, Milliken, 1987.

Three Billy Goats Gruff, illustrated by Dunnington, Children's Press, 1987.

My Bible ABC Book, illustrated by Reed Merrill, Augsburg, 1987.

The Civil Rights Movement in America from 1865 to the Present, Children's Press, 1987, 2nd edition, 1991.

All Paths Lead to Bethlehem, illustrated by Kathryn E. Shoemaker, Augsburg, 1987.

Messy Bessey, illustrated by Richard Hackney, Children's Press, 1987.

The Big Bug Book of Counting, illustrated by Bartholomew, Milliken, 1987.

The Big Bug Book of Opposites, illustrated by Bartholomew, Milliken, 1987.

The Big Bug Book of Places to Go, illustrated by Bartholomew, Milliken, 1987.

The Big Bug Book of the Alphabet, illustrated by Bartholomew, Milliken, 1987.

The Big Bug Book of Things to Do, illustrated by Bartholomew, Milliken, 1987.

Bugs!, illustrated by Martin, Children's Press, 1988.

The Children's ABC Christmas, illustrated by Kathy Rogers, Augsburg, 1988.

Constance Stumbles, illustrated by Dunnington, Children's Press, 1988.

Oh, Happy, Happy Day! A Child's Easter in Story, Song, and Prayer, illustrated by Elizabeth Swisher, Augsburg, 1989.

God Made Something Wonderful, illustrated by Ching, Augsburg, 1989.

Messy Bessey's Closet, illustrated by Hackney, Children's Press, 1989.

James Weldon Johnson: "Lift Every Voice and Sing," Children's Press, 1990.

A Long Hard Journey: The Story of the Pullman Porter, Walker & Co., 1990.

Taking a Stand against Racism and Racial Discrimination, F. Watts, 1990.

W. E. B. DuBois, F. Watts, 1990.

The Story of Booker T. Washington, Children's Press, 1991.

Messy Bessy's Garden, illustrated by Martin, Children's Press, 1991.

"GREAT AFRICAN AMERICANS" SERIES; JUVENILES; WITH FREDRICK L. McKISSACK

Carter G. Woodson: The Father of Black History, illustrated by Ned O, Enslow Publishers, 1991.

Frederick Douglass: Leader against Slavery, illustrated by Ned O, Enslow Publishers, 1991.

George Washington Carver: The Peanut Scientist, illustrated by Ned O, Enslow Publishers, 1991.

Ida B. Wells-Barnett: A Voice against Violence, Enslow Publishers, 1991.

Louis Armstrong: Jazz Musician, illustrated by Ned O, Enslow Publishers, 1991.

Marian Anderson: A Great Singer, Enslow Publishers, 1991.

Martin Luther King, Jr.: Man of Peace, Enslow Publishers, 1991.

Mary Church Terrell: Leader for Equality, illustrated by Ned O, Enslow Publishers, 1991.

Mary McLeod Bethune: A Great Teacher, illustrated by Ned O, Enslow Publishers, 1991.

Ralph J. Bunche: Peacemaker, illustrated by Ned O, Enslow Publishers, 1991.

Jesse Owens, illustrated by Ned O, Enslow Publishers, 1992.

Langston Hughes, illustrated by Ned O, Enslow Publishers, 1992.

Sojourner Truth, illustrated by Ned O, Enslow Publishers, 1992.

Zora Neale Hurston, illustrated by Ned O, Enslow Publishers, 1992.

Satchel Paige, illustrated by Ned O, Enslow Publishers, 1992.

OTHER

(With Mavis Jukes) *Who Owns the Sun?* (film script), Disney Educational Productions, 1991.

Also author, with Fredrick L. McKissack, of "Start Up" series (for beginning readers), four volumes, Children's Press, 1985; editor, with McKissack, of "Reading Well" series, and "Big Bug Books" series, both for Milliken. Writer for preschool series "L Is for Listening," broadcast by KWMU-Radio, 1975-77. Author of radio and television scripts. Contributor of articles and short stories to magazines, including *Friend, Happy Times,* and *Evangelizing Today's Child.*

WORK IN PROGRESS: A book about the McKissack family and several biographies about great African-Americans.

SIDELIGHTS: Patricia C. McKissack's books for children cover a range of topics, including religious stories, and biographies of black historical figures. *Flossie and the Fox,* which *Kirkus Reviews* called "a perfect picture book," is based on a folktale McKissack's grandfather told her as a child. The action surrounds little Flossie Finley as she delivers a basket of eggs to a neighbor and outsmarts the fox who wants the eggs for himself. *Abram, Abram, Where Are We Going?* is a retelling of the biblical stories about Abraham as father to many nations.

McKissack's title *Jesse Jackson: A Biography* was reviewed in the *New York Times* by Rosemary Bray, who wrote: "The complex story [McKissack] tells may seem at odds with the simplicity of the languages she uses. . . . But Patricia McKissack is excellent at conveying sophisticated themes and ideas, so that *Jesse Jackson: A Biography* can be read with pleasure by both children and young adults." In 1991, she wrote her first movie script with award-winning author Mavis Jukes. The movie, titled *Who Owns the Sun?,* won several major film awards and is up for consideration as an Academy Award nominee for short subject.

Patricia C. McKissack told *CA:* "Teaching and writing are compatible careers. My teaching experiences help me identify materials kids like to read and also target what they need to read. I understand the resistance teachers and parents get from the reluctant reader. So, my writing goals are twofold. First, I choose subjects kids need to know about. Second, I try to make the material as interesting as possible. Nothing is more satisfying than a letter from a reader saying, for example, 'Thank you for writing about Paul Laurence Dunbar. I'd never heard of him until I read your book. Now I read his poems.' On days like that the rejection slips seem unimportant. The writer in me pats the teacher in me on the back."

BIOGRAPHICAL/CRITICAL SOURCES:

PERIODICALS

Horn Book, March, 1989, p. 201; September, 1989, p. 613; January, 1990, pp. 87, 125.
Kirkus Reviews, July 15, 1986, p. 1120; November 1, 1988, p. 1607.
New York Times Book Review, November 20, 1988, p. 48; February 25, 1990, p. 32.
School Library Journal, February, 1989, p. 74; May, 1989, p. 88; November, 1989, p. 78; December, 1989, p. 114; January, 1990, p. 125.
Voice of Youth Advocates, December, 1989, pp. 303, 304.

*   *   *

McPHAIL, David M(ichael) 1940-

PERSONAL: Born June 30, 1940, in Newburyport, MA; son of Bernard E. (a salesman) and Rachel (a secretary; maiden name, Cutter) McPhail; married Janis Lazarian, July 2, 1966 (marriage ended); married second wife, Mickey; children: Tristian, Joshua, Gabrian, Jaime. *Education:* Attended Vesper George University, 1957-58, and Boston Museum of Fine Arts School, 1963-66.

ADDRESSES: Home—88 Lime St., Newburyport, MA 01950.

CAREER: Illustrator of books for children, 1967—; author of books for children, 1971—.

AWARDS, HONORS: Sailing to Cythera: And Other Anatole Stories was chosen of American Institute of Graphic Arts' Fifty Books of the Year, 1974; *Boston Globe-Horn Book* honor book for illustration and Caldecott Award consideration, both 1975, both for *The Bear's Bicycle; One Winter Night in August, and Other Nonsense Jingles* was chosen one of *New York Times* Outstanding Books of the Year, 1975; Lewis Carroll Shelf Award, 1977, for *Sailing to Cythera: And Other Anatole Stories,* and 1979, for *The Island of the Grass King: The Further Adventures of Anatole; Captain Toad and the Motorbike* and *Grandfather's Cake* were selected for the American Institute of Graphic Arts Book Show, 1979 and 1980, respectively; *Pig Pig Grows Up* was chosen one of International Reading Association/Children's Book Council's Children's Choices, 1980; *Pig Pig Rides* was chosen one of *School Library Journal*'s Best Books, 1982; Parents' Choice Award for Literature from Parents' Choice Foundation, 1982, for *Great Cat; Farm Morning* and *The Dream Child* were each chosen one of Child Study Association of America's Children's Books of the Year, 1985.

WRITINGS:

FOR CHILDREN; SELF-ILLUSTRATED

In the Summer I Go Fishing, Addison-Wesley, 1971.
The Glerp, Ginn, 1972.
The Bear's Toothache, Little, Brown, 1972.
Oh, No, Go (play), Little, Brown, 1973.
The Cereal Box, Little, Brown, 1974.
Henry Bear's Park, Little, Brown, 1976.
The Train, Little, Brown, 1977.
The Magical Drawings of Moony B. Finch, Doubleday, 1978.
Mistletoe, Dutton, 1978.
Captain Toad and the Motorbike, Atheneum, 1978.
Yesterday I Lost a Sneaker: And Found the Great Goob Sick, Ginn, 1978.
Where Can an Elephant Hide?, Doubleday, 1979.
Grandfather's Cake, Scribner, 1979.
Stanley, Henry Bear's Friend, Little, Brown, 1979.
Pig Pig Grows Up, Dutton, 1980.
Those Terrible Toy-Breakers, Parents Magazine Press, 1980.
Bumper Tubbs, Houghton, 1980.
Alligators Are Awful: And They Have Terrible Manners, Too, Doubleday, 1980.
Surprise!, Houghton, 1981.
A Wolf Story, Scribner, 1981.
Pig Pig Rides, Dutton, 1982.
Great Cat, Dutton, 1982.
That Grand Master Jumping Teacher, Bernard, Meets Jerome, the Great Jumping Glump, Warne, 1982.
Pig Pig Goes to Camp, Dutton, 1983.
Snow Lion, Parents Magazine Press, 1983.
Andrew's Bath, Little, Brown, 1984.
Fix-It, Dutton, 1984.
Lorenzo, Doubleday, 1984.
Sisters, Harcourt, 1984.
The Dream Child, Dutton, 1985.
Emma's Pet, Dutton, 1985.
Farm Morning, Harcourt, 1985.

Pig Pig and the Magic Photo Album, Dutton, 1986.
Emma's Vacation, Dutton, 1987.
Adam's Smile, Dutton, 1987.
First Flight, Little, Brown, 1987.
Something Special, Joy Street, 1988.
David McPhail's Animals A to Z, Scholastic Inc., 1988.
The Story of James, Dutton, 1989.
Goldilocks and the Three Bears: A Retelling of a Classic Tale, Heath, 1989.
Lost, Joy Street, 1990.
The Party, Joy Street, 1990.
Pig Pig Gets a Job, Dutton, 1990.
Sisters, Harcourt, 1990.
Ed and Me, Harcourt, 1990.
Annie & Co., Holt, 1991.

FOR CHILDREN; ILLUSTRATOR

Robert Brooks, *The Run, Jump, Bump Book,* Little, Brown, 1971.
Alma Marchak Whitney, *Leave Herbert Alone,* Addison-Wesley, 1972.
Nancy Willard, *Sailing to Cythera: And Other Anatole Stories,* Harcourt, 1974.
Emilie W. McLeod, *The Bear's Bicycle,* Little, Brown, 1975.
X. J. Kennedy, *One Winter Night in August, and Other Nonsense Jingles,* Atheneum, 1975.
N. Willard, *Stranger's Bread,* Harcourt, 1977.
Marjorie W. Sharmat, *A Big Fat Enormous Lie,* Dutton, 1978.
Nanine Elisabeth Valen, *The Devil's Tail: Based on an Old French Legend,* Scribner, 1978.
X. J. Kennedy, *The Phantom Ice Cream Man: More Nonsense Verse,* Atheneum, 1979.
Genie Iverson, *I Want to Be Big,* Dutton, 1979.
N. Willard, *The Island of the Grass King: The Further Adventures of Anatole,* Harcourt, 1979.
N. Willard, *Uncle Terrible: More Adventures of Anatole,* Harcourt, 1982.
N. Willard, *The Nightgown of the Sullen Moon,* Harcourt, 1983.
Beatrix Potter, *The Tale of Peter Rabbit,* Scholastic Inc., 1986.
Mary Pope Osborne, *Moonhorse,* Knopf, 1988.

ADAPTATIONS: Leave Herbert Alone (filmstrip with cassette or record), BFA Educational Media, 1975; *The Bear's Bicycle* (book and cassette), Live Oak Media, 1986; *Emma's Pet* (book and cassette), Live Oak Media, 1988; *Pig Pig Rides* (book and cassette), Live Oak Media, 1988; *The Bear's Toothache* (cassette), Random House; *Where Can an Elephant Hide?* (filmstrip with cassette), Spoken Arts; *Pig Pig Grows Up* (cassette), Weston Woods; *The Nightgown of the Sullen Moon* (filmstrip with cassette), Random House; *Fix-It* (filmstrip with cassette), Random House; *The Dream Child* (filmstrip with cassette), Random House.

WORK IN PROGRESS: A book for adults, tentatively titled *Confessions of a Children's Book Illustrator.*

SIDELIGHTS: Whether his drawings are of pigs, bears, or children, author-illustrator David M. McPhail excels at filling the pages of his children's books with vivid detail, lively action, and humorous, loveable characters. McPhail once told *CA:* "I wanted to be a 'fine artist,' and it took several years for me to realize and accept that illustrating books *is* a fine art." The numerous awards that he has received for his illustrations of Nancy Willard's "Anatole" adventures (*Sailing to Cythera: And Other Anatole Stories, The Island of the Grass King: The Further Adventures of Anatole,* and *Uncle Terrible: More Adventures of Anatole*) and for his other books are evidence of what many people already consider McPhail's "fine art."

McPhail was born in Newburyport, Massachusetts, in 1940, and remembers growing up in a poor family. "Times were hard in our neighborhood; nobody had that much," he said. "My mother did her best to encourage my sister, my two brothers and myself. She always told us we could do anything we aspired to do." McPhail played in the woods near his home and, from a very young age, he drew. "I always drew from the time I was a child. It was easy for me, but I never took it very seriously. Drawing was something I did for fun, and in my house, work and fun were not supposed to go together. Drawing was always there, however, waiting in the background."

After high school, McPhail worked in a factory making fuses and electronic parts. He recalls: "I hated every minute of my job. My co-workers lived for vacation, retirement, or the next coffee break. It saddened me because most of these people had been working at the factory for twenty-five years. I couldn't see going through life like that." He escaped this gloomy factory job by playing in a rock and roll band and by getting involved in risky business ventures with his brother. Neither diversion was a great success: the rock and roll band "never made much more than ten dollars a night" and the business ventures left him with a surplus of greeting card envelopes and arrows but little money.

McPhail attended Vesper George University on an art scholarship, but was not yet ready to give up his music. He left school to "beat around" for a while, moved to California, and in 1963 sold his convertible in order to return to art school, this time at the Boston Museum of Fine Arts School. "I went into graphics to escape the edict that illustration was not 'art,' " says McPhail, "and also because I wanted to paint what *I* felt. My work from the beginning was illustration. My paintings told stories and were not just landscapes or portraits."

"Gradually," said McPhail, "I realized that I wanted to write and illustrate books. So I screwed up my courage, and wrote and illustrated a story of my own." Though he did not sell the book, the illustrations helped him get some free-lance work. Soon a friend's girlfriend asked if he would be willing to illustrate some textbooks. He was, and illustrated textbooks for several years. Finally he was offered the opportunity to do his own book. McPhail remembers telling his editor "Now I've made it. It's been my ambition for years to publish a trade book. I'm going to be rich." The editor laughed and told him to come back thirty books later and tell her how rich he was. Though he did not become an instant millionaire, McPhail has been busy ever since that time illustrating books for others and writing and illustrating his own books.

One of McPhail's most popular characters, Pig Pig, has appeared in five different books. McPhail conceived of Pig Pig as an old pig who sold his house and bought a boat, but at an editor's suggestion he rewrote the first Pig Pig story to describe the pig's youth. *Pig Pig Grows Up* came so easily that by the time McPhail sat down to write the second book he had almost forgotten what kind of paper, paints, pen and ink he had used. He recalls: "Thankfully, I did not have to establish a new character; I just remembered how I felt about Pig Pig and the drawings came."

McPhail says that he also "loved illustrating the Anatole books because it was a challenge. . . . [Nancy Willard's] stories really hold up to repeated readings." Though McPhail was happy with the award-winning drawings for the first two Anatole books, he was disappointed with the third, *Uncle Terrible: More Adventures of Anatole,* and even considered giving up illustrating altogether. However, meeting Willard for lunch and seeing her drawings for *The Nightgown of the Sullen Moon* changed his mind. Though he feared that he "would be unable to do justice to her highly poetic text," Willard's drawings made him "realize that *Nightgown* is a very lovely, *simple* story, which she had approached in exactly the same way I would have, had I not felt impelled to be esoteric, to make a 'grand statement.' "

McPhail does not consider himself a writer, though he has written well over forty books. He describes his writing as "purely inspirational" and says that "with writing, I get a sudden and wonderful feeling, as if I'm about to win something. There's a story building in my mind and I know I have to open myself to it, because it's about to happen." He adds: "I think everybody has a little transistor radio, which runs on cosmic energy. When you turn this 'radio' on, you tune into stories, and pick them up. Sometimes you get little pieces and then the signal fades out, but sometimes you can actually hear the whole broadcast."

Wherever McPhail gets his stories, they are usually secondary to his drawings, which tell most of the story and which demand more of the author's time. While McPhail's writing starts with inspiration, his drawings usually evolve during the process of working at his drawing board. He says that "the driving force behind my work is a sense of discovery. Until the last stroke of the brush, until the last pen line appears, I'm not really sure what the illustration will be, or if the magic will work. The images are so vague in my head, I can't really say that I am writing *about* the pictures I create."

McPhail says that some of his stories relate to his own childhood, "or in some small way to [his] children." He found that in creating the illustrations for *The Dream Child,* the title character looked very much like his daughter, Jaime, though he didn't set out to use her as a model. McPhail commented that he "had drawn Jaime so often that it was ingrained in me to draw her." McPhail also has many animal characters, which he likes because they "can be genderless. They can have human characteristics, and I can even endow them with bad qualities without reflecting on a particular kind of person." Animal characters can also be put into situations that are dangerous without scaring children, who might sympathize more readily with a human character.

McPhail stated: "I work all the time, even if I'm not at my drawing board. I have many responsibilities, which from time to time impose limits, yet I feel each day is an adventure and each book is a new beginning." His advice for young artists is to "draw from life, and above all, be true to yourself."

BIOGRAPHICAL/CRITICAL SOURCES:

BOOKS

Kingman, Lee, compiler, *Illustrators of Children's Books: 1967-76,* Horn Book, 1978.

PERIODICALS

Los Angeles Times Book Review, January 20, 1985.
New York Times Book Review, August 12, 1984.
Washington Post Book World, November 7, 1982.

—*Sketch by Tom Pendergast*

* * *

MELTZER, Milton 1915-

PERSONAL: Born May 8, 1915, in Worcester, MA; son of Benjamin and Mary (Richter) Meltzer; married Hilda Balinky, June 22, 1941; children: Jane, Amy. *Education:* Attended Columbia University, 1932-36. *Politics:* Independent.

ADDRESSES: Home—263 West End Ave., New York, NY 10023. *Agent*—Harold Ober Associates, 425 Madison Ave., New York, NY 10017.

CAREER: Federal Theatre Project of the Works Projects Administration, New York City, staff writer, 1936-39; Columbia Broadcasting System Inc. (CBS-Radio), New York City, researcher and writer, 1946; Public Relations Staff of Henry A. Wallace for President, 1947-49; Medical and Pharmaceutical Information Bureau, New York City, account executive, 1950-55; Pfizer Inc., New York City, assistant director of public relations, 1955-60; Science and Medicine Publishing Co. Inc., New York City, editor, 1960-68; full-time writer of books, 1968—; historian; biographer. Consulting editor, Thomas Y. Crowell Co., 1962-74, Doubleday & Co. Inc., 1963-73, and Scholastic Book Services, 1968-72; University of Massachusetts, Amherst, adjunct professor, 1977-80; lecturer at universities in the United States and England and at professional meetings and seminars; writer of films and filmstrips. *Military service:* U.S. Army Air Force, 1942-46; became sergeant.

MEMBER: Authors Guild, PEN, Organization of American Historians.

AWARDS, HONORS: Thomas Alva Edison Mass Media Award for special excellence in portraying America's past, 1966, for *In Their Own Words: A History of the American Negro*, Volume 2, *1865-1916;* Children's Literature Award of the National Book Award, finalist, 1969, for *Langston Hughes: A Biography*, 1975, for *Remember the Days: A Short History of the Jewish American* and *World of Our Fathers: The Jews of Eastern Europe,* and 1977, for *Never to Forget: The Jews of the Holocaust;* Christopher Award, 1969, for *Brother, Can You Spare a Dime? The Great Depression, 1929-1933,* and 1980, for *All Times, All Peoples: A World History of Slavery; Slavery: From the Rise of Western Civilization to the Renaissance* was selected one of *School Library Journal*'s Best Books, 1971; Charles Tebeau Award from the Florida Historical Society, 1973, for *Hunted Like a Wolf: The Story of the Seminole War;* Jane Addams Peace Association Children's Book Award Honor Book, 1975, for *The Eye of Conscience: Photographers and Social Change.*

Boston Globe-Horn Book Nonfiction Honor Book, 1976, for *Never to Forget: The Jews of the Holocaust,* and 1983, for *The Jewish Americans: A History in Their Own Words, 1650-1950;* Association of Jewish Libraries Book Award, 1976, Jane Addams Peace Association Children's Book Award, 1977, Charles and Bertie G. Schwartz Award for Jewish Juvenile Literature from the National Jewish Book Awards, 1978, Hans Christian Andersen Honor List, 1979, and selected by the American Library Association as a "Best of the Best Books 1970-1983," all for *Never to*

Forget: The Jews of the Holocaust; Dorothea Lange: A Photographer's Life was selected on the *New York Times* Best Adult Books of the Year, 1978; Washington Children's Book Guild Honorable Mention, 1978 and 1979, and Nonfiction Award, 1981, all for his total body of work; American Book Award finalist, 1981, for *All Times, All Peoples: A World History of Slavery.*

Carter G. Woodson Book Award from the National Council for Social Studies, 1981, for *The Chinese Americans;* Jefferson Cup Award from the Virginia State Library Association, 1983, for *The Jewish Americans: A History in Their Own Words, 1650-1950;* Children's Book Award special citation from the Child Study Children's Book Committee, one of *School Library Journal*'s Best Books for Young Adults, both 1985, and Olive Branch Award from the Writers' and Publishers' Alliance for Nuclear Disarmament, Jane Addams Peace Association Children's Book Award, and New York University Center for War, Peace, and the News Media, all 1986, all for *Ain't Gonna Study War No More: The Story of America's Peace-Seekers;* John Brubaker Memorial Award from the Catholic Library Association, 1986; Golden Kite Award for nonfiction, Society of Children's Book Writers, 1987, for *Poverty in America;* Jane Addams Peace Association Children's Book Award Honor Book, 1989, for *Rescue: The Story of How Gentiles Saved Jews in the Holocaust.*

Many of Meltzer's books have been selected as Library of Congress' Best Children's Books of the Year, Notable Children's Trade Book in Social Studies from the National Council for Social Studies, and *New York Times* Outstanding Children's Books of the Year.

WRITINGS:

NONFICTION FOR YOUNG READERS, EXCEPT AS NOTED

(With Langston Hughes) *A Pictorial History of the Negro in America* (adult), Crown, 1956, 5th revised edition, with C. Eric Lincoln, published as *A Pictorial History of Black Americans*, 1983, revised as *African American History: Four Centuries of Black Life,* Scholastic Textbooks, 1990.

Mark Twain Himself (adult), Crowell, 1960.

(Editor) *Milestones to American Liberty: The Foundations of the Republic* (adult), Crowell, 1961, revised edition, 1965.

(Editor, with Walter Harding) *A Thoreau Profile* (adult), Crowell, 1962.

(Editor) *Thoreau: People, Principles and Politics* (adult), Hill & Wang, 1963.

A Light in the Dark: The Life of Samuel Gridley Howe (ALA Notable Book), Crowell, 1964, Modern Curriculum Press, 1991.

In Their Own Words: A History of the American Negro, Crowell, Volume 1, *1619-1865* (ALA Notable Book),

1964, Volume 2, *1865-1916* (ALA Notable Book), 1965, Volume 3, *1916-1966* (ALA Notable Book), 1967, abridged edition published as *The Black Americans: A History in Their Own Words, 1619-1983,* Crowell, 1984, Trophy, 1987.

Tongue of the Flame: The Life of Lydia Maria Child, Crowell, 1965.

(With August Meier) *Time of Trial, Time of Hope: The Negro in America, 1919-1941* (with teacher's guide), illustrated by Moneta Barnett, Doubleday, 1966, Modern Curriculum Press, 1991.

Thaddeus Stevens and the Fight for Negro Rights, Crowell, 1967.

(With L. Hughes) *Black Magic: A Pictorial History of the Negro in American Entertainment* (adult), Prentice-Hall, 1967, revised as *Black Magic: A Pictorial History of the African-American in the Performing Arts,* introduction by Ossie Davis, Da Capo Press, 1990.

Bread—and Roses: The Struggle of American Labor, 1865-1915, Knopf, 1967, Facts on File, 1991.

Langston Hughes: A Biography (ALA Notable Book), Crowell, 1968.

Brother, Can You Spare a Dime? The Great Depression, 1929-1933 (ALA Notable Book), Knopf, 1969, Facts on File, 1991.

(With Lawrence Lader) *Margaret Sanger: Pioneer of Birth Control,* Crowell, 1969.

Freedom Comes to Mississippi: The Story of Reconstruction, Follet, 1970.

Slavery: From the Rise of Western Civilization to the Renaissance, Cowles, 1971, Volume 2, *Slavery: From the Renaissance to Today,* Cowles, 1972.

To Change the World: A Picture History of Reconstruction, Scholastic Book Services, 1971.

Underground Man (novel), Bradbury Press, 1972, Harcourt, 1990.

Hunted Like a Wolf: The Story of the Seminole War, Farrar, Straus, 1972.

The Right to Remain Silent, Harcourt, 1972.

(With Bernard Cole) *The Eye of Conscience: Photographers and Social Change,* Follett, 1974.

World of Our Fathers: The Jews of Eastern Europe, Farrar, Straus, 1974.

Remember the Days: A Short History of the Jewish American, illustrated by Harvey Dinnerstein, Doubleday, 1974.

Bound for the Rio Grande: The Mexican Struggle, 1845-1850, Knopf, 1974.

Taking Root: Jewish Immigrants in America, Farrar, Straus, 1974.

Violins and Shovels: The WPA Arts Projects, Delacorte, 1976.

Never to Forget: The Jews of the Holocaust (*Horn Book* honor list; with teacher's guide), Harper, 1976, Trophy, 1991.

Dorothea Lange: A Photographer's Life (adult), Farrar, Straus, 1978, reprinted, 1985.

The Human Rights Book, Farrar, Straus, 1979.

All Times, All Peoples: A World History of Slavery (*Horn Book* honor list), illustrated by Leonard Everett Fisher, Harper, 1980.

The Chinese Americans, Crowell, 1980.

(Editor with Patricia G. Holland and Francine Krasno) *The Collected Correspondence of Lydia Maria Child, 1817-1880: Guide and Index to the Microfiche Edition* (adult), Kraus Microform, 1980.

The Truth about the Ku Klux Klan, F. Watts, 1982.

The Hispanic Americans, illustrated with photographs by Morrie Camhi and Catherine Noren, Crowell, 1982.

The Jewish Americans: A History in Their Own Words, 1650-1950 (ALA Notable Book), Crowell, 1982.

(Editor with P. G. Holland) *Lydia Maria Child: Selected Letters, 1817-1880* (adult), University of Massachusetts Press, 1982.

The Terrorists, Harper, 1983.

A Book about Names: In which Custom, Tradition, Law, Myth, History, Folklore, Foolery, Legend, Fashion, Nonsense, Symbol, Taboo Help Explain How We Got Our Names and What They Mean, illustrated by Mischa Richter, Crowell, 1984.

Ain't Gonna Study War No More: The Story of America's Peace-Seekers, Harper, 1985.

Mark Twain: A Writer's Life, F. Watts, 1985.

Betty Friedan: A Voice for Women's Rights (part of the "Women of Our Time" series), illustrated by Stephen Marchesi, Viking, 1985.

Dorothea Lange: Life through the Camera (part of the "Women of Our Time" series), illustrated by Donna Diamond and with photographs by Dorothea Lange, Viking, 1985.

The Jews in America: A Picture Album, Jewish Publication Society, 1985.

Poverty in America, Morrow, 1986.

Winnie Mandela: The Soul of South Africa (part of the "Women of Our Time" series), illustrated by S. Marchesi, Viking, 1986.

George Washington and the Birth of Our Nation, F. Watts, 1986.

Mary McLeod Bethune: Voice of Black Hope (part of the "Women of Our Time" series), illustrated by S. Marchesi, Viking, 1987.

The Landscape of Memory, Viking, 1987.

The American Revolutionaries: A History in Their Own Words, 1750-1800, Crowell, 1987.

Starting from Home: A Writer's Beginnings, Viking, 1988, Puffin, 1991.

Rescue: The Story of How Gentiles Saved Jews in the Holocaust, Harper, 1988, Trophy, 1991.

Benjamin Franklin: The New American, F. Watts, 1988.

American Politics: How It Really Works, illustrated by David Small, Morrow, 1989.

Voices from the Civil War: A Documentary History of the Great American Conflict, Crowell, 1989.

The Bill of Rights: How We Got It and What It Means, Harper, 1990.

Crime in America, Morrow, 1990.

Columbus and the World around Him, F. Watts, 1990.

The American Promise: Voices of a Changing Nation, 1945-Present, Bantam, 1990.

Thomas Jefferson: The Revolutionary Aristocrat, F. Watts, 1991.

The Amazing Potato, HarperCollins, 1992.

Andrew Jackson and his America, F. Watts, in press.

Lincoln: In His Own Words, illustrated by Stephen Alcorn, Harcourt, in press.

Editor of "Women of America" series, Crowell, 1962-74, "Zenith Books" series, Doubleday, 1963-73, and "Firebird Books" series, Scholastic Book Services, 1968-72. Author of introduction for *Learning about Biographies: A Reading-and-Writing Approach,* by Myra Zarnowski, National Council of Teachers of English, 1990.

Also author of documentary films, including *History of the American Negro* (series of three half-hour films), Niagara Films, 1965; *Five,* Silvermine Films, 1971; *The Bread and Roses Strike: Lawrence, 1912* (filmstrip), District 1199 Cultural Center, 1980; *The Camera of My Family,* Anti-Defamation League, 1981; *American Family: The Merlins,* Anti-Defamation League, 1982. Authors of scripts for radio and television.

Contributor to periodicals, including *New York Times Magazine, New York Times Book Review, English Journal, Virginia Quarterly Review, Library Journal, Wilson Library Bulletin, School Library Journal, Microform Review, Horn Book, Children's Literature in Education, Lion and the Unicorn, Social Education, New Advocate,* and *Children's Literature Association Quarterly.* Member of U.S. editorial board of *Children's Literature in Education,* beginning in 1973, and of *Lion and the Unicorn,* beginning in 1980.

SIDELIGHTS: Milton Meltzer is best known for his comprehensive studies of oppressed peoples. Much of his subject matter—poverty, religion, crime, peace, discrimination, slavery—concerns injustices especially common to America. Many critics have praised Meltzer's approach to these complex issues, noting that the author never "talks down" to his audience. In an essay for *Something about the Author Autobiography Series* (*SAAS*), Meltzer explains why he writes about controversial people and themes:

"My subjects choose action. . . . Action takes commitment, the commitment of dedicated, optimistic individuals. I try to make readers understand that history isn't only what happens to us. History is what we *make* happen. Each of us. All of us."

Meltzer has been interested in social issues since his childhood. As a first-generation American, he was able to see firsthand the difficulties faced by many immigrants. (Meltzer's parents, for example, tried to assimilate into American society as much as possible; this action would later cause identity problems for their son.) By the time Meltzer was a young adult, he began to feel a keen sense of loss with regard to his Eastern European/Jewish roots. "Perhaps [my parents] wanted to forget the world they had left behind," he writes in his essay. "Or because they knew I had no interest in their culture. I didn't realize until much later how much meaning their early life would have for me. When at last I had the sense to want to know about it, it was too late. They were gone."

Meltzer has used some key periods and events in his life, such as the Great Depression and his job with the government-sponsored Works Projects Administration, as fodder for books such as *Brother, Can You Spare a Dime?: The Great Depression, 1929-1933* and *Violins and Shovels: The WPA Arts Projects.* Over time, Meltzer has also had the opportunity to explore other concerns, such as racism and black history. While working on these projects, Meltzer has established a reputation for effectively incorporating eyewitness accounts and personal documents, such as diaries, letters, and speeches, into his work. Meltzer notes in *School Library Journal* that "the use of original sources . . . is a giant step out of the textbook swamp. Working with the living expression of an era . . . you get close to reliving those experiences yourself."

Meltzer's choice of material has sometimes come as a surprise to the author himself. "In those first years I wrote books without any great self-conciousness about the subjects I chose," he writes in *SAAS.* "Then one day a reviewer described me as a writer known for his interest in the underdog. A pattern had become obvious. It was not a choice deliberately made." Meltzer has extended his interest in social issues to his private life by joining unions, campaigning for political candidates, parading, and lobbying. "I try to be useful in the same way wherever and whenever I can," he relates in his essay. He adds: "All my writing comes out of my convictions. I've never had to write about anything I didn't believe in."

BIOGRAPHICAL/CRITICAL SOURCES:

BOOKS

Children's Literature Review, Volume 13, Gale, 1987.
Contemporary Literary Criticism, Volume 26, Gale, 1983.

Dictionary of Literary Biography, Volume 61: *American Writers for Children since 1960: Poets, Illustrators, and Nonfiction Authors,* edited by Glenn E. Estes, Gale, 1987, pp. 214-223.
Something about the Author Autobiography Series, Volume 1, Gale, 1986, pp. 203-221.

PERIODICALS

Bulletin of the Center for Children's Books, December, 1985; December, 1986.
Horn Book, October, 1982; January-February, 1986; April-March, 1987.
Los Angeles Times Book Review, April 23, 1989.
New Yorker, October 30, 1978.
New York Times Book Review, August 6, 1978; February 20, 1983.
School Library Journal, October, 1968; September, 1985; December, 1986.

*   *   *

MERRILL, Jean (Fairbanks) 1923-

PERSONAL: Born January 27, 1923, in Rochester, NY; daughter of Earl Dwight and Elsie Almetta (Fairbanks) Merrill. *Education:* Allegheny College, B.A., 1944; Wellesley College, M.A., 1945. *Politics:* Independent. *Avocational interests:* Reading, art, mycology.

ADDRESSES: Home—Angel's Ark, 29 South Main St., Randolph, VT 05060; and R.D., Chelsea, VT 05038 (summer). *Agent*—Dorothy Markinko, McIntosh & Otis, 310 Madison Ave., New York, NY 10017.

CAREER: Scholastic Magazines, Inc., New York City, assistant feature editor, 1945-46, feature editor, 1946-49, *Literary Cavalcade,* associate editor, 1950-51, editor, 1956-57; Bank Street College of Education, Publications Division, New York City, associate editor, 1965-66, consultant, 1967-71; writer for young people. Faculty member of workshops for librarians at Drake University, 1969, and in Hutchinson, KS, 1969.

MEMBER: Authors Guild, Dramatists Guild, Society of Children's Book Writers, American Civil Liberties Union, War Resisters League, North American Mycological Association, League of Vermont Writers, Vermont Council on the Arts, Vermont Institute of Natural Science, Phi Beta Kappa.

AWARDS, HONORS: Fulbright research grant, University of Madras, 1952-53; Fund for the Republic Award, 1956, for one-hour television drama, *The Claws in the Cat's Paw;* Lewis Carroll Shelf Award, 1963, for *The Superlative Horse,* and 1965, for *The Pushcart War;* Boys' Clubs of America Award, 1965, for *The Pushcart War;*

Dorothy Canfield Fisher Memorial Children's Book Award, 1975-76, and Sequoyah Award, 1977, both for *The Toothpaste Millionaire.*

WRITINGS:

FOR CHILDREN; ILLUSTRATED BY RONNI SOLBERT

Henry, The Hand-Painted Mouse, Coward, 1951.
The Woover, Coward, 1952.
Boxes, Coward, 1953.
The Tree House of Jimmy Domino, Walck, 1955.
The Travels of Marco, Knopf, 1955.
A Song for Gar, Whittlesey House, 1955.
The Very Nice Things, Harper, 1959.
Blue's Broken Heart, Whittlesey House, 1960.
Emily Emerson's Moon (verse), Little, Brown, 1960.
Shan's Lucky Knife: A Burmese Folk Tale, W. R. Scott, 1960.
The Superlative Horse: A Tale of Ancient China, W. R. Scott, 1961.
High, Wide & Handsome and Their Three Tall Tales, W. R. Scott, 1964.
The Pushcart War, W. R. Scott, 1964.
The Elephant Who Liked to Smash Small Cars, Pantheon, 1967.
Red Riding, Pantheon, 1967.
The Black Sheep, Pantheon, 1969.
Mary, Come Running, McCall Publishing, 1970.

OTHER

Tell about the Cowbarn, Daddy, illustrated by Lili Wronker, W. R. Scott, 1963.
(Editor with Solbert and author of introduction) Issa Kobayashi, *A Few Flies and I,* translated by R. H. Blyth and Nobuyuki Yuasa, Pantheon, 1969.
Here I Come—Ready Or Not!, illustrated by Frances Scott, A. Whitman, 1970.
How Many Kids Are Hiding on My Block?, illustrated by Scott, A. Whitman, 1971.
Please, Don't Eat My Cabin, illustrated by Scott, A. Whitman, 1971.
The Second Greatest Clown in the World, Houghton, 1971.
The Jackpot, Houghton, 1971.
(Contributor) *Isn't That What Friends Are For?,* (includes one-act play *Tightrope Act*), edited by Bank Street College of Education, Houghton, 1972.
The Toothpaste Millionaire, illustrated by Jan Palmer, Houghton, 1972.
The Bumper Sticker Book, illustrated by Scott, A. Whitman, 1973.
Maria's House, illustrated by Scott, Atheneum, 1976.
The Girl Who Loved Caterpillars, illustrated by Floyd Cooper, Philomel, 1992.

Also author of television drama, *The Claws in the Cat's Paw,* 1956. Associate editor and contributor, "Bank Street Readers" series, Macmillan, 1964-65; contributor to "Adult Reader" series, R & D Corporation, 1968, and to anthologies in the "Discoveries" series, Houghton, 1973. Contributor of short stories, articles, and reviews to various publications.

ADAPTATIONS: The Toothpaste Millionaire aired as an ABC-TV *Afternoon Special* in 1974; *The Superlative Horse* aired on the NBC-TV series *Vegetable Soup* and is available as a 16-mm color film from Phoenix Films. *A Song for Gar* was performed as a children's opera in San Diego, CA, 1970, and was adapted by William J. Adams for Readers Theatre; *Mary Come Running* provided the libretto for a chamber opera by Gwyneth Walker which was first produced in Randolph, VT, 1983. *The Pushcart War* has been broadcast on radio in New York, Boston, MA, and Denmark, and on television in England; stage versions have been performed in Boston, 1978, and Seattle, WA, 1981; a script adaptation by Gregory A. Falls is available from Anchorage Press. *The Elephant who Liked to Smash Small Cars* aired on the radio in 1971. Recordings of *The Travels of Marco, Red Riding,* and *The Elephant Who Liked to Smash Small Cars* have been produced by Random House. *Mary, Come Running* is available as a "talking book," while *The Pushcart War* and *The Toothpaste Millionaire* are available as "talking books" and in Braille.

SIDELIGHTS: "Jean Merrill has earned her solid reputation as a children's writer by the consistently fine quality of her books," Betty Boegehold comments in *Twentieth-Century Children's Writers.* The author is best known for her 1964 book *The Pushcart War,* which tells the story of how the drivers of little pushcarts withstand the bullying attacks of powerful truckers and keep their space on city streets. This "struggle of the small and weak against the strong and mighty" is typical of Merrill's work, according to Boegehold, and is enhanced by the author's mastery of "the subtle art of 'immediacy'—the reader is there and the adventure is happening to him or her."

Merrill's verse story *Emily Emerson's Moon,* for instance, has "wholly natural" relationships "that give the book . . . special charm," a *Horn Book* reviewer comments. In addition, the story "is intriguingly told with . . . catchy rhyme and rhythm," Joan Beck writes in the *Chicago Sunday Tribune. Maria's House,* the story of a poor girl who feels ashamed to draw her home for art class, similarly demonstrates how the author "has a rare gift for creating real characters and letting them develop," David K. Willis says in the *Christian Science Monitor.* The book "ends as the triumph of honesty over deceit, of love over selfishness," and is "so good, so universal in theme, that [it appeals] to the best in all of us."

Merrill's books also contain moral and informative elements in addition to realistic characters. *The Toothpaste Millionaire,* which relates how young Rufus Mayflower creates a big business from his homemade toothpaste, explains such business terms as cost and profit. But these mathematical concepts are "tucked so expertly and unobtrusively into the story that they only heighten the reader's enjoyment," Jennifer Farley Smith remarks in the *Christian Science Monitor. The Black Sheep* similarly brings a delicate touch to the tale of how a maverick sheep teaches his herd to accept individuals and their differences. According to June Meyer Jordan of the *New York Times Book Review,* Merrill's story "is a satisfying sandwich in which the peanut butter, sticky and nourishing, slides down with ease due to judicious use of jelly."

But it is *The Pushcart War,* with its spirited band of cart owners battling big-business truckers, that is "often considered a modern classic," as E. Wendy Saul comments in *School Library Journal.* Presented in the form of a scholarly study, *The Pushcart War* is "one of those rarities—a book that is both humorous and downright funny," a *Horn Book* reviewer states. The war for street space escalates as truckers run over pushcarts and cart owners puncture truck tires. "It's a delightful notion, and an utterly captivating book," Alberta Eiseman writes in the *New York Times Book Review.* The critic adds: "It's rare indeed to find a book for young people with both a point of view and a sense of the ridiculous." "This semi-recognized classic is one of the funniest and most satisfying triumphs of small-and-clever I know," *Washington Post Book World* contributor Noel Perrin claims. "It can be read in [many] different ways, and they are all funny."

"I grew up on an apple and dairy farm on the shores of Lake Ontario in Webster, New York," Merrill once commented, "and most of my waking hours, when I was not in school, were spent out-of-doors: building huts, dams, rafts, forts, making barrel-stave skis, inner-tube guns, roller-skate scooters, bows and arrows, collecting wild flowers and fossil rocks, swimming, tobogganing, climbing silos, riding hay wagons, tumbling in haylofts.

"Dolls, toys and games that came in boxes to be played on boards with set rules bored me swiftly. The only thing that could detain me indoors was a book—though a book could also be carried up into a tree, out to a meadow, down by the lakeside."

The author continued: "My interest in writing children's books may have derived from the great impact certain books had on me as a child, and perhaps a wish to recreate the quality of that experience. Certainly, one of the satisfactions of writing for children is the intensity of caring young readers lavish on the books they like."

BIOGRAPHICAL/CRITICAL SOURCES:

BOOKS

Twentieth-Century Children's Writers, 3rd edition, St. James Press, 1989, pp. 677-679.

PERIODICALS

Chicago Sunday Tribune, November 6, 1960, p. 12.
Christian Science Monitor, July 3, 1974, p. 7; November 6, 1974, p. 11.
Horn Book, October, 1960, p. 399; August, 1964, p. 378.
New York Times Book Review, July 12, 1964, p. 18.
Saturday Review, November 7, 1964, p. 56; January 24, 1970, p. 37.
School Library Journal, April, 1983, p. 30.
Times Literary Supplement, November 23, 1973, p. 1428.
Washington Post Book World, January 14, 1990, p. 11.

*   *   *

MICHAELS, J. Ramsey 1931-

PERSONAL: Born May 1, 1931, in Syracuse, NY; son of Peter (a farmer) and Ethel (a housewife; maiden name, Ramsey) Michaels; married Betty L. Flora (a housewife), July 31, 1954; children: Carolyn Kerr, Linda Donahue, David Kenneth. *Education:* Princeton University, A.B., 1952; Grace Theological Seminary, Th.M., 1956; Harvard University, Th.D., 1962.

ADDRESSES: Home—2706 South Edgewater, Springfield, MO 65804. *Office*—Department of Religious Studies, Southwest Missouri State University, Springfield, MO 65804.

CAREER: Gordon-Conwell Theological Seminary, South Hamilton, MA, instructor, 1958-60, assistant professor, 1960-63, associate professor, 1963-68, professor of New Testament, 1968-84; Southwest Missouri State University, Springfield, professor of religious studies, 1984—.

MEMBER: National Association of Baptist Professors of Religion, Society of Biblical Literature, Catholic Biblical Association, Institute for Biblical Research, Studiorum Novi Testamenti Societas.

AWARDS, HONORS: Burlington Northern Foundation faculty achievement award for scholarship, 1989.

WRITINGS:

(With G. W. Barker and W. L. Lane) *The New Testament Speaks,* Harper, 1969.
Servant and Son: Jesus in Parable and Gospel, John Knox, 1981.
I Peter, Word, Inc., 1988.
John, Hendrickson, 1989.
Interpreting the Book of Revelation, Baker Book, in press.

Contributing translator of *New International Version of the New Testament.* Contributor to theological journals.

SIDELIGHTS: J. Ramsey Michaels told *CA:* "Most of my writing is New Testament scholarship, the outgrowth of my classroom teaching. The object of such writing is, first, the interpretation of the original documents central to Christian faith and, second, the historical understanding of Jesus and Christian beginnings. My purpose is not so much to be a new voice in the present as to make the old voices from the past more clearly understood.

"My random interests outside the New Testament include the French Prophets, an eighteenth century millennarian movement in England, and the stories of Flannery O'Connor."

*   *   *

MIKOLAYCAK, Charles 1937-

PERSONAL: Surname is pronounced "*Mike*-o-lay-chak"; born January 26, 1937, in Scranton, PA; son of John Anthony and Helen (Gruscelak) Mikolaycak; married Carole Kismaric (an editor and writer), October 1, 1970. *Education:* Pratt Institute, B.F.A., 1958; attended New York University, 1958-59. *Avocational interests:* Reading, theatre, films, travel.

ADDRESSES: Home—64 East 91st St., New York, NY 10128.

CAREER: Free-lance illustrator and designer. DuCrot Studios, Hamburg, Germany, illustrator and designer, 1959; Time-Life Books, New York City, designer, 1963-76; Syracuse University, Syracuse, NY, guest instructor, 1976-88. Work represented in exhibits including "The Fine Art of Children's Book Illustrations," Port Washington Public Library, Long Island, NY, 1986; the Kerlan Collection, University of Minnesota; the Festival Art Collection, Keene State College, Keene, NH; the Mazza Collection, Findlay College, Findlay, OH; part of the permanent collection of the International Youth Library, Munich, Germany. *Military Service:* U.S. Army, 1960-62; became sergeant.

MEMBER: Society of Children's Book Writers.

AWARDS, HONORS: American Institute of Graphic Arts Children's Book Show selections, 1967, 1968, 1970, 1973, for *The Feast Day,* 1974, for *Shipwreck,* 1977, 1980, and 1986; Chicago Book Clinic Best of the Year Show selections, 1967, 1971, and 1972; Printing Industries of America Graphic Design Awards, 1967, for *Great Wolf and the Good Woodsman,* 1970, for *Mourka, the Mighty Cat,* 1971, 1972, and 1973; Charles W. Follett Award, 1969, for *Banner over Me;* Society of Illustrators Gold

Medal, 1970, for book art direction; New Jersey Institute of Technology Award, 1970, for *Russian Tales of Fabulous Beasts and Marvels;* works selected for entry in Biennial of Illustrations, Bratislava, by American Institute of Graphic Arts, 1973, for *How the Hare Told the Truth,* and 1984, for *Peter and the Wolf;* Children's Book Showcase selection, Children's Book Council, 1975, for *Shipwreck;* American Library Association (ALA) notable book citations, 1975, for *How Wilka Went to Sea and Other Tales from West of the Urals,* and 1981, for *I Am Joseph;* Brooklyn Museum Art Books for Children citations, 1977, 1978, and 1979, for *Great Wolf and the Good Woodsmen;* New York Graphics award, 1980, for *The Surprising Things Maui Did;* Parents' Choice Award for illustration, 1982, for *Peter and the Wolf,* and 1988, for *The Rumor of Pavel and Paali; New York Times* best illustrated books of 1984 citation, 1984, for *Babushka: An Old Russian Folktale; Horn Book* Fanfare list citation, 1984, for *The Highwayman;* Golden Kite Honor Book Award for illustration, 1986, for *Juma and the Magic Jinn;* University of Minnesota Kerlan Award, 1987, in recognition of singular attainments in the creation of children's literature; National Jewish Book Award for illustration, 1988, for *Exodus.*

WRITINGS:

(Reteller with wife, Carole Kismáric, and illustrator) *The Boy Who Tried to Cheat Death* (Norwegian folktale), Doubleday, 1971.

(Reteller and illustrator) *Babushka: An Old Russian Folktale,* Holiday House, 1984.

(Reteller and illustrator) *Orpheus,* Harcourt, 1992.

ILLUSTRATOR AND/OR DESIGNER OF CHILDREN'S BOOKS

Helen Hoover, *Great Wolf and the Good Woodsman,* Parents Magazine Press, 1967.

Margery Greenleaf, *Banner over Me,* Follett, 1968.

Jacob and Wilhelm Grimm, *Little Red Riding Hood,* C. R. Gibson, 1968.

Grimm and Grimm, *Grimm's Golden Goose,* Random House, 1969.

Jane Lee Hyndman (under pseudonym Lee Wyndham), *Mourka, the Mighty Cat,* Parents Magazine Press, 1969.

Hyndman (under pseudonym Lee Wyndham), *Russian Tales of Fabulous Beasts and Marvels,* Parents Magazine Press, 1969.

Cynthia King, *In the Morning of Time: The Story of the Norse God Balder,* Four Winds, 1970.

Barbara Rinkoff, *The Pretzel Hero: A Story of Old Vienna,* Parents Magazine Press, 1970.

Eric Sundell, *The Feral Child,* Abelard-Schuman, 1971.

Margaret Hodges, reteller, *The Gorgon's Head: A Myth from the Isles of Greece,* Little, Brown, 1972.

Barbara K. Walker, *How the Hare Told the Truth about His Horse,* Parents Magazine Press, 1972.

Edwin Fadiman, Jr., *The Feast Day,* Little, Brown, 1973.

Vera G. Cumberlege, *Shipwreck,* Follett, 1974.

Mirra Ginsburg, translator and editor, *How Wilka Went to Sea and Other Tales from West of the Urals,* Crown, 1975.

Marion L. Starkey, *The Tall Man from Boston,* Crown, 1975.

Jerzy Ficowsky, *Sister of the Birds and Other Gypsy Tales,* translated from the Polish by Lucia Borski, Abingdon, 1976.

Doris Gates, *A Fair Wind for Troy,* Viking, 1976.

Norma Farber, *Six Impossible Things before Breakfast,* Addison-Wesley, 1977.

Avi, *Captain Grey,* Pantheon, 1977.

Farber, *Three Wanderers from Wapping,* Addison-Wesley, 1978.

Barbara Cohen, *The Binding of Isaac,* Lothrop, 1978.

Ewa Reid and Barbara Reid, *The Cobbler's Reward,* Macmillan, 1978.

Richard Kennedy, *Delta Baby and Two Sea Songs,* Addison-Wesley, 1979.

Jay Williams, *The Surprising Things Maui Did,* Four Winds, 1979.

Elizabeth Winthrop, *Journey to the Bright Kingdom,* Holiday House, 1979.

William H. Armstrong, *The Tale of Tawny and Dingo,* Harper, 1979.

Ginsburg, *The Twelve Clever Brothers and Other Fools,* Lippincott, 1979.

Earlene Long, *Johnny's Egg,* Addison-Wesley, 1980.

Cohen, *I Am Joseph,* Lothrop, 1980.

Anne Pellowski, *The Nine Crying Dolls: A Story from Poland,* Philomel Books-U.S. Committee for UNICEF, 1980.

Loretta Holz, *The Christmas Spider: A Puppet Play from Poland and Other Traditional Games, Crafts, and Activities,* Philomel Books-U.S. Committee for UNICEF, 1980.

Anne Laurin, *Perfect Crane,* Harper, 1981.

Bernard Evslin, *Signs and Wonders: Tales from the Old Testament,* Four Winds, 1981.

Sergei Prokofiev, *Peter and the Wolf,* translated from the Russian by Maria Carlson, Viking, 1982, published with cassette, Live Oak Media, 1987.

Jan Wahl, *Tiger Hunt,* Harcourt, 1982.

Winthrop, *A Child Is Born: The Christmas Story,* Holiday House, 1983.

Alfred Noyes, *The Highwayman,* Lothrop, 1983.

Eve Bunting, *The Man Who Could Call Down Owls,* Macmillan, 1984.

Zilpha K. Snyder, *The Changing Maze,* Macmillan, 1985.

Winthrop, editor, *He Is Risen: The Easter Story,* Holiday House, 1985.

Joy Anderson, *Juma and the Magic Jinn,* Lothrop, 1986.

Jane Yolen, editor, *The Lullaby Songbook,* Harcourt, 1986.

Miriam Chaikin, *Exodus,* Holiday House, 1987.

Carole Kismaric, reteller, *The Rumor of Pavel and Paali: A Ukrainian Folktale,* Harper, 1988.

Kismaric, reteller, *A Gift from Saint Nicholas,* Holiday House, 1988.

Lee Bennett Hopkins, compiler, *Voyages: Poems* (by Walt Whitman), Harcourt, 1988.

Yolen, reteller, *Tam Lin: An Old Ballad,* Harcourt, 1990.

Ellin Greene, reteller, *The Legend of the Christmas Rose,* Holiday House, 1990.

Eric A. Kimmel, *Bearhead,* Holiday House, 1991.

Hodges, reteller, *The Hero of Bremen,* Holiday House, 1993.

PICTURE EDITOR AND/OR DESIGNER

Ken Dallison, *When Zeppelins Flew,* Time-Life, 1969.

Fred Freeman, *Duel of the Ironclads,* Time-Life, 1969.

Paul Williams, *The Warrior Knights,* Time-Life, 1969.

Carole Kismaric, *On Leadership,* I.B.M., 1974.

Robert Elson, *Prelude to War,* Time-Life, 1976.

Robert Wernick, *Blitzkreig,* Time-Life, 1976.

Leonard Mosley, *The Battle of Britain,* Time-Life, 1976.

Robert Adams, *Beauty in Photography: Essays in Defense of Traditional Values,* Aperture, 1981.

Adams, *Summer Nights,* Aperture, 1985.

OTHER

Also creator of the Constitution Poster Triptych, a three-poster set celebrating the bicentennial of the U.S. Constitution, 1986.

SIDELIGHTS: Award-winning children's illustrator and book designer Charles Mikolaycak recreates his own boyhood and the historical worlds of others in his works. His drawings deal with everything from biblical stories to the recreations of old folktales and vary in composition from brilliant, lushly colored pictures to more somber black and white depictions. "I have found the perfect vehicle for myself—the picture book," maintains Mikolaycak. "I cast the roles, dress the performers, design the sets, choose the moment to be illustrated and tell a story in visual terms. What an opportunity!"

Born in Scranton, Pennsylvania, Mikolaycak became and remained an only child after his twin brother died a few months following their birth. He remembers making his first drawing in the fourth grade and his interest in illustration increased steadily. By the time he was ten years old, Mikolaycak was drawing more seriously and most, if not all, of his drawings were of movie posters. "Through-out grade school, I drew in my spare time—on the kitchen table with its smooth, cool porcelain surface, on the linoleum floor, on a tablet on the rug in front of the radio," recalls Mikolaycak in an essay for *Something about the Author Autobiography Series (SAAS).* "In the seventh grade I first became aware of drawing as illustration."

Mikolaycak's world opened up even further in high school when he realized that he actually wanted to do something with his drawing ability. Along with taking an art class at school, Mikolaycak's parents also enrolled him in a outside painting class. During these same years, Mikolaycak began accompanying his parents to a nearby summer playhouse, explaining in his *SAAS* essay: "This was a beginning of my love for, and fascination with, the theater." Beginning to think about his future, Mikolaycak noticed a small advertisement for Pratt Institute in the back of the *New York Times Magazine.* He applied and was accepted.

"It was during the years at Pratt I started discovering who I really was and who I was capable of becoming," remarks Mikolaycak in his autobiographical essay. "For the first time in my life I was surrounded by people, friends who had the same interests—not a football player in the crowd." Graduating with a B.F.A. degree, Mikolaycak knew he wanted to illustrate but didn't know for whom or where. This decision was made when he was contacted by Mr. and Mrs. Dudley DuCrot. The couple had a small advertising agency in New Jersey, but wanted to return to Germany, where they had met, and establish a designer's studio. They got Mikolaycak's name from Pratt, and in April of 1960 he sailed for Hamburg. Although the advertising accounts were not very exciting, Mikolaycak planned to stay in Germany for a year before returning to New York to do magazine illustration. His stay was cut short, though, when he was drafted into the Army toward the end of the summer.

Returning home, Mikolaycak discovered that the regional quotas were filled, and not wanting to volunteer, he moved into an apartment in Brooklyn and began illustrating for such teen magazines as *Seventeen, Calling All Girls,* and *Datebook.* The army then decided that they did need Mikolaycak, and following basic training he was assigned to the graphics department in the Pentagon. After being discharged, he spent a summer at home in Pennsylvania before moving back to Brooklyn and beginning his career as a book illustrator. Mikolaycak spent many hours dropping off portfolios before finally receiving calls from Elizabeth Armstrong, who wanted to be his agent, and from Edward Hamilton, who offered him a job as an assistant to the designer at Time-Life Books. So, Mikolaycak began spending his days at Time-Life, using his nights and weekends to do the illustration jobs that Armstrong got for him. After doing his first children's book, *Great Wolf and the Good Woodsman,* Mikolaycak was hooked; and when

Time-Life decided to relocate, he chose to become a full-time illustrator of children's books.

"I am an illustrator because I must illustrate, and I am a book designer because I love books," Mikolaycak once commented. "Obviously the field in which the two meet is the one which makes me most happy—children's books. I can usually find something in most stories which makes me excited; be it a locale or period of time requiring great research, or a sense of fantasy which permits me to exercise my own fantasies pictorially, or great writing which forces me to try to match it in visual images." Although most of Mikolaycak's work consists of illustrating other authors' works, he has written a few of his own books. His 1984 retelling of *Babushka: An Old Russian Folktale* details the story of a peasant woman who was too busy cleaning her house to accompany the three kings as they followed the star. She later repented and spent the rest of her life searching for baby Jesus, leaving gifts for children as she went along. Mikolaycak "has captured the haunting, ethereal qualities of *Babushka*," asserts Lisa Lane in the *Christian Science Monitor*. And Jean F. Mercier, writing in *Publishers Weekly*, concludes: "Mikolaycak's adaptation stands out as an astonishingly original feat."

"I am particularly fond of epics and folk tales," Mikolaycak once remarked. "I don't care how many times they have been illustrated before; the challenge is to find the truth for myself and depict it. When I illustrate I am aware of many things; storytelling, graphic design, sequence of images and my own interests in which I can indulge. I never 'draw-down' to a projected audience. I feel children are most surprisingly capable of meeting a challenge and instinctively understand a drawing. Perhaps it will lead them to ask a question or wonder in silence—either will help them to learn or to extend themselves. I have experienced that if I am satisfied with one of my books, both children and adults will often get from it more than I ever realized I was putting into it."

BIOGRAPHICAL/CRITICAL SOURCES:

BOOKS

Freedman, Russell, *Holiday House, The First 50 Years*, Holiday House, 1985, pp. 96-97.

Mikolaycak, Charles, essay in *Fifth Book of Junior Authors and Illustrators*, edited by Sally Holmes Holtze, H. W. Wilson, 1983, pp. 216-17.

Mikolaycak, essay in *Something about the Author Autobiography Series*, Volume 4, Gale, 1987.

Roginski, Jim, *Behind the Covers*, Libraries Unlimited, Inc., 1985, pp. 138-53.

PERIODICALS

Christian Science Monitor, December 7, 1984, p. B6.

Horn Book, November, 1983; March-April, 1986, pp. 167-73.
Language Arts, October, 1981, pp. 850-57.
Library Journal, November 15, 1971, p. 3902.
New Advocate, spring, 1990, pp. 111-15.
New York Times Book Review, February 19, 1984; November 4, 1984, p. 22; September 25, 1988, p. 51; March 26, 1989; December 9, 1990, p. 30.
Publishers Weekly, September 27, 1971, p. 66; December 14, 1984, p. 54.
School Library Journal, April, 1988, pp. 73-74.
Washington Post Book World, November 7, 1971, p. 4.
Wilson Library Bulletin, February, 1989, pp. 82-83.

*   *   *

MILES, T(homas) R(ichard)   1923-

PERSONAL: Born March 11, 1923, in Sheffield, England; son of Richard (an engineer) and Alice (Miller) Miles; married Elaine Armstrong (a teacher of dyslexic children), August 21, 1951; children: P. J. R. *Education:* Magdalen College, Oxford, M.A., 1945; University College of North Wales, Ph.D., 1963. *Religion:* Society of Friends (Quaker). *Avocational interests:* Lawn tennis (former international and Wimbledon player), golf, playing the cello.

ADDRESSES: Home—Llys-y-Gwynt, Llandegfan, Menai Bridge, Gwynedd, Wales. *Office*—Department of Psychology, University College of North Wales, Bangor, Wales.

CAREER: University College of North Wales, Bangor, assistant lecturer, 1949-52, lecturer, 1952-63, professor of psychology, 1963-87, professor emeritus, 1987—.

MEMBER: Royal Institute of Philosophy (member of council), British Psychological Society (fellow), British Dyslexia Association (vice-president).

WRITINGS:

Religion and the Scientific Outlook, Allen & Unwin, 1959.
Eliminating the Unconscious, Pergamon, 1966.
On Helping the Dyslexic Child, Methuen Educational, 1970.
Religious Experience, Macmillan, 1972.
The Dyslexic Child, Priory Press, 1974.
(With wife, Elaine Miles) *More Help for Dyslexic Children*, Methuen, 1975.
Understanding Dyslexia, Hodder & Stoughton, 1978, Amethyst, 1987.
(With P. Harzem) *Conceptual Issues in Operant Psychology*, Wiley, 1978.
(Editor with G. T. Pavlidis) *Dyslexia Research and Its Applications to Education*, Wiley, 1981.

The Bangor Dyslexia Test, Learning Development Aids, 1982.
(With E. Miles) *Help for Dyslexic Children,* Methuen, 1983.
Dyslexia: The Pattern of Difficulties, Blackwell, 1983.
(With D. E. Gilroy) *Dyslexia at College,* Routledge & Kegan Paul, 1986.
(With E. Miles) *Dyslexia: 100 Years On,* Open University Press, 1990.
(Editor with E. Miles) *Dyslexia and Mathematics,* Routledge & Kegan Paul, 1991.

Contributor to *Quarterly Journal of Experimental Psychology, Mind, Philosophy, British Journal of Educational Psychology, British Journal for the Philosophy of Science, Journal of Child Psychology and Psychiatry, Religious Studies, Annals of Dyslexia,* and other professional journals.

WORK IN PROGRESS: Further research on dyslexia.

SIDELIGHTS: T. R. Miles writes *CA:* "For the last three decades my main research interest has been the study of dyslexia. Originally this was a sideline, but it soon became clear that I had—almost inadvertently—stumbled on something which was of major significance to many people. I have been particularly impressed by the courage displayed by many families despite the fact that dyslexic children are sometimes mistakenly dubbed as 'lazy' or 'careless' and their parents as 'over-fussy'; and in many cases the diagnosis itself can bring overwhelming relief. It therefore seems to me that the spreading of knowledge about dyslexia is important both theoretically and practically. My other interests include the theoretical bases of behaviourism and problems in the relationship between psychology and religion."

*   *   *

MILLER, Sandra (Peden) 1948-
(Sandy Miller)

PERSONAL: Born December 25, 1948, in Horton, KS; daughter of Norman Leslie and Beckie (Wagoner) Peden; married Brian Miller (a writer and vice-president of a boys' ranch), May 18, 1968; children: Benjamin, Jeffery, Philip, Matthew, Elizabeth, Rebecca. *Education:* Attended Washburn University; Northeastern State University, B.A., 1991. *Religion:* Protestant.

ADDRESSES: Home and office—Bethesda Boys Ranch, P.O. Box 311, Mounds, OK 74047.

CAREER: Bethesda Missionary Society, missionary in Jamaica, 1969-71; Bethesda Boys Ranch, Mounds, OK, household coordinator, 1971-85, educational director, 1985—, admissions officer, 1991—. Free-lance writer.

MEMBER: Oklahoma Writers Federation, Tulsa Tuesday Writers (president, 1982), Tulsa Christian Writers (vice-president, 1981).

AWARDS, HONORS: IRA/CBC Award, 1983, for *Two Loves for Jenny,* and 1986, for *Freddie the Thirteenth.*

WRITINGS:

UNDER NAME SANDY MILLER; FOR YOUNG ADULTS

Two Loves for Jenny, New American Library, 1982.
Smart Girl, New American Library, 1982.
Chase the Sun, New American Library, 1983.
Lynn's Challenge, New American Library, 1984.
This Song Is for You, Warner Books, 1984.
Freddie the Thirteenth, New American Library, 1985.
A Tale of Two Turkeys, New American Library, 1985.
Allegra, New American Library, 1987.
(With husband, Brian Miller) *A Piece of the Pie,* Bama Pie Ltd., 1987.

ADAPTATIONS: Two Loves for Jenny was adapted for television and broadcast as *Between Two Loves* by ABC-TV, October 27, 1982.

WORK IN PROGRESS: With Sammie Dennison-Harmon, *Adeline,* an historical adult novel; research on Native Americans for books about the Osage and Cherokee tribes.

SIDELIGHTS: Sandy Miller once told *CA:* "My earliest memories are of sitting on one of my parents' laps while they read Little Golden Books to me, or lying between them in bed as my father read aloud from a novel. As soon as I learned to read for myself at the age of five, that was all I wanted to do. During my early teenage years, I stayed up many nights hiding in my closet with a good book. I always stuck a towel under the crack of the door so my parents wouldn't see the light and tell me to go to bed. I still like to read children's and young adult books. Perhaps that's why I like to write them so much.

"I was an only child for ten years before my parents had four more children. Consequently, I entertained myself. We lived in the country and there were always wonderful things to do, such as climb the windmill, silo, or apple tree. One of my favorite places was a ditch that curved through the length of our pasture. It became all kinds of magical things: a trench for soldiers, a creek for a wagon train crossing the prairie, the yellow brick road leading to Oz. That must be where my imagination got such a productive start, and it's never stopped. I will always love to daydream. When I was eleven, we moved to town. I missed the country, but I built a desk in an elm tree and spent many hours there thinking and writing.

"I began writing poems at the age of seven, and sold the first one, 'My Country,' to *Grit* when I was thirteen. I sold several more poems and two articles when I was a teenager. When I was twenty-seven, I took a correspondence course that started me writing seriously. With six young children, it was hard for me to find time to write, so my first book was written from 4:30 to 6:30 every morning.

"When I write my books, I can remember exactly how I felt when I was a teenager. Though times and situations may change, people's feelings will always be the same. I like to write happy books with uplifting endings because I think it's good for people to read positive, wholesome books."

* * *

MILLER, Sandy
See MILLER, Sandra (Peden)

* * *

MILLMAN, Lawrence 1946-

PERSONAL: Born January 13, 1946, in Kansas City, MO; son of Daniel S. (A lawyer) and Zelma (an artist; maiden name, Lawrence) Millman. *Education:* Washington University, St. Louis, MO, B.A., 1968; Rutgers University, M.A., 1971, Ph.D., 1974. *Politics:* Agrarian. *Religion:* None.

ADDRESSES: Home—Box 1582, Cambridge, MA 02238.

CAREER: University of New Hampshire, Durham, assistant professor of English, 1973-74; writer in western Ireland, 1974-77; University of Minnesota, Minneapolis, assistant professor of English, 1977-78; Tufts University, Medford, MA, lecturer in English, 1979-80; Vermont College, Montpelier, faculty advisor for Goddard M.F.A. in writing program, beginning 1981; affiliated with Harvard University Extension Program, 1985.

AWARDS, HONORS: Grant from International PEN, 1977; Bush Foundation fellowship, 1979-80; Fulbright fellowship to University of Iceland, Reykjavik, 1982; Guggenheim fellowship, 1983-84; finalist, Hemingway Award, 1983; Ludwig Vogelstein fellowship, 1986.

WRITINGS:

Our Like Will Not Be There Again (nonfiction), Little, Brown, 1977.
St. Kilda Amen, Ashplant Press, 1979.
Hero Jesse (novel), St. Martin's, 1982.
Smell of Earth and Clay (Eskimo translations), White Pine, 1985.
Parliament of Ravens (stories), LoonBooks, 1986.

A Kayak Full of Ghosts (Eskimo folktales), Capra Press, 1987.
The Wrong Headed Man (stories), University of Missouri Press, 1988.
Last Places (travel book), Houghton, 1990.
Wolverine Creates the World (folktales), Capra Press, 1992.

SIDELIGHTS: Lawrence Millman told *CA:* "I tend to react eternally against a shady past: a Ph.D. in English. My point of view was formed when I lived in Ireland for two years, among old story-tellers, and listened to the verbal eloquence with which uneducated and illiterate people can speak."

BIOGRAPHICAL/CRITICAL SOURCES:

BOOKS

Brown, George Mackay, *Under Brinkie's Brae,* Gordon Wright, 1980.

PERIODICALS

Atlantic, March, 1990, p. 117.
Boston Globe, March 25, 1990.
Boston Herald, January 28, 1990.
Cambridge Chronicle, December 24, 1987.
Chicago Tribune, October 25, 1987, p. 6.
Kansas City Star, June 5, 1977; January 15, 1989.
Los Angeles Times Book Review, January 21, 1990, p. 6.
New Yorker, February 26, 1990, p. 132.
New York Review of Science Fiction, December, 1991.
New York Times Book Review, June 19, 1977; December 11, 1988, p. 14; June 10, 1990, p. 48.
Orcadian, August 9, 1977; September 6, 1979.
North Shore Magazine, July 12, 1990.
Portsmouth Herald, January 9, 1982.
Times (London), May 21, 1990.

* * *

MOORCOCK, Michael (John) 1939-
(Bill Barclay, William Ewert Barclay, Edward P. Bradbury, James Colvin; Michael Barrington and Philip James, joint pseudonyms; Desmond Reid, house pseudonym)

PERSONAL: Born December 18, 1939, in Mitcham, Surrey, England; son of Arthur and June (Taylor) Moorcock; married Hilary Bailey (a writer), September, 1962 (divorced, April, 1978); married Jill Riches, 1978 (divorced); married Linda Mullens Steele, September, 1983; children: (first marriage) Sophie, Katherine, Max.

ADDRESSES: Home—c/o Sheil, 43 Doughty St., London WC1, England.

CAREER: Writer. Has also worked as a singer-guitarist; editor, *Tarzan Adventures* (juvenile magazine), 1956-58; Amalgamated Press, London, England, editor and writer for the *Sexton Blake Library* and for comic strips and children's annuals, 1959-61; editor and pamphleteer, Liberal Party, 1962; *New Worlds* (science fiction magazine), London, England, editor and publisher, 1964—; works with rock and roll bands Hawkwind and Blue Oyster Cult; member of rock and roll band Michael Moorcock and the Deep Fix.

MEMBER: Authors Guild.

AWARDS, HONORS: Nebula Award, Science Fiction Writers of America, 1967, for *Behold the Man;* British Science Fiction Association award and Arts Council of Great Britain award, both 1967, both for *New Worlds;* August Derleth Award, British Fantasy Society, 1972, for *The Knight of the Swords,* 1973, for *The King of the Swords,* 1974, for *The Jade Man's Eyes,* 1975, for *The Sword and the Stallion,* and 1976, for *The Hollow Lands;* International Fantasy Award, 1972 and 1973, for fantasy novels; Guardian Literary Prize, 1977, for *The Condition of Muzak;* John W. Campbell Memorial Award, 1978, and World Fantasy Award, World Fantasy Convention, 1979, both for *Gloriana; or, The Unfulfilled Queen.*

WRITINGS:

(With James Cawthorn, under house pseudonym Desmond Reid) *Caribbean Crisis,* Sexton Blake Library, 1962.
The Sundered Worlds, Compact Books, 1965, Paperback Library, 1966, published as *The Blood Red Game,* Sphere Books, 1970.
The Fireclown, Compact Books, 1965, Paperback Library, 1966, published as *The Winds of Limbo,* Sphere Books, 1970.
(Under pseudonym James Colvin) *The Deep Fix,* Compact Books, 1966.
The Wrecks of Time (bound with *Tramontane* by Emil Petaja), Ace Books, 1966 (revised edition published separately in England as *The Rituals of Infinity,* Arrow Books, 1971).
The Twilight Man, Compact Books, 1966, Berkley Publishing, 1970 (published in England as *The Shores of Death,* Sphere Books, 1970).
(Under pseudonym Bill Barclay) *Printer's Devil,* Compact Books, 1966, published under name Michael Moorcock as *The Russian Intelligence,* Savoy Books, 1980.
(Under pseudonym Bill Barclay) *Somewhere in the Night,* Compact Books, 1966, revised edition published under name Michael Moorcock as *The Chinese Agent,* Macmillan, 1970.
(Ghostwriter) Roger Harris, *The LSD Dossier,* Compact Books, 1966.

The Ice Schooner, Sphere Books, 1968, Berkley Publishing, 1969, revised edition, Harrap, 1985.
(With wife, Hilary Bailey) *The Black Corridor,* Ace Books, 1969.
The Time Dweller, Hart-Davis, 1969, Berkley Publishing, 1971.
(With James Cawthorn under joint pseudonym Philip James) *The Distant Suns,* Unicorn Bookshop, 1975.
Moorcock's Book of Martyrs, Quartet Books, 1976, published as *Dying for Tomorrow,* DAW Books, 1978.
(With Michael Butterworth) *The Time of the Hawklords,* A. Ellis, 1976.
Sojan (juvenile), Savoy Books, 1977.
Epic Pooh, British Fantasy Society, 1978.
Gloriana; or, The Unfulfilled Queen, Allison & Busby, 1978, Avon, 1979.
The Real Life Mr. Newman, A. J. Callow, 1979.
The Golden Barge, DAW Books, 1980.
My Experiences in the Third World War, Savoy Books, 1980.
The Retreat from Liberty: The Erosion of Democracy in Today's Britain, Zomba Books, 1983.
(With others) *Exploring Fantasy Worlds: Essays on Fantastic Literature,* edited by Darrell Schweitzer, Borgo, 1985.
Letters from Hollywood, Harrap, 1986.
(With James Cawthorn) *Fantasy: The One Hundred Best Books,* Carroll & Graf, 1988.
Mother London, Crown, 1989.
Wizardry and Wild Romance: A Study of Heroic Fantasy, Gollancz, 1989.
Casablanca, Gollancz, 1989.

"ELRIC" SERIES; "ETERNAL CHAMPION" BOOKS

The Stealer of Souls, and Other Stories (also see below), Neville Spearman, 1963, Lancer Books, 1967.
Stormbringer, Jenkins, 1965, Lancer Books, 1967.
The Singing Citadel (also see below), Berkley Publishing, 1970.
The Sleeping Sorceress, New English Library, 1971, Lancer Books, 1972, published as *The Vanishing Tower,* DAW Books, 1977.
The Dreaming City, Lancer Books, 1972 (revised edition published in England as *Elric of Melnibone,* Hutchinson, 1972).
The Jade Man's Eyes, Unicorn Bookshop, 1973.
Elric: The Return to Melnibone, Unicorn Bookshop, 1973.
The Sailor on the Seas of Fate, DAW Books, 1976.
The Bane of the Black Sword, DAW Books, 1977.
The Weird of the White Wolf (contains some material from *The Stealer of Souls, and Other Stories* and *The Singing Citadel*), DAW Books, 1977.
Elric at the End of Time, DAW Books, 1985.
The Fortress of the Pearl, Ace Books, 1989.

"MICHAEL KANE" SERIES; UNDER PSEUDONYM EDWARD P. BRADBURY

Warriors of Mars (also see below), Compact Books, 1965, published under name Michael Moorcock as *The City of the Beast,* Lancer Books, 1970.

Blades of Mars (also see below), Compact Books, 1965, published under name Michael Moorcock as *The Lord of the Spiders,* Lancer Books, 1971.

The Barbarians of Mars (also see below), Compact Books, 1965, published under name Michael Moorcock as *The Masters of the Pit,* Lancer Books, 1971.

Warrior of Mars (contains *Warriors of Mars, Blades of Mars,* and *The Barbarians of Mars*), New English Library, 1981.

"THE HISTORY OF THE RUNESTAFF" SERIES; "ETERNAL CHAMPION" BOOKS

The Jewel in the Skull (also see below), Lancer Books, 1967.

Sorcerer's Amulet (also see below), Lancer Books, 1968 (published in England as *The Mad God's Amulet,* Mayflower Books, 1969).

Sword of the Dawn (also see below), Lancer Books, 1968.

The Secret of the Runestaff (also see below), Lancer Books, 1969 (published in England as *The Runestaff,* Mayflower Books, 1969).

The History of the Runestaff (contains *The Jewel in the Skull, Sorcerer's Amulet, Sword of the Dawn,* and *The Secret of the Runestaff*), Granada, 1979.

"JERRY CORNELIUS" SERIES

The Final Programme (also see below), Avon, 1968, revised edition, Allison & Busby, 1969.

A Cure for Cancer (also see below), Holt, 1971.

The English Assassin (also see below), Allison & Busby, 1972.

The Lives and Times of Jerry Cornelius (also see below), Allison & Busby, 1976.

The Adventures of Una Persson and Catherine Cornelius in the Twentieth Century (also see below), Quartet Books, 1976.

The Condition of Muzak (also see below), Allison & Busby, 1977, Gregg, 1978.

The Cornelius Chronicles (contains *The Final Programme, A Cure for Cancer, The English Assassin,* and *The Condition of Muzak*), Avon, 1977.

The Great Rock n' Roll Swindle, Virgin Books, 1980.

The Entropy Tango (also see below), New English Library, 1981.

The Opium General (also see below), Harrap, 1985.

The Cornelius Chronicles, Volume 2 (contains *The Lives and Times of Jerry Cornelius* and *The Entropy Tango*), Avon, 1986.

The Cornelius Chronicles, Volume 3 (contains *The Adventures of Una Persson and Catherine Cornelius in the Twentieth Century* and *The Opium General*), Avon, 1987.

"KARL GLOGAUER" SERIES

Behold the Man, Allison & Busby, 1969, Avon, 1970.

Breakfast in the Ruins: A Novel of Inhumanity, New English Library, 1972, Random House, 1974.

"CORUM" SERIES; "ETERNAL CHAMPION" BOOKS

The Knight of the Swords (also see below), Mayflower Books, 1970, Berkley Publishing, 1971.

The Queen of the Swords (also see below), Berkley Publishing, 1971.

The King of the Swords (also see below), Berkley Publishing, 1971.

The Bull and the Spear (also see below), Berkley Publishing, 1973.

The Oak and the Ram (also see below), Berkley Publishing, 1973.

The Sword and the Stallion (also see below), Berkley Publishing, 1974.

The Swords Trilogy (contains *The Knight of the Swords, The Queen of the Swords,* and *The King of the Swords*), Berkley Publishing, 1977.

The Chronicles of Corum (contains *The Bull and the Spear, The Oak and the Ram,* and *The Sword and the Stallion*), Berkley Publishing, 1978.

"JOHN DAKER" SERIES; "ETERNAL CHAMPION" BOOKS

The Eternal Champion, Dell, 1970, revised edition, Harper, 1978.

Phoenix in Obsidian, Mayflower Books, 1970, published as *The Silver Warriors,* Dell, 1973.

The Dragon in the Sword, Granada, 1986.

"OSWALD BASTABLE" SERIES

The Warlord of the Air (also see below), Ace Books, 1971.

The Land Leviathan (also see below), Quartet Books, 1974.

The Steel Tsar (also see below), DAW Books, 1983.

The Nomad of Time (contains *The Warlord of the Air, The Land Leviathan,* and *The Steel Tsar*), Granada, 1984.

"THE DANCERS AT THE END OF TIME" SERIES

An Alien Heat (also see below), Harper, 1972.

The Hollow Lands (also see below), Harper, 1974.

The End of All Songs (also see below), Harper, 1976.

Legends from the End of Time, Harper, 1976.

The Transformations of Miss Mavis Ming, W. H. Allen, 1977, published as *A Messiah at the End of Time,* DAW Books, 1978.

The Dancers at the End of Time (contains *An Alien Heat, The Hollow Lands,* and *The End of All Songs*), Granada, 1981.

"CASTLE BRASS" SERIES; "ETERNAL CHAMPION" BOOKS

Count Brass (also see below), Mayflower Books, 1973.
The Champion of Garathorm (also see below), Mayflower Books, 1973.
The Quest for Tanelorn (also see below), Mayflower Books, 1975, Dell, 1976.
The Chronicles of Castle Brass (contains *Castle Brass, The Champion of Garathorm,* and *The Quest for Tanelorn*), Granada, 1985.

"VON BEK FAMILY" SERIES

The War Hound and the World's Pain, Timescape, 1981.
The Brothel in Rosenstrasse, New English Library, 1982, Tigerseye Press, 1986.
The City in the Autumn Stars, Ace Books, 1986.

"COLONEL PYAT" SERIES

Byzantium Endures, Secker & Warburg, 1981, Random House, 1982.
The Laughter of Carthage, Random House, 1984.

SCREENPLAYS

The Final Programme (based on his novel of the same title; removed name from credits after dispute with director), EMI, 1973.
The Land That Time Forgot, British Lion, 1975.

EDITOR

(And contributor under name Michael Moorcock and under pseudonym James Colvin) *The Best of "New Worlds,"* Compact Books, 1965.
Best SF Stories from "New Worlds," Panther Books, 1967, Berkley Publishing, 1968.
The Traps of Time, Rapp & Whiting, 1968.
(And contributor under pseudonym James Colvin) *The Best SF Stories from "New Worlds" 2,* Panther Books, 1968, Berkley Publishing, 1969.
(And contributor under pseudonym James Colvin) *The Best SF Stories from "New Worlds" 3,* Panther Books, 1968, Berkley Publishing, 1969.
The Best SF Stories from "New Worlds" 4, Panther Books, 1969, Berkley Publishing, 1971
The Best SF Stories from "New Worlds" 5, Panther Books, 1969, Berkley Publishing, 1971.
(And contributor) *The Best SF Stories from "New Worlds" 6,* Panther Books, 1970, Berkley Publishing, 1971.
The Best SF Stories from "New Worlds" 7, Panther Books, 1971.
New Worlds Quarterly 1, Berkley Publishing, 1971.
New Worlds Quarterly 2, Berkley Publishing, 1971.
New Worlds Quarterly 3, Sphere Books, 1971.
(With Langdon Jones and contributor) *The Nature of the Catastrophe,* Hutchinson, 1971.
New Worlds Quarterly 4, Berkley Publishing, 1972.
New Worlds Quarterly 5, Sphere Books, 1973.
New Worlds Quarterly 6, Avon, 1973.
Before Armageddon: An Anthology of Victorian and Edwardian Imaginative Fiction Published before 1914, W. H. Allen, 1975.
England Invaded: A Collection of Fantasy Fiction, Ultramarine, 1977.
New Worlds: An Anthology, Fontana, 1983.

RECORDINGS; UNDER NAME "MICHAEL MOORCOCK AND THE DEEP FIX"

The New Worlds Fair, United Artists, 1975.
Dodgem Dude/Starcruiser (single), Flicknife, 1980.
The Brothel in Rosenstrasse/Time Centre (single), Flicknife, 1982.
(With others) *Hawkwind Friends and Relations,* Flicknife, 1982.
(With others) *Hawkwind & Co.,* Flicknife, 1983.

Also composer of songs recorded by others, including *Sonic Attack, The Black Corridor, The Wizard Blew His Horn, Standing at the Edge, Warriors, Kings of Speed, Warrior at the End of Time, Psychosonia, Coded Languages, Lost Chances, Choose Your Masks,* and *Arrival in Utopia,* all recorded by Hawkwind; *The Great Sun Jester, Black Blade,* and *Veteran of the Psychic Wars,* all recorded by Blue Oyster Cult.

OTHER

Contributor, sometimes under pseudonyms, to *Guardian, Punch, Ambit,* London *Times,* and other publications. Writer of comic strips in early 1960s.

ADAPTATIONS: The character Elric is featured in role-playing games from the Avalon Hill Game Company and from Chaosium, in comic books published by Pacific Comics and by Star Reach Productions, and in miniature figures marketed by Citadel Miniatures; the character Oswald Bastable is featured in a computer game.

SIDELIGHTS: Michael Moorcock was associated with the New Wave, an avant-garde science fiction of the 1960s which introduced a wider range of subject matter and style to the science fiction field. As editor of *New Worlds,* the most prominent of the New Wave publications, Moorcock promoted the movement and provided a showcase for its writing.

The New Wave, Donald A. Wollheim writes in *The Universe Makers,* was an "effort to merge science fiction into the mainstream of literature. . . . The charges brought against oldline science fiction were on the basis of both structure and content. Structurally, the charge was made that too much of the writing retained the flavor of the pulps [and] that science fiction writers were not keeping up with the experimental avant-garde. . . . Internally, the charge was made that science fiction actually was dead—because the future was no longer credible. The crises of the twentieth century . . . were obviously insurmountable. We would all never make it into the twenty-first century." In an interview with Ian Covell of *Science Fiction Review,* Moorcock says of the New Wave: "We were a generation of writers who had no nostalgic love of the pulp magazines, who had come to SF as a possible alternative to mainstream literature and had taken SF seriously. . . . We were trying to find a viable literature for our time. A literature which took account of science, of modern social trends, and which was written not according to genre conventions but according to the personal requirements of the individuals who produced it."

Moorcock's own writing covers a wide range of science fiction and fantasy genres. He has written science fiction adventures in the style of Edgar Rice Burroughs's Mars novels, sword and sorcery novels, comic and satirical science fiction, and time-traveling science fiction. Some of Moorcock's fantasy novels have earned him major genre awards and a vaunted position among fans. Tom Hutchinson in the London *Times,* for example, calls Moorcock's sword and sorcery novel *The Chronicles of Castle Brass* "a masterpiece of modern high fantasy."

Yet, despite their continuing popularity, some of these books, Moorcock admits, were written for the money. *New Worlds* was an influential magazine in the science fiction field, but it was never a financial success. When creditors needed to be paid it was Moorcock, as editor and publisher, who was held responsible. He was often forced to write a quick novel to pay the bills. Even so, Charles Platt recounts in his *Dream Makers: The Uncommon People Who Write Science Fiction,* "it was not unusual for the magazine's staff to be found cowering on the floor with the lights out, pretending not to be home, while some creditor rang the bell and called hopefully through the mail slot in the front door—to no avail."

The genre books that brought Moorcock to critical attention, and those that he considers among his most important, combine standard science fiction trappings with experimental narrative structures. His *Breakfast in the Ruins: A Novel of Inhumanity,* for instance, contains a number of historical vignettes featuring the protagonist Karl Glogauer. In each of these, Karl is a different person in a different time, participating in such examples of political violence as the French Revolution, the Paris Commune, a Nazi concentration camp, and a My Lai-style massacre. Interwoven with these vignettes is a homosexual love scene, involving Karl and a black Nigerian, that takes on a mystical connotation as the two lovers seem to

merge into each other's identities. Helen Rogan of *Time* describes the book as "by turns puzzling, funny, and shocking" and Moorcock as "both bizarrely inventive and highly disciplined." Writing in the *New York Times Book Review,* John Deck calls the book "a dazzling historical fantasy."

In the books and stories featuring Jerry Cornelius, Moorcock has experimented with character as well as with narrative structure. Cornelius has no consistent character or appearance. He is, as Nick Totton writes in *Spectator,* "a nomad of the territories of personality; even his skin color and gender are as labile as his accomplishments." Cornelius's world is just as flexible, containing a multitude of alternative histories, all contradictory, and peopled with characters who die and resurrect as a matter of course. Within this mutable landscape, Cornelius travels from one inconclusive adventure to another, trapped in an endless existence. As Colin Greenland maintains in the *Dictionary of Literary Biography,* Cornelius is "an entirely new kind of fictional character, a dubious hero whose significance is always oblique and rarely stable, equipped to tackle all the challenges of his time yet unable to find a satisfactory solution to any of them."

The Condition of Muzak, completing the initial Jerry Cornelius tetralogy, won the Guardian Literary Prize in 1977, bringing Moorcock acceptance by a wider literary world. At the time of the award, W. L. Webb of the *Guardian* wrote: "Michael Moorcock, rejecting the demarcation disputes that have reduced the novel to a muddle of warring sub-genres, recovers in these four books a protean vitality and inclusiveness that one might call Dickensian if their consciousness were not so entirely of our own volatile times." Moorcock, according to Angus Wilson in the *Washington Post Book World,* "is emerging as one of the most serious literary lights of our time. . . . For me his Jerry Cornelius quartet [of novels] assured the durability of his reputation." Ralph Willett, writing in *Science-Fiction Studies,* claims that during the late 1960s and early 1970s, Moorcock became "that rare phenomenon, the popular novelist whose work has also become a cult among the young and the avant-garde." Willett compares Moorcock to experimental novelist William Burroughs, "especially with respect to the Jerry Cornelius books. . . . Moorcock lacks William Burroughs' accurate and devastating satire, and his verbal experiments have been less radical, but in both artists can be observed a basic dissatisfaction with linear methods of representing space and time, a surreal sense of co-existing multiple worlds, and an emphasis on apocalyptic disaster."

Moorcock's literary standing has been substantially enhanced with the publication of *Byzantium Endures* and *The Laughter of Carthage.* These two novels are the closest Moorcock has come to conventional literary fiction, being the autobiography of Russian emigre Colonel Pyat. Pyat was born on January 1, 1900, and so the story of his life is a history of the twentieth century. Pyat survived the Russian revolution, traveled throughout Europe and America, and participated in a number of important historical events. But he is a megalomaniac who imagines himself to be both a great inventor, the equal of Thomas Edison, and a major figure on the stage of world history. He is also an anti-Semite who sees true Christianity, as embodied in the Russian Orthodox Church, in a battle against the Jews, Orientals, Bolsheviks, and other destroyers of order. He likens Western Christianity to Byzantium, his enemies to Carthage. Naturally, Pyat's account of his life is self-aggrandizing and inaccurate.

Byzantium Endures focuses on the first twenty years of Pyat's life, telling of his opportunistic role in the Russian revolution. Pyat survives the upheaval of the revolution and the subsequent civil war by working first for one side and then another. As Frederic Morton writes in the *New York Times Book Review,* his mechanical skills are put to good use "repairing the rifles of anarchist guerrillas, fixing the treads of White Army tanks [and] doctoring the engine in one of Trotsky's armed trains." Pyat claims to have invented the laser gun on behalf of Ukrainian nationalists fighting against the Red Army, but when the electrical power failed, so did his gun. "Pyat's self-serving recollections," Bart Mills states in the *Los Angeles Times Book Review,* "contain a vivid picture of the events of 1917-1920, down to menus, street names and the color of people's moustaches." The novel, writes Robert Onopa in the *Chicago Tribune Book World,* is "utterly engrossing as narrative, historically pertinent, and told through characters so alive and detail so dense that it puts to shame all but a few writers who have been doing this kind of work all along."

The Laughter of Carthage covers Pyat's life from 1920 to 1924, detailing his escape from Communist Russia and subsequent travels in Europe and America. His activities are sometimes unlawful, requiring him to change his residence and name frequently. He meets everyone from Dylan Thomas to Tom Mix and lives everywhere from Constantinople to Hollywood. Because of the scope of Pyat's adventures, *The Laughter of Carthage* is a sweeping picture of the world during the 1920s. "Moorcock provides an exotic itinerary, a robust cast of opportunists and scoundrels, and a series of dangerous adventures and sexual escapades," notes R. Z. Sheppard of *Time.* "This is epic writing," Valentine Cunningham of the *Times Literary Supplement* writes. "As [D. W.] Griffith stuffed his movies with vast throngs and Promethean matter so Pyat's narration feeds hugely on the numerous people he claims to have met, the history he makes believe he has helped to shape, the many places his traveller's tales take him to."

Pyat's narration, because it is colored by his eccentric, offensive views and his distorted sense of self-importance, gives a fantastic sheen to the familiar historical events he relates. "This is Moorcock's achievement: he has rewritten modern history by seeing it in the distorting mirror of one man's perceptions so that the novel has the imaginative grasp of fantasy while remaining solidly based upon recognizable facts," Peter Ackroyd writes in the London *Times.* "Moorcock has here created a fiction," Nigel Andrew writes in the same paper, "that is seething with detailed life at every level—in the headlong narrative, in the bravura passages of scene-setting description, and, particularly, in the rendering of Pyat's vision of the world." Although Richard Eder of the *Los Angeles Times* finds Pyat's narrative an "extremely long-winded unpleasantness" because of his political views, the *New York Times Book Review*'s Thaddeus Rutkowski forgives the "sometimes tedious" nature of Pyat's narration. "Most often," he finds, "Pyat's tirades are beguiling. They are the pronouncements of a singularly innocent intelligence gone awry."

Moorcock combined mainstream fiction with a bit of fantasy in *The Brothel of Rosenstrasse,* a novel set in the imaginary city of Mirenburg. The city's brothel is the center of social life, as well as a "microcosm of *fin de siecle* Central Europe; hedonistic, decadent, deluded and heedless of an inevitable future," as Elaine Kendall writes in the *Los Angeles Times.* Narrated by an aging hedonist who relates the story of his long and dissipated life, the novel follows a handful of decadent characters to their eventual destruction during the bombardment of Mirenburg. Suffering makes the characters finally come alive in a way they have never been before. "They begin to engage our full attention," Kendall concludes, "and earn not only our sympathy but in some cases, our respect. By then it's too late; Mirenburg and all the good and evil it represented has vanished forever. If there's no parable here, surely there's a moral."

In *Mother London,* Moorcock presents a "complex, layered history of London since the war, seen through the stories of a group of psychiatric patients," explains Brian Appleyard in the London *Times.* The novel earned high praise from several critics. Nigel Andrew of the *Listener* calls *Mother London* "a prodigious work of imaginative archaeology. . . . [Moorcock] displays the generosity of spirit, the sweep and sheer gusto of Dickens." Similarly, Gregory Feeley in the *Washington Post Book World* states that *Mother London* "often indulges its author's crotchets and biases, [but] it also proves warm and humane, often surprisingly funny, and moving in a way Moorcock has never before succeeded in being." "If," writes Andrew, "this wonderful book does not finally convince the world that [Moorcock] is in fact one of our very best novelists and a national treasure, then there is no justice."

Moorcock's move from science fiction to mainstream fiction is welcomed by several critics. Observes Gregory Sandow in the *Village Voice:* "It's wonderful to see Moorcock grow from a genre writer into, simply, a writer. . . . A mainstream novel gives him far more scope to nourish the obsessions (and also the passion, zaniness, and eye for detail) that made his science fiction both fun and worthwhile." Moorcock, Andrew allows, "has had to come the long way to literary recognition. But now, with *The Laughter of Carthage,* he can surely no longer be denied his due; this enormous book—with its forerunner, *Byzantium Endures*—must establish him in the front rank of practising English novelists."

Evaluations of Moorcock's career often emphasize the sheer volume and variety of his work. "It is like trying to evaluate an industry," as Philip Oakes explains in the London *Times Magazine.* Throughout his career, Moorcock has shown an impressive ability to write consistently well within a wide range of genres and styles. "I have read about half his prodigious output . . . ," Oakes writes, "and on the strength of that sample Moorcock strikes me as the most prolific, probably the most inventive and without doubt the most egalitarian writer practising today." Speaking in the *Observer* of Moorcock's long career, John Clute describes him as "a figure of revolutionary fervour in the British literary world for nearly 30 years." Wilson calls Moorcock "one of the most exciting discoveries that I have been able to make in the contemporary English novel during the 40 or so years that I have been publishing my own novels and reviewing those of my contemporaries. Exciting for myself and, as is becoming increasingly clear with the appearance of each Moorcock book, for a legion of other readers."

Speaking of his writing, Moorcock told *CA:* "Most of my work recently has been in terms of a moral and psychological investigation of Imperialism (Western and Eastern) seen in terms of fiction. Even my fantasy novels are inclined to deal with moral problems rather than magical ones. I'm turning more and more away from SF and fantasy and more towards a form of realism used in the context of what you might call an imaginative framework. Late Dickens would be the model I'd most like to emulate."

Writing in the *Contemporary Authors Autobiography Series,* Moorcock speaks of the writing life: "The job of a novelist has its own momentum, its own demands, its own horrible power over the practitioner. When I look back I wonder what I got myself into all those years ago when I realised I had a facility to put words down on paper and have people give me money in return. For ages the whole business seemed ludicrous. I couldn't believe my luck. Frequently, I still can't but it seems an unnatural way of earning a living. Of course, it's no longer easy. It's often a struggle. It spoils my health. . . . I suppose it must be an addiction. I'm pretty sure, though I deny it heartily, that I could now no longer give it up. I'm as possessed as any fool I used to mock."

Moorcock continues his work with English rock and roll band Hawkwind, specializing in science fiction-oriented music. The band took its name from a character in one of his novels. He has also formed his own band, Michael Moorcock and the Deep Fix, and has made several recordings. The League of Temporal Adventurers, based in Memphis, Tennessee, is the official Michael Moorcock fan society.

BIOGRAPHICAL/CRITICAL SOURCES:

BOOKS

Bilyeu, R., *Tanelorn Archives,* Pandora's Books, 1979.
Callow, A. J., compiler, *The Chronicles of Moorcock,* A. J. Callow, 1978.
Carter, Lin, *Imaginary Worlds,* Ballantine, 1973.
Contemporary Authors Autobiography Series, Volume 5, Gale, 1987.
Contemporary Literary Criticism, Gale, Volume 5, 1976, Volume 27, 1984 Volume 58, 1990.
Dictionary of Literary Biography, Volume 14: *British Novelists since 1960,* Gale, 1983.
Greenland, Colin, *The Entropy Exhibition: Michael Moorcock and the British "New Wave" in Science Fiction,* Routledge & Kegan Paul, 1983.
Harper, Andrew and George McAulay, *Michael Moorcock: A Bibliography,* T-K Graphics, 1976.
Platt, Charles, *Dream Makers: The Uncommon People Who Write Science Fiction,* Berkley Publishing, 1980.
Walker, Paul, editor, *Speaking of Science Fiction: The Paul Walker Interviews,* Luna Publications, 1978.
Wollheim, Donald A., *The Universe Makers,* Harper, 1971.

PERIODICALS

Amazing Stories, May, 1971.
Analog, February, 1970; March, 1990.
Books and Bookmen, June, 1971; September, 1971; October, 1972; May, 1974; August, 1978.
Chicago Tribune Book World, January 31, 1982.
Commonweal, August 1, 1975.
Detroit News, February 24, 1985.
Encounter, November, 1981.
Extrapolation, winter, 1989.
Guardian Weekly, April 10, 1969.
Harper's Bazaar (British edition), December, 1969.
Ink, August, 1971.

Kensington News, April 18, 1969.

Kensington Post, April 4, 1969.

Listener, June 23, 1988; January 18, 1990.

Locus, May, 1989; November, 1989; February, 1990; March, 1990.

Los Angeles Times, January 9, 1985; November 10, 1987.

Los Angeles Times Book Review, March 7, 1982; February 7, 1988.

Luna Monthly, November, 1975.

New Republic, June 15, 1974.

New Statesman, April 4, 1969; May 18, 1973; June 18, 1976; April 15, 1977.

New Worlds, March, 1969.

New York Times Book Review, April 5, 1970; May 19, 1974; April 25, 1976; February 21, 1982; February 10, 1985; November 23, 1986.

Observer, April 4, 1976; April 3, 1977.

Punch, January 16, 1985.

Saturday Review, April 25, 1970.

Science Fiction Monthly, February, 1975.

Science Fiction Review, January, 1971; January, 1979.

Science-Fiction Studies, March, 1976.

Spectator, April 1, 1969; August 10, 1974; November 20, 1976; April 9, 1977; December 24, 1977; June 27, 1981; February 9, 1985.

Speculation, May, 1970; August, 1970.

Time, August 5, 1974; January 28, 1985.

Time Out, September 17, 1971.

Times (London), September 6, 1984; November 25, 1984; August 5, 1985; June 18, 1988.

Times Literary Supplement, October 27, 1972; November 9, 1973; May 31, 1974; May 7, 1976; June 30, 1978; July 3, 1981; September 7, 1984; July 1, 1988; February 23, 1990.

Times Magazine (London), November 5, 1978.

Tribune Books (Chicago), March 26, 1989.

Village Voice, March 2, 1982.

Virginia Quarterly Review, spring, 1975.

Washington Post Book World, March 21, 1982; December 23, 1984; September 28, 1986; May 14, 1989.

*   *   *

MOORE, Clayton
See BRANDNER, Gary

*   *   *

MOORE, Lilian   1909- (Sara Asheron, a pseudonym)

PERSONAL: Born March 17, 1909, in New York, NY; daughter of Aaron and Sarah (Asheron) Levenson; mar-
ried second husband, Sam Reavin, 1969; children: (first marriage) Jonathan. *Education:* Hunter College, B.A., 1930; graduate study at Columbia University. *Avocational interests:* Chamber music, bicycling, ice skating, gardening, reading, cooking, and travel.

ADDRESSES: Home—Kerhonkson, NY 12446.

CAREER: Writer. Has worked as elementary school teacher in New York City, 1930-37; staff member of New York City Bureau of Educational Research, 1937-50; freelance and editorial consultant for children's books, 1950—; reading specialist and contributor to *Humpty Dumpty's Magazine,* 1952—; Scholastic Book Services, New York City, editor of Arrow Book Club, 1957-67; Grosset & Dunlap, Wonder Books Division, New York City, editor of easy reader series, 1960—; editor of special book project (history and biography series), 1968-69. Has also worked as series editor for Thomas Y. Crowell, New York City, and as director of the Brooklyn Community Counseling Center, Brooklyn, NY.

MEMBER: Council on Interracial Books for Children (founding member), PEN, Authors Guild, Authors League of America.

AWARDS, HONORS: Old Rosie, the Horse Nobody Understood was selected one of *New York Times* Best Books of the Year, 1960; several of Moore's books appeared on Child Study Association of America's list of Children's Books of the Year, including *Just Right,* 1968, *Junk Day on Juniper Street, and Other Easy-to-Read Stories,* 1969, *Sam's Place,* 1973, *To See the World Afresh,* 1974, and *See My Lovely Poison Ivy, and Other Verses about Witches, Ghosts and Things,* 1975; *Sam's Place* was included in the American Institute of Graphic Arts Children's Books Show, 1973; *To See the World Afresh,* 1974, and *Something New Begins,* 1982, were named Notable Books by the American Library Association; *Think of Shadows* was named a Notable Children's Book, American Library Society, 1980; National Council of Teachers of English Award for excellence in poetry for children, 1985.

WRITINGS:

"LITTLE RACCOON" SERIES; FOR CHILDREN

Little Raccoon and the Thing in the Pool, illustrated by G. Fiammenghi, Whittlesey House, 1963.

Little Raccoon and the Outside World, illustrated by Fiammenghi, Whittlesey House, 1965.

Little Raccoon and No Trouble at All, illustrated by Fiammenghi, McGraw, 1972.

Little Raccoon and Poems from the Woods, illustrated by Fiammenghi, McGraw, 1975.

Little Raccoon Takes Charge, illustrated by Deborah Borgo, Western Publishing, 1986.

Little Raccoon's Nighttime Adventure, illustrated by Borgo, Western Publishing, 1986.

OTHER WORKS FOR CHILDREN

(With Leone Adelson) *Old Rosie, the Horse Nobody Understood* (Junior Literary Guild selection), illustrated by Leonard Shortall, Random House, 1952, reprinted, 1960.

(With Adelson) *The Terrible Mr. Twitmeyer* (Junior Literary Guild selection), illustrated by Shortall, Random House, 1952.

The Important Pockets of Paul, illustrated by William D. Hayes, McKay, 1954.

Daniel Boone (biography), illustrated by William Moyers, Random House, 1956.

Wobbly Wheels, illustrated by B. Krush, Abingdon, 1956.

The Snake That Went to School, illustrated by Mary Stevens, Random House, 1957.

Once upon a Holiday, illustrated by Wesley Dennis, Whittlesey House, 1959.

Tony the Pony, illustrated by Dennis, Whittlesey House, 1959.

Bear Trouble, illustrated by Kurt Werth, Whittlesey House, 1960.

Everything Happens to Stuey, illustrated by Stevens, Random House, 1960.

Too Many Bozos, illustrated by Susan Perl, Golden Press, 1960.

A Pickle for a Nickel, illustrated by Perl, Golden Press, 1961.

Once upon a Season, illustrated by Fiammenghi, Abingdon, 1962.

(With L. Adelson) *Mr. Twitmeyer and the Poodle,* illustrated by Shortall, Random House, 1963.

Papa Albert, illustrated by Fiammenghi, Atheneum, 1964.

The Magic Spectacles, and Other Easy-to-Read Stories, illustrated by Arnold Lobel, Parents Magazine Press, 1966.

I Feel the Same Way (poems; Junior Literary Guild selection), illustrated by Robert Quackenbush, Atheneum, 1967.

Just Right, illustrated by Aldern A. Watson, Parents Magazine Press, 1968.

I Thought I Heard the City (poems), illustrated by Mary Jane Dunton, Atheneum, 1969.

Junk Day on Juniper Street, and Other Easy-to-Read Stories, illustrated by Lobel, Parents Magazine Press, 1969.

The Riddle Walk, illustrated by John Pucci, Garrard, 1971.

(Reteller) *The Ugly Duckling by Hans Christian Andersen,* illustrated by Mona Barrett, Scholastic Book Services, 1972.

(Compiler with Lawrence Webster) *Catch Your Breath: A Book of Shivery Poems,* illustrated by Gahan Wilson, Garrard, 1973.

Sam's Place: Poems from the Country, illustrated by Talivaldis Stubis, Atheneum, 1973.

Spooky Rhymes and Riddles, illustrated by Ib Ohlsson, Scholastic Book Services, 1973.

(Reteller) Hans Christian Andersen, *The Ugly Duckling and Two Other Stories,* illustrated by Trina Schart Hyman, Scholastic Book Services, 1973.

(Compiler with Judith Thurman) *To See the World Afresh* (poems), Atheneum, 1974.

(With Remy Charlip) *Hooray for Me!,* illustrated by Vera B. Williams, Parents Magazine Press, 1975.

See My Lovely Poison Ivy, and Other Verses about Witches, Ghosts and Things (Junior Literary Guild selection), illustrated by Diane Dawson, Atheneum, 1975.

(Compiler) *Go with the Poem,* McGraw, 1979.

Think of Shadows (poems), illustrated by Deborah Robison, Atheneum, 1980.

Something New Begins (poems), illustrated by Dunton, Atheneum, 1982.

I'll Meet You at the Cucumbers (first book of trilogy), illustrated by Sharon Wooding, Atheneum, 1988.

Don't Be Afraid, Amanda (second book of trilogy), Atheneum, 1992.

Adam Mouse's Book of Poems (third book of trilogy), Atheneum, 1992.

(Compiler) *Sunflakes: Poems for Children,* Clarion Books, 1992.

Author of the following books, under the name Sara Asheron: *Surprise in the Tree,* 1962; *Will You Come to My Party?; Laurie and the Yellow Curtains; The Surprise in the Story Book; Little Gray Mouse and the Train; How to Find a Friend; Little Gray Mouse Goes Sailing; Little Popcorn; The Three Coats of Benny Bunny; Fraidy Cat;* and *Funny Face at the Window.* Editorial consultant for more than fifty books in the "Easy to Read" series for Grosset and Dunlap. Lilian Moore's works are included in the de Grummond Collection at the University of Southern Mississippi.

Many of Moore's books have been translated into several languages.

ADAPTATIONS: A number of Moore's stories have been adapted into short films, including *Bear Trouble, Too Many Bozos, A Pickle for a Nickel,* and *Tony the Pony.*

SIDELIGHTS: Lilian Moore's interest in reading and telling stories emerged in childhood. Having interviewed Moore for *Language Arts,* Joan I. Glazer reported: "As a child [Moore] was a voracious reader. She would go to the library, leave with an armful of books, and have read two of them before she got home. She simply assumed that she would be a writer when she grew up, and often created stories which she would tell to friends. With utter confidence in the loyalty of her audience, she would stop midway through the tale and announce that it was 'to be continued tomorrow.' "

In college, Moore majored in English in hopes of teaching Elizabethan literature to college students. Instead, having graduated during the economic depression of the 1930s, she found herself teaching truant children how to read. Although she enjoyed the challenge of working with such students, she was frustrated by the lack of easy-to-read books with which to teach them and decided to write her own. She wanted to write books that were both exciting and relatively easy, enabling children with reading problems to know the pleasure of being able to read independently. The numerous children's books that Moore has written since have been generally well received. Critics have praised her ability to write simple sentences using an easy vocabulary. "Lilian Moore is very clever at handling the kind of simple stories that do not discourage those who are still fumbling with the newly acquired ability to read," wrote M. S. Libby of the *New York Herald Tribune Book Review*. A *Bulletin of the Center for Children's Books* writer called *I'll Meet You at the Cucumbers* "one of those rare books that combines quality and appeal (for transitional readers yet). . . . A golden read-aloud."

In addition to her story books, Moore has written several volumes of poetry for children. "Many of the poems have the flavor of haiku and capture the very essence of experience," according to Barbara Gibson's *School Library Journal* review of *I Feel the Same Way*. Writing for *New York Times Book Review*, Alicia Ostriker called Moore "a poet who writes with a child's-eye view that is keen, accurate and full of vitality." In 1985, Moore was awarded the National Council of Teachers of English Award for excellence in poetry for children.

Moore has also been an editor, and she sees similarities between editing and creative writing. She told Glazer: "I believe that editing is a kind of sculpture. If there's a line with a bump in it and you have a sense of form, you smooth it and give it shape. When I was an editor, I was able to help people do that with their manuscripts. I was able to do that with my own stories. And possibly that's what happens with my poetry." In an interview with Rachel Koenig for *Something about the Author*, the author related her advice for writers: "Good writing is clear thinking and honest feeling, murky feeling produces sentimentality, and muddy thinking produces muddy language. This is no different from the way I work on my own poetry. If a line jounces or bucks, I reshape it, as if I were working on a piece of pottery—until I achieve a line that flows for me without interruption."

As the first editor of Scholastic's Arrow Book Club, Moore pioneered a program that made quality paperback books available to elementary school children. Children and teachers alike were enthusiastic about this program that, for the first time, enabled young students to buy many of their favorite books. "Even now I remember the endless wonderful letters from children and teachers," Moore wrote in *Books Are by People: Interviews with 104 Authors and Illustrators of Books for Young Children*. "They made it clear we were irrigating a drought area and raising a whole new crop of readers. Whatever I may have contributed to this program was due in part to my almost total recall of the children I had known and taught. They seemed to haunt me and were specters at my side, vigorously approving or disapproving books we chose for them."

BIOGRAPHICAL/CRITICAL SOURCES:

BOOKS

Moore, Lilian, in *Books Are by People: Interviews with 104 Authors and Illustrators of Books for Young Children*, edited by Lee Bennett Hopkins, Citation Press, 1969.
Something about the Author, Volume 52, Gale, 1988.
Ward, Martha E., and Dorothy A. Marquardt, *Authors of Books for Young People*, 2nd edition, Scarecrow, 1971.

PERIODICALS

Bulletin of the Center for Children's Books, March, 1988, p. 142.
Language Arts, October, 1985, pp. 647-52.
New York Herald Tribune Book Review, April 26, 1959.
New York Times Book Review, November 14, 1982, p. 45.
Parnassus: Poetry in Review, Vol. 8, no. 2, 1980, pp. 63-82.
School Library Journal, September, 1967, p. 111.

*   *   *

MOORE, Tara 1950-

PERSONAL: Born March 4, 1950, in Baltimore, MD; daughter of Egbert Holmes (in real estate) and Helen Louise (an editor; maiden name, Stephenson) Hawkins; divorced, 1986. *Education:* Attended University of New Mexico.

ADDRESSES: Home—Route 1, Box 147K, Queenstown, MD 21658.

CAREER: Artist, 1970—; president, Elephant's Child Productions, Inc., 1983—; president, Cygnus Films Inc., 1990—. Member of board of trustees, Maryland College of Art and Design, 1982-83.

MEMBER: Society of Animal Artists, Academy of the Arts.

WRITINGS:

A Pack of Labs (juvenile), Garrard, 1982.
Elephants (juvenile), Garrard, 1982.
Polar Bears (juvenile), Garrard, 1982.
(And producer and director) *Tusks* (film), produced in 1987.

WORK IN PROGRESS: Burning Passion, a screenplay concerning an artist painting a mural for an eccentric rancher in the Brazilian Amazon; *Shadow in the Shade,* a novel.

SIDELIGHTS: Tara Moore told *CA:* "The motivation behind my writings is a desire to reach and educate people through the means of entertainment. Grabbing people's attention visually with film and paintings helps to tell the story; therefore, more of the public can be reached. Writing sets up the paintings and film.

"Wildlife conservation is my main subject. I have traveled around the world, including the Arctic, Africa, Nepal, and South America, studying natural habitats, with animal scientists and other guides.

"*Tusks* is based on experiences that I have had in the past, but extremely exaggerated, turning the story into total fiction—the story of an artist involved with a poacher, a game warden, and the elephants. It is an adventure story with an animal conservation message. *Tusks* is presently in wide release around the world.

"I transformed myself into a world of fantasy for the purpose of easing pain, guilt and other such unpleasant memories. The next thing I knew a novel was born, *Shadow in the Shade,* unpublished at this writing."

*   *   *

MORRIS, Desmond (John) 1928-

PERSONAL: Born January 24, 1928, in Purton, Wiltshire, England; son of Harry Howe (a writer) and Dorothy Marjorie Fuller (Hunt) Morris; married Ramona Baulch (a writer), July 30, 1952; children: Jason. *Education:* Birmingham University, B.Sc., 1951; Magdalen College, Oxford, D.Phil., 1954. *Politics:* None. *Religion:* None. *Avocational interests:* Painting, archaeology.

ADDRESSES: c/o Jonathan Cape, 32 Bedford Sq., London WC1B 3EL, England.

CAREER: Oxford University, Oxford, England, researcher in animal behavior in department of zoology, 1954-56; Zoological Society of London, London, England, head of Granada TV and Film Unit, 1956-59, curator of mammals, 1959-67; Institute of Contemporary Arts, London, director, 1967-68; full-time writer, 1968—. Oxford

University, research fellow at Wolfson College, 1973-81. Paintings exhibited in England, first in one-man show, London, 1950. Former host of *Zootime* television series, British Broadcasting Corp.

MEMBER: Zoological Society of London (scientific fellow).

AWARDS, HONORS: Statuette with Pedestal, World Organization for Human Potential, 1971, for *The Naked Ape* and *The Human Zoo.*

WRITINGS:

The Reproductive Behaviour of the Ten-Spined Stickleback, E. J. Brill, 1958.
(Editor with Caroline Jarvis) *The International Zoo Yearbook,* Zoological Society of London, Volume 1, 1959-60, Volume 2, 1960-61, Volume 3, 1961-62, Volume 4, 1962-63.
Introducing Curious Creatures, Spring Books, 1961.
The Biology of Art: A Study of the Picture-Making Behaviour of the Great Apes and Its Relationship to Human Art, Knopf, 1962.
(With wife, Ramona Morris) *Men and Snakes,* McGraw, 1965.
The Mammals: A Guide to the Living Species, Harper, 1965.
(With R. Morris) *Men and Apes,* McGraw, 1966.
(With R. Morris) *Men and Pandas,* Hutchinson, 1966, McGraw, 1967, revised edition published as *The Giant Panda,* Penguin, 1981.
(Editor) *Primate Ethology,* Aldine, 1967.
The Naked Ape: A Zoologist's Study of the Human Animal, J. Cape, 1967, McGraw, 1968, revised edition published as *The Illustrated Naked Ape,* J. Cape, 1986.
The Human Zoo, McGraw, 1969.
Patterns of Reproductive Behaviour: Collected Papers (all previously published in journals), J. Cape, 1970, McGraw, 1971.
Intimate Behavior, J. Cape, 1971, Random House, 1972.
Manwatching: A Field Guide to Human Behavior, Abrams, 1977.
(With Peter Collett, Peter Marsh, and Marie O'Shaughnessy) *Gestures: Their Origins and Distributions,* Stein & Day, 1979.
Animal Days, Perigord Press, 1979.
The Soccer Tribe, J. Cape, 1981.
Inrock (fiction), J. Cape, 1983.
The Book of Ages, Viking, 1983.
The Art of Ancient Cyprus, Phaidon, 1985.
Bodywatching: A Field Guide to the Human Species, J. Cape, 1985.
Dogwatching, J. Cape, 1986, Crown, 1987.
Catwatching, Crown, 1987.

The Secret Surrealist: The Paintings of Desmond Morris, Salem House, 1987.

Catlore, Crown, 1988.

(With the Roadshow Team) *The Animals Roadshow,* J. Cape, 1988.

Horsewatching, Crown, 1988.

Animalwatching: A Field Guide to Animal Behavior, Crown, 1990.

FOR CHILDREN

The Story of Congo, Batsford, 1958.

Apes and Monkeys, Bodley Head, 1964, McGraw, 1965.

The Big Cats, McGraw, 1965.

Zoo Time, Hart-Davis, 1966.

OTHER

Author of *The Human Nestbuilders,* 1988. Contributor to journals, including *Behavior, British Birds, New Scientist,* and *Zoo Life.*

ADAPTATIONS: The Naked Ape was filmed by Universal and released in 1973.

WORK IN PROGRESS: Research in human ethology; planning another exhibit of paintings.

SIDELIGHTS: Desmond Morris first came to public attention as the host of *Zootime,* a British Broadcasting Corporation television series featuring the animals of the London Zoo, and as the author of *The Naked Ape,* in which he examines man from a zoologist's perspective. Morris's fascination with animals began in early childhood, when he spent hours at a time in close observation of worms and beetles near his home. As a student, he was drawn to the science of ethology—the study of natural animal behavior. His teachers were some of the founders of this young science, including Konrad Lorenz and Niko Tinbergen. Morris's research in this discipline uncovered such phenomena as homosexuality among the ten-spined stickleback fish and the "divorce" of mated pairs of zebra finches.

His work won him the respect of his peers, but when the opportunity came to trade his academic career for a stint as a television-show host, Morris accepted. *Zootime* was shown live and its animal stars were known for their unpredictable—and often embarrassing—antics. Morris's own popularity was built largely upon his deft, humorous handling of his misbehaving co-stars. In his book *Animal Days,* Morris explains the appeal that a public role holds for him. He was a very shy child and admits that upon entering boarding school, "I often overcompensated and became almost painfully extroverted, as if determined to obliterate my inner relish for privacy. I became a joker, an entertainer. If I am honest, it is a struggle I have never fully resolved, the 'ham' and the academic in me doing

battle with one another, with first one, then the other getting the upper hand." When the program ended, Morris resumed academic "respectability" by becoming curator of mammals at the London Zoo and holding that post for eight years. He resigned when publication of *The Naked Ape* made him wealthy.

In *The Naked Ape,* Morris brings the methods of observation he learned as an ethologist to bear upon his fellow man. He states that man is merely one of many variations within the ape family, and then attempts to explain man's complex behavior by relating it to that of the lesser apes. The result proved fascinating to the general public; the book quickly became a best-seller. Many scientists, however, particularly anthropologists (whose domain is specifically the study of man), have reserved harsh criticism for Morris and *The Naked Ape.*

Saturday Review contributor Morton Fried, for example, believes that Morris is unqualified to write a book on human behavior. Morris, he writes, "has simply given us a naive and scientifically reactionary book. . . . Clearly, he never took even a freshman course in [anthropology], or he flunked it." J. Z. Young similarly faults the book, suggesting that Morris deliberately emphasizes the most provocative aspects of his subject in order to ensure his book's popularity. Young points out in the *New York Review of Books* that while more than one-fourth of *The Naked Ape* describes man's sexual habits, there is no mention whatsoever of language or learning. "It is not fair for any biologist to describe only those aspects of an animal that interest him and titillate his readers, especially if the ones omitted are the essential biological foundations of the success of the species." Other reviewers, however, praise Morris for making scientific material accessible to a wide audience. Peter Williams applauds *The Naked Ape* in *Natural History* for its "brilliant insights" and a *Times Literary Supplement* critic calls it "not only a thoughtful and stimulating book, but also an extremely interesting one." Readers agreed, for *The Naked Ape* was eventually published in twenty-three countries and sold over eight million copies.

Publication of *Animal Days* marked a change in tone. "This time, Morris doesn't try to shock or titillate with . . . theories," notes Peter Gwynne of *Newsweek.* "[*Animal Days*] is a straightforward, unpretentious memoir of his encounters with animals and fellow scientists. And it is a delightful book." Writing in the *New York Times,* Christopher Lehmann-Haupt likewise praises the book for its "gallery of arresting portraits of Mr. Morris's fellow animal behaviorists—the first great generation of them, really." *Animal Days* is "a visit with an engaging raconteur who has spent his life in a fascinating field," a *New York Times Book Review* critic concludes.

In books such as *Dogwatching* and *Catwatching,* Morris applies his ethologist's eye to some of man's favorite pets. The books offer a variety of information about animals, answering questions from why cats seem to prefer women to why dogs bark. "The author turns his attention to animal behavior in just the right tone for pet lovers," notes *Los Angeles Times Book Review* contributor Mordecai Siegal, who commends the books' question-and-answer format as "quite appropriate for the curator of a zoo." Nevertheless, the critic echoes former criticisms of Morris's work, faulting the books for "the absence of information sources." The author refutes this charge in a *Chicago Tribune* interview with Kathy Hacker, explaining that the popular nature of his books precludes the use of extensive citations: "A lot of the statements I make have this huge backup of quantified field work. . . . [Some] do not and are simply based on intuition and anecdotal observation. The agony of writing a pop book is that you can't sort of say which is which. The text has got to flow," Morris continued. "If you put down every detail and every chart and every figure, I suspect people wouldn't read it at all."

Morris's works don't suffer from lack of readers, however. His popularity extends to his other books, which encompass a variety of subjects, from art to soccer. His wide range of interests prompts Gwynne to write of him, "Zoologist Desmond Morris is the epitome of the scholar with interests too lively to hide under an academic bushel." Of himself, Morris told William Overend of the *Los Angeles Times:* "I describe myself as a senile 14-year-old. . . . I get more foolish and frivolous each year. I confess to cultivating immaturity. I don't aspire to maturity because it's so often connected with rigid thought. . . . I really don't want to ever take things too seriously, least of all myself."

BIOGRAPHICAL/CRITICAL SOURCES:

BOOKS

Morris, Desmond, *Animal Days,* Perigord Press, 1979.

PERIODICALS

Best Sellers, December 15, 1969.
Book World, October 12, 1969; February 27, 1972.
Chicago Tribune, January 9, 1986.
Los Angeles Times, March 9, 1984; May 21, 1984.
Los Angeles Times Book Review, June 24, 1979; May 31, 1987.
Natural History, February, 1968; January, 1970.
Newsweek, August 4, 1980.
New York Review of Books, March 14, 1968.
New York Times, July 18, 1980.
New York Times Book Review, February 4, 1968; November 30, 1969; March 5, 1972; November 13, 1977; December 30, 1979; August 10, 1980.
Saturday Review, February 17, 1968; March 4, 1972; July, 1980.
Spectator, October 16, 1971; November 5, 1977.
Time, January 26, 1968; March 13, 1972; January 16, 1978; December 9, 1985.
Times Literary Supplement, November 9, 1967; October 30, 1969; December 7, 1979.
Washington Post, December 8, 1981; March 20, 1984.
Washington Post Book World, August 12, 1979.
Yale Review, summer, 1968.*

*   *   *

MOSELEY, James G(wyn) 1946-

PERSONAL: Born March 24, 1946, in Atlanta, GA; son of James G. (an insurance executive) and Frances (Wilson) Moseley; married Candace Chambers (a Latin teacher), June 28, 1968; children: Emily Ann, James Benjamin. *Education:* Stanford University, B.A., 1968; University of Chicago, M.A., 1971, Ph.D., 1973.

ADDRESSES: Home—2100 Woodmont Dr., Lexington, KY 40502. *Office*—Office of the Dean, Transylvania University, Lexington, KY 40508.

CAREER: New College of the University of South Florida, Sarasota, assistant professor, 1973-79, associate professor, 1979-84, professor of religion, 1984-86, coordinator of American studies, 1973-79, chairman of humanities division, 1979-86; Chapman College, Orange, CA, vice president for academic affairs and dean of the faculty, 1986-89, director of honors program, 1989-91; Transylvania University, Lexington, KY, vice president and dean of the college, 1991—.

MEMBER: American Academy of Religion (Southeastern region chairman of art, literature, and religion section, 1974-76; vice-president, 1978-79; president, 1979-80), American Studies Association (member of Southeastern executive committee, 1983-85).

AWARDS, HONORS: National Endowment for the Humanities, fellow at Princeton University, 1976-77, grants, 1977, 1979, 1982, 1984, 1986, 1990, and 1992.

WRITINGS:

A Complex Inheritance: The Idea of Self-Transcendence in the Theology of Henry James, Sr., and the Novels of Henry James, Scholars Press (Missoula, MT), 1975.
A Cultural History of Religion in America, Greenwood Press, 1981.
Winthrop's World: History as a Story, the Story as History, University of Wisconsin Press, 1992.

Contributor of articles and reviews to theology journals, religious and popular magazines, and newspapers.

SIDELIGHTS: James G. Moseley told *CA:* "My work on the two Henry Jameses, *A Complex Inheritance,* led me to think about the various ways religion is expressed in American culture—thus my book about religion in American history. Investigating religion from the variety of perspectives entailed in that project raised questions about the nature of authority, particularly biblical authority, in American life and about the relations between church and state in America. These latter questions were addressed in several papers and articles, the writing of which generated for me a continuing interest in the life and work of John Winthrop, the subject of my most recent book."

*   *   *

MOSSMAN, Jennifer 1944-

PERSONAL: Born September 8, 1944, in Melksham, England; immigrated to United States, 1951, naturalized citizen, 1956; daughter of Joseph and Ella (Piper) Berger; married Richard Mossman (an attorney), January 2, 1978. *Education:* University of Michigan, B.A., 1966, M.L.S., 1968.

ADDRESSES: Office—Gale Research Inc., Penobscot Bldg., Detroit, MI 48226.

CAREER: San Francisco Public Library, San Francisco, CA, librarian, 1968-69; Eastern Michigan University, Ypsilanti, librarian, 1970-72; Gale Research Inc., Detroit, MI, assistant editor, 1973-77, associate editor, 1977-79, editor, 1979—.

WRITINGS:

(Associate editor) *Eponyms Dictionaries Index,* Gale, 1977, supplement (editor with James A. Ruffner), 1984.
(Editor) *Pseudonyms and Nicknames Dictionary,* Gale, 1980, 3rd edition, 1987, inter-edition supplement published as *New Pseudonyms and Nicknames,* 1988.
(Editor with Donna Wood) *Business Firms Master Index,* Gale, 1985.
(Editor) *Encyclopedia of Geographic Information Sources,* 4th edition, Gale, *U.S. Volume,* 1987, *International Volume,* 1988.
(Editor) *Holidays and Anniversaries of the World,* 2nd edition, Gale, 1990.
(Editor) *Acronyms, Initialisms, and Abbreviations Dictionary,* 16th edition, Gale, 1991.

WORK IN PROGRESS: Editing the 17th edition of *Acronyms, Initialisms, and Abbreviations Dictionary.*

MOTT, Stephen Charles 1940-

PERSONAL: Born April 9, 1940, in Lakewood, OH; son of Royden Cross (an ordained minister) and Katherine (a teacher of retarded children; maiden name, Hyde) Mott; married Sandra Goossen (a professor of nursing), August 21, 1965; children: Adam, Rachel, Sarah. *Education:* Wheaton College, Wheaton, IL, B.A., 1962, B.D., 1965; Harvard University, Ph.D., 1972. *Politics:* Democrat.

ADDRESSES: Home—11 Miller Rd., Beverly, MA 01915. *Office*—Gordon-Conwell Theological Seminary, 130 Essex St., Box 219, South Hamilton, MA 01982.

CAREER: Ordained United Methodist minister, 1965; Gordon-Conwell Theological Seminary, South Hamilton, MA, assistant professor, 1970-75, associate professor, 1975-79, professor of Christian social ethics, 1979—. Delegate to General Conference and member of General Board of Church and Society of the United Methodist Church; president and member of board of directors of North Shore Community Action Programs, 1983—.

MEMBER: Society of Christian Ethics, Society of Biblical Literature, Societe Europeenne de Culture.

WRITINGS:

Biblical Ethics and Social Change, Oxford University Press, 1982.
(With Esther Byle Bruland) *A Passion for Jesus, a Passion for Justice,* Judson, 1983.
Jesus and Social Ethics, Grove, 1984.
Political Visions: A Christian Analysis, Oxford University Press, 1992.

Also contributor to books and to theology journals. Author of column "From the Word," *Christian Social Action,* 1990—.

SIDELIGHTS: Stephen Charles Mott told *CA:* "The central concern in my teaching and writing is that those who stand in the Judeo-Christian tradition understand and be committed to the biblical values of justice. In contrast to the individualism of contemporary Western culture and an acceptance of life as it is, they must seek the changes in institutional life that will raise the disadvantaged to participation in that which is essential for life in community. This should include consideration of more equitable forms of economic life and working through legal processes, as they are empowering and compatible with these ends of justice.

"I understand my role as a professor of social ethics in the context of my deeper call as an ordained minister to strengthen the Christian churches through the preparation of their leadership."

MRABET, Mohammed
See el HAJJAM, Mohammed ben Chaib

*　　*　　*

MUNARI, Bruno 1907-

PERSONAL: Born October 24, 1907, in Milan, Italy; son of a waiter and innkeeper; married wife, Dilma; children: Alberto, Valeria. *Education:* Attended the Technical Institute of Naples (Italy).

ADDRESSES: Home—Via Colonne 39, 20149, Milan, Italy.

CAREER: Painter, sculptor, photographer, illustrator and designer of books, toys, and mobiles. *Exhibitions: Secondo Futurismo,* Galleria Pesaro, Milan, 1927, 1929, 1931; *Biennale di Venezia,* Venice, 1930, 1952; *Quadriennale di Roma,* Rome, 1931; *Secondo Futurismo,* Galerie Renaissance, Paris, 1932; Galleria Tre Arti, Milan, 1933; Public Library, New York City, 1954; *Two Graphic Designers,* Museum of Modern Art, New York City, 1954; Museum of Modern Art, Tokyo, 1966; Howard Wise Gallery, New York City, 1967; Galleria San Fedele, Milan, 1971 (also see below); Galerija Suvremene Umjetnosti, Zagreb, Yugoslavia, 1973; Palazzo Reale, Milan, 1986 (also see below).

AWARDS, HONORS: Gold Medal of the Triennale of Milan; several Golden Compass awards for industrial designs; *New York Times* Best Illustrated Children's Books of the Year awards, 1960, for *Bruno Munari's ABC,* and 1969, for *The Circus in the Mist;* New York Academy of Sciences award, 1974, for *From Afar It Is an Island.*

WRITINGS:

Fotocronache di Munari: dall'Isola dei Tartufi al qui pro quo, Gruppo Editoriale Domus, 1944.
Il Quadrato, All'Insegna del Pesce d'Oro, 1960, translation by Desmond O'Grady published as *The Square,* G. Wittenborn, 1960, published as *Discovery of the Square,* G. Wittenborn, 1963.
Vetrine, negozi Italiani: Modern Design for Italian Show-Windows and Shops (text in Italian, English, and German), Editrice L'Ufficio Moderno, 1961.
Good Design (text in English and Italian), All'Insegna del Pesce D'Oro/Wittenborn, 1963.
Supplemento al dizionario Italiano (text in English, French, Italian, and German), Muggiani, 1963, published as *Supplement to the Italian Dictionary,* G. Wittenborn, 1963.
Il Cerchio, All'Insegna del Pesce D'Oro, 1964, translation by Marcello and Edna Maestro published as *The Discovery of the Circle,* G. Wittenborn, 1965.

Arte come mestiere, Laterza, 1966, translation by Patrick Creagh published as *Design as Art,* Penguin, 1971.
Libro illeggibile, Museum of Modern Art (New York City), 1967.
Design e communicazione visiva: Contributo a una metodologia didattica (title means "Design and Visual Communication"), Laterza, 1968, 4th edition, 1972.
(Editor) *Design Italiano: Mobili* (text in English, French, German, and Italian), C. Bestetti, 1968.
(Editor, with others) *Campo Urbano: Interventi estetici nella demensione collettiva urbanam,* C. Nani, 1969.
Codice ovvio, Einaudi, 1971.
Artista e designer (addresses, essays, and lectures), Laterza, 1971.
Cappuccetto verde (self-illustrated; also see below), Einaudi, 1972.
Cappucetto giallo (also see below), [Turin], 1972.
Alfabetier, [Turin], 1972.
Xerografie originali, Zanichelli, 1977.
Disegnare un albero, Zanichelli, 1978.
La Scoperta del triangolo, Zanichelli, 1978.
La Scoperta del quadrato, Zanichelli, 1978.
(With Rinaldo Donzelli and Piero Polato) *Guida ai lavori in legno,* Mondadori, 1979.
Bruno Munari (addresses, essays, and lectures), introduction by Giulio Carlo Argan, Feltrinelli, 1979.
Disegnare il sole, Zanichelli, 1980.
Il Laboratorio per bambini a faenza, Zanichelli, 1981.
(With Enrica Agostinelli) *Cappuceto rosso, verde, giallo, blu e bainco,* Einaudi, 1981.
Da Cosa nasce cosa: Appunti per una metodologia progettuale, Laterza, 1981.
(With Piero Castiglioni and Davide Mosconi) *Uno Spettacolo di luce,* Zanichelli, 1984.

EXHIBITION CATALOGS

Bruno Munari (Milan exhibition, 1971), Galleria S. Fedele, 1971.
Bruno Munari (Milan exhibition, 1986), Electa, 1986.

FOR CHILDREN; SELF-ILLUSTRATED

I Libri Munari (contains "Mai contenti," "L'Uomo del camion," "Il Prestigiatore verde," "Storie di tre uccellini," "Il Venditore di animali," and "Gigi cerca il suo berretta"; stories later published separately and in English translation; also see below), Mondadori, 1945.
Lorry Driver, Harvill, 1953.
What I'd Like to Be, Harvill, 1953.
Nella notte buia, Muggiani, 1956, translation published as *In the Dark of the Night,* G. Wittenborn, 1961.
Animals for Sale, translation of "Il Venditore di animali" by Maria Cimino, World Publishing, 1957.

Who's There? Open the Door!, translation from the Italian by M. Cimino, World Publishing, 1957.

Tic, Tac, and Toc, translation of "Storie di tre uccellini" by M. Cimino, World Publishing, 1957.

The Elephant's Wish, translation of "Mai contenti," World Publishing, 1959.

The Birthday Present, translation of "L'Uomo del camion," World Publishing, 1959.

Jimmy Has Lost His Cap, Where Can It Be?, translation of "Gigi cerca il suo berretto," World Publishing, 1959.

Alfabetiere secondo il metodo attivo: Facciamo assieme un libro da leggere, Einaudi, c. 1960.

ABC (also known as *Bruno Munari's ABC*), World Publishing, 1960.

Bruno Munari's Zoo, World Publishing, 1963.

Nella nebbia di Milano, Emme Edizioni, 1968, translation published as *The Circus in the Mist,* World Publishing, 1969.

Da Lontano era un'isola, Emme, 1971, adaptation and translation by Pierrette Fleutiaux published as *From Afar It Is an Island,* World Publishing, 1972, published in England as *Search for a Stone,* A. & C. Black, 1972.

A Flower with Love, translation from the Italian by Patricia T. Lowe, Crowell, 1974.

Fantasia (title means "Fantasy"), Laterza, 1977.

Also editor of a collection for children, *Tantibambini.*

ILLUSTRATOR

Gianni Rodari, *Filastrocche in Cielo e in Terra,* Einaudi, 1960.

G. Rodari, *Il Pianeta degli Alberi di Natale,* Einaudi, 1962.

G. Rodari, *Favole al Telefono,* Einaudi, 1962.

G. Rodari, *Il Libro degli Errori,* Einaudi, 1964.

G. Rodari, *La Torta in Cielo,* Einaudi, 1966.

Nico Orengo, *A-Uli-Ule: Filastrocche, Conte, Ninnenanne,* Einaudi, 1972.

OTHER

Also author of *Teoremi sull'arte,* 1961, and editor of *Quaderni di Design.* Contributor to journals and periodicals. Objects designed by Munari have appeared in *Danese* (catalog of objects manufactured by the firm of B. Danese), B. Danese, 1963, and Stefano Casciani's *Industrial Art: Objects, Play, and Thought in Danese Production,* Arcadia, 1988. Munari's drawings have also appeared in *Disegni Astratti,* G. G. Gorlich, 1944. Also creator of several educational games.

Munari's works are collected at the Museum of Modern Art, New York City, and Kaiser Wilhelm Museum, Krefeld, Germany.

ADAPTATIONS: Bruno Munari's ABC was adapted into a filmstrip produced by Weston Woods.

SIDELIGHTS: Bruno Munari is an innovative artist whose talents in painting, sculpting, photography, and other art forms influence his books for children. Employing such devices as cutouts, lift-up flaps, and diminishing page sizes, Munari introduces young readers to the elements of color and geometry. *Bruno Munari's ABC,* a colorful guide to the alphabet, and *The Circus in the Mist,* which recreates a voyage through dense fog to a brightly colored circus in the city, both won *New York Times* Best Illustrated Children's Books awards. In addition to writing children's books, Munari has published works on graphic design, geometry, and the teaching of art.

Munari was born in Milan, Italy, and raised in a small town near Verona where his parents operated an inn. When he was twenty he returned to Milan and started his career as a painter with the futurists, a group of Italian artists, musicians, and writers who attempted to capture the energy and movement of mechanical processes in their works. Since that time he has worked in many artistic media, designing wire mobiles and kinetic sculptures, experimenting with polarized light, and designing objects for the Danese company. A notable achievement in Munari's multifaceted career has been his pioneering efforts in the field of machine art, for which he has served as chief spokesperson. He insists that an artist has a duty to know and understand machines, and to create machine-made products that are aesthetically pleasing. In 1967, he was invited to teach basic design and advanced explorations in visual communications at Harvard University. He drew upon his experiments with teaching design for a book entitled *Design e communicazione visiva: Contributo a una metodologia didattica.*

Munari turned to writing and illustrating children's books when his son Alberto was five years old. The young father despaired at not finding any good books for children, so he decided to create his own. His first collection of stories appeared in Italy in 1945, and the stories were translated and published separately in the United States years later. These books, including *Who's There? Open the Door, Tic, Tac, and Toc,* and *Jimmy Has Lost His Cap, Where Can It Be?,* feature bold full page illustrations in bright flat colors, and flaps which, when opened, change the design on the page and continue the story. Maria Cimino, reviewing Munari's early work for the *Bulletin of the New York Public Library,* says that his "extraordinary originality and his rightness as a creator of children's books rest in turn on the fact that for all his technical proficiency and plastic skills he has been able to retain the fresh eye of childhood and an untrammelled imagination. It is not their formal beauty alone, it is above all their vitality and spontaneity, that make his picture books unforgettable."

In 1960, Munari brought his unique talents to bear on a common book for very young readers: the ABC. Writing in *Horn Book,* Ruth Hill Viguers called *Bruno Munari's ABC* "so truly a work of art that one can look at it again and again and never tire," and a *New Yorker* reviewer noted that "each double-page spread is an experiment in balancing colors, textures, and space. It is as if every letter had produced its own mood and color."

Critics were equally fond of *The Circus in the Mist,* which approximates a walk through a foggy city. The first semi-translucent gray pages reveal distant objects dimly, as if through a cloud. Buses, lamp posts, and a stray cat appear and disappear as the book leads the reader to a park in the center of the city. The fog eventually clears, and the reader comes upon a wildly colored grand circus, complete with clowns and a trapeze. The effect is all the more stunning for the foggy trip. Sada Fretz called *The Circus in the Mist* "a visual toy in book form" in her *School Library Journal* review, and Ingeborg Boudreau, in a review in the *New York Times Book Review,* hailed Munari as "a master at introducing us to the delights of abstraction by playing with color and form."

BIOGRAPHICAL/CRITICAL SOURCES:

BOOKS

Children's Literature Review, Volume 9, Gale, 1985, pp. 121-30.
Kingman, Lee, and others, compilers, *Illustrators of Children's Books, 1956-1966,* Horn Book, 1968.
Miller, Bertha Mahony, and others, compilers, *Illustrators of Children's Books, 1946-56,* Horn Book, 1958.
Tanchis, Aldo, *Bruno Munari,* Idea Books, 1986, translation by Huw Evans published as *Bruno Munari: Design as Art,* MIT Press, 1986.

PERIODICALS

Bulletin of the Center for Children's Books, April, 1975.
Bulletin of the New York Public Library, November/December, 1956, pp. 585-88.
Horn Book, October, 1960, p. 399.
New Yorker, November 19, 1960, p. 223.
New York Times Book Review, December 14, 1969, p. 34.
Saturday Review, March 21, 1970.
School Library Journal, September, 1970, p. 152.*

N

NASH, Father Stephen
　See KAVANAUGH, James J(oseph)

*　　*　　*

NELSON, David Moir 1920-

PERSONAL: Born April 29, 1920, in Detroit, MI; son of James and Elizabeth (Dickie) Nelson; married Shirley Risburg, 1943; children: Amy, Benn, Eric. *Education:* University of Michigan, B.S., 1942, M.S., 1946, graduate study, 1948.

ADDRESSES: Home—114 Briar Ln., Newark, DE. *Office*—College of Physical Education, Athletics, and Recreation, University of Delaware, Newark, DE 19716.

CAREER: Hillsdale College, Hillsdale, MI, director of physical education and athletics, 1946-48; Harvard University, Cambridge, MA, football backfield coach, 1948-49; University of Maine, Orono, head football coach, 1949-51; University of Delaware, Newark, professor of physical education, 1951-60, director of Division of Health, Physical Education, and Athletics, 1951—, athletic director, 1981-83, dean of College of Physical Education, Athletics, and Recreation, 1981-89, special assistant to the president, 1989-90; commissioner of Yankee Conference, 1989—. Has participated in one hundred sports clinics. *Military service:* U.S. Navy, over three years; became lieutenant; awarded Presidential Unit Citation with three battle stars.

MEMBER: National Collegiate Athletic Association (chairman of rules changes committee, 1959-60; member of Hall of Fame committee, 1959-62, editorial committee, 1960, and numerous other committees; secretary of football rules committee, 1962), American Football Coaches Association (trustee), National Association of College Di-

rectors, American Association of Health, Physical Education, and Recreation, Eastern Collegiate Athletic Conference (member of executive council, 1951-53; vice-president, 1958-59; president, 1959-60), Middle Atlantic Athletic Conference (member of executive committee, 1954-56), Phi Beta Kappa.

WRITINGS:

(With Forest Evashevski) *Scoring Power with the Winged-T Offense,* W. C. Brown, 1957.
The Modern Winged-T Play Book, W. C. Brown, 1961.
Football: Principles and Play, Ronald, 1962.
99 Best High School Plays, DuPont Co., 1966.
The Best of High School Defensive Football, DuPont Co., 1967.
Illustrated Football Rules, Doubleday, 1976.
The Anatomy of a Game, NCAA Publishing, 1990.

Contributor to *Championship Football by Twelve Great Coaches,* Prentice-Hall, 1962. Contributor to professional journals. Author of scripts and narration for National Collegiate Athletic Association films *Football Code,* 1962, *Best Plays,* 1963, *Monday Morning Quarterback,* 1967, *Two Platoon Football,* 1968, *Scrimmage Kick Rule,* 1968, *Pass Interference,* 1973, *A Matter of Attitude,* 1981, and *NCAA Football Mechanics in Japanese,* 1989.

SIDELIGHTS: David Moir Nelson coached the North-South Shrine Game in 1959 as well as the All-American Bowl in 1960, 1961, and 1962.

*　　*　　*

NIXON, Joan Lowery 1927-
　(Jaye Ellen)

PERSONAL: Born February 3, 1927, in Los Angeles, CA; daughter of Joseph Michael (an accountant) and Margaret

(Meyer) Lowery; married Hershell H. Nixon (a petroleum geologist), August 6, 1949; children: Kathleen Nixon Brush, Maureen Nixon Quinlan, Joseph Michael, Eileen Marie. *Education:* University of Southern California, B.A., 1947; California State College, certificate in elementary education, 1949. *Religion:* Roman Catholic.

ADDRESSES: Home—10215 Cedar Creek Dr., Houston, TX 77042. *Agent*—Amy Berkower, Writers House Inc., 21 West 26th St., New York, NY 10010.

CAREER: Writer. Elementary school teacher in Los Angeles, CA, 1947-50; Midland College, Midland, TX, instructor in creative writing, 1971-73; University of Houston, Houston, TX, instructor in creative writing, 1974-78; taught creative writing in two parochial schools in Texas.

MEMBER: Authors Guild, Authors League of America, Society of Children's Book Writers (charter member and former member of board of directors), Mystery Writers of America (regional vice-president, Southwest chapter), Western Writers of America, Kappa Delta Alumnae Association.

AWARDS, HONORS: Steck-Vaughn Award, Texas Institute of Letters, 1975, for *The Alligator under the Bed;* Edgar Allan Poe Award for best juvenile novel, Mystery Writers of America, 1980, for *The Kidnapping of Christina Lattimore,* 1981, for *The Seance,* and 1987, for *The Other Side of Dark;* Edgar Allan Poe Award nominee, Mystery Writers of America, 1975, for *The Mysterious Red Tape Gang,* and 1985, for *The Ghosts of Now;* Outstanding Science Trade Book for children, National Science Teachers Association and Children's Book Council Joint Committee, 1979, for *Volcanoes: Nature's Fireworks,* 1980, for *Glaciers: Nature's Frozen Rivers,* and 1981, for *Earthquakes: Nature in Motion;* Crabbery Award, Oxon Hill branch of Prince George's County (MD) Library, 1984, for *Magnolia's Mixed-Up Magic;* Young Hoosier Award, 1988, for *A Deadly Game of Magic;* Golden Spur, Western Writers of America, 1988, for *A Family Apart,* and 1989, for *In the Face of Danger;* Young Hoosier Award, 1989, for *The Dark and Deadly Pool;* Colorado Blue Spruce Young Adult Award, 1988, Virginia Young Adult Silver Cup, 1989, Oklahoma Sequoyah Young Adult Book Award, 1989, Iowa Teen Award, 1989, California Young Readers Medal, 1990, and Utah Young Adult Award, 1991, all for *The Other Side of Dark;* California Young Readers Medal, 1990, for *The Stalker.*

WRITINGS:

Writing Mysteries for Young People, Writer, Inc., 1977.
The Grandmother's Book, Abingdon, 1979.

FICTION; FOR YOUNG PEOPLE

The Mystery of Hurricane Castle, illustrated by Velma Ilsley, Criterion, 1964.
The Mystery of the Grinning Idol, illustrated by Alvin Smith, Criterion, 1965.
The Mystery of the Hidden Cockatoo, illustrated by Richard Lewis, Criterion, 1966.
The Mystery of the Haunted Woods, illustrated by Theresa Brudi, Criterion, 1967.
The Mystery of the Secret Stowaway, illustrated by Joan Drescher, Criterion, 1968.
Delbert, the Plainclothes Detective, illustrated by Philip Smith, Criterion, 1971.
The Alligator under the Bed, illustrated by Jan Hughes, Putnam, 1974.
The Mysterious Red Tape Gang, illustrated by Joan Sandin, Putnam, 1974, published in paperback as *The Adventures of the Red Tape Gang,* illustrations by Steven H. Stroud, Scholastic Inc., 1983.
The Secret Box Mystery (Junior Literary Guild selection), illustrated by Leigh Grant, Putnam, 1974.
The Mysterious Prowler, illustrated by Berthe Amoss, Harcourt, 1976.
The Boy Who Could Find Anything, illustrated by Syd Hoff, Harcourt, 1978.
Danger in Dinosaur Valley (Junior Literary Guild selection), illustrated by Marc Simont, Putnam, 1978.
Muffie Mouse and the Busy Birthday (Junior Literary Guild selection), illustrated by Geoffrey Hayes, Seabury, 1978, also published as *Muffy and the Birthday Party,* Scholastic Inc., 1979..
Bigfoot Makes a Movie, illustrated by S. Hoff, Putnam, 1979.
The Kidnapping of Christina Lattimore, Harcourt, 1979.
Gloria Chipmunk, Star!, illustrated by Diane Dawson, Houghton, 1980, published in paperback with illustrations by G. Hayes, Scholastic Inc., 1980.
Casey and the Great Idea, illustrated by Amy Rowen, Dutton, 1980.
If You Say So, Claude, illustrated by Lorinda Bryan Cauley, Warne, 1980.
The Seance, Harcourt, 1980.
The Spotlight Gang and the Backstage Ghost, Harlequin, 1981.
Days of Fear, photographs by Joan Menschenfreund, Dutton, 1983.
The Specter, Delacorte, 1982, published in England as *The Spectre,* Granada, 1983.
(Under pseudonym Jaye Ellen) *The Trouble with Charlie,* Bantam, 1982.
The Gift, illustrated by Andrew Glass, Macmillan, 1983.
A Deadly Game of Magic, Harcourt, 1983.
Magnolia's Mixed-Up Magic, illustrated by Linda Bucholtz-Ross, Putnam, 1983.

The Ghosts of Now, Delacorte, 1984.

The House on Hackman's Hill, Scholastic Inc., 1985.

Maggie, Too, illustrations by Darrel Millsap, Harcourt, 1985.

The Stalker, illustrations by Wendy Popp, Delacorte, 1985.

And Maggie Makes Three, Harcourt, 1986.

Beats Me, Claude (Junior Literary Guild selection), illustrated by Tracey Campbell Pearson, Viking, 1986.

The Other Side of Dark, Delacorte, 1986.

The Dark and Deadly Pool, Delacorte, 1987.

Fat Chance, Claude, illustrated by T. C. Pearson, Viking Kestrel, 1987.

Haunted Island, Scholastic Inc., 1987.

Maggie Forevermore, Harcourt, 1987.

Secret, Silent Screams, Delacorte, 1988.

The Island of Dangerous Dreams, Dell, 1989.

You Bet Your Britches, Claude, illustrated by T. C. Pearson, Viking, 1989.

Whispers from the Dead, Delacorte, 1989.

That's the Spirit, Claude, Viking, 1990.

Candidate for Murder, Delacorte, 1991.

High Trail to Danger, Bantam, 1991.

Honeycutt Street Celebrities, Dell, 1991.

Mystery Box, Dell, 1991.

Watch Out for Dinosaurs, Dell, 1991.

The Haunted House on Honeycutt Street, Dell, 1991.

A Deadly Promise, Bantam, 1992.

The Weekend Was Murder, Delacorte, 1992.

Will You Give Me a Dream? (picture book), Four Winds Press, 1992.

Land of Hope, Bantam, 1992.

"FIRST READ-ALONE MYSTERIES" SERIES; ILLUSTRATED BY JIM CUMMINS

The New Year's Mystery, Albert Whitman, 1979.

The Halloween Mystery, Albert Whitman, 1979.

The Valentine Mystery, Albert Whitman, 1979.

The Happy Birthday Mystery, Albert Whitman, 1979.

The Thanksgiving Mystery, Albert Whitman, 1980.

The April Fool Mystery, Albert Whitman, 1980.

The Easter Mystery, Albert Whitman, 1981.

The Christmas Eve Mystery, Albert Whitman, 1981.

"KLEEP: SPACE DETECTIVE" SERIES; ILLUSTRATED BY PAUL FRAME

Kidnapped on Astarr, Garrard, 1981.

Mysterious Queen of Magic, Garrard, 1981.

Mystery Dolls from Planet Urd, Garrard, 1981.

"ORPHAN TRAIN" QUARTET

A Family Apart, Bantam, 1987.

Caught in the Act, Bantam, 1988.

In the Face of Danger, Bantam, 1988.

A Place to Belong, Bantam, 1989.

"HOLLYWOOD DAUGHTERS" TRILOGY

Star Baby, Bantam, 1989.

Overnight Sensation, Bantam, 1990.

Encore, Bantam, 1990.

NONFICTION; WITH HUSBAND, HERSHELL H. NIXON

Oil and Gas: From Fossils to Fuels, illustrated by Jean Day Zallinger, Harcourt, 1977.

Volcanoes: Nature's Fireworks, Dodd, 1978.

Glaciers: Nature's Frozen Rivers, Dodd, 1980.

Earthquakes: Nature in Motion, Dodd, 1981.

Land under the Sea, Dodd, 1985.

OTHER

(With others) *This I Can Be* (textbook), Benefic, 1975.

(With others) *People and Me* (textbook), Benefic, 1975.

Five Loaves and Two Fishes: Feeding of Five Thousand for Beginning Readers; John 6:1-15 for Children, illustrated by Aline Cunningham, Concordia, 1976.

Who Is My Neighbor?: The Good Samaritan for Beginning Readers; Luke 10:29-37 for Children, illustrated by A. Cunningham, Concordia, 1976.

The Son Who Came Home Again: The Prodigal Son for Beginning Readers; Luke 15:11-32 for Children, illustrated by A. Cunningham, Concordia, 1977.

When God Listens, illustrated by James McIlrath, Our Sunday Visitor, 1978.

When God Speaks, illustrated by J. McIlrath, Our Sunday Visitor, 1978.

The Butterfly Tree, illustrated by J. McIlrath, Our Sunday Visitor, 1979.

Before You Were Born, illustrated by J. McIlrath, Our Sunday Visitor, 1980.

If You Were a Writer, illustrated by Bruce Degen, Four Winds Press, 1988.

Also author of introduction, *Tales from Ellery Queen's Mystery Magazine: Short Stories for Young Adults,* edited by Cynthia Manson, Harcourt, 1986. Humor columnist for *Houston Post.* Contributor to magazines, including *West Coast Review of Books, Writer, American Home, Parents, Woman's Day,* and *Ms.*

SIDELIGHTS: Joan Lowery Nixon, winner of three Edgar Allan Poe Awards from the Mystery Writers of America, is a prolific author of books for children of every age. Over two-thirds of Nixon's works are young-adult mysteries, noted for their emphasis on both characterization and plot. Nixon's love for mysteries began in childhood, as well as her ability to develop sympathetic characters. She tells an interviewer for *Something about the Author* (*SATA*), that she vividly recalls her own childhood experiences, "how I felt, how I reacted, how I responded to the emotions of happiness, sorrow, excitement, fear . . . so I can understand how a child of today would feel, how he would approach his problems, and how he would identify with the character in a book, who perhaps had the same problems to solve. My characters become a part of me and I feel with them.''

Nixon insists that she had an uneventful childhood, but growing up in Hollywood, California, left her with many interesting and unusual experiences. In her autobiographical sketch in *Something about the Author Autobiography Series* (*SAAS*), Nixon recalls that her parents bragged to their relatives "back east" that "on the same day [they] could play in the snow up in the mountains and enjoy a swim on a sunny beach." She also remembers the excitement of going to a grand opening of a nearby grocery store, "complete with kleig lights, Hollywood starlets, talent shows, and lots of free samples of good things to eat." Nixon says in her *SATA* interview: "I remember one time, a friend and I went for ice cream at a little shop called The Pig'n Whistle next to the Egyptian Theatre. Shirley Temple came in with a friend and sat down at the table next to us. Well, we refused to acknowledge that she was there at all. We didn't want anyone to think us so uncouth as to stare at a movie star.''

Despite the surrounding glamour, Nixon's fondest memories of childhood are of reading, performing puppet plays, and playing in the playroom that connected her parents' house with that of her grandparents. Nixon's mother had been a kindergarten teacher, and she "equipped the room with an upright piano, paints and an easel, and a worktable on which we could create with clay, colored construction paper, crayons, glue, and scissors," the author remembers in *SAAS*. Though her parents and grandparents read to her and her two younger sisters often, Nixon could never get enough, and she says: "I began teaching myself to read, by memorizing words, when I was three, so my mother completed the teaching process, using a combination of the 'look-say' method and phonics.''

Nixon also enjoyed writing from an early age. "I always wanted to become a writer," she maintains in *SAAS*. "My mother told me that at the age of two, before I was old enough to read or write, I would come to her and say, 'Write this down. I have a poem.' " When she published her first poem in *Children's Playmate* at age ten, she knew she had found a career. Her performance in school only encouraged her hopes; though she did poorly in physical education and remembers being teased by boys, she always did well in English classes. Nixon's high-school English teacher, Miss Bertha Standfast, insisted that she had the talent to be a writer, and encouraged her to major in journalism when she went to college.

One week after her high-school graduation, Nixon began college classes at the University of Southern California, majoring in journalism. She found the campus swarming with young sailors who were earning their degrees before joining the troops fighting overseas in World War II. Though she was heavily involved in writing humorous skits for her sorority and attending social events, Nixon found time to meet the man who would become her husband, Hershell Nixon. Nixon graduated before they were married, however, and found that there were few jobs in journalism that paid enough to live on. In her autobiographical sketch, she recounts one particularly bad experience applying for the job of staff writer for a radio program: "I still remember how angry and discouraged I felt when one of these producers looked me up and down and said, 'Why do you want to compete with all the men who write for radio? You're a pretty girl, honey. Why don't you just get married and settle down and raise a family?' I firmly told him that I was a writer and being a woman was going to prove to be an advantage, not a disadvantage." It didn't get her the job, though she soon found a position teaching kindergarten near her parents' home.

Within a few years Nixon was married, living in Texas, and busy raising a family that would include three daughters and a son. But raising a family had not allowed her much time to write, and when she read in the Corpus Christi newspaper about an upcoming Southwest Writers Conference she was eager to go. Leaving the conference, she was intrigued by the idea of writing for children; "I had children, I had taught children, and I have the vivid kind of memory which enables me to remember all the details I saw and the emotions I felt when I was a child," she recalls in *SAAS*. "I made a mental note to myself. Maybe I'd try writing something for children." Her decision was made when her daughters came to her and said: "If you're going to write for children, you have to write a book, and it has to be a mystery, and you have to put us in it." She did all three. *The Mystery of Hurricane Castle*, Nixon's first book, tells the story of two girls left behind during the evacuation of an area just before a hurricane and follows them as they seek shelter in a house that, according to local legend, is haunted. The vivid characterization and fast-moving plot set the tone for the many mystery stories that would follow.

The first book impelled Nixon to continue writing, and she soon found herself busy writing children's books, teaching creative classes at local children's schools, libraries, and colleges, and writing a humor column for the *Houston Post*. Nixon says in *SAAS* that it "soon became apparent that I would have to make a decision about the direction of my career . . . ," for "the careful time I spent on the work from the students in my writing classes subtracted from the time I had for my own writing. It was a difficult decision, but I gave up teaching." This decision allowed her to devote every morning to writing, a hard task, she says in her autobiographical sketch, "but it's such a fulfilling, enjoyable occupation that it's worth all the effort."

Nixon learned much of her discipline as a writer while studying journalism, she comments in her *SATA* interview. "Journalism taught me to focus because I had to sit down and *write,* whether I felt like it or not—no waiting for inspiration. I learned the skill of finding the important facts in a story, and how to isolate them from all of the unnecessary details." Gathering ideas and developing plots for her books, however, requires the different disciplines of imagination and careful research. Her ideas, she continues, are "derived from places I have lived and visited, people I have known, and interesting things I have seen, with the deeper, underlying thoughts which are exclusively mine: my beliefs, my approach to life, my goals, even my own sense of what is humorous, right or good."

Nixon believes that many books for young people are better written than books for adults. "I'm more challenged when I write for young people . . .," she admits in *SATA,* "because when you write for 'children' you write for everyone from a two-year-old to a teenager. There are so many, many different styles and forms for these age groups." Though she has written a number of non-fiction books, Nixon says in *SAAS* that "fiction is my favorite form of writing. The knowledge that as a writer I can create my own characters and take them any place I wish is wonderful, heady, and powerful." And, she affirms, children's writers "can give young people the feeling that although things may be tough *right now,* they will get better and that they have the power to make things get better."

BIOGRAPHICAL/CRITICAL SOURCES:

BOOKS

Lystad, Mary, sketch on Joan Lowery Nixon, *Twentieth-Century Children's Writers,* 3rd edition, St. James Press, 1989, pp. 723-724.
Nixon, Joan Lowery, autobiographical sketch, *Something about the Author Autobiography Series,* Volume 9, Gale, 1990, pp. 267-284.
Something about the Author, Volume 44, Gale, 1986, pp. 131-139.

PERIODICALS

New York Times Book Review, October 9, 1988.
School Library Journal, January, 1987.
School Library Media Quarterly, fall, 1982.
Writer, September, 1972; February, 1977.

—*Sketch by Tom Pendergast*

NOESTLINGER, Christine 1936-

PERSONAL: Born October 13, 1936 in Vienna, Austria; married in 1959; children: two daughters. *Education:* Attended art school in Vienna, Austria.

ADDRESSES: Home—Vienna, Austria.

CAREER: Journalist for a Vienna daily newspaper; writer.

AWARDS, HONORS: Friedrich-Boedecker Prize, 1972, for contribution to children's literature; Buxtehuder Bulle Award, 1973, for *Fly Away Home;* German Youth Literature Prize, 1973, for *The Cucumber King;* Oesterreichischer Staatspreis fuer Kinder- und Jugendliteratur, 1975, for *Achtung! Vranek sieht ganz harmlos aus,* 1979, for *Guardian Ghost,* and 1987, for *A Dog's Life; The Cucumber King* was selected for the International Board on Books for Young People (IBBY) honor list in the translator's category, 1978; Mildred L. Batchelder Award, 1979, for *Konrad;* Kinder- und Jugendbuchpreis der Stadt Wien, 1980, for *Dschi Dsche-i Dschunior; Luke and Angela* was selected as an American Library Association Notable Book, 1981; Hans Christian Andersen Medal from the IBBY, 1984, for body of work; Children's Book Award, City of Vienna, 1987, for *Der geheime Grossvater.*

WRITINGS:

FOR CHILDREN; TRANSLATIONS FROM THE GERMAN BY ANTHEA BELL

Die feuerrote Friedrike, Jugend & Volk, 1970, translated as *Fiery Frederica,* illustrated by David McKee, Abelard-Schuman, 1975.
Die Kinder aus dem Kinderkeller: Aufgeschrieben von Pia Maria Tiralla, Beltz & Gelberg, 1971, translated as *The Disappearing Cellar: A Tale Told by Pia Maria Tiralla, a Viennese Nanny,* illustrated by Heidi Rempen, Abelard-Schuman, 1975.
Mr. Bats Meisterstueck; oder, Die total verjuengte Oma, F. Oetinger, 1971, translated as *Mr. Bat's Great Invention,* illustrated by F. J. Tripp, Andersen Press (London), 1978.
Wir pfeifen auf den Gurkenkoenig, Beltz & Gelberg, 1972, translated as *The Cucumber King: A Story With a Beginning, a Middle, and an End, in Which Wolfgang Hogelmann Tells the Whole Truth,* illustrated by Werner Maurer, Abelard-Schuman, 1975, 2nd edition, 1983, published as *The Cucumber King,* Dutton, 1985.
Der kleine Herr greift ein, illustrated by Rolf Rettich, F. Oetinger, 1973.
Sim Sala Bim, illustrated by Wolfgang Zoehrer, Jugend & Volk, 1973.

Achtung! Vranek sieht ganz harmlos aus (title means "Careful! Vranek Seems to Be Totally Harmless"), Jugend & Volk, 1974.

(With Hans Arnold) *Gugerells Hund,* Betz, 1974.

Iba de guanz oaman Kinda (poem), woodcut illustrated by Thomas Bewick, Jugend & Volk, 1974.

Das Leben der Tomanis, illustrated by Helme Heine, G. Middelhauve, 1974-76.

Konrad; oder, Das Kind aus der Konservenbuechse, F. Oetinger, 1975, translated as *Conrad: The Factory Made Boy,* illustrated by Frantz Wittkamp, Andersen Press, 1976, published as *Konrad,* illustrated by Carol Nicklaus, F. Watts, 1977.

Der kleine Jo (title means "Little Jo"), illustrated by Bettina Anrich-Woelfel, H. Schroedel, 1976.

Das will Jenny haben, illustrated by Anrich-Woelfel, H. Schroedel, 1977.

Lollipop, Beltz & Gelberg, 1977, translation under same title illustrated by Angelika Kaufmann, Andersen Press, 1982.

Pit und Anja entdecken das Jahr: Der Fruehling kommt (title means "Pit and Anja Discover the Year: Spring Comes"), illustrated by Bernadette Parmentier, H. Schroedel, 1978.

Pit und Anja entdecken das Jahr: Im Sommer (title means "Pit and Anja Discover the Year: In the Summer"), illustrated by Parmentier, H. Schroedel, 1978.

Rosa Reidl, Schutzgespenst Jugend & Volk, 1979, translated as *Guardian Ghost,* Andersen Press, 1986.

Dschi Dsche-i Dschunior, Jugend & Volk, 1980.

Einer, illustrated by Janosch, Beltz & Gelberg, 1980.

Der Denker greift ein, Jugend & Volk, 1981, translated as *Brainbox Sorts It Out,* Andersen Press, 1985, published as *Brainbox Cracks the Case,* Bergh, 1986.

Rosalinde hat Gedanken im Kopf (title means "Rosalinde Has Thoughts in Her Head"), Oetinger, 1981.

Gretchen Sackmeier, Oetinger, 1981.

Anatol und die Wurschtelfrau, Jugend & Volk, 1983.

Gretchen hat Haenschen-Kummer: Eine Familiengeschichte, F. Oetinger, 1983.

Jokel, Jula, und Jericho, two volumes, illustrated by Edith Schindler, Beltz & Gelberg, 1983.

Der geheime Grossvater (title means "The Secret Grandfather"), illustrated by Christine Noestlinger, Jr., Jugend & Volk, 1986.

Der Hund kommt!, Beltz & Gelberg, 1987, translated as *A Dog's Life,* illustrated by Jutta Bauer, Andersen Press, 1990.

YOUNG ADULT NOVELS; TRANSLATIONS FROM THE GERMAN BY ANTHEA BELL

Ein Mann fuer Mama, F. Oetinger, 1972, translated as *Marrying Off Mother,* Andersen Press, 1978, Harcourt, 1982.

Maikaefer, flieg! Mein Vater, das Kriegsende, Cohn und ich, Beltz & Gelberg, 1973, translated as *Fly Away Home,* F. Watts, 1975.

Ilse Janda, 14, F. Oetinger, 1974, translated as *Girl Missing,* F. Watts, 1976.

Studentplan, Beltz & Gelberg, 1975, translated as *Four Days in the Life of Lisa,* Abelard-Schuman, 1977.

Die unteren sieben Achtel des Eisbergs, Beltz & Gelberg, 1978.

Luki-live, F. Oetinger, 1978, translated as *Luke and Angela,* Andersen Press, 1979, Harcourt, 1981.

Pfui Spinne!, Beltz & Gelberg, 1980.

Zwei Wochen im Mai: Mein Vater, der Rudi, der Hansi und ich, Beltz & Gelberg, 1981.

But Jasper Came Instead (originally published as *Das Austauschkind,* 1982), Andersen Press, 1983.

SIDELIGHTS: Humor and magic are the main ingredients that Christine Noestlinger adds to her books for children and teenagers. A prominent Austrian author and winner of the 1984 Hans Christian Andersen Medal for her body of work, Noestlinger believes that children should be dealt with honestly, as well as be entertained. "She has said that she sees four elements in writing for children," writes Pat Thomson in *Books for Keeps:* "their love of humour, what they like to read, what they ought to read, and what she feels compelled to write." For younger children this means writing books that "can generally be described as comic fantasy," says Noestlinger's translator, Anthea Bell, in *Junior Bookshelf,* while her stories for young adults also use humor to help relieve the tension in these more realistic stories.

"I grew up in a working-class district of Vienna, where I was considered a 'posh' child, because my mother ran a nursery school and my grandfather had a shop," Noestlinger writes in *Junior Bookshelf.* However, her comfortable family life was destroyed by the onset of World War II. Allied forces bombed Vienna relentlessly, leaving her family homeless and without enough food, clothing, and medicine. The powerful memories of the war would later make their way into some of her books, such as *Fly Away Home.*

Noestlinger's first goal after the war was to become a painter. But before she could finish her studies at an art school in Vienna she married and started a family. Instead of resuming her efforts to become a painter—she did not consider herself to be a very good artist—Noestlinger later took a job with a daily newspaper. One day, she tried writing and illustrating a picture book. "The text won more approval than the pictures," Noestlinger recalls. "As I was very keen on approval at the time, I took to writing."

In her writing, Noestlinger has switched back and forth between juvenile books and young adult books. Magic and fantasy in her stories for younger audiences portray children in new and unexpected ways, often through a reversal of roles between adult and child, or by challenging traditional ideas about how children should act. In *Mr. Bat's Great Invention,* for example, a magic potion turns Robert's grandmother into a six-year-old bratty child. In order to return his grandmother back to normal, Robert has to take charge and use Mr. Bat's time machine. *The Cucumber King* is a book of "teenage rebellion," according to *Growing Point* reviewer Margery Fisher, in which Wolfgang's father helps the tyrannical Cucumber King try to regain power over the other vegetables in the cellar. Because his father is on the wrong side of this bizarre vegetable rebellion, Wolfgang is placed in the uncomfortable position of having to fight against him. Noestlinger offers her readers another kind of twist in her best-known book, *Conrad: The Factory Made Boy,* which is the tale of a made-to-order boy who has perfect manners. Conrad is accidentally delivered to the wrong person, Mrs. Bartolotti, who does not demand perfection from Conrad. When the cold and demanding parents who actually ordered Conrad arrive to pick the boy up, Conrad must quickly learn how to be naughty so that he can stay with Mrs. Bartolotti.

Noestlinger's young adult books tend to be much more realistic, but they retain the author's characteristic use of humor. Even the book *Fly Away Home,* which is set during the final days of World War II, contains a great deal of humor. Based on the author's own experiences, *Fly Away Home* is about the Nazi withdrawal from Austria and the temporary occupation by the Russians. The tension and suffering in the story is relieved by humorous moments, especially those between Christel, the main character, and Cohn, a Russian cook. Critics have praised *Fly Away Home* especially for its "fast realism devoid of self-pity," as one *Booklist* contributor put it. Noestlinger later continued the story in the as yet untranslated book, *Zwei Wochen in Mai: Mein Vater, der Rudi, der Hansi, und ich.*

Other young adult books by Noestlinger are set in the present day and are more directly concerned with the problems of growing up. Comparing *Girl Missing* to *Fly Away Home,* Betsy Hearne writes in *Booklist* that whereas in *Fly Away Home* there is kindness in the middle of strife, here "a time of plenty camouflages bitter struggles among people who hurt each other." This story about a family in conflict follows Erika as she searches for her runaway sister. Although the family in *Girl Missing* remains torn apart, the characters in books like *Luke and Angela* and *But Jasper Came Instead* wind up understanding each other in the end.

As Patricia Crampton acknowledges in a *Bookbird* article, in all of her work the author "is on the side of the children, first, last and all the way." Crampton believes that in

Noestlinger's earlier stories the author may have favored this viewpoint "at the expense of compassion" for her other characters. But in her more recent books "her sympathy now encompasses all her characters, while her themes enrich the reader emotionally and extend his or her understanding, both inwards and outwards." Thomson observes, "Christine Noestlinger speaks very directly to [her] reader[s], involving them in an immediate way. She is antiauthoritarian, writing largely from the child's point of view, but without abdicating adult responsibility. The characters always recognize ultimately that they, too, must contribute to family harmony whatever the parental shortcomings."

Since Noestlinger began her writing career her beliefs about what authors should try to do with their books has changed considerably. In her acceptance speech for the Hans Christian Andersen Medal—reprinted in *Bookbird*—she recalls that in the beginning her philosophy "was quite simple: since children live in an environment which offers them no encouragement to develop Utopias for themselves, we have to take them by the arm and show them how beautiful, cheerful, just and humane this world could be. Rightly done, this will make children long for that better world, and their longing will make them willing to think about what must be got rid of and what must be initiated in order to produce the world they long for."

More recently, though, increasing problems of poverty, famine, pollution, and war have made Noestlinger doubt whether writers can indeed have a positive affect on children's lives. This, along with competition for young audiences from television and videos, has caused Noestlinger to conclude that "there is now less chance than ever of increasing equality of opportunity through reading . . . [unless] everything in the world changes for the better." Still, as Bell notes in *Bookbird,* Noestlinger continues to try to set examples for children in her writing "through the medium of humor."

BIOGRAPHICAL/CRITICAL SOURCES:

BOOKS

Children's Literature Review, Volume 11, Gale, 1987, pp. 179-189.

PERIODICALS

Bookbird, June 15, 1984, pp. 5-6; December 15, 1984, p. 4-8; June 15, 1985, pp. 8-13.
Booklist, September 1, 1975, p. 44; October 15, 1976, pp. 324-325.
Books and Bookmen, June, 1977, pp. 64-66.
Books for Keeps, January, 1984, p. 8; September, 1984, p. 26.
Bulletin of the Center for Children's Books, March, 1986, p. 134.

Economist, December 25, 1976, pp. 90-91.

Growing Point, July, 1975, pp. 2655-2656; January, 1977, p. 3044; September, 1977, p. 3168; July, 1983, pp. 4100-4101; July, 1985, pp. 4463-4464.

Horn Book, January/February, 1989, p. 34.

Junior Bookshelf, August, 1978, p. 192; February, 1984, pp. 35-36; April, 1984, pp. 49-50; October, 1990, pp. 247-248.

Kirkus Reviews, July 1, 1981, pp. 805-806.

The Lion and the Unicorn, June, 1988.

School Librarian, June, 1977, p. 159; September, 1982, p. 236.

School Library Journal, December, 1982, p. 73.

Times Educational Supplement, January 18, 1980, p. 39; June 11, 1982, p. 44; June 3, 1983, p. 43; February 14, 1986, p. 14.

Times Literary Supplement, December 10, 1976, p. 1549; March 25, 1977, p. 358; July 7, 1978, p. 764.*

—Sketch by Kevin S. Hile

*   *   *

NOLL, Mark A(llan) 1946-

PERSONAL: Born July 18, 1946, in Iowa City, IA; son of Francis Arthur (an engineer) and Evelyn Jean (Hummel) Noll; married Ruth Margaret Packer, 1969; children: Mary Constance, David Luther, Robert Francis. *Education:* Wheaton College, B.A., 1968; University of Iowa, M.A., 1970; Trinity Evangelical Divinity School, M.A., 1972; Vanderbilt University, M.A., 1974, Ph.D., 1975. *Religion:* Reformed Protestant.

ADDRESSES: Office—Department of History, Wheaton College, Wheaton, IL 60187.

CAREER: Trinity College, Deerfield, IL, assistant professor of history, 1975-78; Wheaton College, Wheaton, IL, associate professor, 1978-84, professor of history, 1984—. Juniata College, J. Omar Good Visiting Distinguished Professor, 1982-83.

MEMBER: American Historical Association, Organization of American Historians, American Society of Church History, Conference on Faith and History.

WRITINGS:

Christians in the American Revolution, Eerdmans, 1977.

(With Nathan Hatch and John Woodbridge) *The Gospel in America: Themes in the Story of American Evangelicals,* Zondervan, 1979.

(Editor with Hatch, and contributor) *The Bible in America,* Oxford University Press, 1982.

(Co-author and co-editor) *Eerdmans Handbook to Christianity in America,* Eerdmans, 1983.

(Editor) *The Princeton Theology, 1812-1921,* Baker Book, 1983.

Between Faith and Criticism: Evangelicals, Scholarship, and the Bible in America, Harper, 1986, expanded edition, Baker Book, 1991.

(Editor with Roger Lundin) *Voices from the Heart: Four Centuries of American Piety,* Eerdmans, 1987.

One Nation under God? Christian Faith and Political Action in America, Harper, 1988.

(Editor with David Wells) *Christian Faith and Practice in the Modern World: Theology from an Evangelical Point of View,* Eerdmans, 1988.

Princeton and the Republic, 1768-1822: The Search for a Christian Enlightenment in the Era of Samuel Stanhope Smith, Princeton University Press, 1989.

(With Hatch and George Marsden) *The Search for Christian America,* Crossway, 1983, revised edition, Helmers & Howard, 1989.

(Editor) *Religion and American Politics: From the Colonial Period to the 1980s,* Oxford University Press, 1989.

(With Howard Kee and others) *Christianity: A Social and Cultural History,* Macmillan, 1991.

(Editor) *Confessions and Catechisms of the Reformation,* Baker Book, 1991.

A History of Christianity in the United States and Canada, Eerdmans, 1992.

Contributor to books. Contributor to history and theology journals. Associate editor, *Christian Scholar's Review,* 1978-83; member of editorial committee, *Reformed Journal,* 1983-1990.

WORK IN PROGRESS: A book on religion and politics from the mid-eighteenth century to the Civil War.

SIDELIGHTS: Mark A. Noll told *CA:* "My writing arises out of my 'callings' as a historian and a Christian. Sometimes the vocations seem to get in the way of each other, but mostly it is a fruitful combination. The danger of moralizing in historical work and relativizing religion is always present. These are acceptable risks, given the intrinsic satisfaction of the task."

BIOGRAPHICAL/CRITICAL SOURCES:

PERIODICALS

American Historical Review, December, 1978; June, 1983.
Church History, December, 1984.
Publishers Weekly, December 18, 1987.

*   *   *

NORTH, Gary 1942-

PERSONAL: Born February 11, 1942, in San Pedro, CA; son of Samuel William (with the Federal Bureau of Investigation) and Alice M. (Kilgore) North; married Sharon Rose Rushdoony, February 23, 1972; children: Darcy Lynn, Scott Andrew, Lori Michelle, Caleb Allen. *Education:* University of California, Riverside, B.A., 1963, M.A., 1966, Ph.D., 1972; attended Westminster Theological Seminary, 1963-64. *Politics:* "Neo-Puritan." *Religion:* Reformed Episcopal Church.

ADDRESSES: Office—Institute for Christian Economics, P.O. Box 8000, Tyler, TX 75711.

CAREER: Writer. Foundation for Economic Education, Irvington, NY, director of seminars, 1971-73; affiliated with Chalcedon Foundation, Vallecito, CA, 1973-1981; congressional assistant in Washington, DC, 1976; Institute for Christian Economics, Tyler, TX, president, 1977—.

MEMBER: Philadelphia Society (member of board of directors, 1973-76).

AWARDS, HONORS: George Washington Medal, Freedoms Foundation, 1974.

WRITINGS:

Marx's Religion of Revolution, Craig Press, 1968.
Introduction to Christian Economics, Craig Press, 1973.
Puritan Economic Experiments, Remnant Press, 1974.
(Editor) *Foundations of Christian Scholarship,* Ross House, 1976.
None Dare Call It Witchcraft, Arlington House, 1976.
How You Can Profit from the Coming Price Controls, American Bureau of Economic Research, 1977.
Successful Investing in an Age of Envy, Steadman Press, 1981.
Unconditional Surrender: God's Program for Victory, Geneva Divinity School Press, 1981, 3rd edition, 1988.
An Economic Commentary on the Bible, Institute for Christian Economics, Volume 1: *The Dominion Covenant: Genesis,* 1982, 2nd edition, 1987, Volume 2: *Moses and Pharaoh: Dominion Religion vs. Power Religion,* 1985, Volume 3: *The Sinai Strategy: Economics and the Ten Commandments,* 1986, Volume 4: *Tools of Dominion: The Case Laws of Exodus,* 1990.
The Coase Theorem: A Study in Economic Epistemology, Institute for Christian Economics, 1982.
Government by Emergency, American Bureau of Economic Research, 1983.
The Last Train Out, American Bureau of Economic Research, 1983.
(Editor) *Tactics of Christian Resistance,* Geneva Divinity School Press, 1983.
(Editor) *Theology of Christian Resistance,* Geneva Divinity School Press, 1983.
Backward, Christian Soldiers?, Institute for Christian Economics, 1984.

Seventy-five Bible Questions Your Instructors Pray You Won't Ask, Spurgeon Press, 1984.
(Contributor) Robert Clouse, editor, *Wealth and Poverty: Four Christian Views of Economics,* Inter-Varsity Press, 1984.
Conspiracy: A Biblical View, Crossway Books, 1986.
(With Arthur Robinson) *Fighting Chance,* American Bureau of Economic Research, 1986.
Honest Money: Biblical Blueprint for Money and Banking, Thomas Nelson/Dominion Press, 1986.
Unholy Spirits: Occultism and New Age Humanism, Dominion Press, 1986.
Dominion and Common Grace: The Biblical Basis of Progress, Institute for Christian Economics, 1987.
Liberating Planet Earth: Introduction to Biblical Blueprints, Dominion Press, 1987.
Healer of the Nations: Biblical Blueprints for International Relations, Dominion Press, 1987.
Inherit the Earth: Biblical Blueprints for Economics, Dominion Press, 1987.
The Pirate Economy, American Bureau of Economic Research, 1987.
Is the World Running Down?: Crisis in the Christian Worldview, Institute for Christian Economics, 1988.
The Hoax of Higher Criticism, Institute for Christian Economics, 1989.
Political Polytheism: The Myth of Pluralism, Institute for Christian Economics, 1989.
Social Security: The Coming Implosion, American Bureau of Economic Research, 1989.
Trespassing for Dear Life, Dominion Press, 1989.
When Justice Is Aborted, Dominion Press, 1989.
The Implosion Strategy, American Bureau of Economic Research, 1990.
The Judeo-Christian Tradition: A Guide for the Perplexed, Institute for Christian Economics, 1990.
Millennialism and Social Theory, Institute for Christian Economics, 1990.
Victim's Rights: The Biblical View of Civil Justice, Institute for Christian Economics, 1990.
(With Gary DeMar) *Christian Reconstruction,* Institute for Christian Economics, 1991.
(Editor) *Theonomy: An Informed Response,* Institute for Christian Economics, 1991.
Westminster's Confession: The Abandonment of Van Til's Legacy, Institute for Christian Economics, 1991.

Contributor to periodicals, including *Applied Christianity, The Freeman, Human Events, Journal of Political Economy, National Review,* and *Wall Street Journal.* Editor of *Journal of Christian Reconstruction,* 1974-81, *Remnant Review,* 1974—, and *Biblical Economics Today.*

WORK IN PROGRESS: Rotten Wood: How the Liberals Captured the Northern Presbyterian Church; Politically In-

correct: A College Survival Manual; Clean Living: The Biblical View of Environmentalism; Free at Last: The Biblical View of Slavery; and *Boundaries and Dominion: The Political Economy of Leviticus.*

SIDELIGHTS: Gary North once told *CA:* "I write from the perspective of Protestant Christianity in the fields of history, economics, and the social sciences generally." More recently, he added, " 'Of making many books there is no end; and indexing is a weariness of the flesh.' It's a shame I never learned to type properly. I use two fingers; the left index finger depresses the shift key. If I ever learn to type properly, I will be able to crank out a lot more stuff."

O

OAKLEY, Graham 1929-

PERSONAL: Born August 27, 1929, in Shrewsbury, England; son of Thomas (a shop manager) and Flora (Madeley) Oakley. *Education:* Attended Warrington Art School, 1950. *Avocational interests:* Music.

ADDRESSES: Home and office—Kellaways Mill, North Chippenham, Wiltshire, England.

CAREER: Free-lance artist and book illustrator. Scenic artist for English repertory companies, 1950-55; Royal Opera House, designer's assistant, 1955-57; worked at Crawford's Advertising Agency, 1960-62; British Broadcasting Corporation, television set designer for motion pictures and series, including *How Green Was My Valley, Nicholas Nickleby, Treasure Island,* and *Softly, Softly,* 1962-67. *Military service:* Served in the British Army, 1947-49.

AWARDS, HONORS: Kate Greenaway Medal nomination, 1976, and *New York Times* best illustrated children's book of the year citation, 1977, both for *The Church Mice Adrift; Boston Globe-Horn Book* Award illustration special citation, and American Library Association notable book citation, both 1980, both for *Graham Oakley's Magical Changes;* Kate Greenaway Medal nomination, and Kurt Maschler Award runner-up, both 1982, both for *The Church Mice in Action.*

WRITINGS:

SELF-ILLUSTRATED CHILDREN'S BOOKS

Graham Oakley's Magical Changes, Macmillan, 1979, Atheneum, 1980.
Hetty and Harriet, Macmillan, 1981, Atheneum, 1982.
Henry's Quest, Macmillan, 1985, Atheneum, 1986.
Once upon a Time: A Prince's Fantastic Journey, Macmillan, 1990.

SELF-ILLUSTRATED; "CHURCH MICE" SERIES

The Church Mouse (also see below), Atheneum, 1972.
The Church Cat Abroad (also see below), Atheneum, 1973.
The Church Mice and the Moon (also see below), Atheneum, 1974.
The Church Mice Spread Their Wings, Macmillan (London), 1975, Atheneum, 1976.
The Church Mice Adrift, Macmillan, 1976, Atheneum, 1977.
The Church Mice at Bay, Macmillan, 1978, Atheneum, 1979.
The Church Mice at Christmas, Atheneum, 1980.
The Church Mice in Action, Macmillan, 1982, Atheneum, 1983.
The Church Mice Chronicles (contains *The Church Mouse, The Church Cat Abroad,* and *The Church Mice and the Moon*), Macmillan, 1986.
The Diary of a Church Mouse, Macmillan, 1986, Atheneum, 1987.

Also author and illustrator of *The Churchmice and the Ring,* 1992.

ILLUSTRATOR

John Ruskin, *The King of the Golden River,* Hutchinson, 1958.
Hugh Popham, *Monsters and Marlinspikes,* Hart-David, 1958.
Popham, *The Fabulous Voyage of the Pegasus,* Criterion, 1959.
Robert Louis Stevenson, *Kidnapped,* Dent, 1960, with N. C. Wyeth, Crown, 1989.
David Scott Daniell, *Discovering the Bible,* University of London Press, 1961.
Charles Kervern, *White Horizons,* University of London Press, 1962.

Mollie Clarke, adapter, *The Three Feathers: A German Folk Tale Retold,* Hart-Davis, 1963, Follett, 1968.

Richard Garnett, *The White Dragon,* Hart-Davis, 1963, Vanguard, 1964.

Garnett, *Jack of Dover,* Vanguard, 1966.

Patricia Ledward, *Grandmother's Footsteps,* Macmillan, 1966.

Taya Zinkin, *Stories Tole round the World,* Oxford University Press, 1968.

Brian Read, *The Water Wheel,* World's Work, 1970.

Tanith Lee, *Dragon Hoard,* Farrar, Straus, 1971.

Elizabeth MacDonald, *The Two Sisters,* World's Work, 1975.

ADAPTATIONS: *The Church Mouse* was adapted for videocassette by Live Oak Media, 1988.

SIDELIGHTS: British author and illustrator Graham Oakley is recognized for his strong storytelling abilities and his satirical presentation of modern society. The text and elaborate illustrations in his books work together to convey witty and often hilariously comic stories. In his popular "Church Mice" series, for example, Oakley uses the adventures of a group of lively mice and their protector, Sampson the cat, to ridicule such contemporary figures as scientists, the media, and hippies. And in his other works, Oakley uses a similar combination of understated writing and vastly populated pictures—the pictures supplying the story with more meaning than that found in the words alone. "Oakley's witty stories are books to be *enjoyed*—and how often is this vital ingredient missing from children's picture books," points out Edward Hudson in *Children's Book Review.* And Elaine Edelman, writing in the *New York Times Book Review,* maintains: "Oakley is one of the craftiest picture-book people working today."

Born in Shrewsbury, England, Oakley attended the Warrington Art School before beginning his career as a scenic artist for repertory companies in London. He then moved on to the Royal Opera House in Covent Garden where he worked as a design assistant, later joining the British Broadcasting Corporation (BBC-TV) as a television set designer before choosing to become a free-lance author and illustrator. It was while he was working as an illustrator for Macmillan that Oakley first envisioned the fictitious English country town of Wortlethorpe as the setting for a series of children's books. "I was going to open with a high view on top of the town and a series of stories about each building, starting with the church and moving on to the library and the town hall, but the first book, *The Church Mouse* was so successful I never got to the library," explains Oakley in an interview with Barbara A. Bannon for *Publishers Weekly.*

The Church Mouse, the first book in the "Church Mice" series, introduces the mice who populate the church in Wortlethorpe along with their guardian Sampson the cat. This strange alliance between cat and mice is explained by the setting of the story—Sampson has heard so many sermons on brotherly love and meekness that he thinks of mice as his brothers. Originally, there is only one mouse, Arthur, occupying the church, but he goes to the parson and asks if his town friends can live in the church for free if they perform chores and do odd jobs. All is well until Sampson dreams he is back in his mouse hunting days and wakes up to find himself chasing mice around the church. Before the situation can be dealt with, though, a burglar comes to the church that same night and Sampson and the mice save the day. "The story goes with a swing and the slapstick and circumstantial detail are livened with a measure of wit," observes Margery Fisher in *Growing Point.* *The Church Mouse* is filled with "fascinating activities" asserts a *Times Literary Supplement* contributor, adding: "Oakley shows in this book how effectively words and pictures can be grafted together so that our understanding of the story depends on the combination of the two."

The following books in the "Church Mice" series have the occupants of the Wortlethorpe church taking part in a number of equally amusing adventures. In *The Church Cat Abroad,* Oakley has Sampson travelling to an exotic South Sea island to shoot a commercial for cat food in order to earn some money to fix the church's roof. Hudson comments in his review of *The Church Cat Abroad* that it is "a story full of humorous incidents and superb illustrations. Oakley is a true artist of the highest calibre with an ability to create and exploit humorous situations to the full." *The Church Mice in Action,* published in 1982, also has Sampson doing something he'd rather not in order to earn money to fix up the church. This time he's entered a cat show, but events take an unexpected turn when he is kidnapped by horrible men on a tandem bicycle. The mice, who have been arguing over whether or not it's fair to lure the other cats into fights to give Sampson a better chance, are able to rescue him and all is well in the end. "In *The Church Mice in Action,*" assert Donnarae MacCann and Olga Richard in the *Wilson Library Bulletin,* "Oakley creates a book for all ages by combining satiric cartoons, a tongue-in-cheek literary style, and a cleverly improbable story line."

Oakley departs from the town of Wortlethorpe with his 1979 *Graham Oakley's Magical Changes,* in which he "embarks on a technical experiment in picture-book making that is likely to become a landmark in the history of the genre," describes Elaine Moss in *Signal.* The pages of the book contain no words and are split in half horizontally so that they can be mixed and matched in over five hundred different combinations. The images created revolve around six slender cylinders on the left side pages and four thicker ones on the right, creating such surreal combinations as six city gentlemen holding umbrella handles attached to a full clothesline above their heads, and a four poster bed supporting a railway arch with a thundering train racing over it. "By creating such juxtapositions between the ordinary and the fabulous Oakley emphasizes the strangeness of life," relates Jon C. Stott in *World of Children's Books.* "Most books with half pages for flipping are gimmicks; *Magical Changes* is not—it offers an often humorous, often ironic commentary on life." With *Graham Oakley's Magical Changes,* Leigh Dean concludes in *Children's Book Review Service,* "Oakley has touched the eye, the imagination, and the emotions at a depth where words seem inadequate to describe the genius of this book."

Deviating from the "Church Mice" series again in 1981, Oakley presents two hens in *Hetty and Harriet* who are in search of the perfect place to live. The trip is Harriet's idea, and Hetty goes along partly because she is bullied into it, but also because she really has nothing better to do. During the course of their search, the two hens encounter a number of dangers in both the country and the city. Worst of all is the egg production plant, but they manage to escape such threats and end up finding the ideal home—the farmyard from which they began. Writing in the *School Library Journal,* Kenneth Marantz comments that "details of nature, or tongue-in-cheek signs in town, abound. Both text and illustration exude the joy of fine storytelling." Finding the book a "delight," Linda Yeatman concludes in the *British Book News:* "Oakley has developed his own special blend of lifelike representation and fantasy in children's books and *Hetty and Harriet* is a superb example of his skill."

A more recent work, *Henry's Quest,* is set in the future and centers around a young boy's search for a mythical substance—gasoline. The world that Oakley presents is one in which civilization has returned to an age similar to that of medieval times. The country in which Henry lives is surrounded by a large forest, and because the king once read an old copy of *King Arthur and the Knights of the Round Table,* it is alive with the same kinds of things found in the book, such as knights and chivalry. When the king wants to marry off his daughter, he decides to send the suitors on a quest for the substance known as gasoline. Although Henry is only a shepherd-boy and not a knight, he is allowed to participate. He begins his journey through the forest, passing technological gadgets, such as televisions, that have been thrown aside as junk. On the other side of the forest is an evil civilization in which he finds not only gasoline, but also industrialism and corruption. He brings all of these things home, but none, not even the gas, seems to catch on. "The text is very subtle, as funny as it is serious, and the pictures are the stuff of dreams and nightmares, rich with literary and historical illusion," re-

lates Elizabeth Ward in *Washington Post Book World.* "*Henry's Quest* is definitely not a book to be taken too lightly."

BIOGRAPHICAL/CRITICAL SOURCES:

BOOKS

Chevalier, Tracy, editor, *Twentieth-Century Children's Writers,* 3rd edition, St. James Press, 1989, pp. 732-33.

Children's Literature Review, Volume 7, Gale, 1984, pp. 212-23.

Cullinan, Bernice E., Mary K. Karrer, and Arlene M. Pillar, *Literature and the Child,* Harcourt, 1981, pp. 115-60.

Moss, Elaine, *Children's Books of the Year: 1974,* Hamish Hamilton, 1975, p. 54.

PERIODICALS

Bulletin of the Center for Children's Books, June, 1982; May, 1983; March, 1987.

British Book News, spring, 1982, p. 3.

Children's Book Review, spring, 1974, p. 12; spring, 1975, p. 14.

Children's Book Review Service, June, 1980, p. 103.

Growing Point, November, 1972, pp. 2027-28; October, 1973, p. 2245; December, 1974, p. 2541; January, 1979, p. 3450.

Horn Book, June, 1979, p. 294; August, 1983, p. 434.

Junior Bookshelf, April, 1979, pp. 99-100; February, 1982, p. 19.

New York Times Book Review, December 10, 1972, p. 8; May 4, 1975, p. 42; May 2, 1976, p. 46; May 8, 1977, p. 41; May 30, 1982, p. 14.

Publishers Weekly, February 26, 1979, pp. 74-75; February 15, 1980, p. 110; January 9, 1981, p. 76; February 11, 1983, p. 71; February 13, 1987, p. 91.

School Library Journal, May, 1973, pp. 65, 67; December, 1973, p. 44; April, 1975, p. 46; April, 1976, pp. 62-63; April, 1977, p. 56; March, 1979, p. 143; May, 1980, p. 62; October, 1980, p. 162; April, 1982, p. 61; December, 1986, p. 107.

Signal, January, 1980, pp. 3-7.

Times Educational Supplement, November 21, 1980, pp. 29-30; November 19, 1982, p. 32; March 6, 1987, p. 37.

Times Literary Supplement, November 3, 1972, p. 1327; November 23, 1973, p. 1440; December 5, 1975, pp. 1452-53; December 10, 1976, p. 1551; November 28, 1986, p. 1345.

Washington Post Book World, September 14, 1986, p. 11.

Wilson Library Bulletin, October, 1983, p. 131.

World of Children's Books, Volume 6, 1981, p. 26.

—Sketch by Susan M. Reicha

O'CONNOR, Patricia Walker 1931-

PERSONAL: Born April 26, 1931, in Memphis, TN; daughter of Shade Wilson (a college president) and Lillie (Mullins) Walker; married David Evans O'Connor, April 4, 1953 (divorced, 1965); married Anthony M. Pasquariello, February 11, 1978; children: (first marriage) Michael Peter, Erin Anne. *Education:* Attended Florida State University, 1949-51, and University of Havana, summer, 1949; University of Florida, B.A.E., 1953, M.A., 1954, Ph.D., 1962; postdoctoral study at University of Salamance (Spain), 1964. *Avocational interests:* Tennis, piano, minor arts and crafts, play directing, and travel.

ADDRESSES: Home—405 Lafayette Ave., Cincinnati, OH 45220. *Office*—Department of Romance Languages, University of Cincinnati, Cincinnati, OH 45221.

CAREER: University of Cincinnati, Cincinnati, OH, instructor, 1962-63, assistant professor, 1963-67, associate professor, 1967-72, professor of Romance languages, 1972—.

MEMBER: Modern Language Association of America, American Association of Teachers of Spanish and Portuguese, American Association of University Professors, Midwest Modern Language Association, Phi Beta Kappa.

AWARDS, HONORS: Taft grants, 1965 and 1972; American Philosophical Society grant, 1971; Rieveschal Award for creative and scholarly work, 1982; Distinguished Research Professor, 1990; elected to Royal Spanish Academy, 1990.

WRITINGS:

Women in the Theater of Gregorio Martinez Sierra, American Book Co., 1967.
Gregorio and Maria Martinez Sierra, Twayne, 1977.
(Editor with husband, Anthony M. Pasquariello) Antonio Buero Vallejo, *El tragaluz,* Scribner, 1977.
(Editor with Pasquariello) *Contemporary Spanish Theater,* Scribner, 1980.
Plays of Protest from the Franco Era, SGEL, 1981.
Contemporary Spanish Theater: The Social Comedies of the Sixties, SGEL, 1983.
Gregorio y Maria Martinez Sierra: cronica de una colaboracion, La Avispa, 1987.
Dramaturgas espanolas de hoy: una introduccion, Fundamentos, 1988.
Plays of the New Democratic Spain (1975-1990), University Press of America, 1992.

Contributor to Spanish literature journals. Member of editorial staff, *Modern International Drama, Hispanofila,* and *Anales de la novela de posguerra;* editor, *Estreno* (Spanish theater journal).

WORK IN PROGRESS: Research on contemporary Spanish theater, women dramatists, problems of post-Franco theater, women novelists, images of women in Spanish literature, and the contemporary Spanish novel.

SIDELIGHTS: Patricia Walker O'Connor told *CA* that her father was a positive influence in her life. "He was delighted to have a daughter (only child) and never saw—or let me see—gender as a barrier to accomplishment."

*   *   *

O'GRADY, Desmond (James Bernard) 1935-

PERSONAL: Born August 27, 1935, in Limerick, Ireland; son of Leonard Joseph and Elizabeth Anne (Bourke) O'Grady; married Olga Nora Jwaideh, 1957 (divorced); married Florence Tamburro (divorced); children: (first marriage) Deirdre Anne Maria; (second marriage) Leonard John Jules; (with Ellen Beardsley) Gisele Eleanor Anne. *Education:* Attended Cistercian College, Roscrea, Tipperary, Ireland; Harvard University, M.A., 1964, Ph.D., 1982.

ADDRESSES: Home—Rincurran Cottage, Kinsale, Cork, Ireland.

CAREER: Poet; translator. Former English teacher in Paris, France, Rome, Italy, at Roxbury Latin School, West Roxbury, MA, and at Harvard. Distinguished visiting professor at the American University in Cairo, 1971, and visiting poet-in-residence, 1975-76; visiting professor of English literature at Tabriz University, Iran, 1976-77; visiting professor of English literature at University of Alexandria, Egypt, 1978-80. Irish representative to Congress of the Community of European Writers, Florence, 1962, and Rome, 1965; representative to Congress of European Literary Editors and Publishers, Belgrade, 1968. Has given numerous poetry readings in the United States, Europe, and Egypt. Member of Ireland's *Aosdana.*

MEMBER: Amnesty International, Irish Academy of Letters.

WRITINGS:

POETRY

Chords and Orchestrations, Echo Press (Limerick, Ireland), 1956.
(With others) *New Work by Five Poets,* [Rome], 1957.
(With others) *A Reading of New Poems,* [Rome], 1958.
(With others) *Poems,* [Rome], 1959.
Reilly, Phoenix Press (London), 1961.
Professor Kelleher and the Charles River, Carthage Press, 1964.
The Dark Edge of Europe, MacGibbon & Kee, 1967.

Separazioni (poems in English with Italian translations opposite), Editizioni Raporti Europi, 1968.

The Dying Gaul, MacGibbon & Kee, 1968.

Hellas, New Writers' Press (Dublin), 1971.

Separations, Goldsmith Press (Dublin), 1973.

Stations, illustrations by Margo Veillon, American University in Cairo Press, 1976.

Sing Me Creation, Gallery Press (Dublin), 1977.

The Headgear of the Tribe: New and Selected Poems, Brian & O'Keeffe, 1978.

His Skaldcrane's Nest, Gallery Press, 1979.

Alexandrian Notebook, Raven Arts Press (Dublin), 1989.

Tipperary, Salmon Publishing, 1991.

TRANSLATOR

Off Licence, Dolmen, 1968.

The Gododdin, illustrations by Margo Veillon, Dolmen, 1976, Dufour, 1977.

A Limerick Rake, Gallery Press, 1978.

Grecian Glances: Versions from the Classical Anthology, Inkling Press, 1981.

The Seven Arab Odes, Agenda Editions, 1990.

Ten Modern Arab Poets, Dedalus Press (Dublin), 1992.

OTHER

Contributor to anthologies, including *The Norton Anthology of Modern Poetry, The New Irish Poetry, The Castle Poets, The Patrick Kavanagh Anthology,* and *Soundings 72.* Contributor of poetry, reviews, stories, essays, and travelogues to periodicals, including *Transatlantic Review, Botteghe Oscure, Atlantic, Poetry Ireland, Irish Times,* and *Arena.*

WORK IN PROGRESS: The Wandering Celt, a long poem; *Trawling the Tradition,* collected translations; and *Myself Alone,* prose memoirs.

SIDELIGHTS: During a thirty-five year career, Irish poet Desmond O'Grady has published his own verse, has translated others' works, and has taught at schools on four continents. O'Grady's extensive travels and scholarly pursuit of Celtic history and lore have found expression in poems that "explore the connections among a relatively few individuals' present, a whole people's past, and a poet's sense of present and past intermingled," maintains *Dictionary of Literary Biography* contributor William S. Waddell, Jr. Waddell sees O'Grady as a poet who unites his concerns as a contemporary Irishman with a larger, more universal perspective.

O'Grady was born in Limerick, Ireland, and educated by the Irish national schools, the Jesuits, and the Cistercian College, Tipperary. He attended university sporadically in Ireland before leaving to teach English abroad. This vocation led him to Paris, Rome, and Cairo, where he spent much of his free time developing his own poetry. After working a year as a teacher at West Roxbury Latin School in Massachusetts, he enrolled in Harvard University, where he earned a master's degree in Celtic Studies in 1964. Waddell notes: "O'Grady's formal study of Celtic history and literature proved a strong influence on his poetry. Celtic history gave him a tradition and mythology to frame and support the observations of his own experience, finally making history for O'Grady a palimpsest, a layered transparency, much as it had been for his friend Ezra Pound."

Beginning in the mid-1960s, O'Grady found a congenial atmosphere for his work on the Greek island of Paros. There he continued his own writing and began as well to translate poems from the Italian, Armenian, Russian, Greek, Welsh, and Arabic. The 1970s found him teaching at the American University in Cairo, Tabriz University in Iran, and at the University of Alexandria. Not surprisingly, observes Waddell, O'Grady's poetry often explores themes such as "the mystery of the poetic vocation; the life of the voyager, the quester; the complexity and power of contact, relations—inherited, discovered, forsaken, renewed."

Waddell suggests that more recent O'Grady work explores the possibility of reconciliation, not only between the self and others, but with the more universal issues of mortality and desire. The critic finds O'Grady's poetry "full of genuine feeling—nothing shrill and forced, no empty dramatic gesture, but a presence of love, compassion, grief that is sturdy and solid."

O'Grady once told *CA:* "I began writing poems in my Cistercian boarding school in Ireland. At that time I first practiced the styles of Milton and the English and French romantics, later the English and American moderns. The writers who influenced me most in style and technique then were Hopkins, Joyce, Pound and Patrick Kavanagh. I wrote mostly about what concerns young people: nature, love, change or process, death, as I experienced them growing up in the west of Ireland. Through Joyce's influence the architecture of groups or collections of poems became very important to me so that I saw and wrote in interrelated sequences.

"When I left Ireland in the fifties to live on the Continent and in America, themes of social criticism, love, separation, loss, exile concerned me. At that time, too, a reaction to the way of life in Ireland combined with what most young poets ambitiously aspire to—writing the long poem in the shadow of *The Waste Land* and Patrick Kavanagh's *The Great Hunger*—became a preoccupation. *The Dying Gaul* was a personally satisfying attempt.

"Because I have travelled a lot in North Africa, Asia, Europe and America, and read in the literatures of these continents, I began to translate into English some of the poetry of these languages as a way to begin a day's work, or to keep my writing hand moving when not writing poems of my own, or to get closer to the methods of composition of poets who interested me. The intention was to get from under the shadow of Yeats and other Moderns. Again, because I had a serious interest in Celtic literature and culture, I developed a Celtic rather than a Greco-Roman attitude to form for my collections of poems. Making my *The Gododdin* from Welsh into English affected me greatly in this, and Anglo-Saxon poetic devices solved many problems. And because so many of my friends are painters, sculptors, and composers, I developed more of an artist's method of working, of *making,* so that even my translations may hardly be called that but rather my versions of their originals as a painter, sculptor, or a composer would use the work of another—ancient, classical, or modern—to render his own version in his own style or voice.

"For me, therefore, my poem is made as detached from me as a painting, sculpture, musical composition, or vase would be from its maker—no matter how intense the autobiographical element present may be. There are exceptions, where the poem sings itself. But these are rare. I write poems to attempt to order the general chaos of my experience and through that order hopefully understand my life and motives better and also in the hope that I give readers an expression and understanding of our common daily experience. There is a structure of intercyclical and expanding circles that make the whole of my work cohere for me so that I see my total production to date, in verse and verse translation together, as ultimately one book. . . . My prose I intend as a backdrop to my verse. The poems are epiphanic moments in the general narrative of my life.

"My attitude to routine and artistic discipline was formed by a Cistercian monk, Dom. Eugene Boylan, and my attitude to language was formed mostly by Ezra Pound and James Joyce. Every word must work in the line and every line bend its unique tension. My way of seeing things owes much to archeology and anthropology—particularly in collections like *The Dying Gaul, Sing Me Creation,* and *The Wandering Celt,* where the poems, like ruins on an archeological site, may be found under the surface with a little careful digging. I also like to echo or refer back to old poems in the new ones, like artists might in their work, or put faces, places, things that I have been involved with. I believe in the daily effort and in ceaseless revision.

"Looking at the poems and translations I have done since I began to make poems, I see them thematically and not chronologically, and as a single work that will expand spherically as I continue to write. I began with subject matter and in a language drawn from the place and people of my origins in the west of Ireland. I proceeded through various journeyings that constitute a single journey and recorded the experiences of separation from the places, people and paraphernalia encountered on that journey.

"Today I find myself confronted with my own *wyrd* in the sequence of poems called *The Wandering Celt.* It is the *persona* of Reilley, the Wandering Celt, the dying Gaul who journeys. He records the experience of his wanderings of body and mind in an attempt to connect what he left with what he found. . . ."

BIOGRAPHICAL/CRITICAL SOURCES:

BOOKS

Dictionary of Literary Biography, Volume 40: *Poets of Great Britain and Ireland since 1960,* Gale, 1985.

PERIODICALS

New Statesman, September 15, 1967.
Punch, December 25, 1968.
Stony Thursday Book (Limerick, Ireland), Number 6, 1978.

*   *   *

OUTERBRIDGE, David E(ugene) 1933-

PERSONAL: Born August 12, 1933, in New York, NY; son of Kenneth Boyd and Florence (Lockwood) Outerbridge; married Lilia Hollins (a teacher), February 15, 1958; children: Benoni, Oliver, Thomas, Joshua. *Education:* Harvard University, A.B., 1955; New York University, M.A., 1968.

ADDRESSES: Home—RFD 1, Box 673, Belfast, ME 04915.

CAREER: Outerbridge & Lazard, Inc., New York, NY, publisher and editor-in-chief, 1969-74; writer, 1974—. Film director and publisher. *Military service:* U.S. Navy, 1955-58.

MEMBER: Harvard Club (New York City).

AWARDS, HONORS: First prize from American Film Festival, 1974, for directing *The Art of the Potter.*

WRITINGS:

(Editor) *The Potter's Challenge,* Dutton, 1975.
(With Julie Thayer) *The Last Shepherds,* Viking, 1979.
Without Makeup: Liv Ullmann, Morrow, 1979.
The Hangover Handbook, Harmony Books, 1982.
The Art of Wooing, C. N. Potter, 1984.
Bridges, Abrams, 1989.
Easing the Passage, HarperCollins, 1991.

WORK IN PROGRESS: The Gelding of Intelligence: Present-day Educational Practice.

SIDELIGHTS: The Hangover Handbook, David E. Outerbridge's guide to cures for hangover, is an "entertaining survey," Christopher Lehmann-Haupt of the *New York Times* believes. Outerbridge first lists the major physical effects of hangovers and then examines a collection of traditional remedies for them. These remedies range from the two owl's eggs recommended by Pliny the Elder to the Roman cure of eating sheep's lungs to entertainer Dean Martin's advice to just "stay drunk." "You'll find 'The Hangover Handbook' amusing," Lehmann-Haupt promises.

BIOGRAPHICAL/CRITICAL SOURCES:

PERIODICALS

Chicago Tribune, April 15, 1984.
New York Times, January 5, 1982.
New York Times Book Review, October 7, 1979.

*   *   *

OWEN, Jennifer   1936-

PERSONAL: Born November 9, 1936, in Leicester, England; daughter of Frank Alan (a hosiery manufacturer) and Kate (a homemaker) Bak; married Denis Frank Owen (a college lecturer and author), July 12, 1958; children: Richard Frank, Susan Kate. *Education:* Oxford University, B.A. (with honors), 1958; University of Michigan, Ph.D., 1962.

ADDRESSES: Home and office—66 Scraptoft Ln., Leicester LE5 1HU, England.

CAREER: University of East Africa, Kampala, Uganda, demonstrator, 1962-65, lecturer in zoology, 1965-66, curator of Zoology Museum, 1964-66; University of Sierra Leone, Freetown, demonstrator, 1966-69, lecturer in zoology, 1969-70; *Oikos* (ecology journal), Lund, Sweden, editorial assistant, 1971; University of Leicester, Leicester, England, research demonstrator, 1971-74, occasional lecturer in department of adult education, 1971—; Wyggeston Girls' School, Leicester, teacher, 1975-77; Leicester Polytechnic, Leicester, honorary senior research fellow, 1983—. Member of council of Leicestershire and Rutland

Trust for Nature Conservation; Leicester Ecology Trust, director on board of management and chairman of conservation committee.

MEMBER: British Ecological Society.

WRITINGS:

Feeding Strategy, University of Chicago Press, 1982.
Garden Life, Chatto & Windus, 1983.
Marvels and Mysteries of Insect Life, Usborne, 1984.
The Ecology of a Garden, Cambridge University Press, 1991.

Contributor to *Urban Entomology: Interdisciplinary Perspectives,* edited by G. W. Frankie and C. S. Koehler, Praeger, 1983. Contributor to encyclopedias. Contributor to periodicals.

WORK IN PROGRESS: A book on gardening and natural events to accompany television series; research on garden insects and the significance of gardens for conservation.

SIDELIGHTS: Jennifer Owen told *CA:* "My husband, Denis Owen, and I started investigating in detail the flora and fauna (particularly insects) of our Leicester garden in 1971, and the project continues. It is probably fair to claim that more is known about our backyard than about any other area of similar size. Such a high proportion of the British insect fauna occurs in this very ordinary suburban garden that I am convinced that the million acres of English gardens constitute our most important nature reserve, especially because we can manage them to enhance their value as habitats.

"In the United Kingdom there is widespread interest in natural history among people with no formal academic training. Lecturing to and writing for such an audience is very rewarding and, hence, enjoyable. I meet my most enthusiastic audiences when lecturing about garden wildlife, and this has led to my interest in and involvement with urban nature conservation."

P

PALMER, Parker J. 1939-

PERSONAL: Born February 28, 1939, in Chicago, IL; son of Max J. (a business executive) and LaVerne (Hickman) Palmer; married Sarah Ann Hartley, August 18, 1961 (separated, 1988; divorced, 1991); children: Brent, Todd, Carrie. *Education:* Carleton College, B.A., 1961; attended Union Theological Seminary, 1961-62; University of California, Berkeley, M.A., 1965, Ph.D., 1970. *Politics:* "Peace and justice." *Religion:* Quaker.

ADDRESSES: Home and office—P.O. Box 55063, Madison, WI 53705.

CAREER: Pacific School of Religion, Berkeley, CA, director of Bureau of Community Research, 1963-65; Beloit College, Beloit, WI, college examiner and instructor in sociology, 1965-67; Washington Center for Metropolitan Studies, Washington, DC, senior research associate in urban sociology, 1969-74; Georgetown University, Washington, DC, associate professor of sociology, 1972-74; Pendle Hill Quaker Study Center, Wallingford, PA, dean of studies, teacher and writer-in-residence, 1975-85; The Resident Program, Madison, WI, founding director and teacher, 1985-88; independent writer and teacher based in Madison, WI, 1988—. Trustee of Carleton College, 1969-73; co-director of Institute for Public Life, Silver Spring, MD, 1971-74; faculty member of Auburn Theology Seminary, 1979—. Also serves as Senior Associate to the American Association of Higher Education. Consultant to Danforth foundation, 1965-75, and Lilly Endowment, 1978—.

MEMBER: Phi Beta Kappa.

AWARDS, HONORS: Dana Award for personal achievement from Carleton College, 1961; graduate fellowship from Danforth Foundation, 1961; Uhrig Award for excellence in teaching from Beloit College, 1967; grants from Sloane Foundation, 1969-71, Irwin-Sweeny-Miller Foundation, 1971-72, Danforth Foundation, 1972-75, and Lilly Endowment, 1975—; Distinguished Achievement Award, Educational Press Association, 1988; D.HL. from John F. Kennedy University, 1991; *The Company of Strangers* was a "Critic's Choice" in *Commonweal* and *Christian Century; To Know As We Are Known* was selected as one of the ten best books of 1985 by the National Academy of Parish Clergy.

WRITINGS:

(Contributor) Kenneth Underwood, editor, *The Church, the University and Social Policy,* Wesleyan University Press, 1969.
(Contributor) Robert Rankin, editor, *The Recovery of the Spirit in Higher Education,* Seabury, 1980.
The Promise of Paradox, Ave Maria Press, 1980.
The Company of Strangers: Christians and the Renewal of America's Public Life, Crossroad, 1981.
To Know as We Are Known, Harper, 1983.
The Active Life: A Spirituality of Work, Creativity, and Caring, HarperCollins, 1990.
(Editor) *Caring for the Commonweal,* Mercer University Press, 1990.

Contributor of articles and poems to educational, theological, and social change journals, including *Christian Century, Liberal Education, NICM Journal, Friends Journal, Change* and *Warm Wind.* Also author of numerous monographs.

WORK IN PROGRESS: Working on *The Courage to Teach,* on issues relating to leadership, and on the development of a new national fellowship program for gifted entering graduate students who want to become college teachers.

SIDELIGHTS: Parker J. Palmer writes *CA:* "Since 1988, I have been working independently and loving it. I spend half of my time writing, and the other half traveling around the country doing workshops, lectures, and consultations for colleges and universities, religious groups, foundations, and social change organizations. I find this way of working very fulfilling, and at the moment (in the fall of 1991) I am heavily booked into the fall of 1994. I continue my long-time interests in education, community, the inward journey, and non-violent social change."

BIOGRAPHICAL/CRITICAL SOURCES:

PERIODICALS

America, March 13, 1982.
Commonweal, February 26, 1982.

*   *   *

PALMS, Roger C(urtis) 1936-

PERSONAL: Born September 13, 1936, in Detroit, MI; son of Nelson C. and Winifred J. Palms; married Andrea Sisson, 1959; children: Grant Curtis, Andrea Jane. *Education:* Wayne State University, B.A., 1958; Eastern Baptist Theological Seminary, B.D., 1961, M.Div., 1971, D.D., 1977; Michigan State University, M.A., 1971; graduate study at Princeton Theological Seminary.

ADDRESSES: Home—18455 Twilight Trail, Eden Prairie, MN 55346. *Office*—*Decision,* 1300 Harmon Place, Minneapolis, MN 55403.

CAREER: Ordained American Baptist minister, 1961; pastor of Baptist churches in Ronceverte, WV, 1961-64, and Highland Park, NJ, 1964-67; Michigan State University, East Lansing, chaplain of American Baptist Student Foundation, 1967-73; *Decision,* Minneapolis, MN, assistant editor, 1973-74, associate editor, 1975-76, editor, 1976—. President, Evangelical Press Association, 1991-93; lectures extensively; speaker on nationally syndicated radio program *Something for You.*

WRITINGS:

The Jesus Kids, Judson, 1971.
The Christian and the Occult, Judson, 1972.
God Holds Your Tomorrows, Augsburg, 1976.
God's Promises for You, Revell, 1977.
Upon a Penny Loaf, Bethany Fellowship, 1978.
The Pleasure of His Company, Tyndale, 1982.
First Things First, Scripture Press, 1983.
Living under the Smile of God, Tyndale, 1984.
Living on the Mountain, Revell, 1986.
Enjoying the Closeness of God, World Wide Publications, 1989.
Let God Help You Choose, Augsburg, 1989.

SIDELIGHTS: Roger C. Palms once told *CA:* "Teaching other writers is important to me. I teach college and seminary classes, and lecture at schools of writing, schools of evangelism, and other workshops. I've written and taught on six continents."

*   *   *

PARISH, Margaret Cecile 1927-1988
(Peggy Parish)

PERSONAL: Born in 1927, in Manning, SC; died of a ruptured aneurysm, November 19, 1988, in Manning, SC; daughter of Herman and Cecil (Rogers) Parish. *Education:* University of South Carolina, B.A., 1948; graduate study at George Peabody College for Teachers (now of Vanderbilt University), 1950.

CAREER: Writer. Also worked as a teacher in Oklahoma, Kentucky, and Texas; worked as an instructor in creative dancing, 1948-52, and in advertising; Dalton School, New York City, elementary school teacher for fifteen years. Children's book reviewer, *Carolina Today* television show, National Broadcasting Company, Inc. (NBC-TV) affiliate, Columbia, SC.

MEMBER: Authors Guild, Authors League of America, Delta Kappa Gamma.

AWARDS, HONORS: School Library Journal named *Dinosaur Time* one of the best books of the year, 1974; Garden State Children's Book Award, State of New Jersey, 1977, for *Dinosaur Time,* 1980, for *Teach Us, Amelia Bedelia,* and 1988; Palmetto State Award, 1977; Milner Award, City of Atlanta, 1984; Keystone State Children's Book Award, State of Pennsylvania, 1986.

WRITINGS:

UNDER NAME PEGGY PARISH

My Golden Book of Manners, illustrated by Richard Scarry, Golden Press, 1962.
Good Hunting, Little Indian, illustrated by Leonard Weisgard, Young Scott Books, 1962, revised edition published as *Good Hunting, Blue Sky,* illustrated by James Watts, Harper, 1988.
Let's Be Indians, illustrated by Arnold Lobel, Harper, 1962.
Willy Is My Brother, illustrated by Shirley Hughes, W. R. Scott, 1963.
Amelia Bedelia, illustrated by Fritz Siebel, Harper, 1963.
Thank You, Amelia Bedelia, illustrated by Siebel, Harper, 1964.
The Story of Grains: Wheat, Corn, and Rice, Grosset, 1965.
Amelia Bedelia and the Surprise Shower, illustrated by Siebel, Harper, 1966.

Key to the Treasure, illustrated by Paul Frame, Macmillan, 1966.

Let's Be Early Settlers with Daniel Boone, illustrated by Lobel, Harper, 1967.

Clues in the Woods, illustrated by Frame, Macmillan, 1968.

Little Indian, illustrated by John E. Johnson, Simon & Schuster, 1968.

A Beastly Circus, illustrated by Peter Parnall, Simon & Schuster, 1969.

Jumper Goes to School, illustrated by Cyndy Szekeres, Simon & Schuster, 1969.

Granny and the Indians, illustrated by Brinton Turkle, Macmillan, 1969.

Ootah's Lucky Day, illustrated by Mamoru Funai, Harper, 1970.

Granny and the Desperadoes, illustrated by Steven Kellogg, Macmillan, 1970.

Costumes to Make, illustrated by Lynn Sweat, Macmillan, 1970.

Snapping Turtle's All Wrong Day, illustrated by Johnson, Simon & Schuster, 1970.

Sheet Magic: Games, Toys, and Gifts from Old Sheets, illustrated by Sweat, Macmillan, 1971.

Haunted House, illustrated by Frame, Macmillan, 1971.

Come Back, Amelia Bedelia, illustrated by Wallace Tripp, Harper, 1971.

Granny, the Baby, and the Big Gray Thing, illustrated by Sweat, Macmillan, 1972.

Play Ball, Amelia Bedelia, illustrated by Tripp, Harper, 1972.

Too Many Rabbits, illustrated by Leonard Kessler, Macmillan, 1974.

Dinosaur Time, illustrated by Lobel, Harper, 1974.

December Decorations: A Holiday How-To Book, illustrated by Barbara Wolff, Macmillan, 1975.

Pirate Island Adventure, illustrated by Frame, Macmillan, 1975.

Good Work, Amelia Bedelia, illustrated by Sweat, Morrow, 1976.

Let's Celebrate: Holiday Decorations You Can Make, illustrated by Sweat, Morrow, 1976.

Teach Us, Amelia Bedelia, illustrated by Sweat, Morrow, 1977.

Hermit Dan, illustrated by Frame, Macmillan, 1977.

Mind Your Manners!, illustrated by Hafner, Greenwillow, 1978.

Zed and the Monsters, illustrated by Galdone, Doubleday, 1979.

Beginning Mobiles, illustrated by Sweat, Macmillan, 1979.

Amelia Bedelia Helps Out, illustrated by Sweat, Greenwillow, 1979.

Be Ready at Eight, illustrated by Kessler, Macmillan, 1979.

I Can, Can You?, four volumes, illustrated by Hafner, Greenwillow, 1980, published in England as *See and Do Book Bag,* four volumes, MacRae, 1980.

Amelia Bedelia and the Baby, illustrated by Sweat, Greenwillow, 1981.

No More Monsters for Me!, illustrated by Simont, Harper, 1981.

Mr. Adams's Mistake, illustrated by Owens, Macmillan, 1982.

The Cats' Burglar, illustrated by Sweat, Greenwillow, 1983.

Hush, Hush, It's Sleepytime, illustrated by Leonid Pinchevsky, Western Publishing, 1984.

Amelia Bedelia Goes Camping, illustrated by Sweat, Greenwillow, 1985.

Merry Christmas, Amelia Bedelia, illustrated by Sweat, Greenwillow, 1986.

The Ghosts of Cougar Island, Dell, 1986.

Amelia Bedelia'a Family Album, illustrated by Sweat, Greenwillow, 1988.

Scruffy, illustrated by Kelly Oechsli, Harper, 1988.

OTHER

Contributor of book reviews to newspapers. A collection of Parish's manuscripts is housed at the Kerlan Collection, University of Minnesota, Minneapolis.

ADAPTATIONS: Amelia Bedelia, Thank You, Amelia Bedelia, Come Back, Amelia Bedelia, and *Play Ball, Amelia Bedelia* have been adapted as film strips.

SIDELIGHTS: "Children have always been my life," Peggy Parish once commented, "so writing stories for children came naturally." The author of over forty books for children, Parish wrote mysteries, craft books, and the popular "Amelia Bedelia" series. Parish's books sold over seven million copies.

Amelia Bedelia, a maid who takes everything she is told literally, appeared in eleven books for young readers. Amelia's literal mindedness comes from reading cookbooks, where you must do exactly what it says. When Amelia is told to make a sponge cake, she uses real sponges in the recipe. When asked to stuff the Christmas stockings, she fills them with turkey dressing. When requested to dust the furniture, Amelia sprinkles dust on everything. ("At my house we undust the furniture," she says. "But each to his own way.")

According to Nancy Palmer in *School Library Journal,* "Amelia Bedelia is a model of well-intentioned mishap. . . . [She] has become such an institution and a welcome splash of comedy on the easy-reading shelf that one forgives the slightly patronizing domestic set-up." In the course of her adventures, Amelia goes camping (and "pitches the tent" right into the woods), plays baseball (running home after hitting the ball out of the park), and teaching school (yelling "hey, roll!" when the lesson plan says to call roll).

Enormously popular with beginning readers, the Amelia Bedelia books also teach that words can have several meanings. "Young children struggling to master odd usages will find enormous pleasure in Amelia Bedelia's misinterpretations," Judith Gloyer stated in *School Library Journal.* Writing in the *New York Times Book Review,* Cynthia Samuels noted: "No child can resist Amelia and her literal trips through the minefield of the English language—and no adult can fail to notice that she's usually right when she's wrong. Both parents and children can learn, as well, from Amelia's kind employers. Mr. and Mrs. Rogers always come to understand Amelia's confusion and to admit that the language, not the user, is the culprit."

"The things I have Amelia Bedelia do," Parish explained to Richard I. Ammon in *Teacher,* "must be plausible. When I was writing *Good Work, Amelia Bedelia* I thought of having her make a sponge cake in her own inimitable way. So, I spent one afternoon in the kitchen snipping pieces of a sponge into a cake batter. I didn't know whether it would get gooey, burn up or do what I hoped—stay like a sponge. Fortunately, the sponge stayed like a sponge and that's the way it is in the book."

To celebrate Amelia Bedelia's twenty-fifth "birthday" in 1988, her many readers were encouraged to send birthday greetings to Amelia through special mail boxes installed in bookstores and libraries across the country. Paulette C. Kaufmann, director of children's book marketing for Greenwillow, told Edwin McDowell in the *New York Times* about the celebration: "The contents of those mailboxes have been arriving daily—thousands of letters and drawings from children who have read and loved books about Amelia Bedelia."

BIOGRAPHICAL/CRITICAL SOURCES:

BOOKS

Children's Literature Review, Volume 22, Gale, 1990, pp. 152-169.
Norby, Shirley and Gregory Ryan, *Famous Children's Authors,* Dennison, 1988.

PERIODICALS

Bulletin of the Center for Children's Books, July-August, 1985, p. 213.
Kirkus Reviews, July 15, 1986, p. 1123; August 1, 1988, p. 1154.
New York Times Book Review, March 10, 1985, p. 29.
Publishers Weekly, July 23, 1979, pp. 159-160.

School Library Journal, May, 1985, p. 107; October, 1986, p. 111.
Teacher, May-June, 1980, pp. 41-43.

OBITUARIES:

PERIODICALS

New York Times, November 22, 1988.
Publishers Weekly, December 23, 1988.
School Library Journal, January, 1989.*

*   *   *

PARISH, Peggy
    See PARISH, Margaret Cecile

*   *   *

PARKE, Ross D(uke)   1938-

PERSONAL: Born December 17, 1938, in Huntsville, Ontario, Canada. *Education:* University of Toronto, B.A., 1962, M.A., 1963; University of Waterloo, Ph.D., 1965.

ADDRESSES: Home—5421 Glenhaven Ave., Riverside, CA 92506. *Office*—Department of Psychology, University of California, Riverside, CA 92506.

CAREER: University of Wisconsin—Madison, assistant professor, 1965-68, associate professor, 1968-70, professor of psychology, 1970-72; Fels Research Institute, Yellow Springs, OH, chief of social development section, 1972-75; University of Illinois at Urbana-Champaign, professor of psychology, 1975-90; University of California, Riverside, CA, professor and presidential chair in psychology, 1990—. Fels Clinical Professor of Research Pediatrics at University of Cincinnati, 1972-75.

AWARDS, HONORS: Research grants from National Institute of Mental Health, 1965-66, National Science Foundation, 1967-69, 1970-75, 1990-93, and National Institute of Child Health and Human Development, 1978-81, 1981-89.

WRITINGS:

(Editor) *Readings in Social Development,* Holt, 1969.
(Editor) *Recent Trends in Social Learning Theory,* Academic Press, 1972.
(With E. M. Hetherington) *Child Psychology,* McGraw, 1975, 4th edition, 1993.
Fathers, Harvard University Press, 1981.
(Editor) *The Family,* University of Chicago Press, 1984.
(Co-editor with G. Ladd) *Family-Peer Linkages,* Erlbaum, 1992.
(Co-editor with G. Elder and J. Modell) *Children in Time and Place,* Cambridge University Press, 1992.

Associate editor, *Child Development,* 1973-77; editor, *Developmental Psychology,* 1987-92. Former member of editorial board, *Journal of Experimental Child Psychology* and *Human Development;* member of editorial board, *Journal of Social and Personal Relationships* and *Journal of Family Psychology.*

SIDELIGHTS: Unlike many of the recent books dealing with the relationship between a father and his children, Ross D. Parke's *Fathers* provides "documented and reliable information about fathers obtained from scientific and observational studies," writes Raymond E. Lovett in the *Washington Post Book World.* The findings discussed in Parke's book counter the widely accepted theory that mothers have far greater influence on the development of a child than do fathers. Moreover, *Fathers* reveals, Lovett notes, that the father "affects his child's social and intellectual skills from the very beginning and that his degree of involvement has both immediate and far-reaching effects on his child."

BIOGRAPHICAL/CRITICAL SOURCES:

PERIODICALS

Washington Post Book World, July 12, 1981, p. 11.

*   *   *

PATON WALSH, Gillian   1937-
(Jill Paton Walsh)

PERSONAL: Born April 29, 1937, in London, England; daughter of John Llewellyn (an engineer) and Patricia (Dubern) Bliss; married Antony Edmund Paton Walsh (a chartered secretary), August 12, 1961; children: Edmund Alexander, Margaret Ann, Helen Clare. *Education:* St. Anne's College, Oxford, Dip. Ed., 1959, M.A. (honours) in English. *Politics:* None. *Religion:* "Skepticism." *Avocational interests:* Photography, gardening, cooking, carpentry, reading.

ADDRESSES: Home—72 Water Lane, Histon, Cambridge CB4 4LR, England.

CAREER: Enfield Girls Grammar School, Middlesex, English teacher, 1959-62; writer, 1962—. Whittall Lecturer, Library of Congress, Washington, DC, 1978. Visiting Faculty Member, Center for the Study of Children's Literature, Simmons College, Boston, 1978-86. Founder, with John Rowe Townsend, of Green Bay Publishers, 1986.

MEMBER: Society of Authors (member of Management Committee), Children's Writers Group.

AWARDS, HONORS: Book World Festival award, 1970, for *Fireweed;* Whitbread Prize (shared with Russell Hoban), 1974, for *The Emperor's Winding Sheet;* Boston *Globe-Horn Book* Award, 1976, for *Unleaving;* Arts Council Creative Writing Fellowship, 1976-77, and 1977-78; Universe Prize, 1984, for *A Parcel of Patterns;* Smarties Prize Grand Prix, 1984, for *Gaffer Samson's Luck.*

WRITINGS:

JUVENILE FICTION; UNDER NAME JILL PATON WALSH

Hengest's Tale, illustrated by Janet Margrie, St. Martin's Press, 1966.
The Dolphin Crossing, St. Martin's Press, 1967.
Fireweed, Macmillan, 1969, Farrar, Straus, 1970.
Goldengrove, Farrar, Straus, 1972.
Toolmaker, illustrated by Jeroo Roy, Heinemann, 1973, Seabury Press, 1974.
The Dawnstone, illustrated by Mary Dinsdale, London, Hamish Hamilton, 1973.
The Emperor's Winding Sheet, Farrar, Straus, 1974.
The Huffler, Farrar, Straus, 1975 (published in England as *The Butty Boy,* illustrated by Juliette Palmer, Macmillan, 1975).
Unleaving, Farrar, Straus, 1976.
Crossing to Salamis (first novel in trilogy; also see below), illustrated by David Smee, Heinemann, 1977.
The Walls of Athens (second novel in trilogy; also see below), illustrated by David Smee, London, Heinemann, 1977.
Persian Gold (third novel in trilogy; also see below), illustrated by David Smee, Heinemann, 1978.
Children of the Fox (contains *Crossing to Salamis, The Walls of Athens,* and *Persian Gold*), Farrar, Straus, 1978.
A Chance Child, Farrar, Straus, 1978.
The Green Book, illustrated by Joanna Stubbs, Macmillan, 1981, illustrated by Lloyd Bloom, Farrar, Straus, 1982, published as *Shine,* Macdonald, 1988.
Babylon, illustrated by Jenny Northway, Deutsch, 1982.
A Parcel of Patterns, Farrar, Straus, 1983.
Lost and Found, illustrated by Mary Rayner, Deutsch, 1984.
Gaffer Samson's Luck, illustrated by Brock Cole, Farrar, Straus, 1984.
Torch, Viking Kestral, 1987, Farrar, Straus, 1988.
Birdy and the Ghosties, illustrated by Alan Marks, Macdonald, 1989.
Grace, Viking, 1991, Farrar, Straus, 1992.
When Grandma Came (picture book), illustrated by Sophie Williams, Viking, 1992.

OTHER; UNDER NAME JILL PATON WALSH

(With Kevin Crossley Holland) *Wordhoard: Anglo-Saxon Stories,* Farrar, Straus, 1969.
Farewell, Great King (adult novel), Coward McCann, 1972.

(Editor) *Beowulf* (structural reader), Longman, 1975.

The Island Sunrise: Prehistoric Britain, Deutsch, 1975, published as *The Island Sunrise: Prehistoric Culture in the British Isles,* Seabury Press, 1976.

Five Tides (short stories), Green Bay, 1986.

Lapsing (adult novel), Weidenfeld & Nicolson, 1986, St. Martin's, 1987.

A School for Lovers (adult novel), Weidenfeld & Nicolson, 1989.

Some of Paton Walsh's manuscripts and papers may be found in the Kerlan Collection, University of Minnesota, Minneapolis.

SIDELIGHTS: Jill Paton Walsh is noted for her works which deal realistically with life, death and maturation. "Of [the many] skilled and sensitive writers [for young people]," declares Sheila Egoff in *Thursday's Child,* "[Paton] Walsh is the most formally literary. Her writing is studded with allusions to poetry, art and philosophy that give it an intellectual framework unmatched in children's literature." Paton Walsh's works examine eras and topics such as life, death, and honor in Anglo-Saxon England (*Hengest's Tale* and *Wordhoard*), Victorian child labor in England (*A Chance Child*), growing up in World War II England (*The Dolphin Crossing* and *Fireweed*), life in the Early Stone Age (*Toolmaker*), and loyalty in the midst of destruction in fifteenth-century Byzantium (*The Emperor's Winding Sheet*). She has also written several novels that center on the Cornish coast, where she spent part of her childhood.

Jill Paton Walsh was born Jill Bliss, a member of a loving family living in suburban London. Her father was an engineer, one of the earliest experimenters with television, and he and his wife actively stimulated their children to enjoy learning. "For the whole of our childhoods," Paton Walsh writes in her *Something about the Author Autobiography Series (SAAS)* entry, "I, and my brothers and sister—I am the eldest of four—were surrounded by love and encouragement on a lavish scale. . . . And to an unusual degree everyone was without prejudices against, or limited ambitions for, girls. As much was expected of me as of my brothers."

"For five crucial years of my childhood—from the year I was three to the year I was eight—the war dominated and shaped everything around me," Paton Walsh explains in *SAAS,* "and then for many years, until well into my teens, postwar hardships remained." "I do not know if there was a plan of evacuation there when the war began, which my parents did not join in, or if Finchley did not seem a likely target," she continues. Finally her mother's stepfather, upset by a bombing raid, moved the family to his place in Cornwall, in the far west of England. Although Jill's mother soon returned with her younger children to her husband in London, Jill herself remained in Cornwall for the next five years, returning to her family only after her grandmother suffered a fatal heart attack.

"I left St. Ives when I was just eight, and I didn't go back there till I was thirty-six," Paton Walsh explains in *SAAS.* "And it turned out that several people could remember me, and even remember having been in the same class in that little nursery school. A part of me is still rooted on that rocky shore, and it appears again and again in what I write." She stepped out of the comfortable world she had known directly into wartime London. "That first night back," she recalls, "I lay awake listening to the clanging sounds, like dustbins rolling round the night sky, made by German rockets falling somewhere a little distance off."

"The children I talk to nowadays are very interested in the Second World War," Paton Walsh remarks in her *SAAS* essay. "They think it must have been a time of excitement and danger, whereas it was actually dreadfully boring." Wartime restrictions and shortages meant that normal childhood activities—movies, television, radio, and even outdoor play—were severely limited. "I remember, in short, a time of discomfort and gloom, and, above all, upheaval." Part of the upheaval was caused by her mother's relatives, who had been wealthy colonists in Southeast Asia before the war, and who returned to England, newly impoverished, to live with her family. Because they had their own ideas of proper female behavior, Paton Walsh writes, she never knew "whether it was good and clever to give voice to my opinions, or pushy and priggish; not knowing from one day to the next what sort of behaviour would be expected of me." "Yet in the long run," Paton Walsh concludes, "I have benefited greatly from all this. I protected myself. I learned not to care what other people think. I would say what I liked, read what I was interested in, go on my own way, and ignore what the invading hoards of aunts and uncles thought, about me, or about anything else."

Paton Walsh attended a Catholic girl's school in North Finchley, whose environment was quite different from the liberality of her home life. "The nuns who taught me were suspicious of me," she declares in her *SAAS* entry. "They liked girls who worked very hard, not those who found it easy." When Paton Walsh left the school, it was to take a place at Oxford University. "I enjoyed myself vastly at Oxford, made friends, talked late into the night, and even worked sometimes, and work included lectures by both C. S. Lewis and J. R. R. Tolkien. The subject of the lectures and tutorials was always literature or philology—we wouldn't have dared ask those great men about their own work!—but the example they set by being both great and serious scholars, and writers of fantasy and books for children was not lost on me."

By the time Paton Walsh completed her degree, she was engaged to a man she had met at school. She obtained a teaching position, but soon discovered that she disliked being a teacher. "I didn't teach long," she explains in her *SAAS* entry. "I got married in my second year as a teacher, and eighteen months later was expecting a child." The life of a housewife, however, did not suit her either: "I was bored frantic. I went nearly crazy, locked up alone with a howling baby all day and all night. . . . As plants need water and light, as the baby needed milk, I needed something intellectual, cheap, and quiet." So, she says, "I began to write a book. It was a children's book. It never occurred to me to write any other kind."

"Until the moment I began to write I did not know that I was a writer," Paton Walsh explains in *SAAS*. The book she began to work on in those day, she says, "was, unfortunately, a dreadfully bad book. It had twelve chapters of equal length, with a different bit of historical background in each one." Eventually Kevin Crossley Holland, an editor with Macmillan, explained to Paton Walsh that to publish this particular book might be a bad idea. He then offered her an option on her next work. "I set to work joyfully on *Hengest's Tale*," she recalls, "a gory epic retold out of fragments of *Beowulf,* and I stopped work only for a fortnight—between chapter three and chapter four—when my second child, my daughter Margaret, was born. *Hengest's Tale* was my first published book. And I have never forgotten the difference it made to be able to say, to others, certainly, but above all, to myself, 'I am a writer.' "

"This whole question of where ideas for books come from is very intriguing," Paton Walsh states in her *SAAS* entry. "I suppose, 'Where do you get your ideas?' is the question most often asked by the children I meet. I think they are hoping for useful guidance on how to get ideas for their English homework, and I am a bit ashamed to be so hopeless at helping. But I don't really know where I get ideas from; each one in turn seems like an accident. It's a question of being on the lookout for the kind of accident that makes the idea for a book. . . . But I can say that a large part of it is giving loving attention to places; not necessarily beautiful places, just anywhere. Most of my books really have begun with thinking about the places they are set in." For example, she continues, "I went to Greece to find the landscapes for a classical historical novel, written for adults, called *Farewell, Great King,* but when I got there I found Byzantine things, the marvellous mountain-top deserted city of Mistra above all, and the result of that was *The Emperor's Winding Sheet.* And there are more places singing to me. . . ."

Critics celebrate Paton Walsh's ability to evoke both character and setting, and through them to say something meaningful about growing up. She "has an astonishing ability to create appealing personalities," declares Eliza-

beth S. Coolidge in the *Washington Post Book World.* In *Unleaving,* the critic continues, "She has written a book about death, and what this means to a philosopher, a teenager, a grandmother and a very small child. Yet *Unleaving* is in no way a gloomy book, but one that leaves the reader with a warm and optimistic view of humankind." "[Paton] Walsh doesn't tidy up the blight for which man was born," states Alice Bach in a *New York Times Book Review* critique of the same book. "She's too wise to attempt answers about growing, living, dying, ethical choices. She exalts the mystery, the unknowing itself." "As time has gone by," Paton Walsh concludes in her *SAAS* entry, "I have won the friendship of many other writers and readers and book-lovers. I feel lucky in this, beyond my deserts. . . . A writer is what I shall be as long as there is a daydream in my head, and I have strength to sit up and type."

BIOGRAPHICAL/CRITICAL SOURCES:

BOOKS

Children's Literature Review, Volume 2, Gale, 1976.
Contemporary Literary Criticism, Volume 35, Gale, 1985.
Egoff, Sheila A., *Thursday's Child: Trends and Patterns in Contemporary Children's Literature,* American Library Association, 1981, pp. 31-65.
Something about the Author Autobiography Series, Volume 3, Gale, 1987, pp. 189-203.

PERIODICALS

New York Times Book Review, August 8, 1976, p. 18.
Washington Post Book World, May 2, 1976, p. L13.

*   *   *

PATON WALSH, Jill
See PATON WALSH, Gillian

*   *   *

PECK, Richard (Wayne) 1934-

PERSONAL: Born April 5, 1934, in Decatur, IL; son of Wayne Morris (a merchant) and Virginia (a dietician; maiden name, Gray) Peck. *Education:* Attended University of Exeter, 1955-56; DePauw University, B.A., 1956; Southern Illinois University, M.A., 1959; further graduate study at Washington University, 1960-61. *Politics:* Republican. *Religion:* Methodist.

ADDRESSES: Home—155 East 72nd St., New York, NY 10021. *Office*—c/o Delacorte Press, 1 Dag Hammarskjold Plaza, New York, NY 10017. *Agent*—Sheldon Fogelman, 155 East 72nd St., New York, NY 10021.

CAREER: Southern Illinois University at Carbondale, instructor in English, 1958-60; Glenbrook North High

School, Northbrook, IL, teacher of English, 1961-63; Scott, Foresman Co., Chicago, IL, textbook editor, 1963-65; Hunter College of the City University of New York and Hunter College High School, New York City, instructor in English and education, 1965-71; writer, 1971—. Assistant director of the Council for Basic Education, Washington, DC, 1969-70; English-Speaking Union fellow, Jesus College, Oxford University, England, 1973; lecturer. *Military service:* U.S. Army, 1956-58; served in Stuttgart, Germany.

MEMBER: Authors Guild, Authors League of America, Delta Chi.

AWARDS, HONORS: Child Study Association of America's Children's Book of the Year citations, 1970, for *Sounds and Silences,* 1971, for *Mindscapes,* and 1986, for *Blossom Culp and the Sleep of Death;* Writing Award, National Council for the Advancement of Education, 1971; Edgar Allan Poe Award runner-up, Mystery Writers of America, 1974, for *Dreamland Lake;* Best Books of the Year citations, American Library Association (ALA), 1974, for *Representing Super Doll,* 1976, for *Are You in the House Alone?,* and 1977, for *Ghosts I Have Been;* ALA Notable Book citations, 1975, for *The Ghost Belonged to Me,* and 1985, for *Remembering the Good Times;* Friends of American Writers Award (older category), 1976, for *The Ghost Belonged to Me;* Edgar Allan Poe Award for best juvenile mystery novel, 1976, and Author's Award, New Jersey Institute of Technology, 1978, both for *Are You in the House Alone?; School Library Journal*'s Best Books of the Year citations, 1976, for *Are You in the House Alone?,* 1977, for *Ghosts I Have Been,* and 1985, for *Remembering the Good Times; New York Times* Outstanding Book of the Year citation, 1977, for *Ghosts I Have Been;* Illinois Writer of the Year citation, Illinois Association of Teachers of English, 1977; *School Library Journal*'s Best of the Best 1966-1978 citations, for *Dreamland Lake,* and *Father Figure.*

New York Public Library Books for the Teen Age citations, 1980, for *Pictures That Storm inside My Head,* 1981, for *Ghosts I Have Been,* and 1982, for *Are You in the House Alone?* and *Close Enough to Touch;* ALA Best Books for Young Adults citations, 1981, for *Close Enough to Touch,* 1985, for *Remembering the Good Times,* and 1987, for *Princess Ashley; School Library Journal*'s Best Books for Young Adults citations, 1981, for *Close Enough to Touch,* 1983, for *This Family of Women,* and 1985, for *Remembering the Good Times;* ALA's Young Adult Services Division's Best of the Best Books 1970-1983 citations, for *Are You in the House Alone?* and *Ghosts I Have Been;* ALA's Margaret Edwards Young Adult Author Achievement Award, 1990.

WRITINGS:

YOUNG ADULT NOVELS

Don't Look and It Won't Hurt, Holt, 1972.
Dreamland Lake, Holt, 1973, Dell, 1990.
Through a Brief Darkness, Viking, 1973.
Representing Super Doll, Viking, 1974.
The Ghost Belonged to Me, Viking, 1975.
Are You in the House Alone? (with teacher's guide), Viking, 1976.
Ghosts I Have Been (sequel to *The Ghost Belonged to Me*), Viking, 1977.
Father Figure, Viking, 1978.
Secrets of the Shopping Mall, Delacorte, 1979.
Close Enough to Touch, Delacorte, 1981.
The Dreadful Future of Blossom Culp (sequel to *Ghosts I Have Been*), Delacorte, 1983.
Remembering the Good Times, Delacorte, 1985.
Blossom Culp and the Sleep of Death, Delacorte, 1986.
Princess Ashley, Delacorte, 1987.
Those Summer Girls I Never Met, Delacorte, 1988.
Unfinished Portrait of Jessica, Delacorte, 1991.

JUVENILE

Monster Night at Grandma's House, illustrations by Don Freeman, Viking, 1977.

ADULT NOVELS

Amanda/Miranda (Literary Guild selection; Reader's Digest Condensed Book Club selection), Viking, 1980.
New York Time, Delacorte, 1981.
This Family of Women (Literary Guild alternate selection), Delacorte, 1983.
Voices after Midnight, Dell, 1990.

EDITOR

(With Ned E. Hoopes) *Edge of Awareness: Twenty-five Contemporary Essays,* Dell, 1966.
Sounds and Silences: Poetry for Now, Delacorte, 1970.
Mindscapes: Poems for the Real World, Delacorte, 1971.
Leap into Reality: Essays for Now, Dell, 1972.
Urban Studies: A Research Paper Casebook, Random House, 1973.
Transitions: A Literary Paper Casebook, Random House, 1974.
Pictures That Storm inside My Head (poetry anthology), Avon, 1976.

OTHER

(With Norman Strasma) *Old Town, A Complete Guide: Strolling, Shopping, Supping, Sipping,* 2nd edition, [Chicago], 1965.

(With Mortimer Smith and George Weber) *A Consumer's Guide to Educational Innovations,* Council for Basic Education, 1972.

(With Stephen N. Judy) *The Creative Word 2,* (Peck was not associated with other volumes), Random House, 1974.

(Contributor) Kenneth L. Donelson and Alleen Pace Nilsen, *Literature for Today's Young Adults,* Scott, Foresman, 1980.

(Contributor) Donald R. Gallo, editor, *Sixteen: Short Stories by Outstanding Young Adult Writers,* Delacorte, 1984.

(Contributor) D. R. Gallo, editor, *Visions: Nineteen Short Stories by Outstanding Writers for Young Adults,* Delacorte, 1987.

Write a Tale of Terror, Book Lures, 1987.

Anonymously Yours (autobiography), Silver Burdette, 1991.

(Contributor) Gallo, editor, *Connections: Short Stories By Outstanding Writers for Young Adults,* Delacorte, 1989.

Author of column on the architecture of historic neighborhoods for the *New York Times.* Contributor of poetry to several anthologies. Contributor of poems to *Saturday Review* and *Chicago Tribune Magazine.* Contributor of articles to periodicals, including *American Libraries, PTA Magazine* and *Parents' Magazine.*

ADAPTATIONS: Audio cassette versions of Peck's books include *The Ghost Belonged to Me,* Live Oak Media, 1976, *Don't Look and It Won't Hurt* (filmstrip with cassette), Random House, and *Remembering the Good Times* (cassette), Listening Library, 1987. Television movies based on his books include *Are You in the House Alone?,* CBS, 1977, *Child of Glass* (based on *The Ghost Belonged to Me*), Walt Disney Productions, 1979, and *Father Figure,* Time-Life Productions, 1980. Cineville Production Company bought the film rights for *Don't Look and It Won't Hurt* in 1991.

WORK IN PROGRESS: Bel-Air Bambi and the Mall Rats, a novel, 1992.

SIDELIGHTS: Richard Peck's books on such important teen-age problems as suicide, unwanted pregnancy, death of a loved one, and rape have won critical acclaim for their realism and emotional power. Peck has written over a dozen very popular books for young adults, books that assist young readers in the development of self-confidence. He has also written adult novels that show a commitment to eliminating sexual stereotypes. When writing for young adults, he told Roger Sutton in a *School Library Journal* interview, he tries to keep his reader in mind: "As I'm typing I'm trying to look out over the typewriter and see faces. I don't certainly want to 'write for myself' because

I'm trying to write across a generation gap." In books for both age groups, Peck told Jean F. Mercier in *Publishers Weekly,* he tries to "give readers leading characters they can look up to and reasons to believe that problems can be solved." The excellence of his work has been recognized by numerous awards, including the American Library Association's Young Adult Author Achievement Award in 1990.

Peck became familiar with contemporary adolescent problems while teaching high school. He liked his students, but after several years became discouraged and quit, telling *CA* that teaching "had begun to turn into something that looked weirdly like psychiatric social work." Peck decided instead to write books for teenagers that featured the problems he had seen. "Ironically, it was my students who taught me to be a writer, though I had been hired to teach *them,*" he said in a speech published in *Arkansas Libraries.* "They taught me that a novel must entertain first before it can be anything else. I learned that there is no such thing as a 'grade reading level'; a young person's 'reading level' and attention span will rise and fall according to his degree of interest. I learned that if you do not have a happy ending for the young, you had better do some fast talking." He observed that young adults are most concerned with winning approval from their peers and seeking reassurance from their reading material. With these needs in mind, Peck writes about the passage from childhood to adulthood. He believes that in a young adult novel, "the reader meets a worthy young character who takes one step nearer maturity, and he or she takes that step independently."

His first novel, *Don't Look and It Won't Hurt,* was about a teenage pregnancy. Knowing that teens don't identify with protagonists they view as losers, he told the story of alienation and healing from the viewpoint of the young mother's younger sister. The fifteen-year old manages to keep her beleaguered family together, "parenting" her parents in a role reversal that appeals to readers of this age group. She is also instrumental in the sister's recovery after deciding to give the baby up for adoption. Letty Cottin Pogrebin praises the novel's emotional power in the *New York Times Book Review.* The novel received much critical praise and became a popular success, and continues to sell in both paperback and hardcover editions.

Peck's controversial novel about a teenage girl who is raped, *Are You in the House Alone?,* met with critical approval and received the Edgar Allan Poe Award in 1976. Zena Sutherland, writing in the *Bulletin of the Center for Children's Books,* is impressed by the novel's scope: "Peck sees clearly both society's problem and the victim's: the range of attitudes, the awful indignity, the ramifications of fear and shame." Peck explained in his speech, "I did not write the novel to tell the young about rape. They already know what that is." He said he wrote it to warn the young that criminals are regrettably sometimes treated with more respect than victims even though victims of crime live in the shadow of that experience for the rest of their lives. Alix Nelson in the *New York Times Book Review* thinks that Peck "ought to be congratulated for connecting with, and raising the consciousness of, his target audience . . . on a subject most people shun."

Close Enough to Touch, a love story written in response to a young man's request that Peck should write a book about dating, is *"told by a boy,"* the author said in his speech. "It might please some boys to be given this voice. It might surprise some girls that boys have emotions too. Mother never told them. Mothers are still telling daughters that boys only want one thing. How wrong they are. Boys want a great deal." When the boy's first love dies, he suddenly has to cope with the fact that just as no one had prepared him for intimacy with the opposite sex, no one has prepared him to face grief. "There is no sexual content in this book," Peck continued. "This is a novel about the emotions, not the senses."

In 1980 Peck published his first adult novel, *Amanda/Miranda.* It is a romantic story set on the oceanliner *Titanic,* which sank in the Atlantic on its maiden voyage in 1912. Peck explained to Mercier that he didn't want this romance to reflect stereotypical sex roles, despite the fact that "in period novels, women are usually the prizes for men of ingenuity." Instead, Peck made the heroine "the ingenious one in adversity, winner of the male prize, for a change." *Amanda/Miranda* was a bestseller and has been translated into nine languages.

Peck again challenges traditional sexual roles in *This Family of Women,* indicating in publicity material for Delacorte that he wanted to write "about American women who rose in their worlds not because they were born to the right fathers or married the right husbands. I wanted them to rise through their own strengths and needs." *Washington Post Book World* contributor Dennis Drabelle thinks the characters in *This Family of Women* meet Peck's goals, writing that they "summon taciturn strength, flout public opinion, and prosper."

Peck's heroines are known for their independence and individuality. He feels that these qualities are especially important for characters in teenage fiction, writing in *Literature for Today's Young Adults* that we need to "indicate to the young that all of life need not be as cruelly conformist and conservative as adolescence." He concludes that the future of young adult fiction is in "books that invite the young to think for themselves instead of for each other."

Peck believes that American attitudes about public education have resulted in a system that has discouraged young people instead of equipping them for survival in the real world. Addressing other writers in his speech, he said, "Our readers of the 1980's are citizens of the moment not only because they are very young, but because they are no longer taught much history or foreign language or geography or cartography or scripture, which combines history, geography, poetry, and faith. You and I, we people of the word, spend our lives hollering across the famous generation gap, hoping to hear an answering echo." Survivors of the ravaged educational system and permissive parenting are few, he observed. Children raised in permissive homes tend not to look up to others because they view parents and teachers as their servants, Peck told Sutton. They tend to look down on others while viewing themselves as heroes. "There is not anywhere you can go from a permissive home. The rest of the world has rules," he said in his speech.

He concluded that, fortunately, "There is another America, of course, beyond this somber landscape. An America revealed chiefly in books—by novels: of the past, on this year's list, of novels yet to be written. This America is one of self-reliance and coming from behind; of characters who learn to accept the consequences of their actions; of happy endings worked for and almost achieved; of being young in an old world and finding your way in it; of a nation of people hasty and forgetful but full still of hope; of limitless distances and new beginnings and starting over; of dreams like mountaintops, and rivers that run to the sea. We owe our young this record of our dreams, and if you and I do not put that record into their hands, who will?"

When asked what he hopes to accomplish in his books for young adults, Peck told Sutton, "I don't know what books can do, except one point is that I wish every kid knew that fiction can be truer than fact, that it isn't a frivolous pastime unless your reading taste is for the frivolous. I wish they knew that being literate is a way of being successful in any field. I wish they all wanted to pit their own experience against the experiences they see in books. And I wish they had to do a little more of that in order to pass the class in school. But in books you reach an awful lot of promising kids who write back good literate letters and give you hope. So that's the hope I have."

BIOGRAPHICAL/CRITICAL SOURCES:

BOOKS

Children's Literature Review, Volume 15, Gale, 1988, pp. 146-166.
Fifth Book of Junior Authors and Illustrators, Wilson, 1983, pp. 238-240.
Konigsburg, E. L., editor, *In My Own Words Series,* Silver Burdette Press, 1991.

Peck, Richard, in Donelson, Kenneth L. and Alleen Pace Nilsen, editors, *Literature for Today's Young Adults,* Scott, Foresman, 1980, pp. 34-76, 136-171.

Something about the Author Autobiography Series, Volume 2, Gale, 1986, pp. 175-186.

Twentieth Century Children's Writers, St. Martin's Press, 1989, pp. 768-769.

PERIODICALS

American Libraries, April, 1973.

Arkansas Libraries, December, 1981, pp. 13-16.

Bulletin of the Center for Children's Books, March, 1977.

English Journal, February, 1976, pp. 97-99.

Los Angeles Times, April 3, 1981.

New York Times Book Review, June 27, 1971; November 12, 1972, pp. 8, 10; July 27, 1975, p. 8; November 14, 1976, p. 29; December 2, 1979.

Psychology Today, September, 1975, pp. 11, 75.

Publishers Weekly, March 14, 1980.

School Library Journal, May, 1986, pp. 37-39; June, 1990, pp. 36-40 (interview).

Times Literary Supplement, August 21, 1981.

Top of the News, winter, 1978, pp. 173-177; spring, 1987, pp. 297-301.

Washington Post Book World, November 10, 1974, p. 8; May 1, 1983.

Young Adult Cooperative Book Review, February, 1977.

*   *   *

PEDOLSKY, Andrea 1951-

PERSONAL: Born March 13, 1951, in New York, NY; daughter of Milton and Beverly (Finger) Pedolsky. *Education:* Queens College of the City University of New York, B.A., 1975; Columbia University, M.S., 1978.

ADDRESSES: Office—AMACOM Books, 135 West 50th St., New York, NY 10020.

CAREER: Association of the Bar of the City of New York, New York City, research assistant for Drug Law Evaluation Project, 1972-77; Neal-Schuman Publishers, Inc., New York City, managing editor, 1978-88; AMACOM Books, New York City, acquisitions editor, 1988—.

MEMBER: American Library Association, National Organization for Women (member of board of directors, 1981-83).

WRITINGS:

(Editor with Ellen Gay Detlefsen) *National Directory of Mental Health,* Wiley, 1980.

(Editor) *In-House Training and Development Programs,* Gale, 1981.

(Editor) *Continuing Education for Businesspeople,* Gale, 1981.

(Editor with John Ganly and Diane Sciattara) *Small Business Sourcebook,* Gale, 1983.

(Contributor) Betty-Carol Sellen, editor, *Librarian/ Author: A Practical Guide on How to Get Published,* Neal-Schuman, 1985.

(With Betty Turock) *Creating a Financial Plan,* Neal-Schuman, 1992.

Editor of *New York Woman,* 1981-83.

*   *   *

PEET, Bill
See PEET, William Bartlett

*   *   *

PEET, William Bartlett 1915-
(Bill Peet)

PERSONAL: Surname altered to Peet about 1947, though not legally changed; born January 29, 1915, in Grandview, IN; son of Orion Hopkins (a salesman) and Emma (a teacher; maiden name, Thorpe) Peed; married Margaret Brunst, November 30, 1937; children: Bill, Jr., Stephen. *Education:* Attended John Herron Art Institute, 1933-36.

CAREER: Worked briefly as an artist for a greeting card company in the Midwest, 1936-37; Walt Disney Studios, Hollywood, CA, sketch artist and continuity illustrator for motion picture industry, then screenwriter, 1937-64; author and illustrator of children's books.

AWARDS, HONORS: Prizes for paintings at exhibits in Indianapolis and Chicago, 1934-37; John Herron Art Institute citation, 1958, as one of the outstanding students in the history of the school; *Box Office* Blue Ribbon award, 1961, 1964, for best screenplay; Indiana Author's Day award for most distinguished Hoosier book of the year for children, 1967, for *Capyboppy;* Southern California Council on Literature for Children and Young People award for illustration, 1967, for *Farewell to Shady Glade;* named outstanding Hoosier author of children's literature, 1967; Colorado Children's Book Award and California Reading Association Young Reader Medal, both 1976, both for *How Droofus the Dragon Lost His Head;* Little Archer Award from the University of Wisconsin-Oshkosh, 1977, for *Cyrus, the Unsinkable Sea Serpent;* Georgia Picture Book award, 1979, and California Reading Association Young Reader Medal, 1980, both for *Big Bad Bruce;* International Reading Association "Children's Choice" award, 1982, for *Encore for Eleanor;* California Reading Association's Significant Author Award, 1983; George G. Stone Center Recognition of Merit award for body of work, 1985; Caldecott honor book, 1989, for *Bill Peet: An Autobiography,* which also won the Southern California Children's Book Writer's Medal; Annie Award for distinguished contribution to the art of animation.

WRITINGS:

FOR CHILDREN; SELF-ILLUSTRATED; UNDER NAME BILL PEET

Goliath II, Golden Press, 1959.
Chester the Worldly Pig, Houghton, 1965.
Farewell to Shady Glade, Houghton, 1966.
Capyboppy, Houghton, 1966.
Buford, the Little Bighorn, Houghton, 1967.
Jennifer and Josephine, Houghton, 1967.
Fly, Homer, Fly, Houghton, 1969.
The Whingdingdilly, Houghton, 1970.
The Wump World, Houghton, 1970.
How Droofus the Dragon Lost His Head, Houghton, 1971.
The Ant and the Elephant, Houghton, 1972.
The Spooky Tail of Prewitt Peacock, Houghton, 1972.
Merle the High Flying Squirrel, Houghton, 1974.
Cyrus the Unsinkable Sea Serpent, Houghton, 1975.
The Gnats of Knotty Pine, Houghton, 1975.
Big Bad Bruce, Houghton, 1977.
Eli, Houghton, 1978.
Cowardly Clyde, Houghton, 1979.
Encore for Eleanor, Houghton, 1981.
Pamela Camel, Houghton, 1984.
Jethro and Joel Were a Troll, Houghton, 1987.
Cock-a-Doodle Dudley, Houghton, 1990.

CHILDREN'S VERSE; SELF-ILLUSTRATED; UNDER NAME BILL PEET

Hubert's Hair-Raising Adventure, Houghton, 1959.
Huge Harold, Houghton, 1961.
Smokey, Houghton, 1962.
The Pinkish, Purplish, Bluish Egg, Houghton, 1963.
Randy's Dandy Lions, Houghton, 1964.
Ella, Houghton, 1964.
Kermit the Hermit, Houghton, 1965.
The Caboose Who Got Loose, Houghton, 1971.
Countdown to Christmas, Golden Gate, 1972.
The Luckiest One of All, Houghton, 1982.
No Such Things, Houghton, 1983.
The Kweeks of Kookatumdee, Houghton, 1985.
Zella, Zack, and Zodiac, Houghton, 1986.

OTHER; UNDER NAME BILL PEET

Bill Peet: An Autobiography, Houghton, 1989.

Author and illustrator of Walt Disney films *One Hundred and One Dalmations,* 1961, and *The Sword in the Stone,*

1963, and, with others, of *Pinocchio,* 1940, *Dumbo,* 1941, *Fantasia,* 1941, *Song of the South,* 1946, *Cinderella,* 1950, *Alice in Wonderland,* 1951, *Peter Pan,* 1953, *Sleeping Beauty,* 1959, and short subjects.

Peet's books have been translated into many languages, including French, German, Japanese, and Swedish, and many have been issued in Braille.

SIDELIGHTS: William Bartlett Peet's lively drawings were familiar to moviegoers long before he began publishing books for children. As an illustrator for Walt Disney Studios, Peet contributed drawings to such animated classics as *Pinocchio, Fantasia, Cinderella,* and *Peter Pan,* and was the screenwriter for *One Hundred and One Dalmations* and *The Sword in the Stone.* He left Disney in 1964 and since that time has been populating his books with warm animal characters such as Pamela Camel, Buford the Little Bighorn, and Merle the High Flying Squirrel. His children's books, which are all still in print, have won numerous awards and, according to Jim Trelease in the *New York Times Book Review,* "Children in four states have chosen him as their 'favorite author' in annual state polls."

Peet was born in 1915 near Indianapolis, Indiana. Before he was three years old, his father was drafted into the army to serve during World War I. His father had just finished training camp when the war ended, but he never rejoined his family, preferring the life of an itinerant salesman. Peet recalls in *Bill Peet: An Autobiography* that since he had never known his father, he didn't miss him, and he remembers fondly the years he spent living with his grandmother, mother, and brothers. In the attic of his grandmother's home, Peet discovered his love for drawing, a love that would remain with him his entire life.

But drawing sometimes caused Peet trouble. He was not very interested in traditional schoolwork, and constantly drew in the margins of his textbooks, on his desk, and on his ever-present pad of paper. Although the habit irritated many of his teachers, Peet says that "when it came time for the used book sales my illustrated books were best sellers." Peet told *Christian Science Monitor* interviewer Marshall Ingwerson about a teacher who once pleasantly surprised him: "This particular teacher snatched my tablet away just as the others had done and marched to the front of the room with it. Then turning to the class she said, 'I want you to see what William has been doing!' Then with an amused smile the teacher turned the pages for all to see. After returning the tablet she encouraged me with, 'I hope you will do something with your drawing someday.' "

The summer before Peet started high school, his father returned home. It was an unhappy reunion and his beloved grandmother died soon afterward as Peet looked on, helpless. His newly poor family was forced to move frequently, and Peet had to attend one of the country's largest high schools. By the end of his first year he had failed every class except physical education, and his parents' constant quarrelling drove him and his brothers apart. At the suggestion of a childhood friend that he take more art classes, however, Peet dropped some of his academic courses and excelled in each of the art classes he took. His success gave him the momentum to pass his other classes, and in his senior year he received a scholarship to the John Herron Art Institute in Indianapolis. Peet was in his element at the art institute, and comments in his autobiography: "It was all peaches and cream, with no devilish academic problems to boggle my mind."

After leaving school in 1937, "a poor year to start a career as a painter, or a career of any kind for that matter," he remembers, he sold some of his paintings, and filled in the colors on greeting cards for a company in Dayton, Ohio, but still could not make enough money to support a family. However, when Walt Disney Studios responded to a letter he had written, and invited him to report to their California offices for a tryout, Peet shared the roads going west during the Great Depression with many other poor Americans hoping to find jobs in California. He arrived just two days before he was to try out for his new job. All the potential illustrators were placed in a large room where they practiced drawing versions of Mickey Mouse, Donald Duck, and Goofy over and over again, trying to master Disney's roundish drawing style. Peet made the cut, and worked for months as an "in-betweener," the person responsible for filling in all the motion sequences of the characters. His steady job allowed him to marry Margaret, his art-school sweetheart. But the repetitious work soon wore on him. "After drawing [Donald Duck] a few thousand times I had begun to despise [him] . . .," recalls Peet in his autobiography. "It was too much! I went berserk and shouted at the top of my voice, 'NO MORE DUCKS!!!' much to the horror of my fellow in-betweeners." He stormed off the job, swearing not to return.

When Peet returned the next day to retrieve his jacket, he found an envelope on his desk, which he expected to be his dismissal notice. But when he opened it, he found that he was being assigned instead to work on the new Disney movie, *Pinocchio*. This move signalled the beginning of Peet's gradual climb in the Disney organization, for he progressed from creating small background characters to designing progressively larger and more important scenes, and finally to writing the entire screenplay and drawing the story boards for *One Hundred and One Dalmations* and *The Sword in the Stone*. Although Peet certainly had a great deal of success in his twenty-seven year career with Disney, all was not idyllic. Peet, who says in his autobiography that he designed the character of Captain Hook in *Peter Pan* to resemble Walt Disney in looks and in temperament, began to realize in the late 1950s that he needed to escape the stifling demands of adapting someone else's ideas, of continually having his own work changed, and of getting little credit for the work he did. Peet told *Los Angeles Times* writer Myrna Oliver that "Walt was very sensitive about credit. He would say 'Dammit, we are all in this together. But what he meant was 'the credit is all *mine*.' I knew that *we* stood for Walter Elias. Everything came out 'Walt Disney presents' and the rest of our names might as well have been in the phone book."

As Peet's dissatisfaction with Disney grew, he began to devote his free time to developing drawings, characters, and stories of his own. He had no problem with the illustrations, but writing the stories proved difficult. "It finally occurred to me that as long as it was Walt Disney's [story], I could write it," Peet recalls in his autobiography. "But when it came to doing a book for myself, I could never complete one." Peet managed to publish a few books by the time he began designing the animals for the new Disney film, *Jungle Book;* but he and Disney were soon at odds over the voice for a character, and after the short-tempered Disney belittled him, he decided to quit. On his birthday in 1964, Peet became a full-time author of children's books.

Out from under the Disney shadow, Peet was able to develop more inventive stories; his first upon leaving was *Randy's Dandy Lions,* a tale of five timid circus lions too nervous to perform. Although Peet has said that the trainer represents Walt Disney, and he the lions, he is glad that he never worked up the gumption to roar back at the trainer as his lions finally do. However, Peet's favorite book is *Chester the Worldly Pig,* a book that he says in his autobiography "is the one book of mine that reflects my past more than any others." The story traces the adventures of Chester as he leaves the farm to join a circus, only to leave the circus to become a big star on his own.

The author enjoys visiting elementary schools to talk with and draw for children, and once received an idea for a book from them. Peet would often ask the excited students to guess what he was drawing on their blackboard, and they usually knew the answer before he was halfway through. One day, however, Peet outsmarted them by changing the animal as he drew, and soon he had come up with a combination of giraffe, elephant, camel, zebra, reindeer, rhino, and dog that became the basis for *Whingdingdilly,* his story of a dog who wishes to be different, and finds a witch to help him make his dream come true. Children return Peet's attention by writing him thousands of letters. Peet told Oliver: "My favorite compliment from the kids is 'We think your books are funny and make us laugh.' If you are trying to get kids to read, a book should be entertaining. If it isn't fun, it becomes a chore."

Peet's books have attracted much critical attention and have earned him numerous awards. His long experience as an animator shows in his cartoonish drawings; an illustrated page by Peet is always filled with detail and action, and characters come to life before the reader's eyes. Rachel Fordyce notes in *Twentieth-Century Children's Writers* that Peet's books "have an exotic patina of fantasy and realistic detail," and that "the pictures are strong enough to stand on their own." While his characters make the reader laugh, they also draw sympathy. In *American Picture Books from Noah's Ark to The Beast Within*, Barbara Bader calls Peet "the most humane of cartoonists," and Trelease comments that "his characters are less eccentric and have a dollop more warmth than Dr. Seuss' and like Dr. Seuss, Mr. Peet often writes with a message in mind, using animal characters in a fable-like but not didactic fashion." Peet's animal characters are often misfits, but through their resourcefulness and compassion they are able to succeed. Not every critic likes Peet's work, however; Derwent May, writing in *Listener*, insists that the grotesque drawings in *The Whingdingdilly* make it a "coarse and upsetting fantasy," while other critics have complained that Peet's verse is trite and filled with cliches. A *Bulletin of the Center for Children's Books* reviewer contends that children will not be bothered by these elements of Peet's work, for they are having too much fun laughing at Peet's ridiculous drawings.

Peet enjoys the turn that his career has taken, telling Ingwerson: "So my early ambition to illustrate animal stories was finally realized, and a little bit more, since I had never considered writing one. This way I can write about things I like to draw, which makes it more fun than work. And I still carry a tablet around with me and sneak a drawing into it now and then. Sometimes I feel like I'm basically doing the same thing as when I was six years old: drawing lions and tigers in books."

BIOGRAPHICAL/CRITICAL SOURCES:

BOOKS

Bader, Barbara, *American Picture Books from Noah's Ark to The Beast Within*, Macmillan, 1976.
Books for Children, 1960-1965, American Library Association, 1966.
Kingman, Lee, and others, compilers, *Illustrators of Children's Books: 1957-1966*, Horn Book, 1968.
Kingman, L., and others, compilers, *Illustrators of Children's Books: 1967-1976*, Horn Book, 1978.
Larrick, Nancy, *A Parent's Guide to Children's Reading*, 3rd edition, Doubleday, 1969.
Peet, Bill, *Bill Peet: An Autobiography*, Houghton, 1989.
Something about the Author, Volume 41, Gale, 1985, pp. 158-164.
Twentieth-Century Children's Writers, 3rd edition, St. James Press, 1989, pp. 771-772.

PERIODICALS

Bulletin of the Center for Children's Books, June, 1986, p. 194.
Christian Science Monitor, November 9, 1981.
Horn Book, June, 1971.
Library Journal, September, 1970.
Listener, November 11, 1971, p. 665.
Los Angeles Times, December 23, 1990, pp. E1, E14.
New York Times Book Review, March 11, 1984, p. 23; May 21, 1989, pp. 31, 46.

—*Sketch by Tom Pendergast*

*   *   *

PEMBERTON, Margaret   1943-
(Carris Carlise, Christina Marland)

PERSONAL: Born April 10, 1943, in Yorkshire, England; daughter of George Arthur (an architect) and Kathleen (an artist; maiden name, Ramsden) Hudson; married Mike Pemberton (an advertising executive), October 13, 1968; children: Amanda, Rebecca, Polly, Michael, Natasha Christina. *Education:* Attended girls' school in Bradford, Yorkshire, England. *Politics:* "Apolitical."

ADDRESSES: Home—13 Manor Ln., London S.E.13, England. *Agent*—Carol Smith Agency, 25 Hornton Ct., Kensington High St., London W8 7RT, England.

CAREER: Free-lance writer, 1974—. Has worked as a secretary, actress, model, nurse, overseas telegraphist, and catering manager.

MEMBER: Romantic Novelists Association (chairman, 1989-91), Crime Writers Association.

WRITINGS:

Rendezvous with Danger, Macdonald & Jane's, 1974.
The Mystery of Saligo Bay, Macdonald & Jane's, 1975.
Shadows over Silver Sands, Berkeley, 1976.
The Guilty Secret, R. Hale, 1979.
The Lion of Languedoc, Mills & Boon, 1980.
Harlot, Arrow, 1981.
Pioneer Girl, Mills & Boon, 1981.
Some Distant Shore, Pocket Books, 1981.
African Enchantment, Mills & Boon, 1982.
The Flower Garden, F. Watts, 1982.
Flight to Verechencko, Mills & Boon, 1983.
Forever, Fontana, 1983.
The Devil's Palace, Mills & Boon, 1984.
Silver Shadows, Golden Dreams, Macdonald, 1985.
Never Leave Me, Transworld, 1986.
A Multitude of Sins, Transworld, 1988.

(Under pseudonym Carris Carlise) *Party in Peking,* St. Martin's, 1988.

(Under pseudonym Christina Marland) *White Christmas in Saigon,* Transworld, 1990.

WORK IN PROGRESS: A book on lace-making in late medieval France.

SIDELIGHTS: Margaret Pemberton told *CA:* "My main passions in life are Mike Pemberton, smaller Pembertons, Shakespeare, theatre, acting, and travel, in that order. I am a keen amateur actress and will travel anywhere at the slightest excuse. I write because I love it, because it is the only thing I can do!"

*   *   *

PETERS, Linda
See CATHERALL, Arthur

*   *   *

PHILLIPS, Gene D(aniel) 1935-

PERSONAL: Born March 3, 1935, in Springfield, OH; son of Ira Granville (a factory foreman) and Johanna (Davoran) Phillips. *Education:* Loyola University of Chicago, A.B., 1957, M.A., 1959; West Baden College, Ph.L., 1959; Bellarmine School of Theology, S.T.L., 1966; Fordham University, Ph.D., 1970.

ADDRESSES: Home—Faculty Residence, Loyola University, 6525 North Sheridan Rd., Chicago, IL 60626. *Office*—Department of English, Loyola University of Chicago, Chicago, IL 60626.

CAREER: Entered Society of Jesus (Jesuits), 1952, ordained priest, 1965; Loyola University of Chicago, Chicago, IL, 1970—, began as assistant professor, associate professor, 1975-81, professor of film history, fiction, and drama, 1981—.

MEMBER: Society for Cinema Studies, Modern Language Association of America.

AWARDS, HONORS: American Philosophical Society grant, 1971; named Teacher of the Year, Loyola University, 1979.

WRITINGS:

The Movie Makers: Artists in an Industry, Nelson-Hall, 1973, enlarged edition published as *Major Film Directors of the American and British Cinema,* Lehigh University Press, 1990.
Graham Greene: The Films of His Fiction, Teachers College Press, 1974.
Stanley Kubrick: A Film Odyssey, Popular Library, 1975, enlarged edition, 1977.

Evelyn Waugh's Officers, Gentlemen, and Rogues: The Fact behind His Fiction, Nelson-Hall, 1975.
Ken Russell, Twayne, 1979.
The Films of Tennessee Williams, Associated University Presses, 1980.
Hemingway and Film, Ungar, 1980.
John Schlesinger, Twayne, 1981.
George Cukor, Twayne, 1982.
Alfred Hitchcock, Twayne, 1984.
Fiction, Film and Faulkner, University of Tennessee Press, 1988.

Contributor to books, including *Graham Greene: A Collection of Critical Essays,* edited by Samuel Hynes, Prentice-Hall, 1973, *The International Dictionary of Films and Filmmakers,* edited by Christopher Lyon, St. James Press, 1984, and *A Motion Picture Feast: A Filmgoer's Hemingway,* edited by Charles Oliver, Praeger, 1989. Contributor to *Focus On Film, America, Literature/Film Quarterly, Sequences,* and other journals.

WORK IN PROGRESS: Conrad and Cinema.

SIDELIGHTS: Gene D. Phillips told *CA:* "Interviews both here and in England, with directors ranging from Cukor and Kubrick to Losey and Schlesinger, enabled me to write my first book, *The Movie Makers,* about the difficulty of an artist functioning in an industry. (I have since developed the chapters on Kubrick, Russell, Schlesinger, and Cukor into separate books.) Graham Greene's personal cooperation was most helpful in my doing the book on his fiction and films. The publication of Waugh's diaries, and interviews with his family, sparked the book *Evelyn Waugh's Officers, Gentlemen, and Rogues.*"

*   *   *

PIENKOWSKI, Jan (Michal) 1936-

PERSONAL: Born August 8, 1936, in Warsaw, Poland; immigrated to England, 1946; son of Jerzy Dominik and Wanda Maria (a chemist; maiden name, Garlicka) Pienkowski. *Education:* King's College, Cambridge, B.A. (with second class honors), 1957, M.A., 1961. *Religion:* Catholic. *Avocational interests:* Movies, gardening, painting.

ADDRESSES: Home—Oakgates, 45 Lonsdale Rd., Barnes SW13 9JR, England. *Office*—Gallery Five Ltd., 121 King St., London W6 9JG, England. *Agent*—Angela Holder, Gallery Five Ltd., 121 King St., London W6 9JG, England.

CAREER: J. Walter Thompson (advertising agency), London, England, art director, 1957-59; William Collins Sons & Co. (publisher), London, art director in publicity,

1959-60; *Time and Tide,* London, art editor, 1960-61; Gallery Five Ltd. (publisher), London, co-founder and art director, 1961-78, consultant art director, 1978—; Mc-Cann Erickson (advertising agency), London, television producer, 1962-63; author and illustrator of children's books, 1967—. Graphic illustrator for *Watch!,* BBC-TV, 1969-71. Designed sets for stage productions of the *Meg and Mow Show,* 1981-88, and *Beauty and the Beast,* 1986.

MEMBER: Society of Authors, Polish Hearth.

AWARDS, HONORS: Kate Greenaway Medal, British Library Association, 1971, for *The Golden Bird,* 1972, for *The Kingdom under the Sea and Other Stories,* and 1980, for *Haunted House;* Kurt Maschler Award (runnerup), Book Trust, 1984, for *Christmas: The King James Version.*

WRITINGS:

JUVENILE; SELF-ILLUSTRATED

Numbers, Heinemann, 1973, Harvey House, 1975.
Colours, Heinemann, 1973, published in America as *Colors,* Harvey House, 1975.
Shapes, Heinemann, 1973, Harvey House, 1975.
Sizes, Heinemann, 1973, Harvey House, 1975.
Homes, Heinemann, 1979, Messner, 1983.
Weather, Heinemann, 1979, Messner, 1983.
Haunted House, Dutton, 1979.
ABC, Heinemann, 1980, Simon & Schuster, 1981.
Time, Heinemann, 1980, Messner, 1983.
(With Anne Carter) *Dinner Time,* Gallery Five, 1980, published in America as *Dinnertime,* Price Stern, 1981.
(With Helen Nicoll) *The Quest for the Gloop,* Heinemann, 1980.
Robot, Delacorte, 1981.
Gossip, Price Stern, 1983.
(With H. Nicoll) *Owl at School,* Heinemann, 1984.
Christmas: The King James Version, Knopf, 1984.
Farm, Heinemann, 1985.
Zoo, Heinemann, 1985.
Little Monsters, Price Stern, 1986.
I'm Cat, Simon & Schuster, 1986.
I'm Frog, Simon & Schuster, 1986.
I'm Mouse, Simon & Schuster, 1986.
I'm Panda, Simon & Schuster, 1986.
Faces, Heinemann, 1986.
Food, Heinemann, 1986.
Small Talk, Orchard Books, 1987.
Easter: The King James Version, Random House, 1989.
Oh My! A Fly!, Price Stern Sloan, 1989.
Eggs for Tea, Doubleday, 1989.
Pet Food, Doubleday, 1990.

ILLUSTRATOR

Jessie Gertrude Townsend, *Annie, Bridget and Charlie: An ABC for Children of Rhymes,* Pantheon, 1967.
Joan Aiken, *A Necklace of Raindrops and Other Stories,* J. Cape, 1968, Doubleday, 1969, revised edition, 1972.
Nancy Langstaff and John Langstaff, compilers, *Jim Along, Josie: A Collection of Folk Songs and Singing Games for Young Children,* Harcourt, 1970, new edition published as *Sally Go round the Moon,* Revels, 1986.
Edith Brill, *The Golden Bird,* F. Watts, 1970.
J. Aiken, *The Kingdom under the Sea and Other Stories,* J. Cape, 1971, revised edition, Penguin, 1986.
Agnes Szudek, *The Amber Mountain and Other Folk Stories,* Hutchinson, 1976.
Dinah Starkey, *Ghosts and Bogles,* Hutchinson, 1976.
J. Aiken, *Tale of a One-Way Street and Other Stories,* J. Cape, 1978, Doubleday, 1980.
J. Aiken, *Past Eight O'Clock* (stories), J. Cape, 1986, Viking Kestrel, 1987.

ILLUSTRATOR; "MEG AND MOG" SERIES BY HELEN NICOLL

Meg and Mog, Heinemann, 1972, Atheneum, 1973, revised edition, Heinemann, 1977.
Meg's Eggs, Heinemann, 1972, Atheneum, 1973, revised edition, Heinemann, 1977.
Meg on the Moon, Heinemann, 1973, Penguin, 1978.
Meg at Sea, Heinemann, 1973, Penguin, 1978, revised edition, Heinemann, 1979.
Meg's Car, Heinemann, 1975, David & Charles, 1983.
Meg's Castle, Heinemann, 1975, David & Charles, 1983.
Mog's Mumps, Heinemann, 1976, David & Charles, 1983.
Meg's Veg, Heinemann, 1976, David & Charles, 1983.
Meg and Mog Birthday Book, Heinemann, 1979, David & Charles, 1984.
Mog at the Zoo, Heinemann, 1982, David & Charles, 1983.
Mog in the Fog, Heinemann, 1984.
Mog's Box, Heinemann, 1987.

EDITOR AND ILLUSTRATOR; "JAN PIENKOWSKI'S FAIRY TALE LIBRARY" SERIES

Jacob Grimm and Wilhelm Grimm, *Jack and the Beanstalk,* Heinemann, 1977.
J. Grimm and W. Grimm, *Snow White,* Heinemann, 1977.
J. Grimm and W. Grimm, *Sleeping Beauty,* Heinemann, 1977.
Charles Perrault, *Puss in Boots,* Heinemann, 1977.
C. Perrault, *Cinderella,* Heinemann, 1977.
J. Grimm and W. Grimm, *Hansel and Gretel,* Heinemann, 1977.

OTHER

Meg and Mog (play; first produced in London, England at the Unicorn Theatre, 1981), Samuel French, 1984.

Meg and Mog, Meg's Eggs, Meg at Sea, and *Meg on the Moon* have been recorded on audio cassette and released by Cover to Cover, 1985.

SIDELIGHTS: Jan Pienkowski is well-known to young readers for his colorful picture books. Often citing both his Central European background and comic book art as inspirations, Pienkowski specializes in illustrations that feature heavy lines and flat hues. He is also credited with revitalizing the pop-up book with titles such as *Haunted House* and *Dinnertime.* Despite his success, Pienkowski still sees room for improvement in his work. "Sometimes, I think I'm a total failure," he commented in *Books for Keeps.* "When you show what you've done, every single thing you've got is there. And if you've had a little success it gets worse because there's more at stake. . . . I am driven from within by an energy that makes me try harder."

Although he had no formal art training, Pienkowski began designing plays, posters, and greeting cards while attending Cambridge University. After graduation, he held a number of jobs in advertising and publishing. Eventually disillusioned by the business world, Pienkowski started a Christmas card company in 1958. Over time, Pienkowski's card designs became very fashionable. In an interview with Cathy Courtney for *Something about the Author (SATA),* Pienkowski noted: "My designs were right for the moment: I did very bright paper bags, paper clothes were all the rage, and stickers."

Pienkowski became heavily involved in book design when he met Helen Nicoll, a director of children's programming for the British Broadcasting Company (BBC). At Nicoll's request, Pienkowski created the opening and closing credits for the television show *Watch!.* When Nicoll left the BBC to raise a family, she and Pienkowski began the "Meg and Mog" book series. Meg (a witch) and Mog (Meg's pet cat) were based on two very popular characters that Pienkowski had originally drawn as part of the opening and closing credits for *Watch!.* "What appealed to me enormously . . . [in the] 'Meg and Mog' books is the idea that there is no essential difference between the drawing and the writing," Pienkowski told Courtney. "They both convey information and fight for supremacy. Sometimes the writing is important, sometimes the drawing."

Pienkowski produced his first pop-up books in 1979. One of the most popular of these works is *Haunted House,* in which the reader comes face to face with scary creatures and spooky scenes that shift and change. Because of their complex nature, the board books require a great deal of planning and effort. Pienkowski told Tony Bradman of *Publishing News* that "these mechanical books, although they may have my name in big, bold type or lettering on the cover, they're really a team effort, and they're the work of a . . . lot of people."

When not working on new titles, Pienkowski likes to visit schools. Rather than giving prepared speeches, however, he tries to encourage student participation through group art projects. "I like working with other people," Pienkowski related in his *SATA* interview. "I get much better ideas when I do. I don't think I'm as good on my own as when I'm part of a group." Ultimately, Pienkowski is interested in doing one thing for his young audience: entertaining them. He noted for Courtney: "I never discuss my books with children and I don't believe in market research. The most important thing is that it must entertain me, then it's got a chance of entertaining someone else."

BIOGRAPHICAL/CRITICAL SOURCES:

BOOKS

Fourth Book of Junior Authors and Illustrators, edited by Doris de Montreville and Elizabeth D. Crawford, Wilson, 1978, pp. 286-88.
Something about the Author, Volume 58, Gale, 1990.

PERIODICALS

Arts Review, January 29, 1988, p. 50.
Books for Keeps, November, 1981.
New York Times Book Review, November 11, 1984; March 19, 1989, p. 24.
Publishing News, October 16, 1981.
School Library Journal, September, 1983; September, 1987; October, 1987.

*   *   *

PIERARD, Richard Victor 1934-

PERSONAL: Born May 29, 1934, in Chicago, IL; son of Jack P. and Diana F. (Russell) Pierard; married Charlene Burdett, June 15, 1957; children: David Edward, Cynthia Kay. *Education:* Los Angeles State College of Applied Arts and Sciences (now California State University, Los Angeles), B.A., 1958, M.A., 1959; additional graduate study at University of Hamburg, 1962-63; University of Iowa, Ph.D., 1964. *Politics:* Democrat. *Religion:* Baptist.

ADDRESSES: Home—550 Gardendale Rd., Terre Haute, IN 47803. *Office*—Department of History, Indiana State University, Terre Haute, IN 47809.

CAREER: University of Iowa, Iowa City, instructor in history, 1964; Indiana State University, Terre Haute, assistant professor, 1964-67, associate professor, 1967-72, professor of history, 1972—. Visiting professor at Bibelschule Bergstrasse, 1971, Greenville College, 1972-73, Regent College, 1975, Trinity Evangelical Divinity School, 1982, Northern Baptist Theological Seminary, 1987, Fuller Theological Seminary, 1988, 1991, and De Pauw University, 1989. Research fellow, University of Aberdeen, 1978; Fulbright professor, University of Frankfurt, 1984-85, and University of Halle, 1989-90. Democratic Party precinct committeeman, 1978-80, 1990—; member of board of Evangelicals for Social Action, 1978-82; Indiana delegate to White House Conference on Libraries and Information Services, 1979. Member of national advisory committee, Americans United for Separation of Church and State, 1985-92. President, Greater Terre Haute Church Federation, 1987-88; member, Baptist Heritage Study Committee, Baptist World Alliance, 1990-95. *Military service:* U.S. Army, 1954-56; served in Japan.

MEMBER: International Association of Mission Studies, American Historical Association, Conference on Faith and History (secretary-treasurer, 1967—), Evangelical Theological Society (president, 1985), American Society of Church History, American Society of Missiology, Phi Alpha Theta.

AWARDS, HONORS: Fulbright scholar at University of Hamburg, 1962-63; Terre Award for Outstanding Community Service in Religion, 1991.

WRITINGS:

(With Robert G. Clouse and Robert D. Linder) *Protest and Politics: Christianity and Contemporary Affairs,* Attic Press, 1968.

The Unequal Yoke: Evangelical Christianity and Political Conservatism, Lippincott, 1970.

(With Clouse and Linder) *The Cross and the Flag,* Creation House, 1972.

(With Linder) *Politics: A Case for Christian Action,* Inter-Varsity Press, 1973.

(With Linder) *The Twilight of the Saints: Christianity and Civil Religion in Modern America,* Inter-Varsity Press, 1977.

(With Clouse) *Streams of Civilization,* Volume 2, Mott Media, 1980.

Bibliography on the New Christian Right, Department of History, Indiana State University, 1981.

Contributor to numerous books, including *The Lion Handbook of Christian History,* edited by T. Dowley, Lion Press, 1977, 2nd edition, 1990, *Fundamentalism Today,* edited M. J. Selvidge, Brethren Press, 1984, *Biblical Principles and Economics,* edited by R. Chewning, Navpress, 1989, and *Bearing Witness to the Holocaust,* edited by A. L. Berger, Edward Mellen Press, 1991.

Contributor to many reference books, including *Baker's Dictionary of Christian Ethics,* 1973, *The New International Dictionary of the Christian Church,* 1974, *Eerdmans Handbook to the History of Christianity, Brethren Encyclopedia,* 1983, *Baker Dictionary of Theology,* 1984, *Great Lives from History: Twentieth Century,* 1990, and *The American Conservative Press,* 1992. Contributor to periodicals, including *Eternity, Reformed Journal, Christian Century, Review of Religious Research, Covenant Quarterly, Contemporary Education, Christian History,* and *Journal of the Evangelical Theological Society.*

WORK IN PROGRESS: Writing on the German colonial society, the relationship between theological and political conservatism, social concern and Christianity, Christian missions, and the history of Christianity.

*   *   *

PINKWATER, Daniel Manus 1941-
(Manus Pinkwater)

PERSONAL: Born November 15, 1941, in Memphis, TN; son of Philip (a ragman) and Fay (a chorus girl; maiden name, Hoffman) Pinkwater; married Jill Miriam Schutz (a writer and illustrator), October 12, 1969. *Education:* B.A., 1964. *Politics:* "Taoist." *Religion:* "Republican." *Avocational interests:* "Various."

ADDRESSES: Home—111 Crum Elbow Rd., Hyde Park, NY 12538. *Agent*—Dorothy Markinko, McIntosh and Otis.

CAREER: Writer and illustrator of children's books. Art instructor at various settlement houses around New York City. *All Things Considered,* National Public Radio, regular commentator, 1987—. *Exhibitions:* Various small galleries and university shows.

MEMBER: American Federation of Theater and Radio Artists.

AWARDS, HONORS: New Jersey Institute of Technology award, 1975, for *Fat Elliot and the Gorilla;* American Library Association Notable Book award, 1976, for *Lizard Music;* Junior Literary Guild selection, 1977, for *Fat Men from Space;* New York Times Outstanding Book, 1978, for *The Last Guru;* Children's Choice book award from the International Reading Association and the Children's Book Council, 1981, for *The Wuggie Norple Story;* Parents' Choice award (literature), 1982, for *Roger's Umbrella.*

WRITINGS:

FOR CHILDREN

Alan Mendelsohn, the Boy from Mars, Dutton, 1979.

Yobgorgle: Mystery Monster of Lake Ontario, Clarion Books, 1979, revised edition, Bantam, 1981.

The Wuggie Norple Story, illustrated by Tomie de Paola, Four Winds, 1980.

The Worms of Kukumlima, Dutton, 1981.

Slaves of Spiegel: A Magic Moscow Story, Four Winds, 1982.

Young Adult Novel (also see below), Crowell, 1982.

Roger's Umbrella, illustrated by James Marshall, Dutton, 1982.

The Snarkout Boys and the Avocado of Death, Lothrop, 1982.

The Snarkout Boys and the Baconburg Horror, Lothrop, 1984.

Jolly Roger, a Dog of Hoboken, Lothrop, 1985.

Borgel, Macmillan, 1990.

Contributor to *Cricket.*

FOR CHILDREN; SELF-ILLUSTRATED

Wizard Crystal, Dodd, 1973.

Magic Camera, Dodd, 1974.

Lizard Music, Dodd, 1976.

The Blue Thing, Prentice-Hall, 1977.

The Big Orange Splot, Hastings House, 1977.

Fat Men from Space, (Junior Literary Guild selection), Dodd, 1977.

The Hoboken Chicken Emergency, Prentice-Hall, 1977.

The Last Guru, Dodd, 1978.

Return of the Moose, Dodd, 1979.

Pickle Creature, Four Winds, 1979.

The Magic Moscow, Four Winds, 1980.

Tooth-Gnasher Super Flash, Four Winds, 1981.

Attila the Pun: A Magic Moscow Book, Four Winds, 1981.

I Was a Second Grade Werewolf, Dutton, 1983.

Ducks!, Little, Brown, 1984.

Devil in the Drain, Dutton, 1984.

The Moosepire, Little, Brown, 1986.

The Muffin Fiend, Lothrop, 1986.

The Frankenbagel Monster, Dutton, 1986.

Aunt Lulu, Macmillan, 1988.

Guys from Space, Macmillan, 1989.

Uncle Melvin, Macmillan, 1989.

Doodle Flute, Macmillan, 1991.

FOR CHILDREN; UNDER NAME MANUS PINKWATER

The Terrible Roar, Knopf, 1970.

(And illustrator) *Bear's Picture,* Holt, 1972.

Fat Elliot and the Gorilla, Four Winds, 1974.

Three Big Hogs, Seabury, 1975.

(And illustrator) *Blue Moose,* Dodd, 1975.

(And illustrator) *Wingman,* Dodd, 1975.

FOR ADULTS

(With wife, Jill Pinkwater) *Superpuppy: How to Choose, Raise, and Train the Best Possible Dog for You,* illustrated by J. Pinkwater, Seabury, 1977.

Young Adults (three parts; first part based on *Young Adult Novel*), Tor, 1985.

Fish Whistle, Commentaries, Uncommentaries, and Vulgar Excesses, Addison-Wesley, 1990.

Chicago Days, Hoboken Nights, Addison-Wesley, 1991.

ADAPTATIONS:

Wingman (cassette), Listening Library, 1981.

Blue Moose (video cassette), Positive Images, 1982.

The Hoboken Chicken Emergency (television movie), Public Broadcasting System (PBS), 1984.

I Was a Second Grade Werewolf (cassette recording), Live Oak Media, 1986.

WORK IN PROGRESS: "Much."

SIDELIGHTS: Were a blue moose to come striding into Daniel Manus Pinkwater's living room one day and ask for a cup of coffee, Pinkwater should not be at all surprised, for that is exactly the kind of situation he has been describing in his years of writing books for children. From his home in upstate New York, Pinkwater writes and illustrates books about the lives of such characters as Aunt Lulu, the Muffin Fiend, and the Frankenbagel Monster. Though Pinkwater's characters are absurd, his intent in writing is not, and he says in an interview for *Something about the Author* (*SATA*): "I want my readers to feel encouraged and *snarky,* because basically they are kids taking on a hostile and/or indifferent world. My books are about finding favoring signs in the world, about discovering riches—things which are not dead. My stories are about people prevailing."

Pinkwater was born in Memphis, Tennessee in 1941, but grew up in Chicago. He remembers the kids in his neighborhood acting out the stories that they had read in adventure books like *20,000 Leagues under the Sea* and *Three Musketeers,* and he told *SATA:* "We heard about books by word of mouth—the kid next door had an older brother who told me about the *Three Musketeers.* I got to read good books, although mainly adventure stories, because there weren't as many books around at the time." Pinkwater was a self-described oddball as a child, much like the characters in his stories, but was lucky enough to find a group of boys who shared his interests, keeping him from feeling alienated.

During his time at Bard College in Annandale-on-Hudson, New York, Pinkwater decided to become a sculptor in order to become a good writer. By the time he finished college and a three-year apprenticeship with a sculptor, however, he had changed his mind. "I don't want to be a writer," he remembered thinking in *SATA*. "Writer's lives are disgusting, and writing is a horrible unhealthy activity. You get coffee nerves and a bad back, and eye strain. You smoke, and you sit . . . it's terrible." When four years later he returned to writing, he realized he was a better writer for his sculpting experience. Pinkwater advises anyone who wants to write to first learn to do something other than writing.

Pinkwater told *SATA* that he "didn't decide to start doing children's books, [he] floated into it." He had produced a set of illustrations for the book that was to become *The Terrible Roar,* and didn't want to deal with someone else writing the text for the book. So he wrote it himself. Though his first few books were "just a giggle" for him, he soon found them more and more interesting and soon committed himself to writing full-time. "I thought after two or three books I would have saturated my audience, whom I imagined as fat, bespectacled, intellectual boys," he commented to *SATA*. "I often receive photographs from my readers, including good-looking blonde-haired kids, who are captains of their soccer teams. It's not just the sweaty, spotty, stinky, pimply kids who do college physics in middle school who read my work, although, of course those are my favorites."

Pinkwater enjoys writing for children because he thinks they are more honest and more receptive to art than adults. "They are very matter of fact," he explained in *SATA*. "They like something, or they don't, they can use something or they can't. Adults feel an obligation to consider what reflection their artistic preferences will make upon them as people of cultural breeding and intelligence."

Pinkwater's books have been classified as fantasy and science fiction, but Janice Alberghene argues in *Twentieth-Century Children's Writers* that he "is less interested in the creation of a separate secondary world or alternate universe (as in *Alan Mendelsohn: The Boy from Mars,* or *The Worms of Kukumlima*) than he is in the eruption of the fantastic into everyday reality." Pinkwater often introduces extraordinary events into rather ordinary situations, which has the effect of making the ordinary situations stand out. In *Blue Moose,* the title character walks into a restaurant and is hired as a waiter, and later the kitchen floor turns into a spring meadow. In *The Moosepire,* a railroad boxcar operates as a time machine. Both books bring the mundane to life, showing that imagination can make any situation an exciting adventure.

Pinkwater's books are an adventure at least in part because they seem to go off in so many directions at once. Alberghene finds it "par for the course to find James Dean, *The Sorrows of Young Werewolf,* and a giant avocado capable of being modified into a thought-wave producing 'Alligatron' all within the covers of the same book," as in *The Snarkout Boys and the Avocado of Death.* Pinkwater admitted to *SATA* that he actually looks for a book to get out of hand: "The work is like a skateboard that suddenly gets away from me, and the anticipation is that somehow, miraculously, I will finish with the skateboard." It is this sense of play and absurdity that makes children laugh out loud when they read his books.

Some critics, however, think that the absurdity is overdone. Peter Andrews writes in the *New York Times Book Review:* "[Pinkwater] seems to fancy himself as the master surrealist of children's literature, but he sometimes falls into the trap of thinking that if you are writing nonsense you don't have to be logical." John Cech, reviewing *Yobgorgle: Mystery Monster of Lake Ontario* for *Children's Book Review Service,* finds that the continual "weirdness" drains the patience of even the youngest readers, and suggests that the story is "without substance." Alberghene puts these comments in perspective by noting that children have different standards for judging books than adults, and they find Pinkwater's books quite delightful.

Pinkwater is very serious about his work, despite the very un-serious nature of his stories. "I think children's books are the most important thing you can do," Pinkwater told Joann Davis in *Publishers Weekly,* "because these are people who are learning about reading." He says that one of his goals as a writer is to celebrate dying cultural treasures such as beer gardens, used bookstores, old railroad cars, and other aspects of urban life. In addition, Pinkwater doesn't hesitate to mention the names of authors and artists in his works, hoping to encourage young readers to learn more about those people. Though teaching isn't the main focus of his books, Pinkwater says that "it *is* an intention of my books to present the sheer pleasure of the phenomena of civilized life."

Pinkwater told *SATA:* "I also believe it is impossible to make sense of life in this world except through art. That's always been so, but it's more true now than ever before. The only way we can deal with the proliferation of ideas and impetus is to make a story or a picture out of it. At present, there are things happening that I like, as well as things I don't like; by participating I'm able to put some weight on the side of the things I like."

BIOGRAPHICAL/CRITICAL SOURCES:

BOOKS

Children's Literature Review, Volume 4, Gale, 1982.
Landsberg, Michele, *Reading for the Love of It,* Prentice-Hall, 1987.

Marquardt, Dorothy A., and Martha E. Ward, *Authors of Books for Young People,* supplement to the 2nd edition, Scarecrow, 1975.

Something about the Author, Volume 46, Gale, 1987.

Something about the Author Autobiography Series, Volume 3, Gale, 1987.

Twentieth-Century Children's Writers, 3rd edition, St. James Press, 1989, pp. 781-782.

PERIODICALS

Booklist, April 1, 1974; June 1, 1979; April 1, 1982.

Children's Book Review Service, winter, 1980, pp. 68-69.

Christian Science Monitor, May 1, 1974; May 4, 1977.

Graphis 155, Volume 27, 1971-72.

Horn Book, April, 1977; August, 1977; April, 1983; September-October, 1984; May-June, 1986.

New York Times Book Review, April 29, 1979; February 24, 1980; April 25, 1982, p. 51.

People, December 21, 1981.

Publishers Weekly, June 9, 1975; July 18, 1977; August 1, 1977; September 12, 1977; February 27, 1978; October 17, 1980; April 3, 1981; May 7, 1982, pp. 53-54; June 27, 1986.

Science Books and Films, September, 1978.

Science Fiction and Fantasy Book Review, July-August, 1982.

Voice of Youth Advocates, June, 1982; August, 1982; August, 1984.

Washington Post Book World, November 5, 1972; June 10, 1984.

Wilson Library Bulletin, March, 1982.

—*Sketch by Tom Pendergast*

*   *   *

PINKWATER, Manus
    See PINKWATER, Daniel Manus

*   *   *

POLK, Cara Saylor 1945-

PERSONAL: Born August 31, 1945, in Danville, IL; daughter of Harold (a scientist) and Ellen Elizabeth (Forney) Saylor; married James R. Polk (a television network reporter), June 21, 1980; children: Abigail Elizabeth. *Education:* Smith College, B.A., 1965; graduate study at Villanova University, 1965-67. *Politics:* "Eclectic Conservative."

ADDRESSES: Home and office—2929 North Oxford St., Arlington, VA 22207. *Agent*—Robin Rue, Anita Diamant

Literary Agency, 310 Madison Ave., New York, NY 10017.

CAREER: William Morris Agency, New York City, actress and writer, 1967-70; *Iowa REC News,* Des Moines, editor, 1970-71; Muscular Dystrophy Association, New York City, head writer (including material for "Jerry Lewis Telethon"), 1971-76; Hahnemann Medical College and Hospital of Philadelphia, Philadelphia, PA, director of communications, 1976-78; free-lance writer, 1978—.

AWARDS, HONORS: Award from Yale University Drama Festival, 1965, for play "At the Time of Ever."

WRITINGS:

Mr. Charon's Petshop (play), Villanova Playhouse, 1968.
Her Mother's Daughter (novel), Crown, 1982.
Images (novel), St. Martin's, 1986.

Also author of play "At the Time of Ever."

WORK IN PROGRESS: A historical novel, tentatively entitled *No Room for Honor;* a guide for forming cooperative playschools, *United We Buzz;* an adult novel entitled *The Play-group.*

SIDELIGHTS: Cara Saylor Polk told *CA:* "In 1987, to our surprise and delight, our daughter Abigail was born. The 'couple of months off' turned into a few years as I became involved with developing a creative cooperative playschool. As I've designed games, plays, and themes for the 2 to 5 set, the old saw 'Teaching is Learning' came home. As I move towards letting teachers share this joy of learning and returning to story-telling for adults again, I hope my interstices to learn about the moons of Mars, the preferences of fruit bats and the mating calls of polar bears will add texture and humor to the works ahead."

*   *   *

POMERANTZ, Charlotte 1930-

PERSONAL: Born July 24, 1930, in Brooklyn, NY; daughter of Abraham L. (an attorney) and Phyllis (Cohen) Pomerantz; married Carl Marzani (a writer), November 12, 1966; children: Gabrielle Rose, David Avram. *Education:* Sarah Lawrence College, B.A., 1953.

ADDRESSES: Home and office—260 West 21st St., New York, NY 10011.

CAREER: Writer. Has worked as a salesperson, waitress, researcher, copy editor, and editor.

AWARDS, HONORS: Jane Addams Peace Association, Children's Book Award, 1974, for *The Princess and the Admiral,* and Honor Award, 1983, for *If I Had a Paka;* Outstanding Picture Book of the Year, *New York Times,*

1977, for *The Piggy in the Puddle;* one of 10 U.S. books chosen for the "International Year of the Child," IBBY, 1978, for *The Day They Parachuted Cats on Borneo;* selection as a "Notable Book," American Library Association, for *The Tamarindo Puppy and Other Poems;* Christopher Award, 1984, for *Posy;* one of Top Ten Picture Books of 1989, *Boston Globe,* selection for Booklist, American Library Association, 1989, and Parent's Choice Award, 1990, all for *The Chalk Doll;* selection as "A Children's Book of the Year," Library of Congress, 1991, for *How Many Trucks Can a Tow Truck Tow?.*

WRITINGS:

(Editor) *A Quarter-Century of Un-Americana, 1938-1963: A Tragicomical Memorabilia of HUAC, House Un-American Activities Committee,* foreword by H. H. Wilson, Marzani & Munsell, 1963.

JUVENILE FICTION

The Bear Who Couldn't Sleep, illustrated by Meg Wohlberg, Morrow, 1965.

The Moon Pony, illustrated by Loretta Trezzo, Young Scott Books, 1967.

Ask the Windy Sea, illustrated by Nancy Grossman and Anita Siegel, Young Scott Books, 1968.

Why You Look Like You Whereas I Tend to Look Like Me, illustrated by Rosemary Wells and Susan Jeffers, Young Scott Books, 1969.

The Day They Parachuted Cats on Borneo: A Drama of Ecology (play in rhyme), illustrated by Jose Aruego, Young Scott Books, 1971.

The Piggy in the Puddle, illustrated by James Marshall, Macmillan, 1974.

The Princess and the Admiral (adapted from a 13th-century Vietnamese folktale), illustrated by Tony Chen, Addison-Wesley, 1974.

The Ballad of the Long-Tailed Rat (rhyme), illustrated by Marian Parry, Macmillan, 1975.

Detective Poufy's First Case; or, The Missing Battery-Operated Pepper Grinder, illustrated by Marty Norman, Addison-Wesley, 1976.

The Mango Tooth (a Junior Literary Guild selection), illustrated by Marylin Hafner, Greenwillow, 1977.

The Downtown Fairy Godmother, illustrated by Susanna Natti, Addison-Wesley, 1978.

The Tamarindo Puppy and Other Poems (poems in English and Spanish), Greenwillow, 1979.

Noah and Namah's Ark, illustrated by Kelly Carson, Holt, 1980.

If I Had a Paka: Poems in Eleven Languages, illustrated by Nancy Tafuri, Greenwillow, 1982.

Buffy and Albert, illustrated by Yossi Abolafia, Greenwillow, 1983.

Posy (a Junior Literary Guild selection), illustrated by Catherine Stock, Greenwillow, 1983.

Whiff, Sniff, Nibble and Chew: The Gingerbread Boy Retold, illustrated by Monica Incisa, Greenwillow, 1984.

Where's the Bear?, illustrated by Byron Barton, Greenwillow, 1984.

The Half-Birthday Party (a Junior Literary Guild selection), illustrated by DyAnne Di Salvo-Ryan, Clarion, 1984.

All Asleep (lullabies), Greenwillow, 1984.

One Duck, Another Duck, Greenwillow, 1984.

How Many Trucks Can a Tow Truck Tow?, Random House, 1987.

Timothy Tall Feather, Greenwillow, 1987.

The Chalk Doll, illustrated by Frane Lessac, Harper/Collins, 1989.

Flap Your Wings and Try (rhyming verse), Greenwillow, 1989.

The Outside Dog, Harper/Collins, 1992.

You're Not My Friend, Dial Books for Young Readers, 1992.

Serena Katz, Macmillan, 1992.

JUVENILE PLAYS

(Co-author and lyricist) *Eureka!,* produced at Lincoln Center, New York City, 1979.

Rap, Snap: The Electric Gingerbreak Boy ("rap" play; adapted from *Whiff, Sniff, Nibble and Chew: The Gingerbread Boy Retold*), produced in Children's Dance Theater, 1984.

OTHER

Also contributor to anthologies, including *Sounds of a Distant Drum,* Holt, 1967; *Read-Aloud Rhymes for the Very Young,* edited by Jack Prelutsky, Knopf, 1986; and *To the Moon and Back,* compiled by Nancy Larrick, Delacorte, 1991. Contributor to periodicals, including *Ladybug, Humpty Dumpty, New York Times Book Review, Publishers Weekly,* and *Ms.*

Some of Pomerantz's work has been published in French, Japanese, and Afrikaans.

ADAPTATIONS: Several versions of *The Day They Parachuted Cats on Borneo* and *The Princess and the Admiral* have been produced as children's plays at public schools throughout the U.S.

SIDELIGHTS: Charlotte Pomerantz has achieved critical and popular success as the author of children's books. "Although I wrote children's books before I was married or had children," she told *CA,* "I found increasingly that the children provide rich raw material, with the emphasis on *raw.* Many years back my son, then four, was heard to mumble, 'Fee fi fo fum, I smell the blood of an English muffin.' That started me thinking about writing a detective story. It finally became *Detective Poufy's First Case,* published in 1976. *The Mango Tooth* would not have been written had my little girl not been at the age where the tooth fairy was making frequent visits. But the story is fiction."

BIOGRAPHICAL/CRITICAL SOURCES:

PERIODICALS

Chicago Tribune Book World, November 9, 1980; September 5, 1982.
Language Arts, March 15, 1974; February 2, 1976; February 1, 1977; September, 1977; November 1, 1978.
New York Times Book Review, August 15, 1971; May 5, 1984; June 18, 1989.
Saturday Review, May 10, 1969.

*   *   *

POWELL, Ivor 1910-

PERSONAL: Born April 22, 1910, in Crosskeys, Monmouth, Wales; son of James (a mine examiner) and Hephzibah (Terrell) Powell; married Margaret Betty Davies (an evangelist), July 8, 1940. *Education:* Attended South Wales Bible Training Institute. *Avocational interests:* Cinematography and video tape productions.

ADDRESSES: Home and office—612 Surf View Dr., Santa Barbara, CA 93109.

CAREER: Ordained minister of Baptist Union of Wales, 1934; Prince's Street Mission, Barry, Glamorganshire, Wales, pastor, 1936-44; went abroad to serve as official evangelist of Baptist churches in South Africa and Southern Rhodesia, 1948-51, Australia, 1951-54, New Zealand, 1955-56, Canada, 1957-60, and California, 1960—, with current headquarters in Santa Barbara; founder of the Ivor Powell Evangelistic Crusades, Inc., 1967. Producer of more than twenty travel films on mission work.

AWARDS, HONORS: D.D., Training College, Dunedin, FL, 1973.

WRITINGS:

We Saw It Happen, Marshall, Morgan & Scott, 1948.
Black Radiance, Marshall, Morgan & Scott, 1949.
Silent Challenge, Zondervan, 1950.
Bible Cameos, Marshall, Morgan & Scott, 1951.
Bible Pinnacles, Marshall, Morgan & Scott, 1952.
Bible Treasures, Marshall, Morgan & Scott, 1953.
Bible Windows, Marshall, Morgan & Scott, 1954.
Broad Horizons, Marshall, Morgan & Scott, 1955.
God's Little Ones, Marshall, Morgan & Scott, 1956.
This I Believe: The Essential Truths of Christianity, Marshall, Morgan & Scott, 1957.

Bible Highway, foreword by Thomas B. McDormand, Zondervan, 1959.
Don't Lose That Fish!, Zondervan, 1960.
John's Wonderful Gospel, Zondervan, 1962.
Luke's Thrilling Gospel, Zondervan, 1965.
The Rising of the Son, Ivor Powell Evangelistic Crusades, 1973.
Mark's Superb Gospel, Kregel, 1985.
What in the World Will Happen Next?, Kregel, 1985.
Bible Gems, Kregel, 1987.
The Amazing Acts, Kregel, 1987.
Bible Names of Christ, Kregel, 1988.
The Exciting Ephesians, Kregel, 1988.
The Life and Times of David, Kregel, 1990.
Bible Nuggets, Kregel, 1991.

WORK IN PROGRESS: Bible Promises; Bible Oases.

SIDELIGHTS: Ivor Powell told *CA:* "During my travels around the world, I met many young ministers who were experiencing great difficulty in preparing their sermons. Studying in a seminary had been delightful, but the weekly routine of preparing three sermons presented problems. They reminded me of the time when I was a young pastor. I could not find any books to help effectively with the task which became increasingly burdensome. I needed something to give me a start, and regretfully, my homiletics professor in college did not supply what I required. A famous surgeon in Glasgow, Scotland said to me one evening, 'Brother, I love to preach, but all through the week I go from one hospital to another trying to save lives. When Saturday night arrives, I am too tired to think. Why don't you write something to help people like me?' Dr. Manderson's request supplied the inspiration for my first devotional book—*Bible Cameos.* That volume was so well received, I continued my task, and at the present time, seventeen volumes of that type have been completed. I can appreciate the sentiments of Paul who loved to help young men such as Timothy and Titus."

*   *   *

PRELUTSKY, Jack 1940-

PERSONAL: Born September 8, 1940, in Brooklyn, NY; son of Charles (an electrician) and Dorothea (a housewife; maiden name, Weiss) Prelutsky; married wife, Carolynn, 1979. *Education:* Attended Hunter College (now of the City University of New York); has studied voice at several music schools. *Avocational interests:* Making plastic and metal sculptures, bicycling, inventing word games, collecting books and model frogs.

ADDRESSES: Home—Olympia, WA; and c/o Greenwillow Books, 1350 Avenue of the Americas, New York, NY 10019.

CAREER: Poet and singer; worked early in his career as a cab driver, busboy, actor, photographer, furniture mover, potter, sculptor, day laborer, waiter, carpenter, clerk, bookseller, and door-to-door salesman.

AWARDS, HONORS: Nightmares: Poems to Trouble Your Sleep was selected for the Children's Book Showcase of the Children's Book Council and was included in the American Institute of Graphic Arts Book Show, both 1977, and was named one of *School Library Journal*'s Best of the Best Books, 1979; Children's Choice, International Reading Association/Children's Book Council, 1978, for *The Mean Old Mean Hyena; The Headless Horseman Rides Tonight: More Poems to Trouble Your Sleep* was selected one of the *New York Times*'s Outstanding Books of the Year and one of the Best Illustrated Books of the Year, both 1980; *School Library Journal*'s Best Books selections, 1980, for *The Headless Horseman Rides Tonight,* 1981, for *The Wild Baby,* 1983, for *The Random House Book of Poetry for Children* and *The Wild Baby Goes to Sea,* and 1986, for *Read-Aloud Rhymes for the Very Young; Booklist* Children's Reviewers' Choice, 1980, for *The Headless Horseman Rides Tonight; The Random House Book of Poetry for Children* was a Child Study Association Children's Book of the Year and Library of Congress Book of the Year, 1983; Parents' Choice Award, Parents' Choice Foundation, and Garden State Children's Book Award, New Jersey Library Association, both 1986, both for *The New Kid on the Block;* Notable Children's Recording, American Library Association, 1987, for "The New Kid on the Block"; *Something Big Has Been Here* was an Association for Library Services to Children Notable Book and *Booklist* Editor's Choice, both 1990.

WRITINGS:

(Translator) Rudolf Neumann, *The Bad Bear,* illustrated by Eva Johanna Rubin, Macmillan, 1967.

(Translator) Heinrich Hoffman, *The Mountain Bounder,* Macmillan, 1967.

A Gopher in the Garden and Other Animal Poems (also see below), illustrated by Robert Leydenfrost, Macmillan, 1967.

(Translator) *No End of Nonsense: Humorous Verses,* illustrated by Wilfried Blecher, Macmillan, 1968.

Lazy Blackbird and Other Verses, illustrated by Janosch, Macmillan, 1969.

(Translator) *Three Saxon Nobles and Other Verses,* illustrated by Rubin, Macmillan, 1969.

(Translator) James Kruess, *The Proud Wooden Drummer,* illustrated by Rubin, Doubleday, 1969.

The Terrible Tiger, illustrated by Arnold Lobel, Macmillan, 1970.

Toucans Two and Other Poems (also see below), illustrated by Jose Aruego, Macmillan, 1970, published in England as *Zoo Doings and Other Poems,* Hamish Hamilton, 1971.

Circus!, illustrated by Lobel, Macmillan, 1974.

The Pack Rat's Day and Other Poems (also see below), illustrated by Margaret Bloy Graham, Macmillan, 1974.

Nightmares: Poems to Trouble Your Sleep, illustrated by Lobel, Greenwillow, 1976.

It's Halloween, illustrated by Marylin Hafner, Greenwillow, 1977.

The Snopp on the Sidewalk and Other Poems, illustrated by Byron Barton, Greenwillow, 1977.

The Mean Old Mean Hyena, illustrated by Lobel, Greenwillow, 1978.

The Queen of Eene, illustrated by Victoria Chess, Greenwillow, 1978.

Rolling Harvey Down the Hill, illustrated by Chess, Greenwillow, 1980.

The Headless Horseman Rides Tonight: More Poems to Trouble Your Sleep, illustrated by Lobel, Greenwillow, 1980.

Rainy, Rainy Saturday, illustrated by Hafner, Greenwillow, 1980.

(Adapter) Barbro Lindgren, *The Wild Baby,* illustrated by Eva Eriksson, Greenwillow, 1981.

It's Christmas, illustrated by Hafner, Greenwillow, 1981.

The Sheriff of Rottenshot: Poems by Jack Prelutsky, illustrated by Chess, Greenwillow, 1982.

Kermit's Garden of Verses, illustrated by Bruce McNally, Random House, 1982.

It's Thanksgiving, illustrated by Hafner, Greenwillow, 1982.

The Baby Uggs Are Hatching, illustrated by James Stevenson, Greenwillow, 1982.

Zoo Doings: Animal Poems (includes *A Gopher in the Garden and Other Animal Poems, Toucans Two and Other Poems,* and *The Pack Rat's Day and Other Poems*), illustrated by Paul O. Zelinsky, Greenwillow, 1983.

It's Valentine's Day, illustrated by Yossi Abolafia, Greenwillow, 1983.

(Adapter) Lindgren, *The Wild Baby Goes to Sea,* illustrated by Eriksson, Greenwillow, 1983.

(Compiler and editor) *The Random House Book of Poetry for Children,* illustrated by Lobel, Random House, 1983.

It's Snowing! It's Snowing!, illustrated by Jeanne Titherington, Greenwillow, 1984.

What I Did Last Summer, illustrated by Abolafia, Greenwillow, 1984.

The New Kid on the Block, illustrated by Stevenson, Greenwillow, 1984.

My Parents Think I'm Sleeping, illustrated by Abolafia, Greenwillow, 1985.

(Adapter) Lindgren, *The Wild Baby Gets a Puppy,* illustrated by Eriksson, Greenwillow, 1985.

Ride a Purple Pelican, illustrated by Garth Williams, Greenwillow, 1986.

(Adapter) Rose Lagercrantz and Samuel Lagercrantz, *Brave Little Pete of Geranium Street,* illustrated by Eriksson, Greenwillow, 1986.

(Compiler and editor) *Read-Aloud Rhymes for the Very Young,* illustrated by Marc Brown, Knopf, 1986.

Tyrannosaurus Was a Beast: Dinosaur Poems, illustrated by Lobel, Greenwillow, 1988.

(Collector and editor) *Poems of A. Nonny Mouse,* illustrated by Henrik Drescher, Knopf, 1989.

Beneath a Blue Umbrella, illustrated by Williams, Greenwillow, 1990.

Something Big Has Been Here, illustrated by Stevenson, Greenwillow, 1990.

(Compiler and editor) *For Laughing Out Loud,* illustrated by Marjorie Priceman, Knopf, 1991.

Twickham Tweer (from *The Sheriff of Rottenshot*), illustrated by Eldon Doty, DLM, 1991.

Archives of Prelutsky's work are kept in the University of Southern Mississippi's De Grummond Collection and the University of Minnesota's Kerlan Collection.

ADAPTATIONS: Nightmares: Poems to Trouble Your Sleep was made into a record and cassette, Children's Books and Music, 1985; cassettes were also recorded for the following: *It's Thanksgiving,* Listening Library, 1985; *The New Kid on the Block,* Listening Library, 1986; *It's Halloween,* Scholastic, 1987; *It's Christmas,* Scholastic, 1987; *Ride a Purple Pelican,* Listening Library, 1988; *Read-Aloud Rhymes for the Very Young,* Knopf, 1988; *It's Valentine's Day,* Scholastic, 1988; and *Something Big Has Been Here,* Listening Library, 1991. An audio recording has also been produced for *Rainy, Rainy Saturday* (cassette), Random House. Prelutsky's poems have been included in *Graveyard Tales* (record), NAPPS; and *People, Animals and Other Monsters* (record; cassette; includes poems from *The Snopp on the Sidewalk, The Queen of Eene, Rolling Harvey Down the Hill, The Pack-Rat's Day, A Gopher in the Garden,* and *Toucans Two and Other Poems*), Caedmon.

SIDELIGHTS: When Jack Prelutsky was a child the word "poetry" meant to him something dull and irrelevant that teachers forced on their students. So when he decided to become a poet himself, Prelutsky resolved to engage his audience's minds with light, whimsical verses that would stimulate the imaginations of young people. "I realized that poetry was a means of communication, that it could be as exciting or as boring as that person or that experience," Prelutsky tells Raymond Allen in *Early Years.* "Prelutsky's poetry features animals and fantastic beasts which behave in inventive ways," writes *Dictionary of Lit-* *erary Biography* contributor Anita Trout. "He also writes of people and problems familiar to youngsters: dealing with the neighborhood bully, going to school, and being afraid of the dark. Writing in traditional poetic forms, he employs puns, alliteration, and word play in ways which have caused him to be ranked among the masters of contemporary verse for children."

Before he became a poet, Prelutsky was a budding opera singer who gave up his career when he became convinced that he could never compete with the likes of Luciano Pavarotti. He tried various odd jobs after that, including singing folk songs in a Greenwich Village coffeehouse, where he met and became friends with singer Bob Dylan. This musical background is made readily apparent in his verses, which lend themselves well to being sung or read aloud; and Prelutsky has done just that, visiting schools around the country each year to entertain children with his guitar and original compositions.

In addition to Prelutsky's fascination with beasts of all kinds, real and imaginary, his verses often reveal an obsession with food and eating. When these characteristics come together in such collections as *The Terrible Tiger, The Snopp on the Sidewalk and Other Poems, The Baby Uggs Are Hatching,* and *Tyrannosaurus Was a Beast: Dinosaur Poems,* the result is a comical look at fanciful, gluttonous creatures that offers children a unique perspective on their own world. Some of Prelutsky's creations include Baby Uggs, frightful creatures that begin to eat everything—including their mothers—the moment they hatch; a duck-like beast who gobbles up a teacher; a monstrous meath who does its best to satisfy its predatory instincts, but lacks teeth; and Prelutsky's terrible tiger, who receives his due when he slurps down a tailor, scissors and all. In a *New York Times Book Review* article on *Tyrannosaurus Was a Beast,* Myra Cohn Livingston comments that Prelutsky's poems let "children know that this is a dog-eat-dog world in which adults are either ineffective or absent and encourage them to laugh, to meet such a world with hilarity and happy rhymes."

The poet has also written books that recognize a childhood delight in hearing ghost stories that make one afraid of turning the lights off at night. Prelutsky's award-winning collections *Nightmares: Poems to Trouble Your Sleep* and *The Headless Horseman Rides Tonight: More Poems to Trouble Your Sleep* illustrate the author's relish for macabre tales of ghouls and vampires. However, Prelutsky's use of language mitigates the wickedness of his subject matter, just as his other creatures are made less threatening by their very ridiculousness. For example, in "The Ghoul," a poem included in *Nightmares,* the author writes: "Fingers, elbows, hands and knees/And arms and legs and feet—/He eats them with delight and ease,/For every part's a treat."

With collections such as *The Sheriff of Rottenshot, Ride a Purple Pelican,* and *Beneath a Blue Umbrella,* Prelutsky mostly steers clear of monsters while maintaining his love for nonsense rhymes and surprises (one character in *The Sheriff of Rottenshot* literally sneezes his head off). Even when Prelutsky describes situations more familiar to his readers he often ventures into the incredible; or, as one *Kirkus Reviews* critic put it, the poet often "slips into nonsense without your hardly knowing it." *Rolling Harvey Down the Hill,* for example, concerns five friends and the various misadventures they have. Many of their experiences could happen to almost any group of children, except for the unusual prank at the end of the book when Harvey's friends take revenge against him because he pulled down their pants.

In some cases, Prelutsky's choice of subjects has raised concern among critics like *School Library Journal* contributor Marjorie Lewis. Reviewing *Rolling Harvey Down the Hill,* Lewis avers that Prelutsky at times "treads a thin, uneasy line between funny and not-so-funny." Nevertheless, many reviewers have praised the poet's work, and he has remained popular with young audiences. Prelutsky's books consistently win awards, and *Ride a Purple Pelican,* as one *Washington Post Book World* writer notes, "achieved instant-classic status" upon publication. What makes Prelutsky's humorous nonsense poetry so valuable to children, concludes Doris Orgel in her *New York Times Book Review* article on *The Baby Uggs Are Hatching,* is that it is "a powerful antidote to the stuffy, predictable poetry that still gets force-fed to them."

BIOGRAPHICAL/CRITICAL SOURCES:

BOOKS

Children's Literature Review, Volume 13, Gale, 1987.

Cullinan, Bernice E., Mary K. Karrer, and Arlene M. Pillar, *Literature and the Child,* Harcourt, 1981.

Dictionary of Literary Biography, Volume 61: *American Writers for Children since 1960: Poets, Illustrators, and Nonfiction Authors,* Gale, 1987.

Kirkpatrick, D. L., editor, *Twentieth-Century Children's Writers,* 2nd edition, St. Martin's, 1983.

Norton, Donna E., *Through the Eyes of a Child: An Introduction to Children's Literature,* Merrill, 1983.

Prelutsky, Jack, *Nightmares: Poems to Trouble Your Sleep,* illustrated by Arnold Lobel, Greenwillow, 1976.

Shaw, John Mackay, *Childhood in Poetry,* Gale, 1967.

PERIODICALS

Chicago Tribune Book World, October 10, 1982; March 13, 1983.

Children's Literature in Education, Volume 11, number 3, 1980.

Globe and Mail (Toronto), December 13, 1986.

Kirkus Reviews, September 1, 1984.

Los Angeles Times Book Review, August 24, 1980; September 5, 1982; August 5, 1984; January 28, 1990.

New York Times Book Review, April 23, 1978; November 9, 1980; April 25, 1982; November 21, 1982; November 13, 1983; March 26, 1989; November 12, 1989.

Publishers Weekly, July 29, 1988.

School Library Journal, April, 1980.

Times Literary Supplement, February 8, 1985.

Tribune Books (Chicago), November 16, 1986; March 1, 1987.

Washington Post Book World, January 12, 1986; November 6, 1988; February 11, 1990.*

—*Sketch by Kevin S. Hile*

*   *   *

PRICE, Kenneth M(arsden) 1954-

PERSONAL: Born April 22, 1954, in Pomona, CA; son of Marsden (a teacher) and Barbara (Hill) Price; married Renee Hall, August 1, 1981; children: Ashley Marlene, Gillian Barbara. *Education:* Whitman College, B.A. (magna cum laude), 1976; University of Chicago, M.A., 1977, Ph.D., 1981.

ADDRESSES: Home—1107 Edgewood, Bryan, TX 77802. *Office*—Department of English, Texas A&M University, College Station, TX 77843.

CAREER: Texas A&M University, College Station, visiting assistant professor, 1981-82, assistant professor, 1982-87, associate professor of English, 1987—.

MEMBER: Modern Language Association of America, South Central Modern Language Association.

WRITINGS:

(Editor with Dennis Berthold) *Dear Brother Walt: The Letters of Thomas Jefferson Whitman,* Kent State University Press, 1984.

Whitman and Tradition: The Poet in His Century, Yale University Press, 1990.

(Editor with Robert C. Leitz III) *Critical Essays on George Santayana,* G. K. Hall, 1991.

Consulting editor, *The Complete Writings of George Santayana,* twenty volumes, MIT Press, 1990—. Contributor of articles and reviews to literature and library journals. Editor, *South Central Review,* 1988-92.

WORK IN PROGRESS: The Genteel Tradition and International Modernism.

PRIDHAM, Geoffrey 1942-

PERSONAL: Born January 29, 1942, in Guildford, England; son of C.E. and Marian S. Pridham; married Pippa Mason (an education writer), June 15, 1974 (divorced, 1982). *Education:* Trinity Hall, Cambridge, B.A., 1964, M.A., 1968; London School of Slavonic and East European Studies, London, Ph.D., 1969. *Avocational interests:* Travel, reading political thrillers, rambling, music.

ADDRESSES: Office—Department of Politics, University of Bristol, Bristol, England.

CAREER: Foreign Office, London, England, research assistant, 1964-67; Institute of Contemporary History, London, research assistant, 1967-69; University of Bristol, Bristol, England, reader in European politics, 1969-, director, Centre for Mediterranean Studies (CMS), 1987—. Member of Conference Group on Italian Politics and European Consortium for Political Research.

MEMBER: Political Studies Association, Association for the Study of German Politics, University Association for Contemporary European Studies, Association for the Study of Modern Italy, Societa Italiana di Studi Elettorali.

WRITINGS:

Hitler's Rise to Power: The Nazi Movement in Bavaria, 1923-33, Harper, 1973.

(Editor with Jeremy Noakes) *Documents on Nazism, 1919-45,* Viking, 1974.

Christian Democracy in Western Germany: The CDU/ CSU in Government and Opposition, 1945-76, Croom Helm, 1977.

(With Pippa Pridham) *Transnational Party Cooperation and European Integration: The Process towards Direct Elections,* Allen & Unwin, 1981.

The Nature of the Italian Party System: A Regional Case-Study, Croom Helm, 1981.

(With Noakes) *Nazism, 1919-45: A Documentary Reader,* Exeter University Press, Volume I, 1983, Volume II, 1984.

(Editor) *The New Mediterranean Democracies: Regime Transition in Spain, Greece and Portugal,* Frank Cass, 1984.

(Editor) *Conditional Behaviour in Theory and Practice: An Inductive Model for Western Europe,* Cambridge University Press, 1986.

Political Parties and Coalitional Behavior in Italy, Routledge & Kegan Paul, 1988.

(Editor) *Securing Democracy: Political Parties and Regime Consolidation in Southern Europe,* Routledge & Kegan Paul, 1990.

(Editor with F. Mueller-Roumel) *Small Parties in Western Europe: Comparative and National Perspectives,* Sage Publications, 1991.

(Editor) *Encouraging Democracy: The International Center of Regime Transition in Southern Europe,* Leicester University Press, 1991.

WORK IN PROGRESS: Comparative book on democratic transition and consolidation in Southern Europe and Eastern Europe; environmental problems and policies in Southern Europe in the EC context.

*   *   *

PRPIC, George J(ure) 1920-

PERSONAL: Surname is pronounced Per-pich; born November 16, 1920, in Djala, Banat, Yugoslavia; son of Tomislav and Isabella (Toldy) Prpic; married Hilda Hermann, January 20, 1951; children: Francis Thomas, Mary Teresa. *Education:* Real Gymnasium, Pozega, Croatia, Baccalaureate, 1939; Croatian University, Zagreb, Diploma in Jurisprudence (M.A. equivalent), 1944; University of Graz, further study, 1945-49; John Carroll University, M.A., 1956; Georgetown University, Ph.D., 1959. *Religion:* Roman Catholic. *Avocational interests:* Painting and drawing.

ADDRESSES: Home—2615 Charney, University Heights, OH 44118. *Office*—Department of History, John Carroll University, University Heights, OH 44118.

CAREER: John Carroll University, University Heights, OH, instructor, 1958-60, assistant professor, 1960-65, associate professor, 1965-70, professor of history, 1970—.

MEMBER: American Historical Association, American Association for the Advancement of Slavic Studies, American Association for Southeast European Studies, Croatian Academy of America, Donau Institut (Vienna), Institutum Chroatorum Historicum (Rome), American Croatian Academic Society, Phi Alpha Theta.

AWARDS, HONORS: Faculty fellowship award, John Carroll University, 1968-69.

WRITINGS:

Maksimilijan Vanka, La Revista Croata (Buenos Aires), 1958.

French Rule in Croatia: 1806-1813, Institute for Balkan Studies (Salonika), 1964.

Eastern Europe and World Communism, Institute for Soviet and East European Studies, John Carroll University, 1966.

Fifty Years of World Communism, 1917-1967, Institute for Soviet and East European Studies, John Carroll University, 1967.

(Contributor) Joseph P. O'Grady, editor, *The Immigrants' Influence on Wilson's Peace Policies,* University of Kentucky, 1967.

The Croatian Publications Abroad after 1939: A Bibliography, Institute for Soviet and East European Studies, John Carroll University, 1969.

The Croatian Immigrants in America, Philosophical Library, 1970.

A Century of World Communism, Barron's, 1970, revised edition, 1974.

(Contributor) F. H. Eterovich and Christopher Spalatin, editors, *Croatia: Land, People, Culture,* Volume II, University of Toronto Press, 1970.

Posljednji Svibanj (title means "The Last May"; self-illustrated poetry in Croatian), Izdanja Ranjeni Labud (Rome), 1973, revised and enlarged edition, Skolske Novine, 1990.

(With wife, Hilda Prpic) *Croatian Books and Booklets Printed in Exile,* Institute for Soviet and East European Studies, John Carroll University, 1973, new edition, Skolske Novine, 1990.

(With Karl Bonutti) *Selected Ethnic Communication of Cleveland,* Cleveland Urban Observatory, 1974.

The Croatians in Greater Cleveland, Ethnic Heritage Studies Development Program, Cleveland State University, 1976.

South Slavic Immigration in America, Twayne, 1978.

Croatia and the Croatians: An Annotated Bibliography, Associated Book, 1982.

Baklja u Luci—The Torch in the Harbor (poems, notes, drawings), Associated Book, 1989.

WORK IN PROGRESS: Translating the poetry of Walt Whitman into Croatian; *The Immigrants and the American Revolution; The Saga of Joe Magarac.*

*   *   *

PRUCHA, Francis Paul 1921-

PERSONAL: Born January 4, 1921, in River Falls, WI; son of Edward J. (a teacher) and Katharine (Schladweiler) Prucha. *Education:* River Falls State Teachers College (now University of Wisconsin—River Falls), B.S., 1941; University of Minnesota, M.A., 1947; Harvard University, Ph.D., 1950; graduate study, St. Louis University, 1952-54, and St. Mary's College, 1954-58. *Politics:* Democrat.

ADDRESSES: Home—1404 West Wisconsin Ave., Milwaukee, WI 53233. *Office*—Department of History, Marquette University, Milwaukee, WI 53233.

CAREER: Entered Jesuit Order, 1950, ordained Roman Catholic priest, 1957; Marquette University, Milwaukee, WI, 1960—, professor of American history, 1966—, chairman of department of history, 1962-69. *Military service:* U.S. Army Air Forces, 1942-46; became first lieutenant.

MEMBER: American Historical Association, Organization of American Historians (member of executive board, 1980-83), Western History Association (member of council, 1975-78, 1982-85; president, 1983).

AWARDS, HONORS: Faculty research grant, Social Science Research Council, 1959-60; Guggenheim fellow, 1967; National Endowment for the Humanities senior fellow, 1970, 1981; Western History Association prize, 1987.

WRITINGS:

Broadax and Bayonet: The Role of the United States Army in the Development of the Northwest, 1815-1860, State Historical Society of Wisconsin, 1953.

(Editor) G. Croghan, *Army Life on the Western Frontier,* University of Oklahoma Press, 1958.

(Translator and editor with G. Ellard) *Simple Rite of the Restored Order of Holy Week,* Bruce Publishing, 1958.

American Indian Policy in the Formative Years, Harvard University Press, 1962.

A Guide to the Military Posts of the United States, 1789-1895, State Historical Society of Wisconsin, 1964.

The Sword of the Republic, Macmillan, 1968.

Indian Peace Medals in American History, State Historical Society of Wisconsin, 1971.

(Editor) *The Indian in American History,* Holt, 1971.

(Editor) *The Dawes Act and the Allotment of Indian Lands,* University of Oklahoma Press, 1973.

(Editor) *Americanizing the American Indians: Writings by the "Friends of the Indian," 1880-1900,* Harvard University Press, 1973.

(Editor) *Documents of United States Indian Policy,* University of Nebraska Press, 1975, 2nd edition, 1990.

American Indian Policy in Crisis: Christian Reformers and the Indian, 1865-1900, University of Oklahoma Press, 1976.

A Bibliographical Guide to the History of Indian-White Relations in the United States, University of Chicago Press, 1977.

United States Indian Policy: A Critical Bibliography, Indiana University Press, 1977.

The Churches and the Indian Schools, 1888-1912, University of Nebraska Press, 1979.

(Editor) Jeremiah Evarts, *Cherokee Removal: The "William Penn" Essays and Other Writings,* University of Tennessee Press, 1981.

Indian Policy in the United States: Historical Essays, University of Nebraska Press, 1981.

Indian-White Relations in the United States: A Bibliography of Works Published 1975-1980, University of Nebraska Press, 1982.

The Great Father: The United States Government and the American Indians, two volumes, University of Nebraska Press, 1984, abridged edition, 1986.

The Indians in American Society: From the Revolutionary War to the Present, University of California Press, 1985.

Handbook for Research in American History: A Guide to Bibliographies and Other Reference Works, University of Nebraska Press, 1987.

Atlas of American Indian Affairs, University of Nebraska Press, 1990.

Contributor to professional publications.

SIDELIGHTS: Francis Paul Prucha told *CA:* "I continue to be fascinated by the history of the American Indians in the United States. Now that there is considerable new agitation for Indian rights, I insist on the value of careful historical studies for understanding the present situation. Good public policy cannot be built on bad history."

BIOGRAPHICAL/CRITICAL SOURCES:

PERIODICALS

Los Angeles Times Book Review, February 1, 1987, p. 10.
New York Times Book Review, April 20, 1986, p. 23.
Washington Post Book World, January 25, 1987, p. 13.

Q

QUACKENBUSH, Robert M(ead) 1929-

PERSONAL: Born July 23, 1929, in Hollywood, CA; son of Roy Maynard (an engineer) and Virginia (Arbogast) Quackenbush; married Margery Clouser, July 3, 1971; children: Piet Robert. *Education:* Art Center College of Design, B.A., 1956; Center for Modern Psychoanalytic Studies, graduate, 1991.

ADDRESSES: Home—460 East 79th St., New York, NY 10021. *Office*—223 East 78th St., New York, NY 10021.

CAREER: Scandinavian Airlines System, advertising art director in the United States and Stockholm, Sweden, 1956-61; free-lance illustrator, painter, and writer, 1961—; Robert Quackenbush Gallery, New York, NY, owner and teacher of art classes, 1968—; certified psychoanalyst, 1991—. *Military service:* U.S. Army, 1951-53.

MEMBER: Authors Guild, Authors League of America, Mystery Writers Club of America, Society of Children's Book Writers, Holland Society, National Association for the Advancement of Psychoanalysis, Society for Modern Psychoanalysis.

AWARDS, HONORS: American Institute of Graphic Arts Fifty Best Books award, 1963, for *Poems for Galloping;* Society of Illustrators citations, 1965, for *The Selfish Giant,* 1967, for *If I Drove a Truck,* 1969, for *Little Hans, the Devoted Friend* and *The Pilot,* and 1985, for *The Scarlet Letter;* Golden Kite honor book, 1973, for *Red Rock over the River;* American Flag Institute Award for outstanding contribution in the field of children's literature, 1976, 1977, and 1984; Edgar Allan Poe Special Award, 1981, for *Detective Mole and the Halloween Mystery.*

WRITINGS:

SELF-ILLUSTRATED CHILDREN'S BOOKS

Old MacDonald Had a Farm, Lippincott, 1972.

Go Tell Aunt Rhody, Lippincott, 1973.
She'll Be Comin' 'Round the Mountain, Lippincott, 1973.
Clementine, Lippincott, 1975.
There'll Be a Hot Time in the Old Town Tonight: The Great Chicago Fire of 1871 Told with Song and Pictures, Lippincott, 1974.
The Man on the Flying Trapeze, Lippincott, 1975.
Too Many Lollipops, Parents' Magazine Press, 1975.
Animal Cracks, Lothrop, 1975.
Skip to My Lou, Lippincott, 1975.
Pop! Goes the Weasel and Yankee Doodle, Lippincott, 1976.
Pete Pack Rat, Lothrop, 1976.
Take Me Out to the Airfield!: How the Wright Brothers Invented the Airplane, Parents' Magazine Press, 1976, new edition, Houghton, 1991.
Sheriff Sally Gopher and the Haunted Dance Hall, Lothrop, 1977.
The Holiday Song Book, Lothrop, 1977.
Pete Pack Rat and the Gila Monster Gang, Lothrop, 1978.
Mr. Snow Bunting's Secret (Junior Literary Guild selection), Lothrop, 1978.
Calling Doctor Quack, Lothrop, 1978.
Along Came the Model T!: How Henry Ford Put the World on Wheels, Parents' Magazine Press, 1978.
The Most Welcome Visitor, Windmill, 1978.
The Boy Who Dreamed of Rockets: How Robert Goddard Became the Father of Space Travel, Parents' Magazine Press, 1979.
Who Threw That Pie?: The Birth of Movie Comedy, A. Whitman, 1979.
Moose's Store, Lothrop, 1979.
Movie Monsters and Their Masters, A. Whitman, 1980.
Henry's Awful Mistake, Parents' Magazine Press, 1980.
Pete Pack Rat and the Christmas Eve Surprise, Lothrop, 1981.
Henry's Important Date, Parents' Magazine Press, 1981.

The Boy Who Waited for Santa Claus, F. Watts, 1981.

No Mouse for Me, F. Watts, 1981.

City Trucks, A. Whitman, 1981.

Sheriff Sally Gopher and the Thanksgiving Caper, Lothrop, 1982.

Henry Goes West, Parents' Magazine Press, 1982.

First Grade Jitters, Lippincott, 1982.

I Don't Want to Go, I Don't Know How to Act, Lippincott, 1983.

Henry Babysits, Parents' Magazine Press, 1983.

Investigator Ketchem's Crime Book, Avon, 1984.

Funny Bunnies, Clarion, 1984.

Chuck Lends a Paw, Clarion, 1986.

Too Many Ducklings, Western Publishing, 1987.

Mouse Feathers, Clarion, 1988.

Funny Bunnies on the Run, Clarion, 1989.

Robert Quackenbush's Treasury of Humor, Doubleday, 1990.

Benjamin Franklin and His Friends, Pippin Press, 1991.

Henry's World Tour, Doubleday, 1992.

SELF-ILLUSTRATED CHILDREN'S BOOKS; "DETECTIVE MOLE" SERIES

Detective Mole, Lothrop, 1976.

Detective Mole and the Secret Clues, Lothrop, 1977.

Detective Mole and the Tip-Top Mystery, Lothrop, 1978.

Detective Mole and the Seashore Mystery, Lothrop, 1979.

Detective Mole and the Circus Mystery, Lothrop, 1980.

Detective Mole and the Halloween Mystery, Lothrop, 1981.

Detective Mole and the Haunted Castle Mystery, Lothrop, 1985.

SELF-ILLUSTRATED CHILDREN'S BOOKS; "PIET POTTER" SERIES

Piet Potter's First Case, McGraw, 1980.

Piet Potter Returns, McGraw, 1980.

Piet Potter Strikes Again, McGraw, 1981.

Piet Potter to the Rescue, McGraw, 1981.

Piet Potter on the Run, McGraw, 1982.

Piet Potter's Hot Clue, McGraw, 1982.

SELF-ILLUSTRATED CHILDREN'S BOOKS; "MISS MALLARD MYSTERY" SERIES

Express Train to Trouble, Prentice-Hall, 1981.

Cable Car to Catastrophe, Prentice-Hall, 1982.

Dig to Disaster, Prentice-Hall, 1982.

Gondola to Danger, Prentice-Hall, 1983.

Stairway to Doom, Prentice-Hall, 1983.

Rickshaw to Horror, Prentice-Hall, 1984.

Taxi to Intrigue, Prentice-Hall, 1984.

Stage Door to Terror, Prentice-Hall, 1985.

Bicycle to Treachery, Prentice-Hall, 1985.

Surfboard to Peril, Prentice-Hall, 1986.

Texas Trail to Calamity, Prentice-Hall, 1986.

Dog Sled to Dread, Prentice-Hall, 1987.

Danger in Tibet, Pippin Press, 1989.

Lost in the Amazon, Pippin Press, 1990.

Evil Under the Sea, Pippin Press, 1992.

SELF-ILLUSTRATED CHILDREN'S BOOKS; "SHERLOCK CHICK" SERIES

Sherlock Chick's First Case, Parents' Magazine Press, 1986.

Sherlock Chick and the Peekaboo Mystery, Parents' Magazine Press, 1987.

Sherlock Chick and the Giant Egg Mystery, Parents' Magazine Press, 1988.

Sherlock Chick and the Noisy Shed Mystery, Parents' Magazine Press, 1990.

SELF-ILLUSTRATED HUMOROUS BIOGRAPHIES FOR CHILDREN

Oh, What an Awful Mess!: A Story of Charles Goodyear, Prentice-Hall, 1980.

What Has Wild Tom Done Now?!!!, Prentice-Hall, 1981.

Ahoy! Ahoy! Are You There?: A Story of Alexander Graham Bell, Prentice-Hall, 1981.

Here a Plant, There a Plant, Everywhere a Plant, Plant!: A Story of Luther Burbank, Prentice-Hall, 1982.

What Got You Started, Mr. Fulton?: A Story of James Watt and Robert Fulton, Prentice-Hall, 1982.

The Beagle and Mr. Flycatcher: A Story of Charles Darwin, Prentice-Hall, 1983.

Quick, Annie, Give Me a Catchy Line!: A Story of Samuel F. B. Morse, Prentice-Hall, 1983.

Mark Twain? What Kind of Name Is That?: A Story of Samuel Clemens, Prentice-Hall, 1984.

Don't You Dare Shoot That Bear!: A Story of Theodore Roosevelt, Prentice-Hall, 1984.

Who Said There's No Man on the Moon?: A Story of Jules Verne, Prentice-Hall, 1985.

Once Upon a Time!: A Story of the Brothers Grimm, Prentice-Hall, 1985.

Old Silver Leg Takes Over!: A Story of Peter Stuyvesant, Prentice-Hall, 1986.

Who Let Muddy Boots into the White House?: A Story of Andrew Jackson, Prentice-Hall, 1986.

Quit Pulling My Leg!: A Story of Davy Crockett, Prentice-Hall, 1987.

Who's That Girl with the Gun?: A Story of Annie Oakley, Prentice-Hall, 1988.

I Did It with My Hatchet: A Story of George Washington, Pippin Press, 1989.

Clear the Cow Pasture, I'm Coming in for a Landing!: A Story of Amelia Earhart, Prentice-Hall, 1990.

Pass the Quill, I'll Write a Draft: A Story of Thomas Jefferson, Pippin Press, 1990.

Stop the Presses, Nellie's Got a Scoop!: A Story of Nellie Bly, Simon & Schuster, 1992.

ILLUSTRATOR; CHILDREN'S BOOKS

Derrick, Schramm, and Spiegler, editors, *Adventures for Americans,* Harcourt, 1962.

Inez Rice, *A Long, Long Time,* Lothrop, 1964.

Hans Christian Andersen, *The Steadfast Tin Soldier,* Holt, 1964.

Oscar Wilde, *The Selfish Giant,* Holt, 1965.

My City, Macmillan, 1965.

Marie Halun Bloch, *The Two Worlds of Damyan,* Atheneum, 1966.

Robin McKown, *Rakoto and the Drongo Bird,* Lothrop, 1966.

R. McKown, *The Boy Who Woke Up in Madagascar,* Putnam, 1966.

Guy de Maupassant, *The Diamond Necklace,* F. Watts, 1967.

Mary K. Phelan, *Election Day,* Crowell, 1967.

Anthony Rowley, *A Sunday in Autumn,* Singer, 1967.

Margaretha Shemin, *Mrs. Herring,* Lothrop, 1967.

Miriam B. Young, *If I Drove a Truck,* Lothrop, 1967.

Lilian L. Moore, *I Feel the Same Way* (Junior Literary Guild selection), Atheneum, 1967.

M. B. Young, *Billy and Milly,* Lothrop, 1968.

Irma S. Black, *Busy Winds,* Holiday House, 1968.

Eleanor L. Clymer, *Horatio* (Junior Literary Guild selection), Atheneum, 1968.

Stephen Crane, *The Open Boat and Three Other Stories,* F. Watts, 1968.

Herman Melville, *Billy Budd, Foretopsman,* F. Watts, 1968.

Mariana Prieto, *When the Monkeys Wore Sombreros,* Harvey House, 1969.

Natalie S. Carlson, *Befana's Gift,* Harper, 1969.

Era K. Evans, *The Dirt Book: An Introduction to Earth Science,* Little, Brown, 1969.

Wilde, *Little Hans, the Devoted Friend,* Bobbs-Merrill, 1969.

Luther L. Terry and Daniel Horn, *To Smoke or Not to Smoke,* Lothrop, 1969.

Georgess McHargue, *The Baker and the Basilisk* (Junior Literary Guild selection), Bobbs-Merrill, 1970.

M. B. Young, *If I Flew a Plane,* Lothrop, 1970.

Leonore Klein, *D is for Rover,* Harvey House, 1970.

I. S. Black, *Busy Seeds,* Holiday House, 1970.

Charlotte Zolotow, *You and Me,* Macmillan, 1970.

John Stewart, *The Key to the Kitchen,* Lothrop, 1970.

M. B. Young, *Beware the Polar Bear,* Lothrop, 1970.

Guy Daniels, translator, *The Peasant's Pea Patch,* Delacorte, 1971.

Lini R. Grol, *The Bellfounder's Sons,* Bobbs-Merrill, 1971.

Rosemary Pendery, *A Home for Hopper,* Morrow, 1971.

Harry S. George, *Demo of 70th Street,* Walck, 1971.

Jeanette S. Lowrey, *Six Silver Spoons,* Harper, 1971.

Julian May, *Blue River,* Holiday House, 1971.

M. B. Young, *If I Drove a Car,* Lothrop, 1971.

M. B. Young, *If I Sailed a Boat,* Lothrop, 1971.

George Mendoza, *The Scribbler,* Holt, 1971.

M. B. Young, *If I Drove a Train,* Lothrop, 1972.

Ann Cooke, *Giraffes at Home,* Crowell, 1972.

Mindel Sitomer and Harry Sitomer, *Lines, Segments and Polygons,* Crowell, 1972.

M. B. Young, *If I Drove a Tractor,* Lothrop, 1973.

M. B. Young, *If I Rode a Horse,* Lothrop, 1973.

Berniece Freschet, *Prong-Horn on the Powder River,* Crowell, 1973.

Jane Yolen, *Wizard Islands,* Crowell, 1973.

John F. Waters, *Steal Harbor,* Warne, 1973.

M. B. Young, *If I Drove a Bus,* Lothrop, 1973.

Eve Bunting, *A Gift for Lonny,* Ginn, 1973.

M. B. Young, *If I Rode an Elephant,* Lothrop, 1974.

E. Clymer, *Leave Horatio Alone,* Atheneum, 1974.

M. B. Young, *If I Rode a Dinosaur,* Lothrop, 1974.

E. Clymer, *Engine Number Seven,* Holt, 1975.

Natalie Donna, *The Peanut Cookbook,* Lothrop, 1976.

E. Clymer, *Horatio's Birthday,* Atheneum, 1976.

F. N. Mongo, *House on Stink Alley,* Holt, 1977.

E. Clymer, *Horatio Goes to the Country,* Atheneum, 1978.

Walter D. Meyers, *The Pearl and the Ghost or One Mystery after Another,* Viking, 1980.

E. Clymer, *Horatio Solves a Mystery,* Atheneum, 1980.

Charles Keller, compiler, *It's Raining Cats and Dogs: Cat and Dog Jokes,* Pippin Press, 1988.

Also contributor of illustrations to *The Bird Book,* edited by Richard Shaw.

ILLUSTRATOR; ADULT BOOKS

James Fenimore Cooper, *The Pilot,* Limited Editions Club, 1968.

Ann Cornelisen, *Torregreca,* Reader's Digest Condensed Books, 1969.

Mason Weems, *Life of Washington,* Limited Editions Club, 1974.

Pierre Loti, *An Iceland Fisherman,* Reader's Digest Condensed Books, 1978.

Stephen Crane, *Stories,* Franklin Library, 1982.

Norah Lofts, *The Possession of Sister Jeanne,* Reader's Digest Condensed Books, 1983.

Nathaniel Hawthorne, *The Scarlet Letter,* Reader's Digest Association, 1984.

OTHER

(Compiler) *Poems for Counting,* Holt, 1963.

(Compiler) *Poems for Galloping,* Holt, 1963.

The America Songfest (motion picture), Weston Woods, 1976, released as a video cassette, 1990.

Robert Quackenbush School Program Excerpts Plus His Reading of His Book 'Stairway to Doom' (audio tape), Robert Quackenbush Studios, 1985.

On Tour with Robert Quackenbush (video cassette), Robert Quackenbush Studios, 1985.

Dear Mr. Quackenbush: Writing and Illustrating a Mystery, Program 1, (video cassette), Robert Quackenbush Studios, 1989.

The Great American Storybook: The Story of George Washington, Program 1 (video cassette), Robert Quackenbush Studios, 1989.

Too Many Lollipops (coloring book), Robert Quackenbush Studios, 1990.

Also contributor to *Daisy Days,* Scott, Foresman, 1978, *The New York Kid's Book,* Doubleday, 1979, *On Parade,* Scott, Foresman, 1987, *Promises to Keep,* Open Court, 1989, and *Silver Secrets,* Silver Burdett, 1990.

ADAPTATIONS: She'll Be Comin' 'Round the Mountain and *Clementine* were adapted as film strips by Weston Woods, 1975; *The Boy Who Waited for Santa Claus* was adapted as a film strip by Westport Communications Group, 1982.

SIDELIGHTS: Robert Quackenbush is known for his many mystery books for young readers. His detective characters include Miss Mallard, a duck character based on Agatha Christie's famous Miss Marple, and such other sleuths as Detective Mole, Sherlock Chick, and Piet Potter (based on Quackenbush's son). Popular with children, Quackenbush's mysteries have also won awards. In 1981, *Detective Mole and the Halloween Mystery* received an Edgar Allan Poe Special Award as the best juvenile mystery of the year. In addition to his mysteries, Quackenbush has also written and illustrated many other children's books, including a series of humorous biographies of famous people.

Quackenbush told *Something About the Author Autobiography Series (SAAS):* "I am involved in a book for a long time. As I work on a book, many things are going on in my life at the same time. Very often the things that are happening around me find their way into the story and/or illustrations. The characters may take on the personalities and characters of people I've met and am involved with at the moment. Or an idea for a story may be sparked by the recollection of something or someone from my past which also becomes integrated into the book.

"Writers and artists are like that, I am told. They repeat moments in their lives—either consciously or unconsciously—in their creation. I have also heard that writers and artists master their conflicts with their talents and that they replicate themselves, at their deepest and most significant level, in whatever they create. True or not, I am sure of one thing: I enjoy being a writer and illustrator of

books for young readers." Quackenbush added: "My training and experience as a psychoanalyst has been a valuable tool in the creation of my books."

Speaking to *CA,* Quackenbush revealed that many of his books were written with his son, Piet, in mind. "From the day he was born, he put me in contact with a wealth of material—my own childhood experiences—that had been masked and nearly forgotten by time. These early memories and the people involved in them became the basis for such books as *Animal Cracks* and *Detective Mole* [that I] dedicated to Piet. The books seemed to take on a life of their own and the characters in them went on to individual series books that focused on humor."

His son also inspired a series of easy-to-read mysteries. Quackenbush explains in his *SAAS* article: "A series about Piet was created when children wrote and wanted to know about Piet and what he did in New York. Piet became a detective called Piet Potter and our apartment building and the places the real Piet went for amusement became the focus of the action for each mystery."

Quackenbush clarifies in *CA* that other children have also inspired stories: "While it is true that Piet has been a major source of inspiration for my books for young readers, many other children have given me ideas for books. That is why I am in frequent contact with children of all ages. One way is through after school art classes that I offer at my studio. Another is through school visits across the country. [Children's] thoughts, language, and interests change from month to month. So it is very important to be in touch with them. I like listening to them, hearing their ideas, and using their language in my books."

Quackenbush's mother inspired him to write *Henry's Awful Mistake,* the story of how Henry the duck rid his kitchen of an ant but almost destroyed his house in the process. "I got the idea for *Henry's Awful Mistake,*" he explains in *SAAS,* "when I called my mother out in Arizona one Saturday afternoon. I commented that she sounded depressed. She said she was 'feeling low' because she had planned to have friends over for dinner that evening and discovered a roach in her kitchen. She called the exterminator and he literally demolished her kitchen going after that roach, and she had to cancel her dinner party. 'I'm very sorry to hear about that, Mother,' I said, 'but thank you for the story.' " *Henry's Awful Mistake* has sold over 3,500,000 copies.

Another successful Quackenbush project has been his series of humorous biographies of famous people. Each of these books presents the highlights of a prominent person's life, focusing particularly on humorous events, and illustrates them with large, colorful drawings. The series includes such people as Henry Ford, Annie Oakley, the Brothers Grimm, Jules Verne, and Andrew Jackson.

Many of these books are the only biographies on these figures available for young readers.

Quackenbush's artwork is as much appreciated as are his writings. He has illustrated his own books and some sixty other books as well, with artwork ranging from water colors to oil painting, and from pen-and-ink drawings to woodcuts. Richard Calhoun, writing in *Contemporary Graphic Artists,* believes that Quackenbush's woodcuts are his finest work. "Here," Calhoun states, "are lively, detailed creations worthy to stand beside those of such nineteenth- and turn-of-the-twentieth century masters as Howard Pyle and Joseph Pennell, composed with thought and executed by hand and with exceptional quality. Given the impact of technology on graphic art and the current fashionability of minimalism, Quackenbush's work is a comforting reminder of the essential humanity of art."

Over the years, Quackenbush has traveled the world speaking at schools about his books. He has visited schools in Brazil, Thailand, and Germany, as well as throughout the United States. Two days a week he also teaches art classes to adults and children, and he teaches others how to write for children. Quackenbush has a simple rule when he teaches writing. He tells *Something About the Author:* "My basic teaching premise stems from my belief that everyone has a unique story to present and to share with children . . . whether it is told with pictures or with words or both. To awaken these stories within my students, I begin by having them draw or write about the rooms they slept in as children. It is truly exciting to watch people discover their childhood worlds again."

BIOGRAPHICAL/CRITICAL SOURCES:

BOOKS

Contemporary Graphic Artists, Volume 3, Gale, 1988, pp. 167-172.
Fourth Book of Junior Authors, H. W. Wilson, 1978.
Something About the Author Autobiography Series, Volume 7, Gale, 1989, pp. 249-265.

PERIODICALS

American Artist, April, 1965.
Appraisal, winter, 1977; fall, 1978.
Bulletin of the Center for Children's Books, July-August, 1974; March, 1978; May, 1978; March, 1979; June, 1980; May, 1982; October, 1982; January, 1985; May, 1985; July-August, 1985; February, 1986; September, 1986; February, 1987; March, 1988.
Follett Library Newsletter, Spetember, 1987.
Junior Literary Guild, March, 1978.
New York Times Book Review, April 23, 1989.

QUIGLEY, Martin (Schofield), Jr. 1917-

PERSONAL: Born November 24, 1917, in Chicago, IL; son of Martin Joseph (a publisher) and Gertrude Margaret (Schofield) Quigley; married Katherine J. Dunphy (a guidance counselor), 1946; children: Mark, Elin, William, Kevin, Karen, Patricia, John, Mary, Peter, Katherine. *Education:* Georgetown University, A.B. (magna cum laude), 1939; Columbia University, M.A., 1973, Ph.D., 1975. *Politics:* Democrat. *Religion:* Roman Catholic. *Avocational interests:* Sailing.

ADDRESSES: Home—8 Pheasant Run, Larchmont, NY 10538. *Office*—Quigley Publishing Co., 159 West 53rd St., New York, NY 10019.

CAREER: Motion Picture Herald, New York City and Hollywood, CA, reporter, 1939-41; U.S. Office of War Information, New York City, film specialist, 1941-42; Motion Picture Producers and Distributors of America, representative in England, Ireland, and Italy, 1943-45; Quigley Publishing Co., New York City, editor, 1946—, president, 1964—; QWS, Inc. (educational consultants), New York City, president, 1975-80. Teachers College, Columbia University, department of higher and adult education, staff member, 1974-75, adjunct professor, summers, 1979-80 and 1990; adjunct professor of education, Bernard M. Baruch College of the City University of New York, 1977-89, and Seton Hall University, 1981-82. Village of Larchmont, NY, trustee, 1977-79, mayor, 1980-84. Lecturer on motion pictures and on family life issues. Founder and chairman, New York Independent Schools Opportunity Project, 1965-77; member of board of directors, Will Rogers Institute. Consultant to superintendent of schools for New York City Archdiocese, 1962-70.

MEMBER: Foundation for International Cooperation (president, 1960-65; director, 1960-1970), Religious Education Association (treasurer, 1976-80; chairman, 1981-84), Motion Picture Pioneers (member of board of directors), Christian Family Movement (member of executive committee, 1959-62; president of New York chapter, 1960-62; member of national executive committee, 1960-65), Larchmont Yacht Club.

WRITINGS:

Great Gaels, Quigley, 1944.
Roman Notes, Quigley, 1946.
Magic Shadows: The Story of the Origin of Motion Pictures, Georgetown University Press, 1948.
(Editor) *New Screen Techniques,* Quigley, 1953.
(With Edward M. Connors) *Catholic Action in Practice,* Random House, 1963.
(With Richard Gertner) *Films in America, 1929-1969,* Western Publishing, 1970.

Government Relations of Five Universities in Washington, D.C., University Microfilms, 1975.

Peace Without Hiroshima: Secret Action at the Vatican in the Spring of 1945, Madison Books, 1991.

(With Joseph G. E. Hopkins) *Triumphs and Tragedies: A Handbook of the History of Higher Education,* University Press of America, 1992.

Contributor to *Encyclopedia Britannica.*

WORK IN PROGRESS: A book tentatively titled *Secrets no Longer,* about Office of Support Services—O.S.S.—work in neutral Ireland and the Vatican during World War II.

SIDELIGHTS: Quigley told *CANR:* "My long career in the motion-picture trade field was obviously influenced by my father who wrote the Motion Picture Production Code and was a key factor in the Catholic Legion of Decency. Since 1972, my major focus has been on higher education."

*   *   *

QUILL, Barnaby
    See BRANDNER, Gary

R

READ, Piers Paul 1941-

PERSONAL: Born March 7, 1941, in Beaconsfield, England; son of Herbert (a poet) and Margaret (Ludwig) Read; married Emily Boothby, July 28, 1967. *Education:* St. John's College, Cambridge, B.A., 1961, M.A., 1962. *Religion:* Roman Catholic. *Avocational interests:* Travel.

ADDRESSES: Home—Old Byland, Yorkshire, England. *Agent*—Gillon Aitken, Ltd., 17 South Eaton Pl., London SW1 9ER, England.

CAREER: Times Literary Supplement, London, England, sub-editor, 1964-65; writer, 1965—. Adjunct professor of writing, Columbia University, 1980.

AWARDS, HONORS: Ford Foundation fellow in Berlin, 1963-64; Harkness fellow in New York and Lexington, MA, 1967-68; Geoffrey Faber Memorial Prize, 1969, for *The Junkers;* Hawthornden Prize, 1970, for *Monk Dawson.*

WRITINGS:

FICTION

Game in Heaven with Tussy Marx, Weidenfeld & Nicolson, 1966, McGraw, 1967.
The Junkers, Secker & Warburg, 1968, Knopf, 1969.
Monk Dawson, Lippincott, 1970.
The Professor's Daughter, Lippincott, 1971.
The Upstart, Lippincott, 1973.
Polonaise, Lippincott, 1976.
A Married Man, Lippincott, 1979.
The Villa Golitsyn, Harper, 1981.
The Free Frenchman, Random House, 1987.
A Season in the West, Random House, 1989.
On the Third Day, Secker & Warburg, 1990.

NONFICTION

Alive: The Story of the Andes Survivors, Lippincott, 1974.
The Train Robbers, Lippincott, 1978.

OTHER

Also author of television plays produced by British Broadcasting Corporation, including "Coincidence," "The Family Firm," and "The House on Highbury Hill."

SIDELIGHTS: Piers Paul Read is an English novelist whose stylistic works explore caste, crime, and Catholicism in modern society. Although perhaps best known for his nonfiction bestseller *Alive: The Story of the Andes Survivors,* Read has spent the bulk of his time producing fiction and has won several of Britain's most prestigious literary awards. *Commonweal* correspondent Carl Senna notes that Read's works reflect "an unmistakable concern for the moral fate of our affluent culture," adding: "Read's message seems to be that life is not meaningful unless it is rational; and necessity, not possibility, makes it so." *Time* magazine reviewer Melvin Maddocks calls Read "a sad, skilled connoisseur of the moral blindness that occurs when self-righteousness and self-interest try to be one."

The son of poet, essayist, and art critic Herbert Read, Piers Paul Read was born in Beaconsfield, England. He grew up in the rural north of Yorkshire and was educated at Ampleforth College, a Catholic school run by Benedictine monks. He graduated from Ampleforth at sixteen and spent some time traveling in France and Germany before entering St. John's College, Cambridge. There—although he had already decided to be a writer—he studied history and philosophy, earning a B.A. in 1961 and an M.A. in 1962. He spent the following two years in Germany, supporting himself part of the time with a Ford Foundation fellowship.

Read published his first novel, *Game in Heaven with Tussy Marx,* in 1966. *Dictionary of Literary Biography* essayist Philip Flynn contends that even in this experimental piece, Read employs themes that are central to him: "the emptiness of secular society . . . the danger of social stagnation . . . the importance of marital fidelity . . . and the strange connection between Communist and Christian ideals." The tone is ironic, however, and critics note a vein of cynicism and nihilism in the work.

Read's themes became more obvious in subsequent novels such as *The Junkers, Monk Dawson,* and *A Married Man.* Maddocks characterizes these books as "cool little horror stories about decent, well-intentioned people who suddenly find themselves up to their lily-white necks in evil." Religion and morals preoccupy the author in the novels, but he offers more than a tract on the easy solutions offered by orthodox faith. In *London Magazine,* John Mellors writes: "Read sees many of his characters as pilgrims struggling to overcome temptations and win through to the good life. Even non-Catholics are among them. . . . However, to Read, there is only one sure way of fulfilling oneself or saving one's soul, and that is through religion, through Roman Catholicism. It is better to be a monk than to meddle in politics."

Read has also addressed the issue of social class and its petty distinctions in his work. *New York Times Book Review* contributor Jane DeLynn contends that the author "is at his best dissecting the tangle of . . . drives—laziness, greed and desire to impress others—that shape our actions." Also in the *New York Times Book Review,* Malcolm Bradbury writes: "Mr. Read is a realist, a densely social novelist who knows that public and private worlds intersect at every point. . . . But . . . Mr. Read uses realism for irony. The social world, which demands attention, is also a delusion, a source of inexhaustible hypocrisies." This observation provides a theme for several Read novels, including *The Upstart, The Professor's Daughter,* and *A Season in the West.*

"Nearly every Read novel has its lurking snob aristocrat waiting to have the ground slashed away from beneath his feet," claims D. J. Taylor in *Spectator.* " . . . Yet these themes exist only as a backdrop to much wider concerns. Typically a Read novel shifts into gear only when its chief character, having hitherto existed in a fog of cheery complacency, reaches out to grasp the question, 'What are we to do with ourselves?'. . . . By linking these personal crises—the crises of frustrated idealism—with broader political questions, Read manages to bring off profound 'state of the nation' novels."

In 1973 Read turned to nonfiction for the first time and published *Alive: The Story of the Andes Survivors.* The work describes the aftermath of a plane crash in the remote Andes Mountains, where a group of young athletes had to cannibalize the crash victims in order to survive. *Alive* sold more than 250,000 copies in hardcover and over four million paperbacks, earning Read a substantial income in royalties. "I'd always regarded 'Alive' as a means to subsidize the writing of more fiction," Read told the *Washington Post.* "I felt my vocation was as a novelist, and perhaps that's arrogance, but that's what fundamentally interested me—art, trying to express philosophical and moral ideas through fiction."

Read brought these same ideals to the writing in *Alive.* His Roman Catholic background enabled him to understand the moral quandary of the Uruguayan survivors, and he presented their experiences in a religious context. Flynn writes of *Alive:* "This book's religious piety and sacramental vision could not be dismissed by readers as merely the writer's own. These things had really happened, these emotions really had been felt. . . . Distanced by his role as reporter or historian, effective in his sparse prose style, Read seems to let [the survivors'] story tell itself." *Rolling Stone* contributor Michael Rogers concludes: "The lives most of us lead give no hint as to what we may be capable of; the value of stories like *Alive* is the way they remind us of the deepest strengths of the organism. By sighting on that, Read has risen above the sensational and managed a book of real and lasting value."

Modern European history forms the basis for two Read novels, *Polonaise* and *A Free Frenchman.* Both works concern families caught in the political upheavals occasioned by the Second World War: *Polonaise* follows the fortunes of Polish refugees and *A Free Frenchman* explores the divided loyalties in a French family during the years of German occupation. *Newsweek* correspondent Margo Jefferson notes that in *Polonaise* Read "traces the tension between the implacable demands of history and the idiosyncrasies of personality. 'Polonaise' is, in the best sense, a historical novel: the main currents of politics and morality in the first half of the twentieth century are the shaping influences of its characters." In *Spectator,* Anita Brookner notes of *A Free Frenchman:* "Although the novel runs to 570 pages the interest never drifts away from the central conception, which is an examination of the mingled loyalties and disloyalties of Frenchmen, their volatile allegiances, and their frequently appalling recidivism. . . . It is a novel of great scope and considerable understanding . . . more advanced and more comprehensive than anything else on offer this year. It reveals the true skill of the novelist which is to rewrite history, often with more justice and more compassion than the official records can manage."

New York Times correspondent Susan Heller Anderson describes Read as "a tireless traveler with open-minded enthusiasms for strange places." Indeed, Read has traveled much of the world, from Europe and Africa to South America and Southeast Asia. The author teaches an occasional seminar in creative writing, but for the most part he lives quietly in Yorkshire, concentrating on his writing. He told the *New York Times* that he has no desire to court widespread popularity with so-called mainstream work. "I don't think real writers know what bestsellers are," he said. "I believe in integrity. . . . I don't want to succeed as hype. I'm prepared to forgo instant success."

Read's success may not be instant, but his reputation has been building over time as he produces a new novel every two years or so. Taylor calls Read "a profoundly serious contemporary writer whose merits, in an age of . . . mass critical rallying around dubious flags, [is] consistently underrated." Mellors notes: "Read is hardly ever dull. He is a skilled storyteller, with a strong, unfussy narrative style and a good ear for dialogue." Flynn sees Read as the rare modern author who dares to tackle sensitive religious and political themes. The critic concludes that Read "has dealt with the major *isms* of our time on a personal level, with a sharp eye for domestic detail and a keen ear for the rhetoric of moral confusion."

BIOGRAPHICAL/CRITICAL SOURCES:

BOOKS

Contemporary Literary Criticism, Gale, Volume 4, 1975; Volume 10, 1979; Volume 25, 1983.
Dictionary of Literary Biography, Volume 14: *British Novelists since 1960,* Gale, 1983.

PERIODICALS

Books and Bookmen, February, 1977.
Chicago Tribune Book World, February 10, 1980; January 17, 1982.
Commonweal, November 12, 1971.
Encounter, October, 1968.
Listener, November 25, 1976; May 19, 1978.
London Magazine, December, 1973-January, 1974; April-May, 1980; February, 1982.
Los Angeles Times, January 28, 1982.
Los Angeles Times Book Review, February 24, 1980.
New Statesman, June 3, 1966; June 14, 1968; September 7, 1973.
Newsweek, December 27, 1976.
New York Review of Books, May 1, 1980.
New York Times, October 27, 1971; June 16, 1978; December 10, 1979; December 21, 1979; January 19, 1982.
New York Times Book Review, November 7, 1971; June 25, 1978; December 30, 1979; April 12, 1987; August 13, 1989.
Punch, July 17, 1968; January 1, 1969.
Rolling Stone, May 23, 1974.

Spectator, November 20, 1976; June 21, 1968; May 18, 1974; November 24, 1979; September 20, 1986; September 17, 1988; February 24, 1990; October 20, 1990.
Time, October 25, 1971; February 8, 1982.
Times (London), September 25, 1986.
Times Literary Supplement, September 7, 1973; May 19, 1978; October 9, 1981; October 10, 1986; September 9-15, 1988; October 19, 1990.
Washington Post, January 20, 1982; June 28, 1987.
Washington Post Book World, November 28, 1976; June 25, 1978; January 27, 1980.*

—*Sketch by Anne Janette Johnson*

*   *   *

REED, Eliot
See AMBLER, Eric

*   *   *

REID, Desmond
See MOORCOCK, Michael (John)

*   *   *

REID BANKS, Lynne   1929-

PERSONAL: Listed in some sources under Banks; born July 31, 1929, in London, England; daughter of James Reid Banks (a doctor) and Muriel Alexander (an actress; maiden name, Marsh); married Chaim Stephenson (a sculptor), 1965; children: Adiel, Gillon, Omri (sons). *Education:* Attended Queen's Secretarial College, London, 1945-46, Italia Conte Stage School, 1946, and Royal Academy of Dramatic Art, 1947-49. *Religion:* "Practising Atheist." *Hobbies and other interests:* Theater, gardening, teaching ESL abroad.

ADDRESSES: Home—Dorset, England. *Agent*—Sheila Watson, Watson, Little Ltd., 12 Egbert St., London NW1 8LJ, England.

CAREER: Actress in English repertory companies, 1949-54; free-lance journalist, London, England, 1954-55; Independent Television News, London, television news reporter, 1955-57, television news scriptwriter, 1958-62; taught English as a foreign language in Israel, 1963-71; writer, 1971—.

MEMBER: Society of Authors (London).

AWARDS, HONORS: Yorkshire Arts Literary Award, 1976, and Best Books for Young Adults Award, American

Library Association, 1977, both for *Dark Quartet;* West Australian Young Readers' Book Award, Library Association of Australia, 1980, for *My Darling Villain;* Outstanding Books of the Year Award, *New York Times,* 1981, Young Reader's Choice Award, Pacific Northwest Library Association, 1984, California Young Readers Medal, California Reading Association, 1985, Children's Books of the Year Award, Child Study Association, 1986, Young Readers of Virginia Award, 1988, and Arizona Young Readers' Award, 1988, all for *The Indian in the Cupboard;* Parents' Choice Award for Literature, Parents' Choice Foundation, 1986, Notable Books Award, *New York Times,* 1986, Children's Books of the Year Award, 1987, Rebecca Caudill Young Reader's Books Award, Illinois Association for Media in Education, 1988, and Indian Paintbrush Award, Wyoming Library Association, 1989, all for *The Return of the Indian.*

WRITINGS:

JUVENILE

One More River, Simon & Schuster, 1973.

The Adventures of King Midas, illustrated by George Him, Dent, 1976.

The Farthest-Away Mountain, illustrated by Victor Ambrus, Abelard Schuman, 1976.

I, Houdini: The Autobiography of a Self-Educated Hamster, illustrated by Terry Riley, Dent, 1978, Doubleday, 1988.

My Darling Villain, Harper, 1977.

Letters to My Israeli Sons: The Story of Jewish Survival, H. W. Allen, 1979, F. Watts, 1980.

The Indian in the Cupboard, illustrated by Robin Jacques, Dent, 1980, Doubleday, 1981.

The Writing on the Wall, Chatto & Windus, 1981, Harper, 1982.

Maura's Angel, illustrated by Robin Jacques, Dent, 1984.

The Fairy Rebel, illustrated by William Geldart, Dent, 1985, Doubleday, 1988.

The Return of the Indian, illustrated by W. Geldart, Doubleday, 1986.

Melusine: A Mystery, Hamish Hamilton, 1988, Harper, 1989.

The Secret of the Indian, Collins, 1988, Doubleday, 1989.

PLAYS

It Never Rains (produced by BBC, 1954), Deane, 1954.

All in a Row, Deane, 1956.

The Killer Dies Twice (three-act), Deane, 1956.

Already It's Tomorrow (produced by BBC, 1962), Samuel French, 1962.

The Unborn, produced in London, England, 1962.

The Wednesday Caller, produced by BBC, 1963.

The Last Word on Julie, produced by ATV, 1964.

The Gift (three-act), produced in London, 1965.

The Stowaway (radio play), produced by BBC, 1967.

The Eye of the Beholder, produced by ITV, 1977.

Lame Duck (radio play), produced by BBC, 1978.

Purely from Principal (radio play), produced by BBC, 1985.

The Travels of Yoshi and the Tea-Kettle, produced in London, 1991.

OTHER

The L-Shaped Room, Chatto & Windus, 1960, revised edition, Longman, 1977.

House of Hope, Simon & Schuster, 1962, published in England as *An End to Running,* Chatto & Windus, 1962.

Children at the Gate, Simon & Schuster, 1968.

The Backward Shadow, Simon & Schuster, 1970.

The Kibbutz: Some Personal Reflections, Anglo-Israel Association, 1972.

Two Is Lonely, Simon & Schuster, 1974.

Sarah and After: The Matriarchs, Bodley Head, 1975, published as *Sarah and After: Five Women Who Founded a Nation,* Doubleday, 1977.

Dark Quartet: The Story of the Brontes, Weidenfeld & Nicholson, 1976, Delacorte, 1977.

Path to the Silent Country: Charlotte Bronte's Years of Fame, Weidenfeld & Nicholson, 1977.

Defy the Wilderness, Chatto & Windus, 1981.

Torn Country: An Oral History of the Israeli War of Independence, F. Watts, 1982.

The Warning Bell, Hamish Hamilton, 1984.

Casualties, Hamish Hamilton, 1986.

ADAPTATIONS: The L-Shaped Room, starring Leslie Caron, was released by Davis-Royal Films, 1962.

WORK IN PROGRESS: The Magic Hare, twelve stories for young children, publication expected in 1992; *The Mystery of the Cupboard,* in press; *The Crossover* (an adult novel).

SIDELIGHTS: Lynne Reid Banks has written about a number of complex subjects—single parenthood, the Middle East, Zionism—but she is best known to young audiences for her imaginative stories like *The Indian in the Cupboard, The Adventures of King Midas,* and *The Fairy Rebel.* Many of Reid Banks's titles for younger readers, such as the "Indian" books, feature magic as a central theme. Teen readers are attracted to works such as *The Writing on the Wall,* in which Reid Banks deals with typical teenage problems, such as dating and family relationships. In many of all her works, Reid Banks tries to draw on personal experience. "I had learned a fundamental lesson," she wrote in an essay for the *Sixth Book of Junior Authors.* "Nothing is ever wasted. And for a writer, there's something more: nothing one ever experiences or feels is wasted. Even the bad things, the negative emotions. . . . While one is suffering them, I mean at the time, a little voice is saying 'Hold on to it. Remember.' Because one day you may need it."

Reid Banks originally planned on being an actress like her mother. In order to prepare for this career, she attended drama school and worked at various theater-related jobs. "I adored every minute of it. . . . I was going to take the theater world by storm! Little did any of us know the heartbreak and hardships ahead. Very few of us made it. The vast majority left the profession—we simply couldn't make a living," she noted in her essay. While she did not become an actress, Reid Banks later made use of her threatrical training when she taught English to Hebrew-speaking children in Israel. "Every lesson was a performance—how else could I make them understand me?," she remarked. "And it worked. I was more successful at teaching than I ever was on the stage."

Reid Banks's first literary success was the novel *The L-Shaped Room*. The book chronicles the life of unmarried, twenty-seven-year-old Jane Graham who goes to live in a run-down boardinghouse when she becomes pregnant. Janice Elliott of the *New Statesman* called the novel "touching and competent," as well as "ambitious and mature." "Love is the book's theme, developed in bright, warm prose, through diverse and interesting characters," commented Otis Kidwell Burger in the *New York Times Book Review*. Reid Banks eventually wrote two more novels featuring Jane Graham, *The Backward Shadow* and *Two Is Lonely*.

Reid Banks published her first children's book in 1973. Since that time, she has delighted scores of young fans with tales of magical kings, brave fairies, toys that come to life, and intrepid hamsters. Two of her most popular works are *The Indian in the Cupboard* and its sequel, *The Return of the Indian*. In both volumes, a boy's plastic Indian comes to life every time it is locked in a cupboard. Young Omri soon discovers that his toy, Little Bear, has a taste for adventure—sometimes with near-disastrous results. A reviewer for the *Times Literary Supplement* found *The Indian in the Cupboard* to be "original, lively, compulsive writing" that "will well stand through repeated readings."

While Reid Banks enjoys writing for audiences of all ages, she is especially fond of writing tales for the younger set. "Writing for young people is a much pleasanter, and easier, thing than writing for adults," she once commented. "I especially enjoy writing wish-fulfillment tales for younger children. . . . In the end, one has to write what one wants to write, or what one is commissioned to write, and hope for the best. You can't win 'em all."

BIOGRAPHICAL/CRITICAL SOURCES:

BOOKS

Contemporary Literary Criticism, Volume 23, Gale, 1983, pp. 40-43.
Sixth Book of Junior Authors, edited by Sally Holmes Holtze, Wilson, 1989, pp. 22-24.
Twentieth Century Children's Writers, edited by Tracy Chevalier, St. James, 1989, pp. 56-58.

PERIODICALS

Los Angeles Times Book Review, April 23, 1989, p. 10.
New Statesman, July 26, 1968, p. 116.
New York Times Book Review, April 6, 1961, p. 38; May 12, 1968, pp. 40-41; April 16, 1989, p. 26.
Times Literary Supplement, November 21, 1980; December 1, 1988.*

*   *   *

**REILLY, Patrick D.
See ROGERS, Peter D(amien)**

*   *   *

REST, Friedrich Otto 1913-

PERSONAL: Born August 28, 1913, in Marshalltown, IA; son of Karl and Bertha (Leisy) Rest; married Dorothy Schumacher, 1940; children: Paul, Betty, John. *Education:* Elmhurst College, A.B., 1935; Eden Theological Seminary, B.D., 1937; Mission House Theological Seminary, D.D., 1961.

ADDRESSES: Home—827 West Merriweather, New Braunfels, TX 78130. *Office*—172 West Coll St., New Braunfels, TX 78130.

CAREER: Minister of United Church of Christ churches in Jasper, IN, 1937-41, Dayton, OH, 1941-48, Hermann, MO, 1948-55, Evansville, IN, 1955-64, Rochester, NY, 1964-70, and Houston, TX, 1970-75; First Protestant United Church of Christ, New Braunfels, TX, associate pastor, 1975-85; interim pastor of Puula Church in Hawaii, 1985; chaplain, Chandler Memorial Home, 1989—; First Protestant United Church of Christ, New Braunfels, TX, minister of visitation, 1991—. Vice-president, Evangelical and Reformed Church, Missouri Valley Synod, 1954; member of department of worship and arts, National Council of Churches, beginning 1955; president, Evansville Council of Churches, 1962; moderator, South Texas Association, United Church of Christ, 1978-79. Host pastor on television series "Pastor's Study,"

WFIE-TV, 1957-63, WROC-TV, beginning 1964; has appeared on San Antonio, TX, television programs.

MEMBER: New Braunfels Clergy Association, South Central Conference, United Church of Christ.

WRITINGS:

Worship Aids for Fifty-two Services, Westminster, 1951.
Our Christian Symbols, Christian Education Press, 1954.
Worship Services for Church Groups, Christian Education Press, 1962.
A Topical Index of Bible Readings, Church Management, Inc., 1962.
The Cross in Hymns, Judson, 1969.
Our Christian Worship: Resources from Palm Sunday through Easter, C.S.S. Publishing, 1977.
Funeral Handbook, Judson, 1982.
Fourteen Messages of Hope: Thoughts for Funerals and Other Occasions, Baker Book, 1985.
Our Christian Worship: Resources for Advent and Christmastide, C.S.S. Publishing, 1985.
A Month of Family Prayers, Liturgical Press, 1989.
Prayers for Families of Today, Liturgical Press, 1989.
Our Christian Symbolism and Culture, Pilgrim Press, 1992.

Contributor to *Westminster Dictionary of Christian Education,* 1964.

SIDELIGHTS: Friedrich Otto Rest writes *CA:* "Since four of the above books have required additional printings, one now being in the 11th, I'm trying a little harder to make each book have lasting value.

"I like the work I'm doing, but the schedule is a bit shorter than it used to be, so Dorothy and I like to travel (mostly by car) and I'm getting good help from newsletters to manage a modest portfolio of mutual funds."

BIOGRAPHICAL/CRITICAL SOURCES:

PERIODICALS

Evansville Courier, February 2, 1962.
Salem Outlook, September 26, 1963; January 12, 1964.
First Protestant Vision, 1985.

*   *   *

REY, Margret (Elisabeth) 1906-

PERSONAL: Born in May, 1906, in Hamburg, Germany; came to the United States in 1940, naturalized citizen, 1946; married H(ans) A(ugusto) Rey (a writer and illustrator), 1935 (died, 1977). *Education:* Attended Bauhaus, 1927, Dusseldorf Academy of Art, 1928-29, and University of Munich, 1930-31.

ADDRESSES: Home and office—14 Hilliard St., Cambridge, MA 02138. *Agent*—A. P. Watt & Son, 26-28 Bedford Row, London WC1R 4HL, England.

CAREER: Reporter and advertising copywriter in Berlin, Germany, 1928-29; held one-woman shows of watercolors in Berlin, 1929-34; photographer in London, England, Hamburg, Germany, and Rio de Janeiro, Brazil, 1930-35; free-lance writer in Paris, France, 1936-40, in New York City, 1940-63, and in Cambridge, MA, 1963—; writer of children's books, 1937—; Brandeis University, Waltham, MA, instructor in creative writing, 1978—.

AWARDS, HONORS: Children's Book Award from Child Study Association of America, 1966, for *Curious George Goes to the Hospital.*

WRITINGS:

ALL ILLUSTRATED BY HUSBAND, H. A. REY

Pretzel, Harper, 1944.
Spotty, Harper, 1945.
Pretzel and the Puppies, Harper, 1946.
Billy's Picture, Harper, 1948.

WITH H. A. REY; ILLUSTRATED BY H. A. REY

How the Flying Fishes Came Into Being, Chatto & Windus, 1938.
Raffy and the Nine Monkeys, Chatto & Windus, 1939, published as *Cecily G. and the Nine Monkeys,* Houghton, 1942.
Anybody at Home? (verse), Chatto & Windus, 1939, Houghton, 1943.
How Do You Get There?, Houghton, 1941.
Elizabite: The Adventures of a Carnivorous Plant, Harper, 1942.
Tit for Tat (verse), Harper, 1942.
Where's My Baby? (verse), Houghton, 1943.
Feed the Animals (verse), Houghton, 1944.
Mary Had a Little Lamb, Penguin, 1951.
See the Circus (verse), Houghton, 1956.

"CURIOUS GEORGE" SERIES (ALL TITLES PUBLISHED IN ENGLAND AS "ZOZO" SERIES); ILLUSTRATED BY H. A. REY

Curious George (also see below), Houghton, 1941.
Curious George Takes a Job (also see below), Houghton, 1947.
Curious George Rides a Bike (also see below), Houghton, 1952.
Curious George Gets a Medal, Houghton, 1957.
Curious George Flies a Kite (also see below), Houghton, 1958.
Curious George Learns the Alphabet, Houghton, 1963.
Curious George Goes to the Hospital (also see below), Houghton, 1966.

EDITOR, WITH ALLAN J. SHALLECK; BASED ON "CURIOUS GEORGE" FILM SERIES

Curious George and the Dump Truck, Houghton, 1984.
Curious George Goes to the Circus, Houghton, 1984.
Curious George Goes to the Aquarium, Houghton, 1984.
Curious George Goes Sledding, Houghton, 1984.
Curious George Goes Hiking, Houghton, 1985.
Curious George Walks the Pets, Houghton, 1986.
Curious George Plays Baseball, Houghton, 1986.
Curious George Goes to a Costume Party, Houghton, 1986.
Curious George at the Ballet, Houghton, 1986.
Curious George Visits the Police Station, Houghton, 1987.
Curious George Goes Fishing, Houghton, 1987.
Curious George at the Laundromat, Houghton, 1987.
Curious George Visits the Zoo, Houghton, 1988.
Curious George at the Fire Station, Houghton, 1988.
Curious George at the Airport, Houghton, 1988.
Curious George and the Pizza, Houghton, 1988.
Curious George at the Beach, Houghton, 1988.
Curious George at the Railroad Station, Houghton, 1988.
Curious George Goes to a Restaurant, Houghton, 1988.
Curious George Visits an Amusement Park, Houghton, 1988.
Curious George and the Dinosaur, Houghton, 1989.
Curious George Goes to an Ice Cream Shop, Houghton, 1989.
Curious George Goes to School, Houghton, 1989.
Curious George Goes to the Dentist, Houghton, 1989.
Curious George Bakes a Cake, Houghton, 1990.
Curious George Goes Camping, Houghton, 1990.
Curious George Goes to an Air Show, Houghton, 1990.
Curious George Goes to a Toy Store, Houghton, 1990.

OTHER

Contributor, with H. A. Rey, of the "Zozo Page for Children," *Good Housekeeping,* 1951. The Reys' works have been translated into numerous languages.

ADAPTATIONS:

MOVIES AND FILMSTRIPS

Curious George Rides a Bike (motion picture with teaching guide), Weston Woods Studios, 1958.

Curious George Rides a Bike (filmstrip with text), Weston Woods Studios, 1960.

Curious George (filmstrip with record and teaching guide), Teaching Resources Films, 1971.

Curious George Flies a Kite (filmstrip with record and teaching guide), Teaching Resources Films, 1971.

Curious George Gets a Medal (filmstrip with record and teaching guide), Teaching Resources Films, 1971.

Curious George Goes to the Hospital (filmstrip with record and teaching guide), Teaching Resources Films, 1971.

Curious George Takes a Job (filmstrip with record and teaching guide), Teaching Resources Films, 1971.

RECORDINGS

Curious George, and Other Stories about Curious George, read by Julie Harris, Caedmon Records, 1972.

Curious George Learns the Alphabet, and Other Stories about Curious George, read by Harris, Caedmon Records, 1973.

WORK IN PROGRESS: Curious George films for television.

SIDELIGHTS: Born and educated in Germany, Margret Rey studied art at various German schools before moving to Brazil in 1935. While working as a photographer there, she met H. A. Rey, with whom she founded Rio de Janeiro's first advertising agency. The couple subsequently married and moved to Paris, where Margret worked as a free-lance writer while H. A. sold sketches to numerous French publications.

In Paris the Reys began collaborating on children's books, with Margret providing the text for H. A.'s illustrations. The book *Raffy and the Nine Monkeys* inspired their popular "Curious George" series, written in the United States after the Reys fled the Nazi conquest of Paris during World War II.

The Reys commented in *Authors and Illustrators of Children's Books: Writings on Their Lives and Works:* "Among children we seem to be known best as the parents of *Curious George,* the little monkey hero of some of our books. 'I thought you were monkeys too,' said a little boy who had been eager to meet us, disappointment written all over his face." "*Curious George* consistently heads the popularity list of what children themselves call 'funny books,'" notes *Twentieth-Century Children's Writers* contributor James E. Higgins.

Margret Rey once told *CA:* "I now am involved in supervising the production of Curious George films for television and am teaching a course on the craft of writing. I enjoy teaching enormously."

BIOGRAPHICAL/CRITICAL SOURCES:

BOOKS

Children's Literature Review, Volume 5, Gale, pp. 188-200.
Rey, Margret, and H. A. Rey, "Margret and H. A. Rey," in *Authors and Illustrators of Children's Books: Writings on Their Lives and Works,* edited by Miriam Hoffman and Samuel Evans, Bowker, 1972.

Twentieth-Century Children's Writers, 3rd edition, St. James Press, 1989, pp. 820-821.

PERIODICALS

Elementary English, January, 1958, pp. 3-11.

*   *   *

RIPLEY, Alexandra 1934-

PERSONAL: Born January 8, 1934, in Charleston, SC; children: two daughters. *Education:* Vassar College, A.B., 1955.

ADDRESSES: Home—Charlottesville, VA. *Agent*—William Morris Agency, 1350 Avenue of the Americas, New York, NY 10019.

CAREER: Writer.

WRITINGS:

NOVELS

Who's That Lady in the President's Bed?, Dodd, 1972.
Charleston, Doubleday, 1981.
On Leaving Charleston, Doubleday, 1984.
The Time Returns, Doubleday, 1985.
New Orleans Legacy, Macmillan, 1987.
Scarlett: The Sequel to Margaret Mitchell's Gone with the Wind, Warner Books, 1991.

SIDELIGHTS: As the author of *Scarlett: The Sequel to Margaret Mitchell's Gone with the Wind,* Alexandra Ripley found instant fame and was subjected to a large dose of public criticism. Four years of discussion, debate, and sometimes literary warfare preceded the book's simultaneous release in the United States and forty other countries on September 25, 1991. Charles Bremner of the London *Times* noted that Ripley was chosen by the estate of Margaret Mitchell to "follow up those immortal closing lines, 'Tomorrow, I'll think of some way to get him back. After all, tomorrow is another day.' " Yet after the publication of *Gone with the Wind* Mitchell made it clear that, for the purposes of her story, she did not want "tomorrow" to arrive; those most vehemently opposed to the sequel's production trumpeted this at every turn. "Mitchell herself had adamantly refused to write a sequel, insisting that her novel had a 'natural and proper ending,' " John Blades commented in the *Chicago Tribune.* "[Mitchell] felt strongly enough . . . to express in her will a wish that no sequel be undertaken by another hand," Joseph Connolly stated in the *Times.* "But the clause in question has been declared to be 'ambiguous,' and therefore open to the interpretations of would-be entrepreneurs." Mitchell's estate originally agreed to a sequel in 1976, twenty-seven years after Mitchell was killed by a speeding taxi. That

work, a screenplay by novelist Anne Edwards, was never made into the intended film. "An unspecified share" of the profits from Ripley's *Scarlett* will go to the Mitchell estate, Blades said.

Uproar over the book's creation and the " 'moral implications' of a sequel," a worry that the head of one publishing house expressed to Blades, did not prevent Ripley from finding a publisher. The William Morris Agency conducted an auction on her behalf, with Warner emerging as the top bidder. "While most of its $4.94 million bid obviously reflects the hoopla surrounding the sequel to one of the most popular books ever written, part of that amount was bid because Warner's existing relationship with Ms. Ripley persuaded company officials she is an accomplished author," Edwin McDowell explained in the *New York Times.*

The hoopla did not end with the publication of *Scarlett.* While the book debuted at number fifteen on the *Publishers Weekly* bestseller list two weeks after publication and spent the next fifteen weeks at number one, reviewers squared off, blasting the book itself as well as the very idea of a sequel. Many found the plot improbable and the characters unrecognizable. The book begins with the lethargic Ashley Wilkes throwing himself towards his wife's open grave in a fit of emotion. Scarlett reaches to catch him, sparking a scandal which results in her return to Tara, cast out from decent society. From there she travels to various locales, eventually ending up in Ireland. "As Scarlett herself might say, the critics have jumped on this book like ducks on a June bug," Suanne Kelman declared in the *Globe and Mail.* "They blasted it for being bloated, sloppy, meandering, boring and execrably written. It deserves all this abuse and more." Kelman maintained, however, that the book is more a marketing creation than a simple work of fiction, and that Ripley, as "merely the contracted labor" needed to turn out the sequel, "should be judged solely in terms of productivity—her efficiency in manufacturing a story with a minimal expenditure of labour. On that cynical basis, the woman is a genius." Yet Ripley has voiced strong disapproval of this type of system in the publishing industry.

"There are two reasons why I'm doing this book," Ripley told Bremner during the time she was working on *Scarlett.* "I can't resist it and as soon as this is done I will be able to write anything I want to." It was on the strength of that sentiment that Ripley spoke out against "all publishers as a group" at the Southeastern Booksellers Association convention held September 22, 1991, in Atlanta, as Maureen O'Brien reported in *Publishers Weekly.* "I'm going to speak on behalf of all the writers who aren't as lucky as I am," Ripley began. "Thanks to Miss Mitchell and *Scarlett,* right now I can say any damn thing I want to, and people will listen." Ripley criticized the publishing industry for its lack of skilled editors and its emphasis on books as mere products, noting that the first editor to work on *Scarlett* told her, "You have to please me, not those people you keep talking about who love *Gone with the Wind*. *Gone with the Wind* is irrelevant." O'Brien noted Ripley's lament that "almost all the people with experience in editing have had to go freelance. They've been replaced by people with the title of editor whose real skills and experience were gained in sales, marketing or promotion."

Entering into the writing of *Scarlett*, Ripley held the reputation of a skilled historical-romance novelist with an unusual approach. "The most interesting characters in all of Ripley's books are not the most beautiful, in defiance of the conventions of historical romances," Susan Quinn Berneis stated in *Twentieth Century Romance and Historical Writers*. "Instead, the eccentric and the outcast come to life most vividly." Berneis also praised the thoroughness of Ripley's research, particularly in recreating Civil War-era southern cities and fifteenth-century Florence. "Obviously Ripley is a keen student of history," Berneis stated, "for her fictional events are firmly rooted in historical fact."

BIOGRAPHICAL/CRITICAL SOURCES:

BOOKS

Twentieth-Century Romance and Historical Writers, 2nd edition, St. James Press, 1990.

PERIODICALS

Chicago Tribune, May 1, 1988, Section 5, p. 3; August 31, 1990.
Globe and Mail (Toronto), October 5, 1991, p. C10.
Life, November 26, 1988, p. 30.
Los Angeles Times, April 21, 1988; June 5, 1990, pp. E1, E12.
New York Times, April 26, 1988; April 27, 1988; April 29, 1988.
Publishers Weekly, October 4, 1991, p. 10.
Times (London), April 26, 1988; July 18, 1990; September 26, 1991, p. 16.
Washington Post, June 8, 1988.

—*Sketch by Deborah A. Stanley*

*   *   *

ROBBINS, Jane (Borsch) 1939-
(Jane Robbins-Carter)

PERSONAL: Born September 13, 1939, in Chicago, IL; daughter of Reuben August (a lawyer) and Pearl Irene (a housewife; maiden name, Houk) Borsch; married Michael Warren Robbins (a free-lance writer; divorced, 1970); married John M. Carter (a photographer; divorced, 1988);

children: (first marriage) Molly Warren. *Education:* Wells College, B.A. (with distinction), 1961; Western Michigan University, M.L.S., 1966; University of Maryland at College Park, Ph.D., 1972. *Politics:* Democrat. *Religion:* Episcopalian.

ADDRESSES: Home—Madison, WI. *Office*—School of Library and Information Studies, University of Wisconsin—Madison, Madison, WI 53706.

CAREER: University of Pittsburgh, Pittsburgh, PA, assistant professor of library and information science, 1972-73; Emory University, Atlanta, GA, associate professor of library and information management, 1973-74; University of Northern Colorado, Greeley, reference librarian, 1974; Wyoming State Library, Cheyenne, consultant, 1975-77; Louisiana State University, Baton Rouge, associate professor of library science, 1977-79, dean, 1979-81; University of Wisconsin—Madison, professor of library and information studies and director of School of Library and Information Studies, 1981—. Visiting professor at University of Denver, 1974-77, and University of California, Berkeley, 1975.

MEMBER: American Library Association (member of council, 1976-80, 1991-95; chairman of Library Research Roundtable, 1978), American Society of Information Science (chairman of education committee, 1985), Association for Library and Information Science Education (member of board of directors, 1979-81, 1983-85; president, 1984), Wisconsin Library Association (president, 1986).

WRITINGS:

Citizen Participation in Public Library Policy-Making, Scarecrow, 1974.
(Editor under name Jane Robbins-Carter) *Public Librarianship: A Reader*, Libraries Unlimited, 1982.
(With Douglas Zweizig) *Are We There Yet?*, School of Library and Information Science (Madison, WI), 1988.
Evaluation Strategies for Public Library Children's Services, School of Library and Information Sciences, 1989.
(With Zweizig and Debra Johnson) *Libraries: Partners in Adult Literacy*, Ablex Publishing, 1991.

Contributor to library journals. Editor of international journal, *Library and Information Science Research*, 1981—.

WORK IN PROGRESS: Researching financial practice in public libraries.

SIDELIGHTS: Jane Robbins once told *CA:* "Education for the information professions is becoming increasingly diversified and complex. New educational programs for information workers are required. Important new programs, including undergraduate preparation, are being developed at Drexel University, Rutgers University, and Syracuse University.

"Despite very serious concerns related to the education of professional librarians, I believe that the most serious problem facing the field is not the education of professionals—because many changes in professional curricula have already taken place—but rather the education of support staff. Libraries seem to have returned in a significant way to the pre-twentieth-century condition, when virtually all of the education for the skill level of librarianship took place within our libraries. Surely, if professionals are now principally managers, yet the skill work must still be done, then in-house professionals must be training the staff. While I have little doubt that the professional staff of academic libraries are capable of training support staff, I fear that the time that they should be spending on interaction with faculty and students—that is, the delivery of service—is being absorbed by the necessity to train support staff, once again turning the librarians' energies to the production function of the library, not to its service function. I believe the time has come to address the question of the needed education of library support staff."

*   *   *

ROBBINS-CARTER, Jane
See ROBBINS, Jane (Borsch)

*   *   *

ROBOTTOM, John 1934-

PERSONAL: Born January 8, 1934, in Birmingham, England; son of Albert (an engineer) and Kathleen (Carlisle) Robottom; married Molly Barber (a lecturer), November 11, 1956; children: Ellen, Sally, Robert. *Education:* University of Birmingham, B.A. (with honors), 1956.

ADDRESSES: Home—4 Hampton Ln., Solihull B91 2PS, England.

CAREER: Teacher in secondary schools, 1956-65; Bingley College of Education, Yorkshire, England, lecturer in history, 1966-68; Crewe College of Education, Crewe, England, senior lecturer, 1968-73, principal lecturer in history, 1973-76; assistant senior education officer, British Broadcasting Corp., 1976-87; free-lance editor and author, 1987—.

WRITINGS:

Modern China: China in Revolution, Longmans, Green, 1967, published as *China in Revolution,* McGraw, 1969.

Modern Russia, Longmans, Green, 1969.
(Editor) *Making the Modern World,* Longmans, Green, 1970.
Twentieth-Century China, Wayland, 1971.
Nineteenth-Century Britain, Longman, 1976.
(With W. Claypole) *Caribbean Story,* Longman, 1980.
Russia in Charge, Longman, 1984.
Castles and Cathedrals, Longman, 1991.

Also author of *A Social History of Industrial Britain,* Longman.

"LONGMAN MODERN BRITISH HISTORICAL" SERIES

From Manufacturing to Industry, 1720-1850, Longman, 1991.
Transport, 1700-1850, Longman, 1991.
Health and Medicine, 1780-1900, Longman, 1991.
Transport: The Last Hundred Years, Longman, 1991.

*   *   *

RODERUS, Frank 1942-

PERSONAL: Born September 21, 1942, in Pittsburgh, PA; son of Frank James (in sales) and Alice (Hollenshead) Roderus; married Kay Marsh, March 27, 1965 (divorced August, 1977); married Betty Richardson, June 10, 1978; children: Franklin, Stephen, Amanda. *Education:* Attended Emory-at-Oxford Junior College (now Oxford College of Emory University), 1958-60, and St. Petersburg Junior College, 1964-65. *Religion:* Associate Reformed Presbyterian.

ADDRESSES: Home—Sarasota, Florida.

CAREER: Reporter, *Tampa Times,* FL, 1965-66, *Lakeland Ledger,* FL, 1966-68, *Tampa Tribune,* FL, 1968-72, *Waterloo Courier,* IA, 1972-75, *Colorado Springs Gazette Telegraph,* CO, 1979-80; free-lance writer, 1975—. *Military service:* U.S. Army, 1960-63.

MEMBER: Western Writers of America.

AWARDS, HONORS: Spur Award, Western Writers of America, 1983, for *Leaving Kansas.*

WRITINGS:

WESTERN NOVELS

The 33 Brand, Doubleday, 1977.
Journey to Utah, Doubleday, 1977.
Duster (young adult), Independence Press, 1977.
Easy Money, Doubleday, 1978.
The Keystone Kid, Doubleday, 1978.
Home to Texas, Ace Books, 1978.
Hell Creek Cabin, Doubleday, 1979.
The Name Is Hart, Ace Books, 1979.
Sheepherding Man, Doubleday, 1980.

Jason Evers: His Own Story, Doubleday, 1980.
Old Kyle's Boy, Doubleday, 1981.
Cowboy, Doubleday, 1981.
The Ordeal of Hogue Bynell, Doubleday, 1982.
Leaving Kansas, Doubleday, 1983.
The Oil Rig, Bantam, 1984.
The Rain Rustlers, Bantam, 1984.
Reaching Colorado, Doubleday, 1984.
The Video Vandals, Bantam, 1985.
The Turn-Out Man, Bantam, 1985.
The Coyote Crossing, Bantam, 1985.
Finding Nevada, Doubleday, 1985.
Stillwater Smith, Doubleday, 1986.
The Ballad of Bryan Drayne (young adult), New American Library, 1987.
Billy Ray and the Good News, Doubleday, 1987.
Charlie and the Sir, Doubleday, 1988.
The Outsider (young adult), New American Library/Dutton, 1988.
Billy Ray's Forty Days (young adult), Doubleday, 1989.
J. A. Whitford and the Great California Gold Hunt, Doubleday, 1990.
Mustang War, Doubleday, 1991.
His Royal Highness J. A. Whitford, Doubleday, 1992.

WORK IN PROGRESS: Another western novel for Doubleday and *The Way West* for Lynx Books.

SIDELIGHTS: Frank Roderus once told *CA:* "I wrote my first fiction (a western) at age five and never wanted to do anything else. I enjoy researching the American West as well as my travels in the area. My novels are built around my characters, who I like to think are representative of the people who still raise livestock in this great country."

BIOGRAPHICAL/CRITICAL SOURCES:

PERIODICALS

Booklist, October 15, 1989, p. 428.
Kliatt Young Adult Paperback Book Guide, April, 1988, p. 14; January, 1989, p. 16.
Library Journal, June 15, 1990, P. 138.
Publishers Weekly, February 13, 1987, p. 94.
Roundup, spring, 1989, p. 31.
Voice of Youth Advocates, April, 1988, p. 29.

*   *   *

ROGERS, Peter D(amien) 1942-
(Patrick D. Reilly)

PERSONAL: Born December 12, 1942, in Cleveland, OH; son of F. M. (a physician) and Agnes (a nurse; maiden name, Sullivan) Rogers; married Diane L. Burr (a nurse), June 3, 1983; children: Lindsey Erin, Danny, Timmy. *Ed-ucation:* Walsh College, B.A., 1964; University of Tennessee, M.D., 1970; received masters degree from University of North Carolina at Chapel Hill, 1972. *Politics:* Independent. *Religion:* Christian.

ADDRESSES: Home—Chattanooga, TN. *Office*—The Crossroads, 7525 Min Tom Dr., Chattanooga, TN. *Agent*—John Ware, 392 Central Park W., New York, NY 10025.

CAREER: United States Public Health Service, Centers for Disease Control, Atlanta, GA, worked for Epidemic Intelligence Service, 1975-77; pediatrician in private practice in Akron, OH, 1977-84; Northeast Ohio University Colleges of Medicine, Rootstown, OH, assistant professor of pediatrics and community health sciences, beginning 1978; The Crossroads, Chattanooga, TN, currently medical director. Former clinical assistant professor of pediatrics at Case Western Reserve Medical School, Cleveland, OH; faculty member of New York University's Summer Writers Conference, 1985.

MEMBER: American Medical Association, American Society of Addiction Medicine, Impaired Physicians Committee, Ohio State Medical Association.

WRITINGS:

Influenza Alert, F. A. Davis, 1976.
Everyday Problems in Public Health, F. A. Davis, 1977.
(Under pseudonym Patrick D. Reilly) *A Private Practice,* Macmillan, 1984.
Chemical Dependency, F. A. Davis, 1987.
The Substance Abusing Adolescent, Hanley and Belfus, 1992.

SIDELIGHTS: Under the pseudonym Patrick D. Reilly, Peter D. Rogers wrote about his struggle to overcome his drug addiction in *A Private Practice.* After fourteen years of heavy dependence on sedatives, the doctor entered a Toronto facility for substance abuse; his book relates his month of residential treatment and the parallel battles of other members of his therapy group. Daniel X. Freedman wrote in the *New York Times Book Review* that "the suspense of this well-told tale, populated by many characters, is sustained by the uncertain destiny of Dr. Reilly. . . . In the process, the psychology of addiction and recovery is revealed." The reviewer continued: "Dr. Reilly's affecting account helps us to understand the amount of patience and grueling effort needed to sustain sobriety."

Rogers told *CA:* "The major mistake I made after the notoriety I received for *A Private Practice* was that I began to take myself seriously. Fortunately, I survived that with only a mildly bruised ego."

BIOGRAPHICAL/CRITICAL SOURCES:

PERIODICALS

New York Times Book Review, April 29, 1984.

*   *   *

ROGERSON, J(ohn) W(illiam) 1935-
(John Rogerson)

PERSONAL: Born May 16, 1935, in London, England; son of George W. H. (a carpenter and joiner) and Fanny (Page) Rogerson; married Rosalind Ann Fulford, September 11, 1965. *Education:* University of Manchester, B.D., 1961, D.D., 1975; University of Oxford, B.A., 1963, M.A., 1967. *Religion:* Christian.

ADDRESSES: Office—University of Sheffield, Sheffield S10 2TN, England.

CAREER: University of Durham, Durham, England, lecturer, 1964-75, senior lecturer in theology, 1975-79; University of Sheffield, Sheffield, England, professor of biblical studies and chairman of department, 1979—. *Military service:* Royal Air Force, 1953-55.

MEMBER: Society for Old Testament Study (home secretary, 1972-77, president, 1989, foreign secretary, 1990—).

AWARDS, HONORS: Publication Award, Geographic Society of Chicago, 1985.

WRITINGS:

Myth in Old Testament Interpretation, De Gruyter, 1974.
(With J.W. McKay) *Psalms: Cambridge Old Testament Commentaries,* Cambridge University Press, 1977.
Anthropology and the Old Testament, Blackwell/John Knox, 1978.

Contributor to theological and anthropological journals, including *Journal of Theological Studies, Churchman, Theology, Journal of the Anthropological Society of Oxford,* and *Modern Churchman.*

UNDER NAME JOHN ROGERSON

The Supernatural in the Old Testament, Lutterworth, 1976.
(Editor) *Beginning Old Testament Study,* Westminster, 1983.
Old Testament Criticism in the Nineteenth Century, Fortress, 1984.
The Atlas of the Bible, Facts on File, 1985.
(With C. Rowland and B. Lindars) *The Study and Use of the Bible,* Marshall Pickering, 1988.
(With Philip Davies) *The Old Testament World,* Prentice-Hall, 1989.
Genesis I-II, Sheffield Academic Press, 1991.

De Wette: A Critical Biography, Sheffield Academic Press, 1991.

WORK IN PROGRESS: Researching the history of Old Testament criticism; preparing an Old Testament Theology that will address today's world.

SIDELIGHTS: John Rogerson describes his book, *Beginning Old Testament Study,* as a "guide to how to approach the academic study of the Old Testament." In it he explores Old Testament and Israelite history, the world view of the Old Testament, the history of Old Testament scholarship, and the application of the texts to social and moral issues. Anthony Phillips, writing in the *Times Literary Supplement,* determined that *Beginning Old Testament Study* should appear on the "first reading list" of Old Testament students. The critic added: "Conscious of the different spiritual backgrounds from which students come, [Rogerson] exhibits throughout a gentle pastoral touch which in no way blunts the sharpness of his essays."

Rogerson told CA: "I am increasingly concerned with using the Bible to address today's world in the light of the ecological crisis, feminism and theologies of liberation. Academics can no longer ignore the fact that the Bible is a contemporary text."

BIOGRAPHICAL/CRITICAL SOURCES:

PERIODICALS

Times Literary Supplement, July 1, 1983.

*   *   *

ROGERSON, John
See ROGERSON, J(ohn) W(illiam)

*   *   *

RORVIK, David M(ichael) 1946-
(Michael Davidson, M. M. Faraday)

PERSONAL: Born November 1, 1946, in Circle, MT; son of Alan and Frances (Ferch) Rorvik. *Education:* University of Montana, B.A. (with highest honors), 1966; Columbia University, M.S. (with highest honors), 1967.

ADDRESSES: Home—Portland, Oregon. *Office*—Proteus, Inc., P.O. Box 9281, Portland, OR 97207.

CAREER: Time magazine, New York City, reporter, 1967-70; free-lance writer and novelist, 1970—. Lecturer for Future Presentations, Inc., 1978-79; president and founder of Proteus, Inc. (literary agency), 1983—.

AWARDS, HONORS: Pulitzer traveling fellowship, 1968, for study of the press and the politics of apartheid in white-dominated countries; Alicia Patterson Foundation fellowship, 1976-77, for study of the politics of cancer research.

WRITINGS:

(With Landrum B. Shettles) *Your Baby's Sex: Now You Can Choose,* Dodd, 1970, revised edition published as *Choose Your Baby's Sex: The One Sex-Selection That Works,* 1977, revised edition published as *How to Choose Your Baby's Sex,* Doubleday, 1984.

Brave New Baby: Promise and Peril of the Biological Revolution, Doubleday, 1971.

As Man Becomes Machine: The Evolution of the Cyborg, Doubleday, 1971.

(Under pseudonym Michael Davidson) *The Sex Surrogates,* Geis, 1972.

(With O. S. Heyns) *Decompression Babies,* Dodd, 1973.

(With Eleanor Easley and others) *Good Housekeeping Woman's Medical Guide,* Good Housekeeping Books, 1974, revised edition edited by David Devlin, Ebury Press, 1975.

In His Image: The Cloning of a Man, Lippincott, 1978.

(Under pseudonym M. M. Faraday) *The Sharing,* Bantam, 1982, published under own name as *Sabra,* Sphere Books, 1983.

(With Shettles) *Rites of Life: The Scientific Evidence for Life before Birth,* Zondervan, 1984.

(With Bernard Siskin and Jerome Staller) *What Are the Chances?,* Crown, 1989.

Also author of column, "Present Shock," for *Esquire.* Contributor to numerous periodicals, including *Esquire, Good Housekeeping, Ladies Home Journal, New York Times Magazine, Omni, Playboy,* and *Science Digest.*

Rorvik's books have been translated into Spanish, French, German, Norwegian, Portuguese, Japanese, Chinese, Arabic, Italian, Finnish, Danish, Polish, Indian, and Dutch.

SIDELIGHTS: In the controversial *In His Image: The Cloning of a Man,* David M. Rorvik claimed to have helped arrange for the cloning, or exact genetic duplication, of an elderly man who wanted a son exactly like himself. Rorvik provided no documentation to support the claim, yet some reviewers accepted the book's validity or at least the possibility that the cloning process is possible based solely on the book. In the afterword to *In His Image,* Rorvik wrote, "I entertain absolutely no expectation that anyone, scientist or layman, will accept this book as proof of the events described herein. . . . I hope, however, that many readers will be persuaded of the possibility, even the probability, of what I have described and will benefit by this preview of an astonishing development whose time at least in terms of some of the emotional and ethical issues it raises, has apparently not quite yet come."

Max Lerner of the *New York Post* was among the minute percentage who believed *In His Image* as well as admitted their belief in print. "At the risk of being a laughingstock for the rest of my life I want to say that I take seriously the recent book on human cloning," Lerner declared. Most reviewers and scientists, however, rejected the book as a hoax.

Veracity aside, reviews were also mixed as to the book's value as a work of literature. While a reviewer for the *Youngstown Vindicator* described *In His Image* as "an engrossing book written in a readable, non-technical style," In the *New York Times Book Review,* Michael Crichton, author of *The Andromeda Strain,* found the book "stupefyingly dull. The plot is highly unlikely, the characters sketchy and improbably motivated, and the narrator himself is by turns dimwitted and melodramatic." In one way, however, Crichton's views support Rorvik's claim that the book is authentic. Said Rorvik, "If *In His Image* was a novel, it was a failure from my point of view. I don't think I would be capable of writing such poor fiction."

BIOGRAPHICAL/CRITICAL SOURCES:

BOOKS

Rorvik, David M., *In His Image,* Lippincott, 1978.

PERIODICALS

Chicago Tribune, June 30, 1989.
New York Post, March 29, 1978.
New York Times, March 4, 1978; March 11, 1978; March 23, 1978; July 11, 1978.
New York Times Book Review, April 23, 1978.
San Francisco Chronicle, April 3, 1978.
Time, July 24, 1978, p. 47.
Washington Post, March 12, 1978; March 31, 1978.
Youngstown Vindicator, April 16, 1978.

* * *

ROSE, Kenneth Jon 1954-

PERSONAL: Born June 23, 1954, in New York, NY. *Education:* University of Connecticut, B.A., 1976; Marine Biological Laboratory, Woods Hole, MA, 1977; New York University, M.S., 1984, Ph.D., 1989; American University Law School, J.D., 1993.

ADDRESSES: Agent—Barbara Bova Literary Agency, 207 Sedgwick Rd., West Hartford, CT 06107.

CAREER: Woods Hole Oceanographic Institution, Woods Hole, MA, research assistant, 1976-78; free-lance science writer, 1978—; University of California, Irvine, research associate, 1989-90.

MEMBER: American Association for the Advancement of Science, American Intellectual Property Law Association, National Space Society, Society for Neuroscience, New York Academy of Sciences.

AWARDS, HONORS: Distinguished technical communication award, International Audiovisual Competition, and Silver Cindy Award, International Film Producers Association, both 1982, for "The Chemistry of Life: Hormones and the Endocrine System"; finalist, Science Book Prizes, 1989; Best Books for the Teen Age award, New York Public Library, 1989.

WRITINGS:

Classification of the Animal Kingdom, McKay, 1980.
The Body in Time, Wiley, 1988.
Quick Scientific Terminology, Wiley, 1989.
Enemy Ours, Wiley, 1992.
From Head to Toe, J. P. Tarcher, 1992.

Contributor to magazines, including *Analog, Boys' Life, Futurific, Natural History, Omni, Science Digest, Self,* and *Travel and Leisure.*

SIDELIGHTS: Kenneth Jon Rose once told *CA:* "I always enjoyed writing, but didn't start to do it professionally until I had the great fortune to study sharks at Woods Hole. I felt the experience had to be shared. After I had exhausted the subject (some four or five articles later), I left for New York, where the magazine editors there gave me plenty of work.

"As a writer, I have traveled to mummy digs in Chile [and] remote villages in Peru, met with Nobel Prize laureates, senators, astronauts, corporate executives, and television celebrities. I recommend it."

Chicago Tribune reviewer Peter Gorner described *The Body in Time* as "one of those rare works that never fails to inform as it entertains." Examining mysteries such as why heart attacks and strokes are more common in the morning, why babies born in the afternoon are more likely to have medical problems, and why many people are able to wake up seconds before the alarm clock rings, *The Body in Time* uncovers the many timing systems and rhythms within the human body and the ways in which the external world can affect them.

BIOGRAPHICAL/CRITICAL SOURCES:

PERIODICALS

Chicago Tribune, May 25, 1988.
New York Times Book Review, March 27, 1988.*

ROSS, Gary 1948-

PERSONAL: Born October 16, 1948, in Toronto, Ontario, Canada; son of Walter S. and Leila Mary (Walker) Ross. *Education:* University of Toronto, B.A., 1970.

ADDRESSES: Office—Box 45551, Sunnyside Mall, Surrey, British Columbia, Canada V4A 9N3.

CAREER: Weekend Magazine, Toronto, Ontario, senior editor, 1977-79; *Saturday Night,* Toronto, senior editor, 1980-87; Macfarlane Walter & Ross, senior editor (cofounder), 1988—.

MEMBER: PEN International, Writers Union of Canada, Association of Canadian Television and Radio Artists, Writers Guild.

AWARDS, HONORS: E.J. Pratt medal for poetry, 1968, Norma Epstein Award, 1968, Frederic Davison Prize for fiction, 1969, all from University of Toronto; National Magazine Award for fiction, National Magazine Awards Foundation of Canada, 1981, for *Blueberries;* Chatelaine Prize, 1981, for *Open Heart.*

WRITINGS:

Always Tip the Dealer (novel), McClelland & Stewart, 1981, Bantam, 1982.
Stung: The Incredible Obsession of Brian Molony, Stoddart, 1987, General Publishing, 1988.
Tears of the Moon (novel), Viking, 1989.
At Large: The Fugitive Odyssey of Murray Hill and his Elephants (nonfiction), Stoddart, 1992, Random House, 1992.

SIDELIGHTS: Gary Ross told *CA:* "As well as writing books, I edit and publish nonfiction on behalf of Macfarlane Walter & Ross, the Canadian Publishing house which I co-founded in 1988."

*   *   *

ROSTAND, Robert
   See HOPKINS, Robert S(ydney)

*   *   *

ROTH, Henry 1906-

PERSONAL: Born February 8, 1906, in Tysmenica, Galicia, Austria-Hungary (now part of the U.S.S.R.); son of Herman (a waiter) and Leah (Farb) Roth; married Muriel Parker (a musician, composer, and elementary school principal), October 7, 1939; children: Jeremy, Hugh. *Education:* College of the City of New York (now City College of the City University of New York), B.S., 1928. *Politics:* Unaffiliated. *Religion:* None.

ADDRESSES: Home—Los Calinas Retirement Home, 500 Paisano N.E., Albuquerque, NM 87123. *Agent*—Roslyn Targ Literary Agency, 105 West 13th St., New York, NY 10011.

CAREER: Roth says: "in writing and idleness [New York, N.Y.]," 1929-38; with Works Progress Administration (WPA), 1939; substitute high school teacher, Bronx, N.Y., 1939-41; precision metal grinder, New York, N.Y., 1941-45, Providence, R.I., and Boston, Mass., 1945-46; taught in a one-room school in Maine, 1947-48; Augusta State Hospital, Augusta, Me., attendant, 1949-53; waterfowl farmer, 1953-63; tutor in math, and occasionally Latin, 1956-65.

AWARDS, HONORS: Grant from National Institute of Arts and Letters, 1965; Townsend Harris Medal, City College of the City University New York, 1965; D. H. Lawrence fellowship, University of New Mexico, 1968.

WRITINGS:

Call It Sleep (novel), Ballou, 1934, 2nd edition with a history by Harold U. Ribalow, a critical introduction by Maxwell Geismar, and a personal appreciation by Meyer Levin, Pageant, 1960, reprinted, Avon, 1976 (same edition published in England with a foreword by Walter Allen, M. Joseph, 1963).
(Contributor) *The Best American Short Stories, 1967*, Houghton, 1967.
Nature's First Green (memoir), Targ, 1979.
Shifting Landscape: A Composite, 1925-1987, Jewish Publication Society, 1987, new edition, with foreword by Alfred Kazin, Farrar, Straus, 1991.

Contributor to *Atlantic, Commentary, Midstream, New Yorker, Signatures: Work in Progress, Lavender,* and *Studies in American Jewish Literature.* Boston University, which is starting a collection of manuscripts and materials on American Jewish literature, is beginning with a Henry Roth Collection. Preliminary drafts of Roth's *Call It Sleep* are at the New York Public Library.

SIDELIGHTS: First published in the 1930s, *Call It Sleep* received laudatory reviews, Alfred Hayes calling it "as brilliant as [James] Joyce's *Portrait of the Artist,* but with a wider scope, a richer emotion, a deeper realism." The book went into two printings (4,000 copies) and disappeared, leading an underground existence until republication by Pageant in 1960, as a result of the interest of the critic Harold Ribalow. In 1956, the *American Scholar* asked certain notable critics to list the most neglected books of the past twenty-five years. Alfred Kazin and Leslie Fiedler both chose *Call It Sleep,* making it the only book named twice. On October 25, 1961, Irving Howe's

front-page review of *Call It Sleep* in the *New York Times Book Review* marked the first time such space was devoted to a paperback reprint. Howe described the book as "one of the few genuinely distinguished novels written by a 20th-century American, [one which] achieves an obbligato of lyricism such as few American novels can match. . . . Intensely Jewish in tone and setting, *Call It Sleep* rises above all the dangers that beset the usual ghetto novel: it does not deliquesce into nostalgia, nor sentimentalize poverty and parochialism. The Jewish immigrant milieu happens to be its locale, quite as Dublin is Joyce's and Mississippi [William] Faulkner's."

The novel concerns the slum life of a young boy. Haskel Frankel has written, however, that to offer *Call It Sleep* as a tale about "a period in the life of an immigrant Jewish boy in the slums of New York's Lower East Side . . . is to offer a synopsis on a par with Roz Russell's plot summation of *Moby Dick* in the musical *Wonderful Town:* 'It's about this whale.' " The novel has been cited for its political undertones (Roth was close to the Communist Party at the time he wrote the novel; he later repudiated them), its depiction of Jewish domestic life, and its autobiographical aspects.

Howe believes that Roth is especially successful in the way he presents the mind of the young boy. "Yet the book is not at all the kind of precious or narrowing study of a child's sensibility that such a description might suggest. We are locked into the experience of a child, but are not limited to his grasp of it." Roth acknowledges the autobiographical qualities of the novel but emphasizes the methods he used in manipulating events remembered from his childhood. "I was working with characters, situations and events that had in part been taken from life, but which I molded to give expression to what was oppressing me. To a considerable extent I was drawing on the unconscious to give shape to remembered reality. Things which I could not fully understand but which filled me with apprehension played a critical role in determining the form of the novel."

Many critics disagree about the central theme or purpose of *Call It Sleep.* James Ferguson feels that it "is essentially the story of the development of a religious sensibility. Its implications are far more profoundly theological, even metaphysical, than they are social." In *Proletarian Writers of the Thirties,* Gerald Green suggests that Roth did have some social motivation in writing the novel: "Unlike the fashionable terrorists, Roth never loses hope, even if salvation speaks to us through cracked lips." And Walter Allen sees the book as "the most powerful evocation of the terrors of childhood ever written. We are spared nothing of the rawness of cosmopolitan slum life."

Roth once said that "the man who wrote that book at the age of 27 is dead. I am a totally different man. Almost." Some years ago he started another novel. Maxwell Perkins at Scribner thought it was brilliant and gave him an advance, but Roth was dissatisfied and destroyed the manuscript. Bonnie Lyons, writing in the *Dictionary of Literary Biography,* notes that *Call It Sleep* "is so emotionally moving and so artistically elegant that it has made Roth an important literary figure, even though he has never completed another novel."

Roth tells David Bronsen in *Partisan Review* that since the Israeli 1967 war he has begun to write again after many years. The war gave Roth "a place in the world and an origin. Having started to write, it seemed natural to go on from there, and I have been writing long hours every day since then. I am not yet sure what it is leading to, but it is necessary and is growing out of a new allegiance, an adhesion that comes from belonging." He said later: "The surge of partisanship awakened by the '67 war broke the hold of an ossified radicalism."

In a note to *CA,* Roth revealed that he has completed a new novel, *Mercy of a Rude Stream,* "to be published 3 years after my death." Despite his new commitment to writing fiction, Roth's commitment to his domestic life is of primary importance to him. He once said: "I find my greatest pleasure in matrimony, mathematics and puttering about the premises, in that order; I am daily compelled to admiration at the miracle of my wife."

BIOGRAPHICAL/CRITICAL SOURCES:

BOOKS

Allen, Walter, *The Modern Novel,* Dutton, 1965.
Contemporary Literary Criticism, Gale, Volume 2, 1974, Volume 6, 1976, Volume 11, 1979.
Dictionary of Literary Biography, Volume 28: *Twentieth-Century American-Jewish Fiction Writers,* Gale, 1984.
French, Warren, editor, *The Thirties: Fiction, Poetry, Drama,* Everett/Edwards, 1967.
Howe, Irving, *World of Our Fathers,* Harcourt, 1976.
Lyons, Bonnie, *Henry Roth: The Man and His Work,* Cooper Square, 1977.
Madden, Daniel, editor, *Proletarian Writers of the Thirties,* Southern Illinois University Press, 1968.

PERIODICALS

Centennial Review, spring, 1974.
Commentary, August, 1960; August, 1977; September, 1984.
Jewish Social Studies, July, 1966.
Life, January 8, 1965.
Los Angeles Times, December 8, 1987; December 11, 1987.
Los Angeles Times Book Review, January 10, 1988.

Modern Fiction Studies, winter, 1966.
New York Times, April 15, 1971.
New York Times Book Review, October 25, 1964.
Partisan Review, Volume 36, number 2, 1969.
Publishers Weekly, November 27, 1987.
Saturday Review, November 21, 1964.
Shenandoah, fall, 1973.
Studies in American Jewish Literature, spring, 1979.
Studies in the Novel, winter, 1975.
Twentieth Century Literature, October, 1966; January, 1969.
Washington Post, October 25, 1987.
Washington Post Book World, October 3, 1982.

*   *   *

ROUSMANIERE, John 1944-

PERSONAL: Surname is pronounced Ru-ma-*near;* born March 10, 1944, in Louisville, KY; son of James A. (a fundraiser) and Jessie (Pierce) Rousmaniere; married Leah Ruth Robinson; children: William Pierce, Dana Starr. *Education:* Attended University of Pennsylvania, 1962-63; Columbia University, B.S. (with honors), 1967, M.A., 1968; Union Theological Seminary, M.Div., 1988.

ADDRESSES: Home and office—100-23 Hope St., Stamford, CT 06906. *Agent*—Russell & Volkening, Inc., 50 West 29th St., New York, NY 10001.

CAREER: U.S. Military Academy, West Point, NY, assistant professor of history, 1970-72; *Yachting,* New York City, associate editor, 1972-77; *Natural History,* New York City, senior editor, 1978; free-lance writer, editor and consultant, 1978—; Union Theological Seminary, New York City, instructor, 1985-88. Adjunct assistant professor of writing, College of New Rochelle, 1980-83; member of editorial committee, Dolphin Book Club (Book-of-the-Month-Club), 1982—. *Military service:* U.S. Army, 1969-72; became first lieutenant.

MEMBER: Authors Guild, Authors League of America, New York Yacht Club.

WRITINGS:

A Glossary of Modern Sailing Terms, Dodd, 1975, 2nd edition, Putnam, 1989.
(With Dennis Conner) *No Excuse to Lose,* Norton, 1978.
(Editor) *The Enduring Great Lakes,* Norton, 1979
"Fastnet, Force 10," Norton, 1980.
The Luxury Yachts, Time-Life, 1981.
The Annapolis Book of Seamanship, Simon & Schuster, 1983, 2nd edition, 1989.
America's Cup Book, Norton, 1983.
Study Guide to the Annapolis Book of Seamanship, American Sailing Association, 1984.

The Sailing Lifestyle: A Guide to Sailing and Cruising for Pleasure, Simon & Schuster, 1985.

The Golden Pastime: A New History of Yachting, Norton, 1986.

(Editor) *Desirable and Undesirable Characteristics of Offshore Yachts,* Norton, 1987.

The Low Black Schooner: Yacht America, 1851-1945, Mystic Seaport Museum Stores, 1987.

A Picture History of the America's Cup, Mystic Seaport Museum Stores, 1989.

A Bridge to Dialogue, Paulist Press, 1991.

OTHER

The Annapolis Book of Seamanship (video series), Creative Programming, 1987-88.

Also author of numerous articles for major boating periodicals.

WORK IN PROGRESS: A history of the law firm, Davis Polk & Wardwell; a history of the United States in the 1890's.

SIDELIGHTS: John Rousmaniere told *CA:* "I continue to write about a variety of topics, from boating (both historical and instructional) to interfaith relations (*A Bridge to Dialogue*) to American history, in which I am doing an increasing amount of work."

Rousmaniere's "*Fastnet, Force 10*" chronicles the disastrous Fastnet race along the coast of Great Britain and Ireland in August of 1979. Severe weather during the race killed fifteen sailors, sank five yachts and capsized nineteen more, and caused more than half of the field of three hundred participating yachts to retire. Rousmaniere himself was aboard one of the ships during the storm, so he was able to report on the incident with the authority of an observer. Robert Krisch, book critic for the *Los Angeles Times,* calls "*Fastnet, Force 10*" "a narrative worthy of the best sea literature." Peter Jay, in an article for the *Washington Post Book World,* notes: "Rousmaniere's book is a useful, readable and thoroughly sane introduction to the basic facts, individual experiences and underlying issues of the 1979 Fastnet disaster . . . [It] is written in the good muscular style of a competent journalist with all the necessary sailing experience and specialist knowledge."

BIOGRAPHICAL/CRITICAL SOURCES:

BOOKS

Rousmaniere, John, "*Fastnet, Force 10,*" Norton, 1980.

PERIODICALS

Globe and Mail (Toronto), June 4, 1988.
Los Angeles Times, May 16, 1980; July 6, 1980.
Los Angeles Times Book Review, May 5, 1985.
New York Times, August 9, 1980.

Washington Post Book World, May 25, 1980.

*   *   *

RUSTICUS
  See MARTIN, Brian P(hilip)

*   *   *

RUTHIN, Margaret
  See CATHERALL, Arthur

*   *   *

RYAN, Cornelius (John)   1920-1974

PERSONAL: Born June 5, 1920, in Dublin, Ireland; died of cancer, December 23, 1974, in New York City; came to the United States, 1948, naturalized citizen, 1950; son of John Joseph and Amelia (Clohisey) Ryan; married Kathryn Ann Morgan (an author), May 27, 1950; children: Geoffrey John, Victoria Ann. *Education:* Studied violin at the Irish Academy of Music. *Avocational interests:* Golf, fishing, shooting.

CAREER: Writer. Junior secretary to Garfield Weston, Member of Parliament, in London, England, 1940-41; Reuter's News Agency, London, reporter, 1941-42; *Daily Telegraph,* London, war correspondent, 1943-45, reporter on Tokyo bureau, 1945-46, Middle East bureau chief in Jerusalem, 1946-47; *Time,* New York City, contributing editor, 1947-49; *Newsweek* (television show), New York City, member of special projects department, 1949-50; *Collier's,* New York City, associate editor, 1956; *Reader's Digest,* Pleasantville, NY, staff reporter, 1962-65, roving editor, 1965-74. Stringer for *Time* and *St. Louis Post-Dispatch* in Jerusalem, 1946-47. Member of board of directors, Ryan Holdings Co., Connecticut State Bank, and Boys Clubs of America; consultant to Pan American Airways; trustee of Correspondents Fund. Honorary research fellow at University of Manchester, 1964. Notable assignments as reporter include coverage of D-Day landings, General Patton's Third Army in Europe, the opening of *Daily Telegraph's* Tokyo bureau in 1945, post-war atomic bomb tests in the Pacific, and the 1948 Arab-Israeli war.

MEMBER: Society of American Historians, National Press Club (trustee), Authors League of America, Writers Guild, Union Interalliee Club (Paris), Mid-Ocean Club (Bermuda), Dutch Treat Club, Players Club, Silver Spring Country Club (Connecticut).

AWARDS, HONORS: Award for distinguished writing from University of Illinois, 1956; Benjamin Franklin

Award, Overseas Press Club Award, and Christopher Literature Award for best book on foreign affairs, all 1959; Bancarella Prize for literature (Italy), 1962; Eire Society of Boston gold medal for literature, 1966; Medaille de la France Liberee, Legion of Honor; Litt.D. from Ohio University, 1974.

WRITINGS:

(With Frank Kelly) *Star-Spangled Mikado,* McBride, 1948.

(With F. Kelly) *MacArthur: Man of Action,* Doubleday, 1950.

(Editor) Joseph Kaplan and others, *Across the Space Frontier,* Viking, 1952.

(Editor) Wernher Von Braun, *Conquest of the Moon,* Viking, 1952 (published in England as *Man on the Moon,* Sidgwick & Jackson, 1953).

One Minute to Ditch! (story collection), Ballantine, 1957.

The Longest Day: June 6, 1944, Simon & Schuster, 1959.

The Last Battle, Simon & Schuster, 1966.

A Bridge Too Far (Book-of-the-Month Club selection), Simon & Schuster, 1974.

(With wife, Kathryn Morgan Ryan) *A Private Battle,* Simon & Schuster, 1979.

OTHER

Author of screenplay adaptations of *The Longest Day,* 20th Century-Fox, 1962, and *The Last Battle.* Also author of radio scripts and plays in Ireland during the 1940s.

ADAPTATIONS: Ryan's books sold well over 10 million copies and were translated into many foreign languages. *A Bridge Too Far* was filmed by United Artists in 1977.

SIDELIGHTS: Because of the popularity of his World War II histories, Cornelius Ryan was said to be a new breed of historian, one who wrote history with as much emphasis on interest and suspense as he placed on accuracy. Ryan always disagreed with that description: "There is nothing new in what I am doing," he said. "It's only old-fashioned reporting. Regardless of all the talk about this being a new style, it is not. It's being rareified, redefined—but we're doing no more today than fine historians and crime reporters have done, beginning with Thucydides in his history of the Peloponnesian Wars. Take Stendhal's magnificent description of the Battle of Waterloo—when asked why he did it that way he said, 'I simply want to know what happened.' "

While refusing the label of new historian, Ryan admitted that his approach was different from that of his academic contemporaries. One of the reasons he gave for writing *The Longest Day: June 6, 1944* was that he disagreed with the view of war in terms only of the outcome of battles and the movement of huge masses of men. "What was missing was the story of wartime events told in terms of the human

spirit. I wanted to write about the ordinary people who were caught up in a conflict so vast they could perceive an infinitely small segment. What I write about is not war, but the courage of man and the fact that man will prevail. I just use war as the framework to show people at every level in society in all their bravery and compassion."

Paul Montgomery explained how Ryan worked: "Ryan's method was based on an assiduous accumulation of detail, drawing on the experiences in battle of everyone from enlisted man to general. For the D-Day book, for example, he advertised in American, English, Canadian and German newspapers seeking interviews with participants. From 6,300 replies, he culled more than 1,000 interviews; parts of 400 of them appeared in the book, woven together in the writer's suspenseful narrative."

Ryan was well known for his tireless research. For *The Longest Day,* he worked out a complete chronology of D-Day on five to fifteen minute intervals, and he used no detail or anecdote that was not confirmed "by at least four people who were eyewitnesses or who had diary entries to substantiate their statements." While working on *The Last Battle,* Ryan was the first American in over forty years to be allowed access to Russian documents and the first person to interview Otto Gunshe, the man who last saw Adolf Hitler alive.

"To write each one of these books means contacting from 3,000 to 6,000 people," Ryan admitted. "*The Longest Day* dealt with the landing in Normandy, so there were thousands of English, French and so on, and equally thousands of Germans looking down from the defensive positions. Then when they're found, through advertisements or whatever, about 30 per cent turn out to be useless—after all, every man fighting in World War II had his own D-Day, wherever it was and I need several people to describe each incident. *The Longest Day* took ten years of work, and *The Last Battle,* although it's a longer book because the fall of Berlin is the biggest subject, took six. For *The Longest Day* I have 48 drawers of files, and for *The Last Battle,* about 64."

While writing *A Bridge Too Far,* the story of the failed Allied invasion of Arnhem during World War II, Ryan discovered that he had prostate cancer. He insisted on finishing his book. During the day, he refused painkilling drugs in order to keep alert while writing the nearly-600 page book. At the time of his death in November of 1974, *A Bridge Too Far* was number 2 on the nonfiction best-seller list.

Several years after the author's death, his wife, Kathryn, discovered tape recordings and notebooks Ryan had made during his final bout with cancer. She worked the material into a book which includes her own account of the family's struggle with Ryan's illness. "The gritty particularity of this account," wrote Walter Clemons in *Newsweek,* "makes it extraordinarily readable. Ryan was neither a sage not especially eloquent; the prospect of death didn't stir him to profound or magical words-to-live-by. His wife is not a seer or sayer. But the very ordinariness of their joint record is finally very moving."

BIOGRAPHICAL/CRITICAL SOURCES:

BOOKS

Contemporary Literary Criticism, Volume 7, Gale, 1977.
Ryan, Cornelius John and Kathryn Morgan Ryan, *A Private Battle,* Simon & Schuster, 1979.

PERIODICALS

Atlantic, October, 1974, p. 115.
Book World, March 2, 1969.
Christian Science Monitor, October 2, 1974, p. 13.
Collier's, March 17, 1951, p. 66.
Economist, September 28, 1974, p. 108.
National Review, November 22, 1974, p. 1369.
Newsweek, September 16, 1974, p. 86; June 11, 1979, p. 100.
New Yorker, September 30, 1974, p. 131.
New York Herald Tribune, March 27, 1966, p. 1.
New York Times, June 16, 1979.
New York Times Book Review, July 1, 1979, p. 7.
Saturday Review, March 26, 1966, pp. 30-31.
Spectator, November 9, 1974, p. 602; August 16, 1980, p. 17.
Time, September 23, 1974, pp. 95-96; August 6, 1979, p. 83.
Times Literary Supplement, November 1, 1974, p. 1224.
Washington Post Book World, September 15, 1974; July 1, 1979, Section F, p. 4.

OBITUARIES:

PERIODICALS

Newsweek, December 9, 1974, p. 91.
New York Times, November 25, 1974, p. 34.
Publishers Weekly, December 2, 1974, p. 18.
Time, December 9, 1974, p. 107.
Washington Post, November 25, 1974.*

S

SARGESON, Frank 1903-1982

PERSONAL: Born March 23, 1903, in Hamilton, New Zealand; died March 1, 1982. *Education:* Attended University of New Zealand.

CAREER: Writer. Admitted as solicitor of Supreme Court of New Zealand, 1926. New Zealand Public Trust, Wellington, New Zealand, estates clerk, 1928-29; also worked as a journalist.

AWARDS, HONORS: Centennial Literary Competition Prize, 1940; New Zealand Government literary pension, 1947-68; Hubert Church Prize, 1952 and 1968; Katherine Mansfield Award, 1965; D.Litt., University of Auckland, 1974.

WRITINGS:

STORY COLLECTIONS

Conversation with My Uncle and Other Sketches, Unicorn Press (Auckland), 1936.
A Man and His Wife, Caxton Press (Christchurch), 1940.
That Summer and Other Stories, Lehmann, 1946.
Collected Stories, Blackwood & Janet Paul (Auckland), 1964, MacGibbon & Kee, 1964 (New Zealand edition with six pages of bibliography; London edition with introduction by E. M. Forster), revised edition published as *The Stories of Frank Sargeson,* International Publications Service, 1974.
(With others) *Short Stories by New Zealanders,* Longman Paul (Auckland), 1970.

NOVELS

When the Wind Blows, Caxton Press, 1945.
I Saw in My Dream, Lehmann, 1949, new edition, edited and with introduction by H. Winston Rhodes, Oxford University Press, 1974.
I for One . . . , Caxton Press, 1954.

Memoirs of a Peon, MacGibbon & Kee, 1965.
The Hangover, MacGibbon & Kee, 1967.
Joy of the Worm, MacGibbon & Kee, 1969.
Man of England Now [and] *I for One* [and] *A Game of Hide and Seek* (novellas), Caxton Press, 1972.
Sunset Village, Martin Brian & O'Keefe, 1976.
En Route (bound with *Tandem* by Edith Campion), Reed, 1979.

OTHER

(Editor) *Speaking for Ourselves: A Collection of New Zealand Stories,* Caxton Press, 1945.
Wrestling with the Angel (contains *A Time for Sowing,* first produced in Auckland, 1961, and *The Cradle and the Egg,* first produced in Auckland, 1962), Caxton Press, 1964.
Once Is Enough: A Memoir, Reed, 1972, Martin Brian & O'Keefe, 1973.
More Than Enough: A Memoir, Martin Brian & O'Keefe, 1975.
Never Enough!: Places and People Mainly, Martin Brian & O'Keefe, 1977.
Conversation in a Train and Other Critical Writing, Oxford University Press, 1983.

A collection of Sargeson's manuscripts is housed at the Alexander Turnbull Library in Wellington, New Zealand.

SIDELIGHTS: At the time of his death in 1982, Frank Sargeson was "the unquestioned doyen of New Zealand letters," a London *Times* writer commented. Sargeson's characters are alienated and isolated from their society, often because of their sexual orientation, and strive for freedom from a Puritanical society. Many of his characters are also from the lower classes, inarticulate, and violent. According to H. Winston Rhodes, writing in *Landfall Country: Work from "Landfall," 1947-61,* Sargeson's characters "cannot become accustomed to a civilization in which social habits conflict with the promptings of the heart and who, therefore, refuse to adjust themselves." "Sargeson's attitude is one of pity for people who destroy their own capacity for life," Murray S. Martin explained in the *Journal of General Education.* Rhodes claimed that Sargeson's "emphasis on a primitive morality is such that few readers would be able to derive from his stories even a moderate faith in the power of human beings to change the conditions under which men live or to make any substantial progress towards the ideal of the brotherhood of man. His characters do little but crouch down and hold on tight. Their solitude is relieved only by the presence of others in a like predicament. They are the displaced persons whose fate it is to remain for ever rootless, but tormented by vague desires that can never be satisfied."

One of Sargeson's typical characters was described by E. H. McCormick in *New Zealand Literature: A Survey* as "the 'good,' well brought up boy who breaks away from his respectable parents." This character type is found in such novels as *I Saw in My Dream* and *The Hangover.* In *I Saw in My Dream,* follows a middle-class young man, Henry Dave, as he grows to maturity in the New Zealand of the early part of this century. Rhodes, in his introduction to the novel, compares the story to *Pilgrim's Progress*: "Sargeson's 'dream' of a twentieth century, New Zealand pilgrim's progress is no allegory and is less a visionary search for a heavenly goal than a curiously patterned but dramatic portayal of adolescent deprivation culminating in the pursuit of wholeness and the quest for fulfilment."

In *The Hangover,* the young character Alan enters the drug world of the hippies and "loses both his innocence and his sense of belonging," as Martin explained. Speaking of *The Hangover,* Kay Dick once commented that it was "full of fascination and interest, with its straightforward account of a young man gaining maturity through his association with several offbeat characters. Mr. Sargeson is also much concerned to describe the inherent bisexuality of most relationships. He is an expert at tone and mood, and able to switch from conventional illustration . . . to loose philosophical notation." Similarly, Ian Reid of *Australian Book Review* found that, "as in much of his work, Frank Sargeson [in *The Hangover*] directs his unblinking but not uncompassionate eye towards an adolescent struggling to reconcile the disturbing facts of his widening experience with the assumptions derived from a narrow religious upbringing."

In *Memoirs of a Peon,* Sargeson wrote a satirical account of New Zealand middle class respectability. As in his previous books, the focus is on an innocent young character coming of age. Calling Sargeson "a sharp social commentator and a sophisticated literary craftsman," Malcolm Bradbury argued in *Punch* that *Memoirs of a Peon* was "an essentially episodic novel, but since Sargeson is not only a sharp social observer but a writer with an eye for the witty, revealing scene, this works superbly."

Speaking of Sargeson's contribution to New Zealand literature, Bruce King wrote in his *The New English Literatures: Cultural Nationalism in a Changing World:* "in a colonial situation where English middle-class social values are inappropriate, the first really believable characters in fiction are usually the eccentrics and outcasts. It was Frank Sargeson who made such types representative of an authentic New Zealand."

Sargeson once told *CA:* "Personal data of no interest to anyone except self and half a dozen friends. But my publishers think my longest book, *Memoirs of a Peon,* is one of the funniest books written anywhere this century. They may be right."

BIOGRAPHICAL/CRITICAL SOURCES:

BOOKS

Brasch, Charles, editor, *Landfall Country: Work from "Landfall," 1947-61,* Caxton Press, 1962, pp. 412-429.
Contemporary Literary Criticism, Volume 31, Gale, 1985.
Copland, R. A., *Frank Sargeson,* Oxford University Press, 1976.
King, Bruce, *The New English Literatures: Cultural Nationalism in a Changing World,* St. Martin's, 1980, pp. 140-156.
McCormick, E. H., *New Zealand Literature: A Survey,* Oxford University Press, 1959, pp. 108-135.
McEldowney, Dennis, *Frank Sargeson in His Time,* McIndoe (Dunedin), 1976.
Rhodes, H. Winston, *Frank Sargeson,* Twayne, 1969.
Sargeson, Frank, *Once Is Enough: A Memoir,* Reed, 1972, Martin Brian & O'Keefe, 1973.
Sargeson, F., *More Than Enough: A Memoir,* Martin Brian & O'Keefe, 1975.
Sargeson, F., *Never Enough!: Places and People Mainly,* Martin Brian & O'Keefe, 1977.
Shaw, Helen, editor, *The Puritan and the Waif: A Symposium of Critical Essays on the Work of Frank Sargeson,* Hoffmann (Auckland), 1955.

PERIODICALS

Australian Book Review, April, 1968, pp. 110-111.
Books and Bookmen, December, 1965, p. 45; February, 1969, p. 7.
Journal of General Education, September, 1981, pp. 123-134.
Landfall, December, 1950-December, 1951.
Listener, August 7, 1969, p. 193; May 11, 1972, p. 628; May 29, 1975, p. 718; April 29, 1976, p. 549; April 27, 1978, p. 555.
London Review of Books, November 17, 1983, p. 13.

New Statesman, April 2, 1965, p. 538; September 24, 1965, p. 448; August 8, 1969, p. 186; May 12, 1972, p. 648; April 9, 1976, p. 478.

Observer, April 25, 1965, p. 27; September 10, 1967, p.22; August 3, 1969, p. 24; July 2, 1972, p. 31; February 4, 1973, p. 36; June 22, 1975, p. 26; April 4, 1976, p. 26.

Punch, March 31, 1965, p. 484; September 29, 1965, p. 475.

Spectator, April 23, 1965, p. 538; September 24, 1965, p. 388; September 15, 1967, p. 303; August 2, 1969, p. 146.

Times Literary Supplement, June 17, 1965, p. 494; September 16, 1965, p. 795; August 7, 1969, p. 873; July 25, 1975, p. 820; August 20, 1976, p. 1037; April 12, 1985, p. 403.

World Literature Today, spring, 1985, p. 319.

OBITUARIES:

PERIODICALS

Times (London), March 11, 1982.*

*   *   *

SARTORI, Giovanni   1924-

PERSONAL: Born May 13, 1924, in Florence, Italy; son of Dante and Emilia (Quentin) Sartori; married Giovanna Paterno Castello, October 21, 1969; children: Ilaria. *Education:* University of Florence, doctor in political and social sciences, 1946.

ADDRESSES: Office—1430 International Affairs Bldg., Columbia University, 420 West 118th St., New York, NY 10027.

CAREER: University of Florence, Florence, Italy, associate professor of modern philosophy, 1950-57, associate professor of political science, 1957-65, professor of sociology, 1962-65, professor of political science, 1965-76, dean of Faculty of Political Science, 1969-71; Stanford University, Stanford, CA, professor of political science, 1976-79; Columbia University, New York City, Albert Schweitzer Professor in the Humanities, 1979—. Fellow, Center for Advanced Study in the Behavioral Sciences, 1971-72; senior fellow, Hoover Institution, 1976-79.

MEMBER: American Academy of Arts and Sciences.

AWARDS, HONORS: Guggenheim fellow, 1979; Ford Foundation fellow, 1979.

WRITINGS:

Democrazia e Definizioni, Il Mulino, 1957, 6th edition, 1985, translation by the author published as *Demo-*

cratic Theory, Wayne State University Press, 1962, new edition, Praeger, 1965.

A Teoria da Representacao no Estado Representativo Moderno, Universidade de Minas Gerais, 1962.

Il Parlamento Italiano, 1946-1963, Edizioni Scientifiche Italiane, 1963.

Stato e Politica nel Pensiero di B. Croce, Morano, 1966.

Parties and Party Systems: A Framework for Analysis, Cambridge University Press, 1976.

La Politica, SugarCo, 1979.

Teoria dei Partiti e Caso Italiano, SugarCo, 1982.

(Editor and co-author) *Social Science Concepts: A Systematic Analysis,* Sage Publications, 1984.

The Theory of Democracy Revisited, Chatham House, 1989.

Elementi di Teoria Politica, Il Mulino, 1990.

Democrazia, Rizzoli, 1992.

Also contributor to books. Contributor to *International Encyclopedia of the Social Sciences.* Contributor to periodicals. Managing editor, *Rivista Italiana de Scienza Politica,* 1971—.

*   *   *

SCARBROUGH, George (Addison)   1915-

PERSONAL: Born October 20, 1915, in Benton, TN; son of William Oscar (a farmer) and Louise Anabel (McDowell) Scarbrough. *Education:* Attended University of Tennessee, 1935-36, M.A., 1954; attended University of the South, 1941-43; Lincoln Memorial University, B.A., 1947; graduate study at State University of Iowa, 1957. *Politics:* Independent. *Religion:* Unitarian.

ADDRESSES: Home—100 Darwin Lane, Oak Ridge, TN 37830.

CAREER: Newspaperman and farmer in eastern Tennessee, 1937-43; teacher of English at various secondary schools in Tennessee, 1943-64; Hiwassee College, Madisonville, TN, English instructor, 1965-67; Chattanooga City College, Chattanooga, TN, professor of English, 1968; free-lance writer and journalist, 1968—. Has given poetry readings at schools and workshops, including Appalachian State University, State University of New York, Carson-Newman College, and Cumberland Valley Writers Conference.

MEMBER: Poetry Society of America, Southern Appalachian Writers' Co-op, Book Discussion Club (Oak Ridge, TN), Friends of Oak Ridge Library.

AWARDS, HONORS: Pushcart Award nomination for article, "Notes toward a Supreme Regionalism"; actor's award, Lincoln Memorial University, 1947; Carnegie

Foundation grants, 1956, 1975; Borestone Mountain Award, 1961, for "Noon Baptism"; Mary Rugeley Ferguson Poetry Award, *Sewanee Review,* 1964, for "Return: August Afternoon"; PEN grant, 1975; Authors League of America grant, 1976; W. D. Weatherford Award nomination, Berea College, 1978, for *George Scarbrough: New and Selected Poems;* Sheena Albanese Memorial Prize, *Spirit,* 1978-79; Outstanding Tennessean award, governor of Tennessee, 1978; Tennessee governor's proclamation naming June 14, 1978, George Scarbrough Day in Tennessee; Literary Hall of Fame induction, Lincoln Memorial University, 1982; Pulitzer Prize nomination, 1990, for *Invitation to Kim;* Distinguished Tennessee Writer's Award, 1990.

WRITINGS:

POETRY

Tellico Blue, Dutton, 1949.
The Course Is Upward, Dutton, 1951.
Summer So-Called, Dutton, 1956.
George Scarbrough: New and Selected Poems, Iris Press, 1977.
George Scarbrough Chapbook, Spirit Magazine, 1984.
A Summer Ago, St. Luke's Press, 1986.
Invitation to Kim, Iris Press, 1989.

OTHER

Contributor to anthologies, including *Forever the Land,* edited by Russell Lord, Harper, 1950; *The Current Voice: Readings in Contemporary Prose,* edited by Don L. Cook and others, Prentice-Hall, 1971; *Traveling America with Today's Poets,* edited by David Kherdian, Macmillan, 1977; *Southern Poetry: The Post Fugitive Era,* Louisiana State University Press, 1978; *Homewords,* edited by Douglas Paschall, University of Tennessee Press, 1986; and *Practices of the Winds,* edited by David M. Marovich and Nicolaus Washkowsky, Thompson-Shore, 1992. Contributor of poetry to magazines, including *Atlantic, Harper's, Poetry,* and *Saturday Review,* and of articles on travel and conservation to *Appalachian Journal, Land, Mountain Life and Work,* and *Progressive Farmer.* Staff book reviewer, *Chattanooga Times,* 1940-1980.

WORK IN PROGRESS: "Initial volume of the *Journals* to be published by Iris Press, 1992—the first of some 60 volumes. Three volumes of verse awaiting publication by Iris Press."

SIDELIGHTS: George Scarbrough once told *CA:* "As a teacher of creative writing both on the high school and the college level, I have been careful to stress that a poetic renaissance does not happen simply because thousands of people happen to be writing publishable verse. My great ambition is to find a college campus on which I can stress to all interested students the values of language to the would-be writer, a need that is crying in these days of slack attention to the graces of formalized speech, days in which even syntax and correct grammatical forms, not to mention shades of meanings of words, are regarded as old hat and unnecessary to the young scribe. Learning, as such, is adjudged superfluous. All these are reasons I preached, John in the wilderness, that all of us know something, a little, but nobody knows enough. The poetic classroom is disorganized. Poets in America wait for the great one, the teacher, to enter the door.

"As a born dirt farmer, I have dirt, soil, under my nails. I keep it there figuratively, as a reminder. Interstate highways can never quite by-pass the land. It is always there, as is the art of spreading manure on lonely ground between the river and the mountain. And wood doves still call in the remote country places. All this, despite the high smokestacks of Oak Ridge and the atomic honey the bees make from the old flowering pear trees of disappeared farms.

"I am a kind of writing spider that catches only what his net is capable of catching—which means, only, that I am limited to my own time, place, and my sense of values of these. I am not a regional writer. I am a southern writer, with a difference: that difference being that I was born north of the majority of slavery, in the shadow of the southern Appalachians, not of the mountains but nurtured by them. I wish to write out for America what it meant to be such an individual in such a time and in such a place.

"I think the contemporary [literary] scene is too crowded, the notion being that anyone who can put together a simple sentence can write. Very little literature is being produced as a result." Scarbrough advises aspiring writers: "Write if you must, but know there is little reward beyond personal satisfaction. In my own efforts to recreate a county, I have striven to build a remembered place, with little thought of pleasing critics. I write for myself, shunning the pornographic and the stuff that makes for an easy sale. Self-respect is a constant consideration with me, and that is engendered by working as well as I am able. No greater joy is possible for me than the construction of a good English sentence. Language is the size of life. Very few of our younger writers seem to realize that, or indeed to take what they say in a serious fashion. The artist of whatever kind is the fulcrum of a culture; most of today's artists make poor levers for raising the level of the general culture."

BIOGRAPHICAL/CRITICAL SOURCES:

BOOKS

Philips, Robert, editor, *Fifty Southern Writers,* Chapel Hill, 1992.

Rubin, Louis, and others, editors, *The History of Southern Literature,* Louisiana State University Press, 1985.

Seven in Tennessee, University of Tennessee Press, 1968.

Warren, John W., and others, editors, *Tennessee Belles-Lettres: A Guide to Tennessee Literature,* Morrison, 1977.

PERIODICALS

Appalachian Journal, winter, 1975; winter, 1977-78; summer, 1987.

Chattanooga Times, May 22, 1977.

Mossy Creek Journal, spring, 1977.

Select Press Review, summer, 1977.

Sewanee Review, winter, 1978.

Southern Living, October, 1978.

Southern Review, autumn, 1990.

Spirit, fall-winter, 1990.

*   *   *

SCHEICK, William J(oseph)   1941-

PERSONAL: Born July 15, 1941, in Newark, NJ; son of Joseph Edward (an engineer) and Irene (Corvi) Scheick; married Marion Ruth Voorhees, August 3, 1963 (divorced February 29, 1980); children: Jessica Holly, Nathan Andrew. *Education:* Montclair State College, B.A., 1963; University of Illinois, M.A., 1965, Ph.D., 1969.

ADDRESSES: Home—9901 Oak Run Dr., Austin, TX 78758. *Office*—Parlin Hall, University of Texas, Austin, TX 78712-1164.

CAREER: University of Texas at Austin, assistant professor, 1969-74, associate professor, 1974-79, professor of English, 1979-86, J.R. Millikan Centennial Professor, 1986—.

WRITINGS:

The Will and the Word: The Poetry of Edward Taylor, University of Georgia Press, 1974.

The Writings of Jonathan Edwards: Theme, Motif, and Style, Texas A & M University Press, 1975.

Seventeenth-Century American Poetry, G. K. Hall, 1977.

The Slender Human Word: Emerson's Artistry in Prose, University of Tennessee Press, 1978.

The Half-Blood: A Cultural Symbol in Nineteenth-Century American Fiction, University Press of Kentucky, 1979.

(Editor) *Critical Essays on Jonathan Edwards,* G. K. Hall, 1979.

The Splintering Frame: The Later Fiction of H. G. Wells, University of Victoria, 1984.

(Editor) *Contemporary American Women Writers: Narrative Strategies,* University Press of Kentucky, 1985.

H. G. Wells: A Reference Guide, G. K. Hall, 1988.

(Editor) *Two Mather Biographies,* Lehigh University Press, 1989.

Fictional Structure and Ethics: The Turn-of-the-Century English Novel, University of Georgia Press, 1990.

Design in Puritan American Literature, University Press of Kentucky, 1992.

Contributor of over 190 articles and book reviews to academic and literary journals. Member of editorial board of *English Literature in Transition,* 1970—. Editor of *Texas Studies in Literature and Languages,* 1975—.

WORK IN PROGRESS: A study of turn-of-the-century ethical romance.

*   *   *

SCHIFFHORST, Gerald J.   1940-

PERSONAL: Born October 13, 1940, in St. Louis, MO; son of Charles (a stationer) and Helen (Fleming) Schiffhorst; married Lynn Butler, 1987. *Education:* St. Louis University, B.S., 1962, A.M., 1963; University of Illinois, graduate study, 1963-64; Washington University, St. Louis, MO, Ph.D., 1973. *Religion:* Catholic. *Avocational interests:* Travel, golf, music.

ADDRESSES: Home—2444 Forfarshire Dr., Winter Park, FL 32792. *Office*—Department of English, University of Central Florida, Orlando, FL 32816.

CAREER: University of Missouri, St. Louis, instructor in English, 1966-67; University of Central Florida, Orlando, FL, 1970—, began as assistant professor, currently professor of English. Visiting summer instructor, Iowa Wesleyan College.

MEMBER: Modern Language Association of America, Renaissance Society of America, Milton Society of America, South Atlantic Modern Language Association.

AWARDS, HONORS: National Endowment for the Humanities grants, 1974, 1979, and 1986.

WRITINGS:

A Simplified Approach to Theodore Dreiser's 'An American Tragedy,' Barron's, 1965.

(Editor) *The Triumph of Patience,* University Presses of Florida, 1978.

John Milton, Continuum, 1990.

(With John F. Schell) *Short Handbook for Writers,* McGraw, 1991.

Contributor of articles and literary essays to *Milton Studies, South Atlantic Review,* and other journals.

WORK IN PROGRESS: Co-editing *Manifestations of Ideology,* a study of the seventeenth century; researching sexuality and power in seventeenth-century England.

SCHWARZKOPF, LeRoy C(arl) 1920-

PERSONAL: Born December 9, 1920, in Sebewaing, MI; son of Hugo T. and Clara (Sting) Schwarzkopf. *Education:* Yale University, B.A., 1944; University of Michigan, M.A., 1951; Rutgers University, M.L.S., 1967.

ADDRESSES: Home—8429 Greenbelt Rd. #T-2, Greenbelt, MD 20770. *Office*—P.O. Box 232, Greenbelt, MD 20768.

CAREER: Career officer in the U.S. Army, 1944-49, 1951-66; served in the United States, Japan, Korea, and France; retired as lieutenant colonel. University of Maryland at College Park, government documents librarian, 1967-77, head of Documents/Maps Room, 1977-83; freelance writer and consultant, 1983—.

MEMBER: American Library Association (charter member of Government Documents Round Table, 1972—), Special Libraries Association (Geography and Map Division), American Association of Law Libraries, Society of American Archivists, Beta Phi Mu.

AWARDS, HONORS: Documents to the People Award from American Library Association's Government Documents Round Table, 1981.

WRITINGS:

Government Reference Books: A Biennial Guide to U.S. Government Publications (series), four volumes, Libraries Unlimited, 1984-90.
Popular Guide to U.S. Government Publications, Libraries Unlimited, 1985.
Government Reference Serials, Libraries Unlimited, 1988.

Author of "U.S. Government Publications," a bimonthly column in *Booklist,* 1972—; author of "Government Publications and Depository System," an annual article in *ALA Yearbook of Library and Information Services,* 1977-1990; author of "News from Washington," a bimonthly column in *Government Publications Review,* 1983—. Editor of *Documents to the People* and author of its bimonthly column, "Unclassified News from Washington," 1978-82. Contributor to library journals.

SIDELIGHTS: LeRoy C. Schwarzkopf once told *CA:* "My career as a government documents librarian and author has been guided by the theme 'Documents to the People,' which is the motto of the American Library Association's Government Documents Round Table (GODORT) and is also the title of the GODORT official quarterly publication. This motto seeks to increase awareness by the general public of the thousands of useful and interesting publications that are issued annually by government agencies (primarily in the federal government) and are available through the federal depository library program. My writings consist of annotated bibliographies of U.S. government publications and of current news and historical analysis of federal government printing and publishing, as well as information collection and dissemination activities and policies.

"I find that the chore of writing and revising manuscripts has been greatly reduced by the use of an IBM PC compatible computer with the WordPerfect word-processing program and Nutshell Plus, a file management program."

*   *   *

SELBOURNE, David 1937-

PERSONAL: Born June 4, 1937, in London, England; son of Henri Armand Hugh (a physician) and Sulamith (Amiel) Selbourne.

WRITINGS:

PLAYS

The Play of William Cooper and Edmund Dew-Nevett (three-act; first produced in Exeter, England, at Northcott Theatre, January 25, 1968), Methuen, 1968.
The Two-Backed Beast (two-act; first produced in Liverpool, England, at Everyman Theatre, December 4, 1968), Methuen, 1969.
Dorabella (fourteen scenes; first produced in Edinburgh, Scotland, at Traverse Theatre, October 28, 1969), Methuen, 1970.
Samson (first produced in London, England, at Soho Theatre, December, 1971), Calder & Boyars, 1970.
Alison Mary Fagan (first produced in Auckland, New Zealand, at Downside Theatre, 1972), Calder & Boyars, 1972.
The Damned, Methuen, 1972.
Three Class Plays (juvenile; includes three one-act plays), first produced in London at Round House Theatre, December, 1973.
Class Play (one-act; first produced in London at Round House Theatre, December, 1973), Hutchinson, 1975.
Two Plays for Children (includes *What's Acting?* and *Think of a Story, Quickly!,* both one-act; first produced in London at Cockpit Theatre, September, 1977), Edward Arnold, 1977.
A Woman's Trial, first produced in Bengali at People's Little Theatre, Calcutta, India, December, 1982.

Also author of unpublished and unproduced plays "The Tragedy of Miss Rosie Rose," 1975, "Gehenna," 1977, and "Sunday Times," 1978.

NONFICTION

An Eye to China, Black Liberator Press, 1975, 2nd edition, Orient Longman, 1978.

An Eye to India, Penguin, 1977.
The Making of a Midsummer Night's Dream, Methuen, 1982.
Through the Indian Looking Glass, Zed Press, 1982.
Against Socialist Illusion, Macmillan, 1984.
In Theory and in Practice, Oxford University Press, 1985.
Left Behind: Journeys into British Politics, Cape, 1987.
A Doctor's Life, Cape, 1989.
Death of the Dark Hero: Eastern Europe, 1987-90, Cape, 1990.

OTHER

Contributor to journals in England and the United States, including *Guardian, Harper's, Independent, New Society, New Statesman,* and *Times Literary Supplement.*

BIOGRAPHICAL/CRITICAL SOURCES:

PERIODICALS

Times (London), April 28, 1990.
Times Literary Supplement, May 4, 1990, p. 465.

*   *   *

SELSAM, Millicent Ellis 1912-

PERSONAL: Born May 30, 1912, in Brooklyn, NY; daughter of Israel and Ida (Abrams) Ellis; married Howard B. Selsam (a writer), September 1, 1936 (died September 7, 1970); children: Robert. *Education:* Brooklyn College (now part of the City University of New York), B.A., 1932, Columbia University, M.A., 1934. *Avocational interests:* collecting specimens of marine life for aquarium on Fire Island, swimming, dancing, painting, plants.

ADDRESSES: Home—100 West 94th Street, New York, NY 10025.

CAREER: Author of books for young people. New York City Public Schools, high school teacher, 1935-45. Walker & Company Publishers, New York City, juvenile science editor, 1972—.

MEMBER: American Association for the Advancement of Science (fellow), American Nature Study Society, Authors Guild, Authors League of America, National Audubon Society.

AWARDS, HONORS: Gold Medal Award, Boys' Clubs of America, 1963, for *Stars, Mosquitos and Crocodiles: The American Travels of Alexander Von Humboldt;* Eva L. Gordon Award, American Nature Study Society, 1964, for "many contributions to the literature of natural history"; Thomas A. Edison Award for best juvenile science book of the year, 1965, for *Biography of an Atom;* Junior Book Awards certificate, Boys' Clubs of America,

1966-67, for *Benny's Animals and How He Put Them In Order;* Lucky Book Club Four-Leaf Clover Award, 1973, for body of work; Washington Children's Book Guild Nonfiction Award, 1977, for "total body of creative writing"; Garden State Children's Book Award, 1978, for *How Kittens Grow;* nominee for Laura Ingalls Wilder Award, 1980; Garden State Children's Book Award for younger nonfiction, 1981, for *Tyrannosaurus Rex.*

WRITINGS:

Egg to Chick, illustrated by Frances Wells, International Publishers, 1946, revised edition illustrated by Barbara Wolff, Harper, 1970.
Hidden Animals, illustrated by David Shapiro, International Publishers, 1947, revised edition, Harper, 1969.
Play with Plants, illustrated by James MacDonald, Morrow, 1949, revised edition illustrated by Jerome Wexler, 1978.
Play with Trees, illustrated by Fred F. Scherer, Morrow, 1950.
Play with Vines (also see below), illustrated by Scherer, Morrow, 1951.
Play with Leaves and Flowers (also see below), illustrated by Scherer, Morrow, 1952.
All about Eggs, and How They Change into Animals, illustrated by Helen Ludwig, W. R. Scott, 1952, revised edition, Addison-Wesley, 1980.
Microbes at Work, illustrated by Ludwig, Morrow, 1953.
All Kinds of Babies and How They Grow, illustrated by Ludwig, W. R. Scott, 1953, revised edition published as *All Kinds of Babies,* illustrated by Symeon Shimin, Four Winds, 1967.
A Time for Sleep: How the Animals Rest, illustrated by Ludwig, W. R. Scott, 1953, revised edition published as *How Animals Sleep: A Time for Sleep,* illustrated by Ezra Jack Keats, Scholastic, 1969.
How the Animals Eat, illustrated by Ludwig, W. R. Scott, 1955.
The Plants We Eat, illustrated by Ludwig, Morrow, 1955, revised edition, 1981.
(With Betty Morrow) *See through the Sea,* illustrated by Winnifred Lubell, Harper, 1955.
See through the Forest, illustrated by Lubell, Harper, 1956.
Exploring the Animal Kingdom, illustrated by Leo Ames, Doubleday, 1957.
Play with Seeds, illustrated by Ludwig, Morrow, 1957.
See through the Jungle, illustrated by Lubell, Harper, 1957.
See through the Lake, illustrated by Lubell, Harper, 1958.
Nature Detective, illustrated by Theresa Sherman, W. R. Scott, 1958, revised edition published as *How to Be a Nature Detective,* illustrated by Keats, Harper, 1966.
Plants That Heal, illustrated by Kathleen Elgin, Morrow, 1959.

Seeds and More Seeds, illustrated by Tomi Ungerer, Harper, 1959.

(Editor) Charles Darwin, *The Voyage of the Beagle,* Harper, 1959.

Birth of an Island, illustrated by Lubell, Harper, 1959.

Around the World with Darwin, illustrated by Anthony Ravielli, Harper, 1960.

How to Grow House Plants, illustrated by Elgin, Morrow, 1960.

Plenty of Fish, illustrated by Erik Blegvad, Harper, 1960.

Tony's Birds, illustrated by Kert Werth, Harper, 1961.

See along the Shore, illustrated by Leonard Weisgard, Harper, 1961.

Underwater Zoos, illustrated by Elgin, Morrow, 1961.

The Language of Animals, illustrated by Elgin, Morrow, 1962.

(Editor) *Stars, Mosquitos and Crocodiles: The American Travels of Alexander Von Humboldt,* Harper, 1962.

Terry and the Caterpillars, illustrated by Arnold Lobel, Harper, 1962.

The Quest of Captain Cook, illustrated by Ames, Doubleday, 1962.

Plants that Move (contains *Play with Vines,* and *Play with Leaves and Flowers*), Morrow, 1962.

How Animals Live Together, illustrated by Elgin, Morrow, 1963, revised edition, 1979.

Greg's Microscope, illustrated by Lobel, Harper, 1963.

You and the World around You, illustrated by Greta Elgaard, Doubleday, 1963.

The Doubleday First Guide to Wildflowers, illustrated by Wolff, Doubleday, 1964.

The Courtship of Animals, illustrated by John Kaufman, Morrow, 1964.

Birth of a Forest, illustrated by Wolff, Harper, 1964.

Let's Get Turtles, illustrated by Lobel, Harper, 1965.

(With Jacob Bronowski) *Biography of an Atom,* revised edition illustrated by Weimer Pursell, Harper, 1965.

Animals as Parents, illustrated by Kaufman, Morrow, 1965.

Benny's Animals and How He Put Them in Order, illustrated by Lobel, Harper, 1966.

When an Animal Grows, illustrated by Kaufman, Harper, 1966.

The Bug that Laid the Golden Eggs, photographs by Harold Kreiger, illustrated by Kaufman, Harper, 1967.

Questions and Answers about Ants, illustrated by Arabelle Wheatley, Four Winds, 1967.

How Animals Tell Time, illustrated by Kaufman, Morrow, 1967.

Milkweed, photographs by Jerome Wexler, Morrow, 1967.

Maple Tree, photographs by Wexler, Morrow, 1968.

(With George B. Schaller) *The Tiger: Its Life in the Wild,* Harper, 1969.

Peanut, photographs by Wexler, Morrow, 1969.

The Tomato and Other Fruit Vegetables, photographs by Wexler, Morrow, 1970.

How Puppies Grow, Scholastic, 1971, revised edition, photographs by Esther Bubley, Four Winds, 1972.

Is This a Baby Dinosaur? And Other Science Picture Puzzles, Scholastic, 1971.

The Carrot and Other Root Vegetables, photographs by Wexler, Morrow, 1971.

Vegetables from Stems and Leaves, photographs by Wexler, Morrow, 1972.

More Potatoes!, illustrated by Ben Shecter, Harper, 1972.

The Apple and Other Fruits, photographs by Wexler, Morrow, 1973.

Questions and Answers about Horses, illustrated by Robert J. Lee, Four Winds, 1973.

Bulbs, Corms and Such, illustrated by Wexler, Morrow, 1974.

How Kittens Grow, illustrated by Bubley, Four Winds, 1975.

The Harlequin Moth: Its Life Story, illustrated by Wexler, Morrow, 1975.

Animals of the Sea, illustrated by John Hamberger, Scholastic, 1975.

Popcorn, illustrated by Wexler, Morrow, 1976.

Sea Monsters of Long Ago, Scholastic, 1977.

The Amazing Dandelion, photographs by Wexler, Morrow, 1977.

(With Kenneth Dewey) *Up Down and Around: The Force of Gravity,* Doubleday, 1977.

(With Deborah Peterson) *Don't Throw It Grow It Book of Houseplants,* Random House, 1977.

(And illustrator with Les Line), *Land of the Giant Tortoise: The Story of the Galapagos,* Scholastic, 1977.

Sea Monsters of Long Ago, illustrated by Hamberger, Four Winds, 1978.

Mimosa: The Sensitive Plant, illustrated by Wexler, Morrow, 1978.

Tyrannosaurus Rex, Harper, 1978.

Eat the Fruit, Plant the Seed, photographs by Wexler, Morrow, 1980.

Night Animals, Scholastic, 1980.

Also editor of "How Did We Find Out" series by Isaac Asimov, twenty books, Walker, c. 1972; co-editor with Joyce Hunt of "First Look" Series (juvenile science books), Walker, 1972—.

SIDELIGHTS: Millicent Selsam published her first book, *Egg to Chick,* in 1946, and since that time she has become the award-winning author of countless books for children that communicate her excitement over the process of scientific discovery. "I have certain childlike qualities," she once said in Lee Bennett Hopkins' *Books Are By People.* "I love to investigate everything and get great pleasure from growing plants indoors and out. I have always loved to know the *why* of everything. Science is dynamic and exciting, and it has changed the world."

Selsam grew up in New York City, an unusual place in which to develop an interest in nature. Field trips taken in high school inspired her to explore the fields of botany and biology through college study, and eventually led her to obtain advanced degrees in science from Columbia University. She taught high school science classes in New York City until the birth of her son. "I got tired of teaching but still enjoyed the idea of communicating with young people regarding science," she wrote. Looking for another avenue in which to use her science background, Selsam decided to try her hand at writing science books for children.

"To write about science for children an author needs to know science, to know children, and to know how to write—particularly to understand how to communicate with children on their level. Good science books should communicate some of the excitement of discovery—and the triumph that goes with the solution of scientific problems." In her article in *Children's Literature in Education,* she expanded on the important role of science in the education of young people: "When children are taught the elements of the scientific method, they will have a healthy skepticism with regard to prevailing superstitions and exaggerated advertising. They will know that thirteen or any other number is neither unlucky or lucky. If somebody tells them that toads cause warts, or that laetrile cures cancer, they will ask for evidence. And when the radio or television blares out that this product is this or that percentage purer, better, or richer than that of some competitor, the child who has some idea of the scientific method will have his doubts."

BIOGRAPHICAL/CRITICAL SOURCES:

BOOKS

Arbuthnot, May Hill, and Zena Sutherland, *Children and Books,* 4th edition, Scott, Foresman, 1972.
Children's Literature Review, Volume 1, Gale, 1976.
Fenwick, Sara Innis, editor, *A Critical Approach to Children's Literature,* University of Chicago Press, 1967.
Hopkins, Lee Bennett, *Books Are By People,* Citation Press, 1969.

PERIODICALS

Book Week, November 1, 1964; May 16, 1965; May 7, 1967.
Bulletin of the Center for Children's Books, February, 1974, p. 100; April, 1986, p. 157.
Children's Literature in Education, summer, 1980, pp. 82-84.

Christian Science Monitor, May 9, 1963; November 14, 1963; November 5, 1964, p. 108; December 21, 1967.
Fire Island News, May 28, 1966.
Horn Book, October, 1962; June, 1963; August, 1964, p. 391; June, 1965; June, 1977; August, 1977; June, 1978; October, 1978; February, 1979; October, 1980, p. 540.
Natural History, December, 1963; November, 1967.
New York Times Book Review, May 12, 1963; November 10, 1963; July 5, 1964; May 9, 1965; November 7, 1965; May 8, 1966; November 5, 1967, p. 52; April 20, 1969; November 9, 1969; May 9, 1970.
Saturday Review, January 19, 1963; April 22, 1967; November 9, 1968.
School Library Journal, November, 1973.
Times Literary Supplement, June 26, 1969.
Young Reader's Review, October, 1966; May, 1967.

*   *   *

SENNETT, Ted 1928-

PERSONAL: Surname originally Sinitsky; name legally changed, 1955; born March 20, 1928, in Brooklyn, NY; son of Benjamin and Fannie (Friedman) Sinitsky; married Roxane Gerber, February 14, 1954; children: Robert, David, Karen. *Education:* Brooklyn College (now Brooklyn College of the City University of New York), B.A., 1948; Columbia University, M.A., 1949; further study at New York University, 1951-53.

ADDRESSES: Home—31 Patton Lane, Closter, NJ 07624.

CAREER: Charles Scribner's Sons, New York City, director of advertising, 1967-69; Praeger Publishing, New York City, director of promotion, advertising, and publicity, 1969-70; *New York Times,* New York City, promotion manager in Book Division, 1970-71; Crowell-Collier and Macmillan, Inc., New York City, marketing manager in Library Division, 1971-74. *Military service:* U.S. Army, 1953-55.

WRITINGS:

(With Martin Gross) *Are You Sure You're Kosher?,* Ericsson, 1964.
Warner Brothers Presents, Arlington House, 1971.
Lunatics and Lovers, Arlington House, 1974.
(Editor) *The Movie Buff's Book,* Harcourt, 1975.
(Editor) *The Old-Time Radio Book,* Harcourt, 1976.
The Movie Buff's Book 2, Harcourt, 1977.
Your Show of Shows, Macmillan, 1977.
Masters of Menace, Dutton, 1979.
Hollywood Musicals, Abrams, 1981.
Great Hollywood Movies, Abrams, 1983.

Hollywood's Golden Year, 1939: A Fiftieth-Anniversary Celebration, St. Martin's Press, 1989.

Great Hollywood Westerns, Abrams, 1989.

Laughing in the Dark: Movie Comedy from Groucho to Woody, St. Martin's Press, 1991.

WORK IN PROGRESS: Ted Sennett's On-Screen, Off-Screen Movie Guide, for Simon & Schuster.

SIDELIGHTS: Ted Sennett's *Hollywood Musicals,* which he says concentrates on "all important and many less important Hollywood musicals" over a fifty-year range, has been praised for its high-quality illustrations as well as its text, described by Seymour Peck in the *New York Times Book Review* as "a well-organized narrative with largely intelligent, sophisticated opinions—and not just a collection of names, facts and dates." *Newsweek*'s Peter S. Prescott called *Hollywood Musicals* "the quintessential coffee-table production," noting Sennett's liberal use of color and black-and-white photographs. "The layout conveys something of the Holy Moses visual impact of vast production numbers from the films, or the charismatic impact of the stars—Fred and Ginger and Gene and Ruby and all the others," Charles Champlin commented in the *Los Angeles Times Book Review.*

BIOGRAPHICAL/CRITICAL SOURCES:

PERIODICALS

Los Angeles Times Book Review, December 20, 1981, pp. 1, 13; November 20, 1983, p. 18.

Newsweek, December 21, 1981, pp. 78-79.

New York Times Book Review, November 15, 1981, pp. 13, 38; December 4, 1983, p. 72; December 10, 1989, p. 7.

*   *   *

SHELLY, Judith A(llen) 1944-

PERSONAL: Born July 8, 1944, in Washington, DC; daughter of Hugh Arthur, Jr. (in the U.S. Army), and Anne (a secretary; maiden name, Croft) Allen; married James Alfred Shelly (a Lutheran pastor), May 15, 1976; children: Janell MaRee, Jonathan Michael. *Education:* Medical College of Virginia (now Virginia Commonwealth University), B.S.N., 1966; Lutheran Theological Seminary at Philadelphia, M.A.R., 1976. *Religion:* Lutheran.

ADDRESSES: Home and office—P.O. Box 700, Frederick, PA 19435.

CAREER: Mercy Medical Center, Springfield, OH, staff nurse, 1966-67; family practice nurse in Springfield, 1967-70; Nurses Christian Fellowship, Madison, WI, member of campus staff, 1970-74; Lankenau Hospital, Philadelphia, PA, staff nurse, 1974-76; Nurses Christian Fellowship, materials developer, 1976-82, associate director of resources, 1982-84, eastern area director, 1984-86, resource developer, 1987-90.

WRITINGS:

(With Sharon Fish) *Spiritual Care: The Nurse's Role,* with workbook, Inter-Varsity Press, 1978, revised edition, 1983.

Caring in Crisis, Inter-Varsity Press, 1979.

Dilemma: A Nurse's Guide for Making Ethical Decisions, Inter-Varsity Press, 1980.

(Editor and contributor) *The Spiritual Needs of Children,* Inter-Varsity Press, 1982.

(Editor and contributor) *Spiritual Dimensions of Mental Health,* Inter-Varsity Press, 1983.

Not Just a Job: Serving Christ in Your Work, Inter-Varsity Press, 1985.

(Editor) *Teaching Spiritual Care: A Resource Book for Nursing Faculty,* Nurses Christian Fellowship, 1985.

(With Arlene Miller) *Value in Conflict,* Inter-Varsity Press, 1991.

Writing for Publication, Nurses Christian Fellowship, 1991.

Contributor to *Critical Care Update.* Senior editor, *Journal of Christian Nursing,* 1990—.

Shelly's books have been translated into Korean, German, Mandarin Chinese, Norwegian, Portuguese, and Japanese.

SIDELIGHTS: Judith A. Shelly told *CA:* "While working as a nurse I found a vast difference between the quality of technical physical care and the spiritual care that we offered patients. The importance of spiritual care glared at me as I watched patients who were physically doing well lose hope and die for lack of meaningful relationships or purpose in life. As I offered spiritual care—a willingness to discuss spiritual concerns, prayer, encouragement from the Scriptures—I saw a striking improvement in patients' attitudes and physical health. My books are drawn from my own experience and the experiences of my nursing colleagues."

BIOGRAPHICAL/CRITICAL SOURCES:

PERIODICALS

Partnership, March/April, 1984.

*   *   *

SHOWERS, Paul C. 1910-

PERSONAL: Born April 12, 1910, in Sunnyside, WA; son of Frank L. (a music teacher) and M. Ethelyn (a singer;

maiden name, Walker) Showers; married Kay M. Sperry (a psychologist), August 5, 1946 (divorced, 1973); children: Paul Walker, Kate Barger (twins). *Education:* University of Michigan, A.B., 1931; New York University, post-graduate study, 1952-53. *Avocational interests:* music, social history.

ADDRESSES: Home—525 Homer Ave, Palo Alto, CA 94301.

CAREER: Detroit Free Press, Detroit, MI, copyreader, 1937-40; *New York Herald Tribune,* New York City, copy desk staffmember, 1940-41; *New York Times Sunday Mirror,* New York City, writer, copy editor, 1946; *New York Times* New York City, member of Sunday department, 1946-76, assistant travel editor, 1949-61, copy editor of Sunday magazine, 1961-76; free-lance writer, 1976—. *Military service:* U.S. Army, 1942-45; served on staff of *Yank* (army weekly), editor of Okinawa edition; became staff sergeant.

AWARDS, HONORS: Science award, New Jersey Institute of Technology, 1961, for *Find Out by Touching, The Listening Walk* and *In the Night,* 1967, for *How You Talk,* 1968, for *A Drop of Blood, Before You Were a Baby,* and *Hear Your Heart.*

WRITINGS:

"LET'S READ AND FIND OUT SCIENCE BOOK" SERIES; FOR CHILDREN

Find Out By Touching, illustrated by Robert Galster, Trophy, 1961.

In the Night, illustrated by Ezra Jack Keats, Trophy, 1961.

The Listening Walk, illustrated by Aliki, Trophy, 1961.

How Many Teeth?, illustrated by Paul Galdone, Trophy, 1962, revised edition illustrated by True Kelley, 1991.

Look at Your Eyes, illustrated by Galdone, Trophy, 1962.

Follow Your Nose, illustrated by Galdone, Trophy, 1963.

Your Skin and Mine, illustrated by Galdone, Trophy, 1965, revised edition illustrated by Kathleen Kuchera, 1991.

A Drop of Blood, illustrated by Don Madden, Trophy, 1967, revised edition, 1989.

How You Talk, illustrated by Galster, Trophy, 1967, revised edition illustrated by Megan Lloyd, 1990.

(With wife, Kay S. Showers) *Before You Were a Baby,* illustrated by Ingrid Fetz, Trophy, 1968.

Hear Your Heart, illustrated by Joseph Low, Trophy, 1968.

A Baby Starts to Grow, illustrated by Rosalind Fry, Trophy, 1969.

What Happens to a Hamburger?, illustrated by Anne Rockwell, Trophy, 1970, revised edition, 1985.

Use Your Brain, illustrated by Fry, Trophy, 1971.

Sleep Is for Everyone, illustrated by Wendy Watson, Trophy, 1974.

Where Does the Garbage Go?, illustrated by Loretta Lustig, Trophy, 1974.

Me and My Family Tree, illustrated by Madden, Trophy, 1978.

No Measles, No Mumps for Me, illustrated by Harriet Barton, Trophy, 1980.

You Can't Make a Move without Your Muscles, illustrated by Barton, Trophy, 1982.

Ears Are for Hearing, illustrated by Holly Keller, Trophy, 1990.

FOR CHILDREN

Columbus Day, illustrated by Ed Emberly, Crowell, 1965.

Indian Festivals, illustrated by Lorence Bjorklund, Crowell, 1969.

The Bird and the Stars, illustrated by Mila Lazarevich, Doubleday, 1975.

The Moon Walker, illustrated by Susan Perl, Doubleday, 1975.

A Book of Scary Things, illustrated by Perl, Doubleday, 1977.

OTHER

Fortune Telling for Fun and Popularity, New Home Library, 1942, published as *Fortune Telling for Fun,* Newcastle, 1971, and *Fortune Telling for Fun and Profit,* Bell, 1985.

Also contributor of articles and book reviews to *New York Times Book Review;* contributor of humorous verse and short articles to *Life, Judge,* and *Ballyhoo* (national humor magazines). Showers's manuscripts are included in the Kerlan Collection, University of Minnesota.

ADAPTATIONS: All published by Crowell as filmstrip with record and film with cassette: "Look at Your Eyes," 1962, "How Many Teeth," 1962, "Follow Your Nose," 1963, "Your Skin and Mine," 1965, "Drop of Blood," 1967, "How You Talk," 1967, "Hear Your Heart," 1968, "A Baby Starts to Grow," 1969, "What Happens to a Hamburger?" 1970, "Use Your Brain," 1971.

SIDELIGHTS: Showers is a retired newspaperman whose writing for children has always been a part-time occupation. His career in journalism spanned thirty-nine years and found him working for major newspapers in Detroit, Michigan, and New York City. It was while he was a member of the *New York Times* Sunday staff that he was invited by Dr. Franklyn Branley to try his hand at writing a book for children. Dr. Branley, then educational director of the American Museum of Natural History, was preparing to launch the "Let's Read and Find Out" series of nonfiction books, designed for the early grades and originally published by the Thomas Y. Crowell Company.

Showers's initial attempt, a book about the sense of touch, was one of the first titles in the new series, and its success encouraged him to continue with more books, work that has since brought him recognition as a noteworthy author in the field of juvenile nonfiction. While the "Let's Read and Find Out" series was taken over by Harper & Row and subsequently by HarperCollins, Showers has continued to author numerous books on science-related topics in the direct and informal style with which he has been able to engage the curiosity of young readers since the 1960s.

Showers graduated from the University of Michigan in 1931 with the desire to become an actor and playwright. He worked sporadically, accepting bit parts and working "summer stock" theater, but never landed significant roles or had success in finding a producer for plays he wrote. 1934 found Showers at the Chicago World's Fair performing in vignettes from Shakespearean plays on the stage of a replica of England's famous Globe Theater specially constructed for the exhibition. During his years as an actor, he supplemented his meager earnings by doing free-lance writing for several national humor magazines, one of which was *Life*. In 1932, *Life* magazine decided to expand its circulation by creating a novelty crossword feature, a gigantic "cockeyed" puzzle which would cover a two-page spread. Showers recalled his involvement in this new project in his autobiographical sketch for *Something about the Author Autobiography Series* (*SAAS*). "*Life* called its puzzle 'cockeyed' because the definitions were to be outrageously misleading and, whenever possible, to be funny. . . . All words had to be in the average reader's vocabulary; none could be used that required a hunt through the dictionary. This rule was thrown in for the benefit of Westchester commuters, who presumably might buy the magazine at Grand Central [Station] and want to work the puzzle while going home on the train, with no dictionary handy.

"I had just sold a standard-size puzzle to *Life* when the decision was made to give the readers the biggest puzzle then on the market, and I was offered the job at fifty dollars a puzzle. At a time when T-bone steak was selling for twenty-eight cents a pound, an income of fifty dollars a month held definite potential, and I accepted. From that moment on, regardless of what else I might be doing, I made crossword puzzles. Filling in the diagram wasn't difficult. In a way it was fun. Thinking up the definitions was the dismaying part. Each month I had to rack my brains for suitably cock-eyed definitions for a list of between 250 and 300 words. The only one I can now recall was for a four-letter word meaning 'A bender you can take the children on.' The answer was KNEE."

Showers's career as a maker of cross-word puzzles ended in 1936 when *Life* was bought up by *Time* Magazine.

Casting about for a job in publishing, Showers learned of an opening at the *Detroit Free Press* where he took a job on the copy desk, learning the business of editing reporters' written copy and composing headlines. Three years later, he left the Midwest for New York City and a job with the *New York Herald-Tribune*. Showers served three years in the Army during World War II and then returned to New York City. He married and began raising his twin children Paul and Kate, working as an editor for the *New York Times*. He finally submitted his resignation on July 4, 1976. Showers recalled, "It was a once-in-a-lifetime opportunity to make my personal declaration of independence from the newspaper business to work at my own pace as a free-lance writer. That night the occasion was celebrated with a spectacular fireworks display over the Statue of Liberty in New York Harbor!"

The first book that Showers wrote for the "Let's-Read-and-Find-Out" series was *Find Out by Touching*. Book topics relate exclusively to science and are suggested by the series' editorial staff, but Showers has the freedom to compose his texts in an original manner. "I am less interested in writing about science than in putting together books that will appeal to kids who are still learning to read a new language (as kids in kindergarten and the first three grades are doing)," he once commented. After extensive research on his subject, Showers organizes the material in a way that, although elementary in the use of vocabulary and grammar, presents the subject matter with some degree of complexity. Although a child might read at a beginning level, Showers believes that his audience of four-to-eight-year-olds is capable of understanding more advanced concepts than their limited reading vocabulary can express. He finds the task of bridging this gap between language and concept while maintaining interesting and enlightening texts to be the greatest challenge in writing juvenile nonfiction.

Showers believes that conversations among children are an excellent method in which to gauge the readability of his books in terms of how well they will be comprehended. "I wanted to combine a simple vocabulary with recognizable speech patterns, the language ability the beginning reader had already acquired through daily speech," Showers explained in *SAAS*. "We lived in the suburbs and had a house and a garden with a swing in it. The swing was a magnet for the kindergarten set in our neighborhood, and when I was preparing to write a book, I would spend time on weekends working the garden and eavesdropping on the swing crowd. . . . Later, when I sat at my typewriter, I would test each sentence I wrote against my recollection of those conversations. Is this how the kids would have phrased it? If I were talking to them instead of writing it down, is this the way I would say it?

"Repetition and simple sentences may be fine for a beginning reader, but for the writer providing those sentences, they can be a frustrating bore. To relieve the monotony of the endless simplicities, I try mixing in jingles and phonic devices of one sort or another and whenever possible attempt to make a little joke." Showers's sense of humor has not been lost on his young audience. Whether his subject has been heredity, sleep, digestion, hearing, preventative medicine, sight, or blood and its function, his texts have remained popular through several editions, some books selling upwards of eight hundred thousand copies. A critic in *School Library Journal* commended Showers's book *Ears are for Hearing,* calling it, "A delightful book that genuinely succeeds in being informative without being boring." The ability to communicate his affection for his young audience while answering basic questions about science makes Showers's books notable in their field. Sparking the enthusiasm of young children to find out more about the world around them continues to be a fulfilling pastime for this retired newspaperman.

BIOGRAPHICAL/CRITICAL SOURCES:

BOOKS

Children's Literature Review, Volume 6, Gale, 1984, pp. 241-249.
Something about the Author Autobiography Series, Volume 7, Gale, 1989, pp. 285-298.

PERIODICALS

Booklist, April 15, 1980, p. 1210; March 15, 1990, p. 1459; May 1, 1991, p. 1723.
Horn Book, April, 1969; April, 1975; February, 1983, p. 83; September, 1990, p. 631.
New York Times Book Review, November 7, 1965, p. 56.
Redbook, August, 1974.
School Library Journal, August, 1985, p. 57; February, 1990, p. 85; August, 1990, p. 143.
Wilson Library Bulletin, October, 1975.

—*Sketch by Pamela L. Shelton*

*   *   *

SHREVE, Susan Richards 1939-

PERSONAL: Born May 2, 1939, in Toledo, OH; daughter of Robert Kenneth (a broadcaster and writer) and Helen Elizabeth (Greene) Richards; married Porter Gaylord Shreve (a family therapist), May 26, 1962 (divorced); married Timothy Seldes (an agent), February 2, 1987; children: Porter Gaylord, Elizabeth Steward, Caleb Richards, Katharine Taylor. *Education:* University of Pennsylvania, B.A. (magna cum laude), 1961; University of Virginia, M.A., 1969.

ADDRESSES: Home—3319 Newark St. N.W., Washington, DC 20008. *Office*—Department of English, George Mason University, Fairfax, VA 22030. *Agent*—Timothy Seldes, Russell & Volkening, Inc., 50 West 29th St., New York, NY 10001.

CAREER: Teacher of English in private schools in Cheshire, England, 1962-63, Rosemont, PA, 1963-66, Washington, DC, 1967-68, and Philadelphia, PA, 1970-72; Community Learning Center (alternative school), Philadelphia, co-founder, 1972-75; George Mason University, Fairfax, VA, associate professor, 1976-80, professor of literature, 1980—, Jerry McKean Moore chair of writing, 1978—. Columbia University, visiting professor, 1982—;

Princeton University, visiting professor, 1991-92.

MEMBER: PEN/Faulkner Foundation (president), Authors Guild, Authors League of America, Washington Independent Writers, Children's Book Guild, Phi Beta Kappa.

AWARDS, HONORS: Jenny Moore Award, George Washington University, 1978; Notable Book citation, American Library Association (ALA), 1979, for *Family Secrets: Five Very Important Stories;* Best Book for Young Adults citation, ALA, 1980, for *The Masquerade;* Notable Children's Trade Book in the field of social studies citation, National Council for Social Studies and the Children's Book Council joint committee, 1980, for *Family Secrets: Five Very Important Stories;* Guggenheim award in fiction, 1980; National Endowment for the Arts fiction award, 1982; Edgar Allan Poe Award, Juvenile Mystery Category, Mystery Writers of America, 1987, for *Lucy Forever and Miss Rosetree, Shrinks.*

WRITINGS:

FOR CHILDREN

The Bad Dreams of a Good Girl, illustrations by Diane De Groat, Knopf, 1982.
How I Saved the World on Purpose, illustrations by Suzanne Richardson, Holt, 1985.
Lucy Forever and Miss Rosetree, Shrinks, Holt, 1986.
Lily and the Runaway Baby, illustrations by Sue Truesdell, Random House, 1987.

FOR YOUNG ADULTS

The Nightmares of Geranium Street, Knopf, 1977.
Loveletters, Knopf, 1978.
Family Secrets: Five Very Important Stories, illustrations by Richard Cuffari, Knopf, 1979.
The Masquerade, Knopf, 1980.
The Revolution of Mary Leary, Knopf, 1982.
The Flunking of Joshua T. Bates, illustrations by De Groat, Knopf, 1984.

The Gift of the Girl Who Couldn't Hear, Morrow, 1991.
Joshua T. Bates in Charge, Knopf, 1992.
Wait for Me, Morrow, 1992.

ADULT NOVELS

A Fortunate Madness, Houghton, 1974.
A Woman Like That, Atheneum, 1977.
Children of Power, Macmillan, 1979.
Miracle Play, Morrow, 1981.
Dreaming of Heroes, Morrow, 1984.
Queen of Hearts, Linden Press, 1986.
A Country of Strangers, Simon & Schuster, 1989.
Daughters of the New World: A Novel, N. A. Talese/
   Doubleday, 1992.

SIDELIGHTS: American novelist and children's author
Susan Richards Shreve writes about families. In her novels
for adults, Shreve captures "the oxymoronic pull that passion and magic make upon the ordinary working day
world inhabited by her characters," Michael Malone
wrote in the *Washington Post Book World.* Their world,
he added, "is a world where lives of quiet desperation become suddenly (and at times tragically) noisy." Writing
in *Publishers Weekly,* Elizabeth Gleick stated, "In her
novels, the violence of everyday life, what she calls 'the
seeds of extremism,' maintains a precarious balance with
the power of love and fulfillment." In a *Tribune Books* review, Wanda Urbanska commented, "Shreve certainly
adds fireworks to a world of literary fiction that is dominated by small ambitions, small places, and all too often,
imaginative stagnation. . . . She paints on the broad can-
vas of human emotion, creating a world in which her characters' fantasies, unresolved pasts and self-styled moral
codes converge—often explosively—in their intercon-
nected present-day lives."

Shreve contracted polio and two other major illnesses before kindergarten, and entertained herself while bedridden
by imagining dramatic stories involving her dolls. "There
has not been a moment in my life when there was not a
drama going on in my mind," she told Megan Rosenfeld
of the *Washington Post.* Like the author, the polio survivor
Natty Taylor, teen protagonist of *Children of Power,* dares
to try out for cheerleading despite her permanent limp. It
is part of Natty's campaign to resist being defined by her
limitations. Shreve lets Natty explain that when a child's
health suffers early in life, the child can feel excused from
having to do anything more than survive. As Natty says
in *Children of Power,* others feel that "anything she does
is astonishing." Beginning with this disadvantage brings
added joy to Natty's accomplishments.

Shreve knows from personal experience how an unpromis-
ing background can lend a certain exhilaration to achievement. Though at first no one expected Shreve to marry or
have children, there was never any doubt in her mind that

she would. After graduating from the University of Pennsylvania, she married her high school sweetheart and
started her dual career as mother and writer. While raising
four children and working as a schoolteacher, she awoke
before dawn to write at the dining room table. Her determination paid off. Though sales of her first novels were
not remarkable, over time she has come to be recognized
as an important American novelist.

Determination is the subject of *Miracle Play,* which surveys the history of the Howells clan, a family that measures its success in terms of survival. Their "miracle" is
"the family's self-renewal despite the powerful centrifugal
forces exerted by historical and cultural change, and by
the many accidents and ills of life," Julian Moynihan
wrote in the *New York Times Book Review.* The author
skillfully weaves the Howells's personal history with their
country's. Moynihan observed, "In the best parts of *Miracle Play* Susan Shreve can suggest how particular family
events reflect significant social and cultural trends without
losing the rich specificity of individual character and motive." He pointed to the Senator's wife's suicide as such an
event, which her son John recognizes as a political act of
protest against a domineering, male chauvinist husband.
"John is actually reflecting upon the phenomenon of raw
and rank male supremacy, patriarchal and self-
aggrandizing, with attendant victimization of the female,
in earlier American social history. This theme is built up
in the book very fully," Moynihan added.

Dreaming of Heroes belongs to a new genre in fiction, the
story of "a gifted woman's search for a form of service
equal to her gifts," Tom Edwards commented in the *New
York Times Book Review.* The daughter of a war hero,
Jamie survives a meningitis epidemic, which "sets her
compassion and exuberance for humanity and marks her
with a rare inviolability. Death holds neither terror nor
mystery for her," Carol Van Strum noted in the *Washington Post Book World.* A sincere, well-educated faith guides
Jamie through the many battles connected to her work for
the church, a rescue program for child prostitutes that becomes a global human rights crusade. This leader's charismatic power shows its dark side when "at the height of her
career, Jamie discovers in one devastating moment the destructive potential of her power to move others," said Van
Strum. Edwards observed, "Jamie herself is drawn with
considerable tact and delicacy, particularly in the way
Mrs. Shreve suggests a complex mixing of sacred and profane desire in her without any heavy-handed spelling out
of things. And Jamie's experience is made to show not
only the difficulties manmade institutions pose for women
but also the strengths women can bring to the task of participating."

Queen of Hearts exposes the seamier side of life in the
imaginary Massachusetts town of Bethany. Francesca

Woodbine kills her fiance the night before the wedding, and tries to hide her motive—the infidelity of her betrothed. She keeps the secret for years until a second murder sparks new interest in bringing murderers to justice. Jonathan Yardley commented in the *Washington Post Book World* that while *Queen of Hearts* "is indeed, in the best sense of the word, entertaining, it is also a remarkably complex, multi-layered novel in which much more is afoot than the artful untangling of an ingenious plot. At its core it is a novel about that greatest of mysteries, the nature of human character and personality."

Alice McDermott, writing in the *New York Times Book Review,* found that Shreve's skill at drawing an entire cast of memorable characters overshadowed the plot, which she felt was "diminished" by its own complexity. Though some reviewers found the book to be improbable in many places, Shreve's fairy tale of violent passion and retribution is so well-drawn that "resemblance to reality seems beside the point," Kim Hubbard wrote in a *People* magazine review. The lives portrayed in *Queen of Hearts* shed light on the difference between fortune and choice ("Fortune is what happens to you, and choice is what you do about it," says Francesca's father). "It is a struggle as old as humanity," wrote Yardley, "one that gives *Queen of Hearts* the timeless quality of a fable, a story that touches common experience and to which readers can respond." Jack Fuller, writing in *Tribune Books,* commented that *Queen of Hearts* with its strong plot represents the quality that used to be associated with novels properly called romances: "It not only redeems its characters through its story but also helps to redeem the importance and power of story itself." He recommended the novel to readers who have yet to "discover how satisfying a genuine romance [novel] can be."

A Country of Strangers studies the social history of rural America. After the white owner of Elm Grove, a former plantation near Washington, D.C., suddenly disappears, Moses Bellows and his brother Guy—descendants of slaves—move in. While the townspeople eagerly wait for the usurpers to be deposed in the settlement of the owner's estate, the two men are troubled by closer threats to their well-being. Moses develops the dangerous suspicion that his wife and the farm's former owner were lovers; Charley, a white journalist who buys the estate and tries to befriend Moses, takes a dim view of the growing attraction between his new friend and his Danish movie star wife, whose painful past he has not been able to eradicate. Unable to erase the past which haunts Moses, Charley, too, is taken by jealous rage, despite his efforts to combat the racism that surrounds them.

Here, as in the young adult novel *The Bad Dreams of a Good Girl,* a young girl rises through the conflict to the position of peacemaker. Though Prudential, named after

the insurance company and pregnant at thirteen, was sent to be 'tamed' by her aunt Miracle and uncle Moses, "it is Prudential who tames everyone else," Jay Parini noted in the *Times Literary Supplement.* "By the end of the novel, she has taught everyone under the aegis of Elm Grove a lesson in humanity." In light of the birth of her son Simon Peter, conflicts subside and a dream of brotherhood is recalled. "Many such scenes of rich craft and wise feeling" illuminate the novel, said Malone. Citing Shreve's description of the national longing for brotherhood, Malone commented, "Our unending wish to recreate the warm, kind, communal refuge of the first dream of America comes out of our 'inevitable birthright in a country of strangers, of loneliness and isolation and a longing to walk in the company of friends.' "

Shreve's books for young adults are also prized for their memorable characters who achieve understanding against the backdrop of a changing society. *The Revolution of Mary Leary* follows the title character from her confiningly conservative nuclear family into the quirky Cleveland Park household that finally drives her back to security. In *How I Saved the World on Purpose,* the problems of the outside world intrude on nine-year-old Miranda's quiet life in the form of a Cambodian refugee adopted by her neighbors. Her expanded awareness of local and global problems leads her to join a group that serves latchkey children.

The Bad Dreams of a Good Girl presents nine-year-old Lotty, youngest sibling of three ill-behaved brothers, who feels that her parents expect her "to be a paragon of virtue," Merri Rosenberg wrote in the *New York Times Book Review.* Lotty's mostly virtuous responses to their antagonisms provide the framework for lengthy descriptions of her dreams, in which she pays them back without inhibition or remorse. "Shreve sensitively explores Lotty's emotional conflict that results from trying to live up to her parents' expectations, even as her 'bad' feelings surface in her dreams," Rosenberg noted. Rosenberg praised the author's use of "teen language" in her dialogue, saying, "The author's ear is attuned to the cadences of today's breed of hip, wisecracking and smart-aleck kid, just as the realistic illustrations [of Lotty's conflicts] convey the emotional content of these situations with charm and wit."

Shreve is conscious of her work's relevance to contemporary women's issues, but she does not want to be labeled a feminist writer. "If you're a writer, you're a writer, and if you're any good at all you get beyond terms like 'Southern,' or 'feminist,' " she told Gleick. Shreve said she writes about the same kind of woman in each of her novels, one typically having two sides: "One who is ambitious, full of energy, and has a certain amount of self-loathing; and the other who is much more interior and complex, and who is good in almost a conventional sense." The tension created by these two impulses speaks not only for her, she said, but for "my generation of women, who are still tied to another history, yet at the same time are going forward with their own lives."

BIOGRAPHICAL/CRITICAL SOURCES:

BOOKS

Contemporary Authors Autobiography Series, Volume 5, Gale, 1987.

Contemporary Literary Criticism, Volume 23, Gale, 1983.

Shreve, Susan Richards, *A Country of Strangers,* Simon & Schuster, 1988.

Shreve, Susan Richards, *Children of Power,* Macmillan, 1979.

Shreve, Susan Richards, *Queen of Hearts,* Simon & Schuster, 1987.

PERIODICALS

Best Sellers, August 1, 1974, p. 212; December, 1977; June, 1980, p. 119.

Books of the Times, July, 1979, p. 326.

Bulletin of the Center for Children's Books, July, 1985; June, 1987, p. 196; January, 1988, p. 100.

Chicago Tribune Book World, October 18, 1981, section 7, p. 4.

Los Angeles Times Book Review, August 11, 1985, p. 6; March 5, 1989, p. 7.

Maclean's, July 30, 1979, p. 45.

Ms., April, 1984, p. 30.

Newsweek, December 18, 1978, p. 102.

New York Times Book Review, August 4, 1974 p. 27; July 10, 1977, p. 28; June 10, 1979, p. 51; July 1, 1979, p. 12; August 16, 1981, pp. 8, 23; May 16, 1982, p. 29; April 1, 1984, p. 8.

People, March 16, 1987, pp. 13-14.

Publishers Weekly, December 19, 1986, pp. 35-36.

Saturday Review, May 12, 1979, p. 47.

Times (London), March 19, 1987; July 13, 1989.

Times Literary Supplement, September 22, 1978, p. 1056; April 24, 1987, p. 434; November 24, 1989, p. 1313.

Tribune Books (Chicago), January 4, 1987, p. 7; January 8, 1989, p. 6.

Washington Post, February 2, 1987.

Washington Post Book World, December 11, 1977; April 1, 1979, p. E3; May 11, 1980; July 26, 1981, pp. 5, 7; April 11, 1982, p. 11; October 10, 1982, p. 7; March 25, 1984, p. 11; December 14, 1986, p. 3; January 8, 1989, p. 1.

Wilson Library Bulletin, February, 1983.

—*Sketch by Marilyn K. Basel and Deborah A. Stanley*

SHUFFELTON, Frank 1940-

PERSONAL: Born March 10, 1940, in St. Marys, Ohio, son of Frank B. (a postmaster) and Dorothy (a registered nurse; maiden name, Axe) Shuffelton; married Jane Bewail Weiss (a teacher), April 20, 1963; children: Amy Bewail, George Gordon. *Education:* Harvard University, B.A., 1962; Stanford University, M.A., 1968, Ph.D., 1972.

ADDRESSES: Home—51 Fair Oaks Ave., Rochester, NY 14618. *Office*—Department of English, University of Rochester, Rochester, NY 14627.

CAREER: University of Rochester, Rochester, NY, instructor, 1969-72, assistant professor, 1972-77, associate professor, 1977-88, professor of English, 1988—. *Military service:* U.S. Coast Guard, 1962-66; became lieutenant.

MEMBER: Modern Language Association of America, Melville Society, Thoreau Society, American Society for Eighteenth-Century Studies, Northeastern American Society for Eighteenth-Century Studies, American Studies Association.

AWARDS, HONORS: Mellon faculty fellow, University of Rochester, 1977; National Endowment for the Humanities senior fellow, 1988-89.

WRITINGS:

Thomas Hooker, 1586-1647, Princeton University Press, 1977.

Thomas Jefferson: A Comprehensive Bibliography of Writings about Him, Garland Publishing, 1983.

Thomas Jefferson in the 80's: An Annotated Bibliography, Garland, 1992.

(Editor) *A Mixed Race: Ethnicity in Early America,* Oxford University Press, 1992.

Contributor to scholarly journals.

WORK IN PROGRESS: Thomas Jefferson and the Republic of Letters.

SIDELIGHTS: Frank Shuffelton told CA: "I have always been interested in the role that writing plays in the lives of writers and readers, and my own writing has been an attempt to understand the power literature has to order wide ranges of idea and experience. Thomas Hooker and a congregation of Puritan settlers in New England organized a community held together by the power of words, or, as they would have had it, by the power of God's Word.

"I am at the moment particularly interested in the cultural history and literature of the United States in the last half of the eighteenth century. Our founding fathers included among their number a group of remarkable writers. In their political essays, their private letters, and the Declaration of Independence and the Constitution they projected a vision of an American society that was echoed, and sometimes vociferously criticized, by the contemporary poets, novelists, and dramatists.

"Because I am concerned about the possible disintegration or vulgarization of national community in our own time, I am most drawn to thinkers who forcefully attempted in their writings to clarify and create audiences of engaged citizens."

BIOGRAPHICAL/CRITICAL SOURCES:

PERIODICALS

New England Quarterly, December, 1977.

*   *   *

SIMMIE, James Martin 1941-

PERSONAL: Born July 18, 1941, in Oxford, England; son of Walter (an engineer) and Millicent (a fashion buyer; maiden name, Martin) Simmie. *Education:* University of London, B.Sc., 1964, Ph.D., 1979; University of Southampton, M.Phil., 1969. *Avocational interests:* Boating, rugby, squash, tennis, M.G. sports cars, and "my vintage Thames River cruiser."

ADDRESSES: Office—University College, University of London, Gower St., London W.C.1, England.

CAREER: Oxford Polytechnic, Oxford, England, lecturer, 1965-67, senior lecturer in sociology, 1967-70; University of London, University College, London, England, reader in planning and sociology, 1970—. Lecturer, University of California, Berkeley, summer, 1970.

MEMBER: Royal Town Planning Institute.

WRITINGS:

The Sociology of Internal Migration, Centre for Environmental Studies, 1972.
Citizens in Conflict, Hutchinson, 1974.
(Editor) *Sociology, Politics, and Cities,* Macmillan, 1976.
The Sociology of Town Planning: A Bibliography, CPL Bibliographies, 1976.
Power, Property, and Corporation: The Political Sociology of Planning, Macmillan, 1981.
(Contributor) W. Grant, editor, *The Political Economy of Corporatism,* Macmillan, 1985.
(With Susan French) *Corporation, Participation, and Planning: The Case of London,* Pergamon, 1989.
(Editor with Roger King) *The State in Action: Public Policy and Politics,* Pinter Publishers, 1990.

Also author, with J. Dehlsa, of *Yugoslavia in Turmoil,* 1991. Contributor to journals, including *International Journal of Urban and Regional Research.*

SIDELIGHTS: James Martin Simmie told *CA:* "I am a confirmed Californiaphile, and much of my work has been sparked by frequent visits there. I first visited Berkeley in the summer of 1970 and was struck by the differences between the more pluralistic atmosphere in local government there than in the United Kingdom. Subsequently, I have developed specific interests in the ways that changes in production, finance, and government policies affect events at the local level. In general I feel that the United Kingdom tends to be dominated by large corporations that not only have more clout with government at all levels, which I regard as potentially corporatist, but also are mainly responsible for the changing spatial division of labor."

*   *   *

SIMMONS, Jack 1915-

PERSONAL: Born August 30, 1915, in Isleworth, Middlesex, England; son of Seymour Francis and Katharine Lillias (Finch) Simmons. *Education:* Attended Westminster School, London, England; Christ Church, Oxford, B.A., 1937, M.A., 1943. *Avocational interests:* European travel, museums, guide-books, local and regional history.

ADDRESSES: Office—Department of History, University of Leicester, Leicester LE2 1XB, England. *Agent*—David Higham Associates Ltd., 5 Lower John St., Golden Sq., London W1R 4HA, England.

CAREER: Oxford University, Oxford, England, Beit Lecturer in the History of the British Empire, 1943-47; University of Leicester, Leicester, England, professor of history, 1947-75, professor emeritus and honorary archivist, 1975—, pro-vice chancellor, 1960-63, public orator, 1965-68. Member of advisory council, Science Museum, London, 1969-84; chairman, National Railway Museum Committee, York, 1981-84.

MEMBER: Society of Antiquaries (fellow), Leicestershire Archaeological and Historical Society (president, 1966-71).

WRITINGS:

(Editor with Margery Perham) *African Discovery,* Faber & Faber, 1942, 2nd edition, 1957, Northwestern University Press, 1963.
Southey, Collins, 1945, reprinted, Kennikat, 1968.
The Maryport and Carlisle Railway, Oakwood Press, 1947.
(Editor) *From Empire to Commonwealth,* Odhams, 1949.
The City of Leicester, City of Leicester Publications Department, 1951.
(Editor) Robert Southey, *Letters from England,* Cresset, 1951.

(Editor) *Journeys in England,* Odhams, 1951, reprinted, Augusta M. Kelley, 1969.

Parish and Empire: Studies and Sketches, Collins, 1952.

Livingstone and Africa, English Universities Press, 1955, Collier, 1962.

New University, Leicester University Press, 1958.

The Railways of Britain, Routledge & Kegan Paul, 1961, 3rd edition, Macmillan, 1986.

England in Colour, Batsford, 1961.

Transport, Vista Books, 1962.

Britain and the World, Studio Vista, 1965.

St. Pancras Station, Allen & Unwin, 1968.

Transportation: A Tour of Museums, A. S. Barnes, 1970 (published in England as *Transport Museums in Britain and Western Europe,* Allen & Unwin, 1970).

(Editor) *The Birth of the Great Western Railway: Extracts from the Diary and Correspondence of George Henry Gibbs,* Adams & Dart, 1971.

(Editor) *The Railway Traveller's Handy Book of Hints, Suggestions and Advice,* Adams & Dart, 1971.

Life in Victorian Leicester, Leicester Museums, 1971.

(Editor) *A Devon Anthology,* Macmillan (London), 1971.

Leicester Past and Present, two volumes, Eyre Methuen, 1974.

(Editor) Hubert A. Simmons, *Memoirs of a Station Master,* Volume I: *Ernest Struggles,* Adams & Dart, 1974.

Rail 150: The Stockton and Darlington Railway and What Followed, Eyre Methuen, 1975.

(With Colin Dare Bernard Ellis) *History in Leicester: 55 B.C.-A.D. 1976,* 3rd edition, Leicester Recreational and Cultural Services Department, 1976.

The Railway in England and Wales, Volume I: *1830-1914,* Leicester University Press, 1978.

English County Historians, EP Publishing, 1978.

A Selective Guide to England, J. Bartholemew, 1979.

The Railway in Town and Country, 1830-1914, David & Charles, 1986.

The Victorian Railway, Thames & Hudson, 1991.

Editor, *Transactions of the Leicestershire Archaeological and Historical Society,* 1949-61; editor, with Michael Robbins, *Journal of Transport History,* 1953-73; editor, *A Visual History of Modern Britain,* 1961-68.

BIOGRAPHICAL/CRITICAL SOURCES:

PERIODICALS

Times (London), March 23, 1991, p. 23.

*   *   *

SIMONT, Marc 1915-

PERSONAL: Born November 23, 1915, in Paris, France; first came to United States, 1927, but later went back to Europe with parents, returning to America, 1935; naturalized citizen, 1936; son of Josep (an illustrator on staff of *L'Illustration*) and Dolors (Baste) Simont; married Sara Dalton (a teacher), April 7, 1945; children: Marc Dalton. *Education:* Studied art in Paris at Academie Ranson, Academie Julien, and Andre Lhote School, 1932-35, and in New York City at National Academy of Design, 1935-37. *Politics:* Democrat. *Avocational interests:* "Seasonal sports, music (except atonal), improving my Catalan, a good table with friends and Cuban cigars."

ADDRESSES: Home—336 Town St., West Cornwall, CT 06796.

CAREER: Artist and illustrator; since 1939 has worked in portraits, murals, sculpture, prints, and magazine and book illustration; translator and writer of children's books, 1939—. Advocate of community soccer in West Cornwall, CT. *Military service:* U.S. Army, 1943-46; produced visual aids; became sergeant.

MEMBER: American Veterans Committee, Authors Guild, American Civil Liberties Union.

AWARDS, HONORS: Tiffany fellow, 1937; Caldecott honor book citation, 1950, for *The Happy Day; Book World* Spring Book Festival Award, and Child Study Association Book Award, both 1952, both for *Jareb;* Caldecott Medal, 1957, for *A Tree Is Nice;* Steck-Vaughn Award, 1957, for *The Trail Driving Rooster;* citation of merit, Society of Illustrators, 1965; Best Book of the Season citation from the *Today Show,* 1972, for *Nate the Great;* National Book Award finalist, 1976, for *The Star in the Pail;* New York Academy of Sciences Children's Younger Book Award, 1980, for *A Space Story;* New Jersey Institute of Technology Award, 1981, for *Ten Copycats in a Boat and Other Riddles;* New York Times Outstanding Books citation, 1982, for *The Philharmonic Gets Dressed;* Garden State Children's Book Awards, 1984, for *Nate the Great and the Missing Key,* and 1985, for *Nate the Great and the Snowy Trail;* American Institute of Graphic Arts certificate of excellence; Jefferson Cup, 1985, for *In the Year of the Boar and Jackie Robinson;* Parents' Choice award, 1986, for *The Dallas Titans Get Ready for Bed.*

WRITINGS:

SELF-ILLUSTRATED

Opera Souffle: 60 Pictures in Bravura, Schuman, 1950.

Polly's Oats, Harper, 1951.

(With Red Smith) *How to Get to First Base: A Picture Book of Baseball,* Schuman, 1952.

The Lovely Summer, Harper, 1952, revised edition, Doubleday, 1992.

Mimi, Harper, 1954.

The Plumber Out of the Sea, Harper, 1955.

The Contest at Paca, Harper, 1959.

How Come Elephants?, Harper, 1965.

Afternoon in Spain, Morrow, 1965.

(With members of staff of Boston Children's Medical Center) *A Child's Eye View of the World,* Delacorte, 1972.

TRANSLATOR AND ILLUSTRATOR

Federico Garcia Lorca, *The Lieutenant Colonel and the Gypsy,* Doubleday, 1971.

Francesc Sales, *Ibrahim,* illustrations by Eulalia Sariola, Lippincott, 1989. illustrator

Emma G. Sterne, *The Pirate of Chatham Square: A Story of Old New York,* Dodd, 1939.

Ruth Bryan Owens, *The Castle in the Silver Woods,* Dodd, 1939.

Albert Carr, *Men of Power,* Viking, 1940.

Mildred Cross, *Isabella, Young Queen of Spain,* Dodd, 1941.

Charlotte Jackson, *Sarah Deborah's Day,* Dodd, 1941.

Richard Hatch, *All Aboard the Whale,* Dodd, 1942.

Dougal's Wish, Harper, 1942.

Meindert DeJong, *Billy and the Unhappy Bull,* Harper, 1946.

Margaret Wise Brown, *The First Story,* Harper, 1947.

Iris Vinton, *Flying Ebony,* Dodd, 1947.

Robbie Trent, *The First Christmas,* Harper, 1948, new edition, 1990.

Andrew Lang, editor, *The Red Fairy Book,* new edition, Longmans, Green, 1948.

Ruth Krauss, *The Happy Day,* Harper, 1949.

R. Krauss, *The Big World and the Little House,* Schuman, 1949.

Red Smith, *Views of Sport,* Knopf, 1949.

M. DeJong, *Good Luck Duck,* Harper, 1950.

R. Krauss, *The Backward Day,* Harper, 1950.

James Thurber, *The Thirteen Clocks,* Simon & Schuster, 1951.

Marjorie B. Paradis, *Timmy and the Tiger,* Harper, 1952.

Alister Cooke, *Christmas Eve,* Knopf, 1952.

Miriam Powell, *Jareb,* Crowell, 1952.

The American Riddle Book, Schuman, 1954.

Elizabeth H. Lansing, *Deer Mountain Hideaway,* Crowell, 1954.

Jean Fritz, *Fish Head,* Coward, 1954.

E. H. Lansing, *Deer River Raft,* Crowell, 1955.

Fred Gipson, *The Trail-Driving Rooster,* Harper, 1955.

Julius Schwartz, *Now I Know,* Whittlesey House, 1955.

Janice May Udry, *A Tree Is Nice,* Harper, 1955.

J. Schwartz, *I Know a Magic House,* Whittlesey House, 1956.

P. G. Wodehouse, *America I Like You,* Simon & Schuster, 1956.

Thomas Liggett, *Pigeon Fly Home,* Holiday House, 1956.

Chad Walsh, *Nellie and Her Flying Crocodile,* Harper, 1956.

J. Thurber, *The Wonderful "O",* Simon & Schuster, 1957.

Maria Leach, *The Rainbow Book of American Folk Tales and Legends,* World, 1958.

Alexis Ladas, *The Seal That Couldn't Swim,* Little, Brown, 1959.

James A. Kjelgaard, *The Duckfooted Hound,* Crowell, 1960.

R. Krauss, *A Good Man and His Wife,* Harper, 1962.

J. Schwartz, *The Earth Is Your Spaceship,* Whitlesey House, 1963.

David McCord, *Every Time I Climb a Tree,* Little Brown, 1967.

What To Do When There's Nothing To Do, Dell, 1967.

Charlton Ogburn, Jr., *Down, Boy, Down, Blast You!,* Morrow, 1967.

Janet Chenery, *Wolfie,* Harper, 1969.

J. M. Udry, *Glenda,* Harper, 1969.

Edward Fales, Jr., *Belts On, Buttons Down,* Dell, 1971.

D. McCord, *The Star in the Pail,* Little, Brown, 1975.

Beverly Keller, *The Beetle Bush,* Coward, 1976.

Karla Kuskin, *A Space Story,* Harper, 1978.

Faith McNulty, *Mouse and Time,* Harper, 1978.

F. McNulty, *How to Dig a Hole to the Other Side of the World,* Harper, 1979.

Alvin Schwartz, editor, *Ten Copycats in a Boat, and Other Riddles,* Harper, 1979.

F. McNulty, *The Elephant Who Couldn't Forget,* Harper, 1979.

Mitchell Sharmat, *Reddy Rattler and Easy Eagle,* Doubleday, 1979.

D. McCord, *Speak Up: More Rhymes of the Never Was and Always Is,* Little, Brown, 1980.

Marjorie Weinman Sharmat, *Chasing After Annie,* Harper, 1981.

Charlotte Zolotow, *If You Listen,* Harper, 1980.

Peggy Parish, *No More Monsters For Me!,* Harper, 1981.

K. Kuskin, *The Philharmonic,* Harper, 1982.

Julie Delton, *My Uncle Nikos,* Crowell, 1983.

Mollie Hunter, *The Knight of the Golden Plain,* Harper, 1983.

Edward Davis, *Bruno the Pretzel Man,* Harper, 1984.

Bette Bao Lord, *The Year of the Boar and Jackie Robinson,* Harper, 1984.

Joan W. Blos, *Martin's Hats,* Morrow, 1984.

John Reynolds Gardiner, *Top Secret,* Little, Brown, 1984.

Franklyn Mansfield Branley, *Volcanoes,* Crowell, 1985.

M. Hunter, *The Three Day Enchantment,* Harper, 1985.

K. Kuskin, *The Dallas Titans Get Ready for Bed,* Harper, 1986.

F. M. Branley, *Journey into a Black Hole,* Crowell, 1986.

Wendell V. Tangborn, *Glaciers,* Crowell, 1988, revised edition, Harper, 1988.

Sing a Song of Popcorn, Scholastic, 1988.
C. Zolotow, *The Quiet Mother and the Noisy Little Boy,* Harper, 1989.
F. M. Branley, *What Happened to the Dinosaurs?,* Harper, 1989.
J. Thurber, *Many Moons,* Harcourt, 1990.

"NATE THE GREAT" SERIES, BY MARJORIE WEINMAN SHARMAT

Nate the Great, Coward, 1972.
Nate the Great Goes Undercover, Coward, 1974.
Nate the Great and the Lost List, Coward, 1975.
Nate the Great and the Phony Clue, Coward, 1977.
Nate the Great and the Sticky Case, Coward, 1978.
Nate the Great and the Missing Key, Coward, 1981.
Nate the Great and the Snowy Trail, Coward, 1982.
Nate the Great and the Fishy Prize, Coward, 1985.
Nate the Great and the Boring Beach Bag, Coward, 1987.
Nate the Great Stalks Stupidweed, Coward, 1987.
Nate the Great Goes Down in the Dumps, Coward, 1989.
Nate the Great and the Halloween Hunt, Coward, 1989.
(With Craig Sharmat) *Nate the Great and the Musical Note,* Coward, 1990.
Nate the Great and the Stolen Base, Coward, 1992.

ADAPTATIONS: Nate the Great Goes Undercover and *Nate the Great and the Sticky Case* were made into films. The *Nate the Great* books were once optioned for a television series. An excerpt from *Nate the Great* was adapted and is on permanent display at the Museum of Science and Industry, Chicago, Illinois.

WORK IN PROGRESS: A book, *From Sea to Shining Sea,* for Scholastic.

SIDELIGHTS: Marc Simont was born in 1915 in Paris, France, to parents from the Catalonian region of northern Spain. He attended schools in Paris, Barcelona, Spain, and New York City, because his parents kept traveling. Simont's father went to the United States after World War I and decided to become an American citizen. Because that process took five years, Simont lived with his grandfather in Barcelona. During this time he sketched soccer players and bullfighters and while sick in bed with the grippe he learned to write by writing over the text of a picture book called *El Ginesillo.*

This repeated relocation affected his performance as a student. "I was always more concerned with what a teacher looked like than what he said, which didn't do my algebra any good," the illustrator explained in *More Junior Authors.* He didn't graduate from high school, although he became fluent in French, English, Spanish, and Catalonian. On the other hand, the traveling sharpened his skills as an observer—skills important for an artist. He studied art at the Academie Julian and the Academie Ranson in Paris, and in New York City at National Academy of De-

sign. He also studied art with Andre Lohte, but he said his most important art teacher was his father, an illustrator for *L'Illustration* magazine. With a sister and two uncles also making a living as artists, he considers art the family trade.

When he returned to the United States in 1935, Simont worked odd jobs, painted portraits, and drew illustrations for the pulps. Eventually he became an illustrator of picture books for children. Books by many notable children's writers, including James Thurber, David McCord, P. G. Wodehouse, Alistair Cooke, Ruth Krauss, Charlotte Zolotow, and Marjorie Weinman Sharmat, have been published with his illustrations. Simont illustrated Sharmat's book *Nate the Great,* featuring the boy detective who solves neighborhood mysteries, and has won several awards for books in the *Nate the Great* series. Three of them were Junior Literary Guild selections; two were made into films, and the entire series was once optioned for a television series. His illustrations for Janice May Udry's *A Tree Is Nice* won the Caldecott Award in 1957.

Critics have pointed out that Simont's illustrations are perfectly suited to the text in books by a variety of children's authors. George A. Woods comments in the *New York Times Book Review* about Karla Kuskin's *The Philharmonic Gets Dressed:* "Simont has not missed a beat. His musicians are a varied band in terms of age, race and physique. He conveys the awkward stance as well as the graceful pose, the little scenes and moments that are all around us—the hole in the sock, the graffiti inside the subway car as well as the advertising posters." Kenneth Marantz, writing about the same book in *School Library Journal,* notes that Simont's "ability to invest such convincing feelings of life using an almost cartoon-like simplicity is remarkable." *New York Times Book Review* contributor Nora Magid observes that Simont's illustrations in *How to Dig a Hole to the Other Side of the World* have terrific emotional power: "Simont's pictures break the heart. The child voyager is at once intrepid and vulnerable" as he takes an imaginary journey through the earth's crust to China. Other features of Simont's artistic style are a method of composition that gives continuity to the pictures in sequence, and humor that is inviting to readers of all ages.

"I believe that if I like the drawings I do, children will like them also," Simont told Lee Bennett Hopkins for *Books Are By People: Interviews with 104 Authors and Illustrators of Books for Young Children.* He continued, "The child in me must make contact with other children. I may miss it by ten miles, but if I am going to hit, it is because of the child in me."

BIOGRAPHICAL/CRITICAL SOURCES:

BOOKS

Caldecott Medal Books: 1938-1957, Horn Book, 1957.
Kingman, Lee, editor, *Newbery and Caldecott Medal Books: 1956-1965,* Horn Book, 1965.
Klemin, Diana, *The Art of Art for Children's Books,* Clarkson Potter, 1966.
More Junior Authors, Wilson, 1963, pp. 186-187.
Lee Bennett Hopkins, *Books Are By People: Interviews with 104 Authors and Illustrators of Books for Young Children,* Citation Press, 1969, pp. 267-269.

PERIODICALS

Book World, November 5, 1972, p. 4.
Christian Science Monitor, November 11, 1971.
Horn Book, February, 1980, p. 140; April, 1983, p. 158; February, 1984, p. 54; June, 1984, p. 318; May/June, 1985, p. 326; November/December, 1986, p. 737; November/December, 1989, p. 788.
New York Times Book Review, October 31, 1965, p. 56; November 18, 1979, p. 320; October 17, 1982, p. 37; November 6, 1983, p. 43; May 20, 1984, p. 28; November 9, 1986, p. 40.
School Library Journal, August, 1982, p. 99; August, 1984, p. 56; October, 1989, p. 100.
Science Books and Films, November/December, 1988, p. 95.
Time, December 4, 1978, p. 100; December 20, 1982, p. 79.

*   *   *

SINCLAIR, Andrew (Annandale) 1935-

PERSONAL: Born January 21, 1935, in Oxford, England; son of Stanley Charles (in the British Colonial Service) and Hilary (a writer; maiden name, Nash-Webber) Sinclair; married Marianne Alexandre, 1960 (divorced); married Miranda Seymour, October 18, 1972 (divorced June 6, 1984); married Sonia Melchett (a writer), July 25, 1984; children: (first marriage) Timon Alexandre; (second marriage) Merlin George. *Education:* Cambridge University, B.A. (double first honors in history), Trinity College, 1958, Ph.D., Churchill College, 1963.

ADDRESSES: Home—16 Tite St., London SW3 4HZ, England. *Agent*—Gillon Aitken, 29 Fernshaw Rd., London SW10, England.

CAREER: Cambridge University, Churchill College, Cambridge, England, founding fellow and director of historical studies, 1961-63; University of London, London, England, lecturer in American history, 1965-67; managing director, Lorrimer Publishing, London, 1967-89, and

Timon Films, 1969-91. Writer and filmmaker. *Military service:* British Army, Coldstream Guards, 1953-55; became lieutenant.

MEMBER: Association of Cinematographers and Television Technicians, Royal Society of Literature (fellow), Society of American Historians (fellow).

AWARDS, HONORS: Commonwealth fellow, Harvard University, 1959-61; American Council of Learned Societies fellow, 1963-65; Somerset Maugham Literary Prize, 1967, for *The Emancipation of the American Woman;* Venice Film Festival award, 1971, and Cannes Film Festival prize, 1972, both for *Under Milk Wood.*

WRITINGS:

NOVELS

The Breaking of Bumbo (also see below), Simon & Schuster, 1959.
My Friend Judas (also see below), Faber, 1959, Simon & Schuster, 1961.
The Project, Simon & Schuster, 1960.
The Paradise Bum, Atheneum, 1963, published in England as *The Hallelujah Bum,* Faber, 1963.
The Raker, Atheneum, 1964.
Gog, Macmillan, 1967.
Magog, Harper, 1972.
The Surrey Cat, M. Joseph, 1976, published as *Cat,* Sphere, 1977.
A Patriot for Hire, M. Joseph, 1978, published as *Sea of the Dead,* Sphere, 1981.
The Facts in the Case of E. A. Poe, Weidenfeld & Nicolson, 1979, Holt, 1980.
Beau Bumbo, Weidenfeld & Nicolson, 1985.
King Ludd, Hodder & Stoughton, 1988.
The Far Corners of the Earth, Hodder & Stoughton, 1991.

NONFICTION

Prohibition: The Era of Excess, introduction by Richard Hofstadter, Atlantic-Little, Brown, 1962, published as *The Era of Excess: A Social History of the Prohibition Movement,* Harper, 1964.
The Available Man: The Life behind the Masks of Warren Gamaliel Harding, Macmillan, 1965.
The Better Half: The Emancipation of the American Woman, Harper, 1965, published as *The Emancipation of the American Woman,* 1966, reprinted under original title, Greenwood Press, 1981.
A Concise History of the United States, Viking, 1967.
The Last of the Best: The Aristocracy of Europe in the Twentieth Century, Macmillan, 1969.
Che Guevara, Viking, 1970, published in England as *Guevara,* Fontana, 1970.

Dylan Thomas: No Man More Magical, Holt, 1975, published in England as *Dylan Thomas: Poet of His People,* M. Joseph, 1975.

The Savage: A History of Misunderstanding, Weidenfeld & Nicolson, 1977.

Jack: A Biography of Jack London, Harper, 1977.

John Ford: A Biography, Dial, 1979.

Corsair: The Life of J. Pierpont Morgan, Little, Brown, 1981.

The Other Victoria: The Princess Royal and the Great Game of Europe, Weidenfeld & Nicolson, 1981.

(With Ladislas Farago) *Royal Web: The Story of Princess Victoria and Frederick of Prussia,* McGraw, 1982.

Sir Walter Raleigh and the Age of Discovery, Penguin, 1984.

The Red and the Blue: Intelligence, Treason, and the Universities, Weidenfeld & Nicolson, 1985, published as *The Red and the Blue: Cambridge, Treason, and Intelligence,* Little, Brown, 1986.

Spiegel: The Man behind the Pictures, Weidenfeld & Nicolson, 1987, published as *S. P. Eagle: A Biography of Sam Spiegel,* Little, Brown, 1988.

War Like a Wasp: The Lost Decade of the Forties, Hamish Hamilton, 1989, Viking, 1990.

The Need to Give: The Patrons and the Arts, Sinclair-Stevenson, 1990.

PLAYS

My Friend Judas (adapted from author's novel of same title), produced in London at Arts Theatre, 1959.

(Adapter) Dylan Thomas, *Adventures in the Skin Trade* (first produced at Hampstead Theatre Club, 1965; produced in Washington, DC, at Washington Theatre Club, 1970), Dent, 1967, New Directions, 1968.

The Blue Angel (adapted from screenplay of Josef von Sternberg's film of same title), produced in Liverpool, England, at Liverpool Playhouse, 1983.

SCRIPTS

Before Winter Comes (based on Frederick L. Keefe's short story "The Interpreter"), Columbia, 1969.

(And director) *The Breaking of Bumbo* (based on author's novel of same title), Associated British Pictures Corp., 1970.

The Voyage of the Beagle (television script), CBS Films, 1970.

(And director) *Under Milk Wood* (based on Dylan Thomas's play of same title; produced by Timon Films, 1971), Simon & Schuster, 1972.

Malachi's Cove, Timon Films, 1973.

Martin Eden (television script; based on novel by Jack London), RAI, 1981.

Also author of television scripts *The Chocolate Tree,* 1963, and *Old Soldiers,* 1964.

TRANSLATOR

Selections from the Greek Anthology, Weidenfeld & Nicolson, 1967, Macmillan, 1968.

(With Carlos P. Hanserv) *Bolivian Diary: Ernesto Che Guevara,* Lorrimer, 1968.

(With former wife, Marianne Alexandre) Jean Renoir, *La Grande Illusion* Lorrimer, 1968.

Masterworks of the French Cinema, Lorrimer, 1974.

OTHER

(Author of introduction) Homer, *The Iliad,* translated by W. H. D. Rouse, Heron Books, 1969.

Inkydoo, the Wild Boy (children's story), Abelard (London), 1976, published as *Carina and the Wild Boy,* Beaver/Hamlyn, 1977.

(Editor) Jack London, *The Call of the Wild, White Fang, and Other Stories,* introduction by James Dickey, Penguin, 1981.

(Editor and author of introduction) Jack London, *The Sea Wolf and Other Stories,* Penguin, 1989.

(Compiler) *The War Decade: An Anthology of the 1940s,* Hamish Hamilton, 1989.

Contributor to *Atlantic, Harper's, Observer, Guardian, Spectator, New Statesman, Granta, Texas Quarterly, Transatlantic Review,* and other periodicals and newspapers.

SIDELIGHTS: Among Andrew Sinclair's most imaginative works are the allegorical trilogy *Gog, Magog,* and *King Ludd.* A blend of fiction, history, and myth, the books examine Great Britain's past and present through the eyes of half-brothers Gog and Magog, names that evoke the twin giants of British legend whose statues stood guard over London's Guildhall until they were destroyed by German bombs in 1940. As Richard Freedman explains in the *Saturday Review,* Sinclair's modern versions of these age-old figures "symbolize the best and worst people and events from ancient Albion to Labourite Britain."

In the first novel, which begins just after the end of World War II, a seven-foot-tall man is washed ashore on the coast of Scotland, naked and suffering from amnesia. After a brief convalescence, the man—who remembers only that his name is Gog—sets out for London, hoping to learn more about his identity and, therefore, his past. The rest of the novel chronicles his many adventures as he journeys south. In the picaresque tradition, Gog meets a variety of fictional, historical, and mythological characters along the way. Some display concern and offer him assistance and advice; others (including his own wife and half-brother) regard him as "the perfect victim" and derive much pleasure from making him suffer. By the end of the novel, the one-time innocent has developed a less idealistic, more pragmatic attitude toward life, one that acknowledges the existence of evil and corruption and the need for each person to fight his or her own battles.

In their evaluations of *Gog,* critics have tended to rate it in one of two ways: as an unsuccessful attempt at sophisticated satire or as a highly ambitious and imaginative product of genius. An adherent of the former view is *New Statesman* reviewer Kenith Trodd, who characterizes *Gog* as "a series of funny production numbers: droll, but the laughs are hollow where they need to be edgy; the wrong sort of punch." Frank McGuinness also believes *Gog* lacks the proper sort of "punch." Writing in *London Magazine,* McGuinness declares that the book exhibits "perhaps more satirical pretensions than the author's talent for ribald and extravagant inventiveness can finally support. . . . The truth is that if the novel is not without distinction as a study of a mind hovering between sanity and madness, its satirical aims are lost in a welter of scholarly clowning, crude farce and the sort of glib cynicism that is so often mistaken for cold, hard-headed intellectualism."

A similar opinion is expressed by J. D. Scott in the *New York Times Book Review.* "Mr. Sinclair has too much talent to fail to make an impression," the critic begins. "But the impression is confused by too much frenetic action, and softened by long lapses into flat, sometimes merely clever, sometimes merely banal, prose. *Gog* is a monument of myth and slapstick, violence and parody, drama-of-evil and custard-pie comedy. Like some great Gothic folly seen through the mist, it fails to communicate its meaning."

On the other side of the discussion are those reviewers who regard *Gog* as excitingly original and entertaining. Though he thinks the novel is "much too long," Roger Sale comments in the *Hudson Review* that "the end is rich and satisfying, a book the likes of which I have not seen in a long time." In his study *The Situation of the Novel,* Bernard Bergonzi praises Sinclair's "extraordinary imaginative exuberance" and terms *Gog* "an intensely personal book, whose approach could not be followed by writers who do not share Sinclair's preoccupations, knowledge and temperament." Even more enthusiastic is critic Philip Callow, who asserts in *Books and Bookmen:* "[*Gog*] sears and scalds, it's the vision of a cold, planetary eye, and somehow it all founders in the end, goes mad like a cancer and finally smashes in a blind fury of destruction. I'm still reeling. I think there's genius in it."

Rachel Trickett more or less agrees with this assessment of *Gog,* stating in the *Yale Review* that it is "most extraordinary and ambitious. . . . A mixture of traditional genres, the allegory, the romance, and the picaresque tale, it is at once realistic and a fantasy, didactic and mythical, precise and comprehensive. Sinclair complains that most reviewers have misunderstood it, but he can hardly be sur-

prised; it attempts so much. . . . The love of life and a compulsive literary energy are what make *Gog* so impressive a book. . . . Confusion and carelessness are its worst faults, but its inclusiveness is also its strength. Self-indulgent and undisciplined, it nevertheless shows a clumsy but powerful genius which can only leave one astonished, occasionally repelled, but consistently grateful for so much imaginative vigor and breadth."

Magog examines many of the same social, political, and moral issues raised in *Gog,* this time from the point of view of *Gog*'s half-brother and spiritual opposite—Magog, the "symbol of power, authority, centralization, the tyranny of material success and fashion," as Trickett describes him. Like *Gog, Magog* begins in 1945, just after the end of the war. Sinclair portrays his title character as a young civil servant whose promising career with the government comes to an abrupt end when an investigation reveals the extent of his dishonest dealings. Despite this apparent setback, Magog moves on to successively more powerful positions as head of a film production company, an urban developer, and, finally, master of a new college at Cambridge. The focus of the book is on these various stages in Magog's career and on what *Dictionary of Literary Biography* writer Judith Vincent refers to as his ultimate realization "that his material success is hollow and that an inevitably changing order must deprive him of power."

Reviewers have greeted *Magog* with somewhat less enthusiasm than *Gog.* "Gobbling great hunks of time, a vast *dramatis personae;* tossing off puns, inside jokes, bits of mythology; insisting that the life of a man and of an empire have much in common, *Magog* trivializes all it touches," declares Patricia Meyer Spacks in the *Hudson Review.* "It's funny sometimes, sometimes even sad, but the lack of sharp authorial perspective makes it seem purposeless."

Commenting in the *New York Times Book Review,* Anthony Thwaite remarks that *Magog* "suffers, as sequels are apt to do, from the disabilities of its predecessor: lumbering in its episodic movement, spotty in its characterization, arbitrary in its action, and megalomaniac in its overview. . . . This book is not an epic, whatever its author's purpose may have been. Nor, despite its blurb, is it a 'wonderfully sardonic morality tale.' Sinclair's juggled universe bears little resemblance to any known world, no matter how hard he tries to reinforce everything with documentary and travelogue. *Magog* is a febrile, self-indulgent, opinionated and finally rather squalidly boring fling at the picaresque."

Unlike their colleagues, reviewers from the *Times Literary Supplement* and *Books and Bookmen* temper their criticism with praise. The *Times Literary Supplement* critic, for example, believes that "too many events" make *Magog* read like "a first-draft synopsis of a twelve-volume novel series, full of bright ideas, sharp comments and ambitions not yet realized." Nevertheless, the critic adds, "Sinclair is always interesting and convincing about [the] details of high life, which he treats with disdain." Oswell Blakeston also has some positive observations, particularly regarding the author's "ear for civil service dialogue." In general, says Blakeston in *Books and Bookmen,* this makes for "a splendid beginning" to the novel. "But then, alas, [Sinclair] plunges into farce," the critic continues. "[And] after one has laughed at a well-aimed poisoned dart of brilliant criticism, it's hard to accept the old custard pie as a devastating weapon."

Kenn Stitt and Lee T. Lemon are among those whose praise for *Magog* is almost without qualification. In a *New Statesman* article, Stitt describes the novel as "a rich and complex book, mirroring the complexities of the world it is set in, its strands intricately and carefully interwoven." Though he finds the theme somewhat trite, Lemon observes in *Prairie Schooner* that the author "does a fine job of showing the reader the peculiar anguish of the successful but hollow man [and] the intricacies of power." Like several other critics, he also finds that Sinclair "has a talent for the memorable turn of phrase." In short, concludes the reviewer, *Magog* "just might be one of the best novels of the past few years"—even better than *Gog.* "The earlier book was a stumbling romp through the history and mythology of the British Isles," says Lemon. "But *Magog* is a different book. Magog . . . is not hindered by his brother [Gog's] ponderous memories. He is a kind of gadfly of meaningless change. . . . By the end of the novel, Magog the manipulator has learned that time brings new and shrewder manipulators, and that one does not have to manipulate for the things which give satisfaction."

In 1988 *King Ludd,* the last novel in the trilogy, appeared. It begins with the story of the Luddites of the early nineteenth century, British workers who, thrown out of work because of the introduction of machines into factories, began an unorganized rebellion against mechanization. King Ludd was the name given to the mythical leader of the Luddite rebellion. In Sinclair's version of British history, Gog discovers that King Ludd was in reality based on one of his ancestors. Gog also believes that he can hear messages from the old Celtic gods, and he sees vestiges of the ancient Gogam script of the Druids in such present-day activities as cryptography. Gog, D. A. N. Jones explains in the *Times Literary Supplement,* "is a mixo-mythologist." Robert Nye, writing in the London *Times,* states: "What we have here is Gog's version of the history of the Luddites, married to an exhaustive account of the mythology of communications from the time of the Gogam script to the present day." Speaking of the trilogy as a whole, Nye concludes: "Sinclair succeeds in engaging

and holding our attention. I think these books are important, and that they'll last."

Writing in the *Contemporary Authors Autobiography Series,* Sinclair sees *King Ludd* as a story of technology in Britain from the early nineteenth century to the 1980s. The novel covers, Sinclair writes, "the Luddites, who first wrecked the new textile machines, through the story of the printers like Francis Place who defended liberty, on to the sad end of the print unions through new technology. . . . Contemporary events have given *King Ludd* its shape."

In a letter to *CA,* Sinclair comments on the ideas that inspired *Gog* and *Magog* and explains how *King Ludd* completes the trilogy. "*Gog* is based on Eliot's principle that time past and present and future are all the same. It also attempts to bring alive the legendary and mystical history of Britain as seen in the struggle of the people against the power of the government, of London, of King Ludd's town. There is no resolution to the fight of Gog against Magog, of the land against the city, of the ruled against the ruler, but in that fight lies the spirit and the glory of Albion, whatever it may be. *Magog*'s world is the machinations of power, and how its misuse drove Britain down after the end of the Second World War. *King Ludd* deals with England from the time of the Luddites opposing the industrial revolution through the neurosis of the 1930s to the odd conflicts of today, where the descendants of the Tolpuddle martyrs now have their unions and use the workers' power to oppress the rest. When brother fights brother, Magog and King Ludd will always rule."

BIOGRAPHICAL/CRITICAL SOURCES:

BOOKS

Bergonzi, Bernard, *The Situation of the Novel,* University of Pittsburgh Press, 1970.
Contemporary Literary Criticism, Gale, Volume 2, 1974, Volume 14, 1980.
Dictionary of Literary Biography, Volume 14: *British Novelists since 1960,* Gale, 1982.
Morris, Robert K., editor, *Old Lines, New Forces: Essays on the Contemporary British Novel, 1960-1970,* Fairleigh Dickinson University Press, 1976.
Sinclair, Andrew, essay in *Contemporary Authors Autobiography Series,* Gale, Volume 5, 1987.

PERIODICALS

Best Sellers, October 1, 1967.
Books and Bookmen, May, 1967; June, 1967; June, 1972.
Book World, September 24, 1967.
Chicago Tribune Book World, April 1, 1979; October 5, 1981.
Drama, summer, 1967.
Hudson Review, winter, 1967; autumn, 1972.
Listener, April 4, 1968.

London Magazine, June, 1967.

Los Angeles Times, April 7, 1981.

New Statesman, June 9, 1967; May 5, 1972.

New York Times, April 21, 1981.

New York Times Book Review, January 22, 1967; September 10, 1967; October 8, 1967; July 2, 1972; October 12, 1980; March 8, 1987; May 8, 1988.

Observer Review, June 1, 1967; January 1, 1970.

Prairie Schooner, spring, 1974.

Punch, January 20, 1970.

Saturday Review, September 16, 1967.

Spectator, April 25, 1969.

Time, September 1, 1967.

Times (London), January 21, 1982; June 20, 1985; June 29, 1985; October 21, 1989.

Times Literary Supplement, June 8, 1967; July 13, 1967; May 5, 1970; June 26, 1981; July 12, 1985; July 25, 1986; December 18, 1987; September 16, 1988; November 10, 1989.

Variety, January 15, 1969.

Washington Post, April 30, 1981.

Washington Post Book World, February 15, 1987; July 8, 1990.

Yale Review, spring, 1968.

*   *   *

SLAVUTYCH, Yar 1918-

PERSONAL: Surname legally changed in 1954; born January 11, 1918, in Blahodatne, Ukraine; naturalized U.S. citizen in 1954; son of Mykhajlo and Tetiana (Bratunenko) Zhuchenko; married Elwira Cybar, November 10, 1948; children: Bohdan, Oksana. *Education:* Pedagogic Institute of Zaporizzia, diploma, 1940; Ukrainian Free University, Munich, Germany, graduate study, 1945-46; University of Pennsylvania, A.M., 1954, Ph.D., 1955.

ADDRESSES: Home—72 Westbrook Dr., Edmonton, Alberta, Canada T6J 2E1.

CAREER: High school teacher in Zaporizzia, Ukraine, 1940-41, Augsburg, Germany, 1945-49, and Philadelphia, PA, 1950-55; U.S. Army Language School, Monterey, CA, senior instructor in Slavic languages, 1955-60; University of Alberta, Edmonton, assistant professor, 1960-65, associate professor, 1966-79, professor of Slavic languages, 1980—.

MEMBER: Modern Language Association of America, Comparative Literature Association, American Name Society (member of board of directors, 1968-70; member of editorial board, 1971-80), American Association of Teachers of Slavic and East European Languages, American Association for the Advancement of Slavic Studies, Canadian Association of Slavists, Canadian Institute of Onomastic Sciences (secretary, 1966-73; vice president, 1973-76; president, 1976-79), Ukrainian Shakespeare Society (president, 1979—), Ukrainian Free Academy of Sciences, Shevchenko Scientific Society (president of western Canadian branch, 1970-75), Ukrainian Literary and Art Club (president, 1961-65).

AWARDS, HONORS: Literary award, America Press, 1951; Canada Council Award, 1968-69; first and second prizes for poetry, Ivan Franko Foundation, 1981, 1986; Shevchenko Gold Medal, 1974; Poet Laureate, Ukrainian Mohylo-Mazepian Academy of Sciences, 1982.

WRITINGS:

Moderna ukrajins'ka poezija, 1900-1950, America Press, 1950.

The Muse in Prison, Svoboda, 1956.

Vybrani poeziji (translation of poems by John Keats), Ukrainian Publishers, 1958.

Conversational Ukrainian, Gateway Publishers, 1959, 5th edition, 1987.

Oasis (poems; translated into English), Vantage, 1959.

Ukrainian for Beginners, Slavuta, 1962, 7th edition, 1987.

Trofeji, 1938-1963 (poems), Slavuta, 1963.

(Editor) *Pivnichne sjajvo,* five volumes, Slavuta, 1964-71.

Zavojovnyky prerij (poems), Slavuta, 1968.

Mudroshchi mandriw (poems), Slavuta, 1972.

(Editor) *Zakhidnokanads'kyi zbirnyk,* Shevchenko Scientific Society, Volume 1, 1973, Volume 2, 1975.

The Conquerors of the Prairies (poems; contains original Ukrainian versions and translations), translated by R. H. Morrison, Slavuta, 1974, 3rd edition, 1984.

(Editor) *Antolohija ukrajins'koji poeziji v Kanadi, 1898-1973,* Ukrainian Writers' Association, 1975.

Ukrainian Poetry in Canada: A Historical Account, Ukrainian Pioneers' Association of Alberta, 1975.

L'Oiseau de feu (poems), compiled and translated into French by Rene Coulet de Gard, Editions des Deux Mondes, 1976.

Ukrajins'ka poezija v Kanadi, Slavuta, 1976.

Vokal'ni tvory na slova Jara Slavutycha (music to Slavutych's poems), compiled by S. Jaremenko, Slavuta, 1978.

Zibrani tvory, 1938-1978 (poems), Slavuta, 1978.

Valogatott versek (poems), translated by Domokos Sandor, Hungarian Cultural Society of Edmonton, 1983.

Zhyvi smoloskypy (poems), Slavuta, 1983.

An Annotated Bibliography of Ukrainian Literature in Canada, 1908-1983, Slavuta, 1984, 3rd edition, 1987.

Mistsiamy zaporoz'kymy (memoirs), Slavuta, 1985.

Izbrannoe (poems), translated into Russian by Yurij Pustovojtov, Jewish-Ukrainian Society (Jerusalem), 1986.

Standard Ukrainian Grammar, Slavuta, 1987, 2nd edition, 1990.

(Editor) *Ukrajins'ka Shekspiriiana na Zakhodi,* two volumes, Slavuta, 1987-90.

U vyri bahatokul'turnosty (memoirs), Slavuta, 1988.

Oaza tesknoty (poems), translated into Polish by Tadeusz Karabowicz, Slavuta, 1989.

Vybranaie (poems), translated into Belorussian by Masiej Siadniow, Slavuta, 1989.

Slovo pro Zaporoz'ku Sich (poems), Dnipropetrovs'ke (Ukraine), 1991.

Contributor to *Books Abroad, Canadian Slavonic Papers, Jahrbuch der Ukrainekunde, Names, Slavic and East European Journal, Slavic Review, Slavs in Canada, Suchasnist', Ukrainian Quarterly, Ukrainian Review,* and *Vyzvol'nyj shliakh.* Editor of *Kanads'ka Ukrajina,* 1976-78.

WORK IN PROGRESS: Research on Ukrainian literature in Canada and the United States.

BIOGRAPHICAL/CRITICAL SOURCES:

BOOKS

Andrusyshen, C. H., and Watson Kirkconnell, *The Ukrainian Poets, 1189-1962,* University of Toronto Press, 1963.

Balan, Jars, editor, *Yarmarok: Ukrainian Writing in Canada since the Second World War,* University of Toronto Press, 1987.

Mandryka, M. I., *History of Ukrainian Literature in Canada,* Ukrainian Free Academy of Sciences, 1968.

Shcherbak, Mykola, and W. T. Zyla, *Polumjane slovo,* Ukrainian Publishers, 1969.

Slavutych, Vira, compiler, *Bibliohrafija pysan' pro Jara Slavutycha (1978-1985),* Slavuta, 1985.

Zyla, compiler, *Tvorchist'Jara Slavutycha: A Symposium,* Edmonton Jubilee Committee, 1978.

PERIODICALS

Books Abroad, winter, 1971.

*　　*　　*

SMART, Carolyn (Alexandra) 1952-

PERSONAL: Born March 16, 1952, in Kent, England; daughter of Angus Edward (a diplomat and economist) and Jane Elizabeth (a set designer and homemaker; maiden name, Van Tress) Smart; married Kenneth Henri de Kok (a photographer and rancher), May 6, 1983; children: Nicholas Edward, Daniel James. *Education:* University of Toronto, B.A. (with honors), 1973; also attended University of Manitoba.

ADDRESSES: Home—Box 160, Sydenham, Ontario, Canada, K0H 2T0. *Office*—Department of English, Watson Hall, Queen's University, Kingston, Ontario, Canada, K7L 3N6.

CAREER: Doubleday Canada Ltd., Toronto, Ontario, editorial assistant, 1973-74; Macmillan of Canada, Toronto, poetry editor, 1974-75; Government of Manitoba, Winnipeg, conference organizer, 1975-77; free-lance writer and editor, 1977-79; poet and journalist, 1979—; Queen's University, Kingston, Ontario, teacher of creative writing, 1989—. Member of Fireweed Collective; past managing editor of *Fireweed: A Feminist Quarterly.*

MEMBER: PEN International, League of Canadian Poets, Writers' Union of Canada.

WRITINGS:

POEMS

Swimmers in Oblivion, York Publishing, 1981.
Power Sources, Fiddlehead Poetry Books, 1982.
Stoning the Moon, Oberon Press, 1986.
The Way to Come Home, Brick Books, 1992.

Author of "On Craft," a column in *Poetry Canada Review.* Contributor to magazines, including *Tamarack Review, Malahat Review, Canadian Forum,* and *Queen's Quarterly.*

WORK IN PROGRESS: Possessed, a personal prose memoir.

SIDELIGHTS: Carolyn Smart told *CA:* "As a feminist, it is important to me that my work be politically involved. By that I mean to say that day-to-day life as lived by ordinary people is by its own nature a political involvement, and my writing is directed towards that. I attempt to write with a clear, articulate focus with a plain, descriptive language attuned to voice.

"I write for myself, for the purest sense of satisfaction I've ever experienced, but I publish for the contact with others. Living deep in the country of Eastern Ontario I treasure the sense of communion writing and publishing brings to me, and hope that I can somehow greet through written language those other writers I've admired for so long: Carolyn Forche, Galway Kinnell, Margaret Atwood, Michael Ondaatje, and my contemporaries and friends here in Canada who give me such support. As a feminist raising two sons, my work can't help but be politically involved in the true sense, in the way we live our lives."

*　　*　　*

SMITH, Myron J(ohn), Jr. 1944-

PERSONAL: Born May 3, 1944, in Toledo, OH; son of Myron J. and Marion (Herbert) Smith; married Susan

Ballou, June 15, 1968; married Elsie Dennis Pickens, January 9, 1982; children: (first marriage) Myron J. III. *Education:* Attended College of Steubenville, 1962; Ashland College, A.B., 1966; Western Michigan University, M.L.S., 1967; Shippensburg State College, M.A., 1969; additional study at Western Maryland College, University of Maryland, University of Wisconsin, Purdue University, Middle Tennessee State University, and U.S. Air Force Air University.

ADDRESSES: Home—Rte. 2, Box 1760, Chuckey, TN 37641. *Office*—Tate Library, Tusculum College, Box 5087, Greeneville, TN 37743.

CAREER: Mystic Seaport Library, Mystic, CT, research librarian, 1967-68; Western Maryland College, Westminster, assistant librarian, 1969-72; Huntington Public Library, Huntington, IN, director, 1972-76; Salem College, Salem, WV, professor of history and library science, director of libraries, associate director of career aviation program, and R.O.T.C. liaison, 1976-90; Tusculum College, Greeneville, TN, professor of history and library science, and library director, 1990—.

MEMBER: American Library Association, U.S. Naval Institute, U.S. Military Institute, American Committee on the History of the Second World War, Association for the Bibliography of History (national president, 1982), Civil Air Patrol (aerospace education director of West Virginia Wing, 1977-79), Andrew Johnson Historical Association, Professional Football Researchers Association, Stonewall Jackson Civil War Roundtable (vice-president, 1985), Tennessee Library Association, West Virginia Library Association, Alpha Eta Rho, Beta Phi Mu, Phi Alpha Theta, Optimist Club.

AWARDS, HONORS: Named honorary admiral in Texas Navy, 1971, for work on bibliography of Texas Navy; certificate of appreciation, U.S. Navy Department, 1974; named honorary admiral in Georgia Navy, 1975; Distinguished Service Award, Huntington (IN) Centennial Association, 1976; Distinguished West Virginian Award, 1981; achievement certificate, West Virginia Library Association, 1981; first American recipient of the Richard Franck Preis, Bibliothek fuer Zeitgeschichte (Stuttgart), 1981; Litt.D., Cardinal Newman College, 1982.

WRITINGS:

An Indiana Sailor Scuttles Morgan's Raid, Fort Wayne Public Library, 1972.

Sophisticated Lady: The Battleship "Indiana" in World War II, Fort Wayne Public Library, 1973.

(Editor) *Huntington Centennial Handbook and Guide,* Our Sunday Visitor, 1973.

Cloak-and-Dagger Bibliography: An Annotated Guide to Spy Fiction, 1937-1975, Scarecrow, 1975.

The Sea Fiction Guide, Scarecrow, 1976.

World War II at Sea, 1939-1945: A Bibliography of Sources in English, Scarecrow, 1976, Volume 1: *The European Theater,* Volume 2: *The Pacific Theater,* Volume 3, Part 1: *General Works, Naval Hardware, and the All Hands Chronology,* Part 2: *Home Fronts and Special Studies.*

World War I in the Air: A Bibliography and Chronology, Scarecrow, 1977.

The Soviet Navy, American Bibliographic Center/Clio Press, 1979.

Air War Southeast Asia, 1961-1973: An Annotated Bibliography and 16mm Film Guide, Scarecrow, 1979.

War Story Guide: An Annotated Bibliography of Military Fiction, Scarecrow, 1980.

The Secret Wars: A Guide to the Literature of Intelligence, Espionage, Covert Operations, and International Terrorism, three volumes, American Bibliographic Center/Clio Press, 1980-81.

The Soviet Military, three volumes, Regina Books, 1980-82.

Equestrian Studies: The Salem College Guide to Sources in English, 1950-1980, Scarecrow, 1981.

The U.S. Gunboat Carondolet, 1861-1865, U.S.A.F. Historical Foundation, 1982.

Cloak-and-Dagger Fiction, American Bibliographic Center/Clio Press, 1982.

The Mountain State Battleship: U.S.S. West Virginia, West Virginia Book Club Press, 1982.

Mountaineer Battlewagon: U.S.S. West Virginia (BB-48), Pictorial Histories, 1982.

Watergate: An Annotated Bibliography of Sources in English, 1972-1982, Scarecrow, 1983.

Keystone Battlewagon: U.S.S. Pennsylvania (BB-38), Pictorial Histories, 1983.

U.S. Television Network News: A Guide to Sources in English, McFarland & Co., 1984.

The United States Navy and Coast Guard, 1946-1983: A Bibliography of English-Language Works and 16mm Films, McFarland & Co., 1984.

World War II: The European and Mediterranean Theaters, an Annotated Bibliography, edited by Richard L. Blanco, Garland Publishing, 1984.

Golden State Battlewagon: U.S.S. California (BB-44), Pictorial Histories, 1984.

Battleships and Battlecruisers, 1884-1984: A Bibliography and Chronology, Garland Publishing, 1985.

Free State Battlewagon: U.S.S. Maryland (BB-46), Pictorial Histories, 1985.

(Compiler) *Baseball: A Comprehensive Bibliography,* McFarland & Co., 1986.

The Airline Bibliography: The Salem College Guide to Sources on Commercial Aviation, Locust Hill Press,

Volume 1: *The United States,* 1986, Volume 2: *Airliners and Foreign Air Transport,* 1988.

99th Infantry Division Bibliography, U.S. Government Printing Office, 1987.

Passenger Airliners of the United States, 1926-1986: A Pictorial History, Pictorial Histories, 1987, revised edition, 1991.

Brooklyn/Los Angeles Dodgers: A Bibliography, Meckler Books, 1988.

100 Years of Opportunity: A Pictorial History of Salem College, 1888-1988, Walsworth, 1988.

The Pro Football Bio-Bibliography, Locust Hill Press, 1989.

American Warplanes, 1908-1988: A Bibliography, Greenwood Press, 1991.

Pearl Harbor, 1941: A Bibliography, Greenwood Press, 1991.

The Battles of Coral Sea and Midway, 1942: A Bibliography, Greenwood Press, 1991.

Mississippi River Gunboats, 1861-1865: A Pictorial History, Pictorial Histories, 1992.

Writings on Professional Football: The Official Pro Football Hall of Fame Bibliography, Meckler Books, 1992.

Volunteer Battlewagon: U.S.S. Tennessee (BB-43), Pictorial Histories, 1992.

SERIES

"American Naval Bibliography Series, 1775-1941," five volumes, Scarecrow, 1972-74.

"The Air War Bibliography Series, 1939-1945: A Guide to English Sources," five volumes, U.S.A.F. Historical Foundation, 1977-81.

"The Air War Chronology Series, 1939-1945," six volumes, U.S.A.F. Historical Foundation, 1977—.

OTHER

Also co-author with Douglas Reeman of *Strike from the Sea,* 1978. Author of regular column, "HPL: The World of Books," in *Huntington Herald Press,* 1972-76. Contributor of articles and reviews to periodicals, including *Military Affairs, Choice, Journal of Mississippi History, Indiana History Bulletin, Journal of Military History, Log of Mystic Seaport,* and *Civil War History.* Contributing editor, *Military Journal.*

WORK IN PROGRESS: Baseball: A Comprehensive Bibliography—Supplement One, for McFarland & Co.; *The Battle of Guadalcanal: A Bibliography* and *The Battle of the Atlantic, 1939-1945: A Bibliography,* both for Greenwood Press.

SIDELIGHTS: Myron J. Smith, Jr., told *CA:* "I became a librarian because of the job market for historians. History became an avocation and as I became better acquainted with the tools of my profession, it became appar-

ent that I could blend both my hobby and my work through the preparation of bibliographies. Long a student of military affairs, I found that the historical bibliography area of that subject was not well covered and thus a publisher and a market were found for my first outing, *American Civil War Navies.* Although I have strayed from the military to prepare guides to other subjects, e.g., *Watergate, Equestrian Studies,* and my 22,000-entry *Baseball: A Comprehensive Bibliography,* it still continues to amaze me that my original thrust toward the military history market brings publishers willing to produce my work. In addition to nonfiction guides, I have very much enjoyed the preparation of fiction guides, especially the two editions of *Cloak-and-Dagger Fiction* on spy stories, and pictorial histories like my hugely popular *Passenger Airliners of the United States, 1926-1986.*

"My goal as a bibliographer is simple: to provide the most complete coverage available on a subject so as to aid the researcher (student or scholar) who desires a picture of what has already been written in a given area. When compiling, my process is likewise rather basic: all free time available is devoted to scouring libraries with collections bearing on the topic, under examination. Despite the use of a computer, the hardest part, believe it or not, is not the gathering of references, but the preparation of the manuscript. A computer will speed the process, but the difficulties of deciding how to arrange entries, the writing of introductions, and the preparation of indexes remain. For the most part, my works are not translated; however, foreign distribution has been good.

"Bibliographers are not a well-recognized bunch of authors as I've learned over the years; such awards and appreciations as we receive often come from within our own groups. The greatest reward for me has to have been watching a librarian handing one of my tools to a patron or scholar. Indeed, I have received greater return, if that's the correct work, on my smaller text histories of battleships than on all of my bibliographies. Despite a lack of 'big-name recognition,' which would really be a bit of a bother, the satisfaction level in my work is high—and the reviewers have been kind.

"I would offer the following advice to those who might aspire to become bibliographers: learn how to type and find a publisher sympathetic to your project (without those two ingredients, your effort will probably not reach even a limited audience); be complete in your citation gathering; buy a house large enough to store all of your accumulation or a computer with a lot of memory (or lots of discs); and be prepared to devote hours and hours of time to the process, both compilation and manuscript assembly. If you employ a data base, be sure to check the citations carefully as they are sometimes inaccurate (it is just as difficult it seems to change an entry in a data base citation as in an automatic billing system!) and if you can (I haven't learned how yet), take a bit of time occasionally to stop and enjoy nature, TV, a ballgame, mowing the grass, or whatever, not connected with your project. Bibliography is like good mystery; once hooked, it's hard to stop, but halt awhile if you can."

*   *   *

SNOW, Edgar Parks 1905-1972

PERSONAL: Born July 19, 1905, in Kansas City, MO; died February 15, 1972, in Switzerland; son of James Edgar (a printer and editor) and Anna Catherine (Edelman) Snow; married Helen Foster (a writer under pseudonym Nym Wales), 1932 (divorced, 1949); married Lois Wheeler, 1949; children: Christopher, Sian (daughter). *Education:* Attended Junior College of Kansas City (now Metropolitan Junior College—Kansas City), 1923-24, University of Missouri, 1924-26, and Columbia University, 1926-27.

CAREER: Kansas City Star, Kansas City, MO, correspondent, 1927; *New York Sun,* New York City, reporter, 1928; *China Weekly Review,* Shanghai, China, assistant editor, 1929; *Chicago Tribune,* Chicago, IL, correspondent, 1929-30; staff correspondent for Consolidated Press Association, 1930-34; *New York Sun,* New York City, correspondent, 1930-38; *London Daily Herald,* London, England, staff correspondent, 1933-37, chief correspondent in Far East, 1937-41; *Saturday Evening Post,* Indianapolis, IN, world correspondent, 1941-53, associate editor, 1943-52. Lecturer, Yenching University (now Beijing University), early 1930s.

MEMBER: World Academy of Art and Science, Beta Theta Pi, Overseas Press Club, National Press Club, Foreign Correspondents Club.

AWARDS, HONORS: Lawrence S. Mayers Peace Award, 1956.

WRITINGS:

Far Eastern Front, H. Smith & R. Haas, 1933.
Red Star over China, Gollancz, 1937, Random House, 1938, revised edition, Grove, 1968.
Living China: Modern Chinese Short Stories, Reynal, 1937.
(With Norman D. Hanwell) *Wai kuo chi che hsi pei yin shiang chi,* [China], 1937, published as *Mei-huo chi che Chung-kuo hung ch'u yin hsiang chi,* [China], 1949.
Chung-kuo ti hung ch'u, [China], 1938.
The Battle for Asia, Random House, 1941 (published in England as *The Scorched Earth,* Gollancz, 1941).
(Author of introduction) Maung Thein Pe, *What Happened in Burma: The Frank Revelation of a Young Burmese Revolutionary Leader Who Has Recently Emerged from Burma to India,* Kitabistan, 1943.
People on Our Side (Book-of-the-Month Club selection), Random House, 1944 (published in England as *Glory and Bondage,* Gollancz, 1945).
The Pattern of Soviet Power, Random House, 1945.
Stalin Must Have Peace, Random House, 1947.
Random Notes on Red China, Harvard University Press, 1957.
Journey to the Beginning, Random House, 1958.
The Other Side of the River, Random House, 1962, abridged edition published as *China, Russia and the U.S.A.: Changing Relations in a Changing World,* Marzani & Munsell, 1963, abridged edition with new introduction published as *War and Peace in Vietnam,* Marzani & Munsell, 1963, published with a new preface as *Red China Today: The Other Side of the River,* Penguin, 1970, published as *Red China Today,* Random House, 1971, revised and updated edition published as *Red China Today,* Vintage Books, 1971.
One Fourth of Humanity—The China Story (documentary film), 1968.
Mei-huo yu hao jen shih S su-no fang Hua wen chang, [China], c. 1971.
The Long Revolution, Random House, 1972.
Edgar Snow's China, Vintage Books, 1981.

Also author, with others, of *Smash Hitler's International,* 1941, and of *Washington-Tokyo-Peking,* 1969. Contributor to *Asia, Current History, Fortune,* and *Look.*

SIDELIGHTS: Described by the People's Republic of China's ambassador to the United Nations, Huang Hua, as "a true friend of the Chinese people," according to the *Nation,* Edgar Parks Snow devoted some forty years to writing about China. A devoted friend of Mao Tse-tung, Snow was sympathetic to the goals and achievements of the Chinese communist government of China, writing a number of books on the subject.

Snow began his career as a foreign correspondent at the age of twenty-three, first in Central America and Hawaii, and then in the Far East. While visiting China in 1929, he was invited by Dr. Sun Fo, the Minister of Railways and son of the late Dr. Sun Yat-sen, to travel the entire system of government railways in China and Manchuria. From the information Snow gathered during his journeys, he wrote a series of guide books on China.

During the 1930s, Snow covered a number of major news stories in China and the Far East, including Sino-Russian hostilities in Manchuria, the agrarian revolt in Indo-China, a head-hunters uprising in Formosa, and Tharawaddy uprisings against British rule in Burma. He organized a months-long caravan into southwestern China, Burma, and northern India. Together with his wife, Helen Snow, and Rewi Alley, Snow drew up plans for the Chinese Industrial Co-operatives (Indusco), a means whereby China was to quickly rebuild its industrial strength following the war with the Japanese. Helen Snow described the co-operatives in her book *China Builds for Democracy,* published under the pseudonym Nym Wales.

In 1936 Snow traveled with the Chinese Red Army for five months into Soviet China. His photographs and stories in the *London Daily Herald* and the *Saturday Evening Post* broke a news blockade that had existed in this area for nine years. His book *Red Star Over China,* based on these travels, is an account of the rising power of the Chinese communist movement at that time. An international bestseller, the book provided a firsthand look at the Red Chinese army, its war tactics and objectives. It also predicted the final victory of the Chinese communists.

Snow was also granted an interview with Chinese communist leader Mao Tse-tung in 1936, shortly after the famous Long March in which Mao led the Chinese forces in a grueling escape from a superior enemy. Much of their conversation, which took place during several days and nights in a cave near Mongolia, is contained in *Red Star Over China.* The interview began a friendship between the two men which lasted over the next thirty years.

Although Snow was not a communist himself, he sympathized with the communist movement in China, believing that it was "an attempt by the Chinese to rid themselves not only of foreign imperialistic designs but also of centuries of old oppression by bureaucratic officialdom, greedy bankers, and others." Because of his sympathies, Snow found himself in less demand after World War II and the beginnings of the Cold War between East and West. Pressures at the *Saturday Evening Post,* where he was an associate editor, moved him to resign his position. During the 1950s, while Mao took over China and established a communist dictatorship, Snow wrote as a freelancer for a number of news journals, including the *Nation.* Snow was not to return to China until the 1960s, when he made two visits. In 1970 he returned again with his wife. At the time of his death in 1972 Snow was about to visit China again for *Life* magazine, covering President Richard Nixon's historic rapprochement with China.

In *Journey to the Beginning* Snow wrote: "Part of me would always remain with China's tawny hills, her terraced emerald fields, her island temples seen in the early morning mist, a few of her sons and daughters who had trusted or loved me, her bankrupt cheerful civilized peasants who have sheltered and fed me, her brown, ragged, shining-eyed children, the equals and the lovers I had known, and above all the lousy, unpaid, hungry, despised, peasant foot-soldier who in the mysterious sacrifice of his own life alone now gave value to all life and put the stamp

of nobility upon the struggle of a great people to survive and to go forward.

"Yes, I was proud to have known them, to have straggled across a continent with them in defeat, to have wept with them and still to share a faith with them. But I was not and could never be one of them. A man who gives himself to be the possession of an alien land . . . lives a Yahoo life. . . . I was an American."

Even in death Snow is still partly in his beloved China. Some of his remains rest in a garden at Beijing University while the rest are near the Hudson River in New York.

BIOGRAPHICAL/CRITICAL SOURCES:

BOOKS

Snow, Lois Wheeler, *Death with Dignity: When the Chinese Came,* Random House, 1975.

PERIODICALS

Asia, February, 1937.
National Review, January 5, 1973, p. 39.
New York Times, December 10, 1936.
Publishers Weekly, February 12, 1938.
Saturday Review of Literature, January 1, 1938; March 1, 1941.
Time, December 17, 1945; February 28, 1972; September 20, 1976.
Times (London), December 10, 1936; December 12, 1936.

OBITUARIES:

PERIODICALS

Nation, February 28, 1972.
New York Times, February 16, 1972.
Time, February 28, 1972.
Washington Post, February 16, 1972.*

*   *   *

SNYDER, Zilpha Keatley 1927-

PERSONAL: Born May 11, 1927, in Lemoore, CA; daughter of William Solon (a rancher and driller) and Dessa J. (Jepson) Keatley; married Larry Allan Snyder, June 18, 1950; children: Susan Melissa, Douglas; foster children: Ben. *Education:* Whittier College, B.A., 1948; additional study at University of California, Berkeley, 1958-60. *Politics:* Democrat. *Religion:* Episcopalian. *Avocational interests:* "My hobbies seem to change from time to time, but reading and travel remain among the top favorites. And of course writing which, besides being my occupation, is still and always will be my all-time favorite hobby."

ADDRESSES: Home—52 Miller Ave., Mill Valley, CA 94941.

CAREER: Writer. Public school teacher at Washington School, Berkeley, CA, and in New York, Washington, and Alaska, 1948-62; University of California, Berkeley, master teacher and demonstrator for education classes, 1959-61; lecturer.

AWARDS, HONORS: George G. Stone Recognition of Merit from Claremont Graduate School, Lewis Carroll Shelf award, Spring Book Festival first prize, all 1967, and Newbery honor book, 1968, all for *The Egypt Game;* Christopher Medal, 1970, for *The Changeling;* William Allen White Award, Newbery honor book, Christopher Medal, all 1972, and Hans Christian Andersen International honor list of the International Board on Books for Young People, 1974, all for *The Headless Cupid; New York Times* Outstanding Book, 1972, National Book Award finalist and Newbery honor book, both 1973, all for *The Witches of Worm; New York Times* Outstanding Book, 1981, for *A Fabulous Creature;* PEN Literary Award, 1983, and Parent's Choice Award, both for *The Birds of Summer;* Bay Area Book Reviewers Award, 1988, William Allen White Master Reading List, 1989-90, and Georgia Children's Book Award Master List, 1990-91, all for *And Condors Danced;* New Mexico State Award, 1989-90, and on the Notable Trade Books in the Language Arts list of the National Council of Teachers of English, both for *The Changing Maze; Season of Ponies, The Egypt Game, The Headless Cupid, The Witches of Worm,* and *A Fabulous Creature* were all named American Library Association Notable Books; *The Velvet Room* and *The Egypt Game* were named on the *Horn Book* honor list; *The Velvet Room, The Changeling, The Headless Cupid, Below the Root, Until the Celebration,* and *Blair's Nightmare* were all Junior Literary Guild selections; *Blair's Nightmare* was included on state awards master lists in Missouri, Texas, Nebraska, Pacific Northwest, and New Mexico; *Libby on Wednesday* was on the Virginia state award master list.

WRITINGS:

FOR CHILDREN

Season of Ponies, illustrated by Alton Raible, Atheneum, 1964.
The Velvet Room, illustrated by Raible, Atheneum, 1965.
Black and Blue Magic, illustrated by Gene Holtan, Atheneum, 1966.
The Egypt Game, illustrated by Raible, Atheneum, 1967.
Eyes in the Fishbowl, illustrated by Raible, Atheneum, 1968.
Today Is Saturday (poetry), photographs by John Arms, Atheneum, 1969.
The Changeling, illustrated by Raible, Atheneum, 1970.

The Headless Cupid, illustrated by Raible, Atheneum, 1971.
The Witches of Worm, illustrated by Raible, Atheneum, 1972.
The Princess and the Giants (picture book), illustrated by Beatrice Darwin, Atheneum, 1973.
The Truth about Stone Hollow, illustrated by Raible, Atheneum, 1974, published in England as *The Ghosts of Stone Hollow,* Lutterworth, 1978.
Below the Root (first volume in the "Green-sky" trilogy), illustrated by Raible, Atheneum, 1975.
And All Between (second volume in the "Green-sky" trilogy), illustrated by Raible, Atheneum, 1976.
Until the Celebration (third volume in the "Green-sky" trilogy), illustrated by Raible, Atheneum, 1977.
The Famous Stanley Kidnapping Case, illustrated by Raible, Atheneum, 1979.
Come On, Patsy (picture book), illustrated by Margot Zemach, Atheneum, 1982.
Blair's Nightmare, Atheneum, 1984.
The Changing Maze (picture book), illustrated by Charles Mikolaycak, Macmillan, 1985.
The Three Men, Harper, 1986.
And Condors Danced, Delacorte, 1987.
Squeak Saves the Day and Other Tooley Tales, illustrated by Leslie Morrill, Delacorte, 1988.
Janie's Private Eyes, Delacorte, 1989.
Libby on Wednesday, Delacorte, 1990.
Song of the Gargoyle, Delacorte, 1991.

YOUNG ADULT NOVELS

A Fabulous Creature, Atheneum, 1981.
The Birds of Summer, Atheneum, 1983.

ADULT NOVELS

Heirs of Darkness, Atheneum, 1978.

OTHER

Snyder's manuscript collection is kept in the Kerlan Collection, University of Minnesota, Minneapolis.

ADAPTATIONS:

Black and Blue Magic (filmstrip with tape), Pied Piper, 1975.

The Egypt Game (recording and cassette), Miller-Brody, 1975.

The Headless Cupid (from *Newbery Award Cassette* stories; recording and cassette), Miller-Brody, 1976, (filmstrip with tape) Pied Piper, 1980.

The Witches of Worm (recording), Miller-Brody, 1978.

Below the Root (computer game), Spinnaker Software's Windham Classics, 1985.

The Egypt Game was produced as a filmstrip and tape by Pied Piper.

SIDELIGHTS: "I was eight years old when I decided I was a writer," Zilpha Keatley Snyder recalls in Lee Bennett Hopkins's *More Books by More People,* "and in spite of many detours, I never entirely gave up the idea." It was not until after she had become a mother of two and spent nine years working as an elementary school teacher that the author finally found time to write. Inspired by childhood memories and her experiences with children, Snyder decided to write stories that combined typical themes about the problems that children face with an element of fantasy. Snyder's stories, writes Jean Fritz in the *New York Times Book Review,* "suggest that magic lies within the power of imagination itself."

As a child growing up in California, Snyder's imagination was very active. According to her, this was a matter of necessity. "We lived in the country during the Depression and World War II," she says in Hopkins's book. "Due to shortages of such things as gasoline and money, I didn't get around much or do many exciting things. In fact, my world might have been quite narrow and uninteresting if it had not been for two magical ingredients—animals and books." As for animals, the author's family lived in a country house and raised everything from cats, dogs, and rabbits to cows, goats, and horses, so there were plenty of four-legged friends to keep her happy. A nearby library supplied the young Snyder with her other magical ingredient. Having learned to read at the very early age of four years, she borrowed many books from the library, reading about one per day during her first years in school.

When she entered the seventh grade, as she recounts in the *Something about the Author Autobiography Series,* she felt she "was suddenly a terrible misfit" because she had been allowed to skip one grade and was younger than the other children. "So I retreated further into books and daydreams," she later remarked. Snyder began to feel less shy by the time she entered high school. "I became a little less afraid of my peers. I had some good teachers and made some exciting new friends, such as Shakespeare and Emily Dickinson." The author continued to grow as a student at Whittier College, where she also met her husband Larry, who was a music major at the time.

Snyder had romantic dreams of becoming a struggling writer in New York City, but after graduating from Whittier she found that she did not have the money for a ticket to get there, let alone try to live in the city with no dependable income. She took a teaching job instead; and not only did she enjoy teaching elementary school children, but she was so talented at it that she eventually became a master teacher at the University of California at Berkeley. Snyder held several teaching jobs around the United States be-

cause her husband transferred to different graduate schools, and also because he was assigned to several bases while he served in the Air Force during the Korean War. They finally ended up in Berkeley, California, where Larry finished his degree. After moving fifteen times and having two children, the Snyders were finally ready to settle down. "I was still teaching but there seemed to be a bit more time and I caught my breath and thought about writing."

For Snyder the appeal of writing lies in the author's power to create an entire world and populate it with people who have never existed before, so she was naturally drawn toward writing stories that dealt with imagination and fantasy. A large source of her inspiration, especially in her earlier books, has been her childhood memories. "Remembering a dream I'd had when I was twelve years old about some strange and wonderful horses," Snyder says, she sat down to write her first book, *Season of Ponies,* and submitted it to Atheneum for publication. Although the editor there, Jean Karl, did not immediately accept the author's manuscript, she encouraged Snyder to revise the book and, after the author rewrote the story twice, it was accepted.

Other early works like *The Velvet Room* and *The Egypt Game* also originated from Snyder's childhood. *The Velvet Room* echoes experiences Snyder had as a child growing up during the Depression. The story itself is based on one that Snyder wrote when she was only nineteen years old about a migratory worker and his family. Despite the realistic subject, magic enters the tale as it is told through a child's imaginative eyes. The inspiration for *The Egypt Game* came from what Snyder calls the "Egyptian period" of her childhood, a year during which she became completely absorbed in anything having to do with ancient Egypt. "However, the actual setting and all six of the main characters came from my years as a teacher in Berkeley," the author related.

"*The Egypt Game* is probably one of this author's most popular novels, and one of her best," claims *Twentieth Century Children's Writers* contributor Kay E. Vandergrift. "The Egypt game is an elaborate game played in a secret 'temple' and filled with ritualistic gestures. Through his observations of the game, an old professor takes a new interest in life and ultimately saves the children from unexpected danger. Although there is no special note taken of the fact, the players are a mixed group racially and ethnically which was at the time of publication (1967) still somewhat rare in American books for children."

The Egypt Game was published one year after the Snyders adopted their son Ben, a native of Kowloon, China. A few years later, in 1970, the Snyders left their home near Berkeley to tour Europe. When they returned they settled into a century-old farmhouse near Santa Rosa, California. It was here that Snyder wrote many of her books, including the science fiction "Green-sky" trilogy. Mystery and magic continue to be important elements in books like *The Changeling, The Witches of Worm,* and *The Truth about Stone Hollow.* The reappearance of paranormal subjects in these books led a *Dell Carousel* interviewer to ask Snyder whether she was interested in the occult. Snyder responds that she was, "but only because I'm interested in everything that suggests a wider reach to knowledge and experience than what is readily available to the five senses." In Hopkins's book she notes: "A long time ago I accepted the fact that I'm probably incurably superstitious. . . . I've also known for some time that it's not too wise to admit that I still believe in fairy godmothers and some kinds of ghosts and all kinds of magical omens."

Snyder's imagination switched from stories about ghosts and witches to science fiction in the "Green-sky Trilogy," which includes *Below the Root, And All Between,* and *Until the Celebration.* "Like so many of my books," Snyder comments in her autobiographical essay, "the trilogy's deepest root goes back to my early childhood when I played a game that involved crossing a grove of oak trees by climbing from tree to tree, because something incredibly dangerous lived 'below the root.'" The game is first mentioned in *The Changeling,* in which two of the characters play in the trees much as Snyder did, but it is given life in the trilogy. The people of Green-sky, known as the Kindar, are settlers from another planet who live peacefully in the treetops. The only thing they fear are the Erdlings, an evil race who live beneath the trees and capture and enslave Kindar children. The Green-sky books focus on the adventures of three children and are told from the viewpoints of both the Kindar and the Erdlings in an attempt to deliver a message about peace and brotherhood.

Snyder did not at first plan to write a trilogy, but she enjoyed writing *Below the Root* so much that she returned to the world of Green-sky twice more. The same thing happened with Snyder's books about the Stanley family, which include *The Headless Cupid, The Famous Stanley Kidnapping Case, Blair's Nightmare,* and *Janie's Private Eyes.* The five Stanley children—David, Blair, Esther, Janie, and Amanda—are "favorites of mine," Snyder says in a *Junior Literary Guild* article. "Every so often I get an irresistible urge to find out what they're up to now, and the result is another book."

As to what Snyder is up to, in 1985 she finally fulfilled a childhood dream and traveled to Egypt. She also lived for a time in Italy before returning to the United States and settling in Mill Valley near San Francisco, where she continues to write and occasionally gives talks to adults and school children about her work. Her writing has become increasingly diverse, as her more recent books testify.

Since returning to California she has written a historical novel, *And Condors Danced,* a fanciful collection of stories about tiny people called "Tiddlers" in *Squeak Saves the Day and Other Tooley Tales,* a mainstream children's book, *Libby on Wednesday,* and a fantasy novel, *Song of the Gargoyle.*

During one of her lectures a member of the audience asked Snyder why she became an author. Recalling the incident in her autobiographical entry, Snyder responds that "the maximum reward is simply—joy; the storyteller's joy in creating a story and sharing it with an audience. So I write for joy, my own and my imagined audience's—but why for children? Unlike many writers who say that they are not aware of a particular audience as they write, I know that I am very conscious of mine." She later concludes, "I enjoy writing for an audience that shares my optimism, curiosity and freewheeling imagination."

BIOGRAPHICAL/CRITICAL SOURCES:

BOOKS

Chevalier, Tracy, editor, *Twentieth Century Children's Writers,* 3rd edition, St. Martin's, 1989, pp. 903-905.
Contemporary Literary Criticism, Volume 17, Gale, 1981, pp. 469-475.
Hopkins, Lee Bennett, *More Books by More People,* Citation, 1974, pp. 318-322.
Something about the Author Autobiography Series, Volume 2, Gale, 1986, pp. 215-226.

PERIODICALS

Booktalker, September, 1989, p. 9.
Book World, December 3, 1967.
Bulletin of the Center for Children's Books, June, 1974; December, 1979, p. 82; March, 1982; January, 1983; April, 1984; November, 1985; November, 1987; May, 1988.
Catholic Literary World, October, 1976, p. 138.
Children's Book Review, October, 1973, p. 146.
Christian Science Monitor, February 29, 1968.
Commonweal, November 19, 1971, pp. 179-182.
Dell Carousel, fall/winter, 1985-1986.
Growing Point, September, 1976, p. 2939.
Horn Book, June, 1964, p. 284; April, 1965, p. 173; April, 1967, pp. 209-210; April, 1968, pp. 182-183; October, 1970, p. 479; October, 1971; December, 1972; October, 1973, p. 459; August, 1974, p. 380.
Junior Bookshelf, December, 1978, p. 324.
Junior Literary Guild, March, 1975; March, 1984; November 15, 1985, p. 57.
Kirkus Reviews, March 1, 1974, p. 245; March 1, 1975, p. 239; February 1, 1977, p. 95; September 1, 1978, p. 973.

New York Times Book Review, May 9, 1965; July 24, 1966, p. 22; July 23, 1967; May 26, 1968; November 7, 1971, pp. 42-44; December 10, 1972, pp. 8, 10; May 4, 1975, pp. 32, 34; May 23, 1976, p. 16; May 8, 1977, p. 41; July 8, 1984; December 27, 1987.

Publishers Weekly, February 7, 1972; February 27, 1977; February 1, 1991, p. 81.

Saturday Review, May 13, 1967, pp. 55-56.

School Library Journal, April, 1990, p. 124.

The World of Children's Books, fall, 1977, pp. 33-35.

Young Readers Review, May, 1966; May, 1967; May, 1968; October, 1969.

—*Sketch by Kevin S. Hile*

*   *   *

SOBIN, Gustaf   1935-

PERSONAL: Born November 15, 1935, in Boston, MA. *Education:* Brown University, A.B., 1958.

ADDRESSES: Home—New York, NY.

CAREER: Writer.

WRITINGS:

The Tale of the Yellow Triangle (juvenile), Braziller, 1973.
(Translator) Henri Michaux, *Ideograms in China,* New Directions Publishing, 1984.
Venus Blue (novel), Bloomsbury, 1991, Little, Brown, 1992.
Dark Mirrors: A Novel of Provence, Bloomsbury, 1992.

POETRY

Telegrams (booklet), privately printed, 1963.
Ascension (booklet), Ribaute-les-Taverne, 1964.
Wind Chrysalid's Rattle, Montemora Foundation, 1980.
Caesurae: Midsummer (booklet), Shearsman Books, 1981.
Celebration of the Sound Through, Montemora Foundation, 1982.
Ten Sham Haikus (booklet), Grenfell Press, 1983.
The Earth as Air, New Directions Publishing, 1984.
Carnets (booklet), Shearsman Books, 1984.
Nile (booklet), Shearsman Books, 1984.
Voyaging Portraits, New Directions Publishing, 1988.

OTHER

Contributor to anthologies, including *The Best American Poetry, 1990,* Macmillan, 1990, and *New Directions Anthology.* Contributor to periodicals, including *Kayak, Pequod, Sulfur, Temblor, Talisman, Hambone,* and *Conjunctions.*

SIDELIGHTS: Gustaf Sobin told *CA:* "I write in order to extend sense past myself. For me, an accomplished poem is one utterly released, given, offered up to its ever-sought-after 'other.' It's the poem that touches, not the poet. It's the poem that confers.

"In doing so, the poem frees itself of the tyranny of the personal pronoun: of the self, that is, as central, as the mandatory pivot around which all expression must, by debased usage, rotate.

"In the poem, power is redistributed. The center shifts. The poem, in its ongoing movement, extends the significant, reflects it *forward.*"

BIOGRAPHICAL/CRITICAL SOURCES:

BOOKS

Crick, Philip, *Evolving the Idol: The Poetry of Gustaf Sobin,* Shearsman Books, 1984.

PERIODICALS

Parnassus, spring/summer/fall/winter, 1980.
Times (London), January 10, 1991, p. 18.
Village Voice Literary Supplement, June, 1984.

*   *   *

SOBOL, Donald J.   1924-

PERSONAL: Born October 4, 1924, in New York, NY; son of Ira J. and Ida (Gelula) Sobol; married Rose Tiplitz, 1955; children: Diane, Glenn (deceased), Eric, John. *Education:* Oberlin College, B.A., 1948; attended New School for Social Research, 1949-51. *Avocational interests:* Travel, restoring antique cars, boating, fishing, scuba diving, gardening, tennis.

ADDRESSES: Home—Miami, FL. *Agent*—McIntosh & Otis, 310 Madison Ave., New York, NY 10017.

CAREER: Author of fiction and nonfiction for children. *New York Sun,* New York City, reporter, 1946-47; *Long Island Daily Press,* New York City, reporter, 1947-52; R. H. Macy, New York City, buyer, 1953-55; free-lance writer, 1954—. *Military service:* U.S. Army, Corps of Engineers, 1943-46; served in Pacific Theater.

MEMBER: Authors Guild, Authors League of America.

AWARDS, HONORS: Young Readers Choice Award, Pacific Northwest Library Association, 1972, for *Encyclopedia Brown Keeps the Peace;* Edgar Allan Poe Award, Mystery Writers of America, 1975, for entire body of work; Garden State Children's Book Award, 1977, for *Encyclopedia Brown Lends a Hand;* Aiken County Children's Book Award, 1977, for *Encyclopedia Brown Takes the Case;* Buckeye honor citation (grades 4-8 category), 1982, for *Encyclopedia Brown and the Case of the Midnight Visitor.*

WRITINGS:

FOR YOUNG ADULTS

The Double Quest, illustrated by Lili Rethi, Watts, 1957.

The Lost Dispatch, illustrated by Anthony Palombo, Watts, 1958.

First Book of Medieval Man (nonfiction), illustrated by Rethi, Watts, 1959, revised edition published in England as *The First Book of Medieval Britain,* Mayflower, 1960.

Two Flags Flying (biographies of Civil War leaders), illustrated by Jerry Robinson, Platt, 1960.

A Civil War Sampler, illustrated by Henry S. Gilette, Watts, 1961.

The Wright Brothers at Kitty Hawk (nonfiction), illustrated by Stuart Mackenzie, T. Nelson, 1961.

(Editor) *The First Book of the Barbarian Invaders, A.D. 375-511* (nonfiction), illustrated by W. Kirtman Plummer, Watts, 1962.

(With wife, Rose Sobol) *The First Book of Stocks and Bonds* (nonfiction), Watts, 1963.

(Editor) *An American Revolutionary War Reader,* Watts, 1964.

Lock, Stock, and Barrel (biographies of American Revolutionary War leaders), illustrated by Edward J. Smith, Westminster, 1965.

Secret Agents Four, illustrated by Leonard Shortall, Four Winds, 1967.

(Editor) *The Strongest Man in the World,* illustrated by Cliff Schule, Westminster, 1967.

Two-Minute Mysteries, Dutton, 1967.

Greta the Strong, illustrated by Trina Schart Hyman, Follett, 1970.

Milton, the Model A, illustrated by J. Drescher, Harvey House, 1970.

More Two-Minute Mysteries, Dutton, 1971.

The Amazons of Greek Mythology, A. S. Barnes, 1972.

Great Sea Stories, Dutton, 1975.

Still More Two-Minute Mysteries, Dutton, 1975.

True Sea Adventures, T. Nelson, 1975.

(Editor) *The Best Animal Stories of Science Fiction and Fantasy,* Warne, 1979.

Disasters, Archway, 1979.

Angie's First Case, illustrated by Gail Owens, Four Winds, 1981.

The Amazing Power of Ashur Fine: A Fine Mystery, Macmillan Children's Book Group, 1986.

"ENCYCLOPEDIA BROWN" SERIES

Encyclopedia Brown: Boy Detective (also see below), illustrated by Leonard Shortall, T. Nelson, 1963.

Encyclopedia Brown and the Case of the Secret Pitch, illustrated by Shortall, T. Nelson, 1965.

Encyclopedia Brown Finds the Clues, illustrated by Shortall, T. Nelson, 1966.

Encyclopedia Brown Gets His Man, illustrated by Shortall, T. Nelson, 1967.

Encyclopedia Brown Solves Them All, illustrated by Shortall, T. Nelson, 1968.

Encyclopedia Brown Keeps the Peace, illustrated by Shortall, T. Nelson, 1969.

Encyclopedia Brown Saves the Day, illustrated by Shortall, T. Nelson, 1970.

Encyclopedia Brown Tracks Them Down, illustrated by Shortall, T. Nelson, 1971.

Encyclopedia Brown Shows the Way, illustrated by Shortall, T. Nelson, 1972.

Encyclopedia Brown Takes the Case, illustrated by Shortall, T. Nelson, 1973.

Encyclopedia Brown Lends a Hand, illustrated by Shortall, T. Nelson, 1974.

Encyclopedia Brown and the Case of the Dead Eagles, illustrated by Shortall, T. Nelson, 1975.

Encyclopedia Brown and the Eleven: Case of the Exploding Plumbing and Other Mysteries, illustrated by Shortall, Dutton, 1976.

Encyclopedia Brown and the Case of the Midnight Visitor, illustrated by Lillian Brandi, T. Nelson, 1977, Bantam, 1982.

Encyclopedia Brown's Record Book of Weird and Wonderful Facts, illustrated by Sal Murdocca, Delacorte, 1979, illustrated by Bruce Degen, Dell, 1981.

Encyclopedia Brown Carries On, illustrated by Ib Ohlsson, Four Winds, 1980.

Encyclopedia Brown Sets the Pace, illustrated by Ohlsson, Dutton, 1981.

Encyclopedia Brown's Second Record Book of Weird and Wonderful Facts, illustrated by Degen, Delacorte, 1981.

Encyclopedia Brown's Third Record Book of Weird and Wonderful Facts, illustrated by Murdocca, Delacorte, 1981.

Encyclopedia Brown's Book of Wacky Crimes, illustrated by Shortall, Dutton, 1982.

Encyclopedia Brown (omnibus), illustrated by Shortall, Angus & Robertson, 1983.

Encyclopedia Brown's Book of Wacky Spies, illustrated by Ted Enik, Morrow, 1984.

Encyclopedia Brown's Book of Wacky Sports, illustrated by Enik, Morrow, 1984.

(With Glenn Andrews) *Encyclopedia Brown Takes the Cake!: A Cook and Case Book,* illustrated by Ohlsson, Scholastic, 1984.

Encyclopedia Brown and the Case of the Mysterious Handprints, illustrated by Owens, Morrow, 1985.

Encyclopedia Brown's Book of Wacky Animals, illustrated by Enik, Morrow, 1985.

Encyclopedia Brown's Book of the Wacky Outdoors, illustrated by Enik, Morrow, 1987.

Encyclopedia Brown's Book of Wacky Cars, illustrated by Enik, Morrow, 1987.

Encyclopedia Brown and the Case of the Treasure Hunt, illustrated by Owens, Morrow, 1988.

Encyclopedia Brown and the Case of the Disgusting Sneakers, illustrated by Owens, Morrow, 1990.

The Best of Encyclopedia Brown, illustrated by Ohlsson, Scholastic, in press.

Books from the "Encyclopedia Brown" series have been translated into thirteen languages and Braille.

OTHER

Author of syndicated column, "Two Minute Mysteries," 1959-68. Contributor of more than one hundred stories and articles to national magazines under a variety of pen names. Sobol's manuscripts are kept in the Kerlan Collection, University of Minnesota, Minneapolis, MN.

ADAPTATIONS: Filmstrip: *The Best of Encyclopedia Brown* (includes "The Case of the Natty Nut," "The Case of the Scattered Cards," "The Case of the Hungry Hitchhiker," and "The Case of the Whistling Ghost"), with cassette, Miller-Brody, 1977. Esquire Film Productions purchased the television and motion picture rights to the series. These rights were transferred to Howard David Deutsch Productions and Warner Brothers in 1979. *Encyclopedia Brown: Boy Detective* was filmed for Home Box Office in March, 1990. Books from the "Encyclopedia Brown" series have also been made into comic strips.

SIDELIGHTS: American children's mystery author Donald J. Sobol has kept schoolchildren on their toes since 1963 with the publication of the original Encyclopedia Brown book. *Encyclopedia Brown: Boy Detective* began the popular series, which has continued for over three decades. Over the years, Leroy "Encyclopedia" Brown, Sobol's young sleuth, has faced intriguing cases involving everything from dead eagles to disgusting sneakers. Solutions to each case are printed in the back of the book, but children are encouraged to try to solve the cases themselves.

The *Encyclopedia Brown* books each contain ten mysteries presented in readable sentences and enhanced with witty puns and other verbal jokes. It takes careful reading and a variety of methods—deductive reasoning, psychology, and careful observation of physical evidence—to solve the mysteries. "Complexity in writing style is not Sobol's intent, nor is it required for the success of these books," says Christine McDonnell in *Twentieth Century Children's Writers.* "Although the stories are simply written, they are clever and fresh, and seldom obvious or easy to solve."

Ten-year-old Leroy Brown is called "Encyclopedia" because he is so smart that it seems he must have an entire set of encyclopedias crammed into his head. He is so adept at finding clues that he helps his father, the Chief of Police, solve criminal cases. "Readers constantly ask me if Encyclopedia Brown is a real boy. The answer is no," Sobol once said. "He is, perhaps, the boy I wanted to be—doing the things I wanted to read about but could not find in any book when I was ten."

Sobol was born in 1924 in New York City, where he attended the Ethical Cultural Schools. During World War II, he served with the engineer corps in the Pacific, and after his discharge he earned a B.A. degree from Oberlin College. It wasn't until he took a short-story writing course in college that Sobol thought of becoming a writer, and even then he waited several years before making writing his profession. Sobol's first job was as a copyboy for the *New York Sun.* Later he became a journalist for the *Sun* and for the *Long Island Daily News.* "At the age of thirty I quit job-holding for good, married Rose Tiplitz, an engineer, and began to write full time," Sobol once commented, also noting that he has written more than sixty books since then.

For many years, Sobol has received letters from stumped young readers complaining that his mysteries have no proper explanation. These letters are often written by readers who have missed some significant detail. But in 1990, students in a Philadelphia school detected an actual error in the first *Encyclopedia Brown* book. The story about a trickster who bilks his classmates in an egg-spinning contest fails to explain how the cheater managed to get a boiled egg into the dozen before the contestants bought it at the grocery store. After the students wrote to Sobol asking for the explanation, he re-read the story for the first time in nearly thirty years. He admitted the solution should be more fully explained. "This is the first time in a couple of decades where it is really my fault," Sobol told Martha Woodall of the *Detroit Free Press.* "They are really smart kids." The teacher of the first- and second-graders who spotted the error said it has taught the students the importance of questioning the accuracy of what they read. She said they also learned that when something that is incorrect appears in print, there is something they can do about it. New editions including "The Case of the Champion Egg-Spinner" will contain the revised version.

In addition to the boy detective series, Sobol has written many nonfiction books that required him to do extensive research on topics as varied as King Arthur's England (*Greta the Strong*) and Ancient Greece (*The Amazons of Greek Mythology*). His other nonfiction works include biographies of American military leaders of the Revolutionary and Civil Wars: *Lock, Stock and Barrel* and *Two Flags Flying.* Sobol has also written an internationally syndicated newspaper feature, "Two-Minute Mystery Series," hundreds of articles and stories for adult magazines, historical books, and biographies. He is the editor of two history collections, *A Civil War Sampler* and *An American Revolutionary War Reader,* and the author of a book on stocks and bonds.

Sobol told *Pacific Northwest Library Association Quarterly,* "Outwitting you, the reader, is hard, but harder still is making you laugh. I try above all else to entertain. . . . I hope to be making children laugh for decades to come."

BIOGRAPHICAL/CRITICAL SOURCES:

BOOKS

Children's Literature Review, Volume 4, Gale, 1982.
Fourth Book of Junior Authors, Wilson, 1978.
Twentieth Century Children's Writers, St. Martin's Press, 1989.

PERIODICALS

Booklist, February 1, 1983, p. 27; May 1, 1984, p. 1254; March 1, 1991, p. 1382.
Christian Century, December 13, 1967, p. 1602.
Christian Science Monitor, October 5, 1967, p. 10; April 6, 1984, p. B7.
Detroit Free Press, February 12, 1991.
Fantasy Review, May, 1987, p. 795.
Horn Book Guide, July, 1990, p. 79.
New York Times Book Review, November 5, 1967, p. 44; November 11, 1979, pp. 56, 69.
Pacific Northwest Library Association Quarterly, winter, 1973, pp. 18-20.
People, March 12, 1990, pp. 17-18.
School Library Journal, February, 1982, p. 81; August, 1982, p. 107; April, 1984, p. 119; December, 1984, p. 103; April, 1985, p. 93; December, 1985, p. 95; November, 1986, p. 94; April, 1987, p. 104; January, 1988, p. 83; January, 1991, p. 97.
Science Fiction Chronicle, August, 1987, p. 53.
Young Readers' Review, November, 1967; November, 1968.

—*Sketch by Marilyn K. Basel and Deborah A. Stanley*

* * *

SPARKES, Ivan G(eorge) 1930-

PERSONAL: Born April 2, 1930, in Stratton St. Margaret, England; son of Albert William (a butcher) and Gladys Emma (a housewife; maiden name, Price) Sparkes; married Joyce Andrews; children: Geraldine, Elizabeth, Timothy, David. *Education:* Attended technical college and art school in Swindon, Wiltshire, England.

ADDRESSES: Home—8 Barley Colse, Halesworth, Suffolk IP19 8PG, England.

CAREER: Swindon Public Libraries, Swindon, Wiltshire, England, librarian, 1947-53; Thurrock Public Libraries, Thurrock, England, librarian, 1953-65; London Borough of Havering, London, England, reference librarian, 1965-69; Penzance Public Libraries, Penzance, England, borough librarian, 1969-71; High Wycombe Borough Library, High Wycombe, Buckinghamshire, England, borough librarian, 1971-74; High Wycombe Central Library, High Wycombe, librarian, 1974-87. Curator of Wycombe Chair Museum, 1971-88; member of staff at Buckinghamshire County Library Service. Presenter of lectures and slide shows on libraries and local history, High Wycombe and its history, the furniture industry, stagecoaches, and Egypt. Town clerk, High Wycombe Charter Trustees, 1983-87.

MEMBER: Library Association (fellow), Royal Historical Society (associate member).

AWARDS, HONORS: Sir Evelyn Wrench fellowship, 1965; grant from English-Speaking Union, 1965; Senior Librarian's Award from Library Association, 1974.

WRITINGS:

The English County Chair, Spur Publications, 1973, revised edition, 1977.
A Dictionary of Group Terms and Collective Nouns, White Lion, 1974, revised edition, Gale, 1985.
The Windsor Chair, Spur Publications, 1975.
Stagecoaches and Carriages, Spur Publication, 1975.
(With Margaret Lawson) *Victorian and Edwardian Buckinghamshire from Old Photographs,* Batsford, 1976.
Old Horseshoes, Shire Publications, 1976, revised edition, 1989.
High Wycombe as It Was, Hendon Press, 1977.
Woodland Craftsmen, Shire Publication, 1977, revised edition, 1991.
The Book of Wycombe, Barracuda Books, 1979, revised edition, 1984.
English Domestic Furniture, Spur Publications, 1980.
The English Windsor Chair, Shire Publications, 1981.
Yesterday's Town: High Wycombe, Barracuda Books, 1983.
High Wycombe in Old Postcards, European Press, 1983.
Wycombe in Camera, Barracuda Books, 1987.
Around Wycombe in Camera, Barracuda Books, 1988.
Wycombe Chairmakers in Camera, Barracuda Books, 1989.
The Fourposter and Tester Bed, Shire Publications, 1990.
High Wycombe: A Pictorial History, Phillimore, in press.

Author of "Local History Series," thirteen books, self-published, 1963-69. Contributor to periodicals.

WORK IN PROGRESS: Research for *A Bibliography of Furniture History.*

SIDELIGHTS: Ivan G. Sparkes told *CA* that he spent a year in Egypt from 1949 to 1950, which gave him a lasting interest in the country's history and antiquities. He also mentioned the value of his trip to the United States in 1965.

*   *   *

STAAR, Richard F(elix) 1923-

PERSONAL: Born January 10, 1923, in Warsaw, Poland; son of American parents; married Jadwiga Maria Ochota, March 28, 1950; children: Monica Gloria, Christina Marie. *Education:* Dickinson College, A.B., 1948; Yale University, A.M., 1949; University of Michigan, Ph.D., 1954. *Politics:* Republican. *Religion:* Methodist.

ADDRESSES: Home—36 Peter Coutts Cir., Stanford, CA 94305. *Office*—Hoover Institution on War, Revolution, and Peace, Stanford University, Stanford, CA 94305.

CAREER: U.S. Government, Washington, DC, research specialist, 1949-54; Harding College, Searcy, AR, professor of political science, 1954-57; Arkansas State College (now University), Jonesboro, professor, 1957-58; University of Maryland in Germany, lecturer in government, 1958-59; Emory University, Atlanta, GA, professor of political science, 1959-67, chairman of department, 1966-67; National War College, Washington, DC, professor of foreign affairs, 1967-69; Stanford University, Hoover Institution on War, Revolution, and Peace, Stanford, CA, 1969—, began as associate director, currently senior fellow. U.S. Ambassador to the Mutual and Balanced Force Reduction Talks, Vienna, Austria, 1981-83. Board of Visitors at Defense Language Institute, appointed member by Secretary of Defense, chair, 1988-90; International Research and Exchange Board, appointed member to selection committee. U.S. Naval War College, Fleet Admiral Nimitz Professor of Social and Political Philosophy, 1963-64. Voice of America Radio, speaker, 1957—; lecturer in Strasbourg, France, 1958. Consultant to U.S. Department of Defense and U.S. Arms Control and Disarmament Agency. *Military service:* U.S. Marine Corps Reserve; present rank, colonel.

MEMBER: International Studies Association, American Political Science Association, American Association for Advancement of Slavic Studies, Naval Order of the United States, Phi Beta Kappa, Phi Kappa Phi, Pi Gamma Mu, Pi Sigma Alpha, Kappa Sigma.

WRITINGS:

Poland, 1944-62: Sovietization of a Captive People, Louisiana State University Press, 1962.

Communist Regimes in Eastern Europe, Hoover Institution, 1967, 5th edition, 1988.

(Editor and contributor) *Aspects of Modern Communism,* University of South Carolina Press, 1968.

(Editor) Ernest K. Gann, *South Africa: War, Revolution, or Peace?,* Hoover Institution, 1978.

(Editor) Chong-Sik Lee, *Korean Workers' Party: A Short History,* Hoover Institution, 1978.

(Editor) James H. Noyes, *The Clouded Lens: Persian Gulf Security and U.S. Policy,* Hoover Institution, 1979.

(Editor and contributor) *Arms Control: Myth versus Reality,* Hoover Institution, 1984.

U.S.S.R. Foreign Policies after Detente, Hoover Institution, 1985, revised edition, 1987.

(Editor) *Public Diplomacy: U.S.A. versus U.S.S.R.,* Hoover Institution, 1986.

(With William T. Lee) *Soviet Military Policy since World War II,* Hoover Institution, 1986.

(Editor) *The Future Information Revolution in the U.S.S.R.,* Crane, Russak, 1988.

(Editor) *The U.S. and East Europe in the 1990s,* Crane, Russak, 1989.

Foreign Policies of the Soviet Union, Hoover Institution, 1991.

(Editor) *East-Central Europe and the USSR,* St. Martin's/ Macmillan, 1991.

Translator of four books and many articles from German, Polish, and Russian. Editor-in-chief of *Yearbook on International Communist Affairs,* Hoover Institution, 1969—. Contributor to periodicals in the United States and Europe. Member of editorial board, *Current History, Orbis,* and *Strategic Review.* Some of Staar's work has been translated into at least four languages, including Chinese and Polish.

WORK IN PROGRESS: Transition to Democracy in Poland.

SIDELIGHTS: Richard F. Staar speaks or reads Czech, German, Polish, Bulgarian, Ukrainian, and Russian. When Nobel Prize-winning Russian writer Alexander Solzhenitsyn visited the Hoover Institution, Staar served as interpreter on both occasions.

*   *   *

STACEY, Margaret 1922-

PERSONAL: Born March 27, 1922, in London, England; daughter of Conrad Eugene (a printer) and Grace Priscilla (Boyce) Petrie; married Frank Arthur Stacey (a university professor), May 20, 1945 (died, 1977); children: Patricia, Richard, Kate, Peter, Michael. *Education:* London School of Economics and Political Science, B.Sc., 1943. *Politics:* Labour. *Religion:* "Non-aligned."

ADDRESSES: Home—8 Lansdowne Circus, Leamington Spa, Warwickshire CV32 4SW, England. *Office*—Department of Sociology, University of Warwick, Coventry CV4 7AL, England.

CAREER: Royal Ordnance Factory, Glasgow, Scotland, labor officer, 1943-44; Oxford University, Oxford, England, tutor, 1944-51; University College of Swansea, Singleton Park, Swansea, Wales, research officer, 1961-62, research fellow, 1962-63, lecturer, 1963-70, senior lecturer in sociology, 1970-74; University of Warwick, Coventry, England, professor of sociology, 1974-89, professor emeritus, 1989—, chairperson of department, 1974-79. Member, Welsh Hospital Board, 1970-74, and General Medical Council, 1976-84.

MEMBER: British Sociological Association (honorary general secretary, 1968-70; vice-chairperson, 1975-76; chairperson, 1977-79; president, 1981-83).

AWARDS, HONORS: Fawcett Prize, 1982, for *Women, Power and Politics.*

WRITINGS:

Tradition and Change: A Study of Banbury, Oxford University Press, 1960.
(Contributor) K. J. Hilton, editor, *The Lower Swansea Valley Project,* Longmans, Green, 1967.
Methods of Social Research, Pergamon, 1969.
(Editor) *Comparability in Social Research,* Heinemann, 1969.
(Editor) *Hospitals, Children and Their Families: The Report of a Pilot Study,* Routledge & Kegan Paul, 1970.
(With others) *Power, Persistence and Change: A Second Study of Banbury,* Routledge & Kegan Paul, 1975.
(Co-editor) *Health Care and Health Knowledge,* Croom Helm, 1977.
(Co-editor) *Health and the Division of Labour,* Croom Helm, 1977.
(Editor with D. Hall) *Beyond Separation: Further Studies of Children in Hospital,* Routledge & Kegan Paul, 1979.
(With Marian Price) *Women, Power and Politics,* Tavistock Publications, 1981.
The Sociology of Health and Healing: A Textbook, Unwin, 1988.
Regulating British Medicine: The General Medical Council, Wiley Medical, 1992.

Also editor of *Sociology of the NHS,* a sociological review monograph for the University of Keele.

SIDELIGHTS: Margaret Stacey told *CA:* "In earlier years, my main concern was with the individual and soci-

ety. Then this interest led to locality studies and studies of patients in hospitals: my children were a main matter of life importance; my work and writing was undertaken as possible within this consideration.

"In the past decade my work moved increasingly into the area of women's studies and the importance of the gender order in the health care division of labor. Now that I am retired I continue to work in those areas and especially on professional regulation from a socialist-feminist viewpoint."

*   *   *

STANKO, Elizabeth Anne 1950-

PERSONAL: Born December 30, 1950, in Lafayette, IN; daughter of George Louis (a pharmacist) and Catherine J. (a teacher; maiden name, Britt) Stanko. *Education:* Herbert H. Lehman College of the City University of New York, B.A., 1972; Graduate School of the City University of New York, Ph.D., 1977.

ADDRESSES: Home—London, England. *Office*—Department of Law, Brunel University, Oxbridge, Middlesex UB8 3PH, England.

CAREER: Fordham University, Institute for Social Research, Bronx, NY, researcher, 1971-73; Association for the Bar of the City of New York, New York City, researcher, 1974-76; Clark University, Worcester, MA, assistant professor, 1976-83, associate professor of sociology, 1983-90; Brunel University, Oxbridge, England, senior lecturer in the department of law, 1990—. Past president of Daybreak, a shelter for battered women.

MEMBER: American Society of Criminology, National Organization for Women, Sociologists for Women in Society, British Society of Criminology, Law and Society Association.

WRITINGS:

(Editor with Nicole Hahn Rafter) *Judge, Lawyer, Victim, Thief: Women, Gender Roles, and Criminal Justice,* Northeastern University Press, 1982.
Intimate Intrusions: Women's Experience of Male Violence, Routledge & Kegan Paul, 1984.
(Editor with J. Hanmer and J. Radford) *Women, Policing and Male Violence,* Routledge & Kegan Paul, 1989.
Everyday Violence, Pandora Press, 1990.

WORK IN PROGRESS: Research on women's and men's fear of crime and perceptions of safety in the home and on the street; policing and personal safety.

SIDELIGHTS: Elizabeth Anne Stanko told *CA:* "My professional life is devoted to articulating the conditions of women's lives."

STARBIRD, Kaye 1916-
(C. S. Jennison)

PERSONAL: Born June 3, 1916, in Fort Sill, OK; daughter of Alfred A. (a general, U.S. Army) and Ethel (Dodd) Starbird; married James Dalton (deceased); married N. E. Jennison (deceased); children: (first marriage) Kit, Beth; (second marriage) Lee. *Education:* Attended University of Vermont for four years.

CAREER: Professional writer.

AWARDS, HONORS: Bread Loaf Writers' Conference fellowship, 1961; MacDowell Colony fellowships, 1966-70, 1972, 1975, 1976, 1979; Helene Wurlitzer Foundation fellowships, 1967-68; Ella Lyman Cabot Trust grant, 1971; Ossabaw Island Project fellowships, 1971-73, 1975, 1977, 1978, 1980, 1981; Virginia Center for Creative Arts fellowships, 1971-73, 1982; Rhode Island Creative Arts Center fellowships, 1980-82.

WRITINGS:

ADULT NOVELS

Watch Out for the Mules, Harcourt, 1968.
The Lion in the Lei Shop, Harcourt, 1970.

JUVENILE POETRY

Speaking of Cows, Lippincott, 1960.
Don't Ever Cross a Crocodile, and Other Poems, illustrated by daughter, Kit Dalton, Lippincott, 1963.
A Snail's a Failure Socially, illustrated by Dalton, Lippincott, 1966.
The Pheasant on Route Seven, illustrated by Victoria de Larrea, Lippincott, 1968.
The Covered Bridge House and Other Poems, illustrated by Jim Arnosky, Four Winds, 1979.
Grandmother Goose's Recycled Rhymes, Pratt Publishing, 1988.

OTHER

Contributor of poetry to anthologies and periodicals, including *Good Housekeeping, Saturday Evening Post, New York Times, New Yorker,* and *American Mercury.* Also contributor, at times under name C. S. Jennison, of satirical verse, poems, essays, and short stories to magazines, including *Vermont Life, Atlantic, Woman's Day, Reader's Digest, Cosmopolitan, Harper's, Ladies' Home Journal, McCall's,* and *Redbook.*

SIDELIGHTS: Kaye Starbird examines ordinary people and their everyday lives through the light verse which comprises her work for children. Her flowing rhymes present nature in all its glory and introduce a mixture of humorously eccentric characters. "Economically crafted, the poems are appealing not only for their incisive characterization but also for their imaginative wordplay and sense of wonder," remarks Mary M. Burns in *Horn Book.* Fellow *Horn Book* contributor Diane Farrell maintains that Starbird's "shrewd observations give an added dimension to the lives of ordinary people."

Starbird began writing at the age of eight, and sold verse to national magazines such as *Good Housekeeping* and *American Mercury* while in college. Before turning to books in 1960, she also wrote satirical verse and essays for the *Atlantic,* at times under the name C. S. Jennison. *The Pheasant on Route Seven,* Starbird's fourth collection of light verse, introduces the small American town of Pleasantport and its eclectic population. Along with describing the town's surroundings, Starbird also presents a number of humorous characters, including Doctor Ernest Bates, who collects paperweights when he isn't saving lives, and Banjo Scott, the local drunkard. "In this book the village of Pleasantport comes alive," asserts Mary O'Neill in the *New York Times Book Review,* noting of Starbird that her "rhymes never falter; her people are real."

The Covered Bridge House and Other Poems, published in 1979, offers a number of poems dealing with nature and a variety of caricatures. Among the characters described are Little Lenore, who wishes for a Coke machine within easy reach, Artie Dole, who has an overactive imagination, and Miss Flynn, who is the proud owner of thirty cats. The poems in *The Covered Bridge House and Other Poems* "are consistently great fun," comments Daisy Kouzel in the *School Library Journal.* "Young readers will be easily captivated by the gentle humor, the easy musicality of the rhymes, and the upbeat windup of each poem."

Starbird's poems are derived "from experience and also from a galloping imagination that I was born with and for which I claim no credit," she once maintained. This imagination is given "free rein" in most of Starbird's books, the form and content of the works being disciplined at the same time. After deciding on the type of book she wants to do, Starbird once said she writes "eight hours a day until it is completed. Throwing away a lot at the beginning and rewriting until I turn the manuscript in to the publisher. . . . Writing is hard work but I am happier doing it than not doing it. I never Set Out to Be a Writer. I just started writing."

BIOGRAPHICAL/CRITICAL SOURCES:

PERIODICALS

Bulletin of the Center for Children's Books, January, 1980.
Horn Book, October, 1963; October, 1968, p. 568; February, 1980, p. 70.
Library Journal, August, 1970, p. 2721; December, 1976, p. 4526.

New York Times Book Review, November 6, 1966, p. 67; October 27, 1968, p. 42; October 4, 1970, p. 48; November 11, 1979, p. 53.
Publishers Weekly, November 27, 1967, p. 41.
School Library Journal, January, 1980, p. 61.*

*   *   *

STEPHENSON, Maureen 1927-

PERSONAL: Born February 14, 1927, in Manchester, England; daughter of Joseph (a tailor) and Anne (Byrom) Duffy; married Louis John Stephenson (an engineer), August 21, 1954; children: William, David, Sarah. *Education:* Attended high school in London, England. *Religion:* Roman Catholic.

ADDRESSES: Home—Ansley Mill Farm, Ansley, North Warwickshire CV10 0QT, England.

CAREER: Shepperton Studios, London, England, in film continuity, 1944-47; Pinewood Studios, London, in film continuity, 1948-50; Denham Studios, London, in film continuity, 1950-52; Ealing Studios, London, in film continuity, 1952-54; writer, 1977—.

WRITINGS:

Ride the Dark Moors (Gothic novel), Zebra Books, 1977.
The House on Wath Moor (Gothic novel), Zebra Books, 1979.
Flowers of Tomorrow, R. Hale, 1980.
Autumn of Deception, R. Hale, 1982.
Roses Have Thorns, R. Hale, 1983.
The Enchanted Desert, R. Hale, 1986.
I'll Wait Forever, R. Hale, 1987.
Never Too Late, R. Hale, 1990.

Ride the Dark Moors and *The House on Wath Moor* have been published in Germany; *The Enchanted Desert* has been published in Norway.

WORK IN PROGRESS: A novel set in Central America.

SIDELIGHTS: Maureen Stephenson told *CA:* "Born into a second-generation Irish immigrant family, I was never conscious of the lack of money; my father, having a deep love of literature, music, and art, gave a richness to my life which I have always kept.

"My father influenced me to become a writer. I shall never forget his balanced criticisms and kind encouragement. For ten years I worked in the film business. This was another good influence for I found working on film scripts invaluable in learning how to build up a story and a character.

"I wrote short stories from time to time, and the best I achieved was encouraging letters from fiction editors.

Then . . . we bought a historic cottage in a Yorkshire dale that fired my imagination, and I wrote my first novel. From this experience I feel one must live in surroundings that stimulate.

"The authors who have had the greatest influence on me are the Bronte sisters. They achieve a mystical other-worldliness that I admire."

*   *   *

STODDARD, Ellwyn R(eed) 1927-

PERSONAL: Born February 16, 1927, in Garland, UT; son of Roscoe and Mary (Redford) Stoddard; married Elaine Kirby; children: Ellwyn R., Jr., Michael V., Dawn D., Jared Evan, Sunday, Summer; stepchildren: Laura Jane Packham, George H. Packham, R. Kirby Packham. *Education:* Utah State University, B.S., 1952; Brigham Young University, M.S., 1955; Michigan State University, Ph.D., 1961. *Religion:* Church of Jesus Christ of Latter-Day Saints (Mormon).

ADDRESSES: Home—747 Camino Real, El Paso, TX 79922. *Office*—University of Texas, El Paso, TX 79968.

CAREER: Drake University, Des Moines, IA, assistant professor, 1959-63, associate professor of sociology, 1963-65; University of Texas at El Paso, associate professor, 1965-70, professor of sociology and anthropology, 1970—. National Institute of Health Lecturer, College of Osteopathic Medicine and Surgery, 1963-64; New Mexico State University, National Endowment for the Humanities Lecturer, 1969-70, National Institute of Mental Health Lecturer, 1972. Sociological researcher, 1955—. Consultant to over seventy research and action projects involving civil defense, disaster relief, racial awareness, organizational functioning, health and social services delivery systems, and other subjects. Presenter and panelist at numerous professional conferences and workshops. *Military service:* U.S. Coast Guard, Amphibious Corps, 1944-46; served as radioman. U.S. Army, Artillery Corps, 1952-53; served as battalion communications officer.

MEMBER: Association of Borderlands Scholars (founder, past president), PROFMEX-ANUIES Consortium, Rocky Mountain Conference for Latin American Studies (member of executive council, 1970-73), Southwestern Social Science Association, Southwestern Sociological Association, Western Social Science Association, Alpha Kappa Delta, Delta Tau Kappa (life member), Phi Kappa Phi (life member).

AWARDS, HONORS: Southwest Book Award, Border Regional Library Association, 1984, for *Borderlands Sourcebook;* Award for Outstanding Scholarship and Service to the Association of Borderlands Scholars, 1987; Distinguished Faculty Achievement Award in Research, 1990; University of Texas at El Paso, Diamond Jubilee Award, 1990; Burlington Resources Foundation award, 1990.

WRITINGS:

Conceptual Models of Human Behavior in Disaster, Texas Western Press, 1968.
Mexican Americans, Random House, 1973.
Each Man Must Climb His Own Mountain, privately printed, 1980.
A Bibliographical Resource Guide: Ancient and Modern Cultures of Northern Mexico and the Greater Southwest, University of Texas at El Paso, 1981.
(Editor with Richard L. Nostrand and Jonathan P. West) *Borderlands Sourcebook,* University of Oklahoma Press, 1983.
(With John Hedderson) *Patterns of Poverty along the U.S.-Mexico Border* (monograph) New Mexico State University Border Research Institute, 1987.
Maquila: Assembly Plants in Northern Mexico, Texas Western Press, 1987.

Contributor to books, including *Social Aspects of Chronic Illness, Impairment and Disability,* edited by Stephen C. Hey, Gary Kiger and John Seidel, Willamette University, 1984, and *One Border, Two Nations: Policy Implications and Problem Resolutions,* edited by Oscar J. Martinez, Albert E. Utton and Mario Miranda Pacheco, ANUIES, 1988. Contributor of articles and book reviews to journals, including *Journal of Borderlands Studies, American Anthropologist, American Sociologist* and *Policy Perspectives.*

WORK IN PROGRESS: Multidisciplinary coordination of U.S.-Mexico border research, in comparison with African and Eastern European borders; *Contemporary Policy Issues in the U.S.-Mexico Borderlands: Institutional Adaptations in Historical Context; Social Class, Language and Ethnicity Factors in Borderlands Education* and *Differential Funding for Higher Education in Border Texas.*

SIDELIGHTS: Ellwyn R. Stoddard told *CA:* "My professional research and writing converges a multidisciplinary/ multicultural orientation with selected problems of human survival: institutional adaptation to national borders, human colonies in space, disaster behavior and relief efforts, and ethnic minorities. Although this creative experience emerging from the constant interfertilization of concepts born in more than a dozen academic disciplines is personally rewarding, it is a perilous risk for the neophyte scholar, and he should enter such a path forewarned and forearmed. Since our contemporary society lionizes the 'specialist' who is easily categorized and can be plugged into an existing system, the broadly-based generalist finds acceptance within narrow disciplinary confines

somewhat less rewarding than those who remain as mainstream disciples.

"The professional strength required of scientific research pioneers is not gained alone from seeking scientific truth but is a product of self-respect and ethical values, reinforced by security of hearth and home. One is then free from personal ego concerns and can freely explore with objectivity the capacity of mankind to adapt and survive against terrifying odds. Perhaps science progresses best in modest settings wherein grave contemporary problems create the furnace in which the stable traditions of future generations are forged. At least this is the way I have experienced it."

*   *   *

STOKESBURY, James L(awton)   1934-

PERSONAL: Born December 27, 1934, in Derby, CT; son of James E. (a civil servant) and Estelle (Little) Stokesbury; married Elizabeth D'Orsay Dickinson, August 29, 1961; children: Kevin, Brianna, Michael. *Education:* Acadia University, B.A., 1960; University of Western Ontario, M.A., 1962; Duke University, Ph.D., 1968. *Politics:* None. *Religion:* Congregationalist.

ADDRESSES: Home—R.R.1, Wolfville, Nova Scotia, Canada B0P 1X0. *Office*—Department of History, Acadia University, Wolfville, Nova Scotia, Canada B0P 1X0. *Agent*—Ann Elmo Agency, Inc., 60 East 42nd St., New York, NY 10017.

CAREER: Acadia University, Wolfville, Nova Scotia, lecturer in history, 1960-61; University of Western Ontario, London, lecturer in history, 1962; Acadia University, assistant professor, 1964-68, associate professor, 1968-73, professor of history, 1973—. Sessional lecturer at University of Waterloo, 1968. *Military service:* U.S. Navy, 1953-57; became quartermaster first class.

WRITINGS:

(With Martin Blumenson) *Masters of the Art of Command,* Houghton, 1975.
A Short History of World War II, Morrow, 1979.
A Short History of World War I, Morrow, 1981.
Navy and Empire, Morrow, 1983.
A Short History of Air Power, Morrow, 1986.
A Short History of the Korean War, Morrow, 1988.
A Short History of the American Revolution, Morrow, 1991.

Contributor of about forty articles to history journals.

WORK IN PROGRESS: A Short History of the American Civil War, for Morrow.

SIDELIGHTS: James L. Stokesbury told *CA:* "My interests have always been in military and naval history, and by choice I would write about the Napoleonic period. However, by the accidents of the publishing business, most of my publications have been either in colonial American military history or World Wars I and II.

"I have always wanted to write. The particular area in which I like to write lies in the gap between the scholar who writes only for his peers and does not reach any wider audience, and the popular writer who may reach the wider audience but is not up on the latest scholarly advances. There are some real problems in this, and it's rather like being a 'philosophe' instead of a philosopher, but it seems to me a useful thing; I'd be quite happy to have someone think I was a philosophe. Mostly, it's a lot of fun."

Stokesbury's *A Short History of World War I* has been called "an ideal work for the new student of the period" by John Yohalem, writing for the *New York Book Review.* Yohalem, impressed with the thoughtfulness of such a brief treatment of a complicated war, notes: "Remarkable enough that it could be done—astonishing that it is done well." In the *Los Angeles Times,* Robert Kirsch gives similar praise to *A Short History of World War II,* which he believes "fills a need for an overview narrative of the causes, events, and aftermath of the conflict." Kirsch further cites the book for the lessons its topic can teach current generations, commenting: "This is a volume that invites reflection on present-day foreign and strategic policy."

BIOGRAPHICAL/CRITICAL SOURCES:

PERIODICALS

Los Angeles Times, February 13, 1980.
Los Angeles Times Book Review, April 5, 1981.
New York Times Book Review, February 22, 1981.

*   *   *

STONE, Elaine Murray 1922-

PERSONAL: Born January 22, 1922, in New York, NY; daughter of Herman (a banker and diplomat) and Catherine (Fairbanks) Murray-Jacoby; married Frederic Courtney Stone (an electrical engineer), May 30, 1944 (died February, 1985); children: Catherine Rayburn, Pamela Webb, Victoria Richard. *Education:* Attended Juilliard School of Music, 1939-41; New York College of Music, diploma, 1942; Trinity College of Music, licentiate, 1947. *Politics:* Independent. *Religion:* Episcopal. *Avocational interests:* "My favorite occupations are travel, sailing, swimming, surfing, collecting autographs, composing and improvising music, television, Greek, reading, visiting my

grandchildren, conversation, movies, theater, attending concerts, and eating. My favorite composer is Bach; my favorite writer is C. S. Lewis."

ADDRESSES: Home—1945 Pineapple Ave., Melbourne, FL 32935.

CAREER: Musician, composer, television producer, and writer. Organist, choir director, and piano and organ teacher, 1940-70; accompanist with Strawbridge Ballet, 1944-45; *Melbourne Times,* Melbourne, FL, feature writer, 1965-67; Consolidated Cybertronics, Cocoa Beach, FL, vice president, 1968; Cass, Inc., Melbourne, editor-in-chief of educational tape cassettes, 1970-71; WTAI-Radio, Melbourne, director of continuity, 1971-74, host and producer of daily program *Good News,* 1973-74; Engle Realty, Inc., Indialantic, FL, realtor associate, 1975-78; KXTX-TV, Dallas, TX, writer and producer of juvenile news program *Countdown,* 1978-80; host and producer of weekly television show *Focus on History,* TV6, Melbourne, 1982—. Part-time real estate agent, Fountain Cove Condominiums, 1985-86. Diocese of Central Florida, producer of television program *Episcopal Digest,* member of board of evangelism, 1984—. Member of board of promotion of Diocese of Southern Florida, 1960. Cape Kennedy correspondent, 1961-74; Religious News Service correspondent, beginning 1962; board member, Brevard Symphony, Melbourne, FL.

MEMBER: American Society of Composers, Authors, and Publishers, Colonial Dames of America, American Association of University Women, National League of American Penwomen (former president, Cape Canaveral branch; president, Dallas branch, 1980), Women in Communications, Space Pioneers, Daughters of the American Revolution (state chairman of music in Florida, 1964; former vice president, Abigail Chamberlain chapter; former organizing regent; historian, Rufus Fairbanks chapter, 1989—), Florida Space Coast Philharmonic (member of board of directors, 1988—), Florida Space Coast Writers Conference (vice president, 1986-89; member of board of directors, 1991—), Florida Press Women, Florida Penwomen (state chaplain, 1989-91; first vice president, 1991—), Holy Trinity Episcopal Church Women (president, 1989-91).

AWARDS, HONORS: Winner of South Carolina music contest, 1939; first prize in Florida photojournalism contest, 1966, first place book and short story award in Dallas, 1979, first place for *Tekla and the Lion,* 1990, second place for *Kizito, Boy Saint of Uganda,* 1990, and second place for historical essay, 1990, all from National League of American Penwomen; honorary doctorate in communications, World University, 1984; first place in instrumental compositions, National Music Contest, Daughters of the American Revolution, 1988, for piano composition

"The Christopher Columbus Suite"; third place, State Literary Contest of American Association of University Women, Florida, 1990; first place in Georgia black history essay contest, 1990; honorable mention for photo article, "Russian Students," 1991, first place in composition for piano composition, 1991, for "The Christopher Columbus Suite," second place in voice and piano composition, 1991, for "The 23rd Psalm," first place for *Christopher Columbus: His World, His Faith, His Adventures,* and second place for *Kizito, Boy Saint of Uganda,* all from Florida State Convention of National League of American Penwomen.

WRITINGS:

The Taming of the Tongue, Holy Cross Press, 1954.

Love One Another, Holy Cross Press, 1957.

The Examination (play), first produced in Melbourne, FL, at Holy Trinity Episcopal Church, 1962.

Pedro Menendez de Aviles and the Founding of St. Augustine, Kenedy, 1969.

The Melbourne Bicentennial Book, Melbourne Bicentennial Commission, 1976.

Uganda: Fire and Blood, Logos, 1977.

Tekla and the Lion (for children), Association Press, 1981.

Brevard County: From Cape of the Canes to Space Coast, Windsor Publications, 1988.

Kizito, Boy Saint of Uganda (for children), Winston-Derek, 1990.

Christopher Columbus: His World, His Faith, His Adventures (for children), Tyndale, 1991.

Mother Seton, First American Saint, Paulist Press, 1992.

AUDIO TAPE CASSETTES

Bedtime Bible Stories, Cass, Inc., 1970.

Improve Your Business Spelling, Cass, Inc., 1970.

Improve Your Spelling for Better Grades, Cass, Inc., 1970.

Sleepytime Tales, Cass, Inc., 1970.

Tranquility Tapes, Cass, Inc., 1970.

Travel Fun, Cass, Inc., 1970.

OTHER

Author of piano composition, "The Christopher Columbus Suite." Author of more than two hundred scripts for television series *Countdown,* 1978—. Contributor to periodicals, including *Central Florida Episcopalian, Charleston News, Christian Life, Episcopal Churchnews, Guideposts, Holy Cross, Indian River, Living Church, LOGOS,* and *New York Herald Tribune.* Associate editor of *Goodtime Gazette,* 1978-79.

WORK IN PROGRESS: Saints of the New World; A Fifth Avenue Childhood; and *The Widow's Might.*

SIDELIGHTS: Elaine Murray Stone once told *CA:* "I spent the first half of my life on Fifth Avenue in New York as the child of a very successful banker and diplomat. My father was chairman of the board of North American Waterworks, in addition to being president of his own banking concern on Wall Street. He was appointed by Herbert Hoover to represent the United States at the coronation of Haile Selassie [emperor of Ethiopia] in 1930. My parents entertained many of the greats of this century at our home. I attended private schools and in 1939 won the South Carolina state music contest in piano. I then applied to enter the Juilliard School of Music, which I attended from 1939-41. Due to poor health, repeated pneumonia, etc., I changed to the New York College of Music, from which I graduated in 1942. I have composed music since I was nine and have had my works performed all over the United States. After leading such a social life the first half of my existence, my husband and daughters and I moved to Florida for my health in 1950 and lived in the shadow of Cape Canaveral until 1978. We lived in Dallas from 1978-80, then returned to retire in Florida at our riverfront home in Melbourne.

"My interests are very broad. This is fortunate, because the television show I write and produce covers every subject imaginable. I adore research and enjoy tracking down impossible bits of information no one else can find.

"As the space correspondent for Religious News Service, I covered every manned space launch in U.S. history. I was also at the Kennedy Space Center for many other important launches all through the sixties and seventies and hobnobbed with the great newscasters and journalists from every country on earth. I was also in a documentary called 'In the Shadow of the Moon.' I have been interviewed on many television and radio stations about my books *Uganda: Fire and Blood, Brevard County: From Cape of the Canes to Space Coast,* and *Christopher Columbus: His World, His Faith, His Adventures.* I have scrapbooks filled with ads, reviews, and other mementos about each book.

"I guess I've enjoyed being a television producer about as much as anything I've ever done in my life. I had no training in it and learned on the job after I was hired to write the scripts. *Countdown* was aired thirty times per week on the entire CBN network. *Countdown* was a sixty second news show broadcast during the cartooning periods to educate children. We went on location and had guests come to the studio, but mostly we used films and slides to illustrate the story.

"My father, the United States ambassador to Ethiopia, made many trips to Africa. This sparked my interest in the 'Dark Continent' at any early age. This resulted in a book on Uganda and one on Ethiopia. I have traveled extensively myself since I was a small child. I speak French and Spanish. I became unusually devout during my teens, which resulted in the reading of most of the great saints and mystics. Out of this grew over half of my books and all of my published articles. Even though all of my education was in music, I have yet to write on this subject!"

*   *   *

STUART, Reginald (Charles) 1943-

PERSONAL: Born September 1, 1943, in Vancouver, British Columbia, Canada; son of Philip (a draftsman) and Florence (a secretary; maiden name, Jordan) Stuart; married Penelope Warren (a homemaker), August 24, 1969; children: Jonathan. *Education:* University of British Columbia, B.A., 1965, M.A., 1968; University of Florida, Ph.D., 1974. *Religion:* Protestant.

ADDRESSES: Home—115 Hazelholme Dr., Halifax, Nova Scotia, Canada B3M 1N7.

Office—Dean, Humanities and Sciences, Mount Saint Vincent University, Halifax, Nova Scotia, Canada B3M 2J6.

CAREER: University of Prince Edward Island, Charlottetown, lecturer, 1968-74, assistant professor, 1974-81, associate professor, 1981-87, professor of history, 1987-88, chair of department, 1982-88; Mount Saint Vincent University, Halifax, Nova Scotia, professor and Dean of Humanities and Sciences, 1988—.

MEMBER: Organization of American Historians, Society for Historians of American Foreign Relations, Society for Historians of the Early American Republic, Canadian Association for the Study of Higher Education, Phi Beta Kappa, Phi Kappa Phi.

AWARDS, HONORS: Grants from Humanities Research Council, 1977, American Philosophical Society, 1978-79, and Social Sciences and Humanities Research Council of Canada, 1982-84, 1984-86; Albert Corey Prize, 1990.

WRITINGS:

The Half-way Pacifist: Thomas Jefferson's View of War, University of Toronto Press, 1978.
War and American Thought: From the Revolution to the Monroe Doctrine, Kent State University Press, 1982.
The Enlightenment in America, Open Learning Institute, 1985.
(Editor) *Readings in the American Enlightenment,* Open Learning Institute, 1985.
United States Expansionism and British North America, 1775-1871, University of North Carolina Press, 1988.
The First Seventy-Five Years, Canadian Gas Association, 1988.
(Co-author) *The Rise of the Global Village in the Twentieth Century,* McGraw, 1988.

Contributor of articles and reviews to scholarly journals and newspapers. Editorial Board, *Canadian Journal of History.*

WORK IN PROGRESS: The Jefferson Letter and *The Wild Goose* (historical fiction).

SIDELIGHTS: Reginald C. Stuart told *CA:* "Fred Astaire once remarked that however easy his dancing looked to the audience, for him it was 'sweet work.' Writing is like that. As a career academic and university administrator I can only write a bit at a time. Over a year it amounts to something. I'd give it up if I took a shorter view. What counts in the end, after all, is the act of writing and that it leads somewhere.

"My attempts at textbooks and historical fiction developed from my belief that historians should write for a wider readership than one another. We need to bear in mind how most people learn about their past—through myth, folklore, popular literature, the media. My fictitious characters come from and sit in their times and the settings flowed directly from my book on Canadian-American relations. I'm convinced that North Americans do not perceive their similarities and differences properly. They focus on superficial qualities rather than the deep resonances that connect our cultures on this continent. All writing is exploration and along the way I have discovered a unity on my intellectual outlook (even convictions) I was not aware of. Often, what writers learn as they go is just as important personally as what they produce and publish."

Stuart also told *CA* that he felt historians should do more to produce readable history for the public. "This can occur through traditional historical studies, or in fiction, which is why I have tried to branch out as a writer. My characters embody the themes of straddling cultures and being victims, not masters, of their times.

"I am an Anglo-North American as much as a Canadian. As with many who have divided time and thought between two countries, I feel part of both and neither. At times, however, it makes me feel culturally adrift, an outsider, as Colin Wilson used the term. This provides a special vantage point as a writer."

*   *   *

SUHL, Yuri (Menachem) 1908-1986

PERSONAL: Born July 30, 1908, in Podhajce, Austria-Hungary (now part of Poland); immigrated to the United States, 1923; died of cerebral hemorrhage, November 8, 1986, in Martha's Vineyard, MA; son of Shay and Miriam (Fiksel) Suhl; married Isabelle H. Shugars (a librarian),

June 24, 1950. *Education:* Attended Brooklyn College (now Brooklyn College of the City University of New York), 1928-29, and New York University, 1929-30, 1949-53; graduated from Jewish Workers University, 1932. *Religion:* Jewish. *Avocational interests:* Sculpture.

ADDRESSES: Home and office—232 East Sixth St., Apt. 3B, New York, NY 10003. *Agent*—Joan Daves, 59 East 54th St., New York, NY 10022.

CAREER: Writer. During the 1930's worked as an upholsterer, fruit peddler, ditch digger, teacher of Yiddish, and writer on Federal Writers' Project. Teacher of course on Jewish resistance to Nazism at New School for Social Research, beginning 1971; lecturer. Sculpture exhibited in several one-man shows and group exhibitions. *Military service:* U.S. Army, 1942-44.

MEMBER: Authors Guild, Authors League of America.

AWARDS, HONORS: Lewis Carroll Shelf Award, Wisconsin Book Conference, 1972, for *Simon Boom Gives a Wedding;* National Jewish Book Award, Jewish Book Council/Jewish Welfare Board, and Charles and Bertie Schwartz Juvenile Book Award, the Jewish Book Council of America, both 1974, both for *Uncle Misha's Partisans.*

WRITINGS:

JUVENILE FICTION

Der Alter fun Lompaduni un andere meises (title means "The Old Man of Lompaduni and Other Stories"), illustrated by William Gropper, Niedershlesie (Poland), 1948.
Simon Boom Gives a Wedding, illustrated by Margot Zemach, Four Winds, 1972.
Uncle Misha's Partisans, Four Winds, 1973.
The Man Who Made Everyone Late, illustrated by Lawrence di Fiori, Four Winds, 1974.
The Merrymaker, illustrated by Thomas di Grazia, Four Winds, 1975.
On the Other Side of the Gate, F. Watts, 1975.
Simon Boom Gets a Letter, illustrated by Fernando Krahn, Four Winds, 1976.
The Purim Goat, illustrated by Kaethe Zemach, Four Winds, 1980.

JUVENILE NONFICTION

Eloquent Crusader: Ernestine Rose, Messner, 1970.
An Album of Jews in America, F. Watts, 1972.

ADULT FICTION

One Foot in America, Macmillan, 1950.
Cowboy on a Wooden Horse, Macmillan, 1953, published as *You Should Only Be Happy,* Papberback Library, 1969.

ADULT NONFICTION

Ernestine L. Rose and the Battle for Human Rights, Reynal, 1959.
(Editor, translator, and contributor) *They Fought Back: The Story of the Jewish Resistance in Nazi Europe* (documentary anthology), Crown, 1967.

POETRY

Dos Licht oif Men Gass (title means "The Light on My Street"), illustrated by L. Bunin, Signal, 1935.
Dem Tog Antkegen (title means "Toward the Day"), Signal, 1938.
Yisroel Partisan (title means "Israel the Partisan"), Signal, 1942.
A Vort fun Trayst (title means "A Word of Consolation"), YKUF of Mexico, 1952.

OTHER

(Author of book and lyrics) *Benyomen der Dritter* (choral and dance; title means "Benjamin the Third"), produced in New York City at Carnegie Hall, 1938.
Gedenk, Mein Folk (cantata; title means "Remember, My People"), produced in New York City at Town Hall, 1963.

WORK IN PROGRESS: The Restless Dead, a Holocaust novel and a yet-untitled novel based on the author's experiences in the U.S. Army during World War II.

SIDELIGHTS: Until his death in 1986, Yuri Suhl authored English and Yiddish books for children and adults. Suhl's works include Jewish folk tales, several volumes of poetry, and accounts of the Holocaust endured by the Jews under the Nazi conquest of Europe. Born in 1908, in a section of the old Austro-Hungarian empire that is now part of Poland, Suhl recalled his childhood in an essay for *Something about the Author Autobiography Series (SAAS):* "In the summer of 1914, when I was barely six years old, World War I broke out and that part of the southern Ukraine was the first to be occupied by the Russians, an occupation that lasted two years. I have no fond memories of that period. What stands out most vividly in my mind even now is a night of terror when the Cossacks went on a spree of robbing and looting Jewish homes. My parents and grandparents, with whom we then lived, barricaded themselves behind a heap of furniture they had piled up against the door. When the Cossacks approached, shouting commands to open up and pounding on the door, we held our breath in terrified silence until they left."

The author's father was a Talmudic scholar whose temperament was not suited for the business endeavors undertaken to support the family. When Suhl was ten years old, his mother died. "I expressed my grief and sorrow at her loss by fervently saying *Kaddish* (the prayer for the dead) every day for a whole year," said the author. When Suhl was fifteen, he immigrated with his family to Brooklyn, New York. There, he worked during the day and attended high school at night. The author related: "My day began at 6:00 A.M. when I did my homework on the BMT subway during the hour-long ride to my butcher-boy job in Bay Ridge, Brooklyn. Later in the morning when I was out on the bicycle delivering orders, I would compose in my head the writing assignment for my English class that evening. Between deliveries I memorized each sentence and by the end of the day I knew the whole composition by heart and wrote it down from memory." Suhl especially enjoyed writing poetry.

In high school, another student introduced Suhl to Yiddish literature. "He lent me the novel *Noch Alemen (When All Was Said and Done)* by the master of Yiddish prose, David Bergelson," the author related. "Though the story had little plot it held my interest throughout by the sheer beauty of the language. I didn't know that Yiddish could be so rich in nuance and imagery. It was like discovering my mother tongue anew. As soon as I finished reading the book, I was overcome by a desire to write a story in Yiddish." Visiting the public library to find other samples of Yiddish literature, Suhl was especially moved by the poetry of Moishe Leib Halperin.

Suhl worked as an upholsterer and a waiter to earn money for college. He enrolled in New York University (NYU) for a year, but the next year saw the onset of the Great Depression. Unable to make his tuition payments, Suhl left NYU and enrolled in Jewish Workers University, a Marxist school from which he graduated in 1932. He then worked as a Yiddish teacher and wrote poetry. "My first collection of Yiddish poems, *Dos Licht oif Men Gass (The Light on My Street)* was published in 1935, the year that Roosevelt initiated the Works Progress Administration (WPA)," Suhl stated. "It was followed by a number of projects in the arts, of which the Federal Writers Project was one. After a stint of ditch-digging on the WPA, I was assigned to the Jewish Division of the Federal Writers Project."

In 1948, Suhl returned to Poland for the first time since he had emmigrated at age fifteen. The author commented: "After attending the unveiling ceremonies of the Warsaw Ghetto Monument I visited the surviving Jewish communities in Lower Silesia and other parts of Poland on a poetry reading tour sponsored by Jewish communal leaders. This experience marked the beginning of my deep interest in the Holocaust theme. When I returned to Poland a second time, in 1959, it was to do research at the Jewish Historical Insitute of Warsaw and interview surviving resistance leaders for *They Fought Back.*"

Now one of Suhl's best-known works, *They Fought Back: The Story of the Jewish Resistance in Nazi Europe* was initially rejected by publishing companies. "The anthology was five years in the making and was turned down by thirteen publishers on the ground that there would not be a market for it . . . ," the author related. "Six weeks after publication it went into a second printing. Now, [many] years later and after various editions, both here and abroad, the book is still solidly in print."

Suhl's books about the Holocaust stress the activity of the Jewish resistance movement in Eastern Europe during the Nazi occupation. His accounts are often contrasted to those of some authors who have either downplayed the effectiveness of the resistance or denied its existence entirely. M. E. Marty of *Book Week,* for instance, said that *They Fought Back* is "addressed polemically against [Raul] Hilberg's book *The Destruction of European Jews.*" According to Marty, Suhl makes his point by collecting "dozens of stories that contain hundreds of certifying and certifiable names, locations, dates."

One of Suhl's books for young adults, *Uncle Misha's Partisans,* "evolved from a true story, in my documentary anthology *They Fought Back,* about a twelve-year-old boy who joined the Jewish partisans after his family was killed by the Nazis," the author stated in his *SAAS* essay. Another of Suhl's works for young adults, *On the Other Side of the Gate,* is "a factually accurate, modern story that reads like a folktale, and that turns the sufferings of Polish Jews under Nazism into a parable of hope and survival," according to a writer for *Kirkus Reviews.* In a review for the *Bulletin of the Center for Children's Books,* Zena Sutherland noted that *On the Other Side of the Gate* is based on the true story of a young Jewish couple who successfully smuggled their infant son out of the Warsaw ghetto. Sutherland further stated that the book "shows the range of attitudes among Poles from anti-Semitism to defiant compassion. Suhl creates the atmosphere with caustic conviction and constructs the plot and the characters with solidity."

In addition to documenting the injustices perpetrated against Jews in the past, the author took an active interest in contemporary political injustices. In an obituary appearing in the *New York Times,* Edwin McDowell observed that Suhl "publicly protested the persecution of Jews in Poland and the Soviet Union." Suhl also was actively involved in the clemency campaign for Ethel and Julius Rosenberg, relating in his *SAAS* essay: "Like many others in this country and abroad I was disturbed by the cruel and excessive death penalty imposed on two young parents with two small children." Arrested on charges of giving to the Soviet Union classified information regarding nuclear weaponry, the Rosenbergs were executed in 1953. McDowell noted that Suhl became "a trustee of the fund established for the two young sons of Julius and Ethel Rosenberg."

BIOGRAPHICAL/CRITICAL SOURCES:

BOOKS

Authors of Books for Young People, supplement to the second edition, Scarecrow, 1979.
Children's Literature Review, Volume 2, Gale, 1976.
Miller, Wayne, *A Gathering of Ghetto Writers,* New York University Press, 1972.
Something about the Author Autobiography Series, Volume 1, Gale, 1986, pp. 249-268.

PERIODICALS

Book Week, May 14, 1967.
Bulletin of the Center for Children's Books, September, 1975.
Kirkus Reviews, February 1, 1975.
Library Journal, December 15, 1966.
New York Times Book Review, June 1, 1967.
Punch, March 20, 1968.

OBITUARIES:

PERIODICALS

International Herald, November 14, 1986.
New York Times, November 13, 1986.*

*　　　*　　　*

SUK, Julie

PERSONAL: Born in Mobile, AL; daughter of Samuel Palmer, Jr. (an attorney) and Florence (Hollingsworth) Gaillard; married William Joseph Suk; children: Julie Florence, William Gaillard, Palmer Gaillard. *Education:* Attended Stephens College and University of Alabama.

ADDRESSES: Home—845 Greentree Dr., Charlotte, NC 28211.

CAREER: Charlotte Nature Museum, Charlotte, NC, teacher and program coordinator, 1967-78; *Southern Poetry Review,* Charlotte, associate editor and business manager, 1978-90. Queen's College, Charlotte, creative writing teacher in adult education program.

AWARDS, HONORS: Arkansas Poetry Award, 1991, for *The Angel of Obsession.*

WRITINGS:

(Editor with Anne Newman, and contributor) *Bear Crossings* (poems), New South Co., 1978.
The Medicine Woman (poems), St. Andrews Press, 1980.
Heartwood (poems), Briarpatch Press, 1991.

The Angel of Obsession (poems), University of Arkansas Press, 1992.

Contributor of poems to periodicals, including *Georgia Review, Poetry,* and *Southern Humanities Review.*

SIDELIGHTS: Julie Suk told *CA:* "When Anne Newman and I initially began collecting work for *Bear Crossings,* we deliberately avoided any move toward organization. Instead, we let the poems decree their own categories as they fell into place thematically. Even after we became more selective, choice was often arbitrary as we found bears contrary critters, adaptable to more than one of the six sections of the book. Consequently, the short prose quotations, which introduce each group of poems, not only emphasize the various aspects of 'bearness' in man, but also the rich variety of imaginative representation in subject, tone, and technique. Anne wrote the foreword, and I contributed with an introductory poem. Now in its second printing, *Bear Crossings* was a labor or love, and we are more than grateful that *Library Journal* described it as 'the best small press book of this year or any year.'

"As for my own work, the more I write the more humbled I am by the process, and find it difficult to describe poetic views and methods without repeating what others have said better. Perhaps it is best to quote the artist Yves Tanguy: 'It amuses me to imagine what is beyond a hill. I want so much to represent those things I will never see.' I understand that to mean those presences around and within the tangibles of this world, an energy that is our privilege to transform."

*　　　*　　　*

SUVIN, Darko (Ronald) 1932-

PERSONAL: Born July 19, 1932, in Zagreb, Yugoslavia; son of Miroslav (a physician and professor) and Gertrude (Weiser) Suvin; married Nevenka Eric (a teacher), 1961. *Education:* University of Zagreb, M.Sc., 1954, B.A., 1956, Ph.D., 1970; also attended University of Bristol, Sorbonne, and Yale University. *Politics:* Socialist.

ADDRESSES: Office—Department of English, McGill University, 853 Sherbrooke W., Montreal, Quebec, Canada H3A 2T6.

CAREER: Free-lance translator and critic, 1954-59; University of Zagreb, Zagreb, Yugoslavia, assistant lecturer in theatre arts and comparative literature, 1959-67; University of Massachusetts—Amherst, visiting lecturer in English, 1967-68; McGill University, Montreal, Quebec, assistant professor, 1968-70, associate professor, 1970-76, professor of English and comparative literature, 1976—. Visiting associate professor of comparative literature, Indiana University, summer, 1968; visiting professor of English and French, University of Rome, spring, 1982; visiting professor of literary studies, University of Leuven, Belgium, spring, 1986; visiting professor of theatre studies, Ruhr—University of Bochum, Germany, spring, 1989. Member of Croat National Theater Board, 1962-64, and National Library Board, 1963-65; director of national and international colloquia on science fiction, drama, comparative literature, and theory of literature. Union Internationale des Theatres Universitaires, vice-president, 1962-65.

MEMBER: International PEN, International Brecht Society (vice-president, 1984-88), Science Fiction Research Association (member of executive committee, 1970-73; vice-president, 1977-78), Canadian Semiotic Association, Canadian Comparative Literature Association, Modern Language Association of America, Union of Writers of Yugoslavia.

AWARDS, HONORS: Fellowship, Ford Foundation, 1965-66; grants, Canada Council, 1969, 1972, 1973-74, 1975, 1976, 1977-78, 1979, 1980-81, 1986-87, 1990-91; honorary fellow, Clare Hall College, Cambridge, England, 1973-74; grant, Quebec provincial government, 1975-77; Pilgrim Award, Science Fiction Research Association, 1979, for distinguished contributions to the study of science fiction; Outstanding Academic Book of 1979, *Choice* magazine, 1980, for *Metamorphoses of Science Fiction;* honorary fellow, University College, London, 1980-81; second prize, *Amelia* magazine, 1984, for oriental poetry forms poem; research grant, Japan Foundation, summer, 1988; visiting research fellow, Tokyo University, 1990-91.

WRITINGS:

IN ENGLISH

(Editor) *Other Worlds, Other Seas: Science-Fiction Stories from Socialist Countries,* Random House, 1970.

(Editor with M. D. Bristol, and contributor) *A Production Notebook to Brecht's "St. Joan of the Stockyards,"* McGill University, 1973.

Russian Science Fiction, 1956-1974: A Bibliography, Dragon, 1976.

(Editor with R. D. Mullen, and contributor) *Science-Fiction Studies: Selected Articles on Science Fiction, 1973-1975,* Gregg-Hall, 1976.

(Editor with R. M. Philmus, and contributor) *H. G. Wells and Modern Science Fiction,* Bucknell University Press, 1977.

(Editor with Mullen) *Science-Fiction Studies II: Selected Articles on Science Fiction, 1976-1977,* Gregg-Hall, 1978.

Metamorphoses of Science Fiction, Yale University Press, 1979.

Victorian Science Fiction in the United Kingdom: The Discourses of Knowledge and of Power, G. K. Hall, 1983.

To Brecht and Beyond, Barnes & Noble, 1984.

The Long March (poems), Hounslow Press, 1987.

Positions and Presuppositions in Science Fiction, Kent State University Press, 1988.

IN CROATIAN, EXCEPT AS INDICATED

Dva vida dramaturgije (title means "Two Aspects of Dramaturgy"), Razlog, 1965.

Od Lukijana do Lunjika (title means "From Lucian to the Lunik"), Epoha, 1965.

(Editor, translator, and contributor) Bertolt Brecht, *Dijalektika u teatru* (title means "Dialectics in the Theater"), Nolit, 1966.

Uvod u Brechta (title means "Introduction to Brecht"), Skolska Knjiga, 1970.

Pour une poetique de la science-fiction (in French; title means "For a Poetics of Science Fiction"), Presses de l'Universite du Quebec, 1977.

Dramatika Ira Vojnovica (title means "The Dramaturgy of Ira Vojnovic"), Dubrovnik, 1977.

Armirana Arkadija (poems; title means "Armored Arcadia"), Naprijed, 1990.

OTHER

Contributor to books, including *Nebula Award Stories Five,* edited by James Blish, Doubleday, 1970; *Solaris,* by Stanislaw Lem, Walker & Co., 1970; *Brecht,* edited by Erika Munk, Bantam, 1972; *Proceedings of the International Comparative Literature VII Congress,* Bieber, 1979; *Brave New Universe,* edited by Tom Henighan, Tecumseh Press, 1980; *Comparative Studies in Croatian Literature,* edited by Miroslav Beker, Zavod Knjizevnosti, 1981; *Proceedings of the International Comparative Literature IX Congress,* 1982; *Renewals in the Theory of Literary History,* edited by Eva Kushner, Royal Society of Canada, 1984; *Theory of Poetic Form: Proceedings of the International Comparative Literature X Congress,* c. 1985; *Literature and Anthropology,* edited by Jonathan Hall and Ackbar Abbas, Hong Kong University Press, 1986; *Marxism and the Interpretation of Culture,* edited by Cary Nelson and Lawrence Grossberg, University of Illinois Press, 1988; *Fiction—Narratologie—Texte—Genre: Proceedings of the International Comparative Literature XI Congress,* Volume 2, edited by Jean Bessiere, Lang, 1989; *Utopia e modernita,* edited by Giuseppa Saccaro del Buffa and Arthur O. Lewis, Gangemi, 1989; *The Dramatic Touch of Difference: Theatre, Own and Foreign,* edited by Erika Fischer-Lichte and others, Narr, 1990; *Socialism and the Literary Artistry of William Morris,* edited by Florence S. Boos and Carole G. Silver, University of Missouri Press, 1990; *Unconventional Conventions in Theatre Texts,* edited by Gunther Ahrends and Hans Jurgen Diller, Narr, 1990;

Drama und Theatre: Theorie—Methode—Geschichte, edited by Herta Schmid and Hedwig Kral, Sagner, 1991.

Also contributor of over four hundred articles and reviews to literary magazines and theater journals. *Science Fiction Studies,* co-editor, 1973-81, publisher, 1979-81, contributing editor, 1981—; editor, *Literary Research/Recherche litteraire,* International Comparative Literature Association review organ, 1986—; advisory editor, *Wellsian,* 1976-81. Contributor to *Essays on Brecht: Brecht Yearbook 15,* 1990; contributing editor or member of editorial committee of three international journals.

WORK IN PROGRESS: Research on theory of dramaturgy and spectacle (Europe versus Japan) and on cultural theory.

SIDELIGHTS: Darko Suvin once wrote *CA:* "As a critic, I try to contest both the Platonic notion that works of literature and art are a transparency 'expressing' something else (myth, ideology, truth, reality, or what have you), and the notion that they are isolated from social history which, in fact, informs them most intimately. I am equally interested in so-called 'high' and 'low' culture, and consequently in theory-*cum*-history." In 1991 he added, "One of my main preoccupations at the moment is to trace, by means of a differential understanding of the Japanese polytheist tradition, the correlation of monotheism, teleology, and individualism."

BIOGRAPHICAL/CRITICAL SOURCES:

BOOKS

Imbroscio, Carmelina, editor, *Requiem pur l'utopie?,* Libraire goliardica, 1986.
Livres at auteure Quebecois, 1977, Presses de l'Universite Laval, 1978.

PERIODICALS

Essay in Arts and Sciences, August, 1980.
Science Fiction and Fantasy Review, April, 1984.
Science-Fiction Studies, Volume 11, 1984; Volume 12, number 36, 1985, pp. 202-208; Volume 17, number 3, 1990; Volume 18, number 1, 1991.
Times Literary Supplement, May 9, 1980.

T

TARR, Joel A(rthur) 1934-

PERSONAL: Born May 8, 1934, in Jersey City, NJ; married Arlene Green, 1956 (deceased); married Tova Brafman, 1978; children: (first marriage) Michael, Joanna; (second marriage) Maya, Ilana. *Education:* Rutgers University, B.S. (with high honors), 1956, M.A., 1957; Northwestern University, Ph.D., 1963.

ADDRESSES: Office—Department of History, Carnegie-Mellon University, Pittsburgh, PA 15213.

CAREER: Northwestern University, Evanston, IL, instructor in history, 1959-61; Long Beach State College (now California State University, Long Beach), Long Beach, CA, instructor, 1961-63, assistant professor of American history, 1963-66; University of California, Santa Barbara, visiting assistant professor of American history, 1966-67; Carnegie-Mellon University, Pittsburgh, PA, assistant professor, 1967-70, associate professor, 1970-76, professor of history, technology, and urban affairs, 1976-78, professor of history and public policy, 1978—, director of Program in Technology and Humanities, 1975—, codirector of Ph.D. program in applied history and social science, 1977-85, acting dean, School of Urban and Public Affairs, 1986, College of Humanities and Social Science, associate dean 1988-91, acting dean, 1991-92. President of Public Works Historical Society, 1982-83.

MEMBER: Society for the History of Technology, American Association for the Advancement of Science, Sigma Xi.

AWARDS, HONORS: American Philosophical Society grants, 1964, 1966; Scaife Fellow, Carnegie-Mellon University, 1967-69; National Foundation for the Humanities junior fellow, 1969-70; National Science Foundation awards, 1975, 1978, 1983, 1985; awards or grants from Andrew W. Mellon Foundation, 1975, 1980, Exxon Foundation, 1980, and National Oceanic and Atmospheric Administration, 1982, 1983; Abel Wolman Award, American Public Works Association, 1989; Doherty Prize, Carnegie-Mellon University, 1992.

WRITINGS:

A Study in Boss Politics: William Lorimer of Chicago, University of Illinois Press, 1971.
(Consulting editor) *Living in Urban America,* Holt, 1974.
(Editor) *Patterns in City Growth,* Scott, Foresman, 1975.
(Editor) *Retrospective Technology Assessment,* San Francisco Press, 1977.
Transportation Innovation and Changing Spatial Patterns in Pittsburgh, 1850-1934: Essays in Public Works History, Public Works Historical Society, 1978.
(Editor) *Pittsburgh-Sheffield, Sister Cities: Proceedings of the Pittsburgh-Sheffield Symposium on Industrial Cities,* Carnegie-Mellon University Press, 1986.
(Editor) *Technology and the Rise of the Networked City in Europe and America,* Temple University Press, 1989.

Contributor to *Urban Bosses, Machines, and Progressive Reformers,* edited by Bruce Stave, Heath, 1971; *American Urban History,* 2nd edition, edited by Alexander Callow, Oxford University Press, 1973; *The Irish: America's Political Class,* edited by James P. Walsh, Arno, 1976; *The Prairie State,* edited by Robert P. Sutton, Eerdmans, 1976; *Public-Private Partnerships in American Cities,* Lexington Books, 1982; *Energy and Transport: Historical Perspectives on Policy Issues,* edited by Mark Rose and George Daniels, Sage Publications, 1982; *Perspectives on Urban Infrastructure,* edited by Royce Hanson, National Academy of Sciences, 1984; and *Records of the Columbia Historical Society,* edited by J. Kirkpatrick Flack, 1984. Contributor of more than fifty articles to professional journals, including *Agricultural History, American Heritage, Busi-*

ness History, Civil Engineering, History Teacher, Journal of Social History, Public Historian, and *Technology & Culture;* contributor of over fifty reviews to professional journals and national publications.

WORK IN PROGRESS: The Search for the Ultimate Sink: Urban Pollution in Historical Perspective, to be published in "Environmental History" Series, Texas A & M University Press; *Long-Term Pollution Trends in East Coast Estuaries; History of Industrial Waste Disposal.*

SIDELIGHTS: Joel A. Tarr once told *CA:* "My interest for the past few years has been in the interface between technology and society, particularly the city and technology, and technology and the environment. In addition to this area, I have been attempting to use history as a means to shed light upon present day technology-society problems and to aid in anticipating technology impacts."

*   *   *

TAYLOR, Richard S(helley) 1912-

PERSONAL: Born March 30, 1912, in Cornelius, OR; son of Ernest E. (a minister) and Luzena (a writer; maiden name, Shelley) Taylor; married Amy Overby, September 9, 1931 (died January 10, 1983); married Bertha Syverson Gordon (a homemaker), September 12, 1983 (died August, 1991); children: David Richard, Paul Wesley. *Education:* Cascade College, Th.B., 1943; George Fox College, A.B., 1944; Pasadena College (now Point Loma College), M.A., 1945; Boston University, Th.D., 1953.

ADDRESSES: Home—1008 High Ave., Bremerton, WA 98310.

CAREER: Ordained minister of Church of the Nazarene, 1934; pastor of Nazarene churches in Washington, 1931-41, Oregon, 1941-49, Massachusetts, 1949-51, and in Australia, 1954-60; Nazarene Theological Seminary, Kansas City, MO, associate professor, 1961-64, professor of theology and missions, 1965-77, professor emeritus, 1977—. Associate director of Church of the Nazarene Department of Education and Ministry, 1974-77. Professor at Cascade College, 1944-46; president of Nazarene Bible College, Sydney, Australia, 1952-60; visiting professor at Church of the Nazarene Seminary in Japan, 1966-67; interim principal of European Nazarene Bible College in Switzerland, 1969-70.

MEMBER: Evangelical Theological Society, Wesleyan Theological Society (president, 1968-69).

AWARDS, HONORS: Holiness Exponent of the Year Award from Christian Holiness Association, 1978, for *God, Man, and Salvation;* Alumnus of the Year, George Fox College, 1980; D.D., Western Evangelical Seminary, 1991.

WRITINGS:

A Right Conception of Sin (originally published in 1939), revised edition, Nazarene Publishing, 1945.

Talks by the Way, Better Book and Bible House, 1942.

Our Pacific Outposts, Nazarene Publishing, 1956.

The Disciplined Life, Beacon Hill Press of Kansas City, 1962.

Joy for Dark Days, Beacon Hill Press of Kansas City, 1964, revised edition published as *Miracle of Joy,* 1975.

Life in the Spirit, Beacon Hill Press of Kansas City, 1966.

Preaching Holiness Today, Beacon Hill Press of Kansas City, 1968, revised edition, 1987.

Tongues: Their Purpose and Meaning, Beacon Hill Press of Kansas City, 1973.

(Editor) *Timely Sermon Outlines,* Baker Book, 1973.

A Return to Christian Culture, Beacon Hill Press of Kansas City, 1973, published as *The Disciplined Life-Style,* Bethany House, 1980.

The Shape of Things to Come, Beacon Hill Press of Kansas City, 1975, revised edition published as *End Times,* Wesleyan Press, 1976.

(With W. T. Purkiser and Willard H. Taylor) *God, Man, and Salvation,* Beacon Hill Press of Kansas City, 1977.

Biblical Authority and Christian Faith, Beacon Hill Press of Kansas City, 1980.

(Editor) *Beacon Dictionary of Theology,* Beacon Hill Press of Kansas City, 1983.

Exploring Christian Holiness, Volume 3, Beacon Hill Press of Kansas City, 1985.

(Editor) *Great Holiness Classics,* Volume 3: *Leading Wesleyan Thinkers,* Beacon Hill Press of Kansas City, 1985.

Principles of Pastoral Success, Francis Asbury/Zondervan, 1989.

Dimensions of Church Growth, Francis Asbury/Zondervan, 1989.

Also contributor to other books published by Beacon Hill Press of Kansas City, including *Further Insights into Holiness,* edited by K. Geiger, 1963; *The Word and the Doctrine,* edited by Geiger, 1965; *Beacon Bible Commentary,* Volume 10, edited by Albert Harper and Ralph Earl, 1967; *Projecting Our Heritage,* edited by M. Boyd and M. A. Harris, 1969; *Ministering to the Millions,* edited by E. S. Phillips, 1971; *The Holiness of the Pulpit,* edited by James McGraw, 1974; *Family Love in All Dimensions,* edited by J. B. Nelson, 1976; *Great Holiness Classics,* Volume 5: *Holiness, Preachers and Preaching,* edited by William E. McCumber, 1989; and *Biblical Resources for Holiness Preaching,* edited by H. Ray Dunning and Neil B. Wiseman, 1990. Contributor to theology journals. Editor of *Nazarene Pastor,* 1964-72.

SIDELIGHTS: Richard S. Taylor once told *CA:* "I have been motivated by the conviction that all truth is ultimately theological in nature, and that such truth centers in Jesus Christ, and in the religion which bears his name. A further conviction has been that Christ, as a living and risen lord, is adequate as a savior from sin, here and now. Therefore my writing has focused on this available salvation. I have endeavored to expound, as simply and helpfully as possible, its doctrinal, experiential, and practical aspects."

* * *

TAYLOR, Theodore 1921-
(T. T. Lang)

PERSONAL: Born June 23, 1921, in Statesville, NC; son of Edward Riley (a molder) and Elnora Alma (Langhans) Taylor; married Gweneth Goodwin, October 25, 1946 (divorced, 1977); married Flora Gray Schoenleber (a library clerk), April 18, 1981; children: (first marriage) Mark, Wendy, Michael. *Education:* Attended Fork Union Military Academy, VA, 1939-40, U.S. Merchant Marine Academy, Kings Point, NY, 1942-43, and Columbia University, 1948; studied with American Theatre Wing, 1947-49. *Politics:* Republican. *Religion:* Protestant. *Avocational interests:* Ocean fishing and foreign travel.

ADDRESSES: Home—1856 Catalina St., Laguna Beach, CA 92615. *Agent*—Gloria Loomis, Watkins Loomis Agency, Inc., 150 East 35th St., Suite 530, New York, NY 10016.

CAREER: Portsmouth Star, Portsmouth, VA, cub reporter, 1934-39, sports editor, 1941-42; *Washington Daily News,* Washington, DC, copyboy; National Broadcasting Co. Radio, New York City, sports writer, 1942; *Sunset News,* Bluefield, WV, sports editor, 1946-47; New York University, New York City, assistant director of public relations, 1947-48; YMCA schools and colleges, New York City, director of public relations, 1948-50; *Orlando Sentinel Star,* Orlando, FL, reporter, 1949-50; Paramount Pictures, Hollywood, CA, publicist, 1955-56; Perlberg-Seaton Productions, Hollywood, story editor, writer and associate producer, 1956-61; free-lance press agent for Hollywood studios, 1961-68; Twentieth Century-Fox, Hollywood, writer, 1965-68; writer, 1961—. Producer and director of documentary films. *Military service:* U.S. Merchant Marine, 1942-44; U.S. Naval Reserve, active duty, 1944-46, 1950-55; became lieutenant.

MEMBER: Academy of Motion Picture Arts and Sciences, Writers Guild, Authors League of America, Mystery Writers of America, Society of Children's Book Writers.

AWARDS, HONORS: Commonwealth Club of California Silver Medal, 1969, Jane Addams Children's Book Award from Women's International League for Peace and Freedom (returned, 1975), Lewis Carroll Shelf Award, Southern California Council on Literature for Children and Young People Notable Book Award, Woodward Park School Annual Book Award, California Literature Medal Award, and Best Book Award from University of California, Irvine, all 1970, all for *The Cay; Battle in the Arctic Seas* was selected one of *New York Times* Outstanding Books of the Year, 1976; Spur Award for Best Western for Young People, Western Writers of America, and Commonwealth Club of California Silver Medal for the best juvenile book by a California author, both 1977, both for *A Shepherd Watches, a Shepherd Sings;* Southern California Council on Literature for Children and Young People Award, 1977, for distinguished contribution to the field of children's literature and body of work; George G. Stone Center for Children's Books Recognition of Merit Award, 1980, for body of work; Young Reader Medal from the California Reading Association, 1984, for *The Trouble with Tuck;* Jefferson Cup Honor Book, Virginia Library Association, 1987, for *Walking Up a Rainbow: Being the True Version of the Long and Hazardous Journey of Susan D. Carlisle, Mrs. Myrtle Dessery, Drover Bert Pettit, and Cowboy Clay Carmer and Others;* American Library Association Best Book Award, 1989, for *Sniper.*

WRITINGS:

JUVENILE FICTION

The Cay (*Horn Book* honor list), Doubleday, 1969.
The Children's War, Doubleday, 1971.
The Maldonado Miracle, Doubleday, 1973.
Teetoncey, illustrated by Richard Cuffari, Doubleday, 1974.
Teetoncey and Ben O'Neal, illustrated by R. Cuffari, Doubleday, 1975.
The Odyssey of Ben O'Neal, illustrated by R. Cuffari, Doubleday, 1977.
The Trouble with Tuck, Doubleday, 1981.
Sweet Friday Island, Scholastic Inc., 1984.
Walking Up a Rainbow: Being the True Version of the Long and Hazardous Journey of Susan D. Carlisle, Mrs. Myrtle Dessery, Drover Bert Pettit, and Cowboy Clay Carmer and Others, Delacorte, 1986.
The Hostage, illustrated by Darrell Sweet, Delacorte, 1987.
Sniper, Harcourt, 1989.
Tuck Triumphant, Doubleday, 1991.
The Weirdo, Harcourt, 1992.

JUVENILE NONFICTION

People Who Make Movies, Doubleday, 1967.

Air Raid—Pearl Harbor! The Story of December 7, 1941, illustrated by W. T. Mars, Crowell, 1971.

Rebellion Town: Williamsburg, 1776, illustrated by R. Cuffari, Crowell, 1973.

Battle in the Arctic Seas: The Story of Convoy PQ 17 (Junior Literary Guild selection), illustrated by Robert Andrew Parker, Crowell, 1976.

(With Louis Irigaray) *A Shepherd Watches, a Shepherd Sings*, Doubleday, 1977.

The Battle off Midway Island, illustrated by Andrew Glass, Avon, 1981.

H.M.S. Hood vs. Bismarck: The Battleship Battle, illustrated by A. Glass, Avon, 1982.

Battle in the English Channel, illustrated by A. Glass, Avon, 1983.

Rocket Island, Avon, 1985.

ADULT FICTION

The Stalker, D. I. Fine, 1987.
Monocolo, D. I. Fine, 1989.

ADULT NONFICTION

The Magnificent Mitscher (biography), foreword by Arthur W. Radford, Norton, 1954.

Fire on the Beaches, Norton, 1958.

The Body Trade, Fawcett, 1968.

(With Robert A. Houghton) *Special Unit Senator: The Investigation of the Assassination of Senator Robert F. Kennedy*, Random House, 1970.

(With Kreskin) *The Amazing World of Kreskin*, Random House, 1973.

Jule: The Story of Composer Jule Styne, Random House, 1979.

(With Tippi Hedren) *The Cats of Shambala*, Simon & Schuster, 1985.

OTHER

Author of television plays, including *Tom Threepersons* (adult mystery), TV Mystery Theatre, 1964, *Sunshine, the Whale* (juvenile), 1974, and *The Girl Who Whistled the River Kwai*, 1980, and of screenplays, including *Night without End*, 1959, *Showdown*, Universal, 1973, *The Hold-Up*, and seventeen documentaries. Also author of books under the pseudonym T. T. Lang. Contributor of short stories and novelettes to magazines, including *Redbook, Argosy, Ladies' Home Journal, McCall's* and *Saturday Evening Post*. Taylor's manuscripts are held at the Kerlan Collection of the University of Minnesota.

ADAPTATIONS: The Cay was adapted as a movie by NBC-TV, 1974, and as a filmstrip by Pied Piper Productions, 1975. *The Trouble with Tuck* was adapted as a filmstrip by Pied Piper Productions, 1986.

WORK IN PROGRESS: Working on *Francisco and Hernando: A Christmas Story* and *To Dream of Timothy*, both for children, and *To Kill a Pistarckle*, for adults.

SIDELIGHTS: Author Theodore Taylor does not have a very good imagination, or so he contends in his autobiographical sketch in *Something about the Author Autobiography Series* (*SAAS*). The creator of nearly thirty books, both fiction and nonfiction, adult and juvenile, insists that he is "basically a reporter, finding it easier to work from real-life models." Luckily for his readers, his real-life experiences are vast and varied: Taylor has worked for numerous newspapers, been a sailor in two wars, assisted in the production of Hollywood movies, and traveled the world making his own documentary films. These experiences, together with childhood exploits to match those of Huck Finn, provide him with fodder for his many books.

Taylor was born in Statesville, North Carolina on June 23, 1921. His parents were as different as day and night: his father a rough-and-tumble man who went to work in a Pittsburgh foundry at the age of twelve; his mother a delicate, religious woman "who won contests in elocution and would sometimes emote in the kitchen, acting out a part," Taylor remembers in *SAAS*. Taylor and his four sisters "could never understand how these two people got together and got married." Life was never easy for the family, and the Depression sent Taylor's father away in search of work: "I'm not sure where my father went for part-time work," says Taylor in *SAAS*, "but he kept in touch by mail or occasional visits. He in no way ever deserted us; just wisely eliminated another mouth to feed, adding whatever money he could." Taylor did his part as well, selling candy, picking up scrap metal to sell to the junkyard, and delivering newspapers. "It did not occur to me until years later that there was anything exceptional about a boy just shy of ten getting up at four-thirty to walk, not bicycle, to the Vance [a local hotel], pick up sixty-odd newspapers; deliver them by seven; come home, have breakfast and go off to school."

Childhood was not all work for Taylor, however. Though he was not an exceptional student, he says in *SAAS* that he "excelled in the practice of freedom, a brand of which is not known to many of today's children of six or seven. . . . I roamed fields and muddy creeks and other interesting places around and about town: the abandoned headquarters of the volunteer cavalry, soon to burn down; the old brickyard, the strong-smelling building where chewing tobacco had once been manufactured; numerous drainpipes and other places of mystery." When his father got a job in the Naval Yard in Portsmouth, Virginia, Taylor had a whole new world to explore, a world of salt marshes, fishing docks, and coal-burning side-wheeler ferries. Taylor's "unwitting accomplice" in these adventures was his mother; "I do not remember," says Taylor, "at this age of seven and upward, her ever asking, 'Where are you going?' She trusted in God that I'd always be safe."

Taylor recreates this adventurous self-reliance in the characters of many of his books for young people. Ben O'Neal and Teetoncey (from *Teetoncey, Teetoncey and Ben O'Neal,* and *The Odyssey of Ben O'Neal*), Phillip (from *The Cay*), and Jose (from *The Maldonado Miracle*) "are the kind of peer models children can like and respect," Taylor tells *Language Arts* interviewer Norma Bagnall. "All of them are self-reliant; all are self-sufficient. They find their own way without constant reference to adults. I like that kind of kid; I think kids like that kind too, and if it helps them aim toward self-reliance, then I've done a good job."

Taylor got his first writing job when he was thirteen years old. In the spring of 1935 he was offered the chance to write a sports column for the *Portsmouth Star,* reporting on the week's activity in sports at nearby Cradock High. "Never had I thought about writing of any sort," Taylor recalls in *SAAS.* "And, to my knowledge, I had no talent for it. But I was certainly willing to gamble that I could put a story together." His gamble paid off, and as Taylor struggled through high school he kept busy writing sports stories. After graduating he convinced the managing editor of the *Washington Daily News* in Washington, D.C., to hire him as a copyboy. Soon he was writing theater and concert reviews, and within a few months was given the chance to write a profile of a local boxer. He learned about good writing the hard way, for the sports editor hurled this profile, his first big story, in the trash. After not speaking to the young writer for a while, the editor finally gave Taylor some sound advice, as the author recalls in his autobiographical sketch: " 'Ted, you must learn how to write simply. People don't know big words and don't like to read them. . . .' I've never forgotten his advice: *write simply.* Don't use big words to impress readers. You annoy them, not impress them." Taylor says that these newspapers "were to be my college, my seamy-side university, my graduate school. I've often regretted I didn't attend college. City rooms were the substitutes, newsmen were the teachers."

In the fall of 1942, Taylor joined the merchant marine, "having no desire to slog around in army mud nor any great desire for navy discipline," he says in *SAAS,* and at the same time joined the naval reserve. He wasn't involved in any of the big battles that he would write about so effectively in such books as *Air Raid—Pearl Harbor! The Story of December 7, 1941,* and *The Battle off Midway Island,* but during his years of service he developed a love for naval war history that made those books possible. Drew Middleton, writing in the *New York Times Book Review,* says that in *The Battle off Midway Island* "Taylor has provided readers of any age with a splendid picture of the

naval battles that turned the Pacific War around." By carefully selecting revealing episodes in the war of the Pacific, and by providing background on the major figures in those battles, Taylor maintains the kind of pace that, according to Middleton, makes his "depiction of the men, the aircraft and the ships . . . seem as vivid as it was that day when the Navy took its first step on the long road to victory." *Air Raid—Pearl Harbor!* also elicited positive reviews: Wilson Sullivan, reviewing the book in *New York Times Book Review,* comments that "with the scenarist's eye for the effective fadeout, closeup and symbolic detail, Theodore Taylor has presented a vividly credible account of the attack on Pearl Harbor."

Taylor wrote his first book, a biography of Admiral "Pete" Mitscher entitled *The Magnificent Mitscher,* during his five year tour of duty with the naval reserve during the Korean War. Late in that tour he found himself stationed in the Caribbean providing hurricane relief on many of the smaller islands. These experiences also found their way into print, for Taylor says that in the islands he "sponged up background and atmosphere" that he later put into his award-winning book, *The Cay.* The book, which was actually written years after Taylor left the Caribbean, tells the story of a young white boy and an old black West Indian sailor who are marooned on an island together, the only survivors of a shipwreck that left the boy, Phillip, blinded. Despite Phillip's racist upbringing, he comes to rely on and trust Timothy, whose shrewd judgement allows the pair to survive. Eventually Phillip comes to realize that racism is a product of sight, for Timothy feels "neither white nor black." Charles Dorsey, reviewing the book in *New York Times Book Review,* says that *The Cay* is "a story with a high ethical purpose but no sermon." Many critics and reviewers praised the book, citing its fast-paced plot and vivid characterizations. The book also won many awards, including the Jane Addams Children's Book Award and the Lewis Carroll Shelf Award.

However, the book soon came under attack as racist, primarily for what was called "stereotypical" characterization of Timothy, whose dialect Taylor modeled after the West Indian sailors he knew in the Caribbean. The Interracial Council on Children's Books led the attack, and as a result the book was banned in many public libraries. Eventually the Jane Addams Book Award group asked that Taylor return the award, which he did in 1975. Taylor denies the charges of racism leveled against his best-known book, saying in *SAAS* that "*The Cay* is *not* racist, in my firm belief, and the character of Timothy, the old black man, modeled after a real person and several composites, is 'heroic' and not a stereotype." The author told Bagnall that he can't let these criticisms affect the way he writes: " . . . [If] I have to be worried about that kind of thing, I can't write. And the only way I can do it, is simply to forget all that stuff and do my story in the hope that as a human being I'll be fair. I try to do that."

After Taylor left the Navy, he happened into a job as a press agent for a Hollywood film production company. He advanced quickly, becoming a story editor and eventually an assistant to the producer. However, he soon departed Hollywood to make documentary films, many of them "behind-scenes" films for television. Characteristically, he converted these experiences into a book called *People Who Make Movies*, a children's book that explains the movie-making process and describes the many jobs that people perform in the movie industry. But Taylor writes for adults as well, and has published nearly as many adult books as books for children. "The change of pace is important and rejuvenating for me," he remarks in *SAAS*. T. Jefferson Parker, writing in the *Los Angeles Times Book Review*, called the adult suspense novel *The Stalker* "a well-plotted, economical thriller," noting that "Taylor is . . . very good at moving his story along." Taylor has also tackled a study of the assassination of Senator Robert F. Kennedy and biographies of The Amazing Kreskin, the mentalist, and composer Jule Styne. The hard-working author now writes seven days a week—except during football season, when he takes weekends off—in the office of his home three blocks from the Pacific Ocean in California.

BIOGRAPHICAL/CRITICAL SOURCES:

BOOKS

Authors and Artists for Young Adults, Volume 2, Gale, 1989, pp. 223-234.

Marquardt, Dorothy A., and Martha E. Ward, *Authors of Books for Young People*, supplement to the 2nd edition, Scarecrow, 1979.

Something about the Author Autobiography Series, Volume 4, Gale, 1987, pp. 303-320.

Twentieth-Century Children's Writers, 3rd edition, St. James Press, 1989, pp. 953-54.

PERIODICALS

Christian Science Monitor, May 6, 1988; January 25, 1989, p. 13.

Growing Point, January, 1991, pp. 5447-5451.

Horn Book, October, 1974, p. 145; December, 1975, p. 596; April, 1982, p. 170; February, 1984, p. 79; January, 1990, p. 72.

Kirkus Reviews, February 25, 1991, p. 252.

Kliatt, winter, 1982, pp. 57-58.

Language Arts, January, 1980, pp. 86-91.

Los Angeles Times Book Review, June 21, 1987, pp. 3, 8.

New York Times Book Review, September 17, 1967, p. 34; November 3, 1968, p. 53; June 26, 1969, p. 26; July 11, 1971, p. 8; January 9, 1972, p. 8; October 6, 1974, p. 8; October 24, 1976, p. 43; November 15, 1981, pp. 54, 69; March 6, 1983, p. 30.

Publishers Weekly, December 14, 1990, p. 67.

Saturday Review, August 19, 1967, p. 35; June 28, 1969, p. 39; August 21, 1971, p. 27; October 16, 1971, p. 57.

School Library Journal, November, 1984, p. 139; July, 1990, p. 27; March, 1991, p. 196.

Times Educational Supplement, June 10, 1983, p. 22.

Times Literary Supplement, October 30, 1970, p. 1258.

Top of the News, November, 1971; April, 1975.

Voice of Youth Advocates, June, 1984, p. 111; February, 1985, p. 333; December, 1985, p. 336; June, 1986, p. 83; April, 1988, p. 30; June, 1990, pp. 93-94.

Washington Post, May 26, 1979.

—*Sketch by Tom Pendergast*

*   *   *

TENNANT, Emma (Christina) 1937- (Catherine Aydy)

PERSONAL: Born October 20, 1937, in London, England; daughter of Christopher Grey (Lord Glenconner; a businessman) and Elizabeth (Lady Glenconner; maiden name, Powell) Tennant; married three times; children: (first marriage) Matthew, (second marriage) Daisy, (third marriage) Rose. *Education:* Attended St. Paul's Girls' School, London, England. *Avocational interests:* Walking.

ADDRESSES: Home—141 Elgin Cres., London W11, England. *Office*—49 Blenheim Cres., London W11, England. *Agent*—A. D. Peters & Co., Ltd., 10 Buckingham St., London WC2N 6BU, England.

CAREER: Novelist, critic, and editor, 1960—. *Queen*, London, England, travel correspondent, 1963; *Vogue*, London, features editor, 1966; full-time novelist, 1973—.

MEMBER: Royal Society of Literature (fellow).

WRITINGS:

NOVELS

(Under pseudonym Catherine Aydy) *The Colour of Rain*, Weidenfeld & Nicolson, 1963, reprinted under name Emma Tennant, Faber, 1988.

The Time of the Crack, J. Cape, 1973, published as *The Crack*, Penguin, 1978.

The Last of the Country House Murders, J. Cape, 1975, Thomas Nelson, 1976.

Hotel de Dream, Gollancz, 1976.

The Bad Sister, Coward, 1978.

Wild Nights, J. Cape, 1979, Harcourt, 1980.

Alice Fell, J. Cape, 1980.

The Boggart (juvenile), illustrations by Mary Rayner, Granada, 1980.

The Search for Treasure Island (juvenile), illustrated by Andrew Skilleter, Puffin, 1981.

Queen of Stones, J. Cape, 1982.

Woman Beware Woman, J. Cape, 1983, published as *The Half-Mother,* Little-Brown, 1985.

The Ghost Child (juvenile), illustrated by Charlotte Voake, Heinemann, 1984.

Black Marina, Faber, 1985.

The House of Hospitalities, Viking, 1987.

A Wedding of Cousins, Viking, 1988.

The Adventures of Robina, By Herself: Being the Memoirs of a Debutante at the Court of Queen Elizabeth II, Persea Books, 1988.

The Magic Drum, Viking, 1989.

Two Women of London: The Strange Case of Ms Jekyll and Mrs Hyde, Faber, 1989.

OTHER

(Contributor) *Women on Women,* Sidgwick & Jackson, 1974.

(Editor) *Bananas* (anthology), Quartet, 1977, reprinted, Charles River Books, 1988.

(Editor) *Saturday Night Reader,* W. H. Allen, 1979.

(Contributor) John Haffenden, editor, *Novelists in Interview,* Methuen, 1985.

(Contributor) Moira Monteith, editor, *Women's Writing: A Challenge to Theory,* St. Martin's, 1986.

Contributor to numerous periodicals, including *Guardian.* Founding editor, *Bananas* (literary magazine of the British Arts Council), 1975-78; general editor, *In Verse,* 1982—, and *Lives of Modern Women,* 1985—.

WORK IN PROGRESS: A novel, *Grandmother Sea.*

SIDELIGHTS: Emma Tennant's wide-ranging body of fiction offers a satirical but penetrating vision of conditions in modern England. Herself a descendent of Scottish nobility, Tennant turns a novelist's eye on the British upper class, with special emphasis on the uneasy relationships between men and women. "Fantasy, feminism, and political satire are combined in Emma Tennant's novels, which portray humanity's groping, fumbling quest of meaning and purpose today," writes Georgia L. Lambert in the *Dictionary of Literary Biography.* Lambert continues, "The difficulties of distinguishing between illusion and reality are exemplified by Tennant's often comic, dreamlike narratives and her stunning imagery. Her exploration of the imagination and her depiction of the passing of time show exciting originality, and she is a novelist who is inspiring followers of modern fiction."

Tennant's work defies easy categorization. Some of her novels are considered science fiction, others offer a mock Gothic atmosphere, and still others are indebted to Daniel Defoe, James Hogg, and Robert Louis Stevenson. If any theme unites her fiction, it is the state of decay and disreputability plaguing her society in the wake of its grand empire days. *Times Literary Supplement* contributor Carol Rumens writes: "Large, faded country houses and hotels form an important part of the imaginative terrain of Emma Tennant. They seem to provide a metaphor both for the individual human consciousness and for historical change, particularly as it is played out between the generations." In the *London Review of Books,* Margaret Walters concludes that Tennant "has a caricaturist's skill in pinning down social types, and she brings them together in some splendid farcical set-pieces."

Tennant was born in London, the daughter of a wealthy titled businessman. Her father, Lord Glenconner, was of Scotch descent, but the family had long resided in or near London. Just before the outbreak of World War II, however, Lord Glenconner moved his wife and children to the relative safety of Peebleshire, Scotland, where he owned a manor house. In a piece for the *Contemporary Authors Autobiography Series* (*CAAS*), Tennant describes Glen House, the family seat, as "an unfashionable hideosity . . . with [a] labyrinthine basement, freezing halls, and elaborate staircases." It was there, Tennant continues, that she spent her early childhood. "And it is the landscape, both of those hills and burns and moors and of the inside of this surprising house itself, that informs a great deal of my work."

Thus Tennant grew up under the influence of Scottish fairy tales and legends and was especially inspired by the works of James Hogg, author of *The Confessions of a Justified Sinner.* Tennant writes: "As James Hogg knew—and described—it was only too probable that the idle walker would be transformed into a three-legged stool, or a jay, or maybe even a hare. . . . This taking for granted of the magical and the mundane combined did a great deal to provide inspiration in my later years, when I came to understand that I would be a writer. The tales of possession by the devil, of the sinister double who takes over the *Confessions,* had been my earliest landscape. And it was as far from an English landscape, with its realism and irony, as it would be possible to find."

When Tennant was eight her family moved south again to their more comfortable homes in England. There she was raised in a genteel environment, doing "what was expected of a woman of class." At seventeen she had a formal debut, including a presentation at court. The experiences among high society provided Tennant with grist for her fiction—her first novel, *The Colour of Rain,* was written under the pseudonym Catherine Aydy when she was only twenty-four. Lambert describes the work as "a conventional third-person narrative that depicts the English upper-middle class way of life and shows the artificiality and shallowness in their lives and marriages." *Spectator* contributor Susanna Johnston writes: "Although there is an atmosphere of general malevolence in these 115 pages the novel, at its birth, emerged alive and showing promise (subsequently borne out by the development of Miss Tennant's greater talent) as it shone an unsteady torch onto the spoilt ways of upper-crust high-livers."

More than ten years passed before Tennant published another novel, although she wrote constantly. In 1972 she became acquainted with several of England's notable science fiction writers, including J. G. Ballard, John Sladek, and Michael Moorcock. These authors encouraged Tennant to use science fiction conventions to create surrealistic allegories about the hostile environment she perceived around her. The three novels she wrote between 1972 and 1975—*The Time of the Crack, The Last of the Country House Murders,* and *Hotel de Dream*—all offer portraits of England in crisis in the very near future. In these works, notes Harriet Waugh in *Spectator,* "the forces of reality and imagination are let loose on each other, and intermingle destructively."

Spectator correspondent Paul Ableman characterizes Tennant's three science-fiction works as "funny-satirical phantasies [that] show an increasing sureness of touch culminating in the authentically witty *Hotel de Dream.*" Ableman adds that, for a young author, Tennant "demonstrated an authority over satirical comedy rare in contemporary letters." In *Books and Bookmen,* James Brockway observes that in Tennant's particular brand of science-fiction fantasy, "plenty of old English attitudes get murdered . . . and in her own wittily and elegantly lethal way, too."

Tennant writes in *CAAS* that after 1975, "my preoccupations as a writer had turned almost exclusively to the subject of the female psyche, whether pubescent or mature." In works such as *The Bad Sister, Wild Nights,* and *Woman Beware Woman,* Tennant makes the nature and role of women in society a central theme. While a departure from her earlier science fiction, these works abound in mystical and supernatural phenomena, especially the theme of the "double" and the myths and fairy tales that influence the female subconscious. *Spectator* reviewer Francis King observes that the novels are "primarily about the terrible damage that women can inflict on each other."

The Bad Sister, for instance, concerns a troubled young woman who murders her father and his legitimate daughter. Tennant's story is based on Hogg's *The Confessions of a Justified Sinner,* but she substitutes a female character in the central role and then explores feminism carried to the extreme. In her *Village Voice* review of the novel, Sonia Jaffe Robbins writes that the central character's narrative "is a masterful emotional document, plunging us directly into her mind as she is driven mad by the frag-

mentation women often feel in trying to discover who they are. . . . In this story feminism is no answer, for all it denotes is fanaticism."

Tennant's best-known recent work is her series of comic novels of manners, including *The House of Hospitalities, A Wedding of Cousins,* and *The Adventures of Robina, By Herself: Being the Memoirs of a Debutante at the Court of Queen Elizabeth II.* As the titles suggest, the novels offer a social history of the modern British upper class, sometimes from the point of view of its members and at other times from the point of view of a middle-class observer. *New York Times Book Review* correspondent David Sacks claims that in these satires of postwar British aristocracy, Tennant shows the reader "quite a crew: . . . rogues, boors and dimwits, the prey of pimps and con men, in love with bathroom humor and forever poor-mouthing amid ancestral splendors. Totally mercenary, they nevertheless harbor a medieval disdain for commerce, and so they are the worst gold diggers of all." Sacks adds: "Ms. Tennant knows her subject from the inside, . . . offering cruel insights into the mysteries of the ruling class." In the *Times Literary Supplement,* Patricia Craig contends that with *The House of Hospitalities* and *A Wedding of Cousins,* Tennant "is attempting, and in the course of bringing off, . . . an indictment of upper-class exorbitance." Craig concludes that the works "[bristle] with astuteness and animation."

In addition to her fiction writing, Tennant has served as a magazine writer and as founding editor of *Bananas,* a respected English literary magazine. She has also edited several anthologies of women's writing. Brockway outlines the chief attractions of Tennant's own fiction, namely "the agility and ebullience of the humour, the sense of the absurd in human beings, . . . and, best of all, the stylish verve of the writing." In the *New Statesman,* Sara Maitland notes that, at its best, "Tennant's writing can sustain narrative, without losing its poetic quality." Likewise, Rumens cites Tennant for prose that is both "beautifully measured and graceful." One reads Emma Tennant, Rumens concludes, "for the pure pleasure of the style."

BIOGRAPHICAL/CRITICAL SOURCES:

BOOKS

Contemporary Authors Autobiography Series, Volume 9, Gale, 1989.
Contemporary Literary Criticism, Gale, Volume 13, 1980; Volume 52, 1989.
Dictionary of Literary Biography, Volume 14: *British Novelists since 1960,* Gale, 1983.

PERIODICALS

Books and Bookmen, September, 1975; January, 1977; December, 1982.

Globe & Mail (Toronto), February 16, 1985.
London Review of Books, October 13, 1988.
New Review, March, 1975.
New Statesman, July 28, 1978; September 18, 1987.
New York Review of Books, November 9, 1978.
New York Times Book Review, May 12, 1985; April 3, 1988.
Spectator, February 1, 1975; July 24, 1976; July 22, 1978; September 22, 1979; November 26, 1983; October 10, 1987; March 12, 1988.
Times (London), January 12, 1985; October 8, 1987; January 21, 1989; May 18, 1989.
Times Literary Supplement, June 15, 1973; January 31, 1975; July 16, 1976; July 21, 1978; November 7, 1980; November 19, 1982; November 30, 1984; January 25, 1985; June 21, 1985; September 18-24, 1987; September 30, 1988; June 16-22, 1989.
Village Voice, October 16, 1978.*

—*Sketch by Anne Janette Johnson*

*   *   *

TERKEL, Susan N(eiburg) 1948-

PERSONAL: Born April 7, 1948, in Philadelphia, PA; daughter of Sidney A. (in life insurance) and Deborah (a homemaker; maiden name, Burstein) Neiburg; married Lawrence Arthur Terkel (a business executive); children: Ari, Marni, David. *Education:* Cornell University, B.S., 1970.

ADDRESSES: Home—44 West Case Dr., Hudson, OH 44236. *Agent*—Andrea Brown, P.O. Box 429, El Granada, CA 94018-0429.

CAREER: Writer.

MEMBER: Authors Guild, Authors League of America, Society of Children's Book Writers, National Writers' Union.

WRITINGS:

FOR YOUNG PEOPLE

Yoga Is for Me, Lerner Publications, 1981.
(With Janice E. Rench) *Feeling Safe, Feeling Strong: How to Avoid Sexual Abuse and What to Do If It Happens to You,* Lerner Publications, 1984.
Abortion: Facing the Issue, F. Watts, 1988.
Should Drugs Be Legalized?, F. Watts, 1990.
Honest Abe, Harcourt, 1990.
Understanding Child Custody, F. Watts, 1991.
Ethics, Lodestar, 1992.
All about Allergies, Lodestar, 1992.
Colonial Medicine, F. Watts, in press.
Cancer, F. Watts, in press.

IN RUSSIAN

Alexander Johnson, Ariadne, 1992.
The Last Goodbye, Ariadne, 1992.

WORK IN PROGRESS: Works on nonviolence, women in the military, privacy, and vigilantism.

SIDELIGHTS: Susan N. Terkel once told *CA:* "I can still recall the thrill I got when, at the age of six, I completed the last line of my first story. I told myself, 'Susan, you're a writer now.' That conviction has never wavered." Terkel continued, "I love writing because of the chance I get to create my own world, to rewrite my own past, or to share my views about the real world with others, especially with children. Moreover, I like the work conditions that go along with being a writer—working at home, on my own schedule, never having to face retirement.

"There is a great responsibility, particularly when one is writing for our young people today. While I discovered the truth in writing, especially in fiction, that you cannot manipulate your characters into doing things that they wouldn't do if they were real, I also discovered that it is quite possible to infuse in your characters a sense of hope or sense of despair. I hope my work is evidence that I chose to infuse a sense of hope about the world, whether my book is about sexual abuse survivors or about fantasy. I write to tell each child, each reader, that he or she *can* make a difference in the world."

*   *   *

THOMAS, Lewis 1913-

PERSONAL: Born November 25, 1913, in Flushing, NY; son of Joseph S. (a surgeon) and Grace Emma (Peck) Thomas; married Beryl Dawson, January 1, 1941; children: Abigail, Judith, Eliza. *Education:* Princeton University, B.S., 1933; Harvard University, M.D., 1937.

ADDRESSES: Home—333 East 68th St., New York, NY 10021. *Office*—Memorial Sloan-Kettering Cancer Center, 1275 York Ave., New York, NY 10021.

CAREER: Boston City Hospital, Boston, MA, intern, 1937-39; Neurological Institute, New York City, resident in neurology, 1939-41; Boston City Hospital, Tilney Memorial Fellow at Thorndike Laboratory, 1941-42; Rockefeller Institute for Medical Research, New York City, visiting investigator, 1942-46; Johns Hopkins University, Baltimore, MD, assistant professor of pediatrics, 1946-48; Tulane University, New Orleans, LA, associate professor, 1948-50, professor of medicine, 1950, director of Division of Infectious Disease, 1948-50; University of Minnesota, Minneapolis, professor of pediatrics and medicine and director of pediatric research laboratories at Heart Hospital,

1950-54; New York University, New York City, professor of pathology, 1954-69, head of department, 1954-58, director of University Hospital, 1959-66, dean of School of Medicine, 1966-69; Yale University, New Haven, CT, professor of pathology and head of department, 1969-72, dean of School of Medicine, 1971-73; Memorial Sloan-Kettering Cancer Center, New York City, president and chief executive officer, 1973-80, chancellor, 1980-83, emeritus president and member of Sloan-Kettering Institute, 1983—.

Professor at Cornell University; adjunct professor at Rockefeller University (also member of board of trustees); member of board of overseers of Harvard University, 1976—; member of scientific advisory board of C. V. Whitney Laboratory for Experimental Marine Biology and Medicine, at University of Florida, 1976—; member of council of visitors of Bank Street College of Education, 1975—; associate fellow of Ezra Stiles College, Yale University. Pediatrician at Harriet Lane Home for Invalid Children, of Johns Hopkins University, 1946-48; director of medical divisions at Bellevine Hospital, 1958-66, president of Medical Board, 1963-66; chief of pathology at Yale-New Haven Hospital, 1969-73; attending physician at Memorial Hospital; member of scientific advisory committee of Massachusetts General Hospital, 1969-72; member of scientific advisory board of Scripps Clinic and Research Foundation, 1973-78. Member of board of directors of New York City Public Health Research Institute, 1960-69; member of board of trustees of C. S. Draper Laboratory, 1974—, Cold Spring Harbor Laboratory, 1974—, and Hellenic Anticancer Institute (Athens), 1977—; member of scientific advisory committee of Fox Chase Institute for Cancer Research, 1976—; member of scientific council of International Institute of Cellular and Molecular Pathology (Brussels), 1977—. Member of Commission on Streptococcal and Staphylococcal Diseases, of U.S. Department of Defense's Armed Forces Epidemiological Board, 1950-62; member of New York City Board of Health, 1955-60, and Health Research Council, 1974-75 (head of narcotics advisory committee, 1961-63); member of National Advisory Health Council, 1958-62, and National Advisory Child Health and Human Development Council, 1963-67; member of President's Science Advisory Committee, 1967-70; head of National Academy of Sciences committee to review national cancer plan, 1972; member of special medical advisory group to U.S. Veterans Administration. Member of board of trustees of Guggenheim Foundation, 1975—, and board of directors of Squibb Corp., 1969—, and Josiah Macy, Jr. Foundation, 1975—. *Military service:* U.S. Naval Reserve, Medical Corps, active duty, 1941-46; became lieutenant commander.

MEMBER: International Academy of Pathology, Association of American Physicians, American Academy and Institute of Arts and Letters (inducted, 1984), American Pediatric Society, American Association of Immunologists, Society for Experimental Biology and Medicine, American Academy of Microbiology (charter member), American Rheumatism Association, American Society for Clinical Investigation, National Academy of Sciences Institute of Medicine (member of council, 1973-76), American Philosophical Society, American Academy of Arts and Sciences, American Association of University Professors, Peripatetic Clinical Society, Practitioners Society, Harvey Society, Interurban Clinical Club, Phi Beta Kappa, Alpha Omega Alpha, Century Association, Harvard Club.

AWARDS, HONORS: Honorary degrees include M.A. from Yale University, 1969, Sc.D. from University of Rochester, 1974, Princeton University, 1976, Medical College of Ohio, 1976, and Columbia University, 1978, LL.D. from Johns Hopkins University, 1976, L.H.D. from Duke University, 1976, and Reed College, 1977; National Book Award in Arts and Letters, 1974, for *The Lives of a Cell;* distinguished achievement award from *Modern Medicine,* 1975; visiting scholar of Phi Beta Kappa, 1977-78; American Academy and Institute of Arts and Letters award, 1980; American Book Award for science, 1981, for *The Medusa and the Snail.*

WRITINGS:

The Lives of a Cell: Notes of a Biology Watcher, Viking, 1974.

The Medusa and the Snail: More Notes of a Biology Watcher, Viking, 1979.

The Youngest Science: Notes of a Medicine-Watcher, Viking, 1983.

Late Night Thoughts on Listening to Mahler's Ninth Symphony, Viking, 1984.

CONTRIBUTOR

Rheumatic Fever: A Symposium, University of Minnesota Press, 1952.

Gregory Schwartzman, editor, *The Effects of ACTH and Cortisone Upon Infection and Resistance,* Columbia University Press, 1953.

Russell Cecil and R. F. Loeb, editors, *A Textbook of Medicine,* Saunders, 1953.

H. S. Lawrence, editor, *Cellular and Humoral Aspects of the Hypersensitive States,* Paul B. Hoeber, 1959.

Biological Problems of Grafting, Les Congres et Colloques de L'Universite de Liege, 1959.

Streptococcus, Rheumatic Fever, and Glomerulonephritis, Williams & Wilkins, 1964.

W. Braun and M. Landy, editors, *Bacterial Endotoxins,* Rutgers University, Institute of Microbiology, 1964.

The Inflammatory Process, Academic Press, 1965.

The Modern Hospital, McGraw, 1967.

P. A. Miescher, C. Henze, and R. Schett, editors, *The Modern University: Structure, Functions, and Its Role in the New Industrial State,* Georg Thieme Verlag, 1969.

Microbial Toxins, Volume 3, Academic Press, 1970.

G. I. Gallagher, editor, *Immunological Disorders of the Nervous System,* Williams & Wilkins, 1971.

I. Z. Bowers and E. F. Purcell, editors, *Advances in American Medicine: Essays at the Bicentennial,* Josiah Macy, Jr. Foundation, 1976.

Contributor of a poem to *New Yorker.* Contributor of about two hundred articles to medical and scientific journals, including *Science, Nature, Daedalus,* and *Saturday Review of Science.* Author of column, "Notes of a Biology Watcher," in *New England Journal of Medicine,* 1971—. Member of editorial board of *Human Pathology, Journal of Immunology, American Journal of Pathology, Cellular Immunology, Journal of Medicine and Philosophy, Inflammation, Perspectives in Biology and Medicine, Human Nature, Journal of Developmental and Comparative Immunology,* and *Daedalus.*

SIDELIGHTS: The observation of the natural world has long been Lewis Thomas's vocation and avocation. Although his medical specialty is pathology, Thomas's interest has been captured by the range of natural phenomena from the unit of the cell to human social patterns. In 1971 he began contributing a popular column, "Notes of a Biology Watcher," to the prestigious *New England Journal of Medicine.* Some of these essays were collected and published in 1974 as *The Lives of a Cell: Notes of a Biology Watcher.* The book, which according to a *Time* reviewer combined wit and "imagination" with a "bold, encouraging vision of both man and nature," received a National Book Award the same year. Critics were dazzled with Thomas's accomplishment, but he was somewhat embarrassed by his newfound status as a book author. "I mean it's not really fair to have a book with a cover and everything when you never wrote a book, except in such little tiny bits," he told Barbara Yuncker. "I love having it, but it doesn't seem as though I'd earned it."

Symbiosis—the mutually beneficial relationship between organisms—is the main theme of *The Lives of a Cell.* "There is a tendency for living things to join up," explains Thomas, "establish linkages, live inside each other, return to earlier arrangements, get along whenever possible. This is the way of the world." He decries man's attempt to remove himself from nature, and concludes that "the whole dear notion of one's own self-marvelous old free-willed, free-enterprising, autonomous, independent, isolated island of a Self—is a myth."

New Yorker reviewer John Updike noted that Thomas's "absorption in the marvels of symbiotic interconnection intoxicates this scientist, and leads him into flights of what must be fantasy." Some of his ideas, Updike commented, seem "more mystical than demonstrable." He continued: "Dr. Thomas has the mystic's urge toward total unity. He views the earth as a single cell in its membrane of atmosphere. . . . Not that he professes any use for old-fashioned supernaturalist religion. Yet his doctrine of universal symbiosis soars with an evangelical exultation, and it is interesting that even his careful prose lapses into the grammar of teleology."

In the *New York Times Book Review,* Joyce Carol Oates pondered what tack to take in praising Thomas's work. She remarked: "A reviewer who concentrates upon Dr. Thomas's effortless, beautifully-toned style, even to the point of claiming that many of the twenty-nine essays in this book are masterpieces of the 'art of the essay,' would direct attention away from the sheer amount of scientific information these slender essays contain. A reviewer who deals with the book as 'science' would be forced, by Dr. Thomas's marvelous use of paradox, to admit that the book might not yield its wisdom at a single reading." She continued: "One might as well rise to the higher speculation that [this book] anticipates the kind of writing that will appear more and more frequently, as scientists take on the language of poetry in order to communicate human truths too mysterious for old-fashioned common sense."

Since the publication of *The Lives of a Cell,* more of Thomas's essays have been collected in *The Medusa and the Snail: More Notes of a Biology Watcher, The Youngest Science: Notes of a Medicine-Watcher,* and *Late Night Thoughts on Listening to Mahler's Ninth Symphony.* Barbara Brotman writes in the *Chicago Tribune* of *The Medusa and the Snail,* "Despite all his intense concentration through powerful microscopes at minute particles of life, Thomas never has stopped marveling at the Big Picture, how well everything on this Earth works: the civility of the symbiotic relationship between the sea slug and the jellyfish or medusa, the subject of the title essay, the mysterious way warts can actually be *thought* away, the almost always accurate pinpointing and destruction by our antibodies of foreign cells."

Many of Thomas's essays end on an upbeat note. The title essay of *The Lives of a Cell* succinctly expresses Thomas's perception of man's place in the universe and his belief in the continued existence of that universe. He wrote: "We are told that the trouble with Modern Man is that he has been trying to detach himself from nature. He sits on the topmost tiers of polymer, glass, and steel, dangling his pulsing legs, surveying at a distance the writhing life of the planet. In this scenario, Man comes on as a stupendous lethal force, and the earth is pictured as something delicate, like rising bubbles at the surface of a country pond, or flights of fragile birds. But it is an illusion to think that there is anything fragile about the life of the earth; surely this is the toughest membrane imaginable in the universe, opaque to probability, impermeable to death. We are the delicate part, transient and vulnerable as cilia."

BIOGRAPHICAL/CRITICAL SOURCES:

BOOKS

Contemporary Literary Criticism, Volume 35, Gale, 1985.
Thomas, Lewis, *The Lives of a Cell: Notes of a Biology Watcher,* Viking, 1974.

PERIODICALS

Chicago Tribune, July 11, 1979.
Detroit News, May 27, 1979.
Newsweek, June 24, 1974.
New Yorker, July 15, 1974.
New York Post, June 29, 1974.
New York Review of Books, November 28, 1974.
New York Times, April 27, 1979; February 9, 1983; November 5, 1983.
New York Times Book Review, May 26, 1974.
Time, July 22, 1974; May 14, 1979.
Village Voice, June 27, 1974.
Washington Post, August 28, 1979; September 1, 1979.*

* * *

THOMPSON, Jacqueline 1945-

PERSONAL: Born December 4, 1945, in Morristown, NJ; daughter of Bernard Lee Thompson (an advertising executive) and Dorothy Bischoff Hussa. *Education:* Barnard College, B.A., 1969. *Religion:* Protestant.

ADDRESSES: Home and office—10 Bay St. Landing, 7F, St. George, Staten Island, NY 10301.

CAREER: American Bureau of Shipping, New York City, editorial assistant, 1969-70; Peat, Marwick, Mitchell & Co., New York City, editor and writer, 1970-73; free-lance writer and editor, 1973-91; Donaldson, Lufkin & Jeurette, New York City, editor, 1991—. Part-time public relations consultant for Alan Towers Associates, 1976-82, and Carl Byoir Associates, 1983-84.

MEMBER: American Society of Journalists and Authors, New York Macintosh Users' Group.

WRITINGS:

(Contributor) William Albrecht, *Economics* (textbook), Prentice-Hall, 1974.
(Contributor) Daniel T. Pollitoske, *Music* (textbook with study guide, workbook and demonstration record), Prentice-Hall, 1974.

(Contributor) Harold H. Frank, editor, *Women in the Organization,* University of Pennsylvania Press, 1977.
(Compiler and editor) *Directory of Personal Image Consultants,* Editorial Services, 1978-85.
(Contributor) *What to Do with the Rest of Your Life: The Catalyst Career Guide for Women in the '80s,* Simon & Schuster, 1980.
The Very Rich Book: America's Supermillionaires and Their Money—Where They Got It, How They Spend It, Morrow, 1981.
(Editor) *Image Impact: The Aspiring Woman's Personal Packaging Program* (anthology), A & W Publishers, 1981, revised edition published as *Image Impact: The Complete Makeover Guide,* Bristol Books, 1990.
Upward Mobility: A Comprehensive Career Advancement Plan for Women Determined to Succeed in the Working World, Holt, 1982.
Future Rich: The People, Companies and Industries Creating America's Next Fortunes, Morrow, 1985.
(Ghostwriter) J. Nicholson and J. Lewis-Crum, *Color Wonderful: The Revolutionary Color 1 Wardrobe and Makeup Program,* Bantam, 1986.
(Editor) *Image Impact for Men: The Business and Professional Man's Personal Packaging Program* (anthology), Dodd, 1985.
(Ghostwriter) Kenneth Cooper and Mildred Cooper, *The New Aerobics for Women,* Bantam, 1988.
(Ghostwriter) Neil Gordon and Larry Gibbons, *The Cooper Clinic Cardiac Rehabilitation Program,* Simon & Schuster, 1990.
(With Irwin Rosenberg and William Evans) *Biomarkers: The 10 Determinants of Aging You Can Control,* Simon and Schuster, 1991.
(Ghostwriter) Neil Gordon, *The Cooper Clinic Rehabilitation Program for People with . . .* (five book series on diabetes, arthritis, C.F.S., stroke and C.O.P.D.), Human Kinetics, 1992.

Author of scripts for *Family Health News,* WPIX-TV, 1976. Also author of promotional brochures. Contributor of more than seventy feature articles to magazines, including *Us, New York, Gentlemen's Quarterly, Ms., Parade, Working Woman* and *Financial World.*

* * *

THOMPSON, Paul (Richard) 1935-

PERSONAL: Born August 20, 1935, in England; married Thea Vigne; married Natasha Burchardt; children: (first marriage) Stephen, Sarah; (second marriage) Esther. *Education:* Corpus Christi College, Oxford, M.A., 1958; Queen's College, Oxford, D.Phil., 1964.

ADDRESSES: Office—Department of Sociology, University of Essex, Wivenhoe Park, Colchester CO4 3SQ, England.

CAREER: Oxford University, Queen's College, Oxford, England, junior research fellow, 1961-64; University of Essex, Colchester, England, lecturer, 1964-69, senior lecturer in social history, 1969-71, reader, 1971-88, research professor, 1988—. Senior research fellow, Nuffield College, Oxford University, 1968-69; visiting professor, Johns Hopkins University, 1972; Hoffman Wood Professor of Architecture, University of Leeds, 1977-78; director, National Life Story Collection at the National Sound Archive, 1988—.

WRITINGS:

Architecture: Art or Social Service?, Fabian Society, 1963.
(With Peter Kidson and Peter Murray) *A History of English Architecture,* Penguin, 1965, revised edition, 1978.
(Editor) *Close to the Wind: Memoirs of Admiral Sir William Creswell,* Heinemann, 1965.
High Victorian Cultural Achievement, Victorian Society, 1966.
(Editor) *Victorian Rural England,* Victorian Society, 1967.
Socialists, Liberals, and Labour: The Struggle for London, 1885-1914, University of Toronto Press, 1967.
The Work of William Morris, Viking, 1967, 3rd edition, Oxford University Press, 1991.
(Editor) *Victorian Seaport: Liverpool,* Victorian Society, 1969.
(Editor) *Design, 1860-1960,* Victorian Society, 1970.
William Butterfield: Victorian Architect, M.I.T. Press, 1971.
The Edwardians: The Remaking of British Society, Indiana University Press, 1975, 2nd edition, Routledge & Kegan Paul, 1992.
The Voice of the Past: Oral History, Oxford University Press, 1978, 2nd edition, 1988.
(With Gina Harkell) *The Victorians in Photographs,* Holmes & Meier, 1979.
(Editor with Natasha Burchardt) *Our Common History: The Transformation of Europe,* Humanities, 1982.
Living with Fishing, Routledge & Kegan Paul, 1983.
(With Rupert Samuel) *The Myths We Live By,* Routledge & Kegan Paul, 1990.
I Don't Feel Old: The Experience of Later Life, Oxford University Press, 1990.

OTHER

(With Michael Drake) *Memory and History* (recording), Harper, 1974.

Editor, *Victorian Society Conference Reports,* 1963-66, *Oral History,* 1971—, *Life Stories,* 1985-89, and *International Yearbook of Oral History and Life Stories,* 1992—.

BIOGRAPHICAL/CRITICAL SOURCES:

PERIODICALS

Times Literary Supplement, October 26, 1990, p. 1148.

*   *   *

TOLZMANN, Don Heinrich   1945-

PERSONAL: Born August 12, 1945, in Granite Falls, MN; son of Eckhart Heinrich and Pearl (Lundeberg) Tolzmann; married Patricia Ann Himebaugh, March 20, 1971; children: Anna Maria Patricia. *Education:* University of Minnesota, B.A., 1968; Northwestern Lutheran Theological Seminary, graduate study, 1968-71; United Theological Seminary, M.Div., 1972; University of Kentucky, M.A., 1973; University of Cincinnati, Ph.D., 1983. *Religion:* Lutheran.

ADDRESSES: Home—3418 Boudinot Ave., Cincinnati, OH 45211. *Office*—Langsam Library M.L. 33, University of Cincinnati, Cincinnati, OH 45221.

CAREER: University of Cincinnati, Central Library, Cincinnati, OH, 1974—, began as reference librarian and bibliographer, currently senior librarian and director of the German-American Studies Program. Delegate, White House Conference on Ethnicity and the 1980 Census, 1976.

MEMBER: Society for German-American Studies, American Library Association, Immigration History Society, American Historical Association, American Association of Teachers of German, Ohio German Heritage Council.

AWARDS, HONORS: Citation of honor, State of Minnesota, 1972; citation of appreciation, President of the United States, 1972; certificate of merit from Society for German-American Studies, 1973; Tricentennial Medal, Goethe House New York at the University of Cincinnati, 1983; Friendship Award, Federal Republic of Germany, 1986; Ohioana Book Award, 1988; Baldwin-Wallace College Award for Academic Excellence, 1989; German-American of the Year Award, 1989; Bundesverdienstkreuz, Federal Republic of Germany, 1991.

WRITINGS:

German Americana: A Bibliography, Scarecrow, 1975.
America's German Heritage: Bicentennial Minutes, German-American National Congress, 1976.
German-American Literature, Scarecrow, 1977.

Festschrift for the German-American Tricentennial Jubilee: Cincinnati 1983, Cincinnati Historical Society, 1982.

The Cincinnati Germans after the Great War, Verlag Peter Lang, 1987.

The First Description of Cincinnati and Other Ohio Settlements, University Press of America, 1988.

Spring Grove and Its Creator, Ohio Book Store, 1988.

The Catalog of the German-Americana Collection, University of Cincinnati, K. G. Saur, 1990.

The First Mayor of Cincinnati, University Press of America, 1990.

Germany and America, 1450-1700, Heritage House, Inc., 1991.

Editor of "German American Poetry" series. Associate editor of *Journal of German-American Studies,* 1974-80, and *German-American Genealogist,* 1975-76; editor of *Zeitschrift fuer deutschamerikanische literatur,* 1974-78, and *Bulletin of the Society for German-American Studies,* 1977-79.

WORK IN PROGRESS: German-Americana: An Information Guide.

SIDELIGHTS: Don Heinrich Tolzmann told *CA:* "The German-Americana Collection at the University of Cincinnati Blegen Library was established in 1974 and is the nation's largest such collection. It consists of books, pamphlets, documents, journals, and manuscripts of special value to students, scholars, researchers, and the general public interested in the history, literature, and culture of the German-American element. The catalog provides access to the richest and strongest collection of German-Americana in the United States."

*   *   *

TONKIN, Humphrey 1939-

PERSONAL: Born December 2, 1939, in Truro, England; son of George (a businessman) and Lorna (Sandry) Tonkin; married S. Julie Winberg, March 9, 1968; married Jane S. Edwards, October 1, 1983; children: one son, one stepdaughter. *Education:* St. John's College, Cambridge, B.A., 1962, M.A., 1966; Harvard University, A.M. and Ph.D., 1966.

ADDRESSES: Home—85 Bloomfield Ave., Hartford, CT 06105. *Office*—Office of the President, University of Hartford, West Hartford, CT 06117.

CAREER: University of Pennsylvania, Philadelphia, assistant professor, 1966-71, associate professor, 1971-80, professor of English, 1980-83, vice-provost for undergraduate studies, 1972-75, coordinator of international programs, 1976-83, master of Stouffer College House, 1980-83; State University of New York College at Potsdam, president, 1983-88; University of Hartford, West Hartford, CT, president and chancellor of university, 1989—. Visiting professor of English and comparative literature at Columbia University, 1980-81. President, Northern Advanced Technologies Corp., 1984-88; chairperson, Center for Research and Documentation on World Language Problems, Rotterdam and New York, 1983—, Council for the International Exchange of Scholars, 1991—, and Partnership for Service-Learning, 1991—. Member of board, American Forum for Global Education, World Affairs Council of Connecticut, Greater Hartford Arts Council, and Hartford Symphony Orchestra. Former member of board of directors of Pennsylvania Council on International Education and World Affairs Council of Philadelphia.

MEMBER: International Studies Association, Universal Esperanto Association (president, 1974-80, 1986-89; United Nations representative, 1974—), Esperanto Academy, Esperantic Studies Foundation (president, 1991—), Modern Language Association of America, Milton Society of America, Renaissance Society of America, American Council on the Teaching of Foreign Languages, American Comparative Literature Association, Spenser Society (president, 1983-84).

AWARDS, HONORS: Guggenheim fellow, 1975.

WRITINGS:

(Editor) *Sir Walter Ralegh, 1900-1968: Elizabethan Bibliographies Supplements,* Nether Press, 1971.

Spenser's Courteous Pastoral, Clarendon Press, 1972.

(Translator into Esperanto) A. A. Milne, *Winnie-la-pu,* Dutton, 1972.

(Editor) *Esperanto and International Language Problems: A Research Bibliography,* Esperantic Studies Foundation, 1972, 4th edition, 1977.

(With Jane Edwards) *The World in the Curriculum: Curricular Strategies for the Twenty-first Century,* Change Magazine, 1981.

(Contributor) Desmond Fisher and L. S. Harms, editors, *The Right to Communicate: A New Human Right,* Boole Press, 1983.

(Contributor) Francis G. Greco, editor, *Spenser at Kalamazoo 1983,* Clarion University of Pennsylvania, 1983.

(Contributor) George Gerbner and Marsha Siefert, editors, *World Communications: A Handbook,* Longman, 1984.

(Contributor) John M. Darcey, editor, *The Language Teacher: Commitment and Collaboration,* Northeast Conference on the Teaching of Foreign Languages, 1987.

(Contributor) *Serta Gratulatoria in Honorem Juan Regulo,* Volume 2, Universidad de la Laguna, 1987.

The Faerie Queene, Unwin Hyman, 1989.

(Editor with Allison Armstrong Keef) *Language in Religion,* University Press of America, 1989.

(Contributor) Richard K. Greenfield, editor, *Developing International Education Programs,* Jossey-Bass, 1990.

(Contributor) A. C. Hamilton, editor, *The Spenser Encyclopedia,* University of Toronto Press, 1990.

Contributor to *Seventeenth Century News, Comparative Literature Studies, Ohio Review, Centennial Review, Language and Style, PMLA, Modern Philology, Studies in English Literature, World Literature Today, ADFL Bulletin, Language in Society, Journal of Communication, Higher Education Policy, Geolinguistics Language Monthly, Basic Education,* and *Translation Review.* Contributing bibliographer, *MLA International Bibliography,* 1980—. Editor, *International Education Review,* 1978-82, *Esperanto Document,* 1974-89, and *Language Problems and Language Planning.*

WORK IN PROGRESS: Fifth edition of *Esperanto and International Language Problems;* edited volume of Esperanto and interlinguistics.

*   *   *

TOTMAN, Conrad 1934-

PERSONAL: Born January 5, 1934, in Conway, MA; son of Raymond S. (a farmer) and Mildred (Kingsbury) Totman; married Michiko Ikegami (a bilingual teacher), February 10, 1958; children: Kathleen, Christopher. *Education:* University of Massachusetts, B.A., 1958; Harvard University, M.A., 1960, Ph.D., 1964.

ADDRESSES: Home—Northford, CT *Office*—Department of History, Yale University, New Haven, CT 06520.

CAREER: University of California, Santa Barbara, assistant professor of history, 1964-66; Northwestern University, Evanston, IL, assistant professor, 1966-68, associate professor, 1968-72, professor of history, 1972-84, chairman of department, 1977-80; Yale University, New Haven, CT, professor of history, 1984—, acting chair, department of history, 1990-91. Chairman of Council for East Asian Studies, 1985-88. *Military service:* U.S. Army, 1953-56.

MEMBER: Association for Asian Studies (chairman of Northeast Asia Council; member of executive committee, 1978-80; president, New England Conference, 1985-86), Forest History Society.

AWARDS, HONORS: Woodrow Wilson Fellowship; Fulbright grant; National Endowment for the Humanities senior fellow; Japan Foundation fellow.

WRITINGS:

Politics in the Tokugawa Bakufu, 1600-1843, Harvard University Press, 1968.

The Collapse of Tokugawa Bakufu, 1862-1868, University Press of Hawaii, 1980.

Japan before Perry, University of California Press, 1981.

Tokugawa Ieyasu: Shogun, Heian International, 1983.

The Origins of Japan's Modern Forests, University of Hawaii Press, 1985.

The Green Archipelago: Forestry in Preindustrial Japan, University of California, 1989.

Early Modern Japan: 1568-1868, University of California, in press.

Contributor to Asian studies journals.

WORK IN PROGRESS: Japan: A History.

*   *   *

TOULSON, Shirley 1924-

PERSONAL: Born May 20, 1924, in Henley-on-Thames, England; daughter of Douglas Horsfall Dixon (a writer) and Marjorie Brown; married Alan Brownjohn, February 6, 1960 (divorced March, 1969); children: Janet Sayers, Ian Toulson, Steven Brownjohn. *Education:* Birkbeck College, London, B.A., 1953.

ADDRESSES: Home—16 Priest Row Wells, Somerset, England. *Agent*—Bruce Hunter, David Higham Associates, 5-8 Lower John St., Golden Sq., London W1R 4HA, England.

CAREER: Writer. Features editor of *Teacher* (journal of National Union of Teachers), 1967-70; editor of *Child Education,* 1970-74. Teacher of creative writing for adults.

WRITINGS:

Shadows in an Orchard (poems), Scorpion Press, 1960.

Circumcision's Not Such a Bad Thing after All and Other Poems, Keepsake Press, 1970.

All Right, Auden, I Know You're There: A Quick Thought (poems), Offcut Press, 1970.

For a Double Time (poems), Sceptre Press, 1970.

The Fault, Dear Brutus: A Zodiac of Sonnets, Keepsake Press, 1972.

Education in Britain, M. Evans, 1974.

Farm Museums and Farm Parks, Shire Publications, 1977.

(With Fay Godwin) *Drovers' Roads of Wales,* Wildwood House, 1977.

(With John Loveday) *Bones and Angels* (poems), Mid-Day Publications, 1978.

East Anglia: Walking the Leylines and Ancient Tracks, Wildwood House, 1979.

The Drovers, Shire Publications, 1980.

Derbyshire: Exploring the Ancient Tracks and Mysteries of Mercia, Wildwood House, 1980.

The Winter Solstice, Jill Norman & Hobhouse, 1981.

The Moors of the Southwest, Hutchinson, Volume 1, 1983, Volume 2, 1984.

The Mendip Hills: A Threatened Landscape, Gollancz, 1984.

Celtic Journeys, Scotland and the North of England, Hutchinson, 1985.

The Celtic Alternative, Century Hutchinson, 1987.

Walking Round Wales: The Giraldus Journey, Michael Joseph, 1988.

The Companion Guide to Devon, Harper/Collins, 1991.

EDITOR

The Remind-Me Hat and Other Stories (juvenile), M. Evans, 1973.

Dickens, S. Low, 1977.

Kipling, S. Low, 1977.

Milton, S. Low, 1977.

Shakespeare, S. Low, 1977.

WORK IN PROGRESS: A further book about the Celtic church in Britain from the third to the eighth centuries; a county history of Somerset; "I have also worked on a further book on the Welsh drovers' roads, and a study of the Devon/Somerset Blackdown Hills."

SIDELIGHTS: Shirley Toulson told *CA:* "Apart from the social history of the British countryside, my main interest is in contemporary English and American verse. More recently I have been working on the history of the early Celtic church and the places associated with it in Ireland, Scotland, Wales, and the south-west peninsula."

*　　　*　　　*

TRAHERNE, Michael
See WATKINS-PITCHFORD, Denys James

*　　　*　　　*

TREASE, (Robert) Geoffrey 1909-

PERSONAL: Born August 11, 1909, in Nottingham, England; son of George Albert (a wine merchant) and Florence (Dale) Trease; married Marian Haselden Granger Boyer (a teacher), August 11, 1933 (died, 1989); children: Jocelyn Heather (Mrs. Norman Payne). *Education:* Attended Queen's College, Oxford, 1928-29. *Politics:* "Non-partisan, but keenly interested." *Religion:* Church of England. *Avocational interests:* Walking, theater.

ADDRESSES: Home—1 Yomede Park, Newbridge Rd., Bath, Avon BA1 3LS, England. *Agent*— Murray Pollinger, 222 Old Brompton Road, London SW5 0BZ, England.

CAREER: Journalist and social worker in London, England, 1929-32; Clacton-on-Sea, Essex, England, teacher, 1932-33; full-time writer, 1933—. Lecturer on children's literature. *Military service:* British Army, 1942-46; served in India.

MEMBER: Society of Authors (chairman, 1972-73; member of council, 1974—; chairman of children's writers' group, 1963-64, 1968-70), PEN, National Book League, Royal Society of Literature (fellow).

AWARDS, HONORS: Welwyn Festival Award (England), 1939, for *After the Tempest* (play); *New York Herald Tribune* Spring Book Festival Award for Nonfiction, 1966, for *This Is Your Century.*

WRITINGS:

FOR YOUNG PEOPLE; FICTION

Bows against the Barons, illustrations by Michael Boland, International Publishers, 1934, revised edition illustrated by C. Walter Hodges, Meredith Press, 1966.

Comrades for the Charter, illustrations by Boland, Lawrence & Wishart, 1934, revised edition illustrated by Douglas Phillips, Brockhampton Press, 1972.

The Call to Arms, International Publishers, 1935.

Missing from Home, illustrations by Scott, Lawrence & Wishart, 1936.

Red Comet, illustrations by Fred Ellis, Co-operative Publishing Society of Foreign Workers (Moscow), 1936, published in England as *Red Comet: A Tale of Travel in the U.S.S.R.,* Lawrence & Wishart, 1937.

The Christmas Holiday Mystery, illustrations by Alfred Sindall, A. & C. Black, 1937, reprinted as *The Lakeland Mystery,* 1942.

Mystery on the Moors, illustrations by Sindall, A. & C. Black, 1937.

Detectives of the Dales, illustrations by A. C. H. Gorham, A. & C. Black, 1938.

In the Land of the Mogul: A Story of the East India Company's First Venture in India, illustrations by J. C. B. Knight, Basil Blackwell, 1938.

North Sea Spy, Fore, 1939.

Cue for Treason, illustrations by Beatrice Goldsmith, Basil Blackwell, 1940, illustrations by L. F. Grant, Vanguard Press, 1941.

Running Deer, illustrations by W. Lindsay Cable, Harrap, 1941, published as *The Running of the Deer,* illustrations by Maureen Bradley, Hamish Hamilton, 1982.

The Grey Adventurer, illustrations by Goldsmith, Basil Blackwell, 1942.

Black Night, Red Morning, illustrations by Donia Nachsen, Basil Blackwell, 1944.

Army without Banners, Fore, 1945.

Trumpets in the West, illustrations by Joe Krush, Harcourt, 1947, English edition illustrated by Alan Blyth, Basil Blackwell, 1947.

Silver Guard, illustrations by Blyth, Basil Blackwell, 1948.

The Hills of Varna, illustrations by Treyer Evans, Macmillan, 1948, published as *Shadow of the Hawk,* illustrations by Krush, Harcourt, 1949.

The Mystery of Moorside Farm, illustrations by Blyth, Basil Blackwell, 1949.

No Boats on Bannermere, illustrations by Richard Kennedy, Heinemann, 1949, Norton, 1965.

The Secret Fiord, illustrations by H. M. Brock, Macmillan, 1949, illustrations by Krush, Harcourt, 1950.

Under Black Banner, illustrations by Kennedy, Heinemann, 1950.

Web of Traitors: An Adventure Story of Ancient Athens, Vanguard Press, 1952, published in England as *The Crown of Violet,* illustrations by Hodges, Macmillan, 1952.

The Barons' Hostage: A Story of Simon de Montfort, illustrations by Alan Jessett, Phoenix House, 1952, revised edition, Brockhampton Press, 1973, Thomas Nelson, 1975.

Black Banner Players, illustrations by Kennedy, Heinemann, 1952.

The New House at Hardale, Lutterworth, 1953.

The Silken Secret, illustrations by Jessett, Basil Blackwell, 1953, Vanguard Press, 1954.

Black Banner Abroad, Heinemann, 1954, Warne, 1955.

(Editor) *Six of the Best: Stories,* Basil Blackwell, 1955.

The Fair Flower of Danger, Basil Blackwell, 1955.

Message to Hadrian, Vanguard Press, 1956, published in England as *Word to Caesar,* illustrations by Geoffrey Whittam, Macmillan, 1956.

The Gates of Bannerdale, Heinemann, 1956, Warne, 1957.

Escape to King Alfred, Vanguard Press, 1958, published in England as *Mist over Athelney,* illustrations by R. S. Sherriffs and J. L. Stockle, Macmillan, 1958.

The Maythorn Story, illustrations by Robert Hodgson, Heinemann, 1960.

Thunder of Valmy, illustrations by John S. Goodall, Macmillan, 1960, published as *Victory at Valmy,* Vanguard Press, 1961.

Change at Maythorn, illustrations by Hodgson, Heinemann, 1962.

Follow My Black Plume, illustrations by Brian Wildsmith, Vanguard Press, 1963.

A Thousand for Sicily, illustrations by Wildsmith, Vanguard Press, 1964.

The Dutch Are Coming, illustrations by Lynette Hemmant, Hamish Hamilton, 1965.

Bent Is the Bow, illustrations by Charles Keeping, Thomas Nelson, 1965.

The Red Towers of Granada, illustrations by Keeping, Macmillan, 1966, Vanguard Press, 1967.

The White Nights of St. Petersburg, illustrations by William Stobbs, Vanguard Press, 1967.

The Runaway Serf, illustrations by Mary Russon, Hamish Hamilton, 1968.

A Masque for the Queen, illustrations by Krystyna Turska, Hamish Hamilton, 1970.

Horsemen on the Hills, Macmillan, 1971.

A Ship to Rome, illustrations by Leslie Atkinson, Heinemann, 1972.

A Voice in the Night, illustrations by Sara Silcock, Heinemann, 1973.

Popinjay Stairs: A Historical Adventure about Samuel Pepys, Macmillan, 1973, Vanguard Press, 1982.

The Chocolate Boy, illustrations by David Walker, Heinemann, 1975.

The Iron Tsar, Macmillan, 1975.

When the Drums Beat, illustrations by Janet Marsh, Heinemann, 1976, revised edition published as *When the Drums Beat and Other Stories,* Pan Books, 1979.

Violet for Bonaparte, Macmillan, 1976.

The Seas of Morning, illustrations by David Smee, Penguin, 1976.

The Spy Catchers, illustrations by Geoffrey Bargery, Hamish Hamilton, 1976.

The Field of the Forty Footsteps, Macmillan, 1977.

The Claws of the Eagle, illustrations by Ionicus, Heinemann, 1977.

Mandeville, Macmillan, 1980.

A Wood by Moonlight, and Other Stories, Chatto & Windus, 1981.

Saraband for Shadows, Macmillan, 1982.

The Cormorant Venture, Macmillan, 1984.

Tomorrow Is a Stranger, Heinemann, 1987.

The Arpino Assignment, illustrations by Paul Leith, Walker Books, 1988.

A Flight of Angels, illustrations by Eric Stemp, Macmillan, 1988, Lerner Publications, 1989.

Hidden Treasure, illustrations by Chris Molan, Lodestar, 1989.

Shadow under the Sea, Walker Books, 1990.

Calabrian Quest, Walker Books, 1990.

Aunt Augusta's Elephant, illustrations by Jean Foster, Macmillan, 1991.

FOR YOUNG PEOPLE; NONFICTION

Fortune, My Foe: The Story of Sir Walter Raleigh, illustrations by Norman Meredith, Methuen, 1949, published as *Sir Walter Raleigh, Captain and Adventurer,* Vanguard Press, 1950.

The Young Traveller in India and Pakistan, Phoenix House, 1949, published as *The Young Traveler in India and Pakistan,* Dutton, 1956.

Enjoying Books (part of "Excursion Series for Young People"), Phoenix House, 1951, revised edition, 1963.

(Translator) Guillot, *Companions of Fortune,* illustrations by Pierre Collot, Oxford University Press, 1952.

The Young Traveler in England and Wales, Dutton, 1953.

The Seven Queens of England, Vanguard Press, 1953.

(Translator) Rene Guillot, *The King's Corsair,* illustrations by Pierre Rousseau, Oxford University Press, 1953.

Seven Kings of England, illustrations by Atkinson, Vanguard Press, 1955.

The Young Traveller in Greece, Phoenix House, 1955, published as *The Young Traveler in Greece,* Dutton, 1956.

Edward Elgar: Maker of Music, Macmillan, 1959.

Wolfgang Mozart: The Young Composer, Macmillan, 1961, St. Martin's, 1962.

The Young Writer: A Practical Handbook, illustrations by Carl Hollander, Thomas Nelson, 1961.

Seven Stages, Heinemann, 1964, Vanguard Press, 1965.

This Is Your Century, Harcourt, 1965.

Seven Sovereign Queens, Heinemann, 1968, Vanguard Press, 1969.

Byron: A Poet Dangerous to Know, Holt, 1969.

The Phoenix and the Flame: D. H. Lawrence, a Biography, Viking, 1973, published in England as *D. H. Lawrence: The Phoenix and the Flame,* Macmillan, 1973.

Days to Remember: A Garland of Historic Anniversaries, illustrations by Joanna Troughton, Heinemann, 1973.

Britain Yesterday, illustrations by Hodgson, Basil Blackwell, 1975.

Timechanges: The Evolution of Everyday Life, Kingfisher Books, 1985, Watts, 1986.

Living through History: The Edwardian Era, Batsford, 1986.

Hidden Treasure, illustrations by Molan, Hamish Hamilton, 1989.

FOR ADULTS; FICTION

The Unsleeping Sword (short stories), Lawrence, 1934.

Such Divinity (novel), Chapman & Hall, 1939.

Clem Voroshilov: The Red Marshal, Pilot Press, 1940.

Only Natural (novel), Chapman & Hall, 1940.

Snared Nightingale (novel), Macmillan, 1957, Vanguard Press, 1958.

So Wild the Heart (novel), Macmillan, 1958, Vanguard Press, 1959.

FOR ADULTS; NONFICTION

Walking in England, Fenland, 1935.

Tales Out of School: A Survey of Children's Fiction, Heinemann, 1949, revised edition, Heinemann Educational, 1964.

The Italian Story: From the Etruscans to Modern Times, Vanguard Press, 1963, published as *The Italian Story: From the Earliest Times to 1946,* Macmillan, 1964.

The Grand Tour, Holt, 1967.

(Editor) *Matthew Todd's Journal: A Gentleman's Gentleman in Europe, 1814-1820,* Heinemann, 1968.

The Condottieri: Soldiers of Fortune, Thames & Hudson, 1970.

Nottingham: A Biography, Macmillan, 1970.

A Whiff of Burnt Boats: An Early Autobiography, St. Martin's, 1971.

Samuel Pepys and His World, Putnam, 1972.

Laughter at the Door: A Continued Autobiography, St. Martin's, 1974.

London: A Concise History, Scribner, 1975.

Portrait of a Cavalier: William Cavendish, First Duke of Newcastle, Taplinger, 1979.

PLAYS

The Dragon Who Was Different, and Other Plays (juvenile: includes "The Dragon Who Was Different," "The Mighty Mandarin," "Fairyland Limited," and "The New Bird"), Muller, 1938.

After the Tempest (one-act), first produced in Welwyn, Hertfordshire, 1938, produced in London, 1939, published in *Best One-Act Plays of 1938,* edited by J. W. Marriott, Harrap, 1939.

Colony, first produced at Unity Theatre, London, 1939.

The Shadow of Spain, and Other Plays (juvenile; includes "The Shadow of Spain," "The Unquiet Cloister," and "Letters of Gold"), Basil Blackwell, 1953.

Time Out of Mind, first produced on BBC television, January 1, 1959, produced at Comedy Theatre, London, 1967.

Also author of teleplay *Into Thin Air,* 1973; author of radio plays *Mr. Engels of Manchester 'Change,* 1947, *Henry Irving,* 1947, *Lady Anne,* 1949, *The Real Mr. Ryecroft,* 1949, and *Elgar of England,* 1957.

OTHER

Contributor to periodicals, including *Times Literary Supplement, Times Educational Supplement, Horn Book, Junior Bookshelf,* and *Author.* Trease's books have been published in more than twenty countries, including France, Germany, Russia, Estonia, Poland, Romania, Spain, Portugal, Italy, Greece, Israel, Norway, Sweden, Denmark,

Iceland, Holland, and Japan. Author's manuscripts are included in collections in the Nottingham Central Library (England), University of Nottingham Library, and the Kerlan Collection, University of Minnesota.

ADAPTATIONS: Popinjay Stairs was adapted into radio play format and produced for BBC radio in 1973. *Cue for Treason* was adapted for the stage by David Craig and produced by Toronto Young People's Theatre, Canada, 1986.

SIDELIGHTS: "To survey the work of Geoffrey Trease is to write the history of children's books in England for the past fifty-odd years," writes educational author Margaret Meek in her critical study entitled *Geoffrey Trease.* With over one hundred publications now to his credit, and an unflagging dedication to raising the standards of children's literature, Trease indeed looms large in the estimation of educators, critics, and young readers of historical fiction. As one of the first twentieth century children's writers to approach the historical adventure genre seriously, Trease is noted for investing his novels with a strong sense of both historic period and place. His novels have been a source of entertainment for countless people, and his love of the past has motivated many of his young readers to learn more about history.

Trease grew up in Nottingham, England, near Sherwood Forest, home to the legendary Robin Hood. The history and legend of the area captured his boyish imagination, and sparked an early love of history. Trease was further inspired by his teachers at Nottingham High School to excel at academics. At thirteen, his efforts were rewarded when he received a junior scholarship which brought pressure upon him to abandon history and concentrate his studies in Latin and Greek. "I was bitter and rebellious, but I came to see the event as a blessing, very heavily disguised," he later reflected in *Something about the Author Autobiography Series* (*SAAS*). "For nothing could kill my love of history and it is a line of interest you can always follow for yourself, as I have done ever since." "On the other hand," Trease later commented pragmatically, "if I'd continued with my favorite subject, I might have gone straight into academic history—all documents and economics. I probably stopped at the right age for a future adventure story writer."

Before leaving school, Trease won another scholarship, this time to Queen's College, Oxford. Despite his love of academics, Trease resigned his scholarship after only one year. "I had gone to Oxford with the common sense realization that it might not be easy to earn a living as a writer. I was very much attracted to teaching as a second choice. If I'd taken my degree, I'd probably have grumbled for the rest of my teaching life that I hadn't been able to write as many books as I'd wanted." After leaving school, Trease

moved to the East End of London and worked as a social worker for a local youth club, and then went on to work as a publicity journalist. "But I never forgot my determination to become an author," he wrote in *SAAS*. "I finished an eighty-thousand word novel and started sending it round the publishers. Monotonously it came back with a rejection slip, a dozen times. Meanwhile, I was . . . selling small articles to lesser magazines and newspapers, and two obscure newspapers even allowed me to review books. Then—unforgettable moment!—a publisher (I feel sure he was the thirteenth) accepted the novel. A contract was signed. Within a few months my trembling fingers held his new autumn catalogue of forthcoming books, and there was a flattering paragraph about mine. After another few months came the news that the publishing company had gone bankrupt. My book never appeared. My typescript was sent back to me, tattered and dog-eared. For a little while it was like the end of the world."

Trease eventually became a teacher at a private school in Essex, where he met and married his wife Marian. Shortly after their marriage, his desire to write prompted the beginning of what would be his first published book, *Bows against the Barons.* Although considered an adventure story, Trease's earliest novel was unique among its contemporaries within the genre. "Trease began with a big bang," writes Marcus Crouch in *Junior Bookshelf.* "*Bows against the Barons* was a landmark in fictional historical writing, and from it stems not only Trease's later and more sophisticated work but also that of every other writer in this area of fiction."

The close of World War I found writing and bookmaking for children at a low ebb. One reason for this was that the previous decade had given rise to a marketing phenomenon known as "Bumper Books." A Bumper book was a bulky volume compiled of royalty-free stories, poems, and block illustrations reshuffled into various combinations to create books of different appearances containing the same material. They were cheap to produce and consequently profitable to print. The popularity of such books among publishing houses combined with a second factor to produce mediocre children's literature. This was the practice of purchasing book texts for a flat fee. While lucrative from a publisher's standpoint, there was no incentive for writers to produce quality texts with enough long-term appeal to earn royalties on future sales. The short shelf life at bookstores encouraged authors to generate successive books reusing the same plots and characters: the "Serial Book" was born. "Anything at all unusual either in content or style of production was suspect, and it became increasingly difficult for the few firms which continued to produce individual children's books of quality to do so at a profit," writes Frank Eyre in *Twentieth Century Children's Books.* The saturation of the marketplace by such puffy and insubstantial books did a disservice to parents and children, blocking their access to and awareness of older and better books for children.

Trease began his foray into children's literature as a reaction to the dearth of good writing available when the dust of World War I had settled. His first books were prompted or, as he commented in *The Thorny Paradise: Writers on Writing for Children,* "provoked by the sheer badness of the historical fiction then being offered to children." Within the "adventure" genre Trease found nothing bridging the gap between the serial books characteristic of the pre-war years and the weighty fare offered by classic literature. Writers of the stature of Lord Lytton told exciting tales such as *Ben Hur* and *The Last Days of Pompeii,* but these stories were made inaccessible to the post-war generation of young readers due to the small-type versions available and a Victorian prose style difficult to wade through, even in extensively edited versions. Within the serial market the events surrounding World War I had sparked a slew of wildly improbable, escapist stories. "Criminals of various sorts replaced spies and parachutists, but otherwise the slaughter continued unabated and the majority of adventure stories showed little more imagination or intellectual content than the comic strip," according to Eyre.

Bows against the Barons was published in 1934. During the same period, a shift was occurring in attitudes regarding juvenile literature. A movement towards more responsible children's publishing began in America and made its way across the ocean to England due to two factors. First was the introduction of the Carnegie Medal Awards Program initiated by the British Library Association in 1936 to encourage a better standard of writing and book making in the realm of children's publishing. Second was the publication of the premier issue of *Junior Bookshelf,* the British equivalent of *Horn Book Magazine,* devoting itself exclusively to the criticism of literature for children. Trease objected to the romanticism attached to Robin Hood, and he attempted an objective and historically accurate treatment of the man in his first book. He also assumed a higher level of sophistication among his readership than usual by introducing themes of social unrest into his historical action novel. "To [Trease] must go the credit for setting a new style towards a more conscientious, properly researched story of the past that concerned itself as much with the social events of its time, and their effects on the people who lived in them, as with excitement and action," writes Eyre.

"When I became a children's writer . . . children's books were not considered worthy of critical discussion," Trease comments in *The Thorny Paradise.* "And if we search the dusty attics to remind ourselves of what most such books were like in the early 1930s, that attitude becomes understandable. The classics were of course venerated and be-

yond criticism, but contemporary writers did not count. The typical schoolmaster's view was like that of the old cowboy who said, 'The only good Injun is a dead Injun.' The only good author was a dead one. Even today this criterion survives in some quarters—there is a guilty feeling that only the classics are worthwhile. More than once, in my own experience, a teacher has mentioned to her class that she knows me, and the commonest reaction has been an incredulous cry, 'What, is he still alive?' "

Plotting his fast-moving adventure yarns in the book-lined study of his home in Western England, Trease has long been respected for the authenticity and historical accuracy which place his novels well above the "costume-epics" so often serialized by hack writers. His detailed research of his subjects reflects not only his professionalism as a writer, but his love of the process of history. "I am always happiest working with this double kind of inspiration," says Trease in *Children's Literature in Education.* "I love, for instance, the world of Pepys for its own sake. But it is the obvious contemporary comparisons that especially inspire me to weave stories against that background: tales of poor theatre folk battling against unscrupulous property developers, of corrupt contractors blackmailing civil servants, and of adventurous young women striving for professional equality with the men. . . . Children need to know about such things as they grow up into the adult world. The historical novel seems to me to provide analogies from which they can learn agreeably, in their own time, developing their own critical insight."

Crouch explains why Trease has never won a major literary award in his native England: "Trease tells a good story skillfully, but his plots are seldom satisfactory. He seems consumed with the need to keep the pressure up, piling incident upon incident . . . he has not created one entirely memorable character." However, he adds, "Geoffrey Trease has, over a long life, given much pleasure to readers of several generations. . . . We all, whether we are aware of it or not, see history through clearer, less prejudiced eyes because of his achievement."

Tales out of School, published in 1949, was Trease's attempt to set standards of writing in the field of children's literature, contending that children's authors were artists in their own right. He commented in *Children's Literature in Education:* "In our understandable desire to raise critical standards and achieve academic respectability there is a lurking risk that we shall produce books to please teachers and librarians more than the children themselves. We must never forget that, whatever the other valuable elements in a story, the single indispensable one is entertainment. Certainly, children's leisure-time reading is of immense educational importance. I believe that Oscar Wilde once observed, in one of his more serious moments, 'It is what you read when you don't have to that determines what you will be when you can't help it.' True. But how wise, too, was C. S. Lewis's warning against a too self-conscious and schematic approach to imaginative creation: 'I will not say that a good children's book could never be written by someone in the Ministry of Education. But I should lay very long odds against it.' "

BIOGRAPHICAL/CRITICAL SOURCES:

BOOKS

Avery, Gillian, *Author's Choice,* Crowell, 1971.

Blishen, Edward, editor, *The Thorny Paradise: Writers on Writing for Children,* Kestrel, 1975, pp. 13-24.

Doyle, Brian, *The Who's Who of Children's Literature,* Schocken, 1968.

Eyre, Frank, *Twentieth Century Children's Books,* Longmans, Green, 1952.

Fisher, M. T., *Intent upon Reading,* Brockhampton Press, 1961.

Green, Roger Lancelyn, *Tellers of Tales,* Watts, 1965.

Meek, Margaret, *Geoffrey Trease,* Bodley Head, 1960, Walck, 1964.

Root, Shelton, and others, editors, *Adventuring with Books,* Signet, 1966.

Something about the Author Autobiography Series, Volume 6, Gale, 1988, pp. 237-256.

Trease, Geoffrey, *A Whiff of Burnt Boats: An Early Autobiography,* St. Martin's, 1971.

Trease, Geoffrey, *Laughter at the Door: A Continued Autobiography,* St. Martin's, 1974.

White, Dorothy May Neal, *About Books for Children,* Oxford University Press, 1946.

PERIODICALS

Author, summer, 1988, p. 42ff.

Books and Bookmen, May, 1969.

Children's Literature in Education, autumn, 1983, pp. 149-159.

Cricket, February, 1978, p. 45.

Horn Book, June, 1966; June, 1971.

Junior Bookshelf, August, 1989, pp. 151-152.

Times Literary Supplement, July 24, 1981; April 13, 1984.

—*Sketch by Pamela L. Shelton*

TYSON, Joseph B(lake)   1928-

PERSONAL: Born August 30, 1928, in Charlotte, NC; son of Joseph B. (a construction worker) and Lucy (Lewis) Tyson; married Margaret Helms, June 12, 1954; children: Linda S. *Education:* Duke University, A.B., 1950, B.D., 1953; Union Theological Seminary, New York, NY, S.T.M., 1955, Ph.D., 1959. *Religion:* Methodist.

ADDRESSES: Home—8636 Capri Dr., Dallas, TX 75238. *Office*—Department of Religious Studies, Southern Methodist University, Dallas, TX 75275-0202.

CAREER: Southern Methodist University, Dallas, TX, instructor, 1958-60, assistant professor, 1960-65, associate professor, 1965-74, professor of religious studies, 1974—, head of department, 1965-75, 1986—, director, Center for the Study of Religion in the Greco-Roman World, 1983-89.

MEMBER: American Academy of Religion (president of southwestern region, 1968-69), Society of Biblical Literature, Studiorum Novi Testamenti Societas, Catholic Biblical Association.

WRITINGS:

A Study of Early Christianity, Macmillan, 1973.

(Coeditor) *Synoptic Abstract,* Biblical Research Associates, 1978.

The New Testament and Early Christianity, Macmillan, 1984.

The Death of Jesus in Luke-Acts, University of South Carolina Press, 1986.

(Editor) *Luke-Acts and the Jewish People,* Augsburg, 1988.

Images of Judaism in Luke-Acts, University of South Carolina Press, 1992.

(Coeditor) *Cadbury, Knox, and Talbert: American Contributions to the Study of Acts,* Scholars Press, 1992.

Contributor of articles to *Journal of Biblical Literature, New Testament Studies,* and *Novum Testamentum.*

WORK IN PROGRESS: Research on Luke-Acts.

U

ULANOV, Ann Belford 1938-

PERSONAL: Born January 1, 1938, in Princeton, NJ; daughter of Ralph Jones (a surgeon) and Ruth (a nurse; maiden name, Pine) Belford; married Barry Ulanov (a professor and writer), August 21, 1968; children: Alexander; stepchildren: Anne, Nicholas, Katherine. *Education:* Radcliffe College, B.A., 1959; Union Theological Seminary, New York, NY, M.Div., 1962, Ph.D., 1967; graduate of Blanton-Pearle Institutes of Religion and Mental Health, 1965, and C. G. Jung Institute of Analytical Psychology, 1967. *Religion:* Episcopalian.

ADDRESSES: Home—606 West 122nd St., #7E, New York, NY 10027. *Office*—201 West 77th St., #15D, New York, NY 10024.

CAREER: Psychoanalyst in private practice. Union Theological Seminary, New York City, professor of psychiatry and religion, 1966—. Member of board of directors of C. G. Jung Training Center.

MEMBER: International Association of Analytical Psychology, American Association of Pastoral Counselors, American Association of University Professors, American Examining Board of Psychoanalysis, New York Association for Analytical Psychologists, Joint Council for Mental Health.

WRITINGS:

The Feminine in Jungian Psychology and Christian Theology, Northwestern University Press, 1971.
(With husband, Barry Ulanov) *Religion and the Unconscious,* Westminster, 1975.
Receiving Woman: Studies in the Psychology and Theology of the Feminine, Westminster, 1981.
(With B. Ulanov) *Primary Speech: A Psychology of Prayer,* J. Knox, 1982.

(With B. Ulanov) *Cinderella and Her Sisters: The Envied and the Envying,* Westminster, 1983.
Picturing God, Cowley, 1986.
(With B. Ulanov) *The Witch and the Clown: Two Archetypes of Human Sexuality,* Chiron, 1987.
The Wisdom of the Psyche, Cowley, 1988.
(With B. Ulanov) *The Healing Imagination: The Meeting of Psyche and Soul,* Paulist Press, 1991.

Contributor to numerous books, including *Christian Approaches to Human Sexuality,* Seabury, 1975, *Christ and the Bodhisattva,* State University of New York Press, 1986, and *Jung and Christian Spirituality,* Paulist Press, 1989. Contributor of articles and reviews to religion and psychology journals, including *Journal of Religion and Mental Health, Religion in Life, International Journal of Analytical Psychology, American Journal of Psychiatry,* and *Journal of American Academy of Psychoanalysis.*

WORK IN PROGRESS: With husband, Barry Ulanov, *Anima and Animus.*

* * *

ULANOV, Barry 1918-

PERSONAL: Born April 10, 1918, in New York, NY; son of Nathan and Jeanette (Askwith) Ulanov; married Joan Bel Geddes, December 16, 1939; married Ann Belford, August 21, 1968; children: (first marriage) Anne Pietrasanta, Nicholas, Katherine; (second marriage) Alexander. *Education:* Columbia University, A.B., 1939, Ph.D., 1955. *Religion:* Anglo-Catholic.

ADDRESSES: Home—606 West 122nd St., #7E, New York, NY 10027. *Office*—Barnard College, New York, NY 10027.

CAREER: Swing Magazine, New York City, editor, 1939-41; *Listen Magazine,* New York City, editor, 1940-42; *Metronome Magazine,* New York City, editor, 1943-55; Barnard College, New York City, instructor, 1951-56, assistant professor, 1956-59, associate professor, 1959-66, professor of English, 1966-88, McIntosh Professor of English emeritus, 1988—, chairman of department, 1967-71, 1979-82, chairman of program in the arts, 1975-79, 1982-88. Instructor in music, Julliard Institute, 1946; instructor in English, Princeton University, 1950-51; adjunct professor of religion, Columbia University, 1966.

MEMBER: Medieaval Academy, Renaissance Society, Association for American Achievements, Conference on the Humanities (secretary, 1956-57; chairman, 1957-58), St. Thomas More Society (president, 1955-56, 1964-65), Catholic Renascence Society (vice-president, 1956-60; president, 1960-67), The Keys (vice-chairman, 1960).

AWARDS, HONORS: Spiritual Life Award, 1962, for outstanding American spiritual book; Guggenheim fellowship, 1962-63; American Council of Learned Societies grant, 1962-63; Litt.D., Villanova University, 1965; William F. O'Brien Memorial Award, Newman Foundation, 1965, for distinguished contribution to education.

WRITINGS:

The Recorded Music of W. A. Mozart, Resonance, 1942.
Duke Ellington, Creative Age Press, 1946, reprinted, Da Capo Press, 1975.
The Incredible Crosby, McGraw, 1948.
A History of Jazz in America, Viking, 1952, reprinted, Da Capo Press, 1972.
(Translator with Joan Ulanov) Georges Bernanos, *Last Essays,* Henry Regnery, 1955.
A Handbook of Jazz, Viking, 1957, reprinted, Greenwood, 1975.
(Translator with Frank Tauritz) Marie des Douleurs, *Joy Out of Sorrow,* Newman Press, 1958.
Death: A Book of Preparation and Consolation, Sheed, 1959.
Sources and Resources: The Literary Traditions of Christian Humanism, Newman, 1960.
The Way of St. Alphonsus Liguori, Kenedy, 1961.
Makers of the Modern Theater, McGraw, 1961.
Seeds of Hope in the Modern World, Kenedy, 1962.
(With R. C. Roby) *Introduction to Drama,* McGraw, 1962.
Contemporary Catholic Thought, Sheed, 1963.
The Two Worlds of American Art, Macmillan, 1965.
The Making of a Modern Saint: A Biographical Study of Therese of Lisieux, Doubleday, 1966.
(With James B. Hall) *Modern Culture and the Arts,* McGraw, 1967, 2nd edition, 1972.

(With wife, Ann Ulanov) *Religion and the Unconscious,* Westminster, 1975.
(With A. Ulanov) *Primary Speech: A Psychology of Prayer,* J. Knox, 1982.
(With A. Ulanov) *Cinderella and Her Sisters: The Envied and the Envying,* Westminster, 1983.
The Prayers of Saint Augustine, Seabury, 1984.
(With A. Ulanov) *The Witch and the Clown: Two Archetypes of Human Sexuality,* Chiron, 1987.
(With A. Ulanov) *The Healing Imagination: The Meeting of Psyche and Soul,* Paulist Press, 1991.

Columnist for *Down Beat,* 1955-58; associate editor, *The Bridge,* 1955-67.

WORK IN PROGRESS: The Persistence of Grace; with wife, Ann Ulanov, *Anima and Animus.*

SIDELIGHTS: Reviewing Barry Ulanov's *The Making of a Modern Saint* in the *Times Literary Supplement,* Stevie Smith writes: "The book is really excellent and provides an experience of Catholicism one would not miss."

BIOGRAPHICAL/CRITICAL SOURCES:

PERIODICALS

Listener, March 16, 1967.
Times Literary Supplement, March 23, 1967.

*   *   *

UNSWORTH, Walt(er) 1928-

PERSONAL: Born December 16, 1928, in Littleborough, Lancashire, England; married Dorothy Winstanley, 1952; children: Gail, Timothy Duncan. *Education:* Attended Wigan Technical College, 1942-47, and Chester College, 1949-51; Licentiate of the College of Preceptors (L.C.P.), 1956. *Avocational interests:* Mountain climbing, photography, industrial archaeology, general travel.

ADDRESSES: Home—Harmony Hall, Milnthorpe, Cumbria, England.

CAREER: Teacher in Wednesfield, Staffordshire, and in Horwich, Lancashire, England; Worsley Walkden Secondary School, Worsley, Lancashire, head of physics department, 1957-73; editor, *Climber & Rambler* (magazine), 1974-86. Editorial director, Cicerone Press (publishers of specialist guidebooks); has worked as a professional mountain-climbing instructor during summer months. *Military service:* British Army, Royal Artillery, 1947-49; served in Malta and Libya.

MEMBER: Alpine Club, Society of Authors, Lancashire Mountaineering Club (honorary vice-president), British

Guild of Travel Writers, Outdoor Writers' Guild (president).

AWARDS, HONORS: International Prize for Mountain Literature, 1992, for *Everest: A Mountaineering History.*

WRITINGS:

The Young Mountaineer, Hutchinson, 1959.

A Climber's Guide to Pontesford Rocks, Wilding & Son, 1962.

The English Outcrops, Gollancz, 1964.

Matterhorn Man: The Life of Edward Whymper, Gollancz, 1965.

Tiger in the Snow: The Life and Adventures of A. F. Mummery, Gollancz, 1967.

Because It Is There: Famous Mountaineers 1840-1940, Gollancz. 1968.

The Devil's Mill (children's novel), Gollancz, 1968.

The Book of Rock-Climbing, Arthur Barker, 1968.

(Compiler) *Otztal Alps: A Selection of Climbs* (climbing guide), West Col Productions, 1969.

North Face: The Second Conquest of the Alps, Hutchinson, 1969.

Whistling Clough (children's novel), Gollancz, 1970.

(With R. B. Evans) *The Southern Lakes* (climbing guide), Cicerone Press, 1971.

Portrait of the River Derwent, R. Hale, 1971.

The High Fells of Lakeland, R. Hale, 1972.

Colour Book of the Lake District, Batsford, 1974.

Colour Book of the Peak District, Batsford, 1974.

Grimsdyke (children's novel), Gollancz, 1974.

Encyclopaedia of Mountaineering, R. Hale, 1975, revised edition, Hodder & Stoughton, 1992.

Walking and Climbing (for children), Routledge & Kegan Paul, 1977.

Everest: A Mountaineering History, Houghton, 1981, revised edition, Oxford Illustrated Press, 1989.

(Compiler and author of introduction) *Peaks, Passes, and Glaciers: Selections from the Alpine Journal,* Mountaineer Books, 1981.

The Pennine Playground, Penguin Books, 1984.

This Climbing Game, Viking, 1984.

Classic Walks of the World, Oxford Illustrated Press, 1985.

Savage Snows, Hodder & Stoughton, 1986.

Classic Walks of Europe, Oxford Illustrated Press, 1987.

An Illustrated Companion to Lakeland, Oxford Illustrated Press, 1988.

Classic Walks in the Lake District, Oxford Illustrated Press, 1988.

Classic Walks in the Yorkshire Dales, Oxford Illustrated Press, 1989.

Also author of *Everest 72,* the official booklet of the British Mount Everest Expedition, 1972. Contributor to *The Mountaineer's Companion,* Eyre & Spottiswoode, 1966; *Miscellany Four,* Oxford University Press, 1967; *Southern Lakes,* 1971; *The Winding Trail,* Diadem, 1981; *The Book of the Walking Year,* Stephens Ltd., 1988; *The Mountains of Europe,* Oxford Illustrated Press, 1989; and various editions of *Rock Climbs in Lancashire.* Contributor of articles and reviews to magazines, mountaineering journals, and newspapers in Great Britain, the United States, and Australia.

WORK IN PROGRESS: Hold the Heights: The Foundations of Mountaineering, for Hodder & Stoughton.

SIDELIGHTS: Walt Unsworth's book *Everest: A Mountaineering History* tells the story of "the men and the few women who climbed—or didn't succeed in climbing—the mountain, and it shows them to be fully human and often flawed characters," writes Jeremy Bernstein in the *New Yorker.* Unsworth's account of the climbing history of the mountain is based on numerous books written by climbers, the private papers of the British Alpine Club and the Royal Geographical Society, and interviews and letters from those pioneering climbers still living. "By a careful sifting of the records Unsworth has filled in some of the gaps in the Everest story, although he has sometimes been obliged to resort to intelligent guesswork," comments Ronald Faux in the *Times Literary Supplement.* In *Everest,* Unsworth details forty-five expeditions, from the first British expedition in 1921 to the first successful climb without oxygen in 1978. The author offers much new information about George Leigh Mallory and his ill-fated climb in 1924; Unsworth also provides an in-depth look at the events that led to the first successful climb and return from the summit by the New Zealander Edmund Hillary and the Sherpa Tenzing Norgay in 1953. An updated version of *Everest* was published in 1989.

Of Walt Unsworth, whose works have been translated into French, German, Italian, and Japanese, Jan Morris writes in the London *Times,* "No chronicler was ever fairer, more sympathetic or more encyclopedically knowledgeable, but still the sorry conclusion to be drawn from his book is that all in all, with exceptions, the protracted confrontation between mankind and Mount Everest has not been very edifying." Morris adds that the "attempts have been obfuscated by bureaucracy, degraded by chauvinism, soured by private rivalry, cheapened by snobbery of one sort and another or made ridiculous by self importance. Mr. Unsworth dispassionately records it all, motives and manners alike, in a dry, spare and lucid style." Bernstein concludes that *Everest* "is a serious historical study, done in high style, of a world that most of us will never know but that many of us dream about."

BIOGRAPHICAL/CRITICAL SOURCES:

PERIODICALS

Listener, November 14, 1968.
New Statesman, November, 1968.
New Yorker, June 7, 1982.
Times (London), September 24, 1981.
Times Literary Supplement, October 16, 1969; October 30,
    1970; January 1, 1982.

V

VALDES, Nelson P. 1945-
(Ricardo Leyva)

PERSONAL: Born May 19, 1945, in Havana, Cuba; came to the United States in 1961, became U.S. citizen; married Maxine Conant (a poet); children: Ricardo Alberto, Alisa Lynn. *Education:* University of New Mexico, B.A., 1970, Ph.D., 1972. *Politics:* Socialist, anti-bureaucratic. *Religion:* None. *Avocational interests:* Classical music.

ADDRESSES: Home—General Delivery, Bosque, NM 87006. *Office*—Department of Sociology, University of New Mexico, Albuquerque, NM 87106.

CAREER: Former history instructor, University of New Orleans, New Orleans, LA; University of New Mexico, Albuquerque, researcher, 1965-70, instructor, 1970-76, assistant professor of sociology, 1976—.

MEMBER: Latin American Studies Association, American Historical Association.

AWARDS, HONORS: Ford Foundation, National Defense Education Act, and Woodrow Wilson fellowships.

WRITINGS:

EDITOR

(With Rolando Bonachea) *Che: The Selected Works of Ernesto Guevara,* M.I.T. Press, 1969.
(With Edwin Lieuwen) *The Cuban Revolution: A Research Study Guide,* University of New Mexico Press, 1971.
(With Bonachea, and contributor under pseudonym Ricardo Leyva) *Cuba in Revolution,* Doubleday/Anchor, 1972.
(With Bonachea) *Revolutionary Struggle: The Selected Works of Fidel Castro,* Volume 1, M.I.T. Press, 1972.
(With Marshall R. Nason) *Human Rights in Socialist Cuba,* Westview, 1985.

OTHER

Contributor of articles on Cuba to *Aportes* (Paris), *Dissent, Latin American Research Review, New Politics, Science and Society,* and *Worker's Power.*

SIDELIGHTS: Nelson P. Valdes is interested in democratization of Communist regimes, labor movements, anarchism and underdevelopment, and social revolution in Latin America. He once told *CA:* "The writer Leszek Kolakowski and some of [Leon] Trotsky's works have influenced my thinking. Exile has had its effects also."*

*　　　*　　　*

VALGARDSON, W(illiam) D(empsey) 1939-

PERSONAL: Born May 7, 1939, in Winnipeg, Manitoba, Canada; son of Dempsey Alfred Herbert (a fisherman) and Rachel Iris (Smith) Valgardson; married Mary Anne Tooth, May 28, 1960 (divorced); children: Nancy-Rae, Val Dempsey. *Education:* University of Manitoba, B.A., 1961, B.Ed., 1966; University of Iowa, M.F.A., 1969. *Religion:* Lutheran. *Avocational interests:* Rock climbing, hiking, folk dancing.

ADDRESSES: Home—1908 Waterloo Rd., Victoria, British Columbia, Canada V8P 1J3. *Office*—Box 1700, Department of Creative Writing, University of Victoria, Victoria, British Columbia, Canada V8W 2Y2.

CAREER: English teacher in Riverton, Manitoba, 1961-62; art teacher in Transcona, Manitoba, 1963-64; English teacher in Snow Lake, Manitoba, 1964-65, Pinawa, Manitoba, 1965-67, and Tuxedo, Manitoba, 1969-70; Cottey College, Nevada, MO, instructor, 1970-72, assistant professor of English, 1972-74, chairman of department, 1971-74; University of Victoria, British

Columbia, professor, 1974—, chairman of creative writing department, 1982-87.

MEMBER: Saanich International Folkdancers, Writers' Union of Canada, Canadian Authors Association (president, 1985-86), American Writers' Program.

AWARDS, HONORS: First prize, Rochester Festival of Fine Arts, 1968, for poem "Paul Isfeld: Fisherman"; international scholarship to Writer's Workshop, University of Iowa, 1968; Canada Council grant, summer, 1968; honorable mention, Hallmark poetry competition, 1969, for poem "Realization in a Spinning Wheel"; first prize, *Winnipeg Free Press* Non-Fiction Contest, 1969, for article "The Hitchhikers"; second prize, Canadian Author's Association, Manitoba branch, 1970, for poem "Raspberries"; President's Medal, University of Western Ontario, 1971, for short story "Bloodflowers"; Star award, *Kansas City Star*-Hallmark competitions, 1972, for poem "Val Playing"; Bread Loaf scholarship, 1972; first prize, Canadian Broadcasting Corporation Annual Short Story Competition, 1980; best first novel, *Books in Canada*, 1981, for *Gentle Sinners;* drama award, Canadian Authors Association Literary Awards, 1987, for *Granite Point;* Con-Pro Gold Award for best commercial television drama of the year, CKNU-TV, 1983, Golden Sheaf award from Yorkton Short Film and Video Festival, Chris Statuette from Columbus International Film Festival, and Ohio State Award from Institute for Education by Radio-Television, all for *The Catch.*

WRITINGS:

BOOKS

Bloodflowers (short stories), Oberon, 1973.
God Is Not a Fish Inspector (short stories), Oberon, 1975.
In the Gutting Shed (poems), Turnstone Press, 1976, revised edition, 1981.
Red Dust (short stories), Oberon, 1978.
Gentle Sinners (novel), Oberon, 1980.
The Carpenter of Dreams: Poems, Skaldhus Press, 1986.
What Can't Be Changed Shouldn't Be Mourned, Douglas & McIntyre, 1990.

RADIO PLAYS

Bloodflowers, first broadcast by Canadian Broadcasting Corporation (CBC), October 30, 1982.
Granite Point, first broadcast by CBC, October 29, 1983.
The Cave, first broadcast by CBC, December 28, 1985.
An Unacceptable Standard of Cockpit Practice, first broadcast by CBC, 1985.
Seiche, first broadcast by CBC, January 10, 1987.

OTHER

The Catch (television screenplay), broadcast by CKND-TV (Canada), December, 1981.

Contributor to anthologies, including *The Best American Short Stories 1971,* edited by Martha Foley and David Burnett, Houghton, 1971; *Stories from Western Canada,* edited by Rudy Wiebe, Macmillan, 1972; *Sunlight and Shadows,* New English Library, 1974; *New Canadian Stories,* Oberon, 1974; *New Canadian Fiction,* Bantam, 1975; and *Moderne Erzaehler der Welt-Kanada,* Erdman, 1976. Contributor of articles, stories, and poems to literary journals, including *Alphabet, Antigonish Review, Atlantic Advocate, Canadian Forum, Dalhousie Review, Fiddlehead, Inscape, Jeopardy, Midwest Quarterly, New Student Review, Queen's Quarterly, Reader's Quarterly of Icelandic Literature and Thought, Tamarack Review,* and *Windsor Review.*

SIDELIGHTS: W. D. Valgardson's childhood in an Icelandic-Canadian fishing village has provided themes and settings for his stories. He is especially interested in the effects of isolation upon people. Reviewing *God Is Not a Fish Inspector,* Adrian Vale of the *Irish Times* comments that Valgardson's "Manitoba countryside has close affinities with Egdon Heath. There is death and suicide and isolation. These elementals, however, are not dragged in to inflate a final paragraph; they come as hammer-blows, falling inevitably and with complete artistic rightness. Mr. Valgardson is an authoritative writer; he leaves the reader with no inclination to gainsay him or the truth of the events he describes."

Valgardson accepts comparisons of his work to that of authors such as Anton Chekhov. "My writing has been compared to many Russian writers and I think that's fair. The Interlake area is probably similar to some parts of Russia, with people of a similar background, especially Slavs, facing the cold, the poverty, the isolation and so on. I speak out of that environment," Valgardson is quoted as saying by David Jackel in the *Dictionary of Literary Biography.*

Writing does not come easily for Valgardson. Multiple rewrites and the use of "every device available," as he told Jackel, are what enable him to continue. One device he avoids, however, is first-person narrative. "I mistrust the first person very much," he told Jackel. "The first person gives the writer the temptation to fall into writing a summary rather than a story that needs to be dramatized. Also my stories are set in a very small locale, which most readers haven't experienced. That requires a very authoritative tone. I also have a strong Lutheran, and conservative, background that needs to make the statement of belief that the omniscient voice has."

BIOGRAPHICAL/CRITICAL SOURCES:

BOOKS

Dictionary of Literary Biography, Volume 60: *Canadian Writers since 1960, Second Series,* Gale, 1987, pp. 355-358.

PERIODICALS

Books in Canada, November, 1977, pp. 38-39.
Canadian Literature, summer, 1984, pp. 15-34.
Essays on Canadian Writing, fall-winter, 1979-80, pp. 187-190.
Globe and Mail (Toronto), August 30, 1986; July 21, 1990.
Irish Times, July 10, 1976.
University of Toronto Quarterly, summer, 1979, pp. 324-326.

*   *   *

VALIN, Jonathan Louis   1948-

PERSONAL: Born November 23, 1948, in Cincinnati, OH; son of Sigmund and Marcella (Fink) Valin; married Katherine Brockhaus (a poet), January 3, 1971. *Education:* University of Chicago, M.A., 1974; doctoral study at Washington University, St. Louis, MO, 1976-79.

ADDRESSES: Agent—Dominick Abel Literary Agency, 498 West End Ave., New York, NY 10024.

CAREER: Writer, 1979—. University of Cincinnati, Cincinnati, OH, lecturer in English, 1974-76; Washington University, St. Louis, MO, lecturer in English, 1976-79.

MEMBER: Mystery Writers of America, Modern Language Association of America.

AWARDS, HONORS: Norma Lowry Memorial Fund Prize, 1978, for "Replay."

WRITINGS:

"HARRY STONER" MYSTERY NOVELS

Final Notice, Dodd, 1980.
The Lime Pit, Dodd, 1980.
The Celestial Railroad, Dodd, 1981.
Full Fathom Five, Dodd, 1981.
Day of Wrath, Congdon & Weed, 1982.
Dead Letter, Collins, 1982.
The Winter's Tale, Dodd, 1982.
Natural Causes, Congdon & Weed, 1983.
Life's Work, Delacorte, 1986.
Fire Lake, Delacorte, 1987.
Extenuating Circumstances, Delacorte, 1989.
Second Chance, Doubleday, 1991.

OTHER

Work represented in anthologies, including *Subject to Change,* 1978. Contributor to *Writer.*

SIDELIGHTS: Author Jonathan Louis Valin dislikes mystery writers, even though he is one. "I don't read many mysteries," he told *Los Angeles Times* reporter Dick Lochte. The author added, "They're poorly written and even the good ones are predictable. And mystery writers as a whole don't seem to be interested in the same things I'm interested in." Two exceptions to Valin's criticism are Raymond Chandler and Ross Macdonald, authors he admires.

Harry Stoner, private eye, the protagonist in Valin's novels, was created in the tradition of Chandler's Philip Marlowe and Macdonald's Lew Archer. "I've tried to give him a little more character than you normally find in hard-boiled American detectives," Valin told Lochte. "Usually they're just wisecracking voices. I wanted him to be more rounded, to have some sensitivity, not to be just a tough guy. I wanted him to be a recognizable human being rather than a pure type."

"Harry Stoner takes his work very seriously," *New York Times Book Review*'s Marilyn Stasio says in a review of *Second Chance.* The book follows Stoner on his search for an emotionally disturbed college student he has been hired to find. To complicate the search, the psychopath who murdered the young woman's mother has just been released from prison and may be after her as well. "Mr. Valin is very good at turning the screws on a tense situation like this one," Stasio comments. The *Globe and Mail*'s Margaret Cannon finds, "As always, Valin's story is skillfully crafted and the pace keeps the pages flapping to the last paragraph."

BIOGRAPHICAL/CRITICAL SOURCES:

PERIODICALS

Globe and Mail (Toronto), May 11, 1991, p. C6.
Los Angeles Times, June 9, 1983, pp. 1, 17.
New Republic, August 2, 1982, p. 37.
Newsweek, June 7, 1982, p. 71; April 16, 1989, p. 31.
New York Times Book Review, January 25, 1981, p. 26; April 26, 1981, p. 43; January 17, 1982, p. 29; September 4, 1983, p. 20; November 16, 1986, p. 38; November 1, 1987, p. 34; February 12, 1989, p. 32; April 16, 1989, p. 31; July 29, 1990, p. 32; May 19, 1991, p. 45.
Observer, February 26, 1989, p. 47.
Time, April 3, 1989, p. 81.
Times (London), February 4, 1989.
Times Literary Supplement, October 29, 1982, p. 1196; March 30, 1984, p. 354.

Washington Post Book World, July 17, 1983, p. 10; September 21, 1986, p. 6; March 19, 1989, p. 12; April 16, 1989, p. 8; May 19, 1991, p. 8.*

*   *   *

Van ALLSBURG, Chris 1949-

PERSONAL: Born June 18, 1949, in Grand Rapids, MI; son of Richard (a dairy owner) and Chris Van Allsburg; married Lisa Morrison (a self-employed consultant). *Education:* University of Michigan, B.F.A., 1972; Rhode Island School of Design, M.F.A., 1975. *Religion:* Jewish. *Avocational interests:* "When I'm not drawing, I enjoy taking walks and going to museums. I play tennis a few times a week, like to sail—although I have fewer opportunities to do it now (I used to have more friends with boats). I read quite a lot."

ADDRESSES: Office—c/o Houghton-Mifflin, 2 Park St., Boston, MA 02107.

CAREER: Artist; author and illustrator of children's books. Rhode Island School of Design, Providence, RI, teacher of illustration, 1977—. Has exhibited his work at Whitney Museum of American Art, New York, NY; Museum of Modern Art, New York, NY; Alan Stone Gallery, New York, NY; Grand Rapids Art Museum, Grand Rapids, MI; and Port Washington Public Library, NY.

AWARDS, HONORS: New York Times Best Illustrated Children's Books citations, 1979, for *The Garden of Abdul Gasazi,* 1981, for *Jumanji,* 1982, for *Ben's Dream,* 1983, for *The Wreck of the Zephyr,* 1984, for *The Mysteries of Harris Burdick,* 1985, for *The Polar Express,* and 1986, for *The Stranger;* Caldecott Honor Book citation from the American Library Association, and Boston *Globe-Horn Book* Award for illustration, both 1980, and International Board on Books citation for illustration, 1982, all for *The Garden of Abdul Gasazi;* Irma Simonton Black Award from Bank Street College of Education, 1980, for *The Garden of Abdul Gasazi,* and 1985, for *The Mysteries of Harris Burdick; New York Times* Outstanding Books citations, 1981, for *Jumanji,* and 1983, for *The Wreck of the Zephyr;* Caldecott Medal, 1982, for *Jumanji,* and 1986, for *The Polar Express;* Boston *Globe-Horn Book* Award citation for illustration, 1982, for *Jumanji,* and 1986, for *The Polar Express;* Children's Choice from the International Reading Association, and American Book Award for illustration from Association of American Publishers, both 1982, Kentucky Bluegrass Award from Northern Kentucky University, and Buckeye Children's Book Award from Ohio State Library, both 1983, Washington Children's Choice Picture Book Award from the Washington Library Media Association, 1984, and West Virginia Chil-

dren's Book Award, 1985, all for *Jumanji;* Parents' Choice Award for Illustration from the Parents' Choice Foundation, 1982, for *Ben's Dream,* 1984, for *The Mysteries of Harris Burdick,* 1985, for *The Polar Express,* and 1986, for *The Stranger;* Kentucky Bluegrass Award from Northern Kentucky University, 1987, for *The Polar Express.*

Ben's Dream was included in the American Institute of Graphic Arts Book Show in 1983, *The Wreck of the Zephyr* was included in 1984, and *The Mysteries of Harris Burdick* in 1985; *The Wreck of the Zephyr* was chosen one of New York Public Library's Children's Book in 1983, and *The Polar Express* was chosen in 1985; Boston *Globe-Horn Book* Award, 1985, for *The Mysteries of Harris Burdick; The Polar Express* was chosen one of *Redbook*'s Ten Best Picture Books for Kids, and one of Child Study Association's Children's Books of the Year, both 1985; Hans Christian Andersen Award nomination, 1985; *The Stranger* was chosen one of Child Study Association's Children's Books of the Year, 1987.

WRITINGS:

SELF-ILLUSTRATED CHILDREN'S BOOKS

The Garden of Abdul Gasazi, Houghton, 1979.
Jumanji, Houghton, 1981.
Ben's Dream, Houghton, 1982.
The Wreck of the Zephyr, Houghton, 1983.
The Mysteries of Harris Burdick, Houghton, 1984.
The Polar Express, Houghton, 1985.
The Stranger, Houghton, 1986.
The Z Was Zapped: A Play in Twenty-Six Acts, Houghton, 1987.
Two Bad Ants, Houghton, 1988.
Just a Dream, Houghton, 1990.
The Wretched Stone, Houghton, 1991.

ILLUSTRATOR

Mark Helprin, *Swan Lake,* Houghton, 1989.

A selection of Chris Van Allsburg's work is held in the Kerlan Collection at the University of Minnesota.

SIDELIGHTS: Chris Van Allsburg, writes Jim Roginski in *Parents' Choice,* "is one of the most extraordinarily gifted artists working in children's book illustration. His immediately recognizable style—technical genius and startling images—has placed him in the forefront of active illustrators who are advancing the art of book illustration." Although Van Allsburg began his career as a book illustrator as recently as 1979, he has received numerous awards and honors: he "has received," declares Barbara McKee in the *Horn Book,* "the Caldecott Medal two times—for *Jumanji* and for . . . *The Polar Express* (Houghton)—a distinction unprecedented in the history of the award." *The Polar Express* has become a Christmas classic since it first appeared in 1985, and publisher Houghton Mifflin expressed their confidence in Van Allsburg's work when it bought the rights to *Swan Lake,* the artist's 1989 collaboration with author Mark Helprin, for a record $801,000.

"Sometime in the middle of the twentieth century—I like to be mysterious about my age—I was born in Grand Rapids, Michigan," Van Allsburg told Catherine Ruello in an interview for *Something about the Author.* "Growing up, I liked to do normal kid things like playing baseball and building model cars, trucks, and planes. I also used to drive a go-cart on public streets, which was illegal. I lived in a growing suburb with half-built houses, great to spook around in, especially in those with only the stud work sticking out of the top of the foundations. We were not suppose to do this—it was taboo. Obviously parents were afraid we'd hurt ourselves."

"There were open fields, trees, wandering dirt roads," he recalls in an interview with Kim Heron of the *New York Times.* "The houses weren't big—they were nice, small houses for families of four or maybe five. There were still places nearby where I could catch tadpoles, there were places to go sledding, there were fields where you could play baseball—not someplace surrounded by a fence, just open fields. And I rode my bike to school."

"The first book I remember reading is probably the same book many people my age recall as their first," Van Allsburg recalls in his *Horn Book* acceptance speech for the Caldecott Medal. "It was profusely illustrated and recounted the adventures and conflicts of its three protagonists, Dick, Jane, and Spot. Actually, the lives of this trio were not all that interesting. A young reader's reward for struggling through those syllables at the bottom of the page was to discover that Spot got a bath. Not exactly an exciting revelation. Especially since you'd already seen Spot getting his bath in the picture at the top of the page."

"Drawing was a child pleasure that faded away as I got older," Van Allsburg told Ruello. "By the time I was in fourth grade, I really didn't think much about myself as an artist. There were other social considerations and expectations. Little boys were supposed to spend their time and energy learning how to play baseball and football and becoming good little athletes. It wasn't a condition that had anything to do with the teachers at my school, or with my environment being prejudiced against art, or with my parents' attitude. It was just the condition of being a kid growing up.

"I had no idea what I wanted to be when I grew up. I thought I'd be a lawyer, mostly because I couldn't think of anything else. I thought about doing a few other things but never seriously. In high school it was thought okay to study art as a way of expanding cultural horizons, but it was not considered a legitimate career pursuit. So, I studied the usual college prep requirements as math, science, etc. . . . It was understood that I'd go to college, not a decision I had to make, because it was made for me. I still hadn't made a clear choice of what I wanted to do, had no portfolio, and I hadn't studied any of the subjects required for art school. However, because of a bureaucratic oversight, I was accepted into the art school at the University of Michigan. At first it was just a lark. I thought it would be a great way to earn a college degree by goofing around for four years.

"The enthusiasm I had for art as a child was once again rekindled. The first thing I responded to was sculpture, because it was close to the pleasure I had gotten from making things (plastic cars etc.) with my hands, which I did quite a lot until I was eleven years old. I drew only to pass the required courses, spending all my time learning how to cast bronze, carve wood and work in ceramics.

"I began my career as a sculptor and went into painting almost accidentally. It wasn't that I was discouraged with my life as a sculptor. On the contrary, I had already had a couple of well-received shows in New York City. I started drawing in the evening as a hobby, and considered sculpture my real job. A friend of mine who illustrated books saw my drawings and encouraged me to consider illustrations. My wife, who also encouraged me, taught elementary school at the time and occasionally brought home illustrated books. I spent some time working on a little story. My wife took it around to publishers who suggested that I develop it further. I did. The first verse was grim couplets which were a little silly. So, I decided to write prose, instead."

Van Allsburg's first work, *The Garden of Abdul Gasazi,* is the story of a young boy who pursues a runaway dog into a magician's eerie garden of topiary creatures. The artist's evocative, surreal black-and-white pencil illustrations attracted the attention of reviewers. "Critics," writes Laura Ingram in the *Dictionary of Literary Biography,* "hailed *The Garden of Abdul Gasazi* as a graphic masterpiece, praising not only his technical but also his artistic vision"; but, she adds, others felt the author neglected the written elements of the story, allowing them to be overpowered by the illustrations. Van Allsburg told Ruello that he "had no expectations at all. I remember thinking, 'Maybe a few copies will sell; I'll buy the remainder and give them to friends for Christmas.' But *The Garden of Abdul Gasazi* sold quite well." Some of Van Allsburg's original drawings from the book were included in an exhibition of his works at the Alan Stone Gallery in New York City.

After *The Garden of Abdul Gasazi* Van Allsburg published *Jumanji,* the story of two bored suburban children, Judy and Peter, who accidently let loose wild animals in their home while playing a board game. "True to its claim," writes Ingram, "the game dispels the children's listlessness when lions materialize in the living room, monkeys appear on the kitchen table and help themselves to bananas, a volcano erupts, and a herd of rhinos rampage through the house." The game ends when Judy reaches the final destination, and all the animals and other effects of the game mysteriously vanish without a trace. Like *The Garden of Abdul Gasazi, Jumanji*'s illustrations are black-and-white, and they blur the boundary between fantasy and reality. "Van Allsburg's pictures," Ingram states, "which at first glance could be mistaken for photographs, are impressive not only for their realism but for the skill with which he manipulates light and shadow to create a vaguely unsettling mood and for the odd angles which present disconcerting views of common scenes."

Ben's Dream, in which a young boy falls asleep while studying geography and dreams that his house is floating around the world, and *The Wreck of the Zephyr,* the story of a young man who learns to sail his boat through the air, followed *Jumanji* in 1982 and 1983. *The Wreck of the Zephyr* was Van Allsburg's first full-color book, and it received as much acclaim as his black-and-white ventures had. It "was hailed," declares Ingram, "as 'the work of a master; stunning, luminescent and conveying a sense of the mystical and magical.'" But the artist returned to black-and-white for *The Mysteries of Harris Burdick,* perhaps his most idiosyncratic book. It consists of a series of pictures with titles and captions which only suggest the story that might accompany the illustrations. "Designed to challenge even those who claim to have no imagination," Ingram writes, "these pictures possess a haunting quality that hints at unseen mysteries. Though this collection appears on the children's shelves in most libraries and bookstores, Van Allsburg's teasing scenes are sophisticated enough to provoke fantasies in the adult as well as prereaders and school-aged children."

Van Allsburg won his second Caldecott Medal for his second full-color project, *The Polar Express,* published in 1985. "Told as a first-person recollection," declares Heron, "*The Polar Express* is the story of a Christmas Eve long ago, when a little boy boards a mysterious train to the North Pole. There, he meets Santa Claus and gets to choose the first gift of Christmas—a reindeer bell from Santa's sleigh." Unfortunately, he loses the bell through a hole in the pocket of his bathrobe, but it is rediscovered under the Christmas tree the following morning with a cryptic note: "Found this on the seat of my sleigh. Fix that hole in your pocket. Mr. C." The boy, his young sister, and their friends can hear the sound of the bell clearly, while their parents cannot; although, as the young folk grow older, many of them can no longer hear the sound. "But the bell still rings for me," the narrator concludes, "as it does for all who truly believe."

"Van Allsburg," writes Heron, "has frequently observed that *The Polar Express* is about faith—the faith that children, trailing clouds of glory, bring into the world and that is slowly lifted from them during childhood, in the name of growth." "The rationality we all embrace as adults makes believing in the fantastic difficult, if not impossible," Van Allsburg explains in his Caldecott Medal speech. "Lucky are the children who *know* there is a jolly fat man in a red suit who pilots a flying sleigh. We should envy them. And we should envy the people who are so certain Martians will land in their back yard that they keep a loaded Polaroid camera by the back door. The inclination to believe in the fantastic may strike some as a failure in logic, or gullibility, but it's really a gift. A world that might have Bigfoot and the Loch Ness monster is clearly superior to one that definitely does not."

Van Allsburg continues his exploration of the fantastic in works such as *The Stranger:* a mute young man becomes part of Farmer Bailey's family, but his arrival delays the beginning of autumn. *The Z Was Zapped: A Play in Twenty-Six Acts* is "a sort of crazed alphabet book," according to Heron, in which the letters suffer alliterative fates. Other recent works include *Two Bad Ants, Just a Dream,* and *The Wretched Stone.* "A book is a four-and-a-half month commitment," Van Allsburg tells Ruello, "and the challenge is to actually finish it. My problem is maintaining self-motivation after the tenth drawing. There are fourteen to fifteen drawings in a conventionally laid-out book and by the tenth drawing I'm ready to start another project. I've got a 'sketchbook' in my head with thousands of pieces of sculpture and enough descriptions for ten books. But I let those things sit in the back of my mind whereby the weaker ideas settle out by themselves. I would like to be six people at once, so that I could get more of them out of the way."

BIOGRAPHICAL/CRITICAL SOURCES:

BOOKS

Children's Literature Review, Gale, Volume 5, 1983; Volume 13, 1987.
Dictionary of Literary Biography, Volume 61: *American Writers for Children since 1960: Poets, Illustrators, and Nonfiction Authors,* Gale, 1987, pp. 306-13.
Kingman, Lee, editor, *Newbery and Caldecott Medal Books, 1976-1985,* Horn Book, 1986.
Holtze, Sally Holmes, *Fifth Book of Junior Authors and Illustrators,* H. W. Wilson, 1983.
Something about the Author, Volume 53, Gale, 1988.

PERIODICALS

Chicago Tribune Book World, August 1, 1982.

Horn Book, August, 1982, pp. 384-87; July/August, 1986, pp. 420-24, 425-29; September/October, 1986, pp. 566-71.

Los Angeles Times Book Review, March 21, 1982; April 3, 1983.

Newsweek, December 17, 1979.

New Yorker, December 7, 1981.

New York Times, December 24, 1989.

New York Times Book Review, November 11, 1979; November 25, 1979; April 26, 1981; April 25, 1982; June 5, 1983; November 10, 1985; November 9, 1986; November 8, 1987; November 13, 1988.

Parents' Choice, Volume 10, number 3, 1987, pp. 21, 36, 38.

Publishers Weekly, April 8, 1983.

School Library Journal, May, 1982; May, 1988, p. 70.

Time, December 3, 1979; December 21, 1981; December 20, 1982.

Times Literary Supplement, September 18, 1981.

Washington Post Book World, November 11, 1979; July 12, 1981; May 9, 1982; October 14, 1984.

World and I, December, 1991, pp. 252-61.*

*   *   *

Van DUYN, Mona (Jane) 1921-

PERSONAL: Surname is pronounced "van dine"; born May 9, 1921, in Waterloo, IA; daughter of Earl George (a businessman) and Lora G. (Kramer) Van Duyn; married Jarvis A. Thurston (a professor of English), August 31, 1943. *Education:* Iowa State Teachers College (now University of Northern Iowa), B.A., 1942; State University of Iowa, M.A., 1943. *Politics:* Independent. *Religion:* None. *Avocational interests:* "Gardening; sewing; reading recipe books, biographies, autobiographies, poems, travel books, short stories and whodunits."

ADDRESSES: Home—7505 Teasdale Ave., St. Louis, MO 63130.

CAREER: Poet. State University of Iowa, Iowa City, instructor in English, 1945; University of Louisville, Louisville, KY, instructor in English, 1946-50; Washington University, University College, St. Louis, MO, lecturer in English, 1950-67, adjunct professor, 1983, visiting Hurst Professor, 1987; Poet in residence, Breadloaf Writing Conference, MA, 1974 and 1976; lecturer, Salzburg Seminar in American Studies, Salzburg, Austria, 1973; Sewanee Writing Conference, Tennessee, 1990 and 1991; poetry consultant, Olin Library Modern Literature Collection. Judges poetry contests and travels to give readings.

MEMBER: National Institute of Arts and Letters, Academy of American Poets (chancellor, 1985).

AWARDS, HONORS: Eunice Tietjens Memorial Prize, *Poetry,* 1956, for "Three Valentines to the Wide World"; Helen Bullis Prize, *Poetry Northwest,* 1964; National Endowment for the Arts grants, 1966-67 and 1985; Harriet Monroe Memorial Prize, *Poetry,* 1968; Hart Crane Memorial Award, American Weave Press, 1968; first prize, Borestone Mountain Awards, 1968; Bollingen Prize, Yale University Library, 1970; National Book Award for Poetry, 1971, for *To See, To Take;* John Simon Guggenheim Memorial fellowship, 1972-73; Loines Prize, National Institute of Arts and Letters, 1976; Academy of American Poets fellow, 1981; Sandburg Prize, Cornell College, 1982; Shelley Memorial Award, Poetry Society of America, 1987, for body of work; Ruth Lilly Poetry Prize, Modern Poetry Association, 1989; Pulitzer Prize, 1991, for *Near Changes.* D.Litt., Washington University, 1971, Cornell College, 1972, and University of Northern Iowa, 1991.

WRITINGS:

Valentines to the Wide World: Poems (also see below), Cummington Press, 1959.

A Time of Bees (also see below), University of North Carolina Press, 1964.

To See, To Take (also see below), Atheneum, 1970.

Bedtime Stories (also see below), Ceres Press, 1972.

Merciful Disguises: Poems Published and Unpublished (includes new poems, *Valentines to the Wide World, A Time of Bees, To See, To Take,* and *Bedtime Stories*), Atheneum, 1973, reprinted, 1982.

Letters from a Father and Other Poems, Atheneum, 1982.

Near Changes: Poems, Knopf, 1990.

Lives and Deaths of the Poets and Non-Poets, privately published, 1991.

Poems represented in many anthologies including *The New Pocket Anthology of American Verse,* edited by Oscar Williams, Pocket Books, 1957, *Midland,* edited by Paul Engle, Random House, 1961, and *The Honey and the Gall,* edited by Chad Walsh, Macmillan, 1967. Regular contributor of reviews to *Poetry,* 1944-70. Founder and editor with husband, Jarvis Thurston, *Perspective: A Quarterly of Literature,* 1947-67; poetry advisor, *College English,* 1955-57. Contributor of poems, short stories, critical articles, and reviews to numerous periodicals, including *Kenyon Review, Critique, Western Review, Atlantic, New Republic, Yale Review,* and *New Yorker.*

SIDELIGHTS: Distinguished American poet Mona Van Duyn has won a dozen major prizes and awards, including a National Book Award in 1971 for *To See, To Take* and a Pulitzer prize in 1991 for *Near Changes.* Though much celebrated, Van Duyn's work is not widely known because it has been left out of the literary magazines and anthologies by which other important writers have become known to a large audience. Many readers and colleagues regard her as a master of poetic technique. A *Virginia Quarterly Review* contributor writes, "She is a poet of great wisdom, skill, and versatility; she is able to sustain locally intense language over long narrative and meditative poems, in a variety of modes and voices." Using colloquial language arranged in unobtrusive rhyme schemes, she is a poet who finds the extraordinary in the familiar. Elizabeth Frank writes in a *Nation* review that Van Duyn is much like the friend who finds an assembly of cats among the stones in a Parisian graveyard in the poem "At Pere Lachaise." "One of Van Duyn's powers as a poet is just this capacity for finding live cats on marble tombs. . . . She conjures dappled poems out of the graveyard of convention and tradition." Her most frequent subject is the resilience of love and the similar power of art to find meaning and hope in the face of disappointment and loss. A remarkable integrity keeps her from using poetry to mask unpleasant realities with "merciful disguises," which, when they do appear, are always recognized as masks. After domestic strife, or in the shadow of disease and death, she writes to redeem something harmonious from the debris, searching out the possibility of a better future. Frank explains, Van Duyn is "a poet who usually tries harder than any of her contemporaries to coax affirmation out of the waste and exhaustion of modern life."

Van Duyn began to write creatively when very young. "When I was in the second grade I published a poem in a little newspaper," she once told *CA*. "I wrote notebooks full of poems in the fifth, sixth, and seventh grades which I kept secret from everyone. And I've kept on writing for the rest of my life." Neither her parents nor her teachers encouraged her to read poetry, except that she recalls the punishment for misbehaving in gradeschool was to memorize a poem. "I loved nursery rhymes, as I guess all children do. Then I always liked the poems in our readers in school, in the anthologies," she said. Early in life she knew she wanted to write and publish poems or short fiction, and eventually chose poetry because her book of short stories was not accepted by publishers who wanted her to submit novels.

After her first collection of poems, *Valentines to the Wide World,* was published in 1959, she was quickly recognized as a domestic poet. "She is a master . . . of the exasperated-but-loving, intelligent-housewife tone, that, more than the ecstatic, the religious or the nostril-quivering sexual, strikes us as near the center of the way the women we know best and like best are," James Dickey said of her poems in the *New York Times Book Review* in 1965. More recently Thomas H. Landess of the *Sewanee Review* observed, "I can think of no contemporary poet who looks at the world with a steadier eye than does Mona Van

Duyn. . . . Her chief province is the world of everyday experience, of birthdays and minor illnesses, of the pantry and the zoo—a world of feeling which she sees as subtle and various. Yet the feeling she treats is always related to events which are substantial, palpable; and in this respect she is remarkably unspoiled by those abstractions which plague too many of her contemporaries."

Van Duyn contends that her poetry does not fit well into the genre of domestic poetry. As she told *CA,* "I have never written *to* an idea, so to speak, to do a particular kind of thing because I thought it was fashionable. I've just tried to write the way I thought was best and the way I *could* write. I would have to say I've been very satisfied with my work. It does rather irritate me that I'm often called a domestic poet; I think it's simply because I'm a woman. It's not a critical term, but it is a limiting term. I often use domestic imagery to write about everything under the sun, but I would say that only about a fourth of my poems are really domestic poems. I have a man poet friend who writes a great deal more than I do about his home, his wife and children, and he is *never* called a domestic poet. I find it fairly irritating. I think the critical treatment of women poets is improving, though."

Frank agrees that the term "domestic" does not accurately describe Van Duyn's poetry. "To say that Mona Van Duyn is a poet of dailiness and domesticity, of walking the dog and putting up peaches, is to give only a partial account of her world. Though she gives those their due, it is in facing up to the played-out, stale and unrenewable facts of existence that she finds her true voice. . . . When friendship and love have run out of surprises, when what we don't know is what we've decided to ignore, we are in Van Duyn territory," she observes.

Over time, Van Duyn has more accurately been seen as a love poet. The term "love poet" may suggest a romantic viewpoint, but Van Duyn's examination of family relationships is candid about the pitfalls as well as the joys of family life. Herbert Leibowitz of the *New York Times Book Review* explains that she "is a love poet, not of courtship or sexual windfalls, but of the bitter-sweet aftermath, the slow dying of feeling and its fitfull replenishments." The speaker is an intelligent and passionate person who has counted—and paid—the costs of commitment. "The politics of love and marriage" in her poems, says Leibowitz, "are frayed, rife with feud, tedium, insult and a sense of bereavement." Arthur Oberg relates in the *Southern Review,* "Mona Van Duyn fears her capacity to love and knows how love can hallucinate. But she is also one of those few poets who can carry in her poems the convincing impression of a very non-abstract physicality and of that joy before love, and before words, which all important poetry learns to convey." In *Parnassus: Poetry in Review,* Calvin Bedient concurs, "Her poems have the kind of uncalculated balance—of hope and knowingness and love and resignation—that leaves us in the midst of complexity."

Critics remark that Van Duyn is insightful and unsentimental about married love. Commenting on *Merciful Disguises: Published and Unpublished Poems,* a collection representing thirty years of writing, Harriet Zinnes maintains in the *Carleton Miscellany,* "Here Van Duyn shows that to be a woman is not easy and to love is difficult, if not 'harrowing'. . . .[Whether in the role of] wife, poet, friend, godmother, [or] daughter, Mona Van Duyn never loses herself in the infantile, though her lines in their rapid smoothness may appear a bit glib. . . . She knows marriage; knows she is as much victim as victimizer." The poet's careful diction closes self-pity and cynicism out of these deeply personal poems; Leibowitz explains that in all her work, "she keeps the delicate propriety of distance." The reviewer calls her "a brainy poet. Mistrusting stridency, she surveys the 'shifting and lustrous' perimeters of the moral life where passion and reason cross, unearthing motives, defining value, noting how character survives intolerant time."

Van Duyn's poems about her aging parents in *Letters from a Father and Other Poems* also treat emotionally intense material unsentimentally. The title poem lets the father speak for himself about his wife's failing health and the prospect of imminent death. "Harnessed in coarse and grainy slant-rhymes, the vernacular carries everything: the dignity and reality of common life, the sufferings of someone loved and the claustrophobia of love itself," Frank observes. Encouraged by the daughter's gift of a bird feeder, the father relates that their health has improved and both feel obligated to go on feeding the birds indefinitely. Robert Haas remarks in a *Book World* review, "The detail [of their ailments] is potentially gruesome, . . . but there is something in the implied attitude of the daughter—her clear eye, amusement, repugnance, fidelity—that complicates the whole poem and brings it alive, and it gets at an area of human experience that literature—outside of Samuel Beckett—has hardly touched."

For Van Duyn, the activity of writing poems is closely linked to the process of maintaining emotional commitment. When she accepted the National Book Award in 1971, she said, "Poetry honors the formed use of language particularly, being concerned with both its sound and its meaning, and a poet spends his life's best effort in shaping these into a patterned experience which will combine an awareness of earlier patternings with the unique resonance of his own voice. He tries to do so in such a way that the experience may be shared with other people. This effort assumes a caring about other human beings, a caring which is a form of love." Susan Ludvigson says in the *Dic-*

tionary of Literary Biography, "In Mona Van Duyn's world, love and its possibilities are intimately related to the transforming qualities of art. In poetry, as in love, nothing is easy, and perfection is not a realizable goal. Yet, according to Van Duyn, these are the best and finally the most satisfying aims we can have: to love life and each other with commitment; to create art that is rooted in that love."

For Van Duyn, poetry also serves an elegiac purpose. Commenting on painful confrontation after it has ceased, she surveys what can be salvaged from the wreckage. In the act of writing, the poet recalls experience and recreates it, giving shape and harmony to events without escaping into illusion; this kind of writing is an act of redemption that can make the worst aspects of life more endurable. Writing about the poems in *To See, To Take* in *American Poetry Review,* Richard Howard explains, "Here what is required, what is in fact wreaked, is expedience, testimony, formal difference, measurable submission, patience, salvage, adjustment, literalism after dreams and inspirations, charity of the imagination, a room with a clock, intelligent domesticity, chastened rearrangements, storms of fresh possibilities, hinges and disproportions." There is no backing away from loss; rather, as Howard phrases it, in Van Duyn's poetry "loss becomes fruitful."

Van Duyn's use of colloquial language and direct statement give the poems a casual air, but on the level of structure, they are ordered into definite, sometimes elaborate rhyme schemes. Some have traditional forms such as the sestina, but more often the rhyming patterns within stanzas are not repetitive or symmetrical so that the ear does not anticipate them. In the sense that she constructs rhyming verse, she is a formalist. On the other hand, her work has been described as "staunchly unliterary," meaning that it is accessible to readers with little experience in literary appreciation. If unliterary, it is not unsophisticated, for it contains many allusions to Greek mythology, the Bible, nursery rhymes, and the fields of philosophy, psychology, and the arts. Ludvigson says of Van Duyn, "Hers is a generous mixture of the ordinary and the unusual, the natural and the sophisticated."

Some reviewers feel that the "unliterary character" of Van Duyn's work is a liability. In a *Washington Post Book World* review, Marjorie Perloff suggests, "What Mona Van Duyn's poetry lacks, in short, is the quality the Russian Formalists called *factura* or density. If poetry is, as [Ezra] Pound put it, 'language charged with meaning to the utmost possible degree,' hers has a fairly low voltage." In contrast, Louis Coxe maintains in *New Republic* that the lyrics succeed because of the poet's unassuming personal charm: "One's not in this book for a lot of poems nor a series of made objects but for a written-out diary of the poet as one of us: humorous, observant and lively—as we'd all like to think we are. . . . The poems, nearly all of them, are interesting to read because of her company."

For her emotional and intellectual integrity, Van Duyn has often been called "tough-minded." Josephine Jacobsen calls this quality an "illusionless passion" for the real world. Jacobsen observes in a *Poetry* review that in Van Duyn's lyric poems, "there is an utter intention, without safeguards, without the second-thought of good taste and caution, which must just succeed or fail, and which succeeds. If any poetry can free us from the chic bond of with-it verse, this can and does." Writing in the *New York Times Book Review,* Leibowitz explains how the poet's vernacular style helps her to resist covering undesirable realities with a veneer of euphemisms. "As her syntax opens large spaces in which her speculative intelligence can play, as the 'half-demented "pressure of speech"' relaxes into light irony, the textures of experience—the world's 'motley and manifold'—find their comely form. To examine the linked atoms of desire and disguise with clarity of analysis, as Miss Van Duyn does, is to be an expert in moral optics and an artist of 'difficult wholeness.' "

In more than forty years of writing, Van Duyn has added to the literary canon many works memorable for their mastery of craft and hopeful content. "Van Duyn has made distinguished contributions to the observation-and-description poem, that line perfected by Elizabeth Bishop in which a kind of *National Geographic* curiosity and detachment yield detailed celebrations of the external world," writes Frank. The *Virginia Quarterly Review* contributor comments that her long, meditative poems such as "Bedtime Stories," an old woman's tales retold, "make a significant contribution to contemporary poetic narrative." Van Duyn's National Book Award winner, *To See, To Take,* says Oberg in the *Southern Review,* "is an outrageous book in ways that only major books, and major writers, can afford to be. Both Shakespeare and [W. B.] Yeats are prominent here, not so much as literary ghosts, but as sensibilities with whom Mona Van Duyn has much to share. The multiplicity of Shakespeare and that perfect control of tone which Yeats displayed in poems like 'Leda and the Swan,' 'Among School Children,' and 'The Circus Animals' Desertion' find their comparisons in the best poems of this book." *Poetry* contributor Alfred Corn writes that to have maintained her affirmations of the powers of love and art into the 1990s is a notable achievement. Of Van Duyn's recent Pulitzer winner, *Near Changes,* he summarizes, "To be older, tired, and still 'pleasure-hoping'; to be realistic and also subject to transcendent intuitions; to weigh the claims of love along with the claims of poetry; this is the vision informing *Near Changes.* During the past several decades Mona Van Duyn has assembled, in a language at once beautiful and exact, one of the most convincing bodies of work in our

poetry, a poetry that explores, as [Wallace] Stevens put it, ' . . . the metaphysical changes that occur, / Merely in living as and where we live.' "

Van Duyn recently added, "I am not basically a public person, and have consistently avoided all interviews and television appearances, trusting my reviewers and critics (most of them poets themselves) to present my poems to their readers. Rarely, I think, has a poet been rewarded with more affectionate, appreciative praise or more prizes awarded by her fellow poets. And yet . . . and yet . . . I have been waiting a long time for a critic who would discern what has for thirty years seemed to me, and even to my many non-literary readers, one obvious fact. Though I do write domestic poems of marriage, friendship, family, as does nearly every male or female poet, *many* of my poems are extended (domestic) metaphors which deal with a great many other concerns—death, the possibility of atomic destruction, the nature of the human imagination, unsettling scientific experiments, the nature of poetry,the limits of aesthetics, and so on. Perhaps I have used the extended domestic metaphor to explore the complexities of the world more consistently than any other poet presently writing. I don't know. I do know that, reading my poems, the most brilliant and perceptive critics seem to go blind to the subject of the poem. 'Walking the Dog: A Diatribe' is not a descriptive poem about walking the dog ('How do they know what is insufferable in their ignorant gloss?') as a distinguished critic labeled it. 'First Trip through the Automatic Carwash' is not 'about' going through the carwash. The world of my poems is not a world of 'the pantry and the zoo' nor of 'going to the supermarket.' 'Glad Heart at the Supermarket' is a close, complex analysis of love and friendship. When 'I cupboard these pickled peaches in time's despite' I am not talking about pickled peaches. The zoo poem is certainly not 'about' the zoo. 'Death by Aesthetics' uses the extended metaphor of a doctor-patient relationship to explore the defects of aesthetics. 'The Fear of Flying' (the title preceding [Erica] Jong's), is an analysis of my relationship to the world, written in the extended metaphor of a marriage and not a 'confessional' poem about marriage. Both the brilliant poet and editors and my most brilliant poet friends have not hesitated to urge upon me their own re-writings of my poems, destroying the ideas, the subject and the whole careful direction of the poem, reducing it to pure description or a purely 'domestic' attitude, embarrassing me into having to point out to them what the poem is doing.

"I would not, ungratefully, discharge myself of these dissatisfactions with my remarkably generous commentators were it not for 1) the sense that much of my poetry has been in a very significant, a very basic way, misunderstood, and 2) a sense of aging urgency leads me to feel I cannot wait much longer for a critic who will open his or her eyes and read me as he or she reads every other poet, including the infinitely more difficult ones. (I like my own actual domestic poems, as do my critics and friends, but they make up only a portion of my work.)

"Speaking of difficult poets, I might add that for the sake of my many non-poet (even non-literary) friends and readers, I have worked very hard to be as accessible as possible while still keeping faith with an inborn sense of the complexity of experience and the demands of an art which I have loved, read and studies since childhood.

She concluded, "My new work (since *Near Changes,* 1990) consists of about thirty 'minimalist sonnets' in which I have increased both the fun and the difficulty by cutting the sonnet line to either one foot or two feet. There are also long autobiographical poems. Though my books have usually been a mixture of free verse and formal poems, I have been indulging myself in these later years in intensifying the concentration of writing by producing more formal poems than before, usually adding some extra difficulty or challenge to the received or invented form."

BIOGRAPHICAL/CRITICAL SOURCES:

BOOKS

Contemporary Literary Criticism, Gale, Volume 3, 1975; Volume 7, 1977.
Contemporary Poets, St. Martin's Press, 1975.
Dictionary of Literary Biography, Volume 5: *American Poets since World War II,* Gale, 1980.

PERIODICALS

American Poetry Review, November, 1973.
Book World, September 5, 1982.
Carleton Miscellany, spring/summer, 1974.
Nation, May 4, 1970; November 27, 1982.
New Republic, October 6, 1973.
New York Times, January 11, 1971.
New York Times Book Review, November 21, 1965; August 2, 1970; December 9, 1973; March 13, 1983.
Parnassus: Poetry in Review, spring/summer, 1974.
Poetry, June, 1965; June, 1971; October, 1990.
Sewanee Review, winter, 1973.
Southern Review, winter, 1973.
Virginia Quarterly Review, spring, 1965; winter, 1974.
Washington Post Book World, January 6, 1974; September 5, 1982.
Women's Review of Books, January, 1991.

Van SETERS, John 1935-

PERSONAL: Born May 2, 1935, in Hamilton, Ontario, Canada; son of Hugo and Anne (Hubert) Van Seters; married Elizabeth Marie Malmberg, June 11, 1960; children: Peter John, Deborah Elizabeth. *Education:* University of Toronto, B.A., 1958; Yale University, M.A., 1959, Ph.D., 1965; Princeton Theological Seminary, B.D., 1962. *Religion:* Presbyterian.

ADDRESSES: Home—104 Mullin Ct., Chapel Hill, NC 27514. *Office*—Department of Religious Studies, 101 Saunders Hall CB#3225, University of North Carolina at Chapel Hill, Chapel Hill, NC 27599.

CAREER: Waterloo Lutheran University, Waterloo, Ontario, assistant professor of Near Eastern studies, 1965-67; Andover Newton Theological School, Newton Centre, MA, associate professor of Old Testament studies, 1967-70; University of Toronto, Toronto, Ontario, associate professor, 1970-76, professor of Near Eastern studies, 1976-77; University of North Carolina at Chapel Hill, James A. Gray Professor of Biblical Literature, 1977—, chairman of department of religion, 1980-88.

MEMBER: American Oriental Society, American Association of University Professors, American Schools of Oriental Research, Society of Biblical Literature, Society for the Study of Egyptian Antiquities.

AWARDS, HONORS: Woodrow Wilson fellow, 1958; J. J. Obermann fellow, 1962-64; Agusta Hazard fellow, 1964-65; Canada Council research grant, 1973; Guggenheim fellow, 1979-80; National Endowment for the Humanities research fellow, 1985-86; James A. Breasted Prize, American Historical Association, 1985, and American Academy of Religion Book Award, 1986, both for *In Search of History: Historiography in the Ancient World and the Origins of Biblical History;* American Council of Learned Societies research fellow, 1990-91.

WRITINGS:

The Hyksos: A New Investigation, Yale University Press, 1966.
Abraham in History and Tradition, Yale University Press, 1975.
In Search of History: Historiography in the Ancient World and the Origins of Biblical History, Yale University Press, 1983.
Der Jahwist als Historiker (title means "The Yahwist as Historian"), Theologischer Verlag, 1987.

Contributor to journals, including *Biblica, Journal of Biblical Literature, Orientalia, Vetus Testamentum,* and *Zeitschrift fuer die alttestamentliche Wissenschaft.*

WORK IN PROGRESS: "A monograph entitled *Prologue to History: The Yahwist as Historian in Genesis* (Westminster/John Knox Press), dealing with the nature of historiography in the Pentateuch as a sequel to *In Search of History,* will appear in 1992. It will be followed shortly by the Yahwist's 'bibliographical' treatment of the life of Moses in Exodus-Numbers. The so-called 'J' author of the Pentateuch will be viewed as belonging to the intellectual tradition of ancient history writing, with antiquarian interests in national origins, the foundations of social and religious institutions, and politico-religious identity."

SIDELIGHTS: John Van Seters told *CA:* "There is renewed enthusiasm in the historical criticism of the Pentateuch and historical books of the Old Testament, with fundamental changes taking place in these areas of study. My own work has contributed to this reshaping of biblical studies, which has involved a lively dialogue with European scholarship. This is reflected in the fact that Theologischer Verlag of Zurich has published, in German, a preliminary study of my work on the Yahwist and will distribute the European edition of my new book, *Prologue to History.* I have also given many invited lectures in the universities and academic conferences in the U.K. and on the continent. This has been one of the most rewarding and enjoyable results of my writing career."

BIOGRAPHICAL/CRITICAL SOURCES:

PERIODICALS

Times Literary Supplement, April 20, 1967.*

*   *   *

VIPONT, Charles
   See FOULDS, Elfrida Vipont

*   *   *

VIPONT, Elfrida
   See FOULDS, Elfrida Vipont

W

WABER, Bernard 1924-

PERSONAL: Born September 27, 1924, in Philadelphia, PA; son of Henry and Pauline (Fleishman) Waber; married Ethel Bernstein, 1952; children: Paulis, Kim, Jan Gary. *Education:* Attended University of Pennsylvania, Philadelphia College of Art, 1946-50, and Pennsylvania Academy of Fine Arts, 1950-51.

ADDRESSES: Home—3653 Bertha Dr., Baldwin Harbor, NY 11510.

CAREER: Commercial artist for Conde Nast Publications, New York City, and *Seventeen,* New York City, 1952-54; *Life,* New York City, graphic designer, 1955-72; author and illustrator of children's books, 1961—; *People,* New York City, graphic designer, 1974—1988. *Military service:* U.S. Army, 1942-45; became staff sergeant.

AWARDS, HONORS: New York Herald Tribune Children's Spring Book Festival picture book honor, 1962, for *The House on East 88th Street; An Anteater Named Arthur* was selected one of the American Institute of Graphic Arts Children's Books, 1967-68; *Boston Globe-Horn Book* honor book for illustration, 1971, for *A Firefly Named Torchy; Ira Sleeps Over* was included in the Children's Book Showcase of the Children's Book Council, 1973; *But Names Will Never Hurt Me* was selected one of Child Study Association's Children's Books of the Year, 1976; Lewis Carroll Shelf Award, 1979, for *Lyle, Lyle, Crocodile; The Snake: A Very Long Story* was selected one of International Reading Association's Children's Choices, 1979.

WRITINGS:

SELF-ILLUSTRATED

Lorenzo, Houghton, 1961.

The House on East 88th Street, Houghton, 1962, published in England as *Welcome, Lyle,* Chatto, Boyd & Oliver, 1969.
How to Go about Laying an Egg, Houghton, 1963.
Rich Cat, Poor Cat, Houghton, 1963.
Just Like Abraham Lincoln, Houghton, 1964.
Lyle, Lyle, Crocodile, Houghton, 1965.
"You Look Ridiculous," Said the Rhinoceros to the Hippopotamus, Houghton, 1966.
Lyle and the Birthday Party, Houghton, 1966.
Cheese, Houghton, 1967.
An Anteater Named Arthur, Houghton, 1967.
A Rose for Mr. Bloom, Houghton, 1968.
Lovable Lyle, Houghton, 1969.
A Firefly Named Torchy (ALA Notable Book), Houghton, 1970.
Nobody Is Perfick (collection of short stories), Houghton, 1971.
Ira Sleeps Over, Houghton, 1972.
Lyle Finds His Mother, Houghton, 1974.
I Was All Thumbs, Houghton, 1975.
But Names Will Never Hurt Me, Houghton, 1976.
Good-bye, Funny Dumpy-Lumpy, Houghton, 1977.
Mice on My Mind, Houghton, 1977.
The Snake: A Very Long Story, Houghton, 1978.
Dear Hildegarde, Houghton, 1980.
You're a Little Kid with a Big Heart, Houghton, 1980.
Bernard, Houghton, 1982.
Funny, Funny Lyle, Houghton, 1987.
Ira Says Goodbye, Houghton, 1988.

Waber's manuscripts are included in the Kerlan Collection, University of Minnesota.

ADAPTATIONS: The House on East 88th Street (filmstrip with record or cassette), Miller-Brody; *Lovable Lyle* (filmstrip with record or cassette), Miller-Brody; *Lyle, Lyle, Crocodile* (filmstrip with record or cassette), Miller-

Brody; *Lyle and the Birthday Party* (filmstrip with record or cassette), Miller-Brody; *Lyle* (play; based on "Lyle" books), first produced at the McAlpin Rooftop Theatre, 1970; *Ira Sleeps Over* (film), Phoenix/BFA Films; *Ira Sleeps Over* (cassette; filmstrip with cassette), Live Oak Media, 1984; *Lyle, the Musical* (animation), Home Box Office, 1987; *Ira Says Goodbye* (filmstrip with cassette), Live Oak Media, 1989; *Lyle* (musical stage production), first produced in Chicago, 1989; *Lyle* (play), Minneapolis Children's Theater, 1990-91; *Lyle, Lyle, Crocodile* (adapted from *The House on East 88th Street* [videotape]), Hi-Tops Video.

SIDELIGHTS: Bernard Waber is perhaps best known for his books about a crocodile named Lyle. "With aplomb and dazzling showmanship, Lyle entertains and enchants" the family in whose house he appears, according to *Twentieth-Century Children's Writers* contributor Martha J. Fick. Fick also asserts that in the "Lyle" books, "text and illustrations merge dynamically to balance fantasy with the exploration of feelings and relationships." Such balance between story and illustration is noted in some of Waber's other works; commenting on *Ira Says Goodbye,* Alison Teal asserted in *New York Times Book Review* that "the illustrations are delicate and precisely detailed—just like the writing."

During Waber's childhood, his family moved frequently because of business failures. The author once commented: "Each time relocation was necessary, I sought assurance from my parents that a neighborhood library and a motion picture theater existed within rollerskating distance. Availability of prospective playmates was a serious matter too, of course, but by my reasoning the library and cinema were life-giving urgencies, a survival kit for any new neighborhood. . . . When I was about eight years of age, I had the astonishing good fortune to obtain after-school employment in a neighborhood movie theater. It was my job to raise seats and pick up discarded candy wrappers after daily matinee performances. Admission to a movie theater free of charge was living and breathing my own fantasy. It was also my first experience doing work I enjoyed."

Waber credits those early days of movie-watching for beginning his practice of creating stories: "Each day, I raced from school to theater . . . and caught the final ten or fifteen minutes of—in an era of abundant production—a daily new feature film. Following the performance, having seen only the ending, I would try to reconstruct what I imagined to be the middle and beginning. It occurs to me that this was my earliest attempt at plotting, which may or may not account for the frequency with which endings to my own stories come to me before I have realized earlier developments."

Waber also stated: "Although I write and illustrate, I believe if forced to choose between the two, I would choose writing. There is a freedom about writing that appeals to me. You can do it almost anywhere, and I have."

BIOGRAPHICAL/CRITICAL SOURCES:

BOOKS

Kingman, Lee, and others, compilers, *Illustrators of Children's Books: 1957-1966,* Horn Book, 1968.
Kingman and others, compilers, *Illustrators of Children's Books: 1967-1976,* Horn Book, 1978.
Twentieth-Century Children's Writers, 3rd edition, St. James Press, 1989, pp. 1005-1006.
Ward, Martha E., and Dorothy A. Marquardt, *Authors of Books for Young People,* 2nd edition, Scarecrow, 1971.

PERIODICALS

New Yorker, December 16, 1967.
New York Times, March 21, 1970.
New York Times Book Review, February 23, 1969; March 5, 1989, p. 31.
Times Literary Supplement, May 25, 1967; June 26, 1969; April 17, 1970.

*   *   *

WAHL, Jan (Boyer) 1933-

PERSONAL: Born April 1, 1933, in Columbus, OH; son of Russell Rothenburger (a physician) and Nina Marie (Boyer) Wahl. *Education:* Cornell University, B.A., 1953; University of Copenhagen, graduate study, 1954-55; University of Michigan, M.A., 1958. *Religion:* Presbyterian. *Avocational interests:* Collecting old films, particularly animated films by Lotte Reiniger, Ladislas Starevitch, Max Fleisher, Walt Disney, Hugh Harman, and Rudolph Ising; collecting old toys and comic strip and animation art; traveling from the Sahara Desert to Lapland to the Yucatan.

ADDRESSES: Home—6766 Carrietowne Ln., Toledo, OH 43617; and Apartado Postal 33, San Miguel Allende, Guanajuato, Mexico. *Agent*—Mary Jack Wald, 111 East 14th St., New York, NY 10003; Rogers, Coleridge and White, 20 Powis Mews, London W11 1JN, England.

CAREER: Worked with Danish film director Carl Theodor Dreyer during the making of Dreyer's prize-winning *Ordet,* 1954-55; returned to Denmark as secretary to writer Isak Dinesen, 1957-58; later worked with illustrator Garth Williams in Mexico, and with Erik Blegvad in England, 1966-67; writer for young people. Served as correspondent from Copehagen for *Dance* magazine during the 1950s, and worked as a translator of French communiques for two Danish newspapers.

AWARDS, HONORS: Fulbright scholar in Copenhagen, 1953-54; Avery Hopwood Award in fiction, University of Michigan, 1955, for a group of short stories collectively entitled *Seven Old Maids* (the stories appeared in various magazines); Young Critics' award at International Children's Book Fair, Bologna, Italy, 1969, for *Pocahontas in London;* Ohioana Book Award winner, 1970, for *The Norman Rockwell Storybook;* American Library Association (ALA) Notable Book citation, 1974, for *The Woman with the Eggs;* Bowling Green State University, Ohio, declared May 1, 1980, as "Jan Wahl Day"; Parents' Choice literary award, 1982, for *Tiger Watch; Redbook* award, 1987, for *Humphrey's Bear.*

WRITINGS:

CHILDREN'S FICTION

Pleasant Fieldmouse, illustrated by Maurice Sendak, Harper, 1964.

The Howards Go Sledding, illustrated by John E. Johnson, Holt, 1964.

Hello, Elephant, illustrated by Edward Ardizzone, Holt, 1964.

Cabbage Moon, illustrated by Adrienne Adams, Holt, 1965.

The Muffletumps: A Story of Four Dolls, illustrated by E. Ardizzone, Holt, 1966.

Christmas in the Forest, illustrated by Eleanor Schick, Macmillan, 1967.

Pochontas in London, illustrated by John Alcorn, Delacorte, 1967.

Cobweb Castle, illustrated by Edward Gorey, Holt, 1968.

The Furious Flycycle, illustrated by Fernando Krahn, Delacorte, 1968.

Push Kitty, illustrated by Garth Williams, Harper, 1968.

Rickety Rackety Rooster, illustrated by J. E. Johnson, Simon & Schuster, 1968.

Runaway Jonah, and Other Tales (adapted from Biblical stories), illustrated by Uri Shulevitz, Macmillan, 1968, illustrated by Jane Conteh-Morgan, Caedmon, 1985.

The Fisherman, illustrated by Emily Arnold McCully, Norton, 1969.

How the Children Stopped the Wars (fable), illustrated by Mitchell Miller, Farrar, Straus, 1969, illustrated by Gerald Rose, Abelard Schuman, 1975.

May Horses, illustrated by Blair Lent, Delacorte, 1969.

The Norman Rockwell Storybook, illustrated by Norman Rockwell, Windmill, 1969.

A Wolf of My Own, illustrated by Lilian Hoban, Macmillan, 1969.

The Animals' Peace Day, illustrated by Victoria Chess, Crown, 1970.

Doctor Rabbit, illustrated by Peter Parnall, Delacorte, 1970.

The Mulberry Tree, illustrated by Feodor Rojankovsky, Grosset, 1970.

The Prince Who Was a Fish, illustrated by Robin Jacques, Simon & Schuster, 1970.

Abe Lincoln's Beard, illustrated by F. Krahn, Delacorte, 1971.

Anna Help Ginger, illustrated by Lawrence Di Fiori, Putnam, 1971.

Crabapple Night, illustrated by Steven Kellogg, Holt, 1971.

Lorenzo Bear and Company, illustrated by F. Krahn, Putnam, 1971.

Margaret's Birthday, illustrated by Mercer Mayer, Four Winds Press, 1971.

The Six Voyages of Pleasant Fieldmouse, illustrated by P. Parnall, Delacorte, 1971.

The Wonderful Kite, illustrated by U. Shulevitz, Delacorte, 1971.

Cristobal and the Witch, illustrated by Janet McCaffery, Putnam, 1972.

Grandmother Told Me, illustrated by M. Mayer, Little, Brown, 1972.

Magic Heart, illustrated by Trina Schart Hyman, Seabury, 1972.

The Very Peculiar Tunnel, illustrated by S. Kellogg, Putnam, 1972.

Crazy Brobobalou (adapted from *Le Prince spirituel,* by Countess Prince de Beaumont), illustrated by Paula Winter, Putnam, 1973.

S.O.S. Bobomobile! or, The Future Adventures of Melvin Spitznagle and Professor Mickimecki, illustrated by F. Krahn, Delacorte, 1973.

Jeremiah Knucklebones, illustrated by Jane Breskin Zalben, Holt, 1974.

(With Dolores Janes Garcia) *Juan Diego and the Lady/La dama y Juan Diego* (bilingual edition), illustrated by Leonard Everett Fisher, Putnam, 1974.

Mooga Mega Mekki, illustrated by F. Krahn, O'Hara, 1974.

Pleasant Fieldmouse's Halloween Party, illustrated by Wallace Tripp, Putnam, 1974.

The Five in the Forest, illustrated by Erik Blegvad, Follett, 1974.

The Woman with the Eggs (adapted from the poem by Hans Christian Andersen), illustrated by Ray Cruz, Crown, 1974.

Bear, Wolf, and Mouse, illustrated by Kinuko Craft, Follett, 1975.

The Clumpets Go Sailing, illustrated by Cyndy Szekeres, Parents' Magazine Press, 1975.

The Muffletumps' Christmas Party, illustrated by C. Szekeres, Follett, 1975.

The Muffletump Storybook, illustrated by C. Szekeres, Follett, 1975.

The Screeching Door; or, What Happened at the Elephant Hotel, illustrated by J. Winslow Higginbottom, Four Winds Press, 1975.

Follow Me, Cried Bee, illustrated by John Wallner, Crown, 1976.

Grandpa's Indian Summer, illustrated by Joanne Scribner, Prentice-Hall, 1976.

Great-Grandmother Cat Tales, illustrated by C. Szekeres, Pantheon, 1976.

Doctor Rabbit's Foundling, illustrated by C. Szekeres, Pantheon, 1977.

Frankenstein's Dog (also see below), illustrated by Kay Chorao, Prentice-Hall, 1977.

The Muffletumps' Halloween Scare, illustrated by C. Szekeres, Follett, 1977.

The Pleasant Fieldmouse Storybook, illustrated by E. Blegvad, Prentice-Hall, 1977.

Pleasant Fieldmouse's Valentine Trick, illustrated by Marc Brown, Windmill, 1977.

Carrot Nose, illustrated by James Marshall, Farrar, Straus, 1977.

Dracula's Cat (also see below), illustrated by K. Chorao, Prentice-Hall, 1977.

Drakestail (adapted from English folktales), illustrated by Byron Barton, Greenwillow, 1978.

Jamie's Tiger, illustrated by Tomie dePaola, Harcourt, 1978.

Who Will Believe Tim Kitten?, illustrated by C. Szekeres, Pantheon, 1978.

Doctor Rabbit's Lost Scout, illustrated by C. Szekeres, Pantheon, 1979.

Needle Noodle, and Other Silly Stories (English folktales), illustrated by Stan Mack, Pantheon, 1979.

Sylvester Bear Overslept, illustrated by Lee Lorenz, Parents' Magazine Press, 1979.

The Teeny Tiny Witches, illustrated by Margot Tomes, Putnam, 1979.

Button Eye's Orange, illustrated by Wendy Watson, Warne, 1980.

Old Hippo's Easter Egg, illustrated by Lorinda Bryan-Cauley, Harcourt, 1980.

The Cucumber Princess, illustrated by Caren Caraway, Stemmer House, 1981.

Grandpa Gus's Birthday Cake, illustrated by J. Wallner, Prentice-Hall, 1981.

The Little Blind Goat, illustrated by Antonio Frasconi, Stemmer House, 1981.

The Pipkins Go Camping, illustrated by J. Wallner, Prentice-Hall, 1982.

Tiger Watch, illustrated by Charles Mikolaycak, Harcourt, 1982.

More Room for the Pipkins, illustrated by J. Wallner, Prentice-Hall, 1983.

Small One, illustrated by Beth Wiener, Hastings House, 1983.

Peter and the Troll Baby, illustrated by E. Blegvad, Golden Press, 1984.

Cheltenham's Party, illustrated by Lucinda McQueen, Golden Press, 1985.

So Many Raccoons, illustrated by Beth Lee Weiner, Caedmon, 1985.

Rabbits on Roller Skates!, illustrated by David Allender, Crown, 1986.

The Toy Circus, illustrated by Tim Bowers, Gulliver Books-Harcourt, 1986.

Let's Go Fishing, illustrated by Bruce Lemorise, Golden Press, 1987.

Humphrey's Bear, illustrated by William Joyce, Holt, 1987.

Timothy Tiger's Terrible Toothache, illustrated by Lisa McCue, Golden Press, 1988.

Little Dragon's Grandmother, illustrated by L. McQueen, Golden Press, 1988.

Tim Kitten and the Red Cupboard, illustrated by Bruce Degen, Simon & Schuster, 1988.

The Golden Christmas Tree, illustrated by Leonard Weisgard, Golden Press, 1988.

Tales of Fuzzy Mouse: Six Cozy Stories for Bedtime, illustrated by L. Hoban, Golden Press, 1988.

The Adventures of Underwater Dog, illustrated by Tim Bowers, Grosset, 1989.

The Wizard of Oz Movie Storybook, Golden Press, 1989.

Dracula's Cat [and] *Frankenstein's Dog,* illustrated by K. Chorao, Simon & Schuster, 1990.

A Gift for Miss Milo, illustrated by Jeff Grove, Ten Speed Press, 1990.

The Rabbit Club, Harcourt, 1990.

Mrs. Owl and Mr. Pig, illustrated by Eileen Christelow, Lodestar/Dutton, 1991.

Tailypo!, illustrated by Wil Clay, Holt, 1991.

The Sleepytime Book, illustrated by Arden Johnson, Tambourine Books, 1992.

Little Eight John, illustrated by W. Clay, Lodestar/Dutton, 1992.

My Cat Ginger, illustrated by Naava, Tambourine Books, 1992.

CHILDREN'S VERSE

The Beast Book, illustrated by E. W. Eichel, Harper, 1964.

YOUNG ADULT FICTION

Youth's Magic Horn: Seven Stories, Thomas Nelson, 1978.

OTHER

Paradiso! Paradiso! (play), first produced at Cornell University, 1954.

Also author of *Seven Old Maids,* a collection of previously published short stories. Contributor of short stories to a number of literary magazines, such as *Transatlantic Review, Prairie Schooner,* and *Epoch.* Poetry and articles on films have appeared in periodicals in America and abroad.

Wahl's manuscripts are housed in a Jan Wahl Collection at the University of Wyoming, Laramie, at Bowling Green State University, Bowling Green, Ohio, and at the Kerlan Collection at the University of Minnesota, Minneapolis.

ADAPTATIONS: An animated film entitled *Why We Need Each Other: The Animals' Picnic Day,* adapted from *The Animals' Peace Day,* was produced by Bosustow/ Learning Corporation, 1973; a filmstrip with cassette was produced of *The Clumpets Go Sailing* by Listening Library, 1979; an animated film based on *The Furious Flycycle* was produced by Bosustow/Churchill and was later presented on CBS-TV, 1980; an opera based on *How the Children Stopped the Wars* was produced by Northwestern University in 1986, and at Fairfield University in 1991.

WORK IN PROGRESS: New edition of *How the Children Stopped the Wars* for Ten Speed Press.

SIDELIGHTS: Jan Wahl is an imaginative and prolific writer of children's books, many of which are graced by the work of the most notable of illustrators. When he was born in Columbus, Ohio, in 1933, his father was a premedical student at Ohio State University and his mother an art student; therefore, Wahl spent a good portion of the Great Depression years with both sets of grandparents in northwest Ohio improvising stories for his own amusement and later for the amusement of his five other brothers. One of his first literary efforts involved trying to improve upon the story of "Jack and the Beanstalk." At the age of three, though, he remembers being enthralled as his great-grandmother sketched a chicken on what had previously been a blank sheet of paper. "And I believe at that moment I became 'hooked' on art in general," says Wahl in an autobiographical essay in *Something about the Author Autobiography Series.* "Virtually the whole of my adult life has been spent in writing and scribbling so that some artist might make nifty pictures. Much of my life, too, has been spent recalling the freshness of that morning on an Ohio farm where I spent much of my childhood."

As the Great Depression was ending, the family settled in Toledo, Ohio, where Wahl's father had established his medical practice. Since one of his mother's cousins happened to be the music director for a local broadcasting company, Wahl was invited to play on a Saturday morn-

ing radio program and describes his life at the time. "I did puppet shows, magic shows; I pretended to be Danny Kaye and lip-synched his records," recalls Wahl. "I performed before church groups, traveled to other schools, made a buffoon of myself in front of Parent-Teacher groups. And on Saturday mornings did 'The Kiddies' Karnival.' " Wahl also fell in love with the movies, a passion retained in his collection of old films, particularly animated films by Lotte Reiniger, Ladislas Starevitch, Max Fleisher, Walt Disney, Hugh Harman, and Rudolph Ising. Although Wahl, with an early training in piano, wanted to write music for film, he believes that movies have helped him in his career as a writer, enabling him to think visually.

After high school graduation, Wahl entered Cornell University where he began to study creative writing and published stories in a few small magazines. After finishing his bachelor's degree, he won a Fulbright scholarship to Denmark, the land of his ancestors. While studying there, he met several influential people, including writer Isak Dinesen. Also, a fortuitous invitation allowed him to work on director Carl Theodor Dreyer's classic film, *Ordet.* Upon his return to the United States, Wahl accepted a scholarship to earn a master's degree at the University of Michigan and continued his efforts to become a writer, winning the Avery Hopwood Award in fiction for a group of short stories collectively entitled *Seven Old Maids.* Then came an unexpected cable from an ailing Isak Dinesen in Denmark requesting Wahl to join her there so that she could dictate her last tales. Although he was neither a stenographer nor a professional typist, he was eager to assist the writer; however, the arrangement proved unsatisfactory to her and he was soon dismissed. While in Denmark, Wahl also did research for the Danish Film Museum and became correspondent from Copenhagen for *Dance* magazine and worked briefly for Danish newspapers.

Upon his return to the United States, Wahl began work on a novel as well as a few little animal stories for children. "This was a lot more fun. I had found what I could do. I MUST write for children. In a way, I was writing the films I wished I could see. A picture book is related to an animated cartoon." Although his first efforts to publish children's books were unsuccessful, Wahl once commented: "When my first children's book, *Pleasant Fieldmouse,* won reviews such as 'belongs on the same high shelf as Beatrix Potter' and 'not since *Wind in the Willows*' and 'if you buy only one book this year, make it this one,' all my own childhood dreams seemed to come true." In his autobiographical essay, Wahl adds: "My promise to myself was to write in a positive way. To connect with children and their parents through fables and animal stories. To know that truth can be reached via fantasy."

BIOGRAPHICAL/CRITICAL SOURCES:

BOOKS

Authors of Books for Young People, edited by Martha E. Ward and Dorothy A. Marquardt, Scarecrow, 1971.
Something about the Author Autobiography Series, Volume 3, Gale, 1986, pp. 293-311.
Twentieth-Century Children's Writers, 3rd edition, St. James Press, 1989.

PERIODICALS

Book World, December 10, 1967.
Kirkus Reviews, October 15, 1971, p. 1117; March 15, 1986, p. 474; April 15, 1991, p. 540.
National Observer, December 11, 1967.
Newsweek, December 6, 1982.
New York Times Book Review, December 3, 1967; November 7, 1971, p. 46; November 11, 1984, p. 48; August 9, 1987, p. 29.
Ohioana Quarterly, Autumn, 1980.
Publishers Weekly, December 14, 1970, p. 39; February 8, 1971, p. 81; November 11, 1974, p. 48; December 5, 1980, p. 53; January 17, 1986, p. 69; April 25, 1986, p. 72; October 31, 1986, p. 66; April 24, 1987, p. 69; October 13, 1989, p. 56; June 8, 1990, p. 54; May 10, 1991, p. 283.
School Library Journal, January, 1985, p. 48; May, 1986, p. 114; February, 1987, p. 75; August, 1987, p. 76; January, 1990, p. 92; August, 1990, p. 135; September, 1990, p. 232.
School Library Media Activities Monthly, February, 1990, pp. 33-35.

*   *   *

WALKER, Barbara (Jeanne) K(erlin) 1921-
(Beth Kilreon)

PERSONAL: Born October 13, 1921, in Ann Arbor, MI; daughter of Oscar Fahnestock (a school administrator) and Mildred M. (Baldwin) Kerlin; married Warren Stanley Walker (Horn Professor Emeritus of English at Texas Tech University), December 9, 1943; children: Brian, Theresa Sue. *Education:* New York State College for Teachers (now State University of New York at Albany), B.A., 1943, M.A., 1947; Cornell University, graduate courses in folklore. *Religion:* Christian (Disciples of Christ). *Avocational interests:* Storytelling and speaking to children and adults "in schools and libraries and at festivals, conventions, and workshops; field collecting of folktales in Turkey and among Africans close to oral tradition; writing; traveling; advising would-be writers of books for children; designing ethnic costumes; reading."

ADDRESSES: Home—3703 66th St., Lubbock, TX 79413. *Office*—Archive of Turkish Oral Narrative, Texas Tech University Library, Lubbock, TX 79409.

CAREER: Junior high school teacher in Cornwall, NY, 1943-45, and Ithaca, NY, 1948-49; Albany Academy for Girls, Albany, NY, teacher, 1947-48; Cornell University Press, Ithaca, associate editor and first reader, 1949-51; Blackburn College, Carlinville, IL, professor of English and education, 1952-59; Parsons College, Fairfield, IA, instructor in English and education, 1959-61, 1962-64, and college editor, 1962-64; teacher of English as a second language at elementary school in Ankara, Turkey, 1961-62; Texas Tech University, Lubbock, half-time lecturer in undergraduate and graduate children's literature courses, spring, 1973, curator of Archive of Turkish Oral Narrative, 1980—. Member of board of directors, Project Impact, Library-Learning Center, Lubbock; member of advisory board, Lubbock Cultural Affairs Council. Initiated and led first Internationalism in Children's Literature European graduate seminar program, summer, 1973.

MEMBER: International Society for Folk-Narrative Research, Modern Language Association of America, National Association for the Preservation and Perpetuation of Storytelling (NAPPS), National Retired Teachers Association, Society of Children's Book Writers, American Folklore Society, Authors Guild, Authors League of America, Middle East Outreach Council, Middle East Studies Association, American Friends of Turkey, Turkish-American Association, Turkish Studies Association, African Studies Association, Texas Institute of Letters, Texas Folklore Society, Texas Association for Middle Eastern Scholars, Texas Retired Teachers Association, Friends of the Texas Tech University Library, Friends of the Lubbock Public Library, West Texas Turkish-American Association, Phi Kappa Phi, Delta Zeta, Alpha Beta Alpha.

AWARDS, HONORS: Cited by Turkish Ministry of Education for acquainting American children with Turkish culture, 1967; named Texas' most distinguished Delta Zeta alumna, 1970; awarded bronze medal, Institute of Pedagogy, University of Padua, Italy, 1973, for international service to children and literature; commissioned by UNICEF to compile an international children's joke book, 1973; subject of six "Voice of America" broadcasts, 1977-81, for work with Turkish materials for non-Turkish children and adults; Caldecott Medal nominations for *How the Hare Told the Truth about His Horse* and *New Patches for Old;* cited as one of the five most distinguished alumni in 1979 by the State University of New York at Albany; awards from Houston Turkish-American Association, 1986, Arkadas Turkish Folk Ensemble, 1987, and West Texas Turkish-American Association, 1987, for disseminating Turkish culture; elected member of the Ataturk Culture, Language, and History Supreme Council, 1989; Litt.D., Selcuk University, Turkey, 1989; *New York Times Book Review* named *The Dancing Palm Tree and Other Nigerian Folktales* one of its ten best-illustrated children's books published internationally, 1990.

WRITINGS:

FOR ADULTS

(Editor with husband, Warren S. Walker) *Nigerian Folk Tales as Told by Olawale Idewu and Omotayo Adu,* Rutgers University Press, 1961, 2nd edition, Archon Books, 1980.

(Editor with W. S. Walker) *The Erie Canal: Gateway to Empire,* Heath, 1963.

(Editor with W. S. Walker of supplements) W. S. Walker, *Twentieth-Century Short Story Explication: Interpretations, 1900-1975, of Short Fiction since 1800,* Shoe String, 1977, Supplement 1, 1980, Supplement 2, 1984, Supplement 3, 1987, Supplement 4, 1989, Supplement 5, 1991.

(Editor with Mabel Ross) *"On Another Day . . . ": Tales Told among the Nkundo of Zaire,* Archon Books, 1979.

(Editor with W. S. Walker) *Turkish Games for Health and Recreation,* Archive of Turkish Oral Narrative, 1983.

(With Staab, Kaslan, and Griswold) *Turkey: A Precollegiate Handbook,* Turkish Studies Association, 1988.

The Art of the Turkish Tale, Texas Tech University Press, Volume 1, 1990, Volume 2, 1991.

(With W. S. Walker) *Twentieth-Century Short Story Explication, 1961-1991: An Index,* Shoe String Press, 1992.

FOR CHILDREN

Just Say Hic!: A Turkish Silly Tale, Follett, 1965.

Hilili and Dilili: A Turkish Silly Tale, Follett, 1965.

(With Mine Sumer) *Stargazer to the Sultan,* Parents' Magazine Press, 1967.

Watermelons, Walnuts, and the Wisdom of Allah, and Other Tales of the Hoca, Parents' Magazine Press, 1967.

Once There Was and Twice There Wasn't, Follett, 1968.

The Dancing Palm Tree and Other Nigerian Folktales, Parents' Magazine Press, 1968, with woodcuts by Helen Siegl, Texas Tech University Press, 1990.

I Packed My Trunk, Follett, 1969.

Pigs and Pirates: A Greek Tale (Junior Literary Guild selection), David White, 1969.

(With Naki Tezel) *The Mouse and the Elephant,* Parents' Magazine Press, 1970.

The Round Sultan and the Straight Answer, Parents' Magazine Press, 1970.

Korolu, the Singing Bandit, Crowell, 1970.

The Courage of Kazan, Crowell, 1971.

The Ifrit and the Magic Gifts, Follett, 1972.

How the Hare Told the Truth about His Horse, illustrated by Charles Mikolaycak, Parents' Magazine Press, 1972.

New Patches for Old, illustrated by Harold Berson, Parents' Magazine Press, 1974.

Teeny-Tiny and the Witch-Woman, Pantheon, 1975.

Laughing Together: Giggles and Grins from Around the Globe, Four Winds Press, 1977, revised edition, Free Spirit Publishing/UNICEF, 1992.

A Good Fish Dinner, Parents' Magazine Press, 1979.

(With Filiz Erol and Mine Erol) *To Set Them Free: The Early Years of Mustafa Kemal Ataturk,* Tompson & Rutter, 1981.

A Treasury of Turkish Folktales for Children, Linnet Books, 1988.

OTHER

Contributor of more than 375 stories, poems, plays, and articles to newspapers and to folklore, education, and children's periodicals, including *Child Life, Journal of American Folklore, Horn Book, Children's Digest, Cricket, Elementary English, Grade Teacher, Big Book, Faces, Turkish American Gazette,* and *Instructor;* the pseudonym, Beth Kilreon, has been used chiefly in *Humpty Dumpty's Magazine,* for which she supplied the "At Home with the Humpty Dumpty Family" page each month, 1958-70. Walker has recorded *Barbara Walker's Storybags,* Volume 1-4, Kilreon Recordings, 1973, and *Introduction and Twenty Nasreddin Hoca Tales,* Kilreon Recordings, 1985. With Mabel Ross, she produced four filmstrip texts, *African Folk Tales,* Concordia/SVE, 1979, and, with Michael Bragg, *An American Teenager Visits Turkey, 1984* (filmstrip, cassette, and booklet), 1985. Member of editorial board, *New York Folklore Quarterly,* 1948-52, Texas Tech University Press, 1991; yearbook editor, *Lubbock City Panhellenic,* 1969-73.

ADAPTATIONS: Pigs and Pirates and *New Patches for Old* have been filmed by Weston Woods Studios, *Just Say Hic!* by Bailey-Film Associates, and *The Mouse and the Elephant* by Parents' Magazines Enterprises. *Teeny-Tiny and the Witch-Woman* has been produced as a filmstrip by Random House and as a motion picture and videotape by Weston Woods Studios.

WORK IN PROGRESS: A two-volume work entitled *The Art of the Nigerian Tale;* a children's book entitled *African Animal Trickster Tales;* a pilot program for expanding student exposure to Turkey and its culture at three precollege levels through classroom teaching aids (books, tapes, maps, filmstrips, bibliographies, and kits); an expanded edition of *Turkish Games for Health and Recreation;* texts for twelve additional Turkish-based juvenile books.

SIDELIGHTS: Barbara K. Walker and her husband, Warren S. Walker, have been working since 1961 on the Uysal-Walker Archive of Turkish Oral Narrative. Since 1980, she has been curator of the collection, which was donated in 1970 to Texas Tech University and moved to the university library in 1980. The collection includes well over three thousand folktales in Turkish, two-thirds of which have been translated into English. The Walkers began collecting the folktales, children's games, rhymes, and riddles in rural Turkey in 1961 when Warren Walker was Fulbright lecturer in American literature at the University of Ankara, and they plan to continue collecting "as long as we live." Walker spent the summer of 1966 in Turkey gathering materials on Ataturk, worked there again in 1974, 1984, 1986, 1988, and 1989, and plans additional field-collecting visits as opportunity allows.

Walker told *CA* that international understanding is her "primary interest, pursued through writing, through travel in behalf of the International Youth Library (1974, 1976), and through continued support of storytelling as a means of ensuring global understanding. Work on the UNICEF-commissioned children's joke book (1973-76) was exciting and productive, with a harvest of 'funnies' from ninety-eight countries in fifty-six languages, and has prompted more than fourteen thousand letters from readers of all ages. The work with Mabel Ross on Nkundo folktales (1971-77) [was] full of surprises and satisfactions." Because her husband shares her enthusiasm for internationalism, their house has been "home away from home" for visitors from all parts of the world, including Botswana, China, Czechoslovakia, England, India, Japan, Malaysia, Nigeria, Switzerland, West Germany, Yugoslavia, Turkey, and Zaire. "And coming at all hours of the day are children, who regard [me] as both live-in storyteller and branch librarian."

To Set Them Free: The Early Years of Mustafa Kemal Ataturk was adopted by the Turkish Ministry of Education for use in all Turkish schools, and texts of the first twelve of Barbara Walker's Turkish-based children's books were adopted by the Turkish Ministry of Education for use in Turkey's English-as-a-Second-Language school program. Manuscript and production materials of several of Walker's books have been placed on permanent loan to the University of Minnesota library. All of her books for children and all working materials for *How the Hare Told the Truth about His Horse* and *New Patches for Old* are included in the International Youth Library in Munich.

BIOGRAPHICAL/CRITICAL SOURCES:

PERIODICALS

ATA-USA: Bulletin of the Assembly of Turkish-American Associations, Volume 3, number 1, 1982.
Horn Book, February, 1964; June, 1970; December, 1971.

Lamp (Delta Zeta publication), summer, 1970; summer, 1973.
Merhaba (Houston, TX), July-August, 1983.
New York Times Book Review, October 21, 1990.

*   *   *

WALKER, Warren S(tanley) 1921-

PERSONAL: Born March 19, 1921, in Brooklyn, NY; son of Harold Stanley and Althea (Loescher) Walker; married Barbara Jeanne Kerlin (a writer), December 9, 1943; children: Brian, Theresa Sue. *Education:* New York State College for Teachers (now State University of New York at Albany), A.B., 1947, M.A., 1948; Cornell University, Ph.D., 1951.

ADDRESSES: Home—3703 66th St., Lubbock, TX 79413. *Office*—Archive of Turkish Oral Narrative, Texas Tech University Library, Lubbock, TX 79409.

CAREER: Blackburn College, Carlinville, IL, 1951-59, began as faculty member, became chairman of English department; Parsons College, Fairfield, IA, professor and dean of arts and sciences, 1959-64; Texas Tech University, Lubbock, professor of English, 1964-71, Horn Professor of English and director of Archive of Turkish Oral Narrative, 1971—. Fulbright lecturer in American literature at University of Ankara, Ankara, Turkey, 1961-62. Visiting summer professor at New York College for Teachers (now State University of New York at Albany), 1957, State University College of Education (now State University of New York College at Cortland), 1959, and State University of New York College at Oneonta, 1980. Director, Fairfield (IA) Community Fund, 1963-64. Member of advisory board of Texas Cultural Alliance, 1976-84. *Military service:* U.S. Army Air Forces, 1942-45; served in Italy.

MEMBER: International Society for Folk-Narrative Research, Modern Language Association of America, American Folklore Society, American Association of University Professors, National Council of Teachers of English, Middle East Studies Association, Texas Association of Middle East Scholars (member of executive council), Turkish Studies Association, New York Folklore Society, Texas Folklore Society.

AWARDS, HONORS: Citation from Turkish Ministry of Education for contribution to study of Turkish culture, 1967; Texas Writers award, 1967; research grants from Texas Tech University, 1971-74, 1976, 1983, 1984, American Council of Learned Societies, 1973 and 1979, American Philosophical Society, 1974, Republic of Turkey, 1983, and Institute of Turkish Studies, 1984; citation from Turkish Ministry of State for contributions to study of Turkish folklore, 1973; Distinguished Alumnus of State

University of New York at Albany, 1979; Distinguished Lecturer, Southwest Conference Humanities Consortium, 1981; Distinguished Faculty Service Award, Texas Tech Dads Association, 1984; Litt.D., Selcuk University, Turkey, 1989; honorary membership in Ataturk Supreme Council on Turkish Culture, 1989; distinguished research award, Turkish Folklore Research Council, 1989.

WRITINGS:

James Fenimore Cooper: An Introduction and Interpretation, Barnes & Noble, 1962, revised edition, Holt, 1966.

(With Ahmet Uysal) *Tales Alive in Turkey,* Harvard University Press, 1966.

Plots and Characters in the Fiction of James Fenimore Cooper, Archon Books, 1978.

A Bibliography of American Scholarship on Turkish Folklore and Ethnography, Kultur ve Turizm Bakanligi, Milli Folklor Arastirma Dairesi, 1982.

EDITOR

Whatever Makes Papa Laugh: A Folklore Sheaf Honoring Harold W. Thompson, New York Folklore Society, 1958.

(And author of introduction) James Fenimore Cooper, *The Spy,* Hafner, 1960.

(With wife, Barbara K. Walker) *Nigerian Folk Tales as Told by Olawale Idewu and Omotayo Ada,* Rutgers University Press, 1961, 2nd edition, Archon Books, 1980.

(And editor with B. K. Walker of supplements) *Twentieth-Century Short Story Explication: Interpretations, 1900-1960 Inclusive, of Short Fiction since 1800,* Shoe String, 1961, Supplement 1, 1963, Supplement 2, 1965, 3rd edition published as *Twentieth-Century Short Story Explication: Interpretations, 1900-1975, of Short Fiction since 1800,* 1977, Supplement 1, 1980, Supplement 2, 1984, Supplement 3, 1987, Supplement 4, 1989, Supplement 5, 1991.

(With B. K. Walker) *The Erie Canal: Gateway to Empire,* Heath, 1963.

(And author of introduction) Cooper, *The Red Rover,* University of Nebraska Press, 1963.

Prose Lyrics: A Collection of Familiar Essays, Odyssey, 1964.

(And author of introduction) Cooper, *The Sea Lions,* University of Nebraska Press, 1965.

Leatherstocking and the Critics, Scott, Foresman, 1965.

(With Uysal) *Turkish Folktales,* Folkways Records, 1965.

(With Faruk Sumer and Uysal) *The Book of Dede Korkut: A Turkish Epic,* University of Texas Press, 1972.

Archive of Turkish Oral Narrative: Preliminary Catalogue No. 1, Texas Tech Press, 1975.

(With B. K. Walker) *Turkish Games for Health and Recreation,* Archive of Turkish Oral Narrative, 1983.

(With M. Felker and E. Brandt) *Archive of Turkish Oral Narrative: Preliminary Catalogue No. 2—The First 1,000 Tales,* Archive of Turkish Oral Narrative, 1988.

(With B. K. Walker) *Twentieth-Century Short Story Explication, 1961-1991: An Index,* Shoe String Press, 1992.

Contributor to such books as *Underground Empire: Wonders and Tales of New York Caves,* S. Daye, 1948; *James Fenimore Cooper: A Reappraisal,* New York Historical Association, 1954; *The Literature of Emigration and Exile,* Texas Tech Press, 1991; *Proceedings of 4th International Congress on Turkish Folklore,* Turkish Ministry of Culture, 1991. Contributor of more than eighty articles and reviews to professional and folklore journals. Member of editorial board, Center for Editions of American Authors, Cooper Edition, 1968, and "The Works of Joseph Conrad," series, Cambridge University Press. Bibliographer for *Studies in Short Fiction,* 1973—.

WORK IN PROGRESS: Co-writing, with Ahmet Uysal, a book entitled *More Tales Alive in Turkey* for Texas Tech Press. Also compiling a subject index of thirty-eight volumes of Turkish tales from the Archive of Turkish Oral Narrative.

SIDELIGHTS: Warren S. Walker spends summers in Turkey exploring classical sites and collecting Turkish folktales. He reads French, Spanish, and German and has facility in spoken Turkish.

*   *   *

WALLACE, Ian 1950-

PERSONAL: Born March 31, 1950, in Niagara Falls, Ontario, Canada; son of Robert Amiens and Kathleen (Watts) Wallace; married Debra Wiedman. *Education:* Graduated from Ontario College of Art, 1969-73; postgraduate studies, 1973-74. *Avocational interests:* Walking, movies, travel, dining out.

ADDRESSES: Home—184 Major St., Toronto, Ontario, Canada M5S 2L3.

CAREER: Staff writer and illustrator for Kids Can Press, 1974-76; Art Gallery of Ontario, Toronto, Ontario, information officer, 1976-80. Artist. *Exhibitions:* "Chin Chiang and the Dragon's Dance," Art Gallery of Ontario, 1986; "Once upon a Time," Vancouver Art Gallery, 1988; "Canada at Bologna," Bologna Children's Book Fair, 1990.

MEMBER: Writers Union of Canada, Canadian Children's Book Centre.

AWARDS, HONORS: Runner-up for City of Toronto Book Awards, 1976; "Our Choice" Selection, Children's Book Centre, 1977-81; Canada Council grants, 1980, 1981, 1983, 1986, 1987; Imperial Order of Daughters of the Empire Book Award, 1984, Amelia Frances Howard-Gibbon Illustrator's Award, 1984, International Board on Books for Young People Honor List citation, 1986, all for *Chin Chiang and the Dragon's Dance;* Ontario Arts Council grants, 1985, 1988; American Library Association Notable Book citation, 1987, and White Raven Award, International Youth Library, 1987, both for *Very Last First Time;* Mr. Christie Award, and Elizabeth Mrazik Cleaver Award, both for *The Name of the Tree.*

WRITINGS:

JUVENILES

Julie News (self-illustrated), Kids Can Press, 1974.
(With Angela Wood) *The Sandwich,* Kids Can Press, 1975, revised edition, 1985.
The Christmas Tree House (self-illustrated), Kids Can Press, 1976.
Chin Chiang and the Dragon's Dance (self-illustrated), Atheneum, 1984.
The Sparrow's Song (self-illustrated), Viking, 1986.
Morgan the Magnificent (self-illustrated), Macmillan, 1987.
Mr. Kneebone's New Digs (self-illustrated), Groundwood, 1991.

ILLUSTRATOR

Jan Andrews, *Very Last First Time,* Atheneum, 1985, published as *Eva's Ice Adventure,* Methuen, 1986.
Tim Wynne-Jones, *The Architect of the Moon,* Groundwood, 1988, published as *Builder of the Moon,* Macmillan, 1989.
Lottridge, Celia Barker, *The Name of the Tree: A Bantu Folktale,* Macmillan, 1990.
Jam, Teddy, *The Year of the Fire,* Macmillan, 1993.

Contributor to periodicals, including *Canadian Books for Young People.*

SIDELIGHTS: Canadian Ian Wallace both writes and illustrates children's books. He is best known for his award-winning *Chin Chiang and the Dragon's Dance.* "Like most children growing up in Niagara Falls, Ontario in the 1950s," Wallace tells *Something about the Author,* "Sunday afternoons were spent with my family driving leisurely through the countryside counting cows, cars and the many species of trees that my brothers and I could see through the back window of our father's car. This activity was far removed from the one carried out by a fair percentage of large city dwellers of the 80s, many of whom bring their children indoors on Sunday afternoons to expansive spaces we know as art galleries and museums.

Free to roam those hallowed halls, children count the numbers of Renoirs and Modiglianis, or the stuffed horn-rimmed owls and the variety and colour of rare duck's eggs to be found in a single glass case.

"My first exposure to the world of art came not through pictures hung on gallery and museum walls, but through the picture books my brothers and I carted out of our local library. Contained within the covers of each book were worlds so foreign and exciting that we marvelled at the daring of the characters, thrilled to their singular and collective bravery, and were often chillingly jerked back by great waves of fear. For children growing up in small city Ontario, these books and their images carried us out of our sheltered environment to places we never imagined and only discovered within those treasured pages. Just as important, they made us keenly aware of the fact that a painter was not merely someone who, like our father, picked up a brush or roller and stroked or rolled it over the walls of our house whenever the rooms had grown tired around the edges. But rather, an artist was someone who made dreams real.

"My creative life hiccupped along, dropping in and out with unpredictable regularity, until the day at age thirteen when I gave up the notion of being a fireman and announced that I was going to be an artist. My parents' response was not surprising, since they were consistently supportive of my brothers and me, no matter what wild dreams we espoused or what strange predicament we had managed to get ourselves into. 'Of course you will,' they said.

"And that was that. The decision was made. And with it came the unconditional support of my parents, so crucial to anyone risking the possibility of living a creative life. This desire to become an artist did not diminish as my teenage years progressed, but helped to conquer those racing hormones, the battle against teenage angst and love, and the ability to put in countless hours alone in my room with only the sound of a pencil scratching over the surface of stacks of paper.

"My training has been mainly visual, but the single most important lesson I've learned is that everything creative must have a purpose and a reason for its expression. My first three books were labors of love. Writing and illustrating do not come easily to me; the challenge is in the struggle. I have had the opportunity to read to 150,000 children across Canada, and I now understand how important books are to our lives. To watch children laugh or cry at a story with you is achieving a high level of communication."

Chin Chiang and the Dragon's Dance is about a Chinese-Canadian boy who wants to take part in the New Year's Day street dance commemorating the Year of the Dragon, but suffers from stage fright. As Sandra Martin notes on the illustrations in the *Globe and Mail, Chin Chiang,* "complete with an astonishing panoply of 16 watercolor paintings, has taken a quantum leap in production values. The paintings are subtle yet brilliantly colored, particularly in the reds and blues, and for me they pass the acid test: they exist independently of the verbal story and possess enough depth and integrity to tell their own tale. . . . Wallace has painted them with such authenticity and meticulous care that they speak eloquently of centuries of Chinese heritage transplanted onto the Canadian west coast." Wallace explains in *Something about the Author,* "The task of creating this book was not completed in the short term, but over six years. having endured that long gestation, I cannot stress enough the value of time—time to allow the right works to come forth, time to allow the drawings to formulate in the head before they appear on paper, and time to allow both to be as polished as a piece of rare jade"

"As much as I am in need of solitude when I am lost in the activity of writing or illustrating," Wallace tells *Something about the Author,* "I am also a social creature by nature, enjoying the camaraderie of friends and people in general. Writing and illustrating provide me with the former, while storytelling provides me with the latter. At times my life does appear somewhat schizophrenic, but for the most part, I love the balance of the two activities: writing and illustrating or storytelling.

"What a luxury it is to wake up each morning and know that this new day will not be the same as the one before and never the same as those that come after."

BIOGRAPHICAL/CRITICAL SOURCES:

BOOKS

Something about the Author, Volume 56, Gale, 1989, pp. 164-67.
Writers on Writing, Overlea House, 1989.

PERIODICALS

Canadian Children's Literature, number 48, 1987.
Emergency Librarian, February, 1985.
Globe and Mail (Toronto), August 4, 1984; November 1, 1986.
In Review, April, 1979.
New Advocate, spring, 1989.
Quill and Quire, February, 1985.

VIDEO

Ian Wallace, "Meet the Authors" series, Mead Educational [Toronto], 1989.

WALLACH, Janet 1942-

PERSONAL: Born May 4, 1942, in Brooklyn, NY; daughter of George (in business) and Sylvia (Feigen) Weil; married second husband, John P. Wallach (a journalist), June 9, 1974; children: David Alan, Michael Adam. *Education:* Attended Syracuse University, 1959-60; New York University, B.A., 1965.

ADDRESSES: Home—2915 Foxhall Rd., Washington, DC 20016.

CAREER: Herman Geist, New York, NY, designer, 1969-75; Woodward & Lothrop, Washington, DC, fashion coordinator, 1975-76; Garfinckel's, Washington, fashion merchandising director, 1976-80; free-lance writer, 1980—.

MEMBER: Washington Independent Writers.

WRITINGS:

Working Wardrobe, Acropolis Books, 1981.
Looks That Work, Viking, 1987.
Still Small Voices, Harcourt, 1989.
Arafat: In the Eyes of the Beholder, Carol Publishing, 1990.

Contributor to *Washington Post Magazine* and *Stores Magazine.* Contributing editor, *Dossier Magazine.*

SIDELIGHTS: The "capsule concept"—the idea that twelve basic clothing items in two colors and coordinated shapes and fabrics together yield forty different outfits—"is the basic message of one of the few actually useful books about dressing," claims fashion editor Mary Peacock. Reviewing Janet Wallach's book *Working Wardrobe* in *Ms.* magazine, Peacock continues: "Wallach has moved the goal of a workable personal style from theory into practical reality by providing an organizational key, the 'capsule,' which at least partially codified that great intangible, a 'fashion sense.' And the 'capsule concept' works on any level of budget and sophistication, or at any level of dressiness."

Janet Wallach told *CA:* "It has taken me fifteen years to come full circle to my first love, writing, and I'm grateful that my dream has been fulfilled. Writing about fashion seemed like a natural thing to do as I've spent most of my life in that field. It has been gratifying that my book has helped many women come to terms with their clothes and enabled them to make their wardrobes work for them (rather than the reverse). Clothing is important in the way we present ourselves to the world, and it should also be part of the fun of life."

BIOGRAPHICAL/CRITICAL SOURCES:

PERIODICALS

Ms., September, 1981.

* * *

WALSTER, Elaine Hatfield
See HATFIELD, Elaine (Catherine)

* * *

WALTER, Elizabeth

PERSONAL: Born in England.

ADDRESSES: Office—HarperCollins, 77-85 Fulham Palace Rd., Hammersmith, London W6 8JB, England.

CAREER: HarperCollins, London, England, began 1961, currently publisher of Collins Crime Club.

AWARDS, HONORS: Received Scott Moncrieff Translation Prize for *A Scent of Lilies.*

WRITINGS:

The More Deceived, J. Cape, 1960.
The Nearest and Dearest, Harvill, 1962.
Snowfall, and Other Chilling Events, Harvill, 1964, Stein & Day, 1965.
The Sin-Eater, and Other Scientific Impossibilities, Harvill, 1965, Stein & Day, 1967.
Davy Jones's Tale, and Other Supernatural Stories, Harvill, 1971.
Come and Get Me, and Other Uncanny Invitations, Harvill, 1973.
Dead Woman, and Other Haunting Experiences, Harvill, 1975, St. Martin's, 1976.
In the Mist, and Other Uncanny Encounters, Arkham, 1979.
A Christmas Scrapbook (nonfiction), Collins, 1979.
Season's Greetings (nonfiction), Collins, 1980.
A Wedding Bouquet (nonfiction), Collins, 1981.
A Season of Goodwill, Harvill, 1985, Scribners, 1986.
Homeward Bound, Headline, 1990, St. Martin's, 1991.

TRANSLATOR

Claire Gallois, *A Scent of Lilies,* Collins, 1970, Stein & Day, 1971.
Bernard Clave, *Lord of the River,* Little, Brown, 1973.
Janine Boissard, *A Matter of Feeling,* Little, Brown, 1979.

WATERHOUSE, Keith (Spencer) 1929-
(Lee Gibb, a joint pseudonym)

PERSONAL: Born February 6, 1929, in Leeds, England; son of Ernest and Elsie Waterhouse; married Joan Foster, October 21, 1950 (divorced, 1968); children: Penelope, Sarah, Robert. *Educaton:* Attended Osmondthorpe Council School, Leeds.

ADDRESSES: Home—29 Kenway Rd., London SW5 0RP, England. *Agent*—David Hughes Associates, 5-8 Lower John Rd., London W.1, England.

CAREER: Journalist, screenwriter, playwright, novelist.

WRITINGS:

(With Guy Deghy) *Cafe Royal: Ninety Years of Bohemia,* Hutchinson, 1955.
There Is a Happy Land (novel), M. Joseph, 1957.
(With Paul Cave) *Britain's Voice Abroad,* Daily Mirror Newspapers (London), 1957.
The Future of Television, Daily Mirror Newspapers, 1958.
(With Herald Froy [pseudonym of Guy Deghy]) *How to Avoid Matrimony,* Muller, 1958, Day, 1959.
(With Deghy, under joint pseudonym Lee Gibb) *The Joneses: How to Keep Up with Them,* Muller, 1959.
Billy Liar (novel), M. Joseph, 1959, Norton, 1960.
(With Willis Hall) *Billy Liar: A Play in Three Acts* (based on the novel; first produced in London at the Cambridge Theatre, September 13, 1960; first produced in Los Angeles at the Stage Society Theatre, January, 1963), M. Joseph, 1960, Norton, 1961.
(With Deghy, under joint pseudonym Lee Gibb) *The Higher Jones,* Muller, 1961.
(With Hall) *Celebration* (play; first produced in Nottingham, England, at the Nottingham Playhouse, March, 1961; first produced in London at the Duchess Theatre, June 8, 1961), M. Joseph, 1961.
(With Hall) *England, Our England* (play, first produced in London at the Green Hippodrome, April 9, 1962; produced in London at the Prince's Theatre, May 7, 1962), Evans Brothers, 1964.
(With Hall) *All Things Bright and Beautiful* (play; first produced in Bristol, England, at the Bristol Old Vic, October 23, 1962; first produced in London at the Phoenix Theatre, December 13, 1962), M. Joseph, 1963.
(With Hall) *The Sponge Room* and *Squat Betty* (plays; first produced in Nottingham, England, at the Nottingham Playhouse, November 13, 1962; first produced in London at the Royal Court Theatre, December 18, 1962), Evans Brothers, 1963.
(With Hall) *Joey, Joey* (play), first produced in Bristol, England, at the Bristol Old Vic, December 26, 1962; first produced in London at the Saville Theatre, November, 1966.

Jubb (novel), M. Joseph, 1963, Putnam, 1964.

(With Hall) *They Called the Bastard Stephen* (play; first produced in Bristol at the Bristol Old Vic, 1964; first produced in London at the Wimbledon Theatre as *Come Laughing Home,* March 29, 1965), published as *Come Laughing Home,* Evans Brothers, 1966.

(With Hall) *Say Who You Are* (play; first produced in Guildford, England, at the Yvonne Arnaud Theatre, August 3, 1965; first produced in London at the Haymarket Theatre, October 14, 1965; first produced on Broadway at the Booth Theatre as *Help Stamp Out Marriage,* September 29, 1966), Evans Brothers, 1966.

(Editor with Hall) *Writers' Theatre,* Heinemann, 1967.

(With Hall) *Whoops-a-Daisy* (play; first produced in Nottingham at the Nottingham Playhouse, December, 1968), Evans Brothers, 1978.

The Bucket Shop (novel), M. Joseph, 1968, published in America as *Everything Must Go,* Putnam, 1969.

(With Hall) *Children's Day* (play; first produced in Nottingham at the Nottingham Playhouse, July, 1969), Samuel French, 1975.

The Warmongers (television script), British Broadcasting Corp., 1970.

(With Hall) *Who's Who* (play; first produced in Coventry, England, at the Belgrade Theatre, July 6, 1971; first produced in London at the Fortune Theatre, June 27, 1973), Samuel French, 1974.

(With Hall) *The Card* (play; adaptation of novel by Arnold Bennett), first produced in Bristol at the Bristol Old Vic, 1973; first produced in London at the Queen's Theatre, July 23, 1973.

(With Hall) *Saturday, Sunday, Monday* (play; adaptation of play by Eduardo de Filippo; first produced in London at the National Theatre, October 31, 1973), Heinemann, 1974.

The Passing of the Third Floor Buck, M. Joseph, 1974.

Billy Liar on the Moon, M. Joseph, 1975, Putnam, 1976.

Mondays, Thursdays, M. Joseph, 1976.

Office Life, M. Joseph, 1978.

(With Hall) *Filumena* (adaptation of the play by Filippo), Samuel French, 1978.

The Upchat Line (television script), Thames Television, 1978.

The Upchat Connection (television script), Thames Television, 1979.

(With Hall) *The Television Adventures of Worzel Gummidge,* Penguin, 1979.

Rhubarb, Rhubarb, and Other Noises, M. Joseph, 1979.

(With Hall) *Worzel Gummidge* (play), first produced in Birmingham, England, at the Birmingham Repertory Theatre, December 12, 1980.

(With Hall) *More Television Adventures of Worzel Gummidge,* Penguin, 1980.

(With Hall) *Worzel Gummidge at the Fair,* Penguin, 1980.

(With Hall) *Worzel Gummidge Goes to the Seaside,* Penguin, 1980.

(With Hall) *The Trials of Worzel Gummidge,* Penguin, 1981.

Maggie Muggins; or, Spring in Earl's Court, M. Joseph, 1981.

"Daily Mirror" Style, Mirror Books, 1981.

West End Tales (television script), Thames Television, 1981.

In the Mood, M. Joseph, 1983.

Mrs. Pooter's Diary, Corgi, 1984.

Thinks, M. Joseph, 1984.

(With Hall) *Irish Adventures of Worzel Gummidge,* Severn House Publishers, 1984.

Theory and Practice of Lunch, M. Joseph, 1986.

The Collected Letters of a Nobody, M. Joseph, 1986.

(With Hall) *Worzel Gummidge Down Under,* Grafton Books, 1987.

Waterhouse at Large, Grafton Books, 1987.

Our Song, Hodder, 1988.

Jeffrey Bernard Is Unwell (play), first produced in London at the Apollo Theatre, October, 1989.

Bookends (based on Craig Brown's *The Marsh Marlowe Letters*), first produced in London at the Apollo Theatre, November, 1990.

Bimbo, Hodder & Stoughton, 1990.

English, Our English (and How to Sing It), Viking, 1991.

Contributor to *New Statesman, Cosmopolitan, Punch, Observer, Daily Mirror,* and *Queen.*

SCREENPLAYS; WITH WILLIS HALL

Whistle Down the Wind (adaptation of novel by Mary Hayley Bell), AFM-Beaver, 1961.

A Kind of Loving (adaptation of novel by Stan Barstow), BHP-Euro-International, 1962.

The Valiant, BHP-Euro-International, 1963.

Billy Liar, Vic-Waterhall, 1963.

West Eleven (adaptation of novel by Laura del Rivo), Dial Films, 1963.

Man in the Middle (adaptation of novel by Howard Fast), Pennebaker-Belmont, 1964.

Pretty Polly (adaptation of story by Noel Coward), George-Granat-Universal, 1967.

Lock Up Your Daughters (adaptation of play by Bernard Miles), Domino, 1969.

TELEVISION SCRIPTS; WITH WILLIS HALL

Inside George Webley (series), Yorkshire Television, 1968.

Queenie's Castle (series), Yorkshire Television, 1970.

Budgie (series), Weekend Television, 1971-72.

The Upper Crusts (series), London Weekend Television, 1973.

Three's Company (series), BBC, 1973.

Billy Liar (series), London Weekend Television, 1973-74.

RADIO SCRIPTS

The Town That Wouldn't Vote, BBC, 1951.
There Is a Happy Land, BBC, 1962.
The Woollen Bank Forgeries, BBC, 1964.
The Last Phone-In, BBC, 1976.
The Big Broadcast of 1922, BBC, 1979.

SIDELIGHTS: Keith Waterhouse's brilliant satire and caricatures have been cited in discussions of the "Angry Young Men" school of writing, while his heroes have been compared with those of Alan Sillitoe and John Osborne. But he defies classification. Burling Lowrey writes: "He is not visibly anti-Establishmentarian, nor pro-Red Brick, nor a prole. He is himself an original with a talent for exposing hypocrisy, stupidity, and corruption with comic detachment." Waterhouse's novels and plays are marked by what Paul Schlueter in the *Dictionary of Literary Biography* calls "a sardonic, even cynical perspective, in which seemingly doomed characters flounder as they attempt to discover who they are and what they have to offer the world. Waterhouse uses humor, especially exaggeration and wit, as a calculated, objective means of showing his characters to be both psychically and ethically empty."

Billy Liar, a novel about a daydreaming undertaker's assistant who has trouble distinguishing his fantasies from reality, established Waterhouse as a novelist of distinction, and most critics agree with Hubert Saal of *Saturday Review,* who called the book "a brilliant novel, in language fresh and sweet, with characters vivid and singular in an inventive and dynamic story. It teems, it bursts with originality." Judith Thompson notes in the *Dictionary of Literary Biography* that "the combination of humor and pathos in Billy's adolescent fantasies about life in London and his absurd and painful relationship with his social and domestic context was readily translatable onto the stage." The stage version of the story ran for 600 performances in London; a television series based on the book ran on London Weekend Television in 1973-74.

The play *Jeffrey Bernard Is Unwell* is based on the life and writings of *Spectator* writer Jeffrey Bernard, whose column, "Low Life," chronicles his life at the Coach and Horses pub in London's Soho district. The title comes from the euphemistic explanation the *Spectator* runs on those weeks when Bernard is not sober enough to write his column. The play begins with the columnist crawling out from under a table to find himself locked in the Coach and Horses for the night. Once he realizes his predicament, he settles down with a drink and begins to look back over his life, his three marriages, and his many visits to the dog and horse tracks. Bernard is a pub philosopher whose anecdotes, regrets, reminiscences, and observations form the core of the play. *Jeffrey Bernard Is Unwell* ran for nearly

two years, first at the Apollo Theatre and then at the larger Shaftesbury Theatre.

Other Waterhouse works range from the North Country realism of *All Things Bright and Beautiful* to the black comedy of *Jubb.* In his best work, he manages to present characters "on the fringes of society, finely drawing out the pathos and dignity," as Carol Rumens observes in the *Times Literary Supplement.* Alan Hollinghurst, writing in *New Statesman,* finds that Waterhouse "has compacted two kinds of comedy: a relentlessly observant ridicule of the world, and a private systematisation of things carried out by the characters to protect themselves from their uncharitable and ridiculous circumstances." Thompson believes that Waterhouse's versatility may have "denied him some rightful acclaim," but concludes: "He is a man of exceptionally varied talents: his wit, intelligence, and capacity to entertain are fired by an acute and compassionate observation of society and human behavior, a modest humanitarianism which cares deeply that people should have access to beauty—and to laughter."

Speaking to Candida Crewe in the London *Times,* Waterhouse remarks: "I'm a journeyman writer. There were lots in the pre-war days. Shaw used to write magazine articles about how ladies shouldn't wear hats in the cinema. There are a lot of snoots about but, me, I'm ever-grateful to be earning a living from writing."

BIOGRAPHICAL/CRITICAL SOURCES:

BOOKS

Armstrong, W. A., and others, *Experimental Drama,* G. Bell, 1963.
Contemporary Fiction in America and England, 1950-1970, Gale, 1976.
Contemporary Literary Criticism, Volume 47, Gale, 1988.
Dictionary of Literary Biography, Gale, Volume 13: *British Dramatists since World War II,* 1982, Volume 15: *British Novelists, 1930-1959,* 1983.
Gindin, James, *Postwar British Fiction: New Accents and Attitudes,* University of California Press, 1962.
Gray, Nigel, *The Silent Majority: A Study of the Working Class in Post-War British Fiction,* Barnes & Noble, 1973.
Handley, Graham, *Brodie's Notes on Billy Liar,* Pan Books, 1977.
Karl, Frederick R., *The Contemporary English Novel,* Farrar, Straus, 1962.
O'Connor, William Van, *The New University Wits,* Southern Illinois University Press, 1963.

PERIODICALS

Books and Bookmen, January, 1979; July, 1983.
British Book News, December, 1983; October, 1984.
Chicago Sunday Tribune, June 10, 1960.

Critique, Volume 10, number 3, 1968.

Drama, summer, 1966.

Hudson Review, spring, 1961.

Illustrated London News, December 29, 1962.

Listener, November 6, 1975; June 30, 1983; September 6, 1984.

New Statesman, September 12, 1959; September 17, 1960; December 28, 1962; October 4, 1968; June 12, 1981.

Newsweek, April 6, 1964.

New Yorker, March 7, 1964.

New York Times, September 30, 1966; December 13, 1968; December 1, 1989; December 3, 1989.

New York Times Book Review, January 3, 1960; April 5, 1964; January 26, 1969; February 8, 1976.

Observer, November 5, 1978; October 2, 1983; April 13, 1986.

Saturday Review, February 27, 1960; April 4, 1964.

Spectator, September 11, 1959; December 28, 1962; October 25, 1975; October 21, 1989.

Times (London), February 21, 1961; May 8, 1962; October 15, 1965; September 4, 1969; September 6, 1984; April 17, 1986; March 15, 1990; October 20, 1990; March 16, 1991; March 27, 1991.

Times Literary Supplement, September 4, 1959; September 27, 1963; October 25, 1974; May 29, 1981; May 13, 1983; April 18, 1986; March 22, 1990.

Yale Review, March, 1960.

* * *

WATKINS, John G(oodrich) 1913-

PERSONAL: Born March 17, 1913, in Salmon, ID; son of John Thomas and Ethel (Goodrich) Watkins; married Helen Huth, 1971; children: (previous marriage) John Dean, Jonette Alison, Richard Douglas, Gregory Keith, Rodney Phillip; (present marriage) Marvin Huth, Karen Stroobants. *Education:* Attended College of Idaho, 1929-30, 1931-32; University of Idaho, B.S., 1933, M.S., 1936; Columbia University, Ph.D., 1941. *Politics:* Democrat. *Religion:* Unitarian Universalist. *Avocational interests:* Music, boating, public speaking.

ADDRESSES: Home—413 Evans Ave., Missoula, MT 59801. *Office*—Department of Psychology, University of Montana, Missoula, MT 59801.

CAREER: High school teacher in Homedale, Rupert, and Mountain Home (all Idaho), 1933-39; Columbia University, New York City, assistant, 1940; Ithaca College, Ithaca, NY, assistant professor, 1940-41; Alabama Polytechnic Institute (now Auburn University), Auburn, professor, 1941-43; Washington State College (now University), Pullman, associate professor, 1946-49; Veterans Administration Hospital, American Lake, WA, clinical psycholo-

gist, 1949-50; Veterans Administration Mental Hygiene Clinic, Chicago, IL, chief clinical psychologist, 1950-53; Veterans Administration Hospital, Portland, OR, chief clinical psychologist, 1953-64; University of Montana, Missoula, MT, professor of psychology and director of clinical training, 1964-84, professor emeritus, 1984—. Staff member, St. Patrick's Hospital, Missoula, MT.

Diplomate in clinical psychology, American Board of Examiners in Professional Psychology; diplomate in clinical hypnosis, American Board of Psychological Hypnosis (president of board, 1961-63). Acting chief of training in clinical psychology, Illinois Region of Veterans Administration, 1950-51; member of board of directors of Oregon Prison Association, 1957-59; member of Portland Commission on Alcoholism, 1958; president of American Board of Examiners in Psychological Hypnosis, 1959-62; member of Oregon State Board of Psychological Examiners, 1963-64; chairman of Missoula Chamber of Commerce Committee on Mental Health, 1965-67; director of planning and development, International Graduate University, Switzerland, 1974-77. Consulting psychologist, Dammasch State Hospital, Oregon, 1961-64, and Veterans Administration Hospitals and Montana State Prison, 1965-80; part-time practice in psychotherapy and psychological consultation. Lecturer, University of Washington, University of Portland, Northwestern University, Portland State College (now University), and Florida Institute of Technology; visiting professor, University of California, Los Angeles, and State University of New York at Binghamton; lectures and presents workshops in Europe, South America, Australia, and Asia and at numerous institutions throughout the United States. *Military service:* U.S. Army, Quartermaster Corps, 1943-46; served as chief clinical psychologist at Welch Convalescent Hospital, Daytona Beach, FL; became first lieutenant.

MEMBER: International Society for Clinical and Experimental Hypnosis (fellow; executive secretary, 1958-62; president-elect, 1962-64; president, 1965-67), International Society for the Study of Multiple Personality and Dissociation (charter member; fellow), American Society of Clinical Hypnosis (fellow; secretary, 1992), American Psychological Association (fellow; president of Division 30, 1975-76), Society for Clinical and Experimental Hypnosis (fellow; president, 1969-71), Montana Psychological Association, Rocky Mountain Psychological Association (member of board of examiners, 1965-69; chairman of legislative committee, 1967-74), Phi Delta Kappa, Kappa Delta Pi, Phi Mu Alpha, Psi Chi, Sigma Xi.

AWARDS, HONORS: Award for Meritorious Service, U.S. Army, 1946; Raginsky Award, Society for Clinical and Experimental Hypnosis, 1965; Morton Prince Award, Society for Clinical and Experimental Hypnosis and American Board of Psychological Hypnosis, 1971; Outstanding Educators of America award, 1971; Arthur Shapiro Award for Best Book of the Year on Hypnosis, Society for Clinical and Experimental Hypnosis, 1987; Morton Prince Award, International Society for Multiple Personality and Dissociation, 1988; Milton E. Erickson Award, American Journal of Clinical Hypnosis, 1988.

WRITINGS:

Objective Measurement of Instrumental Performance, Columbia University Press, 1942.
Hypnotherapy of War Neuroses, Ronald, 1949.
General Psychotherapy, C. C Thomas, 1960.
The Therapeutic Self, Human Sciences, 1978.
(With R. J. Johnson) *We, the Divided Self,* Irvington, 1982.
Clinical Hypnosis, Irvington, Volume 1: *Hypnotherapeutic Techniques,* 1987, Volume 2, *Hypnoanalytic Techniques,* 1991.

Contributor to *Handbook of Clinical Psychology,* edited by B. B. Wolman, McGraw, 1965; *Introduction to Clinical Psychology,* edited by I. A. Berg and L. A. Pennington, Ronald, 1966; *What's Psychotherapy and Who Needs It?,* edited by H. L. Collier, O'Sullivan Woodside, 1976; *Handbook of Innovative Psychotherapies,* edited by R. Corsini, Wiley, 1982; *The Newer Therapies: A Sourcebook,* edited by L. E. Abt and I. R. Stuart, Van Nostrand, 1982; *The Handbook of Clinical Psychology,* edited by C. E. Walker, Dow Jones-Irwin, 1983; *Encyclopedia of Psychology,* edited by Corsini, Wiley, 1984; *Symposium on Multiple Personality,* Psychiatric Clinics of North America, 1984; *Handbook of States of Consciousness,* edited by Wolman and M. Ullman, Van Nostrand, 1986; *What Is Psychotherapy: Contemporary Perspectives,* edited by J. K. Zeig and W. M. Munion, Jossey-Bass, 1990; and *Creative Mastery in Hypnosis and Hypnoanalysis: A Festschrift for Erika Fromm,* edited by M. L. Fass and D. Brown, Lawrence Erlbaum, 1990.

Contributor of chapters to several other books, including *Medical Hypnosis,* edited by Jerome Schneck; *Hypnosis throughout the World,* edited by Fred Marcuse; *Taboo Topics,* edited by Norman L. Farberow; *Short Term Approaches to Psychotherapy,* edited by H. Grayson; and *Therapy in Psychosomatic Medicine,* edited by F. Antonelli. Contributor of more than 120 articles and reviews to professional journals. Member of editorial boards of four journals.

WORK IN PROGRESS: Work in areas of hypnoanalysis, psychosomatic medicine, psychological theory, multiple personality, and psychotherapy; novels, short stories.

SIDELIGHTS: John G. Watkins once told *CA:* "As a psychologist I am continually trying to understand human behavior, both in myself and others. As a writer I transmit

the results of this search with the hope of promoting the betterment of mankind. I am conceited enough to think that my writings do make a contribution, and trust that when it seems to be otherwise I will have the good sense to stop writing. I read voraciously and am willing to borrow or steal from any source which might improve my contributions—but expect to give proper credit to those whose ideas I have purloined.

"I am also lazy, with islands of intense productivity occasionally looming out of an ocean of non-creative hours. When the time, the place, and the feelings bloom simultaneously, inspirations spring forth, alive with near-ripened fruit. When not, the land is a desert. The hardest job is to sit down and start writing; after that it's easy."

* * *

WATKINS-PITCHFORD, Denys James 1905-1990
(BB, Michael Traherne)

PERSONAL: Born July 25, 1905, in Lamport, Northamptonshire, England; died September 8, 1990; son of Walter (a clergyman) and Edith Elizabeth (Wilson) Watkins-Pitchford; married Cecily Mary Adnitt, August 10, 1939 (died, 1974); children: Angela June, Robin John (deceased). *Education:* Studied art in Paris, 1924; graduated from Royal College of Art.

ADDRESSES: Home—The Round House, Sudborough, Kettering, England. *Agent*—David Higham Associates Ltd., 5-8 Lower John St., Golden Square, London W1R 4HA, England.

CAREER: Writer and illustrator. Assistant art master at Rugby School, 1934-49. Royal College of Art associate. Broadcaster on natural history subjects. *Military service:* City of London Yeomanry Royal Horse Artillery, territorial army, 1925-29; King's Prize, 1928; Captain in the Home Guard during World War II, 1940-46.

MEMBER: Royal Society of Arts (fellow).

AWARDS, HONORS: Carnegie Medal, British Library Association, 1942, for *The Little Grey Men;* honorary M.A., Leicester University, 1986; member of the Order of the British Empire, 1989.

WRITINGS:

FICTION FOR JUVENILES; UNDER PSEUDONYM BB

Wild Lone: The Story of a Pytchley Fox, Eyre & Spottiswoode, 1938.
Manka, the Sky Gipsy: The Story of a Wild Goose, Scribner, 1939, published in England as *Sky Gipsy: The Story of a Wild Goose,* Eyre & Spottiswoode, 1939.

The Little Grey Men: A Story for the Young in Heart, Eyre & Spottiswoode, 1942, Scribner, 1949.

Brendon Chase, Hollis & Carter, 1944, Scribner, 1945.

Down the Bright Stream, Eyre & Spottiswoode, 1948, published as *The Little Grey Men Go Down the Bright Stream,* Methuen, 1977.

The Forest of Boland Light Railway, Eyre & Spottiswoode, 1955, published as *The Forest of the Railway,* Dodd, 1957.

Monty Woodpig's Caravan, Edmund Ward, 1957.

Ben the Bullfinch, Hamish Hamilton, 1957.

Wandering Wind, Hamish Hamilton, 1957, published as *Bill Badger and the Wandering Wind,* Methuen, 1980.

Alexander, illustrations by David Smee, Basil Blackwell, 1958.

Monty Woodpig and His Bubblebuzz Car, Edmund Ward, 1958.

Mr. Bumstead, Eyre & Spottiswoode, 1958.

The Wizard of Boland, Edmund Ward, 1959.

Bill Badger's Winter Cruise, Hamish Hamilton, 1959.

Bill Badger and the Pirates, Hamish Hamilton, 1960.

Bill Badger's Finest Hour, Hamish Hamilton, 1961, published as *Bill Badger and the Secret Weapon,* Methuen, 1983.

Bill Badger's Whispering Reeds Adventure, Hamish Hamilton, 1962.

Lepus: The Brown Hare, Benn, 1962.

Bill Badger's Big Mistake, Hamish Hamilton, 1963.

Bill Badger and the Big Store Robbery, Hamish Hamilton, 1967.

At the Back o' Ben Dee, Benn, 1968.

The Whopper, Benn, 1969, published as *The Monster Fish,* Scholastic, 1972.

Bill Badger's Voyage to the World's End, Kaye & Ward, 1969.

The Tyger Tray, Methuen, 1971.

The Pool of the Black Witch, Methuen, 1974.

Lord of the Forest, Methuen, 1975.

Contributor with A. L. E. Fenton and A. Windsor-Richards to *Stories of the Wild,* Benn, 1975, and with Windsor-Richards to *More Stories of the Wild,* Benn, 1979.

NONFICTION FOR JUVENILES; UNDER PSEUDONYM BB

Meeting Hill: BB's Fairy Book, Hollis & Carter, 1948.

The Wind in the Wood, Hollis & Carter, 1952.

The Badgers of Bearshanks, Benn, 1961.

The Pegasus Book of the Country-side, Dobson, 1964.

NONFICTION FOR ADULTS; UNDER PSEUDONYM BB

The Idle Countryman, Eyre & Spottiswoode, 1943.

Narrow Boat, Eyre & Spottiswoode, 1944.

The Wayfaring Tree, Hollis & Carter, 1946.

A Stream in Your Garden: How the Amateur May Install Running Water in Rock Gardens, and the Construction of Pools, Eyre & Spottiswoode, 1948.

Confessions of a Carp Fisher, Eyre & Spottiswoode, 1950.

Tide's Ending, Scribner, 1950.

Letters from Compton Deverell, Eyre & Spottiswoode, 1950.

Dark Estuary, Hollis & Carter, 1953, revised edition, Boydell Press, 1984.

A Carp Water (Wood Pool) and How to Fish It, Putnam (London), 1958.

The Autumn Road to the Isles, Nicholas Kaye, 1959.

The White Road Westwards, Nicholas Kaye, 1961.

September Road to Caithness and the Western Sea, Nicholas Kaye, 1962.

The Summer Road to Wales, Nicholas Kaye, 1964.

A Summer on the Nene, Kaye & Ward, 1967.

Recollections of a 'longshore Gunner, Boydell Press, 1976.

A Child Alone: The Memoirs of "BB", M. Joseph, 1978.

Ramblings of a Sportsman-Naturalist, M. Joseph, 1979.

The Naturalist's Bedside Book, M. Joseph, 1980.

The Quiet Fields, M. Joseph, 1981.

Indian Summer, M. Joseph, 1984.

The Best of "BB", M. Joseph, 1985.

Fisherman's Folly, Boydell, 1987.

EDITOR; UNDER PSEUDONYM BB

The Sportsman's Bedside Book, illustrations by G. D. Armour, Eyre & Spottiswoode, 1937.

The Countryman's Bedside Book, Eyre & Spottiswoode, 1941.

The Fisherman's Bedside Book, Eyre & Spottiswoode, 1945, Scribner, 1946.

The Shooting Man's Bedside Book, Scribner, 1948.

ILLUSTRATOR

Hesketh V. Prichard, *Sport in Wildest Britain,* Philip Allan, 1936.

Robert G. Walmsley, *Winged Company: Studies in Bird-watching,* Eyre & Spottiswoode, 1940.

Clarence H. Warren, *England Is a Village,* Eyre & Spottiswoode, 1940.

Eric Benfield, *Southern English,* Eyre & Spottiswoode, 1942.

L. T. C. Rolt, *Narrow Boat,* Eyre & Spottiswoode, 1944.

Brian Vesey-Fitzgerald, *It's My Delight,* Eyre & Spottiswoode, 1947.

Arthur Applin, *Philandering Angler,* Hurst & Blackett, 1948.

J. B. Drought, *A Sportsman Looks at Eire,* Hutchinson, 1949.

Arthur G. Street, *Landmarks,* Eyre & Spottiswoode, 1949.

Gerald D. Adams, *Red Vagabond: The Story of a Fox,* Batchworth, 1951.

Mabel C. Carey, editor, *Fairy Tales of Long Ago,* Dutton, 1952.

Henry S. Tegner, *The White Foxes of Gorfenletch,* Hollis & Carter, 1954.

William Mayne, *The Long Night,* Basil Blackwell, 1957.

Elfrida Vipont, *The Secret of Orra,* Basil Blackwell, 1957.

Mayne, *Thirteen O'Clock,* Basil Blackwell, 1959.

Arthur B. W. Richards, *Vix: The Story of a Fox Cub,* Benn, 1960.

Tegner, *Beasts of the North Country: From Whales to Shrews,* Galley Press, 1961.

Andrew Lang, *Prince Prigio and Prince Ricardo,* Dent, 1961.

Richards, *Birds of the Lonely Lake,* Benn, 1961.

Richards, *The Cabin in the Woods,* Friday Press, 1963.

A. R. Channel, *Rogue Elephant,* Macrae Smith, 1963.

Norah A. Burke, *King Todd: The True Story of a Wild Badger,* Putnam (London), 1963.

Frances Brown, *Granny's Wonderful Chair,* Dutton, 1963.

Richards, *The Wild White Swan,* Friday Press, 1965.

Tegner, *To Do with Birds,* Jenkins, 1965.

George Macdonald, *The Lost Princess: A Double Story,* Dutton, 1965.

Channel, *Jungle Rescue,* S. G. Phillips, 1968.

Gerald Summers, *Where Vultures Fly,* Collins, 1974.

OTHER

(Under pseudonym Michael Traherne) *Be Quiet and Go A-Angling* (adult nonfiction), Lutterworth, 1949.

Most works under pseudonym BB were self-illustrated under own name. Contributor under the pseudonym BB of adult fiction to *Five More: Stories,* Basil Blackwell, 1958. Regular contributor to periodicals, including *Country Life, Field,* and *Shooting Times.*

ADAPTATIONS: The Little Grey Men was adapted for a television series by the BBC, 1975, and has been optioned for a film in the United States; *Brendon Chase* was adapted for a radio series, and for a fifteen-episode television series by Southern TV, 1981.

SIDELIGHTS: Denys James Watkins-Pitchford, in an autobiographical essay in *Something About the Author Autobiography Series* (*SAAS*), said he prefaces every book with these words from a Cumbrian gravestone: "The wonder of the world / The beauty and the power, / The shape of things, / Their colours, lights, and shades, / These I saw, / Look ye also while life lasts." His lifelong fascination with and appreciation of nature brought him both joy and sorrow—joy in the remembrance of his own bucolic childhood and sorrow at the pollution that threatens the globe. The personal loss of his wife, Cecily, was added to this sorrow; Watkins-Pitchford maintained that her death re-sulted directly from the application of pesticide to a nearby wheat field. He believed the world could be a paradise if basic rules were observed to keep it intact. Both the events in his life and the pages of his works reflected such a paradise—nature and all its wonders.

Born as a twin, Watkins-Pitchford was the weaker of the two infants and was christened immediately in case he should die. His delicate state kept him from going away to prep school with his brothers, and it was during many hours spent alone that Watkins-Pitchford became an ardent naturalist. Much of his time was spent fishing and hunting near his home, and "I seemed to soon possess the keen nose and ear, and sight too, of a wild animal," continued Watkins-Pitchford in his autobiographical essay. In 1926 he left his country home to study art in London. The noisy streets and crowds of people seemed worlds away from his quiet woodlands and green fields. "At the time of my childhood there were no cars, no aeroplanes, or tractors," he recalled. "No loud noises would be heard in the countryside—only those gentle sounds of nature, the 'tink-tink' of the blacksmith at his forge across the valley from our home, the humming rising and falling of the threshing machine in the fields, the sound of livestock—cows and sheep, the wind in the trees. The countryside of England was then a truly lovely place; much of this peace and beauty has gone forever."

His schooling complete, he "had to look round for a job which suggested teaching, for to live by one's art in my day was definitely dodgy," remarked Watkins-Pitchford in *SAAS.* Taking a job as assistant art master at Rugby School, he stayed sixteen years before moving to a house on a large estate to continue writing and illustrating books. His marriage to Cecily and the births of their two children took place during this time, and the success of his first few books, under the pseudonym BB, prompted the move. It was in this new home that his son Robin died, and for a year thereafter Watkins-Pitchford did no work. Instead he returned to the activities of his childhood, spending his time in the woods and on the lake below the house. The absence of work depleted his finances, however, and Watkins-Pitchford had to give up his country estate for a small village home, fittingly named the Round House. "I designed an iron wild-goose with wings stretched for a weather vane and this made a famous landmark for the villagers, telling them which way the wind was blowing," he described.

Once settled in his new home, Watkins-Pitchford made four tours of Britain with his wife and daughter, writing and illustrating each one. "We were away from home for six to eight weeks at a time. So I was able to enjoy a wild wandering life as well as to write about it, which was a very pleasant state of affairs," he added. While home, Watkins-Pitchford explored the large forest nearby, which was part of the ancient Forest of Rockingham. This was also the forest into which he introduced the purple emperor, considered by many to be the finest of British butterflies. Previously glimpsing the rare butterfly in a forest in Oxfordshire, he collected a number of eggs and placed them in an outdoor muslin cage, bringing them through the winter until they turned into butterflies in late July. By repeating this process every year since the mid-1960s, Watkins-Pitchford managed to establish the purple emperor in a natural habitat. "One sunny day I released over forty males and females in a forest ride. They flew onto the sallow bush and there they displayed in the sun—a wondrous sight indeed, so many gleaming jewels," recounted Watkins-Pitchford in his essay.

Many books followed the move to the Round House, with nature and its "gleaming jewels" often providing the main focus. His personal favorites, *Brendon Chase* and *Wild Lone: The Story of a Pytchley Fox,* involve characters who must fend for themselves in the English woods and countryside. *Brendon Chase* is the story of three boys who run away from home and spend eight months in a nearby ancient forest. During this time they obtain their food and clothing from Brendon Chase, the forest, which sustains them while they are away from home. E. L. Buell wrote in a *New York Times* review that "this curious mixture of moods and styles binds the reader of ten and up in a leisurely unique enchantment." Rufus, the fox in *Wild Lone,* is also alone in the forest, his parents having died when he was a baby. This book tells the story of his life, during which he becomes an almost legendary figure to farmers, hunters, and many others. A *Saturday Review of Literature* contributor, who found Rufus "very close to a poet," added that "the whole volume is an unusually fine piece of bookmaking."

Although not his personal favorite of the more than fifty books written during his long career, *The Little Grey Men* remains Watkins-Pitchford's bestseller. This story of three gnomes recounts the adventures of Baldmoney, Sneezewort, and Dodder as they journey up Folly Brook looking for their lost brother Cloudberry. Many small animals and birds help them along the way, and the book includes three songs. This brook actually ran down the valley near Watkins-Pitchford's childhood home, and in his autobiographical essay he explained that "one fine spring day my brother and I traced the Folly Brook to its source and this gave me the idea for my story." A reviewer in the *New Yorker* maintained that *The Little Grey Men* is "a sylvan fairy story, with a rich, somebre flavor . . . that will probably make a permanent place for itself among imaginative readers."

Watkins-Pitchford once told *CA:* "Like most authors I write with an eye to financial gain. This is certainly not my chief motive. I write chiefly for my own pleasure, re-cording those things I see in nature and the natural world which fill me with perpetual wonder and delight. I am more interested in animals and nature than I am in my fellow men and women for the latter seem to be doing their very best to destroy the world and all those things I hold in such high regard. Perhaps this is because we have not predators to prey upon us. The wild creatures kill to live; we kill each other out of greed and jealousy.

"If I have any advice to give to aspiring authors it is this: Write about those things with which you are familiar and cultivate the most intense awareness of the world about you; try to view things in a fresh and original way. Like the painter who studies the great works of past ages, so you should read the recognized eminent authors, both of the past and the present, but never try to copy them. If submitting manuscript to a publishing house, never serve up a grubby manuscript which has been well thumbed and badly typed. Typing is essential.

"Work habits: I never write unless I feel compelled to do so. What triggers this off I cannot say, it is something quite mysterious. If writing is a physical and mental effort, don't write. To those who are lucky enough to have the spark of genius, writing becomes as natural as breathing!"

BIOGRAPHICAL/CRITICAL SOURCES:

BOOKS

Peppin, Brigid, and Lucy Micklethwait, *Book Illustrators of the Twentieth Century,* Arco, 1984.
Something About the Author Autobiography Series, Volume 4, Gale, 1987.

PERIODICALS

Books and Bookmen, August 1969; November, 1969; November, 1975.
British Book News, October, 1980; July, 1984.
New Yorker, December 3, 1949.
New York Times, November 11, 1945.
Observer (London), December 7, 1969; December 6, 1970; October 25, 1981.
Saturday Review of Literature, December 31, 1938.
Times Literary Supplement, January 28, 1965; March 25, 1967; January 18, 1968; September 28, 1973; March 29, 1974.

OBITUARIES:

PERIODICALS

Times (London), September 12, 1990.*

—*Sketch by Susan M. Reicha*

WEISS, Harvey 1922-

PERSONAL: Born April 10, 1922, in New York City; son of Louis and Bertha (Stern) Weiss; married Miriam Schlein (writer), 1954 (divorced, 1970); married Margaret I. McKinnickinnick, 1981; children: (first marriage) Elizabeth, John. *Education:* Attended University of Missouri, New York University, Rutgers University, Art Students League, National Academy School of Fine Arts; studied sculpture in Paris under Ossipe Zadkine.

ADDRESSES: Home—42 Maple Lane, Green Farms, CT 06463.

CAREER: Free-lance writer, illustrator, sculptor. Adelphi University, Garden City, NY, professor of sculpture. Formerly worked in advertising industry as a production manager. Has had his sculptures exhibited in one-man shows at Paul Rosenberg Gallery, New York City, Fairfield University, Fairfield, CT, Silvermine Guild Arts Center, New Canaan, CT, American Institute of Arts and Letters, and elsewhere; group shows at Sculpture Center Gallery, New York City, Sculptors Guild, New York City, Albright Knox Gallery, Buffalo, NY, and elsewhere. Work represented in permanent collections of Nelson Rockefeller, Joseph Hirschhorn, Kranert Museum, the Ford Foundation, and others. *Military service:* U.S. Air Force.

MEMBER: Authors Guild, Authors League of America, Sculptors Guild (president, 1969-1971), Silvermine Guild.

AWARDS, HONORS: New York Herald Tribune Spring Book Festival Honor Book, 1957, for *A Gondola for Fun,* 1958, for *Paul's Horse, Herman,* and 1961, for *Pencil, Pen, and Brush: Drawing for Beginners;* Ford Foundation purchase award, 1960 and 1961; Olivetti Award, New England Annual Exhibition, 1969; National Institute of Arts and Letters grant, 1970.

WRITINGS:

"BEGINNING ARTISTS LIBRARY" SERIES: JUVENILES; SELF-ILLUSTRATED

Clay, Wood, and Wire: A How-to-Do-It Book of Sculpture, Addison-Wesley, 1956.
Paper, Ink, and Roller: Print-Making for Beginners, Addison-Wesley, 1958, published in England as *The Young Printmaker: Printing with Paper, Ink, and Roller,* Kaye & Ward, 1969.
Pen, Pencil, and Brush Drawing for Beginners, Addison-Wesley, 1961.
Sticks, Spools, and Feathers, Addison-Wesley, 1962.
Ceramics: From Clay to Kiln, Addison-Wesley, 1964.
Paint, Brush, and Palette, Addison-Wesley, 1966.
Collage and Construction, Addison-Wesley, 1970.

Lens and Shutter: An Introduction to Photography, Addison-Wesley, 1971.
How to Make Your Own Movies: An Introduction to Filmmaking, Addison-Wesley, 1973.
Carving: How to Carve Wood and Stone, Addison-Wesley, 1976.
Working with Cardboard and Paper, Addison-Wesley, 1978.

JUVENILES; SELF-ILLUSTRATED

Twenty-four and Stanley, Putnam, 1956.
A Gondola for Fun, Putnam, 1957.
Paul's Horse, Herman, Putnam, 1958.
The Sooner Hound, Putnam, 1960.
The Expeditions of Willis Partridge, Abelard, 1960, reprinted as *The Adventures of Willis Partridge,* Young Readers Press, 1966.
How to Ooze, and Other Ways of Travelling, Abelard, 1961.
Horse in No Hurry, Putnam, 1961.
My Closet Full of Hats, Abelard, 1962.
Very Private Treehouse, Abelard, 1964.
Rocks and Gemstones, Crowell, 1967.
Sailing Small Boats, Addison-Wesley, 1967, published in England as *Better Sailing,* edited by John Chamier, Kaye & Ward, 1969.
The Big Cleanup, Abelard, 1967.
How to Be a Hero, Parents Magazine Press, 1968.
Motors and Engines and How They Work, Crowell, 1969.
The Gadget Book, Crowell, 1971.
Ship Models and How to Build Them, Crowell, 1973.
How to Make Your Own Books, Crowell, 1973.
Model Cars and Trucks and How to Build Them, Crowell, 1974.
Model Airplanes and How to Build Them, Crowell, 1975.
Games & Puzzles You Can Make Yourself, Crowell, 1976.
How to Run a Railroad: Everything You Need to Know about Model Trains, Crowell, 1977.
What Holds It Together, Little-Brown, 1977.
Model Buildings and How to Make Them, Crowell, 1979.
How to Be an Inventor, Crowell, 1980.
Hammer and Saw, Crowell, 1981.
Machines and How They Work, Crowell, 1983
Shelters: From Tepee to Igloo, Crowell, 1988.
Cartoons and Cartooning, Houghton, 1990.
Submarines and Other Underwater Craft, Harper/Collins, 1990.
Maps: Getting from Here to There, Houghton, 1991.

ILLUSTRATOR; JUVENILES

Miriam Schlein, *Here Comes Night,* Albert Whitman, 1957.
David C. DeJong, *The Happy Birthday Umbrella,* Little, Brown, 1959.

Schlein, *The Raggle Taggle Fellow* (Spring Book Festival Honor Book), Abelard, 1959.

Beth Y. Gleick, *Time Is When,* Rand, 1960.

Schlein, *My Family,* Abelard, 1960.

Alice Marriott, *First Comers: Indians of America's Dream,* McKay, 1960.

Norma Simon, *My Family Seder,* United Synagogue Books, 1961.

Simon, *Tu Bishvat,* United Synagogue Books, 1961.

Joan M. Lexau, *Olaf Reads,* Dial, 1961.

DeJong, *The Happy Birthday Egg,* Little, Brown, 1962.

Schlein, *The Pile of Junk,* Abelard, 1962.

Lexau, *Olaf Is Late,* Dial, 1963.

DeJong, *Looking for Alexander,* Little, Brown, 1963.

Schlein, *Who,* Walck, 1963.

Daniel Goldwater, *Bridges and How They Are Built,* Hale, 1965.

DeJong, *Alexander the Money-Sitter,* Little-Brown, 1965.

Marriott, *Black Stone Knife,* Archway, 1968.

Leonore Klein, *Silly Sam,* Scholastic, 1971.

Mel Cebulash, *Willie's Pet,* Scholastic, 1972.

Robert Froman, *Rubber Bands, Baseballs & Doughnuts: A Book About Topology,* Crowell, 1972.

David A. Adler, *3D, 2D, 1D,* Crowell, 1975.

Weiss is also illustrator of numerous other children's books, including *Every Friday Night,* by Norma Simon, United Synagogue Books.

SIDELIGHTS: Harvey Weiss was born in New York City, and he has lived there all his life with the exception of three years he spent in the air force, some travel abroad, and a year of study at the University of Missouri. The broad cultural panorama surrounding him in the city environment exposed young Weiss to many different forms of creative endeavor. The deep enthusiasm for art that resulted has remained with Weiss throughout his life, prompting his exploration into such artistic mediums as sculpture, writing, and drawing. Weiss's varied interests have led him to seek artistic outlets through the many jobs he held in the field of advertising and also to make a series of successful exhibitions as a sculptor. His creative talents have led him finally to a career as the author of a diverse series of nonfiction books for children. Weiss has made a name for himself as an author who can be counted on to inspire and inform young would-be artists and hobbyists with the same enthusiasm that he brings to his own work as a writer and artist.

Weiss discovered the world of books within the doors of the New York Public Library when he was around eleven years old, and he has been an avid reader ever since. "Books have always been very special to me," he once commented in *Something about the Author (SATA)*, "as sources of knowledge, as enlargers of experience, and as means of entertainment. Many of the books I bought and read and treasured as a youngster in school still rest in one of the many bookcases that are scattered through my home and which line the walls of the room where I work. One of the special shelves contains books that I have made myself, strictly for my own amusement. They are sketchbooks and photo albums, unfinished books of poetry, books full of doodles and random thoughts. Some have only a few pages. Others are fairly thick. The bindings are simple and were quickly done. Most of these books are dog-eared and worn from much use, and some, which were experimental, are crude and rather makeshift. But they were all great fun to make and to use. It is nice to have them close at hand where they can be thumbed through at idle moments or shown to friends."

Despite a great love for books and illustration, Weiss came to be an author himself in a round-about fashion. "It wasn't until I had met and married Miriam Schlein in 1954 that I first became aware of the fascination of children's books," he told *SATA*. "I succumbed to the irrepressible urge to write one myself when I began to realize that there was an audience of perceptive, fresh, honest, unspoiled people—children. I had never realized this before. It seemed to me that this was an opportunity for direct and honest art—writing and illustrating—that is rarely found in the commercial world of today. And it had a very close relationship in spirit with the sculpture I had been doing most of my life."

Weiss's other interest-turned-vocation is that of sculpture, which was inspired by the enjoyment of model building as a child. Many of his books for children have been inspired by this hobby, such as *Ship Models and How to Build Them,* and *How to Run a Railroad.* Weiss comments in *Model Cars and Trucks and How to Build Them,* "I find [models] interesting and pleasing by themselves, and I don't really care if they are very accurate or not. They are fun to make. They are fun to have around. . . . I find that my models end up on window sills, the kitchen counter, the coffee table in the living room—in fact, they look fine anywhere at all."

Understanding that the "creative process"—art, ceramics, photography, model making—is of greater importance than the resulting artwork underlies Weiss's "Beginning Artists Library" series. Young artists are given room for experimentation within the technique involved in their new medium, whether it be pencil, paintbrush, pen-and-ink, or print-making, and Weiss's relaxed style allows them time to build confidence in their ability. Whatever subject he chooses, Weiss's books have been consistently commended for their clearly written and well-illustrated texts. As Margaret Sherwood Libby writes in the *New York Herald Tribune,* "Among the many books planned to aid and inspire children [in the arts], our favorites are those by Mr. Weiss."

BIOGRAPHICAL/CRITICAL SOURCES:

BOOKS

Children's Literature Review, Volume 4, Gale, 1982.
Contemporary American Painting and Sculpture, University of Illinois Press, 1961.
de Montreville, Doris, and Donna Hill, *Third Book of Junior Authors,* H. W. Wilson, 1972.
Kingman, Lee, and others, compilers, *Illustrators of Children's Books, 1957-1966,* Horn Book, 1968.
Something about the Author, Volume 27, Gale, 1982, pp. 225-227.
Viguers, Ruth Hill, and others, compilers, *Illustrators of Children's Books, 1946-1956,* Horn Book, 1958.
Weiss, Harvey, *Model Cars and Trucks and How to Build Them,* Crowell, 1974.

PERIODICALS

Booklist, October 15, 1984, p. 316; March 1, 1986, p. 1024; June 1, 1988, p. 1680; March 15, 1990, p. 1460; July, 1990, p. 2096.
New York Herald Tribune, October 7, 1962, p. 14.
School Library Journal, September, 1988, p. 196; April, 1990, p. 138; May, 1990, p. 121.

*   *   *

WEISS, Jess E(dward) 1926-

PERSONAL: Born March 12, 1926, in New York, NY; son of Jerome (a salesman) and Martha (Levy) Weiss; married Shirley Levy, January 17, 1943 (deceased); married Joyce Greco, December 11, 1973; children: (first marriage) Gary Lynn, Gail Susan. *Education:* American University, Veterans Representative Degree, 1947. *Religion:* "Universal."

ADDRESSES: Home—P. O. Box 333, East Norwich, NY 11732-0333.

CAREER: American Veterans Committee, Veterans Claims Service, Washington, DC, director, 1946-52; Aetna Life Insurance Co., New York, NY, claims supervisor, 1952-63; Self Insured Insurance Agency, Baldwin, NY, owner, 1963—. *Military service:* U.S. Army, 1941-46; served in Africa and Europe; received Purple Heart, Silver Star, and Bronze Star.

MEMBER: American Veterans Committee.

WRITINGS:

The Vestibule, Ashley Books, 1972, 3rd edition, 1973.
The Adam and Eve Fantasy, Exposition, 1985.
Overcoming the Fear of Death and Dying, Brookville Books, 1991.

WERSBA, Barbara 1932-

PERSONAL: Born August 19, 1932, in Chicago, IL; daughter of Robert and Lucy Jo (Quarles) Wersba. *Education:* Bard College, B.A., 1954; studied acting at Neighborhood Playhouse and at the Paul Mann Actors Workshop; studied dance with Martha Graham.

ADDRESSES: Home—Box 1892, Sag Harbor, NY 11963. *Agent*—McIntosh and Otis, Inc., 310 Madison Ave., New York, NY 10017.

CAREER: Actress in radio and television, summer stock, Off-Broadway, and touring companies, 1944-59; full-time writer, 1960—. Summer lecturer at New York University; writing instructor at Rockland Center for the Arts.

AWARDS, HONORS: Deutscher Jugend Buchpreis, 1973, for *Run Softly, Go Fast;* American Library Association (ALA) Best Book for Young Adults and Notable Children's Book lists, both 1976, and National Book Award nomination, 1977, all for *Tunes for a Small Harmonica;* ALA Best Book for Young Adults, 1982, for *The Carnival in My Mind;* D.H.L. from Bard College, 1977.

WRITINGS:

FICTION FOR CHILDREN

The Boy Who Loved the Sea, illustrated by Margot Tomes, Coward, 1961.
The Brave Balloon of Benjamin Buckley, illustrated by Tomes, Atheneum, 1963.
The Land of Forgotten Beasts, illustrated by Tomes, Atheneum, 1964.
A Song for Clowns (Junior Literary Guild selection), illustrated by Mario Rivoli, Atheneum, 1965.
Let Me Fall before I Fly, Atheneum, 1971.
Amanda, Dreaming, illustrated by Mercer Mayer, Atheneum, 1973.
The Crystal Child, illustrated by Donna Diamond, Harper, 1982.

POETRY FOR CHILDREN

Do Tigers Ever Bite Kings?, illustrated by Rivoli, Atheneum, 1966.
Twenty-six Starlings Will Fly through Your Mind, illustrated by David Palladini, Harper, 1980.

FICTION FOR YOUNG ADULTS

The Dream Watcher, also see below, Atheneum, 1968.
Run Softly, Go Fast, Atheneum, 1970.
The Country of the Heart, Atheneum, 1975.
Tunes for a Small Harmonica, Harper, 1976.
The Carnival in My Mind, Harper, 1982.
Crazy Vanilla, Harper, 1986.
Fat: A Love Story, Harper, 1987.
Love Is the Crooked Thing, Harper, 1987.

Beautiful Losers, Harper, 1988.
Just Be Gorgeous, Harper, 1988.
Wonderful Me, Harper, 1989.
The Farewell Kid, Harper, 1990.
The Best Place to Live Is the Ceiling, Harper, 1990.
You'll Never Guess the End, Harper, 1992.

OTHER

The Dream Watcher (play; adaptation of her novel of the same title), first produced in Westport, CT, 1975.

Contributor of reviews of children's books to the *New York Times.*

WORK IN PROGRESS: Fiction.

SIDELIGHTS: Barbara Wersba began writing only after a fifteen-year career as an actress, but since that time she has had great success as an author who is able to accurately describe the pains of growing up. While she has published books for children of all ages, her greatest successes have come with her stories for young adults. These often romantic novels describe the difficulties that her characters face ás they struggle to understand their relationships with parents and friends. A trademark of Wersba's work is that the young protagonists often find their way with the help of an older, often quite eccentric character.

Wersba is able to accurately portray the difficulties of youth in part because her own childhood was touched with loneliness and pain. In her autobiographical sketch for the *Something about the Author Autobiography Series* (*SAAS*), she recalls: "I grew up in almost total solitude." Although she did most of the things that children are supposed to do—"attending the local grammar school, joining the Girl Scouts, selling war bonds, and spending every Saturday afternoon at the movies"—she also felt distanced from the roles she was called upon to play. Wersba remembers that she always wanted to be an actress, for as an actress she could assume the life of another person, escaping her own.

When Wersba was eleven years old, her parents ended their tumultuous marriage and she and her mother moved to New York City. The difficulty of the move was compounded by the fact that she was forced to give up her two beloved cats. She writes in *SAAS:* "[T]he first thing I did in New York was to go out and buy a ticket to a play. I had never heard of the playwright or the star, but when the matinee was over, I sat in my seat paralyzed by emotion. The play was *The Glass Menagerie* by Tennessee Williams." This experience further encouraged her acting ambitions, and though her father later encouraged her to go to college at Vassar, she instead chose to attend a small liberal-arts college called Bard. There she immersed her-

self in drama, recalling that "I was like a sponge, trying to absorb it all, acting, directing, stagecraft, dance."

Wersba graduated from college in 1954 and pursued her acting career by moving to New York City and making "the rounds." From her tenement apartment on East Ninth Street she ventured every day to visit theatrical offices, "trying to see someone important, never being allowed to see someone important, and departing in anger," she recalls in *SAAS.* Eventually Wersba got involved with a small touring production, but on her first tour succumbed to the illness that was to end her acting career and begin her career as a writer.

Wersba went to a friend's house on Martha's Vineyard to recuperate from hepatitis, and realized then that she would never return to the theater. In her autobiographical sketch she remembers feeling elated: "No more part-time jobs and making rounds, no more despair over the lack of jobs in the theatre, the cruelty of the theatre. I did not know where I was going, but after fifteen years of struggle I was free. It was then that my hostess said, 'Barbara, why don't you write something?'" The book she wrote was called *The Boy Who Loved the Sea,* and it convinced Wersba that she had the ability and the temperament to begin at age twenty-six a new career as a writer.

Though she enjoyed writing her first few books, it was not until *The Dream Watcher,* published in 1968, that she was able to develop any real characters. She remembers in *SAAS:* "On the day I finished this book I burst into tears, for I knew it to be a milestone in my life." The book tells the story of a fourteen-year-old misfit, Albert Scully, who meets an interesting old lady who, through her descriptions of her illustrious acting career, convinces Albert that he is a worthwhile person. When the lady dies, Albert discovers that all her stories were lies, but that doesn't change his improved self-image. The book received a great deal of critical and popular attention, and Wersba acknowledges "it was only then that I realized that this theme of older person helping younger person had been the underlying theme of my own life. Unable to relate to my parents, I had sought parent substitutes everywhere."

Kay Vandergrift, writing in the *Dictionary of Literary Biography,* notes that "Albert was the first of her sensitive, thoughtful young men of contemporary society who do not fit the expectations for the modern male and who must find the courage to express their own individuality." The second such character was David Marks in *Run Softly, Go Fast.* David immerses himself in the counterculture of the late 1960s—drugs, artiness, free love—in order to escape a deteriorating relationship with his father. David finds happiness only when he can come to terms with his father's impending death. Wersba's 1986 novel *Crazy Vanilla* again shows a young boy becoming whole, this time with the aid of a fifteen-year-old waif who helps him accept his brother's homosexuality. Vandergrift praises the book for containing "one of the most positive images of a homosexual couple in young adult literature," and contends that "this book seems to bring together many of the best and most powerful aspects of Wersba's work—strong and fascinating, somewhat zany characters; a gentle, bittersweet humor with touches of bold laughter; and a believable relationship captured in a language and style that is both engrossing and delightful."

Wersba brings this same skill to her depiction of female characters. In *Fat: A Love Story,* she tells the story of Rita Formica, a fat teenage girl who falls in love with a handsome but conceited boy only to lose that love to her best friend. But Wersba changes this standard story by letting Rita find love with her employer, a thirty-two-year-old cheesecake salesman. This improbable love affair continues in *Love Is the Crooked Thing* and *Beautiful Losers,* as Rita pursues her lover, Arnold, and her ambition to become a writer. The stories provide a roller-coaster ride of emotions and events, but Wersba is able to make the story succeed because, as Cathi Edgerton notes in *Voice of Youth Advocate,* "Rita and Arnold are such delightful, original, authentic characters that their romance never becomes a romantic cliche, despite the happily-ever-after ending."

In *Just Be Gorgeous, Wonderful Me,* and *The Farewell Kid,* Wersba again follows the life of a young girl from ages fifteen through eighteen. In *Just Be Gorgeous,* Heidi Rosenbloom rebels against the wealth and security that her rich parents provide by making friends with a homeless, homosexual street performer named Jeffrey. Heidi discovers her own resourcefulness and abilities when she decides that she will feed and clothe Jeffrey, as well as launch him to stardom. *Wonderful Me* finds Heidi in an odd love affair with her high school English teacher, and *The Farewell Kid* shows her running a dog rescue service—as Wersba herself admits to doing—out of her own apartment. Judy Druse, in her review of *Wonderful Me* for *Voice of Youth Advocate,* says: "Young adults will identify with Heidi's nonconformity, her feelings of inadequacy, her inability to communicate with her divorced parents, and her need for love and affection."

In the Rita Formica books and in others, Wersba deals candidly with sexual relationships between young people and older people. Beth Andersen objects to this kind of situation in a young adult novel in her *Voice of Youth Advocate* review of *Love Is the Crooked Thing,* arguing that Rita's relationship to Arnold and her precocious attitude towards sex are "too adult for readers who should be in the throes of giggly stirrings of boy-awareness that most junior high students usually go through." However, Wersba contends that today's children are exposed to so much

so early in our culture that they need to see sex portrayed honestly, without mystification or moralizing. She writes in *Library Journal* that "I believe that it is up to the children's writer to take a chance and delve deeply into the subject of sex—even if it gets him into trouble."

Wersba is able to portray her characters accurately because so many of them are drawn from situations in her own life. She often sought out older people as friends—whether they be teachers, theatre directors, agents, or actresses—and credits these friends with helping her become the person she is today. The greatest inspiration for Wersba was Carson McCullers, the famous Southern writer to whom she once read twice a week. McCullers, who was almost completely paralyzed at the time, astounded Wersba with her tenacity, her brilliance, and her refusal to quit writing despite enormous pain and inconvenience. Wersba, in her *SAAS* essay, called McCullers "the epitome of the word Writer."

When asked why she writes for children, Wersba responds in *SAAS:* "Because the form is tantalizingly short, and thus tantalizingly difficult. Because the form implies hope. Because those of us who use this form still experience our childhood in strong and passionate ways. There is no chalk line on the sidewalk with childhood on one side and maturity on the other. It is all the same life, it is all one, and the best children's writers know that they are writing for the child in the adult, and the adult in the child."

BIOGRAPHICAL/CRITICAL SOURCES:

BOOKS

Children's Literature Review, Volume 3, Gale, 1977.
Contemporary Literary Criticism, Volume 30, Gale, 1984.
Dictionary of Literary Biography, Volume 52: *American Writers for Children since 1960: Fiction,* Gale, 1986, pp. 374-380.
Something about the Author Autobiography Series, Volume 2, Gale, 1986, pp. 293-304.
Twentieth-Century Children's Writers, 3rd edition, St. James Press, 1989.
Twentieth-Century Children's Writers, St. Martin's Press, 1978.
Ward, Martha E., and Dorothy A. Marquardt, *Authors of Books for Young People,* 2nd edition, Scarecrow Press, 1971.

PERIODICALS

Best Sellers, October, 1982.
Bulletin of the Center for Children's Books, July-August, 1982.
Children's Book News, September-October, 1969.
English Journal, November, 1976.
Horn Book, December, 1971.

Kirkus Reviews, November 1, 1986; July 1, 1987; October 15, 1987.
Kliatt, April, 1991.
Library Journal, September, 1968; February 15, 1973, pp. 620-623.
Los Angeles Times Book Review, August 24, 1980; November 20, 1988.
New York Times Book Review, October 24, 1982.
Observer, April 3, 1988; July 29, 1990.
Publishers Weekly, September 9, 1988; January 13, 1989; March 16, 1990; September 14, 1990; March 15, 1991.
School Library Journal, January, 1971; November, 1986; August, 1987; November, 1988; November, 1990.
Times Literary Supplement, May 23, 1986.
Top of the News, June, 1975.
Voice of Youth Advocate, December, 1986; June, 1987; December 1987, p. 239; April 1988, p. 31; June 1989, p. 108; October, 1990; December, 1990.
Washington Post Book World, August 8, 1982; September 12, 1982.
Young Readers' Review, November, 1968.

—*Sketch by Tom Pendergast*

*　　*　　*

WESTING, Arthur H(erbert) 1928-

PERSONAL: Born July 18, 1928, in New York, NY; son of S. W. (a physician) and Paula (Riesenfeld) Westing; married Carol A. Eck (a teacher), June 5, 1956; children: Jeanne K., Stephen H. *Education:* Columbia University, A.B., 1950; Yale University, M.F., 1954, Ph.D., 1959.

ADDRESSES: Home—Putney, VT. *Office*—Westing Associates in Environment, Security, and Education, RFD 1, Box 919, Putney, VT 05346.

CAREER: U.S. Forest Service, Lansing, MI, research forester, 1954-55; Purdue University, Lafayette, IN, assistant professor of forestry, 1959-64; University of Massachusetts—Amherst, associate professor of tree physiology, 1964-65; Middlebury College, Middlebury, VT, associate professor of biology, 1965-66; Windham College, Putney, VT, associate professor, 1966-71, professor of botany, 1971-76, chairman of department of biology, 1966-75; Stockholm International Peace Research Institute, Solna, Sweden, senior research fellow, 1976-78, 1983-87; Hampshire College, Amherst, professor of ecology and dean of School of Natural Science, 1978-83; International Peace Research Institute, Oslo, Sweden, senior research fellow, 1988-90. Fellow in forest biology, North Carolina State College of Agriculture and Mechanical Arts (now North Carolina State University at Raleigh), 1960; Charles Bullard fellow, Harvard University, 1963-64. Trustee, Vermont Wild Land Foundation, 1966-75; planning commis-

sioner, Town of Westminster, VT, 1968-72. Director of Windham World Affairs Council, 1973-76, 1991—; director of Peace, Security, and the Environment project, United Nations Environment Programme, 1983-90. Advisor and consultant to numerous organizations and publications. *Military service:* U.S. Marine Corps, 1950-52, 1954; became captain.

MEMBER: World Council for the Biosphere (councillor), International Peace Research Association, World Federation of Scientific Workers (corresponding member), International Primate Protection League (scientific advisor), International Society of Naturalists (fellow), Rachel Carson Council (consulting expert), Fauna and Flora Preservation Society, American Association for the Advancement of Science (fellow; director of herbicide assessment commission, 1970-71), Scientists' Institute of Public Information (fellow), Danforth Foundation (associate, 1973—), Vermont Academy of Arts and Sciences (trustee, 1967-71, 1991), Sigma Xi, Xi Sigma Pi.

AWARDS, HONORS: D.Sc. degree from Windham College, 1973; Guggenheim Foundation fellowship, 1973-74; New York Academy Science Award, 1983; Bulgarian Protection of Nature Medal, 1984.

WRITINGS:

(With J. B. Neilands) *Harvest of Death,* Free Press, 1972.
Ecological Consequences of the Second Indochina War, Almqvist & Wiksell, 1976.
Weapons of Mass Destruction and the Environment, Taylor & Francis, 1978.
Warfare in a Fragile World, Taylor & Francis, 1980.
Environmental Warfare, Taylor & Francis, 1984.
Herbicides in War, Taylor & Francis, 1984.
Explosive Remnants of War, Taylor & Francis, 1985.
Global Resources and International Conflict, Oxford University Press, 1986.
Cultural Norms, War, and the Environment, Oxford University Press, 1988.
Comprehensive Security for the Baltic, Sage Publications, 1989.
Environmental Hazards of War, Sage Publications, 1990.

OTHER

Contributor to *Research Problems in Biology,* Doubleday, 1965, 2nd edition, Oxford University Press, 1976; *Ecocide in Indochina: The Ecology of War,* by Barry Weisberg, Canfield Press, 1970; *The Withering Rain: America's Herbicidal Folly,* by Thomas Whiteside, Dutton, 1971; *Gravity and the Organism,* University of Chicago Press, 1971; *Understanding Environmental Pollution,* Mosby, 1971; *The Wasted Nations,* Harper, 1972; *Horticultural Science,* by Jules Janick, 2nd edition, W. H. Freeman, 1972; *Essays Today,* Harcourt, 1972; *Armaments and Disarmament in* the *Nuclear Age,* by Marek Thee, Almqvist & Wiksell, 1977; *Ecological Effects of Pesticides,* by F. H. Perring, Academic Press, 1978; *Future War,* by F. Barnaby, M. Joseph, 1984; *Ecotoxicology and Climate,* by Philippe Bourdeau, J. Wiley, 1989; and *Maintenance of the Biosphere,* by N. Polunin, Edinburgh University Press, 1990. Contributor to *World Book Encyclopedia,* 1983. Contributor of over two hundred articles to scientific journals. Contributing editor to *Vermont Freeman,* 1971-75, and *Horticulture,* 1976-78. Consulting editor to *Environment,* 1978—, *Tree Physiology,* 1985-87, and *Environmental Awareness,* 1989—. Member of editorial board, *Conservation Biology,* 1987-91.

*　　*　　*

WHITNEY, Phyllis A(yame) 1903-

PERSONAL: Born September 9, 1903, in Yokohama, Japan; daughter of U.S. citizens, Charles Joseph and Lillian (Mandeville) Whitney; married George A. Garner, 1925 (divorced, 1945); married Lovell F. Jahnke (a businessman), 1950 (died, 1973); children: (first marriage) Georgia. *Education:* Attended public schools in Chicago, IL. *Avocational interests:* "My only hobby is collecting backgrounds for new books, and that takes most of my time, since I visit these places and do a great deal of research."

ADDRESSES: Agent—McIntosh & Otis, 310 Madison Ave., New York, NY 10017.

CAREER: Author, 1941—. Children's book editor with the *Chicago Sun,* 1942-46, and *Philadelphia Inquirer,* 1946-48. Teacher of juvenile writing at Northwestern University, 1945-46, New York University, 1947-58, and at writers' conferences.

MEMBER: Authors League of America, Mystery Writers of America (member of board of directors, 1959-62; president, 1975), Malice Domestic, American Crime Writers League, Society of Children's Book Writers, Children's Reading Round Table, Midland Authors.

AWARDS, HONORS: Youth Today contest winner, and *Book World*'s Spring Book Festival Award, both 1947, both for *Willow Hill;* Edgar Allan Poe Award for the best juvenile mystery, Mystery Writers of America, 1961, for *Mystery of the Haunted Pool,* and 1964, for *Mystery of the Hidden Hand;* Edgar Allan Poe nominations, 1962, for *The Secret of the Tiger Eyes,* 1971, for *Mystery of the Scowling Boy,* and 1974, for *The Secret of the Missing Footprint;* Sequoyah Children's Book Award, 1963, for *Mystery of the Haunted Pool;* "Today's Woman" citation, Council of Cerebral Palsy Auxiliaries of Nassau County, 1983; Grandmaster Award, Mystery Writers of America,

1988, for lifetime achievement; Malice Domestic Award, 1989, for lifetime achievement.

WRITINGS:

JUVENILE NOVELS

A Place for Ann, illustrated by Helen Blair, Houghton, 1941.

A Star for Ginny, illustrated by Hilda Frommholz, Houghton, 1942.

A Window for Julie, illustrated by Jean Anderson, Houghton, 1943.

The Silver Inkwell, illustrated by Frommholz, Houghton, 1945.

Willow Hill, McKay, 1947.

Ever After, Houghton, 1948.

Linda's Homecoming, McKay, 1950.

Love Me, Love Me Not, Houghton, 1952.

Step to the Music, Crowell, 1953.

A Long Time Coming, McKay, 1954.

The Fire and the Gold, Crowell, 1956.

The Highest Dream, McKay, 1956.

Creole Holiday, Westminster, 1959.

Nobody Likes Trina, Westminster, 1972.

JUVENILE MYSTERIES

Mystery of the Gulls, illustrated by Janet Smalley, Westminster, 1949.

The Island of Dark Woods, illustrated by Philip Wishnefsky, Westminster, 1951, published as *Mystery of the Strange Traveller,* 1967.

Mystery of the Black Diamonds, illustrated by John Gretzer, Westminster, 1954 (published in England as *Black Diamonds,* Brockhampton, 1957).

Mystery on the Isle of Skye, illustrated by Ezra Jack Keats, Westminster, 1955.

Mystery of the Green Cat, illustrated by Richard Horwitz, Westminster, 1957.

Secret of the Samurai Sword, Westminster, 1958.

Mystery of the Haunted Pool, illustrated by H. Tom Hall, Westminster, 1960.

Secret of the Tiger's Eye, illustrated by Horwitz, Westminster, 1961.

Mystery of the Golden Horn, illustrated by Georgeann Helmes, Westminster, 1962.

Mystery of the Hidden Hand, illustrated by Hall, Westminster, 1963.

Secret of the Emerald Star, illustrated by Alex Stein, Westminster, 1964.

Mystery of the Angry Idol, illustrated by Al Fiorentino, Westminster, 1965.

Secret of the Spotted Shell, illustrated by John Mecray, Westminster, 1967.

Secret of Goblin Glen, illustrated by Fiorentino, Westminster, 1968.

Mystery of the Crimson Ghost, Westminster, 1969.

Secret of the Missing Footprint, illustrated by Stein, Westminster, 1970.

The Vanishing Scarecrow, Westminster, 1971.

Mystery of the Scowling Boy, illustrated by Gretzer, Westminster, 1973.

Secret of Haunted Mesa, Westminster, 1975.

Secret of the Stone Face, Westminster, 1977.

ADULT NOVELS

Red Is for Murder, Ziff-Davis, 1943, published as *The Red Carnelian,* Paperback Library, 1965.

The Quicksilver Pool, Appleton, 1955.

The Trembling Hills, Appleton, 1956.

Skye Cameron, Appleton, 1957.

The Moonflower, Appleton, 1958 (published in England as *The Mask and the Moonflower,* Hurst & Blackett, 1960).

Thunder Heights, Appleton, 1960.

Blue Fire, Appleton, 1961.

Window on the Square, Appleton, 1962.

Seven Tears for Apollo, Appleton, 1963.

Black Amber, Appleton, 1964.

Sea Jade, Appleton, 1965.

Columbella, Doubleday, 1966.

Silverhill, Doubleday, 1967.

Hunter's Green, Doubleday, 1968.

The Winter People, Doubleday, 1969.

Lost Island, Doubleday, 1970.

Listen for the Whisperer, Doubleday, 1972.

Snowfire, Doubleday, 1973.

The Turquoise Mask, Doubleday, 1974.

Spindrift, Doubleday, 1975.

The Golden Unicorn, Doubleday, 1976.

The Stone Bull, Doubleday, 1977.

The Glass Flame, Doubleday, 1978.

Domino, Doubleday, 1979.

Poinciana, Doubleday, 1980.

Vermilion, Doubleday, 1981.

Emerald, Doubleday, 1982.

Rainsong, Doubleday, 1984.

Dream of Orchids, Doubleday, 1985.

Flaming Tree, Doubleday, 1986.

Silversword, Doubleday, 1987.

Feather on the Moon, Doubleday, 1988.

Rainbow in the Mist, Doubleday, 1989.

The Singing Stones, Doubleday, 1990.

Woman without a Past, Doubleday, 1991.

The Ebony Swan, Doubleday, 1992.

OTHER

Writing Juvenile Fiction, Writer, Inc., 1947, revised edition, 1960.

Writing Juvenile Stories and Novels: How to Write and Sell Fiction for Young People (contains portions of *Writing Juvenile Fiction*), Writer, Inc., 1976.

Guide to Writing Fiction, Writer, Inc., 1982, 2nd edition, 1988.

Contributor of articles to periodicals, including *Writer.*

SIDELIGHTS: Since the publication of her first novel in 1941, Phyllis A. Whitney has published over fifty mysteries for readers of all ages, giving her the reputation of "America's queen of romantic suspense" and the title of "Grandmaster." Her work is also very popular, with over forty million copies of her novels in print. With a scenic detail sustained by her extensive travels, Whitney brings to life stories of young women whose attempts to unlock secrets and solve puzzles often put them in danger.

Like some of her books, Whitney's early life also featured exotic places and frequent travel. Born in Yokohama, Japan, to American parents, Whitney lived in Japan, China, and the Philippines until the death of her father when she was fifteen. She then came to the United States with her mother, who passed away two years later. Settling in Chicago with an aunt, Whitney finished high school and got married a year after graduation. Already she was writing stories, even though sales to magazines were few and far between. But in 1941 she published *A Place for Ann,* a young adult novel that brought her a measure of success and self-sufficiency.

Shortly after divorcing her husband in 1945, Whitney approached her editor about writing a book involving racial issues. "My editor objected to the story idea," Whitney related in *Library Journal.* "She didn't think I could do it. She doubted that it would sell, and she didn't want to publish it anyway." Whitney went ahead with the project nonetheless, and another publisher brought out *Willow Hill* in 1947. Presenting the story of how a young white girl and her high school friends deal with the integration of a housing project into their community, *Willow Hill* won the Youth Today contest and became one of Whitney's most popular children's books.

Critics have also admired the novel. "For all the problems involved," M. C. Scoggin comments in the *New York Times, Willow Hill* "is not a thesis hung on a clothes-horse of a plot. It is full of flesh-and-blood boys and girls." A *Saturday Review of Literature* critic agrees, noting that "this is a story that comes completely and excitingly to life. . . . A book with a message, it gains rather than loses by its preoccupation." As a result, Bobbie Ann Mason notes in *Twentieth-Century Children's Writers,* "the book seems daringly ahead of its time in its sympathy and in its honest portrayal of race relations."

Soon after *Willow Hill,* the author turned to writing stories of mystery and intrigue because, as she told Diana Gleasner in *Breakthrough: Women in Writing,* "I like mystery novels. It's a difficult form to master because the plotting is so complicated; you have to juggle so many balls at the same time." Whitney's young adult suspense novels "are lively, light mysteries," as Mason describes them, with young female protagonists "who tend to be normal kids with shortcomings and frustrations, rather than sophisticated, independent, idealized heroines. Thus Whitney has been praised for her honesty, realism, and intellectually stimulating themes." As G. P. Lancaster remarks in a *Christian Science Monitor* review of the Edgar-winning *Mystery of the Haunted Pool,* "The author has a fine flair for making her characters likable, lively, and natural."

More recently, Whitney has focused on adult novels of "psychological" or "romantic suspense," stories of young women who must unravel puzzles that often involve mysterious family relationships. But while Whitney's heroines often find romance along the way, they are also "liberated women," according to Barbara Mertz in the *Washington Post Book World.* "They may—and do—end up in the arms of the hero, but they have to solve their own problems before they get there." As Allen J. Hubin similarly notes in the *New York Times Book Review,* "Whitney seeks to create that mood of impending doom . . . without much recourse to the idiotic behavior common to heroines of the genre." The author explained in a *Parade* interview with Pam Proctor: "The girls in my books are out solving their own problems. They've always been women's libbers because I've always been a liberated woman. I've always done whatever I've wanted to do."

Another distinguishing feature of Whitney's mysteries is her striking use of unique settings. *The Stone Bull,* for instance, uses a Catskills setting that combines "mythology, drama, and botany," Irene M. Pompea remarks in *Best Sellers;* with this novel, "Phyllis Whitney has given her public an experience of genuine suspense." More recent offerings eschew exotic locations and time periods for modern situations such as child-custody disputes and kidnappings, a popular singer's widow coping with the press, and psychic phenomena. *Feather on the Moon,* besides including British Columbia's "lush scenery," is "a smoothly written tale," Sherman W. Smith states in *West Coast Review of Books.* "It is indeed an art to glue readers to the pages and Whitney has honed that art to its peak," another *West Coast Review of Books* writer similarly concludes of *Rainsong.*

Whitney once commented: "I have always written because I couldn't help it. From the age of twelve on I loved to make up stories, and I've been doing it ever since. I believe in entertaining my readers, and I also hope to make them

think and feel. I have great respect and admiration for fellow writers in the mystery-suspense field, and I read both to enjoy and to learn. I seem to have been born with a hunger for stories." Although she has been publishing for over fifty years, Whitney shows no signs of slowing down. As she told Sarah Booth Conroy of the *Washington Post:* "These are my happiest years. I always want to live long enough to finish the book I'm working on and see it published. But then I start another book before the previous one is in the stores, so I always have a reason to go on."

BIOGRAPHICAL/CRITICAL SOURCES:

BOOKS

Budd, Elaine, *Thirteen Mistresses of Murder,* Ungar, 1986, pp. 125-135.
Contemporary Literary Criticism, Volume 42, Gale, 1987, pp. 431-438.
Gleasner, Diana, *Breakthrough: Women in Writing,* Walker, 1980, pp. 126-145.
Twentieth-Century Children's Writers, 3rd edition, St. James Press, 1989, pp. 1037-1039.

PERIODICALS

Best Sellers, September, 1977, pp. 173-174.
Christian Science Monitor, May 26, 1960, p. 17; November 23, 1960, p. 11.
Library Journal, October 15, 1963.
New York Times, April 6, 1947, p. 27.
New York Times Book Review, September 29, 1957, p. 41; May 18, 1969, p. 31; November 22, 1970, p. 61; February 20, 1972, p. 27; February 5, 1984, pp. 18-19; May 27, 1990.
Parade, November 2, 1975.
Saturday Review, September 29, 1956.
Saturday Review of Literature, September 6, 1947, p. 34.
Washington Post, September 2, 1991, pp. D1, D9.
Washington Post Book World, January 2, 1983, p. 4; January 6, 1985, p. 11.
West Coast Review of Books, Number 1, 1985, p. 54; Number 6, 1988, p. 27.
Writer, February, 1980, pp. 11-14, 46; June, 1985, pp. 9-12.

*   *   *

WILLIAMS, Vera B. 1927-

PERSONAL: Born January 28, 1927, in Hollywood, CA; immigrated to Canada, 1970; daughter of Albert S. and Rebecca (Porringer) Baker; married Paul Williams (an architect; divorced, 1970); children: Sarah, Jennifer, Merce. *Education:* Black Mountain School, Black Mountain, NC, B.A., 1949; also attended Boston Museum School. *Avoca-*

tional interests: Art, teaching, parenting, food, nature, justice and social issues.

ADDRESSES: c/o Greenwillow Books, 105 Madison Avenue, New York, NY 10016.

CAREER: Writer, graphic artist, educator, political activist. Gate Hill Cooperative Community, Stony Point, NY, co-founder, teacher, and member, 1953-70; Collaberg School (alternative school for children), Stony Point, co-founder and teacher, 1960-69; Everdale School, Ontario, Canada, teacher and cook, 1970-73; author and illustrator of books for children, 1975—; Goddard College, Plainfield, VT, instructor, 1980-82. Member of executive committee of War Resisters League, 1984-87.

MEMBER: PEN, Authors Guild, Authors League of America.

AWARDS, HONORS: Parents' Choice Award for Illustration, Parents' Choice Foundation, 1981, for *Three Days on a River in a Red Canoe; A Chair for My Mother,* 1982, and *Something Special for Me,* 1983, were named among *School Library Journal*'s Best Children's Books; Caldecott honor book citation, American Library Association, 1983, for *A Chair for My Mother,* and 1990, for *"More More More" Said the Baby: 3 Love Stories; Boston Globe-Horn Book* Award for Illustration, 1983, and Other Award, *Children's Book Bulletin,* 1984, both for *A Chair for My Mother; Music, Music for Everyone* was named a Jane Addams Children's honor book, Jane Addams Peace Association, 1985; *Cherries and Cherry Pits* was named a Parents' Choice Award in Literature Notable Book, chosen one of Child Study Association of America's Children's Books of the Year, and selected as one of *New York Times* Best Illustrated Books of the Year, all 1986, and was named a *Boston Globe-Horn Book* honor picturebook, 1987; *Stringbean's Trip to the Shining Sea* was named a *Boston Globe-Horn Book* honor book, 1988.

WRITINGS:

CHILDREN'S BOOKS; SELF-ILLUSTRATED

It's a Gingerbread House: Bake It, Build It, Eat It!, Greenwillow, 1978.
The Great Watermelon Birthday, Greenwillow, 1980.
Three Days on a River in a Red Canoe, Greenwillow, 1981.
A Chair for My Mother, Greenwillow, 1981.
Something Special for Me, Greenwillow, 1983.
Music, Music for Everyone, Greenwillow, 1984.
Cherries and Cherry Pits, Greenwillow, 1986.
My Mother, Leah and George Sand, Greenwillow, 1986.
(With daughter Jennifer) *Stringbean's Trip to the Shining Sea,* Greenwillow, 1988.
"More More More" Said the Baby: 3 Love Stories, Greenwillow, 1990.

CHILDREN'S BOOKS; ILLUSTRATOR

Remy Charlip and Lilian Moore, *Hooray for Me!,* Parents Magazine Press, 1975.
Barbara Brenner, *Our Class Presents Ostrich Feathers: A Play in Two Acts,* Parents Magazine Press, 1978.

ADAPTATIONS: A Chair for My Mother (read-along cassette; filmstrip with cassette), Random House; *Something Special for Me* (cassette), Random House.

SIDELIGHTS: Vera B. Williams "brings to the picture-book genre a uniquely honest and celebratory portrait of working-class culture which has seldom been executed so successfully," according to *Twentieth-Century Children's Writers* contributor Nancy Tillman Romalov, who also asserts that "as much as is possible using the picture-book format, Williams is able to convey a strong sense of working-class life without glossing over the hardships or adjustments her economically disadvantaged characters face."

Williams is perhaps best known for her books about Rosa, a fictional Hispanic child from a family that is loving but poor. Named a Caldecott honor book for its illustrations, *A Chair for My Mother* tells how the girl and her family, with the help of friends, overcome the misfortune of a house fire that destroys their belongings. The story was developed from the author's memories of economic sacrifices made by her family when her mother bought a chair by installment plan payments. In an interview with Marguerite Feitlowitz for *Something about the Author,* Williams declared: "When I got the inspiration for the book, I had the wonderful feeling that I now had the power, as a writer and an illustrator, to change the past into something happier than it really was, and to offer it as a gift to my mother's memory." A *Kirkus Reviews* appraisal of *A Chair for My Mother* asserted that "It's rare to find so much vitality, spontaneity, *and* depth of feeling in such a simple, young book."

Something Special for Me, which is "a visual and emotional treat" according to *School Library Journal*'s Ellen Fader, follows Rosa as she goes on a shopping trip to buy herself a birthday gift with her family's hard-earned money. Eventually, she decides to get an accordian so that her birthday present will also benefit the other members of the family. *Music, Music for Everyone* concludes the series, portraying a fund-raising performance by Rosa and her young musician friends. *New York Times Book Review* writer Josephine Humphreys called *Music, Music for Everyone* "a gently exuberant book."

Williams's familiarity with working-class culture comes from her own childhood. Williams told Feitlowitz that her immigrant parents "politically . . . were left-wing, which is to say, they held dear the original socialist and community aspirations for a better life for the working class."

Williams and her sister were encouraged by their parents to develop artistic talents, and they "became involved with art, dramatics, crafts, games and dance with a student of Isadora Duncan." One of the paintings Williams produced as a child was included in a Works Progress Administration exhibition at the Modern Museum of Art in New York, where the future author stood by her painting and answered questions asked by then first lady Eleanor Roosevelt.

Williams has frequently devoted time to the causes of nonviolence, children, women, and the environment, and she has occasionally been arrested for participating in demonstrations in support of those causes. She told Feitlowitz: "I don't make a point of ending up in jail. But if you try to put your hopes and beliefs for a better life into effect, arrest *is* sometimes a hazard. I am asked if I think any of this helps or works. I say, in the short run, we can't know, but many things we take for granted have been gained by the similar actions of people like myself—the end of child labor, more rights for black people, the vote for women, the end of the Vietnam War are a few. As a person who works for children, who raised three children, who is about to have a grandchild, I have to be able to say I did something to try to save our planet from destruction. It is my faith that we will."

BIOGRAPHICAL/CRITICAL SOURCES:

BOOKS

Children's Literature Review, Volume 9, Gale, 1985.
Something about the Author, Volume 53, Gale, 1988.
Twentieth-Century Children's Writers, 3rd edition, St. James Press, 1989, pp. 1052-1053.

PERIODICALS

Kirkus Reviews, October 1, 1982, p. 1104.
New York Times Book Review, October 21, 1984, p. 35.
School Library Journal, April, 1983, p. 108.*

*   *   *

WILLOUGHBY, Lee Davis
See BRANDNER, Gary

*   *   *

WILSON, David 1942-

PERSONAL: Born August 15, 1942, in Liverpool, England; son of Ronald and Gladys (Griffiths) Wilson. *Education:* Hertford College, Oxford, B.A. (with honors), 1965. *Avocational interests:* The history and politics of modern Greece.

ADDRESSES: Home—4 St. Michaels Gardens, Flat 1, London W.10, England.

CAREER: British Film Institute (BFI), London, England, editor of *Monthly Film Bulletin,* 1966-70, associate editor of *Sight and Sound,* 1970-80, editorial director of BFI Publishing, 1980-90; publishing editor, film writer, and consultant, 1990—.

WRITINGS:

(Translator with Gertrud Mander) Erwin Leiser, *Nazi Cinema,* Secker & Warburg, 1974.
(Editor with Simon Hartog and Hala Salmane) *Algerian Cinema,* British Film Institute, 1976.
(Editor with John Gillett) *Yasujiro Ozu: A Critical Anthology,* British Film Institute, 1976.
(Contributor) Richard Roud, editor, *Cinema: A Critical Dictionary,* Secker & Warburg, 1980.
(Editor and author of introduction) *Sight and Sound: A Fiftieth Anniversary Selection.* Faber & Faber, 1982.
(Editor) *Projecting Britain: Ealing Studios Film Posters,* British Film Institute, 1982.

General editor of "Cinema One" series, British Film Institute. Contributor to magazines and newspapers, including *New Statesman, Times Literary Supplement,* and *Guardian.*

SIDELIGHTS: David Wilson once told *CA:* "I have written frequently about television, especially the way television 'constructs' a view of the world. Are we creating a visual culture whose version of the world is more 'real' than reality? A consensus society in which individuality is drowned by the incessant noise from the screen in the corner? In which people have stopped talking for fear that they will interrupt the talk show?"

*   *   *

WILSON, Jacqueline 1945-

PERSONAL: Born December 17, 1945, in Bath, England; daughter of Harry Albert (a civil servant) and Margaret (Clibbens) Aitken; married William Millar Wilson (a police chief superintendent), August 28, 1965; children: Emma Fiona. *Education:* Attended Carshalton Technical College. *Politics:* None. *Religion:* None.

ADDRESSES: Home—1B Beaufort Rd., Kingston-on-Thames, Surrey, England. *Agent*—Gina and Murray Pollinger, 222 Old Brompton Rd., London SW5 0BZ, England.

CAREER: Journalist, free-lance magazine writer, and author of books and radio plays. Employed by D. C. Thomsons, Dundee, Scotland, 1963-65.

WRITINGS:

SUSPENSE NOVELS

Hide and Seek, Macmillan (London), 1972, Doubleday, 1973.
Truth or Dare, Doubleday, 1973.
Snap, Macmillan (London), 1974.
Let's Pretend, Macmillan (London), 1976.
Making Hate, Macmillan (London), 1977, St. Martin's, 1978.

JUVENILES

Nobody's Perfect, Oxford University Press, 1982.
Waiting for the Sky to Fall, Oxford University Press, 1983.
The Other Side, Oxford University Press, 1984.
The School Trip, Hamilton, 1984.
The Killer Tadpole, Hamilton, 1984.
How to Survive Summer Camp, Oxford University Press, 1985.
Amber, Oxford University Press, 1986.
The Monster in the Cupboard, Blackie & Son, 1986.
Glubbslyme, Oxford University Press, 1987.
The Power of the Shade, Oxford University Press, 1987.
This Girl, Oxford University Press, 1988.
The Left-Outs, Blackie & Son, 1989.
The Party in the Lift, Blackie & Son, 1989.
Falling Apart, Oxford University Press, 1989.

Is There Anybody There?, Armada, 1990, Volume 1: *Spirit Raising,* Volume 2: *Crystal Gazing.*
The Story of Tracy Beaker, Transworld, 1991.
Take a Good Look, Blackie & Son, 1991.
The Werepuppy, Blackie & Son, 1991.
The Dream Palace, Oxford University Press, 1991.
The Suitcase Kid, Transworld, 1992.
Video Rose, Blackie & Son, 1992.
Mark Spark, Hamish Hamilton, 1992.

"STEVIE DAY" SERIES

Supersleuth, Armada, 1987.
Lonelyhearts, Armada, 1987.
Rat Race, Armada, 1987.
Vampire, Armada, 1988.

OTHER

Author of radio plays *Are You Listening, It's Disgusting at Your Age,* and *Ask a Silly Question,* broadcast on British Broadcasting Corp. (BBC), 1982-84. Contributor to *Winter's Crimes,* edited by Virginia Whitaker, Macmillan (London), 1973.

BIOGRAPHICAL/CRITICAL SOURCES:

PERIODICALS

Times Literary Supplement, July 23, 1982; May 29, 1987, p. 589.

Y

YAFFE, Alan
  See YORINKS, Arthur

*   *   *

YORINKS, Arthur 1953-
(Alan Yaffe)

PERSONAL: Born August 21, 1953, in Roslyn, Long Island, NY; son of Alexander (a mechanical engineer) and Shirley (a fashion illustrator; maiden name, Kron) Yorinks; married Adrienne Berg, October 23, 1983. *Education:* Attended New School for Social Research and Hofstra New College, 1971. *Avocational interests:* Opera, theater, dogs, visiting art museums.

ADDRESSES: Home—Hilltop Dr., North Salem, NY 10560. *Office*—The Night Kitchen, 10 East 53rd St., New York, NY 10022. *Agent*—Sheldon Fogelman, 10 East 40th St., New York, NY 10016.

CAREER: Author of children's books; writer for opera, ballet, film, and theater. Cornell University, Ithaca, NY, instructor in theater arts, 1972-79. Writer, teacher, and performer at American Mime Theatre, 1969-79. Associate director of New Works Project in New York City, 1977—; Moving Theatre, founder, artistic director, 1979; co-founder and associate artistic director of national children's theater The Night Kitchen, 1990—.

AWARDS, HONORS: School Library Journal's Best Books of the Year citations, 1980, for *Louis the Fish,* 1988, for *Bravo, Minski,* 1989, for *Oh, Brother,* and 1990, for *Ugh; Booklist* Children's Editor's Choice, 1984, and Biennale of Illustrations plaque (Bratislava, Czechoslovakia), 1985, both for *It Happened in Pinsk;* American Library Association (ALA) Notable Book citation, 1986, Caldecott Medal, 1987, and Kentucky Bluegrass Award, 1988,

all for *Hey, Al; Redbook's* Ten Best Books of the Year citation, and ALA Notable Book citation, both 1988, for *Company's Coming.*

WRITINGS:

CHILDREN'S BOOKS

Sid and Sol (also see below), illustrated by Richard Egielski, Farrar, Straus, 1977.
(Under pseudonym Alan Yaffe) *The Magic Meatballs,* illustrated by Karen B. Anderson, Dial, 1979.
Louis the Fish, illustrated by Egielski, Farrar, Straus, 1980.
It Happened in Pinsk, illustrated by Egielski, Farrar, Straus, 1983.
Hey, Al, illustrated by Egielski, Farrar, Straus, 1986.
Bravo, Minski, illustrated by Egielski, Farrar, Straus, 1988.
Company's Coming, illustrated by David Small, Crown, 1988.
Oh, Brother, illustrated by Egielski, Farrar, Straus, 1989.
Ugh, illustrated by Egielski, Farrar, Straus, 1990.
Christmas in July, illustrated by Egielski, HarperCollins, 1991.

PLAYS

Six (one-act), first produced in New York City at Hunter College Playhouse, November, 1973.
The Horse (one-act), first produced in New York City at Cornelia Street Cafe, November, 1978.
Crackers (one-act), first produced in New York City at Theatre of the Open Eye, June, 1979.
The King (one-act), first produced in New York City at South Street Theatre, July, 1980.
Kissers (one-act), first produced at South Street Theatre, July, 1980.

Piece for a Small Cafe (one-act), first produced at Cornelia Street Cafe, February, 1981.

Piece for a Larger Cafe (one-act), first produced at Cornelia Street Cafe, April, 1982.

OPERA LIBRETTOS

Leipziger Kerzenspiel, first produced at Mt. Holyoke College, 1984.

The Juniper Tree (first produced at the American Repertory Theater, Boston, 1985), music by Philip Glass and Robert Moran, Dunvagen Music, 1985.

(Adaptor with Glass) *The Fall of the House of Usher,* first produced at American Repertory Theater, May, 1988.

OTHER

Sid and Sol (screenplay; adapted from the book of the same title), Four Penny Productions, 1982.

Story by Arthur Yorinks, Pictures by Richard Egielski (video), Farrar, Straus, 1987.

Also author of a full-length story ballet commissioned by the Hartford Ballet; author of screenplay "Making Scents," developed by A & M Films; author, with film director Michael Powell, of screenplay "Usher."

ADAPTATIONS: Louis the Fish was produced as an episode of *Reading Rainbow,* PBS-TV, 1983. *Louis the Fish* and *Sid and Sol* have both been adapted into a cassette with hardcover book by Random House.

WORK IN PROGRESS: "A new picture book set in the old West." Adaptor with Peter Schickele of *Hey Al,* an opera based on the book of the same title, to premiere fall, 1993; adaptor of *Peter Pan,* non-musical version with sets and costumes designed by Maurice Sendak, produced by The Night Kitchen, to premiere fall, 1993.

SIDELIGHTS: "It was because of the influence of a few major artists of this field that I am a writer of children's books today," Arthur Yorinks once said. "Maurice Sendak, William Steig, Tomi Ungerer, Randolph Caldecott, Wilhelm Busch, William Nicholson—I have dedicated myself to this art form in the tradition of those artists who look upon the picture book as a medium where the marriage of words and pictures is all important, and the seam that binds them together is all but invisible. Too many picture books of today have sorry texts used only as vehicles for a set of pictures, like a description attached to a portfolio. That is not what I believe picture books should be. It is a serious art form, most exact. And it is with the responsibility of any artistic pursuit that Richard Egielski (my artist collaborator) and I approach each new work."

Yorinks is best known for his children's books illustrated by Richard Egielski, but he also writes children's plays, opera librettos and plays for adults. His books often fea-

ture themes meaningful to adults as well as younger audiences. For example, an adult reader might recognize the influence of Franz Kafka's *The Metamorphosis* in Yorinks's *Louis the Fish,* the story of a butcher who one day turns into a fish. Yorinks's stories often portray adults in the midst of discovering their true identities. Other themes for young people are played out in the books, including the values of tolerance and self-acceptance.

"Determining the difference between a children's book and a book for adults is often tricky business," said Bill Ott in the *New York Times Book Review.* "After all, many people considered *Huckleberry Finn*—that bible of individualism, perhaps the most delightfully subversive, anti-authoritarian work in American literature—to be a charming children's book. Later generations may be just as surprised to discover that we once classified the mature work of Arthur Yorinks and Richard Egielski as picture books."

Sid and Sol, Yorinks's first book and first collaborative effort with Egielski, tells the story of Sol, a giant who runs amok, and Sid, an unlikely giant-killer. In the *New York Times Book Review,* Maurice Sendak praised the book as a breath of fresh air in the world of children's literature: "*Sid and Sol* is a wonder—a picture book that heralds a hopeful, healthy flicker of life in what is becoming a creatively exhausted genre. The magic rests in the seamless bond of Arthur Yorinks's and Richard Egielski's deft and exciting collaboration."

In a way, Sendak can thank himself for Yorinks's success. Sendak encouraged Yorinks early on and made possible his fortuitous partnership with Egielski. Yorinks once told *Something about the Author* interviewer Marguerite Feitlowitz, "At the age of sixteen, I summoned all the courage I had and did something that was to have an *enormous* effect on my life and work: I showed up at Maurice Sendak's door unannounced. Maurice was them living in Manhattan. It was presumptuous of me, bordering on obnoxious, but my way of learning was always to talk to people I considered among the best at what they did. . . . I walked up to Maurice's door, and as I was about to ring the bell, I lost my nerve. Just as I turned to leave, the door opened and a man (Sendak? I wasn't even certain it was him) said, 'Can I help you?' 'Would you like to see some of my stories?' I blurted out." A lucrative friendship was born.

After *Sid and Sol,* Yorinks wrote *The Magic Meatballs* under his pseudonym, Alan Yaffe. Illustrated by Karen B. Anderson, *The Magic Meatballs* tells the tale of a boy who finds he has turned his family into various food items. He changes them back to human form after they promise to be more considerate of him. Yorinks and Egielski worked together again on *Louis the Fish,* the story of a boy who hates meat but is forced to take over his family's butcher shop. He eventually turns into a fish: "Silvery scales. Big lips. A tail. A salmon," Yorinks writes. Yorinks's and Egielski's "joint pacing and a variety of verbal and visual viewpoints makes *Louis the Fish* an outstanding and refreshingly unusual picture book," said George Shannon in the *School Library Journal*.

Yorinks told Feitlowitz that in creating *Louis the Fish* the pictures flowed easily, but in *It Happened in Pinsk*, his next book with Egielski, they did not. "As we looked at the storyboard, we saw problems," Yorinks said. "What we discovered was that there were some snags we hadn't noticed in the text that were showing up in the pictures. As soon as I fixed those spots in the story, Richard ceased to have problems with the illustrations." Like *Louis the Fish, It Happened in Pinsk* was inspired by another author's story. "*Pinsk* grew out of my reverence for [Nikolay Vasilyevich] Gogol, and particularly my love for his story, 'The Nose,' in which one morning a man wakes up without his nose. As is my habit, when I have read and loved a work by a given author, I read everything he's done, as well as biographies of him. The only way I've really learned to write is to have read authors I admire."

With their reputation for quality children's literature secured, Yorinks and Egielski have continued to produce books praised by both children and adults. *Hey, Al* teaches readers the value of appreciating what they have, not unlike L. Frank Baum's *The Wizard of Oz. Company's Coming* shows the problems created when one group judges another before getting acquainted. *Ugh* is the story of a prehistoric boy who builds a bicycle out of tree limbs and other scraps.

In 1990 Yorinks's friendship with Sendak again produced a lucrative project: the two teamed up to create The Night Kitchen, a national children's theater. The goal of the theater is to fill the need for quality children's plays and operas, not watered-down versions of adult theater, but productions that children will find both entertaining and challenging. Allen Raymond, writing for the teachers' magazine *Teaching Pre K-8* noted that in the announcement introducing the project, Yorinks and Sendak called The Night Kitchen "an extraordinary opportunity to explore many mediums and to extend the boundaries of what is considered suitable for children." The announce-

ment continued, "We hope to reinvigorate all forms of live theater for children with the same energy and passion we bring to our books."

Yorinks's books are often the first exposure a child has to reading and art, and he takes this responsibility very seriously. "Children's first books are often picture books," he once remarked to Feitlowitz. "From picture books, children get their first inkling about literature and visual art. The importance of picture books is therefore profound. The stories and images adults make for children may well say more about a given society than anything else. Children deserve the best we can offer—authentic and uncompromising art."

BIOGRAPHICAL/CRITICAL SOURCES:

BOOKS

Children's Literature Review, Volume 20, Gale, 1990, pp. 213-218.
Sixth Book of Junior Authors and Illustrators, Wilson, 1989, pp. 325-326.
Something about the Author, Volume 49, Gale, 1987.
Yorinks, Arthur, *Louis the Fish*, illustrated by Richard Egielski, Farrar, Straus, 1980.

PERIODICALS

Booklist, October 1, 1979.
Los Angeles Times, October 14, 1979.
Los Angeles Times Book Review, January 1, 1984, p. 7; March 27, 1988, p. 12; December 10, 1989, p. 9.
New York Times, December 8, 1977, p. C21.
New York Times Book Review, December 10, 1978, p. 72; November 23, 1980, p. 36; December 18, 1983, p. 20; January 11, 1987, p. 38; January 10, 1988, p. 3; May 8, 1988, p. 38; May 13, 1990, p. 30.
Publishers Weekly, January 29, 1988, p. 429.
School Library Journal, November, 1980, p. 68; December, 1990, p. 91.
Teaching Pre K-8, November/December, 1991, pp. 51-53.
Time, December 19, 1983, p. 77.
Tribune Books (Chicago), January 25, 1987, p. 4.
Washington Post Book World, February 15, 1987, p. 13; March 13, 1988, p. 10; November 6, 1988, p. 14; December 10, 1989, p. 10; November 4, 1990, p. 18.

—Sketch by Deborah A. Stanley

Z

ZELINSKY, Paul O. 1953-

PERSONAL: Born February 14, 1953, in Evanston, IL; son of Daniel (a professor of mathematics) and Zelda (a medical illustrator; maiden name, Oser) Zelinsky; married Deborah Hallen (a musician), December 31, 1981; children: Anna, Rachel. *Education:* Yale University, B.A., 1974; Tyler School of Art, M.F.A., 1976. *Avocational interests:* Cooking, eating.

ADDRESSES: Office—54 Orange St., Brooklyn, NY 11201.

CAREER: Artist, author, and illustrator of books for children, 1977—.

MEMBER: Graphic Artists Guild, Children's Illustrators and Authors, Society of Children's Book Writers.

AWARDS, HONORS: Best Books Award, *School Library Journal,* 1979, for *How I Hunted the Little Fellows,* 1981, for *The Maid and the Mouse and the Odd-Shaped House: A Story in Rhyme,* 1982, for *Ralph S. Mouse,* and 1986, for *Rumpelstiltskin;* American Institute of Graphic Arts Book Show selection, 1980, for *How I Hunted the Little Fellows,* and 1982, for *The Maid and the Mouse and the Odd-Shaped House: A Story in Rhyme;* Society of Illustrators Show selection, 1982, for *Three Romances,* and 1986, for *Rumpelstiltskin;* Best Illustrated Children's Books of the Year Award, *New York Times,* 1981, for *The Maid and the Mouse and the Odd-Shaped House,* and 1985, for *The Story of Mrs. Lovewright and Purrless Her Cat;* Children's Choice Award, International Reading Association, 1982, for *The Maid and the Mouse and the Odd-Shaped House;* Parents' Choice Award, Parents' Choice Foundation, 1984, for *The Lion and the Stoat,* 1985, for *The Story of Mrs. Lovewright and Purrless Her Cat,* 1986, for *Rumpelstiltskin,* and 1990, for *Hansel and Gretel* (paperback edition); "Graphic Gallery" outstanding picture book se-

lection, *Horn Book,* 1984, for *The Maid and the Mouse and the Odd-Shaped House;* America's Children's Books of the Year Award, Child Study Association, 1985, for *The Story of Mrs. Lovewright and Purrless Her Cat;* Caldecott Honor Book Award, and Bologna International Children's Book Fair exhibition selection, both 1985, both for *Hansel and Gretel;* Ten Best Children's Books Award, *Redbook,* 1986, Caldecott Honor Book Award, 1987, and White Raven Book Award, International Youth Library, all for *Rumpelstiltskin.*

WRITINGS:

JUVENILE; SELF-ILLUSTRATED

(Adapter) *The Maid and the Mouse and the Odd-Shaped House: A Story in Rhyme,* Dodd, 1981.
The Lion and the Stoat, Greenwillow, 1984.
(Reteller) *Rumpelstiltskin,* Dutton, 1986.
(Adapter) *The Wheels on the Bus: A Book with Pictures that Move and Occasionally Pop Up,* Dutton, 1990.

JUVENILE; ILLUSTRATOR

Avi, *Emily Upham's Revenge; or, How Deadwood Dick Saved the Banker's Niece: A Massachusetts Adventure,* Pantheon, 1978.
Boris Zhitkov, *How I Hunted the Little Fellows,* translated from the Russian by Djemma Bider, Dodd, 1979.
Avi, *The History of Helpless Harry: To Which is Added a Variety of Amusing and Entertaining Adventures,* Pantheon, 1980.
Winifred Rosen, *Three Romances: Love Stories from Camelot Retold,* Knopf, 1981.
Naomi Lazard, *What Amanda Saw,* Greenwillow, 1981.
Beverly Clearly, *Ralph S. Mouse,* Morrow, 1982.
Mirra Ginsburg, adapter, *The Sun's Asleep behind the Hill,* Greenwillow, 1982.

David Kherdian, *The Song in the Walnut Grove,* Knopf, 1982.

Rika Lesser, *Etruscan Things* (poetry), Braziller, 1983.

B. Cleary, *Dear Mr. Henshaw,* Morrow, 1983.

Jack Prelutsky, *Zoo Doings: Animal Poems,* Greenwillow, 1983.

R. Lesser, reteller, *Hansel and Gretel,* Dodd, 1984.

Lore Segal, *The Story of Mrs. Lovewright and Purrless Her Cat,* Knopf, 1985.

Pamela Pollock, editor, *The Random House Book of Humor for Children,* Random House, 1988.

B. Cleary, *Strider,* Morrow, 1991.

Hansel and Gretel has been recorded on audio cassette and released by Random House, 1986; *Rumpelstiltskin* has also been recorded and released by Random House, 1988.

SIDELIGHTS: Paul O. Zelinsky is primarily known for his colorful and imaginative illustrations. Whether updating a classic tale, such as *Rumpelstiltskin,* or experimenting with new formats, as in *The Wheels on the Bus,* Zelinsky takes care to match his drawings with the special needs of the text. "I try to make the book talk, as it talks to me, and not worry whether it is in my style or not," he related to Sylvia and Kenneth Marantz in an interview for *Horn Book.* Zelinsky added: "I get a kick out of doing each book differently. I've been pleased that people like the fact that there's a lot of variation in what I do. . . . I figure a style will come on its own."

Zelinsky spent most of his youth in Chicago. He became seriously interested in art while attending Yale University. "I took a course at Yale with Maurice Sendak. . . . He seemed to be making a living at creating books. . . . I thought that making picture books would be something I could do," Zelinsky noted in his interview. Eventually, he decided to get a master's degree in painting. He disclosed: "I went on painting and thought I might teach. Then I got my master's degree in painting and got a short-term teaching job. I found out that I was a lousy teacher and that teaching wasn't what I wanted to do." In spite of this setback, Zelinsky continued to visit publishers with his portfolio; in 1978, Zelinsky's efforts paid off when he was given his first children's book illustration assignment, Avi's *Emily Upham's Revenge.*

In the years since that first project, Zelinsky has expanded the scope of his career by writing and illustrating his own books, such as *The Maid and the Mouse and the Odd-Shaped House* and *Rumpelstiltskin.* A reviewer for *Horn Book* called *The Maid and the Mouse and the Odd-Shaped House* "superb" and "masterful," while Elaine Edelman of the *New York Times Book Review* termed the text "handsomely colored and cleverly designed." And a *Bookbird* reviewer found *Rumpelstiltskin* to be "very dif-

ferent and even more exquisitely wrought. . . . The care of each brush stroke is apparent."

Zelinsky feels the variety of his assignments helps keep his work fresh. In an essay for the *Sixth Book of Junior Authors,* he wrote: "I've been able to illustrate books that are so different from one another that I always get to learn new things: new materials and ways of drawing, all sorts of information." Despite the sometimes difficult nature of his work, Zelinsky has remained enthusiastic about his craft. "It's a great deal of fun," he noted in his essay. "I feel I still get to change my mind all the time about what I want to do—my mind changes with every book I take on. . . . When I realize that there are people all around the country who read my books and (I hope) enjoy the pictures, I think: 'How could I have been so lucky!' "

BIOGRAPHICAL/CRITICAL SOURCES:

BOOKS

Sixth Book of Junior Authors, edited by Sally Holmes Holtze, Wilson, 1989, pp. 326-28.

PERIODICALS

Bookbird, June, 1987.

Horn Book, May-June, 1986, pp. 295-303; November-December, 1986.

Newsweek, December 7, 1981.

New York Times Book Review, September 27, 1981.

Publishers Weekly, January 30, 1987, p. 292.

Time, December 21, 1981, p. 79.

Washington Post, January 8, 1985.

Washington Post Book World, April 8, 1984.

*   *   *

ZEMACH, Margot   1931-1989

PERSONAL: Born November 30, 1931, in Los Angeles, CA; died May 21, 1989, in Berkeley, CA, of Lou Gehrig's disease; daughter of Benjamin (a theatre director) and Elizabeth (an actress; maiden name, Dailey) Zemach; married Ralph Novak, 1953 (died, 1954); married Harvey Fischtrom (an author under pseudonym Harve Zemach), January 29, 1957 (died November, 1974); children: (second marriage) Kaethe Zemach-Bersin, Heidi, Rachel, Rebecca. *Education:* Attended Los Angeles County Art Institute, Jepson Institute of Art, Otis Art Institute, Los Angeles, Kahn Art Institute, Los Angeles, and Chouinard Art Institute, Los Angeles; attended Vienna Academy of Fine Arts, 1955-56.

CAREER: Illustrator and author. *Exhibitions:* Gropper Gallery, Cambridge, MA, 1957.

AWARDS, HONORS: Fulbright scholarship, 1955-56; *Salt, a Russian Tale* received first prize at the *New York*

Herald Tribune Spring Book Festival, 1965; *Mommy, Buy Me a China Doll* was an ALA Notable Children's Book, 1966; *Too Much Nose: An Italian Tale* was an honor book at the *New York Herald Tribune* Spring Book Festival, 1967; *Mazel and Shlimazel: or, The Milk of a Lioness* was an ALA Notable Children's Book, 1967; *When Shliemiel Went to Warsaw, and Other Stories* was an ALA Notable Children's Book, 1968; *The Judge: An Untrue Tale* was a Caldecott Honor Book and an ALA Notable Children's Book, 1970; *A Penny a Look: An Old Story* was an ALA Notable Children's Book, 1971; *Simon Boom Gives a Wedding* was named to the *New York Times'* Best Illustrated Books list, 1972, and received the Lewis Carroll Bookshelf Award; *Duffy and the Devil: A Cornish Tale* was an honor book at the *Book World* Children's Spring Book Festival, 1973, received the Caldecott Medal, 1974, and received the Lewis Carroll Bookshelf Award; *Hush, Little Baby* was chosen to represent the United States by the International Board on Books for Young People, 1978; *It Could Always Be Worse: A Yiddish Folktale* was named to the *New York Times*'s Best Illustrated Books list, 1978, and was a Caldecott Honor Book; *Self-Portrait: Margot Zemach* was an honor book for the Golden Globe/*Horn Book* Award, 1979; United States nominee for the Hans Christian Andersen Award, 1980.

WRITINGS:

SELF-ILLUSTRATED

(Adaptor) *The Three Sillies,* Holt, 1963.
(Editor) *The Little, Tiny Woman, a Folktale,* Bobbs-Merrill, 1965.
(Adaptor) *Hush, Little Baby* (Junior Literary Guild selection), Dutton, 1976.
(Adaptor) *It Could Always Be Worse: A Yiddish Folktale,* Farrar, Straus, 1976.
To Hilda for Helping, Farrar, Straus, 1977.
Self-Portrait: Margot Zemach, Addison-Wesley, 1978.
Jake and Honeybunch Go to Heaven, Farrar, Straus, 1981.
(Adaptor) *The Little Red Hen: An Old Story,* Farrar, Straus, 1983.
(Adaptor) *The Three Witches: An Old Story,* Farrar, Straus, 1986.
(Adaptor) *The Three Little Pigs,* Farrar, Straus, 1990.

ILLUSTRATOR

Harve Zemach, *A Small Boy Is Listening,* Houghton, 1959.
Hannelore Hahn, *Take a Giant Step,* Little, Brown, 1960.
Harve Zemach, *A Hat with a Rose,* Dutton, 1961.
Fleming Lee Blitch, *The Last Dragon,* Lippincott, 1964.
Harve Zemach, adaptor, *Nail Soup: A Swedish Folktale Retold,* Follett, 1964.

Alexei Afansev, adapted by Harve Zemach, *Salt: A Russian Tale,* translation by Benjamin Zemach, Follett, 1965, Farrar, Straus, 1976.
Jay Williams, *The Question Box,* Norton, 1965.
Harve Zemach, adaptor, *Mommy, Buy Me a China Doll,* Follett, 1966, Farrar, Straus, 1975.
Jack Sendak, *The King of the Hermits and Other Stories,* Farrar, Straus, 1966.
Harve Zemach, adaptor, *The Speckled Hen, a Russian Nursery Rhyme,* Holt, 1966.
Harve Zemach, adaptor, *Too Much Nose: An Italian Tale,* Holt, 1967.
Isaac Bashevis Singer, *Mazel and Shlimazel; or, The Milk of a Lioness,* translation by the author and Elizabeth Shub, Farrar, Straus, 1967.
Rose L. Minciel, *Harlequin,* Knopf, 1968.
Isaac Bashevis Singer, *When Shliemel Went to Warsaw and Other Stories,* Farrar, Straus, 1968.
Harve Zemach, *The Judge: An Untrue Tale,* Farrar, Straus, 1969.
Harve Zemach, *Awake and Dreaming,* Farrar, Straus, 1970.
Harve Zemach, *A Penny a Look: An Old Story,* Farrar, Straus, 1971.
Virginia Haviland, *Favorite Fairy Tales Told in Denmark,* Little, Brown, 1971.
Isaac Bashevis Singer, *Alone in the Wild Forest,* Farrar, Straus, 1971.
Yuri Suhl, *Simon Boom Gives a Wedding,* Four Winds Press, 1972.
Harve Zemach, adaptor, *Duffy and the Devil: A Cornish Tale,* Farrar, Straus, 1973.
Lloyd Alexander, *The Foundling and Other Tales of Prydain,* Holt, 1973.
Harve and Kaethe Zemach, *The Princess and Froggie,* Farrar, Straus, 1975.
Isaac Bashevis Singer, *Naftali the Storyteller and His Horse, Sus, and Other Stories,* Farrar, Straus, 1976.
Edward Smith, compiler, *The Frogs Who Wanted a King,* Four Winds Press, 1977.
Randall Jarrell, adaptor, *The Fisherman and His Wife: A Tale from the Brothers Grimm,* Farrar, Straus, 1980.
Zilpha Keatley Snyder, *Come On, Patsy,* Atheneum, 1982.
Alvin Schwartz, *The Cat's Elbow and Other Secret Languages,* Farrar, Straus, 1982.
Kathleen Stevens, *Molly, McCullough and Tom the Rogue,* Crowell, 1983.
Mildred Phillips, *The Sign in Mendel's Window,* Macmillan, 1985.
Yoshiko Uchida, *The Two Foolish Cats,* McElderry Books, 1987.
Mirra Ginsburg, *The Chinese Mirror,* Harcourt, 1988.
Odette Meyers, *The Enchanted Umbrella,* Harcourt, 1988.

Bill Staines, *All God's Critters Got a Place in the Choir,* Dutton, 1989.

OTHER

Some of Zemach's works are included in the Kerlan Collection at the University of Minnesota.

ADAPTATIONS: The Judge: An Untrue Tale, Duffy and the Devil: A Cornish Tale, Mazel and Shlimazel; or, The Milk of a Lioness, It Could Always Be Worse: A Yiddish Folktale and *A Penny a Look: An Old Story* were adapted as film strips by Miller-Brody Productions; *The Princess and Froggie* was adapted as a film strip by Doubleday Multimedia; *Salt: A Russian Tale, Nail Soup: A Swedish Folktale Retold* and *Mommy, Buy Me a China Doll* were adapted as film strips by Weston Woods.

SIDELIGHTS: Margot Zemach was a renowned children's author and illustrator, "a national treasure," as Peter Neumeyer described her in *Parents' Choice.* Winner of the Caldecott Medal and the Lewis Carroll Bookshelf Award, among other prizes, Zemach specialized in adapting folktales for children. Her books included retellings of such classic tales as *The Little Red Hen* and *The Three Little Pigs* as well as stories drawn from Yiddish folklore. "I consider [Zemach]," William Steig stated in the *New York Times,* "the consummate illustrator for children's literature. There's no doubt her work will endure."

Speaking to A. L. Lloyd in *Horn Book* about her illustrations, Zemach remarked: "Children are fascinated by detail. Take a child to the zoo and you may well find that amid all the exotic beasts, it's the pigeon walking around the child's feet that catches the attention. In the most elaborate picture, the chances are that what gives special delight is a little fly or a dropped glove. Children need detail, color, excellence—the best a person can do. I always think, when I'm drawing the view of a town or the inside of a hut: 'Would *I* have liked to live there?' One doesn't need meticulous authenticity of costume or architecture; to a certain extent, one can invent one's own styles of dress and house shapes. But things have to be made real. The food has to be what you'd want to eat, the bed has to be what you'd want to get into right away. But, all in all, I'm not sure that one should consciously bear in mind that the drawings are meant for the gaze of children. If I make a book for children, I draw it the same as I'd draw for grownups."

In an evaluation of Zemach's career for *Horn Book,* Selma G. Lanes stated that right from the start of her career, Zemach was "an artist thoroughly at home between book covers. She used the white page comfortably: it was the air her characters breathed. The artist could show us upstairs and downstairs, indoors and out in a single, uncluttered picture. Her protagonists were in constant, purposeful motion, and the narrative pacing of her illustration never flagged. Here was a born picture book artist."

The first book Zemach illustrated was *A Small Boy Is Listening,* written by her husband, Harve Zemach, and based on the musical life of Vienna. The couple had met while studying in Vienna. While they moved around Europe, living for a time in Italy, Denmark, and England, the pair collaborated on a number of children's books together. Margot also illustrated books by other authors. Eventually, with their four daughters, the Zemachs settled in London, then in Boston—where Harve taught history and social science for several years—and finally in Berkeley, California.

Over the years Zemach illustrated many books based on folktales from around the world. Among her favorites were *Salt: A Russian Tale, Nail Soup: A Swedish Folktale Retold, The Judge: An Untrue Tale, A Penny a Look: An Old Story,* and the tales of Isaac Bashevis Singer, *When Shlemiel Went to Warsaw* and *Mazel and Shlimazel,* based on traditional Yiddish stories. Writing in *Horn Book,* Brian Alderson noted the many sources for the folktales that Zemach illustrated: "Sweden, Denmark, Russia, Italy, Germany—all supplied stories to go with the English tales that Margot chose to illustrate."

It was only natural for Zemach to illustrate folktales. As a young girl learning to draw, she had first drawn pictures to illustrate the fairy tales she enjoyed reading. Later, when her theatrical director father allowed her to play with the costumes from his shows, the young artist began to draw dancers in scenes that were full of movement and bright colors.

Zemach's love of movement is evident in her lively book illustrations. Inspired by her theatrical parents, Zemach saw writing and drawing a picture book in theatrical terms. She wrote in her autobiography, *Self-Portrait: Margot Zemach:* "I can create my own theater and be in charge of everything. When there is a story I want to tell in pictures, I find my actors, build the sets, design the costumes and light the stage. . . . If I can get it all together and moving, it will come to life. The actors will work with each other, and the dancers will hear the music and dance. When the book closes, the curtain comes down."

BIOGRAPHICAL/CRITICAL SOURCES:

BOOKS

Zemach, Margot, *Self-Portrait: Margot Zemach,* Addison-Wesley, 1978.

PERIODICALS

Horn Book, August, 1974, pp. 358-362; September/October, 1989, pp. 597-601; September/October, 1991, pp. 573-579.

New York Times, January 21, 1983.
Parents' Choice, Volume 10, number 4, 1987.
Publishers Weekly, February 18, 1983, p. 60; June 30, 1989.
Top of the News, April, 1971.

OBITUARIES:

PERIODICALS

New York Times, May 23, 1989.
Time, June 5, 1989, p. 63.*

*   *   *

ZOLOTOW, Charlotte S(hapiro) 1915-
(Sarah Abbott, Charlotte Bookman)

PERSONAL: Born June 26, 1915, in Norfolk, VA; daughter of Louis J. and Ella (Bernstein) Shapiro; married Maurice Zolotow (a writer), April 14, 1938 (divorced, 1969); children: Stephen, Ellen (Crescent Dragonwagon). *Education:* Attended University of Wisconsin, 1933-36. *Religion:* Jewish.

ADDRESSES: Home—29 Elm Place, Hastings-on-Hudson, NY 10706. *Office*—HarperCollins Children's Books, 10 East 53rd St., New York, NY 10022.

CAREER: Harper & Row, New York, NY, senior editor of children's book department, 1938-44, 1962-76, vice-president and associate publisher of Junior Books division, 1976-81, consultant and editorial director of Charlotte Zolotow Books division, 1981-91; publisher emerita and editorial advisor, 1991—. University of Indiana Writers' Conference, lecturer, 1961, 1962. Has also lectured at the University of Colorado. Works represented in the Kerlan Collection at the University of Minnesota and the de Grummond Collection at the University of Southern Mississippi.

MEMBER: PEN, Authors League of America.

AWARDS, HONORS: Indian, Indian was named a Spring Book Festival honor book, *New York Herald Tribune,* 1952; American Library Association notable book citations for *Do You Know What I'll Do?, Mr. Rabbit and the Lovely Present, William's Doll,* and *My Grandson Lew; The Storm Book* and *Mr. Rabbit and the Lovely Present* were named Caldecott honor books, 1953 and 1963, respectively; *Mr. Rabbit and the Lovely Present* was named a Newbery honor book, 1962; *New York Times* outstanding book of the year and *School Library Journal* best book of the year awards, both 1972, both for *William's Doll;* Christopher Award, 1974, for *My Grandson Lew;* Harper Gold Medal Award for editorial excellence, 1974; Carolyn W. Field Award, Pennsylvania Library Association

Youth Services Division, 1984, for *Some Things Go Together; Redbook* award, 1984, for *I Know a Lady,* and 1985, for *William's Doll;* Helen C. White tribute, 1982; Kerlan Award, University of Minnesota Children's Literature Research Collections, 1986; LMP Award, R. R. Bowker, 1990; De Grummond Award, 1990; American Library Association tribute, 1991.

WRITINGS:

FICTION

The Park Book, illustrated by H. A. Rey, Harper, 1944.
But Not Billy, illustrated by Lys Cassal, Harper, 1947, illustrated by Kay Chorao, 1983.
The Storm Book, illustrated by Margaret Bloy Graham, Harper, 1952.
The Magic Word, illustrated by Eleanor Dart, Wonder Books, 1952.
Indian, Indian, illustrated by Leonard Weisgard, Simon & Schuster, 1952.
(Under pseudonym Charlotte Bookman) *The City Boy and the Country Horse,* illustrated by William Moyers, Treasure Books, 1952.
The Quiet Mother and the Noisy Little Boy, illustrated by Kurt Werth, Lothrop, 1953, illustrated by Marc Simont, Harper, 1989.
One Step, Two . . . , illustrated by Roger Duvoisin, Lothrop, 1955.
Over and Over, illustrated by Garth Williams, Harper, 1957.
Not a Little Monkey, illustrated by Duvoisin, Lothrop, 1957, illustrated by Michele Chessare, Harper, 1989.
Do You Know What I'll Do?, illustrated by Williams, Harper, 1958.
Sleepy Book, illustrated by Vladimir Bobri, Lothrop, 1958, illustrated by Ilse Plume, Harper, 1988.
The Night When Mother Was Away, illustrated by Reisie Lonette, Lothrop, 1958, published as *The Summer Night,* illustrated by Ben Schechter, Harper, 1974.
The Bunny Who Found Easter, illustrated by Betty Peterson, Parnassus, 1959.
Big Brother, illustrated by Mary Chalmers, Harper, 1960.
The Little Black Puppy, illustrated by Lilian Obligado, Golden Press, 1960.
The Three Funny Friends, illustrated by Chalmers, Harper, 1961.
The Man with the Purple Eyes, illustrated by Joe Lasker, Abelard-Schuman, 1961.
Mr. Rabbit and the Lovely Present, illustrated by Maurice Sendak, Harper, 1962.
Aren't You Glad?, illustrated by Elaine Kurty, Lothrop, 1963.
A Tiger Called Thomas, illustrated by Werth, Lothrop, 1963, illustrated by Catherine Stock, 1988.
The Sky Was Blue, illustrated by Williams, Harper, 1963.

The Quarreling Book, illustrated by Arnold Lobel, Harper, 1963.

The White Marble, illustrated by Lilian Obligado, Abelard-Schuman, 1963, illustrated by Deborah K. Ray, Crowell, 1982.

A Rose, a Bridge and a Wild Black Horse, illustrated by Uri Shulevitz, Harper, 1964, illustrated by Robin Spowart, Harper, 1987.

The Poodle Who Barked at the Wind, illustrated by Duvoisin, Lothrop, 1964, illustrated by June Otani, Harper, 1987.

I Have a Horse of My Own, illustrated by Yoko Mitsuhashi, Abelard-Schuman, 1964.

Someday, illustrated by Lobel, Harper, 1965.

When I Have a Little Girl, illustrated by Hilary Knight, Harper, 1965.

Flocks of Birds, illustrated by Joan Berg, Abelard-Schuman, 1965, illustrated by Ruth Lercher Bornstein, Crowell, 1981.

If It Weren't for You, illustrated by Ben Schecter, Harper, 1966.

Big Sister and Little Sister, illustrated by Martha Alexander, Harper, 1966.

I Want to Be Little, illustrated by Tony De Luna, Abelard-Schuman, 1966, published as *I Like to Be Little,* illustrated by Erik Blegvad, Crowell, 1987.

When I Have a Son, illustrated by Knight, Harper, 1967.

Summer Is . . . , illustrated by Janet Archer, Abelard-Schuman, 1967, illustrated by Bornstein, Crowell, 1983.

My Friend John, illustrated by Schecter, Harper, 1968.

The New Friend, illustrated by Arvis L. Stewart, Abelard-Schuman, 1968, illustrated by Emily A. McCully, Crowell, 1981.

The Hating Book, illustrated by Schecter, Harper, 1969.

(Under pseudonym Sarah Abbott) *Where I Begin,* illustrated by Rocco Negri, Coward-McCann, 1970.

You and Me, illustrated by Robert Quackenbush, Macmillan, 1971, published as *Here We Are,* Macmillan, 1971.

A Father Like That, illustrated by Schecter, Harper, 1971.

The Beautiful Christmas Tree, illustrated by Ruth Robbins, Parnassus, 1972.

(Under pseudonym Sarah Abbott) *The Old Dog,* illustrated by George Mocniak, Coward-McCann, 1972.

Hold My Hand, illustrated by Thomas di Grazia, Harper, 1972.

William's Doll, illustrated by William Pene Du Bois, Harper, 1972.

Janey, illustrated by Ronald Himler, Harper, 1973.

(Editor) *An Overpraised Season: Ten Stories of Youth,* Harper, 1973.

My Grandson Lew, illustrated by Du Bois, Harper, 1974.

The Unfriendly Book, illustrated by Du Bois, Harper, 1975.

May I Visit?, illustrated by Erik Blegvad, Harper, 1976.

It's Not Fair, illustrated by Du Bois, Harper, 1976.

Someone New, illustrated by Blegvad, Harper, 1978.

Say It!, illustrated by James Stevenson, Greenwillow, 1980.

If You Listen, illustrated by Marc Simont, Harper, 1980.

The Song, illustrated by Nancy Tafuri, Greenwillow, 1982.

I Know a Lady, illustrated by Stevenson, Greenwillow, 1984.

Timothy Too!, illustrated by Ruth Robbins, Houghton, 1986.

(Editor) *Early Sorrow: Ten Stories of Youth,* Harper, 1986.

Something Is Going to Happen, illustrated by Catherine Stock, Harper, 1988.

The Summer Night, illustrated by Ben Shecter, Harper, 1991.

This Quiet Lady, illustrated by Anita Lobel, Greenwillow, 1992.

The Seashore Book, illustrated by Wendell Minor, Harper-Collins, 1992.

POETRY

All That Sunlight, illustrated by Walter Stein, Harper, 1967.

Some Things Go Together, illustrated by Sylvie Selig, Abelard-Schuman, 1969, illustrated by Karen Bundersheimer, Crowell, 1983.

River Winding, illustrated by Regina Sherkerjian, Abelard, 1970, illustrated by Kazue Mizumura, Crowell, 1978.

Wake up and Goodnight, illustrated by Weisgard, Harper, 1971.

Everything Glistens and Everything Sings: New and Selected Poems, illustrated by Margot Tomes, Harcourt, 1987.

OTHER

In My Garden, illustrated by Duvoisin, Lothrop, 1960.

When the Wind Stops, illustrated by Lasker, Abelard-Schuman, 1962, illustrated by Howard Knotts, Harper, 1975.

A Week in Yani's World: Greece, photographs by Donald Getsug, Macmillan, 1969.

A Week in Lateef's World: India, photographs by Ray Shaw, Crowell-Collier, 1970.

Contributor to books, including *The Writer's Handbook,* 1968. Contributor to magazines, including *Writer's Yearbook, Prism,* and *McCall's.* Poems, stories, and articles are included in numerous magazines and anthologies for children.

ADAPTATIONS:

FILMS

My Grandson Lew, Barr Films, 1976.

William's Doll, produced and directed by Robert Carlo Chiesa, Phoenix/BFA, 1981.

"Someone New," included in a CBS Library program, *The Wrong Way Kid,* produced by Busustow Entertainment, 1983.

A Father Like That, produced by Phil Marshall, Phoenix Films, 1983.

The Hating Movie (also available as videotape), Phoenix Films and Video, 1986.

FILMSTRIPS

Mr. Rabbit and the Lovely Present, Weston Woods, 1966.

Someday, Educational Enrichment Materials, 1976.

When I Have a Little Girl, Educational Enrichment Materials, 1976.

When I Have a Son, Educational Enrichment Materials, 1976.

The Three Funny Friends, Educational Enrichment Materials, 1976.

A Father Like That, Listening Library, 1978.

The Hating Book was made into a filmstrip by Harper Mediabook.

OTHER

A sound recording of some of Zolotow's stories was made by Vancouver Taped Books Project, 1972; an audiocassette of *Wake up and Goodnight* was made by Caedmon.

SIDELIGHTS: Charlotte Zolotow, author of more than sixty well-received picture books for younger readers, began her career as a writer after having served as a senior editor of Harper & Row's children's book department for several years. Through four decades she has combined her work as an author with her editorial duties, first at Harper & Row and more recently for her own imprint, Charlotte Zolotow Books. In 1974 she was honored with the Harper Gold Medal for editorial excellence, and her stories have received numerous awards, including the 1974 Christopher Award and "honor book" citations from the prestigious Caldecott and Newberry selection committees.

Asserting similarity in the feelings of young and old, Zolotow wrote in *Horn Book:* "We are all the same, except that adults have found ways to buffer themselves against the full-blown intensity of a child's emotions." Later in the article, the author stated that "a grown person's unrequited love evokes misery similar to a child's misery when a big sister or brother goes off without the child. The loss of a wanted job to someone else in the adult world can stir the same sense of rejection that a small child feels when the doll or dog he or she wanted is given to someone else. We are not different from the children we were—only more experienced, better able to disguise our feelings from others, if not from ourselves."

Several critics have indicated that Zolotow's empathy is what attracts the large number of youthful readers to her books. Marcus Crouch of *School Librarian* remarked that Zolotow "writes the kind of poetry that children write. She catches the fleeting moment as it passes and imprisons it in words. Her verses are frail and delicate. One readily acknowledges her sensitivity." May Hill Arbuthnot and Zena Sutherland expressed a similar view in their book *Children and Books:* "Few writers for small children so empathize with them as does Charlotte Zolotow, whose books—with some exceptions—are really explorations of relationships cast in story form and given vitality by perfected simplicity of style and by the humor and tenderness of the stories. . . . [Her] understanding of children's emotional needs and problems, and her ability to express them with candor have made her one of the major contemporary writers of realistic books for small children."

Zolotow, in an essay for *Books Are by People*, discussed the way she begins work on many of her books: "My children and their friends have often reminded me of things from my childhood which become the theme of a book. Sometimes it is a kind of double-exposure—the adult awareness of a phenomenon and the memory of what it seemed to me as a child or seems to the children around me." She also stated that "A good picture book, I think, must be honest and unpretentious and direct. Whether it is funny or poetic (or both) there should be some universal truth or feeling in it, and what Margaret Wise Brown called the 'unexpected inevitable.' "

While working as an editorial assistant to Ursula Nordstrom at Harper & Row, the author drafted an outline for a story which she thought could be well-written by Brown. Nordstrom asked for clarification, and upon receiving a more detailed story, accepted the manuscript as Zolotow's first book. The author has credited her involvement with Nordstrom as the major influence in her writing and editing career. "[Nordstrom] taught me a fundamental lesson—the difference between being an editor and being a writer—early on in my career. . . . An editor *draws out* of an author—doesn't feed the editor's ideas *into* the creative person," Zolotow stated in an essay for *The Calendar.* Zolotow further asserted in an interview with Justin Wintle for *Pied Pipers*: "I have to be careful if I see something isn't working; the temptation's very often there to say how it should be done, which is death to an author. You've got to let him solve his own problems."

In a *Publishers Weekly* interview with Jean Mercier, Zolotow has described the changing focus in children's literature and her position as an editor: "We have to allow authors to put in their books all the information that's valid. We have to allow them to write about abortion, sex encounters, death, divorce and all kinds of problems if these are vital to the story. I don't believe any subject should be taboo if it's handled with taste. We have to tell young people the truth. I don't see how this position can be altered." Discussing what many people feel is the new trend in realism in youth books, Zolotow told Dolores Barclay in the *Los Angeles Times:* "What's called the 'new reality' is just common respect for the child. Young people today are a great deal more sophisticated. Books we used to publish for fourteen-year olds are now being read by ten-year olds. In picture books for younger readers there was a time when death or divorce were never treated and everything worked out well." Writing for *Twentieth-Century Children's Writers,* Mercier noted that Zolotow herself was one of the first authors "to tackle the long-taboo subject of death in a picture book." Zolotow told Barclay, "There's a general implication now that publishers are looking for problem books. . . . We are not seeking controversial books. We are seeking good books."

Many observers feel one reason for Zolotow's success as an editor is her talent for linking the right artist with the right children's author. Zolotow told Mercier: "We look for those who don't follow the text slavishly; they put in their own individual touches, their own viewpoints. Often the illustrators' work means that some of the text or dialogue can be eliminated. But it has to be there in the first place, so they can 'see' what's happening and get ideas." This stress on compatibility between picture and prose has benefitted her authored works as well. For example, Neil Millar wrote in a *Christian Science Monitor* review of *River Winding:* "This is a near-perfect match of poet and illustrator. [The] poems, free verse or formal, are gems, glimpses of a gentle—most rustic—world seen through a gentle child's perception." Zolotow told Wintle: "I used to wish that I could paint myself, but as I've gotten older I've realized that I was very fortunate that I couldn't because I've had a much wider range of other people's talent and imagination than my own could have given me."

BIOGRAPHICAL/CRITICAL SOURCES:

BOOKS

Arbuthnot, May Hill and Zena Sutherland, *Children and Books,* fourth edition, Scott, Foresman, 1972.

Bader, Barbara, *American Picturebooks from Noah's Ark to the Beast within,* Macmillan, 1976.

Children's Literature Review, Volume 2, Gale, 1976.

Dictionary of Literary Biography, Volume 52: *American Writers for Children since 1960: Fiction,* Gale, 1986.

Huck, Charlotte, *Children's Literature in the Elementary School,* Holt, 1976.

Huck, *Children's Literature,* third edition, Holt, 1978.

Rudman, Masha, *Children's Literature,* second edition, Longman, 1976.

Trelease, Jim, *The Read Aloud Handbook,* Penguin Books, 1982.

Twentieth-Century Children's Writers, 3rd edition, St. James Press, 1989, p. 1080-1082.

Zolotow, Charlotte, essay in *Books Are by People,* edited by Lee Bennett Hopkins, Citation Press, 1969.

Zolotow, interview with Justin Wintle for *Pied Pipers,* edited by Wintle and Emma Fisher, Paddington Press, 1974.

PERIODICALS

The Calendar, November, 1981-June, 1982.

Christian Science Monitor, November 13, 1978.

Horn Book, September/October, 1985, pp. 536-540.

Los Angeles Times, February 29, 1980.

Ms., May, 1974.

New Yorker, December 17, 1966.

New York Times Book Review, November 11, 1984.

Publishers Weekly, June 10, 1974.

School Librarian, September, 1971.*